KB186459

한국의 토익 수험자 여러분께,

토익 시험은 세계적인 직무 영어능력 평가 시험으로, 지난 40여 년간 비즈니스 현장에서 필요한 영어능력 평가의 기준을 제시해 왔습니다. 토익 시험 및 토익스피킹, 토익라이팅 시험은 세계에서 가장 널리 통용되는 영어능력 검증 시험으로, 160여 개국 14,000여 기관이 토익 성적을 의사결정에 활용하고 있습니다.

YBM은 한국의 토익 시험을 주관하는 ETS 독점 계약사입니다.

ETS는 한국 수험자들의 효과적인 토익 학습을 돕고자 YBM을 통하여 'ETS 토익 공식 교재'를 독점 출간하고 있습니다. 또한 'ETS 토익 공식 교재' 시리즈에 기출문항을 제공해 한국의 다른 교재들에 수록된 기출을 복제하거나 변형한 문항으로 인하여 발생할 수 있는 수험자들의 혼동을 방지하고 있습니다.

복제 및 변형 문항들은 토익 시험의 출제의도를 벗어날 수 있기 때문에 기출문항을 수록한 'ETS 토익 공식 교재'만큼 시험에 잘 대비할 수 없습니다.

'ETS 토익 공식 교재'를 통하여 수험자 여러분의 영어 소통을 위한 노력에 큰 성취가 있기를 바랍니다.

감사합니다.

Dear TOEIC Test Takers in Korea,

The TOEIC program is the global leader in English-language assessment for the workplace. It has set the standard for assessing English-language skills needed in the workplace for more than 40 years. The TOEIC tests are the most widely used English language assessments around the world, with 14,000+ organizations across more than 160 countries trusting TOEIC scores to make decisions.

YBM is the ETS Country Master Distributor for the TOEIC program in Korea and so is the exclusive distributor for TOEIC Korea.

To support effective learning for TOEIC test-takers in Korea, ETS has authorized YBM to publish the only Official TOEIC prep books in Korea. These books contain actual TOEIC items to help prevent confusion among Korean test-takers that might be caused by other prep book publishers' use of reproduced or paraphrased items.

Reproduced or paraphrased items may fail to reflect the intent of actual TOEIC items and so will not prepare test-takers as well as the actual items contained in the ETS TOEIC Official prep books published by YBM.

We hope that these ETS TOEIC Official prep books enable you, as test-takers, to achieve great success in your efforts to communicate effectively in English.

Thank you.

입문부터 실전까지 수준별 학습을 통해 최단기 목표점수 달성!

ETS TOEIC® 공식수험서
스마트 학습 지원

구글플레이, 앱스토어에서
ETS 토익기출 수험서 다운로드

구글플레이   앱스토어

ETS 토익 모바일 학습 플랫폼!

ETS® 토익기출 수험서 어플

교재 학습 지원
1. 교재 해설 강의
2. LC 음원 MP3
3. 교재/부록 모의고사 채점 및 분석
4. 단어 암기장

부가 서비스
1. 데일리 학습(토익 기출문제 풀이)
2. 토익 최신 경향 무료 특강
3. 토익 타이머

모의고사 결과 분석
1. 파트별/문항별 정답률
2. 파트별/유형별 취약점 리포트
3. 전체 응시자 점수 분포도

ETS TOEIC 공식카페 ▾

etstoeicbook.co.kr

ETS 토익 학습 전용 온라인 커뮤니티!

ETS TOEIC® Book 공식카페

강사진의 학습 지원   토익 대표강사들의 학습 지원과 멘토링

교재 학습관 운영   교재별 학습게시판을 통해 무료 동영상
강의 등 학습 지원

학습 콘텐츠 제공   토익 학습 콘텐츠와 정기시험
예비특강 업데이트

---

www.ybmbooks.com에서도 무료 MP3를 다운로드 받을 수 있습니다.

토익,

실력과 점수를 한 번에!
출제기관이 만든
진짜 문제로 승부하라!

왜
출제기관에서
만든 문제여야
할까요?

2,300명의
시험개발 전문가!

교육, 심리, 통계, 인문학, 사회학 등
2,300여 명의 전문 연구원이 모인 ETS.
토익 한 세트가 완성되려면 문제 설계 및 집필,
내용 검토, 문항의 공정성 및 타당성 검증,
난이도 조정, 모의시험 등 15단계의 개발공정에서
수많은 전문가의 손을 거쳐야 합니다.

2,300

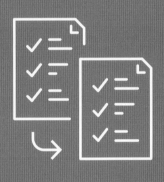

싱크로율 100%

ETS TOEIC 교재의 모든 예문과 문항 및 해설은
100% ETS TOEIC 정기시험 개발부서에서 개발
및 검수되었습니다.
그러므로 사진, LC 음원, 문항 유형 및 난이도 등
모든 면에서 실제 시험과 싱크로율 100%입니다.

100%

최고의 정기시험
적중률!

기출 문항을 변형한 복제 문항이 아닌,
ETS 토익 출제팀이 만든 원본 문항 100%로,
시중의 어느 교재와도 비교할 수 없는 압도적으로
높은 적중률을 보장합니다.

최고의 적중률!

ETS TOEIC

토익 정기시험 기출종합서 RC

발행인 허문호
발행처 YBM

편집 이혜진
디자인 DOTS
마케팅 정연철, 박천산, 고영노, 김동진, 박찬경, 김윤하

초판발행 2021년 11월 8일
4쇄 발행 2023년 10월 2일

신고일자 1964년 3월 28일
신고번호 제 300-1964-3호
주소 서울시 종로구 종로 104
전화 (02) 2000-0515 [구입문의] / (02) 2000-0436 [내용문의]
팩스 (02) 2285-1523
홈페이지 www.ybmbooks.com

ISBN 978-89-17-23861-7

RC 토익 정기시험 기출종합서

PREFACE

Dear test taker,

Here is a test preparation book created to help you succeed in using English as a tool for communication both in Korea and around the world.

This book will provide you with practical steps that you can take right now to improve your English proficiency and your TOEIC® test score. Now more than ever, your TOEIC score is a respected professional credential and an indicator of how well you can use English in a wide variety of situations to get the job done. As always, your TOEIC score is recognized globally as evidence of your English-language proficiency.

With the ETS TOEIC® Official Prep Book, you can make sure you have the best and most thorough preparation for the TOEIC® test. This book contains test questions that have appeared in actual TOEIC® tests, as well as test questions that were developed separately by the same specialists who write the TOEIC® test. It will enable you to master key points of the test at a rapid pace by studying and practicing with actual TOEIC® questions.

The ETS TOEIC® Official Prep Book includes the following key features.
· Questions from actual TOEIC tests
· Analyses of the TOEIC question types and preparation strategies
· Detailed explanations for learners

Use the ETS TOEIC® Official Prep Book to help you prepare to use English in an ever-globalizing workplace. You will become familiar with the test, including the new test tasks, content, and format. These learning materials have been carefully crafted to help you advance in proficiency and gain a score report that will show the world what you know and what you can do.

출제기관이 만든
국내 유일 토익 시험 대비서!

기본기부터 실전까지 가장 빠르고 효과적으로 도달하는 방법, 이 한 권에 모두 담았습니다!

독점제공	출제기관이 제공하는 **기출문제 독점 수록**

최신경향	토익 기출문제로 **정확한 최신 경향 분석**

국내최고	기출 포인트를 꿰뚫는 **명쾌한 분석과 해설**

목차

PART 6

PART 7

WHAT IS THE TOEIC?

TOEIC은 어떤 시험인가요?

Test of English for International Communication (국제적 의사소통을 위한 영어 시험)의 약자로서,
영어가 모국어가 아닌 사람들이 일상생활 또는 비즈니스 현장에서 꼭 필요한 실용적 영어 구사 능력을 갖추었는가를
평가하는 시험이다.

■ 시험 구성

구성	Part		내용	문항수	시간	배점
듣기(LC)	1		사진 묘사	6	45분	495점
	2		질의 & 응답	25		
	3		짧은 대화	39		
	4		짧은 담화	30		
읽기(RC)	5		단문 빈칸 채우기 (문법/어휘)	30	75분	495점
	6		장문 빈칸 채우기	16		
	7	독해	단일 지문	29		
			이중 지문	10		
			삼중 지문	15		
Total	7 Parts			200문항	120분	990점

■ TOEIC 접수는 어떻게 하나요?

TOEIC 접수는 한국 토익 위원회 사이트(www.toeic.co.kr)에서 온라인
상으로만 접수가 가능하다. 사이트에서 매월 자세한 접수일정과 시험 일정 등의
구체적 정보 확인이 가능하니, 미리 일정을 확인하여 접수하도록 한다.

◾ 시험장에 반드시 가져가야 할 준비물은요?

신분증   규정 신분증만 가능
(주민등록증, 운전면허증, 기간 만료 전의 여권, 공무원증 등)

필기구   연필, 지우개 (볼펜이나 사인펜은 사용 금지)

◾ 시험은 어떻게 진행되나요?

09:20	입실 (09:50 이후는 입실 불가)
09:30 - 09:45	답안지 작성에 관한 오리엔테이션
09:45 - 09:50	휴식
09:50 - 10:05	신분증 확인
10:05 - 10:10	문제지 배부 및 파본 확인
10:10 - 10:55	듣기 평가 (Listening Test)
10:55 - 12:10	독해 평가 (Reading Test)

◾ TOEIC 성적 확인은 어떻게 하죠?

시험일로부터 약 10-11일 후, 인터넷과 ARS(060-800-0515)로 성적을 확인할 수 있다. TOEIC 성적표는 우편이나 온라인으로 발급 받을 수 있다(시험 접수시, 양자 택일). 우편으로 발급 받을 경우는 성적 발표 후 대략 일주일이 소요되며, 온라인 발급을 선택하면 유효기간 내에 홈페이지에서 본인이 직접 1회에 한해 무료 출력할 수 있다. TOEIC 성적은 시험일로부터 2년간 유효하다.

◾ TOEIC은 몇 점 만점인가요?

TOEIC 점수는 듣기 영역(LC) 점수, 읽기 영역(RC) 점수, 그리고 이 두 영역을 합계한 전체 점수 세 부분으로 구성된다. 각 부분의 점수는 5점 단위이며, 5점에서 495점에 걸쳐 주어지고, 전체 점수는 10점에서 990점까지이며, 만점은 990점이다. TOEIC 성적은 각 문제 유형의 난이도에 따른 점수 환산표에 의해 결정된다.

학습 스케줄

4 주 완성
학습 플랜

단기간에 토익을
마스터하고자 하는
중급 학습자

8 주 완성
학습 플랜

차근차근 토익을
마스터 하고자 하는
초중급 학습자

4 주 완성 학습 플랜

	☐ Day 1	☐ Day 2	☐ Day 3	☐ Day 4	☐ Day 5
1주	문법 UNIT 01 PART 6 UNIT 01	문법 UNIT 02 PART 7 UNIT 01, 02	문법 UNIT 03 PART 6 UNIT 02	문법 UNIT 04 PART 7 UNIT 03, 04	어휘 UNIT 01~04
	☐ Day 6	☐ Day 7	☐ Day 8	☐ Day 9	☐ Day 10
2주	문법 UNIT 05 PART 6 UNIT 03	문법 UNIT 06 PART 7 UNIT 05, 06	문법 UNIT 07 PART 6 UNIT 04	문법 UNIT 08 PART 7 UNIT 07, 08	어휘 UNIT 05~08
	☐ Day 11	☐ Day 12	☐ Day 13	☐ Day 14	☐ Day 15
3주	문법 UNIT 09 PART 6 UNIT 05	문법 UNIT 10 PART 7 UNIT 09, 10	문법 UNIT 11 PART 6 UNIT 06	문법 UNIT 12 PART 7 UNIT 11, 12	어휘 UNIT 09, 10 TEST 1~12
	☐ Day 16	☐ Day 17	☐ Day 18	☐ Day 19	☐ Day 20
4주	문법 UNIT 13 PART 6 UNIT 07	문법 UNIT 14 PART 7 UNIT 13, 14	문법 UNIT 15 PART 6 UNIT 08	문법 REVIEW 어휘 TEST 1~12	FINAL TEST

8주 완성 학습 플랜

1주	☐ **Day 1** 문법 UNIT 01 PART 6 UNIT 01	☐ **Day 2** 문법 UNIT 01 PART 6 UNIT 01	☐ **Day 3** 문법 UNIT 02 PART 7 UNIT 01, 02	☐ **Day 4** 문법 UNIT 02 PART 7 UNIT 01, 02	☐ **Day 5** 문법 UNIT 03 PART 6 UNIT 02
2주	☐ **Day 6** 문법 UNIT 03 PART 6 UNIT 02	☐ **Day 7** 문법 UNIT 04 PART 7 UNIT 03, 04	☐ **Day 8** 문법 UNIT 04 PART 7 UNIT 03, 04	☐ **Day 9** 어휘 UNIT 01~04	☐ **Day 10** 어휘 UNIT 01~04
3주	☐ **Day 11** 문법 UNIT 05 PART 6 UNIT 03	☐ **Day 12** 문법 UNIT 05 PART 6 UNIT 03	☐ **Day 13** 문법 UNIT 06 PART 7 UNIT 05, 06	☐ **Day 14** 문법 UNIT 06 PART 7 UNIT 05, 06	☐ **Day 15** 문법 UNIT 07 PART 6 UNIT 04
4주	☐ **Day 16** 문법 UNIT 07 PART 6 UNIT 04	☐ **Day 17** 문법 UNIT 08 PART 7 UNIT 07, 08	☐ **Day 18** 문법 UNIT 08 PART 7 UNIT 07, 08	☐ **Day 19** 어휘 UNIT 05~08	☐ **Day 20** 어휘 UNIT 05~08
5주	☐ **Day 21** 문법 UNIT 09 PART 6 UNIT 05	☐ **Day 22** 문법 UNIT 09 PART 6 UNIT 05	☐ **Day 23** 문법 UNIT 10 PART 7 UNIT 09, 10	☐ **Day 24** 문법 UNIT 10 PART 7 UNIT 09, 10	☐ **Day 25** 문법 UNIT 11 PART 6 UNIT 06
6주	☐ **Day 26** 문법 UNIT 11 PART 6 UNIT 06	☐ **Day 27** 문법 UNIT 12 PART 7 UNIT 11, 12	☐ **Day 28** 문법 UNIT 12 PART 7 UNIT 11, 12	☐ **Day 29** 어휘 UNIT 09, 10 TEST 1~12	☐ **Day 30** 어휘 UNIT 09, 10 TEST 1~12
7주	☐ **Day 31** 문법 UNIT 13 PART 6 UNIT 07	☐ **Day 32** 문법 UNIT 13 PART 6 UNIT 07	☐ **Day 33** 문법 UNIT 14 PART 7 UNIT 13, 14	☐ **Day 34** 문법 UNIT 14 PART 7 UNIT 13, 14	☐ **Day 35** 문법 UNIT 15 PART 6 UNIT 08
8주	☐ **Day 36** 문법 UNIT 15 PART 6 UNIT 08	☐ **Day 37** 문법 REVIEW 어휘 TEST 1~12	☐ **Day 38** 문법 REVIEW 어휘 TEST 1~12	☐ **Day 39** FINAL TEST PART 5, 6	☐ **Day 40** FINAL TEST PART 7

점수 환산표 및 산출법

점수 환산표 이 책에 수록된 Final Test를 풀고 난 후, 맞은 개수를 세어 점수를 환산해 보세요.

LISTENING Raw Score (맞은 개수)	LISTENING Scaled Score (환산 점수)	READING Raw Score (맞은 개수)	READING Scaled Score (환산 점수)
96 – 100	475 – 495	96 – 100	460 – 495
91 – 95	435 – 495	91 – 95	425 – 490
86 – 90	405 – 470	86 – 90	400 – 465
81 – 85	370 – 450	81 – 85	375 – 440
76 – 80	345 – 420	76 – 80	340 – 415
71 – 75	320 – 390	71 – 75	310 – 390
66 – 70	290 – 360	66 – 70	285 – 370
61 – 65	265 – 335	61 – 65	255 – 340
56 – 60	240 – 310	56 – 60	230 – 310
51 – 55	215 – 280	51 – 55	200 – 275
46 – 50	190 – 255	46 – 50	170 – 245
41 – 45	160 – 230	41 – 45	140 – 215
36 – 40	130 – 205	36 – 40	115 – 180
31 – 35	105 – 175	31 – 35	95 – 150
26 – 30	85 – 145	26 – 30	75 – 120
21 – 25	60 – 115	21 – 25	60 – 95
16 – 20	30 – 90	16 – 20	45 – 75
11 – 15	5 – 70	11 – 15	30 – 55
6 – 10	5 – 60	6 – 10	10 – 40
1 – 5	5 – 50	1 – 5	5 – 30
0	5 – 35	0	5 – 15

점수 산출 방법 아래의 방식으로 점수를 산출할 수 있다.

 STEP 1

자신의 답안을 수록된 정답과 대조하여 채점한다. 각 Section의 맞은 개수가 본인의 Section별 '실제 점수 (통계 처리하기 전의 점수, raw score)'이다. Listening Test와 Reading Test의 정답 수를 세어, 자신의 실제 점수를 아래의 해당란에 기록한다.

	맞은 개수	환산 점수대
LISTENING		
READING		
총점		

Section별 실제 점수가 그대로 Section별 TOEIC 점수가 되는 것은 아니다. TOEIC은 시행할 때마다 별도로 특정한 통계 처리 방법을 사용하며 이러한 실제 점수를 환산 점수(converted[scaled] score)로 전환하게 된다. 이렇게 전환함으로써, 매번 시행될 때마다 문제는 달라지지만 그 점수가 갖는 의미는 같아지게 된다. 예를 들어 어느 한 시험에서 총점 550점의 성적으로 받는 실력이라면 다른 시험에서도 거의 550점대의 성적을 받게 되는 것이다.

▼

STEP 2

실제 점수를 위 표에 기록한 후 왼쪽 페이지의 점수 환산표를 보도록 한다. TOEIC이 시행될 때마다 대개 이와 비슷한 형태의 표가 작성되는데, 여기 제시된 환산표는 본 교재에 수록된 Test용으로 개발된 것이다. 이 표를 사용하여 자신의 실제 점수를 환산 점수로 전환하도록 한다. 즉, 예를 들어 Listening Test의 실제 정답 수가 61~65개이면 환산 점수는 265점에서 335점 사이가 된다. 여기서 실제 정답 수가 61개이면 환산 점수가 265점이고, 65개이면 환산 점수가 335점 임을 의미하는 것은 아니다. 본 책의 Test를 위해 작성된 이 점수 환산표가 자신의 영어 실력이 어느 정도인지 대략적으로 파악하는 데 도움이 되긴 하지만, 이 표가 실제 TOEIC 성적 산출에 그대로 사용된 적은 없다는 사실을 밝혀 둔다.

PART 5

5

문법편

RC

ETS TOEIC

UNIT 01 주어와 동사

평균 4~7문제 출제

무료인강

● 주어

주어 자리에는 명사 역할을 하는 어구가 오며 동사, 형용사 등은 올 수 없다.

The [**response** / ~~respond~~ / ~~responsive~~] to our new compact car has been positive.
　　　　명사　　　 동사　　　　 형용사

우리의 신형 소형차에 대한 반응은 긍정적이었다.

접속사가 이끄는 절에도 주어가 필요하다.

When **the factory** is complete, it will employ 500 workers.
　　　　접속사가 이끄는 절

공장이 완공되면, 직원 500명을 고용할 것이다.

● 동사

모든 문장에는 주어와 동사가 있다.

The price **increased** (significantly).　가격이 (상당히) 올랐다.
　주어　　　 동사　　　 (수식어)

준동사(to부정사, 동명사, 분사)는 단독으로 동사 자리에 올 수 없다.

Several candidates [**applied** / ~~to apply~~ / ~~applying~~] for the consultant position via e-mail.

몇몇 지원자들이 이메일로 컨설턴트직에 지원했다.

주어와 동사 | ETS 핵심 출제 패턴

우선 문장 구조를 보고 주어 자리와 동사 자리를 파악할 수 있어야 하며 각각의 자리에 올 수 있는 품사를 알고 있어야 한다. 특히 동사 자리의 경우 주어와 수가 일치하는지, 태가 적절한지, 시제가 알맞은지 점검해야 한다.

☑ 주어 자리의 품사를 선택하는 문제

The ------- of the new inventory process has had a significant impact on our management of resources.

(A) adopt   (B) adoption

(C) adopted   (D) adopts

새로운 재고 관리 절차 채택은 자원 관리에 큰 영향을 미쳤다.

핵심 포인트

주어 자리이므로 명사가 들어가야 한다.

▶ 기출공식 1 **p.20**

☑ 동사 자리를 묻는 문제

The Darlingstone Hotel ------- a complimentary breakfast to all of its guests.

(A) offering   (B) be offered

(C) is offering   (D) to offer

달링스톤 호텔은 모든 손님에게 무료로 아침을 제공하고 있다.

핵심 포인트

문장에 동사가 없으므로 동사가 들어가야 한다.

▶ 기출공식 5 **p.22**

☑ 명령문의 동사 형태를 묻는 문제

Please ------- the bottom portion for your records.

(A) retain   (B) retaining

(C) retains   (D) retained

기록용으로 아래 부분을 보관하시기 바랍니다.

핵심 포인트

명령문은 주어 없이 동사원형으로 시작한다.

▶ 기출공식 5 **p.22**

☑ 주어와 동사의 수 일치를 묻는 문제

------- are currently being accepted for the annual office charity drive.

(A) Donates   (B) Donating

(C) Donation   (D) Donations

사무실 연례행사인 자선 모금 운동을 위해 현재 기부금을 받고 있습니다.

핵심 포인트

동사가 복수이므로 주어 자리에 복수명사가 들어가야 한다.

▶ 기출공식 6 **p.22**

기출공식 1 주어 자리에는 명사 역할을 하는 어구가 온다.

명사 **Applications** are available online from July 1. 7월 1일부터 온라인으로 지원할 수 있다.

명사구 **A special luncheon** will be held in honor of the advertising team.
광고팀을 축하하여 특별 오찬이 개최될 것이다.

대명사 **They** will soon finalize the dates for the next staff meeting.
그들은 곧 다음 직원 회의 날짜를 확정할 것이다.

동명사 **Conducting a survey** is the best way to find out about your customers.
설문 조사를 실시하는 것이 고객에 대해 알 수 있는 최선의 방법이다.

to부정사 **To increase employee productivity** is the aim of the new program.
직원 생산성을 높이는 것이 새로운 프로그램의 목표이다.

명사절 **What the builder likes about this contract** is the early completion bonus.
건축업자가 이 계약에서 마음에 들어 한 것은 조기 완공에 대한 보너스이다.

---

1 ------- for changes to the conference program will be considered on November 1.
(A) Requested
(B) Requests
(C) Requesting
(D) To request

2 The mechanics became more efficient as ------- began using the new technology.
(A) themselves
(B) them
(C) their
(D) they

3 ------- for your blender properly will ensure that it continues to function well.
(A) Care
(B) Cares
(C) Cared
(D) Caring

기출공식 2 주어는 동사와 수 일치되어야 한다.

단수주어 <u>The main function</u> of the new electronic notepad **is** Internet use.
　　　　　단수주어　　　　　　　　　　　　　　　　　　　　단수동사
새 전자 노트패드의 주 기능은 인터넷 사용이다.

복수주어 <u>Job openings</u> at Elite Insurance Company **have been posted** on the Web site.
　　　　　복수주어　　　　　　　　　　　　　　　　　　　복수동사
엘리트 보험사의 공석 공고가 웹사이트에 게시되어 있다.

---

4 A key ------- still missing from the upcoming presentation to the client is an estimate of the total project cost.
(A) elementary
(B) element
(C) elements
(D) elemental

5 ------- to Lotus Restaurant have nearly doubled the size of the seating area.
(A) Improved
(B) Improvement
(C) Improvements
(D) Improving

6 The ------- for the MacNeill project is hanging on the wall in the first floor conference room.
(A) schedule
(B) scheduled
(C) schedules
(D) schedulers

기출공식 3 to부정사구, that절 같은 긴 주어는 뒤로 보내고 주어 자리에 가주어 it을 대신 쓴다.

To follow the guidelines for the construction work is important.

= **It** is important **to follow** the guidelines for the construction work.
　　가주어　　　　　　　　　　　　　　진주어

건설 작업에 대한 지침들을 따르는 것이 중요하다.

That mild weather will continue throughout September is likely.

= **It** is likely **that** mild weather will continue throughout September.
　　가주어　　　　　　　　　　　진주어

온화한 날씨가 9월 내내 계속될 듯하다.

7 It is usually most effective ------- a meeting agenda to the attendees in advance.
(A) circulate
(B) circulating
(C) circulates
(D) to circulate

8 Revenue has fluctuated over the last two quarters, so it was a surprise ------- that expenses have nevertheless remained fairly steady.
(A) learned　(B) to learn
(C) learns　(D) is learning

9 Structural engineers have determined that it is technically impossible ------- a building on the proposed site.
(A) construct
(B) to construct
(C) constructed
(D) can construct

기출공식 4 '~이 있다'를 의미하는 There + be / remain / exist 구문에서는 뒤에 오는 명사가 주어이다.

- **There be동사 + 명사(구): ~이 있다**

  There is speculation that Mr. Walker may leave Prince Mart.
  워커 씨가 프린스 마트를 떠날지도 모른다는 추측이 있다.

- **There remain(s) + 명사(구): ~이 남아 있다**

  There remains an issue of production costs. 생산비 문제가 남아 있다.

- **There exist(s) + 명사(구): ~이 있다**

  There exist many proposals for this year's marketing campaign.
  올해 마케팅 캠페인에 대한 많은 제안서가 있다.

  → 주어인 **many proposals**의 수에 맞춰 복수동사인 **exist**를 쓴다.

10 Last year, there was fierce ------- for covered parking in the winter months.
(A) competition
(B) competitions
(C) competitively
(D) competitor

11 When shows are sold out, theater policy is to start a waiting list and call customers if there are -------.
(A) canceled
(B) cancellations
(C) cancels
(D) canceling

12 There have been no major ------- since you last reviewed the report.
(A) revision
(B) revisions
(C) revising
(D) revised

정답 및 해설 p.2

기출공식 5 　모든 문장에는 동사가 반드시 있어야 한다.

The rival company [**introduced** / ~~introduction~~ / ~~introductory~~] a new line of cooking equipment last week.　경쟁사에서 지난주에 신상품 조리기구 제품군을 출시했다.

→ 명사나 형용사는 동사 자리에 올 수 없다.

All employees **can borrow** handbooks from the company library.
전직원은 회사 도서관에서 안내서를 빌릴 수 있다.

→ 조동사 뒤에는 동사원형이 온다.

Please [**leave** / ~~leaving~~ / ~~to leave~~] your hotel key at the front desk when you go out.
외출 시 프런트에 호텔 열쇠를 맡겨 주세요.

→ 명령문은 주어 없이 동사원형으로 시작한다.

---

13 A stay at the Moonlight Tower Hotel ------- an authentic Shanghai breakfast.
(A) including
(B) inclusive
(C) includes
(D) to include

14 Please ------- the enclosed survey and return it to our office as soon as possible.
(A) to complete
(B) complete
(C) completing
(D) completed

15 For performance to be considered satisfactory, production workers must ------- at least 90 percent of the monthly goals assigned by their manager.
(A) to achieve　(B) achieve
(C) achieved　(D) achieving

기출공식 6 　단수주어에는 단수동사, 복수주어에는 복수동사를 써서 수 일치한다.

The manual **provides** a brief overview of the software package.
　　단수주어　　단수동사
설명서에는 소프트웨어 패키지에 관한 간략한 개요가 실려 있다.

→ 주어가 3인칭 단수이므로 동사원형에 -(e)s를 붙인 단수동사를 쓴다.

Visitors (at the center) **are required** to display identification badges at all times.
　복수주어　　　　　복수동사
센터 방문객들은 신분증을 항상 패용해 주십시오.

→ **at the center**는 visitors를 수식하는 말이므로, 복수주어인 **visitors**에 수 일치하여 복수동사인 **are**를 쓴다.

---

16 Rechargeable batteries today ------- almost twice as long as those produced ten years ago.
(A) last
(B) lasts
(C) lasting
(D) lastly

17 Daily guided tours of the warehouse ------- at 10:00 A.M. in the reception area on the first floor.
(A) begin
(B) begins
(C) to begin
(D) beginning

18 Seating in the Bogor Stadium completely ------- the field so that all visitors are afforded excellent views of events.
(A) surround
(B) surrounds
(C) surrounded
(D) surrounding

빈출

기출공식 7　주어가 스스로 행위를 할 때는 능동태, 행위를 받을 때는 수동태를 쓴다.

- **능동태: 주어가 ~하다**

  Makadon Ltd. **manufactures** a variety of tools and equipment.

  마카돈사는 다양한 도구와 장비를 생산한다.

- **수동태: 주어가 ~되다 / 받다**

  All our photo frames **are made** by hand in the artist's studio.

  우리 액자는 모두 장인의 작업실에서 수공으로 제작된다.

19 The Blake X40 is a reliable car, but the passenger space is poorly -------.
(A) design
(B) designed
(C) designer
(D) designing

20 The outstanding balance must ------- promptly or else we will have to close the account.
(A) to pay
(B) be paid
(C) paying
(D) have paid

21 The manufacturer ------- the warranty on its latest camera models by twelve months.
(A) extend
(B) was extended
(C) extending
(D) has extended

빈출

기출공식 8　동사의 시제는 시간 표현에 일치시킨다.

- **현재 시제: 현재의 상태, 현재의 반복되는 습관, 일반적인 사실**

  Aliflora, Inc. **is** now the second largest exporter in the region.

  알리플로라사는 현재 지역에서 두 번째로 큰 수출업체이다.

- **과거 시제: 과거에 일어난 일**

  Ms. Turner **informed** her staff of the dress code two days ago.

  터너 씨는 이틀 전에 직원들에게 복장 규정에 대해서 알렸다.

- **미래 시제: 미래에 예정되거나 계획된 일**

  Starting next week, Steelers Co. **will provide** free online education to its employees.

  다음 주부터 스틸러스사는 직원들에게 무료 온라인 교육을 제공할 예정이다.

22 Dajdor Industries ------- the new product line at a press conference next Monday.
(A) announcing
(B) will announce
(C) announced
(D) being announced

23 Last year, the Hansford Automobile catalog ------- air-conditioning and digital radios as standard features in all automobiles.
(A) listed
(B) list
(C) listing
(D) to list

24 Our team ------- every Monday, so please do not schedule other appointments then.
(A) having met
(B) meeting
(C) meets
(D) met

정답 및 해설 p. 3

1. To ensure prompt return of your laundry, ------- your hotel room number on the tag provided.
   (A) wrote
   (B) written
   (C) write
   (D) writing

2. Civil engineer Lorenzo Raspallo ------- as the guest speaker at the fifth annual Bridge Conservation Colloquium next month.
   (A) to confirm
   (B) to be confirmed
   (C) has been confirmed
   (D) having been confirmed

3. ------- hundreds of technical specialists at the convention in Zurich last month.
   (A) Several
   (B) Many of the
   (C) Having had
   (D) There were

4. People who register for evening classes can fully ------- in all of the activities sponsored by the school.
   (A) participated
   (B) participant
   (C) participate
   (D) participating

5. As the publication date of the sequel to the controversial novel approaches, public ------- is growing exponentially.
   (A) anticipation
   (B) anticipatory
   (C) anticipated
   (D) anticipate

6. Ms. Kimura's employees often ------- her approachable manner and steady leadership.
   (A) to praise
   (B) praising
   (C) praise
   (D) are praised

7. Significant technological ------- have transformed the health-care industry.
   (A) developed
   (B) developmental
   (C) developments
   (D) develops

8. Shan Climbing Gear ------- to open its third retail location in Asia last month but was delayed.
   (A) planning
   (B) is planning
   (C) planned
   (D) was planned

9. The box office at Edger Concert Hall stops selling tickets approximately fifteen minutes after the performances -------.
   (A) had begun
   (B) begin
   (C) to begin
   (D) began

10. Until the computer system is -------, employees should keep track of their hours on the chart in the payroll office.
    (A) repairs
    (B) repaired
    (C) repairing
    (D) repair

11 In designing the interiors for our sleek new trains, we ------- the safety and comfort of passengers.
(A) are prioritized
(B) prioritized
(C) priority
(D) prioritizing

12 Due to safety regulations, visitors are not ------- to enter the factory floor during business hours.
(A) permitting
(B) permitted
(C) permits
(D) permissible

13 A rise in revenue ------- Hashimoto Enterprises to increase its marketing spending.
(A) have been enabling
(B) is being enabled
(C) has enabled
(D) enable

14 When constructing your Eckhart model sailboat, it is important ------- the pieces in quick succession, before the glue has time to dry.
(A) attached
(B) to attach
(C) attaching
(D) attaches

15 Due to new restrictions on international travelers, certain types of plants cannot ------- into most countries without a permit.
(A) bring
(B) be brought
(C) brought
(D) bringing

16 ------- of the management team include improving productivity and reducing annual expenditures.
(A) Priority
(B) Prioritizing
(C) Priorities
(D) Prioritized

17 Mr. Crenshaw ------- the interns to attend the accounting workshop.
(A) encourage
(B) encouraging
(C) encouraged
(D) encouragingly

18 Last year, Entertainment Azusa, Inc., and Sohn Multimedia decided that ------- their expertise and resources would increase profits for both organizations.
(A) combining
(B) combined
(C) combines
(D) combine

19 ------- of homegrown and organic fruits and vegetables, as well as handmade crafts and jewelry, are available for purchase at the Springdale community market.
(A) Varies
(B) Variant
(C) Varieties
(D) Various

20 Every customer service associate is thoroughly ------- to handle all calls regarding delivery options.
(A) train
(B) trains
(C) trained
(D) trainer

목적어 / 보어 / 수식어

평균 4~7문제 출제

무료인강

● 목적어

타동사는 목적어를 가진다.

> The manual explains **the new process**. 그 매뉴얼은 새로운 과정을 설명한다.
> 주어   동사   목적어
>
> → 3형식 동사 뒤에는 목적어가 바로 온다. → explain about (X)
>
> The editor granted **Ms. Porter a deadline extension**. 편집자는 포터 씨에게 마감일 연장을 승인했다.
> 주어   동사   간접목적어   직접목적어
>
> → 4형식 동사의 간접목적어는 '~에게'로 해석되고 직접목적어는 '~을 / 를'로 해석된다.

● 보어

보어는 주어를 보충하거나 목적어를 보충한다.

> Frozen-foods products became **available**. 냉동 식품이 이용 가능해졌다.
> 주어   동사   보어
>
> The information will make your trips **more enjoyable**. 그 정보는 여행을 더욱 즐겁게 만들어 줄 것이다.
> 주어   동사   목적어   목적격 보어

● 수식어

수식어는 문장을 구성하는 필수 성분이 아니므로 긴 문장은 수식어구를 소거하고 파악한다.

> A folk music festival (**with several live performances**) is planned for April 24.
> (몇 가지 라이브 공연이 포함된) 민속 음악 축제가 4월 24일로 예정되어 있다.
>
> → 수식어는 수 일치에 영향을 미치지 않는다.

목적어 / 보어 / 수식어 | ETS 핵심 출제 패턴

목적어 자리에 명사, 보어 자리에 형용사를 넣는 문제가 주로 출제된다. 목적어, 보어, 수식어를 좀 더 잘 이해하려면 동사와 연계하여 학습하는 것도 좋다.

☑ 동사 뒤 목적어 자리를 묻는 문제

Our firm offers excellent ------- as a way to retain its valued employees.

(A) benefits   (B) benefitting

(C) benefitted   (D) beneficial

우리 회사는 소중한 직원들을 붙들어 두기 위한 방편으로 뛰어난 복리후생을 제공한다.

핵심 포인트

동사의 목적어 자리이므로 명사가 들어가야 한다.

▶ 기출공식 1 **p.28**

☑ 전치사 뒤 목적어 자리를 묻는 문제

The mayoral candidates are competing for television -------.

(A) having exposed   (B) exposed

(C) expose   (D) exposure

시장 후보자들은 서로 텔레비전에 많이 나오려고 경쟁하고 있다.

핵심 포인트

전치사의 목적어 자리이므로 명사가 들어가야 한다.

▶ 기출공식 2 **p.28**

☑ 보어 자리를 묻는 문제

The loan application process at Palau Bay Bank is very -------.

(A) efficient   (B) efficiency

(C) efficiently   (D) efficiencies

필라우 베이 은행의 대출 신청 절차는 매우 효율적이다.

핵심 포인트

be동사 뒤 보어 자리이자 부사 뒤 자리이므로 형용사가 들어가야 한다.

▶ 기출공식 5 **p.30**

☑ 수식어 자리를 묻는 문제

------- the foreign delegates visited La Fleur Restaurant, they were served a special mushroom appetizer.

(A) During   (B) Prior to

(C) Even   (D) When

외국 사절단이 라 플뢰르 식당을 방문했을 때, 그들은 스페셜 버섯 전채 요리를 대접 받았다.

핵심 포인트

빈칸 뒤에 완전한 두 문장이 나오므로, 빈칸에는 수식어절을 이끄는 접속사가 들어가야 한다.

▶ 기출공식 8 **p.31**

정답 : (A), (D), (A), (D)

기출공식 1 목적어 자리에는 명사 역할을 하는 어구가 온다.

명사(구)	The JB Hotel provides **ideal meeting spaces** for corporations.
	JB 호텔은 기업들에게 이상적인 회의 공간을 제공한다.
대명사	As Mr. Stone is highly qualified, the committee would like to promote **him**.
	스톤 씨가 자격이 충분하므로 위원회에서는 그를 승진시키고자 한다.
동명사	Ablexar Co. is considering **relocating** their headquarters to the downtown area.
	에이블렉사르사는 도심으로 본사를 이전하는 것을 고려하고 있다.
to부정사	The company is planning **to build** its new plants in this area.
	그 회사는 이 지역에 새로운 공장을 건설하려고 계획하고 있다.
명사절	Mr. Healy agreed **that we should change the design of our Web pages**.
	힐리 씨는 우리의 웹페이지 디자인을 변경해야 한다는 점에 동의했다.

1 Many residents of Alston have expressed ------- to the construction of a new warehouse complex near Fieldspring Lake.
(A) oppose
(B) opposing
(C) opposes
(D) opposition

2 If the discontinued printers are not sold by Friday, Ainley Electronics will offer ------- at 50 percent off.
(A) they
(B) their
(C) them
(D) themselves

3 Vanlin High School is considering ------- solar panels on its roof.
(A) install
(B) to install
(C) installations
(D) installing

기출공식 2 목적어는 타동사 뒤, 전치사 뒤에 온다.

타동사의 목적어	The board of trustees <u>have approved</u> **the budget plan**.
	이사회는 예산 계획을 승인했다.
전치사의 목적어	The date of **expiration** for the manufacturer's warranty is 180 days after purchase.
	제조사의 보증 유효기간은 구입 후 180일입니다

4 Izmit Museum regulations do not permit the ------- of flash photography inside the art gallery.
(A) use
(B) to use
(C) used
(D) usable

5 After much -------, city planning officials determined that the conference center should be built elsewhere.
(A) deliberately
(B) deliberated
(C) deliberate
(D) deliberation

6 Economists note that a change in the price of ------- will not immediately affect consumption levels.
(A) electrify
(B) electrical
(C) electricity
(D) electrically

기출공식 3 긴 목적어는 뒤로 보내고 목적어 자리에 가목적어 it을 대신 쓴다.

Many businesses find to recruit skilled workers difficult.

→ Many businesses find **it** difficult **to recruit skilled workers**.
　　　　　　　　　　　　가목적어　　　　　　　　진목적어

많은 사업체들이 숙련된 일꾼을 구하기 어렵다고 생각한다.

The committee made that it would not postpone the conference clear.

→ The committee made **it** clear **that it would not postpone the conference**.
　　　　　　　　　　　　가목적어　　　　　　　　진목적어

위원회는 총회를 연기하지 않겠다는 점을 분명히 했다.

---

7 The Internet has made ------- easier for vehicle buyers to search for banks that offer the best loans.
(A) they
(B) what
(C) it
(D) us

8 Carlton Clothing's new online store makes it convenient ------- from your home.
(A) shop
(B) shopping
(C) shops
(D) to shop

9 Job applicants will find it useful ------- a candidate profile with a large recruiting agency to help in their employment search.
(A) to complete
(B) completion
(C) are completing
(D) completed

기출공식 4 가목적어 it과 진목적어 사이에는 목적격 보어인 형용사가 온다.

A hybrid vehicle makes it **possible** to reduce greenhouse gases.
　　　　　　　　　　　가목적어 + 형용사 + to부정사구 진목적어

하이브리드 자동차는 온실 가스를 감소시킬 수 있게 해 준다.

The sales director will make it **clear** that we are ready to negotiate a sales contract.
　　　　　　　　　　　　가목적어 + 형용사 + 명사절 진목적어

영업부장은 우리가 판매 계약을 협상할 준비가 되었다는 것을 분명히 밝힐 것이다.

---

10 The AX-5 wireless headset makes it ------- to enjoy music without the use of wires or cables.
(A) possibly
(B) possible
(C) possibilities
(D) more possibility

11 According to recent feedback, some new interns have found it ------- to complete the in-house training program within the one week orientation period.
(A) difficulty
(B) difficult
(C) difficulties
(D) difficultly

12 Unexpected software issues may make it ------- to delay the launch of our new mobile phones to next year.
(A) necessary
(B) necessarily
(C) necessities
(D) necessitating

기출공식 5   보어 자리에는 형용사 또는 명사가 온다.

■ **형용사 보어: 주어/목적어의 상태나 성질을 설명한다.**

형용사	The sports complex is **available** for private functions every weekend. 그 종합운동장은 주말마다 개인 행사에 이용할 수 있다.
현재분사	The audience found the musical **entertaining**. 관객들은 그 뮤지컬이 재미있다고 생각했다.
과거분사	The effectiveness of measures to reduce air pollution remains **limited**. 공기 오염을 줄이기 위한 조치들의 유효성은 여전히 제한적이다.

■ **명사 보어: 주어/목적어와 동격 관계일 때는 명사 보어를 쓴다.**

After years of experience, Mr. Windsor became **the right candidate** for this position.
다년간 경험을 쌓은 후, 원저 씨는 이 직위에 적임자가 되었다. (원저 씨 = 적임자)

---

13 The internship program is mutually ------- to students of Borden College and to local businesses.
(A) benefits
(B) benefited
(C) beneficial
(D) beneficially

14 As a five-time recipient of the Employee of the Month award, Ms. Kuvia was a natural ------- for the new Team Leader position.
(A) choice
(B) choose
(C) choosing
(D) chosen

15 Ms. Itoh from AFT Technology Consulting was ------- in getting everyone familiar with our new computer system.
(A) help
(B) helper
(C) helpful
(D) helpfully

기출공식 6   2형식 동사는 주격 보어를 가진다.

대표적인 2형식 동사: be ~이다 **become** ~이 되다 **remain** ~인 채로 남아 있다 **stay** ~인 채로 있다

According to the reviewers, the concert was very [**impressive** / ~~impressively~~].
평론가들에 따르면 그 콘서트는 아주 인상적이었다.

Your personal information in your résumé remains [**confidential** / ~~confidentially~~].
이력서에 있는 귀하의 개인 정보는 기밀로 유지됩니다.

---

16 Lutzen Department Store hopes your shopping experience will be -------.
(A) enjoy
(B) enjoys
(C) enjoyable
(D) enjoying

17 *The Oliveira Dining Guide*, an online directory of restaurants, is ------- by cuisine type, price range, and location.
(A) search
(B) searcher
(C) searches
(D) searchable

18 We must ------- aware of rapidly changing technology or face a decrease in company profits in the long run.
(A) reach
(B) result
(C) reveal
(D) remain

기출공식 7 5형식 동사는 목적격 보어를 가진다.

대표적인 5형식 동사: make ~하게 만들다 **find** ~라고 생각하다 **keep** ~하게 유지하다 **consider** ~라고 여기다

We keep our prices [**reasonable** / ~~reasonably~~] in order to stay competitive.
우리는 경쟁력을 유지하기 위해 가격을 적정하게 유지한다.

Many biologists consider Dr. Patterson's study [**conclusive** / ~~conclusively~~].
많은 생물학자들이 패터슨 박사의 연구가 결정적이라고 여긴다.

19 Moltor Labs plans to make its departments less ------- by eliminating unnecessary paperwork.
(A) waste
(B) wasteful
(C) wastefully
(D) wasting

20 Speakers can make their seminars more ------- with visual aids.
(A) effective
(B) effects
(C) effect
(D) effectiveness

21 Many students find the suggested reading ------- for understanding the course's content.
(A) usefully
(B) useful
(C) using
(D) use

빈출

기출공식 8 수식어는 문장에서 다양한 위치에 올 수 있다.

전치사구 (**Due to an unexpected system error**), we had problems (**with processing your order**). 예기치 못한 시스템 오류로 귀하의 주문 처리 과정에 문제가 생겼습니다.

to부정사구 The manager's effort (**to meet the customers' needs**) was outstanding.
고객들의 요구를 충족시키려는 부장의 노력은 탁월했다.

분사구 A special sale (**celebrating our fifth anniversary**) will start on March 15.
5주년을 기념하기 위한 특별 세일이 3월 15일에 시작됩니다.

관계사절 The event, (**which was so popular last year**), is expected to draw more visitors this year. 지난해에 무척 인기 있었던 그 행사는 올해 더 많은 방문객을 유치할 것으로 예상된다.

부사절 A check-engine indicator flashes repeatedly (**when maintenance is necessary**).
정비가 필요하면 엔진 점검 표시등이 반복하여 깜박인다.

22 No one is allowed onto the factory floor ------- an identification badge.
(A) without
(B) unless
(C) only
(D) although

23 ------- the initial application form has been received in our office, you will not be required to provide any further documentation.
(A) Whether
(B) Once
(C) As if
(D) Yet

24 ------- better serve our customers, Lipscon Auto is relocating to a larger retail space.
(A) In order to
(B) Due to
(C) With regard to
(D) Owing to

정답 및 해설 p.8

1 Heidt Used Appliance Store guarantees that your purchase will arrive in working -------.
(A) condition
(B) conditional
(C) conditionally
(D) conditioned

2 Analyst Lucy Dumont, from the Switzerland office, has a thorough ------- of European financial markets.
(A) knowledgeable
(B) knowledge
(C) knowing
(D) to know

3 Siam Business Suites has requested a one-month ------- to its building permit.
(A) extend
(B) extending
(C) extension
(D) extended

4 Customers expressed dissatisfaction with the cost of the phone, but complaints about the user interface were relatively -------.
(A) rarest
(B) rare
(C) rarity
(D) rarely

5 Alicia Raini's campaign for mayor will probably be ------- because people approve of her policies.
(A) succeed
(B) successful
(C) successfully
(D) succeeded

6 We could not be ------- that Henrietta Munoz was named the Employee of the Month.
(A) happier
(B) happiest
(C) happiness
(D) happily

7 Taking courses at the Bedford Business Center can lead to greater opportunities for professional -------.
(A) grown
(B) grow
(C) grows
(D) growth

8 Many of our employees have reported that they have found the new computer program to be quite -------.
(A) benefit
(B) benefits
(C) benefitting
(D) beneficial

9 A project manager will be responsible for the information ------- to external team members.
(A) distribute
(B) distribution
(C) distributes
(D) is distributed

10 While remaining ------- to customers who have supported it for decades, McGill Electronics will diversify in all areas of its business.
(A) loyalty
(B) loyalties
(C) loyally
(D) loyal

11 Because the director requested changes to the script, Aachen Pictures has rescheduled the ------- of the documentary for March.
(A) releasable
(B) released
(C) release
(D) releaser

12 In keeping with Barrett International's effort to provide a comfortable work environment, the company's new buildings are ------- and well lit.
(A) spacious
(B) spacing
(C) spaciousness
(D) spaces

13 Mr. Ozuka would like to discuss his ------- of the changes to the most recent budget proposal.
(A) impressionable
(B) impressions
(C) impressive
(D) impress

14 This document certifies that the water samples were collected in accordance with the ------- established by the Clean Air and Water Commission.
(A) proceeds
(B) procedures
(C) proceeding
(D) proceed

15 ------- you decide to have your kitchen renovated, be sure to get cost estimates from several contractors.
(A) When
(B) Would
(C) Always
(D) Near

16 Somwan Games' sales associates follow up with the shipping department when customers have not confirmed ------- of an order.
(A) receive
(B) receives
(C) receipt
(D) received

17 Local manufacturers have been ------- to hire additional employees until productivity improves.
(A) hesitate
(B) hesitation
(C) hesitated
(D) hesitant

18 Mehlway Beverage Ltd. is using unique package designs to make its health drinks ------- to a wider range of consumers.
(A) attracts
(B) attractively
(C) attractive
(D) attracting

19 Frequent changes in the market make it ------- for stereo equipment producers to anticipate demand with much confidence or precision.
(A) hardly
(B) hardness
(C) hard
(D) harden

20 Pack-Pro Company has launched a new Web site ------- part of a rebranding effort.
(A) such
(B) sudden
(C) was
(D) as

UNIT 03 명사

평균 2~3문제 출제

무료인강

● 명사형태

명사는 주로 -tion / -sion / -ment / -ance / -ness / -ship / -ty / -sm / -sis / -ure를 어미로 가진다.

-tion	comple**tion** 완성	addi**tion** 추가	-sion	revi**sion** 개정	expan**sion** 확장
-ment	assign**ment** 임무	ship**ment** 배송	-ance	assist**ance** 지원	mainten**ance** 유지
-ness	fit**ness** 건강	clean**liness** 청결	-ship	owner**ship** 소유(권)	reader**ship** 독자층
-ty	facul**ty** 교수진	proper**ty** 부동산	-sm	enthusia**sm** 열정	touri**sm** 관광
-sis	analy**sis** 분석	ba**sis** 근거, 기준	-ure	fail**ure** 실패	proced**ure** 절차

● 명사의 종류

셀 수 있는지 여부에 따라 가산명사 vs. 불가산명사로 구분된다.

가산명사	셀 수 있으므로 a / an을 붙일 수 있고 복수형이 있는 명사 an item 물건, managers 매니저, a purchase 구매품, refunds 환불 단수 또는 복수 취급할 수 있는 집합명사 committee 위원회, staff 직원들, personnel 직원들
불가산명사	셀 수 없으므로 a / an을 붙일 수 없고 복수형이 없는 명사 access 이용, information 정보, consent 동의

의미에 따라 사람 vs. 사물 / 추상 명사로 구분된다.

사람 명사	a customer 고객, an employee 직원, an investor 투자자 → 사람 명사는 가산명사이다.
사물 / 추상 명사	cooperation 협력, an appliance 장치, a negotiation 협상 → 사물 / 추상 명사는 가산 또는 불가산명사이다.

두 개의 명사를 붙여 쓰는 복합명사가 있다.

명사 + 명사	customer review 고객 후기, product launch 제품 출시, sales department 영업 부서

명사 | ETS 핵심 출제 패턴

주어, 목적어, 보어 자리에 명사를 채워 넣는 문제, 명사의 가산 / 불가산, 사람 / 사물 / 추상 명사를 구별하는 문제, 복합명사 문제가 주로 출제된다.

☑ 주어 자리에 알맞은 품사를 묻는 문제

Fred's superb ------- to detail is his best attribute as a graphic artist.

(A) attends   (B) attended
(C) attendant   (D) attention

세부 사항에 기울이는 프레드의 뛰어난 주의력은 그래픽 아티스트로서 그가 갖춘 최고의 자질이다.

핵심 포인트

주어 자리에 소유격과 형용사의 수식을 받는 명사가 들어가야 한다.

▶ 기출공식 1 **p.36**

☑ 목적어 자리에 알맞은 품사를 묻는 문제

Please review the ------- for new safety procedures, and add your comments.

(A) proposing   (B) propose
(C) proposes   (D) proposal

새로운 안전 절차 제안서를 검토하고 의견을 덧붙여 주세요.

핵심 포인트

동사의 목적어 자리이므로 명사가 들어가야 한다.

▶ 기출공식 1 **p.36**

☑ 사람 명사와 사물 / 추상 명사를 구별하는 문제

------- for the position of Health Inspector must pass an examination given by the City Health Department.

(A) Applications   (B) Applying
(C) Applicants   (D) Applies

위생 검사관직 지원자들은 시 보건국에서 시행하는 시험에 합격해야 한다.

핵심 포인트

주어 자리이므로 명사가 들어가며, 문맥상 사람 명사가 필요하다.

▶ 기출공식 6 **p.38**

☑ 복합명사 문제

Mr. Shmidov hired two lawyers to help with future contract -------.

(A) negotiates   (B) negotiations
(C) negotiator   (D) negotiable

쉬미도브 씨는 향후 계약 협상을 도울 변호사를 두 명 고용했다.

핵심 포인트

전치사의 목적어 자리로 복합명사를 이루는 명사가 들어가야 한다.

▶ 기출공식 8 **p.39**

정답 : (D), (D), (C), (B)

기출공식 1 명사는 주어, 목적어, 보어 역할을 한다.

주어 The [**personality** / ~~personal~~] of each client is reflected in our creative interior designs.
고객 저마다의 개성이 창의적인 인테리어 디자인에 반영된다.

목적어 The billing department <u>has received</u> your [**payment** / ~~payable~~].
동사의 목적어
청구부서에서 귀하가 지불한 돈을 수령했습니다.

The number of people who visit the region <u>for</u> [**pleasure** / ~~pleasant~~] continues to
전치사의 목적어
increase.
그 지역을 관광차 방문하는 사람들의 수가 계속 증가하고 있다.

보어 <u>Ms. Green</u> is a qualified [**employee** / ~~employ~~] considering her expertise.
주어와 동격
전문지식을 고려할 때 그린 씨는 자질이 있는 직원이다.

1 The bridge ------- has caused major traffic delays on River Road and Main Street.
(A) closes
(B) close
(C) closure
(D) closed

2 International experience is the main ------- that separates Mr. Sloan from the other candidates for the position.
(A) qualified
(B) qualification
(C) qualify
(D) qualifying

3 Once the berries are harvested, Green Fields Farms washes and packages the fruit for ------- to retail stores.
(A) distribution
(B) distributional
(C) distributed
(D) distributive

기출공식 2 관사, 소유격, 형용사 뒤에는 명사가 온다.

관사 + 명사 Some of **the equipment** in **the meeting rooms** should be upgraded.
회의실 장비 일부는 업그레이드되어야 한다.

소유격 + 명사 A number of local newspapers have written articles about **her accomplishments.** 많은 지역 신문들이 그녀의 업적에 대한 기사를 썼다.

형용사 + 명사 We have received **positive feedback** concerning the **recent changes** to our Web site. 우리는 웹사이트의 최근 변화에 대해 긍정적인 반응을 받았다.

4 While all her drawings are based on historical photographs, Janis Tierney relies on her ------- to fill in the details.
(A) imagine
(B) imaginative
(C) imagination
(D) imaginary

5 The ------- fee for any of the Logistics Management courses is €25 a person.
(A) enrollment
(B) enroll
(C) enrolled
(D) enrolls

6 Our service department has received numerous ------- about the new TZ-2000 processor overheating.
(A) complain
(B) complaining
(C) complainer
(D) complaints

기출공식 3 명사는 가산명사와 불가산명사로 나뉜다.

혼동하기 쉬운 가산명사	혼동하기 쉬운 불가산명사	기타 빈출 불가산명사	
a plan 계획	planning 기획	information 정보	knowledge 지식
a permit 허가증	permission 허가	advice 조언	change 잔돈
a fund 자금	funding 자금 조달	feedback 의견	research 연구
an approach 접근법	access 접근	equipment 장비	news 뉴스
a certificate 인증서	certification 인증	furniture 가구	damage 손상
a product 제품	production 생산	consent 동의	luggage 수하물
a process 과정	processing 처리	merchandise 상품	baggage 수하물
a seat 좌석	seating 좌석	machinery 기계류	cash 현금

Residents should see the building manager to obtain **a parking** [**permit** / ~~permission~~].
주민은 주차 허가증을 받으려면 건물 관리인을 찾아야 한다.

---

7 The interviewee expressed interest in a marketing job; however, the previous positions on her résumé were exclusively in -------.
(A) accountable
(B) accountant
(C) accounted
(D) accounting

8 To apply for a driving -------, you must show two forms of identification.
(A) permission
(B) permits
(C) permit
(D) permitted

9 Privately-owned companies often have more freedom to focus on long-term -------.
(A) plan
(B) to plan
(C) planned
(D) planning

빈출

기출공식 4 가산명사는 관사가 붙거나 복수형으로 쓰이고, 불가산명사는 복수형이 없다.

관사 + 가산 단수	The firm will place **an advertisement** to find an assistant. 그 회사는 비서를 구하는 광고를 게재할 것이다.
(관사) + 가산 복수	The mailroom employees are required to perform **tasks** that involve heavy lifting. 우편실 직원들은 무거운 것을 들어올리는 작업을 할 수 있어야 한다.
불가산	Mr. Yang's **advice** was very helpful for our business expansion. 양 씨의 조언은 우리의 사업 확장에 큰 도움이 되었다.

→ 불가산명사는 복수형으로 쓸 수 없으며, 앞에 부정관사 a / an이 올 수 없다. (*정관사 the는 올 수 있다)

---

10 Detailed ------- for scanning documents with your Exton scanner are provided on page 9 of the user's manual.
(A) instruct
(B) instructed
(C) instructions
(D) instructors

11 The pharmacy is required to collect ------- at the time prescriptions are filled.
(A) paid
(B) payers
(C) payment
(D) pays

12 The committee accepted the proposal in principle, without having examined the -------.
(A) specifics
(B) specify
(C) specific
(D) specifically

정답 및 해설 p. 12

기출공식 5 한정사 뒤에 오는 명사는 단/복수를 구분해서 써야 한다.

부정관사 a/an	+ 가산명사의 단수	a task, an employee
정관사 the	+ 가산명사의 단·복수/불가산명사	the file(s) 또는 the access
지시형용사 this/that	+ 가산명사의 단수/불가산명사	this result 또는 that advice
지시형용사 these/those	+ 가산명사의 복수	these results, those requests
each/every/another	+ 가산명사의 단수	each product, every month, another job
all/other	+ 가산명사의 복수/불가산명사	all employees 또는 other equipment
any/no	+ 가산명사의 단·복수/불가산명사	any customer(s) 또는 no information

Each room has its own bathroom with **a shower**. 각 방에는 샤워실이 있는 욕실이 있다.

→ 가산명사의 단수 앞에는 한정사가 붙는다.

13 Because the service department is understaffed, it can take five days for customer inquiries to receive a -------.
(A) respond
(B) responding
(C) responded
(D) response

14 All ------- to the auto production plant must register at the security checkpoint before entering.
(A) visit
(B) visitation
(C) visitors
(D) visiting

15 Each seminar ------- should be prepared to discuss his or her career goals.
(A) participant
(B) participants
(C) participation
(D) participated

기출공식 6 사람/사물/추상 명사는 문맥에 맞게 선택해야 한다.

an attendee 참석자	attendance 참석	a competitor 경쟁자	competition 경쟁
an attendant 안내원	attention 주의, 관심	a consumer 소비자	consumption 소비
an inspector 검사자	inspection 검사	an investor 투자자	investment 투자
a participant 참여자	participation 참여	a contributor 기고자	contribution 기여
a distributor 유통업자	distribution 유통, 배포	an architect 건축가	architecture 건축
a critic 비평가	criticism 비평, 비난	a consultant 상담가	consulting 자문

[Inspectors / ~~Inspection~~] from the government will visit tomorrow. 정부 조사관들이 내일 방문할 것이다.

16 Mr. Schweizer has worked under my ------- as an editorial assistant for the past five years.
(A) supervise
(B) supervises
(C) supervised
(D) supervision

17 According to local laws, all restaurants should undergo a health and safety ------- once each year.
(A) inspection
(B) inspect
(C) inspecting
(D) inspector

18 ------- of city buses will attend a training session on new vehicles in the coming months.
(A) Operations
(B) Operators
(C) Operate
(D) Operating

기출공식 7 형용사처럼 보이지만 명사로 쓰이는 어휘들이 있다.

alternative	형 대안	형 대안의	approval 승인	arrival 도착
objective	형 목표	형 객관적인	disposal 처분	rental 임대
representative	형 대표자, 직원	형 대표적인	initiative 계획, 진취성	renewal 갱신
professional	형 전문가	형 전문적인	withdrawal 인출	removal 제거
potential	형 잠재력	형 잠재적인	appraisal 평가	proposal 제안(서)
periodical	형 정기 간행물	형 정기 간행의	referral 소개, 추천	characteristic 특징

Over 3,000 computer [**professionals** / ~~profession~~] will attend the conference.
컴퓨터 전문가 3천여 명이 회의에 참석할 예정이다.

19 A ------- from Jensen-Colmes Corporation will be happy to meet with prospective job applicants at the Westborough Job Fair.
(A) represent
(B) representing
(C) representative
(D) representation

20 Interns in some fields can show ------- by proposing their own projects.
(A) initially
(B) initiated
(C) initiative
(D) initial

21 Napier Corporation consults healthcare ------- when designing its fitness equipment.
(A) profession
(B) professional
(C) professionals
(D) professionally

기출공식 8 복합명사는 '명사 + 명사' 구조이며, 복수형은 뒤 명사에 -(e)s가 붙는다.

rental agreement 임대 계약서 registration fee 등록비 customer satisfaction 고객 만족 employee productivity 직원 생산성 security reason 안전상의 이유	office supplies 사무용품 application form 신청서 job opening 일자리 공석 reference letter 추천서 attendance rate 참석률	retail price 소매가 expiration date 만기일 safety regulation 안전 규정 return policy 환불 정책 job applicant 구직자

[**Safety** / ~~Safe~~] **inspectors** <u>visit</u> us every month. 안전 검사관들이 매달 우리를 방문한다.
→ 형용사가 올 경우 '안전한 검사관'이라는 의미가 되므로 정답이 될 수 없다. 또한 동사는 뒤 명사에 수 일치한다.

22 To increase employee -------, Aelch Medical Supplies rewards employees for outstanding professional contributions.
(A) produced
(B) productivity
(C) productively
(D) will produce

23 Unfortunately, the newly manufactured electronic components do not meet the quality ------- of Gem Associates.
(A) requires
(B) requirements
(C) require
(D) requiring

24 Over the years, businesses have developed and tested various methods to measure employee -------.
(A) performer
(B) performs
(C) performed
(D) performance

정답 및 해설 p. 14

ETS TEST

1. The Manila Wellness Center has part-time and temporary employment ------- for certified nursing attendants in our Makati branch.
(A) opens
(B) openings
(C) openness
(D) opener

2. Referring to the ------- in the user's manual will help you to identify the parts of the workbench.
(A) illustrate
(B) illustrator
(C) illustration
(D) illustrated

3. While Zoulie Studios is a large ------- of animated films, its annual revenues are lower than those of its competitors.
(A) productive
(B) produce
(C) production
(D) producer

4. All of Molina Language Institute's ------- have three or more years of experience and a valid teaching credential.
(A) instructed
(B) instruction
(C) instructing
(D) instructors

5. About 30 percent of our magazine's ------- reside in Singapore.
(A) subscriptions
(B) subscribe
(C) subscribing
(D) subscribers

6. Built in 1885, the Halprin Hill Bridge has been preserved because of its historical -------.
(A) signify
(B) significant
(C) significance
(D) significantly

7. The city council will meet tomorrow to field questions from ------- concerning the new water tower.
(A) resident
(B) residents
(C) residences
(D) residential

8. Our yearlong marketing efforts ensured consumer ------- of the new ice cream flavor.
(A) accept
(B) acceptance
(C) acceptable
(D) accepts

9. The monthly rental fee for the apartment includes the shared cost of ongoing ------- in the surrounding gardens.
(A) maintaining
(B) maintenance
(C) maintained
(D) maintains

10. Earlier today, IGY Corporation released a ------- confirming its plans for expansion in South America.
(A) state
(B) stating
(C) statement
(D) stated

11 All staff members should log in to their time and labor ------- daily to record their hours worked.
(A) accounts
(B) accounted
(C) accountant
(D) accountable

12 The following list details the information Ms. Neylon will need for her ------- of potential corporate clients.
(A) analysis
(B) analyze
(C) analyzed
(D) to analyze

13 For 30 years, Big Top Prop Company has been the premier ------- of circus equipment for troupes around the world.
(A) providing
(B) provision
(C) provider
(D) provides

14 The board of directors of Bridgeworks Corporation will vote on the ------- to modify the company's investment policies.
(A) propose
(B) proposing
(C) proposal
(D) proposed

15 A study found that government ------- on building permits in Clarksburg have led to better city planning.
(A) regulations
(B) regulates
(C) regulating
(D) regulation

16 All pharmacists must sign up to work one eight-hour ------- per week.
(A) shift
(B) shifts
(C) shifted
(D) shifting

17 All members of the Benton Botanical Garden will receive a discount voucher for ------- at the Rosebush Café.
(A) use
(B) useful
(C) usefully
(D) used

18 Evelyn Chu's Web site provides consumers with reviews and price ------- of electronic devices currently on the market.
(A) compare
(B) comparisons
(C) have compared
(D) compares

19 For clients seeking environmentally conscious commercial and residential construction, Green Spaces Ltd. provides an affordable -------.
(A) alternated
(B) alternating
(C) alternatively
(D) alternative

20 ------- will receive a $50 gift card and compensation for travel.
(A) Participating
(B) Participants
(C) Participation
(D) Participant

UNIT 04 대명사

평균 1~2문제 출제

무료인강

● 인칭 대명사의 형태

인칭대명사는 격에 따라 다른 형태를 지닌다.

인칭	수	주격	소유격	목적격	소유대명사
1인칭	단수	I	my	me	mine
	복수	we	our	us	ours
2인칭	단/복수	you	your	you	yours
3인칭	단수	he	his	him	his
		she	her	her	hers
		it	its	it	-
	복수	they	their	them	theirs

● 대명사의 종류

인칭대명사

나, 너, 그녀 등 화자와 청자, 제3자를 가리키는 대명사

재귀대명사

인칭대명사에 -self를 붙여 '~ 자신'이라는 뜻을 가지는 대명사

단수	myself	yourself	himself	herself	itself
복수	ourselves	yourselves	themselves		

지시대명사

이것, 저것 등 대상을 가리키는 대명사

this / these	이것/이것들	This is a formal inspection. 이것은 공식적인 점검입니다.
		These are important files. 이것들은 중요한 서류들입니다.
that / those	그것/그것들	That is an interesting topic. 그것은 흥미로운 주제입니다.
		Those are strictly confidential. 그것들은 극비 사항입니다.

부정대명사

대상이 확실하게 정해지지 않아 막연하게 '어떤 것, 모든 것, 아무것' 등으로 일컫는 대명사

some(one / thing)	어떤 것	Something is not working properly. 무엇인가가 제대로 작동되지 않고 있다.
any(one / thing)	어떤 사람	Anyone can join us. 어떤 사람이든 우리와 합류할 수 있습니다.

대명사 | ETS 핵심 출제 패턴

인칭대명사의 격을 구분하는 문제가 매회 1문제 이상 꾸준히 출제된다. 지시대명사와 부정대명사 문제도 종종 출제된다.

☑ 목적어 자리에 대명사의 알맞은 격을 선택하는 문제

Corvo Graphic Designs will help ------- to create a suitable logo for our newly formed company.

(A) our   (B) ours

(C) us   (D) we

코보 그래픽 디자인스는 우리가 새롭게 설립한 회사에 적합한 로고를 만드는 데 도움을 줄 것이다.

핵심 포인트

동사의 목적어 자리이므로 목적격 인칭대명사가 들어가야 한다.

▶ 기출공식 1 **p.44**

☑ 명사구 앞에 대명사의 알맞은 격을 선택하는 문제

Mr. Aromdee will prepare a dish from ------- hometown of Bangkok.

(A) he   (B) his

(C) him   (D) himself

아롬디 씨는 자신의 고향인 방콕에서 먹는 요리를 준비할 것이다.

핵심 포인트

뒤에 오는 명사를 수식할 수 있는 소유격 인칭대명사가 들어가야 한다.

▶ 기출공식 1 **p.44**

☑ 강조 용법의 재귀대명사를 선택하는 문제

The new guidebook is generously illustrated, and the author took all of the photos -------.

(A) his   (B) himself

(C) him   (D) his own

신간 가이드북은 삽화가 풍부한데 저자가 모든 사진을 직접 찍었다.

핵심 포인트

'직접, 스스로'라는 강조의 의미로 재귀대명사가 들어가야 한다.

▶ 기출공식 2 **p.44**

☑ 지시대명사를 선택하는 문제

Only ------- who have obtained permission from the theater are allowed to take photographs during the play.

(A) those   (B) each

(C) most   (D) another

연극이 진행되는 동안에는 극장의 허가를 받은 사람들만 사진을 찍을 수 있습니다.

핵심 포인트

'사람들'을 의미하는 지시대명사가 들어가야 한다.

▶ 기출공식 3 **p.45**

정답 : (C), (B), (B), (A)

기출공식 1 인칭대명사는 격에 맞게 써야 한다.

주격 New customers are offered a twenty percent discount if **they** register online.
신규 고객은 온라인으로 등록하면 20퍼센트 할인 받는다.

→ 앞에 나온 복수명사 **new customers**를 대신해서 동사 앞에 올 수 있는 주격 **they**를 쓴다.

소유격 Jane Wiseman has **her** own publishing company.
제인 와이즈먼은 본인 소유의 출판사가 있다.

→ 앞에 나온 명사 **Jane Wiseman**을 대신해서, 명사구 앞에 올 수 있는 소유격 **her**를 쓴다.

목적격 Mr. Powell is very creative, and I'd like to ask **him** to work with **us**.
파월 씨가 아주 창의적이므로, 저는 그에게 우리와 함께 일하자고 요청하고자 합니다.

→ 타동사 ask의 목적어로 목적격 **him**, 전치사 with의 목적어로 목적격 **us**를 쓴다.

소유대명사 After he had finished his report, Mr. Abbot helped Ms. Farm complete **hers**.
애벗 씨는 자신의 보고서를 끝낸 뒤 팜 씨가 그녀의 보고서를 작성하는 것을 도왔다.

→ 앞에 나온 명사 **report**가 의미상 중복되므로 **her report**를 대신해서 **hers**를 쓴다.

---

1 Ms. Schwarz advised Mr. Hartmann to publish the results of his current project before ------- requests a promotion.
(A) himself   (B) him
(C) his   (D) he

2 Sales department members must obtain permission from ------- supervisors before applying for travel reimbursement.
(A) they   (B) them
(C) their   (D) theirs

3 Because many proposals were presented to the city council, Mr. Lin and Ms. Jones were pleased when ------- was accepted.
(A) they   (B) them
(C) their   (D) theirs

기출공식 2 재귀대명사(-self)는 재귀, 강조 용법 및 관용 표현이 있다.

재귀 용법 동사의 주체(주어)와 목적어가 동일할 때 목적어 자리에 쓴다.

We pride **ourselves** on the professionalism of our employees.
우리는 직원들의 전문성에 대해 우리 스스로를 자랑스럽게 생각합니다.

강조 용법 주어 뒤나 문장 끝에서 '직접'이라는 의미로 주어를 강조하며, 생략 가능하다.

Director Mark Fielder welcomed the newly recruited employees **himself**.
마크 필더 이사는 신입사원들을 직접 환영했다.

관용 표현 by oneself 혼자서(= on one's own) for oneself 혼자 힘으로, 직접

On the last day of PC training, the intern entered all the data **by herself**.
PC 교육 마지막 날 그 수습사원은 모든 데이터를 혼자서 입력했다.   (= on her own)

---

4 Ki-nam Yi has the expertise needed and so has assigned ------- to the Servoss Limited negotiations.
(A) he   (B) his
(C) him   (D) himself

5 Recently the restaurant's kitchen has been understaffed, so the manager ------- will assist in food preparation this week.
(A) her   (B) herself
(C) hers   (D) her own

6 After three weeks of training, the engineering interns will be asked to develop a new product on -------.
(A) their own   (B) them
(C) themselves   (D) they

기출공식 3   지시대명사는 앞서 언급된 명사를 대신할 때나 '사람들'을 의미할 때 쓴다.

■ **대신하는 명사가 단수이면 that, 복수이면 those를 쓴다. 이때 this, these, them 등은 쓸 수 없다.**

This quarter's sales figures are similar to **those** of the preceding quarter.
<u>(= sales figures)</u>   <u>수식어구</u>

이번 분기 매출액은 지난 분기의 매출액과 비슷하다.

■ **'사람들'을 나타내는 지시대명사는 those이며, 관계사절, 분사구, 전치사구 등의 수식을 받을 수 있다.**

Ms. Lu will mail a copy of the annual report to **those** <u>who cannot attend the meeting.</u>
<u>관계사절</u>

루 씨는 회의에 참석하지 못하는 사람들에게 연례보고서 한 부를 우송할 것이다.

Those <u>experiencing problems with the new software</u> should report to the manager.
<u>분사구</u>

새로운 소프트웨어에 문제가 있는 사람들은 매니저에게 보고해야 한다.

The event is open only to **those** <u>with an invitation.</u> 그 행사는 초대장을 받은 사람들에게만 공개된다.
<u>전치사구</u>

---

7 Reviews posted on the Manipur Footwear Web site, especially ------- relating to product quality, have grown more positive.
(A) few
(B) another
(C) those
(D) anyone

8 ------- who wish to participate in the seminar offered by XMT Consulting must register by Wednesday at 5:00 P.M.
(A) Those
(B) Them
(C) Themselves
(D) Theirs

9 Director Kawamura's position is that ------- with expertise in the field should be responsible for the final hiring decision.
(A) them
(B) those
(C) what
(D) whose

기출공식 4   '-one / -body', '-thing'이 붙는 부정대명사는 제한적인 수식을 받는다.

■ **everyone, everything, anyone, anything, nothing 등은 관계사절, 분사구, 전치사구 등의 수식을 받을 수 있다.**

Anyone <u>who is involved with the project</u> should meet Ms. Kim today.
<u>관계사절</u>
그 프로젝트에 관련된 사람은 누구나 오늘 김 씨를 만나야 한다.

■ **단, 이러한 부정대명사들은 '중에서'를 나타내는 of 앞에서는 쓰지 않는다.**

[**All** / ~~Everyone~~] <u>of the candidates</u> have the necessary skills. 지원자들 중 모두 필수 능력을 갖추고 있다.

---

10 ------- who wants to participate in the seminar on November 12 must contact Ms. Saraswati by Friday.
(A) Others
(B) They
(C) Herself
(D) Anyone

11 ------- of the passengers on flight 246 missed connecting flights in Dublin as a result of the weather delay.
(A) Everybody
(B) Someone
(C) Whom
(D) Several

12 ------- responding to the restaurant survey will receive a $10 gift certificate to the Rangely Café.
(A) Whoever
(B) Whose
(C) Someone
(D) Everyone

정답 및 해설 p.18

- **one은 정해지지 않은 가산 단수명사, ones는 정해지지 않은 복수명사를 대신한다.**

  The laptop was replaced with a new **one**. 그 노트북은 새것으로 교체되었다.

(a new one = a new laptop)

  The lights will be replaced with brighter **ones**. 조명들이 더 밝은 것들로 교체될 것이다.

(brighter ones = brighter lights)

- **another는 앞서 언급한 것을 제외한 '또 다른 하나'를 가리킨다.**

  If you are not satisfied with the design, we can offer you **another**.
  디자인이 마음에 들지 않으면 또 다른 것을 제안하겠습니다. (another = another design)

- **the other는 일정한 수 중에서 나머지 하나를, the others는 일정한 수 중에서 나머지 전부를 가리킨다.**

  Of the two samples, Ms. Porter took one and Mr. Han took **the other**.
  샘플 2개 중에서 포터 씨가 한 개를 가져갔고, 한 씨가 나머지 하나를 가져갔다. (the other = the other sample)

  Just one of the applicants is qualified, so **the others** will not be considered.

(the others = the other applicants)
  지원자들 중에서 단 한 명만 자격을 갖춰서 나머지 지원자들은 고려되지 않을 것이다.

- **others는 수가 정해지지 않은 다수를 가리킨다.**

  Some of our products got excellent reviews, while **others** need improvement.
  우리 제품 일부는 아주 좋은 평가를 받았지만 다른 제품들은 개선이 필요하다. (others = other products)

13 Please use the printers on the third floor for high volume print jobs while ------- on the fifth floor are being repaired.
(A) this
(B) either
(C) the other
(D) the ones

14 After the tremendous success of her first restaurant, Vivienne Blanc decided to open -------.
(A) another
(B) every
(C) other
(D) anyone

15 The tall plant requires more sunlight than ------- in the waiting room.
(A) which
(B) one another
(C) the others
(D) whichever

타동사 뒤 They have known **each other** for years. 그들은 수년간 서로를 알고 있었다.

전치사 뒤 Many buyers and sellers deal with **one another** online.
많은 구매자와 판매자가 온라인으로 거래한다.

→ 주어 자리에는 오지 못하므로 주어 자리 빈칸에서는 오답으로 소거한다.

16 Staff members should work in pairs during the training workshop to help ------- master the procedure for handling customer service inquiries.
(A) one such
(B) each other
(C) yourself
(D) everything

17 The open-plan office will lead employees to interact with ------- more frequently.
(A) ourselves
(B) one another
(C) the other
(D) those

18 While some of the reader comments were critical, ------- were full of praise.
(A) both
(B) someone
(C) each other
(D) others

기출공식 7 수량을 나타내는 부정대명사는 수 일치에 유의해야 한다.

- **all / some / most / half + of the[소유격] + 복수명사 + 복수동사 (단, 불가산명사가 오면 단수동사가 온다.)**
  Most of our facilities are currently unavailable. 우리 시설 중 대부분을 현재 이용할 수 없다.

- **both / (a) few / many / several + of the[소유격] + 복수명사 + 복수동사**
  Several of Mr. Roy's novels are best-selling works. 로이 씨의 소설 중 몇 편은 베스트셀러이다.

- **one / each + of the + 복수명사 + 단수동사**
  Each of the cameras is priced less than $200. 카메라 각각은 가격이 200달러 이하로 책정되었다.

- **either / neither / none of the[소유격] + 복수명사 + 단/복수동사 (단, 불가산명사가 오면 단수동사가 온다.)**
  Neither of the two older models is / are available. 두 구형 모델 모두 구할 수 없다.

19 Before takeoff, flight attendants must ensure that ------- of the passengers is properly seated.
(A) every
(B) all
(C) each
(D) much

20 Unfortunately, ------- of the two venues has the capacity needed to host Tsai Technology's annual banquet.
(A) most
(B) several
(C) neither
(D) some

21 Mr. Eaves requested a window seat, but there were ------- left by that time.
(A) not
(B) none
(C) neither
(D) nobody

기출공식 8 some은 긍정문에, any는 부정문, 조건문, 비교문에 주로 쓰인다.

some
약간, 일부
Many consumers liked the device, but **some** were concerned about its price.
많은 소비자들이 그 기기를 좋아했지만, 일부는 가격에 대해 우려했다.

any
약간, 조금
We need a few more shipping boxes, if the mailroom has **any**.
우편실에 조금이라도 있다면 우리는 배송 상자 몇 개가 더 필요하다.

+만점팁 some / any는 부정형용사로도 쓰인다.

If your DM-7 coffee maker has **any** defects, please return it for replacement.
DM-7 커피 메이커에 어떤 결함이 있다면 반품해서 교환 받으세요.

Our units can be delivered to **any** location. 저희 상품은 어느 지역으로든 배송됩니다.
→ **any는 긍정문에서 '어떤 ~든지'라는 뜻으로 쓰인다.**

22 Please send us more Basahm photo paper if you have ------- in stock.
(A) any
(B) a few
(C) either
(D) other

23 Your insurance would only cover ------- of the costs of the treatment.
(A) some
(B) somehow
(C) someone
(D) sometimes

24 Margaret earned the highest commission of ------- salesperson in the whole company.
(A) such
(B) another
(C) this
(D) any

1 Ms. Dosch collects the interoffice mail in the morning and distributes ------- by 4:00 P.M.
(A) it
(B) him
(C) whose
(D) which

2 An accomplished skater -------, Mr. Loewenstein also coaches the world-champion figure skater Sara Krasnova.
(A) he
(B) him
(C) himself
(D) his

3 Mr. Yamagata is prepared to assist Ms. Hahn's clients while ------- conducts a training seminar in New York.
(A) hers
(B) she
(C) herself
(D) her

4 Architectural surveyors identify historic properties and evaluate ------- physical condition.
(A) which
(B) whose
(C) their
(D) those

5 Answering customer questions is sometimes difficult to do on -------, so we have created a list of frequently asked questions.
(A) yours
(B) yourself
(C) your own
(D) you

6 Café Alta Vista may cancel the reservation of ------- who is more than twenty minutes late.
(A) which
(B) such
(C) other
(D) anyone

7 Although the assistant manager will be transferred next week, the personnel office has not yet found a replacement for -------.
(A) she
(B) herself
(C) her
(D) hers

8 Formerly employed by Chang Architectural, Inc., Jennifer Park started ------- architecture firm last year.
(A) she
(B) hers
(C) her own
(D) herself

9 Joanna Nugent, CEO of Freshest Face, Inc., has earned the respect of virtually ------- in the cosmetics industry.
(A) everyone
(B) anything
(C) whatever
(D) each other

10 Chemem Industry's laminate products are indistinguishable from ------- of its competitors.
(A) that
(B) those
(C) them
(D) theirs

11 The use of umbrellas is prohibited in the sports stadium because they obstruct the view of -------.
(A) others
(B) ones
(C) every
(D) itself

12 If you need ------- special for an event, contact Faith James at fajames@gnt.com.
(A) something
(B) other
(C) itself
(D) whichever

13 In general, model apartments today are furnished more luxuriously than ------- used to be.
(A) their
(B) they
(C) them
(D) themselves

14 Of the five building sites for the new shopping mall, four were too small, while ------- was in a somewhat inconvenient location.
(A) other
(B) each other
(C) the other
(D) one another

15 ------- in the shipping department is required to attend the safety meeting.
(A) Some
(B) These
(C) Everyone
(D) Nothing

16 Mr. Hahn and Ms. Smalls began working at ABCO Corporation at the same time, and ------- hope to be promoted next year.
(A) many
(B) few
(C) one
(D) both

17 The property manager must ensure that renters understand ------- rental agreement.
(A) their
(B) they
(C) theirs
(D) them

18 Mr. Kawano began the research project by ------- but later was assisted by two colleagues.
(A) he
(B) his
(C) him
(D) himself

19 We could not order replacement parts for the packing machine, because the local suppliers have ------- in stock.
(A) any
(B) none
(C) finally
(D) mostly

20 ------- of Ms. Knapp's mail is to be left with a supervisor while she is away on vacation.
(A) Each
(B) Everyone
(C) Such
(D) All

UNIT 05 형용사

평균 2~3문제 출제

무료인강

● 형용사의 형태

형용사는 주로 -able, -ive, -ous, -ful, -ent, -ary, -less, -tial, -ic, -y, -al, -ate를 어미로 가진다.

avail**able** 이용 가능한	posi**tive** 긍정적인	vari**ous** 다양한	success**ful** 성공적인
frequ**ent** 빈번한	tempor**ary** 일시적인	spot**less** 무결점의	essen**tial** 필수적인
histor**ic** 역사적인	hand**y** 편리한	agricultur**al** 농업의	delic**ate** 섬세한

● 형용사의 역할

명사 앞이나 뒤에 놓여 명사의 성질을 한정해 주는 한정적 역할로 쓰인다.

명사 앞에서 수식	The organization received **generous** donations. 그 단체는 후한 기부금을 받았다. → 뒤에 오는 donations를 수식한다.
명사 뒤에서 수식	They offer the cheapest prices **imaginable**. 그들은 상상할 수 있는 최저가를 제공한다. → 앞에 오는 prices를 수식한다.

주어나 목적어의 상태를 보충하는 서술적 역할로 쓰인다.

주어 보충	The intern is **attentive**. 그 수습사원은 세심하다. → 주어인 the intern을 보충 설명한다.
목적어 보충	We keep your information **confidential**. 우리는 귀하의 정보를 기밀로 유지합니다. → 목적어인 your information을 보충 설명한다.

형용사 | ETS 핵심 출제 패턴

형용사의 위치에 관한 문제가 주로 출제된다. 명사 앞에 형용사를 넣거나 주격 보어 자리에 형용사를 넣는 문제가 가장 대표적이다.

☑ 명사 앞 자리의 품사를 선택하는 문제

Most models of the Remagine laptop computer now come with a ------- keyboard.

(A) removability   (B) remove

(C) removable   (D) remover

현재 대부분의 리매진 노트북 컴퓨터 제품에는 탈부착 키보드가 들어 있다.

핵심 포인트

관사 뒤에서 명사를 수식하는 자리이므로 형용사가 들어가야 한다.

▶ 기출공식 1 **p.52**

☑ 주격 보어 자리의 품사를 선택하는 문제

Paychecks are now ------- for pickup at the front desk.

(A) ready   (B) readily

(C) readiness   (D) readies

안내 데스크에서 지금 급료를 찾아가실 수 있습니다.

핵심 포인트

be동사의 보어 자리로 주어를 보충하는 형용사가 들어가야 한다.

▶ 기출공식 2 **p.52**

☑ 알맞은 수량 형용사를 선택하는 문제

------- employees should attend the safety training meeting this afternoon.

(A) Part   (B) All

(C) Total   (D) Every

모든 직원은 오늘 오후에 안전 교육 회의에 참석해야 합니다.

핵심 포인트

뒤에 나온 복수명사를 수식할 수 있는 수량 형용사가 들어가야 한다.

▶ 기출공식 3 **p.53**

☑ 형용사 관용 표현을 묻는 문제

Rates at the West Portal Hotel are ------- to room availability and may change without notice.

(A) plain   (B) public

(C) subject   (D) general

웨스트 포털 호텔의 요금은 객실 이용 가능 여부에 따라 달라질 수 있으며 공지 없이 변경될 수 있습니다.

핵심 포인트

전치사 to와 어울려 문맥상 의미가 통하는 형용사가 들어가야 한다.

▶ 기출공식 7 **p.55**

정답 : (C), (A), (B), (C)

기출공식 1 형용사는 명사를 수식하고 부사의 수식을 받는다.

- **(관사 / 소유격) + 형용사 + 명사**

  The executives thought of the **ideal** solutions for waste management.

  임원들은 쓰레기 관리를 위한 이상적인 해결책을 생각했다.

- **(관사 / 소유격) + 부사 + 형용사 + 명사**

  Last year, Supranda Motors, Inc. developed highly **innovative** hybrid cars.

  지난해 수프란다 자동차사는 고도로 혁신적인 하이브리드 자동차를 개발했다.

- **(관사 / 소유격) + 형용사 + 형용사 + 명사**

  We hired a **professional legal** consultant last month. 우리는 지난달에 전문 법률 상담가를 고용했다.

  → 명사를 수식하는 형용사는 여러 개 겹쳐 쓸 수 있다.

  > **+만점팁** -able, -ible로 끝나는 형용사는 명사를 뒤에서 수식할 수 있다.
  >
  > The marketing team discussed every means **possible**. 마케팅 팀은 가능한 모든 수단을 논의했다.
  > Free Wheel has the newest vehicles **available** for rent. 프리휠은 최신 대여용 차량들을 보유하고 있다.

1 The ------- episode of *City Reporting*, the acclaimed television drama, will be broadcast tonight.
(A) lastly
(B) lasts
(C) lasted
(D) last

2 Passengers should have all ------- boarding documents ready to present to airline personnel.
(A) necessary
(B) necessarily
(C) necessity
(D) necessitating

3 Ana Paskevich has been honored as an ------- talented writer and researcher by her firm.
(A) exceptional
(B) exceptionally
(C) exception
(D) excepted

기출공식 2 형용사는 보어 역할을 한다.

주격 보어를 취하는 동사	be동사 ~이다 stay ~인 채로 있다	become ~이 되다 seem ~처럼 보이다	remain ~인 채로 남아 있다 appear ~처럼 보이다
목적격 보어를 취하는 동사	make ~하게 만들다 consider ~라고 여기다	keep ~하게 유지하다 call ~라고 하다 / 여기다	find ~라고 생각하다 leave ~한 채로 남겨 두다

The city's new plan will become **effective** as of August 1. 시의 새 계획은 8월 1일부로 시행될 예정이다.

We will keep your account [**secure** / ~~securely~~]. 저희가 귀하의 계좌를 안전하게 보관하겠습니다.

→ 해석이 부사처럼 된다고 하여 부사를 쓰지 않도록 유의해야 한다.

4 The security officers at Linde-Abbro Laboratories are ------- by their bright blue uniforms.
(A) identify
(B) identifies
(C) identity
(D) identifiable

5 You will find the manual very ------- in solving any problems you encounter when you first use the software.
(A) help
(B) helpful
(C) helped
(D) helps

6 According to an informal survey, the sales goal set by the management team seems ------- to most of the staff.
(A) realist
(B) realism
(C) realistic
(D) realistically

기출공식 3 수량 형용사는 수 일치에 유의해야 한다.

- another / each / every / either / neither + 가산 단수명사
- many / (a) few / both / several / numerous / various / a number of + 가산 복수명사
- much / (a) little / less / least / a large amount of / a great deal of + 불가산명사
- all / more / most / lots of / a lot of / plenty of / other / some + 가산 복수명사 / 불가산명사
- no / any + 가산 단·복수명사 / 불가산명사

Mr. Kang distributed an agenda to **each** attendee. 강 씨가 참석자 각각에게 안건을 배포했다.

There are **a few** requirements that must be met. 몇 가지 충족해야 할 조건이 있다.

Some information needs to be revised. 몇몇 정보는 수정되어야 한다.

+만점팁 few와 little은 a가 붙을 때 '약간의', a가 붙지 않을 때 '거의 없는'으로 쓰인다.

Few people visited the Web site. 웹페이지 방문자가 거의 없었다.

+만점팁 every, another 뒤에 2 이상의 숫자가 오는 경우 복수명사를 쓴다.

every two weeks 2주마다 another twelve issues 추가 열 두 권

---

7 At 10:15, A.M., ------- skaters competing in the 500-meter race should report to the rink for their five-minute warm-up period.
(A) all
(B) every
(C) entire
(D) whichever

8 Because the sales representatives were late leaving the office, there was very ------- time for us to talk before the client meeting.
(A) little
(B) few
(C) less
(D) hard

9 Customers prefer to shop at Kwon's because the store offers an unconditional guarantee on ------- purchases.
(A) any of
(B) each
(C) all
(D) every

기출공식 4 형태가 유사한 혼동 형용사는 의미를 구분할 수 있어야 한다.

complimentary 무료의	complementary 보완적인	confident 확신하는	confidential 기밀의
considerate 사려 깊은	considerable 상당한	successful 성공적인	successive 연속적인
dependent 의존적인	dependable 신뢰할 만한	reliant 의존적인	reliable 신뢰할 만한
sizable 상당한, 많은	sized (복합어로) 크기가 ~인	favorable 호의적인	favorite 선호하는

The planning team is reviewing a [**confidential** / ~~confident~~] report. 기획팀이 기밀 보고서를 검토 중이다.

---

10 Under more ------- circumstances, the board of trustees would have approved the budget increase, but this year it was not possible.
(A) favorable
(B) favorably
(C) favor
(D) favorite

11 Construction of the new library is ------- on the city's ability to pass a new budget.
(A) depend
(B) depends
(C) dependable
(D) dependent

12 The information you provide on this questionnaire is strictly ------- and will not be shared with any other vendors.
(A) confident
(B) confidential
(C) confidentially
(D) confiding

정답 및 해설 p.23

timely 시기적절한   **orderly** 질서정연한   **likely** ~할 것 같은   **friendly** 친화적인   **costly** 많은 비용이 드는

All expense reports should be submitted to Mr. Tomlinson in a **timely** manner.
모든 비용 보고서는 톰린슨 씨에게 제때 제출되어야 한다.

+만점팁 lively(활기찬, 활기차게)와 횟수를 나타내는 **daily, weekly, monthly, yearly**는 형용사와 부사 둘 다로 쓰인다.

13 Applications for scholarships should be submitted to the selection committee in a ------- manner.
(A) time
(B) timer
(C) timely
(D) timing

14 The county government plans to carry out ------- renovations to Dewey Stadium.
(A) cost
(B) costly
(C) costed
(D) costs

15 Traffic congestion is ------- on Thornhill Street until the roadwork ends.
(A) likeness
(B) liking
(C) likely
(D) liked

빈출

be able to ~할 수 있다 **be eligible to** ~할 자격이 있다 **be likely to** ~할 것 같다 **be hesitant to** ~하기를 꺼리다 **be bound to** 반드시 ~하다	**be about to** 막 ~하려고 하다 **be entitled to** ~할 자격이 있다 **be welcome to** 마음껏 ~하다 **be reluctant to** ~하기를 꺼리다 **be sure to** 반드시 ~하다	**be eager to** ~하고 싶어 하다 **be delighted to** ~하게 되어 기쁘다 **be pleased to** ~하게 되어 기쁘다 **be willing to** 기꺼이 ~하다 **be fortunate to** ~하게 되어 행운이다

All conference attendees **are** [eligible / ~~capable~~] **to** enter the raffle contest.   (to + 동사원형)
회의 참석자 전원은 경품 추첨에 참가할 자격이 있다.
→ 문맥이 맞지 않거나 to부정사와 함께 쓰지 않는 형용사를 넣지 않도록 유의해야 한다.

16 Having achieved considerable success in Asia, Celena Tea Merchants is ------- to enter European markets.
(A) eager
(B) active
(C) busy
(D) firm

17 Jobseekers with highly valued skills are less ------- to navigate complicated hiring processes.
(A) thorough
(B) lengthy
(C) familiar
(D) willing

18 All resort guests are ------- to use the sauna during the designated hours.
(A) welcome
(B) common
(C) inclusive
(D) possible

기출공식 7   'be 형용사 + 전치사 to' 관용 표현이 출제된다.

be beneficial to ~에게 도움이 되다	be equivalent to ~와 동등하다	be subject to ~의 대상이다
be entitled to ~에 대한 자격이 있다	be similar to ~와 비슷하다	be comparable to ~에 필적하다
be responsive to ~에 즉각 반응하다	be resistant to ~에 저항하다	be relevant to ~와 관련이 있다
be adjacent to ~에 인접하다	be limited to ~로 한정되다	be opposed to ~에 반대하다
be dedicated to ~에 헌신하다	be devoted to ~에 헌신하다	be committed to ~에 헌신하다

Amonarth Premium paints **are** highly [**resistant** / ~~cautious~~] **to** most stains.

아모나스 프리미엄 페인트는 대부분의 얼룩에 매우 강하다.   (to + 명사구)

→ 문맥이 맞지 않거나 전치사 to와 함께 쓰지 않는 형용사를 넣지 않도록 유의해야 한다.

19 Each full-time staff member is ------- to three weeks of paid vacation annually.
(A) equivalent
(B) entitled
(C) eager
(D) eligible

20 Drake Technology's new blood-testing device is expected to be very ------- to society.
(A) grateful
(B) approved
(C) beneficial
(D) compatible

21 Payments postmarked after the due date are ------- to a late fee of five percent of the total amount due.
(A) subject
(B) intact
(C) suspect
(D) distinct

기출공식 8   'be 형용사 + 기타 전치사' 관용 표현이 출제된다.

for	be famous/known/renowned for ~으로 유명하다 be responsible/accountable for ~에 책임이 있다 be eligible for ~에 대한 자격이 있다	be suitable for ~에 적합하다 be grateful for ~에 감사하다 be necessary for ~에 필요하다
with	be familiar with ~에 익숙하다 be compatible with ~와 호환 가능하다	be compliant with ~을 따르다, 준수하다 be consistent with ~와 일치하다
of	be appreciative of ~에 감사하다 be capable of ~할 수 있다 be indicative of ~을 나타내다	be aware of ~을 잘 알다 be critical of ~에 비판적이다 be representative of ~을 대표하다
about	be anxious about ~에 대해 염려하다 be nervous about ~에 대해 불안하다	be optimistic about ~에 대해 낙관하다 be enthusiastic about ~에 대해 열광하다

All survey participants **are eligible for** a free sample. 모든 설문 참여자들은 무료 샘플을 받을 자격이 있다.

22 The only downside to the newly released Yari 4200 inkjet printer is that it is not always ------- with older devices.
(A) formal
(B) external
(C) alternate
(D) compatible

23 Candidates for the position of assistant manager must be ------- of assuming a wide range of responsibilities.
(A) capable
(B) enclosed
(C) selected
(D) ready

24 Viewers of *Detective Jones* are ------- with Ms. Khatri's work as a director.
(A) familiar
(B) renowned
(C) compelling
(D) supportive

정답 및 해설 p.25

1 Improvements in irrigation technology throughout the region were followed by ------- gains in corn production.
(A) proportionally
(B) proportional
(C) proportioning
(D) proportions

2 Tax attorney Hyun Chae-Won provides expert advice on ------- issues related to estate planning.
(A) legally
(B) legalize
(C) legal
(D) legalized

3 No more than four passengers are permitted in ------- taxi operated by the Halligan Company.
(A) any
(B) all
(C) some
(D) such

4 Doors to conference rooms should be left ------- at the end of the day for the cleaning staff.
(A) opening
(B) opener
(C) opens
(D) open

5 There will be time for participants to discuss ------- issue presented in the seminar.
(A) most of
(B) all
(C) entire
(D) each

6 Dr. Anita Wiryanto has published numerous articles on the ------- aspects of coral reefs in Indonesia.
(A) beneficially
(B) benefit
(C) beneficial
(D) benefited

7 Devon Motors' ------- new line of fuel-efficient cars has won many prestigious awards from the automobile industry.
(A) impressive
(B) impression
(C) impressing
(D) impress

8 The president of Paterson Industrial Solutions has signed a number of important ------- this month.
(A) contract
(B) contracts
(C) contracted
(D) contracting

9 To be ------- for a position with Ebbesen Research Associates, candidates must have a university degree in economics.
(A) official
(B) eligible
(C) considerate
(D) partial

10 In order to keep prices -------, Kim's Bakery will begin making its breads and cakes on the premises.
(A) reasonable
(B) reasonably
(C) reasoning
(D) reason

11 The local center for Augen Care, Inc.,
   coordinates distribution of its eye glasses
   to a ------- area of the Northwest.
   (A) broadly
   (B) broadness
   (C) broaden
   (D) broad

12 The Castala Theater offers ------- dance
   performances in southern Spain.
   (A) authentic
   (B) authenticate
   (C) authenticity
   (D) authentically

13 Yeoh's Clothing is introducing a new line
   of ------- wool sweaters.
   (A) washable
   (B) washes
   (C) washer
   (D) washing

14 Page 34 lists the ------- suppliers of all
   the major construction equipment that
   can be used in the Ultera pipeline project.
   (A) accept
   (B) accepts
   (C) acceptable
   (D) accepting

15 As head of Neelix Communications,
   Mr. Eames is considered to be an
   unusually ------- leader.
   (A) thoughts
   (B) thoughtful
   (C) thoughtfully
   (D) thoughtfulness

16 While the preliminary research is
   favorable, it may take years for Bogor
   Pharmaceuticals to develop -------
   evidence of the drug's effectiveness.
   (A) conclusion
   (B) concludes
   (C) conclusive
   (D) conclude

17 It is not ------- to enter the manufacturing
   area at Cho Industrial Ltd. without the
   proper safety gear.
   (A) acceptable
   (B) accepting
   (C) accepts
   (D) acceptance

18 Critics of the recent movie with Michelle
   Zhao have called the plot too -------.
   (A) predicting
   (B) predicted
   (C) predictable
   (D) predictably

19 Members of the Young Readers' Book
   Club will receive two new storybooks in
   the mail ------- three weeks.
   (A) many
   (B) every
   (C) most
   (D) less

20 The Moorestown Redevelopment Agency
   is responsible for determining whether
   various properties throughout the
   Township of Moorestown are ------- for
   redevelopment.
   (A) similar
   (B) suitable
   (C) consistent
   (D) accurate

UNIT 06 | 부사

평균 2~3문제 출제

무료인강

● 부사의 형태

부사는 기본적으로 형용사에 **-ly**를 붙여서 만든다.

remarkable 상당한	→ remarkab**ly** 상당히	cautious 주의 깊은	→ cautious**ly** 주의 깊게
domestic 국내의	→ domestical**ly** 국내에서	financial 재정의	→ financial**ly** 재정적으로
general 일반적인	→ general**ly** 일반적으로	adverse 불리한	→ adverse**ly** 불리하게

형태가 불규칙한 부사들도 있다.

together 함께	alone 혼자서	quite 꽤	often 자주	seldom 좀처럼 ~않다	enough 충분히

● 부사의 역할

부사는 다양한 요소를 수식한다.

동사 수식	Our production level has increased **steadily**. 우리의 생산량은 점차 증가했다.
형용사 수식	The blender is **extremely** versatile. 그 믹서기는 매우 용도가 다양하다.
부사 수식	The new audio equipment is **far** too expensive. 새 오디오 장비는 너무 비싸다.
준동사 수식	We expect our guests to arrive **early**. 우리는 손님들이 일찍 도착할 것으로 예상한다.
전치사구 수식	The items are **currently** out of stock. 그 물품은 현재 재고가 없다.
문장 수식	**Fortunately**, our sales improved in spring. 다행히 봄에 판매가 향상되었다.

부사 | ETS 핵심 출제 패턴

문장에서 부사의 알맞은 위치를 묻는 문제가 주로 출제된다. 일부 부사들의 특수 용법을 묻는 문제도 자주 출제된다.

☑ 동사를 수식하는 품사를 선택하는 문제

Dr. Charles Lim, a renowned biologist, has written ------- about marine life in the Gulf of Mexico.

(A) extent
(B) extensive
(C) extensively
(D) extensiveness

유명 생물학자인 찰스 림 박사는 멕시코 만의 해양 생물에 관해 광범위하게 저술해 왔다.

핵심 포인트

빈칸 앞의 동사를 수식할 수 있는 부사가 들어가야 한다.

▶ 기출공식 1 **p.60**

☑ 형용사를 수식하는 품사를 선택하는 문제

Flower arranging is becoming an ------- popular hobby for people of all ages and backgrounds.

(A) increasingly
(B) increasing
(C) increase
(D) increased

꽃꽂이는 나이나 배경과 관계없이 모든 사람들 사이에서 점점 인기 있는 취미로 자리잡고 있다.

핵심 포인트

빈칸 뒤의 형용사를 수식할 수 있는 부사가 들어가야 한다.

▶ 기출공식 2 **p.60**

☑ to부정사를 수식하는 품사를 선택하는 문제

Make sure to fill out the form ------- before submitting it to our office.

(A) complete
(B) completed
(C) completely
(D) completion

우리 사무실에 제출하기 전에 양식을 완벽하게 작성했는지 반드시 확인하세요.

핵심 포인트

빈칸 앞의 to부정사구를 수식할 수 있는 부사가 들어가야 한다.

▶ 기출공식 3 **p.61**

☑ 강조하는 부사를 선택하는 문제

The organizers ask that participants exit the auditorium ------- after Professor Lauter's discussion.

(A) directed
(B) directly
(C) directing
(D) direction

주최측은 참석자들에게 로터 교수의 강연이 끝난 직후 강당을 나가 달라고 요청한다.

핵심 포인트

after 앞에서 after를 강조하며 '직후에'라는 의미를 만드는 강조 부사가 들어가야 한다.

▶ 기출공식 4 **p.61**

정답 : (C), (A), (C), (B)

기출공식 1   부사는 동사를 수식한다.

주어 동사 사이	Ms. Song **previously** published two novels. 송 씨는 이전에 두 소설을 출간했다.
동사 중간	The café can **comfortably** seat twenty guests. 그 카페는 20명의 손님을 편하게 착석시킨다.
	The mall is **finally** opening next Monday. 그 쇼핑몰은 다음 월요일에 마침내 문을 연다.
	The clinic is **conveniently** located near the station. 그 병원은 역 인근에 편리하게 위치한다.
	Mr. Han has **successfully** completed the project. 한 씨는 프로젝트를 성공적으로 완료했다.

→ 조동사와 동사원형 사이, be -ing 사이, be p.p. 사이, have p.p. 사이 모두 부사 자리이다.

동사 뒤	Overall profits have increased **considerably**. 총수익이 상당히 증가했다.
	Ms. Hitchens interviewed the candidates **personally**. 히친스 씨는 구직자들을 직접 면접했다.
	All our products are produced **locally**. 우리 제품은 모두 지역에서 생산된다.
	Please respond **promptly** to the inquiry. 문의에 신속하게 응답해 주세요.

→ 자동사 뒤, 타동사의 목적어 뒤, 수동태 뒤, 자동사와 전치사 사이 모두 부사 자리이다.

---

1 Full-time staff at Dinh and Mann Associates ------- work 37.5 hours in a week.
(A) norm
(B) norms
(C) normal
(D) normally

2 Sales of Seviana Cosmetics have ------- improved since the new marketing campaign began last quarter.
(A) steady
(B) steadily
(C) steadiest
(D) steadied

3 Ms. Lai's draft of Sientech Industries' new mission statement expresses the company's goals -------.
(A) precise
(B) more precise
(C) preciseness
(D) precisely

기출공식 2   부사는 형용사와 또 다른 부사를 수식한다.

형용사 수식	The company's stock price is **relatively** low compared to its annual earnings. 회사의 주가는 연 수익에 비해 비교적 낮다.
부사 수식	Despite a few glitches, the MW-5 mobile phone prototype worked **pretty** well. 몇 가지 사소한 결함에도 불구하고 MW-5 휴대폰 시제품은 꽤 잘 작동했다.

+만점팁 부사는 일반적으로 명사를 수식하지 않지만 '관사 + 명사' 앞에 놓일 때는 강조하는 역할을 할 수 있다.

Even a beginner can operate this camera. 심지어 초보자도 이 카메라를 조작할 수 있다.
The drop in sales was **largely** the result of the recession. 판매 하락은 주로 불황의 결과이다.

---

4 The High Performance weather gauge is ------- accurate in measuring the level of humidity in the air.
(A) surprising
(B) surprisingly
(C) surprised
(D) surprises

5 Mr. Perlmutter has assured the management team that the prototype will be ------- functional by June 9.
(A) complete
(B) completing
(C) completely
(D) completion

6 "Platinum Flyer" status is awarded to those who fly with us ------- frequently.
(A) except
(B) exception
(C) exceptional
(D) exceptionally

기출공식 3　부사는 to부정사/동명사/분사를 수식한다.

to부정사 수식　A new software program was installed to complete the work **efficiently**.
업무를 효율적으로 마무리하기 위해 새로운 소프트웨어 프로그램이 설치되었다.

동명사 수식　By **innovatively** combining various cuisines, the restaurant has created unique dishes. 다양한 요리를 독창적으로 결합함으로써 그 식당은 독특한 메뉴를 개발했다.

분사 수식　**Formerly** known as the "Teen Street", it is now more popular with senior citizens. 이전에 "십대 거리"로 알려졌던 그곳이 지금은 나이 든 시민들에게 더 인기가 많다.

---

7 Mr. Ortega reminded service-desk operators about the importance of listening ------- to customers' concerns.
(A) careful　　(B) caring
(C) carefully　(D) cared

8 Please use this form in order to be reimbursed ------- for last month's travel expenses.
(A) promptly　　(B) prompt
(C) promptness　(D) prompts

9 One responsibility of the position is to ------- update customer information spreadsheets.
(A) regular　　(B) regularities
(C) regularize　(D) regularly

빈출

기출공식 4　숫자 수식 부사와 강조 부사가 출제된다.

숫자 수식 부사　**퍼센트 등의 수치 앞에 놓여 '대략, 최소, 이상' 등을 나타낸다.**

almost/nearly/approximately/roughly/around/about 거의, 대략
more than/over 이상　　at least 최소　　up to 최대　　only/just 겨우, 단지

This facility can accommodate **approximately** 100 participants.
이 시설은 약 100명의 참가자를 수용할 수 있다.

강조 부사　**특정 단어나 표현 앞에서 강조의 의미로 쓰인다.**

even 심지어, ~조차　　(far/much) too 너무　　well 훨씬　　particularly/specifically 특히
only/just/solely/exclusively 오로지 ~만　　simply/just 그저, 단지
right/just/immediately/shortly/directly + before/after ~ 직전에/직후에

The estimate is **well** beyond the allocated budget. 견적이 할당된 예산을 훨씬 초과한다.
→ **well**은 전치사구 앞에 놓여 '훨씬'이라는 의미로 전치사구를 강조한다.

This offer is available **exclusively** to new clients. 이 혜택은 신규 고객에게만 제공됩니다.

There will be a break **right after** the lecture. 강연 직후 휴식 시간이 있습니다.

---

10 The owner of Pergini Builders estimates that the construction in downtown Erlton will take ------- eighteen months to complete.
(A) approximately
(B) slowly
(C) eagerly
(D) spaciously

11 Almost ------- after receiving the necessary tools, our crews began installing telephone cables in the southern part of the county.
(A) precisely
(B) immediately
(C) continually
(D) productively

12 Festival attendees should reserve a hotel room ------- in advance of their arrival next month.
(A) well
(B) so
(C) such
(D) over

정답 및 해설 p. 29

빈도 부사 횟수를 나타내며 be동사, 조동사 뒤, 일반동사 앞에 온다.

| once 한번 | sometimes 때때로 | often/frequently 자주 | usually 보통 | always 늘 |

The company **sometimes** holds team building sessions.
그 회사는 때때로 단합대회를 갖는다.

부정 부사 부정의 의미를 내포하며 다른 부정어와 이중으로 쓰지 않도록 유의해야 한다.

| little/hardly/rarely/scarcely/barely/seldom 거의 ~않다 | never 결코 ~않다 |

We **hardly** [ever / ~~never~~] hold department meetings on Fridays.
우리는 금요일에는 부서 회의를 거의 열지 않는다.

13 Lombard & Cho has ------- been named as the top tax law firm in the area.
(A) frequently
(B) frequent
(C) frequenting
(D) frequents

14 The new coffee shop has become quite popular, even though it is ------- noticeable from the street.
(A) harder
(B) hardly
(C) hard
(D) hardest

15 During the past five years, Marty's Eatery has received a poor review from a food critic just ------.
(A) so
(B) once
(C) about
(D) yet

시간 부사 시간적 의미를 나타내는 부사로, 일부 부사는 특정 위치 또는 시제와 함께 쓰인다.

| already 이미, 벌써 | soon 곧 | still 여전히 | yet 아직 |
| currently 현재 | presently 현재 | shortly 곧 | now 지금 |

The equipment is **still not** functioning. 그 장비는 아직 작동하지 않고 있다.

The contractor has **not yet** finished the project. 하청업자는 아직 프로젝트를 완료하지 못했다.

→ **still**은 부정문에서 쓰일 때 **not** 앞에, **yet**은 **not** 뒤에 쓴다.

We **are currently looking** for volunteers. 저희는 현재 자원봉사자를 찾고 있습니다.

접속부사 두 문장을 의미적인 관계에 따라 연결하는 부사로, **however(그러나), therefore(따라서), moreover(게다가), then(그렇다면, 그 다음에), otherwise(그렇지 않으면)** 등이 있다.

Please submit a receipt. **Otherwise,** no refund can be made.
영수증을 제출하세요. 그렇지 않으면, 환불되지 않습니다.

The device is heavy and **therefore** not portable. 그 장비는 무거워서 휴대성이 좋지 않다.

16 The books we received last week ------- need to be entered into the digital database.
(A) lately
(B) evenly
(C) ever
(D) still

17 If you have already signed up for automatic payments, ------- no further steps are required.
(A) even
(B) additional
(C) then
(D) until

18 The new software will ------- decrease the amount of time it takes to schedule appointments.
(A) soon
(B) recently
(C) lately
(D) very

기출공식 7   -ly가 붙어서 의미가 달라지는 부사가 있다.

close 가까이에	closely 자세히, 면밀히	short 짧게	shortly 곧
hard 열심히	hardly 거의 ~하지 않다	late 늦게	lately 최근에(= recently)
high 높이	highly 매우	near 가까이에	nearly 거의
great 훌륭하게	greatly 대단히	most 가장	mostly 대체로

The client's flight is expected to arrive [late / lately]. 고객의 항공편이 늦게 도착할 것으로 예상된다.

Sales of winter clothing have fallen [late / lately]. 최근 겨울 옷 판매가 감소했다.

19 The artwork for the advertisement was ------- complete when the client requested major changes.
(A) nearly   (B) nearest
(C) nearer   (D) neared

20 The students enrolled in the painting course at the Model Art School have worked exceptionally ------- over the past year.
(A) hard   (B) hardy
(C) hardest   (D) hardly

21 The contractors say they will begin the renovation work ------- before 8 A.M. tomorrow.
(A) short   (B) shorten
(C) shortly   (D) shortest

기출공식 8   특정한 쓰임을 가지는 부사가 있다.

- **very: 형용사·부사의 원급 수식(동사 수식 불가) / much: 형용사·부사의 비교급 수식(원급 수식 불가)**

The corporate event was [very / much] successful. 그 기업 행사는 매우 성공적이었다.

The new logo looked [very / much] clearer. 새 로고는 훨씬 선명해 보였다.

   +만점팁 much 이외에도 even, far, a lot 등이 비교급 수식 부사로 쓰인다.

- **so + 형용사 / 부사 + that 너무 ~해서 …하다**

We are **so** busy **that** we need to hire additional staff. 우리는 너무 바빠서 직원을 더 고용해야 한다.

- **since 이래로 / enough 충분히 / alike 둘 다**

The incorrect figures **have since been** revised. 부정확한 수치는 그 이래로 수정되었다.

   → since는 접속사, 전치사, 부사로 모두 쓰일 수 있다.

The conference room was not **large enough**. 그 회의실은 충분히 크지 않았다.

   → enough는 부사로 쓰일 때 형용사나 부사 뒤에 위치한다.

The area is popular with **tourists and residents alike**. 그곳은 관광객들과 주민들 둘 다에게 인기 있다.

   → alike 앞에는 두 집단이 나온다.

22 Mobile phones have become ------- prevalent that telecommunications companies are establishing service in areas previously thought too remote.
(A) only   (B) such
(C) so   (D) still

23 The prevention of environmental pollution has become an important consideration for small and large businesses -------.
(A) forth   (B) even
(C) alike   (D) beyond

24 The minor concerns that arose during the testing phase of development have ------- been resolved, and the product is ready to progress to assembly.
(A) since   (B) soon
(C) after   (D) often

정답 및 해설 p. 30

1 Mr. White's work has improved ------- since he joined the team, thanks to feedback from his supervisor.
(A) significantly
(B) signifies
(C) significant
(D) signified

2 Your generous donation will go toward the museum's maintenance projects, ------- the restoration of the main entryway.
(A) specific
(B) specifically
(C) specification
(D) specify

3 The company handbook is ------- general so that its policies apply to employees across all divisions.
(A) intent
(B) intention
(C) intentional
(D) intentionally

4 Due to construction delays on Maplewood Avenue, employees will ------- need to find alternate routes.
(A) probable
(B) probably
(C) probability
(D) probabilities

5 Your request has been received, and you will be contacted by one of our agents -------.
(A) lately
(B) shortly
(C) slightly
(D) narrowly

6 Mayor Reynold's views on education ------- established him as a front-runner in the election.
(A) firmer
(B) firmly
(C) firmed
(D) firmest

7 Mr. Solis would be a great project manager, since he has worked with many staff members -------.
(A) collaboratively
(B) collaboration
(C) collaborates
(D) collaborative

8 The courier insisted that the package could not ------- have been damaged during shipment.
(A) possible
(B) possibly
(C) possibility
(D) possibilities

9 The vacation packages the travel agency has been promoting are ------- too expensive for our typical customers.
(A) far
(B) well
(C) quite
(D) pretty

10 The quality of the furniture designed at Oak Valley Company has remained ------- consistent for the 100 years that the firm has operated.
(A) remarks
(B) remarkably
(C) remarkable
(D) remarked

11 The flour mill is operating at a ------- reduced capacity because of a minor mechanical problem.
(A) slightest
(B) slighted
(C) slighting
(D) slightly

12 The executive board sent out a reminder to division heads that all contracts must be ------- reviewed by the legal department before they are signed.
(A) rigor
(B) rigors
(C) rigorous
(D) rigorously

13 New safety glasses will soon be available for use by factory employees and visitors -------.
(A) nearly
(B) quite
(C) alike
(D) cautiously

14 Poleberry Local Marketplace takes pride in carrying only ------- processed dairy products from the region.
(A) nature
(B) natures
(C) natural
(D) naturally

15 For the period ending June 30, the Horizon Stadium Corporation recorded unprecedented revenues from ticket sales, and ------- more from advertising.
(A) all
(B) very
(C) any
(D) even

16 The head chef at Boldoni's Restaurant has been commended for ------- introducing dishes that are both creative and delicious.
(A) continue
(B) continues
(C) continually
(D) continual

17 While Constancio Restaurant employees may exchange shifts, they must ------- receive approval from a manager ahead of time.
(A) already
(B) completely
(C) always
(D) formerly

18 Suburban residents are ------- in favor of expanding Highway 589 to relieve traffic congestion.
(A) overwhelm
(B) overwhelmingly
(C) overwhelming
(D) overwhelms

19 Recipients will ------- be more motivated to open a sales e-mail that has an enticing subject line.
(A) probable
(B) probability
(C) probabilities
(D) probably

20 *Finance Ledger* reports that many small business owners are ------- cautious during their first year of operation.
(A) financially
(B) financed
(C) financing
(D) financial

UNIT 07 전치사

평균 3~4문제 출제

무료인강

● 전치사의 종류

전치사는 명사 앞에 놓여 시간, 장소, 이유, 방법, 목적 등을 나타낸다.

시간	**after** the expiration date 만기일 이후에	**until** further notice 추후 공지 시까지
장소	**throughout** the exhibit hall 전시회장 곳곳에	**at** the technology fair 기술 박람회에서
이유	**due to** construction 공사 때문에	**thanks to** the funding 자금 조달 덕분에
방법	**by** entering a code 암호를 입력하여	**through** television advertising TV 광고를 통해
목적	**for** your reference 참조를 위해	**to** that end 그러한 목적을 위해

● 전치사구와 그 역할

전치사구는 '전치사 + 명사(구)'로, 문장에서 형용사 또는 부사 역할을 한다.

형용사 역할	Decorations **on the ceilings** will be removed soon. 천장에 달린 장식들은 곧 제거될 것이다. → 전치사구 on the ceilings가 앞에 온 명사 Decorations를 수식하는 형용사 역할을 한다. The memo was straightforward and **to the point**. 메모는 간단하고 명료했다. → 전치사구 to the point가 be동사의 보어로 straightforward와 같은 형용사 역할을 한다.
부사 역할	A full schedule is available **on the Web site**. 전체 일정은 웹사이트에서 이용 가능합니다. → 전치사구 on the Web site가 앞에 온 형용사 available을 수식하는 부사 역할을 한다. The renovation project was completed **on schedule**. 개조 작업이 예정대로 마무리되었다. → 전치사구 on schedule이 앞에 온 동사 was completed를 수식하는 부사 역할을 한다.

전치사 | ETS 핵심 출제 패턴

전치사, 접속사, 접속부사의 구별 문제, 각 전치사의 의미와 용법, 전치사가 포함된 다양한 숙어들이 출제된다.

☑ 시점 전치사를 선택하는 문제

Applications received ------- the October 15 deadline will not be processed.

(A) after   (B) already
(C) while   (D) often

10월 15일 마감일 이후에 접수된 지원서들은 처리되지 않을 것이다.

핵심 포인트

문맥상 '10월 15일 마감일 이후에'라는 의미가 되어야 하므로 '~후에'를 뜻하는 전치사가 들어가야 한다.

▶ 기출공식 1 p.68

☑ 위치 전치사를 선택하는 문제

Korean Star Airlines offers daily nonstop flights ------- London and Busan.

(A) aboard   (B) onto
(C) up   (D) between

코리안 스타 항공사는 런던과 부산 사이에 매일 직항 항공편을 제공한다.

핵심 포인트

and와 함께 쓰여 'A와 B 사이에'라는 의미가 되는 전치사가 들어가야 한다.

▶ 기출공식 2 p.68

☑ 기타 전치사를 선택하는 문제

No one is permitted on the factory floor ------- proper safety gear.

(A) following   (B) regarding
(C) unless   (D) without

적절한 안전 장비가 없다면 누구도 작업 현장에 들어갈 수 없다.

핵심 포인트

문맥상 '안전 장비 없이는'이라는 의미가 되어야 하므로 '~ 없이'를 뜻하는 전치사가 들어가야 한다.

▶ 기출공식 3 p.69

☑ 전치사 관용 표현을 묻는 문제

The advertising team made an amazing recovery from a late start to finish the project a week ------- schedule.

(A) ahead of   (B) following
(C) until   (D) on

광고팀은 프로젝트를 예정보다 일주일 앞당겨 끝내기 위해 뒤늦은 시작에도 놀라운 만회를 해냈다.

핵심 포인트

'예정보다 일찍'이라는 의미의 전치사 관용 표현이 들어가야 한다.

▶ 기출공식 6 p.70

정답 : (A), (D), (D), (A)

기출공식 1 시점 전치사와 기간 전치사를 구분해서 써야 한다.

시점	at + 시각 on + 요일/날짜 in + 월/년도 by (완료)/until (계속) ~까지
	after/following ~ 후에 since ~ 이래로 as of/effective/starting/beginning ~부터

The inventory needs to be **completed by** next week. 다음 주까지 재고 조사가 완료되어야 한다.

→ **submit**(제출하다), **complete**(완료하다), **finish**(끝내다)와 같은 완료성 의미를 지닌 동사는 **by**와 함께 쓰인다.

The tournament has been **postponed until** further notice. 시합이 다음 공고가 있을 때까지 연기되었다.

→ **postpone**(연기하다), **continue**(계속하다), **last**(지속되다)와 같은 진행성 의미를 지닌 동사는 **until**과 함께 쓰인다.

기간	for/during/over ~ 동안 in ~ 후에, ~ 만에 throughout 내내 within ~ 이내에

Customers can get a refund [**within** / ~~by~~] **30 days** of the purchase date.
소비자들은 구매일로부터 30일 이내에는 환불 받을 수 있다.

1 Sales ------- weeks four and five will be closely monitored to determine how they will affect first quarter profits.
(A) opposite   (B) beside
(C) during   (D) with

2 River Oaks, Inc., employees must complete the employee satisfaction survey ------- Friday at 5:00 P.M.
(A) as   (B) of
(C) by   (D) in

3 In order to guarantee your room reservation at the Palembang Hotel, please reply to this message ------- twenty-four hours.
(A) within   (B) about
(C) since   (D) into

기출공식 2 다양한 장소 전치사가 출제된다.

장소	at ~에	on ~ 위에, ~에	in ~ 안에	throughout ~ 전역에, ~ 도처에
위치	between (둘) 사이에 above ~ 위에 in front of ~ 앞에	among ~ 사이에 below ~ 아래에 behind ~ 뒤에	within ~ 안에 over ~ 위에 under ~ 아래에	from within ~ 내부에서 beside/next to/by ~ 옆에 around ~ 주위에
방향	to ~로 through ~을 통과하여 across ~을 가로질러	from ~로부터 past ~을 지나서 across from/opposite ~의 맞은 편에	into ~ 안으로 along ~을 따라서	out of ~ 밖으로 toward(s) ~ 쪽으로, ~으로 향하여

The emergency evacuation plans are posted on the wall [**throughout** / ~~into~~] the building.
비상 탈출 계획은 건물 곳곳의 벽에 붙어 있다.

Bourn Communications is **among** the leading providers of telephone service.
본 커뮤니케이션즈는 선도적인 전화 서비스 공급업체에 속한다.

→ **among** 뒤에는 반드시 복수명사가 따른다.

4 All file folders are stored ------- the top shelf of the conference room closet.
(A) out   (B) on
(C) to   (D) for

5 The faculty committee will distribute funds from the research grant ------- its various science departments.
(A) toward   (B) among
(C) after   (D) during

6 The Sook-Joo Gyo Library is located slightly ------- the Green Treat Market on Jacob Avenue.
(A) into   (B) over
(C) among   (D) past

기출공식 3 이유, 양보, 목적, 제외, 추가, 대체 전치사가 자주 출제된다.

이유	because of/due to/owing to thanks to/on account of ~ 때문에	제외	without ~ 없이 except (for)/excluding ~을 제외하고 apart from/aside from ~은 제외하고, ~ 이외에
양보	despite/in spite of/notwithstanding ~에도 불구하고	추가	in addition to/besides ~외에도 including ~을 포함하여
목적	for ~을 위해서	대체	instead of/in exchange for ~ 대신에 in place of ~을 대신하여

Despite high ticket prices, all performances sold out. 비싼 표 가격에도 불구하고 전 공연이 매진되었다.

JB Bank cannot process a loan application **without** the proper documentation.
JB 은행은 적절한 서류 없이는 대출 신청을 처리할 수 없다.

7 ------- the bad weather, the construction of the Acme Cement headquarters was completed on schedule.
(A) Despite
(B) Unless
(C) In order to
(D) As well as

8 ------- significant advances in technology, Hwangbo Automotive has been able to design an exceptionally fuel-efficient vehicle.
(A) Due to
(B) When
(C) Because
(D) In order to

9 The town library is open every day of the week ------- Sundays.
(A) out
(B) except
(C) off
(D) down

기출공식 4 기타 다양한 뜻의 전치사가 출제된다.

주제/연관성	수단/방법/도구	비교/자격/소지/동반	반대/우월/정도
about/as to/on/over regarding/concerning pertaining to ~에 관하여	by ~함으로써, ~을 통해 through ~을 통해 with ~로	(un)like ~처럼/~와 달리 as ~로서 with ~을 가지고 along with ~와 함께	against ~에 반대하여 contrary to ~와 달리 beyond ~을 넘어서는 by (차이, 차액이) ~만큼

This memo outlines policies **regarding** compensation. 이 회람은 보상에 대한 정책을 설명합니다.

Unlike our competitors, we offer a free consultation. 경쟁사와 달리, 저희는 무료 상담을 제공합니다.

10 Ms. Besson is expected to replace Mr. Sikorsky ------- vice president at the end of the month.
(A) about
(B) as
(C) like
(D) out

11 In Ms. Park's absence, all inquiries ------- the Bevington project should be directed to her assistant.
(A) assuming
(B) versus
(C) rather
(D) concerning

12 A completed author's checklist must be submitted ------- your article manuscript.
(A) along with
(B) such as
(C) at
(D) to

정답 및 해설 p. 34

according to ~에 따르면 by means of ~을 통해 in advance of ~에 앞서 in cooperation with ~와 협력하여 in honor of ~을 기념하여 in preparation for ~에 대비하여 prior to ~ 이전에	as a result of ~의 결과로 depending (up)on ~에 따라 in celebration of ~을 축하하여 in excess of ~을 초과하여 in light of ~을 고려하여 in response to ~에 응하여 regardless of ~와 상관없이	as part of ~의 일환으로 in accordance with ~에 따라서 in charge of ~을 책임지고 있는 in favor of ~을 찬성하여 in observation of ~을 준수하여 on behalf of ~을 대표[대신]하여 with the exception of ~을 제외하면

We will proceed with the plan **regardless of** the cost. 비용에 상관없이 우리는 계획을 진행할 것이다.

A party will be held **in honor of** Mr. Wu's promotion. 우 씨의 승진을 기념하여 파티가 있을 것이다.

13 Speaking ------- behalf of the vice president, Alan Lee thanked the employees for their contributions to the fund-raising project.
(A) at
(B) on
(C) by
(D) for

14 In ------- to consumer complaints, assembly instructions for the model 481 bookshelf have been simplified.
(A) control
(B) response
(C) access
(D) expense

15 The Usonne Company makes special parking permits available to employees ------- on their seniority.
(A) depended
(B) depending
(C) depend
(D) depends

on duty 근무 중인[중에] on display 전시 중인 on average 평균적으로 in advance 미리 in writing 서면으로 in effect 시행[발효] 중인 out of stock 재고가 없는	at no cost 무료로 behind schedule 예정보다 늦게 upon arrival 도착하자마자 upon request 요청하는 대로 under construction 공사 중인 beyond repair 수리가 불가능한 within walking distance 도보 거리에	at your earliest convenience 가급적 빨리 ahead of schedule/time 예정보다 일찍 from the date of purchase 구매일로부터 in a timely manner 시기적절하게 until further notice 추후 공지 시까지 under the supervision of ~의 감독하에 on a first-come, first-served basis 선착순으로

An entry fee of $5 must be paid **upon arrival.** 도착하자마자 입장료 5달러가 지불되어야 합니다.

The contractors completed their work **ahead of time.** 하청 업체가 예정보다 일찍 작업을 완료했다.

16 The community swimming pool is not to be used at any time unless a trained lifeguard is ------- duty.
(A) unlike
(B) below
(C) with
(D) on

17 Favorable winds caused Melanesia Airlines Flight 632 to arrive at Honiara Airport ------- schedule.
(A) next to
(B) ahead of
(C) down
(D) aboard

18 On -------, 60,000 listeners tune into Crios Radio each day.
(A) average
(B) averages
(C) averaging
(D) averaged

기출공식 7 자동사 뒤에 알맞은 전치사를 선택하는 문제가 출제된다.

comply with ~을 따르다, 준수하다 deal with ~을 다루다 refrain from ~을 삼가다 consist of ~로 구성되다 refer to ~을 참조하다 specialize in ~을 전문으로 하다 search for ~을 찾다	collaborate with ~와 협력하다 correspond with ~와 부합하다 concentrate on ~에 집중하다 dispose of ~을 처분하다 reply/respond to ~에 답하다 contend with ~와 씨름하다 interfere with ~을 방해하다	coincide with ~와 동시에 일어나다 benefit from ~로부터 혜택을 얻다 depend/rely on ~에 의존하다 participate in ~에 참여하다 account for ~을 설명하다, 차지하다 expand into ~로 확장하다 inquire about ~에 대해 문의하다

The factory **complies with** all of the city's safety regulations. 그 공장은 시의 모든 안전 규정을 준수한다.

Mr. Sanz's visit to Sydney **coincides with** the annual festival. 산스 씨의 시드니 방문은 연례 축제와 겹친다.

19 Soaring Skies Airlines has benefited greatly ------- their acquisition of a competitor.
(A) from
(B) to
(C) on
(D) about

20 Zoticos Clothing, Inc., has acquired two other retail companies as part of a plan to expand ------- Europe and Asia.
(A) each
(B) into
(C) here
(D) already

21 Armstrong Shipping was fined for failing to ------- with environmental regulations for trucks.
(A) fulfill
(B) inform
(C) comply
(D) invest

기출공식 8 명사 뒤에 알맞은 전치사를 선택하는 문제가 출제된다.

impact on ~에 미치는 영향 proficiency in ~에 능숙함 problem with ~에 대한 문제 reliance on ~에 대한 의존 interest in ~에 대한 관심	demand for ~에 대한 수요 drop/decrease in ~의 감소 advantage/edge over ~보다 우위 contribution to ~에 대한 기여 comment on ~에 대한 언급	access to ~에 대한 이용[접근] rise/increase in ~의 증가 dispute over ~에 대한 논쟁 influence on ~에 대한 영향 solution to ~에 대한 해결책

The **demand for** licensed financial planners is increasing. 자격증을 갖춘 재무 설계사에 대한 수요가 늘고 있다.

An ID card is needed to gain **access to** the lab. 연구실 입장을 위해 신분증이 필요하다.

22 In order to keep up with the increasing demand ------- our products, we will have to hire a minimum of four additional workers.
(A) with
(B) during
(C) for
(D) by

23 Cole-Mart's enormous size gives it a competitive edge ------- locally-owned grocery stores.
(A) from
(B) into
(C) through
(D) over

24 Recent government policies have had a positive ------- on housing prices nationwide.
(A) impact
(B) supply
(C) factor
(D) target

정답 및 해설 p. 36

1 ------- Dr. Carrera, who will be in Madrid, the entire surgical team will attend the appreciation gala in Perth.
(A) Except for
(B) Along with
(C) Whereas
(D) Likewise

2 The open access database can be used to search ------- job opportunities at Steinach Publishing.
(A) for
(B) up
(C) as
(D) to

3 ------- the newest trends in the banking industry is the drive toward debt consolidation.
(A) Beside
(B) Except
(C) Through
(D) Among

4 ------- analysts' predictions, McKnight Electronic engineers were able to create a battery capable of lasting twice as long as previous models.
(A) Nevertheless
(B) Provided that
(C) Except
(D) Contrary to

5 In the quarter ------- its purchase of the Sumida factory, Lenir Manufacturing increased production by 15 percent.
(A) follow
(B) follows
(C) followed
(D) following

6 The convention center is located on Market Street, directly ------- Glenview Shopping Center.
(A) opposite
(B) among
(C) apart
(D) nearby

7 Banca Ostrava reports that third-quarter earnings are up 35 percent ------- a year ago.
(A) maybe
(B) under
(C) even
(D) from

8 In twenty-five days, the purchase ------- the Northbridge property will be finalized.
(A) into
(B) to
(C) of
(D) upon

9 The city planning board is undecided ------- whether to allow developers to build an apartment complex on Center Street.
(A) out of
(B) because of
(C) as to
(D) up to

10 All Tegram Company employees, ------- part-time workers, are expected to attend tomorrow's training session.
(A) about
(B) later
(C) nevertheless
(D) including

11   ------- an extensive selection of main
     dishes, the restaurant features a large
     dessert menu with a variety of delicious
     baked goods to choose from.
     (A) Because
     (B) Since
     (C) Besides
     (D) Resulting

12   Passengers must present their passport
     ------- their boarding pass to Lunar
     Airlines' personnel when checking in for
     a flight.
     (A) notwithstanding
     (B) in case
     (C) along with
     (D) in spite of

13   The price of Nara Aluminum stock
     remained stable ------- last week's
     changes in the stock market overall.
     (A) even so
     (B) for example
     (C) although
     (D) despite

14   Visitors to Kensington Corporation must
     obtain guest passes ------- the security
     office prior to entering the facility.
     (A) upon
     (B) from
     (C) toward
     (D) between

15   ------- many accounting software
     programs, Devray Ltd.'s Learnadac Plus
     program is designed to teach basic
     accounting skills to students.
     (A) Unlike
     (B) Still
     (C) Regardless
     (D) Rather

16   Please contact Ms. Blackwell in
     the personnel office if you have not
     received information ------- company
     reimbursement procedures.
     (A) regard
     (B) regards
     (C) regarding
     (D) regarded

17   The public relations team placed a large
     ribbon ------- the building entrance for the
     grand opening celebration.
     (A) like
     (B) across
     (C) while
     (D) than

18   ------- delays in the entryway construction,
     the Orchid Restaurant in Chongqing
     will reopen and provide an alternative
     entrance until all work is complete.
     (A) Furthermore
     (B) Assuming that
     (C) Regardless of
     (D) Subsequently

19   The symphony orchestra's performance
     ------- the new outdoor amphitheater
     drew more than 500 attendees.
     (A) onto
     (B) at
     (C) off
     (D) with

20   As ------- February 6, all employees must
     use the updated identification badge.
     (A) by
     (B) at
     (C) in
     (D) of

UNIT 08

동사의 수 일치 / 태 / 시제

평균 3~4문제 출제

무료인강

● 동사의 수 일치 / 태 / 시제

동사의 형태를 결정하는 요소는 수 일치, 태, 시제 세 가지이다.

| 수 일치 | 단수 | The hotel **is** | The item **has** | The company **specializes** |
| | 복수 | The rooms **are** | The candidates **have** | They **specialize** |

태	'주어가 ~하다'이면 능동태, '주어가 ~되다'이면 수동태이다.	
	능동태	We **hold** a weekly meeting every Monday. 우리는 매주 월요일 주간 회의를 연다.
	수동태	A weekly meeting **is held** (by us) every Monday. 매주 월요일 주간 회의가 열린다.

단순 시제, 진행 시제(be동사 + -ing), 완료 시제(have + p.p.)가 있다.

시제		현재	과거	미래
	단순 시제	visit	visited	will visit
	진행 시제	is / are visiting	was / were visiting	will be visiting
	완료 시제	has / have visited	had visited	will have visited

● 동사의 종류

동사는 목적어를 필요로 하지 않는 자동사와 목적어를 필요로 하는 타동사가 있다.

| 자동사 | rise 오르다 | arrive 도착하다 | remain ~인 채로 남아 있다 |
| 타동사 | address 다루다 | discuss 논의하다 | attend 참석하다 |

The price has risen significantly over the past years. 지난 수년간 가격이 상당히 올랐다.
　　　　　자동사　　　　　　수식어

We should address the concerns immediately. 우리는 그 문제를 즉시 해결해야 한다.
　　　　　타동사　　　목적어

동사 | ETS 핵심 출제 패턴

빈칸이 동사 자리인지 여부를 판단하는 문제, 동사 자리일 때 수 일치, 능/수동태, 시제를 판단하는 문제가 골고루 출제된다.

☑ 주어와 동사의 수 일치 문제

Please use the color printer sparingly, since the ink cartridges it requires ------- currently unavailable.

(A) are　　　　　　(B) is
(C) been　　　　　(D) being

컬러 프린터에 필요한 잉크 카트리지를 현재 구할 수 없으므로 프린터를 아껴서 사용해 주세요.

핵심 포인트

주어가 **the ink cartridges**로 복수이므로 복수동사가 들어가야 한다.

▶ 기출공식 1 **p.76**

☑ 능동태와 수동태를 구분하는 문제

The Oakshore region ------- large numbers of young professionals.

(A) was attracted　　　(B) has been attracted
(C) attracting　　　　　(D) attracts

오크쇼어 지역은 수많은 젊은 전문가들을 매료시킨다.

핵심 포인트

빈칸 뒤에 목적어가 있으므로 동사의 능동태가 들어가야 한다.

▶ 기출공식 5 **p.78**

☑ 알맞은 시제를 선택하는 문제

The plant's output ------- since the introduction of automated assembly.

(A) to double　　　　(B) is doubling
(C) has doubled　　　(D) would have been doubling

자동 조립 도입 이후 공장의 생산량이 두 배가 되었다.

핵심 포인트

빈칸 뒤에 **since**가 '~ 이래로'라는 의미이므로 이와 어울리는 현재완료 시제가 들어가야 한다.

▶ 기출공식 10 **p.80**

☑ 시제 일치의 예외를 묻는 문제

Ms. Park requested that staff ------- the building's back entrance during the lobby construction.

(A) use　　　　　(B) using
(C) to use　　　　(D) used

박 씨는 직원들에게 로비 공사 기간에 건물의 뒷문을 이용하라고 요청했다.

핵심 포인트

요구 동사 **request** 뒤 **that**절에는 **should**가 생략되므로 동사원형이 들어가야 한다.

▶ 기출공식 11 **p.81**

정답 : (A), (D), (C), (A)

기출공식 1 단수주어에는 단수동사, 복수주어에는 복수동사를 써서 수 일치한다.

- **단수주어 + 단수동사**

  The red light **flashes** to show low battery power. 배터리 전력이 부족하면 빨간색 불이 깜박인다.

  Purchasing more supplies **requires** a manager's approval. 추가 물품 구매에는 관리자 승인이 요구된다.

  What the city needs now **is** more parking areas. 시에 현재 필요한 것은 더 많은 주차 공간이다.

  → 단수명사, 동명사구, 명사절은 단수주어이며 단수동사로 수 일치한다.

- **복수주어 + 복수동사**

  Pets **are** not allowed within this complex. 이 단지 내에서는 반려동물이 허용되지 않는다.

  Both **take** responsibility for quality control. 둘 다 품질 관리를 책임지고 있다.

  → 복수명사, 수량 대명사 both, many, (a) few, several 등은 복수주어이며 복수동사로 수 일치한다.

1 Employment figures ------- that the nation's economy is growing at its fastest pace in five years.
(A) confirm
(B) to confirm
(C) confirmation
(D) confirms

2 Event organizers ------- an increase in the number of vendors at this year's art festival.
(A) anticipate
(B) anticipates
(C) anticipating
(D) to anticipate

3 Students are attending the Myerson exhibition at the Wilmington Historical Museum because it ------- authentic dinosaur bones.
(A) feature
(B) features
(C) featured
(D) featuring

기출공식 2 수량 표현이 쓰인 주어는 동사의 수 일치에 유의해야 한다.

단수동사로 수 일치	복수동사로 수 일치	부분 표현의 수 일치
a(n) / one / single 하나의 another 다른 하나의 each 각각의 every 모든 the number of ~의 수	a few 몇몇의 few 적은, 거의 없는 both 둘 다의 several 몇몇의 various 다양한 numerous 수많은 many / a number of 많은	[all / most / some / half] of the + 단수명사 + 단수동사 + 복수명사 + 복수동사 → of 뒤에 오는 명사에 수 일치

One of the candidates [was / ~~were~~] asked to stay. 후보자 중 한 명은 머물러 달라는 요청을 받았다.

A number of factors [is / are] considered in decision-making. 많은 요소들이 결정하는 데 고려된다.

Most of the workers [commute / ~~commutes~~] by car. 대부분의 직원들은 차로 통근한다.

4 Roughly half of the employees at Century Photo Labs ------- to work by bus.
(A) commutes
(B) commute
(C) is commuting
(D) has commuted

5 There are a limited number of visitor parking ------- in front of the building.
(A) spaces
(B) space
(C) spaciously
(D) spaced

6 ------- of our repair technicians complete two weeks of intensive formal training before they begin making house calls.
(A) All
(B) Each
(C) Everyone
(D) Which

기출공식 3 문장 구조에 따라 수 일치에 유의해야 한다.

- **접속사 and로 연결된 주어: 복수동사로 수 일치**

  Both price and durability [is / **are**] the key features of the XB battery.
  가격과 내구성 모두 XB 배터리의 핵심 특징이다.

- **There is: 단수명사로 수 일치 / There are: 복수명사로 수 일치**

  There [is / **are**] **many applicants** wishing to work for MJ Corp.
  MJ사에서 일하고 싶어 하는 지원자들이 많다.

- **관계사절(who, which, that절) 내의 동사: 선행사에 수 일치**

  A brochure which [**contains** / contain] the event schedule is offered at the front desk.
  행사 일정표가 포함된 책자가 안내 데스크에서 제공된다.

7 Tomorrow we will meet with a group of consultants who ------- in staff training and team building.
   (A) specialize
   (B) specializes
   (C) specializing
   (D) specialization

8 There are several ------- in the area that sell the Master Print brand of printer paper.
   (A) store
   (B) stores
   (C) storing
   (D) stored

9 After three years of intense negotiation, Megali Corporation and Liggman Industries ------- finally agreed on the terms of their merger.
   (A) has
   (B) have
   (C) having
   (D) to have

빈출

기출공식 4 수식어는 수 일치에 영향을 주지 않는다.

전치사구   **The computers** (in the library) [is / **are**] regularly checked for disk errors and viruses. (도서관) 컴퓨터들은 디스크 오류와 바이러스를 정기적으로 점검 받는다.

to부정사구 **The team's ability** (to meet sales goals) [**depends** / depend] on its members' commitment. (영업 목표를 달성하는) 그 팀의 능력은 직원들의 헌신에 달려 있다.

분사구   **Our spring items** (manufactured in Malaysia) [is / **are**] currently out of stock.
       (말레이시아에서 제조된) 우리 회사 봄 상품은 현재 재고가 없다.

관계사절   **Those** (who are planning to attend the expo) [is / **are**] using buses to get there.
       (박람회에 참가하고자 하는) 사람들은 버스를 이용해서 갈 것이다.

10 The maintenance supplies for Building B ------- kept in room 132, next to the security desk.
   (A) to be
   (B) are
   (C) is
   (D) being

11 Customers who purchase a new appliance from Mahmud's Home Store ------- up to one month to exchange it.
   (A) has
   (B) having had
   (C) to have
   (D) have

12 Products made by Izmir Vitamins ------- to promote health and well-being.
   (A) are designed
   (B) having designed
   (C) designs
   (D) is designed

정답 및 해설 p. 39

기출공식 5 타동사 뒤에 목적어가 있으면 능동태, 없으면 수동태를 쓴다.

능동태   The city **renovated** the building recently. 시가 최근에 그 건물을 보수했다.
                       주어   동사   목적어

수동태   The building **was renovated** (by the city) recently. 그 건물은 시에 의해 최근에 보수되었다.
                       주어   동사   목적어 없음

+만점팁 완전 자동사는 수동태로 쓰지 않는다.

| rise 오르다 | work 일하다 | arrive 도착하다 | occur 일어나다 | take place 발생하다 |

The production costs **have risen** over the past few years. 지난 몇 년간 생산비가 올랐다.

---

13 Marveo's Supermarket is ------- its services to include an online grocery store and delivery service.
(A) expanded
(B) expanding
(C) expansive
(D) expands

14 A sum of €500,000 ------- anonymously to Galway Hospital earlier this month.
(A) donated
(B) to donate
(C) a donation
(D) was donated

15 Children who are two years old and younger are ------- free of charge to most concerts and films.
(A) admitted
(B) admitting
(C) to admit
(D) admission

기출공식 6 4형식 5형식 동사는 수동태에 유의해야 한다.

■ **4형식 동사는 수동태 뒤에 목적어가 올 수 있다.**

| give 주다 | send 보내다 | offer 제공하다 | grant 주다 | award 수여하다 | issue 발급하다 | charge 부과하다 |

능동태   The manager **gave** Mr. Watson an assignment. 관리자는 왓슨 씨에게 임무를 주었다.
                               간접목적어   직접목적어

수동태   Mr. Watson **was given** an assignment. 왓슨 씨는 임무를 받았다.
                               수동태 뒤에 남아 있는 목적어

■ **5형식 동사는 수동태 뒤에 목적격 보어가 남는다.**

| make 만들다 | keep 유지하다 | find 생각하다 | consider 여기다 | leave 남겨 두다 | name/appoint 임명하다 |

능동태   The committee **named** Mr. Pinto head coach. 위원회는 핀토 씨를 수석 코치로 임명했다.
                               목적어   목적격·보어

수동태   Mr. Pinto **was named** head coach. 핀토 씨는 수석 코치로 임명되었다.
                              수동태 뒤에 남아 있는 목적격 보어

---

16 The inventors of the Spin Gadget ------- first prize in the Family Fun & Games contest for their creative idea.
(A) awards
(B) were awarded
(C) to award
(D) having awarded

17 Checks or money orders in support of the Theater for All project ------- payable to Alio Actors Organization.
(A) to make
(B) are making
(C) should be made
(D) will have made

18 Library patrons who fail to return an item by the due date ------- a fee.
(A) charge
(B) will be charged
(C) have charged
(D) are charging

기출공식 7 다양한 수동태 관용 표현이 출제된다.

be satisfied with ~에 만족하다	be pleased with ~에 기뻐하다	be equipped with ~을 갖추다
be associated with ~와 연관되다	be faced with ~에 직면하다	be covered with ~로 덮이다
be interested in ~에 관심이 있다	be engaged in ~에 종사하다	be involved in ~에 관여하다
be based on ~에 근거하다	be divided into ~로 나뉘다	be exposed to 명사 ~에 노출되다

be [asked/required/requested/encouraged/expected/advised] to부정사 ~하도록 요청[권고]되다

The CEO **was pleased with** the high profits. 최고 경영자는 높은 수익에 기뻐했다.

The tenants **were asked to** pay their rents. 세입자들은 임대료를 지불하도록 요청되었다.

19 Dr. Turner is very ------- with the progress the construction crew has made on his new office.
(A) pleased   (B) pleasant
(C) pleasing   (D) pleasure

20 Applicants for managerial positions at FDJ Finance ------- to possess at least seven years of experience in the field.
(A) require   (B) requires
(C) are required (D) has required

21 The apartments on the lower floors cost less because they are more exposed ------- dust and the noise of traffic.
(A) to   (B) without
(C) from   (D) against

빈출

기출공식 8 동사의 시제는 현재, 과거, 미래로 나뉘며 시간 표현과 함께 출제된다.

현재 **현재의 상태, 반복, 습관, 일반적인 사실을 나타낸다.**

어울리는 부사(구): usually 보통   generally 일반적으로   every + 시점 ex) every month 매달

The city **holds** a music festival every year in Yan Park. 시는 얀 파크에서 매년 음악 축제를 연다.

과거 **과거에 끝난 동작이나 상태를 나타낸다.**

어울리는 부사(구): ago 전에   last + 시점 ex) last week 지난주   recently 최근에   once 한때

Your subscription **expired** a week ago. 귀하의 구독은 1주 전에 만료되었습니다.

미래 **앞으로 발생할 일을 나타낸다.**

어울리는 부사(구): next + 시점   later this + 시점 ex) later this week 이번 주 중으로   soon 곧

A package **will be shipped** later this afternoon. 소포가 오늘 오후 중으로 발송될 것이다.

+만점팁 현재진행 시제(be -ing)도 이미 정해진 미래를 나타낼 수 있다.

22 Mr. Parker ------- office supplies from the warehouse every Wednesday, so please inform him of your needs by Tuesday.
(A) orders
(B) ordered
(C) order
(D) to order

23 Local government officials finally ------- the proposed 2 percent tax increase yesterday.
(A) will be approved
(B) have been approving
(C) are approving
(D) approved

24 Tickets to the golf tournament in Singapore ------- online starting next month.
(A) have been sold
(B) selling
(C) have been selling
(D) will be sold

정답 및 해설 p. 41

- **현재진행(am/are/is -ing): 현재의 한 시점에 진행 중인 일을 나타낸다.**
  Radio Center **is** currently **seeking** a translator fluent in Spanish for its Chicago office.
  라디오 센터는 현재 시카고 지사에서 일할 스페인어에 능통한 번역자를 구하고 있다.

- **과거진행(was/were -ing): 과거의 한 시점에 진행되었던 일을 나타낸다.**
  Mr. Forbes **was attending** a conference in Mexico when one of his clients called.
  고객 한 명이 전화했을 때 포브스 씨는 멕시코에서 회의에 참석하고 있었다.

- **미래진행(will be -ing): 미래의 한 시점에 진행될 일을 나타낸다.**
  Mr. Grove **will be doing** a product demonstration at this time tomorrow.
  내일 이맘때 그로브 씨는 제품 시연을 하고 있을 것이다.

---

25 Magnum Plus cameras ------ very popular right now because they are so easy to use.
(A) became
(B) are becoming
(C) to become
(D) becomes

26 LTD Enterprises is currently ------ an accomplished individual to replace the current director, who will be retiring at the end of the month.
(A) seek　　(B) seeks
(C) sought　(D seeking

27 We are pleased to announce that Ms. Vieri ------ her new position as market analyst on September 30.
(A) has been starting
(B) will be starting
(C) was started
(D) is being started

- **현재완료(have/has p.p.): 현재까지 계속되거나 방금 완료된 일, 과거의 경험 등을 나타낸다.**

  어울리는 부사(구): since ~ 이래로　　for the last[over the past] 지난 ~ 동안　　recently/lately 최근에

  Santorini Bistro **has been** in business since 1986. 산토리니 식당은 1986년 이래로 계속 운영해 왔다.
  Amery & Co. **has** just **released** their new line of footwear. 에이머리사는 신발 신제품군을 막 출시했다.

- **과거완료(had p.p.): 과거의 특정 시점보다 더 먼저 일어난 일을 나타낸다.**
  By the time the document arrived, the planning team **had** already **left** the office.
  서류가 도착했을 무렵 기획팀은 이미 사무실을 나가고 없었다.

- **미래완료(will have p.p.): 미래의 특정 시점에 완료되는 일을 나타낸다.**
  By the end of this year, the construction company **will have completed** the project.
  올해 말이면 건설사가 프로젝트를 끝마쳤을 것이다.

---

28 The executive board has not ------ next year's budget yet.
(A) final
(B) finally
(C) finalized
(D) finalize

29 Dr. Suzuki arrived for the awards ceremony on time even though her train ------ twenty minutes late.
(A) is leaving
(B) will leave
(C) to leave
(D) had left

30 At the end of next month, executive chef Tracy Nakagawa ------ the kitchen at the Hokulea Café for ten years.
(A) has supervised
(B) will have supervised
(C) had been supervising
(D) is supervising

기출공식 11 시제 일치에는 예외가 있다.

- **시간/조건 부사절에서는 현재가 미래를 대신한다.**

  The manager will call us **when** he [**gets** / will get] to the construction site tomorrow.
  관리자가 내일 공사 현장에 도착하면 우리에게 전화할 것이다.

  The factory tour will go ahead next week **if** one more person [**signs** / will sign] up for it.
  한 사람이 더 등록하면 공장 견학은 다음 주에 시작될 것이다.

- **요구/제안의 동사나 당위성을 나타내는 형용사 뒤 that절에는 (should) + 동사원형을 쓴다.**

  ask, request, suggest, recommend/necessary, important, imperative, essential+that절 동사원형

  Ms. Suh **suggested that** the empty office space (should) **be** turned into a staff fitness center. 서 씨는 빈 사무실 공간이 직원 체력단련실로 바뀌어야 한다고 제안했다.

  It is **imperative that** the city council (should) **name** a chairperson.
  시 의회가 빨리 의장을 임명하는 것이 중요하다.

31 The Hong Kong office of Huang Associates will be closed temporarily while renovations -------.
(A) will be complete
(B) are completed
(C) being completed
(D) completing

32 Professional Photographic Arts Studio requests that applicants ------- a portfolio of black-and white photographs.
(A) to submit
(B) submitted
(C) submit
(D) would submit

33 It is imperative that computer passwords ------- kept confidential.
(A) were
(B) be
(C) being
(D) had been

기출공식 12 동사 문제는 수 일치, 태, 시제가 부분적으로 섞인 문제로 주로 출제된다.

동사 문제를 풀 때는 수 일치 → 태 → 시제의 순서로 따져서 정답을 가려내야 한다.

Our marketing promotion for magazine subscriptions ------- positive results last year.
보기: yielded / have yielded / was yielded / will yield

① **수 일치** – 단수명사 our marketing promotion에 수 일치를 해야 하므로 have yielded는 소거한다.
② **태** – 목적어 positive results가 있으므로 수동태인 was yielded는 소거한다.
③ **시제** – 과거 시제의 단서 last year가 있으므로 yielded를 정답으로 선택한다.

34 The Globe Lighting Supply handbook ------- a list of important company telephone numbers.
(A) contain
(B) containing
(C) is contained
(D) contains

35 For the past few months, doughnuts ------- muffins at Marinelle Bakery.
(A) are outsold
(B) will be outselling
(C) have been outselling
(D) would have been outsold

36 Once Ms. Cohen ------- the detailed business plan, she was more receptive to the idea of investing in the new company.
(A) had examined
(B) examines
(C) be examined
(D) was examined

1   Office supplies are to be ------- only when
    conducting business-related tasks.
    (A) used
    (B) uses
    (C) usage
    (D) using

2   Topics at the business communication
    workshop ------- defending an argument,
    synthesizing information, and writing
    precisely and concisely.
    (A) include
    (B) includes
    (C) including
    (D) inclusion

3   Trains for Gruyville ------- at 9:00 A.M.
    from Monday through Friday.
    (A) depart
    (B) is departed
    (C) departs
    (D) is departing

4   Unauthorized individuals are ------- from
    parking their cars in the Jasper Building's
    parking garage.
    (A) prohibit
    (B) prohibitions
    (C) prohibited
    (D) prohibiting

5   The plant supervisor, Mr. Lee, recently
    ------- a tour of the company's main
    production facility for our clients.
    (A) conduct
    (B) conducted
    (C) to conduct
    (D) will conduct

6   Please make sure that Ms. Rossi's order
    ------- before 3:00 P.M. because she is
    leaving the office early today.
    (A) is delivered
    (B) delivery
    (C) is delivering
    (D) delivered

7   Recent research on battery life shows
    that the battery in our newest mobile
    phone ------- better than those in similar
    products.
    (A) perform
    (B) performing
    (C) performs
    (D) performance

8   The court hearing on the boundary
    dispute ------- now that an agreement has
    just been reached.
    (A) to cancel
    (B) canceling
    (C) has canceled
    (D) will be canceled

9   The technician ------- repairs on the
    machinery, so production of the X220 will
    resume when she has finished.
    (A) making
    (B) had made
    (C) will have been made
    (D) has been making

10 Mornesse Hardware ------- free flashlights
    to the first 50 customers during its grand
    opening next Friday.
    (A) is offering
    (B) having offered
    (C) was offered
    (D) to offer

11 While Morgen Copying and Reproduction offers cost-effective rates, Vogel Printing's services better ------- our business needs.
(A) suit
(B) suits
(C) suitable
(D) suitably

12 Horizon Bridge Company won the Innovation Award for its newest suspension bridge project, which ------- by Ms. Kameda, the chief engineer.
(A) is overseeing
(B) was overseen
(C) has overseen
(D) be overseen

13 First City Bank assured its customers that it ------- exceptional service in spite of the ongoing renovations in several branches.
(A) maintaining
(B) maintain
(C) will maintain
(D) to maintain

14 While Ms. Fukui is willing to continue working part-time, she hopes to ------- full-time employment eventually.
(A) be offered
(B) offer
(C) offering
(D) offered

15 Young Automotive plans to launch a new Web site that ------- its customers to access invoices.
(A) has allowed
(B) allow
(C) will allow
(D) allowed

16 Ms. Yakamoto has suggested that the department meeting ------- until everyone returns from vacation.
(A) be postponed
(B) having postponed
(C) will be postponed
(D) to postpone

17 By the time Mr. Schmidt joined our firm as a financial analyst, he ------- in the financial sector for many years already.
(A) has worked
(B) works
(C) will work
(D) had worked

18 This award is designed to recognize employees who ------- exceptional service to our clients.
(A) be provided
(B) provides
(C) provide
(D) providing

19 The warehouse manager at Yamora, Inc., was promoted, so the company ------- for this newly opened position.
(A) recruiting
(B) to recruit
(C) was recruited
(D) is recruiting

20 Aria Fletcher will discuss the advertising budget with the board of directors when they ------- formally next month.
(A) will meet
(B) meet
(C) be meeting
(D) meeting

UNIT 09

to부정사와 동명사

평균 1문제 출제

무료인강

● to부정사(to + 동사원형)와 동명사(동사원형 + -ing)의 역할

to부정사와 동명사의 명사적 역할

Wilson Ltd. plans **to increase** its production. 윌슨사는 생산을 **늘리는 것**을 계획한다.

Increasing the number of customers is a challenge. 고객 수를 **늘리는 것**은 어려운 일이다.

We met our goal without [**increasing** / ~~to increase~~] the cost. 우리는 비용 **증가** 없이 목표를 달성했다.

→ to부정사는 전치사의 목적어로는 쓰지 않는다.

to부정사의 형용사적 역할

The manager created a plan **to increase** sales. 관리자는 판매를 **증가시킬** 계획을 고안했다.

to부정사의 부사적 역할

A new system was introduced **to increase** security. 보안 **향상을 위해** 새 시스템이 도입되었다.

● to부정사와 동명사의 동사에 준하는(준동사적) 성질

보어를 가질 수 있다.

We plan **to remain open** until midnight. 우리는 자정까지 영업할 계획이다.

We are considering **remaining open** until midnight. 우리는 자정까지 영업하는 것을 고려 중이다.

→ remain이 보어를 필요로 하는 동사이므로 to remain / remaining 뒤에 보어가 온다.

목적어를 가질 수 있다.

Company executives convened **to discuss the next steps**. 임원들이 다음 단계를 논의하기 위해 모였다.

Company executives finished **discussing the next steps**. 임원들이 다음 단계 논의를 끝마쳤다.

→ discuss가 목적어를 필요로 하는 동사이므로 to discuss / discussing 뒤에 목적어가 온다.

부사의 수식을 받는다.

We try **to work closely** with other members. 저희는 다른 회원들과 긴밀히 일하려고 노력합니다.

We look forward to **working closely** with other members. 저희는 다른 회원들과 긴밀히 일하기를 기대합니다.

→ work가 자동사로 쓰였으므로 to work / working을 부사가 수식한다.

to부정사와 동명사 | ETS 핵심 출제 패턴

to부정사는 다양한 용법 중 '~하기 위해서'라는 목적의 의미로 쓰이는 to부정사가 가장 많이 출제되며, 동명사는 명사와 구별하는 문제가 자주 출제된다. 그 외에 to부정사와 동명사가 포함된 다양한 표현들도 익혀 두어야 한다.

☑ 목적을 나타내는 to부정사를 완성하는 문제

Our winter clothing is being sold at a discount to ------- room for the new spring merchandise.

(A) making   (B) make
(C) makes   (D) made

봄 신상품을 위한 공간을 마련하기 위해 겨울 옷이 할인가에 판매되고 있다.

핵심 포인트

'공간을 만들기 위해'라는 목적의 의미가 되도록 to부정사가 와야 한다.

▶ 기출공식 1 p.86

☑ 명사를 뒤에서 수식하는 to부정사를 선택하는 문제

The ability ------- the confidence of your clients is essential in a sales job.

(A) to gain   (B) gains
(C) be gained   (D) gain

고객의 신뢰를 얻는 능력은 영업직에서 필수적이다.

핵심 포인트

'~하는 능력'이라는 의미가 되도록 명사를 뒤에서 수식해야 한다.

▶ 기출공식 3 p.87

☑ 주어 자리에 동명사를 선택하는 문제

------- a budget encourages an executive to examine several options before deciding on a course of action.

(A) Prepares   (B) Have prepared
(C) Preparing   (D) Will prepare

예산안 입안은 회사 임원으로 하여금 행동 방침을 결정하기에 앞서 여러 가지 선택 사항을 검토하게 한다.

핵심 포인트

주어 역할을 하면서 목적어 (a budget)를 취할 수 있는 동명사가 들어가야 한다.

▶ 기출공식 6 p.88

☑ 전치사의 목적어 자리에 동명사를 선택하는 문제

The company's goal is to introduce more efficient ways of ------- coal.

(A) burn   (B) burns
(C) burned   (D) burning

회사의 목표는 석탄을 태우는 더 효율적인 방법을 도입하는 것이다.

핵심 포인트

전치사 of의 목적어이자 뒤에 오는 coal을 목적어로 취하는 동명사가 들어가야 한다.

▶ 기출공식 6 p.88

정답 : (B), (A), (C), (D)

기출공식 1 to부정사는 명사, 형용사, 부사로 쓰일 수 있다.

- **to부정사는 역할이 '정해져 있지 않다'하여 부정사라고 한다.**

명사 역할	(목적어나 보어로서) ~하는 것, ~하기	want **to participate** 참석하기를 원하다
형용사 역할	(명사를 수식하여) ~할, ~하는	opportunity **to participate** 참석할 기회
부사 역할	(목적) ~하기 위해, (이유) ~해서	in order **to participate** 참석하기 위해

To encourage cooperation, the director held a meeting between department heads.
협업을 장려하기 위해 이사는 부서장들간의 회의를 개최했다.

→ '~하기 위해'를 뜻하는 부사 역할의 to부정사가 가장 많이 출제되며, **in order to, so as to**로도 쓸 수 있다.

- **긴 to부정사구는 주어로 잘 쓰이지 않으며, 대신 가주어 it을 쓴다.**

To improve the quality of our product is important. 제품 품질을 개선하는 것은 중요하다.

→ It is important **(for us) to improve** the quality of our product.

→ to부정사 앞에 'for + 목적격'을 써서 to부정사의 의미상 주어(주체)를 나타낼 수 있다.

1 The purpose of this government program is ------- schools with better access to new learning technologies.
(A) to provide (B) provides
(C) provided (D) to providing

2 Commissioner Kano has scheduled a time ------- the press statement.
(A) issue (B) issuing
(C) will issue (D) to issue

3 ------- the processing of your claim, include your customer identification number on all correspondence.
(A) Expedite (B) Expedited
(C) To expedite (D) To be expedited

기출공식 2 특정 동사는 to부정사를 목적어나 목적격 보어로 취한다.

- **to부정사를 목적어로 취하는 동사**

want/need to intend to promise to	wish/hope to aim to pretend to	would like to agree to offer to	plan to decide to manage to	expect to afford to fail to

- **to부정사를 목적격 보어로 취하는 동사**

allow 목 to encourage 목 to	expect 목 to ask 목 to	invite 목 to remind 목 to	advise 목 to require 목 to	enable 목 to instruct 목 to

Mr. Moore **agreed to update** the training manual. 무어 씨는 교육 설명서를 업데이트하기로 동의했다.

We **invite** you **to join** our membership. 저희는 귀하께 멤버십에 가입하실 것을 권합니다.

→ You **are invited to** join our membership. → 목적격 보어가 포함된 표현은 수동태로 자주 쓰인다.

4 The company may decide ------- additional staff in order to process the increased volume of orders this holiday season.
(A) hires (B) will hire
(C) must hire (D) to hire

5 Sales in South Asia are expected ------- the majority of the company's revenue this year.
(A) generated (B) generating
(C) will generate (D) to generate

6 Cell Choice marketers are ------- to become familiar with competitors' products and advertising.
(A) encourage (B) encourages
(C) encouraged (D) encouraging

기출공식 3 특정 명사는 to부정사의 수식을 받는다.

ability to ~할 능력	right to ~할 권리	authority to ~할 권한
effort to ~하려는 노력	attempt to ~하려는 시도	decision to ~하려는 결정
way to ~하는 방법	failure to ~하지 못함	opportunity/chance to ~할 기회
time to ~할 시간	plan to ~하려는 계획	proposal to ~하자는 제안

The company reserves the **right to change** the timetable and the fares without notice.
회사는 통보 없이 시간표와 요금을 변경할 권한이 있습니다.

7 Today, Tenopy Tech announced its plans ------- with Shaffly Energy Systems to manufacture solar panels in Quito and Caracas.
(A) to partner
(B) be partnering
(C) is partnered
(D) will partner

8 We at TPG Financial Planning welcome the opportunity ------- you in your business and look forward to a mutually beneficial relationship.
(A) assisting
(B) to assist
(C) assisted
(D) assistant

9 The proposal ------- Greer Trail was approved at the Parks Department's last meeting.
(A) to extend
(B) extension
(C) would extend
(D) is extended

빈출

기출공식 4 to부정사 관용 표현이 자주 출제된다.

- **be동사 + 형용사 + to부정사**

be about to 막 ~하려고 하다	be able to ~할 수 있다	be likely to ~할 것 같다
be eager to ~하기를 열망하다	be willing to 기꺼이 ~하다	be sure to 반드시 ~하다
be due to ~할 예정이다	be ready to ~할 준비가 되다	be hesitant to ~하기를 주저하다
be reluctant to ~하기를 꺼리다	be delighted to ~해서 기쁘다	be pleased to ~해서 기쁘다

- **기타 빈출 표현**

enough to ~하기에 충분히 …하다	too … to 너무 …해서 ~할 수 없다	have[be] yet to 아직 ~하지 않다

Your purchase **is due to** arrive on September 3. 귀하의 구매품은 9월 3일 도착할 예정입니다.

The management **is yet to** determine the criteria for the promotion.
경영진은 아직 승진 기준을 정하지 않았다.

10 Gradeliax, Inc.'s building materials are durable ------- to protect structures against damage from all types of weather conditions.
(A) well
(B) enough
(C) highly
(D) much

11 Many companies are finding that it is ------- expensive to store their paper documents in off-site warehouses.
(A) much
(B) too
(C) far
(D) ever

12 Governor Perez has ------- to confirm that she is running for reelection.
(A) yet
(B) once
(C) soon
(D) finally

정답 및 해설 p. 46

- **사역동사 – have, let, make: 목적어가 ~하도록 만들다 / 시키다**

This software program will **let** <u>staff members</u> **choose** their working hours.
이 소프트웨어 프로그램은 직원들이 근무 시간을 선택할 수 있게 해 줄 것이다.

→ 목적어인 **staff members**와 목적격 보어 '선택하다'의 관계가 능동이므로 원형부정사 choose를 쓴다.

We will **have** <u>the walls</u> **painted** in our office today, so please be careful in the work area.
오늘 사무실 벽에 페인트칠을 하므로 작업 구역에서 유의하시기 바랍니다.

→ 목적어인 **the walls**와 목적격 보어 '칠하다'의 관계가 수동이므로 과거분사 painted를 쓴다.

- **준사역동사 – help: 목적어가 ~하는 것을 돕다**

Mr. Stern's speech **helped** (many students) **(to) set** more ambitious goals.
스턴 씨의 연설은 (많은 학생들이) 더 야심 찬 목표를 세우도록 도왔다.

→ help는 목적격 보어로 원형부정사나 to부정사를 모두 취할 수 있으며, 목적어를 생략하고 쓸 수도 있다.

---

13 The CEO of Vento Cosmetics did not let the recent problems with foreign sales ------- the company's long-term export plans.
(A) to affect
(B) affect
(C) affecting
(D) will affect

14 Resolving customer service issues in a timely and effective manner will help a company ------- a good image.
(A) maintained
(B) be maintained
(C) maintain
(D) is maintaining

15 Montague, Inc. had its new wristwatch ------- by several extreme athletes.
(A) testing
(B) test
(C) tested
(D) that tests

빈출

주어	**Complying with safety rules** is necessary to maintain a safe environment. 안전 규정을 준수하는 것은 안전한 환경을 유지하는 데 필수적이다.
타동사의 목적어	Due to some errors on the Web site, the company <u>suggests</u> **calling** the toll-free numbers. 웹사이트의 몇 가지 오류 때문에 그 회사는 수신자 부담 전화를 이용하라고 제안한다.
전치사의 목적어	By **signing** this form, you agree to the revised terms and conditions. 이 양식에 서명함으로써 개정된 약관에 동의하시게 됩니다.

---

16 ------- a series of trial runs before launching large-scale production of any new product is common practice at Juvo, Inc.
(A) Perform
(B) Performs
(C) Performing
(D) Performed

17 ------- social media to market business services is an inexpensive way to attract new clients.
(A) Usage
(B) Using
(C) Use
(D) Used

18 The management of Eurosan Enterprises is in the process of ------- a new set of guidelines for customer service.
(A) establish
(B) establishes
(C) established
(D) establishing

기출공식 7 동명사는 명사와 달리 목적어를 취할 수 있고 부사의 수식을 받는다.

Ms. Fields will be in charge of [supervision / supervising] this plant.
필즈 씨가 이 공장을 감독하는 일을 담당하게 될 것이다.

→ 뒤에 목적어 'this plant'가 있으므로 명사는 올 수 없다.

[Temporary / Temporarily] postponing the product launch will allow us to do more market research. 제품 출시를 잠시 연기하는 것은 우리가 더 많은 시장 조사를 할 수 있게 할 것이다.

→ 동명사는 동사의 성질을 그대로 가지므로 부사의 수식을 받는다.

＋만점팁 동명사는 부정관사 a / an과 함께 쓰지 않는다.

There was a [decrease / decreasing] in the registration rate for the conference this year.
올해 회의 등록률이 감소했다.

19 We require all visitors to present photo identification prior to ------- the building.
(A) entering
(B) entrance
(C) have entered
(D) being entered

20 Researchers at Gasnite Company have developed an improved method of ------- fuel from industrial waste materials.
(A) extraction
(B) extracts
(C) extracted
(D) extracting

21 The guest speaker highlighted some ideas for ------- introducing change in the workplace.
(A) success
(B) succeed
(C) succeeding
(D) successfully

기출공식 8 특정 동사는 동명사를 목적어로 취한다.

consider -ing ~을 고려하다 include -ing ~을 포함하다 mind -ing ~을 꺼리다	recommend / suggest -ing ~을 제안하다 delay / postpone -ing ~을 미루다 discontinue -ing ~을 중단하다	finish -ing ~을 끝내다 avoid -ing ~을 피하다 enjoy -ing ~을 즐기다

Clerical workers should **avoid sitting** too close to their computer monitors.
사무직 직원들은 컴퓨터 모니터에 너무 가까이 앉으면 안 된다.

22 As part of its new marketing strategy, the company will consider ------- in more international trade shows.
(A) participates
(B) participatory
(C) to participate
(D) participating

23 For the convenience of other passengers, please avoid ------- your bags on the bus's empty seats.
(A) placing
(B) to place
(C) places
(D) place

24 After reviewing our operations, the consultant recommended ------- several departments.
(A) consolidate
(B) consolidation
(C) consolidated
(D) consolidating

정답 및 해설 p. 48

1 Mr. Uemura declined to ------- on rumors about how many medicines the drug manufacturer had in development.
(A) commenting
(B) commentary
(C) comment
(D) comments

2 ------- the range of articles in our publication has undoubtedly helped attract new readers.
(A) Diversity
(B) Diversifying
(C) Diversify
(D) Diversification

3 Geologist Ulia Chernof climbs mountains in Austria ------- the composition of snow on the glacial peaks.
(A) to analyze
(B) analysis
(C) is analyzing
(D) analyzer

4 Tachibana Pharmaceuticals' new method of ------- chemical solutions will increase efficiency in the laboratory.
(A) combine
(B) combinations
(C) combining
(D) combines

5 The Ashford Chamber of Commerce invites visitors ------- the restaurants and theaters on the city's waterfront.
(A) patronize
(B) patronized
(C) to patronize
(D) be patronizing

6 Our database security software has been upgraded ------- maintain the confidentiality of client records.
(A) for
(B) because
(C) so that
(D) in order to

7 The agreement between the two corporations will enable both ------- their businesses.
(A) expanding
(B) expands
(C) to expand
(D) expansion

8 Delemarke's profits are expected ------- steadily over the next ten years as the company begins to offer new services abroad.
(A) to rise
(B) risen
(C) rising
(D) to be risen

9 Melbourne Motors has succeeded in ------- positive publicity for its new line of ecologically friendly automobiles.
(A) generating
(B) generation
(C) generative
(D) generate

10 After ------- failing to win customer support, Tykon's upgraded software program has been withdrawn from the market.
(A) repeat
(B) repetition
(C) repeated
(D) repeatedly

11 Despite ------- declines in revenue over the past six months, the Mori & McGee firm intends to hire three new patent lawyers next year.
(A) will experience
(B) having experienced
(C) has experienced
(D) have been experiencing

12 Some officials still need ------- of the importance of separate playing fields for young football and baseball players.
(A) convince
(B) to be convinced
(C) be convincing
(D) have convinced

13 Mr. Riyadh, a successful local businessman, made his fortune by ------- in real estate.
(A) invests
(B) investing
(C) invested
(D) invest

14 If you wish to cancel your subscription to *The Steele Lake Ledger*, please be sure ------- for four weeks of processing time.
(A) to allow
(B) will allow
(C) be allowing
(D) having allowed

15 Funds raised by the local preservation society have helped ------- the historic Jesenville train station.
(A) restoring
(B) to restore
(C) restored
(D) is restored

16 Despite the opening of several new restaurants in the area, Vitella's Restaurant is still attracting enough customers ------- in business.
(A) stay
(B) to stay
(C) stayed
(D) staying

17 To maintain the laboratory's high standards, employees are required ------- an annual training workshop.
(A) attends
(B) to attend
(C) attending
(D) having attended

18 Count on Heston Roofing to ------- get the job done, no matter the season.
(A) rely
(B) reliable
(C) reliably
(D) relying

19 Based on recent customer feedback, the company may consider ------- its most popular product line.
(A) to expand
(B) expansion
(C) have expanded
(D) expanding

20 The health clinic advises patients that getting sufficient rest can greatly decrease the time it takes ------- from a minor cold.
(A) to recover
(B) will recover
(C) be recovered
(D) has recovered

평균 1문제 출제

무료인강

분사의 형태와 특징

분사는 동사에 '-ing' 또는 '-ed'를 붙여서 만들며 형용사 역할을 한다.

현재분사	demand**ing** 까다로운	exist**ing** 기존의
과거분사	qualifi**ed** 자격을 갖춘	experienc**ed** 경험이 있는

분사는 준동사이므로 동사처럼 보어나 목적어를 가질 수 있고, 부사의 수식을 받는다.

Simon Tech is a company **actively seeking ways** to produce environmentally friendly
products.
목적어 O

사이먼 테크는 친환경 제품을 생산하는 방법을 적극적으로 찾고 있는 회사이다.

→ 분사 **seeking**이 **ways**를 목적어로 받고, 부사 **actively**의 수식을 받고 있다.

분사구문

접속사절에서 접속사와 주어를 생략하고 동사를 분사로 바꾸어 '분사구문'을 만들 수 있다.

<u>Although</u> <u>he</u> <u>interviewed</u> all the applicants, the director could not find any suitable candidates.
   ①   ②   ③

① 접속사를 생략한다.
② 주절과 같은 주어를 생략한다.
③ 동사를 분사로 만든다.

→ Interviewing all the applicants, the director could not find any suitable candidates.
모든 지원자들을 면접했지만, 이사는 적임자를 찾지 못했다.

분사 | ETS 핵심 출제 패턴

명사를 수식하는 자리에서 현재분사와 과거분사를 구별하는 문제가 주로 출제되며, 감정을 나타내는 분사, 분사구문의 올바른 형태를 묻는 문제도 종종 출제된다.

☑ 형용사 자리에 현재분사를 선택하는 문제

Crown Corporation has been the nation's ------- commercial supplier of fabric dyes for over 25 years.

(A) leads
(B) leader
(C) to lead
(D) leading

크라운사는 25년 넘게 국내 굴지의 상용 직물 염색 공급업체이다.

핵심 포인트

빈칸 뒤 명사를 수식하는 형용사 역할을 할 수 있는 현재분사가 들어가야 한다.

▶ 기출공식 1 **p.94**

☑ 현재분사와 과거분사를 구별하는 문제

For a ------- period of time, Merriman-Lewis is offering a 15 percent discount on its entire line of desktop laser printers.

(A) limited
(B) limits
(C) limiting
(D) limitation

한정된 기간에 메리먼-루이스는 데스크톱 레이저 프린터 전 기종을 15퍼센트 할인 판매하고 있다.

핵심 포인트

'한정된 기간'이라는 수동의 의미가 되어야 하므로 과거분사가 들어가야 한다.

▶ 기출공식 2 **p.94**

☑ 명사를 뒤에서 수식하는 과거분사를 선택하는 문제

A thunderstorm ------- by gusty winds is expected to arrive in the northeast region by late afternoon.

(A) will accompany
(B) accompanying
(C) to accompany
(D) accompanied

돌풍이 동반된 뇌우가 오후 늦게 북동 지역에 도착할 것으로 예상된다.

핵심 포인트

빈칸 앞 명사를 수식하는 형용사 역할을 할 수 있는 과거분사가 들어가야 한다.

▶ 기출공식 3 **p.95**

☑ 분사구문을 완성하는 문제

------- for its classic designs, Derby Company is the largest producer of fine stationery in the country.

(A) Know
(B) Known
(C) Having known
(D) Knowing

고전적인 디자인으로 잘 알려진 더비사는 국내 최대의 고급 문구류 생산업체이다.

핵심 포인트

'~로 잘 알려진'이라는 수동의 의미가 되는 과거분사가 들어가야 한다.

▶ 기출공식 7 **p.97**

정답 : (D), (A), (D), (B)

기출공식 1 분사는 형용사 역할을 한다.

명사 앞 수식 Companies should not provide any **misleading** information.
기업들은 허위 정보를 제공해서는 안 된다.

→ 분사 misleading이 형용사처럼 명사 information을 수식한다.

명사 뒤 수식 Any requests **approved** by a supervisor will be processed immediately.
상사의 승인을 받은 어떤 요청이든 즉시 처리될 것이다.

→ 분사 approved가 형용사처럼 명사구 Any requests를 수식한다.

보어 The management was **thrilled** about releasing a new line of clothing.
경영진은 새로운 의류 제품군 출시에 무척 기뻐했다.

→ 과거분사 thrilled가 보어로서 주어인 The management를 보충 설명한다.

+만점팁 단, 순수 형용사와 현재분사의 의미가 비슷한 경우, 순수 형용사가 우선한다.

We received an [**impressive** / ~~impressing~~ / ~~impressed~~] recommendation from Ms. Weller's previous employer.
우리는 웰러 씨의 이전 고용주로부터 매우 인상적인 추천서를 받았다.

---

1 Applicants should allow at least three months to secure a work permit as the process can be quite -------.
(A) complicates
(B) complicated
(C) complicate
(D) complication

2 Summerton Buffet offers a ------- array of entrées, side dishes, and desserts.
(A) satisfying
(B) satisfaction
(C) satisfyingly
(D) satisfies

3 The street maps in Findling's mobile app boast ------- amounts of detail.
(A) impression
(B) impressive
(C) impressed
(D) impressing

기출공식 2 현재분사는 능동, 과거분사는 수동의 의미를 나타낸다.

- **현재분사(동사원형 + -ing): 수식 받는 명사와의 관계가 능동일 때 사용하며, '~하는'으로 해석한다.**
AMC Factory is planning to renovate their [**existing** / ~~exited~~] facilities early next quarter.
AMC 공장은 다음 분기 초에 기존 시설들을 보수할 계획이다.

- **과거분사(동사원형 + -ed): 수식 받는 명사와의 관계가 수동일 때 사용하며, '~된, ~되는'으로 해석한다.**
Mr. Sun is supposed to submit the [~~revising~~ / **revised**] budget by tomorrow.
선 씨는 수정된 예산을 내일까지 제출해야 한다.

---

4 Please accept the ------- coupon book as thanks for opening your personal savings account with South Branch Bank.
(A) enclose
(B) enclosed
(C) enclosing
(D) enclosure

5 The hotel's quiet mountain setting provides a ------- change for visitors who live in a crowded city.
(A) refreshing
(B) refreshment
(C) refreshed
(D) refresh

6 After ------- requests by local residents, the private library was opened to the public.
(A) repeated
(B) repeating
(C) repetition
(D) repeatedly

기출공식 3 분사가 명사 뒤에서 수식할 때는 목적어의 유무로 분사의 형태가 결정된다.

■ **명사 뒤에서 능동의 의미를 가지는 현재분사를 쓰면 목적어가 올 수 있다.**

The steel fence [**surrounding** / ~~surrounded~~] the fountain will be removed.

목적어 O

분수대를 둘러싸고 있는 철제 울타리는 철거될 것이다.

■ **명사 뒤에서 수동의 의미를 가지는 과거분사를 쓰면 목적어가 오지 않는다.**

The activities [~~describing~~ / **described**] in the conference program are subject to change.

목적어 X

회의 프로그램에 설명된 활동들은 변경될 수 있습니다.

7 Orders ------- the weight limit are subject to additional shipping fees.
(A) exceed
(B) exceeded
(C) exceeding
(D) excessive

8 A quarterly survey ------- by *Car Trade* magazine shows that customers prefer fuel-efficiency over size or price when purchasing a new automobile.
(A) performed
(B) to perform
(C) is performed
(D) will perform

9 Employees ------- in joining the company's sports teams should contact Meredith Lo by May 1.
(A) interesting
(B) interests
(C) interest
(D) interested

기출공식 4 일부 분사는 명사 앞에서 주로 현재분사로 쓰인다.

challenging task 힘든 업무 surrounding area 주변 지역 worsening conditions 악화되는 조건 leading supplier 선도적인 납품업체 opposing view 반대 견해 preceding years 지난 몇 년 rewarding experience 가치 있는 경험	contributing author 기고 작가 existing equipment 기존 장비 inviting atmosphere 매력적인 분위기 misleading information 허위 정보 outstanding balance 미지불 잔고 promising candidate 유망한 후보자 encouraging remark 격려의 말	demanding customer 까다로운 고객 growing business 성장하는 사업 lasting impression 지속적인 인상 missing luggage 분실한 짐 outstanding service 뛰어난 서비스 remaining staff 남아 있는 직원 changing market 변화하는 시장

Mateo Rodriguez is a **demanding critic**. 마테오 로드리게스는 까다로운 비평가이다.

10 Mr. Kwon was selected from among other ------- candidates because of his extensive background in international trade law.
(A) promises
(B) to promise
(C) promising
(D) promisingly

11 The building's ------- vacancies include a 5,000-square-foot office on the ground floor.
(A) remainders
(B) remained
(C) remains
(D) remaining

12 Manufacturing waste is a major ------- factor to water pollution around the world.
(A) contributes
(B) contributing
(C) contributed
(D) contribute

정답 및 해설 p. 52

기출공식 5   일부 분사는 명사 앞에서 주로 과거분사로 쓰인다.

accomplished writer 뛰어난 작가	established company 저명한 회사	distinguished scholar 뛰어난 학자
experienced employee 경력 직원	qualified applicant 적격인 지원자	skilled engineer 숙련된 기술자
dedicated employee 헌신적인 직원	motivated worker 적극적인 직원	invited guest 초대받은 손님
attached file 첨부 파일	enclosed form 동봉된 양식	detailed information 자세한 정보
designated area 지정 구역	reserved seat 예약석	desired salary 희망 연봉
damaged goods 파손된 물품	customized product 주문 제작 상품	limited time 제한된 시간
preferred method 선호하는 방식	complicated problem 복잡한 문제	anticipated result 예상되는 결과
proposed site 제안된 부지	written statement 서면 진술	expired coupon 만료된 쿠폰

Please read the **enclosed instructions** before assembling the desk.
책상 조립 전 동봉된 설명을 읽으세요.

13 The museum is seeking private funding for its ------- exhibition on digital art.
(A) propose
(B) proposes
(C) proposed
(D) proposing

14 McKinney Hotel keeps its prices low by offering ------- amenities to guests.
(A) limitation
(B) limiting
(C) limits
(D) limited

15 Enter the code of your ------- product using the vending machine's keypad.
(A) desired
(B) desire
(C) desires
(D) desiring

기출공식 6   감정을 유발하면 현재분사, 감정을 느끼면 과거분사를 쓴다.

confusing 혼란스럽게 하는	confused 혼란스러운	interesting 흥미로운	interested 관심 있는
disappointing 실망스러운	disappointed 실망한	encouraging 고무적인	encouraged 고무된
discouraging 낙담하게 하는	discouraged 낙담한	satisfying 만족스러운	satisfied 만족한
exhausting 지치게 하는	exhausted 지친	fascinating 매력적인	fascinated 매료된
overwhelming 압도적인	overwhelmed 압도된	exciting 흥미진진한	excited 신난, 들뜬
distracting 산만하게 하는	distracted (마음이) 산란한	gratifying 기쁘게 하는	gratified 기쁜

The updated GX-7 mobile phone is [**disappointing** / disappointed] because it has few new features.   최신 GX-7 휴대폰은 새로운 기능이 별로 없어 실망스럽다.
→ 주체(주어)가 감정을 느끼지 못하는 사물이므로 현재분사를 쓴다.

Visit our testimonials page to read what our many [satisfying / **satisfied**] customers have to say.   추천글 페이지를 방문해서 우리의 많은 만족한 고객들의 후기를 읽어 보세요.
→ 수식 받는 대상이 감정을 느끼는 사람이므로 과거분사를 쓴다.

16 We would be ------- to discuss your landscaping needs in detail via e-mail or telephone.
(A) delighting
(B) delighted
(C) delights
(D) delight

17 There are many ------- signs that the quality of education is improving in this country.
(A) encourage
(B) encouraged
(C) encouraging
(D) encouragement

18 The Central City Visitor's Association has produced an ------- new film that promotes the city's top tourist attractions.
(A) excited
(B) exciting
(C) excite
(D) excites

기출공식 7   분사구문의 분사 형태는 목적어의 유무, 주어와의 관계로 결정한다.

[**Providing** / ~~Provided~~] education for children in need, SCR is an important local charity.
<u>목적어 O</u>   주어인 SCR이 교육을 '제공하는' 주체이므로 능동

어려운 아이들에게 교육을 제공하는 SCR은 중요한 지역 자선 단체이다.

→ 목적어가 있고 주어와의 관계가 능동이면 현재분사(-ing 또는 having p.p.)를 쓴다.

[Inspiring / **(Being) inspired**] by a local business owner, Ms. Joo is studying to become a chef.
                                   <u>목적어 X</u>   주어인 Ms. Joo가 영감을 '받는' 대상이므로 수동

지역 업주에게 영감을 받은 주 씨는 요리사가 되기 위해 공부하고 있다.

→ 목적어가 없고 주어와의 관계가 수동이면 과거분사(p.p. 또는 being p.p.)를 쓴다.

| +만점팁 | 자동사는 목적어의 유무에 관계없이 현재분사로 쓴다.

[**Consisting** / ~~Consisted~~] of over 4,000 artworks, the exhibition is expected to draw a large number of visitors.
4,000점 이상의 예술 작품들로 구성된 그 전시회는 수많은 방문객을 끌어들일 것으로 예상된다.

→ consist가 자동사이므로 목적어의 유무로 판단하지 않는다.

---

19 ------- a degree in accounting, Ms. Sakai is considered one of the top candidates for the management position.
(A) Having earned
(B) Earned
(C) Being earned
(D) Earn

20 ------- in the late 1800's, many of the coastline's lighthouses remain standing today, having withstood the forces of nature for decades.
(A) Built   (B) Having built
(C) Building   (D) To build

21 Northband Care limits its budget for office decor, ------- to spend money on quality medical equipment.
(A) prefer
(B) preferred
(C) preferring
(D) preference

빈출

기출공식 8   분사구문에서 명확한 의미를 위해 접속사를 생략하지 않을 수도 있다.

- **주어와의 관계가 능동일 때**

  After we reviewed all the proposals, we decided to implement the new system.

  → **After reviewing** all the proposals, we decided to implement the new system.

  모든 제안서를 검토한 뒤 우리는 새로운 시스템을 구현하기로 결정했다.

- **주어와의 관계가 수동일 때**

  Once it is confirmed, your order will be shipped immediately from our warehouse.

  → **Once confirmed**, your order will be shipped immediately from our warehouse.

  귀하의 주문이 확인되면 주문품이 창고에서 바로 배송됩니다.

---

22 When ------- with potential clients, remember to tell them about Gansen Capital's upcoming promotional event.
(A) spoken   (B) speaking
(C) spoke   (D) to speak

23 Ms. Baxter would like to meet with all members of the hiring committee again after ------- candidates.
(A) interview   (B) interviews
(C) interviewing   (D) interviewed

24 As ------- in the company guidelines, sales agents receive compensation for time spent traveling to meet with clients.
(A) state   (B) stating
(C) statement   (D) stated

정답 및 해설 p.53

1   Production at Peroware's Lima plant has more than doubled since the introduction of ------- assembly.
(A) automate
(B) automatically
(C) automated
(D) automation

2   Adequate storage space is very important to companies ------- large quantities of materials.
(A) produced
(B) produces
(C) produce
(D) producing

3   The opening of new markets in Ghana was cited as an ------- outcome of the business merger.
(A) anticipates
(B) anticipation
(C) anticipating
(D) anticipated

4   Programmers at Ulrich-Ahn Company are responsible for ensuring that software conforms to the ------- system standards.
(A) establish
(B) established
(C) establishing
(D) establishes

5   For proper repair of your Vitera motorcycle, we recommend that you visit one of our ------- dealers.
(A) authorized
(B) authorization
(C) authority
(D) authorize

6   The company has decided to liquidate some of its subsidiaries and invest in areas of research that are clearly more -------.
(A) to promise
(B) promised
(C) promising
(D) promises

7   Mr. Omori is an artist best known for the ------- beauty of his watercolors.
(A) stunning
(B) stunned
(C) stuns
(D) stun

8   At Ben Flores Blinds, first-time customers can benefit from ------- rates of 30 percent off.
(A) introducing
(B) introductions
(C) introduced
(D) introductory

9   Kochi Engineering has proposed the construction of a drainage system ------- to keep the Route 480 highway dry during heavy rain.
(A) was designed
(B) designed
(C) designer
(D) designing

10 Although the reviews of the latest Driscoll computer have largely been favorable, sales of the item have thus far been -------.
(A) disappoint
(B) disappointed
(C) disappointment
(D) disappointing

11 This summer the City of Harsillac Hills will expand its annual food festival, ------- many new business opportunities for local entrepreneurs.
(A) created
(B) create
(C) creates
(D) creating

12 Prices for clothing and furniture items ------- on our Web site are subject to change without notice.
(A) listed
(B) have listed
(C) list
(D) will list

13 Exporters use ------- shipping containers so ships and trailers can be easily loaded and unloaded.
(A) standardize
(B) standards
(C) standardized
(D) standardizing

14 In order to improve customer relations, we need to keep our sales staff ------- of product developments.
(A) informed
(B) information
(C) inform
(D) informant

15 ------- by the product demonstration last week, the operations manager has decided to order several of Handimaid's appliances.
(A) Impressed
(B) Impressive
(C) Impressing
(D) Impression

16 Lexino Publisher's dictionary database allows users to search for entries in ------- languages.
(A) multiplied
(B) multiplying
(C) multiples
(D) multiple

17 ------- in the heart of the city's historical district, Reveille Café is the perfect spot for a meal after a day of sightseeing.
(A) Situating
(B) Situated
(C) Situates
(D) Situate

18 As ------- in yesterday's conference call, the company's annual retreat for managers will be postponed until late July.
(A) discuss
(B) discussion
(C) discussed
(D) discussing

19 Based on the ------- number of advance ticket sales, we expect to see record attendance levels at this year's festival in Donegal.
(A) overwhelm
(B) overwhelms
(C) overwhelming
(D) overwhelmingly

20 Walters, Inc., a natural gas company ------- South Africa's nine provinces, announced on Tuesday that it had sold its eastern division.
(A) serving
(B) served
(C) server
(D) serves

부사절 접속사 / 등위·상관접속사

평균 2~3문제 출제

무료인강

● 부사절 접속사

부사절 접속사는 절과 절을 이어 주는 접속사로, 시간, 이유, 양보, 조건 등을 나타낸다.

Your order will ship **as soon as it becomes available**. 귀하의 주문품은 준비되자마자 발송될 것입니다.
　　　　주절　　　　　　　　부사절

　　　　　　　　　　　　　　→ 전체 문장에서 해당 절이 부사 역할을 한다.

Because the order was placed after the sale had ended, no discount will be given.
부사절 접속사　　　　　　　　　종속절　　　　　　　　　　　주절
주문은 세일이 끝난 이후에 받았기 때문에 할인이 적용되지 않을 것이다.

→ 부사절 접속사가 이끄는 절을 종속절이라고 하며, 부사절을 뺀 나머지 절을 주절이라고 한다.

● 등위·상관접속사

등위접속사는 단어와 단어, 구와 구, 절과 절을 대등하게 연결해 주는 접속사이다.

Arcosa Design Ltd. offers digital **and** print design services.
아르코사 디자인사는 디지털 및 인쇄물 디자인 서비스를 제공한다.

→ 등위접속사로 연결된 단어와 단어, 구와 구, 절과 절은 대등한 구조를 가지며, 이를 병렬구조라고 한다.

Customers can exchange **or** (customers can) return any item with an original receipt.
고객은 원본 영수증이 있으면 어떤 상품이든 교환하거나 반품할 수 있다.

→ 등위접속사로 연결된 구나 절에서 중복된 단어는 생략이 가능하다.

상관접속사는 서로 짝을 이루어 함께 쓰이는 접속사이다.

Both the production plant **and** the warehouse are located outside of the city.
생산 공장과 창고 모두 시 외곽에 있다.

Not only the head chef **but also** the servers attend each cooking seminar.
수석 주방장뿐 아니라 웨이터들도 모든 요리 세미나에 참석한다.

→ 상관접속사로 연결된 단어와 단어, 구와 구, 절과 절도 병렬구조를 가진다.

부사절 접속사 / 등위·상관접속사 | ETS 핵심 출제 패턴

부사절 접속사는 비슷한 의미의 전치사, 또는 접속부사와 비교되어 자주 출제된다. 또한 다양한 부사절 접속사들끼리 의미를 구분하는 문제로도 출제된다. 등위접속사와 상관접속사의 경우 단독 문제도 출제되지만 다른 접속사와의 차이를 묻는 문제도 출제되므로 다양한 접속사에 대한 정확한 이해가 필요하다.

☑ 문맥상 알맞은 부사절 접속사를 선택하는 문제

------- Ms. Bai was not available to lead the board meeting, she was able to find a replacement.

(A) Although   (B) Whether

(C) Instead   (D) Accordingly

배 씨는 이사회 회의를 이끌 수는 없었지만, 대신할 사람은 찾을 수 있었다.

핵심 포인트

완전한 두 문장을 이어 주는 부사절 접속사 자리이며, 문맥상 '비록 ~이지만'이 자연스럽다.

▶ 기출공식 2 **p.102**

☑ 부사절 접속사와 전치사를 구별하는 문제

This special offer on Lumex copy paper is valid at participating stores ------- supplies last.

(A) during   (B) until

(C) while   (D) after

루멕스 복사 용지는 재고가 있는 동안 가맹점에서 특별 할인 가격에 구입할 수 있다.

핵심 포인트

빈칸 뒤 완전한 문장이 나오므로 접속사 자리이며, 문맥상 '~ 동안'이 자연스럽다.

▶ 기출공식 5 **p.104**

☑ 문맥상 알맞은 등위접속사를 선택하는 문제

Ms. Ito would like to extend her study, ------- she does not have the resources available to do so.

(A) but   (B) whether

(C) or   (D) either

이토 씨는 연구를 연장하고 싶어 하지만, 그렇게 하기 위한 자원이 없다.

핵심 포인트

두 문장을 이어 주는 접속사 자리이며, 문맥상 '그러나'가 자연스럽다.

▶ 기출공식 7 **p.105**

☑ 상관접속사의 짝을 선택하는 문제

------- the Chiba office nor the Nagoya office is hiring.

(A) Both   (B) But

(C) Either   (D) Neither

지바 사무실이나 나고야 사무실 모두 직원을 채용하지 않는다.

핵심 포인트

빈칸 뒤 nor과 짝을 이루어 'A도 B도 아닌'을 의미하는 상관접속사가 들어가야 한다.

▶ 기출공식 8 **p.105**

기출공식 1   시간과 이유를 나타내는 부사절 접속사가 자주 출제된다.

시간	when/as ~할 때 while/as ~하는 동안	before ~ 전에 once 일단 ~하면	after ~ 후에 until ~할 때까지	since ~ 이래로 as soon as ~하자마자
이유	because/since/as ~ 때문에		now that ~이므로	in that ~라는 점에서

Once invoices arrive in the office, they should be processed promptly to maintain accurate records. 일단 청구서가 사무실에 도착하면, 정확한 기록을 유지하기 위해 즉시 처리되어야 한다.

The band will play music **as soon as** the keynote speaker appears on the stage.
기조연설자가 무대에 나타나자마자 악단이 음악을 연주할 것이다.

Now that the sales floor has been expanded, we will have room for more new products.
매장이 확장되었으므로 더 많은 신제품을 놓을 공간이 있을 것이다.

1 Construction will begin on the new water park ------- all city permits are authorized.
(A) as soon as (B) due to
(C) during   (D) up to

2 Min-Jung Park will serve as interim vice president ------- a permanent replacement is named.
(A) until   (B) inside
(C) from   (D) within

3 ------- they require greater care in handling and packaging, fragile items are more expensive to transport.
(A) Because (B) In fact
(C) Just   (D) Even

기출공식 2   양보와 조건을 나타내는 부사절 접속사가 자주 출제된다.

양보	although/even though/though 비록 ~이지만 while ~이긴 하지만	even if 설사 ~라고 할지라도 even as ~할 때조차도
조건	if/provided (that)/providing (that) 만약 ~라면 as long as ~하는 한 in case (that) ~하는 경우에 대비해서	unless/if not 만약 ~이 아니라면 assuming/supposing (that) ~라고 가정하면 in the event (that) ~하는 경우에

Although the parking lot is for employees only, today it is open to anyone who visits us.
비록 그 주차장은 직원 전용이지만 오늘은 방문객 누구에게나 개방된다.

Even if sales figures for the next two months are strong, a decline in profits for the year is expected. 설령 향후 두 달간 판매 수치가 좋다 하더라도 여전히 해당 년도 수익 감소가 예상된다.

If we need more part-time workers, posting a job advertisement will be a good idea.
만약 우리에게 시간제 직원이 더 필요하면 구인 광고를 내는 것이 좋겠다.

4 The convenience store around the corner is always open 24 hours a day, ------- it is a national holiday.
(A) even if   (B) whether
(C) not only   (D) except

5 The company's revenue during the next quarter will increase, ------- the lucrative contract with Kang Securities can be finalized before next month.
(A) as if   (B) whereas
(C) whether   (D) assuming that

6 ------- many employees at Vicario Transit indicated interest in the management training program, none have yet enrolled.
(A) As if   (B) Although
(C) But   (D) Nevertheless

기출공식 3 목적과 결과를 나타내는 부사절 접속사가 출제된다.

목적	so that ... can/may/could/would ~할 수 있도록	in order that ~하기 위해서
결과	so/such ~ that ... 너무 ~해서 …하다	

Jason Moore prefers to communicate with clients **so that** he **can** hear real voices from them. 제이슨 무어는 고객들의 생생한 의견을 들을 수 있도록 고객들과 대화하는 것을 좋아한다.

The road was **so** slippery **that** it had to be closed to traffic.
길이 매우 미끄러워서 교통이 통제되어야 했다.

Technology is advancing at **such** a rapid rate **that** many devices are now affordable to everyone. 기술이 너무나 빠른 속도로 발전하고 있어 이제 많은 기기들이 누구나 구입할 수 있을 정도로 저렴하다.

---

7 The building inspection has been postponed until next week ------- that the electrical work can be completed.
(A) also
(B) when
(C) than
(D) so

8 ------- many movie fans wanted to see *Tundra Dwellers* that tickets sold out in three hours.
(A) Too
(B) So
(C) Far
(D) Very

9 Visitors are required to wear special badges ------- they can be easily identified.
(A) except that
(B) rather
(C) anyhow
(D) so that

기출공식 4 기타 다양한 뜻의 부사절 접속사가 출제된다.

고려	considering (that)/given that ~을 고려할 때	대조	whereas/while ~인 반면에
제외	except (that) ~라는 점을 제외하고	비유	as if/as though 마치 ~인 것처럼
양보	whether A or B A이든 B이든 (상관없이)	한정	as far as (범위) ~하는 한

Considering that it has a lot of local competition, Baz's Restaurant is doing very well.
지역 경쟁업체들이 많다는 점을 고려하면 바즈 레스토랑은 아주 잘되고 있다.

All tests will be held on-site, **whereas** some of the interviews will be held remotely.
모든 시험은 현장에서 실시될 것이나 일부 인터뷰는 원격으로 진행될 것이다.

Whether you are an amateur **or** an expert, there are plenty of cooking courses that will suit your needs. 당신이 아마추어이든 전문가이든, 당신의 필요에 맞는 요리 수업이 다양하게 있습니다.

---

10 ------- your windows are angular or rounded, Shadely can make coverings to fit them.
(A) Whether
(B) Currently
(C) Among
(D) According to

11 The workshop went surprisingly well, ------- it was Vince's first time running one.
(A) throughout
(B) given that
(C) after all
(D) whereas

12 ------- patrons had to find on-street parking before, they can now leave their vehicles in the parking area adjacent to the theater.
(A) Until
(B) Unless
(C) Whereas
(D) Whenever

정답 및 해설 p.57

기출공식 5 부사절 접속사는 비슷한 의미의 전치사와 구분해야 한다.

	접속사	전치사
시간	as soon as / once ~하자마자	on / upon ~하자마자
	while ~ 동안	during ~ 동안
	before ~ 이전에 after ~ 이후에	before / prior to ~ 이전에 after / following ~ 이후에
	until ~까지 since ~ 이래로	until ~까지 since ~ 이래로
이유	because / since / as / now that ~ 때문에	because of / due to / owing to / on account of ~ 때문에
양보	although / even though 비록 ~일지라도	despite / in spite of ~에도 불구하고

Loud talking is not allowed [**while** / ~~during~~] speeches are being given.
연설이 진행되는 동안에는 큰 소리로 대화할 수 없습니다.

[**Even though** / ~~Despite~~] ticket prices are increasing, air travel is expected to rise this summer. 항공권 가격이 오르고 있지만 올여름 비행기 여행자 수는 증가할 것으로 예상된다.

13 ------- Ms. Kang's project has been approved, Mauer Consulting needs to hire two new research associates.
(A) If so
(B) Rather than
(C) Owing to
(D) Given that

14 The theater's doors will be closed ------- the performance is taking place.
(A) while
(B) at first
(C) before
(D) during

15 ------- patrons are issued overdue notices, the library does not charge late fees.
(A) Excluding
(B) Although
(C) Despite
(D) Not only

기출공식 6 부사절 접속사 뒤에 문장이 아닌 축약 형태가 올 수 있다.

when + -ing / p.p. ~ 때   while + -ing / p.p. ~ 동안
before / after / since + -ing / being p.p. ~ 전에 / 후에 / 이래로
as / once / if / unless / though / than + p.p. ~ 대로 / 일단 ~하면 / ~라면 / ~하지 않는 한 / ~에도 불구하고 / ~보다

Gary has changed jobs several times **since moving** to New York City.
능동일 때 접속사 + -ing
게리는 뉴욕 시로 이사한 이래로 직업을 수차례 변경했다.

Though confirmed, the expansion plan needs to be grounded in reality.
수동일 때 접속사 + p.p.
비록 승인은 받았지만 확장 계획은 현실에 근거할 필요가 있다.

+만점팁 **if possible**(만약 가능하다면), **while on duty**(근무 동안에)처럼, 접속사 뒤 형용사나 전치사구가 오는 형태도 가능하다.

16 Job seekers are advised to avoid discussing confidential business knowledge acquired ------- working for former employers.
(A) even
(B) beside
(C) while
(D) throughout

17 After ------- their travel reservations online, airline passengers should arrive at the airport at least an hour before departure.
(A) confirmation
(B) confirmed
(C) confirming
(D) have confirmed

18 All Baxmooth appliances come with a standard one-year warranty ------- otherwise noted.
(A) whereas
(B) below
(C) neither
(D) unless

빈출

기출공식 7 등위접속사는 동일한 품사나 구조를 대등하게 연결한다.

and 그리고	or 또는	but / yet 그러나	so 그래서	for 왜냐하면

- **단어와 단어를 연결**

  Passengers remained calm **but** uncertain about what they needed to do afterward.

  승객들은 침착했지만 이후에 어떻게 해야 할지 몰랐다.

- **구와 구 연결**

  Design staff are advised to put the files in a folder **or** on the shelf.

  디자인 직원들은 파일들을 폴더 안이나 선반 위에 놓으세요.

- **절과 절 연결 – 등위접속사 so, for는 단어나 구는 연결할 수 없고, 절과 절만 연결한다.**

  The seminar was very popular last month, **so** you are advised to register in advance.

  그 세미나는 지난달에 인기가 매우 높았으므로 미리 등록하는 편이 좋다.

19 Art Department computers are connected to printers ------- scanners in Area C.
(A) yet
(B) both
(C) and
(D) only

20 We have received your request for an estimate ------- regret that we are unable to process it without documentation.
(A) while
(B) after
(C) then
(D) but

21 Our spring sale begins this week, ------- we should schedule extra staff.
(A) so
(B) but
(C) then
(D) already

빈출

기출공식 8 상관접속사는 짝을 찾는 문제로 출제된다.

both A and B	A와 B 둘 다	either A or B	A와 B 둘 중 하나
not only A but (also) B	A뿐 아니라 B도	neither A nor B	A와 B 둘 다 아닌
= B as well as A	A뿐 아니라 B도	rather A than B	B라기보다는 A
not A but B = B but not A	A가 아니라 B	= A rather than B	B라기보다는 A

Both Mr. Jeong [and / ~~but~~] Ms. Lee have already made hotel reservations.

정 씨와 이 씨 둘 다 이미 호텔을 예약했다.

The results of this customer survey will be revealed **either** tonight [or / ~~and~~] tomorrow morning. 이 고객 설문조사의 결과는 오늘 밤이나 내일 아침에 나올 것이다.

22 Entrance to the laboratory is restricted to those holding ------- an employee identification badge or an official visitor's pass.
(A) both
(B) each
(C) any
(D) either

23 Ms. Choi offers clients ------- tax preparation services and financial management consultations.
(A) only if
(B) either
(C) both
(D) not only

24 Because of elevator repairs, neither the showroom ------- the sales office of Valantin Gowns will be open this Saturday.
(A) so
(B) as
(C) but
(D) nor

정답 및 해설 p. 59

1 The Luxembourg office is closed today ------- the country is observing a national holiday.
(A) as
(B) until
(C) such as
(D) similarly

2 Customers who purchase concert tickets will be charged a service fee ------- they pay by cash or by credit card.
(A) whether
(B) either
(C) even
(D) despite

3 ------- Malone Heating can provide same-day installation of heating units, an extra fee will be charged.
(A) Altogether
(B) While
(C) Despite
(D) Initially

4 The project proposal cannot be accepted ------- both managers have read and approved it.
(A) instead
(B) beyond
(C) until
(D) again

5 Please have your customer account number available for reference ------- calling for service.
(A) when
(B) once
(C) although
(D) because

6 Bus riders can purchase daily ------- weekly Coastal City Transit tickets on any mobile device.
(A) out
(B) still
(C) after
(D) or

7 Employees should submit time sheets by noon today ------- the payroll office can distribute paychecks on schedule.
(A) so that
(B) in order to
(C) that is
(D) in case of

8 ------- this quarter's sales are as high as projected, Hoshiro Designs, Inc., anticipates emerging as the leading graphic design company in Japan.
(A) In case of
(B) After all
(C) Provided that
(D) Subsequent to

9 Students should take entrance exams ------- the term begins and they become busier.
(A) in anticipation of
(B) already
(C) before
(D) so as to

10 ------- Yarggo Press has a new chief editor, the publishing firm plans to keep its focus on cookbooks.
(A) Despite
(B) Whether
(C) Further
(D) Although

11 Southenic Electronics' technicians are on hand 24 hours a day ------- you can be at ease knowing help is always available.
(A) because of
(B) so
(C) everything
(D) until

12 ------- revise the year's sales goal, Mr. Ellis asked each team member to recruit another client by the end of January.
(A) Regarding
(B) Rather than
(C) In summary
(D) Even though

13 The Web site advises customers to review their orders carefully as it is difficult to make changes ------- an order is submitted.
(A) following
(B) once
(C) right away
(D) by means of

14 ------- your return has been received, a refund will be issued to your account within three business days.
(A) In order that
(B) Instead
(C) Now that
(D) Meanwhile

15 ------- spring arrives, a portion of the river will be widened to prevent flooding.
(A) Whether
(B) Besides
(C) Whereas
(D) Before

16 ------- all the preliminary interviews have been completed, the top three applicants for the marketing director position will be contacted.
(A) Compared to
(B) As soon as
(C) So that
(D) Not only

17 ------- Ms. Park appreciated the job offer from Seon Advisory Group, she declined the opportunity because she would have to relocate.
(A) Now that
(B) Only if
(C) While
(D) Whether

18 Knewlbank has decided to open new branches ------- more customers are using online services.
(A) meanwhile
(B) so that
(C) even as
(D) with

19 All passwords must be changed again by Friday ------- you have done so previously.
(A) in that
(B) even if
(C) rather than
(D) not only

20 The electronic time-tracking system indicates regular time ------- extra hours that the employees work.
(A) as well as
(B) in addition
(C) so that
(D) while

UNIT 12 관계사

평균 1문제 출제

무료인강

● 관계대명사

관계대명사는 두 문장을 이어 주는 '접속사 + 대명사' 역할을 한다.

> We met new authors, **and they** signed contracts with us.
>
> 접속사 + 대명사
>
>
>
> We met new authors, **who** signed contracts with us.
>
> 관계대명사
>
> 우리는 신규 저자들을 만났고 그들은 우리와 계약을 맺었다.

관계대명사 앞에서 수식을 받는 명사를 선행사라고 하며, 관계대명사는 선행사에 따라 달라진다.

선행사	주격	소유격	목적격
사람	who	whose	who(m)
사물	which	whose	which
혼용	that	—	that

● 관계부사

관계부사는 두 문장을 이어 주는 '접속사 + 부사' 역할을 한다.

> We met the authors at a café, **and** they signed contracts with us **there**.
>
> 접속사 + 부사
>
>
>
> We met the authors at a café, **where** they signed contracts with us.
>
> 관계부사
>
> 우리는 그 저자들을 카페에서 만났고 그곳에서 그들은 우리와 계약을 맺었다.

관계부사의 선행사는 장소, 시간, 이유, 방법을 나타내는 명사이다.

선행사	관계부사
장소(the place)	where ~하는 장소
시간(the time)	when ~하는 때
이유(the reason)	why ~하는 이유
방법(the way)	how ~하는 방법 *the way와 how는 함께 쓰지 않고 둘 중 하나만 쓴다.

관계사 | ETS 핵심 출제 패턴

관계사는 선행사에 따른 관계사 구분과 격 구분 문제가 주로 출제된다.

☑ 사람 선행사를 받는 관계사를 선택하는 문제

The architect ------- designed the Mori Music Center plans to retire this spring.

(A) who   (B) some

(C) he   (D) also

모리 뮤직 센터를 디자인했던 건축가는 올해 봄에 은퇴할 계획이다.

핵심 포인트

선행사가 architect이므로 사람 선행사를 받는 관계대명사가 들어가야 한다.

▶ 기출공식 1 **p.110**

☑ 사물 선행사를 받는 관계사를 선택하는 문제

The new train line, ------- has been running since March, serves each of the town's six stations.

(A) who   (B) what

(C) where   (D) which

신규 열차 노선은 3월부터 운행되고 있는데 그 도시의 여섯 군데 역에서 운행된다.

핵심 포인트

선행사가 The new train line이므로 사물 선행사를 받는 관계대명사가 들어가야 한다.

▶ 기출공식 1 **p.110**

☑ 관계대명사의 격을 선택하는 문제

Be aware that candidates ------- applications are incomplete will not be considered for an interview.

(A) who   (B) whose

(C) their   (D) they

신청서가 불완전한 지원자들은 면접 대상으로 고려되지 않을 것임을 양지하십시오.

핵심 포인트

빈칸 뒤 명사를 수식하면서 접속사 역할을 하는 관계대명사 소유격이 들어가야 한다.

▶ 기출공식 1 **p.110**

☑ 관계부사를 선택하는 문제

Mayor Williams proudly described the city as a place ------- the citizens are known for their hospitality.

(A) when   (B) where

(C) how   (D) why

윌리엄스 시장은 도시가 시민들이 친절하기로 유명한 곳이라고 자랑스럽게 말했다.

핵심 포인트

빈칸 앞에 place가 나오므로 장소 명사를 선행사로 하는 관계부사가 와야 한다.

▶ 기출공식 5 **p.112**

정답 : (A), (D), (B), (B)

기출공식 1 관계대명사는 선행사와 격에 알맞게 써야 한다.

주격 Ms. Sandusky, **who** is transferring to London in May, will help train the new assistant.
5월에 런던으로 전근하는 샌더스키 씨가 신입 비서 교육을 도울 것이다.

→ **동사 앞 주격 자리에는 who(사람 선행사) 또는 which(사물 선행사)를 쓴다.**

소유격 The historical mansion, **whose** roof was recently replaced, is a major tourist site.
최근에 지붕이 교체된 그 역사적인 저택은 주요 관광지이다.

→ **명사와 명사 사이 소유격 자리에는 선행사에 관계없이 whose를 쓴다.**

목적격 Some employees did not receive the e-mail, **which** Mr. Lee sent yesterday.
일부 직원들은 이 씨가 어제 보낸 이메일을 받지 못했다.

→ **주어와 타동사 앞 목적격 자리에는 whom(사람 선행사) 또는 which(사물 선행사)를 쓴다.**

+만점팁 선행사에 관계없이 who, whom, which 자리에 that을 쓸 수 있으나, 콤마 뒤나 전치사 뒤에는 쓰지 않는다.

1 Tenants ------- plan to vacate the property before the lease expires must provide written notification of their plans.
(A) who
(B) whose
(C) whose own
(D) whoever

2 Tower Apartments plans to add a recreation complex ------- will accommodate a swimming pool and other facilities.
(A) that
(B) who
(C) where
(D) both

3 This year's Middletown Poetry Prize will be awarded to Mie Hasegawa, ------- poem "Venus" was selected from over 500 entries.
(A) which
(B) whom
(C) whose
(D) what

기출공식 2 목적격 관계대명사와 '주격 관계대명사 + be동사'는 생략할 수 있다.

■ **목적격 관계대명사의 생략**

The kitchen tool set **(that)** you ordered is currently out of stock.
귀하가 주문한 주방 조리기구 세트는 현재 재고가 없습니다.

The kitchen tool set [**you** / your / yours] ordered is currently out of stock.

→ **목적격 관계대명사가 생략된 문장에서 주어 자리에 들어갈 대명사의 격을 묻는 문제가 출제된다.**

■ **주격 관계대명사 + be동사의 생략**

Reservations **(which are)** made online will be confirmed via e-mail.
온라인상으로 이루어진 예약은 이메일로 확인될 것이다.

Reservations [**made** / making / make] online will be confirmed via e-mail.

→ **주격 관계대명사 + be동사가 생략된 문장에서 명사 뒤 자리에 들어갈 분사 형태를 묻는 문제가 출제된다.**

4 Province Bank customers are requested to update annually the passwords ------- use for online banking.
(A) they
(B) them
(C) their
(D) themselves

5 Emeliar Ltd. is a company ------- for its extensive employee training and skill development programs.
(A) knowledge
(B) known
(C) knowing
(D) knows

6 Those employees ------- in an assembly area must wear protective gear at all times.
(A) work
(B) have worked
(C) will work
(D) working

기출공식 3 '수량표현 of 목적격 관계대명사' 문제가 출제된다.

- **선행사가 사람일 때**

  We interviewed many applicants, **and all of them** had acceptable qualifications.

  We interviewed many applicants, **all of whom** had acceptable qualifications.

  우리는 많은 지원자들을 면접했고 그들 중 모두가 적절한 자격을 갖추고 있었다.

  → 접속사(and)와 대명사(them) 역할을 동시에 하며, 선행사가 사람이므로 **whom**을 쓴다.

- **선행사가 사물일 때**

  James Lee wrote over 20 books, **and many of them** were published in different languages.

  James Lee wrote over 20 books, **many of which** were published in different languages.

  제임스 리는 20권 이상의 책을 썼고 그 책들 중 다수가 여러 언어로 출간되었다.

  → 접속사(and)와 대명사(them) 역할을 동시에 하며, 선행사가 사물이므로 **which**를 쓴다.

7   Managers often have to decide between several courses of action, none of ------- is completely right or wrong.
(A) that
(B) which
(C) when
(D) where

8   Edward's Plumbing has six company-owned vehicles, two of ------- are now in the repair shop.
(A) whose
(B) which
(C) either
(D) other

9   Ms. Crouse heads a team of ten people, ------- work remotely.
(A) the permission to
(B) most of whom
(C) in spite of her
(D) and also

기출공식 4   관계대명사 앞에 전치사가 올 수 있다.

The city official has not responded yet. + We sent the inquiry **to the city official**.

= **The city official whom** we sent the inquiry **to** has not responded yet.

→ 목적격 관계대명사절에 있는 전치사는 관계대명사 앞으로 끌어올 수 있다.

= **The city official to** [whom / ~~whose~~] we sent the inquiry has not responded yet.

우리가 문의를 보낸 시 공무원은 아직 대답하지 않았다.

→ 선행사는 **the city official**이고 전치사 **to**의 목적어 자리이므로 목적격 관계대명사 **whom**을 쓴다.

There was a board meeting, [~~with~~ / during] **which** the directors talked about the expansion plan.   회의가 있었고 그 회의 동안 임원들은 확장 계획에 대해 논의했다.

→ 선행사는 **a board meeting**이고 '회의 동안'이라는 의미가 되어야 하므로 전치사 **during**을 쓴다.

10   The city council offers entrepreneurs a favorable tax rate, making Mestin a great city in ------- to start a new business.
(A) what
(B) which
(C) where
(D) whose

11   The new radio talk show, ------- which listeners can call in with their questions, will start airing at 10 A.M. next Monday.
(A) even
(B) while
(C) during
(D) between

12   Dr. Kim's acceptance speech is expected to last about ten minutes, after ------- dessert will be served.
(A) them
(B) each
(C) which
(D) where

정답 및 해설 p. 63

기출공식 5   선행사가 장소, 시간, 이유, 방법일 때는 관계부사를 쓴다.

장소   This is the place **where** Baron Holdings held an annual shareholders' meeting.
이곳이 배론 홀딩스에서 연례 주주총회를 개최한 장소이다.

시간   Late autumn is the period **when** we get most of our orders for winter boots.
늦가을은 우리가 겨울 부츠 주문량의 대부분을 받는 시기이다.

이유   Adware programs may be the reason **why** the computers are running slowly.
애드웨어 프로그램이 컴퓨터가 느리게 작동하는 원인일 수 있다.

방법   The seminar will explain **how[the way]** small companies can create a unique brand
image. 세미나는 작은 회사들이 독특한 브랜드 이미지를 만들어 낼 수 있는 방법을 설명할 것이다.

+만점팁 관계부사는 전치사 + 관계대명사로 바꿀 수 있으며, 특히 where 자리에 in[at] which가 빈출된다.

We are familiar with the area **in which[where]** the apartment is located.
우리는 그 아파트가 위치해 있는 지역을 잘 안다.

13 All shipments arrive at the receiving dock, ------- a warehouse worker checks their tracking labels.
(A) who
(B) which
(C) when
(D) where

14 Try to charge your electric vehicle during times of the day ------- electricity costs less.
(A) unless
(B) every
(C) when
(D) or

15 Visitors can view the room ------- Ms. Gibbs wrote her most famous poems.
(A) of
(B) that
(C) as if
(D) in which

기출공식 6   관계대명사 뒤에는 불완전한 절, 관계부사 뒤에는 완전한 절이 온다.

■ **관계대명사 + 불완전한 절**

Credit will be given to Amy Burton **who** won the sales contract last month.
지난달 판매 계약을 따낸 에이미 버튼에게 공적이 돌아갈 것이다.

→ 관계대명사가 관계사절의 주어 역할을 하므로 뒤에는 주어가 빠진 불완전한 절이 온다.

■ **관계부사 + 완전한 절**

The manager asked Chris Bhan **the reason why** he would resign despite many benefits.
부장은 크리스 반에게 많은 혜택에도 불구하고 그만두려는 이유를 물었다.

→ 관계부사는 문장의 주성분에 속하지 않는 부사 역할을 하므로 뒤에는 완전한 절이 온다.

16 Ms. Silva has posted a list of all staff members ------- are expected to attend tomorrow's presentation.
(A) whose
(B) who
(C) where
(D) when

17 The questions ------- are marked with a red asterisk must be answered.
(A) that
(B) why
(C) about
(D) they

18 Each bag is made by hand in Milan, ------- our company is headquartered.
(A) also
(B) where
(C) there
(D) which

기출공식 7   복합관계부사는 부사절을 이끈다.

whenever	언제 ~하더라도(= no matter when)	~하는 언제든지(= at any time when)
wherever	어디서 ~하더라도(= no matter where)	~하는 어디든지(= at any place where)
however	아무리 ~하더라도(= no matter how) + 형용사 / 부사	어떻게 ~하든지(= by whatever means)

Trainees should speak to their instructor **whenever** they need assistance.
실습생들은 도움이 필요하면 언제든 강사에게 알려야 한다.

Fabiola Corp's watches are available **wherever** fine jewelry is sold.
파비올라사의 시계는 귀금속을 판매하는 곳이면 어디서든 구입할 수 있다.

However roughly this tablet device is handled, it never breaks or stops working.
이 태블릿 기기는 아무리 거칠게 다루어도 부서지거나 작동이 멈추지 않는다.

+만점팁 '아무리 ~하더라도'를 의미하는 **however** 뒤에 형용사 또는 부사를 선택하는 문제도 출제된다.

19 ------- uncomfortable they may be, helmets, goggles, and gloves absolutely must be worn by anyone entering the construction zone.
(A) Almost   (B) Nevertheless
(C) Seldom   (D) However

20 Cashiers must put up an "Away" sign ------- they leave their register.
(A) as well as
(B) immediately
(C) whenever
(D) upon

21 City workers spread salt ------- there was ice on the sidewalks.
(A) along
(B) wherever
(C) rather than
(D) otherwise

기출공식 8   복합관계대명사는 부사절 또는 명사절을 이끈다.

whoever	(부사절) 누가 ~하든지(no matter who)	(명사절) ~하는 누구든지(anyone who)
whatever	(부사절) 무엇이 ~하든지(no matter what)	(명사절) ~하는 무엇이든지(anything that)
whichever	(부사절) 어떤 것이 ~하든지(no matter which)	(명사절) ~하는 어떤 것이든지

Whoever completes the survey, he or she will be offered a free appetizer coupon. (부사절)
누가 이 설문지를 작성하든, 그 사람은 무료 전채 요리 쿠폰을 받는다.

You can order our products via Internet or in person, **whichever** is more convenient. (부사절)
인터넷이든 아니면 직접 방문하시든 더 편리한 쪽으로 우리 제품을 주문하실 수 있습니다.

Whoever comes today will be served a free lunch. (명사절)
오늘 오시는 분은 누구든지 무료 점심을 대접 받습니다.

22 Among the sales managers, ------- has the highest sales record by the end of this year will receive the distinguished R. F. Fowler Award.
(A) whose   (B) someone
(C) whoever   (D) nobody

23 Cars from Lefebre Motors come with a warranty lasting 36 months or 60,000 kilometers, ------- comes first.
(A) whichever   (B) either
(C) each other   (D) whoever

24 We will hold the awards ceremony banquet at the Stadni Inn or the Maxtron Suites, ------- is more convenient.
(A) anyone   (B) whichever
(C) both   (D) another

정답 및 해설 p. 65

1 Journalists ------- are registered for next Monday's press conference will receive an admission pass upon registration.
(A) whichever
(B) whoever
(C) who
(D) whose

2 Neatly Apparel sells many fabrics ------- can absorb up to 25 times their weight in water.
(A) but
(B) that
(C) while
(D) than

3 Fong & Haas, Inc., has automated its toothpaste mixing processes, ------- used to take up more than half of the production time.
(A) and
(B) which
(C) though
(D) when

4 The names of the department heads to ------- the monthly reports should be sent are located on the last page of the manual.
(A) whoever
(B) whom
(C) what
(D) where

5 Traditionally, health care practitioners are required to obtain licenses from every country in which ------- practice.
(A) themselves
(B) theirs
(C) their
(D) they

6 The marketing department has announced a new incentive program ------- will begin next week for all of its employees.
(A) that
(B) such
(C) when
(D) until

7 A fine of $200 will be imposed upon any drivers ------- park illegally downtown during the holiday parade.
(A) which
(B) whose
(C) whom
(D) who

8 ------- inexpensive, most batteries available today will last much longer than those produced a decade ago.
(A) Nevertheless
(B) However
(C) Anyway
(D) Yet

9 Harrier Construction employs a group of contractors ------- collective knowledge and experience translate into quality workmanship.
(A) what
(B) whose
(C) which
(D) who

10 Safety boots and protective vests must be worn by all employees ------- duties involve working in the production plant.
(A) who
(B) their
(C) whose
(D) which

11 Of the builders ------- are interested in working on the project, Carlos Sandovar stands out as the best option.
(A) they
(B) some
(C) those
(D) who

12 The latest version of our spreadsheet for tracking expenses, ------- includes updated calculations, is actually quite easy to use.
(A) it
(B) itself
(C) which
(D) whose

13 The safety of employees at Craft Time Ltd. is something ------- will never be compromised.
(A) where
(B) that
(C) when
(D) then

14 Employees are the ones ------- have the most to gain from the new company policies.
(A) whoever
(B) who
(C) whichever
(D) whose

15 It is Mr. Yang's responsibility to notify all office personnel ------- a new computer program is installed.
(A) whenever
(B) however
(C) whoever
(D) whichever

16 Dr. Johnson is offering a three-hour workshop during ------- she will share some perspectives on effective time management.
(A) whose
(B) while
(C) whatever
(D) which

17 Full terms and conditions, ------- may vary from time to time, are listed on the company Web page.
(A) who
(B) which
(C) why
(D) when

18 You may return for full credit any merchandise with ------- you are not satisfied.
(A) who
(B) what
(C) which
(D) whose

19 One of the accomplishments ------- which Ms. Rettson is best known is having started her own fabric design company at the age of 22.
(A) between
(B) from
(C) into
(D) for

20 The manufacturer guarantees that its cosmetic products are good for three years or until the expiration date on the package, ------- is sooner.
(A) what
(B) when
(C) that
(D) whichever

UNIT 13 명사절 접속사

평균 1문제 출제

무료인강

● 명사절의 역할

명사절은 주어, 목적어, 보어 역할을 한다.

주어	**What pleased the clients most** was the effective customer service.
	고객을 가장 만족시킨 것은 효과적인 고객 서비스였다.
타동사의 목적어	We should determine **whether the advertising campaign is effective (or not)**.
	우리는 그 광고 캠페인이 효과적인지 아닌지 알아봐야 한다.
전치사의 목적어	The team had a discussion about **what is needed for the upcoming product launch**.
	그 팀은 다가오는 제품 출시에 무엇이 필요한지에 대해 논의했다.
보어	The fact is **that the team needs additional time to complete the task**.
	과제를 마무리하려면 그 팀에 시간이 더 필요한 것이 사실이다.

● 명사절 접속사의 종류

that, whether / if, 의문사, 복합관계대명사가 명사절 접속사로 쓰인다.

that	~라는 것		
whether / if	~인지 아닌지		
의문사	who 누가 ~하는지	which 어떤 것이(을) ~하는지	what 무엇이(을) ~하는지, ~하는 것
	when 언제 ~하는지	where 어디서 ~하는지	how 어떻게 ~하는지	why 왜 ~하는지
복합관계대명사	whoever 누구든지	whomever 누구든지	whichever 어떤 것이든지	whatever 무엇이든지

● 명사절 vs. 관계사절

명사절 접속사 that은 완전한 문장을 이끌고, 관계대명사 that은 불완전한 문장을 이끈다.

명사절	The survey results indicate **that we need more staff for major projects**.
	주어 동사 목적어
	설문 조사 결과는 주요 프로젝트에 더 많은 직원이 필요하다는 것을 보여 준다.
	→ that절이 목적어로서 명사 역할을 하므로 이때 that은 명사절 접속사이다.
관계사절	Dandar City is the site **that was chosen for the new shopping center**.
	명사 앞서 나온 명사(선행사)를 수식
	단다르 시는 새로운 쇼핑센터 부지로 선정된 곳이다.
	→ that절이 명사(the site)를 수식하는 형용사 역할을 하므로 이때 that은 관계대명사이다.

명사절 접속사 | ETS 핵심 출제 패턴

명사절 접속사 whether, that, which의 출제 빈도가 높다. 문장 구조에 대한 이해와 정확한 해석을 필요로 하는 비교적 높은 난이도의 문제로 출제된다.

☑ 주어 자리에 명사절 접속사를 선택하는 문제

------- manager approves an invoice depends on the area being charged for an expense.

(A) Which   (B) Each

(C) Either   (D) Something

어떤 관리자가 청구서를 승인하는지는 비용이 청구되는 지역에 따라 결정된다.

핵심 포인트

동사 **depends**의 주어 역할을 하는 명사절을 이끄는 접속사가 들어가야 한다.

▶ 기출공식 4 **p.119**

☑ 목적어 자리에 명사절 접속사를 선택하는 문제

The Planning Committee will decide ------- or not to expand the workforce in the branch office.

(A) neither   (B) about

(C) whether   (D) that

기획 위원회는 지점의 인력을 늘릴지 여부를 결정할 것이다.

핵심 포인트

동사 **decide**의 목적어 역할을 하는 명사절을 이끄는 접속사가 들어가야 한다.

▶ 기출공식 3 **p.119**

☑ 명사절을 이끄는 의문사를 선택하는 문제

The employee handbook explains ------- new employees need to know regarding company benefits.

(A) which   (B) where

(C) how   (D) what

직원 안내서에는 회사의 복리 후생과 관련하여 신입직원들이 무엇을 알아야 하는지가 설명되어 있다.

핵심 포인트

명사절 접속사 자리에 들어갈 의문사로 '무엇을 알아야 하는지'라는 의미가 자연스럽다.

▶ 기출공식 4 **p.119**

☑ 명사절을 이끄는 복합관계대명사를 선택하는 문제

------- wants to join the library's book club should register by June 1.

(A) Which   (B) Other

(C) Someone   (D) Whoever

도서관 북클럽에 가입하려는 사람은 누구나 6월 1일까지 등록해야 한다.

핵심 포인트

주어 역할을 하는 명사절을 이끄는 접속사가 들어가야 하며, '누구든지'라는 의미가 자연스럽다.

▶ 기출공식 7 **p.121**

정답 : (A), (C), (D), (D)

기출공식 1   that은 '~라는 것'이라는 의미로 명사절을 이끈다.

주어   **That the musical got excellent reviews** is true. 그 뮤지컬이 좋은 평을 받았다는 점은 사실이다.

> **+만점팁** 긴 명사절 주어 대신 가주어 it을 쓰는 것이 더 일반적이다.

It is true **that the musical got excellent reviews**.

목적어   A research report indicates **(that) consumers prefer quality over low price**.
연구 보고서는 소비자들이 저렴한 가격보다 양질을 더 선호한다는 것을` 보여 준다.

→ 목적어 자리에 오는 that은 생략할 수 있다.

보어   The important thing is **that a manager should know every detail**.
중요한 것은 부장이 모든 세부사항을 알아야 한다는 점이다.

---

1 A recent poll indicates ------- the candidate's popularity has been increasing among voters.
(A) what   (B) that
(C) which   (D) those

2 A major advantage of the Sisfeld Hotel is ------- the rooms feature kitchen facilities and fully equipped work stations.
(A) to   (B) whether
(C) then   (D) that

3 Recent research shows ------- complex projects are completed more rapidly when they are divided into simpler tasks.
(A) either   (B) that
(C) who   (D) something

기출공식 2   명사절 that은 특정 형용사 뒤, 동격을 이루는 명사 뒤에 올 수 있다.

■ **형용사 + that**

be aware that ~을 알고 있다 hopeful/optimistic that ~을 희망/낙관하다 be afraid that 유감스럽게도 ~이다	be confident/sure/certain that ~을 확신하다 be sorry that ~라니 유감이다 be glad/pleased/delighted that ~라니 기쁘다

Mr. Booth is **confident that** the new marketing campaigns will be a great success.
부스 씨는 새로운 마케팅 캠페인이 큰 성공을 거두리라 확신한다.

■ **추상명사 + 동격의 that**

the fact that ~라는 사실 the idea that ~라는 생각 the claim that ~라는 주장	the statement that ~라는 진술, 성명 the speculation that ~라는 추측 the confirmation that ~라는 확인	the opinion that ~라는 의견 the evidence that ~라는 증거 the conclusion that ~라는 결론

The evidence that frequent breaks can help productivity has not been disputed.
잦은 휴식이 생산성에 도움이 된다는 증거에 대해서는 지금까지 이의가 없었다.

---

4 The CEO of Argall Enterprises issued a ------- that the company will open two new stores in the downtown area.
(A) statement   (B) requirement
(C) treatment   (D) enforcement

5 Tallis Engineering is awaiting verification ------- its new water tank designs meet legal specifications.
(A) that   (B) what
(C) from   (D) which

6 Dr. Yoo is ------- that his research results are accurate.
(A) responsible
(B) accustomed
(C) knowledgeable
(D) confident

빈출

기출공식 3 whether/if는 '~인지 아닌지'라는 의미로 명사절을 이끈다.

주어	**Whether we will open a branch office (or not)** is still under discussion. 우리가 지점을 열지 여부는 여전히 논의 중이다. → **whether가 명사절을 이끌 때 or not은 생략할 수 있다.**
타동사의 목적어	Every staff wondered **whether[if] the office would be relocated to Shanghai.** 모든 직원은 사무실이 상하이로 이전될지 여부를 궁금해 했다. → **명사절 접속사 if는 타동사의 목적어 자리에서만 whether 대신 쓸 수 있다.**
전치사의 목적어	A question arose **as to whether we should increase our budget for the project.** 프로젝트 예산을 늘려야 하는지 여부에 대해 의문이 생겼다.
보어	An important issue is **whether we should find a new supplier.** 중요한 문제는 우리가 새로운 납품업체를 찾아야 하는지 여부이다.

7 The fax machine is out of service, and an experienced technician has been called in to see ------- it can be repaired.
(A) if
(B) that
(C) what
(D) though

8 After the Elixis Park apartment complex changes ownership, the building's current maintenance staff can determine ------- they want to work with the new management.
(A) either
(B) whether
(C) instead of
(D) regarding

9 ------- we choose to hold a company outing this Friday will depend on weather conditions.
(A) Whether
(B) Although
(C) Either
(D) Even if

빈출

기출공식 4 의문사는 명사절을 이끌 수 있다.

- **의문대명사 who(m)/what/which + 불완전한 문장**

  The new employee asked the manager **who** will lead the orientation on Thursday.
  신입 사원은 목요일에 누가 오리엔테이션을 이끌지 부장에게 물었다.

  The building supply company asked us **what** we will need for the upcoming construction project. 건축자재 업체는 다가오는 건축 프로젝트에서 우리에게 무엇이 필요한지 물었다.

- **의문부사 when/where/why/how + 완전한 문장**

  We will inform customers **when** our branches will be closed during the first quarter.
  우리는 1사분기 중 언제 지점들이 폐쇄될지 고객들에게 알릴 것이다.

10 The workshop materials describe ------- salespeople can deliver more memorable and more effective presentations to clients.
(A) how
(B) this
(C) so that
(D) as

11 Among other topics, the presenter will tell the forum participants ------- is needed to succeed in the modern workplace.
(A) and
(B) about
(C) what
(D) how

12 The management team will meet on Monday to decide ------- will be recognized as employee of the month.
(A) where
(B) who
(C) which
(D) whose

정답 및 해설 p.68

의문형용사는 명사를 수식하면서 명사절을 이끌 수 있다.

whose Mr. Kim knows **whose desk** the new intern will use.
김 씨는 신입 수습 사원이 누구의 책상을 사용할지 알고 있다.

→ '의문형용사 + 명사' 뒤에 **use**의 목적어가 빠진 불완전한 문장이 나온다.

what Event organizers will decide **what activities** they should add to the program.
행사 기획자들은 프로그램에 어떤 활동을 추가해야 하는지 결정할 것이다.

→ '의문형용사 + 명사' 뒤에 **add**의 목적어가 빠진 불완전한 문장이 나온다.

which Please let me know **which sample** should be returned.
어떤 샘플이 반품되어야 하는지 알려 주세요.

→ '의문형용사 + 명사' 뒤에 **should**의 주어가 빠진 불완전한 문장이 나온다.

13 The course catalog specifies ------- classes are required for each degree.
(A) any other
(B) whom
(C) which
(D) everyone

14 In your message, explain clearly ------- issue you are experiencing with the software.
(A) how
(B) all
(C) and
(D) what

15 As soon as Mr. Shim has reviewed the blueprints and cost estimates, he will determine ------- proposal will be selected.
(A) who
(B) whom
(C) whoever
(D) whose

명사절은 to부정사구로 축약할 수 있다.

We haven't determined **whether we should close** the main entrance during the renovation.
→ We haven't determined **whether to close** the main entrance during the renovation.
우리는 보수 공사 중에 정문을 폐쇄할지 여부를 아직 결정하지 않았다.

The cookbook shows **how you should create** tasty fusion dishes.
→ The cookbook shows **how to create** tasty fusion dishes.
그 요리책은 맛있는 퓨전 요리 만드는 법을 보여 준다.

+만점팁 | **that, if**가 이끄는 명사절은 to부정사구로 축약할 수 없다.

Tomorrow's session will train participants on [**how** / ~~that~~] to prepare containers for overseas shipment.
내일 교육은 참가자들에게 해외 배송 컨테이너를 준비하는 방법에 대해 교육할 것이다.

16 During the workshop, the instructors will explain ------- to prepare and create more effective sales presentations.
(A) excluding
(B) how
(C) try
(D) except

17 Harmony Design consultants can help clients decide ------- to use curtains or blinds when decorating their windows.
(A) if
(B) neither
(C) whether
(D) yet

18 Director Jun Iwata auditioned twenty actors before making the final decision about ------- to cast in the main role.
(A) whom
(B) when
(C) either
(D) whether

기출공식 7　복합관계대명사는 명사절을 이끌 수 있다.

whoever(= anyone who) ~하는 사람은 누구든지	whomever(= anyone whom) ~하는 사람은 누구든지
whatever(= anything that) ~하는 것은 무엇이든지	whichever(= anything that) ~하는 것은 어느 쪽이든지

Whoever(= Anyone who) responds to the survey will receive a $10 gift certificate.
설문 조사에 응하는 사람은 누구든지 10달러짜리 상품권을 받을 것이다.

➔ 복합관계대명사는 '선행사 + 관계대명사'로 바꿀 수 있다.

Our staff will do **whatever** they can to make your special event a success.
저희 직원들은 귀하의 특별한 행사를 성공으로 이끌 수 있도록 할 수 있는 무엇이든지 할 것입니다.

➔ 복합관계대명사는 불완전한 문장을 이끈다.

19 The Wizdaric Plus software program captures ------- appears on your computer screen and saves it in an archive.
(A) wherever
(B) everything
(C) whatever
(D) anyway

20 ------- of the five new editors seems the most experienced with layout will work with Mr. Abdellah on the special edition of the magazine.
(A) Whatever
(B) Whichever
(C) One
(D) Most

21 ------- arrives at the store first is expected to turn on all the lights.
(A) Whoever
(B) Whomever
(C) Whenever
(D) However

빈출
기출공식 8　복합관계대명사와 부정대명사를 비교하는 문제가 출제된다.

[**Whoever** / ~~Anyone~~] books a trip after December 31 will have to pay additional fees.
　　　　　　　　　　　　　　　　　동사　　　　　　　　　　　　　　　　동사

12월 31일 이후 여행을 예약하는 누구든지 추가 수수료를 지불해야 할 것이다.

➔ 동사 개수가 2개이므로 접속사가 필요하다. 따라서 명사절 접속사 역할을 하는 복합관계대명사가 들어가야 한다.

For reasons of safety, [~~whoever~~ / **anyone**] entering the construction area must wear a hard hat.
　　　　　　　　　　　　　　　　　　　　　　분사　　　　　　　　　　　　　　　동사

안전상의 이유로 공사 구역에 들어가는 사람은 누구든지 안전모를 착용해야 한다.

➔ 동사 개수가 1개이므로 접속사가 필요하지 않다. 따라서 접속사 역할이 없는 부정대명사가 들어가야 한다.

22 ------- wishes to donate unwanted electronic items for recycling can do so throughout the months of May and June.
(A) Everyone
(B) Somebody
(C) Those
(D) Whoever

23 Promotions should not automatically be given to ------- has the most seniority.
(A) nobody
(B) whoever
(C) anyone
(D) oneself

24 Stylist Cecilia Wright expertly highlights ------- is most attractive about a client.
(A) their own
(B) herself
(C) whatever
(D) everything

정답 및 해설 p.70

1 The instruction manual shows ------- the camera's lens should be cleaned.
(A) could
(B) not only
(C) either
(D) how

2 Ms. Matsumoto requests ------- all sales employees report their working hours on a weekly basis.
(A) but
(B) which
(C) that
(D) if

3 Yee-Yin Xiong held interviews with numerous clients to determine ------- Echegaray Consulting, Inc., can improve customer service.
(A) unless
(B) in order to
(C) how
(D) as if

4 ------- wants to join the company-sponsored tour of the city's Eastview Technology Park should see Ms. Landers to sign up.
(A) While
(B) Which
(C) Whoever
(D) Anywhere

5 When you subscribe to *News Update*, you can be confident ------- you will receive a reliable analysis of the latest political and economic trends.
(A) that
(B) whether
(C) which
(D) whoever

6 A good résumé tells employers ------- a candidate's qualifications match the job responsibilities.
(A) how
(B) what
(C) which
(D) whose

7 Many readers state that the editorial page of the daily newspaper is more enlightening but admit that ------- they read first is the sports page.
(A) what
(B) these
(C) if
(D) because

8 Ms. Kushida's managers feel ------- she deserves special recognition for her performance in the last sales campaign.
(A) what
(B) that
(C) something
(D) this

9 Ventralcom recently announced ------- Pamela Wang has been named senior vice president of mergers and acquisitions at the company.
(A) what
(B) because
(C) while
(D) that

10 The city council is undertaking a research study to decide ------- to open public beaches all year around.
(A) if
(B) whether
(C) whereas
(D) since

11 Several market research studies indicate ------- product packaging affects consumers' purchasing decisions.
(A) that
(B) but
(C) what
(D) like

12 ------- should impress passengers most is the comfort of the reupholstered seating at Liverpool Regional Airport.
(A) Who
(B) What
(C) When
(D) Where

13 Thanks to today's digital entertainment options, it is rare for individuals to simply sit down and watch ------- appears on the TV screen.
(A) however
(B) anyone
(C) unless
(D) whatever

14 Eun Sung Han, president of Westhaven Glassworks, is considering ------- to renew the contract with Pineford Trucking.
(A) whether
(B) if
(C) what
(D) so

15 Although multiple studies were conducted by market research groups, it is still uncertain ------- customers are ready to purchase their groceries on the Internet.
(A) who
(B) so as to
(C) whether
(D) whichever

16 Passengers should be ------- that the airline is not responsible for lost or stolen items.
(A) aware
(B) aligned
(C) awake
(D) abroad

17 Please indicate on the envelope ------- you would prefer regular or deluxe photo processing for your film.
(A) what
(B) whether
(C) so that
(D) according to

18 Members of the Foster City Historical Society are petitioning to have ------- remains of the courthouse's original architectural elements preserved.
(A) which
(B) that
(C) what
(D) it

19 The Parks and Recreation Department is meeting to discuss ------- implications the extensive sewer work will have for the outdoor summer concert series in Evergreen Park.
(A) what
(B) whether
(C) while
(D) even if

20 The office-supply store's catalog offers many helpful suggestions on how ------- an entire meeting room economically.
(A) furnishing
(B) furnishes
(C) to furnish
(D) furnished

UNIT 14 | 비교 구문

평균 1문제 출제

무료인강

● 원급 / 비교급 / 최상급

두 대상이 동등함을 나타낼 때는 원급을 쓴다.

> The new system is **as effective as** the previous one. 신규 시스템은 이전 시스템만큼 효과적이다.

두 대상 중 하나가 더 우월하거나 열등함을 나타낼 때는 비교급을 쓴다.

> The new system is **more effective than** the previous one. 신규 시스템은 이전 시스템보다 더 효과적이다.
> The new system is **less effective than** the previous one. 신규 시스템은 이전 시스템보다 덜 효과적이다.

셋 이상의 대상 중 하나가 가장 우월하거나 열등함을 나타낼 때는 최상급을 쓴다.

> The new system is **the most effective** to date. 신규 시스템이 지금까지 가장 효과적이다.
> The new system is **the least effective** to date. 신규 시스템이 지금까지 가장 덜 효과적이다.

● 비교 구문의 품사

형용사 vs. 부사 중에서 문장 구조에 따라 알맞은 품사를 선택해야 한다.

> This ladder is as **strong** as the other expensive ones. 이 사다리는 다른 비싼 사다리들만큼 튼튼하다.
> → as ~ as 이하를 뺀 구조에서 is 뒤에 보어가 들어가야 하므로 형용사 자리이다.

> Your order will be delivered as **promptly** as possible. 귀하의 주문품은 가능한 한 빨리 배송될 것입니다.
> → as ~ as 이하를 뺀 구조에서 delivered를 수식하므로 부사 자리이다.

> Smartphones are more **convenient** than a laptop. 스마트폰이 노트북보다 더 편리하다.
> → more ~ than 이하를 뺀 구조에서 are 뒤에 보어가 들어가야 하므로 형용사 자리이다.

> The device analyzes data more **accurately** than expected. 그 장치는 예상보다 더 정확하게 자료를 분석한다.
> → more ~ than 이하를 뺀 구조에서 analyzes를 수식하므로 부사 자리이다.

비교 구문 | ETS 핵심 출제 패턴

비교 구문에서는 비교급을 완성하는 문제가 가장 많이 출제된다. 형용사와 부사 중에서 자리로 판단해야 하는 품사 문제도 출제된다. 또한 원급 / 비교급 / 최상급을 수식하는 수식어와 관용 표현들이 다양하게 출제된다.

☑ 원급 비교 구문의 품사를 선택하는 문제

Customers are advised to be as ------- as possible when describing the problem they have with a product.

(A) specific　　　　(B) specifically
(C) specifies　　　　(D) specified

고객들은 제품의 문제점을 설명할 때 가능한 한 자세하게 설명하도록 권고된다.

핵심 포인트

'가능한 한 자세하게'라는 원급 표현이 들어가야 한다.

▶ 기출공식 1 p.126

☑ 비교급을 완성하는 문제

Francesco Graphics' art department spent ------- time than anticipated on the redesign of the corporate Web site.

(A) again　　　　(B) more
(C) over　　　　(D) above

프란체스코 그래픽스의 미술부는 회사 웹사이트 개편에 예상보다 더 많은 시간을 들였다.

핵심 포인트

빈칸 뒤에 **than**이 있으므로 비교급이 들어가야 한다.

▶ 기출공식 2 p.126

☑ 비교급의 품사를 선택하는 문제

Many educational institutions are switching to recycled paper because it is ------- than new paper.

(A) expensiveness　　　　(B) expense
(C) less expensive　　　　(D) expensively

많은 교육 기관들이 새 종이보다 더 저렴하다는 이유로 재활용 용지로 바꾸고 있다.

핵심 포인트

less와 함께 쓰여 비교급을 완성하는 자리이며, **is**의 보어가 들어가야 한다.

▶ 기출공식 6 p.128

☑ 최상급을 완성하는 문제

The Grady Company has a well-deserved reputation for producing stoves and microwave ovens of the ------- quality.

(A) as high as　　　　(B) highest
(C) highly　　　　(D) heighten

그래디 컴퍼니는 최고 품질의 가스레인지와 전자레인지를 생산한다는 평판을 받는데 그런 평판을 받을 자격이 충분하다.

핵심 포인트

quality를 수식하는 형용사 자리이며, 빈칸 앞에 **the**가 있으므로 최상급이 들어가야 한다.

▶ 기출공식 4 p.127

정답 : (A), (B), (C), (B)

원급 비교를 나타내는 as … as 사이에는 형용사 또는 부사의 원급을 쓴다.

- **as 형용사 / 부사 as: ~만큼 …한**

  The renovation project was just **as urgent as** our new building plan.

  보수 프로젝트는 우리의 신축 계획만큼이나 긴급했다.

  → as ~ as 사이에는 형용사나 부사의 원급이 들어가며, 비교급이나 최상급은 들어갈 수 없다.

- **as 수량 형용사 + 명사 as: ~만큼 많은 / 적은**

  Yoshiko Electronics will introduce **as many products as** they did last year.

  요시코 전자는 지난해에 출시했던 것만큼이나 많은 제품들을 선보일 것이다.

  → 가산명사는 as many … as, 불가산명사는 as much … as와 같이 쓴다.

1 After the disk driver is installed, the protective cover should be replaced as ------- as possible to prevent the accumulation of dust.
(A) quicken
(B) quicker
(C) quickest
(D) quickly

2 The Power Plus Health Club offers new members full use of its weight-training equipment for as ------- as $40 per month.
(A) little
(B) rare
(C) scarce
(D) short

3 Repairing the old copy machine would have cost half as ------- money as buying a new one.
(A) even
(B) quite
(C) still
(D) much

빈출

비교급은 '-er' 또는 more / less로 나타내며 뒤에는 than이 올 수 있다.

- **-er + than: ~보다 더 …한**

  The subway is **faster than** a private vehicle during rush hour.

  러시아워에는 지하철이 승용차보다 빠르다.

- **more / less ~ than: ~보다 더 / 덜 …한**

  This recording software is **more reliable than** the previous one.

  이 녹음 소프트웨어는 이전 것보다 더 신뢰할 수 있다.

  Some new cars are **less expensive than** used cars. 일부 신차는 중고차보다 저렴하다.

  +만점팁 둘을 비교할 때는 비교급 앞에 the를 붙인다.

  Between the B7 and D6 digital cameras, we will take **the simpler of the two** models.

  우리는 B7과 D6 디지털 카메라 중에 더 단순한 모델을 살 것이다.

4 Greenway Airlines is using ------- of its single-engine planes now than ever before.
(A) few
(B) fewer
(C) fewest
(D) a few

5 Mr. Lee takes his job ------- than his predecessor did.
(A) serious
(B) seriously
(C) more seriously
(D) most seriously

6 The last quarterly report showed that TNQ Electronics' earnings were ------- than anticipated.
(A) lowest
(B) lowering
(C) lower
(D) low

빈출

기출공식 3 비교급을 강조하는 부사가 자주 출제된다.

| much / even / still / far / a lot 훨씬
considerably / significantly 상당히 | noticeably 두드러지게, 현저하게
substantially 충분히 |

The new operating system became **far more complicated**. 새로운 운영 시스템은 훨씬 더 복잡해졌다.

→ **very, too는 비교급을 수식할 수 없다.**

The Creaxley racing bicycle is **considerably lighter than** the previous models.
크리엑슬리 경주용 자전거는 이전 모델보다 상당히 가볍다.

→ **비교급 앞에 비교급 강조 부사를 넣거나, 비교급 강조 부사 뒤에 비교급을 넣는 형태로 문제가 출제된다.**

---

7 Because of the relatively cold weather conditions, sales of winter clothing are ------- higher than normal this season.
(A) more
(B) many
(C) as
(D) much

8 The recently-installed CXT-7 order processing software is ------- easier to use than the old program.
(A) consider
(B) considering
(C) considerably
(D) considers

9 The much ------- size of the new picture format will allow us to store hundreds more pictures on each disk.
(A) small
(B) smaller
(C) smallest
(D) smallness

빈출

기출공식 4 최상급은 '-est' 또는 most / least로 나타내며 특정 단서와 함께 잘 어울려 쓰인다.

- **the 또는 소유격 + 최상급 + of / among / in + 집단 / 장소: ~ 중에서 / ~에서 가장 …한**
  The Dtech-Ten is **the fastest of all our laptops.** 디테크-텐은 우리 모든 노트북 중에서 가장 빠르다.

- **the 또는 소유격 + 최상급 + ever / yet / to date: 지금껏 가장 ~한**
  Winning the publishing award is **her most prominent** accomplishment **to date.**
  출판상 수상은 지금까지 가장 두드러진 그녀의 업적이다.

- **[one / two / some] of the 최상급 + 복수명사: 가장 ~한 것들 중 하나 / 둘 / 일부**
  The Rainbow Waterfall is **one of the most popular tourist attractions** on the island.
  레인보우 폭포는 그 섬에서 가장 인기 있는 관광 명소 중 한 곳이다.

- **the 또는 소유격 최상급 + possible / available: 가능한 / 이용할 수 있는 가장 ~한**
  The 2-day "City Tour" is **the cheapest** travel package **available.**
  2일 '시티 투어'는 이용할 수 있는 가장 저렴한 여행 패키지이다.

---

10 Of the subway lines that stop in the central business district, the green line is the ------- to walk to from the Franklin Building.
(A) more easily
(B) easiest
(C) most easily
(D) easy

11 Of all the washing machines we tested, the Swisherette uses water the -------.
(A) most efficiently
(B) more efficient
(C) efficiencies
(D) efficiency

12 The episode on honeybees is the ------- one that *Nature Podcast* has ever released.
(A) most popularly
(B) most popular
(C) popularity
(D) popular

정답 및 해설 p. 74

'the + 최상급' 앞에	'the + 최상급' 사이에	'the + 최상급' 뒤에
even, by far	single, very	ever, yet, possible

This African artifact is **by far the most impressive** one in this museum.
이 아프리카 공예품이 이 박물관에서 단연코 가장 인상적이다.

With locations in more than 50 countries, Colton hotels offer their customers **the very best**
service. 50여 개의 국가에 지점을 가진 콜턴 호텔은 고객들에게 단연 최상의 서비스를 제공한다.

The Vacadar V10 vacuum cleaner is **the company's most powerful ever**.
바카다 V10 진공 청소기는 그 회사에서 역대 가장 강력한 청소기이다.

13 Ms. Vialobos has reported
that the new mobile
telephones are the lightest
------- to be purchased by
the department.
(A) ever
(B) before
(C) quite
(D) well

14 A 20 percent increase in
revenue makes this the most
profitable year ------- for the
Sorvine Hotel Group.
(A) quite
(B) yet
(C) better
(D) enough

15 Our customer service
representatives will make
every effort to bring our
customers the ------- best
experience.
(A) most
(B) enough
(C) very
(D) exactly

빈출

- **형용사 자리 판단하기**
  Helen Kang's presentation was one of the [**most powerful** / ~~most powerfully~~] we had ever
  seen. 헬렌 강의 발표는 우리가 여태까지 본 가장 설득력 있는 발표 중의 하나였다.
  → **be동사의 보어 자리이므로 형용사가 와야 한다.**

- **부사 자리 판단하기**
  The employee handbook [**clearly** / ~~clear~~ / ~~clearer~~ / ~~clearest~~] outlines our company's benefit
  package. 직원 안내서에는 당사의 복리 후생 제도가 명확하게 설명되어 있다.
  → **원급 / 비교급 / 최상급을 판단하기에 앞서, 주어와 동사 사이이므로 부사가 와야 한다.**

16 The advertisement for the
Ecosmart car was more
------- than the one for the
Greenrave car.
(A) memorably
(B) memory
(C) memorize
(D) memorable

17 The architects have found
designing the bridge across
the bay ------- than they had
anticipated.
(A) difficult
(B) difficulty
(C) more difficult
(D) much difficulty

18 The new Prodeliax Pro-6 photo
editing software can be installed
even ------- than previous
versions of the program.
(A) more easily
(B) easier
(C) easing
(D) eased

기출공식 7 비교급 관용 표현이 출제된다.

no longer/not any longer 더 이상 ~ 않다 more than doubled/tripled 두/세 배 이상 늘다 other than ~ 이외에 more than/less than ~ 이상/~ 이하	no later than 늦어도 ~까지 than expected/anticipated/projected 예상보다 더 ~한 the 비교급 ~, the 비교급 ... ~하면 할수록 더 …하다 rather than ~보다는

Brooks Courier Co. will **no longer** transport perishable items.
브룩스 택배사는 부패하기 쉬운 품목들을 더 이상 운송하지 않을 것이다.

Applicants must send in their application forms **no later than** February 2.
지원자들은 늦어도 2월 2일까지는 신청서를 보내야 한다.

19 All members of the design team are expected to submit their completed drafts to Ms. Conroy ------- next Friday.
(A) instead of
(B) no later than
(C) although
(D) otherwise

20 Darjing Food Company has attributed its recent popularity with consumers to changes in its recipes ------- its new packaging.
(A) as for
(B) even so
(C) rather than
(D) after all

21 Due to recent sanitation problems, pets are ------- allowed inside Luna Café.
(A) no sooner
(B) anymore
(C) fewer
(D) no longer

기출공식 8 원급·최상급 관용 표현이 출제된다.

the same ... as ~와 동일한 at least (숫자 수식) 최소한, 적어도 make the most of ~을 최대한 활용하다	as ~ as possible 가능한 한 ~하게 at the latest 아무리 늦어도 at your earliest convenience 가급적 빨리

The new manager will have **the same** responsibilities **as** his predecessor.
신임 부장은 전임자와 동일한 책임을 맡을 것이다.

Please be sure to retrieve your merchandise by October 3 **at the latest**.
아무리 늦어도 10월 3일까지 상품을 찾아 가세요.

22 The new Maxilac M6 mobile phone has the same features ------- the previous models, but it is slightly lighter and thinner.
(A) as
(B) also
(C) to
(D) after

23 In this province, student drivers may not apply for a driver's license until they are ------- 17 years old.
(A) at once
(B) at least
(C) for now
(D) for good

24 Your property's fencing issue must be remedied by August 31 -------.
(A) at the latest
(B) no later than
(C) too late
(D) lately

1 Auron Energy, one of the nation's ------- energy suppliers, delivers electricity to nearly twenty million customers.
(A) largest
(B) more largely
(C) largely
(D) enlarge

2 The survey indicated that people responded even ------- to the taste of the new Factor X Energy Bar than expected.
(A) favorably
(B) most favorable
(C) more favorably
(D) favorable

3 Candidates for positions at Pereira Consulting should answer the questions on the application form as ------- as possible.
(A) accurate
(B) accuracy
(C) accuracies
(D) accurately

4 When *Gadget Guide Weekly* tested the laptops introduced this year, the Star 1000 was rated the -------.
(A) powerful
(B) powerfully
(C) more powerful
(D) most powerful

5 Moving our headquarters to a suburban area would be more convenient and less expensive ------- settling in the congested urban center.
(A) while
(B) but
(C) than
(D) and

6 The product review says that the Cozy Days space heater is ------- to warm up than similar products.
(A) slowest
(B) slower
(C) slowed
(D) slowing

7 Researchers at Firmatek Synthetics are working on a new material that will be twice as ------- as ordinary concrete.
(A) durably
(B) durable
(C) durability
(D) durableness

8 In order for you to receive the early registration rate, your application form must be postmarked ------- Friday, October 28.
(A) in advance
(B) beforehand
(C) previously
(D) no later than

9 Confident that Mr. Takashi Ota was ------- more qualified than other candidates, Argnome Corporation hired him as the new vice president.
(A) much
(B) very
(C) rarely
(D) along

10 Reddell Airlines' second-quarter profits were 25 percent higher than previously -------.
(A) predict
(B) predicted
(C) predicting
(D) prediction

11 During the meeting, the product team insisted that their toaster design was ------- than the competition's latest release.
(A) more efficient
(B) so efficiently
(C) as efficient
(D) most efficiently

12 Because several committee members have been delayed, the accounting report will be discussed ------- than planned at today's meeting.
(A) late
(B) latest
(C) later
(D) lateness

13 The maintenance department replaced the windows with ------- ones to reduce glare in the summer.
(A) darkly
(B) darkness
(C) darker
(D) darkest

14 If Oyola Machines merges with the Menji Corporation, the resulting conglomerate will be ------- of the largest technology companies in the world.
(A) much
(B) some
(C) those
(D) one

15 The red packaging received ------- ratings in customer focus groups than the yellow packaging.
(A) higher
(B) highly
(C) highness
(D) highest

16 Ever since the presentation of the Travercell big-screen television set at the Ghent International Electronics Show, sales have ------- than tripled.
(A) more so
(B) more
(C) mostly
(D) most

17 Nokario Ltd.'s "Core Illumination Solution" has been praised by architects as the ------- lighting system on the market today.
(A) economize
(B) more economically
(C) most economical
(D) economically

18 To meet the audit deadline, accountants at Lyang Associates must submit all financial reports by tomorrow morning at the -------.
(A) latest
(B) lowest
(C) oldest
(D) finest

19 McLellan Associates, the ------- of the two law firms, is presently advertising several job openings for paralegals.
(A) largeness
(B) larger
(C) largely
(D) large

20 The State Street office won a company award because it has been operating ------- than any other branch location.
(A) efficient
(B) most efficient
(C) efficiently
(D) more efficiently

UNIT 15 | 가정법과 도치

평균 1문제 출제

무료인강

● 가정법

가정법은 **if**를 사용하여 나타내며, 가정법의 명칭은 **if**절에 사용된 시제를 따른다.

조건절	if절에 현재형 시제를 쓰며, 실현 가능성이 있는 상황을 나타내는 표현이다. **If** the order **is shipped** on May 8, it will arrive by May 12. 주문품이 5월 8일에 발송되는 경우, 5월 12일까지 도착할 것이다.
가정법 과거	if절에 과거형 시제를 쓰며, 현재 사실의 반대 상황을 가정하는 표현이다. **If** the order **was shipped** on May 8, it would arrive by May 12. 만약 주문품이 5월 8일에 발송된다면, 5월 12일까지 도착할 텐데.
가정법 과거 완료	if절에 과거완료 시제를 쓰며, 과거 사실의 반대 상황을 가정하는 표현이다. **If** the order **had been shipped** on May 8, it would have arrived by May 12. 만약 주문품이 5월 8일에 발송되었다면, 5월 12일까지 도착했을 텐데.
가정법 미래	if절에 'should + 동사원형'을 쓰며, 불확실한 미래를 가정하는 표현이다. **If** you **should wish** to cancel the order, **please contact** us immediately. 혹시라도 주문 취소를 원하실 경우, 저희에게 즉시 연락 주세요.

● 도치

강조하고자 하는 말을 문장 맨 앞으로 빼면 주어와 동사의 어순이 바뀌는데, 이를 도치라고 한다.

be동사 도치 문장	A copy of our most recent annual report is **enclosed**. → **Enclosed** is a copy of our most recent annual report. 가장 최근 연례 보고서가 동봉되어 있습니다.
have p.p. 도치 문장	The organization has **seldom** budgeted money for advertising. → **Seldom** has the organization budgeted money for advertising. 그 단체는 광고를 위해 예산을 편성한 적이 거의 없습니다.
조동사 도치 문장	The safety of employees will **never** be compromised. → **Never** will the safety of employees be compromised. 직원의 안전은 절대 침해되지 않을 것이다.
일반동사 도치 문장	We **rarely** receive complaints about our delivery service. → **Rarely** do we receive complaints about our delivery service. 저희는 배송 서비스에 관해 불만 사항을 접수하는 일이 거의 없습니다. ※ **do/does/did가 주어 앞으로 오고 주어 뒤에는 동사원형이 온다. (의문문 어순)**

가정법과 도치 | ETS 핵심 출제 패턴

가정법은 주로 가정법 공식에 따른 동사의 시제 문제로 출제되므로 공식만 암기하면 쉽게 풀 수 있다. 도치 구문은 가정법 도치, 부정어 도치가 주로 출제되며, 기타 도치 구문도 유형을 익히면 어렵지 않게 문제를 풀 수 있다.

☑ if절의 시제를 채우는 문제

If the red indicator light ------- on, check the electrical connection to the internal rechargeable battery.

(A) comes   (B) coming
(C) had come   (D) to come

만약 빨간색 표시등이 들어오면, 내부 충전 배터리의 전기 연결부를 확인하세요.

핵심 포인트

주절의 시제가 현재형이므로 if절에 현재 시제가 와야 한다.

▶ 기출공식 1 **p.134**

☑ 가정법의 주절 시제를 채우는 문제

If we had ordered the desks last week, we ------- a special discount.

(A) have received   (B) be receiving
(C) will receive   (D) would have received

만약 지난주에 책상을 주문했다면, 우리는 특별 할인을 받았을 텐데.

핵심 포인트

if절의 시제가 과거완료이므로 가정법 과거완료에 맞는 시제가 와야 한다.

▶ 기출공식 3 **p.135**

☑ 가정법 도치 문제

------- you need a paper receipt for your purchases, just request one from the cashier.

(A) After   (B) Throughout
(C) Should   (D) Although

구매에 대한 종이 영수증이 필요하면, 계산원에게 요청하세요.

핵심 포인트

의미상 '만약 ~하다면'의 if가 와야 하므로 가정법 미래가 도치된 것으로 봐야 한다.

▶ 기출공식 5 **p.136**

☑ 보어 도치 문제

------- is a brochure with descriptions of our products.

(A) Enclosure   (B) Enclosed
(C) Enclose   (D) Enclosing

저희 제품에 대한 설명이 담긴 안내 책자가 동봉되어 있습니다.

핵심 포인트

보어 '동봉된'을 강조하기 위해 문장 맨 앞으로 끌어온 보어 도치이다.

▶ 기출공식 6 **p.136**

정답 : (A), (D), (C), (B)

기출공식 1 If절 동사가 현재 시제이면 주절은 '조동사의 원형 + 동사원형' 또는 명령문을 쓴다.

조건절: 만약 ~하면, …할 것이다/하라 (실현 가능성이 있는 상황)

If + 주어 + 동사의 현재 시제 ~, 주어 + 조동사 원형(will, may, can) + 동사원형 (또는 명령문)

If raw material costs **rise**, the retail prices **will increase** accordingly.
만약 원자재 가격이 상승한다면, 소매가가 따라서 오를 것이다.

If you **are** unable to keep your appointment, **please call** us by Wednesday.
만약 예약 시간을 못 지키게 되면, 수요일까지 전화주세요.

---

1 If orders ------- at the current pace all summer, Turramurra Luggage Company will meet its sales goal one month early.
(A) receive
(B) are received
(C) will receive
(D) will be receiving

2 If the toy ------- operate, check that the batteries are inserted correctly and that the switch is in the "on" position.
(A) did not
(B) does not
(C) had not been
(D) were not

3 If you provide the missing receipt, our department ------- your reimbursement request immediately.
(A) would have processed
(B) can process
(C) processed
(D) is processing

기출공식 2 If절 동사가 과거 시제이면 주절은 '조동사의 과거형 + 동사원형'을 쓴다.

가정법 과거: 만약 ~한다면, …할 텐데 (현재 사실과 반대되는 상황)

If + 주어 + 동사의 과거형 ~, 조동사의 과거형(would, should, could, might) + 동사원형

If Mr. Lewis **notified** us earlier, we **would have** enough time to prepare.
만약 루이스 씨가 좀 더 일찍 통지해 준다면, 우리가 준비할 시간이 충분히 있을 텐데.

Ms. Faria **would go** to the theme park if she **were** in the mood to do so.
만약 파리아 씨가 그럴 마음이 있다면, 테마파크로 갈 텐데.

+만점팁 if절에 be동사가 올 때는 단복수와 상관없이 **were**를 쓰는 것이 원칙이나, 현대 영어에서는 **was**를 허용하기도 한다.

---

4 If Douglas Park ------- a playground, more families would go there.
(A) is having
(B) has
(C) had
(D) has had

5 If fares ------- any further, the bus system would not be financially sustainable.
(A) are reduced
(B) will reduce
(C) have reduced
(D) were reduced

6 Departmental meetings ------- more efficient if we determined an agenda in advance.
(A) were becoming
(B) would become
(C) have become
(D) will become

기출공식 3 If절 동사가 과거완료 시제이면 주절은 '조동사의 과거형 + have p.p.'를 쓴다.

가정법 과거완료: 만약 ~했다면, …했을 텐데 (과거 사실과 반대되는 상황)

If + 주어 + had + p.p. ~, 주어 + 조동사의 과거형(would, should, could, might) + have + p.p.

If we **had taken** the earlier flight, we **would have gotten** to the convention site on time.
우리가 좀 더 빠른 비행기를 탔다면, 회의 장소에 제시간에 도착했을 텐데.

+만점팁 혼합가정법

If the staff **had started** the project at the proper time, it **would be finished** by now.
직원들이 프로젝트를 적절한 시기에 시작했더라면 지금쯤 끝나 있을 텐데.

→ '과거에 ~했더라면 지금 … 할 텐데'를 가정법 과거완료와 가정법 과거 시제를 혼합하여 나타낼 수 있다.

7 If the printer had been damaged during shipment, the company ------- to send Mr. Kichida a replacement.
(A) would have offered
(B) has offered
(C) is being offered
(D) would have been offered

8 If Ms. Lee had not helped us out during the proofreading process, we ------- the report deadline.
(A) have missed
(B) would have missed
(C) will be missing
(D) can miss

9 If its proposal ------- more detailed, Donelan Manufacturing might now be our only supplier of steel parts.
(A) has been
(B) had been
(C) was being
(D) were being

기출공식 4 미래의 불확실한 상황을 가정할 때는 if절에 should를 쓴다.

가정법 미래: 혹시라도 ~하면, …할 것이다 / 하라 (불확실한 상황)

If + 주어 + should + 동사원형 ~, 주어 + 조동사 원형(will, may, can) + 동사원형 (또는 명령문)

If we **should be** able to raise £40,000, we **will embark** on an additional renovation project.
우리가 혹시라도 4만 파운드를 모금할 수 있다면, 추가 개조 작업에 착수할 것이다.

If you **should have** further questions, **please feel** free to ask me at any time.
혹시 추가 문의사항이 있으시면, 언제든 주저하지 말고 저에게 문의하세요.

10 If a client ------- moving boxes left over after moving day, Marltac Moving Co. is happy to purchase them back.
(A) have
(B) should have
(C) that has
(D) having

11 The construction company may delay the groundbreaking on its Mall Square-2 project if the ground ------- too wet from recent rainfall.
(A) being
(B) that is
(C) to be
(D) should be

12 If you ------- assistance, simply contact me at this e-mail address.
(A) can require
(B) are required
(C) should require
(D) requiring

정답 및 해설 p. 79

If additional items **should be added** to your order, the bill will be adjusted on the event date.
→ **Should** additional items **be added** to your order, the bill will be adjusted on the event date.
주문에 추가되는 물품이 있는 경우, 계산서가 당일 조정됩니다.

If we **had used** KFX delivery service, our customers might have received their orders in time.
→ **Had** we **used** the KFX delivery service, our customers might have received their orders in time.   우리가 KFX의 배달 서비스를 이용했다면, 우리 고객들은 주문한 상품들을 제시간에 받았을 텐데.

---

13 Mr. Jackson's sales team may work at our exhibit booth at the weekend trade show ------- additional staff be needed during the event.
(A) while
(B) during
(C) should
(D) in addition

14 Had the client given us more time to conduct the market research, we ------- more open-ended questions to the survey forms.
(A) might add
(B) will add
(C) would have added
(D) have added

15 ------- the recruiting team received more responses from the online job posting, the candidate selection process would have lasted longer.
(A) Had
(B) Instead of
(C) Except
(D) Whether

A summary of the recent survey conducted among our local branches is **attached**.
→ **Attached** is a summary of the recent survey conducted among our local branches.
우리 현지 지점들 사이에서 실시된 최근 설문의 요약서가 첨부되어 있다.

→ 보어 attached가 강조되어 문두로 오고 주어와 동사의 자리가 바뀐다.

+만점팁 | 5형식 문장에서는 보어 enclosed가 강조되어 문두로 오고 주어와 동사의 자리는 그대로 유지된다.

You will find a reference letter from the renowned professor **enclosed**.
→ **Enclosed** you will find a reference letter from the renowned professor.
저명한 교수님께 받은 추천장이 동봉되어 있는 것을 찾으실 겁니다.

---

16 ------- is a product catalog that also includes detailed information about our ordering procedure and our shipping policies.
(A) Enclosure
(B) Enclosed
(C) Enclosing
(D) Encloses

17 ------- is an application to participate in the Air Traffic Controller Training Program.
(A) Attach
(B) Attaching
(C) Attached
(D) Attachment

18 ------- in the packet is a guide to eateries near the conference center.
(A) Include
(B) Inclusion
(C) Including
(D) Included

기출공식 7 부정어가 문두에 오면 도치가 된다.

---

hardly / seldom / rarely / scarcely 거의 ~않다   never 결코 ~않다   little 거의 없는[아닌]

We have **never** hired any employees without thoroughly screening them.

→ **Never** have we hired any employees without thoroughly screening them.

우리는 철저한 신원 조사 없이 직원을 고용한 적이 결코 없다.

Mr. Parker would **seldom** hold meetings after 4 P.M. on Fridays.

→ **Seldom** would Mr. Parker hold meetings after 4 P.M. on Fridays.

파커 씨는 금요일 오후 4시 이후에는 회의를 좀처럼 하지 않는다.

19 ------- have market conditions been more ideal for buying a new house.
(A) Seldom
(B) Ever
(C) Appropriately
(D) Moreover

20 ------- is Emiko Imamura a widely published poet, she is also an accomplished painter and sculptor.
(A) Not only
(B) While
(C) If
(D) Due to

21 ------- does Belangier Salon receive negative reviews of its hair care services.
(A) Ever
(B) Sometimes
(C) Rarely
(D) Much

기출공식 8 only, so, neither, 장소 부사구가 문두에 오면 도치가 된다.

- **only 도치: ~해야만 …하다**

  You can get a discount for our new spring session hot items **only with this coupon**.

  → **Only with this coupon** can you get a discount for our new spring session hot items.

  이 쿠폰이 있어야만 새로 나온 봄 인기 상품을 할인 받을 수 있습니다.

  → **only + 부사(구/절)이 강조되어 문두로 오면 주어와 동사가 도치된다.**

- **so 도치: (긍정문에서) ~도 마찬가지이다**

  The financial advisor liked what Mr. Marriot proposed, and **so did the rest of the staff**.

  재정 고문은 메리어트 씨가 제안한 것을 마음에 들어 했고, 나머지 직원들도 마찬가지였다.

- **neither / nor 도치: (부정문에서) ~도 마찬가지이다**

  Ms. Laughton didn't want to be transferred and **neither did Mr. Stewart**.

  (and neither = nor)

  래프톤 씨는 전근을 원하지 않았고, 스튜어트 씨도 마찬가지였다.

- **장소 부사구 도치: ~에 …가 있다**

  Next to the parking lot is a swimming pool. 주차장 옆에 수영장이 있다.

22 Ms. Park will not be able to attend the sales presentation, and ------- will Mr. Jefferson.
(A) also
(B) however
(C) now
(D) neither

23 Critics loved Mr. Ikeda's performance in the film, and ------- did audiences.
(A) as
(B) quite
(C) neither
(D) so

24 Only on "Casual Fridays" can employees stationed at the front desk ------- jeans.
(A) wear
(B) wears
(C) wearing
(D) to wear

정답 및 해설 p. 81

1 Had negotiations not broken down at the last minute, Laureano, Inc., ------- with its main competitor, Trevino-Martin.
(A) has merged
(B) would have merged
(C) had merged
(D) will have merged

2 As the number of local residents' visits to public swimming facilities climbs, ------- the demand for lifeguards to supervise them.
(A) as long as
(B) whereas
(C) so does
(D) as to

3 If the cost of raw materials rises, it ------- the price of the finished product.
(A) will affect
(B) to affect
(C) is affecting
(D) affected

4 ------- you experience any difficulties accessing your online Alaway Bank account, our customer service agents will be happy to assist you.
(A) Than
(B) Should
(C) What
(D) Having

5 If the parts had arrived sooner, we ------- more time to do a careful repair job today.
(A) would have
(B) have had
(C) to have
(D) will have

6 Only after the city built a new stadium did the downtown area ------- popular with out-of-town tourists.
(A) become
(B) became
(C) becoming
(D) had become

7 All tickets will be refunded ------- the soccer game is canceled because of bad weather.
(A) or
(B) if
(C) nor
(D) but

8 Next to the Rostovsky Hotel ------- a luxurious recreational area, complete with a golf course and a swimming pool.
(A) are
(B) is
(C) to be
(D) being

9 Perhaps Ms. Hernandez would not ------- with such criticism if she had made her plans for the company clear to its stockholders.
(A) having confronted
(B) have been confronted
(C) have confronted
(D) had been confronted

10 ------- is Mr. Gariza the award-winning head chef at the Sposo Inn, but he is also an author of four popular cookbooks.
(A) Not only
(B) So
(C) In case
(D) Either

11 Mr. Hernandez is not available at the time the work crew is scheduled to arrive, and ------- is Ms. Hakkonen.
(A) so
(B) also
(C) neither
(D) yet

12 ------- Mr. Park not out of town on a business trip, he would lead today's training session for the new interns.
(A) In fact
(B) Whereas
(C) Only
(D) Were

13 ------- you find the assembly instructions to be unclear, please call our customer support center.
(A) Until
(B) So that
(C) Whether
(D) If

14 Mr. Jung ------- his position as Chief Executive of Cosmic Gaming Company had the merger with Starzan Enterprises succeeded.
(A) is being relinquished
(B) would have relinquished
(C) has been relinquishing
(D) will be relinquished

15 ------- is the latest listing of the distinguished companies and institutions that use our firm's specialized consulting services.
(A) Enclosure
(B) Enclosing
(C) Enclose
(D) Enclosed

16 If we had reserved the large presentation room on the first floor, we ------- holding all our workshops on-site this week.
(A) are
(B) would be
(C) had been
(D) being

17 ------- the staff not worked so enthusiastically on Saturday and Sunday, our weekend book sale would have been a failure.
(A) Whether
(B) Had
(C) Regarding
(D) If

18 ------- you wish to see a complete list of hotel amenities, please refer to the informational binder on the desk in your guest room.
(A) Whether
(B) Despite
(C) If
(D) For

19 If we had seen the new logo designs sooner, we ------- a better idea about ways to market the product now.
(A) could have
(B) have had
(C) have
(D) will have

20 Purchases from any Knott's Hardware store can be returned ------- accompanied by an original receipt.
(A) until
(B) not only
(C) since
(D) only if

PART

5

어휘편

RC

ETS TOEIC

UNIT 01 | ETS 빈출 동사

accommodate (사람을, 의견 등을) 수용하다

빈출표현 **accommodate** a large tour group
단체 관광객을 수용하다
accommodate your request
당신의 요청 사항을 수용하다
파생어 accommodation 숙박, 수용
accommodating 남을 잘 돌보는, 친절한
동의어 seat 수용하다
반의어 refuse 거절하다

afford ~할 여유가 있다

빈출표현 cannot **afford** the expense
그런 비용을 감당할 수 없다
can **afford** a luxury sedan
비싼 세단형 자동차를 살 여유가 있다
cannot **afford** to buy a home
집을 살 여유가 없다
파생어 affordable (가격이) 알맞은
affordability 적당한 가격으로 구입할 수 있는 것

accompany 동반하다, 동행하다

빈출표현 a thunderstorm **accompanied** by gusty
winds 돌풍을 동반한 뇌우
The city official **accompanied** the reporter.
시 공무원은 기자와 동행했다.
반의어 leave 남겨 두다
withdraw 물러나다

allocate 할당하다, 배정하다

빈출표현 **allocate** a team to the project
한 팀에게 그 프로젝트를 배정하다
allocated budget 할당된 예산
파생어 allocation 할당
misallocate 잘못 할당하다
동의어 assign 할당하다

acknowledge 인정하다, 받았음을 알리다

빈출표현 **acknowledge** the support of the event's
sponsors 행사 후원자들의 지원에 사의를 표하다
This is to **acknowledge** receipt of the
following submissions.
이 편지는 다음 제출물들을 수령했음을 알리는 글입니다.
동의어 accept 수락하다 recognize 인정하다
반의어 decline 거절하다

allow 허락하다, 인정하다

빈출표현 **allow** interns to participate
수습 사원들이 참석하도록 허락하다
allow entrance into ~에 출입을 허락하다
파생어 allowable 허락할 수 있는
allowance 허락; 용돈, 수당
동의어 grant, permit 허가하다
반의어 prohibit 금지하다

acquire 얻다, 획득하다, 인수하다

빈출표현 **acquire** additional expertise
추가 전문 지식을 획득하다
acquire a fine company 좋은 회사를 인수하다
파생어 acquisition 획득, 인수, 매입
동의어 gain 얻다
반의어 forfeit 몰수[박탈]당하다

analyze 분석하다, 검토하다

빈출표현 **analyze** the traffic data 교통 데이터를 분석하다
analyze the efficiency of the factories
각 공장의 효율성을 분석하다
promotion to senior **analyst**
선임 애널리스트로 승진
파생어 analysis 분석, 연구 analyst 분석가, 애널리스트

address 연설하다, (일·문제 등을) 처리하다

빈출표현 **address** the audience 청중에게 연설하다
address customers' complaints
고객들의 불만사항을 처리하다
파생어 addressee 수신인 addressor 발신인
동의어 handle, deal with 다루다
반의어 neglect 방치하다

apply 적용하다, 신청하다, 바르다

빈출표현 **apply** for a job transfer 보직 이동을 신청하다
apply paint evenly 페인트를 고르게 바르다
파생어 applicant 지원자
appliance 가전제품
동의어 request 요청하다
반의어 ignore 무시하다

assume 추정하다, 떠맡다; ~인 체하다

빈출표현
assume that traffic is light
교통량이 적으리라 추정하다
assume that the weather is good
날씨가 좋으리라 추정하다

파생어 assumption 가정   assumably 추측하건대
동의어 presume 짐작하다
반의어 disregard 무시하다

complete 완료하다, 작성하다; 완전한

빈출표현
complete a survey 설문지 작성을 완료하다
a **complete** set of dishes 완전한 접시 한 세트

파생어 completion 완성
completed 완성된
동의어 fill out ~을 작성하다
반의어 cease, halt 중단하다

attract ~을 끌어들이다

빈출표현
attract new customers
신규 고객들을 끌어들이다
attract attention from buyers
구매자들의 관심을 끌다

파생어 attractive 매력적인   attraction 매력
동의어 appeal to ~의 마음에 들다
반의어 repel 물리치다

conduct (업무 등을) 행하다; 처신, 행위

빈출표현
conduct market research 시장 조사를 하다
conduct a job interview 채용 면접을 실시하다

파생어 conductor 지휘자
conductive 전도성의
동의어 carry out 수행하다

broaden 넓어지다, 넓히다

빈출표현
broaden production capabilities
생산력을 증대하다
The company **broadened** its presence around
the world. 그 회사는 세계적으로 입지를 넓혔다.

파생어 broad 넓은
동의어 enlarge 확대하다   expand 확장하다
반의어 narrow 좁히다   restrict 제한하다

confirm 확실하게 하다, 확인하다

빈출표현
confirm the reservation 예약을 확인하다
confirm receipt of an order 주문 수령을 확인한다

파생어 confirmation 승인, 확인
confirmed 확인된, 승인된
동의어 approve 승인하다
반의어 invalidate 무효로 하다

certify 인증하다, 확신시키다

빈출표현
certify the building as eco-friendly
그 건물을 환경친화적인 건물로 인증하다
a **certified** agent 공인 중개업자

파생어 certificate 인증서   certified 인증된
동의어 approve 승인하다
반의어 disapprove 반대하다

consult 상의하다, 참고하다

빈출표현
consult an expert 전문가와 상의하다
consult the manual 설명서를 참고하다

파생어 consultant 컨설턴트
consultation 상의
동의어 refer to ~을 참조하다

commend 칭찬하다, 추천하다

빈출표현
commend her for her excellent work
그녀의 훌륭한 업무에 대해 그녀를 칭찬하다
Let me **commend** all of you on your
outstanding work. 여러분의 뛰어난 작업에 대해
여러분 모두를 칭찬해 드리고자 합니다.

파생어 commendable 칭찬할 만한
commendation 칭찬, 인정
반의어 criticize 비판하다
disapprove 못마땅해하다

cost 비용이 들다; 비용

빈출표현
cost less than expected
예상보다 비용이 적게 들다
the **cost** of production 생산비

파생어 costly 값비싼
동의어 charge 청구하다
반의어 be complimentary 무료이다

delegate (권한·업무 등을) 위임하다; 대표자

- 빈출표현 **delegate** projects 프로젝트를 위임하다
  cannot **delegate** responsibility for project safety to third parties
  프로젝트 안전에 대한 책임을 제3자에게 위임할 수 없다
- 파생어 delegation 대표단, 위임
- 동의어 assign 할당하다
  commission 의뢰하다
- 반의어 retract 철회[취소]하다

designate 지정하다, 임명하다

- 빈출표현 **designate** Mr. Bae as a supervisor
  배 씨를 감독관으로 임명하다
  designated parking areas 지정된 주차 구역
- 파생어 designation 지정
  designated 지정된
- 동의어 appoint 임명하다
- 반의어 dismiss 해고하다

determine 결심하다, 밝히다

- 빈출표현 **determine** the best way to solve the problem
  문제를 해결할 최선의 방법을 결정하다
  determine the cause of the delay
  지연 이유를 밝히다
- 파생어 determination 결심
  determined 결심이 확고한
- 동의어 decide 결정하다
- 반의어 hesitate 주저하다

direct 지시하다, (길을) 안내하다; 직접적인

- 빈출표현 Most of the money will be **directed** toward the project.
  대부분의 자금은 그 프로젝트에 투입될 것이다.
  She worked under my **direct** supervision.
  그녀는 내 직속 부하 직원으로 일했다.
- 파생어 director 이사, 감독관
  direction 지시, 방향
- 동의어 instruct 지시하다
- 반의어 follow 따르다

disregard 무시하다, 경시하다; 무관심

- 빈출표현 **Disregard** all previous memos.
  이전 공지들을 모두 무시하십시오.
- 파생어 disregardful 무시하는
- 동의어 ignore 무시하다
- 반의어 attend to ~을 신경 쓰다

enclose 동봉하다, 에워싸다

- 빈출표현 **Enclosed** is a résumé.
  이력서가 동봉되어 있다.
  enclose a garden 정원을 에워싸다
- 파생어 enclosure 동봉, 에워싸인 곳
  enclosed 동봉된
- 동의어 attach 첨부하다
- 반의어 exclude 제외하다

encounter 맞닥뜨리다[부딪히다]

- 빈출표현 **encounter** a problem 문제에 부딪히다
  We are sorry for any problems you may **encounter**.
  혹시 겪게 될지 모르는 문제에 대해 죄송합니다.
- 동의어 run into (곤경 등을) 만나다[겪다]
  come across 접하다[마주치다]
- 반의어 avoid 피하다

endorse 지지하다, (광고 등에서 상품을) 보증하다

- 빈출표현 The actress agreed to **endorse** the new makeup line.
  그 여배우는 새 화장품군을 홍보하기로 동의했다.
- 파생어 endorsement 지지, 보증[홍보]
- 동의어 advocate 옹호하다
- 반의어 criticize 비난하다

enforce 집행하다, 실시하다

- 빈출표현 **enforce** the law 법을 집행하다
  enforce new safety regulations
  새 안전 규정을 실시하다
- 파생어 enforcement 집행, 시행
  enforceable 집행 가능한
- 동의어 carry out, implement 수행하다

exceed 초과하다

- 빈출표현 **exceed** expectations 예상을 초과하다
  exceed the speed limit 제한 속도를 초과하다
- 파생어 excess 초과
  excessive 과도한, 지나친
- 동의어 surpass 초과하다
- 반의어 fall short of 못 미치다

experience 겪다, 경험하다; 경험

- **빈출표현** **experience** difficulties in the new job
  새 직장에서 어려움을 겪다
  a job that requires previous **experience**
  이전 경력이 필요한 일자리
- **파생어** experienced 경험이 많은
- **동의어** undergo ~을 겪다
- **반의어** avoid 피하다

expire 기한이 되다, 만료하다

- **빈출표현** food that will **expire** soon
  곧 유통 기한이 만료되는 음식
  the **expiration** date 만료일
- **파생어** expiration 만기
  expired 기한이 지난
- **동의어** run out 만기가 되다
- **반의어** commence 시작하다

extend 연장하다

- **빈출표현** **extend** its business hours
  영업시간을 연장하다
  extend a meeting 회의를 연장하다
- **파생어** extension 연장; 내선번호
  extensive 광범위한
- **동의어** prolong 연장하다
- **반의어** shorten 단축하다

feature ~을 특징으로 하다, 크게 다루다; 기능

- **빈출표현** **feature** a stylish design
  세련된 디자인을 특징으로 하다
  feature a young talent
  젊은 인재를 크게[특집으로] 다루다
- **파생어** featured 특집의, 주연의
- **동의어** emphasize 강조하다
  characterize ~의 특징이 되다

follow 따르다, ~의 뒤를 잇다

- **빈출표현** A banquet will **follow** the conference.
  회의 뒤에 연회가 있을 것이다.
  follow the instructions 지시에 따르다
- **파생어** follower 추종자
  following 다음의, ~ 이후에
- **동의어** keep, observe 준수하다
- **반의어** precede 앞서다

generate 발생시키다, 만들어 내다

- **빈출표현** **generate** interest 흥미를 불러일으키다
  generate revenue through advertisements
  광고를 통해 수익을 발생시키다
- **동의어** develop 발전시키다
  create, produce 생성하다
- **반의어** destroy 파괴하다
  end 끝내다

host 주최하다, 사회를 맡다; 사회자

- **빈출표현** **host** a TV program
  TV 프로그램의 사회를 맡다
  host a convention 회의를 주최하다
- **동의어** organize (행사 등을) 준비하다
  preside 사회를 보다

illustrate 설명하다, 삽화를 쓰다

- **빈출표현** The chart **illustrates** the process.
  도표는 과정을 설명한다.
  The book is **illustrated** with many pictures.
  이 책에는 많은 그림들이 들어 있다.
- **파생어** illustrator 삽화가
  illustration 삽화, 설명
- **동의어** depict 묘사하다
- **반의어** obscure 불분명하게 하다

implement 시행하다, 이행하다; 도구

- **빈출표현** **implement** the latest data-analysis methods
  최신 데이터 분석 기법을 시행하다
  the **implementation** of some key changes
  몇 가지 주요 변동사항의 이행
- **파생어** implementation 시행, 이행
  implemental 도구의, 도움이 되는
- **동의어** carry out 수행하다

institute (제도 등을) 마련하다, 실시하다; 협회

- **빈출표현** **institute** a policy that allows telecommuting
  재택 근무를 허가하는 정책을 마련하다
  institute a new dress code
  새로운 복장 규정을 마련하다
- **파생어** institution 기관, 제도
- **동의어** establish, initiate, set up 설립하다

interrupt 가로막다, 방해하다

빈출표현 The bus service was **interrupted.**
버스 운행이 중단되었다.
If you have any questions, please **interrupt** me at any time.
질문이 있으면 제가 말하는 중간에 언제든 질문하세요.

파생어 interruption 중단, 방해
interruptive 방해하는

동의어 hinder 방해가 되다

반의어 help, assist 돕다

introduce 소개하다, 출시하다, 도입하다

빈출표현 **introduce** a new car
신차를 출시하다
introduce new technology
새로운 기술을 도입하다

파생어 introduction 소개, 도입
introductory 소개의

동의어 launch, release, roll out 출시하다

locate 위치하다, ~의 위치를 알아내다

빈출표현 the office is **located** in the city
사무실은 도시에 위치하고 있다
locate a leak 새는 곳을 찾아내다

파생어 location 위치
located 위치한

동의어 situate ~에 놓다

maintain 유지하다, 관리하다

빈출표현 **maintain** a building 건물을 관리하다
maintain good health 건강을 유지하다

파생어 maintenance 유지, 보수
maintainable 유지할 수 있는

동의어 keep 유지하다

반의어 discontinue 중단하다

mark 표시하다, 나타내다; 점수

빈출표현 This event **marks** our 10th anniversary.
이 행사는 우리 10주년을 기념하는 것이다.
earn high **marks** 높은 점수를 얻다

파생어 marker 표시하는 것
marking 표시

동의어 indicate 표시하다

반의어 erase 지우다

modify 변경하다, (부분적으로) 수정하다

빈출표현 **modify** the product design
제품 디자인을 손보다
the **modified** agenda
수정된 안건

파생어 modification 수정
modified 수정된

동의어 change 바꾸다

반의어 keep 유지하다

notify 통보하다, 통지하다

빈출표현 **notify** Ms. Suh of her promotion
서 씨에게 승진을 통보하다
notify a customer that a payment is due
고객에게 지급 기일이 되었음을 통지하다

파생어 notification 통지   notice 통지서; 알아차리다

동의어 inform 알리다

반의어 conceal 숨기다

obligate 의무를 지우다

빈출표현 be **obligated** to pay for any damage
모든 파손에 대해 지불할 의무가 있다
be not **obligated** to replace the product
제품을 교환해 줄 의무가 없다

파생어 obligation 의무   obligatory 의무적인, 필수적인

동의어 oblige ~에게 강요하다

반의어 free 자유롭게 하다

offset 상쇄하다

빈출표현 in order to **offset** the increased cost of materials
늘어난 원자재 값을 벌충하기 위해
Losses were **offset** by gains.
손해가 이익으로 상쇄되었다.

동의어 cancel out, set off 상쇄하다

outline 간추려 말하다; 개요

빈출표현 **outline** the year's budget
그 해 예산을 간략히 설명하다
the **outline** of the contract
계약의 개요

동의어 brief, summarize
간략히 설명하다

oversee 감독하다, 감시하다

빈출표현 **oversee** the evening shift
야간 근무조를 감독하다
oversee the company's domestic operations
회사의 내부 운영을 관리하다
파생어 overseer 감독관, 지배인
동의어 supervise 감독하다

postpone 연기하다

빈출표현 **postpone** a meeting 회의를 연기하다
postpone a flight date 비행 일정을 연기하다
파생어 postponement 연기
동의어 delay, put off 연기하다
반의어 continue 계속하다

promote 홍보하다, 촉진하다; 승진시키다

빈출표현 **promote** its new line of products
신제품을 홍보하다
be **promoted** to manager
매니저로 승진하다
파생어 promotion 홍보, 촉진; 승진
promotional 홍보의, 촉진하는
동의어 advertise 광고하다
반의어 demote 강등시키다

recognize 인정하다, 인식하다

빈출표현 Mr. Lee was **recognized** for his work.
이 씨는 맡은 업무로 인정받았다.
recognize Ms. Dale's efforts
데일 씨의 노고를 인정하다
파생어 recognition 인식, 인지
recognizable 인식할 수 있는
동의어 perceive 인지하다
반의어 disregard 무시하다

reflect 반영하다, 반사하다

빈출표현 **reflect** the current trend
현재 경향을 반영하다
reflect the opinions 의견을 반영하다
파생어 reflection 반사
reflective 반사하는
동의어 show, mirror 나타내다, 보여 주다

register 등록하다, 기록하다

빈출표현 **register** for a workshop
워크숍에 등록하다
register at a hotel 호텔 입실 수속을 하다
파생어 registration 등록
registrant 등록자
동의어 sign up, enroll 등록하다

reimburse 상환[환급]하다

빈출표현 The company will fully **reimburse** your travel and daily expenses.
회사가 귀하의 출장 및 일일 경비를 전액 환급할 것입니다.
파생어 reimbursement 상환, 환급
동의어 compensate 보상하다
관련어구 reimbursement request form 환급 신청서

remove 제거하다, 벗다

빈출표현 **remove** a stain from a carpet
카펫에서 얼룩을 제거하다
remove one's shoes[hat]
신발[모자]를 벗다
파생어 removal 제거
removed 제거된
동의어 delete 지우다
반의어 keep, retain 유지하다

replace 교체하다, 대신하다

빈출표현 **replace** a defective item
결함 있는 물건을 교체하다
find a **replacement** for Ms. Choi
최 씨의 후임자를 찾다
파생어 replacement 대체물, 후임자
동의어 exchange 교환하다
반의어 hold, keep 유지하다

represent 대표하다, 대신하다

빈출표현 **represent** a company 회사를 대표하다
represent a manager in the meeting
회의에서 매니저를 대신하다
파생어 representative 대표자, 직원; 대표적인
representation 대표, 표시
동의어 act for ~을 대신하다

require ~을 필요로 하다

[빈출표현] a special license is **required** for
~을 위한 특별한 자격증이 필요하다
require a workforce of 100
100명의 인력이 필요하다
[파생어] requirement 필수 조건
required 필수적인
[동의어] need 필요하다

reserve 예약하다, 비축하다, 유보하다

[빈출표현] **reserve** airline tickets 항공 티켓을 예약하다
reserve a seat 자리를 맡아 두다
[파생어] reservation 예약
reserved 예약된, 따로 떼어 둔
[동의어] book 예약하다
hold 보류하다

retain 유지하다, 보유하다

[빈출표현] **retain** loyal customers 단골 고객을 유지하다
retain dedicated employees by offering
incentives
인센티브를 제공하여 헌신적인 직원을 붙잡아 두다
[파생어] retention 보유
retained 보유한
[동의어] hold, keep 유지하다
[반의어] let go 풀어 주다

retrieve 되찾아오다[회수하다]

[빈출표현] **retrieve** belongings 소지품을 되찾다
Retrieve a package in the main office.
본사에서 소포를 찾아가세요.
[동의어] bring back 되찾다
recover 되찾다
[반의어] lose 잃다
relinquish 포기하다

secure 확보하다, ~을 고정시키다; 안전한

[빈출표현] **secure** a parking space
주차할 곳을 확보하다
secure the lock on the door
문의 잠금 장치를 고정시키다
[파생어] security 안전, 보안
securely 확실하게
[동의어] gain, obtain 얻다, 획득하다
[반의어] lose 잃다

solidify 굳히다[확고히 하다]

[빈출표현] **solidify** the dates 날짜를 확정하다
The merger will **solidify** our position.
합병이 우리의 입지를 굳힐 것이다.
[파생어] solid 단단한, 견고한
[동의어] strengthen 강화하다

specify 상세히 말하다, 구체화하다

[빈출표현] The government has **specified** that ...
정부는 ~을 구체적으로 설명했다
specify the date 날짜를 명확히 하다
[파생어] specification 세부 사항
specific 특정한, 구체적인
[동의어] clarify 명료히 하다
[반의어] generalize 일반화하다

streamline 간소화하다, 능률적으로 하다

[빈출표현] **streamline** the production process
생산 과정을 능률적으로 하다
streamline the office procedures
사무 절차를 간소화하다
[파생어] streamlined 유선형의, 간결한
[동의어] simplify 단순화하다
[반의어] complicate 복잡하게 하다

sustain 지탱하다, 지속하다

[빈출표현] cannot **sustain** that weight
그런 무게를 견딜 수 없다
sustain strong profits 큰 수익을 유지하다
[파생어] sustainability 지속 가능성
sustainable 유지할 수 있는
[동의어] maintain 유지하다
support 떠받치다

undergo 겪다, 경험하다

[빈출표현] **undergo** a medical checkup
건강 검진을 받다
undergo changes 변화를 겪다
undergo a quality check 품질 검사를 받다
[동의어] go through 겪다
experience 경험하다

VOCABULARY PRACTICE

정답 및 해설 p. 85

A 다음 주어진 문장에서 적절한 어휘를 고르세요.

1 Please do not enter the building until you are [(A) notified (B) realized] otherwise.

2 Repairing the machine [(A) paid (B) cost] half as much as buying a new one.

3 The director [(A) evaluated (B) postponed] the meeting because of a scheduling conflict.

4 The company will fully [(A) reimburse (B) advise] your travel expenses.

5 If you have recently renewed your membership, please [(A) expire (B) disregard] this notice.

6 All materials [(A) conducted (B) required] for the upcoming seminar need to be copied.

7 Insadong Images proudly [(A) introduces (B) accomplishes] Machiko Nakamura as its new senior graphics designer.

B 다음 문장의 빈칸에 적절한 어휘를 고르세요.

8 To ------- the Adele's Apparel store that is nearest to you, select your state or country from the pull-down menu.
(A) afford
(B) create
(C) locate
(D) provide

9 Customers of Millor Catering should ------- on the back of this form any special dietary needs they may have.
(A) advise
(B) initiate
(C) specify
(D) permit

10 At the Podell Automotive plant, Ms. Krystle ------- workers who install rebuilt engines in vehicles.
(A) conducts
(B) explains
(C) invests
(D) oversees

11 Ms. Gupta wishes to ------- the terms of her employment contract before signing it.
(A) deprive
(B) respond
(C) modify
(D) assure

12 Emone Motor Company has not ------- any delays in production or delivery to dealerships this quarter.
(A) exerted
(B) submitted
(C) represented
(D) experienced

13 Lim Myung Hee, vice president of public relations, will ------- Kavi Financial at the shareholder meeting on February 14.
(A) represent
(B) furnish
(C) indicate
(D) perform

14 According to the proposal, a large block of rooms in the east wing of the new building will be ------- for storage.
(A) designated
(B) detained
(C) reciprocated
(D) signified

15 Please review the new safety procedures and ------- any questions to Mr. Bae at extension 2528.
(A) inquire
(B) direct
(C) expect
(D) prepare

149

UNIT 02 | ETS 빈출 동사 어구

attribute A to B A를 B의 탓으로 돌리다
- **빈출표현** **attribute** his success **to** his hard work
  그의 성공을 그가 열심히 일한 덕분이라고 생각하다
  The improvement in service **is attributed to** a software upgrade.
  서비스 향상은 소프트웨어 업그레이드 때문이다.
- **동의어** owe A to B, ascribe A to B
  A를 B의 탓으로 돌리다

comment on ~에 대해 언급하다
- **빈출표현** refuse to **comment on** the plan
  계획에 대해 언급하기를 거부하다
  comment on the proposal
  제안에 대해 언급하다
- **동의어** mention, talk[speak] about
  ~에 대해 말하다

break down 고장 나다, 무너지다
- **빈출표현** does not easily **break down**
  쉽게 고장 나지 않는다
  The overloaded elevator **broke down**.
  초과 적재된 엘리베이터가 고장 났다.
- **파생어** breakdown 고장; 명세서
- **동의어** be broken, be out of order 고장 나다
- **관련어구** break into pieces 산산조각 나다
  break out (화재·질병 등이) 발생하다

compare A with[to] B A와 B를 비교하다
- **빈출표현** **compare** the item's price **with** the others
  상품 가격을 다른 상품들과 비교하다
  compare the old model **with** the new model
  신구 모델을 비교하다
- **파생어** comparability 비교 가능성
  comparable 비교할 만한
- **관련어구** compared to ~와 비교해 보면

bring up (문제 따위를) 제기하다
- **빈출표현** have **brought up** a question
  질문을 제기했다
  bring up an issue 문제를 제기하다
- **동의어** pose, raise 제기하다
- **관련어구** bring about ~을 일으키다, 초래하다
  bring along ~을 데려오다, 휴대하다

comply with (법규 등을) 따르다, 지키다
- **빈출표현** **comply with** the legal requirements
  법적 요구 조건들을 따르다
  comply with the client's request
  고객의 요구를 따르다
- **파생어** compliance 준수
- **동의어** conform to, follow, keep, observe 따르다

carry out 실행하다, 수행하다
- **빈출표현** **carry out** a plan 계획을 실행하다
  carry out a survey 설문조사를 실시하다
- **동의어** conduct, implement, put ... into action, put ... into practice 실행하다

consist of ~로 이루어지다[구성되다]
- **빈출표현** **consist of** 2 bedrooms and 2 baths
  2개의 침실과 2개의 욕실로 구성되다
  The committee **consists of** board members, shareholders, and department leaders.
  위원회는 이사진, 주주, 부서장들로 구성되어 있다.
- **동의어** be made up of, comprise ~로 구성되다

coincide with ~와 동시에 일어나다, 일치하다
- **빈출표현** The completion of the project is expected to **coincide with** the building's bicentennial.
  프로젝트의 완공은 건물 200주년과 동시에 있을 예정이다.
- **파생어** coincident 일치하는
  coincidence 우연의 일치, (의견 등의) 일치

contribute to ~에 기여하다, 기부하다
- **빈출표현** **contribute to** the project
  프로젝트에 기여하다
  contribute money **to** a fund 기금에 기부하다
- **동의어** devote oneself to ~에 기여하다
  donate 기부하다

150

deal with ~을 다루다, 해결하다

빈출표현 **deal with** a problem
문제를 다루다
deal with a demanding customer
까다로운 고객에 대처하다
동의어 handle, address 다루다
관련어구 deal exclusively with
전적으로 다루다

hold a ceremony 행사를 열다

빈출표현 The award **ceremony** will be **held** in the ballroom. 시상식은 연회장에서 열릴 것입니다.
hold a ceremony to welcome new employees 신입 사원들을 환영하기 위해 행사를 열다
동의어 take place (행사 등이) 열리다
관련어구 hold a weekly meeting 주간 회의를 개최하다

dispose of ~을 없애다[처리하다]

빈출표현 safely **dispose of** piles of confidential paperwork
기밀 문서 더미를 안전하게 처리하다
We **dispose of** the waste at a regional recycling facility.
우리는 쓰레기를 지역 재활용 시설에 버립니다.
파생어 disposal 처리 disposable 일회용의
동의어 discard 버리다 scrap 버리다, 폐기하다

issue a statement 성명서를 발표하다

빈출표현 will **issue a statement** officially
공식적으로 성명서를 발표할 것이다
관련어구 issue a permit 허가증을 발급하다
issue a ticket 표를 발권하다
the May issue 5월호

distinguish A from B A와 B를 구별하다

빈출표현 **distinguish** real diamonds **from** imitations
진품 다이아몬드와 모조품을 구별하다
distinguished scholars 저명한 학자들
파생어 distinguished 저명한, 특별한
distinguishable 구별할 수 있는
동의어 differentiate A from B, tell A from B
A와 B를 구별하다

lead a session 회의[교육]를 이끌다

빈출표현 **lead a session** in the workshop
워크숍에서 강연을 진행하다
lead the training **session**
교육 훈련을 이끌다
파생어 leader 지도자, 선두업체
leading 선도적인
관련어구 lead a factory tour 공장 견학을 이끌다

engage in ~에 관여하다, ~에 종사하다

빈출표현 **engage in** online sales
온라인 판매에 종사하다
engage in volunteer work
자원봉사 일에 관여하다
파생어 engagement 참여, 약속
engaged 관여된

obtain a pass 출입증을 받다

빈출표현 **obtain a pass** to enter the factory
공장에 들어가기 위해 출입증을 받다
obtain a pass to attend the press conference
기자회견에 참석하기 위해 출입증을 받다
파생어 obtainment 얻기, 획득 obtainable 획득할 수 있는
관련어구 obtain a permit 허가증을 받다
obtain permission from ~로부터 허가를 받다

forward A to B A를 B에게 전달하다

빈출표현 **forward** this letter **to** the manager
이 편지를 매니저에게 전달하다
forward an e-mail **to** the sales person
이메일을 영업사원에게 전달하다
파생어 forwarding 추진, 전달
동의어 send, deliver 발송하다

pass up 거절하다, 포기하다

빈출표현 Don't **pass up** the opportunity.
이 기회를 놓치지 마세요.
Mr. Oh **passed up** the offer.
오 씨는 제안을 포기했다.
동의어 reject 거절하다
give up 포기하다
miss out on ~을 놓치다

permit A to do A가 ~하도록 허가하다

빈출표현 The guide **permitted** us **to** take photos.
가이드는 우리가 사진을 찍도록 허락했다.
Visitors **are** not **permitted to** enter the restricted area.
방문객들은 제한구역에 들어갈 수 없습니다.

파생어 permission 허락 permissible 허용되는

동의어 allow A to do A에게 ~하도록 허락하다
enable A to do A에게 ~하는 것이 가능케 하다

refer to ~을 참조하다

빈출표현 **refer to** the manual first
먼저 설명서를 참고하다
refer to a street map 거리 지도를 참조하다

파생어 reference 추천(서), 참고
referral 소개, 추천

동의어 consult ~을 참조하다

prohibit A from -ing A가 ~하지 못하게 하다

빈출표현 **prohibit** visitors **from** entering
방문객들의 입장을 금지하다
prohibit trucks **from** parking there
트럭이 그곳에 주차하지 못하게 하다

파생어 prohibition 금지

동의어 stop[keep, prevent, inhibit, bar, hinder] A from
-ing A가 ~하지 못하게 하다

refrain from ~을 삼가다

빈출표현 **refrain from** engaging in loud conversations
큰 소리로 대화하는 것을 삼가다
Please **refrain from** using mobile phones.
휴대폰 사용을 삼가 주세요.

동의어 abstain from ~을 삼가다[그만두다]

반의어 indulge in 마음껏 하다

provide A with B
A에게 B를 제공하다(= provide B to A)

빈출표현 **provide** visitors **with** free meals
방문객들에게 무료 식사를 제공하다
be ready to **provide** excellent service
뛰어난 서비스를 제공할 준비가 되어 있다

파생어 provision 제공, (법률 문서의) 조항
provisional 임시의

동의어 present A with B A에게 B를 제공하다

rely on ~에 의존하다

빈출표현 **rely on** customer feedback
고객 피드백에 의존하다
rely on freelance workers
프리랜서들에게 의존하다

파생어 reliability 신뢰성
reliance 의존
reliable 신뢰할 만한

동의어 depend on, count on, rest on ~에 의존하다

qualify for ~에 대한 자격을 갖추다

빈출표현 can **qualify for** a bank loan
은행 대출 자격을 갖추다
She **is qualified to** teach English.
그녀는 영어 교사 자격이 있다.
(= She is qualified for teaching English.)

파생어 qualification 자격 qualified 가격을 갖춘

동의어 be qualified for, be eligible for, be entitled to
~에 자격이 있다

remind A to do A에게 ~하도록 상기시키다

빈출표현 **Remind** me **to** call him this afternoon.
오늘 오후에 그에게 전화하라고 저에게 알려 주세요.
Please be **reminded** that ...
~이라는 점을 명심하세요

동의어 inform A to, notify A to
A에게 ~하도록 알리다

관련어구 remind staff of[about] the picnic
직원들에게 야유회를 상기시키다

raise awareness 인식을 높이다

빈출표현 **raise** public **awareness**
대중의 인식을 높이다
raise awareness among employees about
safety issues
직원들 사이에 안전 문제에 관한 인식을 높이다

파생어 aware ~을 알고 있는

관련어구 be aware of[that] ~을 알고 있다

respond to ~에 응답하다

빈출표현 **respond to** a complaint letter
불만 편지에 답하다
All inquiries were **responded to**.
모든 문의사항에 답변이 되었다.

파생어 respondent 응답자
responsive ~에 응답하는

동의어 react to ~에 반응하다

result in ~라는 결과를 낳다

빈출표현 inadequate training **resulted in** losses
불충분한 훈련으로 손실을 입었다
This great success **resulted from** the good management.
이런 대단한 성공은 훌륭한 경영의 결과다.

관련어구 A(결과) result from B(원인)
A는 B로부터 생기다

strive to do ~하려고 애쓰다, ~에 정진하다

빈출표현 **strive to** be neat
청결하기 위해 노력하다
strive for excellence in service
탁월한 서비스를 위해 노력하다

관련어구 devote oneself to
~에 헌신하다

separate A from B B로부터 A를 분리하다

빈출표현 **separate** personal affairs **from** public affairs
공적인 일과 개인사를 구분하다
They are sold **separately.**
그것들은 따로따로 판매됩니다.

파생어 separation 분리, 별거
separately 떨어져서, 따로따로

동의어 divide 나누다
distinguish 구분 짓다

transfer A to B A를 B로 옮기다[전근시키다]

빈출표현 Ms. Song will **be transferred to** our branch.
송 씨는 우리 지점으로 전근 올 것이다.
transfer $5,000 **to** the account
계좌로 5천 달러를 이체하다

동의어 move, transport 옮기다

관련어구 transfer to ~로 전근 가다, 옮기다

set up 건립하다, 준비하다

빈출표현 **set up** a committee 위원회를 설립하다
set up a party 파티를 준비하다

파생어 setting 환경, 배경

동의어 establish, prepare 마련하다

turn in ~을 제출하다

빈출표현 **turn in** the paper 서류를 제출하다
turn in the application form
지원서[신청서]를 제출하다

동의어 hand in, send in, submit 제출하다

관련어구 turn down (볼륨을) 줄이다, (의견을) 거절하다
turn on[off] ~을 켜다[끄다]

shut down 닫다, 잠그다, 폐쇄하다

빈출표현 **Shut down** your computer before leaving for the day.
컴퓨터를 끄고 퇴근하세요.
shut down the machine 기계를 잠그다

파생어 shutdown 임시 휴업, 조업 중단

동의어 close down 폐쇄하다

urge A to do A에게 ~하도록 촉구하다

빈출표현 **urge** Mr. Son **to** accept the offer
손 씨에게 그 제안을 받아들일 것을 촉구하다

관련어구 prompt A to do A에게 ~하도록 촉구하다
ask A to do A에게 ~하도록 요청하다
encourage A to do A에게 ~하도록 장려하다
would like A to do A가 ~하기를 바라다

specialize in ~을 전문으로 하다, 전공하다

빈출표현 **specialize in** overseas sales
해외 영업을 전문으로 하다
specialize in laptop repairs
노트북 수리를 전문으로 하다

파생어 specialization 전문화, 특수화
specialized 전문화된

waive a fee 요금을 면제하다

빈출표현 **waive the fee** due to our computer error
컴퓨터 오작동으로 인한 요금을 면제하다
waive a late fee 연체료를 면제하다

파생어 waiver 면제, 포기, 면제 증서

관련어구 waive a delivery charge 배송료를 면제하다
waive the tax for small companies
소기업들의 세금을 면제하다

VOCABULARY PRACTICE

정답 및 해설 p. 86

A 다음 주어진 문장에서 적절한 어휘를 고르세요.

1 Ms. Avery will [(A) set up (B) strive to] the videoconference system in the meeting room today.

2 The ventilation system will be [(A) shut down (B) looked out] shortly due to power failure.

3 We [(A) document (B) specialize] in legal issues.

4 Employees are [(A) urged (B) alleged] to take the training class.

5 Keep the receipt in case your smartphone [(A) turns down (B) breaks down].

6 Employees are [(A) commented (B) reminded] to lock the door before leaving for the day.

7 All inquiries should be [(A) forwarded (B) relied] to the director.

B 다음 문장의 빈칸에 적절한 어휘를 고르세요.

8 Radner Laboratories' fourth-quarter report shows that revenues rose nearly 20 percent ------- to the previous quarter.
(A) reminded   (B) considered
(C) compared   (D) preferred

9 Visitors must sign in at the security desk and provide photo identification in order to ------- visitor passes.
(A) obtain   (B) design
(C) require   (D) involve

10 The tasks that Ms. Ogawa must ------- are outlined in her employment agreement.
(A) act   (B) meet
(C) carry out   (D) turn in

11 Out of consideration for other passengers, please ------- from using mobile telephones on the train.
(A) dismiss   (B) prevent
(C) refrain   (D) forbid

12 Ferrelli Steel has ------- in talks with Montag Fabrics to purchase part of its manufacturing business.
(A) involved   (B) engaged
(C) demonstrated   (D) maintained

13 Mr. Oberlin, our corporate benefits manager, will ------- the information sessions for full-time staff on August 12.
(A) lead   (B) invite
(C) raise   (D) regard

14 The awards ceremony will be ------- on the third floor of the Park Station Hotel.
(A) held   (B) raised
(C) taken   (D) granted

15 The CEO of Argall Enterprises is expected to ------- a statement to the press later this week.
(A) act   (B) issue
(C) speak   (D) reply

1. It will be difficult to ------- the safety
    regulations without effective
    monitoring.
    (A) entrust
    (B) enforce
    (C) imply
    (D) implore

2. Fales Bookstores reported a 20 percent
    decrease in net profit this year, which the
    company ------- to fierce competition
    from Yule Booksellers, Inc.
    (A) accused
    (B) presented
    (C) disapproved
    (D) attributed

3. By ------- the furniture shipping process,
    we can lower expenses and cut the
    delivery time in half.
    (A) outpacing
    (B) streamlining
    (C) persevering
    (D) forestalling

4. Wyncote Airlines has announced that
    it will ------- the £15 baggage fee for
    members of its Sky Flyer Club.
    (A) prove
    (B) cost
    (C) waive
    (D) align

5. The advertising campaign should -------
    the public's awareness of the new
    recycling bins in the city parks.
    (A) raise
    (B) reply
    (C) inquire
    (D) react

6. The company's expansion into South
    America will ------- the creation of more
    than 100 jobs.
    (A) return from
    (B) restore to
    (C) research into
    (D) result in

7. Linella Media Group has indicated that
    growth in its new media revenues last
    year helped ------- a decrease in television
    advertising.
    (A) offset
    (B) outplay
    (C) input
    (D) overact

8. In the annual accounts summary, the line-
    graph ------- a further rise in profits over
    the last year.
    (A) determines
    (B) illustrates
    (C) considers
    (D) accounts

9. When he served as president of Delvan
    Manufacturing, Pierre Dunn ------- several
    policies that transformed the company.
    (A) instituted
    (B) relieved
    (C) interviewed
    (D) fabricated

10 All factory visitors must ------- at the front
    desk before entering the production area.
    (A) claim
    (B) distribute
    (C) reveal
    (D) register

11. The legal department will meet this week to discuss the implications of a recent high court decision ------- with manufacturer liability.
(A) dealing
(B) bearing
(C) enacting
(D) separating

12. Upgrading the technological equipment at Mt. Hudson Training Center may ------- to a better learning experience for the students.
(A) offer
(B) submit
(C) donate
(D) contribute

13. The latest microwave oven from Dabato Industries ------- a stainless steel interior and ten different heat settings.
(A) features
(B) produces
(C) implies
(D) appoints

14. No firm can ------- to rely forever only on the strength of its name to sell products.
(A) require
(B) afford
(C) suppose
(D) depend

15. Pronesti Ltd. paid £500 million to ------- the profitable computer software firm XBR Technologies.
(A) acquire
(B) achieve
(C) yield
(D) realize

16. City Council member Elena Torres was asked to identify ways to ------- unnecessary expenses from the Howell City budget.
(A) distribute
(B) exhaust
(C) empty
(D) remove

17. A new lighting system has been installed in the administrative offices, ------- the older, less efficient one.
(A) replacing
(B) comparing
(C) brightening
(D) repairing

18. Ms. Atembe of Hartwick Trucking will conduct a workshop on the best ways to ------- customers' concerns about freight delivery.
(A) inform
(B) address
(C) supervise
(D) promise

19. The employee handbook clearly ------- the procedure for filing expense reports.
(A) purchases
(B) outlines
(C) rations
(D) invests

20. Many of the country's coastal cities have begun to ------- tourism as an important source of revenue.
(A) get in
(B) let down
(C) find out
(D) rely on

21. Employees should feel free to ------- the on-site physician as often as needed.
(A) consult
(B) convert
(C) compare
(D) convince

22. The retirement planning symposium scheduled for July 24 will be ------- by the human resources department.
(A) invited
(B) intended
(C) hosted
(D) excused

23. Initial projections of quarterly earnings have already been ------- with a month still remaining.
(A) exceeded
(B) outdated
(C) overdrawn
(D) impressed

24. Swabian Motors will ------- its current name even after it merges with a rival company.
(A) receive
(B) inquire
(C) grant
(D) retain

25. Executives from the two firms may soon be ready to ------- the terms of the proposed merger.
(A) confirm
(B) converse
(C) commune
(D) collaborate

26. To ------- for the local-shopper discount, customers must show proof of residency.
(A) qualify
(B) award
(C) experience
(D) certify

27. Avery Motors will not ------- on the design of its new line of automobiles until the press release tomorrow.
(A) advance
(B) predict
(C) comment
(D) rely

28. The Soseu Soap Corporation launched an advertising campaign to ------- interest in its new line of cleaning products.
(A) consume
(B) generate
(C) endorse
(D) suppose

29. Mr. Nahm has been promoted to Senior Vice President of Sales and ------- his new role on March 1.
(A) remains
(B) concerns
(C) assumes
(D) participates

30. The original contracts with the Sargasso shipping company have just been shredded because they ------- ten years ago today.
(A) submitted
(B) violated
(C) expired
(D) invalidated

UNIT 03 | ETS 빈출 명사

acceptance 수락, 승인, 동의

빈출표현 Please e-mail me to confirm your **acceptance**.
저에게 이메일을 보내 수락을 확인해 주세요.
Sign below to indicate your **acceptance** of
these terms. 서명하여 이 조건에 동의함을 표시해 주세요.

파생어 accept 받아들이다
acceptable 용인할 수 있는

alternative 대안; 대안의

빈출표현 Renting a car is an **alternative** to using a taxi.
차량 렌트가 택시 이용의 대안이다.
seek an **alternative** 대안을 찾다

파생어 alternation 교대, 교체
alternate 번갈아 하다; 번갈아 하는, 대안의

동의어 substitute 대신하는 사람[것]

access 입장, 접근, 이용

빈출표현 easy **access** to area attractions
지역 명소로의 편리한 접근
The resort offers Internet **access** in each guest
room. 그 리조트는 각 객실 인터넷 사용을 제공한다.

파생어 accessible 이용[접근]할 수 있는

amenity 편의 시설[용품]

빈출표현 guest-room **amenities** 객실 편의 용품
amenities, such as outdoor tennis courts, and
a spa 실외 테니스 코트, 스파 등의 편의 시설
The hotel provides every **amenity** necessary.
그 호텔은 필요한 모든 편의 시설을 제공한다.

advance 발전, 진보; 나아가다; 사전의

빈출표현 a seminar about **advances** in mobile phone
technology 휴대폰 기술 발전에 관한 세미나
give at least 24 hours **advance** notice
적어도 24시간 전에 사전 통지를 하다

파생어 advancement 진전, 승진
advanced 최신의, 진보된

동의어 improvement 향상

반의어 retreat 퇴각, 후퇴

application 지원(서), 신청, 적용; 앱

빈출표현 fill out the **application** form
신청서를 작성하다
develop **applications** for smartphones
스마트폰 앱을 개발하다

파생어 applicant 지원자, 신청자
apply 지원하다, 적용하다, 바르다

affiliation 제휴, 소속기관

빈출표현 have an **affiliation** with foreign banks
외국 은행들과 제휴하다
state your name and **affiliation**
이름과 소속을 말하다

파생어 affiliate 제휴하다; 계열사

동의어 partnership 협력, 제휴

반의어 detachment 분리

appraisal 평가

빈출표현 performance **appraisal**[evaluation]
업무 평가
make an **appraisal** of
~을 평가하다

파생어 appraise 평가하다

동의어 evaluation, assessment 평가

agreement 동의, 계약

빈출표현 reach an **agreement**
합의에 다다르다, 계약을 체결하다
finalize an **agreement**
계약 체결을 마무리하다

파생어 agree 동의하다 agreeable 알맞은, 기분 좋은

동의어 consent 동의

반의어 disagreement 불일치

approach 접근(법)

빈출표현 take a fresh **approach**
새로운 접근법을 취하다
a unique **approach** to healthy eating
건강한 식사에 대한 독특한 접근법

파생어 approachable 접근[이해]하기 쉬운

관련어구 approaching storm 다가오는 태풍
approaching deadline 다가오는 마감

attention 관심, 주의

빈출표현 Recently, shoppers have turned their **attention** to organic foods.
최근에 소비자들은 유기농 음식으로 관심을 돌렸다.

파생어 attend 참석하다
동의어 care 관심
반의어 indifference 무관심

authorization 허가, 승인, 권한 부여

빈출표현 receive the **authorization** from
~로부터 권한을 부여받다
without **authorization** 허가 없이

파생어 authority 권한
authorize 허가하다
동의어 approval 승인
반의어 disapproval 비인가, 반대

blend 혼합, 혼합물; 섞다

빈출표현 a **blend** of old houses and new apartment buildings 오래된 주택과 새 아파트들의 혼재
a **blend** of decorating styles
여러 장식 스타일의 혼합

파생어 blending 혼합
blended 섞인
동의어 mix, mixture 혼합
반의어 separation 분리

caution 경고[주의]; 주의[경고]를 주다

빈출표현 Harmful chemicals should be treated with **caution**.
유해 화학 물질은 주의해서 취급해야 한다.

파생어 cautious 조심스러운, 신중한
cautiously 조심스럽게, 신중하게
관련어구 use[exercise] caution 주의하다
caution against ~하지 말라고 경고하다

certificate 증서, 증명서

빈출표현 a **certificate** good for 10 percent off
10퍼센트 할인증
The **certificate** should be submitted along with your application.
지원서와 함께 자격증이 제출되어야 합니다.

파생어 certify 증명하다, 자격증을 교부하다
certification 증명, 증명서 교부[부여]
관련어구 gift certificate 상품권

circulation 순환, 유통, (신문·잡지의) 판매 부수

빈출표현 a magazine with an impressive international **circulation**
상당한 해외 판매 부수를 올린 잡지

파생어 circulate 유통시키다, 유포되다, (사람들에게) 알리다
관련어구 circulation department 유통 부서

combination 결합, 조합

빈출표현 **combination** lock 번호 자물쇠
combination of all nutrients
모든 영양소의 조합

파생어 combine 결합하다
combined 합쳐진
동의어 mix 혼합
반의어 separation, detachment 분리

complaint 불평, 불만

빈출표현 Some customers had **complaints** about our service.
일부 고객들은 우리 서비스에 불만을 가지고 있었다.
a letter of **complaint** 항의서

파생어 complain 불평하다
complainingly 불평하여
동의어 dissatisfaction 불만족
반의어 compliment, praise 찬사

compliance (법·명령 등의) 준수

빈출표현 in **compliance** with the local laws
지방법을 잘 따라서
ensure **compliance** with its specifications
세부 내역 준수를 확실히 하다

파생어 comply 준수하다
compliant 준수하는, 따르는

concentration 집중, 밀집, 농도

빈출표현 increase the **concentration** of the juice
주스의 농도를 높이다
a **concentration** of population
인구의 집중

파생어 concentrate on ~에 집중하다
concentrated 밀집된, 농축된
동의어 attention 주의
반의어 distraction 주의 산만

concern 걱정, 근심, 관심(사)

빈출표현 a matter of little **concern**
별로 중요하지 않은 문제
have **concerns** about[over]
~에 대해 걱정하다

파생어 concerned 염려하는
concerning ~에 관한

동의어 worry 걱정

반의어 indifference, apathy 무관심

contribution 공헌, 기부(금)

빈출표현 **contribution** to the company
회사에 대한 기여
collect **contributions** from residents
주민들로부터 기부금을 모으다

파생어 contributor 공헌자, 기고가
contribute 기여하다, 기부하다

동의어 donation 기부(금)

coverage 보도[방송], 보상[범위]

빈출표현 receive more press **coverage**
더 많은 언론 보도를 받다
Customers can obtain **coverage** for
replacement and repair of printers.
고객들은 프린터의 교체와 수리에 대한 보상을 받을 수
있습니다.

파생어 cover 다루다, 보도하다, 보상하다

deadline 마감 기한

빈출표현 meet[miss] the **deadline**
마감 기한을 지키다[못 지키다]
extend the **deadline** for one more week
마감 기한을 일주일 더 연장하다
a **deadline** for registration 등록 마감일

동의어 due date 만기일

defect 결함, 하자

빈출표현 find **defects** in the product
제품의 하자를 발견하다
repair a **defect** in manufacturing
제조 과정에서 결함을 고치다

파생어 defective 결함이 있는

동의어 flaw 결점

반의어 perfection, immaculacy 완벽함

deliberation 숙고, 심의

빈출표현 under **deliberation** 숙고 중인
after hours of **deliberation**
수 시간의 심의 후에

파생어 deliberate 숙고하다; 고의의, 숙고한
deliberately 고의로

동의어 consideration 고려, 검토

distraction 주의 산만, 방해물

빈출표현 cause a **distraction**
집중력 저하를 일으키다
distractions due to noise
소음으로 인한 주의 산만

파생어 distract 산만하게 하다
distracting 주의를 산만하게 하는

동의어 confusion 혼란

반의어 concentration 집중

duration 지속, 지속 기간

빈출표현 for the **duration** of the event 행사 기간 동안
events of varying **duration** 다양한 기간의 행사들

파생어 durability 지속성
durable 지속성 있는, 튼튼한

동의어 continuation 계속, 지속

반의어 halt, suspension 중지

estimate 견적(서); 견적을 내다

빈출표현 a free **estimate** 무료 견적
get a cost **estimate** 비용 견적을 받다

파생어 estimation 추정, 판단
estimated 추정되는

동의어 quotation 견적

expertise 전문 지식

빈출표현 **expertise** in advertising campaigns
광고 캠페인 분야에 대한 전문 지식
The new curator will bring his vast **expertise**
to the museum.
새로운 큐레이터는 박물관에 그의 방대한 전문 지식을
가져올 것이다.

파생어 expert 전문가; 전문가의
expertly 훌륭하게, 전문적으로

관련어구 area of expertise 전문 분야

fluctuation 변동, 불안정

빈출표현 **fluctuation** in exchange rates 환율의 변동
fluctuations in the electricity supply
전력 공급의 불안정
파생어 fluctuate 변동하다
fluctuant 불안정한
동의어 variation 변동
반의어 stability 안정

fraction 일부, 작은 부분

빈출표현 at a **fraction** of the cost
비용의 극히 일부분
pay off a **fraction** of the debts
빚의 일부를 갚다
파생어 fractionize 세분하다
동의어 part, portion 일부
반의어 whole 전체

funding 재원, 자금 제공

빈출표현 The city will increase **funding** for cultural
events.
시 정부는 문화 행사를 위한 자금을 증원할 것이다.
receive **funding** from donations
기부금으로 자금을 제공받다
파생어 funds (이용 가능한) 자금, 공채
fund-raiser 모금 행사
fund 자금을 대다
동의어 financing 자금 조달

generosity 관대함, 인심 좋음

빈출표현 show your **generosity**
여러분의 관대함을 보여 주세요
due to your **generosity**
여러분의 관대함 덕분에
파생어 generous 관대한
동의어 leniency 관대
반의어 selfishness 이기적임

implication 암시, 함축, 영향

빈출표현 have serious **implications** for
~에 심각한 영향을 끼치다
the **implications** of the merger
합병의 영향
파생어 implicate 연루시키다, 암시하다
동의어 hint, suggestion 암시
connotation 함축

impression 인상, 감명

빈출표현 leave a good first **impression**
좋은 첫인상을 남기다
a lasting **impression**
지속적으로 남는 인상
파생어 impress 감명을 주다
impressive 감명을 주는
impressed 감명받은
동의어 impact 영향

improvement 향상, 개선

빈출표현 There is room for **improvement.**
개선의 여지가 있다.
the **improvement** of the transportation
system 운송체계의 개선
파생어 improve 향상시키다, 개선시키다
improvable 개선할 수 있는
동의어 enhancement 개선
반의어 deterioration 악화

ingredient 재료, 구성 요소

빈출표현 use fresh **ingredients**
신선한 재료를 사용하다
The **ingredients** are organic.
그 재료들은 유기농이다.
동의어 part 부품
component 구성 요소

initiative 계획, 주도권; 처음의

빈출표현 take the **initiative** 솔선수범하다, 주도권을 쥐다
seize[lose] **initiative** 주도권을 쥐다[잃다]
파생어 initiation 가입, 개시
initiate 시작하다
동의어 plan 계획
action 행동
반의어 inactivity 무기력

innovation 혁신, 획기적인 것

빈출표현 technological **innovation** 기술 혁신
a company famous for **innovation**
혁신으로 유명한 회사
파생어 innovate 혁신하다
innovative 혁신적인
동의어 revolution 변혁
반의어 stagnation 침체

161

inquiry 질문, 문의

빈출표현 **inquiries** regarding the contract
계약에 관한 문의 사항들
forward **inquiries**
문의 사항들을 전달하다

파생어 inquire 질문하다
동의어 question 질문
반의어 answer 답변

inspection 검사, 점검, 검열

빈출표현 pass a safety **inspection**
안전 검사를 통과하다
an **inspection** of the shipment
선적물 검사

파생어 inspector 감사관, 조사관
inspect 점검하다
동의어 investigation 조사

intention 의향, 의도

빈출표현 announce her **intention** to step down
사임 의사를 발표하다
have no **intention** of coming
올 의향이 없다

파생어 intend 의도하다
intentional 의도적인
동의어 intent 의향
purpose, aim 목표

malfunction 오작동; 오작동하다

빈출표현 a **malfunction** of the software
소프트웨어의 오작동
The computer is **malfunctioning**.
컴퓨터가 제대로 작동하지 않다.

파생어 function 기능; 기능하다
동의어 failure 고장

means 수단, 방법

빈출표현 a strong **means** of
~의 강력한 수단
various **means** of payment
다양한 지불 수단

파생어 mean 의미하다
meaningful 의미 있는
동의어 way, method 방법

negligence 부주의, 태만

빈출표현 As the water pipes were installed improperly, the contractor was liable for **negligence.**
수도관들이 부적절하게 설치되어 그 하청업체는 부주의에 대한 책임이 있었다.
negligence in handling the cargo
화물 취급 부주의

파생어 neglect 태만; 소홀히 하다
동의어 disregard 무시(하다)
반의어 attention, care 관심

passion 열정

빈출표현 a **passion** for serving customers
고객들을 잘 응대하려는 열정
a **passion** for teaching
가르침에 대한 열정

파생어 passionate 열정적인
동의어 ardor, fervor 열정
반의어 lethargy 무기력

peak 정점, (산의) 정상; 최고의

빈출표현 at the **peak** of its popularity
인기가 최고조에 있는
the **peak** tourist season
최고의 관광 성수기

파생어 peaky 봉우리가 많은, 뾰족한; 수척해 보이는
동의어 summit 정상

phase 단계[국면]; 단계적으로 하다

빈출표현 help with every **phase** of event planning
행사 기획의 모든 면을 돕다
We will complete the final **phase** of a ten-year project in about one year.
약 1년 후 우리는 10년 프로젝트의 최종 단계를 마무리할 것이다.

동의어 aspect 측면

possession 소유물, 소유

빈출표현 keep your **possessions** in
소지하신 물건은 ~에 보관하십시오
Please pack your **possessions**.
소지품을 챙겨 주세요.

파생어 possess 소유하다
possessive 소유의
동의어 belongings 소지품

potential 잠재력, 가능성; 잠재력이 있는

빈출표현 employees with great **potential**
광장한 잠재력이 있는 직원들
cloudy weather with a **potential** for snow
눈이 올 가능성이 있는 흐린 날씨

파생어 potentially 잠재적으로, 어쩌면

동의어 possibility, likelihood 가능성

promotion 승진, 홍보, 촉진

빈출표현 eligible for the **promotion**
승진할 자격이 있다
a **promotional** strategy 홍보 전략

파생어 promote 승진시키다, 홍보하다
promotional 홍보용의

동의어 advancement 승진

반의어 demotion 강등

practice 관행, 실행, 연습; 실행하다

빈출표현 common **practice** 일반적 관습
put the sales strategy into **practice**
영업 전략을 실행하다

파생어 practical 실제의, 실용적인

동의어 convention 관습
training 연습

ratio 비율, 비례

빈출표현 in reverse **ratio** to ~에 반비례하여
device-to-person **ratio**
기구 대 사람의 비율

파생어 rate 비율; 요금
ration 배급; 할당량

동의어 proportion 비율, 부분

preference 선호, 우선권

빈출표현 **Preference** will be given to
~에게 우선권이 주어질 것이다
food **preference** 음식 선호도

파생어 prefer 선호하다
preferred 선호되는, 우선시 되는

동의어 inclination 경향

반의어 hate, dislike 싫음

reaction 반응

빈출표현 a mixed **reaction** 다양한 반응
an allergic **reaction** to eggs
계란에 대한 알레르기 반응

파생어 react to ~에 반응하다

동의어 response 응답

반의어 request 요청

presence 참석, 입지

빈출표현 in the **presence** of ~의 면전에서
establish the company's **presence** in the
market
시장에서 회사의 입지를 확립하다

파생어 present 현재의, 참석한

동의어 attendance 참석

반의어 absence 부재

reminder 상기시키는 것

빈출표현 This is a **reminder** that ...
이것은 ~을 상기시켜 드리기 위한 것입니다
send **reminder** e-mails
상기시키는 이메일을 보내다

파생어 remind 상기시키다

동의어 indication 표시

반의어 forgetfulness 건망증

priority 우선 사항, 우선 순위

빈출표현 have **priority** over ~보다 우선하다
determine the task's **priority**
과제의 우선 순위를 결정하다

파생어 prior 앞선
prior to ~보다 이전에

동의어 precedence 우위, 우선

resource 자원, 재산, 능력

빈출표현 natural **resources** 천연 자원
human **resources** 인력 자원, 인사부

파생어 resourceful 재치 있는, 자원이 풍부한

동의어 wealth 부유함

반의어 lack, deficiency 부족

responsibility 책임(감), 책무

빈출표현 have **responsibility** for
~에 책임이 있다
take on[assume] a **responsibility**
책임을 떠맡다
파생어 responsible 책임이 있는
동의어 liability 책임
반의어 irresponsibility 무책임

surplus 잉여, 흑자; 잉여의

빈출표현 donate **surplus** supplies
잉여 물품을 기증하다
make use of a budget **surplus**
남은 예산을 사용하다
반의어 lack 부족
deficit 적자

scale 규모, (지도 등의) 축척

빈출표현 produce goods on a small **scale**
소규모로 상품을 생산하다
the **scale** of a map
지도의 축척
파생어 full-scale 전면적인
동의어 size, level 규모
range 범위

transaction 거래, 처리

빈출표현 Our bank charges no fees for most online **transactions**. 저희 은행은 대부분의 온라인 거래에 수수료를 부과하지 않습니다.
Each business **transaction** must be recorded.
각 사업 거래는 기록해야 한다.
파생어 transact 거래하다
transactional 거래의, 업무의

schedule 일정; 일정을 정하다

빈출표현 behind **schedule** 일정에 뒤처진
on **schedule** 일정대로
ahead of **schedule** 일정보다 앞선
파생어 scheduled 예정된
동의어 timetable 일정

transfer 이체, 양도; 옮기다

빈출표현 an unusually large money **transfer**
드물게 큰 금액의 자금 이체
electronic **transfer** 온라인 이체
파생어 transferable 양도 가능한
동의어 move, relocation 이전, 이주

scope 범위, 규모

빈출표현 negotiate the **scope** of the new contract
신규 계약의 범위를 협상하다
The enclosed plan outlines the **scope** of the project.
동봉된 기획안은 프로젝트의 규모를 대략적으로 설명합니다.
동의어 extent 정도[규모]

venture 벤처, 모험적 사업; 위험에 내맡기다

빈출표현 **venture** business 벤처 기업
venture capital 모험 자본
파생어 venturous 모험적인
동의어 enterprise 모험적 사업
반의어 assurance 확실성

selection 선택, 선정된 사람[것]

빈출표현 area's widest **selection** of
이 지역에서 가장 선택의 폭이 넓은 ~
a careful **selection** of employees
엄선된 직원들
파생어 select 선택하다
selective 선별적인
동의어 choice 선택
반의어 rejection 거절

workshop 워크숍, 연수

빈출표현 attend a **workshop** for computer novices
컴퓨터 초보자를 위한 워크숍에 참여하다
register for a **workshop** on public speaking
대중 연설에 관한 워크숍에 등록하다
동의어 training session 연수

VOCABULARY PRACTICE

정답 및 해설 p. 90

A 다음 주어진 문장에서 적절한 어휘를 고르세요.

1 Performing a series of trial runs is common [(A) manner (B) practice].

2 It will be Mr. Ishibashi's [(A) quality (B) responsibility] to review all corporate contracts.

3 We attribute the [(A) improvement (B) expectation] in service to a software upgrade.

4 Visitors are reminded to indicate their meal [(A) preferences (B) implications].

5 The company is liable for [(A) negligence (B) intermission].

6 The health benefits of whole grains come from the [(A) combination (B) proximity] of all the nutrients.

7 Following her [(A) acceptance (B) promotion] to sales director, Ms. Lin assumed responsibility for the firm's marketing activities.

B 다음 문장의 빈칸에 적절한 어휘를 고르세요.

8 After long -------, Bordenton Manufacturing decided not to extend its contract with Tyron Security Systems.
(A) deliberation   (B) impression
(C) conclusion   (D) assumption

9 Due to a rise in revenue, the Easthampton town council has decided to increase ------- for community programs that have not traditionally received much financial support.
(A) preservation   (B) sharing
(C) appraisal   (D) funding

10 Great ------- in tourism levels have had a significant impact on the success of Darling Beach's small businesses.
(A) fluctuations   (B) perceptions
(C) narrations   (D) obligations

11 All interns in the marketing department are encouraged to attend the upcoming -------.
(A) subject   (B) division
(C) workshop   (D) plan

12 Members are a vital part of the Global Musicians' Association, and finding ways to increase membership should be a high -------.
(A) basis   (B) force
(C) direction   (D) priority

13 The ------- behind the initiative is to ensure that all members of our support staff have adequate opportunities for professional development.
(A) resemblance   (B) dependence
(C) intention   (D) retention

14 Ms. Kovac has requested your ------- at the regional meeting that will take place on Thursday of next week.
(A) occurrence   (B) urgency
(C) presence   (D) insistence

15 All members of the sales team are grateful for Michael Dreyman's substantial ------- to the project over the last six months.
(A) assurance   (B) dependence
(C) obligations   (D) contributions

UNIT 04 | ETS 빈출 명사 어구

a variety of 다양한

빈출표현 a wide **variety of** dishes 각양각색의 요리들
a **variety of** tour options 다양한 여행[관광] 옵션들
파생어 various 다양한
varied 다양한
동의어 diverse 다양한
반의어 identical 동일한

a wealth of 많은, 풍부한

빈출표현 a **wealth of** experience 풍부한 경험
Visit our store for **a wealth of** additional books.
많은 추가 도서들을 보시려면 저희 매장을 방문하세요.
동의어 plentiful, ample, abundant 풍부한

advance registration 사전 등록

빈출표현 As this seminar is so popular, **advance registration** is a must.
이 세미나가 매우 인기가 좋아서 사전 등록은 필수이다.
Advance registration is required.
사전 등록을 해야 한다.
파생어 advancement 승진, 진전
advanced 첨단의

as part of ~의 일환으로

빈출표현 **as part of** the effort to reduce noise
소음을 줄이려는 노력의 일환으로
ability to work **as part of** a team
팀의 일원으로 일할 수 있는 능력
establish a base in a new area **as part of** an initiative to expand
확장 계획의 일환으로 신규 지역에 본부를 설립하다

business practice 사업 관행

빈출표현 promoting good **business practices**
모범적인 사업 관행을 장려하다
environmentally responsible **business practices**
환경에 대해 책임 있는 사업 관행
관련어구 common practice 일반적인 관행
routine practice 통상적인 관행

conduct a survey 설문 조사를 하다

빈출표현 regularly **conduct a** customer satisfaction **survey** 정기적으로 고객 만족 설문 조사를 하다
파생어 survey 설문 조사, 설문지; 설문 조사하다
동의어 conduct a poll 여론 조사를 하다
관련어구 survey respondents 설문 조사 응답자

day[night] shift 주간[야간] 근무조

빈출표현 **day shift** on weekdays from 10:00 A.M. to 5:00 P.M.
주중 오전 10시부터 오후 5시까지의 주간 근무
관련어구 morning/evening shift 주간[야간] 근무조
in shifts 교대로

employee productivity 직원 생산성

빈출표현 increase **employee productivity**
직원 생산성을 높이다
have a positive impact on our **employee productivity** and morale
직원 생산성과 사기에 긍정적인 영향을 미치다
관련어구 worker productivity 직원 생산성

give[pay] attention to ~에 관심을 기울이다

빈출표현 No **attention** was **given to** this matter.
이 문제는 관심을 전혀 받지 못했다.
pay attention to details 세부 사항에 유의하다
파생어 attend 출석하다
attentive 관심을 쏟는
동의어 care about 신경 쓰다

have[gain] a (good) reputation for ~에 대해 좋은 평판을 가지다[얻다]

빈출표현 As a CEO, Mr. Na **has a good reputation for** his energy.
사장으로서, 나 씨는 그의 열정에 대해 좋은 평판을 가지고 있다.
파생어 reputable 평판이 좋은
reputedly 평판으로는

in a timely manner[fashion]
시기 적절하게

빈출표현 Any complaints from customers will be dealt
with **in a timely manner**.
고객들의 모든 불만 사항은 시기 적절하게 처리될 것입니다.
finish the project **in a timely manner**
시기 적절하게 프로젝트를 완수하다

동의어 opportunely 시기 적절하게

in charge of ~을 담당하는[책임지는]

빈출표현 Ms. Hamilton is currently **in charge of** the
Marketing Division.
해밀턴 씨는 현재 마케팅 부서를 담당하고 있다.
Ms. Lam will be **in charge of** the project.
램 씨가 그 프로젝트를 담당할 것이다.

파생어 charge 책임, 요금; 청구하다

동의어 responsible 책임지는

in honor of ~에 경의를 표하여, ~을 축하하여

빈출표현 a book festival **in honor of** the late author
고인이 된 작가를 기리는 도서 기념제
a dinner event **in honor of** the new director
신임 이사를 축하하는 저녁 행사

in observance of ~을 기념하여

빈출표현 **in observance of** the national holiday
국경일을 기념하여
a special sale **in observance of** our 20th
anniversary
20주년 기념 특별할인

in the vicinity of ~의 부근에

빈출표현 have a temporary residence **in the vicinity of**
the main office
본사 인근에 임시 거처를 두다
Vehicles will encounter detours **in the vicinity
of** the parade route.
차량들은 행렬 경로 부근에서 우회해야 할 것이다.

동의어 in the proximity of ~의 근처에

make a revision to ~을 수정하다

빈출표현 **make a revision to** the event schedule
행사 일정을 수정하다
make revisions to the manuscript
원고를 수정하다

파생어 revise 수정하다
revised 수정된

동의어 make a change to 수정하다

meet the requirement 필요를 충족시키다

빈출표현 **meet the** job **requirements**
직무 필요 조건에 부합하다

파생어 require 요구하다
required 필수적인

관련어구 meet the demand[needs]
수요를 충족시키다
meet the standard 기준에 부합하다

membership benefits 회원 혜택

빈출표현 a brochure that explains **membership
benefits** 회원 혜택을 설명하는 소책자
take advantage of **membership benefits**
회원 혜택을 이용하다

파생어 benefit 이익, 혜택; ~에게 도움이 되다

관련어구 benefits package 복리후생 제도

on a regular basis 정기적으로

빈출표현 take place **on a regular basis**
정기적으로 개최되다
inspect equipment **on a regular basis**
정기적으로 장비를 검사하다

관련어구 on a monthly basis 매월
on a first-come, first-served basis 선착순으로

on display 전시 중인

빈출표현 keep items **on display** during the sale
할인 기간 동안 물건들을 진열해 놓다
photos **on display** at the art show
전시회에 진열된 사진들

동의어 on exhibition 전시 중인

관련어구 display case 진열장

out of service 고장 난, 작동을 멈춘

빈출표현 The printer is currently **out of service**.
현재 프린터가 고장 나 있다.
Use the stairs if the elevator is **out of service**.
승강기 고장 시 계단을 이용하시오.
파생어 serviceable 유용한, 쓸모 있는
동의어 out of order 고장 난

out of stock 재고가 없는

빈출표현 The item is temporarily **out of stock**.
그 물건은 일시적으로 재고가 떨어졌다.
The item you ordered is **out of stock**.
주문하신 물건은 재고가 없습니다.
파생어 stock 재고; 비축하다
반의어 in stock 재고가 있는

play a role[part] in ~에 역할을 하다

빈출표현 **play a role in** the company's success
기업의 성공에 한몫을 하다
관련어구 role conflict 역할 갈등
role playing 역할 연기

proximity to ~에 가까움, 근접

빈출표현 in close[immediate] **proximity to**
~에 바로 근접한 곳에
offer convenient **proximity to** the airport
공항에서 가까워 편리하다
동의어 be adjacent[contiguous / close] to
~에 가깝다

put[place] an emphasis on
~을 강조하다

빈출표현 a huge **emphasis** will be **placed on**
~에 대해 매우 강조할 것이다
put an emphasis on quality
품질을 강조하다
파생어 emphasize 강조하다
동의어 stress, highlight 강조하다

recommendation letter 추천서

빈출표현 write **recommendation letters**
추천서를 쓰다
파생어 recommend 추천하다
recommendation 추천 (사항)
관련어구 make a recommendation 추천하다

routine maintenance 정기 보수[점검]

빈출표현 Please note that **routine maintenance** of the
server will be performed this weekend.
서버 정기 점검이 이번 주말에 시행됨을 알려 드립니다.
관련어구 routine check 정기 검사
routinely conduct inspections
정기적으로 점검을 시행하다

safety procedure 안전 절차

빈출표현 The workers should follow the **safety
procedures**.
근로자들은 안전 절차를 따라야 한다.
review the **safety procedures**
안전 절차를 검토하다
파생어 safe 안전한
safely 안전하게
관련어구 safety precautions 안전 예방 조치

sales revenue 매출 수익

빈출표현 The company's **sales revenues** rose by 20
percent. 그 회사의 매출 수익이 20% 상승했다.
achieve **sales revenue** goals
판매 수익 목표를 달성하다
동의어 sales figures 매출액
관련어구 sales representative 영업 직원

scheduling conflict 일정 충돌

빈출표현 due to a **scheduling conflict**
일정이 겹쳐서
avoid a **scheduling conflict** with the classes
수업 일정이 겹치는 것을 피하다
관련어구 resolve a conflict 갈등을 해결하다

seating capacity 수용력, 좌석 수

[빈출표현] an auditorium with a **seating capacity** of 500
5백 명을 수용할 수 있는 대강당
increase the stadium's **seating capacity**
경기장의 좌석 수를 늘리다
[파생어] seat 좌석; 수용하다

under one's direction
~의 지도 아래에 있는

[빈출표현] Operators are presently **under Mr. Oh's direction.** 작업자들은 현재 오 씨의 지휘 아래에 있다.
[파생어] director 감독관, 이사
direct 지시하다; 직접적인
[동의어] under one's supervision ~의 감독하에

take a detour 우회하다

[빈출표현] The bridge was blocked, so we had to **take a detour.** 다리가 폐쇄되어 우리는 우회해야 했다.
make a detour around the flooded roads
침수된 도로를 우회하다
[동의어] take a long way around 우회하다
take an alternate route 우회하다

under pressure
압박감을 느끼는, 스트레스를 받는

[빈출표현] All the workers are **under pressure.**
모든 직원들이 압박감을 느끼고 있다.
Deep breathing helps you stay calm **under pressure.** 심호흡은 스트레스를 받을 때 평정을 유지하는 데 도움이 된다.
[동의어] under stress 스트레스를 받는

take a precaution 예방 조치를 취하다

[빈출표현] **take** every possible **precaution** to protect the security of confidential data
기밀 데이터의 보안을 위해 모든 가능한 예방 조치를 취하다
Safety **precautions** must be **taken** by all laboratory employees.
전 실험실 직원들이 안전 예방 조치를 취해야 한다.

winning entry 우승작

[빈출표현] **winning entries** from past competitions
지난 대회 우승작
All **winning entries** will be displayed temporarily.
우승작 전부가 임시로 전시될 것이다.
[관련어구] submit an entry for a contest
콘테스트에 작품을 출품하다

take advantage of ~을 이용하다

[빈출표현] **Take advantage of** this limited opportunity!
이번 한정 기회를 이용하세요!
Take advantage of the end-of-season sale.
시즌 마감 세일을 이용하세요.
[관련어구] have an advantage over
~보다 우위에 있다

with the exception of ~은 예외로 하고

[빈출표현] **with the exception of** personal matters
개인적인 문제들은 제외하고
with the exception of minor errors
사소한 실수들을 제외하고
[파생어] exception 예외, 제외
[동의어] except for, excluding ~을 제외하고
[반의어] without exception 예외 없이

take into account ~을 고려하다, 참작하다

[빈출표현] an ample menu that **takes into account** many dietary restrictions and preferences
많은 식단 제한 및 선호도를 고려한 다양한 메뉴
Weather forecasts should be **taken into account.**
일기 예보를 고려해야 한다.
[동의어] take into consideration ~을 고려하다
allow for 감안[참작]하다

without consent 동의 없이

[빈출표현] **Without** your prior written **consent,** we do not release …
서면 동의 없이 ~을 공개하지 않습니다
[관련어구] mutual consent 상호 합의
give one's consent to ~에 동의하다

A 다음 주어진 문장에서 적절한 어휘를 고르세요.

1 The elevators will be out of [(A) service (B) aid] for the week.

2 The cafeteria serves a [(A) variety (B) type] of sandwiches, soups, and salads.

3 The market-research department conducted a [(A) survey (B) response].

4 The new electronic components do not meet the quality [(A) requirements (B) performances].

5 The panel discussion plays an important [(A) role (B) task] in the annual leadership conference.

6 The monthly rent includes all utilities with the [(A) excess (B) exception] of telephone and cable charges.

7 Assembly-line workers interested in taking overnight [(A) points (B) shifts] next month should inform their managers by Tuesday.

B 다음 문장의 빈칸에 적절한 어휘를 고르세요.

8 Drivers must take a ------- around the construction site until the building is completed in November.
(A) change   (B) view
(C) detour   (D) gap

9 Advance ------- is required for the Northwest Regional Hospital Management conference.
(A) result   (B) registration
(C) respect   (D) regulation

10 Several ------- have been made to the layout of Banham Library's Web site.
(A) revisions   (B) processes
(C) considerations (D) concepts

11 The research and development division at Spiridon Biometrics has improved the quality and scope of its products under Ms. Chang's -------.
(A) disposal   (B) direction
(C) prominence   (D) capacity

12 To ensure that a Web site is effective, it is common ------- to administer a customer feedback survey.
(A) source   (B) practice
(C) topic   (D) supply

13 During the hotel renovation, special ------- was given to the lighting fixtures and decorations.
(A) introduction   (B) attempt
(C) conference   (D) attention

14 Several famous pieces of sculpture are displayed in the ------- of City Hall.
(A) surrounding   (B) standing
(C) vicinity   (D) condition

15 All products on ------- in the store window are available at reduced prices.
(A) example   (B) display
(C) measure   (D) assembly

1. The buildings in the Jamison Complex are open until 7:00 P.M. on workdays, but staff with proper ------- may enter at any time.
(A) reinforcement
(B) participation
(C) competency
(D) authorization

2. The Janug Corporation's newer-model refrigerators use only a ------- of the energy that its older models use.
(A) relation
(B) moderation
(C) fraction
(D) correction

3. At its -------, Checker Enterprises represented over 30 percent of the auto glass manufacturing market.
(A) peak
(B) scale
(C) depth
(D) record

4. If it wishes to become a market leader in electronics, Ribeira Technology, Inc., has no ------- but to diversify its product range.
(A) instance
(B) alternative
(C) preference
(D) reserve

5. Several letters of reference from local community organizations are required for ------- into the Cypress Beach Business Association.
(A) acquisition
(B) acceptance
(C) prospects
(D) improvement

6. Because of ------- regarding noise, the hotel manager has instructed the landscaping staff to avoid operating equipment before 9:30 A.M.
(A) complaints
(B) materials
(C) opponents
(D) symptoms

7. Online communication is an excellent ------- of bringing researchers and practitioners together to discuss practical problems in the field.
(A) technique
(B) approach
(C) instrument
(D) means

8. Payne Carpet's decorative rugs are made from a ------- of synthetic and natural materials.
(A) plan
(B) team
(C) blend
(D) shade

9. The membership ------- should be accompanied by a letter detailing your reasons for wanting to join the association.
(A) guideline
(B) inventory
(C) application
(D) committee

10. With the recent surge in electronic sales, industry analysts are anticipating that the device-to-person ------- will soon surpass earlier predictions.
(A) division
(B) fraction
(C) part
(D) ratio

11. Mr. Yost has decided to rent an apartment for the ------- of his stay in Manchester.
(A) collection
(B) duration
(C) capacity
(D) environment

12. Henriksen Accounting offers a year-end financial summary as ------- of its basic bookkeeping service.
(A) piece
(B) division
(C) section
(D) part

13. Lucio's is a very popular restaurant for weekday lunches, partly because of its ------- to the city's business district.
(A) proximity
(B) location
(C) situation
(D) tendency

14. Safety ------- must be taken by all laboratory employees while working with chemicals that are potentially harmful.
(A) precautions
(B) rules
(C) abilities
(D) guidelines

15. Contributions to our global education ------- will be instrumental in establishing learning opportunities for individuals all over the world.
(A) compartment
(B) opposition
(C) occurrence
(D) initiative

16. Use of this Web site implies ------- with our terms and conditions.
(A) contentment
(B) agreement
(C) placement
(D) development

17. A tax expert will come to our company tomorrow to respond to any ------- you have about recent changes in the law.
(A) components
(B) importance
(C) agreement
(D) concerns

18. The Joseph Wellington Library would like to thank all donors for their ------- during the recent fundraising campaign.
(A) account
(B) privilege
(C) ceremony
(D) generosity

19. This is a ------- to renew your Chamber of Business membership, which expires on August 30.
(A) purpose
(B) conclusion
(C) question
(D) reminder

20. The Produce Growers Association has distributed a pamphlet to area supermarkets that lists fruits and vegetables with the highest ------- of vitamins.
(A) attractions
(B) concentrations
(C) beneficiaries
(D) commands

21. A new law requires manufacturers to put warning labels on products with ingredients known to cause allergic ------- in certain people.
(A) operations
(B) performances
(C) reactions
(D) respondents

22. Ivankoff Industries' venture into experimental technologies will be accomplished by utilizing ------- already available within the company.
(A) purposes
(B) expenses
(C) resources
(D) salaries

23. The Wellborn Science Museum's new astronomy theater has a seating ------- of 250.
(A) aptitude
(B) capacity
(C) demonstration
(D) compliance

24. Lab tests show that a precise combination of the various ------- is necessary for the cleaning compound to be effective.
(A) divisions
(B) prospects
(C) ingredients
(D) compartments

25. With over 50 years of experience, Trust Mutual Bank brings customers the ------- and advice necessary to manage their investments.
(A) inquiry
(B) conversion
(C) expertise
(D) jurisdiction

26. After reviewing the training program for new sales staff, Mr. Vance concluded that more ------- should be placed on networking skills.
(A) appeal
(B) analysis
(C) distinction
(D) emphasis

27. Although our employees did not write the correct address on the shipping form, the machine parts arrived at the dairy farm on -------.
(A) schedule
(B) appointment
(C) authority
(D) condition

28. For applicants seeking employment at Lemnitz Manufacturers, the ------- for submitting materials is May 21.
(A) calendar
(B) intention
(C) deadline
(D) admission

29. In his current role in new product development for Selzern Ltd., Mr. Kumar aims for ------- in new sports equipment.
(A) innovation
(B) implication
(C) consideration
(D) intention

30. The Sanulife Web site brings you news of all the latest ------- in medical research.
(A) novelties
(B) advances
(C) elevations
(D) formations

UNIT 05 | ETS 빈출 형용사

abundant 충분한, 넘치는
- **빈출표현** **abundant** rainfall 풍부한 강수량
  be **abundant** in ~이 풍부하다
- **파생어** abundance 풍부함
  abundantly 충분하게
- **동의어** ample 충분한
- **반의어** insufficient, lacking 부족한

adequate 충분한, 적절한
- **빈출표현** **adequate** amounts of protein 충분한 양의 단백질
  inadequate advertising budget
  불충분한 광고 예산
- **파생어** adequacy 충분함, 적절함
  adequately 충분하게, 적절하게
- **동의어** sufficient 충분한
- **반의어** inadequate 불충분한

accomplished 통달한, 뛰어난
- **빈출표현** an **accomplished** artist 뛰어난 화가
  be **accomplished** at public speaking
  대중 연설에 통달하다
- **파생어** accomplishment 달성, 성취
  accomplish 달성하다, 성취하다
- **동의어** distinguished 뛰어난
- **반의어** incompetent 무능한

affordable 알맞은, 적정한 가격의
- **빈출표현** at an **affordable** price[rate]
  적정한 가격[요금]에
- **파생어** affordability 적당한 가격으로 구입할 수 있는 것
  afford ~할 여유가 있다
- **동의어** reasonable 가격이 적정한
- **반의어** costly, pricey 비싼

accountable 책임이 있는
- **빈출표현** be directly **accountable** to the board of directors
  이사회에 직접 책임이 있다
  be held **accountable** for
  책임이 있는 것으로 간주되다
- **동의어** responsible, in charge of 책임이 있는

appropriate 적절한
- **빈출표현** **appropriate** strategies 적절한 전략들
  It is **appropriate** that she (should) do ...
  그녀가 ~하는 것이 적절하다
- **파생어** appropriately 적절하게
- **동의어** suitable 적절한
- **반의어** inappropriate 부적절한

accurate 정확한
- **빈출표현** make **accurate** records of
  ~을 정확하게 기록하다
  an **accurate** source of information
  정확한 정보 출처
- **파생어** accurately 정확하게
  accuracy 정확(도)
- **반의어** inaccurate 부정확한

attentive 주의 깊은
- **빈출표현** The manager is **attentive** to every detail.
  부장은 모든 세부 사항에 관심을 기울인다.
  The hotel is **attentive** to guests' needs.
  그 호텔은 투숙객들의 요구에 주의를 기울인다.
- **파생어** attention 주의, 관심   attend 참석하다, 신경 쓰다(to)
- **동의어** mindful 신경 쓰는
- **반의어** inattentive 부주의한

additional 추가적인
- **빈출표현** **additional** workers 추가 직원들
  for **additional** information 추가 정보를 위해서는
- **파생어** addition 추가   add A to B A를 B에 추가하다
- **동의어** extra 여분의
  further 더 많은

authentic 진품인, 진짜의
- **빈출표현** **authentic** French cuisine 정통 프랑스 요리
  An **authentic** replacement part is not available.
  정품 교체 부품이 없습니다.
- **파생어** authenticity 진품[진위] 여부

available 이용 가능한, 쓸모 있는

빈출표현 The card is **available** for one year.
이 카드는 1년간 이용이 가능하다.
He is not **available** right now.
그는 지금 바빠서 만날 수 없습니다.

파생어 availability 유용성, 이용할 수 있음
avail 유용하다

동의어 accessible 접근 가능한

반의어 unavailable 이용할 수 없는

brief 간략한; 간략히 보고하다

빈출표현 hold a **brief** meeting
간략한 회의를 하다
fill out a **brief** survey
간결한 설문지를 작성하다

파생어 briefly 간략하게

동의어 concise, succinct 간결한

반의어 lengthy 장황한

competitive 경쟁의, 경쟁심이 강한

빈출표현 **competitive** salary 경쟁력 있는 월급
gain a **competitive** edge from this seminar
이 세미나를 통해 경쟁력을 얻다

파생어 competition 경쟁
compete 경쟁하다

반의어 uncompetitive 경쟁하지 않는, 경쟁력이 없는

complete 완전한, 완성된; 완성하다

빈출표현 The work will be **complete** soon.
그 작업은 곧 끝날 것이다.
hand in the **complete** report
완성된 보고서를 제출하다

파생어 completion 완성
completely 완전히

동의어 finished 마무리된

반의어 incomplete 불완전한

complimentary 무료의

빈출표현 **complimentary** wireless Internet access
무료 무선 인터넷 사용
Complimentary refreshments will be served.
무료 다과가 제공될 예정입니다.

consecutive 연속적인, 계속되는

빈출표현 for three **consecutive**[successive] years
3년 연속으로
for the second **consecutive** month
2개월 연속으로

파생어 consecution 연속
consecutively 연속적으로

동의어 successive 연속하는

반의어 intermittent 간헐적인

contingent 조건으로 하는, 우발적인

빈출표현 **contingent** on[upon]
~을 조건으로 하는

파생어 contingency 비상 상황, 만일의 사태

동의어 accidental 우발적인

deliberate 고의의, 신중한

빈출표현 He is **deliberate** in his actions.
그는 행동에 신중하다.
in a **deliberate** way 신중하게

파생어 deliberation 심사숙고
deliberately 고의로, 신중히

동의어 prudent 신중한

반의어 careless, heedless 부주의한

demanding 지나치게 요구하는, 까다로운

빈출표현 try to satisfy a **demanding** customer
까다로운 고객을 만족시키려고 애쓰다
have a **demanding** job
힘든 직업을 갖고 있다

파생어 demand 수요; 요구하다

동의어 tricky 까다로운

반의어 undemanding 까다롭지 않은

detailed 자세한, 상세한

빈출표현 detailed instructions
상세한 설명서
for more **detailed** information
더 자세한 정보를 얻으려면

파생어 detail 세부사항; 상세히 하다

disappointing 실망스러운

빈출표현 this quarter's **disappointing** revenue
이번 분기의 실망스러운 매출
good food but **disappointing** service
훌륭한 음식이지만 실망스러운 서비스
파생어 disappointment 실망
disappointed 실망감을 느낀
동의어 discouraging 낙담시키는
반의어 satisfactory 만족스러운

due ~하기로 예정된, 지불해야 하는

빈출표현 The next bus is **due** in 10 minutes.
다음 버스는 10분 후에 있습니다.
The report is **due** next Monday.
보고서는 다음 주 월요일까지 제출해야 한다.
동의어 expected, scheduled 예정된
반의어 overdue (지불) 기한이 지난

durable 내구성 있는

빈출표현 a highly **durable** material
매우 내구성이 뛰어난 재료
The product is lightweight, portable, and
durable.
그 제품은 가볍고 휴대 가능하며 내구성이 좋다.
파생어 durability 내구성
동의어 strong, sturdy 튼튼한
반의어 fragile 깨지기 쉬운

enclosed 동봉된, 둘러싸인

빈출표현 the **enclosed** document 동봉된 서류
the **enclosed** parking area
벽으로 둘러싸인 주차장
파생어 enclosure 동봉, 둘러쌈
enclose 동봉하다, 둘러싸다
동의어 attached 첨부된
반의어 open 공개된

equivalent 동일한, 상응하는; 등가물

빈출표현 be **equivalent** to
~에 상응하다, ~와 동일하다
$30 or the **equivalent** amount
30달러 또는 그에 상당하는 액수

essential 필수적인, 중요한

빈출표현 **essential** part
필수적인 부분
It is **essential** that + 주어 + (should) do
필수적으로 ~해야만 한다
파생어 essence 본질, 정수
essentially 필수적으로
동의어 necessary 꼭 필요한
반의어 optional 선택적인

expanded 확충된, 팽창한

빈출표현 offer **expanded** service
확대된 서비스를 제공하다
파생어 expansion 팽창, 확대
expand 확장하다, 발전하다
expansive 팽창력 있는, 발전적인
동의어 enlarged 확대된
반의어 diminished 줄어든

experienced 경험이 많은

빈출표현 **experienced** job candidates
경험이 많은 채용 후보자들
파생어 experience 경험; 경험하다
동의어 seasoned 경험 많은
반의어 inexperienced 경험 없는
관련어구 보통 구인 광고에서 자격 요건을 말할 때,
experienced(경험 많은), dedicated(헌신적인),
motivated(적극적인), qualified(자격을 갖춘)와 같이
과거분사 형태의 어휘를 많이 쓴다.

extensive 광범위한, 폭넓은

빈출표현 have **extensive** experience in the industry
업계에 폭넓은 경험이 있다
embark on **extensive** renovations
대대적인 개조 작업에 착수하다
파생어 extensively 널리, 광범위하게
동의어 broad 폭넓은
반의어 limited 제한된

familiar 익숙한, 잘 알고 있는, 친한

빈출표현 be **familiar** with the rules
그 규칙들에 익숙하다
a touchscreen with a **familiar** layout
익숙한 구조의 터치스크린
파생어 familiarity 익숙함
familiarize oneself with ~을 숙지하다
동의어 acquainted 알고 있는
반의어 unfamiliar 익숙하지 않은

favorable 유리한

빈출표현 The terms of the contract are **favorable** to us.
그 계약 조건은 우리에게 유리하다.
favorable weather conditions
좋은 날씨
파생어 favor 호의; 찬성하다, 좋아하다
favorite 좋아하는
동의어 advantageous 유리한

feasible 실행 가능한, 실현 가능성이 있는

빈출표현 a **feasible** plan 실현 가능한 계획
New technology has made self-driving cars
feasible.
신기술은 자율주행차를 실현 가능하게 만들었다.
파생어 feasibility 실행 가능성

fragile 부서지기[손상되기] 쉬운

빈출표현 **fragile** products 깨지기 쉬운 제품
Please remove any **fragile** or valuable personal
items from your work space.
손상되기 쉽거나 귀중한 개인 물건은 업무 공간에서 치우세요.
동의어 delicate 다치기[부서지기] 쉬운
반의어 durable 견고한

grateful 감사하는, 기분 좋은

빈출표현 I would be **grateful** if … ~라면 감사하겠습니다
All members of the sales team are **grateful**
for … 영업팀 전원은 ~에 대해 감사드립니다
파생어 gratefulness 감사함
gratefully 감사하여
동의어 thankful 감사하는
반의어 ungrateful 배은망덕한

impending 임박한, 곧 일어날

빈출표현 **impending** issues 임박한 문제들
an **impending** conference 임박한 회의
파생어 impendence 임박함
impend 임박하다
동의어 imminent 임박한
upcoming 곧 있을
반의어 past 지난

impressive 인상적인

빈출표현 an **impressive** performance
인상적인 공연
The speech was **impressive.**
연설이 인상적이었다.
파생어 impression 인상, 감명
impress 감동시키다
동의어 notable 주목할 만한
반의어 common 평범한

improper 부적절한, 부도덕한

빈출표현 an **improper** conclusion 부적절한 결론
improper for the occasion 경우에 맞지 않는
파생어 improperness 부당함
improperly 부적절하게
동의어 unsuitable 부적절한
반의어 proper 적절한

innovative 혁신적인

빈출표현 her **innovative** ideas
그녀의 혁신적인 아이디어들
an **innovative** product 혁신적인 제품
파생어 innovation 혁신
innovate 혁신하다
동의어 unprecedented 유례없는, 참신한

lucrative 수익성이 좋은, 유리한

빈출표현 The contract is **lucrative.**
그 계약은 수익성이 좋다.
work in a **lucrative** industry
수익성이 좋은 산업에서 일하다
동의어 profitable 이익이 나는
반의어 unprofitable 이익이 나지 않는

missing 없어진, 놓친, 분실한

빈출표현 a **missing** document 분실한 문서
Missing belongings can be found at the front
desk.
잃어버린 소지품들은 안내 데스크에서 찾으실 수 있습니다.
파생어 miss 놓치다, 빠지다, 그리워하다
동의어 lost 분실된
반의어 found 발견된

operational 작동[가동]하는, 운영상의

- **빈출표현** fully **operational** 완전 가동하는
  operational costs 운영비
- **파생어** operation (기계의) 조작, 운영, 수술
  operate 움직이다, 작용하다, 영향을 미치다
- **동의어** working 작동하는
- **반의어** inoperative 작동하지 않는

principal 주요한, 주된; 학장, 교장

- **빈출표현** **principal** speaker 주요 연사
  principal role 주된 역할
- **동의어** major 주요한
  key 핵심적인

outstanding 뛰어난, 훌륭한; 미납의

- **빈출표현** **outstanding** service 훌륭한 서비스
  outstanding debt 미변제 채무
- **파생어** outstand 눈에 띄다, 돌출하다
  outstandingly 두드러지게
- **동의어** distinguished 뛰어난
  unpaid 미납의
- **반의어** inferior 열등한

probable 가능성 있는, 있음직한; 유망한

- **빈출표현** **probable** rate increases
  가능성 있는 요금 인상
  a **probable** candidate 유망한 후보자
- **파생어** probability 가능성
  probably 아마도
- **동의어** possible 가능한
- **반의어** improbable 가능성이 없는

particular 특정한

- **빈출표현** in particular 특히
  in a **particular** area 특정 분야에서
- **파생어** particularly 특히
  particulars (복수형으로) 세부 사항

receptive 수용하는, 받아들이는

- **빈출표현** He is **receptive** to new ideas.
  그는 새로운 아이디어들에 수용적이다.
  Customers were not **receptive** to the price increase.
  고객들은 가격 인상을 받아들이지 않았다.
- **파생어** reception 연회
  receive 받아들이다
- **동의어** hospitable 환대하는
  open-minded 마음이 열린

perishable 부패하기 쉬운

- **빈출표현** **perishable** food[goods]
  부패하기 쉬운 음식[제품]
  Most **perishable** foods must be refrigerated or frozen.
  대부분의 부패하기 쉬운 음식들은 냉장 또는 냉동되어야 한다.
- **파생어** perish 부패하다, 소멸되다

reliable 믿을 만한, 신뢰할 만한

- **빈출표현** the area's most **reliable** energy supplier
  지역에서 가장 믿을 만한 에너지 공급업체
  reliable service 믿을 만한 서비스
- **파생어** reliability 믿을 만함
  rely (heavily) on[upon] ~을 (몹시) 의존하다
  reliant 의존하는
- **동의어** dependable 믿을 만한
- **반의어** unreliable 믿을 수 없는

preliminary 예비의; 예비 단계

- **빈출표현** **preliminary** tests 예비 시험
  do **preliminary** market research
  사전 시장 조사를 하다
- **동의어** preparatory 예비의
- **반의어** final 최종적인

remote 거리가 떨어진, 희박한

- **빈출표현** at a **remote** distance 멀리 떨어져서
  the possibility is **remote** 가능성이 희박하다
- **파생어** remotely 떨어져서
- **동의어** distant 멀리 떨어진
- **반의어** close, nearby 가까운

rewarding 가치가 있는, 보람 있는

빈출표현 The job is **rewarding**. 그 직업은 보람 있다.
a **rewarding** discussion 가치 있는 토론회
파생어 reward 보상; 보상하다
동의어 worthy 가치 있는
반의어 worthless 가치 없는

straightforward 직접적인, 솔직한

빈출표현 The question is **straightforward.**
그 질문은 직접적이다.
파생어 straightforwardly 직접적으로, 솔직하게
동의어 candid 솔직한
반의어 dishonest 정직하지 않은

rigorous 엄격한, 가혹한

빈출표현 **rigorous** training 엄격한 훈련
be subjected to a **rigorous** test
엄격한 테스트를 거치다
파생어 rigorously 엄격하게
동의어 rigid, thorough 엄격한
반의어 flexible 유연성 있는

stringent 엄격한

빈출표현 a **stringent** inspection process
엄격한 검사 과정
stringent requirements 엄격한 규정
파생어 stringency 엄격함
stringently 엄격하게
동의어 strict, rigorous 엄격한
반의어 lenient 관대한

sensitive 민감한, 섬세한

빈출표현 a **sensitive** device 민감한 기기
She is very **sensitive** to loud noise.
그녀는 큰 소음에 매우 민감하다.
파생어 sensitivity 민감함
동의어 delicate 섬세한
반의어 insensitive 무감각한

subsequent 그 다음의, 그 후의

빈출표현 **subsequent** to ~ 후에, ~ 다음에
subsequent events 그 이후에 일어난 일들
파생어 subsequently 그 뒤에, 나중에
subsequence 뒤에 옴, 이어서 일어나는 것

spacious 넓은, 널찍한

빈출표현 a **spacious** interior 넓은 실내
The hall is **spacious**. 그 홀은 넓다.
파생어 space 공간
spaciously 넓게
동의어 roomy 넓은
vast 광활한
반의어 narrow 좁은

substantial 상당한

빈출표현 receive a **substantial** discount
상당한 할인을 받다
make a **substantial** profit
상당한 이윤을 내다
파생어 substantially 상당히
관련어구 substantially increase 상당히 증가하다
substantially more effective 상당히 더 효과적인

spontaneous 자발적인

빈출표현 make a **spontaneous** decision
자발적인 결정을 하다
spontaneous assistance from local residents
지역 주민들로부터의 자발적인 지원
파생어 spontaneously 자발적으로
유의어 voluntary 자발적인

sufficient 충분한

빈출표현 The fuel in this tank is **sufficient.**
이 탱크의 연료는 충분하다.
without holding **sufficient** discussions
충분한 논의를 거치지 않고
파생어 suffice 충분하다
sufficiently 충분히
동의어 enough 충분한
반의어 insufficient 불충분한

temporary 임시의, 일시적인

- **빈출표현** the **temporary** closing 임시 휴업
  a **temporary** employee 임시 직원
- **파생어** temporarily 임시로
- **동의어** makeshift, provisional 임시 변통의
- **반의어** permanent 영구적인

tentative 잠정적인

- **빈출표현** make a **tentative** reservation 임시 예약하다
  Enclosed is the **tentative** itinerary for your trip to Bangkok.
  귀하의 방콕 여행에 대한 잠정적인 여행 일정이 동봉되어 있습니다.
- **파생어** tentatively 잠정적으로

thorough 철저한, 빈틈없는

- **빈출표현** due to **thorough** management
  철저한 관리 때문에
  A **thorough** inspection is needed.
  철저한 조사가 필요하다.
- **파생어** thoroughly 철저하게
- **동의어** rigorous, stringent 엄격한
- **반의어** lax 느슨한, 허술한

unforeseen 예측하지 못한, 뜻밖의

- **빈출표현** due to **unforeseen** demand
  예상치 못한 수요 때문에
  Unforeseen circumstances sometimes arise.
  예상치 못한 상황이 때때로 발생한다.
- **동의어** unanticipated, unexpected 예상 밖의
- **반의어** predictable 예측 가능한

unprecedented 전례 없는

- **빈출표현** experience **unprecedented** growth
  전례 없는 성장을 경험하다
- **파생어** unprecedentedly 전례 없이
- **반의어** common 흔한
  customary 관례적인
- **관련어구** unprecedentedly high oil prices
  전례 없이 높은 유가

valid 유효한, 타당한

- **빈출표현** **valid** identification card 유효한 신분증
  This is **valid** until June 30.
  이것은 6월 30일까지 유효합니다.
- **파생어** validity 유효성
- **동의어** good, effective 유효한
- **반의어** invalid 유효하지 않은

valuable 가치 있는, 유익한, 값비싼

- **빈출표현** learn a **valuable** lesson 값진 교훈을 얻다
  purchase **valuable** antiques
  가치가 큰 골동품을 구입하다
- **파생어** value 가치
- **유의어** invaluable 매우 귀중한
- **반의어** useless 쓸모 없는

various 다양한, 가지각색의

- **빈출표현** **various** factors 다양한 요소들
  various kinds of software packages
  여러 가지 종류의 소프트웨어 패키지들
- **파생어** variety 다양성
  vary 다양하다
- **동의어** diverse 다양한
- **반의어** similar 유사한

versatile 다재다능한, 다용도의, 다목적의

- **빈출표현** **versatile** enough to provide administrative support
  행정상의 지원을 제공할 만큼 충분히 다재다능한
  The new models are more durable and more **versatile**.
  신규 모델은 더 견고하고 용도가 더 많다.

vulnerable 취약한, 상처받기 쉬운

- **빈출표현** **vulnerable** to staining 착색에 취약한
  more **vulnerable** to changes in the environment
  환경 변화에 더 취약한
- **유의어** sensitive, susceptible 민감한

VOCABULARY PRACTICE

정답 및 해설 p.96

A 다음 주어진 문장에서 적절한 어휘를 고르세요.

1 The most [(A) essential (B) enclosed] task is to finish designing the new corporate logo.

2 We want to maintain a [(A) favorite (B) favorable] reputation at all times.

3 We plan to hire [(A) multiplied (B) additional] workers because of the increased production quota.

4 The success of a product depends on [(A) various (B) useful] factors.

5 Due to the [(A) accidental (B) abundant] rainfall, water levels are much higher.

6 A conservative investment strategy seems [(A) alternative (B) appropriate] in light of the company's current financial situation.

7 As of October 1, all books borrowed from the Queenstown Library will be [(A) due (B) payable] three weeks from the checkout date.

B 다음 문장의 빈칸에 적절한 어휘를 고르세요.

8 A ------- company identification card is required before entering certain restricted areas of the Koles Lumber plant.
(A) relative   (B) consenting
(C) severe   (D) valid

9 Before the laboratory carts can be used to transport ------- materials, technicians must wipe all exposed surfaces with a disinfectant cloth.
(A) vague   (B) passive
(C) sensitive   (D) demonstrative

10 The computer workshop schedule is still considered -------, and we will keep you posted on any changes.
(A) tentative   (B) vigilant
(C) contemporary   (D) infinite

11 The Rutledge Corporation has announced price increases across its entire product line following an ------- rise in the cost of raw materials.
(A) accomplished   (B) abundant
(C) unprecedented   (D) informed

12 The new play received ------- reviews by most of the local theater critics, despite the high number of ticket sales.
(A) disappointing   (B) perceivable
(C) operational   (D) potential

13 Although the possibility of damage in transit is -------, the client has requested that the shipment of equipment to the Vadeleux facility be insured.
(A) contrary   (B) concerned
(C) detached   (D) remote

14 Due to a lack of adequate refrigerated vehicles, Hurst Trucking Co. will no longer transport ------- goods.
(A) durable   (B) spoiled
(C) fragile   (D) perishable

15 Customers concerned about ------- utility rate increases will be given the option of prepaying for three months of service at today's rate.
(A) considerate   (B) instructive
(C) probable   (D) expended

PART 5 어휘 | UNIT 05

UNIT 06 | ETS 빈출 형용사 어구

a broad range of 폭넓은 범위의

빈출표현
A **broad range of** samples will be sent out.
다양한 샘플들이 발송될 것이다.
Our head designer has **a broad range of**
interests. 우리 수석 디자이너는 폭넓은 관심사를 갖고 있다.

파생어 broaden 넓히다 broadly 널리
동의어 a variety of, a wide selection of 다양한

a significant number of 상당수의

빈출표현
a significant number of visitors
상당수의 방문객들
receive **a significant number** of new orders
during the holiday 휴일 동안 상당수의 새 주문을 받다

파생어 significance 중요성 significantly 상당히
동의어 a large number of 아주 많은

be accessible to ~에게 접근이 가능하다

빈출표현
The information **is** easily **accessible to** anyone.
그 정보는 누구나 쉽게 접근이 가능하다.
The research room **is accessible to** all library
users. 연구실은 모든 도서관 이용자들이 출입할 수 있다.

파생어 access 접근, 이용; 접근하다
have access to ~에 접근할 수 있다

be accustomed to
~에 익숙해지다, 적응하다

빈출표현
New employees **are** not **accustomed to**
a new environment.
신입직원들은 새로운 환경에 익숙하지 않다.
Our employees **are accustomed to** working
overtime. 우리 직원들은 초과근무를 하는 데 익숙하다.

파생어 accustom ~을 익숙하게 하다
동의어 be[get] used to ~에 익숙해지다

be acquainted with
~을 알고 있다, 아는 사이다

빈출표현
I have **been** personally **acquainted with**
Dr. Kim for over ten years.
저는 김 박사님과 10년 이상 개인적으로 아는 사이입니다.
be well **acquainted with** photo software
사진 소프트웨어에 대해 잘 알다

파생어 acquaintance 아는 사람, 알고 있음
acquaint 알게 하다, 소개하다

be adaptable to ~에 적응할 수 있다

빈출표현
He **is adaptable to** different work
environments. 그는 다른 근무 환경에 적응할 수 있다.
a recipe **adaptable to** different styles of
cooking 다양한 요리 스타일에 맞출 수 있는 조리법

파생어 adaptation 적응, 각색 adaptability 적응력
adapt to ~에 적응하다

be associated with
~와 관련[연루]되어 있다

빈출표현
The problem **is associated with** the financial
restraints.
그 문제는 재정적 제약과 연관이 있다.

파생어 associate 동료
associate oneself with ~와 친하게 지내다

be aware of[that] ~을 알다

빈출표현
I **am** fully **aware of** the fact that ...
나는 ~라는 사실을 잘 알고 있다
Drivers should **be aware of** sudden weather
changes.
운전자들은 갑작스러운 날씨 변화를 알아야 한다.

파생어 awareness 인식, 앎
동의어 be conscious of, be cognizant of ~을 인식하다

be capable of ~할 수 있다

빈출표현
mobile phones **capable of** browsing
the Internet 인터넷 검색을 할 수 있는 휴대폰
a factory **capable of** producing trucks and
buses 트럭과 버스를 생산할 수 있는 공장

파생어 capability 능력, 수용력
동의어 be able to ~할 수 있다
반의어 incapable ~할 수 없는

be central to ~의 중심을 이루다

빈출표현
Motivating employees **is central to** a
manager's leadership.
직원들에게 동기 부여를 하는 것이 관리자 리더십의
핵심이다.
Online advertising **is central to** the marketing
strategy.
온라인 광고가 마케팅 전략의 중심이다.

파생어 centralize 중심에 모으다

182

be committed to ~에 전념하다, 헌신하다

[빈출표현] **be committed to** satisfying customers
고객을 만족시키는 데 전념하다
[파생어] commitment 전념, 헌신
[동의어] be dedicated to ~에 전념하다
be devoted to ~에 헌신하다
[관련어구] **be dedicated to** the company
회사에 헌신하다

be compatible with ~와 호환되다

[빈출표현] software **compatible with** other systems
다른 시스템과 호환 가능한 소프트웨어
640C printer **is compatible with** most computers.
640C 인쇄기는 대부분의 컴퓨터와 호환된다.
[파생어] compatibility 호환성

be concerned about[over]
~에 대해 걱정하다, 관심을 쏟다

[빈출표현] We **are concerned about** the financial status. 우리는 재정 상태에 대해 우려한다.
[파생어] concern 관심, 걱정; ~와 관련되다
concerning ~에 관한
[반의어] unconcerned 걱정하지 않는

be considerate of ~을 배려하다

[빈출표현] He **is** always **considerate of** his juniors.
그는 항상 부하 직원들을 배려한다.
Please **be considerate of** other users.
다른 사용자들을 배려해 주세요.
[파생어] consider 고려하다
considerately 상냥하게

be consistent with
~와 일치하다, 일관되다

[빈출표현] The figures **are consistent with** the old findings. 이 수치들은 이전에 밝혀진 사실들과 일치한다.
Our store hours **are consistent with** those of other branches. 저희 상점의 영업시간은 다른 지점들의 영업시간과 동일합니다.
[파생어] consistency 일관성
consistently 일관되게
[반의어] inconsistent 일관성이 없는

be dedicated to ~에 헌신하다

[빈출표현] Professor Moon has **been dedicated to** this university during his tenure.
문 교수는 재직 기간 동안 이 대학에 헌신해 왔다.
The Green Parks Club **is dedicated to** protecting the environment.
그린 파크 클럽은 환경보호에 헌신적이다.
[파생어] dedication 헌신
[동의어] be devoted[committed] to ~에 헌신하다

be eager about[to do/that]
~을 갈망하다

[빈출표현] He **is** always **eager about** huge tasks.
그는 늘 큰일을 하고자 갈망한다.
We **are eager to** hear the sales results.
우리는 매출 실적을 꼭 듣고 싶다.
[파생어] eagerness 갈망
eagerly 갈망하여

be eligible for[to do]
~에 대해 자격이 되다

[빈출표현] Ms. Kim **is eligible for** the promotion.
김 씨는 이번 승진에 자격이 된다.
eligible to apply for the manager position
부장직에 지원할 자격이 되는
[파생어] eligibility 적임, 적격
[동의어] be entitled to, be qualified for
~에 자격이 있다

be entitled to ~할 자격[권리]이 있다

[빈출표현] All the customers **are entitled to** a full refund.
모든 고객은 전액 환불을 받을 자격이 있다.
Silver Club members **are entitled to** special discounts.
실버 클럽 회원은 특별 할인을 받을 수 있습니다
[파생어] entitlement 자격, 권리
entitle 자격을 부여하다
[반의어] disentitle 자격을 빼앗다

be equipped with ~을 갖추고 있다

[빈출표현] The conference room **is equipped with** visual aids.
그 회의장은 시각 교구들을 갖추고 있다.
The train station **is equipped with** four elevators.
그 역에는 네 개의 승강기가 갖춰져 있다.
[파생어] equipment 장비
equip ~을 갖추다
[동의어] be outfitted with ~을 갖추고 있다

be exempt from ~로부터 면제되다, 제외되다

빈출표현
be exempt from taxes
세금이 면제되다
be exempt from membership fees
회비가 면제되다

파생어
exemption 면제
exempt 면제하다; 면제되는
exemptible 면제받을 수 있는

be prepared for[to do] ~할 준비가 되다

빈출표현
be prepared to speak at the meeting
회의에서 연설할 준비가 되다
be prepared for the inspection
점검을 받을 준비가 되다

파생어
preparation 준비, 대비
prepare for ~을 준비하다

동의어
be ready to[for] ~할 준비가 되다

be expected to do ~할 것으로 예상되다

빈출표현
The president **is expected to** arrive tomorrow.
회장은 내일 도착하리라 예상된다.
Sales **are expected to** increase this quarter.
이번 분기에는 매출 증대가 예상된다.

파생어
expectation 기대
expect A to do A가 ~하리라 예상하다

동의어
be anticipated[predicted] to
~할 것으로 예상되다

be responsible for
~에 책임이 있다, ~을 관할하다

빈출표현
The manager **is responsible for** supervising assemblers.
관리자는 조립자들을 감독하는 책임을 지고 있다.

파생어
responsibility 책임
take[have] responsibility for ~을 책임지다

동의어
be in charge of ~을 담당하다

be faced with ~에 직면하다

빈출표현
The company **is** currently **faced with** financial difficulties.
그 기업은 현재 재정적 어려움에 직면해 있다.
The manager **is faced with** many challenging decisions. 부장은 많은 어려운 결정들에 직면해 있다.

파생어
face 얼굴; 직면하다
facing ~을 직면하는

동의어
encounter, run into 직면하다

be restricted to ~로 제한되다

빈출표현
This event **is restricted to** the first 50 customers.
이번 행사는 최초 50명의 고객들로 제한된다.

파생어
restriction 규제, 제약, 규정
restrict 제한하다

동의어
be limited to ~로 한정되다

be hesitant to do
~하는 것을 주저하다, 망설이다

빈출표현
He **is hesitant to** apply for a position overseas.
그는 해외 직책에 지원하기를 꺼린다.

파생어
hesitate 주저하다, 망설이다
hesitation 주저, 망설임

동의어
be reluctant to ~을 꺼리다

반의어
be willing to 기꺼이 ~하다

be satisfied with ~에 만족하다

빈출표현
I **was satisfied with** the results.
나는 그 결과에 만족했다.
Most customers **are satisfied with** our delivery service.
대부분의 고객들은 우리의 배달 서비스에 만족한다.

파생어
satisfaction 만족
satisfy 만족시키다
satisfactory 만족스러운

동의어
be pleased[happy/content] with ~에 만족하다

be noted for ~로 유명하다

빈출표현
The car **is noted for** its stylish appearance.
그 자동차는 멋진 외관으로 유명하다.

파생어
note 메모, 지폐; 지적하다
notable 주목할 만한
notably 특히, 현저히

동의어
be known[renowned/famous] for
~로 유명하다

be scheduled to do ~할 예정이다

빈출표현
The speech **is scheduled to** begin at 7.
연설은 7시에 시작할 예정이다.
The delegates **were scheduled to** attend a tour. 대표자들은 견학을 할 예정이었다.

동의어
be expected to, be due to, be slated to, be supposed to ~할 예정이다

be similar to ~와 유사하다, 비슷하다

빈출표현 **be similar to** other towns
다른 도시들과 유사하다
be similar to other artists' works
다른 화가의 작품들과 유사하다

파생어 similarity 유사성

동의어 be analogous to ~와 유사하다

highly qualified 훌륭한 자질을 지닌

빈출표현 The company is known for its **highly qualified** consultants.
그 회사는 훌륭한 자질을 지닌 컨설턴트들로 유명하다.
a caterer with **highly qualified** chefs
훌륭한 요리사들이 있는 출장 연회 업체

파생어 qualification 자격 요건, 능력, 자질
qualify ~에게 자격을 부여하다

be subject to
~의 대상이다, ~을 조건으로 하다

빈출표현 The schedule **is subject to** change without prior notice.
일정은 사전 통보 없이 변경될 수 있습니다.
The budget **is subject to** the executive's approval. 예산은 이사의 승인에 달려 있습니다.

파생어 subject 주제, 과목; 종속하는; 복종시키다

inclement weather 궂은 날씨

빈출표현 in the event of **inclement weather** or any other unforeseen circumstances
궂은 날씨 또는 여타 예상치 못한 상황의 경우
Inclement weather was responsible for the low turnout. 저조한 참석률은 궂은 날씨 때문이었다.

유의어 unfavorable[adverse / bad / poor / severe] weather 궂은 날씨

be suitable for ~에 적합하다

빈출표현 The problem **is suitable for** the meeting agenda.
그 문제는 회의 의제에 적합하다.
This attractive poster **is suitable for** framing.
이 멋진 포스터는 액자로 보관하기에 적합하다.

파생어 suit 어울리다
suitably 적절하게

동의어 be suited[appropriate] for ~에 적합하다

preferred method 선호되는 방식

빈출표현 a **preferred** payment **method**
선호되는 지불 방식
A master's degree will be **preferred**.
석사학위 소유자를 우대합니다.

파생어 preference 선호
preferential 우선의, 선택적인[차별적인]
preferable 바람직한
preferred 선호되는

be willing to do 기꺼이 ~하다

빈출표현 Ms. Sato **was willing to** train the new staff.
사토 씨는 기꺼이 신입 직원들을 교육하고 싶어 했다.
be willing to work overtime
기꺼이 야근하다

파생어 willingness 의향, 의사
willingly 기꺼이

반의어 be unwilling[reluctant] to ~하기를 꺼리다

promising candidate 전도유망한 후보자

빈출표현 be selected from among **promising candidates**
전도유망한 후보자들 중에서 선택되다
One of the most **promising candidates** was eliminated.
가장 유력한 지원자 중 한 명이 제외됐다.

파생어 promised 약속된

generous donation 후한 기부

빈출표현 Your **generous donation** will go toward the library's renovation projects.
귀하의 후한 기부금은 도서관 개조 작업에 사용될 것입니다.

파생어 generously 아낌없이, 관대하게

동의어 lenient 관대한

관련어구 donate[contribute / offer] generously
아낌없이 기증[기여 / 제공]하다

strictly confidential 절대 기밀의

빈출표현 keep customers' personal information **strictly confidential**
고객들의 개인 정보를 절대 기밀로 유지하다
a **strictly confidential** e-mail message
극비 이메일 메시지

파생어 confidentiality 기밀성
confidentially 비밀스럽게

동의어 classified 기밀로 분류된

반의어 open 공개된

A 다음 주어진 문장에서 적절한 어휘를 고르세요.

1 The most [(A) preferred (B) preferential] payment method is cash.

2 Several [(A) promising (B) promised] candidates registered with our job placement agency.

3 Everyone was [(A) satisfied (B) satisfactory] with your idea.

4 The computer is [(A) equipping (B) equipped] with speakers.

5 The information you provide on this questionnaire is strictly [(A) potential (B) confidential].

6 Candidates for the position of assistant manager must be [(A) capable (B) ready] of assuming a wide range of responsibilities.

7 Boats propelled only by oars or paddles are [(A) exempt (B) subject] from state licensing requirements for motor-driven watercraft.

B 다음 문장의 빈칸에 적절한 어휘를 고르세요.

8 City officials determined that Mr. Han is financially ------- for repairing the damaged pavement by his shop.
(A) considerable   (B) responsible
(C) expensive   (D) productive

9 The music hall is supported largely by ------- donations from local companies.
(A) tolerant   (B) thorough
(C) generous   (D) capable

10 Mr. Tomita was pleased that Ms. Arai was ------- to adjust her schedule at the last minute in order to revise the financial report.
(A) busy   (B) willing
(C) changed   (D) timely

11 Marburg Electro Company is ------- to report a significant increase in profits for the year.
(A) earned   (B) outgrown
(C) expected   (D) risen

12 Food exporters are ------- to form business relationships in countries whose economies are growing rapidly.
(A) constructive   (B) eager
(C) relative   (D) delicious

13 Our overseas branch office is ------- to open in Taipei next month.
(A) scheduled   (B) advanced
(C) informed   (D) maintained

14 A ------- number of technical service requests from users prompted Hisocom Corporation to upgrade its Internet servers.
(A) sole   (B) significant
(C) purposeful   (D) capable

15 In the event of ------- weather, the employee recognition ceremony will be relocated from the gardens to the conference room.
(A) vigilant   (B) unfounded
(C) susceptible   (D) inclement

ETS TEST

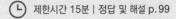

제한시간 15분 | 정답 및 해설 p.99

PART 5 어휘 | UNIT 05&06

1. Almost 60 percent of teachers surveyed reported receiving ------- preparation for their jobs through Stuget University's online courses.
(A) adequate
(B) numerous
(C) thankful
(D) adjacent

2. Sassen Motors' newest car features a stylish dashboard design and a ------- interior.
(A) widespread
(B) plenty
(C) prevalent
(D) spacious

3. Franklin Catering Company offers a ------- range of menu choices for both lunch and dinner.
(A) satisfied
(B) hopeful
(C) dividing
(D) broad

4. The terms and conditions outlined in this document are ------- to change without notice.
(A) dependent
(B) subject
(C) immediate
(D) final

5. The city's water supply must meet ------- water-quality standards set by government health-service agencies.
(A) close
(B) dominant
(C) extended
(D) stringent

6. A report in the *Journal of the Southern Agricultural Society* suggests that consumers are increasingly ------- about where their produce is grown.
(A) exceptional
(B) essential
(C) concerned
(D) significant

7. Recent graduates apply for work at Harnum Corporation because it offers ------- opportunities for advancement.
(A) outgrown
(B) outlying
(C) outstretched
(D) outstanding

8. The warranty on Lelen saucepans does not apply to damages that result from ------- use of cookware.
(A) concise
(B) equivalent
(C) submissive
(D) improper

9. The blueprint for the Sbraga Hotel includes 200 guest rooms, a restaurant, and an ------- parking area.
(A) enclosed
(B) opposite
(C) absent
(D) innocent

10. Our team of specialists works with clients to develop ------- marketing strategies.
(A) unavailable
(B) innovative
(C) resolved
(D) convinced

11. Employees are ------- to take family and medical leave if they have been employed for at least twelve months.
(A) eligible
(B) desirable
(C) preferred
(D) suitable

12. New patients should arrive fifteen minutes before their scheduled appointment time to allow ------- time to complete any paperwork.
(A) sufficient
(B) liberal
(C) thorough
(D) entire

13. Peerplane, Inc., stated yesterday that its new prototype airplane has passed all ------- testing.
(A) undeveloped
(B) foregone
(C) subordinate
(D) preliminary

14. The projected expansion of the apparel division remains ------- on final approval of the necessary budget allocations.
(A) contingent
(B) eventual
(C) hopeful
(D) speculative

15. ------- events showed that the bank's decision to acquire the property adjacent to their main branch had been a good one.
(A) Suspended
(B) Subsequent
(C) Subjective
(D) Sustaining

16. At Energy Coalition, Inc., our primary goal is to make solar energy more ------- to all consumers.
(A) influenced
(B) repeated
(C) affordable
(D) average

17. The directors voted to extend evening hours at local libraries to make them more ------- to patrons who cannot visit them during the day.
(A) educated
(B) capable
(C) appreciative
(D) accessible

18. The street guide to Tompkinsville has been compiled from ------- national and local maps.
(A) decided
(B) delinquent
(C) dependent
(D) detailed

19. Since the labeling machine broke down last night, sending out the deliveries this morning was not -------.
(A) potential
(B) concise
(C) feasible
(D) credible

20. Danner Corporation met its recruitment goals for the third ------- year.
(A) following
(B) consecutive
(C) approximate
(D) absolute

21. Masami Airlines will soon offer ------- service from Nagoya to twelve additional cities throughout Asia and Europe.
(A) accumulated
(B) reinforced
(C) translated
(D) expanded

22. Kyung Bin Yi has been praised for her role in securing several ------- contracts for Dwyer Industries' fledgling mobile-computing division.
(A) arbitrary
(B) spacious
(C) absent
(D) lucrative

23. The managers who took yesterday's tour said that the factory's assembly line is an ------- example of efficiency.
(A) acquired
(B) equipped
(C) indecisive
(D) impressive

24. The Global Marketing Manager is required to travel extensively and so must be ------- to unfamiliar situations.
(A) opposed
(B) versatile
(C) relative
(D) adaptable

25. Some students have complained to the department chairperson that Physics 301, though open to third-year students, is much too ------- for them.
(A) stubborn
(B) demanding
(C) tangled
(D) uneasy

26. The workers from Sanders Plumbing have earned a reputation for ------- and courteous service.
(A) possible
(B) numerous
(C) previous
(D) reliable

27. The full report on the company's budget decisions will not be available until the end of the week, but a ------- memo will be issued sometime today.
(A) constant
(B) momentary
(C) brief
(D) free

28. A well-prepared proposal for a large project will take a ------- amount of time and resources to produce.
(A) substantial
(B) wealthy
(C) consequential
(D) spacious

29. Construction ------- with the replacement of the footbridge will continue to impede the flow of local traffic.
(A) accustomed
(B) associated
(C) coherent
(D) distinct

30. Creative Director Ray Rabelo's unique ideas have been ------- to our reputation as a leading design firm.
(A) main
(B) former
(C) average
(D) central

UNIT 07 | ETS 빈출 부사

accordingly 그에 맞게, 따라서

- **빈출표현** Mr. Kim is a manager, so he should be treated **accordingly**.
  김 씨는 매니저이니까, 그에 따라 대접받아야 한다.
- **파생어** accord 일치; 부합하다(with)
  according to ~에 따라
- **동의어** correspondingly 상응하여 therefore 그러므로

arguably 틀림없이, 단언하건대

- **빈출표현** **arguably** among the best restaurants
  단연 최고 식당 중 하나인
  arguably the most valuable finding
  단연 가장 가치 있는 발견
- **파생어** argue 언쟁하다, 주장하다
  arguable 주장[논증]할 수 있는, 논쟁의 여지가 있는

alike 마찬가지로, 똑같은, 비슷한

- **빈출표현** the performers and the audience **alike**
  연주자들과 청중 모두
- **파생어** alikeness 유사함
- **유의어** likewise 마찬가지로
- **반의어** differently 다르게
- **관련어구** A and B alike A와 B 똑같이

beforehand 미리, 사전에

- **빈출표현** make a reservation **beforehand**
  미리 예약하다
  must apply online **beforehand**
  미리 온라인으로 지원해야 한다
- **동의어** in advance 미리
- **반의어** later, afterward 나중에

altogether 아주, 완전히, 전부 합하여

- **빈출표현** grossed over 1 million dollars **altogether**
  합계 1백만 달러 이상의 수익을 올렸다
  The branch offices employ 160 people **altogether**.
  지점들은 전부 합해 160명의 직원을 고용하고 있다.
- **동의어** completely 완전히
- **반의어** partially 부분적으로

carefully 조심스럽게, 신중히

- **빈출표현** **carefully** deal with ~을 조심스럽게 처리하다
  listen **carefully** to what he says
  그가 말하는 것을 주의 깊게 듣다
- **파생어** care 관심, 돌봄; 신경 쓰다
  careless 부주의한
- **동의어** attentively 주의 깊게
- **반의어** recklessly 부주의하게

annually 해마다, 1년에 한 번

- **빈출표현** be requested to update the passwords **annually**
  비밀번호를 해마다 변경할 것을 요청받다
- **파생어** annual 해마다의, 1년의
- **동의어** yearly 연간의, 매년의
- **관련어구** biannual 한 해 두 번의

collaboratively 합작으로

- **빈출표현** work **collaboratively** to develop a better product 더 좋은 제품 개발을 위해 협업하다
  Rebecca and I **collaborated** on the soundtrack.
  레베카와 나는 사운드 트랙을 공동으로 작업했다.
- **파생어** collaborate 협력하다, 공동 작업하다
  collaboration 협력

approximately 대략, 거의

- **빈출표현** **Approximately** half the flights arrived late.
  항공편 중 대략 절반이 연착했다.
  approximately twice a month
  대략 한 달에 두 번
- **파생어** approximate 대략의
- **동의어** about, around 거의
- **반의어** accurately 정확히

comfortably 편안하게, 불편 없이

- **빈출표현** relax **comfortably** 편안히 쉬다
  comfortably seat up to twenty guests
  20명까지 손님을 불편 없이 앉히다
- **파생어** comfortable 편안한
- **동의어** cozily 아늑하게
- **반의어** uncomfortably 불편하게

commonly 보통, 일반적으로

빈출표현 **commonly** known as 보통 ~로 알려진
items **commonly** sold in second-hand stores
주로 중고품 매장에서 판매되는 상품들

파생어 common 평범한

동의어 generally 일반적으로

반의어 uncommonly 드물게

consistently 지속적으로, 일관되게

빈출표현 **consistently** happening 꾸준히 발생하는
consistently positive reviews
지속적으로 긍정적인 평가

파생어 consist 구성되다(of), 일치하다(with)
consistent 지속적인, 일관적인

동의어 constantly 끊임없이

반의어 inconsistently 모순되게

completely 완전히

빈출표현 **completely** free of charge 완전히 무료로
She was not **completely** satisfied with the product.
그녀는 제품에 완전히 만족하지는 않았다.

파생어 complete 완전한; 완료하다

동의어 absolutely 완전히

반의어 incompletely 불완전하게

definitely 분명히, 반드시, 명확하게

빈출표현 should **definitely** apply for the internship
인턴십에 반드시 신청해야 한다
The rumor is **definitely** true.
그 소문은 분명히 사실이다.

파생어 definite 명확한, 확정된

동의어 clearly 분명히

반의어 indefinitely 무기한으로, 불분명하게

concisely 간결하게

빈출표현 speak clearly and **concisely**
명료하고 간결하게 말하다
answer as **concisely** as possible
가능한 한 간결하게 대답하다

파생어 conciseness 간결함
concise 간결한

동의어 tersely 간결하게

반의어 wordily, lengthily 장황하게

directly 곧장, 직접

빈출표현 send[report] **directly** to ~에게 직접
보내다[보고하다]
book **directly** through a Web site
웹사이트를 통해 직접 예약하다

파생어 direct 직접적인

유의어 straight 곧장, 곧바로

반의어 indirectly 간접적으로

consecutively 연속하여

빈출표현 **consecutively** apply for two promotions
승진을 두 번 연속 신청하다
The two holidays occur **consecutively**.
휴일이 이틀 연속으로 있다.

파생어 consecution 연속, 일관성
consecutive 연속적인

동의어 successively 연속하여

반의어 inconsecutively 연결되지 않게

discreetly 신중하게, 조심스레

빈출표현 handle the dispute **discreetly**
논쟁을 신중하게 처리하다
deal with private customer information
discreetly
사적인 고객 정보를 신중히 다루다

파생어 discreet 신중한, 조심스러운

동의어 deliberately 신중하게

반의어 carelessly 부주의하게

consequently 그 결과, 따라서

빈출표현 **Consequently**, your reservation has now
been placed on hold.
그 결과, 귀하의 예약이 현재 보류 상태입니다.

파생어 consequence 결과

관련어구 unintended consequences
의도치 않은 결과

dramatically 극적으로

빈출표현 **dramatically** increase[decrease]
극적으로 증가[감소]하다

파생어 drama 연극, 드라마
dramatic 극적인

관련어구 sharply, significantly, substantially,
considerably, remarkably, noticeably, markedly
등의 부사가 증감 동사를 수식하는 부사로 자주 출제된다.

efficiently 효율적으로

빈출표현 process orders **efficiently**
주문을 효율적으로 처리하다
An engine that runs **efficiently** can save gas.
효율적으로 가동하는 엔진은 휘발유를 절약할 수 있다.

파생어 efficiency 효율성
efficient 효율적인

동의어 effectively 효과적으로

반의어 inefficiently 비효율적으로

ideally 이상적으로(는)

빈출표현 The complex is **ideally** situated close to shops and restaurants.
그 단지는 상점과 식당에 가까이 이상적으로 위치해 있다.
Ideally, I'd like to make the trip sometime in the next three months.
이상적으로는 향후 3달 중 언젠가 여행하고 싶습니다.

파생어 ideal 이상적인

effortlessly 손쉽게, 어려움 없이

빈출표현 do it **effortlessly** 손쉽게 하다
obtain it **effortlessly** 손쉽게 얻다

파생어 effort 노력
effortless 노력이 필요 없는

동의어 easily 쉽게

반의어 difficultly 어렵게

immediately 즉시

빈출표현 phone the hotel **immediately** upon arriving
도착하자마자 즉시 호텔에 전화하다
tips that can **immediately** be put into practice
즉시 실행에 옮길 수 있는 팁

파생어 immediate 즉각적인

동의어 instantly, promptly 즉각

반의어 later 나중에

exclusively 독점적으로, 전적으로

빈출표현 **exclusively** available 독점적으로 이용 가능한

파생어 exclusion 제외
exclude 제외하다
exclusive 독점적인, 배타적인
excluding ~을 제외하고

동의어 entirely 전적으로

반의어 partially 부분적으로

inadvertently 무심코, 부주의하게

빈출표현 **inadvertently** made a mistake
무심코 실수를 저질렀다
inadvertently omit ~을 의도치 않게 생략하다

파생어 inadvertence 부주의
inadvertent 부주의한

동의어 negligently 태만하게

반의어 carefully 주의 깊게

extremely 몹시, 극도로

빈출표현 **extremely** successful
매우 성공적인
extremely hot weather
극도로 더운 날씨

파생어 extreme 극도의, 극단적인

동의어 highly, very 매우, 몹시

반의어 moderately 알맞게

independently 독립적으로, 따로

빈출표현 handle the project **independently**
독립적으로 프로젝트를 다루다
travel **independently** with a flexible schedule
유연한 일정으로 따로 여행하다

파생어 independence 독립
independent 독립적인

동의어 separately 떨어져서

반의어 collectively 전체적으로

hastily 성급하게

빈출표현 edit the **hastily** made video
성급하게 만든 비디오를 편집하다

파생어 haste 급함; 서두르다
hasty 급한, 성급한

동의어 carelessly, heedlessly 부주의하게
hurriedly 급히, 허둥지둥

반의어 slowly 천천히
prudently 신중하게

instead 그 대신에

빈출표현 **Instead**, he was promoted.
대신에, 그가 승진되었다.
offer the service online **instead**
그 서비스를 온라인으로 대신 제공하다

파생어 instead of ~ 대신에

동의어 alternatively 그 대신에

momentarily 잠시, 곧

빈출표현
pause **momentarily**
잠시 멈추다
The train will leave **momentarily**.
곧 기차가 떠날 것이다

파생어 moment 순간
momentary 순간의, 덧없는

동의어 instantly 즉시

반의어 permanently 영원히

nearly 거의

빈출표현
last **nearly** two hours
거의 두 시간 동안 지속하다
nearly 500 participants
거의 500명의 참석자들

파생어 near 가까이에; 다가가다

동의어 almost, around, about, approximately, roughly 대략

officially 공식적으로

빈출표현
officially assume the position of vice president 공식적으로 부사장직을 맡다
officially recognized 공식적으로 인정받은

파생어 official 공식적인; 관리

동의어 formally 공식적으로

반의어 unofficially 비공식적으로

otherwise 그렇지 않으면, 달리

빈출표현
Otherwise, no refund can be made.
그렇지 않으면 어떠한 환불도 이루어지지 않습니다.
unless **otherwise** indicated
달리 표시되지 않는다면

반의어 likewise 마찬가지로

periodically 주기적으로, 정기적으로

빈출표현
a meeting held **periodically**
정기적으로 열리는 회의

파생어 period 주기, 기간
periodical 정기 간행물; 주기적인
periodic 주기적인

동의어 regularly 정기적으로

반의어 irregularly 불규칙적으로

practically 실제적으로, 사실상

빈출표현
the product, which is **practically** free
사실상 무료인 제품
Mr. Moon is **practically** finished writing the report.
문 씨는 사실상 그 보고서 작성을 마쳤다.

파생어 practical 실제적인

동의어 virtually 사실상

반의어 impractically 비현실적으로

primarily 주로, 무엇보다도 먼저

빈출표현
primarily[mainly] because
주로 ~하기 때문에
We chose the scanner **primarily** due to its low cost.
우리는 무엇보다 저렴한 가격 때문에 그 스캐너를 선택했다.

파생어 primary 주요한

동의어 mainly 주로

반의어 secondarily 부차적으로

promptly 즉각, 신속히

빈출표현
promptly report it to the supervisor
그것을 즉시 상관에게 보고하다
promptly refer to the manual
설명서를 즉각 참고하다

파생어 prompt 신속한; 촉발하다

동의어 immediately, instantly 즉각

반의어 slowly 천천히

publicly 공공연히, 대중 앞에서

빈출표현
speak **publicly** 공공연히 말하다
publicly condemn 공개적으로 비난하다

파생어 public 공공연한; 대중

동의어 openly 공개적으로

반의어 privately 은밀하게, 비공식적으로

rapidly 빠르게

빈출표현
The city will grow **rapidly**.
그 도시는 빠르게 성장할 것이다.
Online sales will **rapidly** increase.
온라인 매출은 빠르게 증가할 것이다.

파생어 rapidity 빠름
rapid 빠른

동의어 quickly, swiftly 빠르게

반의어 slowly 느리게

recently 최근에

빈출표현 if you have **recently** moved
당신이 최근 이사했다면
recently upgraded a building
최근에 건물을 보수했다
파생어 recent 최근의
동의어 lately 최근에(of late)
관련어구 until recently 최근까지

regularly 규칙적으로, 정기적으로

빈출표현 hold meetings **regularly**
정기적으로 회의를 개최하다
regularly meet customers in person
정기적으로 직접 고객들을 만나다
파생어 regularity 규칙적임
regular 정규적인
동의어 periodically 주기적으로, 정기적으로
반의어 irregularly 불규칙적으로

repeatedly 거듭하여

빈출표현 **repeatedly** fail 반복적으로 실패하다
He told me **repeatedly** not to work too fast.
그는 내게 너무 빨리 일하지 말라고 거듭 말했다.
파생어 repetition 반복
repeat 반복하다
repetitive 반복적인, 되풀이되는
동의어 constantly 끊임없이

safely 안전하게

빈출표현 store old files **safely**
예전 파일을 안전하게 보관하다
safely deposit the cash at the bank
현금을 은행에 안전하게 예치하다
파생어 safety 안전
safe 안전한; 금고
동의어 securely 안전하게
반의어 unsafely, insecurely 불안전하게

shortly 곧, 즉시

빈출표현 I'll **shortly** be with you. 곧 가겠습니다.
The recruiter can answer your questions **shortly**.
모집인이 당신의 질문에 곧 답해 줄 것입니다.
파생어 shorten 줄이다
short 짧은
동의어 soon 곧
반의어 later 나중에

skillfully 능숙하게

빈출표현 **skillfully** accomplish any given tasks
어떤 주어진 과제든 능숙하게 완수하다
파생어 skill 기술, 능력
skillful 숙련된
동의어 deftly 빠르게, 능숙하게
반의어 indelicately 거칠게, 섬세하지 않게

slightly 약간, 조금

빈출표현 The screen design **slightly** changed.
스크린의 디자인이 조금 변경되었다.
The menu choices were modified **slightly**.
메뉴판의 품목이 조금 수정되었다.
파생어 slight 조금의
동의어 marginally 아주 조금
반의어 considerably 상당히

smoothly 순조롭게, 매끄럽게

빈출표현 The production process has been running **smoothly**.
생산 과정은 순조롭게 진행되어 왔다.
The interview went very **smoothly**.
면접이 매우 순조롭게 진행되었다.
파생어 smooth 매끄러운

solely 혼자서, 유일하게, 오직

빈출표현 work **solely** from home
집에서 혼자 일하다, 재택근무하다
The manager is **solely** responsible for the manufacturing line.
매니저가 제조 라인에 대해 전적으로 책임진다.
파생어 sole 독점적인, 유일한
동의어 only 오직
반의어 collectively 전체적으로

steadily 꾸준히

빈출표현 **steadily** on the increase[decrease]
꾸준히 증가[감소]하는 추세이다
steadily practice 꾸준히 연습하다
파생어 steady 지속적인; 고정시키다
동의어 constantly 계속해서
반의어 intermittently 간헐적으로

VOCABULARY PRACTICE

정답 및 해설 p.102

A 다음 주어진 문장에서 적절한 어휘를 고르세요.

1 Presidential candidate Christine Witherby spoke [(A) expensively (B) publicly].

2 Ordered items can be shipped [(A) overly (B) directly] from the warehouse.

3 Several teams worked [(A) commonly (B) collaboratively] to design the company's new product line.

4 Ms. Johnson handled the dispute [(A) discreetly (B) remotely] by holding private discussions in her office.

5 Kline Biochemicals is seeking to replace a team of lab technicians with one experienced researcher who is able to handle high-level research projects [(A) independently (B) absently].

6 Mr. Hopkins announced that the company is planning to implement business strategies that will not rely [(A) nearly (B) solely] on labor cost cutting.

7 As the grant application for additional funding cannot exceed five pages, all research must be presented thoroughly yet [(A) concisely (B) evidently].

B 다음 문장의 빈칸에 적절한 어휘를 고르세요.

8 Yuvaves Transit Company drivers should have their vehicles inspected -------.
(A) rather   (B) annually
(C) quite   (D) highly

9 In order to make room for new inventory, stores that ------- would not offer promotional discounts might advertise a limited-time sale.
(A) solely   (B) further
(C) otherwise   (D) fully

10 The legal department has ------- finished its review of company policies and expects to finalize a proposal for changes tomorrow.
(A) slightly   (B) frequently
(C) nearly   (D) continually

11 For five years, our customers have ------- requested online access to their account information, and we have finally provided that service.
(A) repeatedly   (B) incredibly
(C) briefly   (D) exactly

12 Employee performance reviews ------- will be completed by next Wednesday.
(A) ideally   (B) lately
(C) relatively   (D) attractively

13 Sales of Cumberland television sets increased ------- after the manufacturer dropped the price by 25 percent.
(A) accidentally (B) expressively
(C) dramatically (D) eagerly

14 The store ------- charged Ms. Han's credit card twice for the same purchase but quickly corrected its error.
(A) uniformly   (B) potentially
(C) inadvertently (D) functionally

15 Locker Box Software ensures that your personal digital files will remain stored ------- on our online server.
(A) safely   (B) potentially
(C) reportedly   (D) presently

absolutely free 완전 무료로

빈출표현 We'll extend your subscription for 6 months—for **absolutely free**! 완전 무료로 6개월 구독을 연장해 드립니다!
You'll receive a dozen ink cartridges **absolutely free**.
12개의 잉크 카트리지를 완전 무료로 받게 되실 겁니다.

동의어 at no cost 무료로

adversely affect 부정적으로 영향을 미치다

빈출표현 **adversely affect** some regional subscribers
일부 지역 구독자들에게 부정적으로 영향을 미치다

파생어 adversity 역경, 불운
adverse 반대의, 불리한

동의어 unfavorably, negatively 불리하게

반의어 favorably 호의적으로

almost entirely 거의 전적으로

빈출표현 rely **almost entirely** on
거의 전적으로 의존하다

동의어 almost exclusively
거의 전적으로

관련어구 a selection of carpets in almost every color
거의 모든 색상의 다양한 카펫

at the latest (날짜나 요일 뒤에서) 늦어도

빈출표현 Friday **at the latest**
늦어도 금요일까지는(no later than Friday)

동의어 no later than + 날짜[요일] 늦어도 ~까지는

반의어 at the earliest 빨라야

briefly speak 간략하게 말하다

빈출표현 He **spoke** very **briefly** about the sales plan.
그는 판매 계획에 대해 매우 짧게 말했다.

파생어 brief 간략한; 간략히 보고하다

관련어구 directly speak 직접 말하다
speak highly of ~에 대해 칭찬하다

clearly marked 분명하게 표시된

빈출표현 be **clearly marked** in the catalog
카탈로그에 분명히 나와 있다
All sale prices are **clearly marked**.
모든 할인가가 명확히 표시되어 있다.

파생어 clear 맑은, 분명한; 치우다

동의어 explicitly 명시적으로

반의어 ambiguously 모호하게

closely examine 면밀히 조사하다

빈출표현 **closely examine** the records
기록을 면밀히 조사하다
closely examine new proposals
새 사업 제안서들을 면밀히 살펴보다

파생어 closure 폐쇄
close 가까운; 닫다

동의어 thoroughly review 면밀히 검토하다

conveniently located 편리하게 위치한

빈출표현 This site is **ideally situated** for building a hotel.
이 부지는 호텔을 짓기에 이상적인 곳입니다.

파생어 convenience 편리함
convenient 편리한

동의어 ideally, perfectly, agreeably (위치 등이) 좋게

currently available 현재 이용 가능한

빈출표현 The book is **currently** not **available**.
이 책은 현재는 이용할 수 없다.

파생어 current 현재의

반의어 temporarily unavailable
일시적으로 이용 불가능한

evenly distribute 균등하게 나누어 주다

빈출표현 The load needs to be **evenly distributed**.
적재물이 고르게 분배되어야 한다.
Copper **distributes** heat more **evenly**.
구리가 열을 좀 더 고르게 분포시킨다.

관련어구 evenly divide 고르게 나누다

반의어 unevenly 고르지 않게, 불규칙하게

explicitly state 명백히 서술하다

- **빈출표현** The employee handbook **explicitly state** that … 직원 편람은 ~라고 명시하고 있다
- **파생어** explicit 명백한
- **동의어** clearly[expressly] state 명백히 나타내다
- **반의어** implicitly 함축적으로

firmly believe 굳게 믿다

- **빈출표현** The CEO **firmly believes** that the company will keep growing. 최고경영자는 회사가 계속 성장하리라 굳게 믿는다.
- **파생어** firm 확고한, 단단한; 회사
- **동의어** rigidly 단단하게, 엄격하게
  strongly 강력하게

frequently visit 자주 방문하다

- **빈출표현** the most **frequently visited** tourist attractions in this area 이 근방에서 가장 빈번히 방문객들이 찾는 관광명소들
- **파생어** frequency 빈도, 주파수
  frequent 빈번한; ~에 자주 다니다
- **동의어** often, oftentimes 종종
- **반의어** seldom, rarely, hardly, scarcely 거의 ~ 아니다

gradually increasing[decreasing] 점차 증가하는[감소하는]

- **빈출표현** Sales in Europe are **gradually increasing**. 유럽에서 판매량이 점차 증가하고 있다.
- **파생어** gradual 점진적인
- **동의어** progressively 점진적으로
  steadily 꾸준하게
- **반의어** abruptly, suddenly 갑자기

have yet to 아직 ~하지 않다

- **빈출표현** **have yet to** achieve the goal 아직 목표를 달성하지 못하다
  He **has yet to** finish the report. 그는 아직 보고서를 완료하지 못했다.
- **관련어구** not yet 아직 ~ 아니다

highly rated 높은 평가를 받은

- **빈출표현** We carry only **highly rated** items. 우리는 높은 등급의 물건만을 취급합니다.
- **파생어** high 높은, 높게
- **동의어** exceptionally 예외적으로
  greatly 대단하게
- **반의어** unremarkably 평범하게, 하찮게

immediately after[before] ~ 직후[직전]에

- **빈출표현** **immediately after** its introduction 출시 직후에
  immediately before he arrives 그가 도착하기 직전에
- **동의어** right after[before], just after[before], shortly after[before], promptly after[before] ~ 직후[전]에
- **반의어** long after[before] ~의 한참 후[전]에

later this year[week / month] 올해[이번 주 / 이달] 나중에

- **빈출표현** **Later this year,** additional employees will be hired. 올해 나중에 추가 직원들이 고용될 것이다.
- **파생어** late 늦은
- **반의어** earlier this year 올해 이전에

most notably 가장 주목할 만하게

- **빈출표현** **Most notably,** this program is popular among novices. 가장 주목할 만하게, 이 프로그램은 초보자들 사이에서 인기가 있다.
- **파생어** note 주목하다
  notable 주목할 만한
- **동의어** markedly, conspicuously, noticeably 두드러지게
- **반의어** unremarkably 평범하게
  marginally 미미하게

mutually beneficial 상호 이익이 되는

- **빈출표현** The merger between the two airlines will be **mutually beneficial**. 두 항공사의 합병은 상호 이득이 될 것이다.
- **파생어** mutual 상호적인, 서로 관계가 있는
  benefit 혜택; 도움을 주다
  beneficiary 수혜자
- **동의어** favorable 유리한
- **반의어** disadvantageous 불리한

newly hired 신규 채용된

빈출표현 **newly hired** employees
신규 채용 직원

동의어 **newly recruited** 신규 채용된

관련어구 **newly** [released / published / opened]
신규 출시된, 새로 출간된, 새로 개장한

properly function 제대로 작동하다

빈출표현 The equipment is **properly functioning.**
그 장비는 제대로 작동하고 있다.

파생어 proper 적절한

동의어 adequately, appropriately 적절하게

반의어 improperly, inadequately,
inappropriately 부적절하게

not necessarily 반드시 ~하는 것은 아닌

빈출표현 people who do **not necessarily** have the
requisite knowledge
필요한 지식을 반드시 갖고 있는 않은 사람들
The printer does **not necessarily** perform
well enough for a busy office.
그 프린터는 바쁜 사무실에 충분히 적합하게 기능하지는
않는다.

proudly announce 자랑스럽게 발표하다

빈출표현 We **proudly announce** the introduction of
a new system.
새로운 시스템의 도입을 자랑스럽게 발표합니다.

파생어 pride 자부심
proud 자랑스러운

동의어 boastfully 뽐내며

once a month 한 달에 한 번

빈출표현 hold a meeting **once a month**
한 달에 한 번 회의하다

동의어 monthly, every month 매달

관련어구 once a year
일 년에 한 번(yearly, annually, every year)
once every two weeks
2주에 한 번(biweekly, every other week)

randomly choose 임의로 선택하다

빈출표현 The winner will be **randomly chosen.**
당첨자는 무작위로 선정된다.

파생어 random 무작위의

동의어 at random 무작위로

partly because 부분적으로 ~ 때문에

빈출표현 **partly because** the software has some
defects
부분적으로는 그 소프트웨어에 몇 가지 결함이 있기 때문에

반의어 mainly[largely] because 주로 ~ 때문에
due largely to 주로 ~ 때문에

readily available 쉽게 이용 가능한

빈출표현 The information is well documented and
readily available.
그 정보는 잘 기록되어 있고 쉽게 이용 가능하다.

동의어 easily accessible 쉽게 이용[접근] 가능한

관련어구 readily accessible by car or bus
자가용이나 버스로 쉽게 갈 수 있는

prominently placed[displayed]
눈에 띄게 두다[진열하다]

빈출표현 be **prominently placed** along the main route
주요 도로를 따라 눈에 띄게 배치되다
Company logo will be **prominently displayed**
on all promotional materials.
회사 로고는 모든 홍보 자료에 눈에 잘 띄게 게시될 것이다.

관련어구 be prominently posted 잘 보이게 공지되다

reasonably priced 합리적 가격의

빈출표현 The services are **reasonably priced.**
그 서비스는 합리적으로 가격이 책정되어 있다.

파생어 reason 이유, 이성
reasonable 합리적인, (가격이) 알맞은

동의어 logically 논리적으로
rationally 합리적으로

반의어 unfairly 공정치 않게

relatively high[low]
상대적으로 높은[낮은]

[빈출표현] We paid a **relatively low** price for the new copier. 우리는 새 복사기를 상대적으로 낮은 가격에 구입했다.

[파생어] relate 관련시키다
relative 비교적, 친척

[유의어] comparatively 비교적, 어느 정도
comparably 동등하게, 필적할 만큼

than originally predicted
원래 예상했던 것보다

[빈출표현] was higher **than** we **originally predicted**
우리가 원래 예상했던 것보다 높았다

[파생어] prediction 예상
predict 예상하다

[동의어] than originally anticipated 원래 예상보다

[반의어] as predicted[expected] 예상대로

[관련어구] contrary to expectations 예상과 달리

rise significantly 상당히 증가하다

[빈출표현] The demand for this clothing **rose significantly.** 이 의류에 대한 수요는 상당히 증가했다.

[파생어] significant 상당한

[유의어] extremely 매우
quite 꽤

[반의어] insignificantly 사소하게, 하찮게
somewhat 다소
a little 조금

unanimously vote 만장일치로 투표하다

[빈출표현] **voted unanimously** to change the company logo 만장일치로 회사 로고를 변경하기로 투표했다

[파생어] unanimous 만장일치의

[유의어] harmoniously 조화되어
consensually 합의하여

[관련어구] anonymously vote 익명으로 투표하다

routinely check 정기적으로 점검하다

[빈출표현] make it a rule to **routinely check** machinery
기계류를 정기적으로 점검하는 것을 규칙으로 하다

[파생어] routine 일상적인; 진부한 것

[동의어] regularly 정기적으로

[반의어] rarely 거의 ~ 아니다

unless otherwise p.p. 별도로 ~이 없으면

[빈출표현] **unless otherwise** instructed[told]
별도 지시가 없으면
unless otherwise noted[mentioned]
별도 언급이 없으면

[반의어] if so 만약 그렇다면

strongly recommend 강력하게 추천하다

[빈출표현] It is **strongly recommended** that …
~하는 것이 강력하게 추천됩니다
Advance reservations are **strongly recommended.**
선예약이 적극 권장됩니다.

[유의어] strongly encourage 강력하게 권장하다

well attended 참석률이 좋은

[빈출표현] The trade fair was very **well attended.**
무역 박람회는 참석률이 매우 좋았다.

[파생어] attend 참석하다
attendee 참석자
attendance 참석(률)

take ... seriously ~을 진지하게 생각하다

[빈출표현] **take** his suggestion **seriously**
그의 제안을 진지하게 받아들이다
take workplace safety **seriously**
작업장의 안전을 중요하게 여기다

[동의어] sincerely 진심으로, 진지하게

[반의어] casually, lightly 가볍게

well below ~보다 훨씬 못 미치게

[빈출표현] **well below** average
평균보다 훨씬 이하
well above the fixed rate of interest on a loan
대출에 정해진 이자율을 훨씬 넘는

[동의어] fall (far) short of ~에 (훨씬) 못 미치다

[반의어] well above ~을 훨씬 넘는[웃도는]

A 다음 주어진 문장에서 적절한 어휘를 고르세요.

1 Free samples are [(A) precisely (B) currently] available.

2 Housing prices have been [(A) highly (B) gradually] increasing.

3 The samples are [(A) carefully (B) absolutely] free of charge.

4 She was hired [(A) previously (B) immediately] after graduating.

5 Detour signs will be [(A) prominently (B) markedly] placed along the main route to the work site.

6 Pour the cake batter into the pan and shake gently if the batter is [(A) unevenly (B) unwillingly] distributed.

7 The guest speaker for the Jacketti Foundation's symposium will be announced [(A) next (B) later] this week.

B 다음 문장의 빈칸에 적절한 어휘를 고르세요.

8 The unseasonably cold weather has ------- affected the availability of some fruits and vegetables in local supermarkets.
(A) adversely   (B) faithfully
(C) consciously   (D) accurately

9 Yesterday the officers voted ------- to offer large bonuses to high-performing employees.
(A) commonly   (B) increasingly
(C) critically   (D) unanimously

10 Italy's two major airlines have ------- to finalize the details on their cooperative effort to increase tourism.
(A) yet   (B) up
(C) until   (D) else

11 *Risk Takers*, the new thriller filmed ------- entirely on one London street, grossed over ninety million pounds in its first weekend at the box office.
(A) more   (B) almost
(C) near   (D) over

12 The visiting diplomat spoke only ------- at the international conference before returning to Johannesburg.
(A) constantly   (B) frequently
(C) usually   (D) briefly

13 The route to Sandy Shores Inn is ------- marked from exit 262 on the coastal highway.
(A) clearly   (B) freely
(C) deeply   (D) sharply

14 Guest passes to Starville Athletic Center are redeemable for a three-day period ------- a month.
(A) once   (B) soon
(C) formerly   (D) shortly

15 If fuel costs rise -------, the terms of our contract may have to be renegotiated.
(A) mainly   (B) sincerely
(C) freshly   (D) significantly

1. Fordham Stationers recently decided to switch suppliers because Valley Paper has been ------- late in shipping their orders.
(A) steadily
(B) sensibly
(C) exactly
(D) consistently

2. Plumville Library ------- announces the launch of a brand-new Web site.
(A) extremely
(B) proudly
(C) distantly
(D) previously

3. For the annual company dinner, special dietary requests can be accommodated, but only if they are arranged -------.
(A) even
(B) yet
(C) beforehand
(D) meanwhile

4. In my opinion, the company's stock price is ------- low compared to its annual earnings.
(A) audibly
(B) relatively
(C) plentifully
(D) anonymously

5. Because of the large number of tourists in summer months, travelers should plan ------- and make their reservations early.
(A) accordingly
(B) subsequently
(C) conversely
(D) assuredly

6. Advertisements placed by merchants in *The Weekly Roundup* do not ------- imply endorsement by the management of the newspaper.
(A) barely
(B) highly
(C) gradually
(D) necessarily

7. For optimal performance of your Rydor clothes dryer, clean the filter -------.
(A) extremely
(B) regularly
(C) deeply
(D) heavily

8. Photos and related documents were supplied by the author, unless ------- noted.
(A) else
(B) otherwise
(C) instead
(D) rather

9. The Captain's Seafood Restaurant can ------- seat up to twenty guests in its Starboard Lounge.
(A) spaciously
(B) comfortably
(C) abundantly
(D) evenly

10. According to the city planning director, Adelaide's old civic center must be ------- demolished before construction on a new center can begin.
(A) completely
(B) defectively
(C) plentifully
(D) richly

11. Please reply ------- to the invitation for the software training.
(A) closely
(B) promptly
(C) likely
(D) expressly

12. Our e-mail system is ------- known as Fast Track, even though its official name is Fast Mail Delivery and Tracking system.
(A) mutually
(B) relatively
(C) abruptly
(D) commonly

13. The committee members were glad to see how ------- Ms. Park presented the benefits of the incentive program.
(A) privately
(B) apparently
(C) likely
(D) skillfully

14. The Wiltshire Orchestra's concert was ------- three hours long, ending just after 11 P.M.
(A) attentively
(B) approximately
(C) endlessly
(D) comparatively

15. Ms. Borgen changed jobs ------- because her former position provided little flexibility.
(A) partly
(B) financially
(C) widely
(D) relatively

16. There is a coffee machine ------- located on the second floor of the Tabor Building.
(A) conveniently
(B) slightly
(C) considerably
(D) eventually

17. Applications for the receptionist job have come in ------- over the past two weeks.
(A) openly
(B) greatly
(C) exactly
(D) steadily

18. Kristi Driver is a well-known therapist in the area of sports medicine, and her services are very ------- priced.
(A) strongly
(B) internally
(C) reasonably
(D) repeatedly

19. Mariel Castillo's ------- rated radio program will move to a new radio station in the spring.
(A) surely
(B) very
(C) highly
(D) ever

20. Cross Cove is home to several New Zealand artists, most ------- Francis Seward and Kyle McIntyre.
(A) easily
(B) notably
(C) separately
(D) commonly

21. Because she felt that the tourism video appeared to have been ------- made, Ms. Peppin recommended that it be filmed again.
(A) altogether
(B) soon
(C) hastily
(D) repeatedly

22. The impressive floral display at the building entrance is ------- made up of blue flowers, with a few red ones artfully placed throughout.
(A) enough
(B) exclusively
(C) primarily
(D) everywhere

23. Rather than wearing business attire on Thursdays, staff may choose to wear casual clothing -------.
(A) enough
(B) despite
(C) instead
(D) in case

24. For security reasons, all representatives must now register with the receptionist ------- upon arriving at the main building.
(A) suddenly
(B) abruptly
(C) immediately
(D) urgency

25. Upgrades to the order-tracking database will allow staff to process customer purchases more -------.
(A) totally
(B) efficiently
(C) recently
(D) shortly

26. Because we at Credit Pacifica take customer privacy ------- we pledge not to sell your address to outside marketing firms.
(A) soundly
(B) totally
(C) seriously
(D) completely

27. Intergroup Enterprises has ------- negotiated a contract for exclusive rights to distribute Streamflow software in Latin America.
(A) shortly
(B) soon
(C) recently
(D) yet

28. The auditors' training curriculum is ------- revisited to ensure that it reflects current greenhouse-gas emission standards.
(A) formerly
(B) periodically
(C) extremely
(D) simplistically

29. Routine inspections are conducted at the Haldren Paper factory to ensure that all equipment is functioning -------.
(A) properly
(B) officially
(C) literally
(D) rightfully

30. Ms. Rappaport recommends that the manufacturing plant replace the outdated equipment as ------- as possible.
(A) necessarily
(B) definitely
(C) rapidly
(D) predominantly

UNIT 09 | ETS 빈출 전치사

aboard ~을 타고, ~의 안에

 go **aboard** a plane
비행기에 탑승하다
go[climb] **aboard** the cruise ship
유람선에 승선하다

about ~에 관하여[대하여]; 약 ~, ~경에

 about the topic 그 주제에 관하여
meet at **about** 2 o'clock
약 2시경에 만나다
a box weighing **about** 8 kilos
약 8kg 무게의 상자

above [장소] ~ 위에, [수량] ~을 넘는

 a floor **above** us
우리 위층
above average service
평균적인 서비스를 넘는

across ~을 가로질러, 전역에서

 across the bridge
다리를 건너서
products from **across** the world
세계 전역에서 온 제품들

after ~ 후에

 arrive two days **after** the promised date
약속 일자 이틀 후에 도착하다
after graduating from business school
경영 대학원을 졸업한 후에
동의어 following ~ 후에
반의어 before, prior to ~ 전에

against ~에 반대하여, ~에 대비하여

 argue **against** his proposal
그의 제안에 반대하여 주장하다
insurance **against** theft or damage
도난 및 손해에 대비한 보험

along ~을 따라, ~ 도중에

 along the river 강을 따라
along the main hallway 중앙 복도를 따라
along the walking path 인도를 따라
along the way back 돌아오는 도중에

alongside ~ 옆에, ~와 함께, 나란히

 set up **alongside** the rivers 강 옆에 설치하다
work **alongside** the interns 인턴들과 함께 일하다
Their names will appear **alongside** their reviews.
그들의 이름이 후기와 함께 실릴 것이다.

among [셋 이상] ~ 사이에, [최상급] ~ 중 하나

 among employees
직원들 사이에[중에]
Mr. Yu is **among** our best employees.
유 씨는 우리 회사 최고의 직원 중에 하나이다.

around ~의 주변에; 대략, 거의

 sit **around** the speaker
연사 주변에 앉다
around five hundred participants
대략 500명의 참석자들

as [자격] ~로서, ~일 때에

 hired **as** a new financial director
신임 재무 담당관으로 채용된
learned Arabic **as** a boy
소년이었을 때 아랍어를 배웠다

at ~에

 arrived **at** 2 P.M.
오후 2시에 도착했다
located **at** the end of this hall
이 복도 끝에 위치한

before ~ 전에, ~ 앞에

빈출표현
10 days **before** departure 출발 10일 전에
before leaving for the day 퇴근 전에
before a large audience 많은 청중 앞에서
관련어구 before long 머지않아

behind [장소] ~의 뒤편에, [시간] ~보다 늦어

빈출표현
a parking lot **behind** the building
그 건물의 뒤편에 있는 주차장
behind schedule on the renovations
수리가 일정보다 늦어져

below ~ 아래에

빈출표현
below the level 수준 이하의
below the expectations 기대에 못 미치는
far **below** the average
평균보다 훨씬 못 미치는
반의어 above ~ 위에

beneath [위치] ~ 아래에

빈출표현
beneath the ground 땅 아래에
electrical cables **beneath** the road
도로 아래의 전선
There is a parking garage **beneath** the exhibit
hall. 전시홀 아래층에 주차장이 있다.

beside [위치] ~ 옆에, ~와 비교하면, ~을 벗어나

빈출표현
beside the table 테이블 옆에
Beside Ms. Choi, Ms. Wang seems better
qualified. 최 씨와 비교하면, 왕 씨가 더 적임인 듯하다.
beside the point 요점을 벗어나

besides ~뿐 아니라, 게다가

빈출표현
besides working as an intern
인턴으로 일할 뿐 아니라
Besides, we are running short on our budget.
게다가, 우리는 예산도 떨어져 가고 있다.
동의어 in addition to ~에 더하여
in addition 게다가

between 둘 사이에

빈출표현
between the two countries
두 나라 사이에
meal breaks **between** speeches
연설 사이의 식사 시간

beyond [장소, 시간, 범위] ~을 넘어서

빈출표현
beyond the station 역을 지나
The meeting will extend **beyond** noon.
그 회의는 정오 넘어서까지 연장될 것이다.
beyond our budget 예산을 넘은

by [시점] ~까지, [행위의 주체] ~에 의해서, [수단] ~로

빈출표현
by the end of the week 이번 금요일까지
be impressed **by** the product's design
그 제품의 디자인에 감명받다
by bus[subway/train/car]
버스[지하철/기차/차]로

concerning ~에 관하여

빈출표현
some questions **concerning** the topic
그 주제에 관한 몇 가지 질문들
an article **concerning** the current economy
현 경제에 관한 기사
동의어 about, regarding, with[in] regard to
~에 관하여

considering ~을 고려하면

빈출표현
considering the unexpectedly high sales
figures 예상외로 높은 판매 수치를 고려하면
considering the tremendous amount of
income 엄청난 금액의 소득을 고려하면
동의어 given, in light of ~을 고려하면

despite ~에도 불구하고

빈출표현
despite the difficulties
어려움에도 불구하고
despite working overnight
밤새 일했음에도 불구하고
동의어 in spite of, notwithstanding
~에도 불구하고

down ~ 아래쪽으로, ~을 따라

빈출표현
right **down** the street 길 바로 아래쪽으로
rafting trips **down** the rivers
강 따라 급류 타기 여행
march **down** the aisle
통로를 따라 행진하다

given ~을 고려해 볼 때

빈출표현
given the enormous popularity of the show
그 쇼의 어마어마한 인기를 고려해 볼 때
given the unusually hot weather
평소와 달리 더운 날씨를 고려해 볼 때

during [기간] ~ 동안에

빈출표현
during the meeting 회의 동안
shorter operating hours **during** the week
주중 더 짧은 운영 시간
see the factory floor **during** the visit
방문 기간 동안에 공장 작업장을 둘러보다

in [장소] ~ 안에, [시간] ~ 후에, [기간] ~ 동안에, ~ 만에, [관련] ~에 있어서, ~가

빈출표현
in the restricted area 제한 구역 안에서
arrive **in** ten minutes 10분 후에 도착하다
have increased **in** the last three years
지난 3년 동안 증가해 왔다
the first **in** 10 years 10년 만에 처음
three meters **in** length 길이가 3미터

except ~을 제외하고, ~ 외에는

빈출표현
Admission is free **except** Monday.
월요일을 제외하고는 입장이 무료이다.
동의어 except for, excepting ~을 제외하고
관련어구 except in this room 이 방을 제외하고는
except when + 주어 + 동사 ~할 때를 제외하고는
except that + 주어 + 동사 ~라는 점을 제외하고는

including ~을 포함해

빈출표현
including complimentary service
무료 서비스를 포함해
including the delivery cost
배송비를 포함해
반의어 excluding ~을 제외하고

following ~ 뒤에; 다음의

빈출표현
a reception **following** the lecture
강연 후의 연회
Study the **following** example in your workbook.
워크북에 있는 다음의 예를 학습하시오.

inside (~의) 안에, ~ 안으로

빈출표현
look **inside** the shipping box
운반 상자 안을 들여다보다
have plants **inside** the lobby
로비 안에 식물을 두다
Please refrain from bringing food **inside** the library.
도서관 안으로 음식물을 반입하는 것을 삼가 주세요.

for [목적] ~을 위해서, [기간] ~ 동안에

빈출표현
designed our products **for** clients
고객들을 위해 우리 제품들을 설계했다
warranty that lasts **for** a period of one year
1년 동안 유효한 보증서

into [장소] ~ 안으로, [변화] ~로

빈출표현
place packing materials **into** the box
포장 재료를 상자 안에 넣다
convert a building **into** a hotel
건물을 호텔로 개조하다

from [장소, 출처] ~로부터

빈출표현
a souvenir photo **from** Times Square
타임스 스퀘어에서 찍은 기념 사진
a letter of praise **from** a customer
고객으로부터 온 칭찬의 편지

like ~처럼, ~와 마찬가지로

빈출표현
like other customers
다른 고객들처럼
It looks **like** a new car.
그것은 새 차처럼 보인다.
반의어 unlike ~와 달리

near ~ 근처에, 가까이에; 다가가다

빈출표현
place plants **near** the window
창문 근처에 화초를 놓다
vacation period **near** the end of the year
연말 무렵에 있는 휴가 기간

opposite ~ 맞은편에, 맞은편의

빈출표현
the store **opposite** the office
사무실 맞은편 가게
the **opposite** side of the road
도로의 건너편

notwithstanding ~에도 불구하고

빈출표현
notwithstanding some problems
몇몇 문제에도 불구하고
동의어
despite, in spite of
~에도 불구하고

outside ~ 밖에[외에]; 밖의; 바깥쪽

빈출표현
outside the store 상점 밖에
outside working hours 근무 시간 외에
outside the city limits 시외에
반의어
inside ~ 안에

of ~의, ~중에, [동격] ~이라는

빈출표현
the outbreak **of** a disease 질병의 발생
Of the two candidates, Mr. Song is the better.
두 명의 후보자 중 송 씨가 더 낫다.
the field **of** molecular chemistry
분자 화학(이라는) 분야

over [기간] ~에 걸쳐서, [위치, 사물] ~ 위에, ~ 너머로, [대상] ~에 대한

빈출표현
operate from the same location **over** a decade
10년 내내 같은 위치에서 영업하다
lights hanging **over** the table
테이블 위에 걸려 있는 전등

off ~에서 떨어져서

빈출표현
get **off** the train 기차에서 내리다
fall **off** the shelves 선반에서 떨어지다
jump **off** the stage 무대에서 뛰어내리다

past ~을 지나서

빈출표현
drive **past** the post office
우체국을 지나서 차를 몰다
be located slightly **past** the theater
극장을 약간 지나서 위치해 있다

on [날짜, 요일] ~에, [위치] ~ 위에, [접촉] ~에 붙어서, 착용하여

빈출표현
on March 1 3월 1일에
leave it **on** my desk
제 책상 위에 놓아 두세요
cooling vents **on** the ceiling
천장에 붙은 냉방용 송풍구
a bandage **on** his wrist 손목에 찬 붕대

since [시점] ~ 이래로, [이유] ~ 때문에

빈출표현
have been updating the computers **since** noon
정오 이후부터 컴퓨터를 업데이트하고 있다
Since Ms. Lee transferred, we are looking for a replacement.
이 씨가 전근을 갔기 때문에, 우리는 후임을 찾고 있다.

onto ~ 위에, ~ 쪽으로

빈출표현
load the boxes **onto** the shelve
선반 위로 상자를 올리다
turn left **onto** Arthur Avenue
아서 가 쪽으로 좌회전하다

than ~보다

빈출표현
arrive earlier **than** other participants
다른 참가자들보다 더 일찍 도착하다
cost more **than** expected
예상보다 비용이 많이 들다
Improved technology has made online shopping easier **than** ever.
향상된 기술이 온라인 쇼핑을 어느 때보다 더 쉽게 만들었다.

through [위치] ~을 통과하여, [수단, 매체] ~을 통하여, [기간] ~ 내내

빈출표현
walk **through** the tunnel
터널을 통과하여 걷다
discuss the agenda **through** the afternoon
오후 내내 그 안건에 대해 논의하다

until ~까지

빈출표현
will be delayed **until** later
나중으로 연기될 것이다
We will postpone the meeting **until** he comes.
그가 올 때까지 우리는 회의를 연기할 것이다.

throughout [기간] ~ 내내, [장소] ~ 전역에

빈출표현
free festivals **throughout** the summer
여름 내내 열리는 무료 축제
road closures **throughout** the region
그 지역 전역에 걸친 도로 폐쇄

upon ~에, ~하자마자

빈출표현
Ms. Grant will open a clothing boutique **upon** retiring. 그랜트 씨는 은퇴하자마자 옷가게를 열 것이다.
Menu items may vary depending **upon** the availability of ingredients.
메뉴는 재료 유무에 따라 변경될 수 있습니다.

to [방향] ~으로, [목적] ~을 위해

빈출표현
go **to** the reception desk
접수 데스크로 가다
a key **to** success
성공을 위한 열쇠

with ~와 함께, ~한 채로

빈출표현
a meeting **with** a client
고객과의 회의
a meal served **with** bread
빵이 함께 나오는 식사
with his eyes closed
눈을 감은 채로

toward [방향] ~을 향하여, [시점] ~ 무렵, [목적] ~을 위하여

빈출표현
a busy period **toward** the end of the month
월말 무렵의 바쁜 기간
contributed some money **toward** the project
그 프로젝트를 위해 얼마의 돈을 기부했다

within [기간, 장소, 범위] ~ 이내에

빈출표현
guarantee delivery **within** 24 hours
24시간 이내에 배송할 것을 보장하다
tourist attractions **within** the area
그 지역 내의 관광 명소들

반의어 beyond ~을 넘어서

under [위치] ~ 아래에, [진행] ~ 중에, [지시, 지도] ~하에서

빈출표현
under the terms of the warranty
보증서의 조건하에
future sales plans **under** discussion
논의 중인 미래의 판매 계획
a construction project **under** the direction of architect Paul Mullens
건축가 폴 뮬런스의 지휘 아래 진행되는 건설 프로젝트

without ~ 없이, ~가 없다면

빈출표현
offer a replacement or refund **without** delay
지체 없이 교환 및 환불을 제공하다
We cannot finish the project **without** your help.
우리는 당신의 도움 없이는 프로젝트를 완료할 수 없다.

unlike ~와는 달리

빈출표현
unlike large corporations
대기업과는 달리
unlike the previous edition
구판과는 달리

worth ~ 상당의, ~의 가치가 있는

빈출표현
worth considering
고려할 가치가 있는
well **worth** a visit
매우 방문할 가치가 있는
gift certificates **worth** $100
100달러 상당의 상품권

VOCABULARY **PRACTICE**

정답 및 해설 p. 108

A 다음 주어진 문장에서 적절한 어휘를 고르세요.

1 Outbound trains will depart [(A) since (B) from] track twelve.

2 [(A) Upon (B) Within] his arrival, we will resume our meeting.

3 The company's profits have doubled [(A) on (B) in] the last 10 years.

4 All sales reports must be submitted to Mr. Liu [(A) along (B) by] Friday.

5 We will not be open on Saturdays and Sundays [(A) between (B) throughout] the winter.

6 The foundation will contribute money [(A) than (B) toward] the construction.

7 These guidelines should be circulated only [(A) within (B) towards] our department and should not be distributed elsewhere.

B 다음 문장의 빈칸에 적절한 어휘를 고르세요.

8 All office supplies will be kept in a closet ------- the third-floor elevator.
(A) close (B) soon
(C) near (D) onto

9 The Sineville Bridge will be closed ------- the week of June 5.
(A) during (B) between
(C) depending on (D) out of

10 Beginning on May 1, Jasper Clothing will close its physical stores and will operate ------- an online-only retailer.
(A) into (B) as
(C) since (D) during

11 The estimated production costs for the new Pro Tip markers will be $2.15 per set, excluding the cost ------- the packaging.
(A) as (B) at
(C) by (D) of

12 Printer cartridges can be found in the supply cabinet ------- the file folders.
(A) at (B) from
(C) with (D) along

13 Dalytown Hospital offers free classes on nutrition ------- adults and children.
(A) by (B) as
(C) to (D) at

14 Not long ------- leaving the Nisklen company, Mr. Saito began working at a government agency.
(A) around (B) off
(C) over (D) after

15 Mr. Yamaguchi's train was delayed, forcing him to wait ------- the station for over two hours.
(A) at (B) for
(C) to (D) with

UNIT 10 | ETS 빈출 전치사 어구

according to ~에 따르면, ~에 따라

빈출표현
according to a business survey
업계 설문조사에 따르면
if everything goes **according to** plan
만약 모든 일이 계획에 따라 진행된다면

across from ~의 맞은편에

빈출표현
across from the reception desk
안내 데스크 맞은편에
directly **across from** the new sports stadium
새로운 스포츠 경기장 바로 맞은편에

ahead of schedule[time] 일정보다 앞서

빈출표현
complete the construction **ahead of time**
예정보다 일찍 공사를 마치다
arrive at our destination **ahead of schedule**
예정보다 빨리 목적지에 도착하다
동의어 ahead of time 시간보다 앞서
관련어구 behind schedule 일정보다 늦게
on schedule 일정대로

along with ~와 더불어

빈출표현
must present their passport **along with** their boarding pass
탑승권과 더불어 여권을 제시해야 한다

apart from ~을 제외하면, ~와는 별도로

빈출표현
apart from a few minor errors
몇 가지 사소한 실수들을 제외하면
The table is in good condition **apart from** a few small scratches.
그 탁자는 약간의 긁힌 자국을 제외하고는 상태가 좋다.
동의어 aside from ~을 제외하면, ~와는 별도로
except for ~을 제외하면

as a result of ~의 결과로

빈출표현
as a result of the recent merger
최근 합병의 결과로
관련어구 **As a result,** we canceled the appointment.
그 결과, 우리는 약속을 취소했다.

as of ~일자로, ~ 현재

빈출표현
as of today 오늘 현재
as of October 1 10월 1일자로

as opposed to ~에 반대하여, ~와 반대로

빈출표현
as opposed to the plan 그 계획과는 반대로
expanding our present office **as opposed to** relocating
사무실 이전과 반대로 현재의 사무실을 확장하는 것

as to ~에 관해

빈출표현
Please advise us **as to** whether you wish to modify or cancel your order.
주문을 변경하시거나 취소하시기를 원하는지에 대해 저희에게 고지해 주시기 바랍니다.
as to the duration of the CEO's visit
최고 경영자의 방문 기간에 대해

at no cost 무료로

빈출표현
replace damaged goods **at no cost**
파손된 상품을 무료로 교체해 주다
available **at no** extra **cost**
추가 비용 없이 이용 가능한
동의어 at no (additional) charge 추가 비용 없이

away from ~로부터 떨어져서

빈출표현
five kilometers **away from** the town
마을에서 5킬로미터 떨어져서
The food court is just a short distance **away from** our office.
그 푸드 코트는 우리 사무실에서 약간만 떨어져 있다.

because of ~ 때문에

빈출표현
because of its strong brand recognition
탄탄한 브랜드 인지도 때문에
because of the updated processing procedures 변경된 처리 절차 때문에
동의어 due to, owing to, on account of ~ 때문에

by means of ~을 수단으로 하여

 빈출표현 represent one's idea **by means of** pictures
그림을 수단으로 생각을 나타내다
market the product **by means of** Internet advertising
인터넷 광고를 통해 제품을 마케팅하다

in advance 미리, 사전에

빈출표현 book **in advance** 미리 예약하다
register for the seminar at least 5 days **in advance**
적어도 5일 전에 세미나에 등록하다
동의어 beforehand 미리
반의어 afterward 나중에

contrary to ~와는 반대로

 빈출표현 **contrary to** the theory
그 이론과는 반대로
contrary to what he insists
그가 주장하는 바와는 반대로

in case of ~의 경우에

빈출표현 **in case of** an emergency
위기 상황이 발생할 경우
Keep your schedule flexible **in case of** flight delays.
비행기 연착에 대비하여 일정에 융통성을 두십시오.
동의어 in the event of ~할 경우에

depending on ~에 따라

 빈출표현 **depending on** several factors
몇 가지 요인에 따라
Prices vary **depending on** changes in the cost of raw materials.
원자재 가격의 변동에 따라 가격은 달라진다.

in contrast to ~와는 대조적으로

빈출표현 **in contrast to** the competitor
경쟁자와는 대조적으로
in contrast to the earlier version
이전 버전과는 대조적으로

due to ~ 때문에, ~로 인하여

 빈출표현 **due to** the malfunction
오작동 때문에
due to our rising operating costs
운영비 상승으로 인해

in detail 상세하게

빈출표현 discuss a matter **in detail**
문제에 관해 상세히 논의하다
give thorough explanations and answers **in detail**
빈틈없는 설명과 답변을 상세하게 주다

in accordance with ~에 따라

 빈출표현 **in accordance with** the safety precautions
안전 수칙에 따라
hold the staff picnic **in accordance with** park regulations
공원 규정에 맞추어 직원 야유회를 열다

in favor of ~을 찬성하여

 빈출표현 **in favor of** building the new plant
새로운 공장을 건설하는 것에 찬성하여
decide **in favor of** a proposal
제안에 찬성을 결정하다

in addition to ~에 더해서, ~ 외에도

빈출표현 **in addition to** being helped
도움을 받는 것 외에도
in addition to providing the service free of charge
무료 서비스를 제공하는 것 외에도
동의어 besides ~에 더해서, 게다가

in front of ~ 앞에

빈출표현 **in front of** the art museum
미술관 앞에서
in front of a large audience
많은 청중 앞에서

in keeping with ~에 따라, ~을 준수하여

in keeping with their expectations
그들의 기대에 따라
in keeping with the floor plan
평면도에 따라

in spite of ~에도 불구하고

in spite of heavy advertising
대대적인 광고에도 불구하고
in spite of the ongoing renovations
진행 중인 공사에도 불구하고

in light of ~을 고려하여, ~에 비추어

 in light of resident concerns
주민들의 염려를 고려하여
in light of the company's current financial situation
회사의 현 재정 상황을 고려하여

instead of ~ 대신에, ~하지 않고

 instead of renewing the contract
계약을 갱신하는 대신에
purchase the device **instead of** leasing it
장비를 임대하지 않고 구매하다

in line with ~에 부합하는, ~에 따라

 His new job is more **in line with** his ultimate goal.
그의 새로운 직업은 그의 궁극적인 목표에 더 부합한다.
in line with the CEO's request
최고 경영자의 요구에 맞추어

in terms of ~ 면에서, ~에 관하여

빈출표현 vary **in terms of** price, size, and durability
가격, 크기, 견고성 면에서 다르다
show no difference **in terms of** theme
주제 면에서 차이점을 드러내지 않다

in person 직접

 deliver the packet **in person**
그 소포를 직접 배달하다
interview the candidate **in person**
그 후보자를 직접 면접 보다
파생어 personal 개인의
동의어 personally 직접 face-to-face 직접 대면하여
반의어 indirectly 간접적으로

in the event of ~의 경우에

 in the event of severe winter weather
혹독한 겨울 날씨의 경우에
in the event of a power failure
정전이 일어날 경우에

in place of ~ 대신에

 give the talk **in place of** Mr. McDonald
맥도날드 씨 대신에 강연하다
serve tea **in place of** coffee
커피 대신 차를 대접하다

in writing 서면으로

빈출표현 should report it **in writing**
이것을 서면으로 보고해야 한다
file a complaint **in writing**
서면으로 항의 사항을 접수하다

in response to ~에 대한 응답으로

빈출표현 **in response to** his favor
그의 호의에 대한 응답으로
in response to the increasing demand
증가하는 수요에 대응하여

next to ~ 옆에

 right **next to** each other
서로 바로 옆에
The identification numbers appear **next to** the names.
신원 번호는 이름 옆에 적혀 있습니다.

on account of ~ 때문에

 on account of this drastic change
이런 급격한 변화 때문에
an outdoor festival is canceled **on account of** bad weather
악천후 때문에 야외 축제가 취소되다

rather than ~보다는 차라리

 flavor **rather than** price
가격보다는 차라리 맛
blue **rather than** red
붉은색보다는 차라리 파란색

on behalf of ~을 대신하여

 on behalf of our company, I'd like to …
저희 회사를 대신하여 ~하고 싶습니다
on behalf of the president
사장을 대신하여

regardless of ~에 상관없이

 regardless of the cost
비용에 관계없이
Everyone can apply **regardless of** age, religion, and nationality.
나이, 종교, 국적에 관계없이 누구나 지원할 수 있다.
[동의어] irrespective of ~에 관계없이

out of ~의 바깥에, ~이 떨어진

 out of the theater 극장 바깥에
out of sight 눈에서 안 보여
out of stock 재고가 없는

such as 예를 들어 (…와 같은)

 facilities **such as** the patio and pool
테라스, 수영장과 같은 시설들
information **such as** the brand and size
브랜드, 사이즈 등의 정보

owing to ~ 때문에

owing to the illness 병 때문에
owing to his being lazy 그가 게으르기 때문에

thanks to ~ 덕분에[때문에]

thanks to funds from the organization
단체의 기금 덕분에
thanks to this budget increase
예산 인상 덕분에

pertaining to ~에 관한

 additional details **pertaining to** the workshop
워크숍에 관한 추가 세부 정보
topics **pertaining to** health and nutrition
건강과 영양에 관한 주제

until further notice
추후 공지가 있을 때까지

The main branch will remain closed **until further notice**.
본점은 추후 공지가 있을 때까지 폐점입니다.

prior to ~ 전에

 prior to the press release
언론 발표 전에
check the box's contents **prior to** shipping
발송 전에 박스의 내용물을 확인하다
[동의어] before ~ 전에

with[in] regard to ~에 관하여

 The manager will place an ad **with regard to** the job opportunity.
매니저는 구인 광고를 낼 것이다.
[동의어] about, as to, as for, regarding, concerning, with[in] respect[reference] to
~에 관하여

A 다음 주어진 문장에서 적절한 어휘를 고르세요.

1 Office supplies are stored in the copy room, [(A) next to (B) down] the fax machine.

2 We have received many inquiries [(A) with regard to (B) in place of] the new rule.

3 The restoration of the Pratt Theater will be completed [(A) early (B) ahead of] schedule.

4 In order to avoid being misunderstood, you should report it [(A) written (B) in writing].

5 We plan to replace the system [(A) due to (B) because] its frequent malfunctions.

6 [(A) Ahead of (B) Owing to] delays in obtaining the proper construction permits, renovation of the civic center will not resume until Monday.

7 The last shipment was refused by the buyer [(A) according to (B) because of] damage that occurred while the product was in transit.

B 다음 문장의 빈칸에 적절한 어휘를 고르세요.

8 ------- recent studies by a private consulting firm, over 30 percent of the traffic in Springfield is made up of commercial vehicles.
(A) So that
(B) According to
(C) Now that
(D) Even though

9 ------- its main competitor, the ergonomic chair offered by Well Designs is lightweight and comes in a variety of colors.
(A) In contrast to
(B) By way of
(C) Instead of
(D) So as

10 ------- its lack of a large conference center, Stone City is a good choice of location for the Federated Freelancers' yearly meeting.
(A) Instead of
(B) In spite of
(C) Rather than
(D) No sooner than

11 The Harrison Community Bank will open a branch in the center of Harrison, only a kilometer ------- their headquarters in the financial district.
(A) all around
(B) up until
(C) far ahead
(D) away from

12 We accept all applications, ------- whether applicants have previous experience in Internet markets.
(A) regardless of
(B) despite that
(C) except for
(D) considering that

13 Following much deliberation by the designers, the bright orange dress was abandoned ------- one in a more subdued color.
(A) favorable
(B) out of favor
(C) favorite
(D) in favor of

14 Dr. Ravia has made significant contributions to the fields of psychology and neurobiology ------- his earlier work in linguistics.
(A) in as much as
(B) in addition to
(C) in the event of
(D) in either case

15 The advertising campaign for the new Cool Fizz soft drink will feature flavor ------- price.
(A) rather than
(B) in the event of
(C) except for
(D) as for

1. Market researchers reported that customers were most impressed ------- the Vestra Coffeemaker's delayed-start function.
   (A) by
   (B) beyond
   (C) for
   (D) since

2. ------- project manager, Ms. Chung will be directly responsible to the company president.
   (A) Throughout
   (B) Aside
   (C) Plus
   (D) As

3. Today, Saari Travel Agency announced its partnership ------- Colgren Airways, a growing international airline.
   (A) in
   (B) with
   (C) from
   (D) off

4. Flash photography is not permitted ------- the Sakura Museum of Art.
   (A) onto
   (B) among
   (C) inside
   (D) toward

5. The Nevinton Library is open ------- all community residents.
   (A) to
   (B) on
   (C) from
   (D) at

6. HJB Technical School is now accepting applications ------- the upcoming semester in its pharmacy technician and medical administration courses.
   (A) for
   (B) along
   (C) among
   (D) on

7. Renowned violinist Aya Kodura maintained a rigorous practice schedule ------- her national tour.
   (A) during
   (B) among
   (C) aboard
   (D) inside

8. With consumer demand increasing substantially, Lignes Manufacturing must analyze the efficiency ------- its factories.
   (A) until
   (B) when
   (C) of
   (D) how

9. ------- her experience in sales, Ms. Woo has a background in public relations.
   (A) Although
   (B) Besides
   (C) Whether
   (D) Until

10. Please read the instructions ------- start to finish before attempting to replace the air filter yourself.
    (A) of
    (B) from
    (C) by
    (D) during

11. ------- receiving all the applications for the managerial position, the search committee will determine a list of people to be interviewed.
(A) About
(B) Except
(C) After
(D) With

12. Foreign investment has increased steadily over the last five years, largely ------- healthy upturns in several key global markets.
(A) insofar as
(B) thereby
(C) regarding
(D) because of

13. Articles submitted for publication in the *Sinchon Review* should be no more than ten pages ------- length.
(A) under
(B) in
(C) inside
(D) at

14. ------- the hypothesis, the results of the study showed that there was no significant difference in total sleep time between the two groups.
(A) Contrary to
(B) Even though
(C) Except for
(D) In place of

15. Redbury Town Library has received nearly €5,000 in contributions ------- the last twelve months.
(A) above
(B) behind
(C) over
(D) along

16. The number of transport companies competing ------- government contracts has decreased sharply in the last ten years.
(A) along
(B) for
(C) to
(D) near

17. As a result of the merger, all accounts with Sentrala Bank have been transferred to Clarus Trust Ltd. ------- the type of account.
(A) prior to
(B) except for
(C) instead of
(D) regardless of

18. ------- the last decade, Louellen Hospital has been recognized for exemplary patient care and progressive technology.
(A) Throughout
(B) Along
(C) Toward
(D) Beside

19. Mr. Gupta is ------- the few scientists who have been honored by both the Cooperson Society and the Henley Science Committee.
(A) about
(B) from
(C) among
(D) as

20. The organization plans to issue a statement this afternoon ------- the hiring of a well-known marketing strategist.
(A) near
(B) beyond
(C) among
(D) about

21. Ms. Cheon's presentation tried to address investors' unease ------- the negotiations surrounding a potential merger with the Tandell Corporation.
(A) in accordance with
(B) with regard to
(C) in place of
(D) by means of

22. The Vehicle Licensing Agency sends notices to all commercial truck drivers 90 days ------- their license expiration date.
(A) due to
(B) prior to
(C) far from
(D) outside of

23. Optics Eye Care has had all of its brochures and other written materials translated ------- five languages.
(A) on
(B) behind
(C) into
(D) around

24. ------- the large number of résumés received each month, we are unable to respond to every job applicant.
(A) Even if
(B) Other than
(C) Unless
(D) Given

25. ------- a number of inquiries from shareholders, James Hong has issued a formal announcement that his company is doing well.
(A) Following
(B) Beside
(C) Against
(D) Toward

26. Employees at Thompson Labs must wear all the protective gear shown on the poster at the lab entrance, ------- safety regulations.
(A) provided that
(B) extending
(C) in keeping with
(D) by means of

27. Additional details ------- the workshop will be sent to everyone who has expressed interest in attending.
(A) pertaining to
(B) across
(C) in spite of
(D) through

28. Avoid placing the digital scale ------- a source of excessive heat, as this may damage sensitive electronic components.
(A) between
(B) through
(C) despite
(D) near

29. Reference librarians can be reached 24 hours a day ------- Harkley Public Library's online chat service.
(A) through
(B) including
(C) between
(D) such as

30. The strategic planning committee's recommendation was that more emphasis should be put ------- research and development in the coming year.
(A) against
(B) during
(C) for
(D) on

1. Informal attire is not considered ------- for the Advertising Awards dinner.
   (A) useful
   (B) complete
   (C) significant
   (D) appropriate

2. Vista Apparel's ------- regarding the return and exchange of online purchases is detailed on the company Web site.
   (A) policy
   (B) pattern
   (C) order
   (D) supply

3. ------- her time at the university, Dr. LeFleur built a solid reputation for leadership among both students and faculty.
   (A) Into
   (B) Upon
   (C) About
   (D) During

4. If you would like to be considered for a position in our advertising division, please ------- an application to the director of human resources.
   (A) comply
   (B) submit
   (C) urge
   (D) advise

5. In an effort to reduce -------, Barsom Cosmetics has halved its advertising budget.
   (A) values
   (B) expenses
   (C) customs
   (D) refunds

6. Chef Ling's cooking show is ------- to air on public television next month.
   (A) given
   (B) scheduled
   (C) found
   (D) considered

7. In order to keep up with the ------- demand for our products, we will have to hire a minimum of four additional workers.
   (A) elaborating
   (B) useful
   (C) tracking
   (D) increasing

8. Over the last ten years, *Jamaica News* has built a ------- as one of the most reliable current-events programs in the Caribbean.
   (A) privilege
   (B) character
   (C) reputation
   (D) consequence

9. Sinna Motors' sales figures this year were nearly ------- to those recorded in the company's most successful period five years ago.
   (A) equal
   (B) uniform
   (C) even
   (D) fair

10. At Nahoa Media, the performance of junior editors is ------- quarterly.
    (A) evaluated
    (B) understood
    (C) parted
    (D) built

1. At Barna Telecommunications, project leaders are selected based on their expertise in a ------- area.
   (A) granted
   (B) provided
   (C) particular
   (D) substantial

2. Customers can find detailed ------- on repairing wireless problems in the user manual.
   (A) instructions
   (B) computers
   (C) posters
   (D) fixings

3. With its moderate climate and well-qualified workforce, Huntsville is a very ------- location for investors.
   (A) offering
   (B) proposing
   (C) promising
   (D) identifying

4. Based on the information provided, the two job applicants appear ------- qualified for the position.
   (A) punctually
   (B) frequently
   (C) equally
   (D) lately

5. Chin Rentals Group has decided to ------- its agreement with Jenkinson Maintenance.
   (A) proceed
   (B) renew
   (C) urge
   (D) attract

6. The tour group had ------- to be admitted to an area that is usually off-limits to the general public.
   (A) decision
   (B) expense
   (C) request
   (D) permission

7. The technical team is working ------- to restore online access as quickly as possible.
   (A) vastly
   (B) variably
   (C) diligently
   (D) longingly

8. National Bank officials announced that they have taken the necessary steps to ------- another computer system failure.
   (A) upgrade
   (B) ignore
   (C) prevent
   (D) improve

9. Daniel will be checking the report ------- mistakes before it is submitted to the group manager.
   (A) in
   (B) for
   (C) over
   (D) from

10. LTD Enterprises is currently seeking an ------- individual to replace the current director, who will be retiring at the end of the month.
    (A) accomplished
    (B) illustrated
    (C) observed
    (D) influenced

1. Landgrove Real Estate's revenue typically ------- during the winter months and then recovers in the spring.
   (A) declines
   (B) delays
   (C) impacts
   (D) impedes

2. Accountants process a considerable amount of material ------- strict time limits.
   (A) toward
   (B) past
   (C) near
   (D) within

3. To prevent milk and other ------- products from deteriorating, Delio's food delivery trucks are refrigerated.
   (A) plentiful
   (B) perishable
   (C) constructive
   (D) adverse

4. The packaging of Ozigrain cereal will be changed to ------- an even wider market overseas.
   (A) invite
   (B) demand
   (C) call out
   (D) appeal to

5. Havelock Insurance processes a high ------- of claims daily, so it needs efficient employees.
   (A) point
   (B) size
   (C) section
   (D) volume

6. Jane Wiseman has her own publishing company dealing almost ------- with biographies.
   (A) exclusively
   (B) impulsively
   (C) mutually
   (D) generously

7. Construction is ------- 47 percent complete on the Culler Coliseum renovation project.
   (A) far
   (B) now
   (C) once
   (D) quite

8. Ignacio Metal Corporation operates two facilities with a combined floor space ------- 89,000 square meters.
   (A) earning
   (B) processing
   (C) totaling
   (D) completing

9. The new graphic design software program has improved the quality of the designers' work as well as their -------.
   (A) economies
   (B) harvest
   (C) measures
   (D) productivity

10. Tomorrow's training is ------- for employees who have been with the company for less than one year.
    (A) based
    (B) intended
    (C) agreed
    (D) invited

1. After several hours of repair work, the truck was finally ------- to resume its delivery route.
   (A) valuable
   (B) responsible
   (C) able
   (D) possible

2. The Community Center's wellness workshop serves as a ------- for discussing healthful habits.
   (A) selection
   (B) ground
   (C) vision
   (D) forum

3. We will ------- the results of the travel poll with our readers next week on our Web site.
   (A) split
   (B) share
   (C) sample
   (D) suggest

4. Due to technical problems, Nelson's Electronic Auctions is ------- not accepting any picture submissions via e-mail.
   (A) quickly
   (B) currently
   (C) precisely
   (D) temperately

5. Lake Financial agreed to make a $250 million ------- in the news Web site Everydaylive.com.
   (A) investment
   (B) preservation
   (C) requirement
   (D) property

6. Neblus, Inc., will have to add staff if it expects to ------- all of the orders by the end of the year.
   (A) affect
   (B) contain
   (C) fulfill
   (D) mention

7. Mr. Yamanaka prefers that employee expense reports be submitted ------- after the expense has been incurred.
   (A) measurably
   (B) vaguely
   (C) uniquely
   (D) promptly

8. Given the recent boom in new construction, the price of lumber is ------- to climb.
   (A) covered
   (B) sought
   (C) limited
   (D) bound

9. Employees of Reconnaissance Corporation who share rides to work will be eligible for special parking privileges ------- Wednesday.
   (A) outside
   (B) starting on
   (C) afterward
   (D) instead of

10. According to company guidelines, new employees are ------- to receive vacation benefits after three months of full-time employment.
    (A) capable
    (B) variable
    (C) flexible
    (D) eligible

1. All laboratory ------- must annually complete a course in safety practices.
   (A) personnel
   (B) research
   (C) evidence
   (D) network

2. Ayumi Suzuki, an authority on sustainable land use, will be the ------- speaker at the Ninth Agroforestry Conference.
   (A) successive
   (B) principal
   (C) maximum
   (D) immediate

3. The news program's premiere was rescheduled, and it will now be shown on Saturday -------.
   (A) alike
   (B) instead
   (C) already
   (D) seldom

4. When Howland Bakery first began using larger trucks for delivery, all of them were ------- white and brown.
   (A) changed
   (B) painted
   (C) alternated
   (D) transferred

5. Food vendors must ------- with all applicable policies pertaining to sales at special events.
   (A) comply
   (B) achieve
   (C) regulate
   (D) authorize

6. Onsite parking passes are issued ------- the availability of spaces in the garage.
   (A) such as
   (B) adjacent to
   (C) except for
   (D) based on

7. Because our supplies are -------, we can only make this offer to the first fifty customers who come to the store.
   (A) limited
   (B) speedy
   (C) available
   (D) presentable

8. Personnel must sign the register ------- removing any confidential papers from the organization's vaults.
   (A) before
   (B) until
   (C) from
   (D) during

9. Ms. Rivera made it clear that ------- the landowner may authorize improvements to the property.
   (A) only
   (B) easily
   (C) simply
   (D) merely

10. Gryphon Solutions is a growing computer support company ------- to expand its business in East Asia.
    (A) simple
    (B) frequent
    (C) common
    (D) eager

기출 TEST 6

1. Invoices should not be processed ------- the customer's signature.
(A) except
(B) besides
(C) amid
(D) without

2. Please note that the shipping charge for orders under $25, or the ------- amount in local currency, is nonrefundable.
(A) equivalent
(B) profitable
(C) deliberate
(D) controlled

3. The aquarium on Leland Avenue is expected to draw thousands of visitors annually and bring ------- revenue to the city.
(A) modeled
(B) increased
(C) managed
(D) reserved

4. The hotel offers an ------- one-night stay free of charge when guests book two nights.
(A) eager
(B) easy
(C) earliest
(D) extra

5. Ms. Ishimura generously offered to ------- the invitation in person rather than send it through the mail.
(A) respond
(B) benefit
(C) commute
(D) deliver

6. Permits for Gisborne's ------- opened parking garage can be purchased online.
(A) recently
(B) typically
(C) directly
(D) concisely

7. Greene and Burch is a full-service accounting firm that can assist you with a ------- of financial and business needs.
(A) kind
(B) deposit
(C) range
(D) way

8. Workshop participants may choose any seat in the auditorium except those in the front row, which are ------- for the presenters.
(A) chaired
(B) reserved
(C) substituted
(D) performed

9. On Thursday, Ms. Cornado should receive the ------- of the recent survey conducted by the research and development department.
(A) chances
(B) results
(C) matters
(D) events

10. Reports suggest that weather conditions will ------- the July operations of Icehouse Fisheries Ltd.
(A) interfere with
(B) correspond to
(C) fall behind
(D) rely on

1. The Zatcon electronic filing system ensures that all your departmental documents are ------- at a moment's notice.
   (A) competent
   (B) accessible
   (C) constant
   (D) accustomed

2. Some fans lined up outside the box office for as long as fourteen hours to ------- tickets for the concert.
   (A) support
   (B) purchase
   (C) achieve
   (D) replace

3. The new science museum is expected to ------- many tourists to the city.
   (A) attract
   (B) value
   (C) capture
   (D) observe

4. After much -------, it was decided that the company picnic would take place at Sweetwater Park.
   (A) outcome
   (B) precision
   (C) knowledge
   (D) deliberation

5. Every two years, the board of directors ------- a new financial officer to oversee the company's domestic operations.
   (A) deposits
   (B) appoints
   (C) predicts
   (D) operates

6. To take ------- of the company's free software-upgrade program, customers should mail a copy of their receipt to the address provided.
   (A) merit
   (B) service
   (C) advantage
   (D) improvement

7. The maintenance department should ------- be contacted when there is a problem with the air-conditioning.
   (A) exactly
   (B) evenly
   (C) ever
   (D) always

8. Ms. Habib is respected ------- her colleagues and business clients alike.
   (A) plus
   (B) from
   (C) in
   (D) by

9. To avoid leaving anyone behind, the tour operator ------- all the visitors to be in the front lobby by 7 A.M.
   (A) recalled
   (B) memorized
   (C) reminded
   (D) identified

10. Baxter Consulting intends to combine information from various sources in order to provide a single ------- directory of local businesses.
    (A) variable
    (B) apparent
    (C) redundant
    (D) comprehensive

1. Windorn Pharmacy has put significant effort ------- expanding its marketing tools.
   (A) under
   (B) between
   (C) into
   (D) about

2. Holden Enterprises rewards employees who consistently ------- company expectations.
   (A) exceed
   (B) describe
   (C) command
   (D) believe

3. *Searching the Stars* would make a ------- addition to any amateur astronomer's book collection.
   (A) high
   (B) public
   (C) same
   (D) great

4. The full name of the store is The Book Escape for the Imaginative, but it is usually ------- as The Escape.
   (A) referred to
   (B) expanded upon
   (C) balanced
   (D) installed

5. With his superior designs, Mr. Park has already ------- himself from his peers.
   (A) differentiated
   (B) designated
   (C) fashioned
   (D) featured

6. Ms. Croft began working at the Central Library five years ago and has ------- become the director.
   (A) ever
   (B) yet
   (C) so
   (D) since

7. The environmental commission concluded that there is a ------- for immediate funding to repair the dam.
   (A) control
   (B) center
   (C) look
   (D) need

8. The editors of *Caribbean Journal of Engineering* are ------- about which articles they publish.
   (A) prominent
   (B) punctual
   (C) rigorous
   (D) selective

9. *Market Solutions* is one of Europe's leading international business magazines, with ------- in over 50 countries.
   (A) subscribers
   (B) spectators
   (C) witnesses
   (D) participants

10. Real estate agents claim that ------- to the landscape in the Presmont area will encourage buyers to consider homes there.
    (A) continuations
    (B) increments
    (C) deviations
    (D) enhancements

1. Ms. Klein was ------- the grand prize for her routine in the company talent show.
(A) won
(B) awarded
(C) taken
(D) acquired

2. ------- of local businesses for the Readers' Choice Awards must be submitted to the *News-Tribune* by May 20.
(A) Subscriptions
(B) Nominations
(C) Supporters
(D) Venues

3. Employees should make ------- records of travel expenses to avoid delays when requesting reimbursements.
(A) returned
(B) caring
(C) distant
(D) accurate

4. We are ------- seeking volunteers to participate in an upcoming consumer research study for Mayfee Marketing.
(A) significantly
(B) currently
(C) completely
(D) slightly

5. Companies need to provide year-round training to technical support staff due to ------- improvements in technology.
(A) continuous
(B) prosperous
(C) mature
(D) straight

6. The strategic planning meeting will be postponed ------- Mr. Kwon's return.
(A) around
(B) until
(C) from
(D) within

7. The Lafayette Townhome Community is ------- located near a train line that leads to the region's largest shopping mall.
(A) conveniently
(B) consistently
(C) continually
(D) commonly

8. Ms. Kushida's managers feel that she deserves special ------- for her performance in the last sales campaign.
(A) recognition
(B) accomplishment
(C) capability
(D) balance

9. The ------- of the new inventory process has had a significant impact on our management of resources.
(A) habit
(B) adoption
(C) trade
(D) reservation

10. Please ------- the enclosed instructions before attempting to install your new dishwasher.
(A) direct
(B) review
(C) gather
(D) program

1. The head mechanic will ------- the proper method of replacing brake fluid in the Prime SX cars.
(A) demonstrate
(B) respond
(C) inquire
(D) visit

2. Volunteers will help conference participants ------- their way around the convention center.
(A) do
(B) find
(C) put
(D) ask

3. Customers unhappy with the performance of their stereo equipment have two months to request a refund or -------.
(A) complaint
(B) receipt
(C) replacement
(D) promotion

4. ------- among the reasons Ms. Yun is the most qualified candidate is her twelve years of experience as a professor of marketing.
(A) Adept
(B) Proper
(C) Chief
(D) Straight

5. Consumers can ------- enroll online for Wozetco's current marketing study.
(A) very
(B) least
(C) easily
(D) more

6. Sales of the book *Prosperous Investing* have not been ------- to warrant its inclusion in a window display.
(A) many
(B) fair
(C) usual
(D) enough

7. All commercial catering businesses refrigerate perishable food to ------- it from spoiling.
(A) remove
(B) oppose
(C) prevent
(D) forbid

8. Jane Tollen's original manuscript was published last year after Jansen Books obtained her family's -------.
(A) permission
(B) suggestion
(C) comparison
(D) registration

9. We at TPG Financial Planning welcome the opportunity to assist you in your business and look forward to a ------- beneficial relationship.
(A) mutually
(B) punctually
(C) respectively
(D) precisely

10. Our company believes that employees should always work hard, yet they must ------- have time for their families.
(A) altogether
(B) also
(C) alone
(D) almost

1. Ms. Park accepted the internship because it had the ------- to lead to a permanent position.
   (A) preference
   (B) potential
   (C) authority
   (D) ambition

2. The personnel director cannot hire a new sales executive without the CEO's -------.
   (A) success
   (B) advantage
   (C) approval
   (D) benefit

3. The Wooley City Craft Market offers unique handmade items that are not available -------.
   (A) evidently
   (B) elsewhere
   (C) thoroughly
   (D) beyond

4. Drivers must be at least 21 years of age in order to ------- a rental car in Riverside County.
   (A) place
   (B) find
   (C) lease
   (D) turn

5. Next week Zexton Corporation will ------- £1,000 bonuses to employees who exceeded sales quotas last year.
   (A) distribute
   (B) separate
   (C) surprise
   (D) reserve

6. The Hagersville City Council sought to reduce city waste by ------- an extensive recycling program.
   (A) collecting
   (B) implementing
   (C) recruiting
   (D) estimating

7. Kurliss Communications has been our ------- competitor for the past three years.
   (A) full
   (B) numerous
   (C) main
   (D) most

8. Next month, Katie Cooper will be offering a time-management ------- for all employees.
   (A) business
   (B) workshop
   (C) location
   (D) expert

9. At Healthy Tots, we encourage loyalty in our customers by providing quality goods at ------- prices.
   (A) attractive
   (B) primary
   (C) actual
   (D) fortunate

10. Rosine Printing will announce a name change next month as a result of the ------- merger with Burton Paper Company.
    (A) recent
    (B) various
    (C) ready
    (D) frequent

1. Since Kayla's Catering improved its Web site, the number of ------- to the site has increased.
   (A) visitors
   (B) products
   (C) options
   (D) profits

2. Rayford Manufacturing expects to end the year with a budget ------- of one million dollars.
   (A) surplus
   (B) assembly
   (C) launch
   (D) committee

3. Due to the demand for La Paz vacation rental properties, analysts say prices this year will ------- rise.
   (A) firstly
   (B) likely
   (C) tightly
   (D) previously

4. At Exoterrene, all correspondence must be responded to within one week ------- receipt.
   (A) of
   (B) throughout
   (C) about
   (D) by

5. All workers at CPC Builders must take ------- while working in cold weather to keep themselves safe.
   (A) element
   (B) precautions
   (C) advantage
   (D) conditions

6. Typically, most spectators leave the Tellaso Arena shortly after the results of the tournament are -------.
   (A) reduced
   (B) removed
   (C) announced
   (D) continued

7. When Mr. Joshi reviewed his account records, he ------- the monthly charge had not been deleted.
   (A) started
   (B) glanced
   (C) postponed
   (D) noticed

8. Any bicycle parts broken ------- repair during shipment must be promptly reported and returned.
   (A) into
   (B) of
   (C) except
   (D) beyond

9. The waiting room is more inviting and ------- for patients now that it has been remodeled.
   (A) comfortable
   (B) competent
   (C) peculiar
   (D) familiar

10. ------- completion of our online survey earns the respondent credit toward a future purchase.
    (A) Dependent
    (B) Fortunate
    (C) Successful
    (D) Prosperous

PART

6

RC

ETS TOEIC

UNIT 01

대명사 / 지시어 문제

평균 2~4문제 출제

무료인강

출제공식 1 **대명사 / 지시어 문제의 단서는 빈칸 앞 문장에 있다.**

대명사(we, he, it, they 등)와 지시어(this, that, these, such 등) 문제는 가리키는 대상을 지문 내에서 찾는
문제이다. 지칭하는 명사의 단/복수를 꼼꼼히 살펴야 한다.

ETS 예제 이메일

번역 p. 127

Dear Ms. Busby,

Thank you for your message on May 2. Our records indicate
that ① you ordered **two Jollite bicycle tires** (product
JBT1783) through our Web site on April 27 and that **they**
were scheduled to arrive on May 1. ② I am sorry to hear that
you have not yet received ------- . Deliveries usually take no
more than three or four days.

(A) it

(B) one

(C) them

(D) some

핵심내용

① 고객님은 졸리트 자전거 **타이어
2개를** 주문하셨습니다. …
그것들은 5월 1일에 도착할
예정이었습니다.

② 아직 **그것들을** 받지 못하셨다니
죄송합니다.

풀이

①에서 주문한 타이어 2개를
언급했고, ②에서 해당 주문품을
지칭하므로 복수명사이자, 사람/사물
둘 다 지칭할 수 있는 대명사
them으로 받아야 한다.

정답률을 높이는 학습노트

● 인칭대명사 선택 문제

Mr. wolf was awarded the Excellence in Innovation Prize. Let's
congratulate [him / his / us] for receiving the award.

수상자인 Mr. Wolf를 지칭하는
인칭대명사의 목적격 자리이므로 him을
선택한다.

● 지시어/부정대명사 선택 문제

Please update **your address and phone number,** and inform us if
[either / much / these] has changed.

주소와 전화번호 둘 중 어느 하나라도
변경되었으면 알려 달라는 말이므로
둘 중 정해지지 않은 하나를 가리키는
부정대명사 either를 선택한다.
빈칸 뒤에 단수동사 has가 왔으므로
these는 답이 될 수 없다.

1 고객 후기

> **Review of Precicon Worldwide Movers**
>
> Two months ago I unexpectedly learned that I had to move back to Sweden. I had heard about the good reputation of Precicon Worldwide Movers, so I decided to use their service to ship my items from California to Stockholm.
>
> The customer services representative I worked with was excellent; he replied to all e-mails promptly. ------- answers were thorough and helpful. And the price he quoted was quite competitive.

(A) My   (B) His   (C) Both   (D) Their

2 회람

> A recent survey has shown that the number of employees using the company's fitness center has decreased dramatically over the past six months. We understand that, as our business grows, our workers are becoming increasingly busy. Therefore, we have decided to extend the operating hours of the fitness center. Beginning on February 3, ------- will open at 6:00 A.M. and close at 8:30 P.M. We hope that the additional two hours per day will allow employees to take full advantage of the benefits the fitness center offers.

(A) some   (B) each   (C) it   (D) he

3 이메일

> Thank you for inquiring about the procedure for making changes to orders from Finestri Books Online. To answer your question, we cannot change an order placed through our Web site once it has shipped.
>
> However, if your order is still being processed and has not yet been sent out, you may be able to add or remove an item. To do either of ------- , you must speak to a customer service representative.

(A) each   (B) this   (C) that   (D) these

Questions 4-7 refer to the following press release.

Next month, Kenji Lai Ltd. (KLL), Malaysian manufacturer of boldly colored ------- , will
move its national headquarters to 18 Utama Road, where a contemporary ten-story
office building has been renovated. KLL will ------- the top two floors of the building.
There, executive marketing and sales staff will enjoy nearly 35,000 square meters of
new office space. ------- . "This will be an ideal area to display our high-tech ovens and
refrigerators," said company spokesperson Aishah Noor. The company's engineering and
design departments will remain in ------- original location in Taiping, Ms. Noor noted.

4   (A) fixtures
    (B) apparel
    (C) wallpaper
    (D) appliances

7   (A) it
    (B) their
    (C) what
    (D) any

5   (A) sell
    (B) paint
    (C) occupy
    (D) photograph

6   (A) KLL is also leasing retail space on the
        ground floor.
    (B) KLL's products feature cutting-edge
        energy efficiency.
    (C) KLL was listed among the top 50
        places to work in Malaysia.
    (D) KLL's stock price rose after the move
        was announced.

Questions 8-11 refer to the following advertisement.

Enroll in our executive coaching course and gain the ------- needed to mentor business
leaders so they can rapidly develop their managerial abilities. The greatest reward of
executive coaching is in exercising the ability ------- possess to help people in very
practical ways. Imagine the sense of accomplishment when clients leave bad habits
behind and begin to ------- deal with workplace challenges. We train coaches in the art
of supporting clients toward discovering solutions for themselves. ------- . For anyone in
agreement with our philosophy of coaching, this course is a sure way to advance to the
next level.

8 (A) questions
   (B) goals
   (C) skills
   (D) costs

9 (A) you
   (B) he
   (C) she
   (D) it

10 (A) prematurely
   (B) excessively
   (C) barely
   (D) effectively

11 (A) Our financial consultants are in high
       demand.
   (B) In so doing, the client's own
       resourcefulness is affirmed.
   (C) We are looking to fill several
       management positions.
   (D) That is why we offer career counseling
       upon graduation.

UNIT 02 시제 문제

평균 2~4문제 출제

무료인강

출제공식 2 **시제 문제의 단서는 글의 종류, 날짜, 주변 문장의 시제에 있다.**

Part 6에서 시제 문제는 빈칸이 있는 문장만으로는 답을 찾을 수 없는 경우가 많다. 정답의 근거는 이메일이 작성된 날짜, 주변 문장에 쓰인 시제, 글의 종류 등이 될 수 있다. 따라서 이와 같은 요소들을 근거로 하여 시제를 판단해야 한다.

ETS 예제 **이메일**

번역 p. 129

To: Guiyun Lee <glee@grandmoonhotel.com>
From: Everett King <eking@grandmoonhotel.com>
① **Date: 21 August**
Subject: Good afternoon

Guiyun,

I was recently informed of your ② **upcoming promotion.**
Although ③ the new position as general manager in our
Beijing location officially ------- on **3 September,** I wanted
to offer my best wishes to you now. The transition can be
challenging, so feel free to contact me if you need any help.

(A) begins   (B) began
(C) has begun   (D) could begin

핵심내용

① 이메일 작성일: **8월 21일**
② 곧 있을 승진
③ 새 직책 공식 시작일: **9월 3일**

풀이

이메일이 작성된 시점(①)보다 더 미래에 있을 승진(②)과 날짜(③)를 언급하므로 미래를 의미할 수 있는 시제가 필요하다.
현재 시제는 가까운 미래를 나타낼 수 있으므로 begins가 정답이 된다.

정답률을 높이는 학습노트

● **해석에 유의해야 하는 시제**

현재완료(have p.p.)	① ~했다(완료된 상황): **have arrived** (이미) 도착했다
	② ~해 왔다(현재까지 계속되는 상황): **have increased**: (지금껏) 증가해 왔다
현재진행 시제(be -ing)	① ~하고 있는 중이다(현재 상황): **is being repaired** (지금) 수리되고 있는 중이다
	② ~할 것이다 (정해진 미래): **is hosting** (곧) 개최할 것이다
미래진행(will be -ing)	(미래에 진행될 일) We **will be offering** a complimentary dessert to patrons.
	저희는 손님들에게 무료 디저트를 제공할 것입니다.
be to 용법	(예정) The reimbursement **is to be given** within 2 weeks.
	환급은 2주 내에 지급될 예정이다.

ETS CHECK-UP

정답 및 해설 p. 129

1 이메일

It is with great excitement that I inform you that the Komplet Industries Web site is to have a new look and improved functionality. The site ------- several upgraded features such as mobile-device readability and an interactive tour of Komplet facilities. The transition to the new site is scheduled to occur on Saturday, March 31.

(A) included   (B) had included   (C) will include   (D) to include

2 기사

Marvelous Landscapes at High Street Gallery

by Ira Bardsley

LEEDS (7 June)—High Street Gallery's latest exhibition opened last night to an appreciative crowd. The show ------- oil paintings by Jo Wu, watercolours by Trevor Nightingale, and pastels by Casey Feld. Though their styles are distinct, the artists share an interest in capturing the beauty of the local landscape. The works of art complement one another nicely.

(A) will feature   (B) features   (C) featuring   (D) might feature

3 편지

November 5

Dear Ms. Krzezewski,

Thank you for your recent letter. You wanted to know if the Adventurer Jacket from Everwear Clothing would once again become available in the Soft Plum color, as it was last season. In fact, we ------- that color. It has been replaced with the Wild Berry color, which is a shade darker. We did this in response to customer feedback that indicated that dirt showed much less on the darker colors than the lighter ones.

(A) are discontinued   (B) would have discontinued
(C) have discontinued   (D) will have discontinued

Questions 4-7 refer to the following article.

Women's History at the Berkford Museum

Now on display at the Berkford Museum is *She Creates History*. This ------- honors the
4
leaders who earned women the right to vote in the United States. It also focuses -------
5
significant figures in modern American history who earned acclaim in science, literature,
and law. Important documents, photographs, and paintings are on display. Museum
visitors ------- a short film featuring actual footage of early speeches and interviews.
6
------- . *She Creates History* runs through April 20.
7

---

4 (A) article
   (B) award
   (C) exhibit
   (D) documentary

5 (A) by
   (B) on
   (C) with
   (D) after

6 (A) also enjoyed
   (B) can also enjoy
   (C) are also enjoying
   (D) have also enjoyed

7 (A) The museum will be closed for
       maintenance on April 3.
   (B) Unfortunately, the film is no longer
       available.
   (C) Come and learn how these events
       changed history.
   (D) To volunteer, please fill out an
       application at the museum.

Questions 8-11 refer to the following e-mail.

To: dbyeon@mymail.com
From: shipping@anyyouneed.com
Date: January 9
Re: Order #39-AX19Z

Dear Ms. Byeon,

Your order of two portable wireless speakers just left our warehouse. It ------- to 387
8
Parker Avenue, Syosset, New York, on January 12. You may track your order ------- using
9
our live map to view the location of your package.

We hope our ------- meets your expectations. ------- . You can reach our customer service
10 **11**
team from 7:00 A.M. to 7:00 P.M. at (800) 555-0131. Thank you for your business.

Shipping Department

8 (A) has been delivered
   (B) was delivered
   (C) to be delivered
   (D) will be delivered

9 (A) by
   (B) about
   (C) inside
   (D) off

10 (A) class
   (B) document
   (C) product
   (D) music

11 (A) Please contact us with any concerns.
   (B) Note that your payment is now
       overdue.
   (C) Present this e-mail at a local retail
       store.
   (D) We were unable to process your credit
       card.

UNIT 03

접속부사 문제

평균 2~4문제 출제

무료인강

출제공식 3 **접속부사 문제의 단서는 빈칸 앞뒤 문장에 있다.**

접속부사는 문장과 문장을 논리적으로 연결하는 부사이다. 빈칸 앞뒤 문장의 논리적 관계에 따라 역접, 인과, 첨가, 대조 등 알맞은 접속부사를 선택해야 한다. 또한 접속사, 전치사와의 문법적인 차이를 구분할 수 있어야 한다.

ETS 예제 **웹페이지**   번역 p. 131

Violet Sky Rewards

…

① Points can be redeemed to purchase airline tickets, reserve hotel rooms, or rent cars anywhere in the world. ------- , ② the card offers special perks, including free checked bags and priority boarding when members book travel with Tilles Airlines. To get all this for no annual fee, apply at www.vsrewards.com.

(A) Therefore

(B) Regardless

(C) In addition

(D) For instance

핵심내용

① 포인트는 전 세계 어디에서나 항공권 구입, 호텔 객실 예약, 자동차 대여 등에 사용할 수 있습니다.

게다가

② 본 카드는 회원들이 틸레스 항공사로 여행할 때 무료 수하물 수속과 우선 탑승을 포함한 특전을 제공합니다.

풀이

①에서 포인트의 다양한 사용 범위를, ②에서 추가적인 혜택을 언급하므로 첨가의 접속부사 In addition으로 연결하는 것이 자연스럽다.

정답률을 높이는 학습노트

● **빈출 접속부사**

however 그러나	nevertheless 그럼에도 불구하고	still 그럼에도 불구하고	therefore 따라서
then 그 다음에, 그때	consequently 결과적으로	as a result 그 결과	thus 그러므로
in addition 게다가	furthermore 게다가	moreover 게다가	besides 게다가
namely 즉, 다시 말해	on the other hand 반면에	in contrast 대조적으로	likewise 마찬가지로
in fact 사실	otherwise 그렇지 않으면	in short 간단히 말해서	instead 대신
in particular 특히	to that end 그런 목적을 위해	for example 예를 들어	meanwhile 그동안에
in the meantime 그동안에	if not 만약 그렇지 않다면	if so 만약 그렇다면	alternatively 또는

● **접속부사 vs. 접속사 구분하기**

접속부사	The weather conditions were poor. **However,** the event was well attended. 날씨가 열악했다. 그러나	접속부사를 쓸 때는 앞 문장에 마침표를 찍고 두 문장을 독립적으로 쓴다.
접속사	**Although** the weather conditions were poor, the event was well attended. 날씨가 열악했음에도 불구하고	접속사는 두 개의 완전한 절을 하나로 이어 준다.

ETS CHECK-UP

정답 및 해설 p. 131

PART 6 | UNIT 03

1 이메일

Our clients called this morning to inform us that one more person will be joining our meeting at our glass factory this Thursday. This unforeseen change won't affect us in any major way. The clients will still arrive at 10 A.M. to discuss technical matters. That afternoon, we will still take them on an interesting and informative tour of the factory. ------- , before we start the tour, please have safety equipment ready for four, not three, people. This includes an extra hard hat, earplugs, and boots.

(A) Instead
(B) However
(C) Besides
(D) Similarly

2 이메일

Dear Ms. Espino,

Mr. Miyashita, the owner of The Miyashita Gallery of Kyoto, was pleased to display your work as part of the May Modern Artists Celebration. He was particularly impressed with your stunning collection of oil paintings of everyday life in Madrid. He now hopes to present these pieces at his other gallery in Tokyo in September. Are they available for exhibition and sale? Any work that does not sell would be returned to you in October. Please inform us if you are interested and, ------- , we can arrange a meeting to discuss compensation and further details.

(A) even if
(B) if so
(C) so long as
(D) in case

3 보도

SINGAPORE (5 April)—Peytin Tires is planning to greatly increase warehouse capacity at its tire plants in Kuala Lumpur and Bangkok. Larger warehouses are expected to open by the end of the year. The expansion project will improve the company's ability to serve tire dealers throughout Asia.

"The new warehouses will allow us to work more efficiently and save on costs," said Peytin Tires' CEO Xiaolin Cui. "------- , we will be able to better meet the demands of customers across Asia who have reached out to us. This move was made in direct response to their feedback."

(A) If not
(B) Nevertheless
(C) On the contrary
(D) At the same time

241

Questions 4-7 refer to the following e-mail.

To: Bryan Anuru <banuru@brightwing.co.nz>
From: Priscilla Jenkins <pjenkins@blue-depths.org.nz>
Subject: Information
Date: 10 June

Dear Mr. Anuru,

We have received your application for a job as staff photographer at Blue Depths Aquarium. The ------- is still available. ------- .
         4   **5**

I ------- that you have had previous experience working as photographer at an aquarium,
  6
so some of the job duties will be familiar to you. ------- , our facility is unique in many
                                   7
ways, so you would need to learn new procedures here. I have tentatively scheduled an
interview for 17 June at 11:00 A.M. Please call my office at (09) 362 3351 to confirm the
appointment. I look forward to meeting you then.

Sincerely,

Priscilla Jenkins, Personnel Director
Blue Depths Aquarium

---

4 (A) camera
(B) position
(C) picture
(D) document

5 (A) Can you provide me with details about
the compensation at this time?
(B) Specifically, are you familiar with
photo-editing software?
(C) Directions to the facility can be found
on our Web site.
(D) If you remain interested, an on-site
interview will be the next step.

6 (A) see
(B) would see
(C) will see
(D) have been seen

7 (A) Accordingly
(B) Moreover
(C) However
(D) Consequently

November 30—After two years of construction, the largest hotel in Pittsburgh history is almost ready to open. The Rivertop Hotel, on the banks of the Allegheny River, will have 1,012 rooms for visitors. ------- . The first guests will arrive on December 12 as part of a
8
medical technology conference. The project is among four downtown-area hotels ------- .
9
According to Kristofer Walsh, president of the Pittsburgh Hotel & Lodging Association, these new developments are a ------- . "We've had a massive influx of visitors over the
10
past few years," said Mr. Walsh. "------- , almost all the hotels in the city are completely
11
full. Clearly, additional hotel rooms are needed."

8 (A) It is unclear when it will be ready to accept reservations.
(B) Building renovations will begin next month.
(C) It will also have seven meeting rooms for groups of up to 200 people.
(D) There are multiple companies bidding on the job.

9 (A) to construct
(B) are constructing
(C) were constructed
(D) being constructed

10 (A) necessity
(B) nuisance
(C) risk
(D) bargain

11 (A) On the other hand
(B) In other words
(C) In the first place
(D) As a result

UNIT 04 어휘 문제

평균 4~6문제 출제

무료인강

출제공식 4 어휘 문제의 단서는 글 전체 또는 주변 문장에 있다.

Part 6의 어휘 문제는 전체 글을 읽고 주제와 흐름을 파악해야 풀 수 있다. 대부분의 경우, 빈칸을 포함하고 있는
문장만으로는 해결되지 않으며, 앞뒤에 오는 주변 문장에서 단서를 찾아 정답을 결정해야 한다.

ETS 예제 안내문

번역 p. 133

① The community center offers several ------- events throughout the year. The largest and most famous is our annual Fern Fair. All residents are invited to join us on April 12 this year on the Broad Street Pier ② to enjoy the area's best food, crafts, and musical performances while savoring the cool spring breeze.

(A) outdoor
(B) exclusive
(C) athletic
(D) formal

핵심내용

① 커뮤니티 센터는 연중 내내 여러 가지 행사를 제공합니다.

② 시원한 봄바람을 느끼며, 지역 최고의 음식, 공예품, 음악 공연을 즐길 수 있습니다.

풀이

① 보기의 어휘 모두 '행사'를 수식할 수 있는 형용사이므로 해당 문장만으로는 정답을 가려낼 수 없다.

② '시원한 봄바람을 느끼며'라고 했으므로 '실외'라는 단서가 제공된다. 따라서 '야외 행사'가 정답이 된다.

정답률을 높이는 학습노트

● **빈칸 문장 앞에 단서가 있는 경우**

Thank you for agreeing to meet with me on Friday to discuss the acquisition of a TX printer. ... (중략) I look forward to seeing you at the end of the [week / ~~conference~~].

빈칸이 있는 문장만으로는 이번 주 말에 보는지, 회의 말미에 보는지 알 수 없으나, 앞 문장에서 '금요일에 만나기로 약속해 줘서 감사하다'라고 했으므로, 이를 근거로 '이번 주 말'을 선택할 수 있다.

● **빈칸 문장 뒤에 단서가 있는 경우**

I want to let you know that we are holding our [~~first~~ / **annual**] career fair on Saturday, March 2. **This is always our biggest event of the year.**

빈칸이 있는 문장만으로는 첫 번째 박람회인지, 연례 박람회인지 알 수 없으나, 뒤 문장에서 '이 박람회가 늘 한 해 중 가장 큰 행사이다'라고 했으므로, 이를 근거로 '연례 박람회'를 선택할 수 있다.

1 공지

Are you an amateur athlete looking for a ------- ? Get ready for the premier competition of the year. Test your abilities at the Johannesburg Metropolitan Meet of Champions, where athletes from Randburg, Roodepoort, and Sandton will have a chance to represent their hometowns and compete for prizes in a variety of sports. The meet will take place in Roodepoort on 30 March. It is open to athletes 15 years or older. To register, visit jmmchampions.co.za.

(A) trainer

(B) scholarship

(C) teammate

(D) challenge

2 보도

FOR IMMEDIATE RELEASE

TREFFORD CITY (November 18)—The City Waste Management Authority (CWMA) has teamed up with GDA Waste Solutions, a local recycling facility, to collect electronic waste for recycling.

This ------- allows residents to drop off old devices, such as mobile phones and laptop computers, for pickup at the Community Center on Fir Street. Items are accepted during the center's regular hours. Residents are asked not to leave items outside the center after it has closed. "The drop-off program is part of our new 'Clean City' campaign," said CWMA Director Lloyd Ingram.

(A) modification

(B) partnership

(C) separation

(D) law

3 회람

To: All Staff
From: Accounting Department
Date: February 4
Subject: Revised Procedures

Please be advised that the travel compensation procedure for attendance at industry conferences has been modified. ------- , travel expenses were reimbursed several weeks after completion of the trip. Now, employees must submit an Estimated Travel Costs form at least thirty days prior to traveling. All anticipated expenses will be paid by the company, provided that they are reasonable and have been preapproved. Once the travel request has been processed, notification of the approved funding amount will be sent to the employee.

(A) Accordingly

(B) Similarly

(C) Previously

(D) Finally

Questions 4-7 refer to the following article.

LOS ANGELES (April 22)—For a limited time this year, Lunera Coffee Roasters will sell its products in retro packaging dating from fifty years ago, when the brand ------- became famous. This temporary face-lift will not be restricted to Lunera's existing coffees. The company will be introducing cinnamon, ginseng, and dark chocolate coffees, ------- the size of its flavored line; these will also sport vintage-inspired designs.

Lunera president Luz Ortega says the packaging celebrates the brand's history. ------- . "We feel this campaign will resonate with both long-time and new customers," notes Ortega.

Lunera's retro packaging will begin to hit store shelves in June. And its new ------- will debut in July.

4 (A) yet
   (B) it
   (C) first
   (D) all

5 (A) doubling
   (B) had doubled
   (C) will double
   (D) doubles

6 (A) Market research suggests that these flavors will be popular.
   (B) The price of coffee is expected to rise worldwide.
   (C) That is why Lunera has become so famous.
   (D) It also appeals to consumers who long for a simpler time.

7 (A) services
   (B) methods
   (C) devices
   (D) varieties

Questions 8-11 refer to the following press release.

FOR IMMEDIATE RELEASE   Media contact: Albert Yee, (808) 555-0147

The Lopaka Group Welcomes Jo Gacutan

KAPOLEI, HI (August 2)—The Lopaka Group is ------- to announce that it has added
            8

Jo Gacutan as a consultant in the Promotional Services Division. The Lopaka Group

specializes in providing ------- advice and is one of the most successful such firms in the
            9

state.

"Ms. Gacutan is a wonderful addition to the company," said Brent Shimizu, Lopaka

Group's executive vice president of promotions and research. "------- . She knows how
                             10

to help clients find successful ways to advertise to prospective customers," Mr. Shimizu

continued. "Furthermore, she can help clients arrive at the solution that ------- fits
                                                11

their needs by conducting a comprehensive appraisal of the situation from a business

standpoint."

---

8 (A) pleased
  (B) please
  (C) pleasing
  (D) pleases

11 (A) full
   (B) best
   (C) very
   (D) great

9 (A) security
  (B) marketing
  (C) health-care
  (D) energy

10 (A) Her retirement came as a surprise
     to her business partners.
  (B) She plans to help the team to
     develop new software.
  (C) She excels at helping businesses
     to increase overall sales.
  (D) Her decision to start her own team
     came at the right time.

Questions 1-4 refer to the following letter.

10 March

Ms. Norma Barnes
Human Resources Office
Clearview Shopping Mall
2011 Dunston Road
Oakville, ON L6H 6P5

Dear Ms. Barnes,

I am writing to you to report a very ------- experience with one of the mall's parking area

                                    1

attendants. Last Thursday afternoon, I visited the mall to return an item. I was in such a

hurry that I accidentally locked my keys inside my car. I was so upset and was not sure

what to do! ------- , the parking attendant, Mr. Warren Ton, came to my rescue. Within

            2

minutes, he had opened the car door ------- a tool that I had never seen before. He would

                                    3

not accept any gratuity for his trouble. ------- . Could you please convey my thanks to

                                    4

him?

Sincerely,

Eun Joo Kang

---

1 (A) similar
     (B) positive
     (C) amusing
     (D) puzzling

2 (A) Instead
     (B) Generally
     (C) Otherwise
     (D) Fortunately

3 (A) having been used by
     (B) with the use of
     (C) that he used
     (D) for using

4 (A) The parking area is clearly marked.
     (B) It happened again on Friday.
     (C) Mr. Ton is to be commended.
     (D) I did not expect to see so many
         vehicles there.

Questions 5-8 refer to the following article.

Manchester Daily Times Journal

Business Updates

(3 January)—Sky Seek Technology, manufacturer of telescopes and other astronomical instruments, announced today that longtime president Hoshi Nakata will retire next September. Mr. Nakata ------- Sky Seek for more than 20 years. ------- . According
  5   6
to a company press release, his knowledge of astronomy and superb organizational skills made him the perfect candidate for a management position. ------- , he rose to
                                                                                         7
the top post. Derek Grearson, Sky Seek's vice president of operations, said that under Mr. Nakata's leadership, Sky Seek has consistently reaped healthy profits in a highly specialized market. "Mr. Nakata has a remarkable ability ------- new customers," Grearson
                                                                                8
said.

5 (A) has led	**7** (A) However
(B) will lead	(B) Before long
(C) is leading	(C) In other words
(D) had been leading	(D) On the contrary
6 (A) Several firms manufacture telescopes in the UK.	**8** (A) attracts
(B) The company is a favorite of amateurs and professionals alike.	(B) to attract
(C) He began his career in sales at the firm's Tokyo branch.	(C) be attracted
(D) He is a longtime friend of the company's vice president.	(D) of attraction to

Questions 9-12 refer to the following notice.

Sunday Bike Days

Grab your bike, helmet, and a ------- and enjoy the opportunity to cruise the streets of
       9
Pittsburgh. ------- Sunday in October, a different neighborhood will feature its own cycling
    10
route. The route will be open solely to cyclists from 10 A.M. to 5 P.M. It will ------- each
                                                     11
week. For a full listing of the neighborhood cycling routes, visit www.pittsburghsundays.
com. ------- . This year, these include Ayana Cycles, Freel Tires, and Grottendieck's Bike
    12
Studio.

---

9 (A) friendly
    (B) friend
    (C) friendliness
    (D) friendship

10 (A) All
    (B) Every
    (C) Other
    (D) Whatever

11 (A) change
    (B) increase
    (C) show
    (D) break

12 (A) The event will take place rain or shine.
    (B) Helmets are not considered optional for participants.
    (C) Registration is not required for the event.
    (D) Discounted bike rentals are available from participating sponsors.

Questions 13-16 refer to the following e-mail.

To: csc@dobsons.com
From: efuller@seascape.net
Subject: Hapworth Industries Rebate
Date: April 12
Attachment: Store receipt

Dear Dobson's Customer Service Representative,

Impressed with its style and character, I bought a Hapworth deluxe storage unit at -------
 13
store yesterday. I appreciated, moreover, the 30 percent manufacturer's discount that

came with the item. To receive the ------- , I was told I just had to send my receipt and
 14
contact information to Hapworth Industries. Once home, I read the qualifying conditions

more closely and then realized that I was also required to submit a promotional form.

------- . Unfortunately, the clerk did not provide it to me. Therefore, I kindly ------- that the
 15 **16**
form be sent to me. A copy of the receipt is attached to this e-mail.

Thank you for your assistance in this matter.

Sincerely,

Elizabeth Fuller

---

13 (A) your
   (B) our
   (C) their
   (D) his

14 (A) extra part
   (B) survey response
   (C) price reduction
   (D) client number

15 (A) It included assembly instructions.
   (B) It was to be issued at the time of my
       purchase.
   (C) It was highly recommended by my
       manager.
   (D) It is used for electronic payments only.

16 (A) had requested
   (B) requesting
   (C) requested
   (D) request

UNIT 05 | 대명사 / 지시어 활용하기

평균 2~4문제 출제

무료인강

출제공식 5 **대명사와 지시어를 활용하면 문장 넣기의 단서를 얻을 수 있다.**

문장 넣기 문제를 풀 때 주어진 보기 문장 중에 대명사나 지시어(it, they, he, she, this, these)가 있으면 앞 문장에 나온 명사와 인칭 및 단/복수가 일치하는지 확인해야 한다. 또한 빈칸 뒤 문장에 대명사나 지시어가 있다면 보기 문장에 나온 명사와 연결되는지 확인해야 한다. 연결이 적합하지 않은 경우 오답으로 소거한다.

ETS 예제 **지시문**   번역 p.138

Changing Your Password

…

Please note that **strong passwords** are at least ten characters long and include a combination of letters and numbers. ------- . After the system accepts the change, log out and then log back in using your new password.

(A) **They** should not contain names or commonly used words.

(B) Employees must log out of company computers at the end of the day.

(C) You will receive an e-mail when software updates are available.

(D) The Information Technology Department is located on the fifth floor.

핵심내용

보안 강도가 높은 비밀번호는 최소 10자 길이에 문자와 숫자 조합이 들어갑니다.

(보안 강도가 높은 비밀번호는) 이름이나 흔히 사용되는 단어를 포함해서는 안 됩니다.

풀이

앞 문장에서 보안 강도가 높은 비밀번호가 갖추어야 하는 조건을 언급했고, 대명사 they(비밀번호)로 문장을 받아서 비밀번호의 추가 조건을 계속해서 언급하므로 내용이 자연스럽게 연결된다.

정답률을 높이는 학습노트

● 빈칸의 대명사 / 지시어 활용하기

Mr. Pak's promotion will become effective as of 2 June. His new position involves overseeing worldwide marketing strategies, which includes all advertising and brand promotions. **He** will also be responsible for a staff of 25.

빈칸의 대명사 **he**가 앞 문장의 Mr. Pak을 대신하며, 박 씨의 새로운 업무를 소개하는 앞 내용에 이어 추가 업무 내용을 언급하고 있으므로 연결이 자연스럽다.

● 빈칸 뒤의 대명사 / 지시어 활용하기

Keep all vents clear during cooking. The reason for **this** is that blocked air exits will cause the oven to shut down automatically after it is turned on.

빈칸 뒤의 **this**는 '요리하는 동안 모든 통풍구를 열어 두라'는 앞 내용 전체를 지칭하며, 그 이유에 대해 설명하는 내용으로 이어지므로 연결이 자연스럽다.

ETS CHECK-UP

정답 및 해설 p.138

1 광고

Come to the Pebble River Resort, where our three restaurants present culinary adventures for every taste! ------- . Its award-winning chefs offer a classic dining experience influenced by our regional heritage. Should you prefer more casual fare, the Old Sands Grill features seasonal dishes served on the stone terrace. Also, be sure to visit our Sweet Shop to enjoy some handmade chocolates or pastries.

(A) The dining choices vary daily.
(B) Advance reservations are strongly recommended.
(C) Our most formal restaurant is the Riverbank Restaurant.
(D) Favorite dishes include many dessert specialties.

2 이메일

Dear Mr. Pai:

Thank you for your recent order. Although the tan linen suit you ordered is unfortunately not available in your size at this time, we do have the same style in stock in light gray. ------- .

If you order now, we can offer you a 15% discount on the suit, as well as free shipping on your entire order, so you could have the items by next week. If you are interested, please e-mail our customer service department and reference the order number above.

(A) We could send you one of these right away.
(B) Thank you for returning them.
(C) These will be available early next season.
(D) You may exchange your new suits for a larger size.

3 편지

Dear Ms. Lomas,

On Saturday, 18 June, both Cresswell Street and Kookaburra Boulevard will be closed to all traffic between the hours of 8:00 A.M. and 2:00 P.M. for the annual Perth City Triathlon. ------- .

We apologize for the inconvenience. This event has become increasingly popular in recent years. It helps to promote community initiatives for regional publicity and tourism, and local businesses benefit from this. Your cooperation will help us in the continuing success of the Perth City Triathlon.

(A) The deadline for registration is 10 June.
(B) This is to ensure the safety of the athletes.
(C) All residents are being notified of the fare increase.
(D) We thank you for volunteering to assist with the race.

Questions 4-7 refer to the following information.

Web Site Lists Albury Jobs

The Albury Job Directory is an online board for announcing new employment opportunities. It ------- free of charge to Albury residents and helps match them with
4
job openings in the local area. All businesses are welcome to post open positions on the directory at no charge. Employers ------- use the service should be aware that the
5
directory may become temporarily inaccessible for a variety of reasons. ------- . Whenever
6
periodic updates are scheduled, we will do our best to notify users ahead of time. ------- ,
7
the Albury Job Directory assumes no liability in the event that the Web site is completely or partially unavailable.

---

4 (A) is provided
(B) provides
(C) providing
(D) has provided

5 (A) who
(B) any
(C) some
(D) whose

6 (A) The site is funded by the City of Albury.
(B) Volunteers are now being trained.
(C) Others will appear on separate lines within the Directory.
(D) These range from routine maintenance to system malfunction.

7 (A) Again
(B) However
(C) As a result
(D) For example

Questions 8-11 refer to the following announcement.

Excelsior Booksellers is pleased to announce its next Meet the Author event with guest Satoshi Tanaka on Tuesday, May 11, at 7:00 p.m. Mr. Tanaka, ------- work includes over
8
twenty novels, will be releasing his autobiography, *A Lifetime in Writing*, on June 5. In addition to reading an excerpt from this ------- book, Mr. Tanaka will be interviewed by
9
critic Valerie Staley about his entire writing career. ------- .
10

Admission to the event is limited to 100 participants. Guests can reserve their ------- by
11
signing up in advance, free of charge, at www.excelsiorbooksellers.com.

8 (A) his
   (B) its
   (C) who
   (D) whose

9 (A) initial
   (B) fictional
   (C) upcoming
   (D) best-selling

10 (A) He will also take questions from the audience.
   (B) He plans to study writing at the national university.
   (C) The title will be available at a discount.
   (D) A release date has not been announced.

11 (A) time
   (B) price
   (C) seat
   (D) copy

정관사 활용하기

평균 2~4문제 출제

무료인강

출제공식 6 **정관사를 활용하면 문장 넣기의 단서를 얻을 수 있다.**

앞에서 언급된 상황을 뒤에서 재차 언급할 때 '이미 언급된 정해진 상황'을 나타내기 위해 명사 앞에 정관사 the를 붙인다. 따라서 '정관사 + 명사'가 있으면 앞 문장에서 해당 명사와 관련된 상황이 언급되었는지 확인해야 한다. 관련 없는 명사에 the가 붙어 있다면 오답으로 소거하는 것도 정관사를 활용하는 주요 방법이다.

ETS 예제 공지   번역 p. 140

Dear Valued Customer,

Please be advised that the Dellmere Bank branch on Vine Street will be closed on April 5 and 6. During this period, the building will undergo much-needed renovations. These include improvements to the teller line and transaction counters. ------- .

(A) Please complete all transactions early.
(B) The original flooring was kept.
(C) Forms are available in the lobby.
(D) We apologize for **the inconvenience**.

핵심내용

델미어 은행이 4월 5일과 6일 문을 닫는다는 점을 알려 드립니다. 이 기간 동안 건물 보수 공사를 합니다.

...

(그런) 불편을 드려서 죄송합니다.

풀이

앞 문장에서 은행이 특정 날짜에 문을 닫는다고 언급했고, 건물 보수 공사를 이유로 들고 있다. 보기의 'the inconvenience'는 '은행이 문을 닫음으로써 야기되는 불편'이며 이에 대해 사과하는 내용이므로 자연스럽게 연결된다.

정답률을 높이는 학습노트

● **정답 근거로 정관사 활용하기**

When you check in, you will be issued **a parking voucher** to place in your car. Make sure **the slip** is visible through your windshield.
*slip: 전표

빈칸의 **the slip**이 앞 문장의 '주차권(a parking voucher)'을 지칭하며, 해당 주차권이 차량 앞 유리를 통해 보이도록 하라고 설명하고 있으므로 연결이 자연스럽다.

● **오답 소거로 정관사 활용하기**

I'm responding to your request to put some of **your photographs** on display in our coffee shop. ------- .
(A) Thank you for sending us **the samples**. (O)
(B) There are extra fees for ~~the framing service~~. (X)

빈칸의 **the samples**는 앞 문장의 your photographs를 지칭하여, 사진 샘플을 보내 준 것에 감사한다는 내용으로 이어질 수 있다. 빈칸 앞에서 액자 서비스에 대한 언급이 없으므로 '그 액자 서비스(the framing service)'는 오답으로 소거할 수 있다.

1 기사

The Holt City Public Library used book sale will be held this Friday to Sunday during regular library hours. The Holt City Community Council (HCCC) has been gathering used books since July for this annual event. ------- . "Our sale gets more and more popular each year," said organizer Jane Iarricio. "It is a great opportunity for book lovers."

(A) Officials thanked all of the volunteers.

(B) Buyers came from across the city.

(C) The book sale is now in its 8th year.

(D) These discounts are applied automatically.

2 이메일

Dear Ms. Zoldan,

I am writing about your upcoming product presentation to our marketing team on 19 February. Regrettably, I must postpone this appointment. At present, because of budget restrictions, the home accessories department at Millerton's is not in a position to consider new merchandise.

------- . Everyone was interested in learning more about your imported pottery and baskets. They are the types of home decor items that would probably do very well in our store. We would like to reconnect with you in six months.

(A) Note that my sales team and I were looking forward to the meeting.

(B) Remember, my office is now located on the third floor.

(C) Be aware that the store is not open on Sundays.

(D) As you know, we stock a variety of sportswear.

3 전단지

Computer Class Offered at Farmdale Public Library

Farmdale Public Library is pleased to announce it will offer a free computer class sponsored by Varren Computer Services this spring. Class topics will include Internet research, refining word processing skills, and basic computer troubleshooting. Classes will be held on Saturdays at 2:00 P.M. Farmdale residents 18 years and older can register, though space is limited. Sign up at the library's front desk anytime during regular operating hours. ------- . Light refreshments will be served following the opening class.

(A) The librarian will respond to requests soon.

(B) The replacement desk will be delivered on Friday.

(C) The password is posted on the computer room door.

(D) The first class is on March 20.

Questions 4-7 refer to the following Web page.

Zamzara's Gifts & Collectibles – a unique store full of one-of-a-kind items!

Visit our store and find all kinds of treasures—furniture, jewelry, toys, dolls, and more. Carefully crafted by hand, these are the kinds of items that ------- for centuries. Our
4
shelves display the work of 35 artisans from across the region.

------- . We also support a variety of "green" initiatives and sell many products made from
5
recycled materials. Be ------- conscious and purchase an eco-friendly gift from our store
6
today! And don't forget to browse our antiques section. This marvelous collection consists only of ------- items. We never sell any reproductions or replicas.
7

---

4 (A) lasts
  (B) last
  (C) lasting
  (D) to be lasted

5 (A) The classes are still open for registration.
  (B) We strongly believe in "buying local."
  (C) The prize is handed out each October.
  (D) We charge a small fee for these repairs.

6 (A) centrally
  (B) mutually
  (C) environmentally
  (D) collaboratively

7 (A) modern
  (B) imitation
  (C) flawed
  (D) original

POSTED MARCH 3

The Phnom Penh School of Foreign Languages is seeking an experienced French language instructor to ------- our French department. ------- . The successful candidate **8** **9** will assume a managerial role as the head of this small team and be expected to train new instructors. ------- an applicant has a degree in education is not as important as his or her **10** work history. An ideal applicant will have a minimum of five years of teaching experience. Interested parties ------- a résumé and letter of introduction to Ruben Chastain at **11** chastain@ppsfl.ca.ed. A list of references is not needed at this stage of recruitment.

8 (A) close
(B) lead
(C) assess
(D) meet

9 (A) Our students come from diverse backgrounds.
(B) French is an increasingly important global language.
(C) We congratulate Inez Robert on her new position.
(D) The department currently has three full-time teachers.

10 (A) Who
(B) Whereas
(C) Whether
(D) Which

11 (A) sent
(B) have sent
(C) are sending
(D) should send

UNIT 07 | 접속부사 활용하기

평균 2~4문제 출제 · 무료인강

출제공식 7 **접속부사를 활용하면 문장 넣기의 단서를 얻을 수 있다.**

문장 넣기 문제의 보기 또는 보기 뒤 문장에 접속부사가 포함될 때가 있다. 접속부사는 앞뒤 문장의 논리적 관계를 설정해 주는 연결어이므로 정답을 결정하는 중요한 단서가 된다. 접속부사가 있는 경우 앞뒤 문장이 자연스럽게 연결되는지 확인하자.

ETS 예제 **공지** 번역 p. 143

Thank you for your telephone message regarding your missing library book, *Mystery at Windermere*.

(중략)

I did ask staff to check the shelves this morning, in case someone might have found and returned the book. ------- .

If you are unable to locate the book by September 1, we will order a new copy.

(A) All library patrons are invited to attend.
(B) Our catalog can be accessed online.
(C) **Unfortunately,** we were not successful.
(D) However, we are open late on Tuesdays.

핵심내용

분실된 도서관 서적…

…

누군가 해당 서적을 발견해서 반납했을 경우에 대비해, 직원들에게 서가를 확인하라고 지시했습니다.

아쉽게도 책은 찾지 못했습니다.

9월 1일까지 책을 찾지 못하시면 새로 주문하겠습니다.

풀이

빈칸 앞 문장에서 분실된 책을 찾으려는 시도를 했다고 언급했고, 빈칸 뒤 문장에서는 계속 찾지 못할 시 새로 주문하겠다고 했으므로, 책을 찾으려고 했지만 안타깝게도 찾지 못했다는 내용이 와야 앞뒤 문장이 자연스럽게 연결된다.

정답률을 높이는 학습노트

● **빈칸의 접속부사 활용하기**

Ms. Sugimori has held the title of Systems Analyst for four years and earns a salary in the upper range for that post. **In addition,** she earns an annual bonus that is higher than average.

빈칸 앞에서 Ms. Sugimori가 시스템 분석가 직책에서 상위에 속하는 급여를 받고 있다고 했고, **또한** 평균보다 높은 연간 보너스를 받고 있다며 추가 내용이 이어지므로 연결이 자연스럽다.

● **빈칸 뒤의 접속부사 활용하기**

For adventure seekers, there are many activities to keep you busy. Try whale watching, kayaking, or cycling. **Or,** if you prefer, relax and dine at any of our world-class restaurants.

빈칸 뒤에서 '**또는** 원한다면 고급 식당에서 편하게 식사를 하라'는 내용이 이어지므로 빈칸에는 이와 대조되는 다른 활동들(고래 관찰, 카약 타기, 자전거 여행)을 권하는 내용이 오는 것이 자연스럽다.

1 이메일

It's time again for performance reviews, and as always, I expect you to have one-on-one conversations with each of the employees you supervise directly.

As usual, you will provide your employees with feedback.

Prior to meeting with employees, please ask them to send you a summary of their accomplishments. This will allow them to prepare for the conversation and give them confidence about their contributions to the company. ------- .

(A) As you know, this area is restricted to senior staff members.
(B) Unfortunately, hiring a new manager is taking longer than expected.
(C) Additionally, it will help you remember some of their achievements.
(D) The new employees have been hired and will start next week.

2 기사

The Crimson Bay Regional Theater will be extending its run of *Winter in Monterrey*, a play by Edna Riley. The move comes as something of a surprise, given the harsh reviews written by critics following the show's opening on March 2. ------- . The show, however, has suddenly become popular with younger people, many of whom get their news from online sources. They are apparently interested in the play's exploration of economic issues and career choices.

(A) Actors from the show are local residents.
(B) The premiere was attended by local business leaders.
(C) The initial box office sales had also been weak.
(D) Moreover, the theater company has been around for several years.

3 이메일

Thank you for agreeing to work on an article about Veronica Zettici's double role in her recent film as actress and director. By the end of the week, please submit an overview explaining how you plan to focus the interview with her. Once our editors approve your proposal, make sure to confirm the interview day and time with one of our staff photographers. It would be ideal if the article compared the two roles Ms. Zettici played in the production of the film. ------- . I will be available throughout the week if you have any questions.

(A) For example, you might ask her about the next project on her schedule.
(B) Furthermore, it should discuss the distinct skills she brought to each aspect.
(C) In short, your work should be completed in two weeks.
(D) In addition, the article will be published in the April issue.

Questions 4-7 refer to the following e-mail.

To: All Patrons <patronlist@fflibrary.net>
From: Darah Park <d.park@fflibrary.net>
Date: September 3
Subject: Changes

Dear Patrons,

On behalf of the Fulton Falls Library board, I am reaching out to our patrons ------- some
4
changes to our offerings. Due to budget limitations and staffing challenges, we have
made the decision to cut some of our regular ------- . We are unable to ------- the weekly
5 **6**
story time for children as well as the monthly community book club. A new budget will be
approved in January, and we hope to see an increase in funding at that time. ------- . We
7
are always interested in hearing new ideas.

Thanks to all our patrons for your support of Fulton Falls Library.

Sincerely,

Darah Park, Board President
Fulton Falls Library

---

4 (A) along
(B) barring
(C) despite
(D) regarding

5 (A) visits
(B) charges
(C) refreshments
(D) programs

6 (A) continuing to host
(B) continued to host
(C) continue hosting
(D) continuing hosting

7 (A) The library was opened to the
public exactly 26 years ago.
(B) However, the revised schedule is
subject to change without notice.
(C) In the meantime, please let us
know how we can improve our
existing services.
(D) Please accept our apologies for the
delay.

Questions 8-11 refer to the following memo.

To: All Corvallis Motors Sales Staff

From: Alyssa Jacinth, Chief Manufacturing Officer

Date: April 12

Re: New colors for TM300

In response ------- consumer demand, we are introducing new colors for the exterior and
                8
interior of the TM300 sport utility vehicle.

So far, the TM300 has been available only in black, white, silver, and red. But as of today,

production has started on navy blue and jade green versions. The vehicle should be

available in these ------- colors within three weeks.
                9

We are also introducing new interior colors for this model starting next month. ------- .
                                                                            10
Please check the internal Web site for the combinations of exterior and interior colors that

------- .
11

8 (A) after
   (B) for
   (C) on
   (D) to

9 (A) additional
   (B) combined
   (C) complimentary
   (D) adjustable

10 (A) In fact, the price of the TM300
       rose by 5 percent.
   (B) A sales contest is scheduled for
       May 1.
   (C) Specifically, beige and gray are
       being made available.
   (D) The engine of the TM300 should
       be upgraded next year.

11 (A) have been offered
   (B) will be offered
   (C) were offered
   (D) offered

UNIT 08 | 어휘 활용하기

평균 2~4문제 출제

무료인강

출제공식 1   어휘를 활용하면 문장 넣기의 단서를 얻을 수 있다.

보기 어휘들은 해당 문장의 주제를 나타낸다. 전체 글, 또는 빈칸 앞뒤 문장의 주제가 보기에 사용된 어휘와
연결되는지 확인하자. 글의 주제와 전혀 연관성이 없는 어휘가 보기에 있다면 소거하는 것도 주요 활용법이다.

ETS 예제   공지   번역 p. 145

-------. Starting this April, the North-South express train will no longer be stopping at Green Street Station. This will affect the express service only; local train service will continue uninterrupted to all stations on the North-South line, including Green Street Station.

(A) Montego Metro is announcing fare increases.

(B) Note that Green Street Station will soon close.

(C) New station facilities are available on this line.

(D) Please be advised of **a change** to train service.

핵심내용

열차 운행 **변경 사항**에 대해 알려 드립니다.
이번 4월부터 노스-사우스 급행열차는 더 이상
그린 가 역에 정차하지 않습니다.

풀이

빈칸 뒤 문장에 쓰인 'Starting + 시점'은
새로운 변화를 언급하기 위해 쓰인 어휘이며,
no longer(더 이상 ~하지 않다)도 예전과
달라지는 변화를 나타내는 어휘이다. 보기의
change가 주제를 드러내므로 자연스럽게
연결된다.

정답률을 높이는 학습노트

● **정답 근거로 어휘 활용하기**

This is a reminder that you are due for your healthy **eyes examination**. Our records show that you last saw Dr. Lopez eleven months ago. We recommend that all our patients visit their **eye doctor at least once per year**.

환자에게 눈 건강 검진 시기가 도래했음을 알리는
글에서 **eye doctor**, **once per year**와 같은
어휘는 빈칸의 **Dr. Lopez, eleven months
ago**와 연결 고리가 있는 어휘이며, 11개월
전에 마지막으로 진료를 받았고 1년에 최소 한
번은 안과의를 방문하라는 내용으로 자연스럽게
연결된다.

● **오답 소거로 어휘 활용하기**

Your help in setting up the **booths** was particularly appreciated. -------. It was a pleasure to enjoy the great **food** and chat with the vendors.

(A) The set-up fee will be waived. (X)

(B) I visited almost every **food stand**. (O)

빈칸의 **food stand**는 앞 문장의 **booths**, 뒤
문장의 **food**와 연결된다. set-up fee에서 set-
up에 관한 어휘는 있지만 fee(수수료)와 관련된
어휘는 없으므로 수수료가 면제될 것이라는 내용의
보기는 오답으로 소거할 수 있다.

---

1 웹페이지

Beskina Hotel Reservation Policies

Read our reservation and cancellation policy carefully. The following will help you plan your vacation at our hotel. Regularly priced reservations may be canceled for any reason. ------- . For standard reservations, notice of cancellation is required at least 72 hours prior to arrival date. In that case, a full refund will be made.

(A) Specific accommodation requests will be honored depending on hotel capacity.
(B) Beskina Rewards points are not available on special economy packages.
(C) All room rates are for double occupancy, and additional adults will incur a fee.
(D) Discounted rooms require full payment at reservation and may not be canceled.

3 이메일

Dear Member,

The Devray City History Museum is proud to unveil its new Digital Discovery Space, an interactive online museum created to provide the community with free educational resources. To access the site, simply enter the main Web site, www.d-museum.org, and click "Enter Discovery Space." To view the online museum's galleries, go to the menu and click explore our collections. ------- . You can even get a close-up view of a particular exhibit by clicking the camera icon below it.

(A) Member support funded those renovations.
(B) You can then take a virtual museum tour.
(C) Photography is not allowed in any gallery.
(D) Tickets for the event may sell out quickly.

3 기사

New Head at Balmer Industries

Balmer Industries, one of the leading pharmaceutical companies in Switzerland, yesterday announced the appointment of Li Xia Qiao as its newest CEO. The announcement comes nearly two months after Edon Durian, the current head of Balmer, made public that he will retire at the end of the year. ------- . Qiao is well-known in the industry for successfully heading several small pharmaceutical companies. The job at Balmer will be the first position she has held at the helm of an international firm of this size. Qiao, who currently resides in Basel, begins working in Zurich on 28 November.

(A) The company is currently interviewing for the position.
(B) A new CEO will be announced in November.
(C) Balmer then plans to move its headquarters to Basel.
(D) Durian has led the company for seven years.

Questions 4-7 refer to the following letter.

---

5 September

Rachel Hutchinson
8451 Woods Circle
Springfield, IN 62704

Dear Ms. Hutchinson,

Thank you for informing us about the product you purchased recently. We are sorry that the television you ordered did not arrive in perfect condition. In order to meet your ------- , we will send a sales representative to pick up your defective product and drop off
4
a replacement at no additional cost. ------- . Please call the office at 217-555-0121 to
5
------- your delivery time.
6

We strive to make all our customers happy, and hope that you find this ------- satisfactory.
7

Thank you,

Jackson Allarty
Customer Service
Parandon Electronics

---

4 (A) expecting
   (B) expectations
   (C) expects
   (D) expected

5 (A) You will receive the exact same model.
   (B) The serial number is invalid.
   (C) All our televisions are certified energy efficient.
   (D) The product is no longer covered by our warranty.

6 (A) cancel
   (B) change
   (C) arrange
   (D) sign

7 (A) resolution
   (B) discount
   (C) advertisement
   (D) demonstration

Questions 8-11 refer to the following e-mail.

To: carmen.speranza@wyomines.edu
From: mstiveson@blaufeld.com
Date: November 20
Subject: Possible visit

Dear Ms. Speranza,

I was happy to meet you after your very enlightening presentation ------- the mining
8
conference last week. I ------- your research fascinating. As I mentioned then, I would be
9
interested in having you visit Blaufeld Minerals to present to the senior staff here.

Of course, holidays and vacations are coming up. Thus, I imagine it would be ------- for
10
you to fit in your visit in the remainder of the year. Perhaps we might speak soon to settle

on a suitable date after January 1. ------- .
11

Sincerely,

Maxwell Stiveson
President, Blaufeld Minerals

---

8 (A) of
   (B) among
   (C) into
   (D) at

9 (A) found
   (B) will find
   (C) am finding
   (D) would have found

10 (A) insignificant
   (B) attractive
   (C) difficult
   (D) acceptable

11 (A) I am enjoying the holidays with my
       family very much.
   (B) Please let me know if we can talk
       by phone next week.
   (C) Again, I apologize for taking so
       long to get back to you.
   (D) It is my pleasure to include the
       data you requested.

Questions 1-4 refer to the following notice.

April 14

Because of ongoing construction, please use the back door of the building. Ring the bell next to the door when you arrive. ------- will meet you there as quickly as possible to let
1
you in. Please understand that this is a temporary measure ------- to ensure your safety.
2
We expect the ------- to be fully functional starting on June 1. ------- .
3   **4**

Best regards,

The Vulxan Corporation

---

1 (A) They
　　(B) Ours
　　(C) Either
　　(D) Someone

2 (A) implemented
　　(B) to implement
　　(C) it implements
　　(D) implementing

3 (A) kitchen
　　(B) system
　　(C) entrance
　　(D) computer

4 (A) Thank you for your response.
　　(B) We apologize for any inconvenience.
　　(C) Visitors are expected next week after
　　　　3 P.M.
　　(D) This is our favorite time of year.

Questions 5-8 refer to the following e-mail.

To: p.cooper@slixmail.net
From: orders@desertwillowteas.com
Date: May 24
Subject: Thank you

Dear Mr. Cooper,

Thank you for your recent purchase of my specialty tea blends. I hope you are enjoying the teas! If so, I would ------- you to write a positive review on my Web site. If the teas did
5
not meet your expectations, ------- , please let me know what I can do to improve them.
6
I welcome any ------- you are willing to provide.
7

------- . This is a part-time hobby that I am passionate about. I rely on customers like you
8
both to spread the word and to help me continually improve my custom blends of herbs and fruits.

Thank you again for your business.

Sincerely,

Naomi Telkes
Desert Willow Teas

---

5 (A) have liked asking
(B) have liked to ask
(C) like asking
(D) like to ask

6 (A) in other words
(B) for example
(C) therefore
(D) however

7 (A) feedback
(B) evidence
(C) ingredients
(D) donations

8 (A) As you can probably tell from my Web site, I am not a corporate seller.
(B) Because I keep a wide variety of teas in stock, I can accommodate bulk orders.
(C) I apologize if there was a mistake in shipping your order.
(D) My products are not only found online but also in major retail stores.

Questions 9-12 refer to the following e-mail.

To: kayla_jenson@gorbencorp.com
From: meredith.lehman@trackerxpress.com
Date: October 7
Subject: Tracker Xpress
Attachment: Brochure

Dear Ms. Jenson,

Thank you for your inquiry about Tracker Xpress. Our powerful software helps companies streamline the recruitment process, ------- time and money.
9

Please ------- the attached case studies. They feature three well-known companies
10
that have benefitted from Tracker Xpress. As you will see, the ability to browse through résumés based on keywords has been particularly useful to them. ------- , our software
11
makes it easy to find all candidates who live in a particular city or have worked at a specific company. Additionally, since all sorting is done digitally, there is no paper clutter.

------- .
12

Please let me know when we can discuss this further.

Sincerely,

Meredith Lehman
Tracker Xpress Marketing Coordinator

---

9 (A) saved
    (B) saves
    (C) saver
    (D) saving

10 (A) review
    (B) prepare
    (C) discuss
    (D) disregard

11 (A) Afterward
    (B) For example
    (C) As long as
    (D) In keeping with

12 (A) Applicants can submit résumés online or in person.
    (B) Our next software update will address this issue.
    (C) It can be difficult to find qualified candidates for a position.
    (D) All résumés are neatly organized in a computerized database.

Nadja's Ice Cream is Now on the West Side

PROVIDENCE—Nadja's Ice Cream ------- to the West Side. Owner Nadja Kowalski
        13
announced earlier this week that a third location will open July 1 in the ------- Rhodes
                                                                              14
Building. "Customers have been asking us to open a West Side store, but we couldn't

find the right building at first," said Ms. Kowalski. ------- . Though small, the 100-year-old
                                                        15
Rhodes Building features large windows that can be opened in warm weather, and there

is an outdoor space that can be used for additional customer seating in the summer. The

company also plans to sell its ice cream products in grocery stores beginning next year.

"I am very excited about all of this ------- ," remarked Ms. Kowalski.
                                      16

---

13 (A) expansion
 (B) is expanding
 (C) expanded
 (D) has been expanding

14 (A) upcoming
 (B) temporary
 (C) historic
 (D) deteriorated

15 (A) A challenging search for the perfect
  location has ended.
 (B) They are now developing new flavors.
 (C) There is a lot of competition on the
  east side of town.
 (D) Fortunately, business usually improves
  in the summer.

16 (A) growth
 (B) relief
 (C) talent
 (D) value

PART 7

RC

ETS TOEIC

UNIT 01 주제 / 목적 문제

평균 5~6문제 출제

무료인강

출제공식

1 출제빈도가 매우 높은 유형으로, 해당 지문의 첫 번째 문제로 출제된다.

2 글의 주제나 목적은 주로 제목이나 지문의 초반부에서 드러나는 편이다. 다만, 주제가 지문 전반에 걸쳐 제시되는 경우도 있다.

주제 / 목적 문제 유형

- **What** is the **purpose** of the e-mail?   이 이메일의 목적은 무엇인가?
- **What** does the information **mainly discuss**?   이 안내문은 주로 무엇에 대해 다루는가?
- **What** is the article **about**?   이 기사는 무엇에 관한 것인가?
- **Why** was the letter **written**?   이 편지는 왜 쓰였는가?

ETS 예제   이메일

번역 p. 151

+ 풀이 전략

Q. What is the **purpose** of the e-mail?

(A) To ask for feedback
(B) To respond to a request
(C) To apologize for a mistake
(D) To promote a new product

❶ 문제 파악

이메일의 목적을 묻는 문제이다. 글의 첫머리부터 읽어 내려오다가 목적이 드러나는 문장을 포착한다.

To: Juana Reza <juana.reza@delboroughschools.org>
From: Alair Collings <acollings@mansfordsports.com>
Re: Donation
Date: April 7

Dear Ms. Reza:

Thank you for contacting us on behalf of the Delborough School District. As you know, Mansford Sports is a proud supporter of many sports-related activities in our township. **We will be happy to provide the school district with 25 free basketballs, as you requested.** You can pick up the basketballs from our main store on County Line Road on Thursday, April 14, at 2 P.M. (중략)

Sincerely,

Alair Collings, Director of Marketing
Mansford Sports

❷ 지문 해석

연락해 주셔서 감사합니다. (중략) 우리는 귀하께서 요청하신 대로 무료 농구공 25개를 학구에 제공하게 되어 기쁩니다.

❸ 보기 읽고 정답 도출

'연락해 주셔서 감사하다'라는 언급에서 앞서 문의된 내용에 대한 회신임을 알 수 있고, '귀하께서 요청하신 대로 제공하게 되어 기쁘다'라는 언급을 통해 요청 사항을 들어주고 있음을 알 수 있다.

주어진 발췌문을 읽고 정답을 고르세요.

1

Souvenir shops in Krolleen's Old Town are plentiful, and they are not hard to locate. Unfortunately, they are also often overpriced. Tourists are better off purchasing traditional Meledonian handcrafts from individual street vendors, who sell their goods from stalls that line the side streets of the town center.

What is mainly discussed in the excerpt?

(A) How to negotiate prices

(B) Where to make purchases

2

On behalf of the International Architectural Preservation Society, I'd like to invite you to give the opening keynote address at our conference in Budapest from August 31 to September 3. This would be on August 31 at 2:00 P.M. at the Hotel Danube, where the conference will be held.

Why was the letter written?

(A) To request an architectural plan

(B) To invite someone to give a speech

3

Motorists' Alert for Mt. Pleasant Highway: Beginning Monday, April 12, and continuing for the next 15 months, the Mt. Pleasant Highway will undergo repairs. The 40-year-old road has been in great need of repair for many years. In particular, the section around Front Street will undergo major work, and the Front Street exit will be closed for a period of about three weeks while the exit ramp is replaced.

What is one purpose of the notice?

(A) To report on the opening of a new road

(B) To announce the start of a project

4

Welcome to our first edition of the *Healthy Living* Newsletter. We hope you will find the topics both entertaining and beneficial. The newsletter will be sent out every two months and will include articles of special interest, the latest health-care updates, and profiles of the outstanding medical professionals who work here at Tanaka Hospital.

Why was the e-mail sent?

(A) To solicit articles for a new publication

(B) To introduce new services offered by a hospital

5

Rail renovation of the Red Line will start on March 11. The rail section between Nilsen and Voeren (including Pessac and Croix) will not operate from March 12 to March 25. Eastbound trains will stop at Nilsen, and passengers may take a free shuttle bus in order to reach any of the three remaining stations on the line. Passengers who wish to travel west from Voeren, Croix, or Pessac may also take the free bus to the Nilson station.

What is being announced?

(A) Limitations on train service

(B) Plans for new train stations

다음 지문을 읽고 문제의 정답을 고르세요.

Article

This Week in Felhurst

(May 28)—Linfield Utilities will be repairing approximately five kilometers of underground gas pipes in and around downtown Felhurst starting on Monday. The older cast iron pipes will be replaced with durable plastic or coated steel pipes. "These underground pipelines will ensure a safe and reliable gas system for many years into the future," said Jae-Min Lim, director of operations for Linfield Utilities.

During the six-week project, Linfield Utilities is planning to work closely with city transit officials and the Department of Public Works to coordinate the construction. Felhurst police officers will support traffic control, but local residents should be prepared for delays during busy commuting periods.

Linfield Utilities crews will employ standard safety measures including the use of orange traffic cones, roadway signage, and temporary barriers. Felhurst motorists are reminded to reduce their driving speed and to mind detour signs around the construction areas.

1. What is the article about?
(A) A streets beautification project
(B) The replacement of underground pipes
(C) Traffic reduction initiatives
(D) A local company's hiring needs

E-mail

From: Preeti Patel <ppatel@desantech.com>
To: All Employees
Date: October 9
Subject: Painting

I am writing to remind everyone that the lobby will be painted tomorrow, Tuesday, October 10. The work is scheduled to begin at 8 A.M., and it should be finished by 4 P.M. All employees should avoid the lobby while the painters are working. You will need to enter and exit the building through the rear door (from the parking area) and use the staircase located to the right of that doorway.

Thank you for your cooperation. If you have any questions, please contact me at extension 431.

Preeti Patel
Facilities Manager

2. What is the purpose of the e-mail?
(A) To distribute new work schedules
(B) To describe a computer program
(C) To send out a project proposal
(D) To repeat important information

Questions 1-2 refer to the following employee notice.

Nishio Electric Corporation

Training Sessions

- Training sessions will begin and end on time.
- Company uniforms must be worn during all training sessions.
- Trainees must observe all safety precautions established at the beginning of the session. Training leaders are required to review the precautions with the trainees before training begins.
- Food and beverages are restricted to break rooms. None are permitted in laboratories, production areas, or any other training locations.
- Training session participants will keep the training areas tidy. Leaders will ensure that all equipment and work surfaces are cleaned at the end of each session.
- Cell phone use is restricted to business-related calls. Taking personal calls is not permitted. Phones must be set to vibrate during sessions.

1. What is the purpose of the list?
(A) To describe the learning goals of a training class
(B) To notify trainees about laboratory procedures
(C) To communicate rules related to training activities
(D) To explain how to operate equipment in the training locations

2. What is indicated about the cell phone calls?
(A) Calls during training must be taken outside of the room.
(B) Training must pause while a call is being taken by a participant.
(C) Cell phones must be turned off upon entering the training room.
(D) Only calls related to work situations can be taken during training.

Questions 3-5 refer to the following letter.

Guillon Insurance
22 Schoolhouse Lane
Warrington, PA 18976

July 3

Mr. Jack Li
541 Oak Hills Drive
Chalfont, PA 18914

Dear Mr. Li,

Your monthly bill from Guillon Insurance is now available online. — [1] —. Please submit your July car insurance payment of $97 by August 3.

If you have already paid your balance, no further action is required. — [2] —.

To view a printable copy of your statement, request a paper copy, manage your account payment settings, or enroll in our automatic payment plan, visit www.guilloninsurance.com/mypolicy. You will be prompted to log in to your account. — [3] —.

Thank you for choosing Guillon Insurance. — [4] —.

Sincerely,

Denise Hodges

Denise Hodges
Billing Assistant, Guillon Insurance

3. Why did Ms. Hodges contact Mr. Li?
   (A) To remind him to make a payment
   (B) To inform him of a billing error
   (C) To offer him a discount on his insurance
   (D) To request missing account information

4. According to the letter, what is NOT something Mr. Li can do online?
   (A) Access a printable version of his bill
   (B) Request a paper copy of his bill
   (C) Enroll in an automatic payment plan
   (D) Extend a payment deadline

5. In which of the positions marked [1], [2], [3], and [4] does the following sentence best belong?

   "You may need to create a new user profile if you have not yet done so."
   (A) [1]
   (B) [2]
   (C) [3]
   (D) [4]

To:	Kathryn Masur <kmasur@worthco.com.au>
From:	Halim Osman <baharucarrentals.com.my>
Subject:	Your car rental
Date:	23 October

Dear Ms. Masur,

Thank you for renting a car with Baharu Car Rentals. I will be assisting you in resolving your payment issue. The current total charge for the rental is RM375. That includes the RM50 insurance fee and the added RM25 for roadside assistance.

In order to refund the amount to your personal credit card and redirect the charge to your company, we will need to send a separate electronic invoice. As soon as payment is received from your company, I can issue your refund. Could you please supply an e-mail address for the person to whom I should send the invoice?

I would also like to inform you that if your company creates a business account with us, we can offer seamless rentals for you and all company employees. In fact, next month we are offering a 50 percent discount on all car rentals within the month to any business that opens an account with us.

Sincerely,

Halim Osman
Baharu Car Rentals
Kuala Lumpur, Malaysia

6. What is the purpose of the e-mail?
(A) To resolve a safety issue
(B) To approve a client's invoice
(C) To recommend a local business
(D) To help a customer with a refund

7. What is Ms. Masur asked to do?
(A) Call her insurance company
(B) Give contact information
(C) Make a security deposit
(D) Fill out an application

8. What will be offered if Ms. Masur's company opens a business account?
(A) A one-time vehicle upgrade
(B) A complimentary car rental
(C) A lower fee for roadside assistance
(D) A limited-time discount on car rentals

UNIT 02 | 세부 사항 문제

평균 15~20문제 출제

무료인강

출제공식

1 세부 사항 문제는 Part 7에서 가장 높은 비율로 출제된다.

2 질문의 키워드를 정확히 파악하여 지문에서 단서가 있는 부분을 찾고, 패러프레이징된 정답을 선택하면 되는 비교적 쉬운 유형이다.

세부 사항 문제 유형

- **When** was the agreement **modified**?　　계약서는 언제 수정되었는가?
- **Where** is the **IT Department** located?　　IT 부서는 어디에 위치해 있는가?
- **Who** is eligible for a **discount**?　　할인을 받을 수 있는 사람은 누구인가?
- **Why** was the order **delayed**?　　주문은 왜 지연되었는가?

ETS 예제　광고

번역 p. 155

+풀이 전략

Q. What is being offered **at no cost**?

   (A) A laboratory analysis service

   (B) A presentation about a new product

   (C) A delivery of drinking water containers

   (D) A replacement of water treatment equipment

AQUASTI LABS

At Aquasti Labs we specialize in water treatment technologies. We provide state-of-the-art water softeners and equipment for both household and industrial water treatment.

Our **testing facilities** are equipped to determine the equipment best suited to your specific needs. In order to make the most accurate recommendation, **we conduct a water analysis to make a determination of your water pH and iron content.** And now, from July 1 until July 30, **we are offering this service for free** to all customers.

(후략)

❶ 문제 파악

무료로 제공되는 것을 묻는 문제이다. 광고되고 있는 서비스 중에서 질문의 키워드인 'at no cost(무료로)'와 관련된 문구를 포착해야 한다.

❷ 지문 해석

저희 시험 시설은 … 수중 ph(페하)와 철분 함량을 측정하기 위한 수질 분석을 실시합니다. (일정 기간 동안) 저희는 이 서비스를 무료로 제공합니다.

❸ 보기 읽고 정답 도출

키워드인 'at no cost'를 패러프레이징한 'for free'가 지문의 핵심 단서가 된다.
해당 문장의 this service는 앞 문장의 water analysis(수질 분석)를 가리키므로 무료로 제공되는 것은 실험실 분석 서비스이다.

주어진 발췌문을 읽고 정답을 고르세요.

1

A conventional dishwasher consumes 200 to 300 liters of fresh water per use. The Washwave filters the water in its tank for reuse after each cycle. The water in its tank only needs to be changed every other week. This can save the average household 250,000 to 500,000 liters of water annually.

How often should the water in the Washwave be **replaced**?

(A) Once a week

(B) Once every two weeks

2

As a Comtex cardholder, you are automatically covered by the Buyer Protection Plan, which insures purchases made with your credit card for a full 90 days from the date of purchase. The Buyer Protection Plan provides insurance for loss or theft of, and accidental damage to, covered items purchased with your card anywhere in the world.

When does insurance coverage **take effect**?

(A) Ninety days after a credit card is issued

(B) On the day an item is purchased with the card

3

Dear Mr. Beck,

The proceedings of the February Small Business Solutions Conference in San Antonio will be published in August, not in September as originally planned. This means that I will soon be sending out five copies of the volume free of charge to all contributors, and I need to know where your copies should be sent.

Who is Mr. Beck?

(A) The editor of a journal

(B) A contributor to a publication

4

When the editors have finished reviewing the submission, they will notify you as to whether it will be published. Notification can be expected within six months of submission. Please do not contact the Editorial Office for review results. Writers whose stories are published will be compensated at the rate of $20 for each page as the story appears in the final print layout of the magazine.

What will authors **receive** if their pieces are chosen?

(A) Payment according to story length

(B) Reimbursement for postage costs

5

Ms. Theresa Mody has been named as manager of the new office. Prior to coming to Los Angeles, Ms. Mody was in charge of Prime International's Rio de Janeiro branch. Mr. Reginald Shao, senior vice president for United States operations, will be in Los Angeles to celebrate the opening of the new branch and to meet with members of the local business community.

Why is **Mr. Shao** planning to **travel to Los Angeles**?

(A) To make a hiring decision

(B) To make business contacts

ETS PRACTICE

정답 및 해설 p.156

다음 지문을 읽고 문제의 정답을 고르세요.

Memo

MEMO

To: All Hourly Employees
From: Marisa Gomez, President
Date: December 15
Re: Payroll Processing

The accounting department will begin transferring employee information into the new online timekeeping system on or around January 2. The system will be operational beginning on February 1. Starting on that date, all employees must enter their work hours into the online system daily. January 31 is the last date on which the accounting department will accept the old paper timesheets.

Christopher Van Pelt will be loading a tutorial on the new system on Jannuay 15.
To sign up, please call him at ext. 478.

---

1. What are employees being asked to do?
(A) Order paper using a different method
(B) Transfer personal belongings to a new location
(C) Submit employee information online
(D) Ask the accounting department for a new work schedule

Information

Morning Delight

The Morning Delight is a sun-loving plant that produces attractive flowers. Your plant has been packed and shipped with great care, but please inspect our plant to determine that it has arrived safely. Take the following steps to ensure the health of the plant.

Dig a hole in the ground about 15 centimeters deep. When the hole is ready, remove the plant from the carton, including all of its roots. Place the plant in the hole and gently press dirt around it.

The Morning Delight can be watered every other day in mild weather, but must be watered daily when outdoor temperatures are high.

---

2. According to the information, when does a Morning Delight plant require extra attention?
(A) When the flowers are cut
(B) When it is blooming
(C) When it is in a dry storage facility
(D) When the weather is hot

282

Questions 1-2 refer to the following flyer.

Dear Perriman Market shopper,

Thank you for being a loyal customer of the Perriman Market. Our company takes great pride in our staff and our quality products and service. We strive to ensure that you are satisfied with your shopping experience here. Please answer five short questions and become eligible to win one of five $100 gift cards for use in our store. The survey, along with information regarding our business hours, job openings, and in-store discounts, can be found on our Web site, www.perriman.com.

Sincerely,

Kristin Perriman, Owner and General Manager

---

1. What claim does Perriman Market make?
   (A) It cares about customer satisfaction.
   (B) Its prices are the lowest in the area.
   (C) Its business is growing.
   (D) It is planning to start a delivery service.

2. What does the flyer encourage the reader to do?
   (A) Apply for a job
   (B) Respond to a set of questions
   (C) Purchase a gift card
   (D) Attend an event at a market

PART 7 | UNIT 02

Questions 3-5 refer to the following article.

Calista Coffee Moves to Riverside

RIVERSIDE (7 July)—Ten years ago, Daniel Moret founded the Lux Café, the first coffee shop in Riverside to roast its own coffee beans. Now considered the grandfather of Riverside's coffee roasting movement, he welcomes newcomers with open arms. "I love the fact that more and more coffee roasters are moving to our area," declares Mr. Moret.

One such newcomer is Susana Garcia, who recently relocated her family business here from Austin in an attempt to find more reasonable real estate prices. A year-long search landed Ms. Garcia and her Calista Coffee in Riverside.

Ms. Garcia's father served as Calista's CEO until his retirement three years ago. Ms. Garcia began helping out with the roasting process after school while still a teenager, assumed a junior management position in her twenties, and took over for her father when he retired.

Calista Coffee roasts, grinds, and packages organic coffee for bookstore cafés and other small businesses, and there are plans to start supplying hotels next year. The Riverside Chamber of Commerce helped Ms. Garcia find a 2,500-square-foot building on Iris Street to be renovated for coffee roasting. Ms. Garcia has promised to invest $400,000 and eventually create dozens of new jobs.

3. Why did Ms. Garcia decide to move from Austin?
(A) To save money
(B) To work for Mr. Moret
(C) To live closer to her father
(D) To fulfill a promise made to her family

4. What is Ms. Garcia's current job?
(A) Marketing specialist
(B) Junior apprentice
(C) Bookstore owner
(D) Company executive

5. What will Ms. Garcia NOT do in Riverside?
(A) Supply small businesses
(B) Renovate a large building
(C) Sell coffee to hotels
(D) Invest her profits in a new business

Questions 6-9 refer to the following brochure.

Your skills will always be in demand after you attend

Barry's Trade School for Plumbers and Electricians

Do you know that employees in plumbing and electrical work in Tyron County report some of the lowest unemployment rates and some of the highest levels of job satisfaction of any field?

Do you know that by studying part-time for just 10 months (even fewer if you have earned prior credits) you can gain qualification as a Plumber Apprentice or Electrician Apprentice?

At Barry's Trade School, we offer:
❖ Convenient twice-weekly classes that fit into your existing work schedule
    — Group A: Monday and Wednesday, 6:00 P.M. to 10:00 P.M.
    — Group B: Saturday and Sunday, 7:30 A.M. to 11:30 A.M.
❖ Lower tuition rates with proof of residence in Tyron County or surrounding counties
❖ An exciting array of class activities, including shadowing licensed professionals, gaming on our proprietary video-game educational tools, and practicing job interview skills. We guarantee that 75 percent of course time is dedicated to hands-on learning.
❖ Access to the services of our employment specialist to help you secure employment during your first three years after graduation

Ever wonder what a typical electrician or plumber in our area makes?

	Average first-year salary	Average fifth-year salary
Electrician	$43,025	$48,089
Plumber	$41,379	$49,012

For more information, visit our Web site at www.barrystradeschool.com or call 1 (402) 555-0183.

---

6. According to the brochure, what is a benefit of working as a plumber or electrician?
(A) Flexible schedules
(B) Ease of finding jobs
(C) Low cost of needed tools and supplies
(D) Guaranteed annual salary increases

7. Who is eligible for a reduced class cost?
(A) Returning students
(B) Licensed professionals
(C) People who live in the area
(D) Learners with prior credits

8. According to the brochure, what is emphasized about the classes?
(A) They include interview techniques.
(B) They take place online.
(C) They provide extensive review for the licensure exam.
(D) They require students to use textbooks.

9. What is offered by Barry's Trade School?
(A) Job-placement assistance
(B) Instructional videos to take home
(C) An internship position following graduation
(D) Tuition reimbursement for dissatisfied students

Not / True 문제 유형

- What is **true** about Quickstar Airlines?   퀵스타 항공사에 대해 사실인 것은?
- What is **NOT mentioned** in the letter?   편지에서 언급된 것이 아닌 것은?
- What is **stated** about online orders?   온라인 주문에 대해 언급된 것은?
- What is **NOT indicated** about Mr. Palmer?   파머 씨에 대해 명시된 것이 아닌 것은?

ETS 예제   **설명서**   번역 p. 159

Q. What is **NOT** a part of the machine?

(A) A heating element

(B) A cooling fan

(C) A glass container

(D) An electrical plug

Installation Instructions

Quisicup Pro

Model Number: GCM-1624

Volt: 120Vac, 50-60Hz

Wattage: Max. 1800 Watts

Capacity: 20 cups

1. Place machine upright on a hard, flat surface. Insert **plug** into outlet.
2. Leave filter basket empty and slide it into position.
3. Pour cold water (max. 2 liters) into water reservoir.
4. Place the empty **glass carafe** on the **heating plate**.
5. Press the *Brew* button. The *In Use* light will illuminate.
6. Wait 4- 5 minutes for the carafe to fill with hot water.
7. Dispose of hot water and repeat process two more times. This allows hot water to clean the internal parts of the machine before use.

(후략)

+ 풀이 전략

❶ 문제 파악

기계의 부품이 아닌 것을 찾는 문제이다. 나열된 정보에서 언급되지 않은 것을 찾는다.

❷ 지문 해석

1. 기계를 단단하고 평평한 표면에 똑바로 놓고, 콘센트에 플러그를 끼운다.
2. 필터 바스켓을 비운 채로 제자리로 밀어 넣는다.
3. 물통에 찬물(최대 2리터)을 붓는다.
4. 빈 유리 주전자를 열판 위에 놓는다.
5. *끓이기* 버튼을 누르면 *사용 중* 표시등이 켜진다.

❸ 보기 읽고 정답 도출

- heating plate → (A) heating element
- glass carafe → (C) glass container
- plug → (D) electrical plug

냉각 팬에 대한 언급은 없으므로 정답은 (B)이다.

주어진 발췌문을 읽고 정답을 고르세요.

1

> Amazing Cruise offers four days of boating on the rivers and lakes of Alaska, salmon fishing, and enjoying fresh-caught fish around a campfire for dinner. On this trip, participants travel by boat only, and stay in tents set up alongside the rivers and lakes.

What is **NOT mentioned** as a feature of the Amazing Cruise program?

(A) Having a meal around a campfire　　　　(B) Visiting a glacier

2

> Because each region of the world requires different shipping rates, the shipping charges will be calculated separately. Please note that any extra charges resulting from shipping rates in individual regions will be listed in an e-mail sent to you once your order has been processed. Online orders take up to three days to process.

What is **stated** about online orders? ·

(A) They are processed in three days or less.　　(B) They allow the buyer a lower shipping rate.

3

> Because your health is important to us, we would like to remind you that it's time for your examination. We look forward to seeing you!
>
> Your appointment is on Monday, September 12 at 10: 30 A.M. If you cannot keep your appointment, please provide at least 24 hours advance notice or you will be charged a fee.

What is **mentioned** about the doctor's office?

(A) It calls people 24 hours before their visit.　　(B) It charges a fee for late cancellations.

4

> Participation fees are competitive, considering the infrastructure provided at the venue. Forklift operators are available on site to carry the exhibitors' products around the pavilions at no charge. Heavy equipment that does not fit onto a forklift can, for a small fee, be transported by a crane. Each exhibitor is guaranteed free power and water to each booth inside every pavilion.

What is **NOT provided** to exhibitors **for free**?

(A) Electricity　　　　　　　　　　　(B) Crane services

5

> September 1 marks the beginning of the twentieth theatrical season at Shoreline Playhouse in Meadow Lakes, an event that just one year ago few thought would ever take place. The opening of Field Theater in nearby Mooreland City meant that Shoreline Playhouse was no longer the only destination for area theatergoers. In addition, the generous grants given to Field Theater by the Walters Foundation meant larger-scale productions there that had a broader appeal.

What is **true** about Field Theater?

(A) It has been given a significant amount of money.　(B) It is located on Lake Drive.

다음 지문을 읽고 문제의 정답을 고르세요.

Notice

WASTE PREVENTION—HOW YOU CAN HELP

Photocopies

· Eliminate unnecessary photocopies by storing documents on a shared directory.

· Create a central filing system instead of maintaining duplicate files.

· Invest in a program that allows fax transmission directly from your computer.

· Redesign forms and reports to reduce margins (and the number of copies required).

· Prepare executive summaries for lengthy documents. Provide full document only on request.

· Use e-mail and voice mail for interoffice messages.

· Post information on a bulletin board instead of making copies.

---

1. What is NOT a suggested way to reduce photocopying?

(A) Post a list of guidelines for photocopying

(B) Use a shared-document directory

(C) Write executive summaries

(D) Decrease margins on documents

Instructions

IF YOU NEED TO RETURN AN ITEM

1. Wrap the item carefully before placing it in the package.
2. Print the shipping label from www.breezybeluga.co.uk/forms and attach it to the front of the package. A self-adhesive label is recommended. If tape is used to secure the label, make sure that the tape does not cover the bar code.
3. Insure your package before shipping.
4. You may track your package at www.breezybeluga.co.uk/track using your order number.

Please note that these instructions apply to domestic returns only. For international returns, please contact customer service at 0113 496 0836.

---

2. What is indicated about the label?

(A) It must be attached to the package with tape.

(B) It must clearly show the bar code.

(C) It may be written out by hand.

(D) It may be placed anywhere on the package.

Questions 1-2 refer to the following e-mail.

To:	Cara Reilly <carareilly@rphost.ie>
From:	Liam Cassidy <lcassidy@iaw.ie>
Date:	4 March
Subject:	RE: Follow-up on our conversation

Thank you for your message. I will be out of the office from 2 to 9 March, when I will be in Barcelona, Spain, for the International Athletic Goods Trade Show. During this time, I will have limited access to my e-mail. For immediate assistance, please contact Mary Dolan at mdolan@iaw.ie for all matters related to sales and client requests. Otherwise, please expect a response from me upon my return on 10 March.

Kind regards,

Liam Cassidy
Director of Sales, Irish Athletic Wear Ltd.

1. What is indicated about Mr. Cassidy?
   (A) He was recently appointed as director of sales.
   (B) He will be unable to check his e-mail regularly.
   (C) He is working from his office at home.
   (D) He has visited Barcelona before.

2. What are recipients of the message advised to do?
   (A) E-mail the trade show organizers
   (B) Check an event calendar
   (C) Contact Mr. Cassidy's coworker
   (D) Return an order to the sales department

Questions 3-4 refer to the following article.

BUSINESS NEWS: Local Companies in the Wedding Business to Collaborate

Timony Wedding Attire has recently joined other wedding industry businesses to establish a collaborative. Brice Florists, locally known for exquisite bouquets and table arrangements, and Royal Event Designers, a decorating service, have both agreed to participate in a joint enterprise that will ensure that every element of a wedding celebration is coordinated seamlessly. The businesses are located at the Downtown Plaza in Lewisburg. More businesses are planning to join the group soon, including a photographer, a hairstyling salon, and a caterer.

---

3. What does the article describe?
(A) An upcoming wedding
(B) A successful acquisition
(C) A partnering of businesses
(D) A collaboration of investors

4. What type of wedding service is NOT mentioned in the article?
(A) Food
(B) Flowers
(C) Photography
(D) Entertainment

Hotel Competition is Heating Up

Ever since the expansion of the Jenssonville Airport, the city's hotels have been jostling for the increase in guests. The competition is about to become even more intense with the opening of the new Maroon 2 Hotel in the building that was once Jenssonville City Hall. — [1] —.

Twelve years ago, after city hall moved from its downtown location to the historic district's Morning Plaza, an investment group bought the old city hall building and converted it to office space. Then, two years ago, the building was sold to the Maroon 2 Hotel Group.

Maroon 2 has spent the last two years converting the edifice into a hotel and restoring the historical aspects of the early city hall, which have been hidden for decades. For example, the mural of the city's founding, which had been covered by layers of wallpaper, is now a brightly colored feature of the lobby. — [2] —.

The city's only two other hotels that have more than 100 rooms have recently undergone structural changes as well. The 120-room Sonnetters Hotel added an exercise room last month, and around the corner from the Sonnetters, the General's Inn now features an outdoor courtyard restaurant and swimming pool. Of these three hotels, the 146-room Maroon 2 will end up being the most sizable. — [3] —.

General Manager Diego Cordillo is confident that the Maroon 2 brand will attract enough guests to justify the cost of the renovations.

"All the attributes that people associate with the Maroon 2 brand will be here," he said. "Things like the plush robes, exquisite sheets, and, of course, phenomenal service. — [4] —."

5. What is NOT indicated about the mural?
(A) It depicts a historical event.
(B) It is located in the hotel's lobby.
(C) It was created during the renovation.
(D) It had not been viewed for many years.

6. What new feature of the Sonnetters Hotel is mentioned in the article?
(A) A fitness room
(B) A swimming pool
(C) An expanded lobby
(D) An outdoor restaurant

7. What is indicated about all three hotels?
(A) They are brightly colored.
(B) They are located in the historic district.
(C) They were once office buildings.
(D) They have more than 100 rooms.

8. In which of the positions marked [1], [2], [3], and [4] does the following sentence best belong?

"Also, the domed ceiling in the central rotunda has been completely restored to its original state."
(A) [1]
(B) [2]
(C) [3]
(D) [4]

UNIT 04 추론 문제

평균 10~12문제 출제

무료인강

출제공식

1 지문에서 간접적으로 제시된 단서를 근거로 하여 정답을 추론하는 문제 유형이다.
2 지문의 출처나 대상처럼 전반적인 내용을 추론하는 문제와 특정 세부 사항을 추론하는 문제로 구분된다.

추론 문제 유형

- Who most **likely** is Ms. Singh?
- Where does Mr. Hassan **probably** work?
- What is **suggested / implied / inferred / indicated about** the mall?

싱 씨는 누구인 것 같은가?
하산 씨는 아마도 어디서 일하는 것 같은가?
쇼핑몰에 대해 알 수 있는 것은?

ETS 예제 편지

번역 p. 163

Q. What is **suggested about** Ms. Ito?

(A) She has purchased goods from the company in the past.

(B) She moved to Los Angeles during the last year.

(C) She used to work for Brenda Mason.

(D) She has requested a mail-order catalog.

February 15
Tsurumi Ito
11 Almont Street
Los Angeles, CA 90103

Dear Ms. Ito:

Our records indicate that you have not ordered from our seasonal catalogs in the last twelve months. As a company dedicated to maintaining our relationships with previous customers, we would like to offer you a 20 percent discount on all telephone or mail orders, available for 30 days from the date of this letter.
(중략)

Brenda Mason
Vice President of Customer Relations

+ 풀이 전략

❶ 문제 파악

이토 씨에 대해 추론하는 문제이다. 지문 첫머리의 Dear Ms. Ito에서 이토 씨에게 보낸 글임을 알 수 있으므로 편지 전체 내용을 훑어야 한다.

❷ 지문 해석

저희 기록에 따르면, 귀하는 지난 12개월 동안 저희 계절별 상품 카탈로그에서 주문을 하지 않으셨습니다. 이전 고객분들과의 관계를 유지하는 데 정성을 다하는 회사로서 저희는 20퍼센트 할인을 제공하고자 합니다.

❸ 보기 읽고 정답 도출

'12개월 동안 주문을 하지 않았다', '이전 고객과의 관계 유지를 위해 할인을 제공한다'는 언급을 통해 이토 씨의 과거 구매 이력을 유추할 수 있다. 따라서 과거에 해당 업체에서 구매를 한 적이 있다는 (A)가 정답이다.

주어진 발췌문을 읽고 정답을 고르세요.

1

> The Preservation Society is impressed by your leadership in the recent restoration of the Opera Towers in your city. Your commitment to preserving the architectural elements of such an important landmark is a shining example of the best efforts preservationists strive to put forth.

What is **suggested about** the Opera Towers?

(A) They have historical significance.

(B) They are currently under construction.

2

> Manik Bhatta reviewed the calendar for upcoming school group visits to the museum. He has hired an additional staff member, Beverly Thompson, to help him with the work of scheduling the visits so he can concentrate on developing curricula for learning programs and inviting guest lecturers.

Who most **likely** is Mr. Bhatta?

(A) A curator

(B) The education coordinator

3

> Dear Mr. Rhee:
>
> Thank you for your interest in Bartel's food packaging technology. As we discussed in our telephone conversation, Certain Seal is well suited to the needs of a mid-to-large-scale food processing company. It is designed to handle large volumes and can be customized for almost any size or shape of food product.

In what industry does Mr. Rhee **probably** work?

(A) Large-scale agriculture

(B) Food processing

4

> Load the enclosed set of three new UM-3 batteries so that their positive (+) and negative (−) ends are facing as indicated by the markings. These batteries protect transaction information stored in your register's memory when there is a power failure or when you unplug the power adaptor. Be sure to install these batteries before using the machine.

What is **indicated about** the batteries?

(A) They are used when electrical power to the machine is interrupted.

(B) They fit into a compartment on the back of the machine.

5

> Palais Hotel Gets Top Chef
>
> The Palais Hotel, known by insiders as Hong Kong's hidden jewel, is about to become very well-known. The hotel's Jade Restaurant has hired a new executive chef, cooking expert and chef extraordinaire Mei-Yi Gan. Gan, who took over the restaurant last month, has already made her mark by adding some of her signature dishes to the menu.

What is **implied about** the Palais Hotel?

(A) Its restaurant is large.

(B) It is currently not widely known.

다음 지문을 읽고 문제의 정답을 고르세요.

Review

http://www.productreviews.com/outdoor_lighting

Consumer Review: Outdoor Lighting Fixtures
Review posted by: Tony Wivell

My neighbor pays $30 every month for size-D batteries to operate his Dotono motion-activated lights. Even though they emit a lot of light, the cost of operation surprised me. As an alternative, I thought I'd try out F&Q lights, which have a money-back guarantee. To experiment, I purchased only one outdoor wall light just to test it out. I put it out in the sun to charge up for three hours, and that was enough for it to stay lit the whole night! It was also very sensitive to any motion. I've made my choice, and it wasn't even close. I'm sure I'll be happy with more.

1. What did Mr. Wivell probably do after writing his review?
  (A) He asked F&Q for a refund.
  (B) He complained to his neighbor.
  (C) He bought additional F&Q lights.
  (D) He tested a Dotono light.

Article

Malaysian Film Wins

The Mumbai International Film Festival, held yesterday in Mumbai, India, gave top honors to Malaysian director Niu Tan's feature-length film entitled "From the Foothills." The Chinese-language film tells the story of a young man who leaves his rural hometown for the city. The mountains surrounding his hometown are used as a visual metaphor for the difficult, "uphill" emotional journey he undergoes throughout the film.

Director Niu Tan, who was there to accept the Best Feature Film Award, says she is "grateful my work is being honored in this way." She added that she hopes her film will draw "long-overdue, international attention to all the masterful filmmaking taking place in Malaysia and its neighboring countries."

2. What does Ms. Tan suggest about Malaysian films?
  (A) They are often based on novels.
  (B) They are especially popular in India.
  (C) They have received numerous awards.
  (D) They deserve more international recognition.

Questions 1-2 refer to the following online chat discussion.

Winston Huang (9:12 A.M.)
Good morning, Alicia. I've started doing research for my article on the new school buildings being constructed on Madingley Avenue.

Alicia Hernandez (9:14 A.M.)
Great, thanks for getting started so promptly!

Winston Huang (9:15 A.M.)
How long should the article be?

Alicia Hernandez (9:18 A.M.)
We haven't decided whether that article will be published in the print edition or only online, so I don't know what the word limit will be yet. We'll be deciding during our editors' meeting at 10 A.M.

Winston Huang (9:20 A.M.)
OK, let me know after you decide. I have a doctor's appointment at 11 A.M. and plan to start the writing after that.

Alicia Hernandez (9:21 A.M.)
Absolutely!

1. Where do Mr. Huang and Ms. Hernandez most likely work?
   (A) At a research laboratory
   (B) At a construction company
   (C) At a doctor's office
   (D) At a magazine publisher

2. At 9:21 A.M., what does Ms. Hernandez mean when she writes, "Absolutely"?
   (A) She will contact Mr. Huang later.
   (B) She is on her way to a meeting now.
   (C) Mr. Huang should begin his work immediately.
   (D) Mr. Huang should go to Madingley Avenue.

ETS TEST

Questions 3-5 refer to the following e-mail.

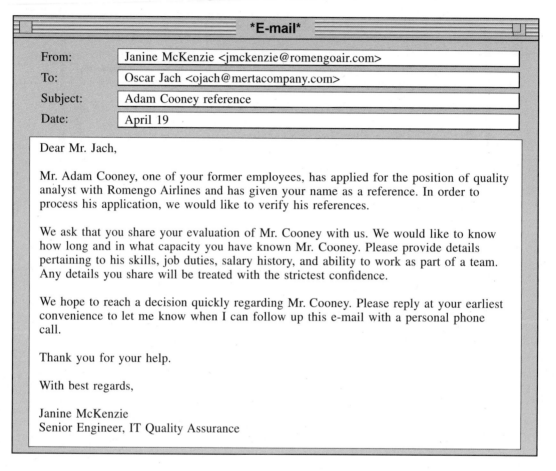

E-mail

From:	Janine McKenzie <jmckenzie@romengoair.com>
To:	Oscar Jach <ojach@mertacompany.com>
Subject:	Adam Cooney reference
Date:	April 19

Dear Mr. Jach,

Mr. Adam Cooney, one of your former employees, has applied for the position of quality analyst with Romengo Airlines and has given your name as a reference. In order to process his application, we would like to verify his references.

We ask that you share your evaluation of Mr. Cooney with us. We would like to know how long and in what capacity you have known Mr. Cooney. Please provide details pertaining to his skills, job duties, salary history, and ability to work as part of a team. Any details you share will be treated with the strictest confidence.

We hope to reach a decision quickly regarding Mr. Cooney. Please reply at your earliest convenience to let me know when I can follow up this e-mail with a personal phone call.

Thank you for your help.

With best regards,

Janine McKenzie
Senior Engineer, IT Quality Assurance

---

3. What is suggested about Mr. Jach?
(A) He once employed Mr. Cooney.
(B) He worked for Romengo Airlines.
(C) He applied for a quality analyst job.
(D) He posted a job advertisement online.

4. What information about Mr. Cooney is NOT requested by Ms. McKenzie?
(A) His last day of work
(B) His job responsibilities
(C) His abilities
(D) His salary

5. What does Ms. McKenzie indicate she wants to do?
(A) Meet with Mr. Jach in person
(B) Send Mr. Jach a follow-up e-mail
(C) Offer Mr. Jach a job at her company
(D) Speak to Mr. Jach by phone

Questions 6-9 refer to the following following product review.

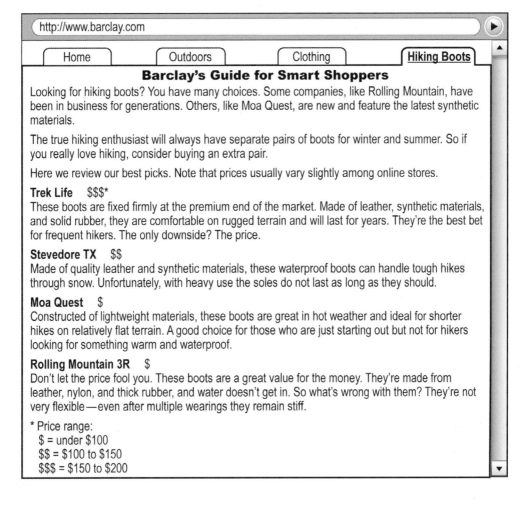

http://www.barclay.com ▶

| Home | Outdoors | Clothing | **Hiking Boots** |

Barclay's Guide for Smart Shoppers

Looking for hiking boots? You have many choices. Some companies, like Rolling Mountain, have been in business for generations. Others, like Moa Quest, are new and feature the latest synthetic materials.

The true hiking enthusiast will always have separate pairs of boots for winter and summer. So if you really love hiking, consider buying an extra pair.

Here we review our best picks. Note that prices usually vary slightly among online stores.

Trek Life $$$*
These boots are fixed firmly at the premium end of the market. Made of leather, synthetic materials, and solid rubber, they are comfortable on rugged terrain and will last for years. They're the best bet for frequent hikers. The only downside? The price.

Stevedore TX $$
Made of quality leather and synthetic materials, these waterproof boots can handle tough hikes through snow. Unfortunately, with heavy use the soles do not last as long as they should.

Moa Quest $
Constructed of lightweight materials, these boots are great in hot weather and ideal for shorter hikes on relatively flat terrain. A good choice for those who are just starting out but not for hikers looking for something warm and waterproof.

Rolling Mountain 3R $
Don't let the price fool you. These boots are a great value for the money. They're made from leather, nylon, and thick rubber, and water doesn't get in. So what's wrong with them? They're not very flexible—even after multiple wearings they remain stiff.

* Price range:
  $ = under $100
  $$ = $100 to $150
  $$$ = $150 to $200

6. What advice is given to buyers who do a lot of hiking?
(A) Buy two pairs of boots
(B) Buy from companies that have been in business many years
(C) Buy only waterproof boots
(D) Buy new hiking boots every year

7. What is one problem with Stevedore TX boots?
(A) They are very heavy.
(B) They are the most expensive boots reviewed.
(C) They are not very comfortable.
(D) They are not very durable.

8. What boots would probably be best for a new hiker?
(A) Trek Life
(B) Stevedore TX
(C) Moa Quest
(D) Rolling Mountain 3R

9. What is suggested about Rolling Mountain 3R boots?
(A) They are reasonably priced.
(B) They are very lightweight.
(C) They are not waterproof.
(D) They cannot be purchased online.

UNIT 05

문장 삽입 문제

평균 2문제 출제

무료인강

출제공식

1 주로 기사문과 이메일/편지의 마지막 문제로 제시된다.

2 지문의 흐름을 파악하고 삽입되는 문장과의 맥락을 고려하여 정답을 선택하는 유형이다. 주어진 문장을 읽고 지문을 해석해 나가다가 흐름이 단절된 부분을 찾고, 해당 위치의 앞뒤 문장과 삽입문이 자연스럽게 이어지는지 확인한다.

문장 삽입 문제 유형

In which of the positions marked [1], [2], [3], and [4] does the following sentence best belong?

"These are free and open to the public but require advance registration."

[1], [2], [3], [4]로 표시된 곳 중에서 다음 문장이 들어가기에 가장 적합한 위치는?

"이는 무료이며 대중에게 공개되지만 사전 등록이 필요합니다."

ETS 예제   회람

번역 p. 168

Q. In which of the positions marked [1], [2], [3], and [4] does the following sentence best belong?

"Where possible, **they** will be accompanied by photographs."

(A) [1]   (B) [2]

(C) [3]   (D) [4]

To: All Employees
From: Audrey Canon
Subject: Coming feature
Date: 2 October

As you may have heard, we are launching a new feature that will appear in the Sunday edition of the paper. It will highlight uplifting and inspiring **stories** that have happened in our region. — [1] —. The decision was motivated by the many requests from readers for just such a feature. — [2] —. The section will appear in both our print and online issues, so it must meet the same high standards as the rest of the newspaper. — [3] —. I will be editing the section with the assistance of reporter Lia Seco. At this time, we have yet to come up with a suitable name for it. — [4] —. Therefore, feel free to submit one, as well as any story ideas you may have.

＋풀이 전략

❶ 문제 파악

주어진 문장을 분석하여 단서를 찾는다.

"지면이 허락하면 그것들은 사진과 같이 실릴 것입니다."

주어진 문장에서 핵심 단서가 되는 'they'를 활용한다. 문장이 삽입될 위치 앞에 놓인 복수명사에 주목한다.

❷ 지문 해석

[1] 앞: 그것은 우리 지역에서 일어난 희망적이고 고무적인 기사들을 중점적으로 다룰 것입니다.

[1] "지면이 허락하면 그것들(기사들)은 사진과 같이 실릴 것입니다."

❸ 오답 소거 및 정답 도출

주어진 문장의 they를 requests(요청들), readers(독자들), standards(기준들)로 받았을 때는 사진과 동반되어 신문 지면에 실린다는 내용이 들어맞지 않게 되므로 [2], [3]을 소거할 수 있다.

[4] 앞에는 복수명사가 오지 않았다. 따라서 stories(기사들)를 they로 받는 [1]이 정답이다.

주어진 발췌문을 읽고 표시된 단서를 활용하여 삽입문이 들어갈 알맞은 위치를 고르세요.

1

I will be resigning from my position as senior lecturer here on May 10. — [1] —. The decision to leave Bernstein Music Academy has been an extremely difficult one, as I have enjoyed teaching at our school tremendously. — [2] —. I believe the position at Montague provides an opportunity for such growth.

"**However**, I feel it is time for me to move on to the next stage of my musical career."

(A) [1]   (B) [2]

2

On December 10 there will be a telephone conference for editors at Plaskett Publishing. — [1] —. Contact Sally Graham, at 877-555-1600 by December 5 to obtain the access code. — [2] —. Also, mark your calendars for January 12, when Konrad Weiss will lead a computer workshop on project management.

"**This** will include employees at the main office in New York and at the plant in Philadelphia."

(A) [1]   (B) [2]

3

The experience that this restaurant provides goes beyond the delicious food. — [1] —. When I visited, opera singer Antonio Bertolli began singing just as I took my seat. — [2] —. The owner said that if this musical entertainment proves popular, he plans to add more performance nights.

"**After his performance**, Mr. Bertolli came over to the tables and introduced himself to the diners."

(A) [1]   (B) [2]

4

A spokesperson for Riester's Food Markets announced yesterday that it will open five new stores over the next two years, starting with one in downtown Swansea this December. — [1] —. The company will next open a Liverpool store in May. — [2] —. The location of the final store has not yet been determined.

"**Two more** will open at sites in Manchester and Edinburgh by summer of next year."

(A) [1]   (B) [2]

5

Lear Heights is a joint venture between the college (a public institution) and the Exner Group (a local property-development firm). It will consist of seven mixed-use buildings. — [1] —. Exner will develop the site and manage the retail operations. "Until recently, most of our students have been commuters," Ms. Afolayan said. "Now we're seeing a sharp increase in the number of applicants who request campus housing. — [2] —.

"**Each** will have retail space at the ground level and student apartments on the two upper floors."

(A) [1]   (B) [2]

다음 지문을 읽고 문제의 정답을 고르세요.

Article

Downtown Business Briefs

Crest Bookstore has purchased the retail space next to the store's original premises at 112 Lark Street in Westford. The popular downtown fixture will use the new space in a much-needed expansion project.

"We opened our doors three years ago and hit the ground running," says Ana Li, founder and co-owner. "We were told that independent bookstores are no longer as successful as they used to be. — [1] —."

According to Li, the revamped Crest Bookstore will be more than double the size of the original. "The grand reopening will take place on October 12," says Li. "— [2] —. We're very excited about the additional space. — [3] —. It means we will now be able to host more events like author appearances, book signings, and meetings of our ever-popular Crest Book Club. — [4] —."

---

1. In which of the positions marked [1], [2], [3], and [4] does the following sentence best belong?
   "We have found the opposite to be true."
   (A) [1]   (B) [2]   (C) [3]   (D) [4]

Review

I am designing a lobby for a commercial high-rise. — [1] —. The project required a fairly large number of upholstered pieces, including multiple couches and lounge chairs. — [2] —. The upholstery company I normally work with does a great job, but since they would have been out of my client's budget, I decided to get estimates from other companies. Ganguly Upholstery gave me a quote that was far below that of its competitors, so I decided to go with them. — [3] —. Clearly, you get what you pay for. While they did finish the job sooner than expected, the work was very sloppy. The fabric I chose had a faint black and gold checkered pattern. — [4] —. When pieces were sewn together, they did not match up correctly. I will not be sending any more work to this company.

— Divya Agrawal

---

2. In which of the positions marked [1], [2], [3], and [4] does the following sentence best belong?
   "I should have known better."
   (A) [1]   (B) [2]   (C) [3]   (D) [4]

Questions 1-3 refer to the following e-mail.

To:	Daniel Bisset <dbisset@goldbear.ca>
From:	Sesi Jones <sjones@greenfieldtheatre.ca>
Subject:	Information
Date:	3 April

Dear Mr. Bisset:

Thank you for your recent online ticket purchase for *Belle in White* at the Greenfield Theatre. This world premiere by Grace Tiong is a highly anticipated event. — [1] —. Your two tickets for the 8:00 P.M. performance on 1 May will be held at the box office. Please come to the box office 30 minutes before the show starts. — [2] —. If this was a student discount purchase, please present a current student ID card. No one will be seated after the first ten minutes of the show.

Please consider becoming a Greenfield Theatre subscriber. — [3] —. You will receive discounts on tickets and parking, as well as invitations to special events. — [4] —. You can find more information on our Web site at www.greenfieldtheatre.ca/subscription.

Sincerely,

Sesi Jones
Box Office Manager

1. Why was the e-mail sent?
(A) To confirm an order
(B) To promote an actress
(C) To advertise a special student production
(D) To bring attention to a new parking area

2. What does the e-mail advise Mr. Bisset to do?
(A) Renew his subscription
(B) Bring his discount coupon
(C) Change a date
(D) Arrive early

3. In which of the positions marked [1], [2], [3], and [4] does the following sentence best belong?

"You will be asked to show identification when you pick up your tickets."
(A) [1]
(B) [2]
(C) [3]
(D) [4]

Questions 4-7 refer to the following article.

Some Job Interview Strategies
By Scott Friedman

Congratulations! — [1] —. You've lined up a job interview. Here are some strategies that will help you feel more confident and increase your chances of being offered the job.

First, research the potential employer. Find out the company's mission, its values and goals, and how it contributes to the industry. — [2] —. Learn about projects it is currently working on. Be prepared to mention what impresses you about the company. Learning something about the hiring manager can help make a connection. Show that you understand what the company is about and that you want to be part of it.

Second, practice answers to typical interview questions. — [3] —. Identify key words in the job posting and incorporate them into your responses. Be ready to provide examples about how you handled past situations that show you have the skills needed for the position.

Third, prepare questions to ask the hiring manager. They may include what advancement opportunities are available and what type of person succeeds in the job you are applying for. You may also ask how you would be evaluated, whether the position involves travel, or whether mentoring is available. Do not raise questions about salary and vacation time; save those for your callback interview.

— [4] —. To reduce your anxiety, allow plenty of time to get to the interview, and plan to arrive fifteen to twenty minutes early to get settled. Greet everyone you see warmly and thank them for their time. Remain calm and confident. You know you can do the job. Make sure your interviewer knows that, too.

4. What is a stated reason for researching a potential employer?
   (A) To know who its competitors are
   (B) To establish how it attracts customers
   (C) To determine its importance to the industry
   (D) To learn about its loyalty toward its employees

5. What is a job interviewee advised to do?
   (A) Schedule a meeting with the hiring manager
   (B) Send the interviewer a thank-you letter
   (C) Prepare responses to usual questions
   (D) Submit work samples

6. According to the article, what should a candidate not ask in a first interview?
   (A) How much the job pays
   (B) How performance is assessed
   (C) Whether mentors are provided
   (D) Whether travel is required

7. In which of the positions marked [1], [2], [3], and [4] does the following sentence best belong?

   "Interviewing can be stressful."
   (A) [1]
   (B) [2]
   (C) [3]
   (D) [4]

GLASTONVILLE (September 2)—Eklectix Entertainment announced today that the venue for its upcoming Open Slate festival has been changed. — [1] —. The event will now take place on October 22 and 23 at the Nooza Cola bottling plant in Glastonville. This change will allow the festival stages to remain open until 12:00 midnight, instead of closing at 10:00 P.M., as previously planned.

The Nooza Cola bottling plant has been a part of Glastonville's skyline for the past 30 years. — [2] —. The plant was refurbished eight years ago as a multievent arena that combines modern comforts with industrial charm in an iconic space. It is quick and convenient to get to the arena. — [3] —. Metro riders should take the Red Line to the Hostra Road Station and then walk three blocks east to the venue.

The Open Slate festival celebrates its fifth anniversary this year with a lineup featuring some of the hottest touring bands in the world. — [4] —. Pop sensation Patti Pinette will be featured on the main stage Friday night, while breakout star Koronas will share the bill Saturday night with jazz legend Cleavon Bell.

Advance discount tickets for this year's Open Slate festival can be purchased at www.eklectix.com/openslate/tickets.

8. Why did the venue change?
(A) To enable longer time periods for performances
(B) To provide more space for attendees
(C) To move the festival closer to public transport
(D) To reduce the festival's budget

9. When did the festival start?
(A) 5 years ago
(B) 8 years ago
(C) 10 years ago
(D) 30 years ago

10. What does the Open Slate festival feature?
(A) International films
(B) Musical performances
(C) Local artists
(D) Fashion designers

11. In which of the positions marked [1], [2], [3], and [4] does the following sentence best belong?

"Drivers can reach the arena by taking the I-9 Highway to Exit 32."
(A) [1]
(B) [2]
(C) [3]
(D) [4]

UNIT 06 | 동의어 문제

평균 1~5문제 출제

무료인강

출제공식

1 지문에 제시된 특정 단어가 문맥에서 의미하는 바가 무엇인지 묻는 문제 유형이다

2 사전적 동의어가 아니라 문장에서의 의미를 묻는 것이므로 보기를 하나씩 대입시켜 문제를 푸는 것이 안전하다.

동의어 문제 유형

In the e-mail, the word **"regular"** in paragraph 1, line 1, is **closest in meaning to**

이메일에서 첫 번째 단락 1행의 "regular"와 의미가 가장 가까운 단어는?

ETS 예제　편지

번역 p.172

Q. In the letter, the word **"issue"** in paragraph 1, line 5, is **closest in meaning to**

(A) bill
(B) benefit
(C) publication
(D) problem

The Edison, *Financial news at your fingertips*

Maxwell Johnstone

600 Regent Industrial Park, Suite 25

Grant, NY 18387

April 1

Dear Mr. Johnstone,

Time passes quickly, and it is now nearly one year since you began receiving *The Edison* each month. This subscription has kept you informed of the latest news from the world of finance. But in just one month, you will receive your final **issue** unless you act now. We hope you will continue your readership without interruption.

(후략)

(+풀이 전략)

❶ 문제 파악

문장 속에서 "issue"와 의미가 가장 가까운 단어를 찾아야 한다.
"issue"가 포함된 문장에서 issue를 대신해서 보기의 단어를 대입했을 때 문장에서 어색함이 없는지, 글의 흐름에 맞는지 확인해야 한다.

❷ 지문 해석

귀하는 이 구독을 통해 금융계의 최신 소식을 계속 접하셨습니다. 그러나 지금 결정하지 않으시면 한 달 뒤 마지막 호를 받게 되실 겁니다.

❸ 보기를 대입하여 정답 도출

〈에디슨〉 구독을 지금 결정하지 않으시면 한 달 뒤 마지막 "발행물"을 받게 되실 겁니다.
발행물을 문장에 대입했을 때 글의 흐름에 맞고 문장에서 가장 적합하므로 (C)가 정답이다.

주어진 발췌문을 읽고 각 문장에 표시된 단어 또는 구의 동의어를 고르세요.

1 The name on the ID must **match** the name in which the reservation was made.

(A) compete with   (B) correspond to

2 The rubber used in the tires is subject to premature **wear**.

(A) clothing   (B) damage

3 Town residents **raised** a significant amount of money in donations through the campaign.

(A) collected   (B) lifted

4 More detailed information is provided in the **succeeding** sections beginning on page 13.

(A) subsequent   (B) accomplishing

5 Please note that the policy allowing a maximum of 30 accumulated leave days is still **in place**.

(A) needed   (B) in effect

6 Tickets that have already been purchased for either airline will be **honored**.

(A) rewarded   (B) accepted

7 Villax Properties will **assume** responsibility for the San Paulo apartment complex on June 15.

(A) suppose   (B) take over

8 The guides **cover** not only the famous, must-see sights, but also many little-known places.

(A) protect   (B) include

9 Thank you for **attending to** this matter in a timely manner.

(A) taking care of   (B) being present at

10 Owner Cheryl Fairley says she's seen business **pick up** dramatically since the park was created.

(A) gather   (B) increase

다음 지문을 읽고 문제의 정답을 고르세요.

Article

I have visited dozens of manufacturing plants in recent years, and often I have left their facilities feeling overwhelmed rather than better informed. A typical tour includes observing a number of complex machines and being introduced to a large group of managers and workers. Many tour guides present too much information. In addition, they use overly technical terms that can confuse visitors.

In order for you to benefit the most from taking a tour like this, keep the following suggestions in mind. First, do preliminary research on the plant prior to the day of the tour. This way, you can ask focused questions about plant operations. Second, make sure you bring the right people from your company, including representatives from senior management as well as production operators—the workers who actually use the manufacturing equipment.

1. The word "focused" in paragraph 2, line 3, is closest in meaning to
   (A) attentive   (B) difficult   (C) specific   (D) final

Letter

Dear Ms. Muthambi,

I would like to be considered for the position of branch manager at the Prime National Bank (PNB) branch office in Chatsworth, Durban, scheduled to open on 2 June. As you know, I have been working in this capacity in our PNB office in Bellville, Cape Town, for the last five years.

Apart from my knowledge and skill set, I bring a particular dimension to the position that others may not: a personal relationship with numerous local residents, including business and community leaders. Until two years ago, my parents owned a popular restaurant in Chatsworth, and I have come to know many local residents. Therefore, I can make a valuable contribution to the company by building our client base.

Thank you for your consideration. I look forward to hearing from you.

2. The word "dimension" in paragraph 2, line 1, is closest in meaning to
   (A) determination   (B) proportion   (C) issue   (D) characteristic

Questions 1-3 refer to the following memo.

MEMO

To: City of Elkston staff
From: Grace Okaro
Date: August 9
Subject: New Web site

We are pleased with the rollout of our new Web site. Now Elkston residents and tourists alike will have easier access to government services and to information about fun things to see and do in our city. The most critical advantage of the new Web platform, however, is that it provides far more protection from malware and cyberattacks than we previously had.

When you go to the sign-in page for the first time, simply follow the steps shown there for setting up a new password. To maintain access to the system, you must remember to update your password every six months. As you approach the six-month mark, the system will automatically e-mail you a reminder.

---

1. According to the memo, why might someone access the Web site?
(A) To order some merchandise
(B) To request a service appointment
(C) To learn about popular locations to visit
(D) To read about how to design Web sites

2. What does Ms. Okaro indicate?
(A) She plans to advertise on social media sites.
(B) She wants staff to reply to her e-mail.
(C) She has had concerns about online security.
(D) She recommends that staff create new user names.

3. The word "mark" in paragraph 2, line 4, is closest in meaning to
(A) limit
(B) symbol
(C) rule
(D) idea

ETS TEST

Questions 4-6 refer to the following e-mail.

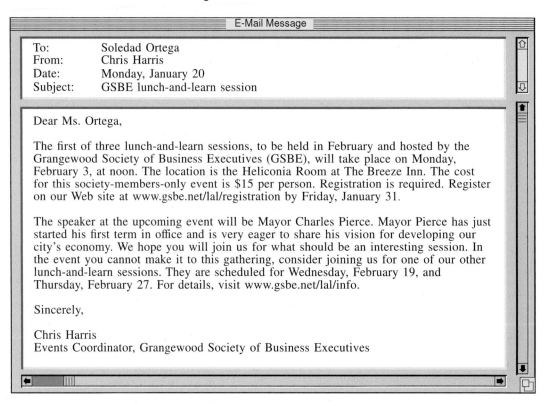

E-Mail Message

To: Soledad Ortega
From: Chris Harris
Date: Monday, January 20
Subject: GSBE lunch-and-learn session

Dear Ms. Ortega,

The first of three lunch-and-learn sessions, to be held in February and hosted by the Grangewood Society of Business Executives (GSBE), will take place on Monday, February 3, at noon. The location is the Heliconia Room at The Breeze Inn. The cost for this society-members-only event is $15 per person. Registration is required. Register on our Web site at www.gsbe.net/lal/registration by Friday, January 31.

The speaker at the upcoming event will be Mayor Charles Pierce. Mayor Pierce has just started his first term in office and is very eager to share his vision for developing our city's economy. We hope you will join us for what should be an interesting session. In the event you cannot make it to this gathering, consider joining us for one of our other lunch-and-learn sessions. They are scheduled for Wednesday, February 19, and Thursday, February 27. For details, visit www.gsbe.net/lal/info.

Sincerely,

Chris Harris
Events Coordinator, Grangewood Society of Business Executives

4. What is stated about the February 3 event?
   (A) It is open to the public.
   (B) It can be attended at no charge.
   (C) It will be held at the GSBE's office.
   (D) It will feature a government official.

5. The word "term" in paragraph 2, line 2, is closest in meaning to
   (A) word
   (B) time period
   (C) condition
   (D) end point

6. A When will the second lunch-and-learn session take place?
   (A) On a Monday
   (B) On a Wednesday
   (C) On a Thursday
   (D) On a Friday

Plotnick Park to be Renovated

By Laura Doriot

ARAMORE (June 17)—Aramore's town council has unanimously approved a resolution to renovate eight-year-old Plotnick Park. The park's renovation was initially proposed two years ago and has been under consideration since. But it was not until Mayor Maya Clark came into office that changes were finally approved. "I told the town that this would be my first major act in office, and I intend to keep that promise," she said in an interview. — [1] —.

After the park was built, its tree-lined three-kilometer path along the lake became Aramore residents' place of choice for an afternoon stroll. It was not long, however, before families realized that the park was not ideal for children. — [2] —.

"We use the trail regularly, but our kids would love to kick a ball around," says town resident Liam Ellis. "The park is lacking the kind of open space that children need to run freely. And we've often thought of bringing a picnic lunch to the park, but there aren't any tables or benches." — [3] —.

The project calls for a major clearing of growth to make way for a large green space for outdoor activities. A playground, picnic tables, and an outdoor volleyball net will be welcome additions. — [4] —. This was a request from the town's running club to accommodate those who prefer to exercise later in the evening. The renovations will take place during the winter months, and the park will be ready for use again next spring.

7. What is indicated about the park's renovation?
(A) It will begin next spring.
(B) Mayor Clark first proposed it.
(C) It will take two years to complete.
(D) All the council members agreed to it.

8. The word "intend" in paragraph 1, line 10, is closest in meaning to
(A) plan
(B) agree
(C) attempt
(D) communicate

9. How have residents been using the park?
(A) To eat lunch
(B) To play sports
(C) To go for walks
(D) To swim in the lake

10. In which of the positions marked [1], [2], [3], and [4] does the following sentence best belong?

"And the council has also agreed to have lampposts installed along the park's trail."
(A) [1]
(B) [2]
(C) [3]
(D) [4]

정답이 보이는 동의어 리스트

account

1. 계좌 = bank account
   to open / close an **account**
   계좌를 개설 / 해지하다
2. 설명 = description, report
   a detailed **account** of the meeting
   회의에 관한 자세한 설명

acknowledge

1. 인정하다 = admit, recognize
   acknowledge one's mistakes
   실수를 인정하다
2. 감사를 표하다 = express thanks
   acknowledge contributions
   공헌에 감사를 표하다

address

1. 말하다, 연설하다 = deliver a speech
   address the audience 청중에게 말하다
2. 다루다, 처리하다 = deal with, handle
   address a concern 걱정거리를 해결하다
3. 보내다 = direct, refer
   address all inquiries to the administrative
   staff 모든 문의 사항을 행정 직원에서 보내다

appreciate

1. 감사하다 = give thanks for
   We **appreciate** your feedback.
   의견 감사합니다.
2. 이해하다 = understand
   I **appreciate** your concern.
   귀하의 우려 사항을 이해합니다.

assume

1. 떠맡다, 책임지다 = take over, take on
   assume the role of spokesperson 대변인 역할을 맡다
2. 추정하다 = suppose
   assumed it would take a few days
   며칠 걸릴 것으로 예상했다

balance

1. 균형 = ability to remain upright
   sense of **balance** 균형 감각
2. 잔액 = remainder
   the current **balance** in my account
   내 계좌의 현재 잔액

bear

1. 참다, 견디다 = endure
   bear the strain 부담감을 견디다
2. 띠다, 간직하다 = carry
   The mall **bears** the name of its owner.
   그 쇼핑몰의 이름은 소유주의 이름을 띠고 있다.
3. (책임 등을) 떠맡다, 감당하다 = be responsible for
   bear 50 percent of the costs
   50퍼센트의 비용을 부담하다

carry

1. 나르다, 들고 있다 = take somewhere
   carry a suitcase
   여행용 가방을 나르다
2. 취급하다, 구비하다 = have in stock
   carry a range of home appliances
   다양한 가전 제품을 취급하다

certain

1. 확실한, 틀림없는 = sure
   not **certain** when it will take place
   언제 일어날지 확실하지 않다
2. 특정한 = specific
   exceed a **certain** weight 일정 무게를 초과하다

command

1. 명령(하다), 지휘(하다) = order
   give the **command** 명령하다
2. (언어) 구사력 = ability
   a brilliant **command** of Chinese
   훌륭한 중국어 구사력

commitment

① 약속(한 일), 책무 = duty, responsibility
take on a new **commitment** 새로운 책무를 맡다
make a **commitment** to help 돕기로 약속하다

② 헌신 = devotion, dedication
show an outstanding **commitment**
두드러진 헌신성을 보이다

concern

① 걱정, 우려 = worry, anxiety
growing **concern** about the impact of the oil shock
석유 파동 충격에 대한 점점 커지는 우려

② 관심사 = interest
a matter of **concern** 관심사

condition

① 상태 = state
be in excellent **condition**
상태가 아주 좋다

② 조건 = requirement
a necessary **condition**
필요 조건

contain

① 포함하다 = include, consist of
The survey **contains** 10 questions.
설문은 10개의 질문을 포함하고 있다.

② 억제하다, 제어하다 = hold back, control
help **contain** production costs
생산 비용을 제어하는 것을 돕다

cover

① 덮다, 가리다, 숨기다 = hide, protect, conceal
a mountain **covered** with snow
눈으로 덮인 산

② 다루다, 포함하다 = deal with, include
The session will **cover** the company policy.
그 시간에는 회사 정책에 대해 다룰 것입니다.

③ 비용을 대다 = provide for
cover the cost of construction
건축비를 대다

credit

① 신용, 신용 거래 = trust
a person of high **credit** 신용도가 높은 사람

② 칭찬 = praise
take all the **credit** for the project
그 프로젝트에 대한 모든 공을 인정받다

③ ~을 …의 덕분으로 여기다 = attribute
credit something to a person

④ 입금하다, 적립하다 = add money
$100 was **credited** to your account.
100달러가 귀하의 계정으로 입금되었습니다.

decline

① 거절하다 = reject, refuse
decline the invitation 초대를 거절하다

② 감소(하다) = decrease, fall, drop
a rapid / significant **decline** 급격한 / 상당한 감소

degree

① 정도 = level
a high **degree** of professionalism 높은 수준의 프로 정신

② 학위 = qualification
a bachelor's **degree** 학사 학위

dimension

① 치수 = size, measurement
store **dimension** 매장 면적

② 특징, 측면 = characteristic, aspect
add another **dimension** to 또 다른 특징을 더하다

direct

① 직행의 = without stopping
a **direct** flight 직항

② 지시하다, 지휘하다 = supervise, control
direct a film 영화를 감독하다

③ 보내다 = address, refer
direct questions to the customer service
department 고객 서비스 부서로 질문을 보내다

정답이 보이는 동의어 리스트

draw
① 그리다 = illustrate, sketch
hand-**drawn** flyers
손으로 그린 전단지
② 당기다, 끌다 = attract, pull
draw a lot of people
많은 사람들을 끌어모으다

entry
① 입력 = putting information
data-**entry** error 데이터 입력 오류
② 입장, 출입 = admission
free **entry** to attractions 관광 명소 무료 입장
③ 출품작 = submission to a contest
the winning **entry** 우승작

extend
① 연장하다, 늘리다 = continue
extend a deadline 마감 기한을 연장하다
② 주다 = offer
extend an invitation to a banquet 연회 초대장을 주다

fairly
① 상당히, 꽤 = quite
fairly large 상당히 큰
② 정당하게, 공평하게 = impartially
treat **fairly** 공평하게 처우하다

figure
① 수치 = number
sales **figures** 판매 수치
② 인물 = person
a prominent **figure** 거물, 저명인사
③ 모습, 형상 = shape

fine
① 좋은, 건강한, 멋진 = good
fine clothes 좋은 옷
② 벌금 = monetary penalty
fine for speeding 과속 범칙금

follow
① 따라가다, 뒤따르다 = go after
A be **followed** by B A 다음에 B
② 지켜보다 = monitor
follow with great interest
많은 관심을 갖고 지켜보다

function
① 기능 = role
key **functions** of the new software
새 소프트웨어의 핵심 기능
② 행사 = event, gathering
banquet room for business **functions**
비즈니스 행사를 위한 연회장

hold
① 보유하다, 유지하다 = have, keep
hold a degree in accounting
회계학 학위를 갖고 있다
② 열다, 개최하다 = **hold** a meeting 회의를 개최하다
③ 여기다, 간주하다 = be **held** responsible 책임이 있다

issue
① 쟁점, 문제 = topic, matter
a controversial **issue** 논란의 여지가 있는 쟁점
② (발행물의) 호 = edition
preview of the March **issue** 3월호 미리보기
③ 발행하다 = publish, give out
issue a certificate 증명서를 발급하다

keep

❶ 계속하다 = continue
Keep checking your e-mail.
이메일을 계속 확인하세요.

❷ 유지하다 = stay in state
Keep quiet. 조용히 하세요.

❸ (약속 등을) 지키다 = maintain without change
keep an appointment 약속을 지키다

last

❶ 마지막의 = final
Her **last** day will be March 15.
그녀의 마지막 근무일은 3월 15일입니다.

❷ 최근의, 지난 = most recent
for the **last** few weeks 지난 몇 주 동안

❸ 지속되다 = continue, keep on
The meeting **lasted** for 2 hours.
회의는 2시간 동안 지속되었다.

level

❶ 수준[정도] = amount, degree
minimize the noise **level** 소음 수준을 최소화하다
a high **level** of job satisfaction 높은 수준의 직업 만족도

❷ 수준[단계] = standard of ability
entry-**level** position 신입직

mark

❶ 표시하다 = write
marked price 표시된 가격

❷ 기념하다 = celebrate
mark the 10th anniversary
10주년을 기념하다

measure

❶ 조치 = action
take every **measure** 모든 조치를 취하다

❷ 척도[기준] = standard, criteria
measures to determine annual salary increases
연봉 인상을 결정하기 위한 척도

note

❶ 메모, 필기 = memo
take **notes** 메모하다

❷ 말하다 = say, mention
as **noted** 언급된 대로

❸ 유념하다 = realize
Please **note** that there are a few requirements.
몇 가지 조건이 있다는 점을 유념하세요.

notice

❶ 공고 = announcement
post a **notice** on the board 공지문을 게시판에 게시하다

❷ 통보 = notification
give 2 weeks **notice** 2주 전에 통보하다

❸ 알아차리다, 주목하다 = become conscious
I **noticed** that I was charged too much.
제게 너무 많은 금액이 부과된 것을 발견했습니다.

observe

❶ 관찰하다, 주시하다 = watch, monitor
The patient was **observed** for 2 weeks.
그 환자는 2주 동안 관찰되었다.

❷ (법을) 준수하다 = follow, comply with
The procedures must be **observed**.
그 절차들은 준수되어야 한다.

outstanding

❶ 뛰어난 = excellent
an **outstanding** tenor 뛰어난 테너

❷ 미지불된 = remaining
the **outstanding** balance 미지불 잔액

performance

❶ 공연 = show, concert
the evening **performance** 저녁 공연

❷ 실적 = record
sales **performance** 판매 실적

promotion

1 승진 = advancement
   promotion to marketing manager
   마케팅 매니저로 승진

2 판촉(활동) = bargain
   special **promotions** 특별 할인

raise

1 올리다 = increase, move upwards, lift
   raise salaries 봉급을 올리다

2 (자금, 사람 등을) 모으다 = collect
   raise money for charity 자선 기금을 모으다

3 불러일으키다, 야기하다 = cause
   raise doubts 의심을 불러일으키다

4 양육하다 = bring up, take care of
   raise children 아이들을 키우다

rate

1 속도, 비율
   at a **rate** of 10 miles an hour 시속 10마일로

2 요금, 가격 = price, an amount of money
   at a reduced **rate** 할인된 가격으로

3 평가하다 = judge
   be highly **rated** 높은 평가를 받다

reach

1 도달하다, ~에 이르다 = arrive
   reach one's destination 목적지에 도착하다

2 연락하다 = contact
   can be **reached** 24 hours a day
   24시간 연락 가능하다

recognize

1 알아보다 = identify, remember
   recognize the model number 모델 번호를 식별하다

2 알다 = understand, acknowledge
   recognize the frustration 고객의 불만을 이해하다

3 (공을) 인정하다 = honor, acknowledge
   recognize the individual achievements
   개인의 업적을 인정하다

reservation

1 예약 = booking
   make a **reservation** 예약하다

2 의구심, 우려 = concern, doubt
   reservations about the mechanical elements
   기계적인 요소들에 대한 우려

respect

1 존경, 존중 = admiration
   show one's **respect** for
   ~에 대해 존경을 표하다

2 점, 사항 = aspect, point
   in this **respect** 이런 점에서

response

1 반응 = reaction
   response to the product 그 제품에 대한 반응

2 답변 = answer
   frequently asked questions and **responses**
   자주 묻는 질문과 답변

rest

1 나머지 = remainder
   the **rest** of the day 하루 중 남은 시간

2 휴식 = break
   take a **rest** 휴식을 취하다

run

1 작동하다, 기능하다 = function
   The engine **runs** well. 엔진이 잘 작동한다.

2 계속되다, 지속되다 = continue
   The meeting is to **run** until 11 A.M.
   회의는 오전 11시까지 계속될 예정이다.

3 운영하다, 경영하다 = manage
   run a clothing store 의류점을 운영하다

secure

① 안전한 = certain, safe
secure job 안정적인 직업

② 확보하다 = obtain
secure one's place 자리를 확보하다

③ 보호하다 = protect
secure environment 환경을 보호하다

sensitive

① 세심한 = thoughtful, delicate
sensitive asset management 세심한 자산 관리

② 민감한, 약한 = fragile, easily affected
sensitive to chemicals 화학 물질에 약한

③ 기밀을 요하는 = confidential
retrieve **sensitive** corporate data
기밀 기업 자료를 복구하다

serve

① 제공하다 = offer
Light refreshments will be **served**.
가벼운 다과가 제공됩니다.

② 근무하다 = work
serve as marketing director for 2 years
마케팅 이사로 2년 동안 근무하다

step

① 단계 = stage
step by **step** 차근차근

② 걸음 = footstep
make a **step** forward 앞으로 한 걸음 전진하다

③ 조치 = measures, actions
take **steps** 조치를 취하다

④ 계단 = stair

stock

① 비축(물), 저장 = supply
have in **stock** 재고가 있다

② 주식 = share
stock market 주식 시장

succeed

① 성공하다 = do well
succeed in business 사업에서 성공하다

② 계승하다, 뒤를 잇다 = follow
succeeding generations 다음 세대들

suggest

① 제안하다, 추천하다 = recommend
I **suggest** that you take the train.
기차를 타실 것을 추천합니다.

② 암시하다 = imply
The reports **suggested** there were safety
concerns.
보고서는 안전에 대한 우려가 있었음을 암시했다

take off

① 이륙하다 = leave the ground, depart
My flight **took off** an hour late.
제 비행기가 한 시간 늦게 출발했어요.

② 옷을 벗다 = remove clothing
Take off your shoes. 신발을 벗으세요.

③ 유행하다, 인기를 얻다 = become successful
His business has really **taken off**.
그의 사업이 크게 번창하고 있다.

term

① 용어, 말 = word
technical **term** 전문 용어

② 기간 = period
short **term** parking 단기 주차

③ 조건, 조항 = conditions
terms of the lease 임대 계약의 조항

wear

① (옷 등을) 입다, 착용하다 = have something on
wear contact lenses
콘택트렌즈를 끼다

② 낡다, 닳다 = gradually decay
worn-out parts 낡은 부품

UNIT 07 이메일 / 편지

평균 3~4문제 출제

무료인강

이메일/편지 지문 유형

- 주로 격식을 갖춘 업무 관련 서신이 출제된다.
- 고객과 업체간, 회사와 직원간, 혹은 업체간 이메일 출제 빈도가 가장 높다.
- 축하, 감사, 사과, 추천, 홍보, 지시 및 요청, 답신을 목적으로 하는 지문이 대부분이다.

ETS 예제 이메일

번역 p. 177

수발신	To: Mario Gonzalez <mgonz@protemp.com>
	From: Estela Morales <emorales@caixadirectcorp.com>
제목	Subject: Application
날짜	Date: July 20
받는이	Dear Mr. Gonzalez,
인사말	Thank you for your application for the junior accounting position here at Caixa Direct.
세부사항	All applications and résumés are first reviewed by two of our senior staff members. If you are selected for an interview following that review, you will be contacted by our personnel officer, Ricardo Martinez, who will set up an appointment. At that time, we will ask for names and contact information for three references.
요청사항	
첨부파일	Attached is a copy of our most recent annual report, as you requested. Thank you again for your interest in Caixa Direct Corporation.
	Yours truly,
글쓴이	Estela Morales, Office Manager
직책/소속	Caixa Direct Corporation

✚ 지문 파악하기

① 주로 서두에서 주제와 목적이 드러난다.

제목: 지원서
카익사 다이렉트의 하급 회계직에 지원해 주신 것에 감사드립니다.

② 중/후반부에는 세부 정보가 제공된다.

검토 후 면접 대상자로 선정되면 인사부 담당자 리카도 마르티네즈가 연락해서 약속 시간을 잡을 것입니다.

③ 첨부파일 등의 추가 내용이 덧붙는다.

첨부된 파일은 귀하께서 요청하신 우리 회사의 최신 연례 보고서 사본입니다.

✚ 문제풀이

글의 목적 ①	**What is the purpose of the e-mail?** 이 이메일의 목적은?	▶ **To confirm receipt of an application** 지원서 수령 확인
세부 사항 ②	**Who will contact Mr. Gonzalez to arrange a meeting?** 회의 일정을 잡기 위해 누가 곤잘레스 씨에게 연락할 것인가?	▶ **The personnel officer** 인사 담당자
첨부된 것 ③	**What is being sent with the e-mail?** 이메일과 함께 전달된 것은?	▶ **A company report** 회사 보고서

이메일 / 편지 | 정답이 보이는 단서

주제

⊙ 제목을 통해 주제를 한눈에 파악할 수 있다.

Subject: Performance reviews	제목: 업무 평가
Subject: Web designer position	제목: 웹디자이너직
Subject: RE: Service request	제목: 회신: 서비스 요청

목적

⊙ 주로 초반부에서 글을 쓴 목적을 밝힌다.

I am writing to invite you to speak at the annual conference.	~ 차 편지를 드립니다
We are pleased to introduce the terms of a new payment plan.	~하게 되어 기쁩니다
This letter is to confirm the prices we discussed.	~하기 위한 편지입니다
I would like to extend my gratitude to all staff members.	~하고자 합니다

요청 / 요구

⊙ Please 명령문, 또는 공손한 표현 'if you could(혹시 해 주신다면)' 등을 사용한다.

Please let me know which one you prefer.	~을 알려 주세요
I would appreciate if you could review the documents.	~해 주시면 감사하겠습니다
I wonder if you could come by the store today.	~해 주실 수 있는지 궁금합니다
Should you choose to accept, **make sure you** complete the forms.	~하는 경우, 반드시 ~하셔야 합니다

첨부 사항

⊙ attach, enclosed, included 등의 표현에 주목한다.

Please refer to **the attached** documents for more details.	첨부된 문서를 참조 바랍니다
Enclosed is a questionnaire we want you to complete.	설문지가 동봉되어 있습니다
I will **send** the brochure **along with** some coupons.	쿠폰과 함께 책자를 드립니다
Please consult the map **included** in the packet.	세트에 포함된 지도를 참조하세요

연락 방법

⊙ 글의 말미에 요청문의 형태로 제시된다.

Please visit our Web site if you have any questions.	웹사이트를 방문하세요
For more information, you may **contact me at ext.** 5810.	내선번호로 연락주세요
I will be reachable by phone for all your inquiries.	전화로 문의주세요.
Please direct any questions **to** the floor manager.	매니저에게 질문을 보내 주세요
We request that you **RSVP** at your earliest convenience.	가능한 빨리 회신주세요

이메일 / 편지 빈출 어휘

● 주문

account 계정, 계좌
bill 청구하다
charge 요금(을 부과하다)
clarify 명확하게 하다
confirm 확인하다, 확정하다
due 회비; 지불 기일이 된
estimate 견적(= quote)
fee 요금
in stock 재고가 있는
in transit 수송 중인
in writing 서면으로
no later than 늦어도 ~까지
outstanding balance 미지불 잔액
ship 배송하다, 수송하다
statement 명세서
submit 제출하다

● 구매 / 할인

affordable 가격이 적당한
at no cost 무료로(= free of charge)
clearance sale 창고 정리 세일
extend 늘리다, 연장하다
gift certificate 상품권
giveaway 증정품, 경품
installment 할부(금)
inventory 재고, 재고 목록
markdown 가격 인하
range 범위(가 ~에 이르다)
redeem 현금이나 상품으로 바꾸다
retail price 소매가
special offer 특별 할인
take advantage of ~을 이용하다
voucher 할인권, 상품권

● 사업

acquire 획득하다
approve 승인하다
bid 입찰에 응하다
brand awareness 상표 인지도
(= brand recognition)
district 지역(= territory)
endorse 보증하다, 지지하다
establishment 설립, 기관
generate 산출하다, 만들어 내다
overview 개요
patent 특허
profitable 수익성 좋은(= lucrative)
prototype 시제품
provision 조항, 준비
put[run, place] an ad 광고를 내다
thrive 번영하다(= flourish)

● 감사 / 사과

apology 사과
as a token of appreciation
감사의 표시로
compensate 보상하다
complimentary 무료의
courteous 공손한, 정중한
defective 결함 있는(= faulty, have a flaw)
delay 미루다, 지연시키다(= postpone)
delighted 기쁜(= glad, happy, pleased)
grateful 감사하는, 고마워하는
gratitude 감사
on behalf of ~을 대표하여, 대신하여
patronage 애용
recognize ~을 인정하다, 인식하다
regretful 유감스러운
valuable 귀중한(= invaluable, valued)

● 서비스

appointment 약속, 예약
around the clock 24시간 내내
atmosphere 분위기
courtesy 무료의, 서비스의
exemplary 본보기가 되는
expire 만료되다
extensive 광범위한
hospitality 서비스업, 환대
maintenance 유지, 보수
meet demands 수요를 충족시키다
requirement 요구 사항, 필요 조건
subscribe 구독하다
substitute 대체하다; 대체자
termination 종결
under the terms of ~의 조항에 따라

● 자금

asset 재산
assign 할당하다
contribution 기부, 공헌
deposit 보증금; 입금하다
exceed 초과하다
financial 금융의, 재무의
fundraising 모금
generous 후한, 너그러운
monetary donation 금전적 기부
possess 소유하다
property 재산, 부동산
reimburse 상환하다, 변제하다
retain 보유하다, 유보하다
revenue 수익, 수입
transfer 송금하다, 옮기다
withdraw 인출하다

● 축하 / 기념

anniversary 기념일
attire 복장
cater 음식을 공급하다
celebrate 축하하다
consecutive 연이은
grand opening 개업식
honor 명예(를 주다)
in advance 사전에, 미리(= ahead of time)
judge 심사위원, 판사
luncheon 오찬
plaque 명판, 상패
refreshments 다과
register 등록하다(= enroll, sign up)
retirement 은퇴
retreat 연수, 야유회
venue 장소

● 추천

attitude 태도
certificate 증명서
considerate 신중한, 사려 깊은
consistently 끊임없이, 항상
cooperation 협동, 협력
enthusiastic 열성적인
expertise 전문 지식
potential 잠재력 있는; 잠재력
promote 승진시키다, 홍보하다
prospective 장래성 있는, 유망한
qualification 자격 요건
recruit 채용하다; 신입 사원
referral 소개
supervise 감독하다
work ethic 직업 윤리

● 건강 / 보험

count on ~을 믿다, ~에 의지하다
coverage 보상 (범위)
diagnosis (병원) 진단, 진찰
disease 질병
immune 면역성이 있는
insure 보험에 들다[가입하다]
over the counter 처방전 없이 살 수 있는
pharmaceutical 제약(의)
physician 내과의사
plan (의료 보험, 연금 등의) 제도
prescription 처방(전)
proof of insurance 보험증서
recovery 회복
remedy 치료(법)
symptom 증상
vaccinate 예방 접종하다

Questions 1-2 refer to the following e-mail.

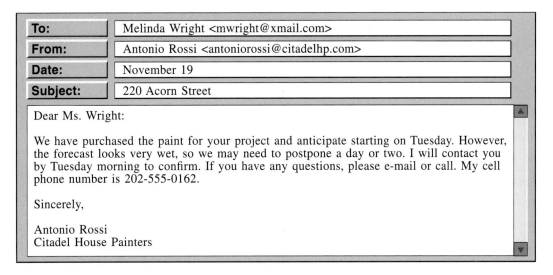

To:	Melinda Wright <mwright@xmail.com>
From:	Antonio Rossi <antoniorossi@citadelhp.com>
Date:	November 19
Subject:	220 Acorn Street

Dear Ms. Wright:

We have purchased the paint for your project and anticipate starting on Tuesday. However, the forecast looks very wet, so we may need to postpone a day or two. I will contact you by Tuesday morning to confirm. If you have any questions, please e-mail or call. My cell phone number is 202-555-0162.

Sincerely,

Antonio Rossi
Citadel House Painters

1. What is the purpose of the e-mail?
(A) To revise a price estimate
(B) To respond to feedback
(C) To provide an update
(D) To confirm an order

2. What does Mr. Rossi indicate about the project?
(A) It is halfway done.
(B) It could be delayed by rain.
(C) It was finished on Tuesday.
(D) It will require additional paint.

Questions 3-6 refer to the following e-mail.

To:	m.chae@newmail.co.uk
From:	info@fantastisoft.co.uk
Date:	15 February
Subject:	Fantastisoft Premium pricing

Dear Ms. Chae,

Because you are a past subscriber of Fantastisoft Premium, we wanted to let you know that now is the perfect time to revisit our product and increase your knowledge of software and soft skills. Our users now have access to some amazing new features, such as a smartphone app with on-the-go access to lessons for essential business skills. Learners can also now choose from a greater range of topics for lessons, prerecorded videos, and games.

However, with these great new features comes new pricing. Starting on 12 April, a monthly subscription will be £12 rather than the current £9, and the annual subscription will increase to £110 from £90. The updated prices better reflect the value that Fantastisoft Premium offers to our learners. Visit www.fantastisoft.co.uk/premium before 12 April and you can subscribe to Fantastisoft Premium at today's lower prices!

Read what Fantastisoft Premium customers have to say:

"I upgraded to Fantastisoft Premium a few months ago, and the lessons and games quickly became part of my daily routine. I have learned so many new skills, and I'm sure that's why I was promoted at work. Premium is so worth it!" —Gustav Roland

"Since I became a Fantastisoft Premium user, I start every morning with a Fantastisoft lesson to keep my skills fresh. I'm so much more confident. Premium has really helped me take my business to the next level!" —Monica Tahseen

The Fantastisoft Team

3. What is the purpose of the e-mail?
(A) To advertise an upcoming sale
(B) To collect a customer testimonial
(C) To ask a current user to make a payment soon
(D) To encourage a previous user to subscribe again

4. What feature was recently added to Fantastisoft Premium?
(A) Virtual partners for skills practice
(B) Easier access to lessons
(C) Enhanced graphics in educational games
(D) Live business videos

5. How much will Fantastisoft Premium cost per year after April 12 ?
(A) £9
(B) £12
(C) £90
(D) £110

6. What is true about both Mr. Roland and Ms. Tahseen?
(A) They run their own businesses.
(B) They use Fantastisoft Premium every day.
(C) They were recently promoted.
(D) They think Fantastisoft Premium should cost less.

Morehouse Suppliers
Leeds, England

Dear Customer,

We are delighted to be delivering your recent order to you. Please ensure that all items listed on the attached packing slip are included in this package. — [1] —.

Because you have taken advantage of our alterations service, please note that the size label on your garment no longer reflects the current measurements. Also, the shirt sleeves we shortened will appear to be longer than requested by up to 1.5 centimetres. — [2] —. It was done to account for normal shrinkage. To enable the sleeves to assume the desired length, simply put the shirt through the laundry cycle three times.

For future orders, please note that we offer all of the following standard customisation services:
• Adding a shirt cuff monogram
• Adding a pocket
• Shortening trousers
• Shortening shirt sleeves
• Replacing buttons (for most items)

— [3] —. For a complete list of our alteration services, including prices and restrictions, see the chart at the back of either our Spring or Winter catalogues. — [4] —. If you would like to receive our most recent catalogue, please access the form on the Customer Service section of our Web site where you can provide us with your mailing address.

Thank you,

Frederick Garza
Frederick Garza
Tailoring Director

7. What kind of business is Morehouse Suppliers?
(A) A construction materials producer
(B) An art supplies store
(C) A furniture manufacturer
(D) A clothing company

8. What does Mr. Garza suggest that the customer do?
(A) Check a product for defects
(B) Wash an item several times
(C) Remove a price tag
(D) Submit comments about a service

9. According to the letter, where can customers obtain more details about alteration services?
(A) In a catalog
(B) On a Web site
(C) In a promotional e-mail
(D) On an enclosed packing slip

10. In which of the positions marked [1], [2], [3], and [4] does the following sentence best belong?

"This is not an error."
(A) [1]
(B) [2]
(C) [3]
(D) [4]

UNIT 08 광고

평균 1~2문제 출제

무료인강

광고 지문 유형

- 업체 광고 – 업체 상품 및 서비스의 특장점, 구매 혜택, 부가 서비스, 구매처 등의 내용이 전개된다.
- 구인 광고 – 모집 직책, 담당 업무, 자격 요건, 회사 복지 혜택, 지원 방법 등의 내용이 전개된다.
- 행사 광고 – 행사 목적, 행사 일시 및 장소, 출연자 소개, 진행 일정, 신청 방법 등의 내용이 전개된다.

ETS 예제 광고

번역 p.179

ARTISTICS, INC., GRAND OPENING!

업체명	Artistics, Inc., is proud to announce that our store has reopened at a new location, 2416 Whalley Avenue. We
전문 분야	will continue to specialize in business cards, flyers, posters, menus, catalogs, and other promotional materials. In addition, our bigger space now allows us
서비스 특장점	to offer the services of an expanded team of graphic designers who can work with you to conceptualize and design your product in order to achieve maximum visual appeal.
취급 상품	We invite you to visit our store and take a look at hundreds of sample cards, mailers, and brochures, all of which can be customized for your specific products
구매 혜택	or services. If you make a purchase of $200 or more in printing services in the month of April, you will receive a complimentary 100-count box of business cards (a $25 value).

+ 지문 파악하기

❶ 광고되는 상품과 업체명이 소개된다.

명함, 전단지, 포스터, 메뉴, 카탈로그, 홍보 자료를 전문적으로 취급합니다.

❷ 상품이나 업체의 특장점이 언급된다.

이제 넓어진 매장 덕분에 보강된 그래픽 디자이너팀의 서비스를 제공해 드릴 수 있게 되었습니다.

❸ 부가 서비스 및 구매 혜택이 제시된다.

200달러 이상 인쇄 서비스를 이용하시면 무료로 100장들이 명함 한 통(25달러 상당)을 받으실 수 있습니다.

+ 문제풀이

업체 종류 ❶	What type of business is Artistics, Inc.? 아티스틱스사는 어떤 종류의 업체인가?	▶ A printing company 인쇄 회사
업체 특성 ❷	What is indicated about Artistics, Inc.? 아티스틱스사에 대해 알 수 있는 것은?	▶ It has hired additional staff. 추가 직원을 고용했다.
구매 혜택 ❸	What is offered with a purchase of $200 or more? 200달러 이상 구매하면 무엇이 제공되는가?	▶ A set of business cards 명함 세트

광고 | 정답이 보이는 단서

관심 유도
⊙ 소비자의 관심을 끌기 위해 질문으로 광고를 시작할 수 있다.

Do you need to safely store confidential paperwork?	기밀 문서 보관 장치 광고
Do you find many of your clothes do not fit anymore?	옷 수선 서비스 광고
Do you want to build stronger partnerships with international clients?	비즈니스 세미나 광고

광고 분야 및 내용 소개
⊙ 상품 및 서비스, 구인 광고가 대표적이다.

We are proud to **announce our special sales event**.	특별 할인 행사 안내
We are pleased to **introduce the debut of a low-cost internet plans**.	저가 인터넷 요금제 출시 소개
We **specialize in kitchen design, fabrication, and installation**.	부엌 디자인, 제작, 설치 작업
We are **looking for an instructor** to lead our fitness program.	피트니스 강사 구인
We are currently **seeking an assistant editor**.	편집 보조 구인

제품 및 서비스 특장점
⊙ feature / boast / now / 비교급 / 최상급 등의 표현에 주목하자.

This model **features** adjustable lamp and sizable seating area.	~을 특징으로 합니다
We **boast** a number of high-profile part-time instructors.	~을 자랑합니다
Our display room **now** has **brighter** lighting and **bigger** space.	신규 또는 변화된 것
The shopping mall has the state's **largest** food court.	특장점

조건 / 제한 사항
⊙ if / only / exclusive / limited 등의 표현에 주목하자.

If you make a purchase of $100 or more, you will receive a free bag.	일정 금액 이상 구매 시
For a limited time only, we offer 50% discount.	기간 한정
Only for our new customers, we can deliver your order at no charge.	신규 고객 특전
These giveaway items are **on a first-come, first-served basis**.	선착순

자격 요건
⊙ 필수 조건과 그렇지 않은 조건을 구분해야 한다.

Job applicants **must/should** possess a valid driver's license.	필수 조건
Relevant work experience is **required/necessary/mandatory**.	필수 조건
Certification in quality assurance is **ideal but not essential**.	우대 사항
A master's degree in computer science is **preferred**.	우대 사항

● 부동산

commercial 상업적인; 광고
flat 아파트
floor plan 평면도
fully-furnished 내부가 완비된
landlord 임대주
lease 임대하다
real estate agent 부동산 중개인
rent 임대료; 임대하다
residential 거주용의
separate 분리된
situated ~에 위치한(= located)
studio 원룸 형태의 공간
tenant 세입자
utility (전기·수도와 같은) 공익 서비스
within walking distance 도보 거리 이내

● 식당

appetite 식욕
assortment 모듬
conveniently located 위치가 좋은
cuisine 요리(법)
culinary 요리의, 주방의
dip (소스 등에) 담그다
entrée 주요리
flavor 향, 맛
ingredient 재료, 성분
made-to-order 주문 제작된
marvelous 놀라운
one serving 1인분
patron 고객
platter 대형 접시, 여러 음식을 차려 놓은 요리
signature dish 대표 요리

● 항공사

airfare 항공료
aisle seat 통로 쪽 좌석
baggage allowance 수하물 허용치
boarding pass 탑승권
book 예약하다(= reserve)
cardholder 카드 소지자
carry-on bag 기내용 가방
comfort 안락
courtesy 무료의, 서비스의
expand routes 노선을 확대하다
frequent flyer 자주 여행하는 고객
overhead compartment 머리 위 짐칸
passenger 승객
priority seating 우대석
round trip 왕복 여행
via ~을 경유하여

● 상품

apparel 옷
artifact 공예품, 인공물
browse 둘러보다
bulk order 대량 주문
compact 소형의
craft 공예
durable 내구성이 좋은
energy efficient 에너지 효율이 좋은
exquisite 정교한, 매우 아름다운
flexibility 융통성, 유연함
portable 휴대용의
present a coupon 쿠폰을 제시하다
replica 복제품
specification 사양
versatile 다재다능한, 다용도의

● 서비스

a range of 다양한(= a variety of)
accommodate 수용하다
customized 맞춤식의(= tailored)
exclusively 독점적으로
facilitate 용이하게 하다
freight 화물
packaging 포장(재)
practical 실용적인
promotional material 홍보 자료
reasonable price 적당한 가격
reliable 믿을 만한(= solid)
renew 갱신하다
specialize in ~을 전문으로 하다
superior 우수한
testimonial 추천의 글

● 구인

applicant 지원자
assess 평가하다
benefits 복지 혜택
candidate 후보자
certified 공인된
competitive salary 경쟁력 있는 연봉
cover letter 자기소개서
credential 경력, 자격 증명서
deadline 마감일(= due date)
degree 학위
desirable 바람직한
fluent 유창한
hire 고용하다(= employ)
human resources 인사과(= personnel)
job opening 공석
multi-lingual 여러 언어를 구사하는

● 행사

award-winning 수상 경력이 있는
ceremony 의식, 예식
compilation 편집, 모음집
drawing 추첨, 제비뽑기(= raffle)
entry 입장, 출품(작)
feature 특집; 포함하다
flat rate 고정 요금
foster 촉진하다, 조성하다
function 행사, 연회
last-minute 막바지의
mark 기념하다(= celebrate)
present 소개하다, 제시하다
prestigious 명망 있는, 일류의
recognized 인정 받은
spectator 관중

● 관광

accommodation 숙소
attraction 관광 명소
companion 동반인
depart 출발하다
destination (여행 등의) 목적지, 행선지
excursion 여행
expert 전문가
landscape 풍경
lodge 산장
picturesque 그림 같은
scenic 경치가 좋은
spectacular 장관인
stunning 놀랄 만큼 멋진, 훌륭한
vacancy 빈방
year-round 일 년 내내

● 구인

perform tasks 업무를 수행하다
permanent 정규직의
preference 우선권, 선취권
primary duty 주요 업무
proficiency 능숙함
qualified 자격을 갖춘
reference 추천서
relevant 관련된(= related)
replacement 교체, 후임자
required 필수적인
résumé 이력서
seek 구하다, 찾다
shift 교대 근무조
stationed 배치된
temporary 임시의, 임시직의
willingness 기꺼이 하는 마음

ETS TEST

🕐 제한시간 9분 | 정답 및 해설 p.180

Questions 1-2 refer to the following advertisement.

Euro Teletalk

Are you looking to connect with your clients while in Europe? Euro Teletalk gets you immediate mobile service with no contract and no hidden fees! With plans starting as low as $40, we have options to fit every budget.

Start by going to euroteletalk.ca to activate your account and simply choose the plan that suits your travel needs. Then download our $1.99 app to your mobile phone to access your user profile and to enjoy the convenience of your Euro Teletalk talk, text, and data package while doing business overseas. Set your account to Automatic Pay to skip the hassle of missing a payment. Cancel anytime without penalty.

www.euroteletalk.ca

---

1. For whom is the advertisement intended?
(A) University students
(B) Business travelers
(C) Government officials
(D) People on vacation

2. What is indicated about the Euro Teletalk service?
(A) It requires a contract.
(B) It includes a cancellation fee.
(C) It offers a variety of plan options.
(D) It includes a free mobile phone.

Questions 3-5 refer to the following advertisement.

Come Join Us!

Victoria Hospitality Deluxe is looking for career-minded individuals. We have openings in sales and marketing, public relations, and information technology at our world headquarters in Melbourne. And at our many hotels here in Australia and in countries across the globe, we have openings in culinary arts, landscape design, event services, and facility management.

Along with a competitive salary and benefits package, we also offer relocation assistance, a wellness program, and leadership training. Call 1800 160 401 to take the first step toward becoming one of our team members, each of whom is vital to our success.

---

3. What is suggested about Victoria Hospitality Deluxe?
(A) It is being reorganized.
(B) It owns hotels around the world.
(C) It has relocated its headquarters.
(D) It gives staff some free hotel stays.

4. Who would probably be most interested in the advertisement?
(A) An electrical engineer
(B) A medical technician
(C) An athletic trainer
(D) A pastry chef

5. The word "vital" in paragraph 2, line 3, is closest in meaning to
(A) essential
(B) persuasive
(C) energetic
(D) literal

Questions 6-9 refer to the following advertisement.

TRY BINLER FITNESS PRODUCTS BEFORE YOU BUY!

Whether you are a seasoned athlete or an enthusiastic beginner, new fitness equipment can be a pricey investment. But now, with Binler Fitness's hassle-free equipment rental program, you can experience what it's like to train in your own personal gym without the long-term commitment and heavy up-front expense. Rent numerous types of exercise machines, such as treadmills, ellipticals, and free weights from top brand names, and use them in the comfort of your home.

Some other great features of our exclusive program:
- Flexible rental agreements, with terms starting at just three months
- An option to purchase equipment or extend the length of the rental at any time
- Rental payments are applied to purchase price
- A team of professionals available to deliver and set up your equipment
- Continued warranty and service options available with equipment purchase

We have hundreds of items to offer that will help you meet your fitness goals. Visit us online at www.binlerfitness.com.au and explore our inventory today!

---

6. Who is the target audience of the advertisement?
(A) Private trainers who are in search of new clients
(B) People who have just joined a gym
(C) People who are interested in trying new fitness equipment
(D) People who would like to receive a fitness catalog

7. The word "seasoned" in paragraph 1, line 1, is closest in meaning to
(A) flavored
(B) experienced
(C) periodic
(D) softened

8. What is NOT mentioned as a feature of the program?
(A) Equipment is delivered to homes.
(B) Contracts can easily be extended.
(C) Personal trainers are available to guide workout sessions.
(D) Previous rental payments can be counted toward purchases.

9. According to the advertisement, how can information about products be obtained?
(A) By accessing a Web site
(B) By going to a store showroom
(C) By calling a customer service line
(D) By signing up to receive promotional e-mails

UNIT 09 공지 / 회람

평균 2~3문제 출제

무료인강

공지 / 회람 지문 유형

- 회람(memo) – 전직원 또는 특정 부서를 대상으로 하는 기업 회람이 대부분이다.
- 사내 공지 – 정책 변경, 인사 이동, 사내 행사, 업무 지원 요청 등을 공지한다.
- 일반 공지 – 보수 / 점검, 서비스 중단 / 종료, 사무실 이전, 세미나, 강연 등의 각종 행사를 공지한다.

ETS 예제 · 공지

번역 p. 182

제목 행사명	**Korost Iron and Steel Company Awards Dinner**
행사 일정	The Korost Iron and Steel Company's awards dinner will take place as planned on Monday, 1 June, from 6:00 P.M.- 9:30 P.M. However, the event location has been changed due to construction. It will no longer be held at the Colona Building, but at the Whitwell Center on Sheridan Road.
주요 정보 변동 사항	
세부 정보 길 안내	**Directions from Korost headquarters:** Head south on Marlin Street, which turns into Crescent Drive. Make a right onto Arthur Avenue, continue on for six blocks and then turn left onto Sheridan Road. The Whitwell Center is the first building on your right, number 552. The dinner will be held on the second floor.
추가 정보 주차 안내 권장 사항	**Parking information:** Parking is available at the Whitwell Center in a private area. The entrance to the area is to the right of the building. To avoid paying a fee, please bring your awards dinner invitation to show the parking attendant.

+ 지문 파악하기

❶ 주요 공지 사항이 서두에 등장한다.

공사로 인해 행사(시상식 만찬) **장소가 변경**되었습니다.

❷ 공지 세부 사항이 중반부에 등장한다.

코로스트 본사에서 오시는 길: **말린 가에서** 남부 방향으로 진출하여 크레슨트 로로 진입하십시오.

❸ 추가 정보 및 요청 사항이 제시된다.

주차료를 납부하는 일이 없도록 시상식 만찬 초대장을 지참하여 주차 요원에게 제시하십시오.

+ 문제풀이

변동 사항 ❶	What has been changed about the event? 행사에서 변경된 것은 무엇인가?	▶ The place 장소
세부 정보 ❷	Where is the Korost headquarters located? 코로스트 본사는 어디에 위치하는가?	▶ On Marlin Street 말린 가
추가 정보 ❸	What is indicated about Whitwell Center parking? 휘트웰 센터 주차장에 관해 알 수 있는 것은?	▶ It is free to certain visitors. 특정 방문객들에게는 무료이다.

공지 / 회람 | 정답이 보이는 단서

제목

➡ 공지 / 회람의 제목은 주제 또는 공지 대상을 드러낸다.

Delivery Rejection Notice	배송 거부 통지
Leave for Exceptional Performance	포상 휴가
Attention West Paragon Residents	웨스트 파라곤 입주민들께

목적 / 업종 / 장소

➡ 공지 목적을 묻는 문제, 업종 또는 공지 장소를 유추하는 문제가 출제된다.

We are **looking to hire an office assistant** in a fast-paced environment.	목적: 구인
Our customers often ask about **the status of their parcels**.	업종: 배송
Put on goggles and gloves before using machines.	장소: 공장

행사 / 공사 관련

➡ 행사 / 공사 일정 및 내용 안내, 변경 및 유의 사항 등이 공지된다.

A panel discussion on online publishing will be held **after lunch**.	행사 일정 및 내용
Elevators will be out of service for half an hour **starting from 2 P.M.**	공사 일정 및 내용
Regrettably, the last performer **has been replaced**.	변경 사항
Children under the age of 12 **must** be accompanied by an adult.	유의 사항

업무 관련

➡ 사내 신규 시스템 및 정책 안내, 협조 요청 사항 등이 공지된다.

Next week **new cash registers will be installed**.	신규 시스템 도입 알림
Supervisor approval is necessary to work overtime.	규정 안내
Please note the **travel reimbursement procedure has been modified**.	정책 변경 안내
All personnel **are advised to use the north entrance**.	협조 요청

서비스 관련

➡ 신규 서비스 도입, 기존 서비스 종료, 서비스 이용 안내 등이 공지된다.

We will now be offering mobile phone service to customers.	신규 서비스 안내
Effective May 1, the following products **will be discontinued**.	제품 생산 중단 안내
The food courts will be unavailable while work is being completed.	일시적 이용 중단 안내
Canceling on the same day will result in no refund.	환불 안내

공지 / 회람 빈출 어휘

● 정책 변경

activate 작동시키다, 활성화시키다
adopt a system 시스템을 도입하다
alternative entrance 대체 출입구
appraisal 평가
compensation 보상
concern 관심, 걱정
expenditure 지출
immediate supervisor 직속 상관
install 설치하다
mandatory 의무적인, 필수적인
obtain 얻다, 획득하다
policy 정책
reimburse 상환하다, 변제하다
sign up 등록하다
tutorial 교육
violation 위반

● 회의

address 다루다, 취급하다
agenda 안건[의제]
committee 위원회
look forward to ~을 고대하다
minutes 회의록(= proceedings)
nomination 지명, 임명
nominee 후보
objective 목적, 목표
outline 약술하다
party 일행, 무리
performance 실적
refreshments 다과
shareholder 주주(= stockholder)
the board of directors 이사회
unanimous 만장일치의

● 공사

aim 목표; 겨냥하다
annex 부속 건물
break ground 공사를 시작하다
building supervisor 건물 관리자
develop 개발하다
interrupt 방해하다, 중단시키다
launch 시작하다
phase 단계
plumbing 배관 (작업)
prolonged 장기화된, 오래 끄는
put into action 조치를 취하다
repave 도로를 재포장하다(= resurface)
resume 재개하다
setback 차질
upon completion 완공 시에

● 인사 이동

accomplishment 성취, 업적
acknowledge (공을) 인정하다
administrative 관리의, 운영의
assume 떠맡다
be named 임명되다(= be appointed)
CFO 최고재무이사
chair 의장(을 맡다)
deliberation 심사숙고
headquarters 본사(= main office)
interim 임시의
oversee 감독하다
predecessor 전임자
retire 은퇴하다
serve as ~로서 역할을 하다
smooth transition 순조로운 전환
tenure 재임 기간

● 전시

admission 입장(= entrance)
artificial 인공적인
collection 소장품, 수집품
commemorate 기념하다
contemporary art 현대 미술
critic 비평가
curator 큐레이터(전시 책임자)
exhibition 전시
existing 현존하는
extend an invitation 초대장을 보내다
feature 특집; 포함하다
host 주최하다
needless to say 말할 필요도 없이
showcase 전시, 진열; 전시하다
sculpture 조각품

● 대회

award 상; 수여하다
be suitable for ~에 적합하다
ceremony 예식
competition 경쟁, 대회
content 내용
counterpart 상대(= rival)
depict 묘사하다
entry 입장, 출품작
fierce 치열한
foremost 가장 중요한, 맨 앞의
judge 심사위원
on a first-come, first-served basis 선착순으로
precede ~에 앞서다
stand out 두드러지다

● 회사 생활

absence 부재, 결석
achieve 달성하다
attendance record 출석 기록
colleague 동료(= coworker)
demonstration 시연
division 부서
extension 내선번호
fast-paced 업무 템포가 빠른
fluent 능숙한(= competent)
job description 직무기술서
labor 근로, 노동
on duty 근무 중인
performance evaluation 업무 평가
sort out 분류하다
task 업무
trainee 훈련생

● 지역 사회

cause 대의 명분
city council 시의회
collective 공동의, 집단의
grant 승인하다; 보조금
initiative (새로운) 계획
mayor 시장
municipal 시의, 지방 자치의
occupied 사용 중인
outreach 지원[봉사] 활동
prestigious 명망 있는
proceeds 수익금
publicize 홍보하다
recycle 재활용하다
town hall 시청
volunteer 자원하다; 자원봉사자

● 환경

climate change 기후 변화
conservation 보존, 보호
contamination 오염
dispose of ~을 버리다, 처분하다
endangered 멸종 위기에 처한
environmentally conscious 환경을 신경 쓰는
extinction 멸종, 소멸
fossil fuel 화석 연료
pollutant 오염 물질
preserve 보존하다, 지키다
solar power 태양열
species 종
waste 쓰레기(= litter, garbage)
wildlife 야생 동물

Questions 1-3 refer to the following announcement.

Attention Clients of Doyle, Inc.

While waiting for its permanent headquarters to be completed, architectural and engineering firm Doyle, Inc., will be moving its offices just down the street as of September 1. The move from 1102 Main Street to 813 Main Street will be temporary (until the completion of the firm's new permanent headquarters at the Odessa Business Center). We would like to assure you that business will continue as usual and none of our current projects will be delayed as a result of this move. Please note, however, that our involvement with the university's architectural intern program will be postponed this summer and will not resume until next year.

1. What is being announced?
   (A) The relocation of a company
   (B) The opening of a university
   (C) The closing of a firm
   (D) The merger of two organizations

2. Where are the offices of Doyle, Inc., currently located?
   (A) At the local university
   (B) At 813 Main Street
   (C) At the Odessa Business Center
   (D) At 1102 Main Street

3. What will be delayed?
   (A) The construction of a business center
   (B) The completion of architectural plans
   (C) A company's participation in a program
   (D) A company's annual meeting

Questions 4-6 refer to the following notice.

DELIVERY REJECTION NOTICE

This notice is submitted to verify our rejection of the following item(s):

Delivery date	Product	Invoice	Delivery address
April 2	Klorep latex paint, Royal Blue, 10 gallons	8996510	Portswood Construction 367 Meridian Road Ketchikan, AK 99901

Our records show that you accepted payment for the item(s) in the following form:

Date	Credit card	Amount	Paid to
March 30	Ending in 4617	$230.50	Branch Paint Company

Reasons:

When the order was placed on March 15, delivery was promised on or before March 28. Another source has been found for the paint.

Please advise us regarding the return of the rejected goods at your expense. A full refund for the paint and the delivery fee is expected within 10 business days.

Regards,

Westin Sloan
Bookkeeper
Portswood Construction

---

4. What is indicated about the paint?
(A) It was ordered in March.
(B) It was delivered to a customer's home.
(C) It was supplied by Mr. Sloan.
(D) It was shipped in two containers.

5. Why was the delivery rejected?
(A) It arrived too late.
(B) It cost more than expected.
(C) An item was damaged.
(D) An item was missing.

6. According to the notice, what should Branch Paint Company do?
(A) Extend a payment deadline
(B) Send another delivery immediately
(C) Provide an explanation for the problem
(D) Pay for return shipping charges

Questions 7-10 refer to the following memo.

MEMO

To: New Products Department
From: Arianna Lee, Focus Group Coordinator
Date: October 12
Subject: Focus group number 4829

On October 10, I conducted a formal taste test of the four new bottled iced tea drinks developed as summer specials. The flavors tested were: Summer Raspberry, Fresh Mint, Fresh Mint with Lemon, and Hint of Peach. Several of you have been asking about the taste test, so I'd like to provide a brief summary.

Two groups with twelve participants each from the local area were selected at random. They met during the day of October 10th at an off-site location. Participants in the first group were given a sample of each flavor and asked to rate each sample on a scale of 1 to 10, with 1 signifying that the drink was not enjoyable at all and 10 signifying that the drink was highly enjoyable. Participants in the second group were given the same sample, but the samples were labeled by name. They were then asked to rate the samples on two scales from 1 to 10: how much they enjoyed the drink, and how well it satisfied the expectation created by its name. The purpose of this test was to determine if the flavors of the drinks actually match the expectation created by the name of the product.

Results of the group taste test are being processed and analyzed and will be available next week. As always, the results are confidential, so my assistant will hand-deliver a paper copy of the report directly to your offices rather than sending it as an e-mail attachment. Remember, our competition is eager to find out the results. If you think you need to share any details with anyone outside our department, please check with me first.

---

7. What is the purpose of the memo?
   (A) To share details about a product test
   (B) To provide an opinion of one of the drinks
   (C) To explain the results of a customer satisfaction survey
   (D) To recommend changes to focus group procedures

8. The word "rate" in paragraph 2, line 3, is closest in meaning to
   (A) price
   (B) judge
   (C) deserve
   (D) understand

9. What is NOT mentioned about the study?
   (A) Its participants were divided into groups.
   (B) It was conducted by Ms. Lee's assistant.
   (C) Its participants were selected by chance.
   (D) It was held away from the corporation's offices.

10. According to the memo, what will occur next week?
   (A) More people will sample the drinks.
   (B) The drinks will be put on the market.
   (C) The procedure will be redesigned.
   (D) Results of the study will be available.

UNIT 10 기사 / 안내문

평균 2~3문제 출제

무료인강

기사 / 안내문 지문 유형

- 기사 – 보도 자료 형태로 출제되며 지역, 기업, 인물, 문화 등 다양한 분야의 주제를 다룬다.
- 안내문 – 제품 매뉴얼, 약정서, 시설 안내, 행사 순서, 각종 절차 및 방법 안내 등을 다룬다.

ETS 예제   기사

번역 p. 184

제목 / 주제	Geoffery's Gets a Makeover
발행지역 발행일 업체 소개 주요 소식	TORONTO (16 July)—Two years ago, Canadian design firm Inteligami was given the task of redesigning Geoffery's, the store chain with 60 locations in countries across the Americas and the Caribbean. Just last week the Geoffery's in Mexico City was the twenty-second to undergo a makeover by Inteligami, and all stores are scheduled to be redesigned by January of next year.
핵심 정보 세부 정보	— [1] —. Visitors to updated Geoffery's stores may be pleasantly surprised to find that the grocery section has been moved to the front of the store. — [2] —. Other elements of the redesign effort project a feeling of ordered, open space. The floors have been stripped of their tile down to the concrete and polished to a gleaming shine. — [3] —. The walls have been covered in oak paneling. And LED lighting has replaced the harsh fluorescent light. — [4] —. All these changes create a more pleasant and efficient shopping experience.

+ 지문 파악하기

① 주요 소식과 업체 정보가 소개된다.

"제프리즈, 새롭게 단장하다"
제프리즈는 미주 및 카리브해 전역에 걸쳐 60개의 지점을 두고 있는 체인형 매장이다.

③ 핵심 정보가 전개된다.

새롭게 단장한 제프리즈 매장 이용객들은 식품 코너가 매장 전면으로 이동한 모습을 보고 반색할 듯하다.

※ 핵심 정보가 세부 정보보다 먼저 제시되지만, 문장 삽입 문제는 항상 세트의 마지막 문제로 등장한다.

② 세부 정보가 제시된다.

바닥은 타일을 벗겨내고 콘크리트에 윤이 나도록 광을 냈다.

+ 문제풀이

업체 정보 ❶	What is indicated about Geoffery's? 제프리즈에 대해 명시된 것은?	▶ It operates in several different countries. 여러 국가에서 영업한다.
세부 정보 ❷	What type of flooring do the redesigned stores have? 개조된 매장은 어떤 종류의 바닥재를 쓰는가?	▶ Concrete 콘크리트
핵심 정보 문맥 완성 ❸	In which of the positions marked [1], [2], [3], and [4] does the following sentence best belong? "This change is appreciated by the many customers who stop in only to buy food." 다음 문장이 들어가기에 가장 적절한 위치는?	▶ [2] "이러한 변화는 식품만 사기 위해 들르는 많은 고객들에 의해 높이 평가 받고 있다."

기사 / 안내문 | 정답이 보이는 단서

제목

➡ 기사의 제목을 통해 주제와 주요 골자를 파악할 수 있다.

Two Prominent Law Firms to Merge	굴지의 두 로펌 합병하기로
Botanic Gardens to Reopen Soon	식물원 곧 재개장 예정
Fisko Odometer Recall	피스코, 주행기록계 리콜
Public Opinion Divided over Water	물 문제로 분열된 여론
Change in Leadership at Komptex, Inc.	콤프텍스사, 경영진 교체

육하원칙

➡ 기사는 육하원칙에 따라 주요 소식을 전한다.

Fagan Law and Hinton & Associates will join forces.	누가 / 무엇을
The **Italian garden downtown** will officially reopen **next week**.	어디서 / 언제
Construction projects now **take longer, due to stricter regulations**.	어떻게 / 왜

인용문

➡ 기사는 인용문을 이용한 문제를 종종 출제한다.

"**By combining our areas of expertise, we can better serve our clients**."	○○가 언급한 합병의 장점은?
"We use the park's trail regularly **for an afternoon stroll**."	주민들의 공원 사용 목적은?
"I had only **played before a small audience," Mr. Ray explained**.	레이는 누구일 것 같은가?
"I expect next year's show to **draw even larger crowds**."	올해 행사는 어땠겠는가?
"We believe **our pricing practice gives us a competitive advantage**."	제품에 대해 알 수 있는 것은?

안내

➡ 안내문은 안내 목적과 대상을 묻거나, 안내된 장소를 유추하는 문제가 자주 출제된다.

This guide provides **instructions about how to use your new phone**.	목적: 전화기 사용 방법 안내
When submitting a reimbursement form, please follow the steps.	대상: 환급을 받고자 하는 직원
Do not perform maintenance on a **machine** while it is **in operation**.	장소: 공장

유의 사항

➡ 안내문에서는 별표(*)나 유의를 요하는 문구(please note, make sure 등)에서 문제가 나올 확률이 높다.

*Delivery may take longer due to high volume of orders.	배송에 대해 명시된 것은?
Please note that these instructions apply to domestic returns only.	환불에 대해 사실인 것은?
Make sure that everything is included in the box.	설치 전에 해야 할 일은?

PART 7 | UNIT 10

335

기사 / 안내문 빈출 어휘

● 경제

account for (부분·비율을) 차지하다
analyze 분석하다
commerce 상업
debt 빚, 부채
expenditure 지출
figure 수치
fluctuate 변동을 거듭하다
generate 발생시키다, 만들어 내다
investment 투자
lack 부족(하다)
market share 시장 점유율
monetary 통화의, 화폐의
offset 상쇄(하다)
recession 불황
stable 안정적인
statistics 통계
upswing 호전, 상승

● 도로 / 교통

be advised ~을 권고 받다(= be encouraged)
be held up in traffic 교통체증에 막히다(= be stuck in traffic)
boulevard 대로
caution 조심; 주의시키다
circulation 순환
commuter 통근자
duration 기간
encounter 직면하다, 맞닥뜨리다
fine 벌금, 과태료
fleet 전체 차량[수송기]
flood 홍수
improvement 개선
intersection 교차로

● 건물 / 건설

expansion 확장
habitat 거주지, 서식지
insulation 단열
landmark 주요 지형지물
mural 벽화
phase 단계, 양상
proximity 인접, 근접
put on hold 보류하다
real estate 부동산
refurbish 재단장하다
restoration 복구, 복원
story 층 **multi-storied** 복층의
structure 구조
transform 변형시키다
wing 별관, 부속 건물

● 경영

accounting 회계
aid 원조, 지원; 돕다
ambitious 야망 있는
aspiring 장차 ~이 되려는
associate 제휴하다, 결합시키다; 사원
boost 북돋우다
bring about ~을 야기하다, 초래하다
chairperson 의장
commission 위원회, 수수료, 위임(하다)
competitor 경쟁사
corporation 기업, 법인
distributor 배급업체, 유통회사
entrepreneur 기업가
executive 임원; 행정의
expand 확장하다
founder 설립자
implement 실시하다

● 도로 / 교통

lane 길, 차선
motorist 운전자
opposition 반대
overhaul 점검(하다)
pedestrian 보행자
permit 허가증; 허가하다
public transportation 대중교통
ramp 경사로
relieve 경감시키다, 낮추다
ridership 이용자 수, 승객 수
road closure 도로 폐쇄
suburban 시외 지역
traffic congestion 교통체증
transit authority 교통 당국
undergo 겪다, 경험하다(= experience)

● 문화 / 예술

acclaimed 호평 받는
appreciate (작품 등을) 감상하다
artwork 예술 작품
authentic 진짜인
celebrity 유명인사, 명사
commemorative 기념하는
cultural heritage 문화 유산
depict 묘사하다
distinctive 특유의, 특이한
diverse 다양한
enlightening 계몽적인
exceptional 예외적인, 특출한
expose 드러내다
influential 영향력 있는
recognition 인정

● 경영

merger and acquisition 합병과 인수 (M&A)
morale 근로 의욕, 사기
motivate 동기를 부여하다
obstacle 장애물
occupy 차지하다, 사용하다, (직책을) 맡다
operate 운영하다
pioneer 개척자
primary 주된, 주요한, 최초의
promising 전도유망한
prosperous 번영하는, 번창하는
quarter 분기
revenue 수익(= profit)
reward 보상(하다)
step down 물러나다
strategy 전략
workforce 노동력

● 건물 / 건설

abandoned 버려진
adjacent 인접한
ancient 고대의
archaeologist 고고학자
architect 건축가
be buried 매장되다
belong to ~에 속하다
capacity 수용력, 능력
complex 복합 단지
consist of ~로 구성되다
convert 전환하다
demolish 철거하다
deterioration 악화, 하락
establish 설립하다
excavation 발굴

● 문화 / 예술

innovative 혁신적인
inspire 영감을 주다
literature 문학
manuscript 원고, 필사본
metaphor 은유
playwright 극작가
production (영화, 연극) 제작, 작품
publicity 홍보, 평판
pursue 추구하다
release 발표하다, 개봉하다
renowned 유명한(= famed, noted)
reputation 명성
respected 훌륭한, 존경받는
unveil 공개하다, 발표하다
virtual 가상의, 사실상의

Questions 1-3 refer to the following press release.

FOR IMMEDIATE RELEASE   CONTACT: Celia Perkins,
                                          +27 11 555 1823

JOHANNESBURG (3 May)—Southern Oceans Airlines (SOA), the long-time South African carrier, is proud to announce its latest route linking Durban, South Africa, with Perth, Australia. —[1]—.

Flights are set to begin on 3 June, providing the only nonstop service between these two vibrant cities and saving time for thousands of business travelers. —[2]—. Australian travelers will have ready access to Durban's world-class beaches, and South African travelers will be able to enjoy Perth's outstanding water sports scene.

SOA flight 72 will leave Durban daily at 16:00 and arrive in Perth at 11:45 the next day. The return flight, SOA 73, will leave Perth daily at 14:30 and arrive in Durban at 19:30 the same day. —[3]—. Flights in both directions will feature a modern Eco Widebody EW-1555 aircraft, seating 52 passengers in business class and 216 in economy class.

The fastest growing airline in Africa and one of the fastest growing airlines in the world, SOA is proud to lead among world carriers in on-time departures. —[4]—.

---

1. What is the press release about?
(A) A new international airline route
(B) Improvements to in-flight entertainment
(C) An airport renovation in Johannesburg
(D) An airline's updated luggage policy

2. What is SOA known for?
(A) Low costs
(B) Few delays
(C) Lightweight aircraft design
(D) High passenger numbers

3. In which of the positions marked [1], [2], [3], and [4] does the following sentence best belong?

"Vacationers will also benefit."
(A) [1]
(B) [2]
(C) [3]
(D) [4]

PART 7 | UNIT 10

Questions 4-6 refer to the following information.

> **Takashi Fujioka**
> *Kyoto at Twilight*
> Oil on canvas
> 114.3 cm x 99.06 cm
>
> This work is the first in Takashi Fujioka's *Kyoto Nightfall* series, which gained international recognition. Works from this series of paintings have been exhibited in museums and galleries around the world, including the Moto Contemporary Art Museum in Tokyo, the Fontaine-Shields Gallery in New York City, and the Starlit Art Gallery in London. *Kyoto at Twilight* was featured on the cover of *Modern Painting* magazine the year it was painted. It was bought four years ago by Thomas Chester Gaines for his private collection and was sold to the Clarkson-Walker Museum for our permanent collection two years ago. It has remained here with us since. Mr. Fujioka famously called this painting "my finest hour."

4. Where is the information posted?
(A) At the Moto Contemporary Art Museum
(B) At the Fontaine-Shields Gallery
(C) At the Starlit Art Gallery
(D) At the Clarkson-Walker Museum

5. Who most likely is Mr. Gaines?
(A) A painter
(B) An art critic
(C) An art collector
(D) An exhibition director

6. What is NOT stated about *Kyoto at Twilight* ?
(A) The artist created it over a period of two years.
(B) It has had more than one owner.
(C) It appeared on the cover of *Modern Painting* magazine.
(D) The artist considers it to be one of his best works.

Study Shows Complexities

July 20—According to a recent report, office and warehouse rents in the city of Harbor Point are nearly 24 percent above the national average. — [1] —. The study found that, in recent years, an influx of technology firms has been creating high demand for space. Simultaneously, uncertainty in the regional economy has discouraged many building contractors from launching new construction projects. — [2] —. For example, only seven new developments have been completed in Harbor Point during the last two years. — [3] —. Moreover, construction projects now take longer to complete, thanks in part to stricter environmental requirements. — [4] —. The combination of factors is restricting supply and raising rental prices.

Just behind Harbor Point in the trend are the nearby cities of Summit and Midville. In the last nine months, the two cities have seen 10 percent and 8.5 percent increases in commercial rents, respectively.

7. What does the article describe?
(A) A reduction in environmental restrictions
(B) A shortage of commercial space
(C) Building projects left unfinished
(D) Apartments that are too expensive

8. According to the article, why does it take extra time to complete a building project in Harbor Point?
(A) Technologies need to be updated.
(B) Contractors are already overbooked.
(C) Some rules have been changed.
(D) Many work sites are difficult to access.

9. What does the article suggest about Harbor Point, Summit, and Midville?
(A) They have income growth above the national average.
(B) They are declining in population.
(C) They have busy construction industries.
(D) They are in the same region.

10. In which of the positions marked [1], [2], [3], and [4] does the following sentence best belong?

"The rents are the highest in the nation."
(A) [1]
(B) [2]
(C) [3]
(D) [4]

CH. 02 | 지문 유형별 공략

UNIT 11

웹페이지 /
기타 양식

평균 2~3문제 출제

무료인강

웹페이지/기타 양식 지문 유형

● 웹페이지 – 기업이나 단체의 홈페이지를 주로 다루며, 제품 소개, 리뷰, 안내 사항을 주 내용으로 한다.
● 양식 – 영수증, 주문서, 신청서, 증명서, 초대장, 설문지, 쿠폰 등의 다양한 실용문 형태를 띤다.

ETS 예제 온라인 양식(주문 내역서)   번역 p. 187

업체 정보

Betaphasic Solutions
965 Hayward Boulevard
Des Moines, IA 50047

주문 내역

Customer Type: New
Customer Name: Jing-Wen Lee
Phone Number: 515-555-0144
E-mail Address: jlee@comptravel.com
Project Name: Color Flyers
Contact Preference: E-mail
Attach specifications document here:
COMPTRAVEL_AD

주문 세부 요청 사항

Add any additional information here:

I recently started a travel company called Comp Travel, and I will be going to a trade show next month to promote my business.

I will need 250 copies of the file I've attached on high-quality color photo paper, so that I can hand them out at the trade show. Please provide me with a price estimate for this job.

＋지문 파악하기

❶ 요청 사항은 글의 목적과 연결된다.

이 작업에 대한 **견적서를 보내 주십시오.**

❷ 주문 세부 내역을 파악해야 한다.

고객 이름: 리징웬
저는 최근에 컴프 트래블이라는 여행사를 시작했고 제 사업을 홍보하기 위해 다음 달에 무역 박람회에 갈 예정입니다.

❸ 내역을 통해 업체 정보를 알 수 있다.

작업명: 컬러 전단지
고급 컬러 인화지로 첨부한 파일 **250 장**이 필요합니다.

＋문제풀이

글의 목적 ❶	Why did Ms. Lee fill out the online form? 이 씨는 왜 온라인 양식서를 작성했는가?	▶ To ask for information 정보를 요청하려고
주문 정보 ❷	What is indicated about Ms. Lee? 이 씨에 대해 알 수 있는 것은?	▶ She is a new business owner. 신규 사업주이다.
업체 종류 ❸	What kind of business most likely is Betaphasic Solutions? 베타페이직 솔루션즈는 어떤 업체이겠는가?	▶ A printing company 인쇄 회사

웹페이지 / 기타 양식 | 정답이 보이는 단서

웹페이지 탭

➡ 홈페이지에서 표시된 탭 정보를 통해 글의 주제와 목적을 가늠할 수 있다.

Home / About Us	회사 전반 소개
Our Products / Services / Menu / Work Samples	서비스 종류 및 특장점 소개
Reviews / Testimonials	고객 후기 소개
Membership / Join Us / Register / Sign Up	회원 가입 혜택 소개

영수증 / 주문서

➡ 주문 물품을 통한 업종 유추, 요금 및 결제 정보 등과 관련된 문제가 출제된다.

Item: Oak **Table** 2 / White Flexible **Desk** 4 / Metal **Cabinet** 2	어떤 종류의 업체인가?
Transportation to the hotel: $10 / **Equipment rental**: $30 / **Lunch** $20	경비에 포함되지 않는 것은?
Free delivery is available **within 15 kilometers of Kensington**.	배송비가 지급된 이유는?
Amount Paid: $15.00 deposit / **Amount Due** on Arrival: $30.00	지불해야 할 총 금액은?

쿠폰 / 전단지

➡ 할인 조건, 혜택 기간, 서비스 제외 품목, 다양한 요금제 등과 관련된 문제가 출제된다.

Bring this coupon for $5 off **a purchase of $10 or more**.	고객은 어떻게 할인을 받는가?
Valid throughout January.	2월에는 무슨 일이 있겠는가?
Not valid on / Cannot be used on / Exclude all fashion accessories.	할인이 적용되지 않는 품목은?
Gold Class: All the services of our **Silver Class plus free delivery**.	골드 등급에 포함된 서비스는?

설문지

➡ 서비스 항목, 평점, 개선 및 제안 사항 등과 관련된 문제가 출제된다.

Toiletries: ★★★☆ / Laundry: ★★★★ / Internet access: ★★☆☆	언급된 서비스가 아닌 것은?
Cleanliness: Not satisfied / Satisfied / Very satisfied	OO의 진술과 일치하는 것은?
I was **particularly pleased with** the friendliness of the staff.	OO가 특히 만족하는 것은?
Comment: ... I felt that two hours is not enough to cover the topic.	워크숍에 대해 사실인 것은?

초대장

➡ 행사 종류와 대상을 유추하는 문제, 행사 정보의 사실 관계 확인 문제 등이 출제된다.

Lecture topic: How to deal with upset customers	누가 초대장을 받겠는가?
You can **enjoy live performances** by local musicians **after dinner**.	식사 후에 일어날 일은?
Seating is limited. Please RSVP by August 11.	행사에 대해 알 수 있는 것은?

웹페이지 / 기타 양식 빈출 어휘

● 청구 / 결제

back-order 이월 주문하다
balance 잔액
billing address 청구 주소
deduct 빼다, 공제하다
deposit 보증금, 착수금(선불금)
estimate 견적(액); 어림잡다
in installment 할부로
incidental expense 부대 비용
invoice 주문서
measurement 치수, 측정
overdue 기한이 지난, 늦은
partial payment 부분 지불
reduction 할인
reimbursement 환급, 상환
shipping address 배송지 주소
subtotal 소계
waive a fee 요금을 면제해 주다

● 공연

audience 청중
autograph 서명(하다)
choir 합창단
composer 작곡가
conclusion 결말, 종결
coordinator 진행 담당자
costume (무대) 의상, 복장
current 현재의
flawless 결점이 없는
impeccable 흠잡을 데 없는
intermission 중간 휴식 시간
masterpiece 명작, 걸작
outstanding 뛰어난
overwhelming 압도적인
passion 열정

● 초대

anonymously 익명으로
banquet 연회
broadcast 방송하다
charity 자선 (단체)
compassionate 인정 많은, 동정적인
cordially 진심으로, 다정하게
credit 칭찬, 인정
decent 괜찮은, 품위 있는
devote 바치다, 헌신하다
donor 기증자
former 이전의
fundraiser 모금행사
in honor of ~을 기념하여

● 여행

amenity 생활 편의 시설
archive 기록 보관소
botanic garden 식물원
budget 예산; 값이 싼
business trip 출장
civic 시의
conduct a tour 투어를 안내하다
courtesy bus 무료 버스
customs 세관
departure 출발
dining establishment 식사 시설
exotic 이국적인
expedition 탐험
explore 답사[탐험]하다
group rate 단체 요금
house 수용하다
immigration 출입국 관리소

● 공연

play 연극
poem 시, 운문 **poet** 시인
premiere 개봉, 초연
preview 시사회
production 제작, 상연 작품
prohibit 금지하다
remarkable 주목할 만한
reveal 드러내다
sequel 속편
stage 무대(에 올리다)
star 주연(을 맡다)
string 줄, 현악기
theatergoer 극장을 자주 가는 사람
troupe 공연단
usher (극장 등의) 안내인

● 초대

judging committee 심사위원단
light refreshments 간단한 다과
local resident 지역 주민
moderate 사회를 보다
monument 기념비
network 인맥을 형성하다
open to the public 대중에게 개방하다
organization 단체, 기관
panel discussion 공개 토론회
recipient 수상자
retiree 은퇴자
RSVP (초대에) 회답 바랍니다.
solicit a donation 기부금을 요청하다

● 여행

itinerary 여행 일정표
memorable 기억에 남는
native 원산의, 토박이의
off season 비수기
outskirts 변두리, 교외
overseas 해외의; 해외로
peak season 성수기(= busy season)
restriction 제한
ruins 폐허, 유적
rural 시골풍의(= rustic)
sightseeing 관광
souvenir 기념품
stopover 경유, 단기간 체류
tourist attraction 관광 명소
travel arrangements 여행 준비
vessel 선박, 배
voyage 항해(하다)

● 전자제품 / 가구

antique 골동품; 골동품의
appliance 가전제품
compatible 호환이 되는
cutting-edge 최신식의
easy to assemble 조립하기 쉬운
finish 마감재
furnishing 가구
in working condition 정상 작동하는
instructions 설명(서), 지시
light fixture 조명
outlet 콘센트
upholstery 가구용 덮개[커버]
valid 유효한
warehouse 창고
warranty 품질 보증(서)

● 의생활

alteration 수선, 변경
athletic apparel 운동복
bleach 표백제
detergent 세제
footwear 신발
garment 의복(= clothing, clothes)
laundry 세탁
measurement 치수, 측정
ready-to-wear 기성복의
shrink 줄어들다
soak 흠뻑 적시다, 담그다
textile 섬유(= fabric)
wardrobe 옷, 옷장

Questions 1-2 refer to the following Web site.

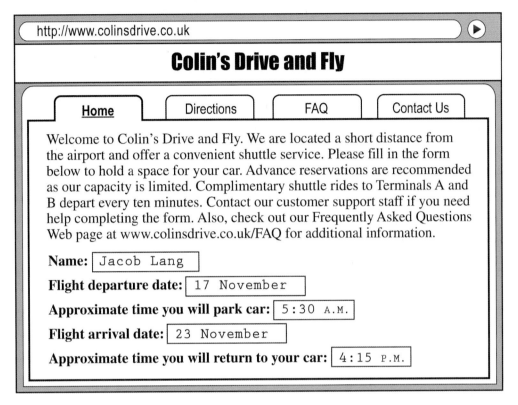

http://www.colinsdrive.co.uk ▶

Colin's Drive and Fly

| __Home__ | Directions | FAQ | Contact Us |

Welcome to Colin's Drive and Fly. We are located a short distance from the airport and offer a convenient shuttle service. Please fill in the form below to hold a space for your car. Advance reservations are recommended as our capacity is limited. Complimentary shuttle rides to Terminals A and B depart every ten minutes. Contact our customer support staff if you need help completing the form. Also, check out our Frequently Asked Questions Web page at www.colinsdrive.co.uk/FAQ for additional information.

Name: Jacob Lang

Flight departure date: 17 November

Approximate time you will park car: 5:30 A.M.

Flight arrival date: 23 November

Approximate time you will return to your car: 4:15 P.M.

1. What is the form used for?
   (A) Requesting a hotel's transportation service
   (B) Scheduling a driver for an airport pickup
   (C) Reserving a parking location
   (D) Giving feedback about a service

2. What is indicated about the shuttle?
   (A) It waits ten minutes at each terminal.
   (B) There is an additional fee to use it.
   (C) Seats should be reserved a day before.
   (D) It runs multiple times an hour.

Questions 3-5 refer to the following form.

STARR Transportation

Thank you for using Starr Transportation. In a concerted effort to better serve our customers, we'd like your opinion about your most recent experience with us. Please take a moment to fill out the following survey and mail it to us in the enclosed self-addressed, stamped envelope by May 28.

Date: <u>May 20</u>   Customer Name: <u>V.N. Chen</u>   Phone: <u>603-555-0143</u>

Date and description of service:
<u>April 12-transport from Carroll Corporation to Franklin Airport.</u>
<u>April 25-transport from Franklin Airport to my home in Centerville, NH.</u>

Please rate the following on a scale of 1 to 4, 1 being "poor" and 4 being "excellent."
Service

Friendliness	1	2	3	(4)
Reservation Process	1	2	(3)	4

Vehicle

Spaciousness	1	2	(3)	4
Cleanliness	1	2	3	(4)

Would you use our services again?   YES NO (MAYBE)

Would you recommend our services to others?   YES NO (MAYBE)

Comments:
<u>I use Starr Transportation often for business travel and have always been</u>
<u>satisfied. This time when I arrived at Franklin Airport after a long flight from</u>
<u>Lima, Peru, the driver was nowhere to be found. The airplane had arrived at a</u>
<u>different terminal than scheduled, but the driver should have checked the</u>
<u>flight's arrival status well beforehand. I ended up waiting for him when I could</u>
<u>have taken a bus.</u>

---

3. How will Starr Transportation most likely use information they collect from the form?
(A) To create effective marketing materials
(B) To plan time-saving driving routes
(C) To determine employee promotions
(D) To improve customer service

4. What did Mr. Chen indicate about the vehicle?
(A) It was a bus.
(B) It was very clean.
(C) It was too large.
(D) It was difficult to drive.

5. What does Mr. Chen indicate about the service he received?
(A) The trip from Centerville took too long.
(B) The reservation process was confusing.
(C) The driver arrived later than scheduled.
(D) The vehicle was too small to fit his luggage.

Questions 6-9 refer to the following report.

Gandall Fashions

Weekly Status Report for March 12–17
Prepared by: Sam Hodgkins, Project Manager

This week's accomplishments:
- Contacted five manufacturing companies in Gujarat, India, with experience making handbags. — [1] —. Provided them with drawings of our new bag design and asked questions about minimum order quantity, production and shipping costs, and turnaround time. — [2] —.
- Based on initial responses, Kadsan Industries seems to be the manufacturer that is best suited to our needs. — [3] —. Also, Dulari Roy, an account manager, phoned me right away. She was very professional, personable, and gave me straightforward responses to all my questions. I can see us developing a good business relationship with her.
- The four other companies contacted were either unable to accommodate our schedule or could not meet our pricing requirements. — [4] —. Therefore they will no longer be considered.

Plans for the week of March 20–24:
- Continue discussions with Kadsan Industries about project needs and payment terms.
- Have the design team document final measurements, fabrics, and colors and then outline the steps of the production process. Submit this information to Kadsan Industries so that a sample can be made.

6. What is suggested about Gandall Fashions?
(A) It is relocating to India.
(B) It is hiring a project manager.
(C) It is developing a new product.
(D) It is merging with another company.

7. According to the report, what did Mr. Hodgkins do during the week of March 12 ?
(A) He developed shipping schedules.
(B) He acquired construction permits.
(C) He trained temporary factory employees.
(D) He evaluated possible business partners.

8. What is mentioned about Ms. Roy?
(A) She met Mr. Hodgkins in person.
(B) She is part of the design team.
(C) She asked many questions.
(D) She is easy to work with.

9. In which of the positions marked [1], [2], [3], and [4] does the following sentence best belong?

"It is not as large as some of the other companies, but it is willing to hire additional staff to complete our order."
(A) [1]
(B) [2]
(C) [3]
(D) [4]

UNIT 12 문자 메시지 / 온라인 채팅

평균 2문제 출제

무료인강

문자 메시지 / 온라인 채팅 지문 유형

- 신속한 업무 처리를 위해 즉석에서 주고받는 정보나 의견 전달이 주를 이룬다.
- 문자나 채팅 특성상 구어체 표현이 자주 등장한다.
- 특정 문장의 의도를 묻는 의도 파악 문제가 반드시 포함된다.

ETS 예제 문자 메시지

번역 p. 190

화제 언급	**Ann Daniels [11:00 A.M.]** Hello, Kenneth. I just want to let you know that the latest surveys are being sent out to our customers today.
업무 진행 상황 공유	**Kenneth Jutras [11:03 A.M.]** Great! The last time we did a survey, we received high ratings for having a wide variety of items in stock, particularly our kitchen accessories and apparel. Our fitting rooms were described as cramped and cluttered, though.
관련 피드백	**Ann Daniels [11:04 A.M.]** Let's see the ratings now that the remodeling has been completed. Management assured me that they would not cut corners.
처리 결과 공유	**Kenneth Jutras [11:05 A.M.]** The fitting rooms do look very nice now.
	Ann Daniels [11:06 A.M.] That's what I've heard. I haven't seen them yet myself.
추가 전달 사항	**Kenneth Jutras [11:07 A.M.]** Yesterday I walked through the entire place, from the jewelry area to electronics. It all looks great!

+ 지문 파악하기

① 대화를 통해 인물 관계 및 관련 업종을 유추할 수 있다.

지난번 설문에서 우리는 **다양한 품목들**, 특히 **주방용품**과 **의류**를 구비하고 있다는 점에서 높은 평가를 받았어요. 탈의실은 비좁고 어수선하다는 평이었지만요.

② 특정 문장의 의도는 대화의 흐름 속에서 파악할 수 있다.

"지금은 탈의실이 정말 근사해 보여요."
"저도 그렇게 들었어요"

+ 문제풀이

업체 종류 ❶	For what type of business do the writers most likely work? 글쓴이들은 어떤 업계에 종사하고 있겠는가?	▶ A department store 백화점
의도 파악 ❷	At 11:06 A.M., what does Ms. Daniels most likely mean when she writes, "That's what I've heard"? 오전 11시 6분에 대니얼스 씨가 "저도 그렇게 들었어요"라고 쓴 의도는?	▶ She understands that the fitting rooms have been improved. 탈의실이 개선되었다는 것을 알고 있다.

동의 / 수락

➡️ 의견, 제안, 요청에 대한 동의 / 수락의 표현이 출제된다.

Can you set up a payment account? / **Absolutely!(= Certainly!)**	지불 계좌를 개설해 줄 수 있다.
What about the following Monday? / **That works.**	다음 주 월요일에 시간이 된다.
Make sure you send an e-mail to our clients. / **Got it.**	고객들에게 이메일을 보내겠다.
Let me know if you spot an error. / **Will do.**	오류가 있으면 알리겠다.
We'd like to move in by May 31. / **Shouldn't be a problem.**	5월 31일까지 이사할 수 있다.
I can't believe the project was completed so soon. / **I know.**	일처리가 예상보다 빨리 끝났다.
Would you be able to work extra shifts tomorrow? / **I'd be happy to.**	추가 근무를 할 수 있다.
I'm looking forward to learning more about the program. / **Same here.**	프로그램에 대해 더 알고 싶다.
I forgot to bring my access card. Can you help? / **Sure thing.**	도움을 제공할 수 있다.
It'll be good to have the latest equipment. / **No question about it.**	최신 장비를 갖추는 것이 좋다.
Instead of repairing it again, let's get a new one. / **That makes sense.**	장비를 구입하는 것이 낫겠다.
Can I send you the picture by e-mail instead? / **Even better.**	이메일로 받는 것이 더 편하다.

의구심 / 반대 / 부정

➡️ 동의하지 않음, 거절, 부정 등을 나타내는 표현도 출제된다.

Should I wear formal business attire for the event? / **No need.**	정장을 입지 않아도 된다.
Do you think 10 minutes is enough to cover everything? / **I doubt it.**	10분은 충분하지 않다.
Finding a venue for the event could be a problem. / **Not necessarily.**	장소 섭외가 어렵지만은 않다.
Have you had any luck finding a place for the luncheon? / **Not really.**	좋은 장소를 찾지 못했다.
I will set up more chairs in case more people come. / **Don't bother.**	의자를 더 가져오지 않아도 된다.

기타 구어체 표현

➡️ 기타 자주 등장하는 구어체 표현들을 익혀 두면 좋다.

Does anybody want to go to the new Italian restaurant? / **I'm in.**	저도 합류할게요.
Should we drive to the site or walk there? / **Your call.**	당신이 결정하세요.
I will send out the invitations right away. / **Take your time.**	천천히 하세요.
All other fees are included in your registration. / **That's a relief.**	다행이네요.
Could you bring the reports to my office? / **On my way.**	가고 있어요.
We only have ten pairs of safety goggles. / **That will do.**	그거면 돼요.
The show starts in just 10 minutes. / **I can't make it on time.**	제시간에 못 갈 것 같아요.
We need two more microphones and a projector. / **Is that it?**	그게 다예요?

문자 메시지 / 온라인 채팅 빈출 표현

● 업무 관련

act up (기계 등이) 말을 안 듣다
approval 승인
area of expertise 전문 분야
audiovisual equipment 시청각 장비
authorize 권한을 주다
behind schedule 예정보다 늦은
by end of day 퇴근 때까지
commission 수수료
configure (기기의) 환경을 설정하다
crew 작업반
delivery slip 배송장
do a rush job 서둘러 작업하다
existing customer 기존 고객
expedite 신속하게 처리하다

finance 자금을 대다
firm date 확정 일자
general overview 대강의 개요
go smoothly 순조롭게 진행되다
high-profile 인지도가 높은
in-house 내부의, 사내의
in the long run 장기적으로
increase morale 사기를 높이다
load a truck 트럭에 짐을 싣다
loading dock 하역장
look into 알아보다, 조사하다
look over 검토하다
mechanical problem 기계적 결함
new hire 신입 사원

office supply room 비품실
preliminary 예비의
progress 진척[진행]
proofread 교정하다
put on hold ~을 보류하다, 연기하다
remotely 원격으로
sales territory 영업 활동 지역
shred 파쇄하다
spreadsheet 데이터 문서
stretch a budget 예산을 늘리다
switch shifts 근무 시간을 바꾸다
virtual meeting 가상 회의
work around ~을 피해서 일하다
work remotely 재택근무하다

● 일상생활

ample room 충분한 공간
appropriate 적절한
banquet 연회
be about to 막 ~하려고 하다
be held up 지체되다
be supposed to ~하기로 되어 있다
booked solid 모두 예약된
caterer 출장 요리 업체
concession stand 구내 매점
courier 택배 회사
donation drive 기부 운동
eatery 음식점
eye-catching 눈길을 끄는
flat tire 펑크 난 타이어
get started 시작하다

give a hand 거들어 주다
grab 급히 챙기다
halfway (거리·시간상으로) 중간에
hear back from ~로부터 소식을 듣다
in place 준비된
make an exception 예외로 하다
manage to ~을 해내다
on my end 내 쪽에서
on short notice 갑자기, 촉박하게
parcel 소포
pose a problem 문제를 일으키다
prior engagement 선약
pros and cons 장단점, 찬반
pull in 차를 세우다
reach out to ~에게 연락을 취하다

return a favor 호의에 답례하다
run out of ~이 바닥나다
set aside 따로 떼어 두다
show up 등장하다
shut off 멈추다
spot 발견하다
stick around 머무르다
stuck in a traffic jam 교통 체증에 갇힌
take a detour 우회하다
take care of 처리하다
take the initiative 솔선수범하다
tentatively 잠정적으로
the other day 며칠 전에
travel insurance 여행 보험
wrap up 마무리 짓다

● 기타 표현

(by) any chance (의문문에서) 혹시라도
30 minutes from now 30분 후
Absolutely. / Certainly. 물론입니다.
at the last minute 막판에
back out (하기로 했던 일에서) 빠지다
be backed up with ~로 밀리다, 뒤처지다
come up with 생각해 내다
follow up 후속 조치하다, 더 알아보다
get ~ off the ground ~을 실행에 옮기다
get back to ~에게 나중에 다시 연락하다
get called away 불려 가다
Good to know. 다행이네요.
head out 출발하다
Hold on. 잠깐만요.

I'll get it sorted out. 제가 처리할게요.
I'm heading there. 그쪽으로 가고 있어요.
in an hour or so 한 시간 정도 후에
It can't be helped. 어쩔 수 없네요.
just in case 만일에 대비하여
Keep me posted. 계속해서 알려 주세요.
keep track of 기록하다, 계속 파악하다
Magnificent. / Fabulous. 훌륭하네요.
mind if ~해도 괜찮을까요?
Never mind. 신경 쓰지 마세요.
not necessarily 반드시 ~한 것은 아니다
On my way. 가고 있는 중이에요.
Possibly. 아마도요.
run ~ past[by] ~을 보여 주다

run into (곤경 등을) 겪다
run through 리허설하다
see to something ~을 맡아 처리하다
sort through 자세히 살펴보다
take turns 교대로[차례로 돌아가며] 하다
that way 그런 식으로
That would work out. 그러면 되겠네요.
That's a thought. 괜찮은 생각이네요.
That's it. 그게 다입니다.
touch base 다시 연락[접촉]하다
Understood. 알겠습니다.
what if ~라면 어쩌죠?
What's the rush? 왜 서두르시나요?
wire the money 전신 송금하다

Questions 1-2 refer to the following text-message chain.

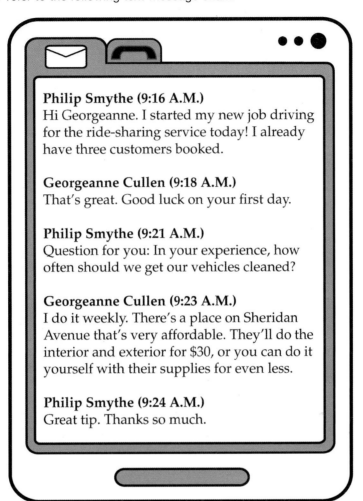

Philip Smythe (9:16 A.M.)
Hi Georgeanne. I started my new job driving for the ride-sharing service today! I already have three customers booked.

Georgeanne Cullen (9:18 A.M.)
That's great. Good luck on your first day.

Philip Smythe (9:21 A.M.)
Question for you: In your experience, how often should we get our vehicles cleaned?

Georgeanne Cullen (9:23 A.M.)
I do it weekly. There's a place on Sheridan Avenue that's very affordable. They'll do the interior and exterior for $30, or you can do it yourself with their supplies for even less.

Philip Smythe (9:24 A.M.)
Great tip. Thanks so much.

1. According to Ms. Cullen, what can Mr. Smythe do on Sheridan Avenue?
(A) Shop for supplies
(B) Find a parking area
(C) Pick up passengers
(D) Have a car washed

2. At 9:24 A.M., what does Mr. Smythe most likely mean when he writes, "Great tip"?
(A) He received extra money from a customer.
(B) He is pleased that Ms. Cullen's company hired him.
(C) He appreciates Ms. Cullen's giving him advice.
(D) He is available to drive customers this week.

Questions 3-6 refer to the following online chat discussion.

Phoebe DePaul [8:18 A.M.]: Good morning. I'm just following up to see if Technical Support got my e-mail from yesterday.

Nick Reece [8:19 A.M.]: Hi, Ms. DePaul. Yes, I read it at the end of the day. Sorry for not getting back to you sooner. The problem is your computer monitor, right?

Phoebe DePaul [8:20 A.M.]: Yes. Late yesterday afternoon my screen suddenly went extremely bright. It was really uncomfortable to work, so I decided to report it.

Nick Reece [8:21 A.M.]: Would you mind if I add my manager to this conversation?

Phoebe DePaul [8:22 A.M.]: That's OK.

Nick Reece [8:23 A.M.]: Hi, Yihui. I'm chatting with Phoebe DePaul about her monitor. She says it's unusually bright, and I think it could be an outdated display driver.

Yihui Li [8:24 A.M.]: Possibly. Ms. DePaul, have you tried adjusting the display settings?

Phoebe DePaul [8:25 A.M.]: I did yesterday, with no luck. I even asked my colleague Mr. Ahn for help when I got here this morning. He's great with technology, but the problem is still there.

Yihui Li [8:28 A.M.]: I suggest that you reinstall her display driver, Nick. Could you please see to it?

Nick Reece [8:32 A.M.]: Sure—thanks, Yihui. Ms. DePaul, it will take another ten minutes to do this. Do you have the time now?

3. Who was most likely the first to be notified of Ms. DePaul's problem?
(A) Her secretary
(B) Her manager
(C) Mr. Reece
(D) Mr. Ahn

4. At 8:24 A.M., what does Mr. Li imply when he writes, "Possibly"?
(A) He hopes that Mr. Reece will answer e-mails promptly.
(B) He believes that Mr. Ahn could help Ms. DePaul.
(C) He is still unsure about the cause of a monitor issue.
(D) He thinks a new monitor should be purchased.

5. What does Ms. DePaul suggest about Mr. Ahn?
(A) He recently repaired his own monitor.
(B) He forgot to install a program.
(C) He has an extra monitor she could use.
(D) He was unable to find a solution.

6. What will Mr. Reece most likely do next?
(A) Confirm a model number
(B) Reinstall some software
(C) Test a device for problems
(D) Replace Ms. DePaul's hardware

Questions 7-10 refer to the following text-message chain.

> **Henry Deerings [9:22 P.M.]** Brianna, the conveyer on line 3 here at the factory has stopped. I think the production run for Kraler Stationery has finished. Do you want me to start the next run?
>
> **Brianna Pemmer [9:24 P.M.]** You just have to make sure the run is completely finished and that it didn't stop for another reason.
>
> **Henry Deerings [9:26 P.M.]** OK, I haven't done this before. How do I check?
>
> **Brianna Pemmer [9:28 P.M.]** Look at the screen on the main control panel for line 3. What does it say?
>
> **Henry Deerings [9:31 P.M.]** It says, "End Run 2,500."
>
> **Brianna Pemmer [9:34 P.M.]** Above the screen, you should see a printout posted that lists all of today's production runs. Does the number on the screen match the number in the production-run quantity column for Kraler?
>
> **Henry Deerings [9:36 P.M.]** Yes, 2,500.
>
> **Brianna Pemmer [9:38 P.M.]** Then it's complete. Look at the next line down on the chart and it will tell you the next production run. I just texted Charles to double-check it.
>
> **Charles Marcus [9:41 P.M.]** The next run is for Juanita Miller's order. 1,500 of item 345 in blue.
>
> **Henry Deerings [9:42 P.M.]** Precisely.
>
> **Brianna Pemmer [9:45 P.M.]** Good, go ahead and start it. We need to have it packed up for them by tomorrow night. I'll be back there in about an hour or so. I have a little more work here at the warehouse.

7. For what type of industry do the writers work?
   (A) Travel
   (B) Finance
   (C) Manufacturing
   (D) Communications

8. Who most likely is the newest employee of the company?
   (A) Juanita Miller
   (B) Henry Deerings
   (C) Charles Marcus
   (D) Brianna Pemmer

9. At 9:42 P.M., what does Mr. Deerings imply when he writes, "Precisely"?
   (A) He sees the information that Mr. Marcus has provided.
   (B) The numbers on the screen and the printout match.
   (C) He will send Ms. Pemmer updated information.
   (D) The conveyor is working as expected.

10. Where is Ms. Pemmer when she writes her text messages?
    (A) At her home
    (B) In a warehouse
    (C) On a factory floor
    (D) At a stationery store

정답이 보이는 패러프레이징 리스트

discount
할인
→ reduced price[rate]
할인가

a coupon for 10% off your next order
다음 주문에 대한 10퍼센트 할인 쿠폰
→ a discount on a future purchase
차후 구매에 대한 할인

monetary donation[grant / funds]
금전적 기부[보조금 / 자금]
→ financial contribution[support]
재정적 기여[후원]

has headquarters in
본사를 ~에 두고 있다
→ is based in
~에 본거지[본사]를 두다

will open a branch overseas
해외 지사를 열 것이다
→ will expand internationally
국외로 확장할 것이다

job openings
일자리 공석
→ vacant positions
비어 있는 직책

sold out[out of stock]
매진된 / 재고가 없는
→ currently not available
현재 이용 가능하지 않은

discontinue
생산을 중단하다
→ no longer available
더 이상 이용 가능하지 않은

on a daily[weekly / monthly / yearly] basis
매일[매주 / 매달 / 매년]
→ regularly / periodically
정기적으로

available at any branch
어느 지점에서나 이용 가능한
→ has more than one location[multiple locations] 하나 이상의[다수의] 지점을 가지고 있다

free of charge[at no cost]
무료로
→ complimentary[without paying a fee]
무료로[비용 지불 없이]

friend[former coworker / business contact] 친구[예전 동료 / 업무상 연락하는 사람]
→ acquaintance
지인

rival company[counterpart]
경쟁사[상대자]
→ competitor
경쟁사

your last order / our previous[former] customer 귀하의 지난번 주문 / 저희의 이전 고객
→ purchased before[previously used the service] 전에 구매한 적이 있다[이전에 서비스를 이용했다]

those who attended last year's event
지난해 행사에 참석한 사람들
→ past participants
과거 참석자들

certified in
~에 자격증이 있다
→ has familiarity with
~을 잘 알고 있다

used for many years
수년간 사용했다
→ has sufficient experience
풍부한 경험이 있다

proficiency in
~에 능숙함

→ **competency with**
~에 대한 능력

fluent in English and one additional language 영어와 추가 제 2외국어에 능통한

→ **has knowledge of multiple languages**
다수의 언어에 지식을 갖고 있다

take international business trips
해외 출장을 가다

→ **travel abroad for work**
업무차 해외로 나가다

previously worked as an engineer
이전에 엔지니어로서 일했다

→ **has a background in engineering**
공학 기술 분야 경력이 있다

strong interpersonal skills
우수한 대인 관계 능력

→ **ability to relate well with others**
타인과 관계를 잘 맺는 능력

the successful applicants
합격하는 지원자

→ **selected candidates**
선발된 지원자

a recommendation letter
추천서

→ **a letter of reference**
추천서

work overtime[work an extra shift]
초과 근무를 하다

→ **work extra[additional] hours**
추가 시간을 일하다

over a decade
10년 이상

→ **more than 10 years**
10년 이상

family member[sister/brother/cousin…]
가족[언니, 형, 사촌…]

→ **relative**
가족, 친지

annual conference
연례 회의

→ **the conference is held every year**
회의가 매년 개최된다

once every two years
2년마다 한 번

→ **every other[second] year**
2년마다

banquet[workshop/seminar/conference]
연회/워크숍/세미나/회의

→ **(business/social) function[event/gathering]**
(비즈니스/사교) 행사

available around the clock[open 24 hours a day] 24시간 이용할 수 있는[24시간 운영하는]

→ **can access at any time**
언제든지 이용할 수 있다

voucher[coupon]
상품권[쿠폰]

→ **gift certificate**
상품권

has a fitness center on the premises
건물 내에 피트니스 센터가 있다

→ **has an on-site gym**
구내 체육 시설이 있다

restaurant/bistro/café
식당/카페

→ **eating establishment**
식사 시설

magazines / documents
잡지 / 문서
→ reading materials
읽을거리

flyers / product catalogs[brochures]
전단지 / 제품 카탈로그[책자]
→ promotional materials
홍보 자료

the dress code
복장 규정
→ guidelines for appropriate clothing
적절한 복장에 대한 지침

should wear formal business attire
정장을 입어야 한다
→ need to comply with specific dress codes
특정한 복장 규정을 준수해야 한다

personalized / customized / custom-made / tailored 개인 맞춤형의, 맞춤 제작의
→ can accommodate individual requests
개별 요청을 수용해 주다

timetable[itinerary]
시간표[일정]
→ schedule
스케줄

snacks and beverages[food and drinks] / appetizers 간식과 음료 / 애피타이저
→ refreshments
다과

request for a vacation
휴가 신청
→ request for time off
휴가 신청

delayed[postponed] / prolonged
지연된[연기된] / 장기화된
→ took longer than expected
예상보다 오래 걸렸다

would like your ideas[input / feedback]
의견을 원하다
→ solicit opinions
의견을 구하다

this offer expires soon
이 혜택은 곧 만료된다
→ the promotional period will end
판촉 기간이 끝난다

provide technical support
기술 지원을 제공하다
→ offer assistance with technical difficulties
기술적 문제에 대해 도움을 주다

will debut in retail locations early next year 소매점에 내년 초 선보일 것이다
→ not yet available in stores
현재 매장에서 이용 가능하지 않은

drew a sizeable crowd
많은 대중을 끌어들였다
→ was well attended[was very popular]
참석률이 좋았다[인기가 매우 좋았다]

will say a few words
몇 마디 할 예정이다
→ will give[deliver] a short speech
짧은 연설을 할 예정이다

included in the admission fee
입장료에 포함되어 있는
→ covered by the admission fee
입장료에 포함되어 있는

updated every week
매주 업데이트 되는
→ change weekly
매주 변경되다

launch an advertising campaign
광고 캠페인을 시작하다

→ start a promotion
홍보를 시작하다

to keep electronic documents safe
전자 문서를 안전하게 보관하기 위해서

→ to securely store documents
문서를 안전하게 보관하기 위해

show you how to install the equipment
장비를 어떻게 설치하는지 보여 주다

→ demonstrate an installation process
설치 과정을 보여 주다

provide services internationally[overseas]
해외로 서비스를 제공하다

→ is a global company
글로벌 기업이다

a follow-up study
후속 연구

→ additional research
추가 연구

can have access to high-speed Internet
고속 인터넷을 이용할 수 있다

→ are equipped for Internet access
인터넷을 갖추고 있다

should come in through the rear door
후문을 통해 들어와야 한다

→ should use a different entrance
다른 입구를 사용해야 한다

parts of the item are missing
상품의 부품이 누락되다

→ some pieces were not included
일부 부품이 포함되지 않았다

to better serve our customers
고객을 더 잘 응대하기 위해

→ to improve customer service
고객 서비스를 향상시키기 위해

stay open longer hours
더 긴 시간을 운영하다

→ extend hours of operation
운영 시간을 연장하다

offer rides
차편을 제공하다

→ provide transportation
교통편을 제공하다

plan to expand its range of services
서비스의 범위를 확장할 계획이다

→ will broaden its offerings
제공을 늘릴 것이다

experienced attorneys
경험 많은 변호사들

→ accomplished legal professionals
뛰어난 법률 전문가들

has outlets across the country
국내 곳곳에 매장이 있다

→ has branches nationwide
전국 곳곳에 지점이 있다

all sales are final
모든 판매는 환불이 불가능하다

→ does not accept returns
반품을 받지 않는다

received an award from
~로부터 상을 받다

→ was recognized by
~로부터 인정을 받았다

named one of the state's Top Ten
Companies 국내 10대 기업 중 하나로 지명되다

→ is highly rated
높이 평가된다

정답이 보이는 패러프레이징 리스트

proceeds will go toward ...
수익금은 ~에 쓰일 것이다

→ funds will be used to ...
자금은 ~하기 위해 사용될 것이다

the amount due should be paid
지급액이 납부되어야 한다

→ the bill must be settled
지불금이 정산되어야 한다

is a loyal subscriber
오랜 구독자이다

→ has been a customer for an extended period 장기간 고객이었다

menu selections vary by season
메뉴는 계절별로 다르다

→ the dining choices change seasonally
메뉴가 계절마다 변한다

produce faster and more efficiently
더 빠르고 효율적으로 생산하다

→ improve a manufacturing process
제조 과정을 향상시키다

the road will be repaved
도로가 재포장될 것이다

→ maintenance work will be performed
도로 유지 보수 작업이 실시될 것이다

has a prior engagement
선약이 있다

→ has a scheduling conflict
일정이 겹친다

give instructions on where to ship
어디로 배송할지 방법을 알려 주다

→ provide a mailing address
우편 주소를 제공하다

profiles of the musicians
뮤지션 프로필

→ performer biographies
공연자 약력

run a business
사업을 운영하다

→ is an owner[proprietor]/entrepreneur
사업주[소유주]/기업가이다

can be converted into
~로 변신할 수 있다

→ is adjustable
조절이 가능하다

already reached its maximum capacity
최대 수용 인원에 도달하다

→ is already full
정원이 다 차다

relatively inexpensive
비교적 비싸지 않은

→ reasonably priced
저렴한 가격의

plan to finish the first stage
첫 단계를 마무리할 계획이다

→ part of a plan will be completed
계획의 일부가 마무리될 것이다

collaborate with
~와 협력[합작]하다

→ work closely with
~와 긴밀히 일하다

keep the information confidential
정보를 기밀로 유지하다

→ the information is kept private
정보는 비공개로 유지된다

open from Monday to Friday
월요일부터 금요일까지 연다

→ is closed on weekends
주말에는 닫는다

356

will be entered in a contest to win ...
~을 탈 수 있는 경품 행사에 응모될 것이다

→ have a chance to win ...
~을 탈 수 있는 기회를 가지다

enter a raffle
추첨에 응모하다

→ enter a contest
경품 행사에 참여하다

show little enthusiasm
열의를 거의 보이지 않다

→ are reluctant to do
~하기를 꺼리다

complete a survey
설문지를 작성하다

→ fill out a questionnaire
설문지를 작성하다

contract / lease
계약(서) / 임대 계약(서)

→ (rental) agreement
(임대) 계약서

a contemporary interior décor
현대적인 인테리어 장식

→ modern look
현대적인 모습

a discount for bulk purchases
대량 구매에 대한 할인

→ a special offer for large orders
대량 주문에 대한 특가 판매

is adjacent to ... [is within walking distance] ~에서 가깝다[도보 거리에 있다]

→ is conveniently located[is located nearby]
편리하게[근처에] 위치해 있다

non-refundable deposit is required
환불이 안 되는 보증금이 요구된다

→ cannot get the deposits back
보증금을 돌려받을 수 없다

will implement a new process
새로운 절차를 시행할 것이다

→ a new procedure will go into effect
새로운 절차가 시행될 것이다

do not block the aisles
통로를 막지 않다

→ keep walkways clear
통로를 비워 두다

an expanded selection of supplies
더 다양해진 물품

→ a wider range of products
더 많은 종류의 상품들

periodic reminders
정기 알림 메시지

→ regular notification
정기적인 통지

verify the information
정보를 확인하다

→ confirm the details
세부 사항을 확인하다

has been named the new vice president
새로운 부사장으로 임명되었다

→ announced change in a company's leadership 회사의 지도자 변화를 발표했다

reduce the impact on the environment
환경에 미치는 영향을 줄이다

→ is environmentally conscious
환경을 신경 쓰다

energy-efficient
에너지 효율이 좋은

→ consume less electricity
더 적은 전기를 소비하다

이중 지문의 연계 문제 공식

- 서로 관련 있는 지문 두 개를 한 세트로 하며, 세트당 5문항으로 구성된다.
- 반드시 1문항은 정답의 단서가 두 지문에 걸쳐 있으며, 5문항 중 연계 문제가 나오는 순서는 랜덤이다.
- 첫 번째 지문에서 1차 정보, 두 번째 지문에서 2차 정보를 찾아 두 단서를 종합해야 정답이 도출된다.

ETS 예제 **이메일 + 쿠폰**

번역 p. 193

Dear Mr. Patel:

I am sorry to hear about your recent experience at the Timpane Star Sydney Hotel on 18 September. I understand that although you had a confirmed reservation, the room you had booked was unavailable. I am happy to learn, however, that the dedicated front desk staff members were able to find you alternative accommodations.

From what I have been able to discover, there was a computer software malfunction that caused particular rooms to be listed as available when, in fact, they had already been reserved. Your visit to Sydney coincided with two international conferences in the area of the hotel, resulting in an unusually high number of guests. Unfortunately, this caused some unintentional overbooking.

I apologize for the inconvenience, and on behalf of Timpane Hotels, I would like to offer you a complimentary one-night stay at any of our locations in Australia (Sydney, Perth, Melbourne, or Brisbane).

Please see the attached voucher for details.

Sincerely,

Samantha Johnston, Vice President of Guest Services → STEP 2
Timpane Hotel Corporation

Timpane Hotels **Voucher** # X3445

This voucher is good for a complimentary stay of one night in a standard room at either the Timpane Star Sydney, the Timpane Seaview Perth, the Timpane High Square Melbourne, or the Timpane Guest Suites Brisbane. The room must be booked in advance. Meals are not included.

Guest Signature _____ Date _____

If you have questions, please contact Guest Services. → STEP 3
By e-mail: guestservices@timpanehotels.com.au
By phone: 1800 160 401
By post: 14 Chesler Rd., **Brisbane** QLD 4000, Australia

---

1 글의 목적

존스턴이 이메일을 보낸 이유는?
- 고객님께서 9월 18일 팀페인 스타 시드니 호텔에서 최근 겪으신 일을 듣게 되어 유감입니다.
- 제가 알아본 바로는 컴퓨터 소프트웨어 장애가 있었습니다.
- 불편을 드려 죄송하며, 팀페인 호텔을 대표하여 무료 1일 숙박권을 제공해 드리고자 합니다.
→ 정답: 불만 사항에 대해 대응하기 위해

2 세부 사항

존스턴이 9월 18일에 발생했다고 한 일은?
하지만 전담 프런트 직원들이 대체할 숙소를 찾았다고 하니 다행입니다.
→ 정답: 직원들이 문제를 해결했다.

3 추론

파텔 씨에 대해 암시되는 것은?
손님께서는 예약이 확정되었음에도 예약한 방을 쓰실 수 없었다고 알고 있습니다.
→ 정답: 미리 방을 예약했었다.

4 동의어

쿠폰의 'good'과 의미상 가장 가까운 단어는?
이 쿠폰은 일반실 1일 무료 숙박에 유효합니다.
→ 정답: 유효한

5 연계 문제

존스턴 씨의 사무실이 위치한 곳은?
지문 ❶ 사만다 존스턴, 고객 서비스부 부장
지문 ❷ 문의 시 고객 서비스부로 연락하십시오. 주소: 체슬러 가 14번지, 브리즈번, 퀸즐랜드 주, 호주
→ 정답: 브리즈번

1 Why did Ms. Johnston send the e-mail?

(A) To confirm a reservation

(B) To respond to a complaint

(C) To help with conference arrangements

(D) To ask about Mr. Patel's plans

2 What does Ms. Johnston indicate happened on September 18 ?

(A) Hotel staff members resolved a problem.

(B) Hotel staff members installed some new software.

(C) Mr. Patel arrived earlier than expected.

(D) New front desk receptionists were trained.

3 What is suggested about Mr. Patel?

(A) He was in Sydney to attend a conference.

(B) He requested a change in his room.

(C) He had reserved a room in advance.

(D) He had previously stayed at other Timpane-owned hotels.

4 In the voucher, the word "good" in paragraph 1, line 1, is closest in meaning to

(A) high quality

(B) lucky

(C) well behaved

(D) valid

5 Where most likely is Ms. Johnston's office located? → (STEP 1)

(A) In Sydney

(B) In Perth

(C) In Melbourne

(D) In Brisbane → (STEP 4)

이중 연계 문제 이렇게 푼다

(STEP 1) 연계 문제 파악하기

5문항 중 반드시 1문항은 연계 문제이므로 순차적으로 문제를 풀면서 한 지문으로 문제가 풀리지 않는 경우 연계 문제라고 판단해야 한다.

(STEP 2) 1차 단서 찾기

질문에서 존스턴 씨의 사무실 위치를 묻고 있으므로 첫 번째 지문에서 존스턴 씨에 대한 정보가 있는 곳을 스캔한다. 이메일 마지막에 이메일 발신자인 존스턴 씨의 이름과 직책, 부서명(Guest Service)을 확인한다.

(STEP 3) 2차 단서 찾기

첫 번째 지문인 이메일에서 Guest Service(고객 서비스 부서)의 위치를 알 수 없으므로 두 번째 지문인 쿠폰에서 관련 정보를 추가로 확인한다. 두 지문의 연결 고리가 되는 고객 서비스 부서에 대한 정보가 마지막 줄에 명시되어 있다.

(STEP 4) 정답 도출

존스턴 씨는 고객 서비스부에서 일한다. + 고객 서비스부는 브리즈번에 위치해 있다.

= 존스턴 씨의 사무실은 브리즈번에 위치해 있다.

● ETS 연계 문제 출제 패턴

● 수치나 날짜, 표와 관련된 세부 정보 연계 문제가 가장 많은 비율을 차지한다.

이메일 + 이메일

지문 **❶**
수신: 관계자께
발신: 톰 포드
저희 업체 상품을 신문 광고에 싣고 싶습니다.
90자 광고는 월 가격이 얼마입니까?

➕

지문 **❷**
월 패키지 안내

패키지 #1	70자 미만 광고	월 150달러
패키지 #2	100자 미만 광고	월 300달러
패키지 #3	150자 미만 광고	월 400달러

Q 포드 씨는 얼마짜리 광고에 관심이 있는가? → 월 **300달러**

웹페이지 + 고객 후기

지문 **❶**
저희 베스트 티켓은 고객이 원하는 티켓을 저렴한 가격에
디자인해 드립니다. 티켓 장당 가격은 아래와 같습니다.

150~500장	장당 50센트
501~1000장	장당 30센트
1001~1500장	장당 10센트

➕

지문 **❷**
리뷰 작성자: 레이
저는 베스트 티켓에서 **700장의 티켓**을 주문했습니다.
디자인 세부 요청 사항이 많았지만 친절하게 응대해
주셔서 매우 만족스러웠고 다음에도 이용할 생각입니다.

Q 레이 씨에 대해 알 수 있는 것은? → 티켓 한 장에 **30센트**를 지불했다.

웹일정표 + 이메일

지문 **❶**
JP 타워 창문 교체 일정

11월 20일	7층
11월 21일	8층
11월 22일	9층
11월 23일	10층

➕

지문 **❷**
수신: 클레어 터너
발신: JP 타워 건물 관리팀
터너 씨께,
귀하의 사무실 창문 교체 공사가 **11월 21일**로 예정되어
있습니다. 원활한 공사를 위해 창문 주변에 놓인 물건들을
모두 치워 주시기 바랍니다

Q 터너 씨에 대해 암시된 것은? → **8층** 사무실을 사용한다.

● 두 지문에 흩어진 단서들을 보기와 하나씩 대조해서 찾는 문제 유형도 있다.

웹사이트 + 공지

지문 **❶**
웰링턴 지역 커뮤니티에 오신 것을 환영합니다.
• 웰링턴 주요 정부 청사 둘러보기
• 휴양 코스로 유명한 자전거 도로 둘러보기

➕

지문 **❷**
웰링턴 주민들께 알립니다.
올해 지역 연례 축제는 새롭게 단장한 화단으로 더욱
화사해진 자전거 도로에서 시작됩니다.

Q 웰링턴 가에 대해 언급되지 않은 것은?
(A) 정부 건물이 있다.
(B) 연례 행사를 개최한다.
(C) 자전거 도로가 있다.
(D) 지역 체육 대회로 유명하다. (X)

다음 지문을 읽고 문제의 정답을 고르세요.

Letter + Schedule

Dear WHKK Radio,

I heard a wonderful symphony on my car radio last Tuesday morning around 10 A.M. Unfortunately I got to work before the host announced the composer and name of the piece. I would like to have this information because I think a recording of this music would make an excellent birthday present for my wife.

As long as I am writing, let me add that I moved to the area recently and have been delighted by the variety of types of music that your station plays. Also, is it possible to get a list of your programs and the times they are broadcast?

Yours,

Joseph Bernard
Joseph Bernard

WHKK Radio Broadcast Schedule for July

	Monday-Friday	Saturday & Sunday
8 A.M.-11 A.M.	Morning Classical with Todd Hampton	Local and National News
11 A.M.-1 P.M.	Classic Jazz with Roger Freed	Latin Rhythms with José Campo
1 P.M.-5 P.M.	Rock (host varies)	Oldies
5 P.M.-7 P.M.	National News	Night Talk with Randall Tyler

For more information about the music played on any program, call the station at 555-9765 and ask to speak to the host of the program. Subscribe to our newsletter for advance notice of concerts and other events by calling 555-9766.

---

1. To whom should Mr. Bernard probably speak for more information?
   (A) Todd Hampton
   (B) Roger Freed
   (C) Randall Tyler
   (D) José Campo

PART 7 | UNIT 13

361

Notice + Calendar

Lunchtime Walking Club

On May 17, the Asher Recreation Board approved the creation of the Lunchtime Walking Club at Asher Community Park. The walking club will meet from Monday through Friday, noon-1 P.M., and the activity will run all year long. The club will meet at the trailhead by the park's north entrance at Hunter Street. Each participant should wear comfortable walking shoes and bring a bottle of drinking water. Interested residents should call or visit the park's Recreation Office to register. The club will officially meet after a minimum of seven members have joined. Please check the calendar for any updates or changes. For more information, contact club coordinator Shreya Kamdar at 215-555-0193.

Weekly Activities Calendar for the Month of July Asher Community Park

Mondays	12:00 P.M.	**Lunchtime Walking Club** (North Trail)
	5:30 P.M.	**Community Volleyball** (West Court)
Tuesdays	12:15 P.M.	**"Learn at Lunch"**: Butterflies (Pavilion) $7 fee, includes lunch
Wednesdays	12:00 P.M.	**Lunchtime Walking Club** (North Trail)
	5:30 P.M.	**Community Volleyball** (West Court)
Thursdays	12:15 P.M.	**"Learn at Lunch"**: Fungi (Pavilion) $7 fee, includes lunch
	5:30 P.M.	**Bird Watching** (2nd & 4th weeks) (Recreation Arena)
Fridays	12:00 P.M.	**Lunchtime Walking Club** (North Trail)
	5:30 P.M.	**Community Volleyball** (West Court)
Saturdays	10:00 A.M.	**"Nature and Art"**: Painting (Recreation Building) $10 fee, includes supplies
	2:00 P.M.	**Tour of Asher Park Lake** (Boathouse) $15 boat rental fee

For more detailed information about any of the events listed above, please contact the park's Recreation Office at 215-555-0102

---

2. What is suggested about the walking club in July?

   (A) It meets less frequently than originally planned.

   (B) Its coordinator is being replaced.

   (C) It provides bottled water to participants.

   (D) It meets at a different location each day.

Weekly New Business Spotlight: Revitalize Renovations

John and Bradley Nichols' one-year-old company, Revitalize Renovations, is changing the climate of the real estate market in central Sydney. The small firm works with existing landlords in the city to refurbish older apartments. This pair of consultants evaluates properties to determine what improvements would most efficiently increase value and rental income potential. From outdoor landscaping to indoor floor installation, Revitalize Renovations then selects and manages skilled laborers in completing the project. So far, all of their work has been concentrated in central Sydney.

A local landlord, Whitney Grey, recently contracted the Nichols brothers to refurbish her city-centre apartment building. "After working with Revitalize Renovations, I saw my rental profits go up by 11 percent thanks to both increased tenant demand and the reduced costs for power and water. I received numerous calls from tenants about how much they enjoy the fresh air and panoramic views from the new rooftop terrace. I will certainly seek advice from Revitalize Renovations again," said Grey.

The Nichols brothers can be contacted through their Web site, revren.com.au, where interested parties can learn more about the company and submit details of a proposed project.

From: Tania Ferreira <tferreira@quintext.com.au>
To: John Nichols <jnichols@revren.com.au>
Re: New Renovation Proposition
Date: January 2

Mr. Nichols,

I am writing because I recently purchased a building in Point Piper, a seaside town near Sydney. I thought you might be interested in the project. The building is not currently in habitable condition, so it had a very low sale price. However, it is close to public transportation, which is a major advantage. Within the next few months, I want to turn this building into a nice living space and put the fifteen apartments in the building up for rent.

I have limited experience in construction and could benefit greatly from your help. Additionally, I would like to learn about compliance with new energy guidelines and how this may affect potential improvements to the electrical wiring. Please let me know if you would be available to discuss this with me.

Thank you,

Tania Ferreira

3. How is Ms. Ferreira's proposal different from typical jobs for Revitalize Renovations?
   (A) The work would be done outside Sydney.
   (B) Ms. Ferreira would organize the construction.
   (C) The fee would be paid before the project begins.
   (D) There would be strict time constraints.

Questions 1-5 refer to the following e-mail and online form.

To:	Undisclosed Recipients
From:	Linda Voigt
Date:	30 April
Subject:	Seeking your feedback

Good afternoon,

Thank you for attending the Leeds Technology Conference at the Orini Event Centre on Friday, 13 April, through Sunday, 15 April. We were thrilled by everyone's enthusiasm and by the record number of attendees!

Please take a few minutes to complete our online comment form: ltc.co.uk/feedback. We will use your responses to make next year's conference even better. To show our appreciation for your honest input, if you submit comments by 31 May, you will receive a free video download of Friday's keynote address by the renowned physician and award-winning author, Dr. Charlie Whitley.

Kind regards,

Linda Voigt
Conference Organiser

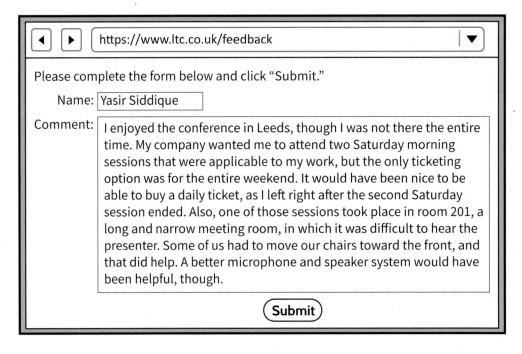

https://www.ltc.co.uk/feedback

Please complete the form below and click "Submit."

Name: Yasir Siddique

Comment: I enjoyed the conference in Leeds, though I was not there the entire time. My company wanted me to attend two Saturday morning sessions that were applicable to my work, but the only ticketing option was for the entire weekend. It would have been nice to be able to buy a daily ticket, as I left right after the second Saturday session ended. Also, one of those sessions took place in room 201, a long and narrow meeting room, in which it was difficult to hear the presenter. Some of us had to move our chairs toward the front, and that did help. A better microphone and speaker system would have been helpful, though.

Submit

1. According to the e-mail, how did the most recent conference differ from previous ones?
   (A) It had more people in attendance.
   (B) It covered more topics.
   (C) It took place in a larger building.
   (D) It lasted one day longer.

2. In the e-mail, what is offered in exchange for feedback?
   (A) A video recording of a speaker
   (B) A signed copy of a book
   (C) A discount on next year's ticket
   (D) An invitation to a special event

3. What is one complaint that Mr. Siddique notes in the online form?
   (A) That one of the classrooms was difficult to find
   (B) That a session he attended was not relevant to his work
   (C) That the schedule should have been finalized earlier
   (D) That a one-day ticket should have been available

4. What can be concluded about Mr. Siddique?
   (A) He left the conference on April 15.
   (B) He did not attend Dr. Whitley's lecture.
   (C) He attended the conference with some colleagues.
   (D) He spoke with Ms. Voigt during the conference.

5. In the form, what does Mr. Siddique indicate about room 201?
   (A) It was far away from the main hall.
   (B) It had comfortable seating.
   (C) It needed a better audio system.
   (D) It was too warm.

Questions 6-10 refer to the following chart and e-mail.

Golden Crunch Snack Company—Marketing Campaign Analysis					
Campaign Name	Dates	Description	SocialFriend.com # Shares	VoteTally.com # Votes	Goldencrunch.com # Visits
Health Benefits	April 29–May 20	Pop-up ads reminded customers to get annual checkups and eat more Healthy Bite Crackers.	92	N/A	1,112
New Flavors	May 23–June 14	Customers were invited to vote for one of six proposed cracker seasoning concepts.	N/A	873	34
Puzzle Challenge	June 20–July 29	Customers were given clues to a puzzle on product boxes and asked to post answers online.	1,865	N/A	216
Free Box	August 1–August 31	Customers were offered a free box for every friend they introduced to Healthy Bite Crackers.	430	N/A	889

To:	dbenson@gcsnackco.com
From:	lcortez@multiplicityadvisors.com
Date:	September 6
Subject:	New campaign

Dear Mr. Benson,

Thanks for sending me your idea for your October marketing campaign. At first glance, it looks good. Your customers have responded well to challenge-style campaigns before. Also, it really suits your brand image to link Healthy Bite Crackers to individual exercise.

There is one consideration to keep in mind, however. In general, we have found that Web page traffic does not necessarily translate into strong sales numbers. And the data gathered on your past campaigns bear this out. Those statistics indicate a strong correlation between sales and social media engagement. Therefore, I would caution against using your Web page to launch the next campaign. A more effective strategy might be to introduce the campaign on a social media platform, like SocialFriend.com or VoteTally.com. When customers give feedback and voice their opinions online, this can lead to the strongest levels of brand loyalty.

By the way, I recommend that we consult with Erin Dupree on our product research team—she is a health expert and has been a great resource for us in the past.

Best,

Lynette Cortez
Multiplicity Advisors

6 What were customers asked to do during the marketing campaign that began in May?
(A) Come up with original flavor suggestions
(B) Choose between several product ideas
(C) Answer a questionnaire about health
(D) Solve a difficult puzzle

7. In the e-mail, the word "consideration" in paragraph 2, line 1, is closest in meaning to
(A) kindness
(B) factor
(C) meditation
(D) payment

8. What marketing campaign probably generated the most sales?
(A) Health Benefits
(B) New Flavors
(C) Puzzle Challenge
(D) Free Box

9. What is suggested about the marketing campaign being planned for October?
(A) It will involve a personal fitness challenge.
(B) It will involve questions related to sports history.
(C) It will be launched in magazines and newspapers.
(D) It will distribute information gathered in a previous campaign.

10. What does Ms. Cortez want to do next?
(A) Conduct a marketing survey
(B) Contact a health expert
(C) Redesign the company's Web site
(D) Review some health data

Questions 11-15 refer to the following e-mail and employee time sheet.

From:	Alejandra Quintana
To:	Le Wei Tsang
Subject:	Time sheet adjustment
Date:	Monday, December 10

Dear Mr. Tsang,

Thank you for submitting your time sheet for the last pay period on time. I am writing to let you know that I made an adjustment to your form before sending it to payroll. I know that you took half a day as paid time off last week, but your time sheet did not reflect this. All your hours for the week were coded to either 001 project time, 002 administrative time, or 003 nonproject time. For future reference, whenever you take paid time off, please charge the time to the associated code 004 under the "Pay Code" column.

I've amended your form for you this time. Please confirm the change when you have a spare moment. Remember, as a full-time financial advisor with Grossberg Consulting, you have flexibility to set your own schedule and are entitled to ten paid days off per year.

I would like to express my appreciation for the excellent job you are doing. You've gotten off to a great start with the clients these past two weeks and have made a seamless transition to your position here at Grossberg Consulting.

Sincerely,

Alejandra Quintana, Managing Director
Grossberg Consulting

Grossberg Consulting Employee Time Sheet
Le Wei Tsang–Financial Advisor, Salem Office　　GC

Pay Code	Monday Dec-3	Tuesday Dec-4	Wednesday Dec-5	Thursday Dec-6	Friday Dec-7	Total for Pay Period
[001]	3.00	7.75	6.50	7.75	4.00	29.00
[002]	4.00		1.00			5.00
[003]	1.00	0.25	0.50	0.25		2.00
[004]					4.00	4.00

11. Why does Ms. Quintana contact Mr. Tsang?
(A) To approve his request for time off
(B) To alert him to an error he made
(C) To reassign him to another team
(D) To congratulate him on a job promotion

12. What does Ms. Quintana ask Mr. Tsang to do?
(A) Inform the payroll department of changes to his work schedule
(B) Update his calendar to show the hours he works each day
(C) Verify a change that was made to his time sheet
(D) Submit a proposal to clients for their approval

13. In the e-mail, the word "set" in paragraph 2, line 3, is closest in meaning to
(A) position
(B) arrange
(C) deposit
(D) obtain

14. What is implied about Mr. Tsang?
(A) He recently joined the full-time staff at Grossberg Consulting.
(B) He has taken more days off than what is allowed.
(C) He is a human resources professional.
(D) He has transferred to a different Grossberg Consulting location.

15. When did Mr. Tsang take paid time off?
(A) On Monday
(B) On Wednesday
(C) On Thursday
(D) On Friday

Questions 16-20 refer to the following e-mail and catalog listing.

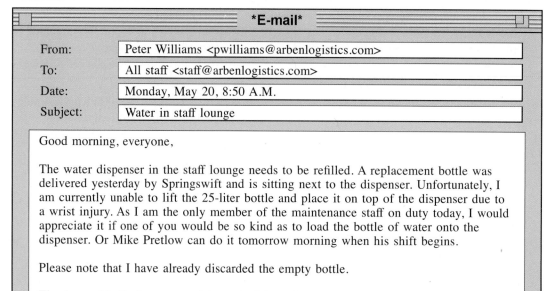

From:	Peter Williams <pwilliams@arbenlogistics.com>
To:	All staff <staff@arbenlogistics.com>
Date:	Monday, May 20, 8:50 A.M.
Subject:	Water in staff lounge

Good morning, everyone,

The water dispenser in the staff lounge needs to be refilled. A replacement bottle was delivered yesterday by Springswift and is sitting next to the dispenser. Unfortunately, I am currently unable to lift the 25-liter bottle and place it on top of the dispenser due to a wrist injury. As I am the only member of the maintenance staff on duty today, I would appreciate it if one of you would be so kind as to load the bottle of water onto the dispenser. Or Mike Pretlow can do it tomorrow morning when his shift begins.

Please note that I have already discarded the empty bottle.

Thank you kindly for your assistance in this matter.

Peter Williams
Maintenance Department, Arben Logistics

Springswift Drinking Water

Springswift water undergoes a rigorous ten-step quality assurance process and is lightly enhanced with minerals to ensure that it is healthy and refreshing.

Springswift water
• can be safely stored and consumed for two months from the date of bottling.
• comes in a sealed, tamper-proof 25-liter bottle.
• contains ozonated water and minerals (magnesium sulfate, potassium bicarbonate).

Why not subscribe to our convenient water delivery service? We will bring your bottles to you once a month on your chosen day. You just need to load them onto your cooler.

Note: Delivery service is only available within 15 kilometers of Wellington.

16. What is the purpose of the e-mail?
(A) To inquire about the delivery of an item
(B) To announce a work schedule change
(C) To request assistance with a task
(D) To notify employees of a new policy

17. What does the e-mail suggest about Mr. Pretlow?
(A) He repairs broken water dispensers.
(B) He has injured his wrist.
(C) He is usually scheduled to work at night.
(D) He is a member of the maintenance team.

18. In the e-mail, the word "discarded" in paragraph 2, line 1, is closest in meaning to
(A) ignored
(B) rejected
(C) thrown away
(D) brought into

19. What is suggested about Arben Logistics?
(A) It recently started a water delivery service.
(B) It is located within fifteen kilometers of Wellington.
(C) It has multiple water dispensers in its office.
(D) It is recruiting maintenance workers.

20. What is a stated feature of Springswift water?
(A) Its protective packaging
(B) Its affordable price
(C) Its flavor choices
(D) Its range of sizes

Questions 21-25 refer to the following information and permit.

Gulverton Parks Management

Obtaining event permits

To hold an event at any public park within the city of Gulverton, you must submit an application for a permit with the Gulverton Parks Management Division. When planning your event and filling out the required permit application, please pay attention to the following policies.

Parks

- The city has designated areas for events of different sizes and types. Occasionally the requested location is deemed unsuitable based on the nature of your event. In this case an approval may be granted for an alternate site chosen at our discretion.

- The application must be submitted at least 30 days prior to the event. Late applications are considered to be "rush requests" and require a nonrefundable $50 fee.

- Events that feature live music or outside food vendors will require additional permits. These are issued by other city divisions, and it is your responsibility to obtain such approvals. For guidance on this and any other questions, contact the Gulverton Parks Management Division at parksmanagement@gulverton.gov.

City of Gulverton

Event Permit #: 4571

Status: Rush Request

The Gulverton Parks Management Division hereby grants the Starlite Melodies Foundation, represented by Quentin Pelletier, permission to use the facilities as outlined, subject to the terms and conditions of this agreement.

Event Information

Event Applicant: Quentin Pelletier   **Phone:** 228-555-0132

Event Name/Details: "Starlite Sounds" is an outdoor evening concert that is free and open to the public. It will include three different stages and live musical performances.

Estimated Attendance: 800–1,000

Location: Mayor Collins Park–Oceanside Promenade

Date and Times of Use:
Starting: Saturday, October 12 5:00 P.M., **Ending:** Saturday, October 12 10:00 P.M.

Approved by: Riona Ozaki

Approval date: Wednesday, September 23

21. For whom is the information most likely intended?
(A) Park officials
(B) Visitors to Gulverton
(C) Event coordinators
(D) Local musicians

22. What is indicated about the city of Gulverton?
(A) It has several event venues.
(B) It is a popular tourist destination.
(C) It has recently expanded its Parks Management Division.
(D) It is known for its music festivals.

23. What is suggested about Mr. Pelletier?
(A) He needs to sell 800 tickets.
(B) He was charged a $50 fee.
(C) He lives in Gulverton.
(D) He held a meeting with Ms. Ozaki.

24. What will the Starlite Melodies Foundation need to do before October 12 ?
(A) Obtain an additional permit
(B) Renew an expired license
(C) Move to a larger location
(D) Recruit food vendors

25. Where does Ms. Ozaki work?
(A) In the Gulverton Parks Management Division
(B) At a Mayor Collins Park restaurant
(C) At the Oceanside Promenade
(D) At the Starlite Melodies Foundation

Questions 26-30 refer to the following note and page from a catalog.

Tagens Booksellers
Summer Catalog

A Note to Customers:

We hope you will enjoy looking through our latest catalog. Beginning on page 3, in our "Travel and Tourism" section, you will find phrase books and travel guides to help you no matter where you go this summer. Our "Food and Drink" section on page 5 includes titles of interest for food lovers and amateur cooks with both large and small home kitchens. Leading experts highlight new trends in residential and commercial construction in the "Architecture and Design" titles beginning on page 7. For all the latest in the "Business and Management" section, see our selection of course books and reference materials, including the *Encyclopedia of Business Marketing*, winner of the Henderson Prize (page 8).

This catalog contains just a small sample of our most recent acquisitions. For a full listing of our titles, go to www.tagensbooks.com. If you are in the Minneola area, be sure to visit our store for a wealth of additional books—including hundreds that are not available on our Web site.

Tagens Booksellers

Business Analysis Textbook
by Stephen Y. Correia and Jane S. Yamashiro

A clear and readable introduction to finance management, full of suggested learning activities and entertaining cartoons illustrating essential points. Teachers are free to reproduce sheets for group activities. Condition: Very good with limited signs of use. $49.95

New Century Finance Management
by Amelie Goranson

This invaluable book combines solid financial theory with practical applications. Goranson highlights theoretical principles with real-life examples and case studies. Recommended for both students and business owners. Condition: Like new. $34.95

Accounting for Small Businesses
by Alicia D. Koh

Essential reading for owners of small companies who wish to take care of their own accounting and tax obligations. Condition: Fair with some wear to corners and edges. $29.95

Encyclopedia of Business Marketing
by Andrew Opalinsky

Any novice will appreciate this book, with its more than 2,500 definitions of key terms in business and marketing. A must-have for anyone entering the world of business. Condition: Good with signs of cover wear. $35.95

Tagens Booksellers

26. Based on the note, what book would
    Tagens Booksellers most likely have in
    stock?
    (A) A biography of a famous photographer
    (B) A history of space travel
    (C) A review of top vacation spots in
        Europe
    (D) A textbook for professional chefs

27. In the note, the word "wealth" in
    paragraph 2, line 3, is closest in meaning
    to
    (A) value
    (B) expense
    (C) fortune
    (D) abundance

28. What is suggested about the catalog?
    (A) It advertises used books.
    (B) It is a comprehensive listing.
    (C) It includes mainly academic texts.
    (D) It is published once a year.

29. Who received an award?
    (A) Mr. Correia
    (B) Ms. Goranson
    (C) Ms. Koh
    (D) Mr. Opalinsky

30. What feature is NOT mentioned among
    the descriptions of the books on the
    catalog page?
    (A) Material that may be photocopied
    (B) Checklists for starting a new company
    (C) Examples drawn from real life
    (D) Drawings to clarify key points

Questions 31-35 refer to the following chart and e-mail.

Nydoka.com Web Site – Visitor Analysis Week of June 1		
Web page	Percentage of guests who left Web site after this page	Possible reasons guests did not visit other pages
Home	46%	Too many links to advertisements on the home page
Products	34%	Poor layout
Contact Us	31%	Limited customer service hours
Sales	13%	No follow-up with customers who leave items unpurchased
Checkout	5%	Successful transactions

E-mail

To:	ernest.bram@nydoka.com
From:	lservin@nydoka.com
Date:	June 12
Subject:	RE: Web site visitor analysis

Dear Ernest,

Thanks for forwarding your Web site visitor analysis report. Let me offer some insights I can derive from the data. We can talk about my observations when we meet tomorrow.

• I think the most pressing need is to address the links issue. It seems we are alienating our visitors by sending them to other sites rather than keeping them with us. I could communicate with our marketing department about this.

• One possible solution to the products page problem would be to list items separately rather than showing similar products together. For example, on our products page for audio devices, we could list headphones and speakers separately. I'll have our Web designer Vijay Rajasthan make modifications to the page.

• I'd like to request that Web developer Umeka Tatsuno add a pop-up message to the sales page to remind customers that they have items in their virtual shopping cart when they try to leave the Web page.

Looking forward to our discussion,

Lydia Servin

31. What percent of visitors to the Web site purchase something?
(A) 46 percent
(B) 34 percent
(C) 31 percent
(D) 5 percent

32. What Web page is Ms. Servin most concerned about?
(A) Home
(B) Products
(C) Contact Us
(D) Sales

33. What does Nydoka, Inc., most likely sell?
(A) Clothing and accessories
(B) Sound equipment
(C) Kitchen appliances
(D) Office supplies

34. What will Mr. Rajasthan most likely do?
(A) He will fix some links.
(B) He will redesign a page layout.
(C) He will revise a contract.
(D) He will launch a new study.

35. What will Ms. Tatsuno be asked to create?
(A) An e-mail response
(B) An eye-catching logo
(C) A new payment option
(D) An automated alert

삼중 지문의 연계 문제 공식

● 서로 관련 있는 지문 세 개를 한 세트로 하며, 세트당 5문항으로 구성된다.

● 반드시 2문항은 정답의 단서가 두 지문에 걸쳐 있으며, 5문항 중 연계 문제가 나오는 순서는 랜덤이다.

● 첫 번째와 두 번째 지문, 두 번째와 세 번째 지문, 혹은 첫 번째와 세 번째 지문이 연계되어 출제된다.

ETS 예제   기사 + 전단지 + 광고   번역 p.205

AUCKLAND (1 February)—Australia's Z&W Foods is expanding. The supermarket chain announced that throughout next year it will be opening twenty new stores in New Zealand and South Africa. "Z&W is committed to opening stores around the world. We believe our pricing practice gives us a competitive advantage in new and existing markets," said spokesperson Maya Kapil in a telephone interview.

In addition, the new regional vice president of Z&W Foods, Daniel Stephenson, said that several existing stores will be remodeled. "We are aiming for our stores to have a more modern and inviting design and to implement features that are environmentally friendly," he explained. Locally, the Z&W Foods store on Hawkins Street in Auckland is expected to close on 1 March for the renovations. It will be closed for about three months, with a reopening planned for 18 May. → STEP 2

Grand Reopening Celebration Z & W Foods
673 Hawkins St., Auckland Saturday, 2 May → STEP 2

Join manager Rose Enoka and employees for the ribbon-cutting ceremony at 9:00 A.M. → STEP 2   Enjoy complimentary snacks, cakes, and beverages along with chances to win prizes. The Fourth Street School Children's Choir will perform at 10:00 A.M.

Come see the changes we have made to the store.
• Remodeled soup-and-salad bar
• On-site bakery, open seven days a week
• Expanded customer service area
• New pharmacy with a consultation area
Coming in June—in-store cafe and coffee bar!

HELP WANTED
Z & W Foods
673 Hawkins St., Auckland
• Counter staff for in-store cafe
• Bakers for overnight shift (experience required)
• Cashiers, full-time or part-time
• Maintenance
See store manager for details. → STEP 2

---

1 글의 목적

기사의 목적은?
슈퍼마켓 체인점이 내년 뉴질랜드와 남아프리카에 20개의 신규 매장을 개점한다고 발표했다.
→ 정답: 회사의 계획 보도

2 추론

기사는 Z&W사의 제품에 대해 타 업체 제품과 비교해서 어떻다고 암시하는가?
"저희의 가격 관행은 저희의 시장 경쟁력입니다."
→ 정답: 제품이 덜 비싸다.

3 연계 문제

전단지에서 추론할 수 있는 것은?
지문 ❶ 3월 1일에는 공사로 인해 폐점하며 **5월 18일** 새롭게 오픈할 예정이다.
지문 ❷ 개업식: **5월 2일**
→ 정답: 공사가 예정보다 일찍 끝났다.

4 사실 관계

전단지가 상점에 대해 명시하는 것은?
매장내 베이커리, 연중무휴
→ 정답: 베이커리가 매일 연다.

5 연계 문제

누가 구직자들에게 더 자세한 내용을 제공할 수 있는가?
지문 ❸ 세부 정보는 매장 **매니저**에게 문의하세요.
지문 ❷ 오전 9시, 리본 커팅식에 매니저 **로즈 에노카**와 직원들과 함께해 주십시오
→ 정답: 에노카 씨

1 What is the purpose of the article?

(A) To discuss the promotion of an executive
(B) To highlight some new products
(C) To report on a company's plans
(D) To explain regional business trends

2 What does the article suggest about Z&W's products compared with those of other vendors?

(A) They are less expensive.
(B) They are of higher quality.
(C) They represent a wider selection.
(D) They are environmentally friendly.

3 What can be inferred from the flyer? → STEP 1

(A) The ceremony is closed to the public.
(B) Refreshments will be sold at a discount during the event.
(C) The school choir received a prize.
(D) A renovation project was completed ahead of schedule. → STEP 3

4 What does the flyer indicate about the store?

(A) It no longer carries medication.
(B) Its bakery is open every day.
(C) Its prices have been lowered.
(D) Its business hours have changed.

5 Who can provide job applicants with more details? → STEP 1

(A) Mr. Stephenson
(B) Ms. Enoka → STEP 3
(C) The head baker
(D) The senior cashier

삼중 연계 문제 이렇게 푼다

STEP 1 **첫 번째 연계 문제 파악**

3번 문제는 전단지를 읽고 답을 구해야 하므로 첫 번째 기사 지문을 모두 읽은 후, 두 번째 지문인 전단지 내용까지 읽는다.

STEP 2 **1차 + 2차 단서 조합하기**

전단지 제목에 표기된 개업식 행사일자와 첫 번째 기사문에 나온 공사 후 재개장 예정일이 차이가 나는 것을 알 수 있다.

STEP 3 **정답 도출**

공사 마감 후 5월 18일 재개장 예정
+ 실제 개업식: 5월 2일
= 공사가 예정보다 일찍 끝났다.

STEP 1 **두 번째 연계 문제 파악**

질문의 키워드인 더 많은 정보(more details)를 언급하고 있는 지문을 찾는다.

STEP 2 **1차 + 2차 단서 조합하기**

세 번째 지문에서 키워드 'details'를 그대로 사용한 문장이 있고, 매니저에 대한 정보는 두 번째 지문에서 언급된 바 있다.

STEP 3 **정답 도출**

세부 정보는 매니저에게 문의하라
+ 매니저 이름: 로즈 에노카
= 세부 정보는 에노카 씨가 제공할 수 있다.

● ETS 연계 문제 출제 패턴

● 지문 1과 지문 2, 지문 2와 지문 3이 순차적으로 연계되는 유형이 가장 자주 출제된다.

공지 + 이메일 + 이메일

지문 ❶

재택근무 신청 시 **부서장**에게 알리시오.

➕

지문 ❷

터너 씨, 내일 재택근무를 신청합니다. 예정되어 있던 회의는 다음 주가 어떨까요? 저는 **월, 화, 목요일** 시간이 비어 있습니다.

➕

지문 ❸

레이 씨, 다음 주에는 내가 **화, 수요일**만 회사에 출근합니다. 다음 주에 봅시다.

Q1 터너 씨는 누구인 것 같은가? → **지문 1 + 지문 2** = 부서장

Q2 터너와 레이는 언제 회의를 할 것 같은가? → **지문 2 + 지문 3** = 화요일

공지 + 문자 메시지 + 이메일

지문 ❶

공식 앱으로 열차편을 예약한 경우, 일정 변동 시 **문자 알림 메시지가 발송**됩니다.

➕

지문 ❷

웰러 씨, 귀하의 열차편이 40분 뒤로 미뤄진 10시 40분 출발로 변경되었음을 알려 드립니다. 목적지 **도착 시간은 2시**입니다.

➕

지문 ❸

레이첼 씨, 제 열차편이 연착되어 **회의가 시작하는 시간에는 여전히 열차에 있을 것 같습니다.** 먼저 진행하고 계시면 도착하는 대로 합류하겠습니다.

Q1 웰러 씨에 대해 알 수 있는 것은? → **지문 1 + 지문 2** = 공식 앱으로 열차를 예약했다.

Q2 회의에 대해 사실인 것은? → **지문 2 + 지문 3** = 2시 이전에 시작한다.

광고 + 문자 메시지 + 가격표

지문 ❶

세탁 서비스, **오전 8시까지 맡길** 시 추가 비용 없이 **당일 서비스** 가능

➕

지문 ❷

포터 씨, 요청하신 **단일 아이템**의 **당일 세탁** 총 서비스 요금은 **45달러**입니다.

➕

지문 ❸

면 - $5, 청바지 - $10, 자켓, 코트 - $30, 모피, 실크류 - $40, **이불 - $45**

Q1 포터 씨에 대해 알 수 있는 것은? → **지문 1 + 지문 2** = 오전 8시까지 세탁물을 맡겼다.

Q2 포터 씨가 맡긴 세탁물은 무엇인가? → **지문 2 + 지문 3** = 이불

● 지문 1과 지문 3, 지문 2와 지문 3이 연계되는 유형도 가끔 출제된다.

공지 + 웹사이트 + 기사

지문 ❶

그린빌 박물관의 신규 전시관이 **10월 1일 개관**할 예정입니다.

➕

지문 ❷

그린빌 박물관에서 우리 지역을 테마로 한 **지역 작가**의 작품을 수집합니다. 선정된 작품들은 **신규 전시관에 전시될 예정**입니다.

➕

지문 ❸

지역 최대 규모의 그린빌 박물관의 신규 전시관이 **11월 개관**했다. **제임스 리**를 비롯한 유명 아티스트의 작품을 감상할 수 있다.

Q1 신규 전시관에 대해 사실인 것은? → **지문 1 + 지문 3** = 예정보다 늦게 개관했다.

Q2 제임스 리에 대해 알 수 있는 것은? → **지문 2 + 지문 3** = 지역 작가이다.

다음 지문을 읽고 문제의 정답을 고르세요.

Web page + Advertisement + E-mail

Services	**People**	Press	Careers

Plimpton Financial Services

Country: United States   Branch: Dallas

If you would like to contact one of our leading experts for more information, please e-mail us.

Partner: b.green@plimptonfs.com
Director: j.waters@plimptonfs.com
Audit Manager: k.bean@plimptonfs.com
Senior Accountant: l.framel@plimptonfs.com

Entry-level Tax Accountant

Plimpton Financial Services is seeking an entry-level tax accountant to join our international team in Dallas. The candidate should be a team player with some experience with preparation of international tax accounting documents. Bilingual candidates are preferred. We offer excellent health benefits and opportunities for career advancement. Please send your résumé, cover letter, and three references to Janice Waters at j.waters@plimptonfs.com.

From: Maurice Williams <maury@gomail.com>
To: Janice Waters <j.waters@plimptonfs.com>
Subject: Tax Accountant Position
Attachments: Documents

Dear Ms. Waters:

I'm writing in regards to the entry-level tax accountant position. I believe I would be a good match for the job, as my current duties at Chesterfield Financial Group in London are focused on tax accounting. Once I have completed this internship, I will be back in Dallas on February 2. I have attached all the support documents you requested. I look forward to hearing from you.

Sincerely,

Maurice Williams

1. What is Janice Waters' position at Plimpton Financial Services?
   (A) Director
   (B) Senior Accountant
   (C) Partner
   (D) Audit Manager

2. What has Mr. Williams NOT attached to his e-mail?
   (A) References
   (B) Tax receipts
   (C) A résumé
   (D) A cover letter

Web page + Article + Letter

Title: *Put a Penny in the Bank*   Author: Harper Lyons
Book Description
Harper Lyons opens her second book with wise words from her father. "Every penny you put in the bank," her father says, "is a penny toward a future investment." Lyons took her father's advice and put her money into successful businesses and stocks. In her new book, Lyons shares her thoughts, strategies, and warnings on investing money.

Product Details   Format: Hardcover   Price: $19.99   On sale: November 4

HARPER LYONS RELEASES NEW BOOK

Boston—Harper Lyons, the best-selling author of *What a Dollar Can Do*, has finally released her highly anticipated book, *Put a Penny in the Bank*. The 187-page book, which describes how to invest money wisely, has already sold over one million copies. According to economist Aiden Henry, Lyons has written a book "people can relate to and learn from."

Next month, Lyons will embark on a national book tour that will run for two weeks. Lyons is scheduled to be in Boston on December 4 at Margot Bookstores. For more information about the tour, visit the Owl & Parrot Publishers Web site.

November 17

Dear Ms. Lyons,

I am pleased to inform you your promotional book tour is set to begin on December 1. I have included a finalized copy of your itinerary. Please note two details have been added since you last looked at the schedule.

On December 4, a book signing event has been added to your appearance at Margot Bookstores. It will take place after you read a short excerpt from *Put a Penny in the Bank*. Also, your interview on the radio program *Ventura News* has been confirmed. Therefore, a flight to Los Angeles on December 12 has been included in your agenda. If you have any questions, please do not hesitate to contact me.

Best regards,

Logan Parkinson, Editor, Business and Money
Owl & Parrot Publishers

---

3. What is NOT indicated about *Put a Penny in the Bank*?
   (A) It sells for more than twenty dollars.
   (B) It offers investment advice to readers.
   (C) It contains fewer than 200 pages.
   (D) It was written by a best-selling author.

4. What will most likely occur in Boston?
   (A) A promotional tour will begin.
   (B) An author will read an excerpt from *What a Dollar Can Do*.
   (C) A writer will sign copies of a new book.
   (D) A radio interview will be recorded.

To: Thiago Franco <franco@cooperdenton.com>
From: Zainab Wasem <wasem@cooperdenton.com>
Subject: Web site announcements
Date: May 31

Thiago,

There are a couple of announcements I would like you to post on our museum Web site. First, we should publicize our special three-month exhibition, *Great Flights*, in Edgar Hall. I have details about the aviation exhibition in my office, so you can pick up the information at your earliest convenience. Also, please notify visitors of the Wright Hall closure. Thanks.

Sincerely,

Zainab Wasem
Cooper Denton Museum Director

NOTICE

Posted June 5

Starting July 1, Wright Hall will be temporarily closed as part of an ongoing preservation project. The museum will be protecting and conserving the objects in the hall. The rest of the museum will remain accessible to the public. Wright Hall will reopen on August 1.

Rating ★ ★ ★ ☆
Posted by: Gabriel Yi

I visited the Cooper Denton Museum last week, and I had a great time. Our tour guide, Natalie, was knowledgeable and friendly. *Great Flights* was a spectacular exhibition that showcased different types of aircraft used for exploration. I had to buy another ticket on top of the general admission ticket to get in, but it was worth it. The only downside of my visit was I couldn't see space suits and equipment astronauts used in space because the hall they are displayed in, Wright hall, was temporarily closed.

5. What is true about the exhibition in Edgar Hall?
(A) It was curated by Thiago Franco.
(B) There is an extra entrance fee.
(C) It is intended for children.
(D) It features some video exhibits.

6. In what month did Mr. Yi visit the museum?
(A) May
(B) June
(C) July
(D) August

Questions 1-5 refer to the following e-mails and schedule.

From:	Agnes Harpenden <aharpenden@findleycommunitycentre.ca>
To:	Kevin Bockman <kbockman@westbanklaw.ca>
Subject:	Sponsorship opportunity
Date:	14 December

Dear Mr. Bockman,

Over the years, you have authorized funding on behalf of your legal firm, Westbank Law Partners, for several of the educational opportunities that we at Findley Community Centre have offered free of charge to residents of our community. Now we are inviting you to consider becoming a corporate sponsor for our annual lecture series that will take place again this coming February and March. We can assure you that these lectures have been well attended in each of the six years that we have hosted them. If you should choose to financially support this lecture series, we would be proud to identify your firm's sponsorship on all related publications and signs. I look forward to hearing your response.

Sincerely,

Agnes Harpenden
Events Coordinator
Findley Community Centre

Findley Community Centre Wednesday Lecture Series
Sponsored by Westbank Law Partners

February 6: Astrid Coulomb
The owner of local clothing store Astrid's Touch, Ms. Coulomb will discuss the problems and joys of the fashion industry and business ownership.

February 20: Lucas Carrel
A professionally trained chef, Mr. Carrel will talk about his experiences working in and owning a restaurant.

March 6: Hayir Khatana
The owner of Arrangements for You, Mr. Khatana will share how he launched his successful flower store franchising business.

March 20: Eva Rubio
A certified financial planner, Ms. Rubio will discuss financial issues, including budgeting and saving for retirement.

All events begin at 6:30 P.M. in the Findley Community Centre's auditorium and are open to the public. Admission is free, but registration is required. Complimentary coffee, tea, and light snacks are provided. For more information about the series, please contact our events coordinator, Agnes Harpenden, at 416-555-0179, ext. 43, or e-mail her at <aharpenden@findleycommunitycentre.ca>.

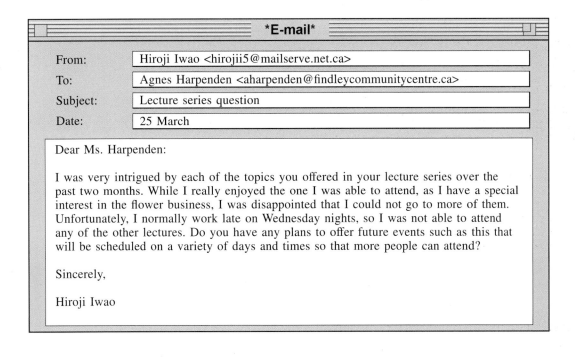

E-mail

From:	Hiroji Iwao <hirojii5@mailserve.net.ca>
To:	Agnes Harpenden <aharpenden@findleycommunitycentre.ca>
Subject:	Lecture series question
Date:	25 March

Dear Ms. Harpenden:

I was very intrigued by each of the topics you offered in your lecture series over the past two months. While I really enjoyed the one I was able to attend, as I have a special interest in the flower business, I was disappointed that I could not go to more of them. Unfortunately, I normally work late on Wednesday nights, so I was not able to attend any of the other lectures. Do you have any plans to offer future events such as this that will be scheduled on a variety of days and times so that more people can attend?

Sincerely,

Hiroji Iwao

---

1. What is mentioned in the first e-mail about Findley Community Centre?
(A) It plans to hire a marketing company to advertise its services.
(B) It is having difficulty finding lecturers willing to give speeches.
(C) It invites vendors to come on-site to sell products to attendees.
(D) It has held several of the lecture-series events in past years.

2. What can be concluded about Mr. Bockman?
(A) He approved a financial gift for the Wednesday lecture series.
(B) He gives legal advice to international companies.
(C) He meets with Ms. Harpenden regularly.
(D) He will teach a class at a community center.

3. What is indicated about the lecture series?
(A) It requires a fee to attend.
(B) It includes free food and drinks.
(C) Its original location was changed.
(D) Its target audience is lawyers.

4. Whose presentation did Mr. Iwao most likely attend?
(A) Ms. Coulomb's
(B) Mr. Carrel's
(C) Mr. Khatana's
(D) Ms. Rubio's

5. What problem does Mr. Iwao mention?
(A) He arrived late to an event.
(B) He did not receive the item he ordered.
(C) He is usually busy on Wednesday evenings.
(D) His work does not offer much variety.

Questions 6-10 refer to the following job listing and e-mails.

Copywriter – Curious Cat Analytics

Curious Cat Analytics is looking for a talented marketing copywriter to join our dynamic team. Our copywriters create concise, engaging content to promote our brand and services.

Job Responsibilities
- Collaborate with our marketing team by writing and editing content for articles, blog posts, and e-mails
- Maintain style guides while developing the voice of Curious Cat Analytics

Desired Qualifications
The ideal candidate should
- have at least 3 years of marketing experience,
- possess strong writing and editing skills, and
- enjoy working on a team in a fast-paced environment.

Interested job seekers should send a cover letter and résumé to Sara Chow, schow@cca.com.

From:	Jeba Singh <j.singh@swiftbox.com>
To:	Sara Chow <schow@cca.com>
Date:	December 18
Subject:	Copywriter position
Attachment:	🖇 Résumé

Dear Ms. Chow:

I am writing to apply for the position of marketing copywriter at Curious Cat Analytics. As a longtime travel writer and outdoor group excursion leader, I am confident that I would be a productive and innovative contributor to your team. Please find my résumé attached.

My travel blog, Wander Earth, has a large following and shows the effectiveness of my writing. It represents over a decade of travel writing experience. I continue to produce three or four new posts each week that showcase my strong curiosity about other cultures and customs.

I am also a strong team-builder. I spent three years coordinating programs and leading tour groups for SEA Travel, and I excel at forging relationships between people of different backgrounds while helping clients feel at home. I look forward to meeting with you to explore the contributions I could make to Curious Cat Analytics.

Sincerely,

Jeba Singh

To:	Jeba Singh <j.singh@swiftbox.com>
From:	Sara Chow <schow@cca.com>
Date:	December 26
Subject:	Your application

Dear Mr. Singh,

Thank you for applying for the copywriter position. Our hiring committee was impressed with your cover letter and résumé. Your reference, Ms. Dunbar, spoke particularly highly of you based on her experience leading backpacking excursions in Vietnam with you.

In moving you to the next step in your candidacy for this position, we request that you compose and submit a 500-word blog post on the importance of using search engine optimization to best reach a target market. Once we review your submission, we will reach out to you regarding a potential interview.

Kind regards,

Sara Chow

6. According to the job listing, what will Mr. Singh need to do if he is hired?
(A) Move to another city
(B) Work alone most of the time
(C) Post some of his work online
(D) Hold sales meetings with potential clients

7. What kind of work does Ms. Chow most likely do?
(A) Product development
(B) Financial analysis
(C) Staff recruitment
(D) Customer service

8. What could prevent Mr. Singh from being considered for the position?
(A) He submitted his cover letter late.
(B) His educational background is not strong enough.
(C) His cover letter was sent to the wrong person.
(D) He does not have enough marketing experience.

9. In the first e-mail, what is suggested about Mr. Singh?
(A) He has stopped writing his blog.
(B) He enjoys working with other people.
(C) He has never traveled abroad before.
(D) He has a background in data analytics.

10. What is most likely true about Ms. Dunbar?
(A) She is a hiring manager.
(B) She was recently promoted.
(C) She was Mr. Singh's colleague at SEA Travel.
(D) She is a copywriter for Curious Cat Analytics.

ETS TEST

Questions 11-15 refer to the following article, Web page, and interview transcription.

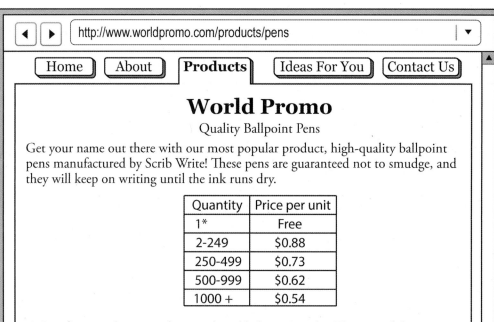

PROMOTIONAL ITEMS ATTRACT CUSTOMERS

Why should your company use promotional items? There are many reasons. Large corporations have used giveaways effectively for many years. Although some items, like sweatshirts, are too expensive for small businesses, you can reach many potential customers by giving out cheaper products, such as calendars. Including your logo on the item builds brand recognition; if your contact information is written on the item, it can then act as a business card.

When deciding what type of item to buy, be sure to choose something that customers will use daily for many months. Companies with bigger budgets can try a more creative product. Everyone likes to receive gifts. Make them work for your business!

---

http://www.worldpromo.com/products/pens

[Home] [About] [**Products**] [Ideas For You] [Contact Us]

World Promo
Quality Ballpoint Pens

Get your name out there with our most popular product, high-quality ballpoint pens manufactured by Scrib Write! These pens are guaranteed not to smudge, and they will keep on writing until the ink runs dry.

Quantity	Price per unit
1*	Free
2-249	$0.88
250-499	$0.73
500-999	$0.62
1000 +	$0.54

* One free sample per product can be added to any order. The cost of shipping is additional.

Return to the main Products page to view more World Promo products—shirts, cups, tote bags, calendars, and more.

Transcription of October 18 radio broadcast of *Business Today*. Host Nida Varma interviewed Al Rubin, owner of Renew with Rubin.

Ms. Varma: So tell me about your business.

Mr. Rubin: We design and install kitchens. We work with customers to create the look they want at a price they can afford.

Ms. Varma: How did you build your base of customers?

Mr. Rubin: Word-of-mouth, mostly. But we also attend home shows, trade shows, and local festivals.

Ms. Varma: You have been in business a long time, more than four decades. What advice do you have for new businesses?

Mr. Rubin: Your business may take time to become profitable. Make contacts. Give away items that people want to keep and use on a daily basis.

Ms. Varma: You mean like promotional giveaways?

Mr. Rubin: Exactly. In fact, we ordered 600 pens from World Promo to take to our last trade show, and we gave them all away. Many people came to our booth just for the pens! They may not be ready to install a new kitchen when we meet them, but if we give them a pen with our name, they will remember us when they're ready.

11. What does the article suggest that small businesses could give away?
    (A) Sweatshirts
    (B) Calendars
    (C) Business cards
    (D) Informational videos

12. What is indicated on the Web page?
    (A) Pens are the only item available at World Promo.
    (B) Various methods of payment are accepted.
    (C) Shipping is included in the purchase price.
    (D) Items are cheaper in larger quantities.

13. What is indicated about Mr. Rubin's business in the interview?
    (A) It organizes trade shows.
    (B) It plans to change its name.
    (C) It was profitable from the start.
    (D) It was founded over 40 years ago.

14. On what piece of advice do the author of the article and Mr. Rubin agree?
    (A) Wrap your item in gift packaging.
    (B) Keep logo designs as simple as possible.
    (C) Give out items that are used regularly.
    (D) Include a business card with your item.

15. How much did Renew with Rubin pay for each pen?
    (A) 54 cents
    (B) 62 cents
    (C) 73 cents
    (D) 88 cents

Questions 16-20 refer to the following notice, online form, and article.

MONTEGO BAY TRANSPORT CORPORATION
Introduction of Electronic Ticketing Machines

The Montego Bay Transport Corporation (Mobay Transcorp) is considering the introduction of electronic ticketing machines (ETMs) as well as a monthly bus pass. Both of these options for commuters would be similar to those currently used by the Kingston Urban Transit Authority (KUTA) in the country's capital. Marking five decades of service just last month, Mobay Transcorp desires to improve its interactions with customers as well as provide more convenient ticketing.

The proposed introduction date of the ETMs and monthly bus pass is 1 October. Residents are invited to view details of the proposed initiatives and submit comments and suggestions at www.mbtc.com.jm/etmprop.

As all comments will be made public, respondents are advised to omit personal data from their comments or suggestions. Those wishing to include confidential information should submit their comments on paper, addressed to Denise Samuda, Communications Director, Montego Bay Transport Corporation, 123 Henderson Road, Montego Bay. Electronic as well as paper submissions must be received by 30 March at 11:59 P.M.

---

www.mbtc.com.jm/etmprop   🗕 🗖 X

Name:

Orlando Grange

Date:

9 March

Comments or complaints:

I have experienced firsthand the unintended consequences that may come with the introduction of ETMs. Last month I was in Kingston for a family gathering, and I took a bus operated by the Kingston Urban Transit Authority (KUTA), which just last year had introduced ETMs. KUTA drivers are required to punch in certain codes into the ETM before a passenger can be issued a ticket. But since the ETM on the bus I was on had malfunctioned, the driver had to punch in those codes repeatedly for quite a few passengers. As a result, I arrived ten minutes later than planned at that gathering. Imagine how the delay might have affected me had I been going to a job interview. I understand, moreover, that repair of the equipment tends to be time-consuming, particularly when technicians lack adequate training to perform repairs. I therefore urge Mobay Transcorp to stick to the current method of issuing bus tickets.

(Submit)

Mobay Transcorp to Overhaul Electronic Ticketing System

MONTEGO BAY (24 September)—On 1 December, Mobay Transcorp will debut electronic ticketing machines (ETMs) on its buses. The company is making this change despite concerns expressed by local citizens who worry that the machines are a costly investment that offers little benefit. Many of the comments Mobay Transcorp received from the public referenced problems that the Kingston Urban Transit Authority (KUTA) is experiencing with its own ETM system.

Mobay Transcorp Communications Director Denise Samuda stated that the company has implemented a set of measures to minimize the problems ETMs may pose.

To reduce wear and tear on the equipment and to further simplify the ticketing process, the company will introduce daily, weekly, and monthly bus passes. Moreover, company technicians have received extensive training in ETM repair to ensure that any equipment failure is addressed in a timely fashion.

Mobay Transcorp has also entered into a partnership with the Dutch multinational company Damsko Integrated Systems, which will supply Mobay Transcorp with new ETMs every three years. In April of next year, both companies will evaluate the efficacy of the new ticketing system and make adjustments as needed.

16. What is one purpose of the notice?
(A) To announce the launch of a Web site
(B) To invite public commentary
(C) To address employee concerns
(D) To announce bus route changes

17. According to the notice, what did Mobay Transcorp recently do?
(A) It celebrated its fiftieth year of service.
(B) It changed the way it records data.
(C) It partnered with KUTA.
(D) It decided to hire Montego Bay residents only.

18. What is true about Mr. Grange?
(A) He regularly attends conferences.
(B) He recently had a job interview.
(C) He experienced a travel delay.
(D) He used to be a KUTA bus driver.

19. What is suggested about Mobay Transcorp?
(A) It has replaced its communication director.
(B) It will introduce ETMs later than originally planned.
(C) It has increased the price of its bus passes.
(D) It has signed a two-year contract with Damsko Integrated Systems.

20. What concern of Mr. Grange did Mobay Transcorp address?
(A) Wrong codes
(B) Outdated equipment
(C) Excessive costs
(D) Staff training

Questions 21-25 refer to the following Web page, press release, and article.

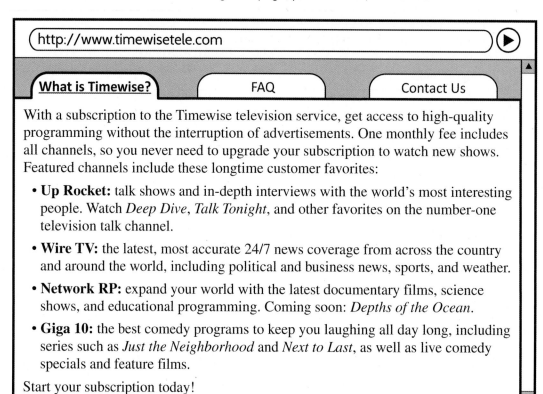

http://www.timewisetele.com ▶

| **What is Timewise?** | FAQ | Contact Us |

With a subscription to the Timewise television service, get access to high-quality programming without the interruption of advertisements. One monthly fee includes all channels, so you never need to upgrade your subscription to watch new shows. Featured channels include these longtime customer favorites:

- **Up Rocket:** talk shows and in-depth interviews with the world's most interesting people. Watch *Deep Dive*, *Talk Tonight*, and other favorites on the number-one television talk channel.

- **Wire TV:** the latest, most accurate 24/7 news coverage from across the country and around the world, including political and business news, sports, and weather.

- **Network RP:** expand your world with the latest documentary films, science shows, and educational programming. Coming soon: *Depths of the Ocean*.

- **Giga 10:** the best comedy programs to keep you laughing all day long, including series such as *Just the Neighborhood* and *Next to Last*, as well as live comedy specials and feature films.

Start your subscription today!

For immediate release

March 18—WTB Studios has announced that its hit series *What's Here* has been renewed for another season. For the past decade, the popular show has kept its many fans laughing with its quirky characters and sharp wit. Jenna Gervis and Anwar Saeed return as the hilarious main characters, Anna and Lucas. The show will also welcome a new star, Dennis Lam, who plays the couple's new next-door neighbor. The season premiere is scheduled for September 9 at 8:00 P.M. and is available through the television subscription service Timewise.

What's Dennis Lam Doing?

April 5—Dennis Lam has been busy. After moving to Hollywood nearly ten years ago, he landed the leading role as a basketball star on the popular television show *Next to Last*. After several seasons, he left that role to explore other opportunities. Mr. Lam's talents have proved to be diverse. He starred in two feature-length films and then went on to write a play for the Sencha Theater. Mr. Lam recently announced that he will leave his current job at Up Rocket's *Deep Dive* at the end of the month. He plans to return to acting with a role created just for him on the popular show *What's Here*.

"I am looking forward to acting again," Mr. Lam said. "It is such a great show, and I cannot wait to be part of it." Look for Mr. Lam this fall in the season premiere of *What's Here*.

—by Catalina Barros

21. What is the purpose of the information on the Web page?
(A) To attract new customers
(B) To promote an offer to upgrade
(C) To sell television advertising time
(D) To announce recently added channels

22. On what channel will Timewise most likely broadcast *What's Here* ?
(A) Up Rocket
(B) Wire TV
(C) Network RP
(D) Giga 10

23. According to the press release, how will *What's Here* be different in the fall?
(A) It will be set in Hollywood.
(B) It will introduce a new character.
(C) It will be on television after Deep Dive.
(D) It will change its broadcast time.

24. According to the article, why did Mr. Lam leave *Next to Last* ?
(A) His role on the show ended.
(B) His family moved to another city.
(C) He wanted to try other jobs in his field.
(D) He decided to pursue a basketball career.

25. What most likely is Mr. Lam's current job?
(A) Talk show host
(B) Movie director
(C) News reporter
(D) Theater manager

ETS TEST

Questions 26-30 refer to the following e-mail, invoice, and review.

To:	Liam Dugan
From:	Deirdre Corrigan
Date:	Thursday, 15 September, 9:15 A.M.
Subject:	Shopping
Attachment:	📎 Invoice

Dear Chef Liam,

Please find attached my invoice from the Finnan Street Market for this morning's shopping trip. The market was completely sold out of the parsnips for this evening's soup, so we will have to switch to carrot soup instead. I'm heading over now to McKeown's Grocery to purchase the remaining ingredient for the carrot soup. By the way, Finnan Street Market was selling leafy greens at a marked-down price, so I bought 5 kilos each of two different kinds. I hope you'll be able to find a use for them. I found everything else you requested.

See you this evening.

Best,

Deirdre

Finnan Street Market
Invoice

Purchaser: Café de Liam
Date: 15 September

Item	Amount	Price per Kilo	Total
Spinach	5 kilos	€1.00	€5.00
Green leaf lettuce	5 kilos	€1.00	€5.00
Figs	18 kilos	€4.00	€72.00
Red potatoes	20 kilos	€2.00	€40.00
Carrots	25 kilos	€1.50	€37.50
Onions	30 kilos	€0.95	€28.50
Grand Total			**€188.00**

Restaurant Review: Café de Liam Continues to Impress

by Bridget Traynor

KILLARNEY (16 September)—Café de Liam has been a hidden gem of the Killarney dining scene for a long time. Now, thanks to Chef Liam's best-selling vegetarian cookbook, the restaurant has begun to see increased table reservations and long lines. I visited the café last night to see if the quality of its offerings had suffered as a result. I am happy to report that despite its newfound fame, Café de Liam has lost none of its attention to quality.

My starter of fresh baked bread with butter and fig jam was excellent, and the curried carrot soup with coconut yogurt was especially flavourful. I also enjoyed the main course: a hearty corn soufflé with roasted grapes. But the real showstopper was the date cake with caramel sauce. I never would have expected such a simple dish to be so delicious.

I wholeheartedly recommend Café de Liam for a wonderful night out. Reservations can be made by calling the café at 020 912 0155 or by visiting the Web site at cafedeliam.ie.

26. Why did Ms. Corrigan send the e-mail?
(A) To request a recipe from the chef
(B) To inform the chef of a problem
(C) To give her opinion of a store
(D) To offer a cooking suggestion

27. According to the invoice, how many kilograms of onions did the café purchase?
(A) Eighteen
(B) Twenty
(C) Twenty-five
(D) Thirty

28. What item was sold at a discounted price?
(A) Spinach
(B) Figs
(C) Potatoes
(D) Carrots

29. What ingredient for the carrot soup did Ms. Corrigan most likely obtain from McKeown's Grocery?
(A) Butter
(B) Jam
(C) Yogurt
(D) Carrots

30. What was the reviewer's favorite dish?
(A) The starter
(B) The soup
(C) The main course
(D) The dessert

Questions 31-35 refer to the following notice and e-mails.

Prepare for Winter Storms and Be Safe!

Attention all Janz Engineering employees:

We are entering the coldest part of the season and weather conditions can become challenging. When a major winter storm is forecast within a projected 24-hour period, remember to take laptop computers and any critical documents home with you as you leave the workplace. This is in case travel conditions become unsafe as a storm progresses.

In addition, make every effort to reschedule meetings or plan to conduct video meetings. There are several options that may be taken based on individual situations. The options are: travel to the office if it is safe to do so, work from home, or use an earned vacation day. Above all, stay safe and keep your immediate supervisor informed of your plan.

E-mail

To:	Faride Adeh <fadeh@janzengineering.com>
From:	Darryl Peterson <dpeterson@janzengineering.com>
Date:	January 7
Subject:	Schedule update

Hello, Ms. Adeh,

Per company policy, I just wanted to let you know that because of the weather predicted for tomorrow, I am planning to work from home. Also, how would you like to proceed with the meeting that you and I have scheduled for tomorrow? Would you like me to arrange a videoconference, or do you want to postpone the meeting to another day? My schedule is open on Monday, Tuesday, Thursday, and Friday next week.

Also, I was wondering about the Farrow River project now that Nick Garrity has left our company. What is the status of hiring his replacement? Is the project on track to be completed in May?

Thanks,

Darryl Peterson

```
┌─────────────────────────────────────────────────────────────┐
│ ▍▍══════════════════════ *E-mail* ═══════════════════════▍▍ │
├─────────────────────────────────────────────────────────────┤
│  To:      │ Darryl Peterson <dpeterson@janzengineering.com>  │
│  From:    │ Faride Adeh <fadeh@janzengineering.com>          │
│  Date:    │ January 7                                        │
│  Subject: │ RE: Schedule update                              │
├─────────────────────────────────────────────────────────────┤
│  Hi, Mr. Peterson,                                            │
│                                                               │
│  Let's plan to meet in person next week. I will be in the     │
│  office only on Tuesday and Wednesday because I need to make  │
│  several off-site visits. You ask a good question about the   │
│  status of the Farrow River project. We have interviewed      │
│  some job candidates and have narrowed the search down to     │
│  three individuals. A job offer will be extended soon, with   │
│  a new project manager on board by the end of the month, so   │
│  the project will proceed as originally planned.              │
│                                                               │
│  Faride Adeh                                                  │
└─────────────────────────────────────────────────────────────┘
```

31. What are employees asked to do in case of forecasts for severe weather?
- (A) Leave important paperwork at the office
- (B) Plan to arrive to work early
- (C) Take computers home
- (D) Use public transportation

32. Who most likely is Ms. Adeh?
- (A) A department supervisor
- (B) A company trainee
- (C) A Janz Engineering client
- (D) A payroll coordinator

33. What is indicated about Mr. Garrity?
- (A) He will oversee work at project sites.
- (B) He is a former employee of Janz Engineering.
- (C) He has completed an important project.
- (D) He is interviewing prospective managers.

34. When will Mr. Peterson and Ms. Adeh most likely hold their next meeting?
- (A) On Monday
- (B) On Tuesday
- (C) On Thursday
- (D) On Friday

35. In the second e-mail, what is indicated about the Farrow River project?
- (A) It will be completed as expected.
- (B) It has become costly to the company.
- (C) It involves an unusual engineering design.
- (D) It will begin in May.

ETS

FINAL TEST

READING TEST

In the Reading test, you will read a variety of texts and answer several different types of reading comprehension questions. The entire Reading test will last 75 minutes. There are three parts, and directions are given for each part. You are encouraged to answer as many questions as possible within the time allowed.

You must mark your answers on the separate answer sheet. Do not write your answers in your test book.

PART 5

Directions: A word or phrase is missing in each of the sentences below. Four answer choices are given below each sentence. Select the best answer to complete the sentence. Then mark the letter (A), (B), (C), or (D) on your answer sheet.

101. Ms. Yu will not be attending the sales meeting because ------- has another commitment that day.
(A) she
(B) her
(C) hers
(D) herself

102. The Jin Zan Group received Ms. Ellibe's application and will contact her about the position ------- .
(A) shortly
(B) shorter
(C) shortness
(D) short

103. The Darel Company ------- unexpectedly strong revenue growth in the third quarter.
(A) wrote
(B) insisted
(C) commented
(D) reported

104. The Curls Galore hair product line will be on store ------- in April.
(A) shelf
(B) shelves
(C) shelved
(D) to shelve

105. To reserve a conference room or to find out which rooms are -------, contact Building Services.
(A) widespread
(B) consistent
(C) instructive
(D) available

106. Cardholders purchasing tickets with their reward points should refer ------- the list of restrictions on the Web site.
(A) in
(B) at
(C) by
(D) to

107. Experienced hikers are ------- able to navigate the Hoping Mountain trail system.
(A) softly
(B) easily
(C) sharply
(D) precisely

108. The CEO at Hartford Produce ------- that standardizing the protocols at all storage facilities should be a top priority.
(A) was believed
(B) to believe
(C) believes
(D) a belief

109. In honor of Mr. Shin's -------, the team plans to gather at The Center Bistro at noon on Friday.

(A) revision
(B) adjustment
(C) refinement
(D) promotion

110. CEO Alma Cabanag will meet with ------- administration team next Tuesday.

(A) we
(B) us
(C) our
(D) ours

111. Following their planning session, the advertising specialists at Hobart Media Group ------- their best ideas for the client.

(A) measured
(B) afforded
(C) based
(D) summarized

112. ------- for the conference begins on May 1 and can be completed on our Web site.

(A) Register
(B) Registers
(C) Registered
(D) Registration

113. Andover Software is seeking qualified candidates ------- the position of quality assurance analyst.

(A) as
(B) for
(C) out
(D) from

114. The design for the T-shirts was ------- complete when the client called with a last-minute change.

(A) nearest
(B) nearness
(C) nearly
(D) nearer

115. ------- loading the truck, the driver must take the permit that allows for transport of materials beyond the border.

(A) Instead
(B) Whether
(C) After
(D) Since

116. Each month, the employee ------- has the highest sales figures will receive a prize.

(A) why
(B) where
(C) who
(D) whose

117. If you encounter any issues when using the software application, notify the technical team -------.

(A) commonly
(B) formerly
(C) unnecessarily
(D) immediately

118. Passengers are ------- to bring video cameras and binoculars on the whale watch.

(A) encouragement
(B) encouraged
(C) encouraging
(D) encouragingly

119. All visitors must present valid ------- at the front desk before entering the building.

(A) communication
(B) reception
(C) identification
(D) graduation

120. Mr. Okabe is hoping to see ------- results in the next data report by Mori Analytics.

(A) improve
(B) improved
(C) improves
(D) to improve

Go on to the next page

121. The new employee evaluation process simplifies determining ------- an employee is meeting standards.
    (A) whether
    (B) due to
    (C) so that
    (D) either

122. Cleaning the parts ------- increases both the brewing quality and life span of the coffee maker.
    (A) periodically
    (B) period
    (C) periodic
    (D) periods

123. We offer a range of high-quality promotional items, including ------- pens, brochures, and stickers.
    (A) customize
    (B) customizes
    (C) customizer
    (D) customized

124. Weissinger Realty plans to open three new office locations ------- the next several months.
    (A) within
    (B) going
    (C) whichever
    (D) most

125. Clean Suds Company respects the environment by employing scientists ------- nonpolluting soaps.
    (A) to formulate
    (B) formulate
    (C) will formulate
    (D) have formulated

126. Beginning in June, Finch Airways will allow the use of mobile phones ------- in flight.
    (A) along
    (B) while
    (C) beside
    (D) over

127. Turnet Tea's new location on Gellam Lane is much more ------- than its original Bank Street store.
    (A) careful
    (B) urgent
    (C) spacious
    (D) gradual

128. Biolmaz, Inc., is ------- to enhance the online customer-service experience by adding a live chat feature.
    (A) regarding
    (B) viewing
    (C) looking
    (D) serving

129. The Roig Foundation has ------- announced that it will fund the town's reading project.
    (A) plus
    (B) just
    (C) but
    (D) prior

130. Book publisher Pitner Press quickly embraced new trends in popular fiction and ------- led the industry in sales last year.
    (A) however
    (B) despite
    (C) therefore
    (D) unless

Directions: Read the texts that follow. A word, phrase, or sentence is missing in parts of each text. Four answer choices for each question are given below the text. Select the best answer to complete the text. Then mark the letter (A), (B), (C), or (D) on your answer sheet.

Questions 131-134 refer to the following e-mail.

To: All Staff
From: Rosita Gomez
Date: September 30
Re: Shredding event

To help protect your sensitive information, we have arranged for an on-site shredding event with Van Winkle Shredding on October 30. This ------- is being offered to all employees free of
131.
charge. Before Van Winkle's visit, you will receive up to three boxes for any personal papers.
------- . Place them outside of ------- office no later than noon on October 30. Between 1:00
132.   133.
and 2:00 P.M., employees of Van Winkle will go around the building and ------- your materials
134.
for shredding. For confidential company documents, we request that you continue to use the secure blue bins in the photocopier areas.

Best,

Rosita

131. (A) service
     (B) training
     (C) experience
     (D) performance

132. (A) Information breaches can be costly.
     (B) Please use only the boxes provided.
     (C) Another shredding event will take place in May.
     (D) Van Winkle Shredding has been in business for over forty years.

133. (A) his
     (B) her
     (C) your
     (D) their

134. (A) produce
     (B) develop
     (C) promote
     (D) collect

Go on to the next page →

Questions 135-138 refer to the following advertisement.

At Fawnville Wholesale Linens, providing people with a good night's sleep is our business.

------- , we sell only to hotels, inns, and resorts. But throughout the month of April, we open
135.

our online store to the general public. This is a great opportunity for consumers we do not

typically serve ------- on our high-quality sheets, pillows, comforters, and blankets. We offer a
136.

variety of sizes, colors, and materials. ------- . So take advantage of this offer to outfit every
137.

------- in your home with our luxurious products!
138.

135. (A) Nevertheless
     (B) However
     (C) Normally
     (D) Accordingly

136. (A) to stock up
     (B) stocking up
     (C) it stocked up
     (D) that stocks up

137. (A) This year marks our tenth anniversary.
     (B) Please ensure that all items are well
         packaged.
     (C) Our products are scented with natural
         blends of pure essential oils.
     (D) You are guaranteed to find whatever
         suits your style and preference.

138. (A) bed
     (B) floor
     (C) table
     (D) window

Questions 139-142 refer to the following e-mail.

To: Ramesch Nandiraju <rnandiraju@tsag.in>

From: Pratima Dharmapuri <pratima@dharmapurievents.in>

Date: 21 February

Subject: Gym rental

Dear Mr. Nandiraju,

I would like to know if Towering Sports and Gymnasium is available to be rented. I ------- an
139.
event planner, and one of my corporate clients is interested in holding the company's annual

family event at a gym and picnic area. ------- , my client is looking for a facility with basketball
140.
courts for games and other indoor and outdoor activities. ------- .
141.

My client would like to hold the event on either the second or third Sunday in May. Please let

me know if this plan is ------- . If so, please let me know what the cost would be for an event
142.
that runs from 11 A.M. to 4 P.M.

Sincerely,

Pratima Dharmapuri

Dharmapuri Event Planning

---

139. (A) am
(B) was
(C) have been
(D) will be

140. (A) As you expected
(B) Unfortunately
(C) In any case
(D) Specifically

141. (A) Please contact me to discuss your
proposal.
(B) Yours meets those criteria perfectly.
(C) They are considering investing in your
business.
(D) We would be happy to coordinate your
special event.

142. (A) better
(B) possible
(C) avoidable
(D) underway

Go on to the next page

Questions 143-146 refer to the following letter.

Winslow Financial Advisers • 4215 31st Street • New York, NY 10003

November 1

Wendy Gendelman
22 Avenue E
New York, NY 10009

Dear Ms. Gendelman,

It is very important to safeguard the money you earn. ------- the knowledge and tools provided
143.
by Winslow Financial Advisers, you can manage your money to support your lifestyle and save

for the future. ------- . Using the information you provide, we create a personalized financial
144.
plan to enable you to safely spread out your investments. We explain all the ------- to you.
145.
These include investments, savings, insurance, and tax strategies.

Contact Winslow Financial Advisers now at (212) 555-0100 to get started making safe, -------
146.
financial decisions.

Sincerely,

Barak Kamara, Financial Adviser

143. (A) Yet
     (B) With
     (C) Except
     (D) Besides

144. (A) We listen to your needs.
     (B) Our company helps many new clients.
     (C) Let us tell you about affordable
         housing.
     (D) Saving money is very hard.

145. (A) studies
     (B) options
     (C) changes
     (D) problems

146. (A) information
     (B) informing
     (C) informs
     (D) informed

PART 7

Directions: In this part you will read a selection of texts, such as magazine and newspaper articles, e-mails, and instant messages. Each text or set of texts is followed by several questions. Select the best answer for each question and mark the letter (A), (B), (C), or (D) on your answer sheet.

Questions 147-148 refer to the following e-mail.

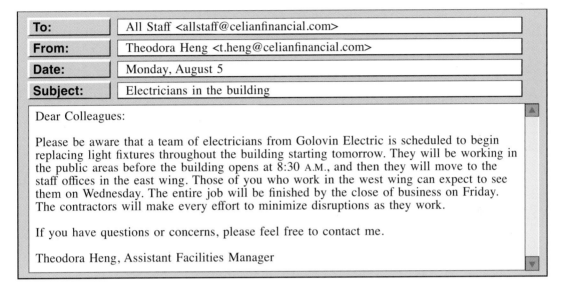

To:	All Staff <allstaff@celianfinancial.com>
From:	Theodora Heng <t.heng@celianfinancial.com>
Date:	Monday, August 5
Subject:	Electricians in the building

Dear Colleagues:

Please be aware that a team of electricians from Golovin Electric is scheduled to begin replacing light fixtures throughout the building starting tomorrow. They will be working in the public areas before the building opens at 8:30 A.M., and then they will move to the staff offices in the east wing. Those of you who work in the west wing can expect to see them on Wednesday. The entire job will be finished by the close of business on Friday. The contractors will make every effort to minimize disruptions as they work.

If you have questions or concerns, please feel free to contact me.

Theodora Heng, Assistant Facilities Manager

---

147. What is indicated about the scheduled work?

(A) It will affect the east wing only.
(B) It will begin before the building opens for the day.
(C) It will be carried out by staff in Ms. Heng's department.
(D) It will require employees to move to a different location.

148. When will the work be completed?

(A) On Monday
(B) On Tuesday
(C) On Wednesday
(D) On Friday

Go on to the next page

Stay at the Palm Frond Motel

The Bentson family has been welcoming guests to the Palm Frond Motel for generations. Located just a two-minute drive from U.S. Highway 40, the Palm Frond Motel features updated rooms with comfortable beds, large-screen televisions, and coffee makers. In addition to free Wi-Fi and parking, we offer on-site laundry service at affordable rates. Small pets are welcome for an additional fee.

Call 760-555-0157 or reserve online at reservations@palmfrondmotel.com.

149. What is suggested about the Palm Frond Motel?

(A) It has operated for many years.
(B) It features a full-service restaurant.
(C) It leases two-room suites.
(D) It hosts business conferences.

150. Where is the Palm Frond Motel?

(A) Near an airport
(B) Close to a highway
(C) At a theme park
(D) In a downtown area

151. What do guests have to pay extra for?

(A) Wi-Fi access
(B) Coffee service
(C) Pet accommodation
(D) Vehicle parking

Questions 152-153 refer to the following book proposal.

Book Proposal Overview

Title: *The Architect of Heinsburg*
Author: Celeste Serre

Description: This book will be based on a story I covered as a reporter for Channel 10 News. It traces the life of Mariana Dell, a woman whose family moved to the city of Heinsburg in 1897. Her parents bought a farm on the outskirts of the city and became active in local politics. Ms. Dell eventually was elected mayor of Heinsburg and spearheaded the creation of the city's famous botanical gardens. Ms. Dell is a crucial historical figure, but she is not well-known. My research will involve municipal records, old newspaper articles archived at the Heinsburg Public Library, and interviews with local historians.

152. What most likely is Ms. Serre's profession?

(A) Librarian
(B) Architect
(C) Gardener
(D) Journalist

153. What type of book is being proposed?

(A) A biography
(B) A mystery novel
(C) A travel guide
(D) A series of personal essays

Go on to the next page

```
*E-mail*
```

To:	Marketing Team Distribution List
From:	Eric Mushimba
Subject:	Vacation
Date:	June 12

Dear Marketing Team:

I will be on vacation beginning on June 26 and returning on July 10. I will have limited access to the Internet and will not be checking e-mail during this time.

In terms of support while I am away, Yenay Chen will be covering for me. Ms. Chen is up-to-date on our ongoing projects, and she will be answering my e-mails and voice messages. Please contact her directly with any unresolved client issues. I will inform key clients of my absence, and my out-of-office e-mail response will include relevant contact information.

Good luck on the Datafine Technologies presentation. I look forward to hearing about it when I return.

Best,

Eric Mushimba
Marketing Director

154. Why did Mr. Mushimba send the e-mail?

(A) To inform his team about an Internet disruption

(B) To provide an update on the Datafine Technologies presentation

(C) To explain a new vacation policy

(D) To describe the plan for when he is out of the office

155. What is indicated about Ms. Chen?

(A) She will soon return from vacation.

(B) She prefers voice messages to e-mails.

(C) She is familiar with current team projects.

(D) She recruited a major new client.

Questions 156-157 refer to the following online chat discussion.

Mayumi Tamaki (9:20 A.M.)
Good morning. We've interviewed five people for the accountant position.
Two of them will have follow-up interviews next week. Robert Fletcher strongly
prefers one candidate, and I'm leaning toward the other. Would you like to sit in
on both interviews?

Henry Crouse (9:22 A.M.)
If I'm here. I'm going to Brussels tomorrow. I'll be back next Wednesday.
When are the interviews?

Mayumi Tamaki (9:23 A.M.)
We don't have exact dates for them yet, but I can schedule both around your trip.
We'd really like to get your input before we make a final decision.

Henry Crouse (9:24 A.M.)
Perfect.

156. What is indicated about Ms. Tamaki?

(A) She disagrees with Mr. Fletcher about
an applicant.
(B) She wants to review more applications.
(C) She has asked Mr. Fletcher to go to
Brussels on business.
(D) She is preparing a new job
advertisement.

157. At 9:24 A.M., what does Mr. Crouse most
likely mean when he writes, "Perfect"?

(A) He agrees to schedule a meeting with
Mr. Fletcher.
(B) He appreciates being included in the
interviews.
(C) He is available on the date suggested.
(D) He is confirming his travel plans.

Go on to the next page

Questions 158-160 refer to the following e-mail.

To:	Millbury Office Staff
From:	Technology Team
Date:	Monday, May 18
Subject:	Network server

Please be advised that on Friday, May 22, the server at the Millbury office will be taken off-line for repair. As a result, employees at this location will be unable to access the Internet or any of the files on that server.

Millbury office staff will be allowed to work from home that day. Alternatively, staff can be accommodated at our Northborough office. Please inform your manager no later than Wednesday, May 20, which option you will choose. We anticipate that everything will run properly on Monday, May 25.

The Technology Team

158. Who is affected by the problem mentioned in the e-mail?

(A) Only remote employees
(B) Only technology team members
(C) Millbury office employees
(D) Northborough office employees

159. What is provided in the e-mail?

(A) An apology for an inconvenience
(B) Instructions for employees
(C) Appreciation for contributions
(D) An estimate for cost of services

160. The word "run" in paragraph 2, line 3, is closest in meaning to

(A) function
(B) hurry
(C) flow
(D) change

To:	Research and Development Division
From:	Eva Tangen
Date:	July 20
Subject:	Teamwork

Hello, everyone,

I wanted to express my gratitude to you all for hosting my farewell party today. What a lovely surprise! — [1] —. It was a reminder of what I have enjoyed the most about working for Sanmerke these past 14 years: the extraordinary team. — [2] —.

As difficult as it is to say goodbye, I am excited to begin a new phase of my career, moving into the regulation side of our industry. — [3] —. Since the responsibilities at my new post are related to the health-care work we do here, I know I will continue to meet with many of you in the future.

— [4] —. My personal e-mail address will be the best way to reach me: eva.tangen@lmnmail.com.

Warmly,

Eva Tangen
Vice President of Research and Development
Sanmerke Industries

161. What is the purpose of the e-mail?

(A) To thank colleagues for hosting an event
(B) To remind employees of a company regulation
(C) To announce the hiring of a new employee
(D) To request assistance with a project

162. What is indicated about Ms. Tangen?

(A) She is retiring.
(B) She has worked in health care for over a decade.
(C) She is the founder of Sanmerke Industries.
(D) She will be managing a new branch office of Sanmerke Industries.

163. In which of the positions marked [1], [2], [3], and [4] does the following sentence best belong?

"I hope to stay in touch."

(A) [1]
(B) [2]
(C) [3]
(D) [4]

Go on to the next page

Lehine Partners, one of the nation's largest sports law firms, is searching for a talented and driven social media expert. We specialize in sports law, particularly as it applies to athletes and contract negotiations. We want our social media presence to reflect our legal expertise as well as our engagement in the sports industry. — [1] —. Candidates with a background in both fields will be given priority in the hiring process.— [2] —.

Candidates must have a bachelor's degree in communications or journalism and a minimum of five years of professional experience in social media. — [3] —. Familiarity with a range of sports is preferred but not required. Knowledge of the legal field is a plus. Interested candidates should send a résumé and a cover letter to admin@lehinepartners.com. — [4] —. Personal interviews with select candidates will be conducted before a final decision is made.

---

164. What is indicated about Lehine Partners?

(A) It is a relatively small law firm.
(B) It represents athletes in contract negotiations.
(C) It specializes in only a few sports.
(D) It must update its social media policy.

165. What is a requirement of the position?

(A) A law degree
(B) A background in sports
(C) A prior job in social media
(D) A familiarity with legal procedures

166. How should interested candidates apply for the job?

(A) By attaching application materials to an e-mail
(B) By filling out an online application form
(C) By uploading work samples to a Web site
(D) By signing up for a personal interview

167. In which of the positions marked [1], [2], [3], and [4] does the following sentence best belong?

"Please be sure to include contact information for two professional references."

(A) [1]
(B) [2]
(C) [3]
(D) [4]

MEMO

To: All staff
From: Keith Ahern
Date: May 4
Subject: Reminder

Our office moving day is coming up this Friday, May 8. Employees are responsible for packing their own files, office supplies, books, and personal items, such as any artwork or plants. Computer towers, monitors, and keyboards can remain where they are; the moving team will pack these. Please have all boxes packed and marked by the end of the workday on Thursday, May 7. Ensure that your name and new location are clear. We will dispose of any unpacked items on Friday morning.

The day of the move is a company holiday, so enjoy the long weekend. We expect you to be in the office as usual on Monday, May 11. Please use that day to unpack your belongings and break down boxes. Make sure you leave any empty boxes outside your workstation or office to be picked up by maintenance staff.

Keith Ahern
Office Manager, Fambisa Public Relations

---

168. What is the purpose of the memo?

(A) To request volunteers for a special project
(B) To describe an upgrade to company equipment
(C) To announce plans for an upcoming relocation
(D) To remind employees of a scheduled cleaning

169. What items should employees leave in place?

(A) Books
(B) Electronic equipment
(C) Office supplies
(D) Artwork

170. The word "marked" in paragraph 1, line 5, is closest in meaning to

(A) labeled
(B) revised
(C) graded
(D) proposed

171. According to the memo, when will employees have a day off?

(A) On Monday
(B) On Tuesday
(C) On Thursday
(D) On Friday

Go on to the next page

Bella Bottorf (8:45 A.M.) Hi, everyone. I have created a folder called "Prospective Clients" on our shared drive. It includes a list of our potential clients and the slide presentation that gives an overview of our Internet marketing services.

Greg Ybarra (8:50 A.M.) I saw that, but when I click on it, I'm redirected to the folder where all my personal documents are.

Katie Armbruster (8:54 A.M.) That's strange, Greg. I'm able to open the folder.

Greg Ybarra (8:56 A.M.) It seems I don't have authorization to do so. Maybe the file sharing settings need to be changed.

Katie Armbruster (9:01 A.M.) Greg, I just e-mailed you a copy of the slide presentation. You might need it for your upcoming meeting with Chronos Jewelers.

Greg Ybarra (9:03 A.M.) Actually, I may need some additional documents for that meeting, but I'll let you know.

Bella Bottorf (9:05 A.M.) Greg, you'd know best. I know you've already spoken with them a few times.

Katie Armbruster (9:08 A.M.) Well, what about sharing data from our marketing campaign for Bech Fashion? I have a great graph showing their revenue both before and after they partnered with us. Since they're my client, I could ask them if we could share that graph.

Greg Ybarra (9:12 A.M.) Thank you. That's exactly the kind of detail I need to present to Chronos Jewelers to get them on board with us.

Katie Armbruster (9:14 A.M.) OK! I'll message Bech Fashion today.

172. For what type of company do the writers most likely work?

(A) A technical support services firm
(B) A marketing agency
(C) An Internet service provider
(D) A software development company

173. What is Mr. Ybarra having difficulty doing?

(A) Contacting a client
(B) Accessing a folder
(C) Researching a product
(D) Remembering a password

174. At 9:05 A.M., what does Ms. Bottorf most likely mean when she writes, "I know you've already spoken with them a few times"?

(A) A decision is taking longer than anticipated.
(B) Sometimes it is necessary to send multiple reminders to potential clients.
(C) Mr. Ybarra should try to gather information more efficiently.
(D) Chronos Jewelers is already familiar with the company's services.

175. Why will Ms. Armbruster contact one of her clients?

(A) To renegotiate a contract
(B) To relate some positive news
(C) To confirm some recent revenue statistics
(D) To ask for permission to share some information

Go on to the next page

Questions 176-180 refer to the following memo and e-mail.

MEMO

To: Sales Team
From: Sarah Lancers, Sales Manager
Date: March 30
Subject: Philabux Corporation announcement

All members of the sales team are required to attend a meeting on Wednesday, April 7, at 9:00 A.M. At that time, company president Adnan Mahmoudi will make an important announcement about the company's anticipated merger with Livas National in Dallas, Texas. He will also introduce a Dale Relocation Services representative who will discuss the plan for the team's seamless move to Dallas.

The meeting will take place in the Arnett Building conference room. Attendance is mandatory.

E-mail

From:	dan@dalerelocation.com
Sent:	April 10
To:	slancers@philabux.com
Subject:	Appointment

Hello, Ms. Lancers:

As previously arranged, you have a scheduled appointment for a home inspection and sales consultation at 457 Oakland Street in Philadelphia on Wednesday, April 12, at 9:15 A.M. We will discuss pricing your house to sell quickly and make sure that no major repairs need to be completed before putting it on the market. Then we can talk about where to focus our search for your new home.

I appreciate your time and understand that your availability may change. If you need to reschedule this appointment, please call the office and speak with the receptionist directly.

We look forward to seeing you on April 12.

Sincerely,

Dan Wolenski
Dale Relocation Services
(301) 555-0186

176. What is indicated about Philabux Corporation?

(A) It is about to hire a new chief executive officer.
(B) It is likely to change its marketing strategy.
(C) It is planning to renovate its facilities.
(D) It is preparing to merge with another firm.

177. What does the memo state about the meeting?

(A) It is a monthly event.
(B) It will last for about an hour.
(C) It will be led by the head of the company.
(D) It will include several board members.

178. What is the purpose of the e-mail?

(A) To arrange a series of appointments
(B) To send a reminder
(C) To reschedule a meeting
(D) To verify contact information

179. In the e-mail, the word "appreciate" in paragraph 2, line 1, is closest in meaning to

(A) value
(B) increase
(C) comprehend
(D) applaud

180. What is suggested about Ms. Lancers?

(A) She has hired a company to make home repairs.
(B) She has a scheduling conflict on April 12.
(C) She is an employee of Dale Relocation Services.
(D) She will be relocating to Dallas.

Go on to the next page

Tamino Group

Company: Golden Crown Educational Consultants

Order Date: November 22   **Order Confirmation:** No. 432886

Product Number	Item	Cost	Quantity	Total	Delivery Method	Estimated Delivery Date
TG433	Jakex toner for Titan Star printer (model 433x)	$98.49	2 boxes	$196.98	Ground–expedited	November 25
TG214	Cakel paper (size A4)	$32.99	4 cases	$131.96	Ground–regular	November 29
TG558	Montan staples (standard size)	$3.49	6 packs	$20.94	Ground–economy	December 4
TG232	Perker paper clips (medium)	$2.49	12 boxes	$29.88	Ground–economy	December 4
		Shipping		$50.00		
		Total Cost		**$429.76**		

From:	Albert Huang <albert.huang@goldencrownec.com>
To:	Help Desk <help@taminogroup.com>
Date:	November 23 11:00 A.M.
Subject:	Order Number 432886

To Whom It May Concern:

I am sorry to trouble you, but apparently I made a few errors on my order. I spoke to a customer service representative on the phone earlier, and she told me to e-mail the help desk so you could confirm the changes I made with her and to ask you to put in the code to change my shipping method for one of the items.

This was my first time using your online ordering system, and I seem to have made the wrong printer selection from the menu. I need toner for the model 430x printer—not the 433x. Additionally, I would now like to speed up the paper order to "ground–expedited" so that it will arrive with the toner. Also, please add two more packs of staples for a total of eight packs, and adjust the total price of the order accordingly. Thank you for your assistance.

Regards,

Albert Huang, Office Manager
Golden Crown Educational Consultants

181. According to the invoice, when will the paper clips be delivered?

(A) On November 22
(B) On November 25
(C) On November 29
(D) On December 4

182. What is the purpose of the e-mail?

(A) To request confirmation of changes made to an order
(B) To cancel delivery of certain office supplies
(C) To order additional cases of paper
(D) To get information about the company's Web site

183. In the e-mail, the word "trouble" in paragraph 1, line 1, is closest in meaning to

(A) warn
(B) urge
(C) bother
(D) confuse

184. What is indicated about Mr. Huang?

(A) He is upset with the slow speed of delivery.
(B) He spoke with a Tamino Group employee.
(C) He is unsure as to which model of printer he has.
(D) He was not satisfied with the service he received on the phone.

185. What is the product number of the item Mr. Huang asked to have shipped more quickly?

(A) TG433
(B) TG214
(C) TG558
(D) TG232

Go on to the next page

Wildport Has New Director

SPRINGDALE (May 21)—Wildport Gallery, the popular art space in Springdale, announced yesterday that Ms. Rell Manon has been appointed as its director. Most recently, Ms. Manon was associate professor in the Department of Visual Arts at Lochdale Arts Academy and served as the department's chair.

Ms. Manon graduated from Matlin University, where she studied sculpting. Her works have been on display in galleries and museums across the world. Her most recent exhibit, held last January, took her to Kuala Lumpur, Malaysia.

She is also the author of several books and articles on modern and contemporary art and has served as an adviser on the sets of several film and theatrical productions.

Wildport Gallery
presents
Days of Summer

A multimedia exhibit featuring the works of:

- **Aliyah Suharli**—abstract sculptures (on view June 8–26)
- **Henri Holland**—watercolor paintings (on view July 5–24)
- **Abel Ngozi**—ceramic pottery tableware (on view August 9–28)
- **Martha Torres**—black-and-white photographs (on view September 6–25)

An opening reception, with welcome remarks from the artist, will be held for each exhibit. Gallery hours: Monday–Friday, 12:30–8:30 P.M., and Saturday, 10:00 A.M.–6:00 P.M. Admission is free.

221 East Hickory Street | Springdale | 555-0179 | www.wildportgallery.com

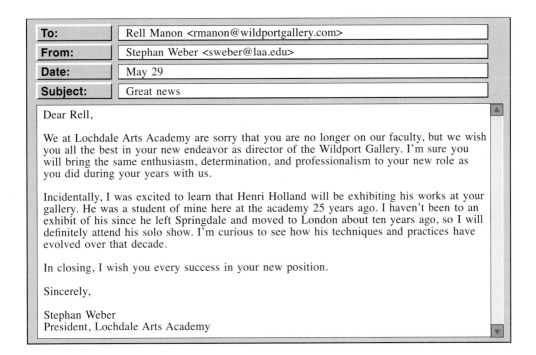

To:	Rell Manon <rmanon@wildportgallery.com>
From:	Stephan Weber <sweber@laa.edu>
Date:	May 29
Subject:	Great news

Dear Rell,

We at Lochdale Arts Academy are sorry that you are no longer on our faculty, but we wish you all the best in your new endeavor as director of the Wildport Gallery. I'm sure you will bring the same enthusiasm, determination, and professionalism to your new role as you did during your years with us.

Incidentally, I was excited to learn that Henri Holland will be exhibiting his works at your gallery. He was a student of mine here at the academy 25 years ago. I haven't been to an exhibit of his since he left Springdale and moved to London about ten years ago, so I will definitely attend his solo show. I'm curious to see how his techniques and practices have evolved over that decade.

In closing, I wish you every success in your new position.

Sincerely,

Stephan Weber
President, Lochdale Arts Academy

186. According to the article, what was one of Ms. Manon's previous jobs?

(A) Gallery owner
(B) University president
(C) Film consultant
(D) Movie actor

187. What is indicated about the exhibitions?

(A) They feature multilingual audio guides.
(B) They can be attended for a fee.
(C) They will include a speech on the first day.
(D) They are open to the public seven days a week.

188. When will Mr. Weber most likely attend an exhibition at the Wildport Gallery?

(A) In June
(B) In July
(C) In August
(D) In September

189. What is the purpose of the e-mail?

(A) To inquire about an employment opportunity
(B) To express interest in purchasing a work of art
(C) To offer congratulations on an accomplishment
(D) To request tickets for a future exhibit

190. What is suggested about Mr. Holland?

(A) He was a classmate of Ms. Manon's.
(B) He is known for using innovative techniques.
(C) He started his professional career 25 years ago.
(D) He used to live in the city that Ms. Manon works in now.

Go on to the next page

Questions 191-195 refer to the following letter, e-mail, and advertisement.

Raucher Office Complex
456 Jade Street, Moncton, New Brunswick E1G 9Z9

Dear Business Owner,

Say good-bye to long leases, high rents, and costly equipment rentals. Your small but growing business can now rent shared office space on an as-needed basis at a convenient downtown location. You'll enjoy a modern building with all the benefits of well-established company facilities—including printer/copiers, Internet access, and comfortable meeting rooms—at very reasonable monthly rates. Just bring your laptop computers and you'll be open for business!

Work Shift	Single Office	Double Office	Triple Office
Day (7 A.M.–6 P.M.)	$350	$500	$750
Evening (6 P.M.–midnight)	$250	$400	$550
Overnight (midnight–7 A.M.)	$150	$300	$450
24 hours a day	$600	$900	$1,300

Please contact me at 506-555-0163 or at arthur@raucherofficecomplex.ca to discuss your needs.

Sincerely,

Arthur Raucher

Arthur Raucher

To:	arthur@raucherofficecomplex.ca
From:	mlangenbach@frogpod.ca
Date:	April 20
Subject:	Frog Pod

Dear Mr. Raucher,

I learned about the Raucher Office Complex from Maria Shelby, who is renting space there. I am interested in doing the same. I'd like to meet with you to discuss an unusual use for an office space and find out if you are willing to accommodate it.

My plan is to offer a service that is a podcast centre, called Frog Pod. Essentially, I would like to rent a double office for 24 hours a day and outfit one of the offices with my basic recording equipment. Then I would sublet this mini recording studio by the hour to anyone who wants to make their own audio or video productions. Please let me know what you think.

Thank you,

Marc Langenbach

Frog Pod
456 Jade Street, Moncton, New Brunswick E1G 9Z9

Get a jump on your broadcasting career! Hop on over to Frog Pod to record your very own podcasts.

Step 1: Rent our recording space by the hour. We are located at the Raucher Office Complex.

Step 2: Make your podcast. Talk about whatever you like—sports, arts, entertainment, news ... anything!

Step 3: Relax and let Frog Pod do the rest of the work! We will distribute your podcast on all major social media platforms.

Visit us at frogpod.ca to learn more!

---

191. What is the purpose of Mr. Raucher's letter?

(A) To inquire about renovating an office space

(B) To survey rental costs in downtown Moncton

(C) To promote a service to business owners

(D) To describe the benefits of working in Moncton

192. What is indicated about Ms. Shelby?

(A) She leases space at the Raucher Office Complex.

(B) She owns an office building in Moncton.

(C) She is an employee of Mr. Langenbach's.

(D) She enjoys listening to podcasts.

193. How much would Mr. Langenbach most likely pay each month for his desired work space?

(A) $400
(B) $600
(C) $900
(D) $1,300

194. How did Mr. Raucher respond to an inquiry he received on April 20 ?

(A) He purchased a new printer.
(B) He lowered his rental rates.
(C) He changed Internet providers.
(D) He agreed to a proposal.

195. What does Frog Pod primarily offer?

(A) Training materials for broadcasters

(B) Access to media production technology

(C) Financing for the purchase of office space

(D) Design and maintenance of Web sites

Go on to the next page

Sanspore Corporation
Singapore - New York - Toronto

Management Training Program in Human Resources

Sanspore Corporation invites applications for a six-month management training program in Human Resources, to begin in September of this year. The training involves a variety of assignments (rotations) throughout the company. Upon successful completion of the program, trainees will be considered for full-time positions as associate human resources officers in our company. The program curriculum encompasses the following.

PROGRAM MONTH	ROTATION TOPICS
September	General Policies and Hiring
October	Compensation and Payroll
November	Employment Law and Disputes
December	Benefits
January	The Telecommunications Industry
February	Communication and Marketing

For further information and an application, contact Minh Nguyen at mnguyen@sanspore.com.

To:	John Rossano <jrossano@otil.com>
From:	Minh Nguyen <mnguyen@sanspore.com>
Date:	May 27
Subject:	Management training program
Attachment:	📎 Application form

Dear Mr. Rossano,

Thank you for your inquiry about the management training program at Sanspore Corporation. Your university degree in psychology provides a solid foundation for a career in human resources. The coursework you completed in telecommunications, your secondary field of study, is an advantage as well and could mean that you would be excused from participating during the month of that rotation topic. Please complete the application form I have attached to this e-mail and submit it by July 18, along with a transcript of your coursework and two letters of recommendation. We will notify applicants of our decision by August 10.

Best wishes,

Minh Nguyen, Human Resources Director

July 18

Mr. Minh Nguyen
Sanspore Corporation
12 Forty-Sixth Street
New York, NY 10017

Dear Mr. Nguyen,

I would like to strongly recommend John Rossano to your management training program. I have known Mr. Rossano for four years. He worked for my company on a part-time basis while he studied at Hartland University.

While completing special projects for me, he demonstrated that he is a quick learner who works well with others and contributes effective ideas for system improvements. As a supervisor of many staff members over the years, I believe Mr. Rossano holds outstanding promise for the successful completion of your program.

Sincerely,

Ellyn Karen Peters
Ellyn Karen Peters, President
EKP Consulting, Inc.

196. What is the purpose of the announcement?

(A) To invite job seekers to an industry conference
(B) To recruit potential employees for a special program
(C) To remind employees of professional development requirements
(D) To publicize a change in a series of classes

197. What was the main focus of Mr. Rossano's study?

(A) Management
(B) Business finance
(C) Telecommunications
(D) Psychology

198. What does the e-mail suggest about Mr. Rossano?

(A) He meets the requirements for Sanspore Corporation's training program.
(B) He has previously applied for a job at Sanspore Corporation.
(C) He submitted an application on May 27.
(D) He attended university with Mr. Nguyen.

199. In what month might Mr. Rossano be excused from a rotation?

(A) September
(B) October
(C) January
(D) February

200. What is most likely true about the letter?

(A) It was sent on the day of the application deadline.
(B) It was sent with a work sample.
(C) It was submitted by a former professor of Mr. Nguyen's.
(D) It includes a job offer from EKP Consulting, Inc.

Stop! This is the end of the test. If you finish before time is called, you may go back to Parts 5, 6, and 7 and check your work.

ANSWER SHEET

Final Test

수험번호

응시일자 : 20 년 월 일

성명	한글
	한자
	영자

LISTENING (Part I ~ IV)

(answer bubbles for questions 1–100, options ⓐ ⓑ ⓒ ⓓ)

1 2 3 4 5 6 7 8 9 10 11 12 13 14 15 16 17 18 19 20
21 22 23 24 25 26 27 28 29 30 31 32 33 34 35 36 37 38 39 40
41 42 43 44 45 46 47 48 49 50 51 52 53 54 55 56 57 58 59 60
61 62 63 64 65 66 67 68 69 70 71 72 73 74 75 76 77 78 79 80
81 82 83 84 85 86 87 88 89 90 91 92 93 94 95 96 97 98 99 100

READING (Part V ~ VII)

(answer bubbles for questions 101–200, options ⓐ ⓑ ⓒ ⓓ)

101 102 103 104 105 106 107 108 109 110 111 112 113 114 115 116 117 118 119 120
121 122 123 124 125 126 127 128 129 130 131 132 133 134 135 136 137 138 139 140
141 142 143 144 145 146 147 148 149 150 151 152 153 154 155 156 157 158 159 160
161 162 163 164 165 166 167 168 169 170 171 172 173 174 175 176 177 178 179 180
181 182 183 184 185 186 187 188 189 190 191 192 193 194 195 196 197 198 199 200

ETS TOEIC®

기출문제 한국 독점출간

RC 토익 정기시험

기출종합서

정답 및 해설

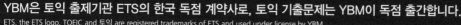

YBM은 토익 출제기관 ETS의 한국 독점 계약사로, 토익 기출문제는 YBM이 독점 출간합니다.
ETS, the ETS logo, TOEIC and 토익 are registered trademarks of ETS and used under license by YBM.

RC 토익 정기시험 기출종합서

정답 및 해설

PART 5 GRAMMAR

CHAPTER 01 | 문장의 구조

UNIT 01	주어와 동사

기출공식 1	본책 p. 20
1 (B) **2** (D) **3** (D)	

1

해설 **주어 자리:** 빈칸은 동사 will be considered의 주어 자리
이다. 따라서 주어 역할을 할 수 있는 명사인 (B) Requests
가 정답이다. 동명사인 (C) Requesting과 to부정사
인 (D) To request도 문장의 주어 역할을 할 수 있으나,
request는 타동사이므로 전치사 for 없이 바로 목적어
(changes)가 와야 한다.

번역 회의 프로그램 변경 요청은 11월 1일에 검토될 예정입니다.

어휘 conference 회의   consider 검토하다, 고려하다
request 요청; 요청하다

2

해설 **주어 자리:** 접속사 as가 이끄는 절의 주어가 들어갈 자리이
므로 주격 대명사인 (D) they가 정답이다.

번역 정비공들은 신기술을 사용하기 시작하면서 더욱 능률이 높
아졌다.

어휘 mechanic 정비공   efficient 능률적인   technology
기술

3

해설 **주어 자리:** 동사 will ensure 앞에는 문장의 주어가 필요하
며, '믹서기를 적절하게 관리하는 것'이라는 의미를 나타낼
수 있는 동명사 (D) Caring이 정답이다. 부사 properly의
수식을 받고 있으므로 일반 명사가 아닌 동명사를 선택해야
한다.

번역 믹서기를 적절하게 관리하는 것은 계속 잘 작동하는 것을
보장해 줄 것이다.

어휘 properly 적절하게   ensure ~하도록 보장하다
continue to 계속 ~하다   function 작동하다

기출공식 2	본책 p. 20
4 (B) **5** (C) **6** (A)	

4

해설 **주어와 동사의 수 일치:** 빈칸은 주어로 쓰일 명사가 들어갈
자리인데 앞에 부정관사 a가 있으며, 동사가 is이므로 단
수형인 (B) element를 써야 한다. key element는 '핵심
요소'란 뜻이다.

번역 곧 있을 고객 대상 발표에서 여전히 누락된 핵심 요소는 전
체 프로젝트 비용에 대한 견적서이다.

어휘 key 핵심적인   missing 누락된   estimate 견적서
elementary 초보의, 기본적인   elemental 기본적인

5

해설 **주어와 동사의 수 일치:** 빈칸은 주어로 쓰일 명사가 들어갈
자리인데, 뒤에 복수동사인 have가 나오므로 복수명사인
(C) Improvements가 정답이 된다. (D) Improving은
동명사로 주어 역할을 할 수 있지만 목적어가 필요하므로
빈칸에 들어갈 수 없다.

번역 로터스 레스토랑은 개량 공사로 좌석 구역을 거의 두 배로
확장했다.

어휘 double 두 배로 만들다   seating 좌석, 자리   improve
개선하다, 나아지다   improvement 개선

6

해설 **주어와 동사의 수 일치:** 빈칸은 문장의 주어 자리이고, 동사
는 단수동사인 is이다. 따라서 단수명사인 (A) schedule
이 정답이다.

번역 맥닐 프로젝트 일정은 1층 회의실 벽에 걸려 있다.

어휘 hang 걸리다   first floor 1층

기출공식 3	본책 p. 21
7 (D) **8** (B) **9** (B)	

7

해설 **가주어 it 구문:** It은 가주어 역할을 하고 있으며, 빈칸에는
진주어 역할을 할 수 있는 말이 들어가야 한다. 따라서 보기
중 to부정사인 (D) to circulate이 정답이다.

번역 일반적으로 회의 참석자들에게 사전에 회의 안건을 돌리는
것이 가장 효과적이다.

어휘 effective 효과적인   agenda 의제, 안건   attendee
참가자   in advance 사전에,   circulate 유포하다,
회람하다

8

해설 **가주어 it 구문:** it이 가주어이고 빈칸은 진주어 자리이다.
따라서 진주어 역할을 할 수 있는 to부정사구인 (B) to
learn이 정답이다.

번역 지난 두 분기에 걸쳐 수익 변동이 컸는데도 지출에는 그다지 변화가 없었다는 사실은 놀라운 일이었다.

어휘 revenue 수익, 수입 fluctuate 변동[등락]을 거듭하다 quarter (1/4)분기 nevertheless 그럼에도 불구하고 fairly 상당히, 꽤 steady 꾸준한, 안정된

9

해설 **가주어 it 구문:** that 이하의 절에서 it은 가주어이고 빈칸 이하가 진주어로 쓰였다. 따라서 빈칸에는 진주어로 쓰일 수 있는 to부정사구가 필요하므로 (B) to construct가 정답이다.

번역 구조 공학자들은 제안된 부지에 건물을 짓는 것이 기술적으로 불가능하다는 것을 밝혀냈다.

어휘 determine 결정하다 proposed 제안된

기출공식 4		본책 p. 21
10 (A)	**11** (B)	**12** (B)

10

해설 **There 구문:** there 구문에서는 'there + 동사' 뒤에 주어가 온다. 따라서 빈칸에는 주어인 명사가 필요한데, 동사가 단수(was)이므로 단수명사인 (A) competition이 와야 한다. 가산명사인 (D) competitor는 앞에 관사나 소유격이 필요하므로 답이 될 수 없다.

번역 지난해 겨울철에는 지붕이 있는 주차장에 대한 경쟁이 치열했다.

어휘 fierce 맹렬한, 심한 covered 지붕이 덮인 competition 경쟁 competitively 경쟁적으로 competitor 경쟁 업체

11

해설 **There 구문:** 빈칸에는 주어인 명사가 와야 하는데, 동사가 복수(are)이므로 복수명사인 (B) cancellations가 정답이 된다.

번역 공연이 매진되면 대기자 명단을 만들기 시작해 취소가 생기면 고객에게 연락하는 것이 극장의 정책이다.

어휘 policy 정책 waiting list 대기자 명단 cancel 취소하다 cancellation 취소

12

해설 **There 구문:** 빈칸에는 주어인 명사가 와야 하는데, 동사가 복수(have been)이므로 복수명사인 (B) revisions가 정답이다.

번역 당신이 마지막으로 보고서를 검토한 이후로는 중요한 수정 사항이 없습니다.

어휘 revision 수정 revise 수정하다

기출공식 5		본책 p. 22
13 (C)	**14** (B)	**15** (B)

13

해설 **동사 자리:** A stay (at the Moonlight Tower Hotel)이 문장의 주어이고, 빈칸이 동사인 문장이다. 따라서 단수 동사인 (C) includes가 정답이다. 동명사 혹은 현재분사인 (A) including이나 to부정사인 (D) to include는 문장의 본동사 자리에 들어갈 수 없다.

번역 문라이트 타워 호텔 숙박에는 정통 상하이식 조식이 포함됩니다.

어휘 stay 숙박; 머무르다 authentic 진짜의, 정통의 include 포함하다 inclusive (가격에 경비가) 포함된, 포괄적인

14

해설 **명령문:** 주어 없이 동사로 시작하는 명령문에는 동사원형을 쓴다. 따라서 (B) complete가 정답이다.

번역 동봉한 설문서를 작성해서 가능한 한 빨리 저희 사무실로 반송해 주십시오.

어휘 enclosed 동봉된 survey 설문서 complete 작성하다

15

해설 **조동사 + 동사원형:** 조동사 must 뒤에는 동사원형이 와야 하므로, (B) achieve가 정답이다.

번역 실적이 만족스럽다는 평가를 받으려면, 생산직 근로자들은 최소한 관리자가 할당한 월간 목표의 90퍼센트를 달성해야 한다.

어휘 performance 성과, 실적 satisfactory 만족스러운 assign (일 등을) 할당하다 achieve 성취하다

기출공식 6		본책 p. 22
16 (A)	**17** (A)	**18** (B)

16

해설 **주어와 동사의 수 일치:** 빈칸은 문장의 동사가 들어갈 자리인데, 주어가 복수 batteries이므로 (A) last가 정답이다.

번역 오늘날의 충전지는 10년 전에 생산된 충전지보다 거의 2배는 오래간다.

어휘 rechargeable battery 충전지 last 지속되다 lasting 영구적인 lastly 마지막으로

17

해설 **주어와 동사의 수 일치:** Daily guided tours of the warehouse가 주어이고, 동사는 없다. 빈칸에는 동사가 와야 하는데, 주어가 Daily guided tours로 복수이므로, 정답은 (A) begin이다.

번역 안내원을 동반한 일일 창고 견학은 1층 접빈실에서 오전 10시에 시작한다.

어휘 daily 매일의, 나날의 guided tour 안내원이 동반하는, 안내원이 딸린 warehouse 창고, 저장소 reception area 응접실, 접빈실

18

해설 **주어와 동사의 수 일치:** 문장의 동사가 필요한 자리이고 주어가 단수이므로 (B) surrounds가 정답이다.

번역 보고르 주경기장의 좌석은 경기장을 완전히 둘러싸고 있어서 모든 방문객이 경기를 아주 잘 관람할 수 있다.

어휘 completely 완전히 afford 주다, 제공하다 surround 둘러싸다, 에워싸다

기출공식 7		본책 p. 23
19 (B)	**20** (B)	**21** (D)

19

해설 **수동태:** the passenger space가 주어이고, 좌석 공간은 설계되는 수동적인 입장이므로 수동의 의미를 지닌 과거분사가 들어가야 한다. 따라서 (B) designed가 정답이다.

번역 블레이크 X40은 신뢰할 만한 자동차이지만 탑승자를 위한 공간은 잘못 설계되어 있다.

어휘 reliable 신뢰할 만한, 믿을 만한 passenger 승객, 탑승객 space 공간

20

해설 **수동태:** 조동사인 must 뒤에는 동사원형이 와야 하며, 주어 The outstanding balance(미지불 잔액)는 pay(지불하다)의 주체가 아니라 대상이므로 '잔액이 지불되어야 한다'라는 수동의 의미가 적절하다. 따라서 (B) be paid가 정답이다.

번역 미지불 잔액은 즉시 지불되어야 하며, 그렇지 않으면 우리는 계좌를 폐쇄해야 합니다.

어휘 outstanding balance 미지불 잔액 promptly 즉시 or else 그렇지 않으면

21

해설 **능동태:** 동사 자리 뒤에 목적어 the warranty가 있으므로 능동태인 (D) has extended가 정답이다.

번역 그 제조사는 최신 카메라 모델들의 품질 보증을 12개월까지 연장했다.

어휘 manufacturer 제조자, 제조사 warranty 품질 보증 extend 연장하다

기출공식 8		본책 p. 23
22 (B)	**23** (A)	**24** (C)

22

해설 **미래 시제:** Dajdor Industries가 주어, 빈칸이 동사인 문장이다. 문장 끝에 미래의 시점을 나타내는 표현인 next Monday(다음 주 월요일)가 있으므로, 미래 시제인 (B) will announce가 정답이다.

번역 다즈도 산업은 다음 주 월요일 기자회견에서 신제품 라인을 발표할 예정이다.

어휘 product line 제품군, 제품 라인 press conference 기자회견

23

해설 **과거 시제:** 빈칸은 문장의 동사가 필요한 자리이다. Last year가 과거를 의미하므로 과거 시제인 (A) listed를 써야 한다.

번역 지난해 한스퍼드 자동차회사 카탈로그에서는 에어컨과 디지털 라디오가 전 차종의 기본 사양으로 포함되었다.

어휘 automobile 자동차 air-conditioning 에어컨 장치 feature 특징, 기능 list 리스트[목록]에 언급하다[포함시키다]

24

해설 **현재 시제:** 빈칸은 주어 Our team의 동사 자리이므로 동사 역할을 할 수 없는 (A) having met과 (B) meeting은 제외된다. every Monday라는 표현이 있고, 뒤에 오는 명령문과 함께 문맥상 '매주 월요일에 회의를 하므로 약속을 잡지 마세요'라는 의미가 되어야 하므로 반복되는 일을 나타낼 때 쓰는 현재 시제 (C) meets가 정답이다.

번역 우리 팀은 매주 월요일에 회의를 하므로, 그때는 다른 약속을 잡지 마세요.

어휘 appointment 약속

ETS **TEST**				본책 p. 24
1 (C)	**2** (C)	**3** (D)	**4** (C)	**5** (A)
6 (C)	**7** (C)	**8** (C)	**9** (B)	**10** (B)
11 (B)	**12** (B)	**13** (C)	**14** (B)	**15** (B)
16 (C)	**17** (C)	**18** (A)	**19** (C)	**20** (C)

1

해설 **동사 자리:** 주어 없이 동사로 시작하는 명령문에서 동사의 형태는 동사원형인 (C) write로 쓴다.

번역 확실하게 귀하의 세탁물을 즉각 돌려받으시려면, 제공된 꼬리표에 호텔 객실 번호를 써 주십시오.

어휘 ensure 보장하다 prompt 즉각적인 laundry 세탁물 tag 꼬리표, 번호표

2

해설 **동사 자리:** Civil engineer Lorenzo Raspallo가 주어이고 빈칸이 동사인 문장이다. 따라서 문장에서 본동사 역할을 할 수 있는 (C) has been confirmed가 정답이 된다.

번역 토목 기사인 로렌조 라스팔로가 다음 달에 있을 제5회 연례 교량관리 학회의 초청 연사로 확정되었다.

어휘 civil engineer 토목 기사 guest speaker 초청 연사 annual 연례의, 일년마다의 conservation 보존, 보호 colloquium 전문가 회의, 학회

3

해설 **There 구문:** 모든 문장에는 동사가 있어야 하는데 동사가 없는 문장이다. 따라서 '~이 있다'를 의미하면서 문장의 동사를 갖추게 되는 (D) There were가 정답이다.

번역 지난달 취리히에서 열린 회의에 수백 명의 기술 전문가들이 있었다.

어휘 specialist 전문가

4

해설 **조동사 + 동사원형:** 조동사 can 뒤에는 동사원형이 와야 하므로 (C) participate가 정답이다. fully는 조동사와 본동사 사이에 들어간 부사이다.

번역 저녁 수업에 등록한 사람들은 학교에서 주관하는 모든 활동에 전부 참여할 수 있다.

어휘 register for (수업 등에) 등록하다 activity 활동 sponsor 주관하다, 후원하다

5

해설 **주어 자리:** 빈칸은 동사 is growing 앞 주어 자리이며, 빈칸 앞 형용사 public의 수식을 받고 있다. 따라서 명사인 (A) anticipation이 정답이다.

번역 논란이 많은 소설의 속편 출간일이 다가오면서 대중의 기대가 기하급수적으로 증가하고 있다.

어휘 publication 출판 sequel 속편 controversial 논란이 많은 novel 소설 approach 다가오다 exponentially 기하급수적으로 anticipation 예상, 기대

6

해설 **능동태:** 빈칸 앞의 Ms. Kimura's employees는 주어이고 빈칸 뒤의 her approachable manner and steady leadership은 목적어로 절에 반드시 필요한 동사가 보이지 않으므로 빈칸은 동사 자리이다. 또한, 빈칸 뒤에 목적어가 있으므로 능동태 동사인 (C) praise가 정답이다.

번역 기무라 씨의 직원들은 종종 그녀의 다가가기 쉬운 태도와 한결 같은 리더십을 칭찬한다.

어휘 approachable 접근 가능한 manner 태도 steady 한결 같은 praise 칭찬하다

7

해설 **주어 자리:** 빈칸은 동사 have transformed의 주어 자리이고, 형용사 significant technological의 수식을 받고 있으므로 명사가 들어가야 한다. 따라서 '발전'이라는 뜻의 명사인 (C) developments가 정답이다.

번역 상당한 기술 발전이 의료산업을 바꾸어 놓았다.

어휘 significant 상당한 transform 바꾸어 놓다

8

해설 **능동태 + 과거 시제:** 빈칸은 Shan Climbing Gear의 동사 자리로, 뒤에 있는 to부정사구(to open its third retail location)를 목적어로 취해 '세 번째 소매점을 열 계획'이라는 의미가 되어야 자연스러우므로 능동태 동사가 와야 한다. (B) is planning과 (C) planned가 가능한데, last month라는 과거 시점 표현이 있으므로 (C) planned가 정답이다.

번역 샨 등산장비는 지난달 아시아에 세 번째 소매점을 열 계획이었으나 연기되었다.

어휘 retail 소매

9

해설 **동사 자리 + 현재 시제:** 빈칸은 after절(시간 부사절)의 동사 자리이며, 주어는 the performances이다. 따라서 본동사 역할을 할 수 없는 (C) to begin은 제외된다. 주절의 동사가 stops(현재)이며, '공연 시작 약 15분 후에는 티켓 판매를 중단한다'라는 일반적인 사실을 나타내고 있으므로 현재 시제인 (B) begin이 정답이 된다.

번역 에저 콘서트 홀의 매표소에서는 공연 시작 약 15분 후에는 티켓 판매를 중단한다.

어휘 box office 매표소 approximately 약, 대략 performance 공연, 작업

10

해설 **수동태:** 주어인 컴퓨터 시스템은 '수리하다'를 뜻하는 repair의 주체가 될 수 없으므로 수동태인 (B) repaired가 정답이다.

번역 컴퓨터 시스템이 수리될 때까지 직원들은 경리과에 있는 차트에 본인의 근무 시간을 기록해야 합니다.

어휘 **keep track of** ~을 기록하다, ~을 파악하다 **payroll office** 경리과 **repair** 수리(하다)

11

해설 **능동태:** 빈칸 앞의 we는 주어이고 빈칸 뒤의 the safety and comfort는 목적어로 절에 반드시 필요한 동사가 보이지 않으므로 빈칸은 동사 자리이다. 또한, 빈칸 뒤에 목적어가 있으므로 능동태 동사인 (B) prioritized가 정답이다.

번역 날렵한 새 열차의 내부를 설계하는 데, 우리는 승객의 안전과 편안함을 우선시했다.

어휘 **sleek** 매끈한 **safety** 안전 **comfort** 편안함 **passenger** 승객 **prioritize** 우선으로 하다

12

해설 **수동태:** be동사 뒤에는 현재분사(permitting), 과거분사(permitted), 형용사(permissible)가 올 수 있는데, 문맥상 '방문객은 출입이 허용되지 않는다'라는 수동의 의미가 되어야 자연스러우므로 수동태를 만들어주는 과거분사 (B) permitted가 정답이다. 빈칸 뒤에 목적어가 없으므로 능동태를 만드는 (A) permitting은 답이 될 수 없고, (D) permissible은 '(객체나 행위 등이) 허용되는'을 뜻하며 사람을 주어로 취하지 않는다.

번역 안전 규정상 방문객은 근무 시간 중 공장 작업장 출입이 금지된다.

어휘 **regulation** 규정 **factory floor** 공장 작업장 **permit** 허가하다

13

해설 **수 일치 + 능동태:** 빈칸은 주어 a rise의 동사 자리이고 뒤에 목적어 Hashimoto Enterprises가 있으므로, 단수주어와 수 일치가 되면서 목적어를 취할 수 있는 능동태 단수 동사가 답이 되어야 한다. 따라서 (C) has enabled가 정답이다.

번역 매출 증가로 하시모토 엔터프라이즈는 마케팅 지출을 늘릴 수 있게 되었다.

어휘 **revenue** 매출 **increase** 늘리다 **spending** 지출 **enable** 가능하게 만들다

14

해설 **가주어 it 구문:** it이 가주어이고 빈칸이 진주어인 문장이므로 빈칸에는 진주어 역할을 할 수 있는 to부정사인 (B) to attach가 적절하다.

번역 엑카트 모형 보트를 조립할 때는 접착제가 마르기 전에 조각들을 빠르게 연달아 붙이는 것이 중요합니다.

어휘 **in succession** 연달아 **glue** 접착제 **dry** 마르다 **attach** 붙이다, 첨부하다

15

해설 **조동사 + 동사원형:** 조동사 cannot 뒤에는 동사원형이 와야 하며, 주어인 certain types of plants는 bring의 행위자가 아니라 대상이므로 수동태인 (B) be brought가 정답이다. 뒤에 목적어가 없으므로 능동태로는 쓰일 수 없다.

번역 해외 여행객들에 대한 신규 규제 때문에 어떤 종류의 식물들은 허가 없이 대부분의 나라에 반입될 수 없다.

어휘 **due to** ~ 때문에 **restriction** 제한, 규제 **certain** 어떤, 일정한 **permit** 허가, 허가증

16

해설 **주어 자리:** 빈칸은 복수동사 include의 주어 자리이다. 따라서 복수동사에 수 일치되는 복수명사인 (C) Priorities가 정답이다.

번역 관리팀의 우선순위는 생산성을 향상시키는 것과 연간 지출을 줄이는 것을 포함한다.

어휘 **include** 포함하다 **improve** 향상시키다 **productivity** 생산성 **reduce** 줄이다 **expenditure** 지출 **priority** 우선순위 **prioritize** 우선순위를 매기다

17

해설 **주어와 동사의 수 일치:** 문장에 동사가 없으므로 빈칸은 동사 자리이며, 주어가 3인칭 단수 Mr. Crenshaw이므로 동사 과거형인 (C) encouraged가 정답이다. (A) encourage는 수 일치가 맞지 않으므로 오답이다.

번역 크렌쇼 씨는 인턴들에게 회계 워크숍에 참석하라고 독려했다.

어휘 **accounting** 회계 **encourage** 독려하다

18

해설 **주어 자리:** 빈칸은 that절의 일부로 동사 would increase의 주어 역할을 하고 있다. 빈칸 뒤 목적어 their expertise and resources를 취하면서 주어 역할을 할 수 있는 품사는 준동사인 동명사이다. 따라서 (A) combining이 정답이다.

번역 지난해 엔터테인먼트 아주사사와 손 멀티미디어는 그들의 전문 지식과 자원을 합하는 것이 양쪽 기관 모두의 이윤을 증가시킬 것이라고 결론지었다.

어휘 **expertise** 전문 지식 **resource** 자원 **profit** 이윤 **combine** 결합하다

19

해설 **주어 자리:** 빈칸부터 동사 are 앞까지가 전부 문장의 주어이므로 빈칸에는 of 이하의 수식을 받는 명사가 와야 한다. 따라서 '종류, 다양한 품종'이라는 의미의 명사인 (C) Varieties가 정답이다.

번역 스프링데일 지역 시장에서는 수제 공예품과 보석뿐만 아니라 집에서 재배한 다양한 품종의 유기농 과일과 채소를 구할 수 있다.

어휘 organic 유기농의　handmade 손으로 만든, 수제의　craft 공예(품)　available 구할 수 있는　purchase 구매　vary 다르다　various 다양한

20

해설 **수동태:** Every customer service associate가 주어이며 빈칸에는 be동사와 함께 동사의 형태를 완성해야 하는 자리이다. 문맥상 '고객 서비스 담당자 전원은 철저히 교육 받는다'라는 의미가 되어야 하므로, is와 함께 동사의 수동태를 이루는 (C) trained가 정답이 된다.

번역 고객 서비스 담당자 전원은 배송 선택 사항과 관련된 모든 전화를 처리할 수 있도록 철저히 교육 받습니다.

어휘 associate 동료 (직원)　thoroughly 철저하게　handle 다루다, 처리하다　regarding ~에 관한　delivery 배송, 운송

UNIT 02　목적어 / 보어 / 수식어

기출공식 1		본책 p. 28
1 (D)	**2** (C)	**3** (D)

1

해설 **동사의 목적어 자리:** 동사 express의 목적어 자리이므로 명사인 (D) opposition이 정답이다.

번역 알스톤의 많은 주민들이 필드스프링 호수 주변의 새 창고 단지 건설에 반대를 나타냈다.

어휘 resident 거주자　warehouse 창고　complex 복합 건물, 단지　oppose 반대하다　opposition 반대

2

해설 **동사의 목적어 자리:** 빈칸 앞에 있는 동사 offer의 목적어가 필요한 자리이므로 목적격인 (C) them이 정답이다. 여기서 them은 if절에 있는 복수명사 the discontinued printers를 가리킨다.

번역 단종된 프린터들이 금요일까지 팔리지 않으면 에인리 전자는 50퍼센트 할인한 가격으로 판매할 계획이다.

어휘 discontinue (생산을) 중단하다

3

해설 **동사의 목적어 자리:** 빈칸 앞에 온 is considering이 문제 해결의 단서로, consider는 동명사를 목적어로 취하는 동사이다. 따라서 동명사인 (D) installing이 정답이다. 명사인 (C) installations는 뒤에 오는 목적어 solar panels를 받을 수 없으므로 오답이다.

번역 밴린 고등학교는 지붕에 태양열 전지판을 설치하는 안을 고려하고 있다.

어휘 consider 고려하다　solar panel 태양열 전지판　install 설치하다　installation 설치

기출공식 2		본책 p. 28
4 (A)	**5** (D)	**6** (C)

4

해설 **타동사의 목적어 자리:** 타동사 permit의 목적어 자리로, 빈칸 앞의 정관사 the와 뒤에 오는 of 전치사구의 수식을 받을 수 있는 것은 명사이므로, (A) use가 정답이다.

번역 이즈미트 미술관에서는 규정상 미술관 안에서 플래시 촬영을 허용하지 않는다.

어휘 regulation 규정　permit 허용하다　flash photography 플래시 촬영　art gallery 미술관　used 중고의　usable 사용 가능한, 쓸 수 있는

5

해설 **전치사의 목적어 자리:** 빈칸은 전치사 after의 목적어 자리이므로, 목적어 역할을 할 수 있는 명사가 들어가야 한다. 따라서 '심사숙고'라는 의미의 명사인 (D) deliberation이 정답이다.

번역 심사숙고 끝에 도시 계획 공무원들은 회의장을 다른 곳에 지어야 한다고 결정했다.

어휘 official 간부, 공무원　determine 결정하다, 판단하다　conference 회의, 총회　elsewhere 다른 곳에서　deliberation 심사숙고

6

해설 **전치사의 목적어 자리:** 빈칸은 of 뒤에 있으므로 전치사의 목적어 역할을 하는 명사 자리이다. 따라서 정답은 (C) electricity이다.

번역 경제학자들은 전기요금의 변화가 당장 소비량에 영향을 미치지 않을 것이라고 말한다.

어휘 economist 경제학자　note 주목하다, 언급하다　immediately 즉시　affect 영향을 미치다　consumption level 소비량

7 (C)   **8** (D)   **9** (A)

7

해설   **가목적어 it 구문:** 'make + 목적어 + 목적보어(easier)' 구문으로, 목적어가 너무 길어 목적어 자리에 가목적어 it을 쓰고, 진목적어인 to부정사구(to search 이하)는 문장 뒤로 보낸 형태이다. 따라서 (C) it이 정답이다.

번역   인터넷으로 인해 차량 구매자들이 최고의 대출을 제공하는 은행을 찾는 게 더 쉬워졌다.

어휘   vehicle 차량   loan 대출

8

해설   **가목적어 it 구문:** 동사 makes 뒤에 가목적어 it이 있으므로 빈칸에는 진목적어가 들어가야 한다. 따라서 to부정사인 (D) to shop이 정답이다. 참고로, 목적어 역할을 하는 to부정사 구문이 길면 흔히 그 자리에 가목적어 it을 쓰고 to부정사 구문을 문장 뒤로 보낸다는 점을 알아 두자.

번역   칼턴 의류사의 새 온라인 상점은 집에서 쇼핑하는 것을 편리하게 해 준다.

어휘   convenient 편리한

9

해설   **가목적어 it 구문:** 빈칸은 find의 진목적어 자리이므로, 진목적어 역할을 할 수 있는 to부정사인 (A) to complete이 정답이다.

번역   구직자들은 일자리를 찾을 때 대형 채용업체의 도움을 받아 지원자 프로필을 작성하는 것이 유용하다고 생각할 것이다.

어휘   job applicant 구직자   candidate 지원자 employment 일자리, 취업

10 (B)   **11** (B)   **12** (A)

10

해설   **목적격 보어 자리:** to enjoy 이하가 진목적어, it이 가목적어 역할을 하는 문장이다. 가목적어 it이 동사 makes의 목적어이며, 빈칸은 목적격 보어 자리이다. 따라서 '가능한'이라는 의미의 형용사인 (B) possible이 정답이다.

번역   AX-5 무선 헤드셋은 선이나 케이블을 사용하지 않아도 음악을 즐길 수 있게 해준다.

어휘   wireless 무선의   wire 선   cable 케이블   possibly 아마도   possible 가능한   possibility 가능성

11

해설   **목적격 보어 자리:** to complete 이하가 진목적어, it이 가목적어 역할을 하는 문장이다. 가목적어 it이 동사 have found의 목적어이며, 빈칸은 목적격 보어 자리이다. 따라서 형용사인 (B) difficult가 정답이다.

번역   최근 피드백에 따르면, 일부 신입 수습사원들은 일주일 오리엔테이션 기간 내에 사내 교육 프로그램을 수료하는 것이 어렵다고 생각했다.

어휘   complete 완료하다   in-house 사내의   period 기간

12

해설   **목적격 보어 자리:** to delay 이하가 진목적어, it이 가목적어 역할을 하는 문장이다. 가목적어 it이 동사 make의 목적어이며, 빈칸은 목적격 보어 자리이다. 따라서 '필연적인, 불가피한'이라는 의미의 형용사인 (A) necessary가 정답이다.

번역   예기치 못한 소프트웨어 문제로 우리의 새 휴대전화 출시를 내년으로 미루는 것이 불가피할지도 모른다.

어휘   unexpected 예기치 못한   issue 문제, 사안   delay 미루다   launch 출시   necessarily 필연적으로

13 (C)   **14** (A)   **15** (C)

13

해설   **보어 자리_형용사:** be동사의 보어 자리에 올 형용사가 필요하므로 정답은 (C) beneficial이다. mutually는 be동사와 형용사 사이에 들어간 부사이다.

번역   그 인턴쉽 프로그램은 모든 컬리지의 학생들과 지역 사업체들 상호간에 이득이 된다.

어휘   mutually 상호 간에   beneficial 유익한

14

해설   **보어 자리_명사:** 빈칸에는 be동사의 주격 보어로 쓰일 형용사나 명사가 필요하다. 빈칸 앞에 부정관사 a가 있으므로 명사인 (A) choice가 정답이다. 이때 choice는 명사 주격 보어로 주어인 Ms. Kuvia와 동격 관계이다.

번역   쿠비아 씨는 이달의 직원상을 다섯 번이나 받은 수상자로, 신임 팀장 자리에 선택된 것은 당연했다.

어휘   recipient 수령자

15

해설   **보어 자리_형용사:** be동사 뒤에는 주어를 보충 설명하는 주격 보어로 형용사가 와야 한다. 따라서 (C) helpful이 정답이다. 사람을 뜻할 수 있는 (A) help나 (B) helper가 오려면 관사가 필요하므로 오답이다.

번역　AFT 기술 컨설팅에서 온 이토 씨는 모든 사람이 우리 새 컴퓨터 시스템에 익숙해지도록 하는 데 도움이 되었다.

어휘　familiar with ~에 익숙한, 친숙한

기출공식 6　　　　　　　　　　　　본책 p. 30

16 (C)　　**17** (D)　　**18** (D)

16

해설　**주격 보어 자리:** be동사 뒤에 보어 역할을 할 수 있는 형용사가 와야 하므로 (C) enjoyable이 정답이다.

번역　루첸 백화점은 고객님들이 즐겁게 쇼핑하시기를 바랍니다.

어휘　shopping experience 쇼핑 경험　enjoy 즐기다 enjoyable 즐거운

17

해설　**주격 보어 자리:** 빈칸은 be동사 is 뒤에 보어로 쓰이는 형용사 자리이므로 '검색 가능한'이라는 뜻의 (D) searchable 이 정답이다.

번역　온라인 식당 주소록인 〈올리베이라 다이닝 가이드〉는 요리 종류, 가격대 및 위치별로 검색이 가능하다.

어휘　directory 주소록, 안내 책자　cuisine 요리　price range 가격대

18

해설　**주격 보어를 가지는 동사:** 빈칸 뒤에 형용사인 aware가 오므로 빈칸에는 주격 보어를 가지는 2형식 동사가 와야 한다. 따라서 정답은 (D) remain이다.

번역　우리는 급속하게 변화하는 기술을 인지하고 있어야 하며, 그렇지 않을 시 장기적으로 회사 이윤 하락에 직면할 것이다.

어휘　aware ~을 알고[자각하고] 있는　rapidly 급속히　face 직면하다　decrease 감소　profit 이윤　in the long run 장기적으로

기출공식 7　　　　　　　　　　　　본책 p. 31

19 (B)　　**20** (A)　　**21** (B)

19

해설　**목적격 보어 자리:** its departments는 make의 목적어이며, 빈칸은 목적격 보어 자리이다. 문맥상 '몰터 랩스는 사내 부서들이 낭비를 덜 하도록 만들 계획이다'라는 의미가 되어야 하므로, '낭비적인'이란 의미의 형용사인 (B) wasteful이 정답이 된다. (D) wasting은 '소모성의'라는 의미이므로 빈칸에 적절하지 않다.

번역　몰터 랩스는 불필요한 문서 업무를 없애서 부서들의 낭비를 줄일 계획이다.

어휘　department 부서　eliminate 없애다　unnecessary 불필요한　paperwork 문서 업무, 서류 작업 wastefully 헛되이

20

해설　**목적격 보어 자리:** their seminars는 동사 make의 목적어이며, 빈칸은 목적격 보어 자리이다. 따라서 '효과적인'이라는 의미의 형용사인 (A) effective가 정답이다.

번역　연설자들은 시각 자료로 세미나를 좀 더 효과적으로 만들 수 있다.

어휘　visual aids 시각 자료　effective 효과적인

21

해설　**목적격 보어 자리:** the suggested reading은 동사 find 의 목적어이며, 빈칸은 목적격 보어 자리이다. 따라서 '유용한'이라는 의미의 형용사인 (B) useful이 정답이다.

번역　많은 학생들이 추천도서가 강좌 내용을 이해하는 데 유용하다고 생각한다.

어휘　suggested reading 추천도서　content 내용 useful 유용한

기출공식 8　　　　　　　　　　　　본책 p. 31

22 (A)　　**23** (B)　　**24** (A)

22

해설　**수식어_전치사:** 빈칸 앞에 완전한 절이 왔고, 뒤에는 an identification badge라는 명사구가 왔으므로, 빈칸에는 전치사가 들어가야 한다. 또한 문맥상 '신분증 없이는 작업장 출입이 허용되지 않는다'라는 내용이 되어야 하므로, '~ 없이'라는 의미의 전치사인 (A) without이 정답이 된다. (B) unless와 (D) although는 접속사이므로 뒤에는 '주어 + 동사'를 갖춘 절 앞에서 쓰이며, (C) only는 부사이므로 뒤에 오는 명사구를 문장에 연결하는 자리에는 맞지 않다.

번역　신분증 없이는 누구도 작업장 출입이 허용되지 않습니다.

어휘　allow 허용하다, 허락하다　factory floor (공장) 작업장 identification 신분증, 신분확인(서)

23

해설　**수식어_접속사:** 두 문장을 이어 주는 접속사 자리이며, 문맥상 '1차 신청 서류가 본사에 접수되면, 추가 서류를 제출할 필요가 없다'라는 의미가 되어야 하므로, (B) Once가 가장 적절하다.

번역 1차 신청 서류가 본사에 접수되면, 추가 서류를 제출할 필요가 없습니다.

어휘 initial 처음의, 1차적인   application form 신청서

24

해설 **수식어_to부정사:** 빈칸 뒤에 부사 better와 동사원형인 serve가 왔고, 문맥상 '더 나은 서비스를 제공하기 위하여'라는 의미가 되어야 하므로 빈칸에는 목적의 의미를 나타내는 to부정사 표현이 와야 한다. 따라서 정답은 (A) In order to이다. (B) Due to(~ 때문에), (C) With regard to(~에 관해서는), (D) Owing to(~ 때문에)는 모두 전치사구이므로, 뒤에 동사원형이 올 수 없다.

번역 립스콘 오토는 고객님들께 더 나은 서비스를 제공하기 위해 더 큰 소매 공간으로 이전할 예정입니다.

어휘 serve (서비스 등을) 제공하다   relocate 이전하다   retail 소매의; 소매

본책 p. 32

ETS TEST

1 (A)	**2** (B)	**3** (C)	**4** (B)	**5** (B)
6 (A)	**7** (D)	**8** (D)	**9** (B)	**10** (D)
11 (C)	**12** (A)	**13** (B)	**14** (B)	**15** (A)
16 (C)	**17** (D)	**18** (C)	**19** (C)	**20** (D)

1

해설 **전치사의 목적어 자리:** 빈칸은 전치사 in의 목적어 자리로, '(정상적으로) 작동하는'을 의미하는 형용사 working의 수식을 받는 명사가 들어가야 한다. 따라서 정답은 (A) condition이다.

번역 하이트 중고 전자제품 상점은 여러분의 구매품이 작동하는 상태로 도착할 것을 보장합니다.

어휘 used 중고의   appliance 전자제품   purchase 구매(품)   condition 상태, 조건

2

해설 **타동사의 목적어 자리:** 빈칸은 동사 has의 목적어 자리이고, 앞에 부정관사 a와 형용사 thorough가 있으므로 명사가 들어가야 한다. 따라서 '지식'이라는 뜻의 명사인 (B) knowledge가 정답이다.

번역 스위스 사무소의 분석가 루시 듀몽은 유럽 금융시장에 대한 빈틈없는 지식을 가지고 있다.

어휘 thorough 빈틈없는   financial market 금융시장   knowledgeable 아는 것이 많은

3

해설 **타동사의 목적어 자리:** 빈칸은 동사 has requested의 목적어 자리이며 부정관사 a 뒤에는 반드시 단수명사가 와야 하므로 명사인 (C) extension이 정답이다.

번역 샴 비즈니스 스위트는 건축 허가를 한 달 연장해 달라고 요청했다.

어휘 building permit 건축 허가   extension 연장

4

해설 **주격 보어 자리:** 빈칸은 be동사 뒤 주격 보어 자리로, 부사 relatively의 수식을 받는 형용사가 들어가야 한다. 따라서 정답은 (B) rare이다.

번역 고객들은 전화기 비용에 불만을 표현했지만, 사용자 인터페이스에 대한 불만은 상대적으로 드물었다.

어휘 express 표현하다   dissatisfaction 불만족   complaint 불만, 항의   relatively 상대적으로   rare 드문   rarity 진귀한 사람[것]   rarely 거의 ~않다

5

해설 **주격 보어 자리:** 빈칸은 동사 will be의 보어 자리로, 문맥상 '선거 운동은 성공적일 것이다'라는 의미가 되어야 자연스러우므로 '성공적인'이라는 뜻의 형용사 (B) successful이 정답이다. 과거분사 (D) succeeded는 '계승하다, 뒤를 잇다'라는 뜻의 타동사 succeed에서 파생되어 '계승된'이라는 의미가 되므로 문맥상 오답이다.

번역 알리샤 라이니의 시장 선거 운동은 사람들이 그녀의 정책을 지지하기 때문에 아마도 성공할 것이다.

어휘 campaign 선거 운동   approve 지지하다   policy 정책

6

해설 **주격 보어 자리:** 빈칸은 be동사 뒤 보어 자리로, 문맥상 '이보다 더 기쁠 수 없다'가 되어야 자연스러우므로 형용사인 (A) happier가 정답이다. (B) happiest는 형용사의 최상급이므로 앞에 the를 붙여서 써야 하며, (C) happiness는 주어인 we와 동격이 될 수 없으므로 오답이다.

번역 우리는 헨리에타 무노즈가 이달의 사원으로 지명되어 더없이 기쁩니다.

어휘 name 지명[임명]하다

7

해설 **전치사의 목적어 자리:** 빈칸은 전치사 for의 목적어 자리이자 형용사 professional의 수식을 받는 자리이므로 명사인 (D) growth가 정답이다.

번역 베드포드 비즈니스 센터에서 강의를 듣는 것이 직업적 성장의 더 큰 기회로 이끌 수 있다.

어휘 course 강의, 강좌   professional 전문가의, 전문적인
growth 성장

8

해설 **보어 자리:** 빈칸은 be동사의 보어 자리로, 부사 quite의
수식을 받는 형용사가 들어가야 한다. 따라서 '유익한'이라
는 의미의 (D) beneficial이 정답이다. (C) benefitting
이 답이 되려면 뒤에 목적어가 필요하다.

번역 우리 직원들의 상당수는 새 컴퓨터 프로그램이 매우 유익하
다고 보고했다.

어휘 benefit 이익을 얻다, ~에게 이롭다   beneficial 유익한,
이로운

9

해설 **전치사의 목적어 자리:** 빈칸은 전치사 for의 목적어 자리로
명사가 와야 하므로, 앞에 온 명사 information과 결합하
여 복합명사를 이루는 (B) distribution이 정답이다. 나머
지 보기들은 모두 동사의 형태이므로 오답이다.

번역 프로젝트 관리자는 외부 팀원들에게 정보를 배포할 책임을
맡게 될 것입니다.

어휘 responsible 책임이 있는, (업무를) 담당하는   external
외부의   distribution 배포, 배분, 유통

10

해설 **주격 보어 자리:** While이 이끄는 절의 동사 remain은
2형식 동사로 형용사 보어가 필요하므로, 빈칸에는 '충실
한, 충성스러운'을 뜻하는 (D) loyal이 들어가야 한다.

번역 맥길 일렉트로닉스는 수십 년 동안 자사를 지원해 준 고객들
에게 계속 충실하면서 모든 사업 분야를 다각화할 것이다.

어휘 remain 여전히 ~이다   for decades 수십 년 동안
diversify 다각[다양]화하다   loyalty 충성, 충실

11

해설 **타동사의 목적어 자리:** 빈칸은 동사 reschedule의 목적
어 자리로, 명사가 들어가야 한다. 문맥상 '개봉'이라는 뜻
이 필요하므로, 정답은 (C) release이다.

번역 감독이 대본 수정을 요청했기 때문에 아헨 픽처스는 다큐멘
터리의 개봉을 3월로 변경했다.

어휘 script 대본, 원고   reschedule 일정을 변경하다
releasable 석방할 수 있는, 양도할 수 있는   release
개봉[출시]; 개봉[출시]하다

12

해설 **주격 보어 자리:** 빈칸은 be동사의 보어 자리로, 주어
buildings를 수식하는 형용사가 와야 한다. 따라서 '공간
이 넓은'이라는 뜻의 (A) spacious가 정답이다. 참고로,
and 뒤에 온 well lit은 '채광이 좋은'이라는 의미로 쓰인
또 다른 보어로, and 앞뒤는 같은 품사끼리 대등하게 병렬

구조를 이룬다.

번역 쾌적한 근무 환경을 제공하려는 바렛 인터내셔널의 노력에
맞게, 회사의 신사옥은 넓고 채광이 좋다.

어휘 in keeping with ~와 어울려   work environment
근무 환경   spacing 간격   spaciousness 널찍함

13

해설 **타동사의 목적어 자리:** 빈칸에는 동사 discuss의 목적어
역할을 하며 소유격대명사 his의 수식을 받는 명사가 들어
가야 한다. 따라서 '생각, 인상'이라는 의미의 명사인 (B)
impressions가 정답이다.

번역 오주카 씨는 가장 최근의 예산안 수정에 대한 자신의 생각
을 이야기하고 싶어 한다.

어휘 recent 최근의   budget proposal 예산안
impression 인상, 생각

14

해설 **전치사의 목적어 자리:** 빈칸은 전치사 with의 목적어 자리
이므로, '절차'라는 의미의 명사인 (B) procedures가 정
답이다.

번역 이 서류는 물의 샘플들이 청정 대기 및 수질 위원회가 정한
절차에 따라 수집되었음을 증명한다.

어휘 document 서류, 문서   certify 증명하다   in
accordance with ~에 따라서, ~과 일치하여
established 확립된, 확정된   proceed 나아가다,
계속하여 ~하다

15

해설 **수식어_부사절:** 빈칸 뒤에 완전한 절이 나오고, 콤마 뒤에
명령문이 나오면서 두 문장이 접속사 없이 연결되어 있으므
로 빈칸에는 접속사가 들어가야 한다. 따라서 정답은 '~할
때'라는 뜻의 부사절 접속사 (A) When이다. When부터
콤마까지가 전부 빠져도 문장은 성립하므로 부사절은 전체
문장에서 수식어 역할을 한다고 볼 수 있다.

번역 주방을 수리하기로 결정할 때는 반드시 여러 도급업체에서
비용 견적서를 받으십시오.

어휘 renovate 수리하다   estimate 견적(서)   contractor
도급업체

16

해설 **동사의 목적어 자리:** 빈칸은 have confirmed의 목적어
자리이다. 따라서 정답은 명사인 (C) receipt이다. 참고로,
receipt는 가산명사로 쓰일 때는 '영수증', 불가산명사로
쓰일 때는 '수령'을 뜻한다.

번역 섬완 게임즈의 영업 직원들은 고객들이 주문품의 수령 여부
를 확인하지 않으면 발송부에 연락해 후속 조치를 취한다.

sales associate 영업 직원 follow up ~을 추적하다,
후속 조치를 취하다 shipping department 발송 부서
confirm 확인하다 order 주문, 주문품

17

해설 **주격 보어 자리:** 빈칸은 be동사의 주격 보어 자리이며, 빈
칸 뒤에 온 to부정사와 함께 '~하기를 주저하다'라는 의
미가 되어야 하므로 '주저하는'이라는 뜻의 형용사 (D)
hesitant가 정답이다. '주저하다'를 뜻하는 동사 hesitate
는 수동태로 쓰지 않으므로 (C) hesitated는 오답이다.

번역 현지 제조업체들은 생산성이 향상될 때까지 추가적인 인력
채용을 꺼려 왔다.

어휘 local 현지의 manufacturer 제조업체 additional
추가의 productivity 생산성 hesitation 망설임

18

해설 **목적격 보어 자리:** 5형식 동사 make 뒤에 목적어인 its
health drinks가 왔으므로, 빈칸은 make의 목적격 보
어 자리이다. 따라서 '매력적인'이라는 의미의 형용사인 (C)
attractive가 정답이다.

번역 멜웨이 음료사는 건강 음료를 더 다양한 소비자들에게 매력
적으로 만들기 위해 독특한 포장 디자인을 사용하고 있다.

어휘 unique 독특한 package 포장, 소포 a wide
range of 다양한 attract 끌어모으다 attractively
매력적으로

19

해설 **목적격 보어 자리:** 5형식 동사 make 뒤에 목적어로 it이
왔으므로, 빈칸은 make의 목적격 보어가 와야 한다. 따라
서 정답은 형용사인 (C) hard이다. 이때 it은 가목적어이며
뒤에 나오는 to부정사가 make의 진목적어이므로, 해석할
때는 make의 목적어 자리에 to부정사를 넣어, '예측하는
것(to anticipate)을 어렵게(hard) 만든다(make)'와 같
이 해석한다.

번역 시장의 잦은 변동은 스테레오 장비 생산업체들이 자신 있게
혹은 정확하게 수요를 예측하는 것을 어렵게 만든다.

어휘 frequent 빈번한 producer 생산업체 anticipate
예상하다 demand 수요 precision 정확함

20

해설 **수식어_전치사:** 빈칸 앞에 완전한 절이 있고 뒤에 part라
는 명사가 나오므로 명사를 절에 연결할 수 있는 전치사가
필요하다. 따라서 정답은 (D) as이다. as 이하는 전체 문장
에서 수식어 역할을 한다.

번역 팩-프로사는 브랜드 이미지 쇄신 노력의 일환으로 새로운
웹사이트를 개설했다.

어휘 launch 개설하다 rebranding 브랜드 이미지 쇄신
effort 노력

CHAPTER 02 | 품사

UNIT 03	명사

기출공식 1	본책 p. 36
1 (C) **2** (B) **3** (A)	

1

해설 **명사의 역할_주어:** 빈칸까지가 주어이고, has caused가
동사인 문장으로 빈칸에는 명사가 들어가야 한다. 따라서
명사인 (B) close와 (C) closure가 가능한데, (B) close
는 단수로 쓰여 '끝, 종결, (문을) 닫기'라는 의미이고, (C)
closure는 '폐쇄'라는 의미이므로, bridge와 어울려 쓰이
는 (C) closure가 정답이 된다.

번역 다리 폐쇄로 리버 가와 메인 가의 교통이 많이 지체되었다.

어휘 cause 유발하다 traffic delay 교통 지체

2

해설 **명사의 역할_보어:** 빈칸은 동사 is의 보어 자리로, 정관사
the와 형용사 main의 수식을 받으므로 빈칸에는 명
사가 들어가야 한다. 따라서 '자격'이라는 의미의 (B)
qualification이 정답이다.

번역 슬로운 씨가 그 직책에 지원한 다른 지원자들과 차별되는
주요한 자격 요건은 바로 국제 경험이다.

어휘 separate A from B A를 B로부터 분리[구분]하다
candidate 후보자, 지원자 position 직위 qualified
자격 있는, 적임의 qualify ~에게 자격을 주다

3

해설 **명사의 역할_전치사의 목적어:** 전치사 for 다음에는 명사
가 와야 한다. 따라서 '유통, 배분'이라는 의미의 (A)
distribution이 정답이다.

번역 일단 베리를 수확하면, 그린 필즈 농장은 소매점에 유통하
기 위해 수확물을 세척하고 포장한다.

어휘 once 일단 ~하면 berry 베리(딸기류의 열매) harvest
수확하다; 수확, 추수 package 포장하다, 싸다

기출공식 2	본책 p. 36
4 (C) **5** (A) **6** (D)	

4

해설 **명사 자리_소유격 뒤:** 전치사 on의 목적어 역할로 소유격
뒤 명사가 와야 하므로, 빈칸은 명사 자리이다. 따라서 '상
상, 상상력'이라는 의미의 명사인 (C) imagination이 정
답이다.

번역 재니스 티어니의 모든 그림은 역사적인 사진들을 바탕으로 하지만, 그녀는 세부적인 것들은 상상력에 의존해 채운다.

어휘 drawing 그림, 도면 be based on ~을 바탕으로 하다 rely on ~에 의존하다

5

해설 **명사 자리_관사 뒤:** 관사 뒤에는 명사가 오는데, 문맥상 뒤에 온 명사 fee와 함께 쓰여 '등록비'를 의미하는 복합명사를 만들 수 있는 (A) enrollment가 정답이다.

번역 물류 관리 과정의 등록비는 1인당 25유로다.

어휘 logistics 물류 enrollment 등록 enroll (이름을) 명부에 올리다, 등록하다

6

해설 **명사 자리_형용사 뒤:** 동사 has received의 목적어 역할로 형용사 뒤 명사가 와야 하므로 (D) complaints가 정답이다. '수많은'을 의미하는 numerous 뒤에 가산명사의 복수형이 온다는 사실을 알아도 complaints를 선택할 수 있다.

번역 우리 서비스부는 신형 TZ-2000 프로세서의 과열과 관련하여 수많은 불만을 접수했다.

어휘 numerous 다수의, 수많은 processor (컴퓨터의) 프로세서 overheating 과열 complain 불평하다, 항의하다 complaint 불평, 불만

기출공식 3 본책 p. 37

7 (D) **8** (C) **9** (D)

7

해설 **가산명사와 불가산명사:** 빈칸은 전치사 in의 목적어 자리이므로 명사가 들어가야 한다. 전치사 in은 분야와 함께 쓰이므로 '회계'라는 분야를 나타낼 수 있는 불가산명사인 (D) accounting이 정답이다. '회계사'를 뜻하는 (B) accountant는 가산명사이므로 한정사와 함께 쓰여야 한다.

번역 그 면접자는 마케팅 자리에 관심을 표했으나 그녀의 이력서 상의 이전 경력은 오로지 회계 부문이었다.

어휘 interviewee 면접을 받는 사람 previous 이전의 résumé 이력서 exclusively 독점적으로, 오로지

8

해설 **가산명사와 불가산명사:** 빈칸 앞에 온 driving과 함께 쓰여 '운전 면허증'이라는 의미의 가산명사를 만들 수 있는 (C) permit이 정답이다. driving 앞에 부정관사 a가 있으므로 복수형인 (B) permits는 쓸 수 없다. (A) permission은

'허락, 허가'라는 의미의 불가산명사이므로 부정관사 a와 함께 쓸 수 없다.

번역 운전면허증을 신청하려면 두 가지 형태의 신분증을 보여 주어야 한다.

어휘 apply for ~을 신청하다 identification 신분증 permit 허가증

9

해설 **가산명사와 불가산명사:** 빈칸은 전치사 on의 목적어 자리이고 형용사 long-term의 수식을 받고 있으므로 명사가 들어가야 한다. 따라서 (A) plan과 (D) planning 중 하나를 선택해야 하는데, 빈칸 앞에 관사나 소유격이 없으므로 가산명사인 plan은 들어갈 수 없고 불가산명사인 (D) planning이 정답이다.

번역 사기업들은 종종 장기적인 계획에 집중할 수 있는 자유가 더 많다.

어휘 privately-owned company 사기업 long-term 장기적인

기출공식 4 본책 p. 37

10 (C) **11** (C) **12** (A)

10

해설 **가산명사와 불가산명사:** 빈칸에는 '자세한'이라는 뜻의 형용사 detailed의 수식을 받는 명사가 필요하다. 보기 중 (C) instructions와 (D) instructors가 명사인데, 문맥상 주어 부분은 '자세한 설명'이라는 의미가 적절하므로 '설명'이라는 뜻의 (C) instructions가 정답이다.

번역 엑스턴 스캐너로 문서를 스캔하는 것에 대한 자세한 설명이 사용설명서 9페이지에 나와 있습니다.

어휘 detailed 상세한, 자세한 provide 제공하다, 주다 user's manual 사용설명서 instruct 가르치다, 지시하다 instructor 강사

11

해설 **가산명사와 불가산명사:** 빈칸은 앞에 온 to부정사(to collect)의 목적어 자리이므로, 명사가 들어가야 한다. 보기 중 명사는 (B) payers와 (C) payment인데, payer는 '지급인, 납부자'라는 의미의 사람명사이고, payment는 '지불금'이라는 의미의 사물명사이다. 문맥상 '대금을 회수하다'라는 의미가 되어야 하므로, (C) payment가 정답이다.

번역 약국은 처방약을 조제할 때 대금을 회수해야 한다.

어휘 pharmacy 약국 be required to ~하도록 요구되다 collect payment 대금을 회수하다 fill prescriptions 처방약을 조제하다

12

해설 **가산명사와 불가산명사:** 빈칸은 having examined의 목적어 역할을 하고 있으므로 명사 자리이다. 따라서 '세부 사항'이라는 의미의 명사인 (A) specifics가 정답이다. 참고로 '세부 사항'을 의미할 때는 항상 복수형으로 쓰인다.

번역 위원회는 상세한 내용은 검토하지 않은 채 원칙적으로 그 제안을 수용했다.

어휘 accept 수용하다   in principle 원칙적으로, 대체로   specify 명시하다   specific 구체적인, 특정한   specifically 명확하게, 특별하게

기출공식 5   본책 p. 38

13 (D)   **14** (C)   **15** (A)

13

해설 **한정사 + 명사:** 빈칸 앞에 부정관사 a가 있으므로 동사 receive의 목적어로 쓰일 단수명사가 필요하다. 따라서 (D) response가 정답이다. 동명사인 (B) responding도 목적어 역할을 할 수 있지만, 동명사는 부정관사와 함께 쓰지 않으므로 정답이 될 수 없다.

번역 서비스부에 직원이 부족하기 때문에 고객 문의에 대한 답변을 받는 데 5일이 걸릴 수 있습니다.

어휘 understaffed 인원이 부족한   inquiry 문의   respond 대답하다, 응답하다

14

해설 **한정사 + 명사:** 빈칸 앞에 가산 복수명사 또는 불가산명사와 함께 쓰는 한정사 all이 있으므로 (C) visitors가 정답이다. 사람명사가 아닌 다른 명사 보기는 '등록해야 한다(must register)'의 주체가 될 수 없으므로 오답이다.

번역 자동차 생산 공장을 찾는 방문객은 모두 안으로 들어가기 전에 반드시 보안 검문소에 등록해야 한다.

어휘 register 등록하다   security checkpoint 보안 검문소   visit 방문; 방문하다   visitation 방문, 시찰   visitor 방문객

15

해설 **한정사 + 명사:** 빈칸 앞에 가산 단수명사와 함께 쓰는 한정사인 each가 있으므로 (A) participant가 정답이다.

번역 모든 세미나 참가자는 자신의 진로 목표에 대해 이야기할 준비가 되어 있어야 한다.

어휘 prepared 준비된   career goal 진로 목표   participation 참가   participate 참가하다

기출공식 6   본책 p. 38

16 (D)   **17** (A)   **18** (B)

16

해설 **추상명사:** 소유격 뒤 명사 자리이므로 (D) supervision이 정답이다. under one's supervision은 '~의 감독[지휘]하에'라는 의미로 자주 출제되니 통째로 암기해 두자.

번역 슈바이처 씨는 지난 5년간 나의 감독하에 편집 보조로 일해 왔다.

어휘 editorial 편집의   assistant 조수, 보좌역   supervise 감독하다, 지휘하다

17

해설 **추상명사:** 동사 undergo는 '겪다, 받다'의 목적어로 사람명사가 아닌 추상명사가 어울린다. 따라서 '조사'라는 의미의 (A) inspection이 정답이다.

번역 지방 법규에 따르면, 모든 식당은 매년 한 번씩 보건 및 안전 조사를 받아야 한다.

어휘 undergo 겪다, 받다   inspector 조사관

18

해설 **사람명사:** 빈칸은 주어 역할을 하는 명사 자리이다. 문장의 동사 '참석할 것이다(will attend)'의 주체로는 사람명사가 어울리므로 (B) Operators가 정답이다.

번역 시내 버스 운영자들은 다음 달 신형 차량에 대한 연수 교육에 참석할 것이다.

어휘 city bus 시내 버스   training session 연수 교육   operation 운영   operator 운영자

기출공식 7   본책 p. 39

19 (C)   **20** (C)   **21** (C)

19

해설 **-tive형 명사:** will 앞까지 문장의 주어로, 빈칸에는 주어 역할을 하는 명사가 와야 한다. '회사에서 나온 대표 직원'이라는 의미를 가지며 will be happy의 주체가 되어야 하므로 사람을 지칭하는 (C) representative가 정답이다.

번역 젠슨-콤즈사의 직원은 기꺼이 웨스트보로우 취업 박람회에서 유망한 구직자들을 만날 것이다.

어휘 corporation 주식회사   prospective 유망한, 기대되는   job applicant 구직자   job fair 취업 설명회[박람회]   representative 직원, 대리인   representation 표시, 표현

20

해설 **-tive형 명사:** 빈칸은 동사 can show의 목적어 자리이므로 명사가 와야 한다. 문맥상 '진취성을 보여줄 수 있다'라는 의미가 되어야 자연스러우므로 '진취성'이라는 뜻의 명사인 (C) initiative가 정답이다. (D) initial도 명사이기는 하나 '이름의 첫 글자'라는 의미로 문맥에 어울리지 않고, 가산명사이므로 한정사와 함께 쓰거나 복수형으로 써야 한다. 참고로 take the initiative(주도권을 쥐다)도 빈출 표현이므로 알아 두는 것이 좋다.

번역 일부 분야의 인턴들은 자신만의 프로젝트를 제안해 진취성을 보여줄 수 있다.

어휘 propose 제안하다   initially 처음에   initiate 주도하다   initial 원래의

21

해설 **-al형 명사:** 문맥상 '의료 전문가와 상담한다'라는 의미가 되어야 하므로, '전문가'라는 의미의 (C) professionals가 정답이다.

번역 네이피어사는 피트니스 장비를 설계할 때 의료 전문가와 상담한다.

어휘 healthcare 의료; 의료의   equipment 장비   profession 직업   professional 직업의; 전문가

기출공식 8	본책 p. 39
22 (B) **23** (B) **24** (D)	

22

해설 **복합명사:** to increase의 목적어 자리이므로, 빈칸에는 명사가 들어가야 한다. employee는 가산명사인데 앞에 관사도 없고 복수형도 아니므로 단독으로 명사 자리에 올 수 없으며, 뒤에 따르는 명사와 함께 복합명사를 이루어야 한다. 따라서 '생산성'이라는 의미의 명사인 (B) productivity가 정답이다. employee productivity는 대표적인 복합명사로 '직원 생산성'을 의미한다.

번역 직원 생산성을 증진시키기 위해 앨취 의학 용품점은 직업적 기여를 한 우수 직원들에게 포상을 한다.

어휘 reward 상을 주다, 포상을 하다   outstanding 뛰어난   professional 직업의, 전문가의   contribution 공헌, 기여

23

해설 **복합명사:** meet의 목적어이자, 빈칸 앞의 quality와 함께 쓰여 '품질 요구 조건을 충족시키다'라는 의미의 복합명사를 만들 수 있는 (B) requirements가 정답이다.

번역 유감스럽게도, 새로 제조된 전자 부품들은 젬 어소시에이츠의 품질 요구 조건을 충족시키지 못한다.

어휘 unfortunately 유감스럽게도   manufactured 제조된   component 부품   meet 충족시키다   require 요구하다

24

해설 **복합명사:** 빈칸 앞의 employee와 함께 쓰여 '직원 업무 성과'라는 의미의 복합명사를 만들 수 있는 (D) performance가 정답이다.

번역 수년간 회사들은 직원 업무 성과를 측정할 다양한 방법들을 개발하고 시험해 왔다.

어휘 various 다양한   method 방법   measure 측정하다   performer 연기자   perform 이행하다

ETS **TEST**				본책 p. 40
1 (B)	**2** (C)	**3** (D)	**4** (D)	**5** (D)
6 (C)	**7** (B)	**8** (B)	**9** (B)	**10** (C)
11 (A)	**12** (A)	**13** (C)	**14** (C)	**15** (A)
16 (A)	**17** (A)	**18** (B)	**19** (D)	**20** (B)

1

해설 **복합명사:** 빈칸에는 동사 has의 목적어 역할을 하며 employment와 함께 복합명사를 이루는 명사가 와야 한다. 문맥상 '취업 자리'라는 의미가 적절하므로 '일자리, 공석'을 뜻하는 (B) openings가 정답이다.

번역 마닐라 웰니스 센터에는 우리 마카티 지점의 공인 간호조무사직의 시간제 및 임시 취업 자리가 있다.

어휘 part-time 시간제의   temporary 임시의   certified 공인의   nursing attendant 간호조무사   openness 솔직함, 개방성

2

해설 **추상명사 vs. 사람명사:** 빈칸 앞에 관사 the가 있으므로 빈칸은 명사 자리이다. 문맥상 '사용자 설명서의 삽화를 참조하는 것'이라는 의미가 되어야 하므로, '삽화'라는 뜻의 추상명사 (C) illustration이 정답이다.

번역 사용자 설명서의 삽화를 참조하는 것은 작업대 부품을 확인하는 데 도움이 될 것이다.

어휘 refer to 참조하다   identify 알아보다, 확인하다   workbench 작업대   illustrate 삽화를 넣다   illustrator 삽화가   illustration 삽화

3

해설 **추상명사 vs. 사람명사:** 빈칸은 동사 is의 보어 자리로, 부정관사 a와 형용사 large의 수식을 받고 있으므로 빈칸에는 명사가 들어가야 한다. 또한 주어인 '줄리 스튜디오'와 동격을 이루어야 하므로 '제작사'라는 뜻의 (D) producer가 정답이다.

번역 줄리 스튜디오는 큰 애니메이션 제작사이지만, 연간 수익은 경쟁사들에 비해 낮다.

어휘 animated 만화 영화로 된 annual 연간의 revenue 수익 competitor 경쟁자

4

해설 **추상명사 vs. 사람명사:** 빈칸 앞에 소유격('s)이 있고 뒤에는 동사 have가 있으므로, 빈칸에는 주어 역할을 할 수 있는 명사가 들어가야 한다. 동사 have의 주체가 되며 수가 일치하는 사람명사 (D) instructors가 정답이다.

번역 모든 몰리나 어학원의 강사들은 3년 이상의 경력과 유효한 교사 자격증을 가지고 있다.

어휘 language institute 어학원 valid 유효한 credential 자격, 보증서 instruction 설명(서) instructor 강사

5

해설 **추상명사 vs. 사람명사:** 소유격 다음에는 소유격의 수식을 받는 명사가 반드시 필요하고, 문맥상 '우리 잡지의 구독자'라는 의미가 되어야 자연스러우므로 '구독자'라는 뜻의 (D) subscribers가 정답이다.

번역 우리 잡지 구독자의 약 30%는 싱가포르에 거주한다.

어휘 about 약 reside 거주하다

6

해설 **명사 자리_형용사 뒤:** 빈칸에는 소유격 대명사 its 및 형용사 historical의 수식을 받는 명사가 들어가야 한다. 따라서 '중요성, 의의'라는 뜻의 명사인 (C) significance가 정답이다.

번역 1885년에 건설된 핼프린 힐 다리는 역사적 의의 때문에 보존되어 오고 있다.

어휘 preserve 보존하다 historical 역사적인 signify 의미하다 significant 중요한, 의미 있는 significantly 상당히

7

해설 **사물명사 vs. 사람명사:** 빈칸은 전치사 from의 목적어로 명사가 와야 한다. 해석상 '주민들로부터 온 질문'이라고 하는 것이 자연스러우며, resident는 가산명사이므로 한정사가 붙거나 복수형으로 써야 한다. 따라서 정답은 (B) residents이다.

번역 시 의회는 새로운 급수탑에 관한 주민들의 질문을 처리하기 위해 내일 만날 것이다.

어휘 council 의회 field (질문을) 처리하다 concerning ~에 관한 water tower 급수탑 residence 집 residential 거주의

8

해설 **복합명사:** 빈칸은 동사 ensured의 목적어 자리이며, 앞에 온 명사 consumer가 가산명사임에도 앞에 한정사가 붙거나 복수 형태로 쓰이지 않았으므로 빈칸 자리에는 또 다른 명사가 와서 복합명사를 이루어야 한다. 따라서 '소비자 수용'이라는 의미의 복합명사를 만들 수 있는 (B) acceptance가 정답이다.

번역 우리의 1년에 걸친 마케팅 활동으로 새로운 아이스크림 맛에 대한 소비자 수용이 확실해졌다.

어휘 yearlong 1년간 계속되는 ensure 확실하게 하다 consumer 소비자 flavor 맛 acceptance 수용 acceptable 수용할 수 있는

9

해설 **명사의 역할_전치사의 목적어:** 빈칸은 전치사 of의 목적어 역할을 하며 형용사 ongoing의 수식을 받는 명사 자리이므로, 정답은 (B) maintenance이다. 참고로, maintain은 타동사로서 동명사로 쓰일 경우 목적어를 취해야 하므로 (A) maintaining은 정답이 될 수 없다.

번역 아파트의 월세에는 계속 진행되는 인근 정원 관리 분담금이 포함되어 있다.

어휘 rental fee 임대료 shared cost 분담금 ongoing 계속 진행 중인 maintenance 관리, 유지 및 보수 surrounding 주변의, 인근의

10

해설 **명사 자리_관사 뒤:** 빈칸에는 관사 뒤에 올 수 있는 명사가 들어가야 하는데, '사업 확장 계획을 확인하는 성명'이 되는 것이 자연스러우므로 정답은 (C) statement이다.

번역 IGY사는 오늘 아침 남아메리카에서의 사업 확장 계획을 확인하는 성명을 발표했다.

어휘 release 발표하다 confirm 확인하다, 인증하다 expansion 확장 state 진술하다 statement 성명, 내역서

11

해설 **추상명사 vs. 사람명사:** 빈칸은 '~에 로그인하다'라는 뜻의 동사구 'log in to'의 목적어 자리이며, 문맥상 '시간 및 근로 계정에 로그인해야 한다'는 의미가 되어야 하므로, '계정'이라는 의미의 (A) accounts가 정답이다.

번역 모든 직원들은 근무한 시간을 기록하기 위해 매일 시간 및 근로 계정에 로그인해야 한다.

어휘 record 기록하다 account 계정; 설명하다(for)
accountant 회계사 accountable 책임이 있는

12

해설 **명사 자리_소유격 뒤:** 빈칸은 전치사 for의 목적어로 소유격의 수식을 받는 명사 자리이다. 따라서 '분석'이라는 뜻의 (A) analysis가 정답이다.

번역 다음 목록에는 네일런 씨가 잠재적 기업 고객을 분석할 때 필요한 정보가 상세히 나와 있습니다.

어휘 following 다음의, 다음에 나오는 detail 자세히 말하다; 세부 사항 potential 잠재적인; 잠재력
corporate client 기업 고객

13

해설 **추상명사 vs. 사람명사:** 빈칸은 has been의 보어 자리로, 앞에 온 형용사 premier의 수식을 받는 명사 자리이다. 따라서 업체명인 주어와 동격을 이루는 명사 (C) provider가 정답이다. (B) provision은 조항, 준비라는 뜻이므로 주어와 동격이 될 수 없다.

번역 30년 동안, 빅 탑 프롭 컴퍼니는 전 세계 극단들을 위한 최고의 서커스 장비 제공 업체였다.

어휘 prop(property) 소도구 premier 최고의 troupe
공연단, 극단

14

해설 **명사 자리_관사 뒤:** 빈칸 앞에 정관사 the가 있으므로 빈칸은 명사 자리이다. 따라서 '제안'이라는 뜻의 명사 (C) proposal이 정답이다.

번역 브리지윅스사의 이사회는 회사의 투자 정책을 수정하자는 제안을 표결에 부칠 것이다.

어휘 board of directors 이사회 vote 투표하다 modify
수정하다 investment 투자 policy 정책

15

해설 **복합명사:** that절의 주어 자리에 온 명사 government는 가산명사임에도 앞에 한정사가 붙거나 복수 형태로 쓰이지 않았으므로 빈칸 자리에는 또 다른 명사가 와서 복합명사를 이루어야 한다. 또한 동사가 have led로 복수동사이므로 빈칸에는 복수명사가 와야 한다. 따라서 정답은 (A) regulations이다.

번역 한 연구에서 클라크스버그에서 건축 허가에 대한 정부 규정으로 인해 도시 계획이 더 개선되었다는 것을 밝혀냈다.

어휘 building permits 건축 허가(증) city planning 도시
계획 regulate 규제하다, 통제하다

16

해설 **명사 자리_한정사 뒤:** 빈칸은 to부정사 to work의 목적어로 쓰일 명사가 들어갈 자리이고, 빈칸 앞에 한정사 one이 있으므로 단수명사인 (A) shift가 정답이다.

번역 약사는 전원 일주일에 한 번 8시간 교대 근무를 하도록 신청해야 한다.

어휘 pharmacist 약사 sign up 신청하다

17

해설 **명사의 역할_전치사의 목적어:** 빈칸은 전치사 for의 목적어 자리이므로 명사인 (A) use가 정답이다.

번역 벤튼 식물원 회원 전원은 로즈부시 카페에서 사용할 수 있는 할인권을 받게 된다.

어휘 voucher 할인권 for use 사용할 수 있는 useful
유용한

18

해설 **복합명사:** 빈칸 앞에 온 명사 price는 가산명사인데 앞에 한정사가 붙거나 복수 형태로 쓰이지 않았으므로 빈칸 자리에는 또 다른 명사가 와서 복합명사를 이루어야 한다. 따라서 빈칸 앞의 명사 price와 함께 쓰여 '가격 비교'라는 의미의 복합명사를 만들 수 있는 (B) comparisons가 정답이다.

번역 에블린 추의 웹사이트에서는 현재 시판 중인 전자제품에 대한 평가와 가격 비교를 소비자들에게 제공한다.

어휘 consumer 소비자 electronic device 전자 기기
on the market 시중에 판매되고 있는

19

해설 **-tive형 명사:** 빈칸은 동사 provides의 목적어 자리이며 형용사 affordable의 수식을 받는 자리이므로 명사인 (D) alternative가 정답이다.

번역 환경 의식적 상업 및 주거용 건축을 추구하는 고객들을 위해서 그린 스페이스사는 합리적인 대안을 제공한다.

어휘 environmentally conscious 환경 의식적인
commercial 상업용의 residential 주거용의
affordable (가격이) 합리적인 alternate 번갈아
나오다 alternative 대안; 대체의

20

해설 **추상명사 vs. 사람명사:** 빈칸은 주어 자리이며 동사 will receive의 주체가 되어야 하므로 사람명사가 와야 한다. 또한 participant는 가산명사이므로 한정사 없이 단독으로는 단수형으로 쓸 수 없다. 따라서 (B) Participants가 정답이다.

번역 참가자는 50달러의 상품권과 이동 경비를 받게 됩니다.

어휘 gift card 상품권 compensation 보상(금)
participate 참가하다 participation 참가

UNIT 04 | 대명사

기출공식 1   본책 p. 44

1 (D)   **2** (C)   **3** (D)

1

해설 **인칭대명사_주격:** 접속사 before절에서 동사 requests의 주어가 와야 하는 자리이므로, 정답은 주격인 (D) he이다.

번역 슈바르츠 씨는 하트만 씨에게 승진 요청을 하기 전에 현 프로젝트의 결과를 발표하라고 조언했다.

어휘 publish 발표하다, 출판하다   current 현재의
request 요청하다; 요청   promotion 승진

2

해설 **인칭대명사_소유격:** 빈칸에는 명사 supervisors를 수식할 수 있는 소유격이 들어가야 한다. 따라서 정답은 (C) their가 정답이다.

번역 영업부 직원들은 출장비 환급을 신청하기 전에 자신들의 상사들로부터 허가를 받아야 한다.

어휘 obtain 얻다, 획득하다   permission 허가
supervisor 상사, 감독관   apply for ~을 신청하다
reimbursement (경비 등의) 상환

3

해설 **인칭대명사_소유대명사:** 접속사 when절에서 동사 was accepted의 주어가 와야 하는 자리이므로, 빈칸에는 주격이면서 단수 취급되는 대명사가 들어가야 한다. 따라서 정답은 소유대명사인 (D) theirs이다. 이때 theirs는 their proposal을 의미한다.

번역 시의회에 많은 제안서가 제출되었기 때문에, 린 씨와 존스 씨는 자신들의 제안서가 수락되자 기뻐했다.

어휘 proposal 제안(서)   present 제출하다   city council 시의회   accept 수락하다, 받아들이다

기출공식 2   본책 p. 44

4 (D)   **5** (B)   **6** (A)

4

해설 **재귀대명사_재귀 용법:** 빈칸은 동사 has assigned의 목적어 자리이므로 목적격 인칭대명사인 (C) him과 재귀대명사인 (D) himself 중에서 선택해야 한다. 문맥상 '이기남

씨는 필요한 전문 지식을 갖추고 있어 스스로 서보스사 협상을 맡기로 했다'는 의미가 적절하므로 동작의 대상이 되는 목적어가 주어 자신(Ki-nam Yi)이 된다. 따라서 재귀대명사인 (D) himself가 정답이다.

번역 이기남 씨는 필요한 전문 지식을 갖추고 있어 스스로 서보스사 협상을 맡기로 했다.

어휘 expertise 전문지식   assign (일, 문건 등을) 배당하다
negotiation 협상

5

해설 **재귀대명사_강조 용법:** 빈칸이 없어도 완전한 문장이므로 강조 용법의 재귀대명사가 필요하다. 따라서 (B) herself가 정답이다.

번역 최근 그 식당의 주방에는 일손이 부족해서 이번 주에는 매니저가 직접 요리 준비를 도울 것이다.

어휘 understaffed 일손이 부족한   preparation 준비

6

해설 **대명사_관용 표현:** '3주간의 교육 후에'라는 내용으로 보아, 빈칸이 포함된 절은 엔지니어링 인턴들이 교육 후 '직접' 신제품을 개발하라는 요청을 받을 것이라는 내용이 되어야 자연스럽다. 따라서 정답은 전치사 on과 함께 쓰여 '스스로'의 의미를 강조하는 (A) their own이다.

번역 3주간의 교육 후 엔지니어링 인턴들은 스스로 신제품을 개발하라는 요청을 받을 것이다.

어휘 develop 개발하다   new product 신제품   on one's own 스스로, 직접

기출공식 3   본책 p. 45

7 (C)   **8** (A)   **9** (B)

7

해설 **지시대명사_those:** Reviews ~ Web site가 주어이고 have grown이 동사, 그리고 especially ~ quality는 동격의 삽입구이다. 앞뒤로 especially와 relating to product quality의 수식을 받고 있는 빈칸에는 Reviews를 대신하는 대명사가 필요하다. 보기 중 복수명사를 대신할 수 있는 대명사는 (C) those뿐이다.

번역 매니퍼 풋웨어 웹사이트에 게시되는 상품평, 특히 제품 품질과 관련된 것들은 갈수록 더 긍정적이 되었다.

어휘 review 논평, 비평   post (웹사이트에 자료를) 올리다, 게시하다   footwear 신발류   relate to ~와 관련되다
product quality 제품 품질   grow 점차 ~하게 되다
positive 긍정적인

8

해설 **지시대명사_those:** 주격 관계대명사 who 앞에서 '사람들'이라는 뜻으로 쓰일 수 있는 대명사는 (A) Those이다.

번역 XMT 컨설팅이 주최하는 세미나에 참석하기를 희망하는 분들은 수요일 오후 5시까지 등록해야 합니다.

어휘 participate in ~에 참가[참석]하다   register 등록하다

9

해설 **지시대명사_those:** 빈칸이 that절의 주어 자리이며, 문맥상 '그 분야의 전문 지식을 가진 사람들'이라는 의미가 되어야 하므로 (B) those가 정답이다.

번역 카와무라 이사의 견해는 그 분야의 전문 지식을 가진 사람들이 최종 채용 결정을 내려야 한다는 것이다.

어휘 expertise 전문성, 전문 지식   be responsible for ~을 책임지다

기출공식 4		본책 p. 45
10 (D)	**11** (D)	**12** (D)

10

해설 **부정대명사_anyone:** 빈칸을 수식하는 관계사절의 동사가 wants로 단수이며, 문맥상 '세미나에 참석하고 싶은 사람은 누구나'라는 의미가 가장 적절하므로, 정답은 (D) Anyone이다. 참고로 those who를 쓰는 경우에는 동사가 want가 되어야 한다.

번역 11월 12일에 있는 세미나에 참석하고 싶은 사람은 누구나 금요일까지 사라스와티 씨에게 연락해야 한다.

어휘 participate in ~에 참여하다

11

해설 **부정대명사_several:** 문장의 주어 역할을 하면서 뒤의 명사 passengers를 받는 부정대명사가 필요하므로 '~ 중의 몇몇'을 나타내는 (D) Several이 정답이다.

번역 246편의 일부 승객들이 날씨로 인한 연착의 결과로 더블린에서 연결 항공편을 놓쳤다.

어휘 miss 놓치다   connecting flight 연결 항공편

12

해설 **부정대명사_everyone:** 빈칸은 분사의 수식을 받으며 주어 역할을 하는 명사 자리이다. 문맥상 '설문 조사에 응하는 모든 사람'이라는 의미가 되어야 자연스러우므로, (D) Everyone이 정답이 된다.

번역 식당 설문 조사에 응답하는 모든 사람은 랭글리 카페의 10달러 상품권을 받을 것이다.

어휘 respond to ~에 대답[응답]하다   gift certificate 상품권

기출공식 5		본책 p. 46
13 (D)	**14** (A)	**15** (C)

13

해설 **부정대명사_ones:** while절의 주어 역할을 하는 동시에 주절에 언급된 복수명사 the printers를 받는 부정대명사가 필요하므로 (D) the ones가 정답이다.

번역 5층 프린터들이 수리되는 동안 대량 인쇄 작업은 3층 프린터들을 사용하시기 바랍니다.

어휘 high-volume 대량의   repair 수리하다; 수리

14

해설 **부정대명사_another:** 빈칸은 open의 목적어 자리이다. 첫 식당을 성공한 후에 '또 다른 하나'를 열기로 했다는 의미이므로 부정대명사 (A) another가 정답이다. 참고로 (C) other는 형용사로만 쓰인다.

번역 첫 식당이 크게 성공한 후, 비비엔 블랑은 식당을 하나 더 열기로 결정했다.

어휘 tremendous 엄청난, 대단한

15

해설 **부정대명사_the others:** 빈칸은 전치사 than의 목적어 자리이며, 문맥상 키가 큰 식물들을 대기실의 나머지 다른 식물들과 비교하는 의미가 되어야 하므로 '나머지들'을 뜻하는 부정대명사 (C) the others가 정답이다.

번역 키가 큰 식물은 대기실에 있는 나머지 다른 식물들보다 햇빛이 더 많이 필요하다.

어휘 require 필요하다

기출공식 6		본책 p. 46
16 (B)	**17** (B)	**18** (D)

16

해설 **상호대명사_each other:** 빈칸은 동사 help의 목적어 자리이고, 빈칸 앞에 짝을 지어 일한다(work in pairs)는 내용이 나오므로 '서로'를 의미하는 상호대명사인 (B) each other가 정답이다.

번역 직원들은 연수 기간 동안 짝을 지어 일하면서 고객 서비스 문의 사항들을 처리하는 과정을 완벽히 익힐 수 있도록 서로 도와야 한다.

어휘 in pairs 짝을 지어   master 완전히 익히다   procedure 절차   handle 다루다, 처리하다   inquiry 문의

17

해설 **상호대명사_one another:** 빈칸은 전치사 with의 목적어 자리이고, 문맥상 '서로 더 자주 소통하도록'이라는 내용이 되어야 자연스러우므로 '서로'를 의미하는 상호대명사인 (B) one another가 정답이다.

번역 개방형 사무실은 직원들이 서로 더 자주 소통하도록 유도할 것이다.

어휘 open-plan office 개방형 사무실 interact with ~와 소통하다 frequently 자주

18

해설 **부정대명사_others:** 앞에 나온 some이 문제 해결의 단서로, some과 others는 일부와 다른 일부를 대조하는 내용에서 자주 함께 쓰인다. 문맥상 '일부 의견들은 비판적이지만, 다른 의견들은 칭찬 일색이었다'는 의미가 되어야 하므로 (D) others가 정답이다. 상호대명사인 (C) each other는 주어 자리에 오지 못하므로 오답이다.

번역 일부 독자의 의견은 비판적이지만, 다른 의견들은 칭찬 일색이었다.

어휘 critical 비판적인 praise 칭찬

기출공식 7	본책 p. 47
19 (C) **20** (C) **21** (B)	

19

해설 **수량을 나타내는 부정대명사:** 빈칸은 that절의 주어 자리로 단수동사 is와 수가 일치하며, 'of + 복수명사' 구조와 함께 쓸 수 있는 대명사가 들어가야 한다. 따라서 정답은 (C) each이다. (A) every는 형용사이므로 every of는 불가능하며, (B) all은 동사와 수 일치가 맞지 않다. 또한 much는 'of + 불가산명사'와 함께 써야 하므로 오답이다.

번역 이륙 전 승무원들은 반드시 각 승객이 제대로 착석했는지 확인해야 한다.

어휘 takeoff 이륙 ensure 반드시 ~하게 하다

20

해설 **수량을 나타내는 부정대명사:** 빈칸은 문장의 주어 자리로 단수동사 has와 수가 일치하며, '둘 중에서'를 뜻하는 'of the two' 구조와 함께 쓸 수 있는 대명사가 들어가야 한다. 따라서 '둘 다 아닌'을 뜻하는 (C) neither가 정답이다. (A) most, (B) several, (D) some은 'of the two'와 어울리지 않으며, 'of the 복수명사'와 함께 쓸 때는 복수동사로 수 일치를 해야 하므로 오답이다.

번역 유감스럽게도 두 장소 중 어떤 곳도 차이 테크놀러지의 연례 연회를 개최하는 데 필요한 좌석 수를 갖추지 못했다.

어휘 venue 장소 capacity 수용 능력, 정원 banquet 연회

21

해설 **수량을 나타내는 부정대명사:** 빈칸은 'There + be동사' 구문 뒤의 주어 자리이므로 복수동사에 수 일치하는 복수명사가 와야 한다. 따라서 단수와 복수 둘 다를 의미할 수 있는 (B) none이 정답이다. (A) not은 부사이므로 주어 자리에 올 수 없고, (C) neither는 '하나를 요청했는데 둘 다 없었다'라는 의미가 되므로 맞지 않으며, (D) nobody는 단수명사이므로 오답이다.

번역 이브즈 씨가 창가 자리를 요청했지만, 그때는 남아 있는 것이 없었다.

기출공식 8	본책 p. 47
22 (A) **23** (A) **24** (D)	

22

해설 **부정대명사_any:** 빈칸은 동사 have의 목적어 자리이며, 문맥상 '재고가 조금이라도 있으면'이라는 의미가 되어야 하므로 조건문에서 '조금이라도'를 의미하는 대명사인 (A) any가 정답이다. 빈칸은 불가산명사로 쓰인 photo paper를 대신하므로 복수명사를 나타내는 (B) a few는 오답이다.

번역 재고가 조금이라도 있으면 바삼 사진 전용 인화지를 우리에게 더 보내 주세요.

어휘 in stock 재고가 있는

23

해설 **부정대명사_some:** 빈칸은 동사 cover의 목적어 자리이며, 문맥상 '치료비 일부'라는 의미가 되어야 자연스러우므로 '일부'를 뜻하는 대명사인 (A) some이 정답이다.

번역 귀하의 보험은 치료비 일부만 보험처리 됩니다.

어휘 insurance 보험 treatment 치료

24

해설 **부정형용사_any:** 빈칸 뒤의 단수명사인 salesperson을 수식하는 형용사를 고르는 문제이다. 보기 모두 단수명사와 쓸 수 있으므로 문맥상 적절한 형용사를 골라야 한다. any가 최상급과 함께 쓰여, '어떤 영업 사원 중에서도 가장 높은'이라는 의미를 이루므로 정답은 (D) any이다.

번역 마가렛은 회사 전체 어떠한 영업 사원 중에서도 가장 높은 수수료를 받았다.

어휘 earn 받다 commission 수수료 such 그러한

ETS TEST

본책 p. 48

1 (A)	2 (C)	3 (B)	4 (C)	5 (C)
6 (D)	7 (C)	8 (C)	9 (A)	10 (B)
11 (A)	12 (A)	13 (B)	14 (C)	15 (C)
16 (D)	17 (A)	18 (D)	19 (B)	20 (D)

1

해설 **인칭대명사_목적격:** 빈칸에는 the interoffice mail이라는 단수 사물명사를 받는 대명사가 필요하므로 정답은 (A) it이다.

번역 도쉬 씨는 아침에 사내 우편물을 수거하여 그것을 오후 4시까지 나눠 준다.

어휘 collect 모으다, 수거하다 interoffice 회사 내의, 각 부서 간의 distribute (사람들에게) 나누어 주다, 분배하다

2

해설 **재귀대명사_강조 용법:** 주어인 An accomplished skater 뒤에서 주어를 강조하는 자리이므로 빈칸에는 재귀대명사가 들어가야 한다. 따라서 (C) himself가 정답이다.

번역 뛰어난 스케이터인 로웬스타인 씨는 세계 챔피언 피겨 스케이터인 사라 크라스노바를 지도하기도 한다.

어휘 accomplished 기량이 뛰어난 coach 코치하다, 지도하다

3

해설 **인칭대명사_주격:** 빈칸 뒤에 동사가 있으므로 동사 앞에서 주어 역할을 하는 주격 인칭대명사를 써야 한다. 따라서 (B) she가 정답이다.

번역 야마가타 씨는 한 씨가 뉴욕에서 연수 세미나를 진행하는 동안 그녀의 고객들을 도울 준비가 되어 있다.

어휘 assist 돕다 conduct 진행하다 training 교육, 연수

4

해설 **인칭대명사_소유격:** evaluate가 동사이고 빈칸 뒤의 physical condition이 목적어이므로, 빈칸에는 단수명사를 수식할 수 있는 한정사가 들어가야 한다. 문맥상 '역사적인 건물들을 파악하고 그것들의 물리적 상태를 평가한다'는 내용이 되어야 하므로, 소유격 대명사 (C) their가 정답이 된다. 참고로, (D) those는 복수형 명사(구)를 수식하므로 정답이 될 수 없다.

번역 건축 감정인들은 역사적인 건물들을 파악하고 물리적 상태를 평가한다.

어휘 architectural 건축학(술)의 surveyor 감정인, 감독관 identify 식별하다, 확인하다 property 부동산, 건물 evaluate 평가하다 physical 물리적인

5

해설 **대명사_관용 표현:** 문맥상 '고객문의에 혼자 답변하는 것이 힘든 일이라 자주 묻는 질문 목록을 만들었다'라는 의미가 되는 것이 가장 자연스러우므로, 빈칸에는 전치사 on과 함께 쓰여 '혼자서, 스스로'의 의미를 강조하는 (C) your own이 들어가야 한다.

번역 고객 문의에 혼자서 답변하는 것이 때때로 힘들어서, 우리는 자주 묻는 질문 목록을 만들었다.

어휘 frequently asked questions 자주 묻는 질문들(FAQ) on one's own 혼자서, 스스로

6

해설 **부정대명사_anyone:** 빈칸에는 관계사절(who is more than twenty minutes late)의 수식을 받으며 전치사 of의 목적어 역할을 하는 명사나 대명사가 들어가야 한다. 관계대명사 who는 사람 선행사를 수식하므로 사람을 뜻하는 대명사인 (D) anyone이 정답이다.

번역 카페 알타 비스타는 20분 이상 늦는 사람은 누구나 예약을 취소할 수 있다.

어휘 reservation 예약

7

해설 **인칭대명사_목적격:** the assistant manager에 대한 대명사 목적격이 필요한 자리이므로 (C) her가 정답이다.

번역 그 대리가 다음 주에 전근되는데도 인사과는 아직 그녀의 후임을 구하지 못했다.

어휘 assistant manager 대리 transfer 전근시키다 personnel office 인사과 replacement 대체, 후임자

8

해설 **인칭대명사_소유격:** 빈칸은 건축 회사(architecture firm)를 수식하는 소유격 자리이므로 her를 쓸 수 있는데, 소유의 의미를 강조하기 위해 own을 붙여서 '본인 소유의 건축 회사'라고 나타낼 수 있으므로 정답은 (C) her own이다.

번역 전에 창 아키텍처럴사에서 일했던 제니퍼 박은 작년에 자신의 건축 회사를 설립했다.

어휘 formerly 이전에, 예전에 employ 고용하다 architectural 건축의, 건축술의 architecture firm 건축 회사

9

해설 **부정대명사_everyone:** 빈칸은 전치사 of의 목적어 자리로, 명사나 대명사가 들어가야 한다. 문맥상 '화장품 업계에서 거의 모든 사람의 존경을 받는다'는 의미가 되어야 하므로, (A) everyone이 정답이다. (B) anything과 (C) whatever는 사물을 나타내므로 오답이며, (D) each other는 '서로'라는 의미로 문맥상 어색하다.

번역 프레쉬스트 페이스의 최고 경영자인 조안나 뉴전트는 화장품 업계에서 거의 모든 사람들의 존경을 받아 왔다.

어휘 **earn** 얻다, 받다 **respect** 존경 **virtually** 거의, 사실상 **cosmetics industry** 화장품 업계

10

해설 **지시대명사_those:** 빈칸은 앞서 언급된 복수명사 laminate products를 반복해서 사용하는 것을 피하기 위해 쓰는 지시대명사 자리이다. 따라서 정답은 (B) those이다. 체멤 산업의 제품들과 경쟁업체의 제품들은 각각 다른 대상이므로, 정확히 동일한 대상을 지칭할 때 쓰는 인칭대명사 (C) them은 오답이다.

번역 체멤 산업의 라미네이트 제품들은 경쟁업체의 라미네이트 제품들과 분간할 수 없다.

어휘 **indistinguishable** 분간할 수 없는 **competitor** 경쟁업체

11

해설 **부정대명사_others:** 문맥상 '다른 사람들의 시야'가 적절하므로 '다른 사람들[것들]'을 뜻하는 대명사 (A) others가 정답이다. (B) ones는 사람들을 뜻할 수 있지만 '어떤' 사람들인지 한정해 주는 수식어가 없을 때는 일반 사람들을 통칭하는 대명사이며, (C) every는 형용사이므로 오답이다.

번역 우산은 다른 사람들의 시야를 가로막으므로 경기장 안에서 사용이 금지된다.

어휘 **prohibit** 금지시키다 **obstruct** 막다 **view** 관점, 시야

12

해설 **부정대명사_something:** 빈칸은 동사 need의 목적어 자리이며, 빈칸 뒤에 온 형용사 special의 수식을 받아 '특별한 무언가'라는 의미를 이루는 (A) something이 정답이다. '-thing'으로 끝나는 대명사는 형용사가 후치 수식한다는 점을 알아 두자.

번역 이벤트에 특별한 무엇인가가 필요할 때는 페이스 제임스에게 fajames@gnt.com으로 연락 주세요.

13

해설 **인칭대명사_주격:** 빈칸 뒤에 동사구 used to be가 왔으므로 빈칸에는 주어가 와야 한다. 따라서 인칭대명사의 주격 (B) they가 정답이다.

번역 대체로 요즘 모델 하우스는 예전에 비치되었던 것보다 더 호화롭게 가구가 비치되어 있다.

어휘 **in general** 대체로 **furnish** 가구를 비치하다 **luxuriously** 호화롭게 **used to** (과거에) ~이었다

14

해설 **부정대명사_the other:** 다섯 곳 중에 네 곳은 너무 작았다고 했으므로 while절의 주어 자리에는 '나머지 하나'를 뜻하는 대명사가 들어가야 한다. 따라서 '나머지 하나'를 의미하는 (C) the other가 정답이다.

번역 새 쇼핑몰을 위한 다섯 곳의 건축 부지 중에서, 네 곳은 너무 작았고, 나머지 하나는 다소 불편한 위치에 있었다.

어휘 **building site** 건축 부지 **somewhat** 다소, 약간 **inconvenient** 불편한

15

해설 **부정대명사_everyone:** 빈칸은 단수 동사 is required의 주어 자리이므로 단수 대명사가 필요하다. 또한 '회의에 참석해야 한다'는 의미로 보아, 주어 자리에는 사람이 들어가야 의미가 자연스러우므로 사람을 뜻하는 단수 대명사인 (C) Everyone이 정답이다.

번역 배송부 전원이 안전 회의에 참석해야 한다.

어휘 **shipping** 배송 **be required to** ~해야 한다

16

해설 **수량을 나타내는 부정대명사:** 앞에서 언급한 '두 사람 모두'를 의미하는 대명사인 (D) both를 써야 한다. (C) one은 대명사일 때 단수동사로 받으므로 hope와 수 일치가 되지 않는다.

번역 한 씨와 스몰즈 씨는 동시에 ABCO사에서 일하기 시작했고 둘 다 내년 승진을 희망한다.

어휘 **promote** 승진시키다, 홍보하다

17

해설 **인칭대명사_소유격:** 동사 understand의 목적어로 복합명사 rental agreement가 나왔으므로 명사를 수식할 수 있는 소유격이 들어가야 한다. 따라서 (A) their가 정답이다.

번역 부동산 자산 관리자는 반드시 임차인들이 자신의 임대 계약을 이해하도록 해야 한다.

어휘 **property** 부동산 **ensure** 보장하다, 반드시 ~하게 하다 **renter** 임차인, 임대 업자 **rental** 임대 **agreement** 계약

18

해설 **재귀대명사_관용 표현:** '연구 프로젝트를 혼자 시작했다'라는 내용이 와야 but 뒤의 상반되는 내용과 자연스럽게 연결된다. 따라서 전치사 by와 함께 쓰여 '혼자서, 직접'이라는 의미의 관용 표현을 이루는 (D) himself가 정답이다.

번역 카와노 씨는 혼자 연구 프로젝트를 시작했지만 이후 동료 두 사람의 도움을 받았다.

어휘 research 연구　assist 돕다　colleague 동료

19

해설 **부정대명사_none:** 빈칸은 because절의 동사인 have의 목적어 자리이므로 목적어 역할을 할 수 있는 명사나 대명사가 들어가야 한다. 문맥상 '재고가 없어서 교체 부품을 주문할 수 없었다'라는 의미가 되어야 하므로 부정의 의미를 이루는 (B) none이 정답이다. (A) any는 부정문에서 쓰여야 동일한 뜻을 이룬다.

번역 지역 공급업체에 재고가 없어서 포장기 교체 부품을 주문할 수 없었다.

어휘 replacement 교체　packing 포장　supplier 공급업체　in stock 재고가 있는

20

해설 **수량을 나타내는 부정대명사:** 빈칸은 문장의 주어 자리이자 of Ms. Knapp's mail의 수식을 받는 자리이다. 불가산 명사 mail이 문제 해결의 핵심 단서로, 빈칸에는 불가산 명사와 함께 쓸 수 있는 수량 대명사가 와야 한다. 따라서 정답은 (D) All이다. (A) Each는 each of로 쓰일 때 복수명사와 함께 써야 하므로 오답이다.

번역 냅 씨가 휴가로 자리를 비우는 동안 그녀의 모든 우편물은 관리자에게 맡겨 두어야 합니다.

어휘 supervisor 관리자, 상사　on vacation 휴가 중인

UNIT 05	형용사

기출공식 1　　　　　　　　　　본책 p. 52

1 (D)　　**2** (A)　　**3** (B)

1

해설 **형용사의 역할_명사 수식:** 빈칸은 뒤에 온 명사 episode를 수식하는 형용사 자리이다. 따라서 '마지막의'라는 의미의 형용사인 (D) last가 정답이다.

번역 평이 좋은 텔레비전 드라마 〈시티 리포팅〉의 마지막 에피소드가 오늘 밤 방송됩니다.

어휘 acclaimed 칭찬[호평] 받는　broadcast 방송하다

2

해설 **형용사의 역할_명사 수식:** 빈칸 뒤의 명사구 boarding documents를 수식하는 자리이므로 형용사인 (A) necessary가 정답이다. 빈칸 앞의 all은 boarding documents를 수식하는 한정사이다.

번역 승객들은 모든 필요한 탑승 서류를 항공사 직원에게 제시할 준비를 하고 있어야 한다.

어휘 passenger 승객　boarding document 탑승 서류　present 제시하다, 제출하다　personnel 직원　necessity 필요, 필수품

3

해설 **부사의 역할_형용사 수식:** 빈칸은 뒤에 온 형용사 talented를 수식하는 부사 자리이므로, '굉장히, 특별히'라는 의미의 부사인 (B) exceptionally가 정답이다.

번역 애나 파스케비치는 특출하게 재능 있는 작가이자 연구자로 회사에서 존경받아 왔다.

어휘 honor 존경하다; 명예　talented 재능이 있는　researcher 연구자　firm 회사, 기업　exceptional 특출한, 예외적인　exception 예외　except 제외하다

기출공식 2　　　　　　　　　　본책 p. 52

4 (D)　　**5** (B)　　**6** (C)

4

해설 **형용사의 역할_주격 보어:** 빈칸은 주어인 security officers에 대해 설명하는 주격 보어 자리이다. 따라서 '알아볼 수 있는, 인식 가능한'을 의미하는 형용사인 (D) identifiable이 정답이다. 명사도 보어 역할을 할 수 있으나, 이 경우에는 보어가 주어와 동격이어야 하므로 '신원, 독자성'을 의미하는 단수 추상명사인 (C) identity는 정답이 될 수 없다.

번역 린데-아브로 래버러토리스의 경비원들은 밝은 청색 유니폼으로 식별이 가능하다.

어휘 security office 경비원, 안전요원　laboratory 실험실　identify 식별하다, 확인하다

5

해설 **형용사의 역할_목적격 보어:** 동사 find는 목적격 보어로 형용사나 형용사 역할을 하는 분사를 취한다. 따라서 형용사인 (B) helpful이 정답이다.

번역 그 소프트웨어를 처음 사용할 때 부딪히는 문제를 해결하는 데 안내 책자가 아주 유용할 것이다.

어휘 encounter (우연히) 만나다　helpful 유용한, 도움이 되는

6

해설 **형용사의 역할_주격 보어:** 2형식 동사 seem 뒤에는 주격 보어가 와야 하므로, 형용사인 (C) realistic이 정답이다.

번역 비공식적인 조사에 따르면, 경영팀에서 정한 판매 목표가 대부분의 직원들에게 현실적으로 보이는 듯하다.

어휘 **informal** 비공식의   **survey** 설문 조사   **sales goal** 판매 목표

기출공식 3		본책 p. 53
7 (A)	**8** (A)	**9** (C)

7

해설 **수량 형용사 + 가산 복수명사:** 빈칸 뒤에 복수명사인 skaters가 왔으므로 (A) all이 정답이다. (B) every는 단수명사와 함께 쓰이고, (C) entire는 정해진 전부를 가리키는 경우, 주로 정관사 the 또는 소유격과 함께 쓰인다. 또한 두 문장을 연결하는 접속사 기능을 하는 (D) whichever는 동사가 하나뿐인 문장에서 답이 될 수 없다.

번역 오전 10시 15분에, 500미터 경주에 참가하는 모든 스케이터들은 5분 준비 운동 시간을 위해 링크로 나와야 한다.

어휘 **compete** 경쟁하다   **report to** ~에 출두하다

8

해설 **수량 형용사 + 불가산명사:** time을 수식할 수 있는 형용사를 찾아야 한다. time이 불가산명사로 쓰였으므로 (A) little이 정답이다. (B) few는 복수명사와 함께 써야 하며, (C) less는 little의 비교급으로 very와 함께 쓸 수 없으므로 오답이다.

번역 영업 사원들이 사무실을 늦게 빠져나갔기 때문에, 우리가 고객과의 회의 시간 전에 논의할 시간이 거의 없었다.

어휘 **sales representative** 영업 사원   **client** 고객

9

해설 **수량 형용사 + 가산 복수명사:** 빈칸은 명사 purchases를 수식해 주는 형용사가 들어가야 한다. 따라서 가산 복수명사를 수식할 수 있는 수량 형용사인 (C) all이 정답이다. '수량 대명사 + of' 구조를 쓸 때는 of 뒤에 'the + 명사'와 같은 형태로 명사 앞에 한정사가 필요하므로 (A) any of는 답이 될 수 없다. 또한 (B) each와 (D) every는 가산 단수명사와 함께 쓰이므로 오답이다.

번역 고객들은 권스(상호명)가 모든 구매 상품에 대해 조건 없는 보증 서비스를 제공하기 때문에 그곳에서 쇼핑하는 것을 선호한다.

어휘 **unconditional** 무조건적인   **guarantee** 보증   **purchase** 구매한 물건, 구매

기출공식 4		본책 p. 53
10 (A)	**11** (D)	**12** (B)

10

해설 **혼동하기 쉬운 형용사:** 빈칸 뒤에 명사 circumstances를 수식하는 형용사 자리이다. 보기 중 형용사는 (A) favorable과 (D) favorite인데, 문맥상 '좋은 환경'이라는 의미가 적절하므로 정답은 (A) favorable이다.

번역 좀 더 유리한 환경에서라면 이사회에서 예산 인상을 승인했겠지만, 올해는 가능하지 않았다.

어휘 **circumstance** 환경, 상황   **board of trustees** 이사회   **budget** 예산   **favorable** 호의적인, 유리한   **favorably** 호의적으로   **favor** 호의, 친절   **favorite** 마음에 드는, 좋아하는

11

해설 **혼동하기 쉬운 형용사:** 동사 is 뒤 빈칸은 보어 역할을 할 수 있는 형용사나 명사가 들어가야 한다. 보기 중 형용사는 (C) dependable과 (D) dependent인데, 문맥상 '새 예산안을 통과시킬 역량에 달려 있다'라는 의미가 되어야 하므로, 뒤에 온 전치사 on과 함께 쓰여 '~에 달려 있는, ~에 의존하는'의 의미를 나타내는 (D) dependent가 정답이다. (C) dependable은 '신뢰할 수 있는, 의지할 수 있는'이라는 의미로 빈칸에 적절하지 않다.

번역 새 도서관 건설은 시에 새 예산안을 통과시킬 역량이 있는지에 달려 있다.

어휘 **construction** 건설, 공사   **pass** 통과시키다   **budget** 예산(안)

12

해설 **혼동하기 쉬운 형용사:** 동사 is 뒤 빈칸은 보어 자리이다. and 뒤의 will not be shared with any other vendors가 문제 해결의 단서로, 문맥상 '이 질문지에 제공한 정보는 기밀이다'라는 의미가 되어야 한다. 따라서 '기밀의'라는 의미를 지닌 형용사 (B) confidential이 정답이다.

번역 이 질문지에 제공하신 정보는 엄격히 기밀 사항이며 다른 어떤 납품업체에게도 공유되지 않을 것입니다.

어휘 **questionnaire** 질문서, 설문지   **strictly** 엄밀히, 절대적으로   **share** 공유하다   **vendor** 납품업체, 판매인   **confident** 자신감 있는, 확신하는

<table>
<tr><td>기출공식 5</td><td>본책 p. 54</td></tr>
<tr><td colspan="2">**13** (C)　　**14** (B)　　**15** (C)</td></tr>
</table>

13

해설　-ly로 끝나는 형용사: 빈칸 뒤에 manner라는 명사가 왔으므로 빈칸에는 형용사가 들어가야 한다. 따라서 '시기적절한'이라는 의미의 (C) timely가 정답이다.

번역　장학금 신청서는 선정 위원회에 제때 제출해야 한다.

어휘　application 지원(서)　scholarship 장학금

14

해설　-ly로 끝나는 형용사: 빈칸 뒤에 renovations라는 명사가 왔으므로 빈칸에는 형용사가 들어가야 한다. 따라서 '비용이 많이 드는'이라는 의미의 (B) costly가 정답이다.

번역　카운티 정부는 듀이 스타디움에 비용이 많이 드는 개보수 공사를 수행할 계획이다.

어휘　carry out 수행하다　renovation 개보수 공사　cost 비용; 비용이 들다

15

해설　-ly로 끝나는 형용사: 빈칸은 be동사 is의 보어 자리이므로 형용사나 명사가 들어갈 수 있다. 문맥상 '교통체증이 있을 것 같다'는 내용이 되어야 자연스러우므로 '~할 것 같은, 있음 직한'이라는 뜻의 (C) likely가 정답이다. (A) likeness는 주어인 traffic congestion과 동격이 아니므로 오답이며, (B) liking은 빈칸 앞의 is와 함께 현재 진행시제가 되는데, 감정동사 like는 진행형으로 쓰지 않으므로 답이 될 수 없다. 또한 (D) liked는 앞의 is와 함께 수동의 의미가 되어 문맥상 적절하지 않으므로 오답이다.

번역　도로공사가 끝날 때까지 손해 가는 아마도 교통체증이 심할 것 같다.

어휘　congestion 체증　likeness 유사성, 외관

<table>
<tr><td>기출공식 6</td><td>본책 p. 54</td></tr>
<tr><td colspan="2">**16** (A)　　**17** (D)　　**18** (A)</td></tr>
</table>

16

해설　be동사 + 형용사 + to부정사: 문맥상 '유럽 시장 진출을 갈망한다'가 적합하므로, 정답은 (A) eager이다. 'be eager to부정사'는 '~하는 것을 갈망하다'라는 의미로 자주 쓰이는 표현이니 암기해 두자. 참고로, (B) active를 활용한다면 be active in entering 형태로 써야 한다.

번역　아시아에서 상당한 성공을 거둔 셀레나 차 판매 회사는 유럽 시장 진출을 갈망하고 있다.

어휘　achieve 성취하다　considerable 상당한　active 적극적인　firm 단단한, 확고한

17

해설　be동사 + 형용사 + to부정사: 문맥상 '복잡한 절차를 잘 거치려 들지 않는다'는 의미가 되어야 적합하므로, 정답은 (D) willing이다. 'be willing to부정사'는 '기꺼이 ~하다'는 의미로 자주 쓰이는 표현이므로 알아 두자. 참고로, (C) familiar는 뒤에 전치사 with와 자주 함께 쓰인다.

번역　각광받는 역량을 가진 구직자들은 복잡한 채용 과정을 기꺼이 거치려고 하지 않는다.

어휘　jobseeker 구직자　navigate 거치다, 다루다　complicated 복잡한　thorough 철저한　lengthy 긴　familiar 익숙한

18

해설　be동사 + 형용사 + to부정사: 문맥상 '사우나를 자유롭게 이용해도 좋다'는 의미가 되어야 적합하므로, 정답은 (A) welcome이다. 형용사 welcome은 뒤에 to부정사와 함께 '자유롭게 ~해도 좋은'이라는 뜻으로 자주 쓰이므로 알아 두자. (D) possible은 사람을 주어로 쓰지 않고 주로 가주어 it을 써서 'it is possible (for + 사람) + to부정사' 형태로 쓴다는 것도 알아 두자.

번역　모든 리조트 고객은 지정된 시간에 사우나를 자유롭게 이용해도 좋습니다.

어휘　designated 지정된　welcome ~해도 좋은　common 흔한　inclusive ~이 포함된

<table>
<tr><td>기출공식 7</td><td>본책 p. 55</td></tr>
<tr><td colspan="2">**19** (B)　　**20** (C)　　**21** (A)</td></tr>
</table>

19

해설　be동사 + 형용사 + 전치사 to: 빈칸에는 be동사 is의 보어이자 전치사 to와 어울려 쓰이는 형용사가 들어가야 한다. 문맥상 '1년에 3주간 유급 휴가를 받을 자격이 있다'는 내용이 되어야 자연스러우므로 '~할 자격이 있는'이라는 뜻의 (B) entitled가 정답이다. (A) equivalent는 전치사 to와 함께 쓸 수는 있지만 '~와 동등한'이라는 의미로 문맥에 어울리지 않는다. (D) eligible은 be eligible to부정사 또는 be eligible for + 명사(구)의 형태로 쓰이므로 정답이 될 수 없다.

번역　모든 정규직 직원은 1년에 3주간 유급 휴가를 받을 자격이 있다.

어휘　paid vacation 유급 휴가　annually 1년에　equivalent 동등한　entitled to ~할 자격이 있는　eager 열심인　eligible 자격이 있는

20

해설 **be동사 + 형용사 + 전치사 to:** 빈칸에는 to부정사로 쓰인 be동사의 보어이자 뒤에 온 전치사 to와 어울려 쓰이는 형용사가 들어가야 한다. 문맥상 '사회에 유익할 것으로'라는 의미가 되어야 하므로 전치사 to와 함께 쓰여 '~에 유익한'이라는 뜻의 (C) beneficial이 정답이다. (A) grateful도 전치사 to와 함께 쓰이기는 하나 '~에게 감사하는'이라는 뜻으로 문맥에 어울리지 않는다.

번역 드레이크 테크놀러지의 새로운 혈액검사 기기는 사회에 매우 유익하리라 예상된다.

어휘 **device** 기기 **be expected to** ~하리라 예상되다 **beneficial** 유익한 **grateful** 감사하는 **approved** 승인된 **compatible** 호환되는

21

해설 **be동사 + 형용사 + 전치사 to:** 빈칸에는 be동사 is의 보어이자 전치사 to와 어울려 쓰이는 형용사가 들어가야 한다. 문맥상 '마감일이 지난 납부금이 연체료의 대상이 된다'라는 의미가 가장 적절하므로 '~의 대상이 되다'라는 뜻의 be subject to를 이루는 (A) subject가 정답이다.

번역 납부 마감일 이후의 소인이 찍힌 금액은 총납부액의 5퍼센트가 연체료로 붙습니다.

어휘 **postmark** (우편물의) 소인을 찍다 **due date** (납부) 마감일 **late fee** 연체료 **amount due** 지불 금액, 납부액 **intact** 온전한, 손상되지 않은 **distinct** 뚜렷한, 분명한

기출공식 8		본책 p. 55
22 (D)	**23** (A)	**24** (A)

22

해설 **형용사 관용어구:** 빈칸에는 be동사 is의 보어이자 전치사 with와 어울려 쓰이는 형용사가 들어가야 한다. 문맥상 '더 오래된 기기들과 항상 호환이 되는 것은 아니다'라는 내용이 되는 것이 가장 적절하므로 '호환이 되는'이라는 의미의 (D) compatible이 정답이다.

번역 최근 출시된 야리 4200 잉크젯 프린터의 유일한 단점은 더 오래된 기기들과 호환이 안 될 수도 있다는 점이다.

어휘 **downside** 불리한 면, 단점 **release** 출시하다, 공개하다 **device** 기기 **formal** 공식적인 **external** 외부의 **alternate** 번갈아 생기는, 대안의

23

해설 **형용사 관용어구:** 빈칸에는 be동사 is의 보어이자 전치사 of와 어울려 쓰이는 형용사가 들어가야 한다. 문맥상 '책무를 맡을 수 있어야 한다'는 의미가 가장 적절하므로 '~할 수

있는'이라는 의미의 (A) capable이 정답이다.

번역 부지배인 직책의 지원자들은 아주 다양한 책무를 맡을 수 있어야 한다.

어휘 **assume** (책임 등을) 떠맡다, 담당하다 **a wide range of** 아주 다양한 **responsibility** 책임, 책무 **enclosed** 에워싸인, 동봉된

24

해설 **형용사 관용어구:** 빈칸에는 be동사 are의 보어이자 전치사 with와 어울려 쓰이는 형용사가 들어가야 한다. 문맥상 '카트리 씨의 작품을 잘 알고 있다'는 내용이 되어야 자연스러우므로 be familiar with의 형태로 자주 쓰이는 '~을 잘 알다'라는 뜻의 (A) familiar가 정답이다.

번역 〈형사 존스〉 시청자들은 감독으로서 카트리 씨의 작품을 잘 알고 있다.

어휘 **viewer** 시청자 **detective** 형사 **director** 감독 **familiar** 잘 아는 **renowned** 유명한 **compelling** 저항하기 어려운 **supportive** 지원하는

ETS **TEST**				본책 p. 56
1 (B)	**2** (C)	**3** (A)	**4** (D)	**5** (D)
6 (C)	**7** (A)	**8** (B)	**9** (B)	**10** (A)
11 (D)	**12** (A)	**13** (A)	**14** (C)	**15** (B)
16 (C)	**17** (A)	**18** (C)	**19** (B)	**20** (B)

1

해설 **형용사의 역할_명사 수식:** 빈칸은 by 전치사구에서 명사 gains를 수식하는 형용사 자리이다. 따라서 정답은 (B) proportional이다.

번역 지역 내 관개 기술의 발전은 옥수수 생산량의 비례적인 증가로 이어졌다.

어휘 **improvement** 개선 **irrigation** 관개 **gain** 증가, 이익 **corn** 옥수수 **production** 생산(량) **proportional** (~에) 비례하는

2

해설 **형용사의 역할_명사 수식:** 빈칸은 뒤에 온 명사 issues를 수식하는 형용사 자리이므로 '법적인'이라는 의미의 형용사인 (C) legal이 정답이다. 과거분사인 (D) legalized도 명사를 수식할 수 있으나, '합법화된, 인증된'이라는 의미로 문맥상 어울리지 않으므로 오답이다.

번역 현채원 세무사는 자산 계획과 관련된 법률 문제에 대해 전문적인 조언을 제공한다.

어휘 **expert** 전문적인 **related to** ~와 관련된 **estate** 자산 **legal** 법적인 **legalize** 합법화하다

3

해설 **수량 형용사:** 문장은 '어떤 택시에서도 허락되지 않는다'라는 부정문이므로 빈칸에는 '어떤 ~도 아니다'라는 의미를 완성하면서, 가산 단수명사 taxi를 수식할 수 있는 (A) any가 정답이다.

번역 헬리건사에서 운영하는 어떤 택시에서도 4명 이상의 승객이 허락되지 않는다.

어휘 permit 허락하다 operate 운영하다 such 그러한

4

해설 **형용사의 역할_목적격 보어:** leave는 5형식 동사로 'leave + 목적어 + 목적격 보어'로 쓰는데, 목적어 doors가 주어로 와서 수동태 구조가 되었으므로 빈칸에는 목적격 보어가 와야 한다. 따라서 정답은 '문이 열린 채로 남겨져 있어야 한다'라는 의미를 이루는 형용사 (D) open이다.

번역 회의실로 가는 문은 청소 직원을 위해 일과가 끝날 때 열어두어야 한다.

어휘 leave (~을 …한 상태로) 남겨두다 cleaning staff 청소 직원 opening 빈 일자리, 개장 opener 병따개, 첫 행동

5

해설 **수량 형용사:** 빈칸 뒤에 가산명사의 단수형인 issue가 왔으므로 정답은 (D) each이다. (A) most of는 가산 복수명사 또는 불가산명사와 함께 쓰이며, of 뒤에 명사를 쓸 때는 'most of the issues'와 같이 한정사를 붙여서 써야 한다. (B) all은 가산명사와 함께 쓰일 때 반드시 복수형과 쓰이며, (C) entire는 주로 the나 소유격 뒤에 온다.

번역 참가자들이 세미나에서 제시된 각 문제에 대해 토론할 시간이 있을 것이다.

어휘 present 제시[제출]하다

6

해설 **형용사의 역할_명사 수식:** 빈칸은 정관사와 명사 사이에서 명사 aspects를 수식하는 형용사 자리이다. 따라서 '유익한, 이로운'이라는 의미의 형용사인 (C) beneficial이 정답이다. 과거분사도 명사를 수식하는 형용사 역할을 할 수 있으나, aspects는 benefit의 대상이 아닌 주체이므로 (D) benefited는 정답이 될 수 없다.

번역 아니타 위리얀토 박사는 인도네시아 산호초의 유익한 측면에 관한 많은 논문들을 발표해 왔다.

어휘 publish 발표[출판]하다 numerous 많은 article 논문, 기사 aspect 측면 coral reef 산호초

7

해설 **형용사의 역할_명사 수식:** 빈칸은 명사구 new line을 수식하는 형용사 자리이므로, '인상적인'이라는 의미의 형용사인 (A) impressive가 정답이다.

번역 데본 자동차의 연료 효율이 좋은 인상적인 신형차 라인은 자동차 업계로부터 많은 권위 있는 상을 받았다.

어휘 fuel-efficient 연료 효율이 좋은 prestigious 권위 있는

8

해설 **수량 형용사:** a number of 뒤에는 가산 복수명사가 와야 한다. 따라서 (B) contracts가 정답이다.

번역 패터슨 인더스트리얼 솔루션즈의 사장은 이 달에 많은 중요한 계약서에 서명했다.

어휘 contract 계약(서); 계약하다

9

해설 **형용사 관용어구:** 빈칸에는 be동사의 보어이자 전치사 for와 어울려 쓰이는 형용사가 들어가야 한다. 주절에 '학사 학위를 소지해야 한다'라는 자격 요건이 나왔으므로, to부정사구는 '에베센 리서치 어소시에이츠에서 근무할 자격이 되려면'이라는 내용이 되는 것이 가장 적절하다. 따라서 '~할 자격이 있는'이라는 의미의 형용사인 (B) eligible이 정답이다.

번역 에베센 리서치 어소시에이츠에서 근무할 자격이 되려면 지원자는 경제학 학사 학위를 소지해야 한다.

어휘 position 직위, 일자리 Research Associates 연구 협회 candidate 지원자, 후보자 university degree 학사 학위

10

해설 **형용사의 역할_목적격 보어:** 5형식 동사 keep의 목적어로 prices가 왔으므로 빈칸에는 keep의 목적격 보어가 와야 한다. 따라서 '가격을 적정하게 유지하기 위해서'라는 의미를 이루는 형용사 (A) reasonable이 정답이다.

번역 적정 가격을 유지하기 위한 노력의 일환으로 김 제과점은 빵과 케이크를 점포에서 만들기 시작할 것이다.

어휘 on the premises 점포 내에서

11

해설 **형용사의 역할_명사 수식:** 빈칸 앞에는 부정관사, 뒤에는 명사 area가 있으므로 명사를 수식하는 형용사 (D) broad가 정답이다.

번역 아우겐 케어사의 지역 센터는 광범위한 북서부 지역의 안경 유통을 총괄한다.

어휘 coordinate 총괄하다, 조정[조율]하다 distribution 분배, 유통 broaden 넓어지다, 넓히다

12

해설 **형용사의 역할_명사 수식:** 빈칸은 뒤에 온 복합명사 dance performances를 수식하는 형용사 자리이다. 따라서 '진짜인, 정통의'라는 의미의 형용사인 (A) authentic이 정답이다.

번역 카스탈라 극장은 스페인 남부에서 정통 무용 공연을 제공한다.

어휘 performance 공연 southern 남쪽의
authenticate 진짜임을 증명하다 authenticity
확실성, 진짜임

13

해설 **형용사의 역할_명사 수식:** 빈칸은 뒤에 온 복합명사 wool sweaters를 수식하는 형용사 자리이고, 문맥상 '물빨래가 가능한 모직 스웨터'라는 의미가 되어야 자연스러우므로 '물빨래가 가능한'이라는 의미의 형용사인 (A) washable이 정답이다. 전치사 of의 목적어 역할을 하면서 뒤의 복합명사 wool sweaters를 목적어로 취할 수 있는 동명사도 들어갈 수는 있으나 '모직 스웨터를 세탁하는 것'이라는 의미로 문맥상 어색하므로 답이 될 수 없다.

번역 여오 의류는 물빨래 가능한 모직 스웨터 신제품군을 선보이고 있다.

어휘 washable 물빨래 가능한

14

해설 **형용사의 역할_명사 수식:** 빈칸은 뒤에 온 명사 suppliers를 수식하는 형용사 자리이고, '괜찮은 공급업체들'이라는 의미가 되어야 자연스러우므로 '그런대로 괜찮은'이라는 뜻의 형용사인 (C) acceptable이 정답이다.

번역 34쪽에는 울테라 파이프라인 프로젝트에 사용될 수 있는 모든 주요 건설 장비를 공급하는 괜찮은 업체들이 열거되어 있다.

어휘 list 열거하다 supplier 공급업체 major 주요한
construction 건설 equipment 장비 acceptable
그런대로 괜찮은

15

해설 **형용사의 역할_명사 수식:** 빈칸 앞에 부정관사 an과 부사 unusually, 빈칸 뒤에 명사 leader가 있는 것으로 보아 빈칸은 명사를 수식하면서 부사의 수식을 받는 형용사 자리이다. 따라서 (B) thoughtful이 정답이다.

번역 닐릭스 커뮤니케이션즈의 책임자로서, 임스 씨는 대단히 사려 깊은 리더로 여겨진다.

어휘 head 책임자 unusually 대단히, 특이하게
thoughtful 사려 깊은

16

해설 **형용사의 역할_명사 수식:** to develop의 목적어로 온 명

사 evidence를 수식하는 자리이므로 '결정적인'이라는 뜻의 형용사 (C) conclusive가 정답이다.

번역 예비 연구가 순조롭더라도 보고르 제약 회사가 그 약의 효능에 대한 확증을 도출하기까지 수년이 걸릴 수도 있다.

어휘 preliminary 예비의 favorable 순조로운, 우호적인
pharmaceutical 제약의, 조제의 evidence 증거,
근거 conclusive 결정적인, 최종적인

17

해설 **형용사의 역할_주격 보어:** 빈칸은 가주어 it의 보어 자리이므로 정답은 형용사인 (A) acceptable이다.

번역 적절한 안전 장비를 갖추지 않고 조 인더스트리얼사의 공장에 들어갈 수 없습니다.

어휘 manufacturing 제조(업) proper 적절한 safety
gear 안전 장비 acceptable 용인되는, 받아들일 수
있는 acceptance 수락, 승인

18

해설 **형용사의 역할_목적격 보어:** 5형식 동사 called 뒤에 목적어 the plot이 왔으므로 빈칸은 부사 too의 수식을 받으면서 목적격 보어 역할을 하는 형용사 자리이다. 문맥상 '줄거리가 너무 뻔하다고 말했다'라는 의미가 되어야 하므로, '예측할 수 있는, 뻔한'이라는 의미의 (C) predictable이 정답이다.

번역 평론가들은 미셸 자오 씨가 출연한 최근 영화에 대해 줄거리가 너무 뻔하다고 말했다.

어휘 critic 평론가 plot (소설·영화 등의) 구성, 줄거리
predict 예측하다 predictable 예측할 수 있는, 뻔한
predictably 예상대로

19

해설 **수량 형용사:** 문맥상 '3주마다'라는 의미가 적절하므로 정답은 (B) every이다. every는 단수명사와 함께 쓰지만, 명사 앞에 숫자가 오는 경우 복수명사가 올 수 있다.

번역 영 리더스 북 클럽의 회원들은 3주마다 우편으로 두 권의 새 동화책을 받게 됩니다.

어휘 storybook 동화책 in the mail 우편으로 every 매~,
~마다 most 대부분의

20

해설 **형용사 관용어구:** 문맥상 '재개발에 적합한지'라는 의미가 적절하므로, 빈칸 앞에 온 be동사, 빈칸 뒤의 for와 결합하여 '~에 적합하다'라는 뜻을 이루는 형용사 (B) suitable이 정답이다.

번역 무어스타운 재개발국은 무어스타운 군구의 다양한 부동산이 재개발에 적합한지 여부를 결정하는 책임을 맡고 있다.

어휘 redevelopment 재개발 agency (정부) 기관, ~청, ~국 determine 결정하다 property 재산, 부동산 township 군구(행정 구역 단위) consistent 지속적인 accurate 정확한

UNIT 06	부사

기출공식 1   본책 p. 60

1 (D)   **2** (B)   **3** (D)

1

해설 **부사의 역할_동사 수식:** Full-time staff (at Dinh and Mann Associates)가 주어이고, work가 동사이며, 빈칸은 동사 work를 수식하는 부사 자리이다. 따라서 '보통, 통상적으로'라는 의미의 부사인 (D) normally가 정답이다.

번역 딘 앤 만 어소시에이츠의 상근직 직원들은 보통 일주일에 37.5시간 근무한다.

어휘 Associates 여러 사람이 공동 운영하는 회사명에 쓰이는 단어 norm 표준, 규범 normal 보통의, 평범한

2

해설 **부사의 역할_동사 수식:** 빈칸은 have와 p.p. 사이에 있으므로 동사를 수식하는 부사 자리이다. 따라서 정답은 (B) steadily이다.

번역 세비아나 코스메틱스의 판매량은 지난 분기 새로운 마케팅 캠페인을 시작한 이후로 꾸준히 향상되었다.

어휘 sales 판매(량) improve 개선되다, 나아지다 quarter 분기 steady 꾸준한

3

해설 **부사의 역할_동사 수식:** Ms. Lai's draft (of Sientech Industries' new mission statement)가 주어, expresses가 동사, the company goals가 목적어인 완전한 문장이다. 빈칸에는 동사 expresses를 수식할 부사가 들어가야 하므로, (D) precisely가 정답이다.

번역 라이 씨가 쓴 시엔텍 산업의 새로운 강령 초안은 회사의 목표를 명확하게 나타내고 있다.

어휘 draft 초안 mission statement (회사의) 강령 precise 명확한 preciseness 명확성

기출공식 2   본책 p. 60

4 (B)   **5** (C)   **6** (D)

4

해설 **부사의 역할_형용사 수식:** 빈칸은 보어 역할을 하는 형용사 accurate를 수식해 주는 부사 자리이므로, 정답은 (B) surprisingly이다.

번역 고성능 날씨 측정기는 공기 중 습도의 정도를 측정하는 데 놀라울 정도로 정확하다.

어휘 performance 성능 gauge 측정기 accurate 정확한 measure 측정하다 humidity 습도

5

해설 **부사의 역할_형용사 수식:** 빈칸 뒤의 형용사 functional을 수식하는 자리이므로 '완전히'를 의미하는 부사 (C) completely가 정답이다.

번역 펄무터 씨는 관리팀에게 시제품이 6월 9일까지는 완전히 가동될 것이라고 장담했다.

어휘 assure 장담하다, 확신시키다 management team 관리팀, 경영팀 prototype 원형, 시제품 functional 가동되는 complete 완전한, 완벽한; 완료하다, 끝마치다

6

해설 **부사의 역할_부사 수식:** 빈칸은 앞에 완전한 절이 있고, 뒤에 온 부사 frequently를 수식하는 역할을 하는 자리이다. 따라서 '특별히, 이례적으로'를 뜻하는 부사 (D) exceptionally가 정답이다.

번역 '플래티넘 플라이어' 지위는 당사 비행기를 특별히 자주 이용하는 사람들에게 부여된다.

어휘 status 지위 award 부여하다 frequently 자주 except 제외하다 exception 예외 exceptional 예외적인

기출공식 3   본책 p. 61

7 (C)   **8** (A)   **9** (D)

7

해설 **부사의 역할_동명사 수식:** 빈칸에는 동명사로 쓰인 listening to를 수식할 수 있는 부사가 필요하므로 (C) carefully가 정답이다.

번역 오르테가 씨는 서비스 센터 상담원들에게 고객의 관심사를 주의 깊게 경청하는 일이 중요하다고 상기시켰다.

어휘 remind 상기시키다, 일깨우다 operator 상담원, 교환원 listen to ~을 경청하다 concerns 관심사, 용무 carefully 주의 깊게, 세심하게

8

해설 **부사의 역할_to부정사 수식:** 빈칸이 없어도 완전한 문장을 이루고 있으므로, 빈칸에는 앞에 나온 to부정사에 쓰인 동사 be reimbursed를 수식하는 부사가 들어가야 한다. 따라서 정답은 '즉시'를 의미하는 부사인 (A) promptly이다.

번역 지난달 여행 경비를 즉시 상환 받으려면 이 양식을 사용하십시오.

어휘 reimburse 상환하다　travel expenses 여행 경비
prompt 즉각적인; 촉발하다, 유도하다　promptness
신속

9

해설 **부사의 역할_to부정사 수식:** 빈칸은 to부정사의 to와 동사 사이에서 to부정사를 수식하는 역할을 하므로 부사가 들어가야 한다. 따라서 '주기적으로'를 의미하는 부사인 (D) regularly가 정답이다.

번역 이 직책의 한 가지 책무는 고객 정보 데이터 문서를 주기적으로 업데이트하는 것이다.

어휘 responsibility 책무　spreadsheet 데이터 문서
regular 주기적인　regularity 규칙성　regularize
규칙적으로 하다

기출공식 4	본책 p. 61
10 (A)　**11** (B)　**12** (A)	

10

해설 **숫자 수식 부사:** 빈칸 뒤에 숫자가 있으므로, 주로 숫자 앞에 쓰여 '대략, 거의'라는 의미를 나타내는 부사인 (A) approximately가 정답이다.

번역 페르지니 건축사 사장은 얼튼 시내의 공사를 완료하는 데 대략 18개월 정도 걸릴 것으로 추정한다.

어휘 estimate 추정하다, 어림잡다　take 시간이 걸리다
eagerly 열망하여　spaciously 넓게

11

해설 **강조 부사:** 빈칸 뒤의 after와 어울릴 수 있는 부사를 찾는 문제이다. 문맥상 '도구들을 받은 직후'라는 의미가 적절하므로 빈칸에는 (B) immediately가 알맞다.

번역 필요한 도구들을 받은 직후에 우리 작업반이 카운티의 남부 지역에 전화 케이블을 설치하기 시작했다.

어휘 crew 작업반, 팀, 조　install 설치하다　telephone
cable 전화 케이블　precisely 꼭, 정확히
immediately 즉시　continually 계속, 끊임없이
productively 생산적으로

12

해설 **강조 부사:** 빈칸 뒤에 오는 전치사구 in advance of의 의미를 강조하면서 수식할 수 있는 부사가 들어가야 한다. 따라서 전치사구 앞에 놓여 '훨씬'이라는 의미로 전치사구를 강조하는 부사 (A) well이 정답이다.

번역 축제 참가자들은 다음 달 도착에 훨씬 앞서 호텔 방을 예약해야 한다.

어휘 attendee 참석자, 참가자　reserve 예약하다
in advance 미리, 사전에

기출공식 5	본책 p. 62
13 (A)　**14** (B)　**15** (B)	

13

해설 **빈도 부사:** 빈칸은 has와 p.p. 사이에 있으므로 동사를 수식하는 부사 자리이다. 따라서 '자주'라는 의미의 빈도 부사 (A) frequently가 정답이다.

번역 롬바드 앤 조는 지역 최고의 세무 법률 회사로 자주 이름이 거론된다.

어휘 name 명명하다　tax law firm 세무 법률 회사
frequent 잦은; 자주 다니다

14

해설 **부정 부사:** 빈칸 뒤 형용사 noticeable을 수식하는 자리이므로 부사가 필요하다. 보기 모두 부사가 될 수 있는데 문맥상 '눈에 띄지 않지만 인기가 높다'라는 의미가 적절하므로 부정 부사인 (B) hardly가 정답이다.

번역 새로 생긴 커피숍은 거리에서 눈에 거의 띄지 않지만 아주 인기가 높아졌다.

어휘 noticeable 눈에 띄는, 두드러진

15

해설 **빈도 부사:** '지난 5년 동안'이라는 특정 기간이 나오고 '지금까지 받았다'는 의미로 현재완료 has received가 쓰였으므로, 혹평을 받은 횟수에 대한 내용이 오는 것이 가장 자연스럽다. 빈칸 앞에 just가 있으므로, '한 번'을 의미하는 빈도 부사인 (B) once가 정답이 된다.

번역 지난 5년 동안 마티스 이터리는 음식 비평가들로부터 단 한 번 혹평을 받았다.

어휘 eatery 식당　poor review 혹평　critic 비평가

기출공식 6	본책 p. 62
16 (D)　**17** (C)　**18** (A)	

16

해설 **시간 부사:** 빈칸에 적절한 부사를 선택하는 문제이다. 해당 부분은 '지난주에 받은 책들(The books we received last week)이 디지털 데이터베이스에 입력되어야 한다 (need to be entered)'라는 내용이므로, 여전히 해야 할 일로 남아 있다는 의미로 need와 함께 쓰여 '여전히 필요하다'라는 뜻을 이루는 (D) still이 가장 적절하다.

번역 지난주에 우리가 받았던 책들은 여전히 디지털 데이터베이스에 입력되어야 한다.

어휘 receive 받다   lately 최근에   evenly 고르게

17

해설 **접속부사:** 빈칸은 문장 전체를 수식하는 부사 자리이며, '그렇다면'이라는 의미의 (C) then이 정답이다. then은 if와 함께 자주 쓰인다는 것도 알아 두자.

번역 이미 자동 납부를 신청했다면, 추가 조치를 할 필요는 없습니다.

어휘 sign up for ~을 신청하다   automatic payment 자동납부   further 더 이상의, 추가의   step 단계, 조치   required 필수의, 필요로 하는

18

해설 **시간 부사:** 빈칸에는 미래에 대한 일을 이야기할 때 쓰이는 조동사 will과 어울려 쓰이는 시간 부사가 들어가야 한다. 문맥상 '새 소프트웨어 덕분에 약속 일정을 잡는 데 걸리는 시간이 곧 줄어들 것이다'라는 의미가 되어야 하므로, 정답은 '곧'을 의미하는 시간 부사 (A) soon이다. 참고로, (B) recently는 과거 또는 현재완료 시제와 함께 쓰이며, (C) lately는 주로 현재완료 시제와 함께 쓰이므로 답이 될 수 없다. 또한 (D) very는 동사가 아닌 형용사나 부사를 수식한다.

번역 새 소프트웨어 덕분에 곧 약속 일정을 잡는 데 걸리는 시간이 줄어들 것이다.

어휘 decrease 줄다, 줄이다   schedule 일정을 잡다; 일정   appointment 약속, 예약

19

해설 **-ly가 붙어서 의미가 달라지는 부사:** 빈칸은 '완성된'을 의미하는 형용사 complete을 수식할 부사 자리이다. 따라서 완성 정도에 대해 이야기할 때 쓰이는 '거의'라는 뜻의 (A) nearly가 정답이다. 참고로, 부사로 쓰이는 near는 '가까이에'라는 뜻이다.

번역 광고 삽화가 거의 완성되었을 때 고객이 대폭 수정을 요구했다.

어휘 artwork 삽화, 미술품   major 중대한, 주요한   change 수정

20

해설 **-ly가 붙어서 의미가 달라지는 부사:** 빈칸은 동사 have worked를 수식하며 부사 exceptionally의 수식을 받는 부사 자리이다. 문맥상 '열심히 노력했다'라는 의미가 적절하므로 '열심히'라는 의미의 부사인 (A) hard가 정답이다. (D) hardly는 '거의 ~하지 않다'라는 부정의 의미를 지닌 부사이므로 오답이다.

번역 모델 미술 학교의 미술 강좌에 등록한 학생들은 지난해에 특별히 열심히 노력했다.

어휘 enroll 등록시키다, 등록하다   painting 그림 그리기, 화법   exceptionally 예외적으로, 특별히, 유별나게

21

해설 **-ly가 붙어서 의미가 달라지는 부사:** 빈칸에는 before 앞에 쓰여 '직전에'라는 의미를 나타낼 수 있는 부사가 들어가야 한다. 따라서 '즉시, 곧'을 의미하는 (C) shortly가 정답이다. shortly before는 '직전에', shortly after는 '직후에'라는 뜻으로 쓰인다.

번역 계약업자들은 내일 오전 8시 직전에 공사를 시작할 것이라고 말한다.

어휘 contractor 계약업체, 계약자   renovation 수리, 개축

22

해설 **특정한 쓰임을 가지는 부사:** '너무 ~해서 …하다'라고 표현할 때는 'so + 형용사/부사 + that절'의 형태가 된다. 따라서 빈칸에는 (C) so가 정답이다. 참고로 (B) such의 경우 'such + (a(n)) + (형용사) + 명사+that절'의 형태가 된다는 것에 유의하자.

번역 휴대폰이 널리 보급되어 정보 통신 회사들은 예전에는 너무 멀다고 여겨졌던 곳에도 서비스를 확충하고 있다.

어휘 prevalent 널리 퍼진, 보급된, 유행하고 있는   telecommunications 원격 통신   establish 설립하다   previously 이전에   remote 멀리 떨어진, 외진

23

해설 **특정한 쓰임을 가지는 부사:** 문맥상 '중소기업과 대기업 둘 다에게'라는 의미가 적절하므로 두 집단 뒤에 쓰여 '둘 다'를 나타낼 수 있는 (C) alike가 정답이다.

번역	환경 오염 예방은 중소기업과 대기업 둘 다에게 중요한 고려 사항이 되었다.	
어휘	prevention 예방, 방지 environmental 환경의 pollution 오염 consideration 고려 사항 forth ~ 쪽으로; 앞으로	

24

해설 **특정한 쓰임을 가지는 부사:** 현재완료 사이에 들어갈 부사를 묻는 문제로 빈칸에는 '그 이래로'를 의미하는 since가 들어가야 가장 자연스럽다. 따라서 정답은 (A) since이다.

번역 개발 시험 단계에서 발생했던 사소한 우려 사항들은 그 이후로 해결되었고, 해당 제품은 조립 단계로 넘어갈 준비가 되어 있다.

어휘 minor 작은, 사소한 concern 우려 사항, 걱정 arise 발생하다 testing phase 시험 단계 resolve 해결하다 progress 진행하다, 나아가다 assembly 조립

ETS TEST
본책 p. 64

1 (A)	2 (B)	3 (D)	4 (B)	5 (B)
6 (B)	7 (A)	8 (B)	9 (A)	10 (B)
11 (D)	12 (D)	13 (C)	14 (D)	15 (D)
16 (C)	17 (C)	18 (B)	19 (D)	20 (A)

1

해설 **부사의 역할_동사 수식:** 빈칸은 동사 has improved를 수식하는 자리이므로 '상당히'를 뜻하는 부사 (A) significantly가 정답이다. 참고로, 같은 의미로 향상 정도를 수식할 수 있는 기타 부사로는 considerably, noticeably, remarkably, dramatically, substantially가 있다.

번역 상사의 조언 덕분에, 팀에 합류한 후 화이트 씨의 업무는 크게 향상되었다.

어휘 thanks to ~ 덕분에 signify 의미하다, 뜻하다 significant 중요한, 의미 있는

2

해설 **부사의 역할_명사구 강조:** 부사는 일반적으로 명사를 수식하지 않지만 '관사 + 명사' 앞에 놓일 때는 강조하는 역할을 할 수 있다. 문맥상 '특히 정문 입구 통로 복원 공사'라는 의미로 명사를 강조할 수 있는 부사 (B) specifically가 정답이다.

번역 귀하의 후한 기부금은 박물관의 보수 프로젝트, 특히 정문 입구 통로 복원 공사에 쓰일 것입니다.

어휘 generous 후한, 너그러운 donation 기부, 기부금 go toward ~에 도움이 되다 restoration 복원, 복구 entryway 입구 통로 specific 구체적인, 특정한 specifically 분명히, 특별히 specification 명세, 세목 specify 명시하다

3

해설 **부사의 역할_형용사 수식:** 빈칸은 be동사와 형용사 사이에서 형용사를 수식하는 부사 자리이므로 '의도적으로'라는 뜻의 (D) intentionally가 정답이다.

번역 회사 편람은 회사 정책이 모든 부서에 걸쳐 직원들에게 두루 적용되도록 의도적으로 보편적인 내용을 다루고 있다.

어휘 policy 정책 apply to ~에 적용되다 division 부서 intent 의도 intention 의도 intentional 의도적인

4

해설 **부사의 역할_동사 수식:** 빈칸은 조동사와 일반동사 사이에서 동사를 수식하는 부사 자리이다. 따라서 정답은 (B) probably이다.

번역 메이플우드 가의 공사 지연 때문에, 직원들은 아마 다른 길을 찾아야 할 것이다.

어휘 due to ~ 때문에 construction 공사 alternate 교체의, 다른 probable 일어날 것 같은 probably 아마도 probability 가능성

5

해설 **시간 부사:** 동사의 시제가 미래이므로 '곧 연락을 받을 것이다'라는 의미를 이루는 부사 (B) shortly가 정답이다. shortly는 short(짧은)에 '-ly'가 붙어서 의미가 달라지는 부사이므로 뜻에 유의해야 한다.

번역 귀하의 요청이 접수되었으며, 곧 저희 직원으로부터 연락을 받으실 겁니다.

어휘 receive 접수하다 agent 직원, 외판원 shortly 곧 lately 요즘 slightly 약간 narrowly 가까스로

6

해설 **부사의 역할_동사 수식:** 빈칸에는 주어 Mayor Reynold's views와 동사 established 사이에서 동사를 수식하는 부사 자리이다. 따라서 '확고히'라는 의미의 부사인 (B) firmly가 정답이다.

번역 레이놀드 시장의 교육에 관한 견해는 그를 선거의 선두 주자로 확실히 자리매김하게 했다.

어휘 view 견해 education 교육 establish 확고히 하다 front-runner 우승 후보 election 선거

7

해설 **부사의 역할_동사 수식:** 빈칸 앞에서 완전한 문장이 끝났으므로 빈칸은 부사 자리이다. 따라서 '협력하여'라는 뜻의 부사로 동사 has worked를 수식하는 (A) collaboratively가 정답이다.

번역 솔리스 씨는 많은 직원들과 협력해서 일해 왔기 때문에 훌륭한 프로젝트 매니저가 될 것이다.

8

해설 **부사의 역할_동사 수식:** 빈칸은 조동사와 일반동사 사이 부사 자리이다. 따라서 정답은 (B) possibly이다. 참고로, possibly는 can't, couldn't가 쓰인 부정문에서 '도저히'라는 의미로 쓰인다.

번역 배달원은 소포가 도저히 배송 중에 파손되었을 리는 없다고 주장했다.

어휘 courier 택배 회사, 배달원　insist 주장하다　package 소포　damage 손상하다; 파손　shipment 배송

9

해설 **강조 부사:** 빈칸 뒤에 온 부사 too가 문제 해결의 단서로, 빈칸에는 too를 강조하는 부사가 들어가야 한다. 따라서 '너무'라는 의미의 (A) far가 정답이다. 참고로 much나 way 또한 too를 강조하는 강조 부사로 쓸 수 있다.

번역 그 여행사가 판촉하고 있는 휴가 패키지 상품들은 일반 고객층에게는 너무 고가이다.

어휘 vacation package 휴가 패키지 상품　travel agency 여행사　promote 촉진하다, 증진[장려]하다　typical 전형적인, 대표적인

10

해설 **부사의 역할_형용사 수식:** 2형식 동사 remained 뒤에 보어로 형용사인 consistent가 왔으므로 형용사를 수식하는 부사가 와야 한다. 따라서 (B) remarkably가 정답이다.

번역 오크 밸리사에서 디자인한 가구는 회사가 100년 동안 사업을 해 오는 동안 놀라울 정도로 한결같은 품질을 유지하고 있다.

어휘 quality 품질　consistent 한결같은, 일관된　firm 회사　operate 영업하다　remark 논평, 언급; 언급하다, 논평하다　remarkably 두드러지게, 현저하게　remarkable 놀라운, 주목할 만한

11

해설 **부사의 역할_분사 수식:** 빈칸에는 형용사 역할을 하는 과거분사 reduced를 수식하는 부사가 들어가야 한다. 따라서 정답은 '약간, 다소'라는 의미의 부사인 (D) slightly이다.

번역 제분소는 사소한 기계 결함 때문에 가동력이 약간 떨어진 상태로 운영되고 있다.

어휘 flour mill 제분소　operate 운영하다　reduced 감소된　capacity 생산 능력, 가동력　minor 작은, 사소한　mechanical 기계의

12

해설 **부사의 역할_동사 수식:** 빈칸은 be동사와 p.p. 사이로 동사를 수식하는 부사 자리이다. 따라서 '철저히, 엄격하게'라는 뜻의 (D) rigorously가 정답이다

번역 이사회는 모든 계약서는 서명 전에 법무 부서에 의해 철저히 검토되어야 한다는 것을 명심하라는 메모를 부서장들에게 발송했다.

어휘 executive board 이사회　send out ~을 발송하다　reminder 상기시키는 메모[조언]　division head 부서장　legal 법률의, 법률에 관한　rigor 엄함, 엄격　rigorous 엄격한, 철저한

13

해설 **특정한 쓰임을 가지는 부사:** 문맥상 '직원과 방문객 둘 다'라는 의미가 적절하므로 두 집단 뒤에 쓰여 '둘 다 모두'를 나타낼 수 있는 (C) alike가 정답이다.

번역 공장 직원들과 방문객들이 모두 사용할 수 있는 새로운 보안경이 곧 이용 가능해질 것이다.

어휘 safety glasses 보안경　available 이용할 수 있는

14

해설 **부사의 역할_분사 수식:** 빈칸 뒤 과거분사인 processed를 수식하는 부사 (D) naturally가 정답이다.

번역 폴베리 지역 장터는 지역에서 천연 가공한 유제품만을 취급한다는 것에 자부심을 가지고 있다.

어휘 local 지역의　marketplace 시장, 장터　take pride in ~을 자랑하다　carry 취급하다　process 가공하다, 처리하다　dairy product 유제품　region 지역

15

해설 **비교급 강조 부사:** 빈칸 뒤의 비교급 more가 문제 해결의 단서로, 빈칸에는 비교급 수식 부사가 들어가야 한다. 따라서 정답은 '훨씬'이라는 뜻으로 비교급을 수식하는 (D) even이다.

번역 6월 30일로 종료되는 기간 동안, 호라이즌 스타디움사는 티켓 판매로 전례 없는 수익을 기록했고, 광고에서는 훨씬 많은 수익을 올렸다.

어휘 corporation 기업, 회사　record 기록하다　unprecedented 전례 없는　revenue 수익, 수입

16

해설 **부사의 역할_준동사 수식:** 빈칸 앞에 전치사가 있고, 뒤에 전치사의 목적어로 온 명사가 있으므로 동명사를 수식하는 부사 (C) continually가 정답이다.

번역 볼도니 레스토랑의 주방장은 창의적이면서도 맛있는 요리들을 끊임없이 선보이는 것으로 칭찬이 자자하다.

어휘 head chef 주방장 commend 칭찬하다 introduce 소개하다 creative 창의적인

17

해설 **빈도 부사:** 빈칸은 must receive를 수식하는 자리로, 직원들이 지켜야 할 수칙을 설명하는 내용이므로 '항상 승인을 받아야 한다'라는 의미를 완성하는 빈도 부사 (C) always가 정답이다.

번역 콘스탄시오 레스토랑 직원들은 교대 근무 시간을 서로 바꿀 수 있지만, 항상 사전에 지배인으로부터 승인을 받아야 한다.

어휘 exchange 교환하다 shift 교대 근무 (시간) approval 승인 ahead of time 미리, 사전에 completely 완전히 formerly 이전에

18

해설 **부사의 역할_전치사구 수식:** 전치사구는 문장에서 형용사나 부사 역할을 하는데, 여기서는 in favor of가 '찬성하는'이라는 의미로 be동사의 보어로 쓰였다. 따라서 빈칸은 보어로 온 전치사구를 수식하는 부사 자리이므로 정답은 '압도적으로'라는 뜻의 (B) overwhelmingly이다.

번역 교외 지역 주민들은 교통 혼잡을 줄이기 위해 589 고속도로를 확장하는 것에 압도적으로 찬성한다.

어휘 suburban 교외 지역의 relieve 완화시키다 congestion 혼잡

19

해설 **부사의 역할_동사 수식:** 빈칸은 조동사와 be동사 사이에서 동사를 수식하는 부사 자리이다. 따라서 정답은 (D) probably이다.

번역 수신자들은 아마도 마음을 끄는 제목이 있는 판매 이메일을 더 열어 보고 싶을 것이다.

어휘 motivated to ~하고 싶은 enticing 마음을 끄는 probable 개연성 있는 probability 개연성

20

해설 **부사의 역할_형용사 수식:** 빈칸은 뒤에 온 형용사 cautious를 수식하는 부사 자리이므로, '재정적으로'라는 의미의 부사인 (A) financially가 정답이다.

번역 〈파이낸스 레저〉는 많은 소기업 소유주들이 영업 첫 해에는 재정적으로 신중하다고 보도한다.

어휘 report 보도하다, 발표하다 cautious 신중한 operation 운영, 영업

UNIT 07	전치사

기출공식 1   본책 p. 68

1 (C)   **2** (C)   **3** (A)

1

해설 **기간 전치사:** 빈칸 뒤의 weeks four and five와 함께 어울려 쓸 수 있어야 하며, 문맥상 '네 번째 및 다섯 번째 주 동안의 매출'이라는 내용이 되어야 한다. 따라서 '~ 동안'이라는 뜻의 (C) during이 정답이다.

번역 네 번째 및 다섯 번째 주 동안의 매출을 면밀하게 추적 관찰해 1분기 수익에 어떤 영향을 미치는지 판단할 것이다.

어휘 closely 면밀하게, 유심히 monitor 관찰하다, 감시하다 determine 판단하다, 결심하다 profit 수익

2

해설 **시점 전치사:** 동사 complete와 함께 쓰여 '금요일까지'라는 완료의 의미를 나타내는 전치사인 (C) by가 정답이다.

번역 리버 오크스사의 직원들은 금요일 오후 5시까지 직원 만족 설문지를 완료해야 한다.

어휘 complete 완료하다 satisfaction 만족

3

해설 **기간 전치사:** 시간 표현과 함께 쓰여 '~ 이내에'를 의미하는 전치사인 (A) within이 정답이다.

번역 귀하의 팔렘방 호텔 객실 예약을 확실히 하기 위해서 24시간 이내에 이 메시지에 회답해 주십시오.

어휘 guarantee 보장하다, 확실히 하다 reply to ~에 회답하다

기출공식 2   본책 p. 68

4 (B)   **5** (B)   **6** (D)

4

해설 **장소 전치사:** 빈칸은 뒤에 오는 the top shelf와 결합하여 동사 are stored를 수식하고 있다. '파일 폴더가 맨 위 선반 위에 보관되어 있다'라는 의미가 되어야 하므로 정답은 (B) on이다.

번역 모든 파일 폴더는 회의실 수납장의 맨 위 선반에 보관되어 있다.

어휘 store 보관하다 conference room 회의실

5

해설 **위치 전치사:** 동사가 '분배하다'라는 뜻의 distribute이고 빈칸 뒤에 '다양한 학과들'이라는 복수명사 various science departments가 나오므로 '다양한 학과들 사이에 자금을 배분하다'라는 범주의 의미를 이루는 (B) among이 정답이다. (A) toward은 '~을 향해'라는 뜻으로 운동 방향이나 목적을 나타내므로 적합하지 않으며, (C) after는 시점, (D) during은 기간 표현과 쓰이므로 오답이다.

번역 교수 위원회는 연구 보조금에서 나온 기금들을 여러 이학부 학과들 사이에 분배할 것이다.

어휘 faculty (대학 학부의) 교수진, 교직원   research grant 연구 보조금   science departments 이학부 학과들

6

해설 **방향 전치사:** 빈칸 앞의 동사 is located와 빈칸 뒤에 온 장소 명사 the Green Treat Market와 함께 어울려 쓸 수 있는 전치사를 선택해야 한다. 문맥상 '숙주 교 도서관은 그린 트리트 마켓을 조금 지나서 위치해 있다'라는 내용이 되어야 하므로, '~을 지나서'라는 의미의 (D) past가 정답이 된다.

번역 숙주 교 도서관은 제이콥 가의 그린 트리트 마켓을 조금 지나서 위치해 있다.

어휘 located 위치한, 자리한   slightly 조금, 약간

기출공식 3   본책 p. 69

7 (A)   **8** (A)   **9** (B)

7

해설 **양보 전치사:** 빈칸은 뒤에 온 명사구 the bad weather를 목적으로 취하는 전치사 자리이다. 콤마 앞에서 악천후를 언급했으나, 뒤따르는 절에서 예정대로 완공되었다고 했으므로, '~임에도 불구하고'를 의미하는 전치사 (A) Despite가 정답이 된다.

번역 악천후에도 불구하고, 아크메 시멘트 본사는 예정대로 완공되었다.

어휘 construction 공사, 건설   headquarters 본사 complete 완성하다   on schedule 예정대로

8

해설 **이유 전치사:** 빈칸은 뒤에 온 명사구 significant advances in technology를 목적어로 취하는 전치사 자리이다. 따라서 보기 중 유일한 전치사인 (A) Due to가 정답이다. (B) When과 (C) Because는 접속사이고, (D) In order to는 to 뒤에 동사원형이 와야 하므로 빈칸에 들어갈 수 없다.

번역 상당한 기술 발전에 힘입어 황보 오토모티브는 굉장히 연비가 좋은 자동차를 설계할 수 있었다.

어휘 significant 상당한, 중요한   advance 진보, 발전 automotive 자동차의   exceptionally 굉장히, 특별히 fuel-efficient (자동차) 연비가 좋은, 연료 절약형의

9

해설 **제외 전치사:** 문맥상 '일요일을 제외하고 매일'이라는 의미가 되어야 자연스러우므로 (B) except가 정답이다. 참고로 all, every, always나 no 뒤에는 except가 자주 사용되며, '~을 제외하고 모두[항상]', 또는 '~만 제외하고 ~하지 못한다'라는 내용이 된다.

번역 마을 도서관은 일요일을 제외하고 일주일 동안 매일 문을 연다.

기출공식 4   본책 p. 69

10 (B)   **11** (D)   **12** (A)

10

해설 **자격 전치사:** 보기가 모두 전치사이므로 문맥상 가장 적합한 단어를 골라야 한다. 직책 앞에 쓰여 '부사장으로서'라는 자격의 의미를 나타내는 (B) as가 정답이다.

번역 월말에 베송 씨가 시코르스키 씨를 대신하여 부사장 직을 맡을 예정이다.

어휘 be expected to ~하기로 되어 있다   vice president 부사장   replace 대신하다

11

해설 **주제 / 연관성 전치사:** 문맥상 '베빙튼 프로젝트에 관한 모든 문의 사항'이라는 의미가 되어야 하므로, '~에 관한'이라는 의미로 주제를 나타낼 수 있는 전치사 (D) concerning이 정답이다.

번역 박 씨의 부재 시에, 베빙튼 프로젝트에 관한 모든 문의 사항은 그녀의 비서에게 보내야 한다.

어휘 absence 결석, 부재   inquiry 질문   direct to ~에게 보내다   assuming 가령 ~라면   versus ~대, ~에 비해 rather 꽤

12

해설 **동반 전치사:** 문맥상 '논문 원고와 함께 제출되어야 한다'는 내용이 되어야 자연스러우므로 '~와 함께'라는 뜻의 (A) along with가 정답이다.

번역 저자가 기입을 완료한 일람표는 논문 원고와 함께 제출되어야 한다.

어휘 author 저자   submit 제출하다   article 논문 manuscript 원고

13 (B)   **14** (B)   **15** (B)

13

해설 **전치사구:** 빈칸 뒤에 온 behalf of가 문제 해결의 단서로, behalf of는 전치사 on과 함께 쓰여 '~을 대신하여'라는 의미를 이룬다. 따라서 (B) on이 정답이다.

번역 앨런 리 씨는 부사장을 대신해 연설하는 자리에서 직원들이 기금 모금 운동에 힘써 준 데 감사를 표했다.

어휘 **vice president** 부사장 **contribution** 기여 **fund-raising** 자금 조달(의), 모금(의)

14

해설 **전치사구:** 문맥상 '고객 불만에 대한 반응으로'라는 의미가 되어야 하므로, 전치사구 in response to를 완성하는 (B) response가 정답이다.

번역 고객 불만에 대한 반응으로, 481 책꽂이 모델에 대한 조립 설명서가 단순화되었다.

어휘 **assembly** 조립 **instruction** 설명서 **simplify** 단순화하다 **control** 통제 **access** 접근 **expense** 비용

15

해설 **전치사구:** 문맥상 '직급에 따라'라는 의미가 되어야 적절하므로 전치사 on과 함께 쓰여 '~에 따라'라는 의미를 이루는 (B) depending이 정답이다.

번역 우손사는 근속 연수에 따라 직원들이 특별 주차권을 이용할 수 있도록 한다.

어휘 **permit** 허가증 **available** 이용할 수 있는 **seniority** (근속 연수에 따른) 서열

16 (D)   **17** (B)   **18** (A)

16

해설 **전치사 관용 표현:** 빈칸 뒤에 온 명사 duty가 문제 해결의 단서로, 명사 duty는 전치사 on과 함께 쓰여 '근무 중'이라는 의미를 나타낸다. 따라서 (D) on이 정답이다.

번역 훈련 받은 구조원이 근무하지 않는 경우에는 지역 수영장을 사용할 수 없다.

어휘 **community** 지역사회 **trained** 훈련 받은

17

해설 **전치사 관용 표현:** 빈칸 뒤의 schedule이 문제 해결의 단서로, 문맥상 '예정보다 일찍 도착했다'라는 의미가 되어야

하므로 정답은 (B) ahead of이다.

번역 순풍으로 인해 멜라네시아 항공편 632가 호니아라 공항에 예정보다 일찍 도착했다.

어휘 **favorable wind** 순풍 **cause** 야기하다

18

해설 **전치사 관용 표현:** 빈칸 앞의 전치사 on과 함께 쓰여 '평균적으로'라는 의미의 관용 표현을 만드는 단수명사 (A) average가 정답이다.

번역 평균 6만 명의 청취자가 매일 크리오스 라디오를 청취한다.

어휘 **tune into** (라디오나 TV를) 듣다, 시청하다

19 (A)   **20** (B)   **21** (C)

19

해설 **자동사 + 전치사:** 빈칸에는 동사 benefit와 함께 쓰여 '~로부터 이익을 얻다, ~에서 이득을 보다'라는 의미를 나타내는 전치사가 들어가야 한다. 따라서 정답은 (A) from이다.

번역 소어링 스카이즈 항공은 경쟁사를 인수해서 크게 이득을 보았다.

어휘 **soar** 치솟다, 오르다 **greatly** 크게 **acquisition** 인수 **competitor** 경쟁사, 경쟁자

20

해설 **자동사 + 전치사:** 빈칸 앞의 동사 expand와 결합하여 '~로 확장하다, ~로 진출하다'라는 뜻으로 방향을 나타내며, 빈칸 뒤에 오는 명사를 목적어로 취할 수 있는 것은 전치사 (B) into이다. 참고로 expand는 '~을 확장하다'라는 뜻의 타동사로도 출제되니 알아 두자.

번역 조티코스 의류사는 유럽과 아시아로 확장하려는 계획의 일환으로 두 개의 다른 소매업체를 인수했다.

어휘 **acquire** 얻다, 취득하다 **retail** 소매 **as part of** ~의 일환으로 **expand** 확대하다, 확장하다

21

해설 **자동사 + 전치사:** 빈칸에는 전치사 with와 어울려 '준수하다'라는 뜻을 이루는 동사가 와야 한다. 따라서 (C) comply가 정답이다. (A) fulfill도 '준수하다'라는 의미가 있지만 타동사이므로 전치사와 함께 쓰지 않는다.

번역 암스트롱 배송은 트럭에 대한 환경 규정을 준수하지 않아 벌금이 부과되었다.

어휘 **fine** 벌금을 부과하다 **environmental** 환경의 **regulation** 규정 **fulfill** 이행하다, 준수하다 **inform** 알리다 **invest** 투자하다

기출공식 8	본책 p. 71
22 (C) **23** (D) **24** (A)	

22

해설 **명사 + 전치사:** 빈칸 앞에 온 명사 demand가 문제 해결의 단서로, 명사 demand는 전치사 for와 함께 쓰여 '~에 대한 수요'라는 의미를 나타낸다. 따라서 (C) for가 정답이다.

번역 우리 제품에 대한 수요 증가에 맞추기 위해 최소 4명의 직원을 추가로 고용해야 할 것이다.

어휘 **keep up with** ~에 맞춰 나가다, ~에 뒤떨어지지 않다 **additional** 추가의, 부가의

23

해설 **명사 + 전치사:** 빈칸 앞의 a competitive edge와 뒤의 ~ stores가 문제 해결의 단서로, 문맥상 '지역 식료품점 대비 경쟁 우위를 제공한다'라는 의미가 되어야 자연스럽다. 따라서 어떤 대상에 비해 우위를 차지할 때 '~보다, ~을 능가하여'의 의미를 나타내는 (D) over가 정답이다.

번역 콜마트의 어마어마한 규모는 지역 기반 식료품점 대비 경쟁 우위를 제공한다.

어휘 **enormous** 어마어마한 **competitive edge** 경쟁 우위 **locally-owned** 지역 기반의, 동네의

24

해설 **명사 + 전치사:** 빈칸 뒤에 온 전치사 on이 문제 해결의 단서로, 명사 impact는 전치사 on과 함께 쓰여 '~에 미치는 영향'이라는 의미를 나타낸다. 따라서 (A) impact가 정답이다.

번역 최근의 정부 정책은 전국 주택 가격에 긍정적인 영향을 미치고 있다.

어휘 **policy** 정책 **positive** 긍정적인 **housing price** 집값 **nationwide** 전국에 **supply** 공급 **factor** 요인

ETS **TEST**				본책 p. 72
1 (A)	**2** (A)	**3** (D)	**4** (D)	**5** (D)
6 (A)	**7** (D)	**8** (C)	**9** (C)	**10** (D)
11 (C)	**12** (C)	**13** (D)	**14** (B)	**15** (A)
16 (C)	**17** (B)	**18** (C)	**19** (B)	**20** (D)

1

해설 **제외 전치사:** 빈칸은 뒤의 명사 Dr. Carrera를 목적어로 취해 수식어구를 형성하는 전치사 자리이다. 문맥상 '카레라 박사를 제외하고'라는 의미가 되어야 자연스러우므로 '~을 제외하고'라는 뜻의 (A) Except for가 정답이다.

번역 마드리드에 있을 카레라 박사를 제외한 외과팀 전체가 퍼스에서 열리는 감사 행사에 참석할 예정이다.

어휘 **entire** 전체의 **surgical** 외과[수술]의 **attend** 참석하다 **appreciation** 감사 **gala** 축하 행사 **along with** ~에 덧붙여 **whereas** (접속사) 반면 **likewise** (접속부사) 또한

2

해설 **자동사 + 전치사:** 문맥상 '개방형 접속 데이터베이스는 취업 기회를 검색하기 위해 사용될 수 있다'는 내용이 되어야 하므로, 빈칸에는 search와 함께 쓰여 '~을 검색하다, 찾다'라는 의미를 나타내는 전치사가 들어가야 한다. 따라서 정답은 (A) for이다.

번역 개방형 접속 데이터베이스를 사용해 슈타이나흐 퍼블리싱의 취업 기회를 검색할 수 있다.

어휘 **access** 접근, 접속, 이용 **opportunity** 기회 **publishing** 출판(사)

3

해설 **위치 전치사:** 빈칸 뒤 명사 the newest trends와 어울려 가장 자연스러운 의미를 만드는 전치사를 택해야 한다. '은행업계의 최신 동향 중에'라는 범주의 의미가 되어야 하므로 (D) Among이 정답이다. 보어 역할을 하는 전치사구(Among the newest trends in the banking industry)가 문장 앞으로 나가서 주어(the drive toward debt consolidation)와 동사(is)가 도치된 문장 구조임을 알아두자.

번역 은행업계의 최신 동향들 중에 부채 정리 운동이 있다.

어휘 **drive** 운동 **debt** 채무 **consolidation** 통합, (부채 등의) 정리

4

해설 **대조 전치사:** 빈칸은 analysts' predictions라는 명사구를 목적어로 취하는 전치사 자리이며, '예상과 달리'라는 의미가 적절하므로 정답은 '~와 반대로'라는 뜻의 (D) Contrary to이다. (C) Except는 전치사와 접속사 둘 다로 쓰일 수 있지만 문맥이 맞지 않아 오답이다.

번역 전문가들의 예상과 반대로 맥나이트 전자의 기술자들은 이전 모델보다 두 배나 오래 지속되는 건전지를 만들 수 있었다.

어휘 **prediction** 예상 **capable** ~할 수 있는 **last** 지속되다 **previous** 이전의 **nevertheless** (접속부사) 그럼에도 불구하고 **provided that** (접속사) 만약 ~라면

5

해설 **시점 전치사:** 빈칸 뒤에 명사구 its purchase of the Sumida factory가 있고, 문맥상 '공장을 매입하고 난 다음 분기에'라는 의미가 되어야 한다. 따라서 빈칸에는 '~ 후에'라는 의미의 전치사인 (D) following이 정답이다.

번역 수미다 공장을 매입하고 난 다음 분기에 레니르 매뉴팩처링의 생산량은 15퍼센트 증가했다.

어휘 **quarter** 1분기(1년의 4분의 1) **manufacturing** 제조업 **production** 생산, 생산량

6

해설 **장소 전치사:** 빈칸 뒤 장소 명사 Glenview Shopping Center가 왔으므로 정답은 '쇼핑센터 맞은편에'라는 의미를 이루는 (A) opposite이다. (C) apart는 부사, (D) nearby는 형용사 또는 부사이며, (B) among 다음에는 복수명사가 와야 하므로 오답이다.

번역 컨벤션 센터는 글렌뷰 쇼핑센터 바로 맞은편인 마켓 가에 위치해 있다.

어휘 **directly** 바로 **opposite** ~의 반대편에 **apart** 떨어져서 **nearby** 근처의, 가까이에

7

해설 **비교 전치사:** 문맥상 '1년 전보다 35% 올랐다'는 의미가 되어야 자연스러우므로, 비교 대상 앞에 쓰여 변화 추이를 나타낼 수 있는 전치사 (D) from이 정답이다. 비교/차이를 나타낼 때 different from을 쓰는데 이와 유사한 쓰임이라는 것을 알아 두자.

번역 방카 오스트라바는 3분기 수익이 1년 전보다 35% 증가했다고 보고했다.

어휘 **quarter** 분기 **earnings** 수익

8

해설 **기타 전치사 어휘:** 문맥상 '부동산의 매입'이라는 의미가 되어야 자연스러우므로 (C) of가 정답이다.

번역 25일 후면 노스브리지 부동산 매입이 마무리될 것이다.

어휘 **purchase** 매입 **property** 부동산 **finalize** 마무리하다

9

해설 **주제/연관성 전치사:** 빈칸 뒤 whether가 문제 해결의 핵심 단서로, '~인지 아닌지에 관해'라는 의미를 이루는 (C) as to가 정답이다. as to whether 구문을 통째로 암기하면 좋다.

번역 도시계획국은 개발자들이 센터 가에 아파트 단지를 건설하도록 허가할지에 대해 아직 결정하지 않은 상태이다.

어휘 **city planning board** 도시계획국 **allow** 허가하다 **developer** 개발자 **apartment complex** 아파트 단지

10

해설 **포함 전치사:** 빈칸은 뒤의 명사구 part-time workers와 결합하여 수식어구를 만드는 자리이므로 전치사가 들어가

야 한다. 문맥상 '시간제 직원을 포함해 전 직원'이라고 해석되어야 자연스러우므로 (D) including이 정답이다.

번역 내일 교육 세션에는 시간제 직원을 포함, 테그램사 전 직원이 참석해야 한다.

어휘 **be expected to** ~해야 한다 **nevertheless** 그럼에도 불구하고 **including** ~을 포함해

11

해설 **추가 전치사:** 문맥상 '광범위한 주요리 외에도 후식이 있다'라는 의미가 적절하므로 '~ 외에도'라는 추가의 의미를 지닌 전치사 (C) Besides가 가장 적절하다.

번역 광범위한 주요리 외에도 그 식당은 갖가지 맛 좋은 제빵류와 더불어 다양한 후식 메뉴를 고를 수 있는 특징이 있다.

어휘 **extensive** 광범위한 **selection** 선택 **main dish** 주요리 **feature** 특징으로 하다 **a variety of** 다양한 **baked goods** 제빵류

12

해설 **동반 전치사:** 문맥상 '탑승권과 함께 여권을 제시해야 한다'라는 의미가 적절하므로 '~와 함께'라는 동반의 의미를 지닌 전치사 (C) along with가 정답이다.

번역 승객들은 비행기에 탑승 수속을 할 때 루나 항공사 직원들에게 탑승권과 함께 여권을 제시해야 한다.

어휘 **passport** 여권 **boarding pass** 탑승권 **personnel** 인원, 전 직원 **check in** 탑승 수속을 하다 **notwithstanding** (전치사) ~에도 불구하고 **in case** (접속사) ~인 경우에 대비하여 **in spite of** (전치사) ~에도 불구하고

13

해설 **양보 전치사:** 빈칸 앞에 완전한 절이 있고 뒤에 last week's changes라는 명사구가 나오므로 명사구를 절에 연결할 수 있는 전치사가 필요하다. 따라서 '~에도 불구하고'라는 양보의 의미의 지닌 전치사 (D) despite가 정답이다.

번역 지난주 증시 전반의 변화에도 불구하고 나라 알루미늄 주가는 안정세를 유지했다.

어휘 **stock** 주식 **stable** 안정적인 **overall** 전반적인 **even so** (접속부사) 그렇다고 하더라도

14

해설 **출처 전치사:** 문맥상 '보안 사무실에서 받아야 한다'라는 의미가 되어야 하므로, 출처를 나타내는 전치사 (B) from이 정답이다.

번역 켄싱턴사 방문자들은 시설에 입장하기 전에 보안 사무실에서 방문자 통행증을 받아야 한다.

어휘 **obtain** 얻다 **pass** 통행증 **security** 보안 **prior to** ~하기 전에 **facility** 시설

15

해설 **비교 전치사:** 빈칸 뒤로 명사구가 왔으므로 빈칸은 전치사 자리이다. 따라서 유일한 전치사로 '~와는 달리'라는 비교의 의미를 지닌 (A) Unlike가 정답이다. 나머지 보기들은 모두 부사이므로 오답이다.

번역 많은 회계 소프트웨어 프로그램과는 달리, 데브레이사의 런어닥 플러스 프로그램은 학생들에게 기본적인 회계 기술을 가르치기 위해 고안되었다.

어휘 accounting 회계   be designed to ~하기 위해 고안되다   skill 기술   regardless 상관없이

16

해설 **주제/연관성 전치사:** 빈칸 앞에 완전한 절이 있고 뒤에 company reimbursement procedures라는 명사구가 나오므로 명사구를 절에 연결할 수 있는 전치사가 필요하다. 따라서 정답은 '~에 관하여'라는 주제/연관성의 의미를 지닌 전치사 (C) regarding이다.

번역 회사 환급 절차에 관한 정보를 받지 못했다면 인사과의 블랙웰 씨에게 연락하세요.

어휘 personnel office 인사과   reimbursement 환급, 상환   procedure 절차, 방법   regard 여기다, 간주하다

17

해설 **장소 전치사:** 빈칸 앞에 완전한 절이 있고 뒤에 the building entrance라는 명사구가 나오므로 명사구를 절에 연결할 수 있는 전치사가 필요하다. 문맥상 '건물 입구를 가로질러'라는 내용이 되어야 자연스러우므로, '~을 가로질러'라는 의미로 장소와 함께 어울려 쓸 수 있는 전치사인 (B) across가 정답이다.

번역 홍보팀은 성대한 개막 축하행사를 위해 건물 입구를 가로질러 대형 리본을 달았다.

어휘 public relations 홍보   entrance 입구   celebration 축하(행사)

18

해설 **전치사구:** 빈칸에는 뒤에 나온 명사구를 목적어로 취하는 전치사가 들어가야 한다. 따라서 정답은 유일한 전치사로 '~와 관계없이'라는 의미를 지닌 (C) Regardless of이다.

번역 입구 통로 공사의 지연과 상관없이, 충청의 오키드 레스토랑은 재개장할 것이며, 모든 작업이 완료될 때까지 대체 출입구를 제공할 것입니다.

어휘 entryway (건물) 입구의 통로   alternative 대안(의)   entrance 출입문   complete 완성된   furthermore (접속부사) 게다가   assuming that (접속사) ~라는 것을 가정하면   subsequently 그 이후에

19

해설 **장소 전치사:** 문맥상 '신설 야외 원형극장(new outdoor amphitheater)에서 열린 교향악단의 연주'라는 내용이 되어야 하므로, 빈칸에는 장소와 함께 어울려 쓸 수 있는 전치사가 들어가야 한다. 따라서 정답은 (B) at이다.

번역 신설 야외 원형극장에서 열린 교향악단의 연주에 500명 이상의 참석자가 몰렸다.

어휘 symphony orchestra 교향악단   performance 공연   amphitheater 원형극장   draw 끌어들이다, 유치하다   attendee 참석자

20

해설 **시점 전치사구:** 빈칸 뒤에 나온 시점 February 6가 문제 해결의 단서로, as와 함께 쓰여 '특정 시점부터'라는 의미를 이루는 (D) of가 정답이다. 참고로, 빈출 어구 'as of today(오늘부터)'도 함께 암기해 두자.

번역 2월 6일부터 모든 직원은 개선된 신분증을 사용해야 한다.

어휘 identification 신분 증명   as of ~부터

CHAPTER 03 | 동사

UNIT 08	동사

기출공식 1		본책 p. 76
1 (A)	**2** (A)	**3** (B)

1

해설 **복수주어 + 복수동사:** 주어가 Employment figures로 복합명사이므로 뒤에 위치한 명사에 맞춰 동사의 수를 일치시켜야 한다. 따라서 복수명사인 figures에 어울리는 복수동사 (A) confirm이 정답이다.

번역 고용률은 그 나라의 경제가 5년 사이에 가장 빠른 속도로 성장하고 있음을 입증한다.

어휘 employment figure 고용률   confirm 확인하다, 입증하다   pace 속도, 박자

2

해설 **복수주어 + 복수동사:** 주어가 Event organizers로 복수명사이므로 복수동사 (A) anticipate가 정답이다.

번역 행사 주최자들은 올해 예술 축제에서 판매상의 수가 늘어날 것으로 예상한다.

어휘 event organizer 행사 주최자, 기획자   increase 증가; 증가하다   vendor 판매상, 행상인   anticipate 예상하다

3

해설 **단수주어 + 단수동사:** because절의 주어가 3인칭 단수인 it이고, 해당 절이 현재 박물관이 무엇을 전시하고 있는지 설명하는 내용이므로 '특별히 포함하다, 특징으로 하다'라는 의미의 (B) features가 정답이 된다.

번역 진짜 공룡 뼈를 전시하기 때문에 학생들은 윌밍턴 역사 박물관에서 열리는 마이어슨 전시회에 참석하고 있다.

어휘 **attend** 참석하다 **exhibition** 전시(회) **authentic** 진짜의

4 (B)   **5** (A)   **6** (A)

4

해설 **수량 표현이 쓰인 주어의 수 일치:** half of the employees (at Century Photo Labs)가 문장의 주어이고, 빈칸이 동사인 문장이다. half of와 같이 부분을 나타내는 표현은 of 뒤의 명사에 수를 일치시킨다. 여기서는 복수명사인 the employees가 왔으므로 복수동사인 (B) commute가 정답이다.

번역 센추리 현상소에서 근무하는 직원의 대략 절반이 버스로 통근한다.

어휘 **roughly** 약, 대략 **photo lab** 현상소 **commute** 통근하다

5

해설 **수량 표현이 쓰인 주어의 수 일치:** a number of 뒤에는 복수명사가 와야 한다. 따라서 복수명사인 (A) spaces가 정답이다.

번역 그 건물 앞에는 제한된 수의 방문객용 주차 공간이 있다.

어휘 **a limited number of** 제한된 수의 **visitor parking space** 방문객용 주차 공간

6

해설 **수량 표현이 쓰인 주어의 수 일치:** 동사가 complete로 복수동사이므로 of 뒤에 오는 복수명사와 함께 쓰여 복수동사로 수 일치해야 하는 (A) All이 정답이다. (B) Each는 'each of 복수명사'가 주어인 경우 단수동사로 수 일치해야 하므로 오답이다.

번역 우리의 모든 수리 기술자들은 2주간의 강도 높은 공식 교육 과정을 완수한 후 방문 출장을 시작한다.

어휘 **complete** 완성하다 **intensive** 강도 높은 **house call** 가정 방문 **make house calls** 왕진하다, 방문 출장하다

7 (A)   **8** (B)   **9** (B)

7

해설 **관계사절 내 동사의 수 일치:** 관계사절의 동사는 선행사에 수를 일치시키는데, 선행사인 a group of consultants가 복수이므로 빈칸에도 복수동사가 들어가야 한다. 따라서 정답은 (A) specialize이다.

번역 내일 우리는 직원 교육 및 팀 빌딩을 전문으로 하는 컨설턴트 팀을 만날 것이다.

어휘 **consultant** 컨설턴트, 고문 **staff training** 직원 교육 **team building** (조직개발 기법) 팀워크 향상 **specialize in** ~을 전문으로 하다

8

해설 **There 구문의 수 일치:** There 구문에서는 동사와 뒤에 오는 명사의 수가 일치해야 하는데, 동사가 are이므로, 빈칸에는 복수명사가 들어가야 한다. 따라서 정답은 (B) stores이다. several 뒤에는 항상 복수명사가 온다는 것도 알아 두자.

번역 그 지역에는 마스터 프린트 상표의 인쇄용지를 파는 매장이 여러 곳 있다.

어휘 **several** 몇몇의 **printer paper** 인쇄용지

9

해설 **and로 연결된 주어의 수 일치:** Megali Corporation and Liggman Industries가 문장의 주어이므로 빈칸은 복수동사 자리이다. 따라서 (B) have가 정답이다.

번역 3년간의 열띤 협상 끝에 메갈리사와 리그먼 산업은 합병 조건에 최종적으로 합의했다.

어휘 **intense** 격렬한, 치열한 **agree on** ~에 합의하다 **terms** (계약 등의) 조건 **merger** 합병

10 (B)   **11** (D)   **12** (A)

10

해설 **수식어가 있는 문장의 수 일치_전치사구:** 복수명사인 The maintenance supplies가 문장의 주어이고, 빈칸은 동사 자리이다. 따라서 복수동사인 (B) are가 정답이다. 전치사구 for Building B는 수 일치에 영향을 주지 않는다.

번역 B 건물의 유지 보수용 비품은 보안 창구 옆에 있는 132호실에 보관되어 있습니다.

어휘 **maintenance** 유지 보수 **supplies** 공급품, 비품 **next to** ~ 옆에 **security desk** 보안 창구

11

해설 **수식어가 있는 문장의 수 일치_관계사절:** 복수명사인 Customers가 문장의 주어이고, who ~ Store는 주어인 Customers를 수식하는 관계사절이며, 빈칸은 동사 자리이다. 관계사절은 수 일치에 영향을 주지 않으므로 복수동사인 (D) have가 정답이다.

번역 마흐무드 홈 스토어에서 새 가전제품을 구매하는 고객들은 최대 1개월까지 제품을 교환할 수 있다.

어휘 appliance 가전제품   exchange 교환하다

12

해설 **수식어가 있는 문장의 수 일치_분사구:** 복수명사인 Products가 문장의 주어이고, made by Izmir Vitamins는 주어인 Products를 수식하는 분사구이며, 빈칸은 동사 자리이다. 분사구는 수 일치에 영향을 주지 않으므로 복수동사인 (A) are designed가 정답이다.

번역 이즈미르 비타민사가 제조한 제품들은 건강과 행복을 증진하기 위해 기획된 것이다.

어휘 product 상품, 제품   promote 홍보하다, 촉진시키다

기출공식 5 본책 p. 78

13 (B)   **14** (D)   **15** (A)

13

해설 **능동태:** 빈칸 뒤에 온 목적어 its services가 문제 해결의 단서로, 목적어가 있으므로 능동태 문장임을 알 수 있다. 따라서 be동사 뒤에서 진행형 문장을 만들 수 있는 현재분사 (B) expanding이 정답이다. 참고로 expand는 자동사, 타동사 둘 다로 사용될 수 있다.

번역 마베오스 슈퍼마켓은 온라인 식료품점과 배달 서비스를 포함하기 위해 서비스를 확대하고 있다.

어휘 include 포함하다   grocery 식료품   delivery 배달   expand 확대하다

14

해설 **수동태:** A sum of €500,000가 주어, 빈칸이 동사인 문장으로, 빈칸 뒤에 목적어가 아닌 부사 anonymously가 왔으므로 정답은 수동태인 (D) was donated이다. 문맥상으로도 A sum of €500,000가 donate의 주체가 아니므로 능동태는 적절하지 않다.

번역 이번 달 초에 골웨이 병원에 익명으로 50만 유로가 기부되었다.

어휘 sum 돈, 합계   anonymously 익명으로   donate 기부하다

15

해설 **수동태:** 주어는 Children이고, 빈칸은 are 뒤 현재분사나 과거분사를 써서 동사의 형태를 완성시켜야 하는 자리이다. 빈칸 뒤 목적어가 아닌 부사구 free of charge(무료로)가 나오므로, 수동태를 이루는 (A) admitted가 정답이다.

번역 두 살 이하 어린이는 대부분의 콘서트와 영화관에 무료로 입장된다.

어휘 free of charge 공짜의, 무료의   concert 콘서트, 음악회   film 영화

기출공식 6 본책 p. 78

16 (B)   **17** (C)   **18** (B)

16

해설 **4형식 동사의 수동태:** 주어는 The inventors (of the Spin Gadget)이고 빈칸은 동사 자리이다. 목적어로 first prize가 나오므로 능동태라고 생각하기 쉽지만 들어갈 동사가 4형식 동사 award이므로 문맥을 따져야 한다. 주어로 온 발명가들이 1등상을 주는 것이 아니라 받는 것이므로 수동의 의미를 이루는 (B) were awarded가 정답이다.

번역 스핀 개지트를 발명한 사람들은 가족 오락 및 게임 경연대회에서 창의적인 아이디어로 1등상을 받았다.

어휘 inventor 발명가   award 상; 수여하다(주다)

17

해설 **5형식 동사의 수동태:** 5형식 동사 make가 들어갈 자리에서 빈칸 뒤로 목적어가 없으므로 수동태가 와야 한다. 'make + 목적어 + payable' 구조에서 목적어가 주어로 가면서 수동태가 된 형태이다. 따라서 정답은 (C) should be made이다.

번역 '모두를 위한 극장' 프로젝트를 후원하는 수표나 우편환은 알리오 연기자 협회 앞으로 발행되어야 한다.

어휘 check 수표   money order 우편환   in support of ~을 지지[후원]하여   be made payable to (수표 등이) ~ 앞으로 발행되다

18

해설 **4형식 동사의 수동태:** 주어는 Library patrons이고 주어를 수식하는 관계사절 뒤 빈칸에는 동사가 와야 하는데, 목적어로 a fee가 나오므로 능동태라고 생각하기 쉽다. 그러나 들어갈 동사가 4형식 동사인 charge이므로 문맥을 따져야 한다. 주어로 온 도서관 이용객들이 수수료를 청구하는 것이 아니라 청구 받는 것이므로 수동의 의미를 이루는 (B) will be charged가 정답이다.

번역 반납일까지 책을 반납하지 못한 도서관 이용객들은 수수료를 물게 된다.

어휘 patron 고객 due date 반납 기한, 마감일 fee 수수료 charge (요금을) 청구하다

기출공식 7   본책 p. 79

19 (A) **20** (C) **21** (A)

19
해설 **수동태 관용 표현:** 주어인 Dr. Turner가 '진전 상황에 기뻐한다'라는 의미가 되어야 하므로 'be pleased with'라는 수동태 관용 표현을 이루는 (A) pleased가 정답이다.

번역 터너 박사는 공사 인부들이 그의 새 사무실에 한 작업의 진전 상황에 대해 굉장히 기뻐하고 있다.

어휘 progress 진전, 진행 construction crew 공사 인부

20
해설 **수동태 관용 표현:** 문맥상 '지원자들은 해당 분야에 적어도 7년 이상의 경력을 보유해야 한다'는 의미가 되어야 하며, 지원자들이 해당 사항을 요구 받는 입장이므로 'require + 목적어 + to부정사'가 수동형으로 쓰여야 한다. 따라서 정답은 (C) are required이다.

번역 FDJ 파이낸스의 관리직에 지원하는 사람들은 해당 분야에서 적어도 7년 이상의 경력을 보유해야 한다.

어휘 applicant 지원자 managerial position 관리직 possess 보유하다, 갖추다 field 분야

21
해설 **수동태 관용 표현:** 빈칸 앞에 온 exposed가 문제 해결의 단서로, '~에 노출되다'라는 의미를 이루는 수동태 관용 표현은 'be exposed to'이다. 따라서 정답은 (A) to이다.

번역 저층 아파트들은 먼지나 차량의 소음에 더 많이 노출되기 때문에 더 저렴하다.

어휘 dust 먼지 traffic 차량(들), 교통(량)

기출공식 8   본책 p. 79

22 (A) **23** (D) **24** (D)

22
해설 **현재 시제:** 빈칸이 포함된 절에 '수요일마다'라는 반복의 의미를 나타내는 every Wednesday라는 표현이 있으므로, 빈칸에는 현재 반복되는 사실을 나타낼 수 있는 현재형이 들어가야 한다. 따라서 3인칭 주어에 수 일치되는 (A) orders가 정답이 된다.

번역 파커 씨가 매주 수요일에 창고에서 사무 용품을 주문하니, 화요일까지 그에게 필요한 것을 알려 주세요.

어휘 office supplies 사무 용품 warehouse 창고 needs 요구 사항, 필요로 하는 것

23
해설 **과거 시제:** 문장의 맨 끝에 과거를 나타내는 시간 부사 yesterday가 나왔으므로 동사는 과거 시제가 되어야 한다. 따라서 (D) approved가 정답이다.

번역 어제 마침내 그 지역 공무원들은 제안된 2퍼센트 세금 인상을 승인했다.

어휘 local 지역의, 현지의 government official 공무원 proposed 제안된 tax increase 세금 인상 approve 승인하다, 찬성하다

24
해설 **미래 시제:** 문장 끝에 next month라는 미래 표현이 있으므로 미래 시제인 (D) will be sold가 정답이다.

번역 싱가포르 골프 선수권 대회 입장권은 다음 달부터 온라인으로 판매될 예정입니다.

어휘 golf tournament 골프 선수권 대회

기출공식 9   본책 p. 80

25 (B) **26** (D) **27** (B)

25
해설 **현재진행 시제:** 주어는 복수명사인 Magnum Plus cameras이고 빈칸에는 동사가 필요하다. '지금'을 의미하는 now가 있고 '인기가 아주 높아지고 있다'라는 의미가 되어야 하므로, 현재진행 시제인 (B) are becoming이 정답이 된다.

번역 매그넘 플러스 카메라는 사용하기 매우 쉬워서 현재 인기가 아주 높아지고 있다.

어휘 easy to use 사용하기 쉬운

26
해설 **현재진행 시제:** 현재 또는 현재진행 시제와 어울려 쓰이는 부사 currently가 문제 해결의 단서로, 빈칸 앞에 동사 is가 있으므로 현재진행 시제를 완성하는 (D) seeking이 정답이다.

번역 LTD 엔터프라이즈는 이달 말에 은퇴하는 현직 이사의 후임으로 지금 기량이 뛰어난 사람을 모집하고 있다.

어휘 **accomplished** 기량이 뛰어난, 숙련된 **individual** 개인, 사람 **replace** ~의 후임자가 되다 **current** 현재의 **director** 이사, 임원 **retire** 은퇴하다

27

해설 **미래진행 시제:** 빈칸은 that절의 동사가 들어갈 자리로, September 30이라는 특정 시점에 진행되고 있을 일을 나타낸 미래진행 시제 (B) will be starting이 정답이다. 빈칸 뒤에 new position이라는 목적어가 있으므로 수동 태인 (C) was started와 (D) is being started는 오답이다. 또한 '새로운 직책을 시작해 오고 있는 중이다'라는 어색한 의미를 만드는 현재완료진행 시제 (A) has been starting도 문맥상 답이 될 수 없다.

번역 비에리 씨가 9월 30일자로 시장 분석가직을 새로 맡게 될 것임을 발표하게 되어 기쁩니다.

어휘 **position** 일자리, 직위 **analyst** 분석가

기출공식 10   본책 p. 80

28 (C)	**29** (D)	**30** (B)

28

해설 **현재완료 시제:** 빈칸 앞에 has와 not이 있고, 문장 끝에 '아직'이라는 의미의 부사 yet이 있으므로, '아직 확정하지 않았다'라는 의미를 이루는 현재완료 시제가 적절하다. 따라서 정답은 (C) finalized이다.

번역 이사회는 아직 내년 예산안을 확정하지 못했다.

어휘 **executive board** 이사회 **budget** 예산(안)

29

해설 **과거완료 시제:** 기차가 20분 늦게 출발한 것은 스즈키 박사가 시상식에 도착한 것보다 더 먼저 일어난 일이므로 과거완료 시제인 (D) had left가 정답이다.

번역 스즈키 박사는 기차가 20분 늦게 출발했는데도 시상식에 제시간에 도착했다.

어휘 **awards ceremony** 시상식 **on time** 제시간에

30

해설 **미래완료 시제:** 미래의 특정 시점인 '다음 달 말'을 의미하는 at the end of next month가 문제 해결의 단서로, 다음 달 말이 되면 감독한 지 10년째가 될 것임을 나타내고 있다. 따라서 미래완료 시제인 (B) will have supervised 가 정답이다.

번역 다음 달 말이면 수석 요리사 트레이시 나카가와 씨가 호쿨레아 카페의 주방을 감독한 지 10년이 된다.

어휘 **executive** 관리(직)의 **supervise** 감독하다, 지휘하다

기출공식 11   본책 p. 81

31 (B)	**32** (C)	**33** (B)

31

해설 **시제 일치의 예외:** while은 '~하는 동안'이라는 뜻으로 시간 부사절을 이끄는 접속사이다. 시간 부사절에서는 현재 시제가 미래 시제를 대신하므로 (B) are completed가 정답이다.

번역 후앙 어소시에이츠의 홍콩 사무소는 개조 공사가 완료되는 동안 일시적으로 문을 닫을 것이다.

어휘 **temporarily** 일시적으로 **renovation** 개조[보수] 공사 **complete** 완료하다; 완벽한, 완전한

32

해설 **시제 일치의 예외:** '요구하다'라는 뜻의 동사 requests 뒤 that절에서는 '(should) + 동사원형'을 써야 하므로, 빈칸에는 동사원형 (C) submit이 와야 한다.

번역 전문 사진 아트 스튜디오에서는 지원자들에게 흑백 사진으로 된 작품집을 제출할 것을 요구한다.

어휘 **request** 요구하다 **applicant** 지원자, 신청자 **portfolio** 작품집, 포트폴리오 **black-and-white** 흑백의 **submit** 제출하다

33

해설 **시제 일치의 예외:** 가주어 It으로 시작하는 구문에서 be동 사 뒤에 당위성을 나타내는 형용사 imperative가 나오므로 that절에 '(should) + 동사원형'이 와야 한다. 따라서 (B) be가 정답이다.

번역 컴퓨터 비밀번호는 반드시 기밀로 유지해야 한다.

어휘 **imperative** 긴요한 **confidential** 기밀의

기출공식 12   본책 p. 81

34 (D)	**35** (C)	**36** (A)

34

해설 **수 일치 + 태:** 동사가 필요한 자리이며, 단수주어에 수 일치 하여 단수동사를 써야 한다. 또한 빈칸 뒤에 목적어 a list 가 있으므로 능동태가 와야 한다. 따라서 (D) contains가 정답이다.

번역 글로브 조명 공급의 편람에는 중요 기업들의 전화번호 목록 이 포함되어 있다.

어휘 **contain** 포함하다

35

해설 **태 + 시제:** doughnuts가 주어, 빈칸이 동사, muffins가 목적어인 문장이므로, 빈칸에는 목적어를 취할 수 있는 능동태 동사가 와야 한다. 또한 '지난 몇 달 동안'이라는 의미의 for the past few months는 현재완료 시제의 단서가 되므로, 능동태이면서 현재완료 시제인 (C) have been outselling이 정답이다.

번역 지난 몇 달 동안 마리넬 제과점에서는 도넛이 머핀보다 더 많이 팔리고 있다.

어휘 outsell 더 많이 팔다[팔리다]

36

해설 **태 + 시제:** 빈칸 뒤 목적어가 있으므로 빈칸에는 목적어를 취할 수 있는 능동태 동사가 와야 한다. 또한 시간상으로 볼 때, 코헨 씨가 계획서를 검토한 후에 투자 계획에 수용적으로 된 것이므로 계획안을 검토한 것이 주절 시제인 과거보다 먼저 일어난 일이 된다. 따라서 정답은 능동태이면서 과거완료 시제인 (A) had examined이다.

번역 코헨 씨는 세부적인 사업 계획을 검토하자 새 회사에 투자하는 계획에 대해 더욱 수용적이 되었다.

어휘 detailed 상세한 receptive 수용적인, 받아들이는 examine 살펴보다, 검사하다

ETS **TEST**				본책 p. 82
1 (A)	**2** (A)	**3** (A)	**4** (C)	**5** (B)
6 (A)	**7** (C)	**8** (D)	**9** (D)	**10** (A)
11 (A)	**12** (B)	**13** (C)	**14** (A)	**15** (C)
16 (A)	**17** (D)	**18** (C)	**19** (D)	**20** (B)

1

해설 **수동태:** 빈칸은 be동사와 함께 동사를 완성하는 자리로 현재분사 또는 과거분사가 들어갈 수 있는데, 빈칸 뒤 목적어가 없으므로 수동태를 만드는 과거분사 (A) used가 정답이다.

번역 사무용품은 업무와 관련된 과제를 수행할 때만 사용되어야 한다.

어휘 office supplies 사무용품 conduct 수행하다, 실시하다 business-related 업무와 관련된 task 과제, 임무

2

해설 **수식어가 있는 문장의 수 일치_전치사구:** 복수명사인 Topics가 주어이므로 복수동사인 (A) include가 정답이다. at이 이끄는 전치사구는 수식어구이므로 수 일치에 영향을 주지 않는다.

번역 비즈니스 의사소통 워크숍의 주제는 논지 방어하기, 정보 종합하기, 정확하고 간결한 글쓰기를 포함한다.

어휘 defend 방어하다 synthesize 종합하다 precisely 정확하게 concisely 간결하게

3

해설 **수식어가 있는 문장의 수 일치_전치사구:** 복수명사인 Trains가 주어이고, for Gruyville이 주어를 수식하는 전치사구이므로 복수동사인 (A) depart가 정답이다.

번역 그뤼빌행 열차는 월요일부터 금요일까지 오전 9시에 출발한다.

어휘 depart 출발하다

4

해설 **수동태:** '허가 받지 않은 사람들'을 뜻하는 Unauthorized individuals가 주어이며, 타동사 prohibit의 목적어가 오지 않았으므로 '금지된다'라는 의미의 수동태 문장이 와야 한다. 따라서 정답은 과거분사인 (C) prohibited이다. 'A가 -ing하는 것을 막다'라는 뜻의 'prohibit A from -ing' 구문을 수동태로 쓴 것이다.

번역 허가를 받지 않은 사람들은 재스퍼 빌딩의 주차장에 주차하는 것이 금지된다.

어휘 unauthorized 승인[허가] 받지 않은 individual 사람, 개인 parking garage 주차장(건물)

5

해설 **과거 시제:** 빈칸은 동사 자리이며, 시간 부사 recently가 문제 해결의 단서이다. recently는 과거 또는 현재완료 시제와 함께 쓰는 부사이므로 정답은 (B) conducted이다.

번역 공장 관리자인 이 씨는 최근에 고객들을 위한 주요 생산 시설 견학을 진행했다.

어휘 supervisor 관리자 facility 시설 conduct 수행하다, 안내하다

6

해설 **수동태:** that절의 주어는 Ms. Rossi's order이며 빈칸은 동사 자리인데, 타동사 deliver의 목적어가 오지 않았으므로 정답은 수동태인 (A) is delivered이다.

번역 로시 씨가 오늘 일찍 퇴근할 예정이니 반드시 3시 전에 그녀의 주문품이 배달되게끔 하세요.

어휘 make sure 반드시 ~하도록 하다 order 주문(품) leave the office 퇴근하다

7

해설 **수식어가 있는 문장의 수 일치_전치사구:** that절에 단수주어 the battery가 나오므로 단수동사인 (C) performs가 정답이다. 전치사구 in our newest mobile phone은 수식어구이므로 수 일치에 영향을 주지 않는다.

번역 배터리 수명에 대한 최근 연구는 우리 최신 휴대전화 배터리가 유사 제품들보다 더 좋은 성능을 발휘한다는 것을 보여 준다.

어휘 similar 비슷한, 유사한   perform 수행하다, 성능을 발휘하다

8

해설 **수동태:** 두 문장을 연결하는 접속사 now that 앞에 동사가 없으므로 빈칸은 동사 자리인데, 타동사인 cancel의 목적어가 나오지 않았으므로 정답은 수동태인 (D) will be canceled이다.

번역 이제 합의에 이르렀기 때문에 토지 경계 분쟁에 대한 법원 심리는 취소될 것이다.

어휘 court hearing 법원 심리   boundary 경계, 영역   dispute 분쟁, 논쟁   now that ~이므로   agreement 합의, 계약   reach 도달하다

9

해설 **태 + 시제:** The technician이 주어이고 빈칸이 동사인 문장이다. 빈칸 뒤 목적어가 있으므로 능동태가 와야 하며, so 이하에서 그녀가 마무리하면 생산이 재개될 것이다 (production ~ finished)라고 했으므로 아직 수리가 마무리되지 않았음을 알 수 있다. 따라서 과거부터 현재까지 쭉 수리가 진행 중임을 나타내는 현재완료진행 시제가 와야 하므로 정답은 (D) has been making이다.

번역 기술자가 기계를 수리하고 있으므로, 그녀가 수리를 마치면 X220의 생산이 재개될 것이다.

어휘 technician 기술자   machinery 기계류   production 생산   resume 재개하다   make repairs 수리하다

10

해설 **태 + 시제:** 빈칸 뒤에는 free flashlights라는 목적어가 있으므로 능동태 문장이 되어야 하며, next Friday로 미루어 미래를 나타낼 수 있어야 한다. 현재진행 시제로 정해진 미래의 일을 나타낼 수 있으므로, (A) is offering이 정답이다.

번역 모르네세 하드웨어는 다음 주 금요일 개점 때 선착순 50명의 고객들에게 무료 손전등을 제공할 예정이다.

어휘 free 무료의   flashlight 손전등   grand opening 개장, 개점   offer 제공하다

11

해설 **복수주어 + 복수동사:** Vogel Printing's services가 주어이고, 빈칸은 부사 better의 수식을 받으며 our business needs를 목적어로 취하는 동사 자리이다. 주어가 복수이므로, 복수동사인 (A) suit가 정답이다.

번역 모겐 카핑 앤 리프로덕션이 비용 효율적인 요금을 제시하긴 하지만, 보겔 프린팅의 서비스가 우리의 사업적 요구에 더 잘 맞는다.

어휘 reproduction 복사, 재생산   cost-effective 비용 효율이 높은, 가성비가 좋은   rate 요금, 가격   needs 요구 사항   suit 부합하다

12

해설 **수동태:** 빈칸 뒤의 by Ms. Kameda가 문제 해결의 단서로, 'by + 행위자'는 수동태 문장에서 뒤따르는 전치사구이므로 정답은 (B) was overseen이다. (D) be overseen도 수동태이지만 조동사 없이 원형으로 쓸 수 없는 구조이므로 오답이다.

번역 호라이즌 브릿지 컴퍼니는 최근에 수석 엔지니어인 카메다 씨가 감독했던 현수교 프로젝트로 혁신상을 수상했다.

어휘 innovation 혁신   suspension bridge 현수교   oversee 감독하다

13

해설 **수 일치:** 빈칸은 that절의 동사 자리이므로 3인칭 단수주어 it에 수 일치해야 한다. 따라서 조동사와 함께 쓰여 수 일치의 제약을 받지 않는 (C) will maintain이 정답이다. (B) maintain은 수 일치가 맞지 않으므로 오답이다.

번역 퍼스트 시티 뱅크는 여러 지점에서 진행되고 있는 보수공사에도 불구하고 변함없이 탁월한 서비스를 제공할 것을 고객들에게 약속했다.

어휘 assure 보장하다   exceptional 뛰어난, 우수한   renovation 수리, 보수   maintain 유지하다

14

해설 **4형식 동사의 수동태:** 빈칸에는 동사 hopes의 목적어로 to부정사가 와야 하는데 offer는 4형식 동사이므로 빈칸 뒤에 오는 목적어의 유무만으로는 능/수동을 파악할 수 없다. 따라서 문맥으로 태를 결정해야 하는데, Ms. Fukui는 현재 part-time으로 일하고 있고, full-time 채용을 '제의 받고자 희망한다'라는 의미가 적절하므로 정답은 '제안하다'의 수동태인 (A) be offered이다.

번역 푸쿠이 씨는 계속해서 파트타임으로 일할 용의가 있지만 궁극적으로는 정규직 채용 제의를 받았으면 한다.

어휘 be willing to 기꺼이 ~하다   part-time 시간제로, 파트타임으로   full-time 전임의, 풀타임의   employment 고용, 채용   eventually 결국, 궁극적으로

15

해설　**수 일치 + 시제:** 빈칸은 관계사절의 동사 자리이므로 선행사인 a new Web site에 수 일치하여 단수동사가 와야 하며, '웹사이트를 개설할 계획이다'라는 주절 내용으로 보아 Web site는 아직 개설되지 않았음을 알 수 있으므로 미래 시제인 (C) will allow가 정답이다.

번역　영 오토모티브는 고객들이 송장을 볼 수 있게 해 줄 새로운 웹사이트를 개설할 계획이다.

어휘　launch 출시하다, 개시하다　access 접근하다, 이용하다; 접근, 이용　invoice 송장, 청구서　allow 허락[허가]하다

16

해설　**시제 일치의 예외:** 주장, 제안, 요구의 동사 뒤에 온 that절에서는 '(should) + 동사원형'을 쓰므로 정답은 should가 생략된 형태인 (A) be postponed이다.

번역　야카모토 씨는 휴가에서 모두 돌아올 때까지 부서 회의를 연기하자고 제안했다.

어휘　department 부서　postpone 연기하다

17

해설　**과거완료 시제:** By the time절에 과거 시제가 왔으므로 주절에는 과거완료 시제가 와야 한다. 따라서 정답은 (D) had worked이다.

번역　슈미트 씨가 우리 회사에 재무 분석가로 입사했을 무렵 그는 이미 수년 간 금융 분야에서 근무해왔던 상태였다.

어휘　financial analyst 재무 분석가　sector 분야, 부문

18

해설　**수식어가 있는 문장의 수 일치_관계사절:** 관계사절의 동사는 선행사에 수를 일치시킨다. 선행사가 employees로 복수이므로 정답은 복수동사인 (C) provide이다.

번역　이 상은 우리 고객들에게 특별한 서비스를 제공한 직원들의 공로를 인정하기 위해 만들어진 것이다.

어휘　design 만들다, 설계하다　recognize (공로를) 인정하다　exceptional 뛰어난

19

해설　**능동태:** 빈칸은 so 이하 절에서 주어 the company의 동사 자리이다. 동사 recruit는 자동사와 타동사 둘 다로 쓰이는데, 문맥상 '회사가 구인 중이다'라는 능동 의미가 자연스러우므로 능동태 동사인 (D) is recruiting이 정답이다.

번역　야마라사의 창고 관리자가 승진하여, 회사에서 새로 비어 있는 이 직책에 사람을 구하고 있다.

어휘　warehouse 창고　promote 승진시키다　position 직책　recruit 모집하다

20

해설　**시제 일치의 예외:** when은 '~할 때'라는 뜻으로 시간 부사절을 이끄는 접속사이다. 해당 절에 next month가 있으므로 미래를 나타내야 하지만, 시간 부사절에서는 현재 시제가 미래 시제를 대신하므로 (B) meet이 정답이다.

번역　아리아 플레처 씨는 다음 달 공식 회의에서 이사회와 광고 예산을 논의할 것이다.

어휘　discuss 논의하다　advertising budget 광고 예산　board of directors 이사회　formally 공식적으로

CHAPTER 04 | 준동사

UNIT 09	to부정사와 동명사

기출공식 1　　　　　　　　　　　　본책 p. 86

1 (A)　　**2** (D)　　**3** (C)

1

해설　**to부정사의 역할_명사:** 주어가 purpose, objective, goal 등과 같은 '목표, 목적'이라는 뜻의 명사일 때 주격 보어로는 '~하는 것'이라는 뜻의 명사 역할의 to부정사가 온다. 따라서 정답은 (A) to provide이다.

번역　이 정부 프로그램의 목적은 학교들에게 새로운 학습 기술에 대해 좀 더 쉽게 접근할 수 있도록 하는 것이다.

어휘　better access to ~에 더 용이한 접근　provide A with B A에게 B를 제공하다

2

해설　**to부정사의 역할_형용사:** Commissioner Kano가 주어, has scheduled가 동사, a time이 목적어인 완전한 문장에서, 명사 time을 수식하면서 빈칸 뒤에 오는 명사구인 the press statement를 목적어로 받을 수 있는 것은 to부정사이므로 (D) to issue가 정답이다.

번역　카노 위원은 언론 성명 발표를 위한 일정을 잡았다.

어휘　commissioner 위원　schedule 일정을 잡다　press statement 언론 성명　issue 발표하다, 발부하다

3

해설　**to부정사의 역할_부사:** 문맥상 '신속히 처리하기 위해'라는 능동의 의미가 자연스러우므로 to부정사의 부사적 용법으로 '목적'을 나타내는 (C) To expedite가 정답이다.

번역　귀하의 청구를 신속히 처리하기 위해 모든 서신에 고객 식별 번호를 포함하시오.

어휘　processing 처리　claim (보상금 등에 관한)

청구, 신청 identification number 식별 번호
correspondence 서신 expedite 신속히 처리하다

기출공식 2   본책 p. 86

4 (D)   **5** (D)   **6** (C)

4

해설 **to부정사를 목적어로 취하는 동사:** 문장의 동사는 may decide인데, decide는 to부정사를 목적어로 취하는 동사이므로 빈칸에는 (D) to hire가 들어가야 한다.

번역 회사는 이번 휴가철에 늘어난 주문량을 처리하기 위해 직원을 더 채용하기로 결정할 수도 있다.

어휘 additional 추가의 process 처리하다 increased 증가한 volume 양

5

해설 **to부정사를 목적격 보어로 취하는 동사:** expect는 목적격 보어로 to부정사를 취하는 동사로, 주어진 문장은 'expect + 목적어 + to부정사'가 수동태로 된 문장이다. 따라서 정답은 (D) to generate이다. 'be expected to부정사'는 '~할 것으로 예상되다'라는 의미로 자주 쓰이는 표현이니 익혀 두자.

번역 남아시아 매출이 올해 회사 수익의 대부분을 창출할 것으로 예상된다.

어휘 majority 대부분, 대다수 revenue 수익 generate 생성하다, 만들어내다

6

해설 **to부정사를 목적격 보어로 취하는 동사:** encourage는 목적격 보어로 to부정사를 취하는 동사로, 주어진 문장은 'encourage + 목적어 + to부정사'가 수동태로 된 문장이다. 따라서 정답은 (C) encouraged이다.

번역 셀 초이스 마케팅 담당자들은 경쟁사의 제품과 광고에 정통해지도록 권장 받는다.

어휘 familiar 친숙한, 정통한 competitor 경쟁업체
advertising 광고

기출공식 3   본책 p. 87

7 (A)   **8** (B)   **9** (A)

7

해설 **to부정사의 수식을 받는 명사:** 빈칸에는 앞에 온 명사 plans를 수식할 to부정사가 들어갈 자리이다. 따라서 (A) to partner가 정답이다. 문장에는 본동사인 announced가 있으므로 동사 형태인 나머지 보기들은 답이 될 수 없다.

번역 테노피 테크는 퀴토와 카라카스에서 태양열 패널을 생산하기 위해 섀플리 에너지 시스템스와 제휴하려는 계획을 오늘 발표했다.

어휘 manufacture 생산하다 partner 제휴[협력]하다

8

해설 **to부정사의 수식을 받는 명사:** 빈칸에는 앞에 온 명사 opportunity를 수식할 to부정사가 들어갈 자리이다. 따라서 (B) to assist가 정답이다.

번역 저희 TPG 재무 기획은 귀하의 사업을 도울 기회를 환영하며 상호 유익한 관계를 고대합니다.

어휘 opportunity 기회 look forward to ~을 고대하다
mutually 서로, 상호간에 assist 돕다

9

해설 **to부정사의 수식을 받는 명사:** 빈칸에는 앞에 온 명사 proposal을 수식할 to부정사가 들어갈 자리이다. 따라서 (A) to extend가 정답이다.

번역 그리어 트레일을 연장하자는 제안은 공원부의 마지막 회의에서 승인되었다.

어휘 proposal 제안 trail 산길, 오솔길 approve 승인하다
extend 연장하다 extension 연장

기출공식 4   본책 p. 87

10 (B)   **11** (B)   **12** (A)

10

해설 **to부정사 관용 표현:** 문맥상 '보호할 정도로 충분히 내구성이 강하다'라는 의미가 되어야 하므로, '~하기에 충분히 … 하다'라는 의미를 이루는 'enough + to부정사'가 적절하다. 따라서 (B) enough가 정답이다. 참고로 enough는 형용사나 부사를 수식할 때 형용사나 부사보다 뒤에 와야 하므로 형용사인 durable 뒤에 위치한다는 것도 알아 두자.

번역 그레이드리악스사의 건축 자재는 모든 날씨 상태에서 오는 손상으로부터 구조물을 보호하기에 충분할 정도로 내구성이 강하다.

어휘 material 재료 durable 내구성이 있는 protect
보호하다 structure 구조, 구조물 damage 손상

11

해설 **to부정사 관용 표현:** 형용사나 부사 앞에 쓰여, '너무 ~해서 …할 수 없다'라는 의미를 이루는 'too … to부정사'가 적절하다. 따라서 (B) too가 정답이다.

번역 많은 회사가 외부 창고에 종이 서류를 보관하는 것이 너무 비용이 많이 든다고 생각하고 있다.

어휘 store 저장하다, 보관하다 off-site 외부의
warehouse 창고

12

해설 **to부정사 관용 표현:** 빈칸 앞에 온 has와 뒤의 to부정사가
문제 해결의 단서로, '아직 ~하지 않다'라는 의미를 이루는
'have(has) + yet + to부정사'가 적절하다. 따라서 (A)가
정답이다.

번역 페레스 주지사는 재선을 위해 출마한다고 아직 공식 확인하
지 않았다.

어휘 governor 주지사 confirm 공식 확인하다 run
출마하다 reelection 재선

기출공식 5   본책 p. 88

13 (B)   **14** (C)   **15** (C)

13

해설 **사역동사_let:** 빈칸은 사역동사 let의 목적격 보어 자리로,
원형부정사가 와야 한다. 따라서 동사원형인 (B) affect가
정답이다.

번역 벤토 화장품의 CEO는 해외 판매의 최근 문제점들이 회사
의 장기적 수출 계획에 영향을 끼치지 않도록 했다.

어휘 long-term 장기적인 export 수출 affect 영향을
끼치다

14

해설 **준사역동사_help:** 빈칸은 준사역동사 help의 목적격 보어
자리로, to부정사와 원형부정사가 올 수 있다. 따라서 동사
원형인 (C) maintain이 정답이다.

번역 시기적절하고 효과적인 방법으로 고객 서비스 문제를 해결
하는 것은 회사가 좋은 이미지를 유지하는 데 도움이 될 것
이다.

어휘 resolve 해결하다 timely 시기적절한 effective
효과적인 manner 방식 maintain 유지하다

15

해설 **사역동사_have:** 빈칸은 사역동사 have의 목적격 보어 자
리로, 목적어와의 관계가 능동이면 원형부정사를 쓰고 수
동이면 과거분사를 쓴다. 여기서는 목적어가 its new
wristwatch라는 사물로 '테스트를 받는 대상'이므로, 수
동 관계를 나타내는 과거분사인 (C) tested가 정답이다.

번역 몬터규사는 익스트림 스포츠 선수 몇 명에게 새로운 손목시
계를 테스트하게 했다.

어휘 wristwatch 손목시계 extreme athlete 익스트림
스포츠 선수

기출공식 6   본책 p. 88

16 (C)   **17** (B)   **18** (D)

16

해설 **동명사의 역할_주어:** is가 동사인 문장에서 빈칸에는 문장
의 주어 역할을 하는 동시에 a series of trial runs
를 목적어로 취할 수 있는 동명사가 들어가야 하므로 (C)
Performing이 정답이다.

번역 모든 신상품을 대량 생산하기 전에 일련의 시연을 행하는
것은 주보사의 일반적인 관행이다.

어휘 a series of 일련의, 연속되는 trial run 시연, 시행
launch 착수하다 large-scale 대규모의 common
practice 일반적인 관행 perform 행하다

17

해설 **동명사의 역할_주어:** is가 동사인 문장에서 빈칸에는 문장의
주어 역할을 하는 동시에 social media를 목적어로 취할
수 있는 동명사가 들어가야 하므로 (B) Using이 정답이다.

번역 사업 서비스를 광고하기 위해 소셜 미디어를 사용하는 것은
새로운 고객을 유인하는 저렴한 방법이다.

어휘 market 광고하다 inexpensive 저렴한 attract
끌어모으다

18

해설 **동명사의 역할_목적어:** 빈칸에는 전치사 of의 목적어 역할
을 하며, 빈칸 뒤에 오는 명사구 a new set of guidelines
를 목적어로 취할 수 있는 동명사가 들어가야 한다. 따라서
정답은 (D) establishing이다.

번역 유로산 엔터프라이지즈의 경영진은 고객 서비스에 대한 새
로운 방침을 세우는 과정에 있다.

어휘 management 경영진 enterprise 기업, 회사
process 과정 establish 수립하다

기출공식 7   본책 p. 89

19 (A)   **20** (D)   **21** (D)

19

해설 **동명사 vs. 명사:** 빈칸은 전치사구 prior to의 목적어 자리
이므로 명사나 동명사가 들어갈 수 있다. 그런데 빈칸 뒤에
the building이라는 목적어가 나오므로, 목적어를 취할
수 있는 동명사가 들어가야 한다. 따라서 (A) entering이
정답이다.

번역 우리는 모든 방문객들에게 건물에 들어오기 전에 사진이 부착된 신분증을 제시하도록 요구합니다.

어휘 photo identification 사진이 붙은 신분증 prior to ~에 앞서 entrance 입구, 입장

20

해설 **동명사 vs. 명사:** 빈칸은 전치사 of의 목적어 자리이므로 명사나 동명사가 들어갈 수 있다. 그런데 빈칸 뒤에 fuel이라는 목적어가 나오므로, 목적어를 취할 수 있는 동명사가 들어가야 한다. 따라서 (D) extracting이 정답이다. (C) extracted는 분사로 문법적으로는 명사 앞에 들어갈 수 있지만 '추출된 연료의 방법'이라는 어색한 의미를 만들므로 오답이다.

번역 가스나이트사의 연구원들은 산업 폐기물에서 연료를 추출하는 보다 개선된 방법을 개발했다.

어휘 researcher 연구원 develop 개발하다 improved 개선된 method 방법, 방식 fuel 연료 industrial 산업의, 공업의 waste 폐기물 material 자료, 자재 extraction 추출 extract 추출하다

21

해설 **준동사 수식_부사:** 빈칸은 전치사 for 뒤의 자리로 얼핏 봐서는 명사나 동명사가 와야 하는 자리로 보이지만, 빈칸 뒤에 introducing이라는 동명사가 있다. 따라서 빈칸에는 동명사 introducing을 수식할 수 있는 부사가 와야 하므로, (D) successfully가 정답이다.

번역 초청 연사는 성공적으로 직장에 변화를 도입하기 위한 몇 가지 아이디어를 강조했다.

어휘 guest speaker 초청 연사 highlight 강조하다 introduce 도입하다, 소개하다 workplace 직장, 작업장

기출공식 8		본책 p. 89
22 (D)	23 (A)	24 (D)

22

해설 **동명사를 목적어로 취하는 동사:** 빈칸 앞에 온 consider가 문제 해결의 단서로, consider는 동명사를 목적어로 취하는 동사이다. 따라서 동명사인 (D) participating이 정답이다.

번역 새로운 마케팅 전략의 일환으로 그 회사는 더 많은 국제 무역 박람회에 참가하는 것을 고려할 것이다.

어휘 strategy 전략 consider 고려하다 international 국제적인 trade show 무역 박람회 participate in ~에 참가하다 participatory 참여하는

23

해설 **동명사를 목적어로 취하는 동사:** 빈칸 앞에 온 avoid가 문제 해결의 단서로, avoid는 동명사를 목적어로 취하는 동사이다. 따라서 동명사인 (A) placing이 정답이다.

번역 다른 승객들의 편의를 위해 버스의 빈자리에 가방을 놓는 일을 삼가기 바랍니다.

어휘 convenience 편의 passenger 승객 avoid 피하다 empty 비어 있는 place 놓다

24

해설 **동명사를 목적어로 취하는 동사:** 빈칸 앞에 온 recommend가 문제 해결의 단서로, recommend는 동명사를 목적어로 취하는 동사이다. 따라서 동명사인 (D) consolidating이 정답이다.

번역 운영을 검토한 후 컨설턴트는 여러 부서를 통합하라고 권유했다.

어휘 operation 운영 recommend 권유하다 department 부서 consolidate 통합하다 consolidation 통합

ETS TEST				본책 p. 90
1 (C)	2 (B)	3 (A)	4 (C)	5 (C)
6 (D)	7 (C)	8 (A)	9 (A)	10 (D)
11 (B)	12 (B)	13 (B)	14 (A)	15 (B)
16 (B)	17 (B)	18 (C)	19 (D)	20 (A)

1

해설 **to부정사를 목적어로 취하는 동사:** decline은 to부정사를 목적어로 취해 '~하기를 거절하다'로 쓰이므로 빈칸은 to부정사를 완성하는 동사원형이 와야 한다. 따라서 정답은 (C) comment이다.

번역 우에무라 씨는 그 제약사가 얼마나 많은 의약품을 개발 중이었는지에 대한 소문에 대해 언급하는 것을 거부했다.

어휘 rumor 소문, 루머 medicine 의약품 drug 약 manufacturer 제조회사 development 개발 comment 의견을 말하다; 의견 commentary 논평, 해설

2

해설 **동명사의 역할_주어:** 빈칸은 뒤에 오는 명사 range를 목적어로 취하면서, 동사 has의 주어 역할을 하는 자리이므로 동명사인 (B) Diversifying이 정답이다.

번역 우리 출판물의 기사 범위를 다양화한 것이 신규 독자 유치에 확실히 도움이 되었다.

어휘 undoubtedly 의심의 여지없이, 확실히 attract 끌다, 유치하다

3

해설 **to부정사의 역할_부사:** 빈칸 앞에 완전한 절이 있고 빈칸 뒤에 명사구가 왔으므로, 빈칸에는 앞에 나온 완전한 절을 수식하면서 뒤에 온 명사구를 목적어로 취할 수 있는 to부정사가 와야 한다. 따라서 정답은 (A) to analyze이다.

번역 지질학자 울리아 체르노프는 빙하로 덮인 산봉우리에 있는 눈의 성분을 분석하기 위해 오스트리아 산맥을 등반한다.

어휘 **geologist** 지질학자   **composition** 성분   **glacial** 빙하의   **analyze** 분석하다   **analysis** 분석

4

해설 **동명사 vs. 명사:** 빈칸은 전치사 of의 목적어 자리인데, 빈칸 뒤에 목적어 chemical solutions가 있으므로, 목적어를 취할 수 있는 동명사인 (C) combining이 정답이다. 명사는 목적어를 받을 수 없으므로 (B) combinations는 오답이다.

번역 타치바나 제약 회사의 화학 용액을 결합하는 새로운 방법은 실험실의 효율성을 증가시킬 것이다.

어휘 **pharmaceuticals** 제약 회사   **chemical** 화학의   **solution** 용액, 용해   **efficiency** 효율성   **laboratory** 실험실   **combine** 결합하다

5

해설 **to부정사를 목적격 보어로 취하는 동사:** invite는 to부정사를 목적격 보어로 취하여 'invite + 목적어 + to부정사'의 형태로 쓴다. 따라서 to부정사인 (C) to patronize가 정답이다.

번역 애쉬포드 상공회의소는 방문객들이 도시의 해안가에 있는 식당과 극장들을 이용하도록 권한다.

어휘 **invite** 요청하다   **patronize** 거래하다, 단골로 삼다

6

해설 **to부정사의 역할_부사:** 빈칸 뒤에 동사원형이 온 것이 문제 해결의 단서로, 보기 중에서 동사원형이 바로 뒤에 올 수 있는 것은 to부정사가 들어간 표현밖에 없다. 따라서 '~하기 위해서'라는 목적의 의미를 지니는 (D) in order to가 정답이다.

번역 의뢰인의 기록을 기밀로 유지하기 위해 데이터베이스 보안 소프트웨어를 개선했습니다.

어휘 **security** 보안   **maintain** 유지하다, 지키다   **confidentiality** 기밀(성)

7

해설 **to부정사를 목적격 보어로 취하는 동사:** enable은 to부정사를 목적격 보어로 취하는 동사이므로 빈칸에는 (C) to expand가 들어가야 한다.

번역 두 기업 간의 협약으로 양사 모두 사업을 확장할 수 있을 것이다.

어휘 **agreement** 협약, 협정   **enable** 가능하게 하다   **expand** 확장하다

8

해설 **to부정사를 목적격 보어로 취하는 동사:** expect는 to부정사를 목적격 보어로 취하여 'expect + 목적어 + to부정사' 형태로 쓰이며, 특히 수동태 구조로 자주 쓰인다. 따라서 'be expected to'를 완성하는 (A) to rise가 정답이다. rise는 완전 자동사이며, 수동태로 쓰지 않으므로 (D) to be risen은 오답이다.

번역 델레마르케의 수익은 해외에 새로운 서비스를 제공하기 시작하면서 향후 10년 동안 꾸준히 성장할 것으로 예상된다.

어휘 **profit** 수익   **steadily** 꾸준히

9

해설 **동명사 vs. 명사:** 빈칸은 전치사 in의 목적어 자리이므로 명사나 동명사가 들어갈 수 있는데, 빈칸 뒤에 positive publicity라는 목적어가 있으므로 정답은 동명사인 (A) generating이다.

번역 멜버른 모터스는 새로운 친환경 자동차 라인에 대한 긍정적 평가를 이끌어 내는 데 성공했다.

어휘 **succeed in** ~에 성공하다   **publicity** 평판, 광고, 홍보   **ecologically friendly** 친환경적인, 생태에 이로운   **generate** 만들어 내다, 이끌어 내다

10

해설 **준동사 수식_부사:** 빈칸 앞에 전치사 after가 있고, 빈칸 뒤에는 전치사의 목적어가 되는 동명사 failing이 있다. 동명사는 동사의 성질이 있기 때문에 형용사가 아닌 부사의 수식을 받는다. 따라서 정답은 동명사를 수식하는 부사 (D) repeatedly이다.

번역 고객의 사랑을 얻는 데 계속 실패한 후, 타이콘의 업그레이드된 소프트웨어 프로그램은 시장에서 철수되었다.

어휘 **win** 얻다, 획득하다   **support** 지지, 성원   **upgraded** 업그레이드된   **withdraw** 철수하다, 회수하다   **repetition** 반복   **repeated** 반복된   **repeatedly** 반복해서

11

해설 **동명사의 역할_목적어:** 빈칸은 전치사 despite의 목적어 자리이므로 동명사 형태를 하고 있는 (B) having experienced가 정답이다. 전치사 뒤에는 동사가 올 수 없으므로 나머지 보기들은 모두 오답이다.

번역 지난 6개월 동안 수익 감소를 겪었음에도 불구하고 모리 앤 맥기사는 내년에 3명의 특허 전문 변호사를 신규 채용할 계획이다.

어휘 despite ~에도 불구하고   decline 감소, 하락
revenue 수익   intend to부정사 ~하려고 의도하다
patent 특허

12

해설 **to부정사를 목적어로 취하는 동사:** need는 to부정사를 목적어로 취하여 '~할 필요가 있다'라는 의미로 쓰인다. 따라서 (B) to be convinced가 정답이다.

번역 몇몇 임원들은 젊은 축구 선수와 야구 선수들에게 필요한 개별 경기장의 중요성에 대해 아직까지도 확신하지 못하고 있다.

어휘 official 임원, 간부   separate 별개의   playing field 경기장, 운동장   be convinced of ~을 확신하다

13

해설 **동명사의 역할_목적어:** 빈칸은 전치사 by의 목적어 자리이므로 정답은 (B) investing이다. by -ing는 '~함으로써'라는 의미로 사용 빈도가 높은 표현이니 암기해 두자.

번역 리야드 씨는 성공한 지역 사업가로 부동산에 투자함으로써 재산을 모았다.

어휘 make a fortune 재산을 모으다   real estate 부동산   invest in ~에 투자하다

14

해설 **to부정사 관용 표현:** 빈칸 앞의 be sure가 문제 해결의 단서로, '반드시 ~하다'라는 의미의 to부정사 관용 표현인 'be sure to부정사'를 완성하는 (A) to allow가 정답이다.

번역 〈더 스틸 레이크 레저〉지 구독을 해지하시려면 반드시 4주 간의 처리 시간을 감안해 주십시오.

어휘 cancel 해지하다, 취소하다   subscription 정기 구독   process 처리하다; 공정, 과정

15

해설 **준사역동사_help:** 동사 help는 'help + 목적어 + 목적격 보어' 구조로 쓸 수 있으며, 목적격 보어로 to부정사나 원형부정사를 취한다. 또한 목적어를 생략하고 목적격 보어만 남길 수 있는 특수한 구조로도 쓸 수 있다. 해당 문장은 후자의 경우로, 빈칸에는 help의 목적격 보어가 와야 한다. 따라서 정답은 (B) to restore이다.

번역 지역 보존 협회에서 모금한 자금은 역사적으로 중요한 제이슨빌 기차역 복원에 도움이 되었다.

어휘 preservation 보호   historic 역사적으로 중요한

16

해설 **to부정사 관용 표현:** 빈칸 앞에 나온 enough가 문제 해결의 단서로 '~하기에 충분한'이라는 관용 표현을 완성하는 (B) to stay가 정답이다.

번역 그 지역에 식당 여러 곳이 신장개업했지만 비텔라즈 레스토랑은 여전히 사업을 유지하기에 충분한 고객들을 유치하고 있다.

어휘 opening 개업, 개점   attract 끌다, 유치하다

17

해설 **to부정사를 목적격 보어로 취하는 동사:** require는 to부정사를 목적격 보어로 취하여 'require + 목적어 + to부정사' 형태로 쓴다. 이 문장을 수동태 문장으로 바꾸면 'be required to부정사'의 형태가 되므로, 정답은 (B) to attend이다.

번역 연구소의 높은 수준을 유지하기 위해 직원들은 연례 연수 워크숍에 참석해야 한다.

어휘 maintain 유지하다   laboratory 연구소   standard 기준   annual 연례의   attend 참석하다

18

해설 **준동사 수식_부사:** to부정사는 동사의 성질을 지니므로 부사의 수식을 받는다. 빈칸은 to부정사를 수식하는 자리이므로 정답은 부사인 (C) reliably이다.

번역 계절에 상관없이 일을 확실하게 해내는 헤스턴 루핑을 믿으세요.

어휘 count on ~을 믿다   rely 믿다   reliable 믿을 수 있는   reliably 확실하게

19

해설 **동명사 vs. 명사:** 빈칸은 동사 consider의 목적어 자리로, 명사와 동명사가 올 수 있다. 빈칸 뒤에 its most popular product line이라는 명사구가 있으므로, 명사구를 목적어로 취할 수 있는 동명사 (D) expanding이 정답이다.

번역 최근 고객 의견에 근거하여 그 회사는 가장 인기 있는 제품 군을 확대하는 것을 고려할 수 있다.

어휘 based on ~에 근거하여   feedback 의견, 반응   consider 고려하다   popular 인기가 있는   expand 확대하다   expansion 확대

20

해설 **to부정사의 역할_진주어:** 빈칸이 포함된 절은 목적격 관계대명사가 생략된 채 앞에 나오는 명사구 the time을 수식해 주고 있다. 해당 절에서 it이 가주어가 되고, '가벼운 감기에서 회복하는 것'이 진주어가 되어야 하므로, 빈칸에는 to부정사가 들어가야 한다. 따라서 정답은 (A) to recover이다.

번역 진료소는 환자들에게 충분한 휴식을 취하는 것이 가벼운 감기에서 회복하는 데 걸리는 시간을 크게 줄여줄 수 있다고 충고한다.

어휘 **advise** 충고하다, 권고하다 **sufficient** 충분한
decrease 줄여주다, 감소하다 **recover** 회복하다

UNIT 10	분사

기출공식 1　　　　　　　　　　本책 p. 94

1 (B)　　**2** (A)　　**3** (B)

1

해설 **분사의 역할_보어:** as가 이끄는 부사절에서 be동사는 주격 보어가 필요한 동사로, 빈칸에는 명사 또는 형용사가 들어가야 한다. 따라서 '복잡한'이라는 의미의 분사형 형용사인 (B) complicated가 정답이다. 명사인 (D) complication은 주어인 the process와 동격 관계가 아니므로 정답이 될 수 없다.

번역 지원자들은 과정이 아주 복잡할 수 있으므로 취업 허가를 받는 데 최소한 3개월은 잡아야 한다.

어휘 **applicant** 지원자 **allow** 허용하다, (계산하여) 잡다 **complicate** 복잡하게 만들다 **complication** 문제, 합병증

2

해설 **분사의 역할_명사 수식:** 빈칸 앞에 부정관사 a가 있고 뒤에 array라는 명사가 나오므로 빈칸은 형용사가 들어갈 자리이다. 따라서 '충분한'이라는 뜻의 현재분사 (A) satisfying이 정답이다.

번역 서머튼 뷔페는 충분히 다양한 앙트레와 곁들임 요리, 디저트를 제공한다.

어휘 **an array of** 다양한 **entrée** (주요리 또는 주요리 앞에 나오는) 앙트레 **satisfaction** 만족 **satisfyingly** 만족스럽게 **satisfy** 만족시키다

3

해설 **형용사 vs. 분사:** 빈칸은 뒤에 오는 명사 amounts를 수식하는 형용사 자리이다. 문맥상 '대단한 양의 세부 정보'라는 의미가 되어야 자연스러우므로, '대단한, 인상적인'이라는 뜻의 순수 형용사 (B) impressive가 정답이다. (C) impressed는 '감명 받은'이라는 의미로 사람이 느끼는 감정을 나타내므로 오답이다.

번역 파인들링의 모바일 앱에 있는 거리 지도는 대단히 많은 세부 정보를 자랑한다.

어휘 **boast** 자랑하다 **impression** 인상 **impress** 깊은 인상을 주다

기출공식 2　　　　　　　　　　本책 p. 94

4 (B)　　**5** (A)　　**6** (A)

4

해설 **수동을 나타내는 과거분사:** 빈칸은 복합명사인 coupon book을 수식하는 형용사 자리이다. 보기 중 과거분사인 (B) enclosed와 현재분사인 (C) enclosing이 형용사 역할을 할 수 있는데, coupon book은 동봉되는 대상이므로 수동적 의미의 (B) enclosed가 정답이 된다.

번역 사우스 브랜치 은행에서 개인 보통예금 계좌를 개설하신 데 대한 감사의 표시로 동봉된 쿠폰북을 받아 주십시오.

어휘 **savings account** 보통예금 계좌 **enclose** 동봉하다 **enclosure** 동봉된 것

5

해설 **능동을 나타내는 현재분사:** 빈칸 앞에 부정관사 a가 있고 뒤에 명사가 나오므로 빈칸은 형용사가 들어갈 자리이다. 형용사 역할을 할 수 있는 현재분사 (A) refreshing과 과거분사 (C) refreshed 중에 선택해야 하는데, '신선한 변화'라는 의미가 되어야 하므로, (A) refreshing이 정답이 된다. (C) refreshed는 '(기분이) 상쾌한'이라는 의미로 사람이 느끼는 감정을 나타내는 형용사로 쓰인다.

번역 조용한 산에 위치한 그 호텔은 혼잡한 도시에 사는 방문객들에게 신선한 변화를 제공한다.

어휘 **setting** (자연의) 환경, 배경 **crowded** 혼잡한 **refreshment** 원기 회복 **refresh** 상쾌하게 하다

6

해설 **수동을 나타내는 과거분사:** 빈칸은 명사 requests를 수식하는 형용사 자리이다. 요청은 사람에 의해서 반복되는 대상이므로, 수동의 의미를 나타내는 과거분사인 (A) repeated가 정답이 된다.

번역 지역 주민들의 반복된 요청을 받고 나서 그 사설 도서관은 대중에게 공개되었다.

어휘 **request** 요청 **private library** 사설 도서관 **repeating** 반복하는 **repetition** 반복 **repeatedly** 반복적으로

기출공식 3　　　　　　　　　　本책 p. 95

7 (C)　　**8** (A)　　**9** (D)

7

해설 **분사의 역할_명사 후치 수식:** 문장에 본동사 are가 있으므로 빈칸에는 앞의 명사 Orders를 수식하는 동시에 the weight limit를 목적어로 취하는 분사가 들어가야 한다. 따라서 현재분사인 (C) exceeding이 정답이다.

번역 중량 제한을 초과하는 주문품은 추가 배송비를 내야 한다.

어휘 order 주문, 주문품   weight limit 중량 제한   be subject to ~의 대상이다   additional 추가의   shipping fee 배송비

8

해설 **분사의 역할_명사 후치 수식:** 문장에 본동사 shows가 있으므로 빈칸에는 앞의 명사 survey를 수식하는 분사가 들어가야 한다. 빈칸 뒤에 목적어가 나오지 않았으므로 수동 형태인 과거분사 (A) performed가 정답이다.

번역 〈카 트레이드〉지에서 실시한 분기별 조사에서 고객들은 새 차량을 구매할 때 크기나 가격보다 연비 효율성을 더 선호하는 것으로 나타났다.

어휘 quarterly 분기별의   fuel-efficiency 연비 효율성   over (비교) ~에 비해, ~보다

9

해설 **분사의 역할_명사 후치 수식:** 문장에 본동사 should contact가 있으므로 빈칸에는 앞의 명사 Employees를 수식하는 분사가 들어가야 한다. 빈칸 뒤에 목적어가 나오지 않았으므로 수동 형태인 과거분사 (D) interested가 정답이다.

번역 회사 스포츠팀 가입에 관심 있는 직원들은 5월 1일까지 메리디스 로에게 연락하십시오.

어휘 contact 접촉하다, 연락하다   interested in ~에 관심 있는

기출공식 4		본책 p. 95
10 (C)	**11** (D)	**12** (B)

10

해설 **현재분사 + 명사:** 빈칸은 뒤따라오는 명사 candidates를 수식하는 형용사 자리로, '유망한'이란 뜻의 현재분사인 (C) promising이 정답이다.

번역 권 씨는 국제 무역법 분야에서의 폭 넓은 경험 덕분에 유망한 지원자들 중에서 선발되었다.

어휘 extensive 폭 넓은   promising 유망한

11

해설 **현재분사 + 명사:** 빈칸은 뒤따라오는 명사 vacancies를 수식하는 형용사 자리로, '남아 있는'이라는 뜻의 현재분사인 (D) remaining이 정답이다. 자칫 '남겨진'이라고 해석하여 과거분사를 선택하지 않도록 유의해야 한다. 명사를 수식할 때는 'remaining' 형태로만 쓰인다는 것을 알아 두자.

번역 그 건물의 나머지 공실에는 1층에 있는 5천 제곱피트의 사무실이 포함된다.

어휘 vacancy 공실   remainder 나머지   remain 남다

12

해설 **현재분사 + 명사:** 빈칸은 뒤따라오는 명사 factor를 수식하는 자리로, '기여하는, ~의 원인이 되는'이라는 의미의 현재분사인 (B) contributing이 정답이다.

번역 제조 폐기물은 전 세계 수질 오염의 원인이 되는 중요한 요인이다.

어휘 manufacturing 제조   factor 요인   pollution 오염   contribute 기여하다, ~의 원인이 되다

기출공식 5		본책 p. 96
13 (C)	**14** (D)	**15** (A)

13

해설 **과거분사 + 명사:** 빈칸은 소유격인 its와 명사 exhibition 사이에서 명사를 수식하는 자리이므로 분사가 들어갈 수 있다. exhibition은 제안이 되는 대상이므로 수동의 의미를 나타내는 과거분사 (C) proposed가 정답이다.

번역 박물관은 제안된 디지털 예술 전시회를 위해 민간 자금을 구하고 있다.

어휘 seek 구하다   exhibition 전시(회)

14

해설 **과거분사 + 명사:** 빈칸은 뒤따라오는 명사 amenities를 수식하는 형용사 자리로, '제한된'이라는 의미의 과거분사 형태의 형용사 (D) limited가 정답이다.

번역 맥키니 호텔은 투숙객에게 제한된 편의시설을 제공해 가격을 낮게 유지한다.

어휘 amenity 편의 시설   limitation 제한   limit 제한; 제한하다

15

해설 **과거분사 + 명사:** 빈칸은 소유격인 your와 명사 product 사이에서 명사를 수식하는 자리이므로 '원하는'이라는 뜻의 과거분사 (A) desired가 정답이다. 자칫 해석이 능동으로 된다고 하여 현재분사를 선택하지 않도록 유의해야 한다. 명사 앞에서 과거분사로 쓰이는 분사들은 형태 그대로 암기해 두는 것이 좋다.

번역 자동판매기의 키패드를 이용해 원하는 제품의 코드를 입력하세요.

어휘 vending machine 자동판매기

16 (B)   **17** (C)   **18** (B)

16

해설   **감정을 나타내는 분사:** 인칭대명사인 주어 We와 호응하는 보어가 필요한 자리인데, 문맥상 사람이 느끼는 감정을 나타내는 형용사가 와야 하므로, 과거분사인 (B) delighted가 정답이 된다.

번역   고객님의 조경에 필요한 사항에 대해 이메일이나 전화를 통해 자세히 논의할 수 있으면 기쁘겠습니다.

어휘   discuss 논의하다   landscaping 조경   needs 요구 사항   be delighted to ~하게 되어 기쁘다

17

해설   **감정을 나타내는 분사:** 빈칸 뒤의 사물명사인 signs를 수식하는 자리이므로 형용사 역할을 할 수 있는 분사가 빈칸에 들어가야 한다. 문맥상 '희망적인 조짐'이라는 의미가 되어야 하며, signs가 감정을 유발하고 있으므로 현재분사인 (C) encouraging이 정답이 된다.

번역   이 나라에서 교육의 질이 개선되고 있다는 많은 희망적인 조짐들이 있습니다.

어휘   sign 징후, 조짐   encourage 격려하다, 장려하다   encouraging 희망을 주는, 고무적인

18

해설   **감정을 나타내는 분사:** 빈칸 뒤의 사물명사인 new film을 수식하는 자리이므로 현재분사인 (B) exciting이 정답이다.

번역   센트럴 시티 방문자 협회는 도시의 최고 관광 명소를 홍보하는 멋진 새 영화를 제작했다.

어휘   produce 제작하다   promote 홍보하다   tourist attraction 관광 명소

19 (A)   **20** (A)   **21** (C)

19

해설   **분사구문:** 주어가 Ms. Sakai이고, 동사가 is considered인 문장으로, 보기 중에서 동사 형태인 (D) Earn은 제외시킨다. 빈칸 뒤에 목적어 a degree가 있으므로 능동태 분사구문인 (A) Having earned가 정답이다. (B) Earned와 (C) Being earned는 수동형 분사로 목적어를 취할 수 없으므로 오답이다. 참고로 having p.p.는 주절에 쓰인 시제보다 앞서 일어난 일을 표현할 때 쓸 수 있다.

번역   회계학 학위를 취득한 사카이 씨는 관리직에 유력한 후보자들 중 한 명으로 고려된다.

어휘   degree 학위   accounting 회계학   consider 간주하다, 고려하다   candidate 후보, 지원자   earn 얻다, 벌다

20

해설   **분사구문:** 주어가 lighthouses이고, 동사가 remain인 문장으로, 보기는 모두 수식 역할을 하는 준동사로 구성되어 있다. 빈칸 뒤에 목적어가 없고, lighthouses는 '건축된' 대상이므로 준동사의 수동태가 들어가야 한다. 따라서 정답은 (A) Built이다.

번역   대부분 1800년대 후반에 건축된 해안가의 등대들은 수십 년에 걸쳐 비바람을 견디며 오늘날까지 건재하다.

어휘   coastline 해안선   lighthouse 등대   withstand 견디다, 버티다   force of nature (폭풍·지진 등의) 자연의 힘   decade 10년

21

해설   **분사 구문:** 빈칸 앞에 완전한 절이 왔고 접속사가 없는 문장이므로, 분사구문이 되어야 한다. 빈칸 뒤에 명사 형태의 목적어가 없으므로 자칫 분사의 수동태가 들어간다고 생각하기 쉽지만, prefer는 to부정사를 목적어로 취하는 동사이며, 빈칸 뒤에 오는 to부정사가 목적어로 온 것이다. 또한 주어와의 관계를 따져볼 때, 주어인 노스밴드 케어는 동사 '선호하다(prefer)'의 능동적인 주체이다 따라서 정답은 현재분사인 (C) preferring이다.

번역   노스밴드 케어는 사무실 장식에 드는 예산을 제한하며, 고급 의료 장비에 돈을 쓰는 것을 선호한다.

어휘   limit 제한하다   quality 양질의, 고급의   prefer to ~하기를 선호하다

22 (B)   **23** (C)   **24** (D)

22

해설   **부사절 접속사 + 분사:** 주절이 remember로 시작하는 명령문인 것으로 보아 생략된 주어는 you이다. 따라서 '(당신이) 잠재 고객들과 이야기를 나눌 때'라는 능동의 의미가 되어야 하므로, 정답은 (B) speaking이다. 참고로 speak는 언어명이 목적어로 올 때는 타동사로 쓰이고 '~와 이야기하다'일 때는 자동사로 쓰인다.

번역   잠재 고객들과 이야기를 나눌 때, 곧 있을 간센 캐피탈의 판촉 행사에 대해 알리는 것을 잊지 마십시오.

어휘   potential 잠재적인, 유망한   client 고객   upcoming 다가오는, 곧 있을   promotional 판촉의

23

해설 **부사절 접속사 + 분사:** after절에서 생략된 주어가 Ms. Baxter이므로 '백스터 씨가 지원자들을 면접하다'라는 능동의 의미가 필요하다. 따라서 정답은 (C) interviewing 이다.

번역 백스터 씨는 지원자들의 면접을 본 후에 인사 위원회의 모든 위원들을 다시 만나고 싶어 한다.

어휘 hiring committee 인사[채용] 위원회 candidate 지원자, 후보자

24

해설 **부사절 접속사 + 분사:** 문맥상 '회사 수칙에 언급되어 있듯이'라는 수동의 의미가 되어야 하므로, 과거분사인 (D) stated가 정답이다. 'as + p.p.'는 '~되어 있듯이, ~된 바와 같이'라는 뜻으로 자주 쓰이는 구조이니 암기해 두자.

번역 회사 수칙에 언급되어 있듯이 판매 사원들은 고객을 만나기 위해 시간을 낸 출장에 대해 보상을 받는다.

어휘 guideline 가이드라인, 지침, 수칙 sales agent 판매 대리점, 판매 사원 compensation 보상

ETS **TEST**				본책 p. 98
1 (C)	**2** (D)	**3** (D)	**4** (B)	**5** (A)
6 (C)	**7** (A)	**8** (D)	**9** (B)	**10** (D)
11 (D)	**12** (A)	**13** (C)	**14** (A)	**15** (A)
16 (D)	**17** (B)	**18** (C)	**19** (C)	**20** (A)

1

해설 **분사의 역할_명사 수식:** 명사 assembly를 수식하는 자리이므로 형용사로 쓸 수 있는 분사인 (C) automated가 정답이다.

번역 페로웨어의 리마 공장에서의 생산은 자동화된 조립 공정을 도입한 이후 두 배 이상이 되었다.

어휘 double 두 배가 되다 introduction 도입, 소개 assembly 조립 automate 자동화하다[되다] automatically 자동적으로 automation 자동 조작, 자동화

2

해설 **분사의 역할_명사 후치 수식:** 빈칸은 명사 companies를 뒤에서 수식하는 자리로, 명사를 수식할 수 있는 현재분사와 과거분사 중에서 선택해야 한다. 명사를 후치 수식하는 분사를 고를 때는 목적어의 유무가 중요한 단서가 되는데, 빈칸 뒤에 large quantities of materials라는 목적어가 있으므로 능동의 의미인 현재분사가 와야 한다. 따라서 정답은 (D) producing이다.

번역 충분한 저장 공간은 자재를 대량 생산하는 기업들에 매우 중요하다.

어휘 adequate 충분한 storage 저장, 보관 large quantities of 대량의

3

해설 **과거분사 + 명사:** 빈칸의 위치가 부정관사와 명사 사이에 있으므로, 빈칸에는 명사를 수식하는 형용사가 들어가야 한다. 따라서 '예상되는 결과'라는 수동의 의미를 완성하는 과거분사 (D) anticipated가 정답이다.

번역 기업 합병의 예상되는 결과로 가나에 새로운 시장이 열리는 것을 예로 들었다.

어휘 cite 언급하다, (이유·예를) 들다 outcome 결과 merger 합병 anticipate 예상하다 anticipation 예상

4

해설 **과거분사 + 명사:** 빈칸의 위치가 정관사와 명사 사이에 있으므로, 빈칸에는 명사를 수식하는 형용사가 들어가야 한다. 따라서 '확립된 표준'이라는 수동의 의미를 완성하는 과거분사 (B) established가 정답이다. '확립된'이라는 것은 이미 정해져 있음을 의미하기도 하므로 established 자체를 '기성의'라는 뜻의 형용사로 알아 두는 것도 좋은 방법이다.

번역 울리치-안사의 프로그래머들은 소프트웨어가 반드시 기성 시스템 표준에 따르도록 할 책임이 있다.

어휘 ensure 반드시 ~하게 하다 conform to ~에 따르다, 합치하다 standard 기준, 표준 established 확립된, 기성의

5

해설 **과거분사 + 명사:** 빈칸의 위치가 소유격과 명사 사이에 있으므로, 빈칸에는 명사를 수식하는 형용사가 들어가야 한다. 따라서 '공인된 판매점'이라는 수동의 의미를 완성하는 과거분사 (A) authorized가 정답이다.

번역 귀하의 비테라 오토바이를 제대로 수리받으려면, 저희 공식 판매점 중 한 곳에 방문할 것을 권고드립니다.

어휘 proper 적절한 recommend 권고하다 dealer 판매자[처] authorized 공인된

6

해설 **분사의 역할_보어:** 빈칸에는 be동사의 보어가 와야 하며, 부사 clearly의 수식을 받는 자리이므로 형용사가 와야 한다. 문맥상 '더 유망한 연구 분야'라는 의미가 적절하므로 '유망한'이라는 뜻의 (C) promising이 정답이다.

번역 이 회사는 몇몇 자회사들을 청산하고 확실히 더 유망한 연구 분야에 투자하기로 결정했다.

어휘 liquidate (사업체를) 청산[정리]하다, (빚을) 청산하다
subsidiary 자회사 invest 투자하다 research 연구
clearly 분명히, 확실히 promise 약속하다

7
해설 **감정을 나타내는 분사:** stun은 '감동시키다'라는 감정 유발 동사이며, 빈칸에는 뒤에 오는 명사 beauty를 수식하는 형용사가 와야 하므로 '감동적인, 굉장한'이라는 의미의 감정 분사인 (A) stunning이 정답이다. (B) stunned는 '(사람이) 놀란'이라는 뜻이므로 어울리지 않는다.
번역 오모리 씨는 굉장한 매력을 가진 수채화로 가장 잘 알려진 화가이다.
어휘 known for ~으로 유명한 beauty 아름다움, 매력

8
해설 **형용사 vs. 분사:** 빈칸은 '가격'이라는 뜻으로 쓰인 명사 rates를 수식하는 자리이며, '출시 특가'라는 의미를 완성하려면 '출시용의, 소개용의'라는 뜻의 형용사가 와야 한다. 따라서 정답은 (D) introductory이다. 분사도 명사를 수식할 수 있지만 의미가 맞지 않으므로 오답이다. 참고로, '입문자용 수업'은 'introductory courses'로 표현한다는 것도 알아 두자.
번역 벤 플로어스 블라인즈에서, 최초 고객들은 출시를 기념하기 위한 30퍼센트의 할인 혜택을 받을 수 있다.
어휘 benefit from ~로부터 이익을 얻다 rates 비율
introductory 출시를 기념하기 위한, 소개용의

9
해설 **분사의 역할_명사 후치 수식:** 빈칸은 명사 a drainage system을 뒤에서 수식하는 자리로, 명사를 수식할 수 있는 현재분사와 과거분사 중에서 선택해야 한다. 빈칸 뒤에 목적어가 오지 않았으므로 '고안된 시스템'이라는 수동의 의미가 되어야 한다. 따라서 정답은 과거분사인 (B) designed 이다.
번역 코치 엔지니어링은 폭우가 내릴 때 루트 480 고속도로의 물기를 제거하기 위해 고안된 배수 시스템을 구축하자고 제안했다.
어휘 construction 건설, 공사 drainage 배수 heavy rain 큰비, 폭우 design 설계하다

10
해설 **감정을 나타내는 분사:** 빈칸은 be동사의 보어 자리이며, disappoint는 감정을 유발하는 동사이므로 수식 관계를 따져서 현재분사와 과거분사 중에서 선택해야 한다. 주어가 상품의 판매량(sales of the item)이므로 감정을 느끼는 주체가 될 수 없다. 따라서 정답은 (D) disappointing 이다.

번역 드리스콜사의 최신 컴퓨터에 대한 후기는 대체로 호의적이지만, 해당 상품의 판매량은 지금까지 기대에 못 미치고 있다.
어휘 largely 대체로, 크게 favorable 호의적인
disappoint 실망시키다 disappointment 실망

11
해설 **분사구문:** the City of Harsillac Hills가 주어이고, will expand가 동사인 문장으로, 문맥상 '하실락 힐스 시는 연례 먹거리 축제를 확대할 계획으로 이로 인해 지역 기업가들에게 많은 새로운 사업 기회가 생길 것이다'라는 의미가 되어야 한다. 따라서 앞 문장의 내용이 사업 기회를 만들어 낸다는 능동적 의미가 되어야 하므로, 현재분사인 (D) creating이 정답이다.
번역 올여름 하실락 힐스 시는 연례 먹거리 축제를 확대할 계획으로, 이로 인해 지역 기업가들에게 많은 새로운 사업 기회가 생길 것이다.
어휘 expand 확대하다 annual 연례의 opportunity 기회
entrepreneur 기업가

12
해설 **분사의 역할_명사 후치 수식:** Prices가 주어이고 are가 동사이므로, 빈칸에는 명사를 뒤에서 수식해 줄 수 있는 분사가 와야 한다. 따라서 '웹사이트에 기재된'이라는 의미를 완성하는 과거분사 (A) listed가 정답이다. 나머지 보기들은 동사이므로 오답이다. (C) list는 명사로도 쓰일 수 있지만 앞에 나온 명사 items와 함께 복합명사를 이루지는 못한다.
번역 우리 웹사이트에 기재된 의류 및 가구 품목의 가격은 예고 없이 변경될 수 있다.
어휘 be subject to ~의 대상이다 notice 예고[통지]

13
해설 **과거분사 + 명사:** 빈칸은 복합명사 shipping containers를 수식하는 형용사 자리이다. 선적 컨테이너는 사물로서 표준화의 대상이 되므로, 수동의 의미를 나타내는 과거분사인 (C) standardized가 정답이다.
번역 수출업자들은 선박 및 트레일러를 쉽게 하역할 수 있도록 표준화된 선적 컨테이너를 사용한다.
어휘 exporter 수출업자 shipping 선적 trailer 트레일러
load (짐을) 싣다 unload (짐을) 내리다

14
해설 **분사의 역할_보어:** 빈칸은 동사 keep의 목적격 보어 자리로, 목적어와 목적격 보어의 관계가 능동이면 현재분사를 쓰고 수동이면 과거분사를 쓴다. 여기서는 목적어가 our sales staff(사람)으로, '숙지하게 되는 대상'이다. 따라서 과거분사인 (A) informed가 정답이다.

번역 고객관리를 개선하기 위해 우리는 영업 사원들에게 제품 개발에 대해 숙지하도록 해야 한다.

어휘 customer relations 고객관리   product development 제품 개발

15

해설 **분사구문:** 문장의 주어는 the operations manager이며 impress는 '깊은 인상을 주다'라는 감정 동사이다. 분사구문에서 분사의 형태는 주어와의 관계를 따져야 하는데, 주어인 manager가 감동을 '받은' 것이므로 수동의 의미를 나타내는 과거분사 (A) Impressed가 정답이다. 빈칸 뒤에 나온 전치사 by 또한 수동태라는 단서를 제공해 준다.

번역 지난주 제품 시연으로 인해 깊은 인상을 받은 업무팀장은 핸디메이드의 가전제품 몇 개를 주문하기로 결정했다.

어휘 demonstration 시연   operation 경영, 운용
appliance 가전제품   impress 깊은 인상을 주다
impressive 인상적인   impression 인상

16

해설 **형용사 vs. 분사:** 빈칸은 전치사구에서 명사 languages를 수식하는 형용사 자리로, 문맥상 '다양한 언어들'이라는 의미가 되어야 한다. 따라서 (D) multiple이 정답이다.

번역 렉시노 출판사의 사전 데이터베이스는 사용자들이 다양한 언어로 된 항목을 검색하도록 허락해 준다.

어휘 dictionary 사전   entry 항목   multiply 늘리다,
다양화하다   multiple 다양한

17

해설 **분사구문:** 문장의 주어는 Reveille Café이고 '~에 위치해 있다'는 be located[situated] in으로 표현한다. 따라서 '시의 역사 지구 중심부에 위치해 있는 카페'라는 의미를 완성하는 (B) Situated가 정답이다.

번역 그 도시의 역사 지구 중심부에 위치해 있는 레벌리 카페는 온종일 관광한 후에 식사하기에 완벽한 장소이다.

어휘 historical 역사적인   district 지구   spot 장소   meal
식사   sightseeing 관광   situate 위치시키다

18

해설 **부사절 접속사 + 분사:** as는 과거분사와 결합하여 '~된 대로'라는 관용 표현을 이룬다. 따라서 '논의된 대로'라는 수동의 의미를 완성하는 과거분사 (C) discussed가 정답이다.

번역 어제 전화 회의에서 논의된 대로 회사의 연례 간부급 연수회가 7월 말까지 미뤄질 예정이다.

어휘 conference call 전화 회의   annual 연례의   retreat
연수회   manager 관리자   postpone 연기하다

19

해설 **분사의 역할_명사 수식:** 빈칸의 위치가 정관사 the와 명사 사이에 있으므로, 빈칸에는 명사를 수식하는 형용사가 들어가야 한다. overwhelm은 '압도시키다'라는 뜻의 감정 유발 동사로, 수식 받는 명사로 온 number가 감정의 주체가 될 수 없으므로 현재분사 형태인 (C) overwhelming이 정답이다.

번역 압도적인 티켓 예매 수치에 근거하여 우리는 도니골에서 열릴 올해의 축제에서 기록적인 참석률을 기대하고 있다.

어휘 based on ~에 근거하여   advance ticket sale 티켓
예매   record 기록적인   attendance 참석, 출석률

20

해설 **분사의 역할_명사 후치 수식:** 빈칸이 포함된 부분은 주어인 Walters, Inc.의 동격으로 명사구가 되어야 한다. 따라서 빈칸은 앞에 나온 명사 company를 수식해 주는 분사가 들어가야 한다. 빈칸 뒤에 목적어(South Africa's nine province)가 있고, company가 serve의 주체가 되므로, 현재분사인 (A) serving이 정답이다.

번역 남아프리카의 아홉 개 주에서 서비스를 제공하는 천연 가스 회사인 월터스사가 동부 지부를 매각했다고 화요일에 발표했다.

어휘 natural gas 천연 가스   province 주, 지방
announce 발표하다, 알리다   division 부(서)   serve
(상품, 서비스를) 제공하다

CHAPTER 05 | 접속사

UNIT 11	부사절 접속사 / 등위 · 상관접속사

기출공식 1		본책 p. 102
1 (A)	**2** (A)	**3** (A)

1

해설 **부사절 접속사_시간:** 빈칸 앞뒤로 주어와 동사를 갖춘 완전한 절이 나오므로 빈칸에는 접속사가 들어가야 한다. 따라서 '~하자마자'라는 시간의 의미를 나타내는 부사절 접속사인 (A) as soon as가 정답이다. 나머지 보기들은 모두 전치사로 문장과 문장을 연결시키지 못하므로 오답이다.

번역 모든 시 허가서들을 인가받는 대로 새로운 수상 공원의 건설이 시작될 것이다.

어휘 construction 건설   permit 허가증, 인가서
authorize 정식으로 허가하다

2

해설 **부사절 접속사_시간:** 빈칸 앞뒤로 주어와 동사를 갖춘 완전한 절이 나오므로 빈칸에는 접속사가 들어가야 한다. 따라서 '~까지'라는 시간의 의미를 나타내는 부사절 접속사인 (A) until이 정답이다. until은 접속사와 전치사 둘 다로 사용되지만 나머지 보기들은 모두 전치사로만 사용되므로 오답이다.

번역 박민정 씨는 상임 후임자가 임명될 때까지 임시 부회장으로 일하게 됩니다.

어휘 **serve as** ~로 일하다 **interim** 임시의, 중간의 **permanent** 영구적인, 상임의 **replacement** 대체[자]

3

해설 **부사절 접속사_이유:** 빈칸 뒤로 주어와 동사를 갖춘 완전한 두 절이 나오므로 빈칸에는 접속사가 들어가야 한다. 따라서 '~때문에'라는 이유의 의미를 나타내는 부사절 접속사인 (A) Because가 정답이다. (B) In fact는 접속부사, (C) Just와 (D) Even은 부사이므로 오답이다.

번역 깨지기 쉬운 제품은 처리와 포장에 더 많은 주의가 필요하기 때문에 운송비가 더 비싸다.

어휘 **require** 필요하다, 요구하다 **handle** 다루다 **packaging** 포장 **fragile** 부서지기 쉬운 **transport** 수송하다; 수송

기출공식 2 본책 p. 102

4 (A) **5** (D) **6** (B)

4

해설 **부사절 접속사_양보:** 빈칸 앞뒤로 주어와 동사를 갖춘 완전한 절이 나오므로 빈칸에는 접속사가 들어가야 한다. 문맥상 '비록 국경일이라 할지라도'라는 의미가 적절하므로 '비록 ~일지라도'라는 양보의 의미를 나타내는 (A) even if가 정답이다.

번역 모퉁이에 있는 편의점은 국경일이라 할지라도 하루 24시간 내내 영업한다.

어휘 **convenience store** 편의점 **national holiday** 국경일

5

해설 **부사절 접속사_조건:** 주절에서는 다음 분기에 수익이 증가할 것이라고 추측하고 있고, 빈칸 이하는 그런 추측의 근거로 강 증권사와의 수익성 좋은 계약이 마무리되는 경우를 가정하고 있으므로 '~라고 가정하면'이라는 뜻의 조건의 의미를 나타내는 (D) assuming that이 정답이다.

번역 다음 달 이전에 강 증권사와의 수익성 좋은 계약이 마무리된다고 가정하면, 다음 분기에 이 회사의 수익은 증가할 것이다.

어휘 **revenue** 수익, 수입 **lucrative** 수익성이 좋은 **finalize** 마무리 짓다, 완결하다 **whereas** ~에 반하여

6

해설 **부사절 접속사_양보:** 부사절에서 '많은 직원들이 프로그램에 관심을 보였다'라고 했지만, 주절에서 '아직 아무도 등록하지 않았다'라고 했으므로, '비록 ~이지만'이라는 양보의 의미를 나타내는 (B) Although가 정답이다.

번역 비카리오 운송의 많은 직원들이 경영 교육 프로그램에 관심을 보였지만, 아직 아무도 등록하지 않았다.

어휘 **employee** 직원 **indicate** 나타내다 **management** 경영, 운영 **enroll** 등록하다

기출공식 3 본책 p. 103

7 (D) **8** (B) **9** (D)

7

해설 **부사절 접속사_목적:** 빈칸 뒤에 오는 that과 that절에 온 조동사 can이 문제 해결의 단서로, 빈칸은 that과 결합하여 '~하기 위하여'라는 목적의 의미를 나타내는 접속사를 완성시키는 (D) so가 정답이다. so that 뒤에는 can, may, could, would와 같은 조동사가 잘 따라붙는다는 것도 알아 두자.

번역 건물 조사는 전기 작업이 완료될 수 있도록 다음 주로 연기되었다.

어휘 **inspection** 조사 **postpone** 미루다, 연기하다 **electrical** 전기의

8

해설 **부사절 접속사_결과:** 문장 중의 that이 문제 해결의 단서로, 문맥상 '너무 많은 팬들로 인해 3시간 만에 표가 매진되었다'라는 내용이 되어야 한다. 따라서 that과 함께 쓰여 '너무 ~해서 …하다'라는 결과의 의미를 이루는 (B) So가 정답이다.

번역 너무 많은 영화 팬들이 〈툰드라 거주자들〉을 보고 싶어 해서 3시간 만에 표가 매진되었다.

어휘 **dweller** 거주자

9

해설 **부사절 접속사_목적:** 빈칸 앞뒤로 주어와 동사를 갖춘 완전한 절이 나오므로 빈칸에는 접속사가 들어가야 한다. 문맥상 '방문자가 쉽게 식별될 수 있도록'이라는 목적의 의미를 나타내므로 '~할 수 있도록'이라는 뜻의 (D) so that이 정답이다.

번역 방문자는 쉽게 식별될 수 있도록 특수한 배지를 착용해야 한다.

어휘 be required to ~해야 한다 identify 식별하다
so that ~ can ~가 …할 수 있도록

기출공식 4   본책 p. 103

10 (A)   **11** (B)   **12** (C)

10

해설 **부사절 접속사_양보:** 빈칸 뒤로 주어와 동사를 갖춘 완전한 두 절이 나오므로 빈칸에는 접속사가 들어가야 한다. 뒤에 오는 or가 문제 해결의 단서로, 'A이든 B이든'이라는 양보의 뜻을 이루는 접속사 (A) Whether가 정답이다. (B) Currently는 부사, (C) Among과 (D) According to는 전치사이므로 오답이다.

번역 창문이 각이 지든 둥글든, 셰이들리는 창문에 맞는 가리개를 만들 수 있다.

어휘 angular 각진 fit 맞다 currently 현재 according to ~에 의하면

11

해설 **부사절 접속사_고려:** 빈칸 앞뒤로 주어와 동사를 갖춘 완전한 절이 나오므로 빈칸에는 접속사가 들어가야 한다. '이번 워크숍이 빈스의 첫 번째 진행이라는 점을 감안하면'이라는 내용이 되어야 자연스러우므로 '~을 감안하면'이라는 뜻의 접속사인 (B) given that이 정답이다. (A) throughout은 전치사, (C) after all은 부사구이므로 오답이며, (D) whereas는 두 가지 사실을 비교·대조할 때 쓰는 접속사이므로 의미가 적절하지 않다.

번역 이번 워크숍은 빈스의 첫 번째 진행이라는 점을 감안하면 놀라울 정도로 순조로웠다.

어휘 surprisingly 놀라울 정도로 throughout ~ 내내
after all 결국 whereas ~인 반면에

12

해설 **부사절 접속사_대조:** 보기가 모두 부사절 접속사로 쓰일 수 있으므로 문맥상 가장 적합한 접속사를 선택해야 한다. 'before'와 'now'를 대조하는 내용이므로 '~인 반면에'를 의미하는 (C) Whereas가 정답이다.

번역 전에는 고객들이 노상주차 공간을 찾아야 했던 반면에, 지금은 차를 극장에 인접한 주차장에 둘 수 있다.

어휘 patron (상점 등의) 단골손님, 고객 on-street parking 노상 주차 vehicle 차량 adjacent to ~에 인접한 unless ~하지 않는 한

기출공식 5   본책 p. 104

13 (D)   **14** (A)   **15** (B)

13

해설 **부사절 접속사 vs. 전치사:** 빈칸 뒤로 주어와 동사를 갖춘 완전한 두 절이 나오므로 빈칸에는 접속사가 들어가야 한다. 따라서 '~라는 것을 고려할 때'를 의미하는 (D) Given that이 정답이 된다. (A) If so는 '만약 그렇다면'이라는 뜻의 부사구로 쓰이므로 절과 절을 연결하지 못하며, (C) Owing to는 '~ 때문에'라는 뜻의 전치사이므로 오답이다.

번역 강 씨의 프로젝트가 승인되었다는 것을 고려할 때, 마우어 컨설팅은 두 명의 연구원을 새로 고용해야 한다.

어휘 approve 승인하다 research associate 연구원

14

해설 **부사절 접속사 vs. 전치사:** 빈칸 뒤에 주어와 동사가 있으므로 접속사가 필요하다. '공연이 진행되는 동안에'라는 내용이 되어야 적절하므로 '~하는 동안'이라는 뜻의 접속사 (A) while이 정답이다. (D) during도 '~ 동안'이라는 뜻이지만 전치사이므로 절을 이끌 수 없어 오답이다.

번역 공연이 진행되는 동안에는 극장 문이 닫힐 것이다.

어휘 performance 공연

15

해설 **부사절 접속사 vs. 전치사:** 빈칸 뒤에 주어와 동사를 갖춘 완전한 절이 있으므로 접속사가 필요하다. 따라서 '(비록) ~이긴 하지만'이라는 뜻의 양보 부사절을 이끄는 접속사 (B) Although가 정답이다. (C) Despite도 양보의 의미가 있지만 전치사이므로 절을 이끌 수 없어 오답이다.

번역 이용자들에게 연체 안내문이 발급되지만 도서관은 연체료를 부과하지 않는다.

어휘 patron 이용자, 고객 issue 발급하다 overdue 연체된, 기한이 지난 charge 부과하다 late fee 연체료 excluding ~을 제외하고

기출공식 6   본책 p. 104

16 (C)   **17** (C)   **18** (D)

16

해설 **부사절의 축약:** '일하는 동안 습득된 기밀 사업 정보'라는 의미가 적합하므로 while they are working을 축약한 while working이 되어야 한다. 따라서 정답은 '~ 동안'이라는 의미의 접속사 (C) while이다.

번역 구직자들은 예전 직장에서 일하면서 알게 된 기밀 사업 정보를 말하지 않도록 권장된다.

어휘 **job seeker** 구직자 **confidential** 기밀의 **acquire** 습득하다, 얻다 **former** 이전의 **employer** 고용주, 고용 사업체

17

해설 **부사절의 축약:** '예약을 확인한 후에'라는 의미가 적합하므로 After they confirm their travel reservations을 축약한 After confirming이 되어야 한다. 따라서 (C) confirming이 정답이다.

번역 온라인으로 여행 예약을 확인하고 나서, 항공기 탑승객들은 적어도 출발 시간 한 시간 전에 공항에 도착해야 한다.

어휘 **reservation** 예약 **at least** 적어도, 최소한 **departure** 출발 **confirmation** 확인 **confirm** 확인하다

18

해설 **부사절의 축약:** 빈칸 뒤 otherwise noted가 문제 해결의 단서로, 'unless otherwise p.p.'는 '별도로 ~되지 않는다면' 즉, unless otherwise stated(별도로 언급되지 않는다면), unless otherwise indicated(별도로 표시되지 않는다면)' 등과 같이 활용되는 주어와 be동사를 생략한 부사절 축약 형태의 관용 표현이다. 따라서 정답은 '만약 ~이 아니라면'이라는 뜻의 (D) unless이다.

번역 별도의 언급이 없으면 모든 백스무스 가전제품에는 기본 1년 보증서가 제공됩니다.

어휘 **appliance** 가전 **warranty** 보증(서)

기출공식 7   본책 p. 105

19 (C)   **20** (D)   **21** (A)

19

해설 **등위접속사_and:** 빈칸 앞의 명사 printers와 빈칸 뒤의 명사 scanners를 연결할 등위접속사가 필요하다. '컴퓨터들이 프린터와 스캐너에 연결되어 있다'는 내용이므로, 비슷한 속성끼리 대등하게 연결하는 (C) and가 정답이다.

번역 미술부 컴퓨터들은 C 구역의 프린터 및 스캐너와 연결되어 있습니다.

어휘 **connect to** ~에 연결하다

20

해설 **등위접속사_but:** 문맥상 '요청은 받았지만 처리할 수 없어 유감이다'라는 내용이 되어야 하므로, 상반되는 의미로 연결할 때 쓰이는 등위접속사인 (D) but이 정답이 된다.

번역 견적서에 대한 귀하의 요청을 받았지만, 유감스럽게도 서류 없이는 그 요청을 처리할 수 없습니다.

어휘 **request** 요청 **estimate** 추정, 견적서 **regret** ~하여 유감이다 **process** 처리하다 **documentation** 서류

21

해설 **등위접속사_so:** 문맥상 '할인이 곧 시작되므로 추가 인원이 필요하다'라는 내용이 되어야 하므로 '따라서'라는 의미의 등위접속사 (A) so가 정답이다.

번역 이번 주부터 봄 할인이 시작되니 추가 직원의 일정을 잡아야 한다.

기출공식 8   본책 p. 105

22 (D)   **23** (C)   **24** (D)

22

해설 **상관접속사_either A or B:** or가 문제 해결의 단서로, 문맥상 '직원 신분증과 공식 방문객 출입증 중 하나'라는 의미가 되어야 한다. 따라서 or와 상관접속사를 이루는 (D) either가 정답이 된다.

번역 실험실 출입은 직원 신분증이나 공식 방문객 출입증을 가지고 있는 사람만 가능하다.

어휘 **entrance** 입장, 출입구 **laboratory** 실험실 **be restricted to** ~로 제한되다 **identification badge** 신분증 **pass** 출입증

23

해설 **상관접속사_both A and B:** and가 문제 해결의 단서로, 문맥상 '세금 준비와 재무 경영 자문을 둘 다 제공한다'는 의미가 되어야 한다. 따라서 and와 상관접속사를 이루는 (C) both가 정답이다.

번역 최 씨는 고객들에게 세금 준비 서비스와 재무 경영 자문을 둘 다 제공한다.

어휘 **financial** 재무의, 금융의 **consultation** 상담, 자문

24

해설 **상관접속사_neither A nor B:** 빈칸 앞의 neither가 문제 해결의 단서로, neither와 함께 'neither A nor B'의 형태로 'A도 아니고 B도 아닌'이라는 의미를 나타내는 (D) nor가 정답이다.

번역 엘리베이터 수리 때문에 전시장과 발란틴 가운 영업소 모두 이번 토요일에 문을 열지 않습니다.

ETS TEST

본책 p. 106

1 (A)	**2** (A)	**3** (B)	**4** (C)	**5** (A)
6 (D)	**7** (A)	**8** (C)	**9** (C)	**10** (D)
11 (B)	**12** (B)	**13** (B)	**14** (C)	**15** (D)
16 (B)	**17** (C)	**18** (C)	**19** (B)	**20** (A)

1

해설 **부사절 접속사_이유:** 빈칸 뒤에 주어(the country)와 동사(is observing)를 갖춘 완전한 절이 왔으므로 빈칸에는 접속사가 들어가야 한다. 또, 문맥상 '국경일을 준수하여'라는 의미가 되어야 자연스러우므로, '~하여, ~하므로'라는 뜻의 (A) as가 정답이다.

번역 룩셈부르크 사무소는 국경일을 준수하여 오늘 문을 닫습니다.

어휘 observe 준수하다 national holiday 국경일

2

해설 **부사절 접속사_양보:** 빈칸에는 두 문장을 연결할 수 있는 부사절 접속사가 와야 하며, 빈칸 뒤에 온 or가 문제 해결의 단서이다. or와 함께 쓸 수 있는 접속사는 (A) whether와 (B) either가 있는데, 부사절을 이끌 수 있는 접속사가 와야 하므로 정답은 (A) whether이다. 'whether A or B'는 부사절을 이끌어 'A이든 B이든 상관없이'라는 양보의 의미로 쓰인다. 참고로, whether가 부사절을 이끌 때는 반드시 or가 뒤따른다. (B) either는 or와 함께 상관접속사로 쓰이며, 두 문장을 이어 주는 부사절 역할은 하지 못하므로 오답이다.

번역 콘서트 표를 구매하는 고객들은 현금으로 지불하든 신용카드로 지불하든 수수료를 내야 할 것이다.

어휘 purchase 사다, 구매하다 charge (대가나 요금을) 청구하다 service fee 수수료 pay by cash 현금으로 지불하다

3

해설 **부사절 접속사_양보:** 빈칸 뒤에 주어와 동사를 갖춘 완전한 절이 왔으므로 빈칸에는 접속사가 들어가야 한다. 따라서 부사절 접속사인 (B) While(~이긴 하지만)이 정답이다.

번역 물론 난방은 당일에 난방기를 설치할 수는 있지만, 추가 수수료가 청구될 것이다.

어휘 installation 설치 charge 청구하다 altogether 전적으로 initially 처음에, 원래

4

해설 **부사절 접속사_시간:** 빈칸 앞뒤로 완전한 문장이 있으므로 빈칸에는 접속사가 들어가야 한다. 따라서 부사절 접속사인 (C) until이 정답이다. (A) instead와 (D) again은 부사, (B) beyond는 전치사이므로 오답이다.

번역 두 관리자가 모두 읽고 승인해야 프로젝트 제안이 수락될 수 있다.

어휘 proposal 제안(서) accept 수락하다 approve 승인하다 not A until B B하고서야 A하다

5

해설 **부사절의 축약:** 부사절 접속사는 주어가 생략되고 동사가 분사 형태로 변형된 분사구를 연결할 수 있는데, 문맥상 '서비스를 요청하실 때'라는 의미가 되어야 가장 자연스러우므로 '~할 때'라는 뜻의 (A) when이 정답이다.

번역 서비스를 요청하실 때는 참조할 수 있도록 고객 계정 번호를 준비해 주십시오.

어휘 account 계정 available 이용할 수 있는 reference 참조

6

해설 **등위접속사_or:** 빈칸 앞의 형용사 daily와 뒤의 형용사 weekly를 대등하게 연결할 등위접속사가 필요하다. 문맥상 '1일 또는 1주짜리 승차권'이라는 의미가 되어야 하므로, '~ 또는, 혹은'이라는 뜻의 등위접속사인 (D) or가 정답이다.

번역 버스 승객은 모든 모바일 기기에서 1일 또는 1주짜리 코스털 시티 교통 승차권을 구입할 수 있습니다.

어휘 purchase 구매[매입]하다; 구매(품) transit 운송, 교통 mobile device 모바일 기기

7

해설 **부사절 접속사_목적:** 빈칸 뒤에 주어 the payroll office와 동사 can distribute가 나오므로, 빈칸에는 절을 이끄는 접속사가 와야 한다. 따라서 '~할 수 있도록'이라는 목적의 의미를 나타내는 접속사인 (A) so that이 정답이다. 참고로, 조동사 can, may, could, would가 so that 뒤에 자주 쓰인다는 것을 알아 두면 문제 해결의 단서로 이용할 수 있다.

번역 직원들은 경리과 사무실에서 일정대로 급료를 나누어 줄 수 있도록 오늘 정오까지 근무 시간 기록표를 제출해야 한다.

어휘 submit 제출하다 payroll office 경리과 사무실 distribute 분배하다, 나누어 주다 paycheck 급료 on schedule 일정에 맞추어 that is 즉, 다시 말해서

8

해설 **부사절 접속사_조건:** 빈칸 뒤에 주어와 동사를 갖춘 절이 왔으므로, 빈칸에는 접속사가 들어가야 한다. 따라서 '~라면'이라는 조건의 의미를 나타내는 (C) Provided that이 정답이다.

번역 이번 분기의 매출이 예상만큼 높다면 호시로 디자인스사는 일본 선두의 그래픽 디자인 회사로 발돋움할 것으로 예상한다.

어휘 　project 예상하다, 전망하다　leading 선두의
　　　in case of ~ 경우를 대비하여　after all 결국, 마침내
　　　subsequent to ~ 뒤에, ~에 뒤이어

9

해설 　**부사절 접속사 _시간:** 빈칸 앞뒤에 주어와 동사를 갖춘 완
　　　전한 절이 왔으므로 빈칸에는 접속사가 들어가야 한다. 문
　　　맥상 '학기가 시작되고 바빠지기 전에'라는 내용이 되어야
　　　하므로, '~ 전에'라는 의미의 부사절 접속사인 (C) before
　　　가 정답이다.

번역 　학생들은 학기가 시작되어 더 바빠지기 전에 입학시험을 봐
　　　야 한다.

어휘 　entrance exam 입학시험　term 학기, 임기, 기간　in
　　　anticipation of ~을 내다보고, ~을 기대하고　already
　　　이미, 벌써　so as to ~하기 위하여

10

해설 　**부사절 접속사 _양보:** 빈칸은 완전한 절을 연결하는 자리이
　　　므로, 접속사가 들어가야 한다. 따라서 부사절 접속사인
　　　(D) Although가 정답이다. (B) Whether는 부사절 접속
　　　사로 쓰일 경우 or을 수반해야 하므로 오답이다.

번역 　비록 야고 프레스에 편집장이 새로 부임했지만, 출판사는
　　　계속 요리책에 초점을 맞출 계획이다.

어휘 　chief editor 편집장

11

해설 　**등위접속사 _so:** 빈칸 앞뒤에 완전한 절이 나오므로 빈칸에
　　　는 접속사가 와야 한다. 문맥상 빈칸 앞의 내용이 원인이며
　　　빈칸 뒤에 결과가 뒤따르므로 정답은 '따라서'라는 의미의
　　　등위접속사 (B) so이다. 참고로, 등위접속사 so는 완전한
　　　두 문장만 연결할 수 있다는 것도 알아 두자.

번역 　사우더닉 전자의 기사들은 하루 24시간 대기하고 있으므
　　　로, 여러분은 도움을 언제나 받을 수 있다는 것을 알고 안심
　　　하실 수 있습니다.

어휘 　electronics 전자 제품　technician 기술자, 기사
　　　on hand (도움을) 구할 수 있는, 대기하여　at ease
　　　안심하고　available 이용 가능한

12

해설 　**상관접속사 _rather than:** 빈칸 뒤의 동사원형 revise가
　　　문제 해결의 단서로, 주어를 생략하고 같은 품사나 구조끼
　　　리 대등하게 연결할 수 있는 등위접속사나 상관접속사가
　　　빈칸 자리에 올 수 있다. 따라서 '~하기보다, ~ 대신'이라
　　　는 의미의 상관접속사 (B) Rather than이 정답이다. 이때
　　　revise는 주절의 to recruit와 병렬 구조를 이루며, to부
　　　정사끼리 병렬 구조를 이룰 때는 주로 to를 생략한다.

번역 　엘리스 씨는 연간 판매 목표를 수정하는 대신 각 팀원에게
　　　1월 말까지 새 고객을 모집하라고 요청했다.

어휘 　revise 수정하다　goal 목표　recruit 모집하다,
　　　채용하다　client 고객

13

해설 　**부사절 접속사 _시간:** 빈칸 뒤에 완전한 절이 나오므로 빈
　　　칸에는 접속사가 와야 한다. 따라서 '일단 ~하면'이라는 의
　　　미의 (B) once가 정답이다. (A) following과 (D) by
　　　means of는 전치사, (C) right away는 부사이므로 오답
　　　이다.

번역 　일단 주문서가 제출되면 변경하기 어려우므로 웹사이트는
　　　고객들에게 주의 깊게 주문을 검토하도록 조언한다.

어휘 　advise 조언하다　as ~ 때문에　following ~ 이후에
　　　once 일단 ~하면　right away 즉각, 즉시　by means
　　　of ~을 이용해서

14

해설 　**부사절 접속사 _이유:** 빈칸 뒤에 주어와 동사가 나오므로
　　　빈칸에는 절을 이끄는 접속사가 와야 한다. 문맥상 '당신
　　　의 반환품이 수령되었기 때문에'라고 하는 것이 자연스러
　　　우므로 정답은 (C) Now that이다. (B) Instead와 (D)
　　　Meanwhile은 부사이므로 오답이다.

번역 　당신이 반환하신 물품이 도착했으므로, 환불금이 영업일 기
　　　준 3일 이내에 당신의 계좌로 지급될 것입니다.

어휘 　return 반환(품)　refund 환불(금)　issue 발급하다,
　　　지급하다　account 계좌　in order that ~하기
　　　위해　instead 대신에　now that 이제 ~하니까
　　　meanwhile 그동안에, 한편

15

해설 　**부사절 접속사 _시간:** 빈칸 뒤에 주어와 동사를 갖춘 완전
　　　한 절이 왔으므로 빈칸에는 접속사가 들어가야 한다. 또, 문
　　　맥상 '봄이 오기 전에'라는 의미가 되어야 자연스러우므로,
　　　'~하기 전에'라는 뜻의 (D) Before가 정답이다.

번역 　봄이 오기 전에, 강의 일부가 홍수를 예방하기 위해 확장될
　　　것이다.

어휘 　portion 일부[부분]　widen 넓히다　prevent 예방하다
　　　flooding 홍수

16

해설 　**부사절 접속사 _시간:** 빈칸은 두 문장을 이어 주는 부사절
　　　접속사 자리이다. 문맥상 '예비 면접이 모두 끝나는 대로,
　　　지원자 상위 3명에게 연락할 것이다'라는 내용이 되어야 자
　　　연스러우므로, '~하자마자'라는 의미의 접속사인 (B) As
　　　soon as가 정답이다.

번역 　예비 면접이 모두 끝나는 대로 마케팅 이사직 지원자 상위
　　　3명에게 연락할 것입니다.

어휘 　preliminary 예비의　applicant 지원자　contact
　　　연락하다

17

해설 **부사절 접속사 _양보:** 앞 문장에서는 일자리 제안에 감사했다는 내용이 나오고, 뒤 문장에서는 거절했다는 내용이 나오므로 '감사했지만 거절했다'라는 양보의 의미를 지니는 부사절 접속사 (C) While이 정답이다.

번역 박 씨는 선 자문그룹에서 온 일자리 제안에 감사했지만, 지역을 옮겨야 하기 때문에 그 기회를 거절했다.

어휘 appreciate 감사하다 advisory 자문의, 고문의
decline 거절하다 opportunity 기회 relocate
이전하다 now that 이제 ~하니까 only if ~하기만
한다면 while ~인 반면에, ~이긴 하지만 whether
~인지 아닌지, ~이든지

18

해설 **부사절 접속사 _양보:** 빈칸 뒤에 완전한 절이 나오므로 빈칸에는 접속사가 들어가야 한다. '더 많은 고객들이 온라인 서비스를 이용하고 있는 와중에도'라는 내용이 되어야 자연스러우므로 '~할 때조차도'라는 시간과 양보의 의미를 지니는 부사절 접속사 (C) even as가 정답이다.

번역 더 많은 고객들이 온라인 서비스를 이용하고 있는 와중에도 뉴을뱅크는 신규 지점을 개설하기로 결정했다.

어휘 decide 결정하다 customer 고객

19

해설 **부사절 접속사 _양보:** 빈칸 뒤에 완전한 절이 왔으므로 빈칸에는 접속사가 들어가야 한다. '이전에 했더라도 또 해야 한다'라는 의미가 자연스러우므로, '(비록) ~이지만, ~일지라도'의 의미로 양보의 뜻을 나타내는 접속사 (B) even if가 정답이다. 참고로, done so는 '그렇게 했다'라는 뜻이며, 해당 문장에서 '그렇게 했다'라는 것은 '암호를 변경했다'라는 의미가 된다.

번역 이전에 변경했다고 해도 금요일까지 모든 암호를 다시 변경해야 합니다.

어휘 previously 이전에, 과거에

20

해설 **상관접속사 _as well as:** The electronic time-tracking system이 주어, indicates가 동사, regular time과 extra hours가 목적어인 문장이다. 따라서 빈칸에는 목적어인 두 명사구를 이어 주는 접속사가 들어가야 한다. 문맥상 '정규 시간뿐만 아니라 추가 시간까지도 표시해 준다'라는 의미가 되어야 하므로, '~뿐만 아니라 ~도'란 의미의 상관접속사 (A) as well as가 정답이 된다.

번역 전자 시간 추적 시스템은 직원들이 근무한 정규 시간뿐만 아니라 추가 시간도 표시해 준다.

어휘 electronic 전자의 indicate 나타내다, 표시하다
regular time 정규 시간 employee 직원, 근로자

UNIT 12	관계사

기출공식 1	본책 p. 110
1 (A) **2** (A) **3** (C)	

1

해설 **관계대명사 _주격:** 선행사가 사람(Tenants)이며, 관계사절에서 동사 plan의 주어 역할을 하고 있으므로, 주격 관계대명사인 (A) who가 정답이다. plan을 '계획'이라는 명사로 잘못 이해한 경우 (B) whose를 정답으로 잘못 고를 수 있으니 유의하자.

번역 임대가 끝나기 전에 집을 비울 계획인 세입자들은 반드시 서면으로 계획을 통지해야 한다.

어휘 tenant 세입자, 입주민 vacate 비우다 property
재산, 소유 lease 임대 expire 기간이 만료하다
notification 통지

2

해설 **관계대명사 _주격:** 선행사가 사물(a recreation complex)이며, 관계사절에서 will accommodate의 주어 역할을 하고 있으므로, 주격 관계대명사 (A) that이 정답이다.

번역 타워 아파트는 수영장과 기타 시설을 제공하는 휴양 단지를 추가할 계획이다.

어휘 recreation complex 휴양 단지 accommodate
제공하다, 수용하다 facility 시설

3

해설 **관계대명사 _소유격:** 선행사가 Mie Hasegawa이며, 관계사절에서 명사 poem을 수식하는 자리이므로, 소유격 관계대명사인 (C) whose가 정답이다.

번역 올해 미들타운 시 문학상은 500편이 넘는 출품작 중에서 선정된 시 '비너스'를 쓴 미에 하세가와에게 수여될 것이다.

어휘 award 주다, 수여하다 poem (한 편의) 시 select
선정하다, 선택하다 entry 출품작, 참가작

기출공식 2	본책 p. 110
4 (A) **5** (B) **6** (D)	

4

해설 **목적격 관계대명사의 생략:** 빈칸 이하는 the passwords를 수식하는 관계사절로 빈칸 앞에는 목적격 관계대명사인 that이 생략되어 있다. 빈칸 뒤에 동사 use가 왔으므로, 빈칸은 주어 자리임을 알 수 있다. 따라서 주격 인칭대명사인 (A) they가 정답이다.

번역 프로빈스 은행 고객들은 온라인 뱅킹을 이용하기 위해 사용하는 암호를 매년 갱신하도록 요청 받는다.

어휘 update 갱신하다 annually 매년

5
해설 **주격 관계대명사 + be동사의 생략:** 문맥상 '~으로 알려진 회사'라는 의미로 빈칸 앞에 나오는 명사 a company를 수식하는 것이 적절하므로, which is가 생략되어 과거분사만 남은 (B) known이 정답이다.

번역 에멜리아사는 포괄적인 직원 훈련과 역량 개발 프로그램으로 알려진 회사이다.

어휘 extensive 포괄적인 development 개발, 발전 knowledge 지식 be known for ~로 알려져 있다

6
해설 **주격 관계대명사 + be동사의 생략:** 문맥상 '조립 구역에서 일하는 직원들'이라는 의미로 빈칸 앞에 나오는 명사 Those emplóyees를 수식하는 것이 적절하므로, who are가 생략되어 현재분사만 남은 (D) working이 정답이다.

번역 조립 구역에서 일하는 직원들은 항상 보호장비를 착용해야 한다.

어휘 assembly 조립 protective gear 보호장비

기출공식 3	본책 p. 111
7 (B) 8 (B) 9 (B)	

7
해설 **수량표현 + of + 관계대명사:** 선행사가 several courses of action이고 of의 목적어 역할을 하는 관계대명사 자리이므로 정답은 목적격 관계대명사 (B) which이다. (A) that은 목적격 관계대명사로 쓰이지만 콤마 뒤와 전치사 뒤에서는 쓰지 않으므로 오답이다.

번역 관리자들은 종종 몇 가지 행동 방침들 사이에서 결정을 해야 하는데, 어느 것도 전적으로 옳거나 틀리지 않다.

어휘 course of action 행동방침 completely 전적으로, 완전히

8
해설 **수량표현 + of + 관계대명사:** 문장에서 has와 are가 동사이며, 동사가 두 개인 문장에서 접속사가 없으므로 접속사 역할을 할 수 있는 관계대명사가 들어가야 한다. 빈칸은 전치사 of 뒤 목적격 자리이며, 선행사가 vehicles이므로 정답은 목적격 관계대명사 (B) which이다.

번역 에드워즈 플러밍은 여섯 대의 회사 소유 차량을 가지고 있으며, 그 중 두 대는 지금 정비소에 있다.

9
해설 **수량표현 + of + 관계대명사:** 문장에서 heads와 work가 동사이며, 동사가 두 개인 문장에서 접속사가 없으므로 접속사 역할을 할 수 있는 것을 보기 중에서 선택해야 한다. 따라서 ten people을 선행사로 하여 관계대명사로 연결되는 (B) most of whom이 정답이다. (D) and also에서 and 또한 접속사 역할이 가능하지만 주어가 Ms. Crouse이므로 동사의 수 일치가 맞지 않는 work로 연결할 수 없으므로 오답이다.

번역 크루즈 씨는 10명으로 구성된 팀을 이끌고 있는데, 그들 대부분은 원격으로 일한다.

어휘 head 이끌다 remotely 원격으로

기출공식 4	본책 p. 111
10 (B) 11 (C) 12 (C)	

10
해설 **전치사 + 관계대명사:** 빈칸에는 전치사와 함께 쓰일 수 있는 관계대명사가 들어가야 한다. 선행사가 a great city이며 전치사 in의 목적어가 들어갈 자리이므로, 목적격 관계대명사인 (B) which가 정답이다. 참고로, 빈칸 뒤의 구조는 관계사절을 to부정사구로 바꾼 것이며 이때 in which를 생략해도 문장은 성립된다.

번역 시의회는 사업가들에게 유리한 세율을 제공하는데, 이는 메스틴을 창업하기 좋은 도시로 만들고 있다.

어휘 city council 시의회 entrepreneur 사업가, 기업가 favorable 유리한, 호의적인

11
해설 **전치사 + 관계대명사:** 관계대명사 앞에 쓰일 전치사를 선택하는 문제로, 선행사가 The new radio talk show이므로 '새로운 라디오 토크 쇼 중에'라는 의미를 이루는 (C) during이 정답이다.

번역 방송되는 동안 청취자가 전화로 질문할 수 있는 새로운 라디오 토크 쇼가 다음 주 월요일 오전 10시부터 방송된다.

어휘 listener 청취자 air 방송하다[되다]

12
해설 **전치사 + 관계대명사:** 빈칸에는 전치사와 함께 쓰일 수 있는 관계대명사가 들어가야 한다. 선행사가 ten minutes이며 전치사 after의 목적어가 들어갈 자리이므로, 목적격 관계대명사인 (C) which가 정답이다.

번역 김 박사의 수락 연설은 10분 정도 진행될 것으로 예상되며, 그 후에 후식이 제공될 것이다.

어휘 **acceptance speech** 수락 연설 **last** 지속되다, 계속되다

기출공식 5   본책 p. 112

13 (D) **14** (C) **15** (D)

13

해설 **관계부사 _where:** 빈칸 이하는 장소 선행사인 the receiving dock을 부연 설명하는 관계사절로, 빈칸 뒤에 완전한 절이 왔으므로 관계부사 (D) where이 정답이다.

번역 모든 운송품은 하역장으로 도착하며, 그곳에서 창고 담당자가 운송품의 추적 라벨을 확인한다.

어휘 **shipment** 운송(품) **receiving dock** 하역장 **warehouse** 창고 **tracking** 추적

14

해설 **관계부사 _when:** 빈칸 이하는 시간 선행사인 times of the day를 부연 설명하는 관계사절로, 빈칸 뒤에 완전한 절이 왔으므로 관계부사 (C) when이 정답이다.

번역 하루 중 전기요금이 저렴한 시간대에 전기차를 충전하도록 하세요.

어휘 **electric vehicle** 전기차 **electricity** 전기

15

해설 **전치사 + 관계대명사:** 빈칸 이하는 장소 선행사인 the room을 부연 설명하는 관계사절로, 빈칸 뒤에 완전한 절이 왔으므로 관계부사 where을 대신할 수 있는 '전치사 + 관계대명사'가 들어가면 된다. 따라서 (D) in which가 정답이다. 관계대명사 (B) that은 완전한 절을 이끌 수 없고, 부사절 접속사 (C) as if는 '마치 ~인 것처럼'이라는 의미로 문맥에 어울리지 않는다.

번역 방문객들은 깁스 씨가 자신의 가장 유명한 시들을 쓴 방을 볼 수 있다.

기출공식 6   본책 p. 112

16 (B) **17** (A) **18** (B)

16

해설 **관계대명사 + 불완전한 절:** 빈칸 뒤에 불완전한 절이 왔으므로 관계대명사가 들어가야 한다. 빈칸 뒤에 동사 are expected to가 나오므로, 주격 관계대명사인 (B) who가 정답이다.

번역 실바 씨는 내일 프레젠테이션에 참석하기로 예정되어 있는 모든 직원들의 명단을 게시했다.

어휘 **be expected to** ~하기로 예정되어 있다 **attend** 참석하다

17

해설 **관계대명사 + 불완전한 절:** 빈칸 뒤에 불완전한 절이 왔으므로 관계대명사가 들어가야 한다. 빈칸 뒤에 동사 are marked가 나오므로, 주격 관계대명사인 (A) that이 정답이다.

번역 붉은 별표로 표시된 질문에는 반드시 답해야 한다.

어휘 **asterisk** 별표

18

해설 **관계부사 + 완전한 절:** 빈칸 뒤에 완전한 절이 왔으므로 관계부사가 들어가야 한다. 선행사가 Milan이라는 장소를 나타내므로 정답은 (B) where이다.

번역 모든 가방은 회사 본사가 있는 밀라노에서 수작업으로 제작된다.

어휘 **headquarter** 본사를 두다

기출공식 7   본책 p. 113

19 (D) **20** (C) **21** (B)

19

해설 **복합관계부사 _however:** 빈칸 뒤의 구조 '형용사 + 주어 + 동사'가 문제 해결의 단서로, 빈칸에는 해당 구조를 이끌 수 있는 부사절 접속사가 와야 한다. 따라서 (D) However가 정답이다. 복합관계부사 however는 형용사나 부사 바로 앞에 놓여 '아무리 ~할지라도'라는 의미로 쓰인다. 나머지 보기는 모두 부사이므로 오답이다.

번역 아무리 불편하더라도 헬멧과 보안경, 장갑은 공사 구역에 출입하는 사람은 누구나 반드시 착용해야 한다.

어휘 **uncomfortable** 불편한 **goggles** 고글, 보안경 **absolutely** 절대적으로, 무조건적으로 **construction zone** 공사 구역 **almost** 거의 **nevertheless** 그럼에도 불구하고 **seldom** 좀처럼 ~ 않는

20

해설 **복합관계부사 _whenever:** 빈칸 뒤에 완전한 절이 왔으므로 접속사가 필요하고, 문맥상 '금전등록기를 떠날 때마다'라는 의미가 되어야 자연스러우므로 복합관계부사인 (C) whenever가 정답이다.

번역 계산원은 금전등록기가 있는 곳을 떠날 때마다 '자리 비움' 팻말을 붙여야 한다.

어휘 **register** 금전등록기 **immediately** 즉시 **whenever** ~할 때마다

21

해설 **복합관계부사 _wherever:** 빈칸 뒤에 완전한 절이 왔으므로 접속사가 필요하고, 문맥상 '얼음이 있는 곳이면 어디든'이라는 의미가 되어야 자연스러우므로 복합관계부사인 (B) wherever가 정답이다. 상관접속사인 (C) rather than은 '~라기보다는'이라는 의미로 문맥에 어울리지 않는다.

번역 시 작업자들은 인도에 얼음이 있는 곳이면 어디든 소금을 뿌린다.

어휘 sidewalk 인도

기출공식 8 본책 p. 113

22 (C)   **23** (A)   **24** (B)

22

해설 **명사절을 이끄는 복합관계대명사:** will receive의 주어 역할을 하며, has ~ this year를 문장의 주어가 될 수 있도록 명사절로 만들어 주는 접속사가 필요하므로, '~한 사람은 누구든지'를 의미하는 복합관계대명사인 (C) whoever가 정답이다. (B) someone, (D) nobody는 접속사 역할을 할 수 없으며, (A) whose는 주격 자리에 올 수 없으므로 오답이다.

번역 판매 담당자들 중에서 연말까지 최고의 매출을 기록한 사람은 누구든지 유명한 R. F. 포울러 상을 받을 것이다.

어휘 distinguished 유명한, 저명한

23

해설 **부사절을 이끄는 복합관계대명사:** 빈칸 앞에 완전한 문장이 나오고, 빈칸 뒤에 동사 comes가 나오므로 빈칸에는 접속사가 들어가야 한다. 빈칸 앞에 선택 범위(36 months or 60,000 kilometers)가 주어지므로 '어떤 것이든지'라는 뜻으로 쓰여 부사절을 이끄는 (A) whichever가 정답이다.

번역 르페브르 모터스 자동차에는 36개월과 6만 킬로미터 중에서 어느 쪽이 먼저 채워지든 그때까지 보증하는 보증서가 딸려 있다.

어휘 come with ~이 딸려 있다   warranty (품질) 보증서

24

해설 **부사절을 이끄는 복합관계대명사:** 빈칸 앞에 완전한 문장이 나오고, 빈칸 뒤에 동사 is가 나오므로 빈칸에는 접속사가 들어가야 한다. 따라서 부사절을 이끄는 복합관계대명사 (B) whichever가 정답이다. 나머지 보기는 모두 접속사 역할을 하지 못하므로 오답이다.

번역 우리는 스태드니 인이나 맥스트론 스위트 중에서 어느 쪽이든 더 편리한 곳에서 시상식 연회를 개최할 것이다.

어휘 hold 개최하다   awards ceremony 시상식
banquet 연회   convenient 편리한

ETS **TEST** 본책 p. 114

1 (C)	**2** (B)	**3** (B)	**4** (B)	**5** (D)
6 (A)	**7** (D)	**8** (B)	**9** (B)	**10** (C)
11 (D)	**12** (C)	**13** (B)	**14** (B)	**15** (A)
16 (D)	**17** (B)	**18** (C)	**19** (B)	**20** (D)

1

해설 **관계대명사 _주격:** 빈칸 이하는 선행사 Journalists를 수식하는 관계사절로, 빈칸 뒤에 동사가 나오므로, 주격 관계대명사 (C) who가 정답이다. (B) whoever는 주격 자리에 올 수 있지만 선행사를 포함하는 복합관계대명사이므로 선행사 뒤에 올 수 없다.

번역 다음 월요일 기자회견에 등록된 기자들은 등록 시 입장권을 받게 될 것이다.

어휘 register 등록하다, 기재하다   press conference 기자회견   admission pass 입장권   registration 등록

2

해설 **관계대명사 _주격:** 빈칸 이하는 선행사 fabrics를 수식하는 관계절로, 빈칸 뒤에 동사가 나오므로 주격 관계대명사 (B) that이 정답이다.

번역 니틀리 어패럴은 무게의 최대 25배까지 물을 흡수할 수 있는 많은 원단을 판매한다.

어휘 fabric 천   absorb 흡수하다   weight 무게

3

해설 **관계대명사 _주격:** 빈칸 이하는 선행사 mixing processes를 수식하는 관계절로, 빈칸 뒤에 동사가 나오므로 주격 관계대명사 (B) which가 정답이다.

번역 퐁 앤 하스사는 생산 시간의 절반 이상을 차지했던 치약 혼합 공정을 자동화했다.

어휘 automate 자동화하다   toothpaste 치약   process 공정, 과정

4

해설 **전치사 + 관계대명사:** 빈칸 앞에 전치사 to가 있으므로 빈칸에는 목적격 관계대명사가 들어가야 한다. 선행사가 사람 명사인 department heads(부서장)이므로 (B) whom이 정답이다. to는 뒤 문장의 should be sent에 수반되어 '~에게 보내다'로 쓰이는 전치사인데 동사 뒤에 오는 전치사를 관계대명사 앞으로 끌어올 수 있기 때문에 to whom이 된 것이다.

번역 월간 보고서가 발송될 부서장들의 이름은 직원 편람 마지막 장에 적혀 있다.

어휘 department head 부서장   be located 위치해 있다

5

해설 **인칭대명사_주격:** in which가 이끄는 관계사절에 주어와 동사가 필요하다. 빈칸은 동사 practice의 주어 역할을 하는 주격 대명사 (D) they가 정답이다. 이때 they는 practitioners를 가리킨다.

번역 전통적으로, 의사들은 자신들이 일하는 모든 나라로부터 자격증을 얻어야 한다.

어휘 **health care** 의료 서비스, 보건 **practitioner** 의사 **obtain** 얻다 **practice** (의사, 변호사 등이) 개업하다, 영업하다

6

해설 **관계대명사_주격:** 빈칸 이하는 선행사 a new incentive program을 수식하는 관계절로, 빈칸 뒤에 동사가 나오므로 주격 관계대명사 (A) that이 정답이다.

번역 그 마케팅 부서는 전 직원을 위해 다음 주에 시작할 새로운 보너스 프로그램을 발표했다.

어휘 **incentive** 인센티브, 수당, 장려금

7

해설 **관계대명사_주격:** 빈칸 이하는 선행사 drivers를 수식하는 관계절로, 빈칸 뒤에 동사가 나오므로 주격 관계대명사 (D) who가 정답이다. 선행사가 사람이므로 (A) which는 오답이다.

번역 축제 퍼레이드 동안에 시내에 불법으로 주차하는 운전자들에게는 200달러의 벌금이 부과될 것이다.

어휘 **fine** 벌금, 과태료 **impose A upon[on] B** B에게 A를 부과하다 **park** 주차하다 **illegally** 불법적으로

8

해설 **복합관계부사_however:** 빈칸 뒤에 나온 형용사 inexpensive가 문제 해결의 단서로, 형용사나 부사 앞에 놓여, '아무리 ~할지라도'라는 양보의 의미를 이루는 복합관계부사 (B) However가 정답이다.

번역 아무리 저렴할지라도, 오늘날 구입할 수 있는 대부분의 건전지들은 10년 전에 생산된 건전지들보다 훨씬 오래간다.

어휘 **inexpensive** 저렴한 **available** 구입할 수 있는, 입수할 수 있는 **last** 지속[존속]하다, 계속하다 **decade** 10년

9

해설 **관계대명사_소유격:** 빈칸 이하는 선행사 a group of contractors를 수식하는 관계절로, 빈칸 뒤에 명사구 (collective knowledge)가 나오므로 명사구를 수식할 수 있는 소유격 관계대명사 (B) whose가 정답이다. 소유격은 선행사가 사람이든 사물이든 관계없이 whose를 쓴다.

번역 해리어 건설은 공동의 지식과 경험을 훌륭한 기술로 전환시키는 도급업자들을 고용한다.

어휘 **contractor** 계약업체, 계약자 **workmanship** 기술, 솜씨

10

해설 **관계대명사_소유격:** 빈칸 이하는 선행사 all employees를 수식하는 관계절로, 빈칸 뒤에 명사구가 나오므로 명사구를 수식할 수 있는 소유격 관계대명사 (C) whose가 정답이다.

번역 생산 공장에서 일하는 것이 직무에 포함된 모든 직원은 반드시 안전화와 보호 조끼를 착용해야 한다.

어휘 **safety boots** 안전화 **protective vest** 보호 조끼 **duty** 의무, 직무 **production plant** 생산 공장

11

해설 **관계대명사_주격:** 빈칸 이하는 선행사 builders를 수식하는 관계절로, 빈칸 뒤에 동사가 나오므로 주격 관계대명사 (D) who가 정답이다.

번역 이 프로젝트 진행에 관심 있는 건축업자들 중에서 카를로스 산도바가 단연 가장 유력한 후보로 두각을 나타낸다.

어휘 **builder** 건축업자, 건축 회사 **work on** ~에 착수하다 **stand out as** ~으로 두드러지다

12

해설 **관계대명사_주격:** 빈칸 이하는 선행사 The latest version of our spreadsheet을 수식하는 관계절로, 빈칸 뒤에 동사가 나오므로 주격 관계대명사인 (C) which가 정답이다.

번역 갱신된 계산 기능을 포함해, 경비 추적을 위한 최신판 스프레드시트는 실제로 사용하기가 매우 쉽습니다.

어휘 **latest** 최신의 **version** 판, 버전 **track** 추적하다 **expense** 경비, 비용 **include** 포함하다 **calculation** 계산, 산출 **actually** 실제로

13

해설 **관계대명사_주격:** 빈칸 이하는 선행사 something을 수식하는 관계절로, 빈칸 뒤에 동사가 나오므로 주격 관계대명사인 (B) that이 정답이다.

번역 크래프트 타임사에서 직원 안전은 결코 타협될 수 없는 문제이다.

어휘 **safety** 안전 **employee** 직원 **compromise** 타협하다, 양보하다

14

해설 **관계대명사_주격:** 빈칸 이하는 선행사 the ones를 수식하는 관계절로, 빈칸 뒤에 동사가 나오므로 주격 관계대명사인 (B) who가 정답이다. 복합관계대명사인 (A) whoever와 (C) whichever는 주격으로 쓸 수 있으나 선행사를 포함하고 있으므로 선행사 the ones 뒤에 올 수 없다.

번역 새로운 회사 정책으로 가장 얻을 것이 많은 사람들은 직원들이다.

어휘 employee 직원   gain 얻다, 획득하다; 이익   policy 정책, 방침

15

해설 **복합관계부사_whenever:** 빈칸 뒤에 완전한 문장이 왔으므로 복합관계부사가 들어가야 한다. 문맥상 '새 컴퓨터 프로그램이 설치될 때마다'라는 의미가 되어야 하므로 (A) whenever가 정답이다.

번역 새 컴퓨터 프로그램이 설치될 때마다 모든 사무 직원들에게 통지하는 것은 양 씨의 책임이다.

어휘 responsibility 책임, 맡은 일   personnel 직원들   install 설치하다

16

해설 **전치사 + 관계대명사:** 빈칸 앞에 전치사 during이 있으므로 빈칸에는 목적격 관계대명사가 들어가야 한다. 선행사가 a three-hour workshop이므로 (D) which가 정답이다.

번역 존슨 박사는 효율적인 시간 관리에 대해 논의할 세 시간짜리 워크숍을 개최한다.

어휘 offer 제공하다, 개설하다   share 나누다, 공유하다   perspective 견해, 관점   effective 효율적인   time management 시간 관리

17

해설 **관계대명사_주격:** 빈칸 이하는 선행사 terms and conditions를 수식하는 관계절로, 빈칸 뒤에 동사가 나오므로 주격 관계대명사인 (B) which가 정답이다. 선행사가 사물이므로 (A) who는 오답이다.

번역 전체 약관은 그때그때 바뀔 수 있으며 회사 웹페이지에 게시된다.

어휘 terms and conditions 약관   vary 바뀌다

18

해설 **전치사 + 관계대명사:** 빈칸 앞에 전치사 with가 있으므로 빈칸에는 목적격 관계대명사가 들어가야 한다. 선행사가 merchandise이므로 (C) which가 정답이다. with는 뒤 문장의 satisfied에 수반되어 be satisfied with로 쓰이는 전치사인데 동사 뒤에 오는 전치사를 관계대명사 앞으로 끌어올 수 있기 때문에 with which가 된 것이다. 참고로, 이 문장에서 return의 목적어는 any merchandise인데 관계절의 수식을 받아 길어지므로 짧은 전치사구인 for full credit이 긴 목적어와 자리를 바꾼 구조이다.

번역 귀하가 만족하지 못하는 물건은 어떤 것이라도 반품하면 전액 환불 받을 수 있습니다.

어휘 full credit (다음 구매 시 물건값에서 빼주는 형식으로 돌려주는) 전액 환불   be satisfied with ~에 만족하다

19

해설 **전치사 + 관계대명사:** 관계절 문장에 수반되는 전치사는 관계대명사 앞으로 끌어와서 쓸 수 있는데, be known과 함께 쓰이는 전치사는 'be known for(~로 알려져 있다)'이므로 정답은 (D) for이다.

번역 렛슨 씨의 가장 많이 알려진 업적 중의 하나는 22세 때 자신 소유의 직물 디자인 회사를 차렸다는 것이다.

어휘 accomplishment 업적, 성과   be best known for ~로 가장 잘 알려져 있다   fabric 천, 직물   at the age of ~의 나이에

20

해설 **복합관계대명사_whichever:** 빈칸은 문장을 연결할 수 있는 접속사 자리이며, 빈칸 앞에 온 문장에서 선택 범위(3년 또는 제품 용기에 표시된 유효 기간)가 주어지므로 '둘 중 어느 쪽이 더 빠르든지'를 의미하여 부사절을 이끌 수 있는 복합관계대명사 (D) whichever가 정답이다.

번역 그 제조업체는 자사에서 제조한 화장품이 3년 또는 제품 용기에 표시된 유효 기간 중, 어느 쪽이 더 빠르든, 더 빠른 날짜까지 사용 가능하다고 보장한다.

어휘 manufacturer 제조업체   guarantee 보장[보증]하다   cosmetic product 화장품   good 유효한   expiration date 유통 기한   package 포장, 용기   whichever 어느 것이 ~하든

UNIT 13	명사절 접속사

기출공식 1		본책 p. 118
1 (B)	**2** (D)	**3** (B)

1

해설 **명사절 접속사_that:** 빈칸은 동사 indicates의 목적어 역할을 하는 명사절을 이끄는 접속사 자리로, '~라는 것을 나타낸다'라는 의미가 되어야 하므로 정답은 (B) that이다.

번역 최근에 한 여론 조사는 유권자들 사이에서 그 후보자의 인기가 올라갔다는 것을 보여 준다.

어휘 poll 여론 조사, 투표   indicate 보여 주다, 나타내다   candidate 후보자, 지원자   popularity 인기   increase 증가하다   voter 유권자, 투표자

2

해설 **명사절 접속사_that:** 빈칸 이하는 동사 is의 보어 역할을 하는 명사절을 이끄는 접속사 자리로, '호텔의 장점은 ~라는 점이다'라는 의미가 되어야 하므로 정답은 (D) that이 정답이다.

번역 시스펠드 호텔의 가장 큰 장점은 객실에 주방 시설과 완비된 업무 공간이 있다는 점이다.

어휘 advantage 장점 feature ~을 특징으로 하다 facility 시설, 설비 fully equipped 완비된

3

해설 **명사절 접속사_that:** 빈칸에는 shows의 목적어 역할을 하는 명사절을 이끄는 접속사 자리로, '~라는 것을 보여 준다'라는 의미가 되어야 하므로 정답은 (B) that이다.

번역 최근 연구는 복잡한 프로젝트가 더 간단한 업무로 세분되었을 때 더 빨리 완료된다는 사실을 보여 준다.

어휘 complex 복잡한 complete 완료하다 rapidly 빨리 divide into 나누다 task 일, 과제

기출공식 2	본책 p. 118
4 (A) 5 (A) 6 (D)	

4

해설 **동격의 that:** 빈칸은 동사 issue의 목적어 자리로, that 뒤에 완전한 문장으로 온 것으로 볼 때 동격의 접속사 that과 함께 쓰는 추상명사 자리이다. 따라서 정답은 (A) statement이다. 이때 '신규 매장 두 개를 열 것'이라는 내용이 곧 '성명' 내용이므로 둘은 동격을 이룬다.

번역 아르갈 엔터프라이즈의 CEO는 회사가 도심 지역에 신규 매장 두 개를 열 것이라는 성명을 발표했다.

어휘 issue 발표하다 statement 성명 requirement 요건 treatment 치료, 처리 enforcement 시행

5

해설 **동격의 that:** 빈칸 앞에 '확인'이라는 뜻의 추상명사 verification이 있고 빈칸 뒤에 완전한 문장이 나오므로, verification과 동격을 이루는 명사절 접속사 (A) that이 정답이다. 이때 '디자인이 합법적인 사양을 충족시킨다'라는 내용이 곧 '확인' 사항이므로 둘은 동격을 이룬다.

번역 탤리스 엔지니어링사에서는 자사의 신제품인 물탱크 디자인이 합법적인 사양을 충족한다는 확인을 기다리고 있다.

어휘 await 기다리다 verification 검증, 확인 water tank 물탱크, 수조 meet 충족시키다 legal 법률의, 합법적인 specification 사양

6

해설 **형용사 + that:** 빈칸은 be동사의 보어 자리로, 빈칸 뒤에 온 that절과 함께 쓸 수 있는 형용사가 와야 한다. 따라서 정답은 'that 이하 내용을 확신하다'라는 뜻을 이루는 (D) confident이다.

번역 유 박사는 자신의 연구 결과가 정확하다고 확신한다.

어휘 result 결과 accurate 정확한 responsible 책임 있는 accustomed 익숙한 knowledgeable 박식한

기출공식 3	본책 p. 119
7 (A) 8 (B) 9 (A)	

7

해설 **명사절 접속사_if:** 빈칸 이하는 to see의 목적어 역할을 하는 명사절로, 문맥상 '수리가 가능한지 알아보기 위해'라는 의미가 되어야 한다. 따라서 '~인지 아닌지'라는 의미의 명사절 접속사 (A) if가 정답이다.

번역 팩스기가 고장 났는데, 수리가 가능한지를 알아보기 위해 노련한 기술자를 불렀다.

어휘 out of service 작동하지 않는, 고장 난 experienced 경험 많은, 숙련된 technician 기술자 call in ~을 부르다

8

해설 **명사절 접속사_whether:** 빈칸 이하는 동사 determine의 목적어절로, 문맥상 '~인지 아닌지 여부를 결정하다'라는 의미가 되어야 한다. 따라서 동사 determine과 함께 쓰여 '~인지 아닌지'라는 의미를 나타내는 명사절 접속사인 (B) whether가 정답이다.

번역 엘릭시스 파크 아파트 단지의 소유주가 바뀐 후로 그 건물의 현재 유지보수 직원들은 새 경영진과 함께 일할지 말지를 결정할 수 있다.

어휘 ownership 소유, 소유권 current 현재의 maintenance 유지보수 management 경영진 regarding ~에 대하여

9

해설 **명사절 접속사_whether:** 빈칸부터 Friday까지가 문장의 주어이므로 빈칸에는 명사절을 이끄는 접속사가 필요한데, 문맥상 '~인지 아닌지'라는 의미가 되어야 하므로 (A) Whether가 정답이다.

번역 우리가 이번 금요일에 회사 야유회를 하기로 할지는 날씨 상태에 달려 있을 것이다.

어휘 outing 야유회 depend on ~에 달려 있다 condition 상태, 조건

10 (A)   **11** (C)   **12** (B)

10

해설 **명사절을 이끄는 의문사_how:** 빈칸에는 describe의 목적어 역할을 할 수 있는 명사절을 이끄는 접속사가 필요한데, 뒤에 주어와 동사가 있는 완전한 문장을 이끌면서, 문맥상 '어떻게 하면 영업 사원들이 고객에게 더 기억에 남고 더 효과적인 발표를 전할 수 있는지'라는 의미가 되어야 하므로 '어떻게'라는 의미의 의문사인 (A) how가 정답이다.

번역 그 워크숍 자료는 어떻게 하면 영업 사원들이 고객에게 더 기억에 남고 더 효과적인 발표를 전할 수 있는지가 설명되어 있다.

어휘 **material** 자료 **describe** 서술하다 **deliver** 전달하다 **memorable** 기억에 남는 **effective** 효과적인

11

해설 **명사절을 이끄는 의문사_what:** 4형식 동사로 쓰인 tell의 직접 목적어가 빠져 있는 구조이며, 빈칸이 이끄는 절은 '무엇을'에 해당하는 직접 목적어가 된다. 빈칸 뒤에 주어가 빠진 불완전한 문장이 나오므로 (C) what이 정답이다. (D) how는 완전한 문장을 이끄는 명사절 접속사이므로 오답이다.

번역 나머지 주제들 중에서 그 발표자는 포럼 참가자들에게 현대 사회의 직장에서 성공하는 데 무엇이 필요한지 말해 줄 것이다.

어휘 **presenter** 발표자 **participant** 참가자 **succeed** 성공하다 **workplace** 직장, 일터

12

해설 **명사절을 이끄는 의문사_who:** 빈칸에는 to decide의 목적어 역할을 할 수 있는 명사절을 이끄는 접속사가 필요한데, 빈칸 뒤에 주어가 빠진 불완전한 문장이 있고 문맥상 '누가 이달의 직원으로 선정될지'라는 내용이 되어야 자연스러우므로, 명사절 접속사 (B) who가 정답이다.

번역 경영진은 월요일에 만나 누가 이달의 직원으로 선정될지를 결정할 것이다.

어휘 **management** 경영(진) **recognize** (공로를) 인정[표창]하다

13 (C)   **14** (D)   **15** (D)

13

해설 **명사절을 이끄는 의문형용사_which:** 빈칸은 동사 specifies의 목적어인 명사절을 이끄는 접속사 자리이다.

또한 뒤에 온 명사 classes를 수식하는 역할을 해야 하므로 '어떤 강의들'이라는 의미를 이루는 의문형용사 (C) which가 정답이다.

번역 강좌 카탈로그는 각 학위에 어떤 강의들이 요구되는지 명시하고 있다.

어휘 **specify** 명시하다 **degree** 학위

14

해설 **명사절을 이끄는 의문형용사_what:** 빈칸은 동사 explain의 목적어인 명사절을 이끄는 접속사 자리이다. 빈칸 뒤에 가산명사인 issue가 관사 없이 단독으로 왔으므로, 빈칸에는 issue를 수식할 수 있는 의문형용사가 필요하다. 따라서 (D) what이 정답이다. issue는 동사 are experiencing의 목적어로 형용사 역할로 쓰인 명사절 접속사 what과 함께 명사절의 앞쪽으로 옮겨진 상태이다.

번역 메시지에서 소프트웨어로 어떤 문제를 겪고 있는지 명확히 설명하세요.

어휘 **explain** 설명하다 **experience** 겪다

15

해설 **명사절을 이끄는 의문형용사_whose:** 빈칸은 동사 determine의 목적어인 명사절을 이끄는 접속사 자리이다. 빈칸 뒤에 가산명사인 proposal이 관사 없이 단독으로 왔으므로, 빈칸에는 proposal을 수식할 수 있는 의문형용사가 와야 한다. 따라서 정답은 (D) whose이다.

번역 심 씨는 도면들과 가격 견적서들을 검토한 후 곧 누구의 제안서를 선택할지 결정할 것이다.

어휘 **review** 검토하다 **blueprint** 청사진, 도면 **estimate** 견적서 **determine** 결정하다 **proposal** 제안서

16 (B)   **17** (C)   **18** (A)

16

해설 **명사절 접속사 + to부정사:** 빈칸은 바로 뒤에 온 to부정사구와 결합하여 동사 will explain의 목적어 역할을 할 수 있어야 한다. 따라서 정답은 to부정사와 결합하여 명사구를 이룰 수 있는 명사절 접속사 (B) how이다.

번역 워크숍 중에 강사들은 더 효과적인 판매 프레젠테이션을 어떻게 준비하고 제작하는지 설명할 것이다.

어휘 **instructor** 강사 **explain** 설명하다 **prepare** 준비하다 **effective** 효과적인

17

해설 **명사절 접속사 + to부정사:** 빈칸은 바로 뒤에 온 to부정사구와 결합하여 동사 decide의 목적어 역할을 할 수 있어

야 한다. 따라서 정답은 to부정사와 결합하여 명사구를 이룰 수 있는 명사절 접속사 (C) whether이다. 'decide/determine + whether to'는 '~할지 결정하다'라는 뜻으로 자주 출제되는 구조이다.

번역 하모니 디자인 컨설턴트들은 고객들이 창을 장식할 때 커튼을 이용할지 블라인드를 이용할지 결정하는 데 도움을 줄 수 있다.

어휘 help A to부정사 / 원형부정사 A가 ~하는 것을 돕다

18

해설 **명사절 접속사 + to부정사:** 빈칸은 바로 뒤에 온 to부정사구와 결합하여 전치사 about의 목적어 역할을 할 수 있어야 한다. 문맥상 '누구에게 주연을 맡길지'라는 의미가 자연스러우므로 정답은 (A) whom이 정답이다.

번역 준 이와타 이사는 누구에게 주연을 맡길지에 대한 최종 결정을 내리기 전에 20명의 연기자를 심사했다.

어휘 audition 심사하다, 오디션을 하다   cast 배역을 정하다[맡기다]   main role 주연

기출공식 7	본책 p. 121
19 (C) **20** (B) **21** (A)	

19

해설 **명사절을 이끄는 복합관계대명사:** 빈칸 이하가 동사 captures의 목적어이므로 명사절을 이끄는 접속사가 필요하다. 따라서 정답은 복합관계대명사인 (C) whatever이다. (A) wherever는 복합관계부사로 부사절을 이끈다. 복합관계대명사는 명사절과 부사절을 이끌 수 있고, 복합관계부사는 부사절을 이끈다는 점을 알아 두자.

번역 위즈대릭 플러스 소프트웨어 프로그램은 컴퓨터 화면에 나타나는 것은 무엇이나 캡처해서 아카이브에 저장한다.

어휘 capture 포착하다, 캡처하다   archive (컴퓨터) 아카이브, 저장소

20

해설 **명사절을 이끄는 복합관계대명사:** 빈칸부터 layout까지가 전부 will work의 주어이므로 빈칸에는 명사절 접속사가 들어가야 한다. '다섯 명의 새로운 편집자 중에서(of the five new editors)'라는 선택 범위가 주어지므로 '~중 어느 쪽이든'이라는 뜻의 (B) Whichever가 정답이다. 참고로, whichever는 사물과 사람을 모두 지칭할 수 있다.

번역 다섯 명의 편집자들 중 레이아웃에 관해 어느 사람이든 경험이 가장 많은 사람이 압둘라 씨와 그 잡지의 특별호를 작업할 것이다.

어휘 editor 편집자   layout 레이아웃, 지면 배정   special edition 특별판

21

해설 **명사절을 이끄는 복합관계대명사:** 빈칸부터 first까지가 전부 is의 주어이므로 빈칸에는 명사절 접속사가 들어가야 한다. 빈칸은 명사절 안에서 동사 arrive의 주어 자리이므로 정답은 주격 복합관계대명사인 (A) Whoever이다.

번역 누구든 매장에 처음 도착하는 사람이 조명을 모두 켜야 한다.

어휘 be expected to ~해야 한다

기출공식 8	본책 p. 121
22 (D) **23** (B) **24** (C)	

22

해설 **복합관계대명사 vs. 부정대명사:** 문장에 동사가 wishes와 can do로 두 개이므로 빈칸에는 접속사가 들어가야 한다. 보기 중에서 접속사 역할을 하는 것은 복합관계대명사밖에 없으므로 정답은 (D) Whoever이다. (A) Everyone은 Everyone who와 같이 접속사 역할을 하는 관계대명사를 함께 써야 복합관계대명사와 같은 역할을 할 수 있다.

번역 재활용을 위해 불필요한 전자 제품을 기부하고 싶은 사람은 누구든지 5월과 6월 내내 그렇게 할 수 있다.

어휘 donate 기부하다   unwanted 원치 않는   electronic 전자의   recycling 재활용

23

해설 **복합관계대명사 vs. 부정대명사:** 빈칸은 전치사 to의 목적어인 명사절을 이끄는 접속사 자리이다. 빈칸은 명사절에서 동사 has의 주어 자리이므로, 주어와 명사절 접속사 역할을 동시에 할 수 있는 복합관계대명사 (B) whoever가 정답이다. (C) anyone은 anyone who로 써야 복합관계대명사와 같은 역할을 할 수 있다.

번역 근속 연수가 가장 높은 사람에게 승진이 자동으로 부여되면 안 된다.

어휘 promotion 승진   seniority 근속 연수

24

해설 **복합관계대명사 vs. 부정대명사:** 빈칸은 동사 highlights의 목적어인 명사절을 이끄는 접속사 자리이다. 따라서 명사절 접속사인 복합관계대명사 (C) whatever가 정답이다. (D) everything은 everything that으로 써야 복합관계대명사와 같은 역할을 할 수 있다.

번역 스타일리스트 세실리아 라이트는 고객의 가장 매력적인 부분을 능숙하게 강조한다.

어휘 expertly 능숙하게   attractive 매력적인

ETS TEST

본책 p. 122

1 (D)	**2** (C)	**3** (C)	**4** (C)	**5** (A)
6 (A)	**7** (A)	**8** (B)	**9** (D)	**10** (B)
11 (A)	**12** (B)	**13** (D)	**14** (A)	**15** (C)
16 (A)	**17** (B)	**18** (C)	**19** (A)	**20** (C)

1

해설 **명사절을 이끄는 의문사_how:** 빈칸은 동사 show의 목적어 역할을 하는 명사절을 이끄는 접속사 자리이다. 완전한 형태의 명사절을 이끌 수 있는 의문사가 들어가야 하므로 정답은 (D) how이다.

번역 그 사용 설명서는 카메라 렌즈를 어떻게 닦아야 하는지 보여 준다.

2

해설 **명사절 접속사_that:** 빈칸에는 동사 request의 목적어 역할을 하는 명사절을 이끄는 접속사가 필요하다. request는 목적어로 that절을 받으며 that절은 '주어 + (should) + 동사원형' 형태로 쓰인다. 따라서 정답은 (C) that이다.

번역 마츠모토 씨는 모든 영업 직원들이 일주일 단위로 근무 시간을 보고하도록 요청한다.

어휘 on a weekly basis 주 단위로, 매주

3

해설 **명사절을 이끄는 의문사_how:** 빈칸 뒤에 주어와 동사를 갖춘 절이 나오므로 빈칸은 접속사 자리이다. 빈칸 앞 동사 determine의 목적어 역할을 하는 명사절을 이끄는 접속사가 필요하므로, (C) how가 정답이다.

번역 이인 시웅 씨는 어떻게 에체가라이 컨설팅사가 고객 서비스를 향상시킬 수 있는지 밝히기 위해 수많은 고객들과 면접을 했다.

어휘 numerous 수많은 determine 알아내다, 결정하다 improve 개선하다 unless ~하지 않는다면 in order to ~하기 위해 as if 마치 ~인 것처럼

4

해설 **명사절을 이끄는 복합관계대명사:** should see 앞에 오는 문장 전체는 should see의 주어가 되어야 하므로 빈칸부터 Park까지를 명사절 접속사가 이끌어야 한다. 빈칸 뒤에 동사 wants가 오므로 주격이 와야 하며, should see의 주체가 되는 사람이 주어로 와야 하므로 '~하는 누구든지'를 뜻하는 복합관계대명사 (C) Whoever가 정답이다.

번역 회사가 후원하는 시내 이스트뷰 기술단지 견학에 참가하고 싶은 사람은 누구든지 랜더스 씨를 만나서 등록해야 합니다.

어휘 sponsor 후원하다 sign up 등록하다

5

해설 **형용사 + that:** 빈칸 앞에 온 be confident가 문제 해결의 단서로, be confident 뒤에 that절이 와서 '~을 확신하다'라는 의미를 나타낼 수 있다. 따라서 (A) that이 정답이다.

번역 〈뉴스 업데이트〉 지를 구독하면, 최신 정치와 경제 동향에 대한 신뢰할 만한 분석을 받아볼 것임을 확신할 수 있다.

어휘 subscribe to ~을 구독하다 be confident that ~을 확신하다 latest 최신의

6

해설 **명사절을 이끄는 의문사_how:** tell이 4형식 동사로 쓰여 간접목적어 뒤 직접목적어가 올 자리이므로, 빈칸에는 빈칸 이하의 절을 이끌어 줄 명사절 접속사가 와야 한다. 빈칸 뒤에 완전한 문장이 나오므로 완전한 문장을 이끄는 명사절 접속사 (A) how가 정답이다.

번역 좋은 이력서는 지원자의 자격요건들이 어떻게 책무에 적합한지를 고용주에게 보여 준다.

어휘 qualification 자격요건 match 어울리다

7

해설 **명사절 접속사_what:** admit의 목적어로 온 that절에 동사 is가 있으므로 빈칸부터 first까지가 is의 주어가 되어야 한다. 명사절이 they read first로 끝나고, read의 목적어가 없는 불완전한 문장이므로 불완전한 문장을 이끄는 명사절 접속사 (A) what이 정답이 된다. 이때 what은 '~하는 것'으로 해석된다.

번역 많은 독자들은 일간 신문의 사설 면이 더 교육적이라고 말하지만 그들이 처음 읽는 것은 스포츠 면이라는 점을 인정한다.

어휘 state 말하다 editorial 사설 enlightening 가르침을 주는, 교육적인

8

해설 **명사절 접속사 that:** 빈칸 이하는 동사 feel의 목적어 역할을 하는 명사절이다. 빈칸 뒤에 완전한 문장이 나오므로 완전한 문장을 이끄는 명사절 접속사 (B) that이 정답이다. (A) what은 불완전한 문장을 이끄는 명사절 접속사이므로 오답이다.

번역 쿠시다 씨의 관리자들은 그녀가 지난 영업 캠페인 동안 올린 실적에 대해 특별한 인정을 받을 자격이 있다고 생각한다.

어휘 deserve ~을 받을 만하다 recognition (공로 등에 대한) 인정, 표창 performance 실적, 성과 sales campaign 영업 캠페인

9

해설 **명사절 접속사 that:** 빈칸에는 동사 announced의 목적어 역할을 하는 명사절을 이끄는 접속사가 들어가야 한다. 따라서 완전한 문장을 이끄는 명사절 접속사 (D) that이 정답이다.

번역 벤트랄콤은 회사에서 인수 합병을 담당할 상임 부사장으로 파멜라 왕이 임명되었다고 최근 발표했다.

어휘 announce 발표하다, 알리다　name 임명하다　merger 합병　acquisition 인수

10

해설 **명사절 접속사 + to부정사:** 빈칸 뒤에 온 to open이 문제 해결의 단서이다. 명사절 접속사 whether와 의문사는 to부정사와 결합할 수 있는 특징이 있으므로 (B) whether가 정답이다. (A) if는 명사절 접속사로 쓰일 때 whether와 같은 뜻이지만 to부정사와 결합할 수 없으므로 오답이다.

번역 시의회는 공공 해수욕장을 연중 내내 개장할지 여부를 결정할 조사 연구를 수행하고 있다.

어휘 city council 시의회　undertake 수행하다, 떠맡다

11

해설 **명사절 접속사 that:** 빈칸에는 indicate의 목적어 역할을 할 수 있는 명사절을 이끄는 접속사가 필요한데, 빈칸 뒤에 완전한 문장이 나오므로 (A) that이 정답이다.

번역 몇몇 시장 조사 연구는 제품 포장이 소비자의 구매 결정에 영향을 미친다는 사실을 보여 준다.

어휘 indicate 나타내다, 보여 주다　packaging 포장　affect 영향을 미치다　purchasing decision 구매 결정

12

해설 **명사절 접속사 what:** 빈칸부터 most까지가 is의 주어가 되어야 하므로 빈칸에는 명사절 접속사가 필요한데, 빈칸 뒤에 주어가 빠지고 동사부터 나오므로 불완전한 문장을 이끄는 명사절 접속사가 와야 한다. 주어는 보어인 the comfort와 동격이 되어야 하므로 '~하는 것'이라는 의미를 이루는 (B) What이 정답이다. (A) Who도 불완전한 문장을 이끄는 명사절 접속사로 쓸 수 있지만 the comfort와 동격이 될 수 없는 절을 이끌게 되므로 오답이다.

번역 리버풀 지역 공항에서 승객들을 가장 감동시키는 것은 속을 다시 채운 좌석의 편안함이다.

어휘 impress 감동시키다　comfort 편안함　upholster 의자에 속을 넣고 천을 씌우다

13

해설 **복합관계대명사_whatever:** 빈칸에는 동사 watch의 목적어 역할을 하는 동시에 동사 appears의 주어 역할을 할 수 있는 명사절 접속사가 와야 한다. 빈칸 뒤가 불완전하므

로 불완전한 문장을 이끄는 복합관계대명사 (D) whatever가 정답이다. (A) however는 완전한 문장을 이끄는 복합관계부사이므로 명사절 접속사 역할을 할 수 없다.

번역 오늘날 취사 선택할 수 있는 디지털 오락 매체들 덕분에 사람들이 그냥 앉아서 무엇이든 TV 화면에 나오는 것을 보는 일은 드물다.

어휘 entertainment 오락　option 선택(권), 취사 선택할 자유　rare 드문　individual 개인　appear 나타나다

14

해설 **명사절 접속사 + to부정사:** 빈칸은 is considering의 목적어 자리이며 빈칸 뒤에 온 to renew가 문제 해결의 단서이다. 명사절 접속사 중에서 whether와 의문사는 to부정사와 결합할 수 있는데, '계약을 연장할지 말지를 고려 중이다'라는 내용이 적절하므로 정답은 (A) whether이다.

번역 웨스트헤이븐 글래스웍스의 한은성 사장은 파인포드 트럭킹과의 계약을 연장할지 말지를 놓고 숙고하고 있다.

어휘 glassworks 유리 공장　consider 고려하다, 숙고하다　renew (계약 등을) 갱신하다, 연장하다　trucking 트럭 수송(업)

15

해설 **명사절 접속사_whether:** 빈칸 앞에 있는 uncertain이 문제 해결의 단서로, uncertain은 '불확실한'을 뜻하므로 '~인지 아닌지 불확실하다'라는 내용으로 연결되는 것이 자연스럽다. 따라서 정답은 (C) whether이다.

번역 많은 연구가 시장 조사 단체들에 의해 수행되었지만, 고객들이 인터넷을 통해 식료품을 구입할 의향이 있는지 여부는 여전히 불확실하다.

어휘 conduct 수행하다　grocery 식료품

16

해설 **형용사 + that:** 빈칸은 be동사의 보어 자리로 that절과 함께 쓸 수 있는 형용사가 와야 한다. 따라서 '~을 알다'라는 뜻의 be aware that을 완성하는 (A) aware가 정답이다.

번역 승객들은 분실하거나 도난당한 물품에 대해서 항공사 측에 책임이 없음을 알아야 한다.

어휘 be responsible for ~을 책임지다, ~에 책임이 있다　aligned 조절된, 맞춰진　awake 깨어 있는　abroad 해외에, 해외로

17

해설 **명사절 접속사_whether:** 빈칸 뒤에 오는 or가 문제 해결의 단서로, or와 함께 쓰여 'A 혹은 B, 둘 중 하나'를 뜻하는 (B) whether가 정답이다. 참고로, whether가 이끄는 명사절은 동사 indicate의 목적어인데, 영어 문장은 짧은 것을 앞에, 긴 것을 뒤에 놓는 습성이 있으므로 긴 목적어와 짧은 전치사구(on the envelope)가 자리를 바꾼 구조이다.

번역 필름을 보통 인화로 할지, 아니면 고급 인화로 할지 봉투에 표시해 주십시오.

어휘 indicate 나타내다, 표시하다 envelope 봉투
regular 보통의, 규칙적인 deluxe 고급의, 호화로운

18

해설 **명사절 접속사 what:** '사역동사 have + 목적어 + 목적격 보어(p.p.)' 구조가 보여야 풀 수 있는 고난이도 문제이다. 사역동사 have 뒤로 '목적어를 보존되게 하다'라는 내용이 와야 하는데, 빈칸부터 elements까지가 목적어이므로 빈칸에는 명사절 접속사가 와야 한다. 문맥상 '남아 있는 것을 보존되게 하다'가 적절하므로 '~하는 것'이라는 의미로 불완전한 문장을 이끄는 명사절 접속사 (C) what이 정답이다.

번역 포스터 시티 사학회의 회원들은 법원 청사의 독창적인 건축 요소들 중 남아 있는 것이 보존되도록 청원하고 있다.

어휘 historical society 사학회 petition 탄원하다, 청원하다 remain 남다, 잔존하다 courthouse 법원 청사 original 독창적인 architectural 건축학의
preserve 보존하다

19

해설 **명사절을 이끄는 의문형용사_what:** 빈칸에는 discuss의 목적어로 명사절을 이끄는 접속사가 와야 하는데, 빈칸 뒤에 명사 implications가 나오므로 명사를 수식하면서 명사절을 이끌 수 있는 의문형용사 (A) what이 정답이다.

번역 공원 및 오락 시설 담당부서는 광범위한 하수도 공사가 에 버그린 공원에서 열리는 야외 여름 콘서트에 어떤 영향을 미칠지 논의하기 위해서 회의를 할 것이다.

어휘 implication 영향 extensive 넓은, 광범위한 sewer 하수(도) outdoor 야외의

20

해설 **명사절 접속사 + to부정사:** 빈칸에는 전치사 on의 목적어로 온 명사절 접속사 how와 결합할 수 있는 구조가 와야 한다. 의문사와 whether는 주어 동사를 갖춘 명사절을 이끌기도 하지만 to부정사와도 결합할 수 있다. 따라서 정답은 (C) to furnish이다.

번역 그 사무용품점의 카탈로그는 회의실 전체에 가구를 경제적으로 비치하는 방법에 관해 많은 유용한 제안을 해준다.

어휘 office-supply store 사무용품점 helpful 도움이 되는, 유용한 entire 전체의 economically 경제적으로 furnish (가구를) 비치하다

CHAPTER 06 | 특수 구문

UNIT 14	비교 구문

기출공식 1   본책 p. 126

1 (D)   **2** (A)   **3** (D)

1

해설 **원급 비교:** '가능한 ~한[하게]'라는 의미로 as와 as possible 사이에는 형용사나 부사의 원급이 온다. 여기서는 동사 be replaced를 수식하는 부사가 필요하므로 (D) quickly가 정답이다.

번역 먼지가 쌓이는 것을 막기 위해 디스크 드라이버가 설치된 후 보호용 커버는 가능한 빨리 교체되어야 한다.

어휘 replace 교체하다 prevent 막다, 예방하다
accumulation 축적, 쌓임

2

해설 **원급 비교:** as ... as 사이에 40달러라는 금액 명사와 어울리는 표현이 들어가야 하므로 (A) little이 정답이다.

번역 파워플러스 헬스클럽은 신규 회원들에게 한 달에 40달러밖에 안 되는 적은 회비로 클럽 내의 모든 웨이트 트레이닝 시설을 이용할 수 있도록 제공해 준다.

어휘 weight-training equipment 웨이트 트레이닝 장비
rare 드문, 희귀한 scarce 부족한, 희귀한

3

해설 **원급 비교:** as ... money as 사이에 명사 money를 수식할 수 있는 형용사가 들어가야 하므로 수량 형용사인 (D) much가 정답이다.

번역 낡은 복사기를 수리하는 데는 새것을 구입하는 비용의 절반이 들었을 것이다.

어휘 repair 수리하다 cost 비용이 들다

기출공식 2   본책 p. 126

4 (B)   **5** (C)   **6** (C)

4

해설 **비교급 + than:** than ever before가 문제 해결의 단서로, 빈칸에는 than과 함께 쓰이는 비교급이 들어가야 한다. 따라서 정답은 (B) fewer이다.

번역 현재 그린웨이 항공이 그 어느 때보다 단발 항공기를 더 적게 활용하고 있다.

어휘 single-engine plane (기관을 하나만 장착한) 단발
항공기 **fewer** 더 적은 것[사람]; 더 적은

5

해설 **비교급 + than:** 빈칸 뒤에 than이 온 것으로 미루어 빈칸
에는 비교급 형태가 들어가야 한다는 것을 알 수 있으므로
(C) more seriously가 정답이다.

번역 리 씨는 자신의 업무를 전임자보다 더 진지하게 생각한다.

어휘 **predecessor** 전임자, 선배

6

해설 **비교급 + than:** 빈칸 뒤에 온 than이 문제 해결의 단서로,
빈칸에는 비교급이 들어가야 한다. 따라서 형용사 low
의 비교급 형태인 (C) lower가 정답이다. '비교급 + than
anticipated'는 '예상했던 것 보다 덜 / 더 ~한'이란 의미로
자주 쓰이는 표현이니 암기해 두자.

번역 지난 분기 보고서에 따르면 TNQ 전자의 수익은 예상보다
낮았다.

어휘 **quarterly** 분기의, 계간의 **earnings** 소득, 수익
anticipate 예상하다

기출공식 3	본책 p. 127
7 (D) **8** (C) **9** (B)	

7

해설 **비교급 강조 부사:** 빈칸은 비교급 higher를 강조하는 부사
자리이다. 따라서 비교급 앞에서 '훨씬 더'라는 의미로 비
교급을 강조하는 부사인 (D) much가 정답이다. 빈칸 뒤
에 오는 than만 보고 (A) more를 고르지 않도록 유의하
자. 형용사 high에 '-er'을 붙여 비교급이 되었으므로 또
more를 붙일 수 없다.

번역 상대적으로 추운 날씨 상태 때문에 이번 시즌 겨울 옷 매출
은 평상시보다 훨씬 더 높았다.

어휘 **relatively** 상대적으로 **condition** 상태, 조건 **normal**
정상의, 보통의

8

해설 **비교급 강조 부사:** 빈칸은 비교급 easier를 강조하는 부사
자리이다. 따라서 '상당히'라는 의미로 비교급을 강조하는
부사인 (C) considerably가 정답이다.

번역 최근 설치된 CXT-7 주문 처리 소프트웨어는 기존 프로그
램보다 사용하기가 상당히 쉽다.

어휘 **recently-installed** 최근 설치된 **order processing**
주문 처리 **consider** 고려하다

9

해설 **비교급 강조 부사:** 빈칸 앞에 비교급 강조 부사 much가 문
제 해결의 단서로, 빈칸에는 '훨씬 더 작은'이라는 의미를
완성하는 비교급을 써야 한다. 따라서 정답은 (B) smaller
이다.

번역 새로운 사진 포맷의 훨씬 더 작은 용량 덕분에 한 장의 디스
크에 수백 장의 더 많은 사진을 저장할 수 있게 될 것이다.

어휘 **store** 저장하다

기출공식 4	본책 p. 127
10 (B) **11** (A) **12** (B)	

10

해설 **the + 최상급:** 다수의 지하철 노선 중에서(Of the subway
lines) 하나(green line)를 선택하여 설명하고 있으며, 빈
칸 앞에 정관사 the가 있으므로 빈칸에는 '가장 편리한 (노
선)'을 의미하는 최상급이 들어가야 한다. 따라서 정답은
(B) easiest이다.

번역 중심 업무 지구에 정차하는 지하철 노선 중 녹색 노선이 프
랭클린 빌딩에서 걸어가기에 가장 편리한 노선이다.

어휘 **central business district** 중심 업무 지구

11

해설 **the + 최상급:** 테스트한 모든 세탁기 중에서(Of all the
washing machines we tested) 하나(the
Swisherette)를 선택하여 설명하고 있으며, 빈칸 앞에 정
관사 the가 있으므로 빈칸에는 '가장 효율적으로'를 의미
하는 최상급이 들어가야 한다. 따라서 정답은 (A) most
efficiently이다.

번역 우리가 테스트한 모든 세탁기 중에서 스위셔렛이 물을 가장
효율적으로 사용한다.

어휘 **washing machine** 세탁기 **efficiently** 효율적으로
efficient 효율적인 **efficiency** 효율

12

해설 **the + 최상급:** 빈칸은 부정대명사 one을 수식하는 형용사
자리이다. 빈칸 앞의 정관사 the와 뒤의 ever가 문제 해
결의 단서로, 문맥상 '지금껏 공개한 것 중 가장 인기 있
다'는 내용이 되어야 하므로 최상급 형용사인 (B) most
popular가 정답이다. 참고로, ever는 '지금까지'라는 뜻으
로 최상급 표현 뒤에서 최상급을 강조하는 부사로 자주 쓰
인다.

번역 〈네이처 팟캐스트〉가 공개한 에피소드 중 꿀벌에 관한 에피
소드가 가장 인기 있다.

어휘 **release** 공개하다 **popular** 인기 있는 **popularity**
인기

13

해설　**최상급 강조 부사:** 빈칸 앞에 the lightest라는 최상급이 나오므로, 최상급 뒤에서 그 말을 강조하여 '이제까지, 지금까지'라는 의미로 쓰이는 부사 (A) ever가 정답이다.

번역　비알로보스 씨는 새로 구입한 핸드폰들이 그 부서에서 이제껏 구입한 핸드폰 중 가장 가볍다고 보고했다.

어휘　report 보고하다　mobile telephone 휴대전화, 핸드폰　purchase 사다, 구매하다　department 부

14

해설　**최상급 강조 부사:** 빈칸 앞에 the most profitable이라는 최상급이 나오므로 최상급 뒤에서 강조할 수 있는 강조 부사가 와야 한다. 따라서 정답은 최상급과 함께 쓰여 '지금까지 가장 ~한'이라는 의미를 이루는 (B) yet이다.

번역　수입이 20퍼센트 증가하여 소르빈 호텔 그룹은 올해 지금까지 중 가장 많은 수익을 냈다.

어휘　revenue 수입, 소득

15

해설　**최상급 강조 부사:** 빈칸은 정관사 the와 최상급 best 사이에서 최상급을 수식하는 부사 자리이므로, 최상급을 강조하는 (C) very가 정답이다.

번역　저희 고객 서비스 직원들은 고객들께 단연 최고의 경험을 드리기 위해 갖은 노력을 기울일 것입니다.

어휘　representative 대표자, 직원

16

해설　**비교 구문의 품사 판단:** The advertisement가 문장의 주어이고 동사는 was이므로 빈칸에는 보어 역할을 할 수 있는 형용사가 들어가서 비교급을 완성해야 한다. 따라서 정답은 (D) memorable이다.

번역　에코스마트 자동차 광고는 그린레이브 자동차 광고보다 더 기억에 남을 만한 것이었다.

어휘　advertisement 광고　memorably 기억에 남도록　memory 기억　memorize 암기하다

17

해설　**비교 구문의 품사 판단:** 빈칸 뒤에 온 than이 문제 해결의 단서로, 빈칸에는 found의 목적격 보어 역할을 하는 형

용사의 비교급 형태가 들어가야 한다. 따라서 (C) more difficult가 정답이다.

번역　건축가들은 만을 가로지르는 다리를 디자인하는 것이 예상했던 것보다 더 어렵다고 생각하게 되었다.

어휘　architect 건축가　bay 만

18

해설　**비교 구문의 품사 판단:** 빈칸 뒤에 than이 있으므로 비교급을 써야 하는데, 빈칸은 동사 can be installed를 수식하는 자리이므로 부사의 비교급으로 들어가야 한다. 따라서 (A) more easily가 정답이다.

번역　새로 나온 프로델리악스 프로-6 사진 편집 소프트웨어는 이전 버전의 프로그램보다 훨씬 더 쉽게 설치될 수 있다.

어휘　install 설치하다　previous 이전의

19

해설　**비교급 관용 표현:** 빈칸 뒤의 시점 표현 next Friday가 문제 해결의 단서로, '늦어도 다음 주 금요일까지'라는 의미를 이루는 비교급 관용 표현인 (B) no later than이 정답이다.

번역　모든 디자인 팀원들은 늦어도 다음 주 금요일까지는 완성된 초안을 콘로이 씨에게 제출해야 한다.

어휘　submit 제출하다　draft 원고, 초안　instead of ~ 대신에　otherwise 만약 그렇지 않으면

20

해설　**비교급 관용 표현:** 빈칸 앞뒤로 its recipes와 its new packaging이라는 대등한 명사구가 나오며, 문맥상 '새로운 포장보다는 조리법의 변화를 인기의 이유로 꼽았다'라는 내용이 되어야 한다. 따라서 '~보다는'이라는 의미의 (C) rather than이 정답이다.

번역　다징 푸드사는 최근 소비자들에게 인기가 높은 이유로 새로운 포장보다는 조리법의 변화를 꼽았다.

어휘　attribute A to B A를 B의 결과로[덕분으로] 보다　recent 최근의　popularity 인기　consumer 소비자　recipe 조리법　packaging 포장

21

해설　**비교급 관용 표현:** 문맥상 '애완동물은 더 이상 허용되지 않는다'는 내용이 되어야 하므로 '더 이상 ~않다'는 뜻의 비교급 관용 표현인 (D) no longer가 정답이다.

번역　최근에 있었던 위생 문제 때문에 애완동물은 더 이상 루나 카페 안에 들어올 수 없습니다.

어휘　due to ~ 때문에　sanitation 위생

기출공식 8	본책 p. 129
22 (A) **23** (B) **24** (A)	

22

해설 **원급 관용 표현:** 빈칸 앞에 온 the same이 문제 해결의 단서로, 'the same ~ as'는 '~와 동일한'이라는 원급 표현이다. 따라서 (A) as가 정답이다.

번역 새로 나온 맥실락 M6 휴대전화는 기존 모델과 동일한 기능을 가지고 있지만, 좀 더 가볍고 두께가 얇다.

어휘 feature 기능 previous 이전의 slightly 약간

23

해설 **최상급 관용 표현:** 빈칸 뒤 숫자가 문제 해결의 단서로, 숫자 앞에서 '적어도'라는 의미로 숫자를 수식하는 (B) at least가 정답이다.

번역 이 지역에서 학생 운전자들은 최소 17세가 될 때까지는 운전 면허를 신청할 수 없다.

어휘 province 지역 apply for ~을 신청하다 at once 당장, 동시에 for now 우선은, 현재로서는 for good 영원히

24

해설 **최상급 관용 표현:** 빈칸 앞의 시점 표현 by August 31가 문제 해결의 단서로, '늦어도 8월 31일까지'라는 의미를 이루는 최상급 관용 표현인 (A) at the latest가 정답이다. (B) no later than은 같은 의미로 쓰이지만 'no later than + 시점'과 같이 시점 표현이 관용 표현 뒤에 위치해야 하므로 오답이다.

번역 늦어도 8월 31일까지는 당신 부지의 울타리 문제가 해결되어야 한다.

어휘 property 부지 remedy 해결하다; 해결책 lately 최근에

ETS **TEST**				본책 p. 130
1 (A)	**2** (C)	**3** (D)	**4** (D)	**5** (C)
6 (B)	**7** (B)	**8** (D)	**9** (A)	**10** (B)
11 (A)	**12** (C)	**13** (C)	**14** (D)	**15** (A)
16 (B)	**17** (C)	**18** (A)	**19** (B)	**20** (D)

1

해설 **the + 최상급:** '가장 ~한 것들 중 하나'라는 의미를 나타내는 'one of the/소유격 최상급 + 복수명사'를 알면 풀 수 있는 문제이다. 빈칸에는 최상급 표현이 들어가야 하므로 (A) largest가 정답이다.

번역 국내 최대의 에너지 공급업체 중 하나인 오론 에너지는 거의 2천만 명의 고객에게 전기를 공급한다.

어휘 deliver 전달하다, 배달하다 electricity 전기

2

해설 **비교급 + than:** 빈칸 뒤의 than과 함께 비교급을 이루는 (C) more favorably가 정답이다.

번역 그 설문조사는 사람들이 새로운 팩터 X 에너지 바의 맛에 대해 예상보다 훨씬 더 호의적으로 응답했음을 나타냈다.

어휘 respond 대답하다 favorably 호의적으로 favorable 호의적인

3

해설 **비교 구문의 품사 판단:** 'as + 형용사/부사 + as possible'은 '가능한 ~한'이라는 의미로 관용구처럼 쓰인다. 따라서 빈칸에는 형용사나 부사가 와야 하는데, 빈칸 앞에 '타동사 + 목적어'가 왔으므로 빈칸에는 동사 answer를 수식하는 부사가 와야 한다. 따라서 정답은 (D) accurately이다. 만약 be동사처럼 보어를 취하는 불완전자동사가 쓰이면 'as ~ as' 사이에 형용사가 온다.

번역 페레이라 컨설팅에 지원하는 구직자들은 지원서 질문 사항에 가능한 한 정확하게 답변해야 한다.

어휘 candidate 후보자, 지원자 position 직위 application form 신청서, 지원서 accurate 정확한 accuracy 정확(도) accurately 정확하게

4

해설 **the + 최상급:** 빈칸 앞에 정관사 the가 있고, 올해 출시된 여러 노트북 컴퓨터를 비교 대상으로 하는 것이므로 빈칸에는 최상급 형용사인 (D) most powerful이 정답이다.

번역 〈가제트 가이드 위클리〉가 올해 출시된 노트북 컴퓨터를 테스트했을 때 스타 1000이 성능이 가장 뛰어난 것으로 평가되었다.

어휘 laptop 노트북 컴퓨터 rate 평가하다

5

해설 **비교급 + than:** 빈칸 앞에는 비교급인 more convenient와 less expensive, 빈칸 뒤에는 비교 대상이 나오므로, '~보다'라는 의미의 (C) than이 정답이 된다.

번역 본사를 교외로 이전하는 것이 혼잡한 도심에 자리잡는 것보다 더 편리하고 저렴할 것입니다.

어휘 headquarters 본사 suburban 교외의 settle in ~에 자리잡다, 적응하다 congested 혼잡한 urban 도시의

6

해설 **비교급 + than:** 빈칸 뒤에 than이 있으므로 비교급 형용사인 (B) slower가 정답이다.

번역 제품 평가에서는 코지 데이즈 실내 난방기가 예열하는 것이 유사 제품들에 비해 느리다고 한다.

어휘   review 검토, 평가   warm up 예열하다, 준비 운동을
          하다   similar 비슷한

7

해설   **비교 구문의 품사 판단:** 'as + 형용사/부사 + as'는 '~만
         큼'이라는 뜻으로 동등 비교를 나타낸다. 빈칸에는 형용사
         나 부사가 와야 하는데, 동사가 보어를 취하는 불완전자동
         사인 be동사이므로 'as ~ as' 사이에 형용사가 온다. 따라
         서 정답은 (B) durable이다. 참고로, 동사가 타동사인 경
         우에는 부사가 온다.

번역   퍼머텍 화학의 연구원들은 일반 콘크리트보다 내구성이 2
         배 강한 새로운 물질을 연구하고 있다.

어휘   synthetics 합성 화학 (공업)   material 물질,
         원료   ordinary 평상의, 보통의   concrete 콘크리트
         durable 오래 견디는, 튼튼한

8

해설   **비교급 관용 표현:** 빈칸 뒤의 시점 표현 Friday, October
         28가 문제 해결의 단서로, '늦어도 10월 28일 금요일까
         지'라는 의미를 이루는 비교급 관용 표현인 (D) no later
         than이 정답이다.

번역   조기 등록비 혜택을 받으시려면, 신청서에 10월 28일 금요
         일자 이전의 소인이 찍혀야 합니다.

어휘   registration 등록, 기재   rate 비율, 요금
         application form 신청서, 신청 양식   postmark
         (수동형으로) 소인을 찍다   in advance 사전에
         beforehand 미리, 벌써   previously 이전에

9

해설   **비교급 강조 부사:** 빈칸 뒤에 온 비교급 표현 more
         qualified가 문제 해결의 단서로, 빈칸에는 비교급 강조
         부사가 들어가야 한다. 따라서 정답은 (A) much이다. '훨
         씬'이라고 해석하는 비교급 강조 부사에는 much, even,
         still, far, a lot 등이 있다.

번역   타카시 오타 씨가 다른 후보자들보다 훨씬 더 적임이라고 확
         신했기 때문에, 아그놈사는 그를 신임 부사장으로 채용했다.

어휘   confident 확신하는   qualified 적임인, 자격 있는
         candidate 후보자   vice president 부사장   rarely
         거의 ~않다   along ~을 따라

10

해설   **비교급 관용 표현:** 앞에 온 비교급 표현 higher than과 함
         께 '예상되었던 것보다 더 높은'이라는 의미를 완성할 수 있
         는 (B) predicted가 정답이다. than 뒤에 주어와 be동
         사가 생략되었기에 과거분사가 들어가야 하며, predicted
         대신 expected/anticipated도 쓰일 수 있다는 점도 함
         께 알아 두자.

번역   레델 에어라인의 2분기 수익은 일전에 예상되었던 것보다
         25% 더 높았다.

어휘   quarter (1/4)분기   profit 수익   previously 일전에,
         예전에   predict 예상하다

11

해설   **비교급 + than:** 빈칸은 be동사의 보어 자리이며, 빈칸 뒤
         에 than이 있으므로 형용사의 비교급이 와야 한다. 따라서
         정답은 (A) more efficient이다.

번역   회의를 하는 동안 제품 팀은 경쟁사의 최신 제품보다 자신
         들의 토스터 디자인이 더 효율적이라고 주장했다.

어휘   insist 주장하다   competition 경쟁, 경쟁자[사]
         latest 최신의   release 발매, 출시품   efficient
         효율적인

12

해설   **비교급 + than:** 빈칸 뒤에 than이 있으므로 비교급인 (C)
         later가 정답이다.

번역   몇몇 위원들이 지체되었기 때문에, 회계 보고서는 오늘 회
         의에서 예정보다 늦게 논의될 것입니다.

어휘   several 몇몇의   committee member 위원
         accounting 회계

13

해설   **비교 구문의 품사 판단:** 빈칸은 뒤에 나온 명사 ones를 수
         식하는 자리이므로 형용사가 와야 한다. 따라서 정답은 형
         용사의 비교급인 (C) darker이다. (D) darkest도 형용사
         이지만 최상급 앞에 붙어야 하는 소유격이나 the가 없으므
         로 빈칸에 오지 못한다. 참고로, than이 있는 문장에는 비
         교급을 반드시 써야 하지만, 비교급을 쓴다고 해서 반드시
         than이 수반되어야 하는 것은 아니다.

번역   관리부는 여름에 눈부심을 완화하기 위해 창문을 더 어두운
         것으로 교체했다.

어휘   maintenance 유지 보수, 관리   replace 교체하다
         reduce 줄이다, 완화하다   glare 환한 빛, 눈부심

14

해설   **one of the + 최상급:** 최상급과 어울리는 표현으로 가장 ~
         한 것들 중 하나'라는 의미를 나타내는 'one of the 최
         상급 + 복수명사'를 알면 풀 수 있는 문제이다. 따라서 정
         답은 '가장 큰 기술 회사들 중에 하나'라는 의미를 완성하
         는 (D) one이다. 나머지 보기들은 주어인 the resulting
         conglomerate와 동격을 이루지 못하므로 오답이다.

번역   오율라 기계가 멘지사와 합병한다면 그 결과로 출현하는 재
         벌 기업은 전 세계에서 가장 큰 기술 회사 중 하나가 될 것
         이다.

어휘   merge 합병하다   conglomerate 재벌 기업

15

해설 **비교급 + than:** 빈칸은 명사 ratings를 수식하는 형용사 자리이고 빈칸 뒤에 than이 나오므로, 형용사의 비교급 형태인 (A) higher가 정답이다.

번역 빨간색 포장은 고객 포커스 그룹에서 노란색 포장보다 더 높은 등급을 받았다.

어휘 packaging 포장 rating 등급 focus group 포커스 그룹(시장 조사를 위해 각 계층을 대표하도록 뽑은 사람들로 이뤄진 그룹)

16

해설 **비교급 + than:** 빈칸 뒤에 than이 있으므로 비교급인 (B) more가 정답이다. more than은 배수를 나타내는 동사인 double, triple 등의 앞에서 '~배 이상'이라는 의미를 나타낸다.

번역 겐트 국제 가전 전시회에서 트래버셀 대형 스크린 TV 세트가 발표된 이후 매출이 3배 이상 증가했다.

어휘 ever since ~이후로 계속 presentation (신제품 등의) 발표, 설명, 프레젠테이션 sales 매출 triple 3배가 되다, 3배로 만들다

17

해설 **the + 최상급:** 빈칸 앞에 정관사 the가 있고, 문맥상 '오늘날 시장에서 가장 경제적인 조명 시스템'이라는 의미가 되어야 한다. 따라서 형용사의 최상급 표현인 (C) most economical이 정답이다.

번역 노카리오사의 "코어 일루미네이션 솔루션"은 오늘날 시장에서 가장 경제적인 조명 시스템으로 건축가들에게 찬사를 받았다.

어휘 illumination 조명 praise 칭찬하다 architect 건축가 lighting system 조명 시스템 economize 절약하다 economically 경제적으로

18

해설 **최상급 관용 표현:** 문맥상 '아무리 늦어도 내일 오전까지'가 적합하므로 빈칸에는 (A) latest가 정답이다. at the latest는 특정한 시점 표현 바로 뒤에서 '아무리 늦어도'라는 뜻으로 쓰인다.

번역 회계 감사 기한을 맞추기 위하여 량 어소시에이츠의 회계사들은 아무리 늦어도 내일 오전까지는 모든 재무 보고서를 제출해야 한다.

어휘 meet a deadline 기한을 맞추다 audit 회계 감사 accountant 회계사 submit 제출하다 financial report 재무 보고서

19

해설 **the 비교급 + of the two:** '둘 중에서 더 ~한'이라는 의미로 두 개의 대상을 비교할 때는 'the + 비교급 + of the two'

구문을 쓴다. 따라서 정답은 비교급 형태인 (B) larger이다.

번역 두 법률 사무소 중 더 큰 곳인 맥럴랜 어소시에이츠는 현재 보조원을 몇 명 구한다는 구인 광고를 냈다.

어휘 law firm 법률 사무소 presently 지금, 현재 job opening 공석, 일자리 paralegal (변호사 및 법무사 사무실에서 법률 업무를 보조하는) 법률가 보조원

20

해설 **비교급 + than:** 빈칸 뒤에 than이 있으므로, 비교급 형태인 (D) more efficiently가 정답이다.

번역 스테이트 스트리트 사무소는 다른 어떤 지사보다 더 효율적으로 운영되고 있다는 이유로 회사 상을 받았다.

어휘 award 상 operate 운영되다 efficient 효율적인

UNIT 15	가정법과 도치

기출공식 1   본책 p. 134

1 (B)   **2** (B)   **3** (B)

1

해설 **조건절:** 주절의 동사가 미래 시제이므로, if절의 동사 자리인 빈칸에는 현재 시제가 들어가야 한다. 또한 빈칸 뒤 목적어가 없으므로 수동태이자 현재 시제인 (B) are received가 정답이다. 조건과 시간의 부사절에서는 현재가 미래를 대신하므로 will을 포함하고 있는 나머지 보기들은 오답이다.

번역 여름 내내 현재 속도로 주문이 들어온다면 투라무라 러기지 사는 매출 목표를 한 달 일찍 달성할 수 있을 것이다.

어휘 current 현재의 pace 페이스, 속도 meet 충족시키다, 맞추다 receive 받다, 접수하다

2

해설 **조건절:** 주절이 check로 시작하는 명령문이므로, if절의 동사 자리인 빈칸에는 현재 시제가 들어가야 한다. 따라서 (B) does not이 정답이다.

번역 만약 장난감이 작동하지 않으면 배터리가 제대로 들어 있는지, 그리고 스위치가 "on" 자리에 가 있는지 확인하세요.

어휘 operate 작동하다 insert 삽입하다 correctly 제대로

3

해설 **조건절:** if절의 동사가 현재 시제이므로, 주절의 동사 자리인 빈칸에는 '조동사의 원형 + 동사원형', 또는 명령문이 올 수 있다. 따라서 정답은 (B) can process이다.

번역 분실한 영수증을 제공하면 우리 부서에서 즉시 환급 요청을 처리할 수 있습니다.

어휘 receipt 영수증 reimbursement 환급
immediately 즉시 process 처리하다

기출공식 2	본책 p. 134
4 (C) **5** (D) **6** (B)	

4

해설 **가정법 과거:** 주절의 동사가 would go이므로 if절의 동사 자리인 빈칸에는 과거 시제가 들어가야 한다. 따라서 (C) had가 정답이다.

번역 만약 더글라스 공원에 놀이터가 있다면, 더 많은 가족들이 그곳에 갈 것이다.

어휘 playground 놀이터

5

해설 **가정법 과거:** 주절의 동사가 would not be이므로 if절의 동사 자리인 빈칸에는 과거 시제가 들어가야 한다. 따라서 (D) were reduced가 정답이다.

번역 만약 요금이 더 인하된다면, 버스 시스템은 재정적으로 버틸 수 없을 것이다.

어휘 fare 요금 financially 재정적으로 sustainable 버틸 수 있는 reduce 인하하다

6

해설 **가정법 과거:** if절의 동사가 과거 시제이므로, 주절의 동사 자리인 빈칸에는 '조동사의 과거형 + 동사원형'이 들어가야 한다. 따라서 정답은 (B) would become이다.

번역 우리가 안건을 미리 정하면 부서 회의 능률이 더 높아질 것이다.

어휘 efficient 능률이 높은 determine 결정하다 agenda 안건 in advance 미리

기출공식 3	본책 p. 135
7 (A) **8** (B) **9** (B)	

7

해설 **가정법 과거완료:** if절의 동사가 과거완료 시제이므로, 주절의 동사 자리인 빈칸에는 '조동사의 과거형 + have + p.p.'가 들어가야 한다. 또한 빈칸 뒤 주어인 the company가 동사 offer의 주체가 되므로 능동태인 (A) would have offered가 정답이다. offer는 to부정사를 목적어로 취하는 동사이며, 빈칸 뒤 to부정사가 offer의 목적어 역할을 하고 있다.

번역 만약 프린터가 배송 중에 파손되었다면, 회사는 키치다 씨에게 대체품을 보내 주겠다고 제안했을 것이다.

어휘 damage 파손하다 shipment 배송 replacement 대체, 대신하는 사람[것]

8

해설 **가정법 과거완료:** if절의 동사가 과거완료 시제이므로, 주절의 동사 자리인 빈칸에는 '조동사의 과거형 + have + p.p.'가 들어가야 한다. 따라서 정답은 (B) would have missed이다.

번역 만약 이 씨가 교정 과정에서 우리를 도와주지 않았더라면 우리는 보고서 마감일을 맞출 수 없었을 것이다.

어휘 proofreading 교정, 교열 process 과정 deadline 마감(일), 마감 기한

9

해설 **혼합가정법:** 주절의 동사가 might be인데 혼합가정법의 힌트가 될 수 있는 부사 now가 함께 쓰인 것으로 보아 if절의 동사 자리인 빈칸에는 과거완료 시제가 들어가는 것이 적합하다. 따라서 정답은 (B) had been이다.

번역 그 제안서가 더 자세했더라면, 도넬란 메뉴팩처링은 지금 우리 철강 부품의 유일한 공급업체일지도 모른다.

어휘 detailed 상세한, 자세한 supplier 공급업자

기출공식 4	본책 p. 135
10 (B) **11** (D) **12** (C)	

10

해설 **가정법 미래:** 빈칸은 if절의 동사 자리이므로 온전한 동사의 형태를 갖춘 (A) have와 (B) should have 중에서 선택해야 한다. (A) have는 3인칭 주어인 a client에 수 일치가 되지 않으므로 정답은 (B) should have이다. if절에 should를 쓴 가정법 미래이다.

번역 고객에게 혹시라도 이사 날 이후에 남은 이삿짐 상자가 있다면, 말탁 이사업체는 기꺼이 환불해 드리겠습니다.

어휘 moving box 이삿짐 상자 leave over ~을 남겨두다 purchase 구매하다

11

해설 **가정법 미래:** 빈칸은 if절의 동사 자리이므로 온전한 동사의 형태를 갖춘 (D) should be가 정답이다.

번역 혹시라도 땅이 최근 내린 비로 너무 젖어 있다면, 그 건설회사는 몰 스퀘어-2 프로젝트의 착공을 미룰 수 있다.

어휘 construction 건설 delay 미루다 groundbreaking 착공; 획기적인 rainfall 강우(량)

12

해설 **가정법 미래:** 주절이 '나에게 연락하라'라는 명령문이며, 빈칸은 '혹시라도 도움이 필요하다면'이라는 미래 상황에 대해 가정하는 내용이 와야 하므로, 정답은 (C) should require이다.

번역 혹시라도 도움이 필요하면, 이 이메일 주소로 저에게 연락만 하세요.

어휘 assistance 도움   require 필요하다

기출공식 5   본책 p. 136

13 (C)　　**14** (C)　　**15** (A)

13

해설 **가정법 도치:** 주절에 조동사 may가 있고, 조건절의 주어인 additional staff 다음에 be needed가 왔으므로, if가 생략되어 주어와 조동사가 도치된 가정법 미래 구문이라는 것을 알 수 있다. 따라서 (C) should가 정답이다. 참고로, 가정법 미래 구문의 주절에는 will 이외에도 shall, can, may가 쓰일 수 있다.

번역 행사 기간에 추가로 직원이 필요하다면, 잭슨 씨의 영업팀이 주말 무역 박람회의 우리 전시 부스에서 일할 수 있다.

어휘 exhibit 전시   trade show 무역 박람회   additional 추가적인

14

해설 **가정법 도치:** 'Had + 주어 + p.p.'로 문장이 시작되므로 가정법 과거완료의 도치 구문임을 알 수 있다. 따라서 주절의 동사는 '조동사의 과거형 + have + p.p.' 형태가 되어야 하므로 (C) would have added가 정답이다.

번역 의뢰인이 시장 조사를 할 시간을 더 많이 주었더라면, 우리는 설문 양식에 개방형 질문을 더 많이 추가할 수 있었을 것이다.

어휘 conduct 실시하다   open-ended question 개방형 질문   survey 설문

15

해설 **가정법 도치:** 주절의 동사가 'would + have + p.p.'이므로 if절에는 과거완료 시제가 와야 한다. 빈칸 뒤의 the recruiting team이 주어이며 동사의 일부분 received가 있으므로, 빈칸은 도치된 조동사가 와야 한다. 따라서 정답은 과거완료 시제를 만드는 조동사 (A) Had이다.

번역 채용팀이 온라인 채용 공고에서 더 많은 회신을 접수했더라면, 지원자 선발 과정이 더 길어졌을 것이다.

어휘 recruiting 채용   response 응답, 회신   job posting 채용 공고   candidate 지원자, 후보자   selection 선택, 선발   last 계속되다

기출공식 6   본책 p. 136

16 (B)　　**17** (C)　　**18** (D)

16

해설 **보어 도치:** 보어가 도치되어 문장 앞에 쓰이는 경우에는 '보어 + 동사 + 주어'의 어순이 된다. 따라서 보어 역할을 할 수 있는 형용사 (B) Enclosed가 정답이다. 명사인 (A) Enclosure는 '동봉된 것'을 나타낼 때 가산명사로 쓰이므로 관사 없이 쓸 수 없다.

번역 저희 주문 절차와 배송 정책에 대한 상세 정보도 포함된 제품 카탈로그를 동봉합니다.

어휘 detailed 상세한   procedure 절차   shipping 배송 policy 정책

17

해설 **보어 도치:** an application 이하가 문장의 주어이고 is가 동사, 빈칸은 보어 자리로 해당 문장은 보어 도치 구문이다. 신청서가 '첨부되어 있는'이라는 의미가 적절하므로 과거분사인 (C) Attached가 정답이다. 명사인 (D) Attachment는 '첨부된 것'을 나타낼 때 가산명사로 쓰이므로 관사 없이 쓸 수 없다.

번역 항공교통 관제사 교육 프로그램에 참여하기 위한 신청서를 첨부합니다.

어휘 application 신청(서)   participate in ~에 참여하다 air traffic controller 항공교통 관제사   attach 첨부하다   attachment 첨부(한 것)

18

해설 **보어 도치:** a guide 이하가 문장의 주어이고 is가 동사, 빈칸은 보어 자리로 해당 문장은 보어 도치 구문이다. 꾸러미에 '포함되어 있는'이라는 의미가 적절하므로 과거분사인 (D) Included가 정답이다. 명사인 (B) Inclusion은 '포함된 것'을 나타낼 때 가산명사로 쓰이므로 관사 없이 쓸 수 없다.

번역 이 꾸러미에는 콘퍼런스 센터 인근 식당에 대한 안내가 포함되어 있다.

어휘 packet 꾸러미   eatery 식당   include 포함하다 inclusion 포함(된 것)

기출공식 7   본책 p. 137

19 (A)　　**20** (A)　　**21** (C)

19

해설 **부정어 도치:** market conditions가 문장의 주어이고, have been이 동사인데, have가 주어 앞으로 도치된 문

장이다. 따라서 문두에 놓여 주어와 동사를 도치시킬 수 있는 부정 부사 (A) Seldom이 정답이다.

번역 신규 주택을 구입하기에 시장 상황이 이렇게 좋았던 적은 거의 없었다.

어휘 condition 여건, 조건   ideal 이상적인

20

해설 **부정어 도치:** 빈칸 뒤에 주어와 동사가 도치된 구조가 문제 해결의 단서로, 빈칸에는 부정어가 들어갈 수 있다. 따라서 정답은 (A) Not only이다.

번역 에미코 이마무라는 작품이 널리 출간된 시인일 뿐 아니라 뛰어난 화가이자 조각가이다.

어휘 publish (책 등을) 출간하다   poet 시인
accomplished 기량이 뛰어난, 재주가 많은   sculptor 조각가

21

해설 **부정어 도치:** 빈칸 뒤에 주어와 동사가 도치된 구조가 문제 해결의 단서로, 빈칸에는 부정어가 들어갈 수 있다. 따라서 정답은 부정 부사 (C) Rarely이다. 참고로, 일반동사가 쓰인 문장의 도치 구문에서는 do/does/did가 주어 앞으로 오고 주어 뒤에 동사원형이 온다.

번역 벨랑지에 살롱은 머리손질 서비스에 대해 부정적인 평가를 받는 경우가 좀체 없다.

어휘 receive 받다   rarely 좀체 ~하지 않는

기출공식 8		본책 p. 137
22 (D)	**23** (D)	**24** (A)

22

해설 **neither 도치:** 빈칸 뒤에 동사 will과 주어 Mr. Jefferson이 도치되어 있는 어순이 문제 해결의 단서로, 빈칸에는 so 또는 neither를 쓸 수 있다. 해당 문장은 not을 포함한 부정문이므로 (D) neither가 정답이다.

번역 박 씨는 제품 소개에 참석할 수 없는데, 제퍼슨 씨 역시 참석할 수 없을 것이다.

어휘 sales presentation 제품 소개

23

해설 **so 도치:** 빈칸 뒤에 동사 did와 주어 audiences가 도치되어 있는 어순이 문제 해결의 단서로, 빈칸에는 so 또는 neither를 쓸 수 있다. 해당 문장은 긍정문이므로 (D) so가 정답이다. 참고로, (A) as는 접속사 and와 so의 역할을 동시에 할 수 있으므로 and가 없는 문장에서 정답이 될 수 있다.

번역 평론가들은 영화에서 이케다 씨의 연기를 좋아했고 관객들도 마찬가지였다.

어휘 critic 평론가   performance 연기   audience 관객

24

해설 **only 도치:** only가 이끄는 부사구 Only on "Casual Fridays"가 문두로 가면서 주어인 employees stationed at the front desk와 조동사 can이 도치된 문장이다. 조동사 뒤에는 동사원형이 들어가야 하므로 (A) wear가 정답이다.

번역 프런트에 배치된 직원들은 '평상복 입는 금요일'에만 청바지를 입을 수 있다.

어휘 station 배치하다

ETS **TEST**				본책 p. 138
1 (B)	**2** (C)	**3** (A)	**4** (B)	**5** (A)
6 (A)	**7** (B)	**8** (B)	**9** (B)	**10** (A)
11 (C)	**12** (D)	**13** (D)	**14** (B)	**15** (D)
16 (B)	**17** (B)	**18** (C)	**19** (A)	**20** (D)

1

해설 **가정법 과거완료:** 'Had + 주어 + p.p.'로 문장이 시작되므로 가정법 과거완료의 도치 구문임을 알 수 있다. 따라서 주절의 동사는 '조동사의 과거형 + have + p.p.' 형태가 되어야 하므로 (B) would have merged가 정답이다.

번역 협상이 막판에 결렬되지 않았다면 로레아노사는 주요 경쟁사인 트레비노-마틴과 합병했을 것이다.

어휘 negotiation 협상, 교섭   break down (계획·교섭 등이) 실패하다   at the last minute 마지막 순간에, 막판에   competitor 경쟁자, 경쟁 기업   merge 합병하다

2

해설 **so 도치:** 접속사 as가 이끄는 종속절과 빈칸이 있는 주절로 이루어진 문장인데, 주절에 본동사가 없으므로 보기 중 (대)동사가 있는 (C) so does가 정답이 된다. 여기서 does는 climbs를 대체하며, so와 함께 쓰여 '수요도 늘고 있다'라는 의미를 완성시킨다. 'So + (대)동사 + 주어'는 긍정의 진술에 덧붙여 '~도 또한 …하다'라는 뜻으로 쓰인다.

번역 공공 수영 시설을 방문하는 지역 주민 수가 늘어남에 따라 그들을 감독할 인명 구조원에 대한 수요 또한 늘고 있다.

어휘 resident 주민   facility 시설   climb 오르다, 상승하다   lifeguard (수영장의) 인명 구조원   supervise 감독하다   as long as ~하는 한   whereas ~에 반하여   as to ~에 관하여

3

해설 **조건절:** if절의 동사가 현재 시제(rises)이므로, 주절에는 현재 또는 미래 시제가 가능하다. 따라서 정답은 (A) will affect이다.

번역 원자재 비용이 상승하면 완제품의 가격에 영향을 미칠 것이다.

어휘 **raw material** 원료, 원자재 **finished product** 완제품 **affect** 영향을 미치다

4

해설 **가정법 도치:** 주절의 미래 시제와 호응하려면 종속절은 '혹시라도 어떠한 일이 생긴다면'이라는 의미의 가정법 미래가 되어야 한다. 가정법의 if절에서 if가 생략되면 조동사와 주어가 도치되므로 정답은 (B) Should이다.

번역 앨러웨이 은행의 온라인 계좌에 접속하는 데 어려움이 있다면 저희 고객서비스 담당자가 기쁜 마음으로 도와 드릴 것입니다.

어휘 **difficulty** 어려움, 장애 **access** 접속하다 **account** 계좌, 계정

5

해설 **혼합가정법:** if절의 동사가 had p.p.로 과거완료인데 주절에 혼합가정법의 힌트가 될 수 있는 부사 today가 쓰인 것으로 보아 빈칸에는 'would + 동사원형'이 와야 한다. 따라서 정답은 (A) would have이다.

번역 부품이 더 일찍 도착했다면 우리가 오늘 면밀하게 수리할 시간이 더 많을 텐데.

어휘 **part** 부품 **careful** 면밀한, 꼼꼼한 **repair** 수리

6

해설 **only 도치:** only가 이끄는 부사절(Only after ~ stadium)이 문장 맨 앞으로 가면서 주절의 주어 the downtown area와 조동사 did가 도치된 문장이다. 따라서 빈칸에는 동사원형이 들어가야 하므로, (A) become이 정답이다.

번역 그 도시가 새 경기장을 지은 후에야 도심 지역이 타지에서 온 관광객에게 인기를 끌게 되었다.

어휘 **stadium** 경기장 **popular** 인기가 있는 **out-of-town** 타지에서 온

7

해설 **조건절:** 빈칸 앞 절에서 모든 표가 환불될 것이라고 했으므로, 문맥상 뒤에 오는 절이 '경기가 취소된다면'이라는 가정 상황 및 조건을 나타내야 자연스럽다. 따라서 '만일 ~한다면'을 의미하는 (B) if가 정답이다.

번역 만일 악천후로 축구 경기가 취소된다면, 모든 표를 환불해 드릴 것입니다.

어휘 **refund** 환불하다 **cancel** 취소하다

8

해설 **장소 부사구 도치:** 부사구인 Next to the Rostovsky Hotel이 문두로 오면서 주어 a luxurious recreational area와 빈칸 자리에 올 동사가 도치된 문장이다. 주어가 a luxurious recreational area로 단수이므로 빈칸에는 단수동사인 (B) is가 적절하다.

번역 로스토브스키 호텔 옆에는 골프장과 수영장이 완비된 호화로운 휴양 시설이 있다.

어휘 **next to ~** 옆에 **luxurious** 사치스러운, 호화로운, 고급스러운 **complete with** ~이 완비된[갖춰진] **golf course** 골프장

9

해설 **가정법 과거완료:** if절의 동사가 과거완료 시제이므로, 주절의 동사 자리인 빈칸에는 '조동사의 과거형 + have + p.p.'가 들어가야 한다. 또한 빈칸 뒤에 목적어가 오지 않았으므로 수동태인 (B) have been confronted가 정답이다.

번역 만약 헤르난데스 씨가 회사를 위한 자신의 계획안들을 주주들에게 명확히 밝혔더라면 아마도 그런 비난에 직면하지 않았을 것이다.

어휘 **criticism** 비판 **stockholder** 주주 **be confronted with** ~에 직면하다

10

해설 **부정어 도치:** 콤마 뒤의 but ~ also가 문제 해결의 단서로, 'not only A but (also) B' 구조가 와야 한다. 따라서 정답은 (A) Not only이며, 부정어구가 문두로 오면서 도치된 문장이다.

번역 가리자 씨는 수상 경력이 있는 스포소 인의 주방장일 뿐 아니라 인기 있는 요리책 4권의 저자이기도 하다.

어휘 **award-winning** 수상한, 수상 경력이 있는 **cookbook** 요리책

11

해설 **neither 도치:** 빈칸 뒤에 동사 is와 주어 Ms. Hakkonen이 도치되어 있는 어순이 문제 해결의 단서로, 빈칸에는 so 또는 neither를 쓸 수 있다. 해당 문장은 not을 포함한 부정문이므로 (C) neither가 정답이다.

번역 헤르난데스 씨는 작업반원들이 도착하기로 예정된 때에 시간이 나지 않으며, 하코넨 씨도 마찬가지이다.

어휘 **not available** (누군가가) 시간이 나지 않는, 바쁜 **crew** (같은 일에 종사하는) 반, 조

12

해설 **가정법 도치:** 주절에 '조동사의 과거형 + 동사원형'이 왔으므로, 가정법 과거 구문이라는 것을 알 수 있다. 따라서 빈칸이 포함된 절이 'If + 주어 + 과거 동사'의 형태가 되어야 하는데 if가 생략되었으므로, 빈칸에는 주어(Mr. Park)와 도치된 be동사 (D) Were가 들어가야 한다.

번역 | 박 씨가 타 지역으로 출장을 가지 않는다면, 그가 신입 수습 사원들을 위한 오늘 연수 교육을 이끌 텐데.

어휘 | out of town 도시를 떠나서 lead 이끌다 training session 연수 교육

13

해설 | **조건절:** 주절인 명령문에서 '고객 지원 센터에 전화하세요'라고 했으므로, 빈칸으로 시작하는 절이 '조립 설명서가 명확하지 않다고 생각되면'이라는 가정 상황 및 조건을 나타내야 자연스럽다. 따라서 '만일 ~한다면'을 의미하는 (D) if가 정답이다.

번역 | 조립 설명서가 명확하지 않다고 생각된다면 고객 지원 센터에 전화하세요.

어휘 | assembly 조립 instructions 설명, 지시 unclear 명확하지 않은 support 지원

14

해설 | **가정법 과거완료:** 문장 중간에 'had + 주어 + p.p.' 구조가 온 것으로 보아 가정법 과거완료의 도치 구문임을 알 수 있다. 따라서 주절의 동사는 '조동사 과거형 + have p.p.'의 형태가 되어야 하므로, (B) would have relinquished가 정답이다.

번역 | 스타잔 엔터프라이지즈와의 합병이 성공했더라면 정 씨는 코스믹 게이밍사의 최고경영자직을 그만두었을 것이다.

어휘 | merger 합병 relinquish 포기하다, 내주다

15

해설 | **보어 도치:** 보어가 문두에 와서 주어 the latest listing과 동사 is가 도치된 문장이다. 문맥상 '최신 목록이 동봉되다'라는 수동의 의미가 되어야 하므로 과거분사인 (D) Enclosed가 정답이다.

번역 | 우리 회사의 전문 컨설팅 서비스를 이용하는 명망 있는 회사 및 단체의 최신 목록을 동봉합니다.

어휘 | listing 목록, 명단 institution 단체, 기관 firm 회사 specialized 전문화된, 전문적인 consulting service 자문 서비스 enclosed 동봉한

16

해설 | **혼합가정법:** if절의 동사가 had p.p.로 과거완료인데 주절에 혼합가정법의 힌트가 될 수 있는 부사구 this week가 쓰인 것으로 보아 빈칸에는 'would + 동사원형'이 와야 한다. 따라서 (B) would be가 정답이다.

번역 | 만약 우리가 1층 대형 설명회장을 예약했더라면, 이번 주에 하는 모든 워크숍을 사내에서 진행할 수 있을 텐데.

어휘 | reserve 예약하다 hold 개최하다 on-site 내부의, 현장의

17

해설 | **가정법 도치:** 주절의 동사가 'would + have + p.p.'이므로 if절에는 과거완료 시제가 와야 한다. 빈칸 뒤의 the staff가 주어이며 동사의 일부인 worked가 있으므로, 빈칸은 도치된 조동사가 와야 한다. 따라서 정답은 과거완료 시제를 만드는 조동사 (B) Had이다.

번역 | 직원들이 토요일과 일요일에 그렇게 열성적으로 일하지 않았더라면, 우리의 주말 도서 매출은 실패였을 것이다.

어휘 | enthusiastically 열성적으로 failure 실패 regarding ~에 대하여

18

해설 | **조건절:** 빈칸은 완전한 절을 이끄는 접속사 자리이며, 주절이 명령문으로 왔으므로 '만약 ~하고 싶으면 …하라'라는 조건의 의미를 이루는 (C) If가 정답이다.

번역 | 호텔 편의 시설의 전체 목록을 보고 싶으시면, 귀하의 객실 책상 위의 정보 바인더를 참조하세요.

어휘 | complete 전부의, 완전한 amenities 편의 시설 refer to 참조하다 informational 정보의 binder (종이 등을 함께 묶는) 바인더 guest room 객실

19

해설 | **혼합가정법:** if절의 동사가 had p.p.로 과거완료인데 주절에 혼합가정법의 힌트가 될 수 있는 부사 now가 쓰인 것으로 보아 빈칸에는 '조동사의 과거형 + 동사원형'이 와야 한다. 따라서 (A) could have가 정답이다.

번역 | 만약 우리가 새 로고 디자인을 더 일찍 보았더라면, 지금쯤 그 제품을 광고하는 방법에 대해 더 좋은 아이디어를 갖고 있을 텐데.

어휘 | market 광고하다

20

해설 | **조건절:** 빈칸 앞 주절에서 '구매한 상품은 반품이 가능하다'라고 했으므로, 빈칸으로 시작하는 절이 '영수증 원본이 동반되는 경우에만'이라는 유일한 조건을 진술해야 자연스럽다. 따라서 정답은 (D) only if이다. 참고로, if절은 주어와 be동사가 생략되고 과거분사(accompanied)만 남긴 부사절 축약 구조이다.

번역 | 모든 노츠 하드웨어 가게에서 구매한 상품은 영수증 원본이 동반되는 경우에만 반품이 가능하다.

어휘 | hardware store 철물점 return 반품하다 accompany 동반하다 original 원본의

PART 5 VOCABULRARY

UNIT 01 ETS 빈출 동사

VOCA PRACTICE
본책 p. 149

1 (A)	2 (B)	3 (B)	4 (A)	5 (B)
6 (B)	7 (A)	8 (C)	9 (C)	10 (D)
11 (C)	12 (D)	13 (A)	14 (A)	15 (B)

1

별도로 **통지를 받기(notified)** 전에는 건물에 들어오지 마십시오.

어휘 otherwise 달리, 다르게 realize 깨닫다

2

기계 수리 비용은 새 제품 구입보다 절반의 **비용이 들었다(cost)**.

어휘 half as much as 절반만큼

3

이사는 일정이 겹쳐 회의를 **연기했다(postponed)**.

어휘 director 임원, 이사 scheduling conflict 일정 겹침 evaluate 평가하다

4

회사가 당신의 출장 경비를 전액 **환급해 줄 것이다(reimburse)**.

어휘 fully 완전히 travel expense 출장 경비

5

만약 최근에 멤버십을 갱신하셨다면 이 통지를 **무시해 주세요 (disregard)**.

어휘 renew 갱신하다 expire 만료되다, 만기가 되다

6

다음 세미나에 **필요한(required)** 모든 자료들은 복사해야 한다.

어휘 material 자료, 재료 upcoming 다가오는, 곧 있을

7

인사동 이미지스에서는 마치코 나카무라를 새로운 선임 그래픽 디자이너로 자랑스럽게 **소개합니다(introduces)**.

어휘 proudly 자랑스럽게 accomplish 완수하다, 성취하다

8

해설 '가까운 곳을 찾는다'는 의미로 '~의 위치를 알아내다'는 뜻의 (C) locate가 정답이다. 수동태 표현인 be located at[in](~에 위치해 있다)도 자주 나온다.

번역 가장 가까운 아델레 의류점을 찾으려면 풀다운 메뉴에서 당신의 주 또는 국가를 선택하세요.

어휘 pull-down 접는 식의, 펼쳐지는 afford ~할 여유가 있다

9

해설 '특이 사항을 상술하라'는 뜻으로 (C) specify가 정답이다. 이때 on the back ~ form은 전치사구로, specify의 목적어는 any special dietary needs임에 주의한다.

번역 밀러 케이터링의 고객들은 특별히 필요한 음식이 있으면 양식서 뒷면에 기재해야 합니다.

어휘 form 양식서 dietary 음식물의, 규정식의 initiate 시작하다 permit 허용하다

10

해설 빈칸 뒤 목적어와 의미가 가장 자연스럽게 통하는 동사를 선택한다. '직원들을 감독한다'는 의미의 (D) oversees가 정답이다. (B) explains의 목적어로는 설명하고자 하는 내용이 와야 하며, '직원들에게 설명한다'는 explain to workers로 표현한다.

번역 포델 자동차 공장에서, 크리스틀 씨는 리빌트 엔진을 자동차에 설치하는 직원들을 감독한다.

어휘 automotive 자동차의 plant 공장 install 설치하다 rebuilt 다시 조립된 conduct 수행하다 explain 설명하다 invest 투자하다 oversee 감독하다

11

해설 '계약하기 전에 조건들을 수정하다'라는 의미로 (C) modify가 정답이다. modify는 '부분적으로 변경[수정]하다'라는 뜻이다.

번역 굽타 씨는 자신의 고용계약서에 서명하기 전에 조건들을 수정하길 희망한다.

어휘 terms 조건 deprive 빼앗다 respond to ~에 응답[반응]하다 assure A of[that] A에게 ~을 확신시키다

12

해설 '지연 따위의 문제를 겪지 않았다'는 뜻으로 '겪다'라는 뜻의 (D) experienced가 정답이다.

번역 에몬 모터사는 이번 분기에 생산이나 대리점 배송에서 어떠한 지연도 겪지 않았다.

어휘 exert (힘 따위를) 쓰다 submit 제출하다 represent 대표하다

13

해설 '~을 대표[대신]하다'라는 뜻으로 (A) represent가 정답이다.

번역 홍보 담당 부사장인 임명희는 2월 14일 주주총회에서 카비 파이낸셜을 대표하게 될 것이다.

어휘 shareholder 주주 furnish 가구를 비치하다, 공급하다 indicate 나타내다 perform 행하다

14

해설 '방이 ~ 용도로 지정되다'라는 의미로 (A) designated가 정답이다.

번역 그 계획안에 따르면 새 건물의 동쪽 별관에 있는 상당수의 방이 저장소로 지정될 것이다.

어휘 wing 별관 storage 저장 detain 붙들다, 지체하게 하다 reciprocate ~에 보답하다 signify 의미하다, 나타내다

15

해설 전치사 to가 해결의 단서로 'direct A to B'는 'A를 B로 보내다'라는 뜻이다. 따라서 '질문을 배 씨에게 보내다'라는 뜻으로 (B) direct가 정답이다. 참고로, 이때의 동의어는 address, refer가 있다.

번역 새 안전 절차를 검토한 후 궁금한 점이 있으면 내선번호 2528번으로 배 씨에게 문의하세요.

어휘 safety procedures 안전 절차 inquire 질문하다

UNIT 02	ETS 빈출 동사 어구

VOCA PRACTICE
본책 p. 154

1 (A)	2 (A)	3 (B)	4 (A)	5 (B)
6 (B)	7 (A)	8 (C)	9 (A)	10 (C)
11 (C)	12 (B)	13 (A)	14 (A)	15 (B)

1
애버리 씨는 오늘 회의실에 화상 회의 시스템을 **준비할 것이다**(set up).

어휘 videoconference 영상[화상] 회의 strive to ~하려고 분투하다 애쓰다

2
정전 때문에 환기 시스템이 곧 **멈출 것이다**(shut down).

어휘 ventilation 통풍, 환기 shortly 곧 power failure 정전 look out (경고하는 말로) 조심해라

3
저희는 법률 문제를 **전문으로 다룹니다**(specialize).

어휘 legal 법률과 관련된, 합법적인 document 기록하다; 문서

4
직원들은 그 교육 강좌를 들으라고 **재촉을 받는다**(urged).

어휘 allege 혐의를 제기하다[주장하다]

5
스마트폰이 **고장 날**(breaks down) 경우에 대비해 영수증을 보관하세요.

어휘 receipt 영수증, 수령 in case ~인 경우에 대비하여 turn down 거절하다

6
직원들은 문을 잠그고 퇴근하라고 **알림을 받는다**(reminded).

어휘 leave for the day 퇴근하다 comment 논평하다; 논평

7
모든 문의 사항은 책임자에게 **전달되어야 한다**(forwarded).

어휘 inquiry 문의 director 책임자, 관리자 rely (on/upon) 의지하다

8
해설 '이전 분기에 비해'가 적합하므로 (C) compared가 정답이다.

번역 래드너 연구소가 발표한 4분기 보고서에 따르면, 총수익은 이전 분기 대비 약 20퍼센트 늘어났다.

어휘 quarter 4분의 1, 분기(1년의 4분의 1) revenue 수익, 수입 previous 이전의

9
해설 '통행증을 받다'라는 뜻으로 (A) obtain이 정답이다.

번역 방문객들은 방문자 통행증을 받으려면 보안 창구에서 서명하고 사진이 부착된 신분증을 제시해야 한다.

어휘 security 보안 photo identification 사진이 부착된 신분증 require A to B A로 하여금 B하게 하다 be involved in ~에 관여하다

10
해설 '수행해야 하는 업무'가 적합하므로 '수행하다'라는 뜻의 (C) carry out이 정답이다.

번역 오가와 씨가 수행해야 하는 임무는 그녀의 고용 계약서에 설명되어 있다.

어휘 outline 설명하다 employment agreement 고용 계약(서) turn in 돌려 주다, 반납하다

11

해설 '사용을 삼가라'는 내용이 적합하므로 from과 함께 쓰는 (C) refrain이 정답이다. '금지하다'라는 뜻의 prevent와 forbid는 타동사로, 'prevent[forbid] A from B'와 같이 쓴다.

번역 다른 승객들에 대한 배려로 열차에서는 휴대폰 사용을 삼가기 바랍니다.

어휘 out of consideration ~에 대한 배려로 dismiss 해고하다 forbid 금지하다

12

해설 '회담에 가담하다'라는 의미가 적절하므로 in과 함께 쓰여 '~에 관여하다'라는 뜻이 되는 (B) engaged가 정답이다. (A) involved는 be involved in(~에 관여하다)처럼 수동태로 써야 가능하다.

번역 퍼렐리 철강은 제조업체 일부를 매입하기 위해 몬테그 섬유와 협의해 왔다.

어휘 manufacturing 제조 demonstrate 입증하다 maintain 유지하다

13

해설 '회의를 이끌다'라는 lead a session이 기본 표현으로, (A) lead가 정답이다. lead는 '사람[단체]을 이끌다'라는 뜻으로도 쓰이며, 자동사인 경우 lead to(~라는 결과를 낳다)처럼 쓰이기도 한다.

번역 우리 회사 복리 후생 담당자인 오버린 씨는 정규직 직원들을 위해 8월 12일에 설명회를 열 것이다.

어휘 benefits 복지 혜택 full-time 정규직의 regard 간주하다

14

해설 '식을 거행하다'는 표현은 hold a ceremony이다. 이 구문의 수동태 문장으로 (A) held가 정답이다.

번역 시상식은 파크 스테이션 호텔 3층에서 열릴 것이다.

어휘 awards ceremony 시상식 raise ~을 올리다 grant ~을 허가하다, 수여하다

15

해설 '성명서를 발표하다'라는 뜻의 issue a statement를 완성하는 (B) issue가 정답이다.

번역 아갈사의 최고 경영자는 이번 주 나중에 언론에 성명서를 발표할 것으로 예상된다.

어휘 be expected to ~할 것으로 예상되다 the press 언론 later this week 이번 주 나중에 act as ~로서 행동하다 speak to[with] A about B A에게 B에 관해 말하다

ETS TEST
본책 p. 155

1 (B)	2 (D)	3 (B)	4 (C)	5 (A)
6 (D)	7 (A)	8 (B)	9 (A)	10 (D)
11 (A)	12 (D)	13 (A)	14 (B)	15 (A)
16 (D)	17 (A)	18 (B)	19 (B)	20 (D)
21 (A)	22 (C)	23 (A)	24 (D)	25 (A)
26 (A)	27 (C)	28 (B)	29 (C)	30 (C)

1

해설 '안전 규정을 시행하다'라는 의미가 적절하므로 '시행하다'라는 뜻의 (B) enforce가 정답이다.

번역 효율적인 감시 없이 안전 규정을 시행하는 건 어려울 것이다.

어휘 safety regulations 안전 규정 effective 효과적인 monitor 모니터하다, 감시하다 entrust (일을) 맡기다 imply 암시하다, 내포하다 implore 애원하다, 간청하다

2

해설 '순수익이 떨어진 것을 타사와의 치열한 경쟁 탓으로 돌렸다'라는 의미가 적절하므로 'attribute A to B(A를 B의 탓으로 돌리다)'를 완성하는 (D) attributed가 정답이다.

번역 페일스 북스토어스는 올해 순이익이 20퍼센트 하락했다고 발표했는데, 이 회사는 이것을 율 북셀러스사와의 치열한 경쟁에서 기인한 결과로 보았다.

어휘 net profit 순이익 fierce 치열한, 극심한 competition 경쟁 accuse 고발하다, 비난하다 present 제시하다, 제출하다 disapprove 못마땅해하다, 불만을 나타내다

3

해설 목적어인 '절차(process)'와 호응하는 '간소화하다'가 가장 적절하다. 따라서 (B) streamlining이 정답이다.

번역 가구 운송 절차를 간소화함으로써, 우리는 비용을 낮추고 배송 시간을 절반으로 줄일 수 있다.

어휘 outpace ~을 능가하다 persevere 인내하다 forestall 미연에 방지하다

4

해설 목적어는 '수하물 비용(baggage fee)'이다. 클럽 회원들을 위해서라면 그 '비용을 받지 않고 면제한다'는 뜻이 어울리므로 (C) waive가 정답이다.

번역 와인콧 항공은 자사의 스카이 플라이어 클럽 회원에게는 15파운드의 수하물 비용을 면제해 줄 것이라고 발표했다.

어휘 prove (to be) ~라는 것이 입증되다 cost A B A에게 B의 비용이 들다 align 정렬하다

5

해설 '인식을 높이다'라는 의미가 적합하므로 (A) raise가 정답이다.

번역 이 광고 캠페인은 시 공원의 새로운 분리 수거함에 대한 대중의 인식을 높여야 한다.

어휘 recycling bin 재활용 수거함 reply to ~에 대답하다 inquire ~을 묻다 react to ~에 반응하다

6

해설 회사의 확장으로 인해 일자리가 창출될 것이므로 '~한 결과를 낳다'라는 의미의 (D) result in이 정답이다. 참고로, '~의 원인이다'라고 할 때는 result from을 쓴다.

번역 그 기업의 남미 지역으로의 확장은 100개 이상의 일자리를 창출할 것이다.

어휘 expansion 확장 creation 창조 restore A to B A를 B로 되돌리다 research into ~을 조사하다

7

해설 '성장(growth)'이 '감소(decrease)'를 '상쇄하다'가 적합하므로 '상쇄하다'라는 뜻의 (A) offset이 정답이다.

번역 리넬라 미디어 그룹은 작년에 새로운 미디어 분야의 수익 성장이 텔레비전 광고의 감소를 상쇄하도록 도와주었음을 시사했다.

어휘 growth 성장, 발전 revenue 수입 outplay 패배시키다 input 입력하다 overact 지나치게 행동하다

8

해설 '그래프가 추가 상승을 보여 주다'가 적합하므로 '(도표·삽화 등으로) 보여 주다'를 뜻하는 (B) illustrates가 정답이다.

번역 연간 회계 요약에서 선 그래프는 지난해에 걸쳐 수익이 추가 상승했음을 보여 준다.

어휘 determine 알아내다, 결정하다 consider 간주하다 account (for) ~을 설명하다

9

해설 '여러 정책을 시행하다'가 적합하므로 '실시하다'라는 뜻의 (A) instituted가 정답이다. 참고로, 정책이나 규칙 등과 함께 쓰여 '실시하다'로 쓸 수 있는 기타 동사로는 enforce, implement가 있다.

번역 피에르 던은 델번 제조사의 사장으로 근무할 때, 회사를 변화시킨 여러 가지 정책을 실시했다.

어휘 serve as ~의 역할을 하다 transform 바꾸다 relieve 완화하다, 줄이다 fabricate 조립하다, 제작하다

10

해설 빈칸 뒤에 목적어가 없으므로 보기 중 자동사를 찾아야 한다. '등록하다'라는 뜻의 자동사 (D) register가 정답이다. 나머지 보기들은 주로 타동사로 쓰이는 동사들이다.

번역 모든 공장 방문객은 생산 구역으로 들어가기 전 반드시 안내 데스크에서 등록해야 한다.

어휘 claim ~을 주장하다 distribute 나누어 주다 reveal 드러내다

11

해설 전치사 with와 함께 사용하는 자동사로 '~을 처리하다, 다루다'를 의미하는 (A) dealing이 정답이다.

번역 법무팀은 제조업체의 책임에 관해 최근 고등법원의 판결이 의미하는 바를 토의하기 위해 이번 주에 회의를 할 것이다.

어휘 legal department 법무팀 implication 함축, 함의 high court 고등법원 liability 책임 bear with ~을 견디다, 참다 enact 제정하다 separate 분리하다

12

해설 전치사 to와 함께 '~에 기여하다'라는 의미를 이루는 (D) contribute가 정답이다. 참고로, contribute는 자동사와 타동사의 쓰임이 모두 출제된다. 나머지 보기들은 모두 타동사로 출제된다.

번역 마운트 허드슨 수련원의 기술 장비 업그레이드는 학생들을 위한 더 나은 학습 경험에 기여할 것이다

어휘 offer ~을 제공하다 submit ~을 제출하다 donate ~을 기부하다

13

해설 빈칸 뒤에 주어인 전자레인지에 대한 두 가지 특징이 나열되고 있으므로 '특징으로 하다'라는 뜻의 동사 (A) features가 정답이다.

번역 다바토 산업에서 나온 최신 전자레인지는 스테인리스강 내부와 10개의 가열 메뉴가 특징이다.

어휘 microwave oven 전자레인지 produce 생산하다 imply 암시하다 appoint 임명하다, (시간·장소 등을) 정하다

14

해설 목적어로 나온 to부정사가 문제 해결의 단서로, 목적어로 to부정사를 취할 수 있는 동사를 선택해야 한다. 따라서 '~할 수 있다'라는 뜻의 (B) afford가 정답이다.

번역 어떤 회사도 제품을 팔기 위해 브랜드 파워에만 영원히 의존할 수는 없다.

어휘 strength 힘 be required to ~해야 한다 be supposed to ~할 예정이다 depend on ~에 의존하다

15

해설 목적어로 회사명이 나오므로, 회사를 '인수하다'라는 뜻의 (A) acquire가 정답이다. acquire는 '지식, 목표' 등의 명사가 목적어로 올 때는 '획득하다'라는 의미로도 쓰인다. 참고로, 회사명과 함께 쓰여 '합병하다'라는 뜻을 나타내는 merge with도 알아 두자.

번역 프로네스티사는 수익성 있는 컴퓨터 소프트웨어 회사인 XBR 테크놀러지를 인수하기 위해 5억 파운드를 지불했다.

어휘 profitable 수익성이 있는 achieve (성과·목적 등을) 달성하다 yield 산출[생산]하다

16

해설 '불필요한 지출을 없애다'가 적합하므로 '제거하다'라는 뜻의 (D) remove를 쓴다.

번역 시의회 의원인 엘레나 토레스는 호웰 시 예산에서 불필요한 지출을 없애는 방법을 찾도록 요청 받았다.

어휘 identify 찾다, 파악하다 unnecessary 불필요한 expense 경비, 지출 distribute 분배하다 exhaust 다 써버리다 empty 비우다

17

해설 새롭게 설치된 것은 이전 것을 '대체하는' 것이다. 따라서 정답은 (A) replacing이다.

번역 새로운 조명 시스템이 총무과에 설치되어, 낡고 비효율적인 조명을 대체했다.

어휘 compare A with[to] B A를 B에 비교[비유]하다 brighten 밝게 하다 repair 수리하다

18

해설 목적어로 나온 '염려, 우려 사항(concerns)'과 호응하는 '다루다, 처리하다'라는 뜻의 동사 (B) address가 정답이다. address는 concern뿐만 아니라 issue, problem과도 짝을 이루어 잘 쓰인다.

번역 하트윅 운송의 아템브 씨는 화물 운송에 대한 고객들의 우려를 처리해 줄 가장 좋은 방법들에 관한 워크숍을 열 것이다.

어휘 inform A of B A에게 B에 대해 알리다 supervise 관리[감독]하다

19

해설 '안내서는 절차를 설명한다'가 적합하므로 '개요를 서술하다'라는 뜻의 (B) outlines가 정답이다.

번역 직원 안내서는 경비 보고서 제출 절차를 명확히 설명한다.

어휘 clearly 명확히, 분명히 procedure 절차 file (증서나 서류를) 정식으로 제출하다 ration 배급하다 invest 투자하다

20

해설 매출의 근원지로 '관광에 의존하다'가 적합하므로 (D) rely on이 정답이다. 동의어로 depend on(= rest on, count on)도 쓰이며, on을 upon으로 바꾸어 쓰기도 한다.

번역 그 나라의 많은 해안 도시들은 주요 수입원으로 관광 산업에 의존하기 시작했다.

어휘 coastal 해안의 source of revenue 수입원 get in ~에 들어가다, 도착하다 let down ~을 실망시키다 find out ~을 알아내다

21

해설 to부정사의 목적어로 사람 목적어인 physician이 있고, 문맥상 '~와 상담하다'가 적절하므로 정답은 (A) consult이다. 참고로, '~와 상담하다'로 쓰일 때는 consult with도 가능하다.

번역 직원들은 필요 시마다 사내 상주 의사에게 마음 놓고 상담해도 된다.

어휘 on-site 현장의 convert 전환시키다[개조하다] convince 확신시키다

22

해설 '학술회를 인사부가 주최한다'는 내용이 적합하므로 '주최하다'의 수동태 구조를 이루는 (C) hosted가 정답이다.

번역 7월 24일로 예정된 은퇴 계획에 관한 심포지엄은 인사부에 의해 주최될 것이다.

어휘 intend ~을 의도하다 excuse ~을 용서하다, ~에 대해 변명하다

23

해설 '분기 예상 수입액이 이미 ~했다'라는 의미가 되어야 한다. 따라서 '초과하다'라는 의미의 (A) exceeded가 정답이다.

번역 분기 말까지 아직 한 달이 남았는데 애초에 예상했던 분기 예상 수입액이 이미 초과되었다.

어휘 initial 처음의, 초기의 projection 예상, 예측 quarterly 연 4회의, 분기마다의 outdate 시대에 뒤지게 하다 overdraw (수표나 어음을) 잔액 이상으로 초과 발행하다

24

해설 '지금의 회사명을 계속 유지하다'가 적합하므로 (D) retain이 정답이다.

번역 스와비안 모터스는 경쟁사와 합병한 후에도 현 사명을 그대로 유지할 것이다.

어휘 even 심지어 merge with ~와 합병하다 rival 경쟁하는 inquire 문의하다, 묻다 grant 주다, 수여하다

25

해설 '계약 조건을 확정하다'의 의미가 적합하므로 (A) confirm 이 정답이다. 나머지 보기들은 모두 자동사이며 주로 전치사 with와 어울려 쓰인다.

번역 두 회사의 임원들은 곧 제안된 합병의 조건들에 대해 확정할 것이다.

어휘 be ready to ~할 준비가 되다 term 조건, 임기 merger 합병 converse 대화하다 commune 교제하다, 이야기하다 collaborate 협력하다

26

해설 빈칸 뒤 전치사 for와 함께 쓰여 '~에 대한 자격을 갖추다'라는 의미를 이루는 (A) qualify가 정답이다. 유사한 의미로 be eligible for도 알아 두자.

번역 지역 소비자 할인을 받을 자격이 되려면 고객들은 거주 증명서를 제출해야 한다.

어휘 proof of residency 거주(자) 증명 award 수여하다 certify 보증하다, 증명하다

27

해설 '공식 발표(press release)가 있을 때까지는 언급하지 않겠다'라는 내용이 적합하므로 전치사 on과 함께 쓰여 '~에 대해 언급하다'라는 의미를 이루는 (C) comment가 정답이다.

번역 에이버리 모터스는 내일 공식 발표 전까지는 신차 라인의 디자인에 대해 언급하지 않을 것이다.

어휘 press release 공식 발표, 언론 보도 advance 전진시키다 predict 예상하다

28

해설 목적어로 나온 interest와 어울려, '흥미를 유발하다, 관심을 불러일으키다'라는 뜻을 완성하는 (B) generate가 정답이다.

번역 소세우 숍사는 새로 출시된 청소용품에 대한 관심을 불러일으키기 위하여 광고 캠페인을 시작했다.

어휘 launch 시작하다, 착수하다 advertising campaign 광고 캠페인 cleaning product 청소용품 consume 소비하다, 소모하다 generate 일으키다, 초래하다 endorse 지지하다, 승인하다 suppose 가정하다

29

해설 role, responsibility, position 등과 같은 책무나 직급 명사를 목적어로 하여 '역할, 책임 등을 떠맡다'라는 의미로 쓰이는 (C) assumes가 정답이다.

번역 남 씨는 영업 담당 수석 부사장으로 승진했으며 3월 1일에 새 업무를 맡는다.

어휘 be promoted to ~으로 승진하다 senior vice president 수석 부사장 concern 걱정시키다, 관련되다 assume (역할·책임을) 맡다

30

해설 '계약서가 만료되었다'라는 의미가 적합하므로 '만료되다'라는 뜻의 (C) expired가 정답이다.

번역 사르가소 운송사와의 계약은 10년 전 오늘 만료되었으므로 원본 계약서는 막 파기되었다.

어휘 contract 계약(서) shred 파쇄하다 violate 위반하다 invalidate 무효로 만들다

UNIT 03 ETS 빈출 명사

VOCA PRACTICE				본책 p. 165
1 (B)	2 (B)	3 (A)	4 (A)	5 (A)
6 (A)	7 (B)	8 (A)	9 (D)	10 (A)
11 (C)	12 (D)	13 (C)	14 (C)	15 (D)

1

일련의 시험 가동을 하는 것은 일반적 **관행(practice)**이다.

어휘 a series of 일련의 trial run 시험 가동, 시행 manner 방식

2

모든 기업의 계약들을 검토하는 것은 이시바시 씨의 **책무(responsibility)**가 될 것이다.

어휘 corporate 기업의 contract 계약(서) quality 질

3

우리는 서비스의 **개선(improvement)**을 소프트웨어 업그레이드 덕분으로 돌린다.

어휘 attribute (~을 …의) 결과로[덕분으로] 보다 expectation 예상, 기대

4

방문객들은 그들의 메뉴 **선호도(preferences)**를 표시하도록 알림을 받는다.

어휘 remind 상기시키다 indicate 나타내다 implication 영향[결과], 암시

5

그 회사는 **부주의(negligence)**에 대해 법적 책임이 있다.

어휘 liable 법적 책임이 있는 intermission 중간 휴식 시간

6

통곡물이 주는 건강상의 이로움은 모든 영양소의 **조합**(combination)에서 나온다.

어휘 **benefit** 혜택, 이득 **whole grain** 통곡물, 미정제 곡물 **nutrient** 영양소, 영양분 **proximity** 가까움[근접]

7

린 씨는 영업 이사로 **승진**(promotion)한 후에 회사의 마케팅 활동에 대한 책임을 떠맡았다.

어휘 **assume** (권력·책임을) 맡다 **responsibility for** ~에 대한 책임 **firm** 회사 **activity** 활동 **acceptance** 받아들임[수락]

8

해설 빈칸 앞 형용사 long의 수식을 받는 명사 자리이다. 문맥상 '오랜 고민을 한 후에'라고 하는 것이 자연스럽다. 정답은 (A) deliberation이다.

번역 오랜 심사숙고 끝에 보든턴 제조사는 타이론 보안 시스템즈와 계약을 연장하지 않기로 결정했다.

어휘 **manufacturing** 제조업 **extend** 연장하다 **contract** 계약 **security** 보안 **deliberation** 심사숙고 **impression** 인상, 느낌 **conclusion** 결론, 결말 **assumption** 가정

9

해설 '세입이 증가(rise in revenue)'했으므로 자금 조달을 늘리기로 했다는 의미가 적합하다. 따라서 (D) funding이 정답이다.

번역 세입 증가로 이스트햄튼 시 의회는 통상적으로 대규모 재정 지원을 받지 못했던 지역 프로그램의 자금을 늘리기로 결정했다.

어휘 **revenue** 매출, 세입 **traditionally** 예전부터, 통상적으로 **preservation** 보존 **sharing** 공유 **appraisal** 평가

10

해설 관광객 수의 '변동'이 성공에 영향을 끼친다는 의미가 되는 (A) fluctuations가 정답이다.

번역 관광객 수의 큰 변동은 달링 비치 영세업체들의 성공에 중대한 영향을 끼쳐 왔다.

어휘 **have an impact on** ~에 영향을 끼치다 **significant** 중대한 **fluctuation** 변동 **perception** 인식, 인지 **narration** 서술 **obligation** 의무

11

해설 빈칸 앞의 동사 attend(참석하다)와 어울리는 명사로 (C) workshop이 정답이다.

번역 마케팅부의 모든 수습사원들은 다가오는 워크숍에 참석하도록 권장된다.

어휘 **be encouraged to** ~하도록 권유받다 **subject** 주제, 과목 **division** 사업부

12

해설 회원을 늘리는 것이 '제일 중요하다, 우선 사항이다'라는 뜻으로 (D) priority가 답이다.

번역 회원들은 세계 음악가 협회의 매우 중요한 부분이며, 회원 수를 늘릴 방법을 찾는 것이 최우선 과제가 되어야 한다.

어휘 **vital** 필수적인 **increase** 늘리다 **basis** 기준 **force** 힘 **direction** 방향 **priority** 우선 사항

13

해설 그 계획 이면의 '의도'라는 의미로 '보장하는 것(to ensure)'과 동격을 이루는 (C) intention이 정답이다. 참고로, intention처럼 목적이나 목표를 의미하는 goal, purpose, objective, aim 등이 주어로 오면 '목표는 ~하는 것이다'라는 뜻을 이루기 위해 to부정사가 보어로 오는 구조가 흔히 쓰인다.

번역 그 계획 이면의 의도는 우리 지원팀의 모든 직원들이 직무 능력 개발을 위한 적절한 기회를 갖도록 보장해 주는 것이다.

어휘 **initiative** (목적 달성을 위한) 계획 **ensure** 보증하다, 보장하다 **support staff** 지원팀 직원들 **adequate** 적절한, 충분한 **resemblance** 닮음, 유사함 **dependence** 의존, 의지 **intention** 의도, 목적 **retention** 보유, 유지

14

해설 회의에 참석해 달라는 내용이 되어야 자연스러우므로 '참석'을 뜻하는 (C) presence가 정답이다.

번역 코백 씨가 다음 주 목요일에 열릴 지역 회의에 당신의 참석을 요청했습니다.

어휘 **regional** 지역의 **take place** 열리다 **occurrence** 발생 **urgency** 긴급 **presence** 참석, 존재 **insistence** 주장

15

해설 '프로젝트에 기여한 것에 대해 감사하다'는 내용이 적합하므로 (D) contributions가 정답이다.

번역 영업팀원 모두가 마이클 드레이먼이 지난 6개월 동안 프로젝트에 상당히 기여한 데 대해 감사하고 있다.

어휘 **grateful** 감사하는 **substantial** 상당한 **assurance** 확언 **dependence** 의존 **obligation** 의무 **contribution** 기여

VOCA PRACTICE
본책 p. 170

1 (A)	2 (A)	3 (A)	4 (A)	5 (A)
6 (B)	7 (B)	8 (C)	9 (B)	10 (A)
11 (B)	12 (B)	13 (D)	14 (C)	15 (B)

1

엘리베이터가 그 주에는 **운행(service)**되지 않을 것이다.

어휘 out of service 고장 난, 작동을 멈춘 aid 원조, 지원

2

그 구내식당은 **다양(variety)**한 샌드위치, 수프, 샐러드를 제공한다.

어휘 serve (식당 등에서 음식을) 제공하다

3

시장 조사 부서에서 **설문 조사(survey)**를 실시했다

어휘 conduct 실시하다 response 대답, 응답

4

새로운 전자 부품은 품질 **요구 사항(requirements)**을 충족시키지 않는다.

어휘 electronic 전자의 component 부품 meet the requirement 요구 사항을 충족시키다 performance 실적, 성과

5

패널 토론은 국가의 연례 리더십 회의에서 중요한 **역할(role)**을 한다.

어휘 panel 패널, 토론 참석자 discussion 토론 annual 연례의 play a role 역할을 하다

6

월 임차료는 전화와 케이블 요금을 **제외(exception)**한 모든 공과금을 포함한다.

어휘 rent 집세, 임차료 utility (수도·전기·가스 등) 공익 서비스 charge 요금 excess 초과, 과잉

7

다음 달 철야 **근무(shifts)**를 희망하는 조립 라인 직원들은 화요일까지 매니저에게 알려야 한다.

어휘 assembly-line 조립 라인의 overnight 야간의 inform 알리다

8

해설 '공사 현장 주변으로 우회하다'라는 의미가 되어야 하므로 (C) detour가 정답이다.

번역 11월에 건물이 완공될 때까지 운전자들은 공사 현장 주변으로 우회해야 합니다.

어휘 construction site 공사[건설] 현장 complete 완료하다, 완성하다 view 시야 gap 틈, 공백

9

해설 형용사 Advance와 연결되어 문맥에 맞는 주어가 될 수 있는 명사가 들어가야 하므로 (B) registration가 정답이다.

번역 노스웨스트 지역 병원 경영 콘퍼런스에는 사전 등록이 요구된다.

어휘 advance registration 사전 등록 respect 존중 regulation 규정, 규제

10

해설 make revisions to(~을 수정하다)라는 표현이 수동태가 된 것으로 정답은 (A) revisions이다.

번역 밴햄 도서관 웹사이트의 배열이 여러 번 수정되었다.

어휘 layout 배열, 설계 process 과정, 절차 consideration 고려 concept 콘셉트, 기본 테마

11

해설 under one's direction은 '~의 지도 아래'라는 뜻이다. 정답은 (B) direction이다. 유사한 표현으로 under the supervision of나 under the control of, under the management of 등이 있다.

번역 스피리든 바이오메트릭스의 연구개발부는 창 씨의 지도 하에 제품의 품질과 영역을 개선해 왔다.

어휘 research and development 연구개발 quality 품질 scope 범주 disposal 처분 prominence 탁월, 두드러짐 capacity 수용력, 능력

12

해설 '일반적인 관행'을 뜻하는 표현으로 common practice를 쓴다. 따라서 정답은 (B) practice이다.

번역 웹사이트가 효과적일 수 있도록 하려면 고객 피드백 설문 조사를 실행하는 것이 일반적이다.

어휘 ensure 보장하다 effective 효과적인 administer 관리하다, 시행하다 source 출처 supply 공급

13

해설 원래 give attention to(~에 관심을 기울이다)라는 표현인데, 목적어인 attention이 주어가 되면서 수동태가 된 것이다. 정답은 (D) attention이다.

번역 호텔 개보수 작업 중 특히 주의를 기울인 부분은 조명 기구와 실내 장식이었다.

어휘 lighting 조명 fixture 기구 decoration 장식 attempt 시도

14
해설 '~의 부근에, 근처에'를 의미하는 표현으로 in the vicinity of를 쓴다. 따라서 정답은 (C) vicinity이다.

번역 여러 유명 조각품이 시청 근처에서 전시되어 있다.

어휘 sculpture 조각 (작품) surrounding (명사 앞에서) 인근의, 주위의

15
해설 '전시 중인, 진열 중인'이라는 뜻으로 전치사 on과 어울리는 표현인 (B) display가 정답이다. 동의어로는 on exhibition이 있다.

번역 진열장에 전시되어 있는 모든 상품들은 할인가로 구매할 수 있다.

어휘 available 이용 가능한 reduced price 할인가 example 예 measure 조치; 측정하다 assembly 조립

ETS **TEST**			본책 p. 171	
1 (D)	**2** (C)	**3** (A)	**4** (B)	**5** (B)
6 (A)	**7** (D)	**8** (C)	**9** (C)	**10** (D)
11 (B)	**12** (D)	**13** (A)	**14** (A)	**15** (D)
16 (B)	**17** (D)	**18** (D)	**19** (D)	**20** (B)
21 (C)	**22** (C)	**23** (B)	**24** (C)	**25** (C)
26 (D)	**27** (A)	**28** (C)	**29** (A)	**30** (B)

1
해설 '출입을 위해서 허가가 필요하다'라는 의미가 적절하므로 정답은 '허가'를 의미하는 (D) authorization이다. 동의어로는 permission이 있다.

번역 재미슨 단지의 건물들은 근무일에 저녁 7시까지 열려 있지만, 적절한 허가를 받은 직원들은 언제든지 들어올 수 있다.

어휘 complex 복합 건물, (건물) 단지 workday 근무일 proper 적절한 reinforcement 강화 participation 참여 competency 능숙함

2
해설 '에너지를 더 적게 사용한다'라는 의미가 적절하므로 '적은 양, 일부'를 뜻하는 (C) fraction이 정답이다.

번역 자너그사의 신형 냉장고 모델들은 그 회사의 구형 모델들이 사용하는 에너지 양의 극히 일부만을 사용한다.

어휘 refrigerator 냉장고 relation 관계 moderation 적당함, 절제 correction 정정, 수정

3
해설 '전성기에 시장의 30퍼센트를 점유했다'라는 의미가 적절하므로 '절정, 정상'을 의미하는 (A) peak가 정답이다.

번역 체커사는 전성기 때 자동차용 유리 제조 시장의 30퍼센트 이상을 점유했다.

어휘 represent ~에 해당하다 over ~ 이상 scale 규모 depth 깊이

4
해설 '~할 수밖에 (다른 선택권이) 없다'라는 뜻으로 have no choice but to를 쓴다. 빈칸에는 choice의 동의어가 들어가는 것이 적절하므로 '대안'이라는 뜻의 (B) alternative가 정답이다.

번역 전자업계에서 시장 주도 기업이 되기를 원한다면 리베이라 테크놀러지사는 제품의 범위를 다각화하는 수밖에 없다.

어휘 diversify (사업을) 다각화하다 instance 사례, 경우 alternative 대안 preference 선호 reserve 보존, 비축; 보유하다

5
해설 전치사 into에는 '~안으로'라는 진입의 의미가 있고, into의 목적어로 비즈니스 협회(Business Association)가 나오므로 '협회로의 가입 승인'이라는 의미가 적절하다. 따라서 '가입 승인'이라는 뜻의 (B) acceptance가 정답이다.

번역 사이프러스 비치 비즈니스 협회의 가입 승인을 위해서는 지역 사회 단체들의 추천서들이 요구된다.

어휘 a letter of reference 추천서 local 현지의 acquisition 습득 prospect 전망, 가능성 improvement 개선

6
해설 9시 30분 전에는 기계 작동을 피하라고 지시했다는 내용으로 볼 때, '소음에 관한 항의 때문'이라는 내용이 적절하다. 따라서 정답은 '불만, 항의'라는 뜻의 (A) complaints이다.

번역 소음과 관련된 항의 때문에, 호텔 매니저는 조경 직원에게 오전 9시 30분 이전에는 장비를 작동시키는 것을 피하도록 지시했다.

어휘 regarding ~에 관한 noise 소음 instruct 지시하다 landscaping 조경 avoid 피하다 operate 작동시키다 equipment 장비 material 재료 opponent 상대, 반대자 symptom 증상

7

해설 빈칸은 be동사의 보어 자리로 주어인 온라인 통신(Online communication)과 동격을 이루는 명사가 와야 한다. 'a means of'는 '~의 수단'이라는 뜻으로 쓰여, '연결의 수단'이라는 의미를 이룬다. 따라서 정답은 (D) means이다.

번역 온라인 통신은 분야별 실질적인 문제를 논의하도록 연구자들과 실무자들을 연결해 주는 훌륭한 수단이다.

어휘 communication 통신 excellent 훌륭한 bring together 연결[집합] 시키다 practitioner 실무자 practical 실질적인 approach 접근 instrument 기구[도구]

8

해설 of 뒤에 합성 재료와 천연 재료가 나오므로 그 두 가지를 섞어서 만들었다고 하는 것이 적절하다. 따라서 '혼합'이라는 의미의 (C) blend가 정답이다.

번역 페인 카펫의 장식용 양탄자는 합성 재료와 천연 재료의 혼합으로 제조된다.

어휘 decorative 장식용의 synthetic 합성의, 모조의 shade 그늘

9

해설 '협회에 가입하려는 이유(reasons wanting to join the association)'라는 말이 있으므로 회원 신청서 작성에 관한 내용임을 알 수 있다. 따라서 정답은 '신청서'를 의미하는 (C) application이다.

번역 회원 신청서에는 귀하가 이 협회에 가입하려는 이유를 자세히 적은 편지가 동봉되어야 한다.

어휘 accompany 동반하다, 함께하다 detail 상세히 기술하다 guideline 지침 inventory 재고(품) committee 위원회

10

해설 device-to-person은 '장비 대 사람'을 뜻하며 가령, 이 비율이 2:1인 경우 1인당 장비가 두 대라는 뜻이 된다. 이와 같이 몇 대 몇으로 표현하는 것이 비율 개념이므로 정답은 '비율'이라는 뜻의 (D) ratio이다.

번역 전자제품 판매량의 최근의 급등과 더불어, 업계 분석가들은 1인당 장비 비율이 앞선 예상치를 곧 넘어설 것이라고 예상하고 있다.

어휘 surge 급증 analyst 분석가 surpass 능가하다 prediction 예상(치) division 분할, 부문 fraction 부분 ratio 비율

11

해설 빈칸 뒤에 온 '그의 체류(his stay)'와 호응하여 '체류 기간 동안'이라고 해야 적절하다. 따라서 '기간'을 의미하는 (B) duration이 정답이다.

번역 요스트 씨는 맨체스터에 머무르는 동안 아파트를 빌리기로 결심했다.

어휘 rent 빌리다 collection 수집, 소장품 capacity 수용력, 능력 environment 환경

12

해설 재무 요약본을 제공하는 것이 '서비스의 일환'이라는 내용이 적합하다. 따라서 '~의 일환으로'라는 뜻의 as part of를 완성하는 (D) part가 정답이다.

번역 헨릭슨 회계는 기본적인 회계 서비스의 일환으로 연말 재무 요약본을 제공한다.

어휘 year-end 연말의 bookkeeping 부기, 회계 piece 조각, 일부분 division 사업부 section 부분, 부

13

해설 식당의 인기 이유 중 하나로 상업 지구와의 근접성을 드는 것이 적절하므로, 전치사 to와 함께 쓰여 '~와의 근접성'을 나타내는 (A) proximity가 정답이다. (B) location은 to 이하를 쓰지 않고 단순히 (좋은) 위치 때문에 인기가 좋다고는 할 수 있으나, 전치사 to 이하와 호응을 이루지 않으므로 오답이다.

번역 루시오는 주중 점심 식사로 매우 인기 있는 식당인데, 부분적인 이유는 시의 상업 지구와 가깝기 때문이다.

어휘 partly because 부분적으로 ~ 때문에 proximity to ~에 가까움 location 위치, 지점 situation 위치, 상황 tendency 경향

14

해설 동사 take가 문제 해결의 단서로, 빈칸에 오는 주어는 take와 함께 쓸 수 있는 명사여야 한다. take는 '조치'를 뜻하는 action, step, measure와 함께 쓰여 조치를 '취하다'로 쓰이며, '예방 조치를 취하다'라고 할 때는 take precautions를 쓴다. 따라서 정답은 (A) precautions이다. (B) rules, (D) guidelines는 follow와 주로 짝을 이룬다.

번역 위험 소지가 있는 화학 물질을 다루는 동안 모든 실험실 직원은 안전 예방책을 준수해야 한다.

어휘 laboratory 실험실 chemical 화학 물질 potentially 잠재적으로 harmful 위험한, 해로운 precaution 예방책 ability 능력 guideline 가이드라인, 지침

15

해설 빈칸은 앞에 나온 명사 education과 복합명사를 이루는 자리이며, '글로벌 교육 계획'이 가장 적합하므로 정답은 '(목적 달성을 위한) 계획'을 뜻하는 (D) initiative가 정답이다. initiative는 계획이라는 뜻 외에도 '주도권, 진취성'이라는 의미로도 출제된다.

번역 우리의 글로벌 교육 계획에 대한 기여는 전 세계 사람들에게 학습 기회를 만들어 주는 데 도움이 될 것이다.

어휘 **contribution** 기여, 공헌, 기부 **instrumental** 중요한, 도움이 되는 **compartment** 객실, 칸 **opposition** 반대 **occurrence** 사건, 발생

16

해설 전치사 with와 함께 쓰여 '약관에 동의함을 나타낸다'라는 의미가 적절하므로 '동의'라는 뜻의 (B) agreement가 정답이다. agreement는 '계약', 또는 '계약서'를 의미할 때도 있다.

번역 이 웹사이트 이용은 우리의 약관에 동의함을 의미합니다.

어휘 **imply** 의미하다, 암시하다 **terms and conditions** 약관[조건] **contentment** 만족 **placement** 배치 **development** 발달

17

해설 '대답하다(respond to)'의 목적어 자리이므로 '귀하의 우려 사항에 대해 답변하다'라는 의미가 가장 적절하다. 따라서 '염려, 우려'를 뜻하는 (D) concerns가 정답이다.

번역 세금 전문가가 최근의 법규 변경에 관한 귀하의 우려 사항에 답변을 주기 위하여 내일 우리 회사를 방문할 것이다.

어휘 **respond to** ~에 응답하다 **component** 요소, 부품 **importance** 중요성 **agreement** 합의, 계약(서)

18

해설 '기부자들의 관대함'에 감사한다는 내용이므로 '관대함, 후한 기부'를 뜻하는 (D) generosity가 정답이다. 참고로, '후한 기부'를 뜻하는 generous donation과 generous contribution도 짝을 이루어 자주 쓰인다.

번역 조셉 웰링턴 도서관은 최근 기금 모금 행사에 참여해 주신 모든 기부자들의 관대한 기부에 감사드립니다.

어휘 **donor** 기부자 **fundraising campaign** 기금 모금 행사 **account** 계좌, 계정 **privilege** 특권 **ceremony** 의식

19

해설 약속이나 해야 할 일 등을 상기시켜 주려는 목적으로 메시지를 보낼 때, 첫머리에 자주 쓰이는 표현이 'This is a reminder to ~'이다. '이 글은 ~하라고 알려 드리는 공지입니다'라는 의미이다. 따라서 정답은 '알림'을 뜻하는 (D) reminder이다.

번역 8월 30일자로 기한이 만료되는 상공회 회원권을 갱신하셔야 한다는 것을 알려 드립니다.

어휘 **renew** 기한을 연장하다, 갱신하다 **expire** 만료되다 **purpose** 목적 **conclusion** 결론

20

해설 과일과 채소에 비타민이 많이 함유되어 있다는 내용이 적절하므로 '농축'을 의미하는 (B) concentrations가 정답이다. concentration은 '집중'이라는 뜻으로도 출제된다.

번역 농산물 재배자 협회는 비타민이 가장 많이 든 과일과 채소 목록이 있는 소책자를 지역 슈퍼마켓들에 배포했다.

어휘 **produce** 농작물 **grower** 재배자 **association** 협회 **distribute** 배포하다, 배급하다 **list** 기록하다, 목록으로 만들다; 목록 **attraction** 매력 **beneficiary** 수혜자, 수익자 **command** 명령, 지휘

21

해설 빈칸 앞의 형용사 allergic이 핵심 단서로, '알레르기 반응'이라고 하는 것이 가장 적절하다. 따라서 '반응'을 뜻하는 (C) reactions가 정답이다.

번역 새 법안은 제조사들로 하여금 특정한 사람들에게 알레르기 반응을 일으키는 것으로 알려진 성분이 포함된 상품에는 경고 문구를 부착하도록 요구한다.

어휘 **manufacturer** 제조사 **warning label** 경고 문구 **ingredient** 성분 **cause** 일으키다, 유발하다 **operation** 작동 **performance** 성과 **respondent** 응답자

22

해설 '이용하다'를 뜻하는 utilize의 목적어로 '자원을 이용하다'라는 의미를 이루는 (C) resources가 정답이다. 참고로, resources는 인력 자원(human resources)을 의미하기도 한다.

번역 이반코프 산업의 실험적 기술들에 대한 투자는 회사 내 기존 가용 자원들을 활용함으로써 달성될 것이다.

어휘 **venture** 모험, 투기 **experimental** 실험적인 **accomplish** 완수하다, 성취하다 **utilize** 활용하다 **purpose** 목적 **expense** 비용 **salary** 급료

23

해설 빈칸은 앞에 나온 명사 seating과 복합명사를 이루는 자리이며, 250이라는 수치가 최대 좌석 수를 의미하므로 '최대 수용치'를 뜻하는 (B) capacity가 정답이다.

번역 웰본 과학박물관의 새로운 천문 극장은 250명을 수용할 수 있는 좌석 규모를 갖추었다.

어휘 **astronomy** 천문학 **aptitude** 소질, 적성 **demonstration** 시연 **compliance** 준수, 따름

24

해설 '다양한 재료의 정확한 배합'이라는 의미가 적절하므로 '재료'를 뜻하는 (C) ingredients가 정답이다.

번역 실험실 테스트는 청정제가 효과적이기 위해서는 다양한 원료들의 정확한 조합이 필요하다는 것을 보여 준다.

어휘 precise 정확한 combination 조합, 결합
compound 혼합물, 화합물 effective 효과적인
division 분할, 부문 prospect 가능성 ingredient
재료, 성분 compartment 칸, 객실

25
해설 은행이 고객들에게 투자 관리와 관련해 '전문 지식과 조언'을
제공한다는 의미가 적절하므로, and 뒤에 오는 명사 advice
에 상응하는 '전문 지식'이라는 뜻의 (C) expertise가 정
답이다.

번역 50년 이상의 경험을 바탕으로 트러스트 뮤추얼 은행은 고
객에게 투자를 관리하는 데 필요한 전문 지식과 조언을 제
공합니다.

어휘 manage 관리하다 investment 투자 inquiry 문의
conversion 전환 jurisdiction 관할권

26
해설 빈칸 뒤에 나온 동사 place와 전치사 on이 핵심 단서로,
'~에 주안점을 두다, 강조하다'라는 의미의 place[put]
emphasis on을 완성하는 (D) emphasis가 정답이다.

번역 반스 씨는 신입 영업 사원을 위한 교육 프로그램을 검토한
후에, 네트워킹 기술에 좀 더 주안점을 두어야 한다고 결론
내렸다.

어휘 conclude 결론 내리다 networking 네트워킹, 개인적
인맥[정보망]의 형성 appeal 애원, 호소 analysis
분석 distinction 구별

27
해설 빈칸 앞의 on과 함께 쓰여 '예정대로'라는 의미를 이루는
(A) schedule이 정답이다. 참고로, '예정보다 늦게'
는 behind schedule, '예정보다 일찍'은 ahead of
schedule로 표현한다는 것도 알아 두자.

번역 우리 직원들이 배송 양식에 정확한 주소를 쓰지 않았지만,
기계 부품들은 예정대로 낙농장에 도착했다.

어휘 form 서식, 양식 part 부품 dairy farm 낙농장
appointment 약속 authority 권위, 권한

28
해설 빈칸 뒤 보어로 '5월 21일'이라는 날짜가 나오므로 주어는
해당 날짜와 동격을 이룰 수 있는 명사여야 한다. 따라서
'마감일'이라는 뜻의 (C) deadline이 정답이다.

번역 렘니츠 제조업체에 취업하려는 지원자의 경우 자료 제출 마
감일은 5월 21일이다.

어휘 applicant 지원자 employment 취업 material
자료 intention 의도 admission 입장

29
해설 동사로 '목표로 하다(aim for)'가 나왔고 전치사 in 뒤에
'새로운 스포츠 장비'라는 분야가 나왔으므로, '새로운 스포
츠 부문의 혁신을 목표로 하다'가 적합하다. 따라서 정답은
'혁신'을 뜻하는 (A) innovation이다.

번역 셀젠사에서 현재 신제품 개발을 담당하는 쿠마르 씨는 새
스포츠 장비의 혁신을 목표로 한다.

어휘 aim for ~을 목표로 하다 implication 함축, 암시
consideration 고려 intention 의도

30
해설 전치사 in 뒤에 '의료 연구(medical research)'라는 분야
가 나왔으므로 '의료 연구 분야의 발전'이라는 의미를 완성
하는 (B) advances가 정답이다.

번역 사누라이프 웹사이트는 여러분께 의학 연구 분야의 모든 최
신 발전에 대한 소식을 알려 드립니다.

어휘 novelty 새로움, 신기함 elevation 격상, 높이
formation 형성, 대형

UNIT 05	ETS 빈출 형용사

VOCA **PRACTICE**			본책 p. 181	
1 (A)	**2** (B)	**3** (B)	**4** (A)	**5** (B)
6 (B)	**7** (A)	**8** (D)	**9** (C)	**10** (A)
11 (C)	**12** (A)	**13** (D)	**14** (D)	**15** (C)

1
가장 **필수적인**(essential) 과제는 새로운 회사 로고 디자인을 끝
내는 것이다

어휘 task 일, 과제 corporate 기업의 enclosed 동봉된,
둘러싸인

2
저희는 **좋은**(favorable) 평판을 항상 유지하고자 합니다.

어휘 maintain 유지하다 reputation 평판, 명성 at all
times 항상 favorite 마음에 드는

3
생산 할당량이 증가해서 우리는 **추가**(additional) 직원들을 고
용할 계획이다.

어휘 increased 증가한 production 생산 quota 할당량
multiplied 증식된, 다양화된

4

제품의 성공은 **여러 가지**(various) 요소에 좌우된다.

어휘 depend on ~에 달려 있다[~에 의해 결정되다] factor 요소, 요인

5

풍부한(abundant) 강우량 때문에 수위가 훨씬 높다.

어휘 rainfall 강우(량) water level 수위 accidental 우연한

6

보수적인 투자 전략은 회사의 현재 재정 상황을 고려할 때 **적절한** (appropriate) 것 같다.

어휘 conservative 보수적인 investment 투자 strategy 전략 in light of ~에 비추어, ~을 고려하여 current 현재의 financial 재정의

7

10월 1일자로, 퀸스타운 도서관에서 대출한 모든 도서는 대출일로부터 3주 후 **반납되어야**(due) 합니다.

어휘 as of ~일자로 checkout 대출 payable (돈을) 지불해야 하는, 지불할 수 있는

8

해설 '유효한' 신분증이어야 효력이 있는 것이다. 정답은 (D) valid이다.

번역 콜스 목재 공장의 특정 제한구역에 들어가기 전에 유효한 회사 신분증이 필요합니다.

어휘 identification card 신분증 restricted 제한된 relative 상대적인; 친척 consenting 동의하는 severe 심한, 엄한

9

해설 빈칸의 수식 대상인 명사 materials와 의미가 가장 잘 통하는 형용사를 선택해야 한다. '민감한 물질'이라고 해석하는 것이 가장 자연스러우므로 정답은 (C) sensitive이다.

번역 실험실 카트가 민감한 물질들을 수송하는 데 사용되기 전에, 기술자들이 소독용 천으로 모든 노출된 면을 닦아야 한다.

어휘 transport 나르다, 수송하다 material 물질 wipe 닦다 exposed 노출된 surface 표면 disinfectant 소독용의 vague 모호한 passive 수동적인 demonstrative 숨기지 않는, 드러내고 표현하는

10

해설 변경이 있을 시 공지하겠다는 내용으로 보아 일정이 잠정적인 것임을 알 수 있다. 따라서 '잠정적인'이라는 뜻의 (A) tentative가 정답이다.

번역 컴퓨터 워크숍 일정은 잠정적인 것으로 간주되며 변경이 있을 시 계속 공지해 드리겠습니다.

어휘 post 공지하다 vigilant 방심하지 않는 contemporary 현대의 infinite 무한한

11

해설 '(가격의) 상승'이라는 명사를 수식하기에 적절한 형용사로 '전례 없는'이라는 뜻의 (C) unprecedented가 정답이다.

번역 러틀리지사는 전례 없는 원자재 가격의 상승에 따라 전 제품군에 걸친 가격 인상을 발표했다.

어휘 announce 발표하다 entire 전체의 rise 인상 raw material 원자재 accomplished 기량이 뛰어난 abundant 풍부한 informed 잘 아는

12

해설 '~에도 불구하고'라는 의미의 despite가 이끄는 전치사구가 나오므로, 빈칸에는 문맥상 전치사구의 내용과 반대되는 형용사가 와야 적절하다. '실망스러운 평가'가 적절하므로 (A) disappointing이 정답이다.

번역 새 연극은 표가 많이 팔렸지만, 대다수 지역 연극 평론가들에게는 실망스러운 평가를 받았다.

어휘 theater critic 연극 평론가 perceivable 지각할 수 있는 operational 가동상의, 운영상의 potential 가능성이 있는, 잠재적인

13

해설 remote의 기본 의미는 '거리가 멀리 떨어진'이지만, 가능성(possibility)에 관해 말할 때는 '희박하다'는 뜻이다. 따라서 정답은 (D) remote이다.

번역 운송 중 손상 가능성은 희박하지만, 그 고객은 바델루 시설로 장비를 배송하는 데 보험을 들어 줄 것을 요청했다.

어휘 possibility 가능성 in transit 운반 중에 insure 보험에 들다 contrary 반대의 concerned 걱정하는 detached 분리된

14

해설 냉동 차량의 부족으로 인해 운송이 어려울 만한 상품을 연관지어 판단해야 한다. 따라서 정답은 '부패하기 쉬운'이라는 뜻의 (D) perishable이다.

번역 냉동 차량이 부족하기 때문에 허스트 트러킹사는 부패하기 쉬운 제품은 더 이상 운송하지 않는다.

어휘 adequate 충분한 refrigerated vehicle 냉동 차량 transport 운송하다

15

해설 요금 인상의 '가능성이 있는'이라는 의미가 적절하므로 (C) probable이 정답이다.

번역 공공요금 인상 가능성을 걱정하는 고객들에게는 현재 요금으로 3개월치 서비스 비용을 선납하는 선택권을 줄 것이다.

어휘 concerned about ~에 대해 걱정하는 utility rate 공과금 prepay 선불하다 considerate 사려 깊은 instructive 교육적인 expended 지출된

UNIT 06	ETS 빈출 형용사 어구

VOCA PRACTICE 본책 p. 186

1 (A)	2 (A)	3 (A)	4 (B)	5 (B)
6 (A)	7 (A)	8 (B)	9 (C)	10 (B)
11 (C)	12 (B)	13 (A)	14 (B)	15 (D)

1

가장 **선호되는(preferred)** 지불 방식은 현금이다.

어휘 payment 지불 method 방식, 방법 preferential 우선권[특혜]을 주는

2

전도유망한(promising) 지원자 여러 명이 우리 구직 알선 기관에 등록했다.

어휘 several 몇몇의 candidate 지원자 register 등록하다 job placement agency 직업소개소

3

당신의 아이디어에 전원이 **만족(satisfied)**했습니다.

어휘 satisfactory 만족스러운, 충분한

4

그 컴퓨터는 스피커를 **갖추고(equipped)** 있다.

5

귀하께서 설문지에 제공하신 정보는 절대 **기밀(confidential)**입니다.

어휘 questionnaire 설문지 strictly 엄격히, 절대적으로 potential 가능성이 있는, 잠재적인

6

보조 관리자직 지원자는 다양한 책무를 떠맡을 **수 있어야(capable)** 한다.

어휘 assume 떠맡다 a wide range of 광범위한, 다양한

7

오로지 노로만 추진되는 보트들은 모터 구동 선박용 국가 면허 취득 의무에서 **제외(exempt)**된다.

어휘 propel 추진하다, 나아가게 하다 oar 노 paddle 노 motor-driven 모터로 움직이는 watercraft 선박

8

해설 '한 씨가 보도 수리에 재정적으로 책임이 있다'라는 내용이 자연스러우므로 전치사 for와 함께 쓰이는 (B) responsible이 정답이다.

번역 시 관계자들은 한 씨가 그의 가게 주변의 파손된 보도를 수리하는 데 재정적으로 책임이 있다고 결정했다.

어휘 official (고위) 공무원 determine 결정하다 financially 재정적으로 damaged 손상된 pavement 보도 considerable 상당한 productive 생산적인

9

해설 명사 '기부(donations)'를 수식할 가장 적절할 형용사가 필요하므로 '넉넉한, 후한'이라는 뜻의 (C) generous가 정답이다.

번역 이 뮤직홀은 주로 지역 기업체들의 후한 기부에 의해 지원받고 있다.

어휘 largely 대부분, 주로 donation 기부 tolerant 관대한, 관용하는 thorough 빈틈없는 capable ~을 할 수 있는, 유능한

10

해설 '기꺼이 ~하다'는 표현인 be willing to가 적절하다. 따라서 정답은 (B) willing이다.

번역 토미타 씨는 아라이 씨가 재무 보고서를 수정하기 위해서 막판에 자신의 일정을 기꺼이 조정해 준 것에 대해서 기뻐했다.

어휘 be pleased that ~을 기뻐하다 adjust 조정하다 at the last minute 막판에 timely 시기적절한

11

해설 '~할 것으로 예상되다'라는 be expected to가 어울리므로, 정답은 (C) expected이다.

번역 마버그 일렉트로사는 올해 상당한 이윤 증가를 보고할 것으로 예상된다.

어휘 significant 상당한 increase 증가 profit 이익 earn 벌다 outgrow ~보다 더 빨리 성장하다

12

해설 뒤에 나온 to부정사가 문제 해결의 단서로, '~을 하고 싶어하다'라는 뜻의 be eager to를 써서 '업자들이 관계를 형성하고 싶어 한다'는 내용을 이루는 (B) eager가 정답이다.

번역 식품 수출업자들은 경제가 빠르게 성장하고 있는 국가에서 사업 관계를 형성하기를 원하고 있다.

어휘 **exporter** 수출업자 **form** 형성하다 **rapidly**
빠르게 **constructive** 건설적인 **relative** 상대적인
delicious 맛있는

13

해설 '~할 예정이다'라고 할 때 'be scheduled to부정사'를 쓴
다. 따라서 정답은 (A) scheduled이다. be due to도 동
의어로 알아 두자.

번역 우리의 해외 지사가 다음 달 타이베이에서 문을 열 예정이다.

어휘 **overseas** 해외의 **advance** 나아가다, 발전하다
inform 알리다, 통지하다 **maintain** 유지하다

14

해설 수를 수식하는 표현으로 '상당한 수'를 의미하는 (B)
significant가 정답이다.

번역 이용자들로부터 상당수의 기술 서비스 요청이 있어서, 히소
콤사는 인터넷 서버를 업그레이드하게 되었다.

어휘 **prompt A to B** A로 하여금 B하게 하다 **a significant
number of** 상당수의 **sole** 유일한 **purposeful** 목적
의식이 있는, 결단력 있는 **be capable of** ~할 수 있다

15

해설 날씨를 수식하여 궂은 날씨를 나타내는 형용사로, bad,
poor, unfavorable, adverse, inclement 등이 있다.
따라서 (D) inclement가 정답이다.

번역 날씨가 좋지 않은 경우 직원 포상식은 야외 시설에서 회의
실로 이전될 것이다.

어휘 **recognition** 포상 **relocate** 이전하다 **gardens**
(의자·테이블이 있는) 야외 (식당) 시설

ETS **TEST**				본책 p. 187
1 (A)	**2** (D)	**3** (D)	**4** (B)	**5** (D)
6 (C)	**7** (D)	**8** (D)	**9** (A)	**10** (B)
11 (A)	**12** (A)	**13** (D)	**14** (A)	**15** (B)
16 (C)	**17** (D)	**18** (D)	**19** (C)	**20** (B)
21 (D)	**22** (D)	**23** (D)	**24** (D)	**25** (B)
26 (D)	**27** (C)	**28** (A)	**29** (B)	**30** (D)

1

해설 온라인 수업을 통해 '충분한 대비'를 했다는 의미가 적절하
므로 '충분한'이라는 의미의 (A) adequate이 정답이다.
(B) numerous는 복수명사와 함께 쓰인다는 것도 알아
두자.

번역 설문에 응답한 교사 중 60퍼센트는 스투겟 대학교의 온라
인 강좌들을 통해 업무에 대한 충분한 대비를 했다고 밝
혔다.

어휘 **numerous** 수많은 **thankful** 감사하는 **adjacent**
인접한

2

해설 자동차에 대한 설명으로, '내부(interior)'를 수식하는 형용
사 사이므로 '넓은'을 뜻하는 (D) spacious가 정답이다.

번역 새손 모터스의 신차는 멋진 계기판 디자인과 넓은 실내 공
간이 특징이다.

어휘 **feature** 특징을 이루다 **dashboard** (자동차의) 계기판
widespread 널리 퍼진 **plenty** 풍부한 **prevalent**
만연한

3

해설 '다양한'을 나타내는 표현으로 a range[variety] of를 쓰
는데, 명사를 강조하여 a broad range of, a wide
variety of 등으로 쓸 수 있다. 따라서 정답은 (D) broad
이다.

번역 프랭클린 출장 연회 회사는 점심과 저녁 모두 다양한 메뉴
선택권을 제공한다.

어휘 **catering** 요식 조달업, 출장 연회업 **satisfied** 만족하는
dividing 나누는, 구분하는

4

해설 '약정이 변경될 수 있다'라는 표현은 '~의 대상이다, ~을 조건
으로 하다'라는 뜻의 be subject to를 써서 be subject
to change로 쓴다. 따라서 정답은 (B) subject이다. 이
때 to는 전치사, change는 명사라는 것을 알아 두자.

번역 이 문서에 기술된 계약 조건들은 사전 공지 없이 변경될 수
있다.

어휘 **terms and conditions** (거래·계약 등의) 조건
outline (개요를) 서술하다, 기술하다 **without notice**
예고 없이 **dependent** 의존하는 **immediate**
즉각적인

5

해설 '엄격한 수질 기준에 맞추다'라는 의미가 적절하므로 '엄격
한'이라는 뜻의 (D) stringent가 정답이다.

번역 이 도시의 상수도는 정부의 보건 기관들이 정한 엄격한 수
질 기준에 맞춰야 한다.

어휘 **water supply** 물 공급 **meet** (필요·요구 등을) 맞추다,
충족시키다 **water-quality** 수질 **set** 정하다, 결정하다
dominant 우세한, 지배적인 **extended** (기간을)
연장한, 장기간의

6

해설 '소비자들이 농작물의 재배 지역에 관심을 갖는다'라는 의미
가 적절하므로 '~에 대해 걱정하다, 관심을 가지다'라는 뜻의
be concerned about을 완성하는 (C) concerned가
정답이다.

번역 〈남부 농업 협회지〉에 실린 한 보고서에 따르면, 소비자들은 갈수록 농산물의 재배 지역에 관심을 쏟고 있다.

어휘 increasingly 점점 더 produce 농산물
exceptional 예외적인 essential 필수적인
significant 중요한

7

해설 '기회(opportunities)'를 수식하는 형용사로 '좋은 기회'를 의미할 수 있는 '뛰어난'이라는 뜻의 (D) outstanding이 정답이다.

번역 최근의 졸업생들은 좋은 승진 기회를 제공받기 때문에 하넘사에 지원한다.

어휘 apply for ~에 지원하다 advancement 승진
outgrown 너무 커서 맞지 않게 된 outlying 외딴, 외진
outstretched 죽 뻗은

8

해설 '잘못된 사용으로 인한 파손은 품질 보증이 적용되지 않는다'라는 의미가 적절하므로 명사 use를 수식하는 형용사로 '잘못된, 적절하지 않은'을 뜻하는 (D) improper가 정답이다.

번역 르렌 냄비의 품질 보증은 요리 기구의 부적절한 사용에 따른 파손에는 적용되지 않습니다.

어휘 warranty 품질 보증 saucepan 냄비 apply to ~에 적용되다 damage 파손 result from ~에서 기인하다
cookware 취사도구 concise 간결한 equivalent 동등한, 상응하는 submissive 순종하는, 복종하는

9

해설 '주차 구역(parking area)'을 수식하는 형용사로, 장소 앞에 쓰여 '(벽·담·울타리 등으로) 둘러싸인'이라는 뜻으로 쓰이는 (A) enclosed가 정답이다.

번역 스브라가 호텔의 청사진은 200개의 객실, 식당 하나, 둘러막힌 주차 구역을 포함한다.

어휘 blueprint 청사진 opposite 반대의 absent 결석한
innocent 순진한, 순수한

10

해설 '마케팅 전략을 개발한다'는 말을 보면 빈칸에는 긍정적 의미의 형용사가 어울린다. 적절한 형용사는 '혁신적인'이라는 뜻의 (B) innovative이다.

번역 우리 전문가팀은 혁신적인 마케팅 전략을 개발하기 위해 고객과 협력한다.

어휘 work with ~와 함께 일하다 strategy 전략
unavailable 이용[입수]할 수 없는 resolved 굳게 결심한 convinced 확신하는

11

해설 '휴가를 받을 자격이 있다'가 적절하므로 '~할 자격이 있다'를 의미하는 be eligible to를 써야 한다. 따라서 (A) eligible이 정답이다. 참고로, be entitled to도 같은 뜻으로 쓸 수 있으며, be eligible to와 달리 to를 to부정사와 전치사로 모두 활용할 수 있다.

번역 직원들은 12개월 이상 근무했다면 가족 휴가와 보건 휴가를 갈 자격이 있다.

어휘 leave 휴가 desirable 바람직한, 호감이 가는
preferred 우선의 suitable 적합한

12

해설 서류 작성을 위해 '충분한 시간을 갖도록'이라는 의미가 적합하므로 '충분한'을 뜻하는 (A) sufficient가 정답이다.

번역 새 환자들은 서류 작성에 필요한 충분한 시간을 가질 수 있도록 진료 예약 시간 15분 전에 도착해야 한다.

어휘 appointment (진료) 약속 allow (돈·시간 따위를) 주다 liberal 자유로운, 자유주의의 entire 전체의

13

해설 시제품이 '예비 검사'를 통과했다는 의미가 적합하므로 '예비의'를 뜻하는 (D) preliminary가 정답이다.

번역 피어플레인사는 새로운 비행기 시제품이 모든 예비 검사를 통과했다고 어제 발표했다.

어휘 state 언급하다 prototype 원형, 표본
undeveloped 개발되지 않은 foregone 이미 정해진
subordinate 종속된, 부하의

14

해설 '계획이 최종 승인에 달려 있다'는 의미가 적절하므로 전치사 on과 함께 쓰여 '~에 달려 있다'라는 의미를 이루는 (A) contingent가 정답이다. remain 대신 be, become을 써도 되며, contingent도 쉬운 형용사인 dependent로 바꾸어 쓸 수 있다.

번역 의류사업부 확장 계획은 소요 예산 배분에 대한 최종 승인에 달려 있다.

어휘 expansion 확장, 확대 approval 승인, 결재
budget allocation 예산 배정[할당] eventual 최종적인 speculative 이론적인, 투기적인

15

해설 '뒤이어 일어난 일들'이라는 문맥이 어울리므로 (B) Subsequent가 정답이다. the following도 가능하다.

번역 뒤이어 일어난 일들을 보면, 그 은행이 본사 근처의 부지를 인수한 결정은 옳았다.

어휘 acquire 인수하다, 획득하다 property 부동산
suspended 보류된, 정지된 subjective 주관적인
sustaining 지탱하는, 유지하는

16

해설 모든 소비자가 살 수 있는 태양 에너지로 만들고자 한다는 내용이 적합하므로 '가격이 알맞은'을 뜻하는 (C) affordable이 정답이다.

번역 저희 에너지 코올리션사의 주요 목표는 모든 소비자에게 태양 에너지를 더 저렴한 가격에 제공하는 것입니다.

어휘 primary 주요한   solar 태양열을 이용한   consumer 소비자   influenced 영향을 받은   average 평균적인

17

해설 저녁 열람 시간 연장은 이용자들이 지역 도서관들을 더 잘 이용할 수 있게 만들고자 함이므로 '접근[이용] 가능한'을 뜻하는 (D) accessible이 정답이다.

번역 이사들은 투표를 통해, 낮 시간에 지역 도서관을 방문할 수 없는 이용자들을 위해 도서관의 저녁 열람 시간을 연장하기로 했다.

어휘 vote to ~할 것을 투표하다   extend 연장하다   patron 이용객, 고객   appreciative 고마워하는

18

해설 '지도(map)'를 수식하는 형용사로 '상세한'을 뜻하는 (D) detailed가 정답이다.

번역 톰킨스빌 도로 안내서는 상세한 전국 지도와 지방 지도를 바탕으로 편찬되었다.

어휘 compile 편찬하다, 편집하다   decided 단호한   delinquent 미불인, 태만한   dependent 의존하는

19

해설 어젯밤에 기계가 고장 났다는 내용으로 보아 오늘 아침에 발송하는 것은 '실현 가능성이 없다'는 문맥이 어울린다. 따라서 정답은 '실현 가능한'이라는 뜻의 (C) feasible이다.

번역 라벨 붙이는 기계가 어젯밤 고장 난 탓에 오늘 아침에 배송하는 것은 불가능했다.

어휘 break down 고장 나다   potential 잠재력 있는   concise 간결한   feasible 실현 가능한   credible 믿을 수 있는

20

해설 '3년 연속으로 목표를 이루었다'라는 의미가 적절하므로 '연속적인'이라는 뜻의 (B) consecutive가 정답이다. 참고로 '서수(third) + consecutive year' 혹은 '기수(three) + consecutive years'로 표현한다.

번역 대녀사는 3년 연속 신입 사원 채용 목표를 이루었다.

어휘 meet (기준·목표를) 맞추다, 충족시키다   recruitment 신입 사원 모집[채용]   following 그 다음의   approximate 거의 정확한, 대략의   absolute 절대적인

21

해설 12개의 추가 도시로 서비스를 제공한다는 내용이 있으므로 '확대된 서비스 제공'이 문맥상 적절하다. 따라서 '확대된'이라는 뜻의 (D) expanded가 정답이다.

번역 마사미 항공은 확대된 서비스를 나고야에서 아시아와 유럽에 걸친 12개의 추가 도시로 곧 제공할 것이다.

어휘 additional 추가적인   accumulated 축적된, 누적된   reinforced 강화된   translated 해석된

22

해설 계약을 따내 칭찬을 받았다는 내용이 있으므로, '계약 (contracts)'을 수식하여 '수익성이 좋은'을 뜻하는 (D) lucrative가 정답이다. 동의어 profitable도 답이 될 수 있다.

번역 이경빈은 드와이어 산업의 신규 모바일 컴퓨팅 부서에서 수익성 좋은 여러 계약을 확보하는 데 역할을 해 칭찬을 받았다.

어휘 praise 칭찬하다   secure 확보하다   fledgling 시작한 지 얼마 안 된   arbitrary 임의적인, 제멋대로인   spacious 넓은   absent 부재한

23

해설 '예(example)'를 수식하는 형용사로 '효율성을 보여 주는 좋은 예'라는 의미가 적절하므로, 긍정의 의미로 '인상적인'이라는 뜻의 (D) impressive가 정답이다.

번역 어제 견학을 다녀온 관리자들은 공장의 조립 라인이 효율성을 보여 주는 인상적인 본보기였다고 말했다.

어휘 assembly line 조립 라인   efficiency 효율성   acquired 습득한   equipped 장비를 갖춘   indecisive 우유부단한

24

해설 익숙하지 않은 환경에 잘 적응할 수 있어야 한다는 내용이 적절하므로 '~에 적응하다'라는 뜻의 be adaptable to를 완성하는 (D) adaptable이 정답이다.

번역 해외 마케팅 매니저는 널리 출장 다니는 것이 요구되므로, 익숙하지 않은 상황에 잘 적응할 수 있어야 한다.

어휘 extensively 광범위하게   unfamiliar 익숙하지 않은   be opposed to ~에 반대하다   versatile 다용도의, 다재다능한   relative 상대적인

25

해설 '3학년에게 개설되어 있지만'이라는 내용에 이어서 '그들에게는 너무 어렵다'로 연결되는 것이 자연스러우므로 '까다로운'이라는 의미의 (B) demanding이 정답이다. 동의어로 challenging도 알아 두자.

번역 일부 학생들은 물리학 301 과목이 3학년생들이 수강할 수 있도록 되어 있지만 너무 어렵다고 학과장에게 불평했다.

어휘 complain 불평하다 department chairperson 학과장 stubborn 고집이 센 tangled 뒤얽힌, 복잡한 uneasy (마음이) 불편한

26

해설 '정중한(courteous)'이라는 단어와 함께 service를 수식하기에 적절한 단어를 골라야 한다. 따라서 '믿을 수 있는'이라는 의미의 (D) reliable이 정답이다.

번역 샌더스 배관의 직원들은 믿을 수 있고 정중한 서비스로 명성을 얻었다.

어휘 earn 얻다 reputation 명성 courteous 정중한 numerous 많은

27

해설 '전체 보고서(full report)'와 대조적인 의미이면서 '메모(memo)'를 수식하는 형용사로 '간략한'이라는 뜻의 (C) brief가 정답이다.

번역 회사의 예산 결정에 대한 전체 보고서는 이번 주말까지 완성되지 않겠지만, 간략한 회람은 오늘 중에 발표될 것이다.

어휘 issue 발표하다 constant 끊임없는 momentary 순간적인

28

해설 양, 총액(amount)을 수식하는 형용사로 '상당한 양의 시간'이라는 뜻을 이루는 (A) substantial이 정답이다.

번역 대형 프로젝트를 위해 잘 준비된 제안서는 작성하는 데 상당한 시간과 자원이 소요될 것이다.

어휘 proposal 제안(서) resource 자원 wealthy 부유한 consequential 결과적인 spacious 넓은

29

해설 전치사 with와 함께 쓰여 '육교 교체와 관련된 공사'라는 의미가 되는 (B) associated가 정답이다.

번역 육교 교체와 관련된 공사는 지역 교통의 흐름을 계속 지연시킬 것이다.

어휘 replacement 교체 footbridge 육교 impede 지연시키다 flow 흐름[이동] be accustomed to ~에 익숙하다 coherent 일관성 있는 distinct 뚜렷이 다른

30

해설 '독특한 아이디어가 선도 업체라는 명성에 핵심 역할을 했다'는 내용이 적절하므로 전치사 to와 함께 쓰여 '~에 중심이 되다'라는 뜻의 be central to를 이루는 (D) central이 정답이다.

번역 크리에이티브 디렉터 레이 라벨로의 독특한 아이디어는 선도적인 디자인 회사로서 당사의 명성에 구심점이 되어 왔다.

어휘 reputation 명성 leading 선도적인 former 이전의

102

| UNIT 07 | ETS 빈출 부사 |

VOCA PRACTICE 본책 p. 195

1 (B)	2 (B)	3 (B)	4 (A)	5 (A)
6 (B)	7 (A)	8 (B)	9 (C)	10 (C)
11 (A)	12 (A)	13 (C)	14 (C)	15 (A)

1

대선 후보인 크리스틴 위더비는 **대중 앞에서(publicly)** 연설했다.

어휘 presidential candidate 대선 후보 expensively 비싸게

2

주문된 물건들은 창고에서 **직접(directly)** 배송될 수 있다.

어휘 warehouse 창고

3

여러 팀이 회사의 새 제품군을 디자인하기 위해 **협업해서(collaboratively)** 일했다.

어휘 commonly 흔히, 보통

4

존슨 씨는 자신의 사무실에서 비공개 토론을 열어 그 분쟁을 **신중히(discreetly)** 처리했다.

어휘 dispute 분쟁, 논쟁 private 비공개의 remotely 멀리서, 원격으로

5

클라인 바이오케미컬즈는 고난도 연구 프로젝트를 **독자적으로(independently)** 처리할 수 있는 한 명의 경험 많은 연구원으로 실험실 전문가팀을 대체하려고 하고 있다.

어휘 seek to ~하려고 노력[시도]하다 replace 대신[대체]하다 absently 멍하니, 무심코

6

홉킨스 씨는 회사가 **오로지(solely)** 인건비 절감에만 의존하지 않는 비즈니스 전략을 시행할 계획이라고 발표했다.

어휘 implement 시행하다 strategy 전략 rely on ~에 기대다, 의존하다 labor cost 인건비 nearly 거의

7

추가 자금 조달을 위한 보조금 신청서는 5페이지를 넘길 수 없으므로, 모든 연구 내용은 철저하지만 **간결하게(concisely)** 제시되어야 한다.

어휘 **grant application** 보조금 신청서 **exceed** 넘어서다[초과하다] **present** 제시[제출]하다 **thoroughly** 철저히 **yet** 그렇지만 **evidently** 분명히

8

해설 '해마다 점검 받는'이라고 하는 것이 가장 자연스러우므로 정답은 (B) annually이다.

번역 유바베스 수송 회사 운전자들은 자신들의 차량을 해마다 점검 받아야 한다.

어휘 **transit** 수송 **inspect** 점검하다 **rather** 꽤, 상당히 **quite** 꽤, 상당히 **highly** 매우

9

해설 (C) otherwise는 앞에 나온 말을 받아서 '그렇지 않으면'이라는 뜻을 가진다. 이 문장에서도, '재고를 위해 공간을 만드는 게 아니라면'이라는 의미이다. 특히 가정법을 만드는 would와 잘 쓰인다.

번역 새로운 상품들을 놓아둘 공간을 마련하기 위해서, 그렇지 않으면 판촉 할인을 하지 않을 상점들이 한시 할인 광고를 할 것이다.

어휘 **make room for** ~을 위한 공간을 만들다 **limited-time** 제한된 시간의 **solely** 유일하게 **further** 추가적으로 **fully** 완전히

10

해설 '끝냈다'라는 의미의 동사 has finished를 수식하여 '거의 끝마쳤다'는 의미가 가장 적합하므로 정답은 (C) nearly이다.

번역 법무팀은 회사 정책 검토를 거의 끝마쳤고 변경 제안을 내일 마무리할 것이다.

어휘 **legal department** 법무팀 **finalize** 마무리 짓다 **proposal** 제안(서) **slightly** 약간 **frequently** 자주 **continually** 계속해서

11

해설 빈칸 뒤의 우리가 '마침내 그 서비스를 제공하게 되었다'는 문맥과 호응하려면 '반복해서 요청해 왔다'가 적절하므로 '반복적으로'라는 뜻의 (A) repeatedly가 정답이다.

번역 5년 동안 우리 고객들은 계정 정보의 온라인 이용을 반복적으로 요청했고, 마침내 우리는 그 서비스를 제공하게 되었다.

어휘 **access** 이용 **account** 계정, 계좌 **finally** 마침내 **incredibly** 믿을 수 없을 정도로 **briefly** 잠시

12

해설 '다음 주 수요일까지 완료하는 것'이 가장 바라는 결과라는 것을 나타내기 위해 '이상적으로는 수요일까지 완료할 것이다'라고 말할 수 있다. 따라서 '이상적으로'라는 뜻의 (A) ideally가 정답이다.

번역 이상적으로는 다음 주 수요일까지 직원 성과 평가를 완료할 것이다.

어휘 **employee performance review** 직원 성과 평가 **complete** 완료하다 **lately** 최근에 **relatively** 비교적 **attractively** 매력적으로

13

해설 증감 동사 increased를 수식하므로 '극적으로, 급격히'라는 뜻의 (C) dramatically가 정답이다.

번역 컴버랜드의 TV 판매는 제조업체가 가격을 25% 내린 뒤 급격하게 증가했다.

어휘 **manufacturer** 제조사 **drop** 떨어뜨리다 **accidentally** 우연히 **expressively** 의미심장하게 **eagerly** 열렬히

14

해설 동일한 제품에 대해서 대금을 두 번 청구한 것이므로 '부주의하게 청구했다'가 적절하다. 따라서 정답은 (C) inadvertently이다.

번역 그 매장은 같은 구매품에 대해서 한 씨의 신용카드에 부주의하게 대금을 두 번 청구했지만, 신속히 실수를 정정했다.

어휘 **charge** 청구하다 **twice** 두 번 **purchase** 구매(품) **correct** 정정하다 **uniformly** 균일하게 **potentially** 잠재적으로 **functionally** 기능상

15

해설 파일이 서버에 '안전하게' 저장된다는 의미가 적절하므로 (A) safely가 정답이다.

번역 락커 박스 소프트웨어는 여러분의 개인 디지털 파일들이 우리의 온라인 서버에 안전하게 저장될 것을 보장합니다.

어휘 **ensure** 확실하게 하다 **remain** ~한 상태로 남아 있다 **reportedly** 보도된 바에 따르면 **presently** 현재

UNIT 08	ETS 빈출 부사 어구

VOCA PRACTICE 본책 p. 200

1 (B)	2 (B)	3 (B)	4 (B)	5 (A)
6 (A)	7 (B)	8 (A)	9 (D)	10 (A)
11 (B)	12 (D)	13 (A)	14 (A)	15 (D)

1

무료 샘플들은 **현재**(currently) 이용 가능합니다.

어휘 **precisely** 정확하게

2

주택 가격이 **점차(gradually)** 상승하고 있다.

어휘 **highly** 매우 (*highly는 증감 동사를 수식하지 못한다.)

3

그 샘플들은 **완전(absolutely)** 무료입니다.

어휘 **free of charge** 무료의; 무료로 **carefully** 조심스럽게, 신중히

4

그녀는 졸업 **바로(immediately)** 후에 채용되었다.

어휘 **previously** 이전에

5

우회 표지판이 작업 현장으로 가는 주 도로를 따라 **눈에 띄게 (prominently)** 배치될 것이다.

어휘 **detour** 우회; 우회하다 **place** 놓다[두다], 배치하다 **along** ~을 따라 **markedly** (증감 동사를 수식하여) 현저하게, 두드러지게

6

케이크 반죽을 팬에 붓고 반죽이 **고르지 않게(unevenly)** 퍼지면 살살 흔드세요.

어휘 **pour** 붓다 **batter** 케이크 반죽 **gently** 부드럽게, 살살 **distribute** 배분하다, 분포시키다 **unwillingly** 마지못해

7

재킷티 재단의 학술회 초청 연사는 **이번 주 나중에(later)** 발표될 것이다.

어휘 **foundation** 재단 **symposium** 학술 토론회

8

해설 추운 날씨가 '불리하게 영향을 끼쳤다'는 의미가 적절하므로 동사 has affected를 꾸미는 부사로 (A) adversely 가 정답이다.

번역 계절에 맞지 않게 추운 날씨가 현지 슈퍼마켓의 일부 과일과 채소 수급에 안 좋은 영향을 끼쳤다.

어휘 **unseasonably** 계절에 맞지 않게 **affect** 영향을 끼치다 **availability** 이용 가능성 **consciously** 의식하고 **accurately** 정확하게

9

해설 '투표했다(voted)'를 수식하는 부사로 '만장일치로'라는 뜻의 (D) unanimously가 정답이다.

번역 어제 간부들은 성과가 뛰어난 직원들에게 큰 상여금을 주는 안건에 만장일치로 찬성했다.

어휘 **high-performing** 성과가 뛰어난 **commonly** 흔히, 보통 **increasingly** 점점 **critically** 비판적으로

10

해설 '세부 사항을 아직 마무리 짓지 못했다'라는 내용이 적절하므로, '아직 ~하지 않았다'라는 뜻의 'have yet to부정사' 표현을 완성하는 (A) yet이 정답이다.

번역 이탈리아의 두 주요 항공사는 관광 산업을 증대시키기 위한 협력에 관한 세부 사항을 마무리 짓지 못했다.

어휘 **major** 주요한 **finalize** 마무리 짓다 **details** 세부 사항 **cooperative** 협력하는 **effort** 노력

11

해설 100퍼센트는 아니지만 100퍼센트에 가깝다는 것을 의미하기 위해, '전부'를 뜻하는 단어 앞에 almost(거의)를 붙일 수 있다. 따라서 entirely(전부)를 수식하는 부사로 (B) almost가 정답이다.

번역 거의 다 런던의 한 거리에서 촬영된 신작 스릴러 영화 〈모험가들〉은 개봉 첫 주말 박스 오피스에서 9천만 파운드 이상의 수익을 올렸다.

어휘 **thriller** 스릴러물 **film** (영화를) 촬영하다 **entirely** 전적으로 **gross** ~의 수익을 올리다

12

해설 spoke를 수식하고 only의 수식을 받고 있으므로, '간략하게만 말했다'라는 의미가 적절하다. 따라서 '간략하게'를 뜻하는 (D) briefly가 정답이다.

번역 방문한 외교관은 국제회의에서 단지 간략하게만 말하고 요하네스버그로 되돌아갔다.

어휘 **diplomat** 외교관 **return to** ~로 되돌아가다 **constantly** 끊임없이 **frequently** 빈번히

13

해설 '분명하게 표시되어 있다'라는 문맥이 적합하므로 '분명하게'를 뜻하는 (A) clearly가 정답이다.

번역 샌디 쇼어즈 모텔로 가는 길은 연안 간선도로 262번 출구부터 명확히 표시되어 있다.

어휘 **mark** 표시하다 **coastal** 해안[연안]의 **freely** 자유롭게 **deeply** 깊게 **sharply** 날카롭게, 급격히

14

해설 '한 달에 한 번'이라는 뜻이 적합하므로, 정답은 '한 번'을 뜻하는 (A) once이다.

번역 스타빌 체육 센터의 게스트 입장권은 한 달에 한 번 3일간만 사용 가능하다.

어휘 **redeemable** 보상이 가능한, (현금 등과) 교환할 수 있는 **formerly** 이전에 **shortly** 곧

15

해설 증감 동사 중의 하나인 rise(오르다)를 수식하는 부사 자리이므로 '상당히'를 의미하는 (D) significantly가 정답이다.

번역 연료비가 크게 상승한다면 우리 계약 조건을 재교섭해야 할지도 모른다.

어휘 fuel cost 연료비   term 조건   renegotiate 재교섭하다   mainly 주로   sincerely 성실히, 진심으로

ETS TEST   본책 p. 201

1 (D)	**2** (B)	**3** (C)	**4** (B)	**5** (A)
6 (D)	**7** (B)	**8** (B)	**9** (B)	**10** (A)
11 (B)	**12** (D)	**13** (D)	**14** (B)	**15** (A)
16 (A)	**17** (D)	**18** (C)	**19** (C)	**20** (B)
21 (C)	**22** (C)	**23** (C)	**24** (C)	**25** (B)
26 (C)	**27** (C)	**28** (B)	**29** (A)	**30** (C)

1

해설 업체를 바꾸기로 결정한 이유로 배송이 늦는다는 내용이 왔으며, '늦은(late)'을 수식하는 부사로는 '지속적으로 늦은'이 어울린다. 따라서 정답은 (D) consistently이다. (A) steadily는 발달 전개의 지속성을 나타내므로 increase, decrease 등과 같은 증감 동사를 수식하는 부사로 출제된다.

번역 포드햄 문구는 밸리 제지가 지속적으로 주문 배송에 늦어서 최근 공급업체를 교체하기로 결정했다.

어휘 switch 바꾸다   supplier 공급업체   shipping 선적, 배송   sensibly 현저히, 현명하게   exactly 정확하게

2

해설 '발표하다(announces)'를 수식하는 부사로, 좋은 소식을 전할 때 '자랑스럽게 발표하다'라는 표현을 쓴다. 따라서 정답은 (B) proudly이다.

번역 플럼빌 도서관은 새로운 웹사이트를 개설한 것을 자랑스럽게 발표합니다.

어휘 launch 개시, 출시   brand-new 새로운, 신품의   extremely 극단적으로, 지극히   distantly 멀리, 떨어져서   previously 이전에

3

해설 특별한 요청을 할 때는 '미리 예약할 때만 가능하다'라는 내용이 적합하므로 '사전에, 미리'를 의미하는 부사 (C) beforehand가 정답이다.

번역 회사 연례 만찬을 위해 특별 식단 요청이 수용될 수는 있지만, 미리 예약 신청을 할 때만 가능하다.

어휘 annual 연례의   dietary 식사의   request 요청   accommodate (의견을) 수용하다, (공간에) 수용하다   arrange 마련하다   meanwhile 그동안에

4

해설 '~와 비교하여(compared to)'라는 표현과 어울려 '상대적으로 낮은'이라고 표현하는 것이 자연스럽다. 따라서 정답은 '상대적으로'라는 의미의 (B) relatively이다.

번역 내 의견으로는, 이 회사의 주가는 연간 수익과 비교해 상대적으로 낮다.

어휘 stock price 주가   earnings 소득, 이익   audibly 들을 수 있게   plentifully 풍부하게   anonymously 익명으로

5

해설 '계획해야 한다(should plan)'를 수식하는 부사로, 관광객이 많으므로 그에 맞게 계획해야 한다는 내용이 자연스럽다. 따라서 '그에 따라'라는 뜻의 (A) accordingly가 정답이다.

번역 여름철에는 관광객이 아주 많으므로 여행객들은 그에 따라 계획을 세우고 일찍 예약해야 한다.

어휘 subsequently 결과적으로   conversely 역으로, 반대로   assuredly 확실히, 틀림없이

6

해설 '반드시 ~하지는 않다'는 부분 부정의 표현으로 not necessarily를 쓴다. 광고된 내용이 반드시 경영진이 지지하는 내용이라고는 볼 수 없다는 내용이 적절하므로 정답은 (D) necessarily이다.

번역 〈위클리 라운드업〉지에 상인들이 게재한 광고들은 반드시 저희 경영진의 지지를 나타내지는 않습니다.

어휘 merchant 상인, 무역상   imply 암시하다   endorsement 지지, (유명인이 광고에 나와 하는 상품에 대한) 보증, 홍보   barely 간신히, 가까스로   gradually 서서히

7

해설 필터를 '주기적으로 청소하다'가 적합하므로 '정기적으로'라는 뜻의 (B) regularly가 정답이다.

번역 라이더 의류 건조기가 최적의 성능을 발휘하도록 필터를 정기적으로 청소하세요.

어휘 optimal performance 최적의 성능   extremely 아주, 극단적으로   deeply 깊이, 심각하게   heavily 상당히

8

해설 '달리 명시되어 있지 않다면'이라는 의미가 되어야 하므로, '그렇지 않다면'을 뜻하는 (B) otherwise가 정답이다. 'unless otherwise p.p.'로 암기해 두는 것이 좋다.

번역 달리 명시되어 있지 않다면, 사진과 관련 서류들은 저자에 의해 제공되었다.

어휘 document 문서, 서류 supply 제공하다

9

해설 '불편 없이, 편안하게 앉히다'가 적절하므로 '편안하게'를 뜻하는 (B) comfortably가 정답이다.

번역 캡틴즈 시푸드 레스토랑은 스타보드 라운지에 최대 20명의 손님을 편안하게 수용할 수 있다.

어휘 seat ~을 앉히다 up to ~까지 abundantly 풍부하게 evenly 고르게

10

해설 '철거되어야 한다(should be demolished)'를 수식하여 '완전히 철거되어야 한다'라는 의미가 적절하므로 '완전히' 라는 뜻의 (A) completely가 정답이다.

번역 도시 계획 책임자에 따르면, 애들레이드의 구 도심 지역은 신 도심 건설 작업이 시작하기 전에 완전히 철거되어야 한다.

어휘 city planning 도시 계획 director 책임자, 관리자 civic center 도심 demolish 철거하다 construction 건설 defectively 불완전하게 plentifully 풍부하게 richly 화려하게, 풍부하게

11

해설 '대답하다(reply to)'를 수식하여, '즉시 대답하다'라는 의미를 이루는 (B) promptly가 정답이다.

번역 소프트웨어 연수 초대장에 즉시 회답해 주세요.

어휘 closely 자세히, 긴밀하게 likely ~할 것 같은 expressly 특별히, 명백히

12

해설 '~로 알려져 있다(be known as)'를 수식하여 일반적으로 '패스트 트랙'이라는 이름으로 알려져 있다는 의미가 적합하므로 '일반적으로'를 뜻하는 (D) commonly가 정답이다.

번역 우리 이메일 시스템의 정식 명칭은 '패스트 메일 딜리버리 앤 트래킹' 시스템이지만, 보통 '패스트 트랙'으로 알려져 있다.

어휘 official 공식적인 mutually 서로, 상호간에 relatively 상대적으로, 비교적 abruptly 갑자기, 불쑥

13

해설 '발표하다(present)'를 수식하여 '능숙하게 발표하다'가 적절하므로 (D) skillfully가 정답이다.

번역 위원회 위원들은 박 씨가 인센티브 프로그램의 혜택들을 얼마나 능숙하게 발표했는지를 알게 되어 기뻤다.

어휘 be glad to ~하게 되어 기쁘다 privately 사적으로, 비공개로 apparently 보기에, 분명히

14

해설 숫자(three)를 수식하는 부사 자리이므로 '대략'을 뜻하는 (B) approximately가 정답이다.

번역 윌트셔 오케스트라의 콘서트는 대략 3시간 길이였고, 밤 11시가 막 지나서 끝났다.

어휘 three hours long 3시간 길이의 just after ~ 직후에 attentively 세심하게 endlessly 끝없이 comparatively 비교적

15

해설 이유를 수식하는 부사로 '부분적으로 ~ 때문이다'라는 의미를 이루는 (A) partly가 정답이다. 참고로, '주로 ~ 때문이다'라고 할 때는 largely나 primarily를 쓸 수 있다.

번역 보르겐 씨가 이직한 이유는 부분적으로 이전 직책에 유연성이 없었기 때문이다.

어휘 flexibility 융통성, 유연성 financially 재정적으로 widely 널리 relatively 상대적으로

16

해설 '~에 위치해 있다(be located on)'를 수식하여, 왕래하기 편리한 위치에 있다는 의미로 '편리하게'를 뜻하는 (A) conveniently가 정답이다.

번역 커피 기계가 테이버 건물의 2층의 편리한 곳에 위치해 있다.

어휘 conveniently 편리하게 slightly 약간 considerably 상당히, 많이 eventually 결국

17

해설 '지난 2주간 지원서가 꾸준히 들어왔다'는 의미가 적합하므로 '꾸준히, 지속적으로'를 뜻하는 (D) steadily가 정답이다.

번역 접수 담당자 직책에 대한 지원서가 지난 2주에 걸쳐 꾸준히 들어왔다.

어휘 application 지원(서) come in ~에 들어오다 openly 터놓고, 솔직하게 greatly 크게, 대단히 exactly 정확하게

18

해설 '합리적으로 가격이 책정된'이 적합하므로 (C) reasonably 가 정답이다.

번역 크리스티 드라이버는 스포츠 의학계에서 유명한 치료사로, 치료 비용도 매우 합리적으로 책정되어 있다.

어휘 therapist 치료사 internally 내부적으로 repeatedly 반복해서

19

해설 '높이 평가 받았다'라는 의미가 적합하므로 정답은 (C) highly이다.

번역 상당히 호평 받았던 마리엘 카스틸로 씨의 라디오 프로그램은 봄에 새 라디오 방송국으로 옮길 것이다.

20

해설 앞 내용을 받아 '그중에도 특히'라고 할 때 '가장 주목할 만하게'라는 뜻으로 most notably를 쓴다. 따라서 정답은 (B) notably이다.

번역 크로스 코브는 많은 뉴질랜드 예술가들의 본산인데, 그중에 특히 프란시스 슈어드와 카일 매킨타이어가 유명하다.

어휘 separately 각각, 개별적으로 commonly 공통적으로

21

해설 다시 촬영해야 한다는 내용이 뒤따르므로 영상이 성급하게 제작되었다는 의미가 적절하다. 따라서 '서둘러, 급하게'를 뜻하는 (C) hastily가 정답이다.

번역 페핀 씨는 관광 안내 동영상이 급하게 제작되었다고 느꼈기 때문에, 다시 촬영해야 한다고 권했다.

어휘 appear to ~해 보이다 recommend 권하다 altogether 완전히, 통틀어

22

해설 '~로 구성되다(be made up of)'를 수식하여, '주로 파란 꽃으로 구성되어 있다'라는 의미가 적합하다. 따라서 정답은 '주로'를 뜻하는 (C) primarily이다. '오로지, 전적으로'라는 뜻의 (B) exclusively는 '~로만 구성되어 있다'라는 의미가 되는데, 빨간 색 꽃도 섞여 있다고 했으므로 답이 될 수 없다.

번역 건물 입구에 있는 인상적인 꽃 장식은 주로 파란 꽃으로 이루어져 있고, 빨간 꽃 몇 송이가 주변에 솜씨 있게 배치되었다.

어휘 impressive 인상적인 floral display 꽃 장식 artfully 기교 있게 throughout 도처에

23

해설 '정장(business attire)' 대신에 '간편한 복장(casual clothing)'을 입을 수 있다는 의미가 적절하므로 정답은 (C) instead이다.

번역 매주 목요일에 비즈니스 정장을 입지 않고, 직원들은 대신 간편한 옷을 입는 것을 선택할 수 있다.

어휘 rather than ~ 대신에 attire 복장 casual 간편한 in case ~일 경우에 대비하여

24

해설 빈칸 뒤 'upon -ing'는 '~하자마자'를 뜻하므로 '하자마자 즉시'라는 의미를 이루는 (C) immediately가 정답이다.

번역 보안상의 이유로, 이제 모든 대리인들은 본관에 도착하자마자 즉시 접수계원에게 신고해야 한다.

어휘 security 보안 representative (판매) 대리인, 대표자 register 등록하다 urgency 긴급, 위급

25

해설 시스템을 업그레이드하여 더욱 '효율적으로' 업무를 처리할 거라는 문맥이다. 따라서 정답은 (B) efficiently이다.

번역 주문 추적 데이터베이스의 업그레이드로 직원들은 고객의 구매를 더 효율적으로 처리할 수 있을 것이다.

어휘 track ~을 추적하다 process 처리하다; 과정, 절차 purchase 구매, 구입품 totally 완전히 shortly 곧

26

해설 고객의 사생활을 중시한다는 의미로 take와 함께 쓰여 '~을 중시하다'라는 뜻을 이루는 (C) seriously가 정답이다.

번역 저희 크레딧 패시피커는 고객의 개인정보를 중시하므로, 귀하의 주소를 외부 마케팅 대행사들에 판매하지 않을 것을 약속드립니다.

어휘 pledge 맹세하다 soundly 견실하게 totally 완전히 completely 전적으로

27

해설 현재완료(has negotiated)를 수식하는 부사 자리이므로 (C) recently가 정답이다. (A) shortly와 (B) soon은 '곧'이라는 뜻으로 미래 시제와 잘 어울리고, (D) yet은 '아직 ~하지 않았다'라는 의미로 'have yet to부정사'를 쓴다.

번역 인터그룹사는 최근 라틴 아메리카에 스트림플로우 소프트웨어를 유통시킬 독점권 계약을 협상했다.

어휘 negotiate 협상하다 contract 계약 exclusive 독점적인 right 권한 distribute 유통시키다

28

해설 빈도부사는 현재 시제를 수식하는 부사로 자주 출제된다. 문맥상 '주기적으로 검토되고 있다'로 자연스러우므로 '주기적으로'라는 의미의 (B) periodically가 정답이다.

번역 현행 온실가스 배출 기준을 반영할 수 있도록 감사관의 교육 과정을 주기적으로 재검토하고 있다.

어휘 auditor 감사관 curriculum 교육 과정 revisit (어떤 아이디어·주제를) 다시 논의하다 ensure 보장하다 reflect 반영하다 current 현재의 greenhouse 온실 emission 배출 formerly 이전에 simplistically 단순화하여

29

해설 '작동하고 있다(is functioning)'를 수식하여 '장비가 제대로 작동하다'라는 의미를 이루는 (A) properly가 정답이다.

번역 홀드런 제지 공장에서는 모든 장비가 제대로 작동하는지 확인하기 위해 정기 점검이 수행된다.

어휘 routine inspection 정기 검사 conduct 실시하다
ensure 보장하다 equipment 장비 function
기능하다 officially 공식적으로 literally 문자 그대로
rightfully 정당하게

30

해설 구식 장비를 가능한 한 빨리 교체하라는 의미가 적절하므로
'빨리, 신속하게'를 뜻하는 (C) rapidly가 정답이다.

번역 래퍼포트 씨는 제조 공장이 가능한 빨리 구식 장비를 교체
할 것을 권고한다.

어휘 recommend 권장하다 manufacturing 제조업
plant 공장 replace 교체하다 outdated
구식인 equipment 장비 definitely 분명히
predominantly 주로

UNIT 09	ETS 빈출 전치사

VOCA PRACTICE
본책 p. 209

1 (B)	2 (A)	3 (B)	4 (B)	5 (B)
6 (B)	7 (A)	8 (C)	9 (A)	10 (B)
11 (D)	12 (C)	13 (C)	14 (D)	15 (A)

1

하행 열차들은 12번 트랙**에서(from)** 출발할 것입니다.

어휘 outbound 떠나는, 하행의 depart 출발하다

2

그가 도착**하자마자(Upon)** 우리는 회의를 재개할 것이다.

어휘 arrival 도착 resume 재개하다

3

그 회사의 수익이 지난 10년 **동안(in)** 두 배가 되었다.

어휘 profit 이익, 수익 double 두 배로 되다; 두 배의

4

모든 판매 보고서는 류 씨에게 금요일**까지(by)** 제출되어야 한다.

어휘 submit 제출하다

5

저희는 겨울 **내내(throughout)** 토요일과 일요일에는 문을 열지
않을 것입니다.

6

그 재단은 공사를 **위해(toward)** 돈을 기부할 것이다.

어휘 foundation 재단 contribute 기부하다, 기여하다

7

이 지침들은 우리 부서 **내에서(within)**만 회람되어야 하며, 다른
곳으로 유출되면 안 된다.

어휘 circulate 돌리다, 유포하다 distribute 배포하다
elsewhere 다른 곳으로

8

해설 the third-floor elevator라는 장소 명사 앞에서 '엘리베
이터 근처에'라는 의미로 쓸 수 있는 (C) near가 정답이다.
(A) close는 전치사 to를 붙여 close to와 같이 써야 정
답이 될 수 있다.

번역 모든 사무용품들은 3층 엘리베이터 근처에 있는 벽장에 보
관될 것이다.

어휘 office supplies 사무용품 closet 벽장

9

해설 the week of June 5가 6월 5일부터 1주일을 나타내는
기간 명사이므로 기간 전치사 (A) during이 정답이다.

번역 시네빌 교량은 6월 5일부터 한 주 동안 폐쇄될 것이다.

10

해설 오프라인 매장을 닫는다는 앞 내용으로 볼 때, online-only
retailer(온라인 전용 소매업체)로서만 운영할 것이라고 연
결해야 자연스러우므로 자격을 나타내는 전치사 (B) as가
정답이다.

번역 5월 1일부터 재스퍼 의류는 오프라인 매장을 닫고, 온라인
전용 소매업체로만 운영할 것이다.

어휘 beginning on ~부터 physical store 오프라인 매장

11

해설 '포장에 대한 비용'이라는 의미가 적합하므로 '~에 대한'을
뜻하는 (D) of가 정답이다.

번역 새로운 프로 팁 마커펜의 예상 생산비는 포장 비용을 제외
하고 세트당 2달러 15센트가 될 것이다.

어휘 estimated 예상되는 per ~당 exclude 제외시키다

12

해설 '비품 캐비닛'과 '파일 폴더'의 관계를 연결하려면, 파일 폴
더가 들어 있는 비품 캐비닛이 가장 적합하므로 소유와 부
속 개념을 나타낼 수 있는 (C) with가 정답이다.

번역 프린터 카트리지는 파일 폴더가 들어 있는 비품 캐비닛에서
찾을 수 있다.

13

해설 동사 offer의 목적어로 free classes가 있고, 빈칸 뒤에
는 adults and children이라는 대상이 나왔으므로 '~에
게 제공하다'가 적합하다. 따라서 정답은 (C) to이다.

번역 데일리타운 병원은 성인들과 아이들을 대상으로 영양에 관한 무료 수업을 제공한다.

어휘 free 무료의   nutrition 영양(물)   adult 성인

14

해설 '머지않아'를 뜻하는 not long은 ago, before, after 등의 시간 부사(구/절)와 결합하여 '얼마 전, 얼마 후' 등을 나타낸다. 따라서 정답은 '떠난 후 얼마 지나지 않아'라는 의미를 완성하는 (D) after이다.

번역 니스클렌사를 떠난 후 얼마 지나지 않아 사이토 씨는 정부 기관에서 일하기 시작했다.

15

해설 '역에서 기다리다'라는 의미가 적절하므로 장소 전치사 (A) at이 정답이다. wait는 뒤에 기다리는 대상이 올 때는 for를 쓰므로 의미 파악 없이 (B) for를 고르지 않도록 유의해야 한다.

번역 야마구치 씨는 기차가 지연되어 역에서 두 시간 넘게 기다려야만 했다.

어휘 force ~하게 만들다

UNIT 10 ETS 빈출 전치사 어구

VOCA PRACTICE 본책 p. 214

1 (A)	2 (A)	3 (B)	4 (B)	5 (A)
6 (B)	7 (B)	8 (B)	9 (A)	10 (B)
11 (D)	12 (A)	13 (D)	14 (B)	15 (A)

1

사무용품은 팩스기 **옆(next to)**의 복사실에 보관된다.

어휘 office supply 사무용품   store 저장[보관]하다

2

우리는 새로운 규칙에 **관한(with regard to)** 많은 문의들을 받았다.

어휘 inquiry 문의   in place of ~ 대신에

3

프라트 극장의 복구 작업은 일정보다 **미리(ahead of)** 완료될 것이다.

어휘 restoration 복원, 복구

4

오해 받는 것을 피하기 위해 **서면으로(in writing)** 보고해야 한다.

어휘 misunderstand 오해하다

5

잦은 오작동 **때문에(due to)** 우리는 시스템을 교체할 계획이다.

어휘 replace 교체하다   frequent 잦은, 빈번한   malfunction 오작동, 고장

6

적합한 공사 허가증 획득이 지연되었기 **때문에(Owing to)**, 시민 회관 개조 작업은 월요일이 되어서야 재개될 것이다.

어휘 obtain 얻다, 획득하다   proper 적절한   permit 허가(증)   renovation 수리   civic 시민의   resume 재개하다   not A until B B하고서야 A하다   ahead of ~보다 앞선

7

마지막 선물은 상품 수송 중에 발생한 파손 **때문에(because of)** 구매자에 의해 거부되었다.

어휘 refuse 거절[거부]하다   occur 일어나다, 발생하다   in transit 수송 중에

8

해설 '사설 컨설팅 회사의 최근 연구에 따르면'이라는 의미가 적절하므로, (B) According to가 정답이다. 나머지 보기들은 모두 접속사이므로 오답이다.

번역 사설 컨설팅 회사의 최근 연구에 따르면, 스프링필드 교통량의 30퍼센트 이상이 상업용 차량으로 이루어져 있다.

어휘 be made up of ~로 구성되다   commercial 상업의   now that ~이므로   even though 비록 ~일지라도

9

해설 '경쟁사와 달리'라는 문맥이 적절하므로 정답은 (A) In contrast to이다.

번역 주요 경쟁사와 달리, 웰 디자인스가 제공하는 인체공학적 의자는 가볍고 다양한 색상으로 출시된다.

어휘 competitor 경쟁자   ergonomic 인체공학적인   lightweight 가벼운   come in ~로 나온다   by way of ~을 거쳐[경유하여]

10

해설 '부족'을 의미하는 lack과 '좋은 선택'을 의미하는 'good choice'가 내용상 상반되므로 '부족하지만 좋은 선택이다'로 연결될 수 있도록 대조의 의미의 전치사가 들어가는 것이 적합하다. 따라서 정답은 (B) In spite of이다.

번역 스톤 시티는 대규모 콘퍼런스 센터가 부족하지만 프리랜서 연합의 연례 회의를 개최하기에 좋은 장소이다.

어휘 lack 부족, 결여   no sooner A than B A하자마자 B하다

11
해설 '본사에서 1킬로미터 떨어진'이라는 거리 의미가 적합하므로 (D) away from이 정답이다.

번역 해리슨 지역 은행은 금융 지구에 있는 본사에서 단 1킬로미터 떨어진 해리슨의 중심지에 지점을 열 것이다.

어휘 branch 지점, 지사 headquarters 본사 all around 도처에 up until ~에 이르기까지 far ahead 멀리, 앞쪽에

12
해설 whether가 이끄는 명사절을 연결하는 자리이므로 전치사가 필요하다. 또한 '모든' 지원서를 받는다고 했으므로 '~에 상관없이'가 들어가야 문맥이 자연스럽다. 따라서 (A) regardless of가 정답이다.

번역 우리는 지원자가 인터넷 시장에 사전 경험이 있는지 여부에 상관없이 모든 지원서를 받는다.

어휘 accept 받아 주다 application 지원서 applicant 지원자 previous 이전의

13
해설 오렌지 색상 드레스가 폐기되었다는 내용 뒤에 '더 은은한 색상을 선호하여'라는 내용이 오는 것이 적합하므로 '~을 찬성하여'라는 뜻의 (D) in favor of가 정답이다.

번역 디자이너들이 많이 숙고한 끝에 더 은은한 색상의 드레스를 선호하여 밝은 오렌지색 드레스는 폐기되었다.

어휘 deliberation 숙고, 심의 abandon 버리다, 폐기하다 subdued 부드러운, 은은한

14
해설 박사가 기여한 분야가 psychology, neurobiology라고 나왔고 빈칸 뒤에 linguistics라는 또 다른 분야가 나오므로 '~ 외에도'를 뜻하는 (B) in addition to가 정답이다.

번역 라비아 박사는 초창기 언어학 분야의 업적 외에도 심리학과 신경 생물학 분야에서도 상당한 공헌을 했다.

어휘 significant 상당한, 중요한 contribution 공헌, 기부 psychology 심리학 neurobiology 신경 생물학 in as much as ~인 점을 고려하면 in either case 어느 경우에나

15
해설 빈칸 앞뒤로 맛과 가격이라는 대등한 요소가 대치되는 구조이므로 '가격보다는 맛'이라는 의미로 (A) rather than이 정답이다.

번역 신제품 음료 쿨피즈의 광고 캠페인은 가격보다는 맛을 특징으로 삼을 것이다.

어휘 feature 특징으로 하다; 특징 flavor 맛

ETS TEST
본책 p. 215

1 (A)	2 (D)	3 (B)	4 (C)	5 (A)
6 (A)	7 (A)	8 (C)	9 (B)	10 (B)
11 (C)	12 (D)	13 (B)	14 (A)	15 (C)
16 (B)	17 (D)	18 (A)	19 (C)	20 (D)
21 (B)	22 (B)	23 (C)	24 (D)	25 (A)
26 (C)	27 (A)	28 (D)	29 (A)	30 (D)

1
해설 '~에 의해' 감명받았다는 뜻으로 행위의 주체를 나타내는 (A) by가 정답이다. since는 접속사일 때 '~ 때문에'라는 의미도 있어서 문맥에 어울릴 수도 있지만, 빈칸 뒤는 명사구이므로 전치사만 올 수 있다.

번역 시장조사 연구원들의 보고에 따르면, 고객들은 베스트라 커피메이커의 예약 타이머 기능을 가장 인상적으로 느꼈다고 한다.

어휘 be impressed by ~에 인상을 받다 delayed-start 시작 시간 예약의 beyond ~을 넘어서 for ~을 위해 since ~ 이래로, ~ 때문에

2
해설 '프로젝트 매니저로서'가 적합하므로 자격을 나타내는 (D) As가 정답이다.

번역 프로젝트 매니저로서 정 씨는 회사 사장 직속이 될 것이다.

어휘 be directly responsible to ~의 직속이다, ~의 명령을 직접 받다 aside 옆쪽에, 한쪽으로

3
해설 명사 '제휴(partnership)'와 어울리는 전치사로 '~와'를 의미하는 (B) with가 정답이다.

번역 금일 사리 여행사는 성장하고 있는 국제 항공사인 콜그렌 항공과 제휴한다고 발표했다.

어휘 announce 발표하다 partnership 동업 관계, 제휴, 협력 growing 성장하는

4
해설 '박물관 내에(서)'가 적합하므로 (C) inside가 정답이다.

번역 사쿠라 미술관 안에서는 플래시를 이용한 사진 촬영은 허가되지 않는다.

어휘 permit 허락하다 onto ~ 위로 among (셋 이상) ~의 사이에 toward ~ 쪽으로

5
해설 '~에게'로 대상을 나타낼 때는 전치사 (A) to를 쓴다. be open to(~에게 개방되다)로 암기해 두자.

번역   네빈튼 도서관은 지역 주민 모두에게 개방된다.

어휘   resident 주민

6

해설   '현재 다음 학기 지원서를 받고 있다'라는 의미를 이루어야 하는데, applications는 the upcoming semester를 위한 지원서이므로 '목적, 용도'의 전치사인 (A) for가 정답이다.

번역   HJB 공업 학교가 현재 약사 보조원과 의료 행정 과정의 다음 학기 지원서를 접수하고 있습니다.

어휘   accept 받아들이다   application 지원, 지원서   upcoming 다가오는   semester 학기   pharmacy technician 약사 보조원   medical administration 의료 행정

7

해설   '전국 순회(national tour)'라는 기간을 나타내는 명사 앞이므로 기간 전치사 (A) during이 정답이다. (B) among 뒤에는 복수명사가 온다는 것을 함께 알아 두자.

번역   유명한 바이올린 연주자인 아야 코두라는 전국 순회공연 동안에도 엄격한 연습 일정을 유지했다.

어휘   renowned 저명한   maintain 유지하다   rigorous 엄격한, 정확한

8

해설   전치사인 보기 (A) until과 (C) of 중에서, '공장의 효율성'이라는 의미가 적합하므로 (C) of가 정답이다.

번역   소비자 수요가 상당히 증가함에 따라, 리그네스 제조사는 공장의 효율성을 분석해야만 한다.

어휘   demand 수요   substantially 상당히, 많이   analyze 분석하다   efficiency 효율성

9

해설   전치사인 (B) Besides와 (D) Until 중에서, 경력이 두 가지 언급되므로 '영업 경력 외에도'라고 하는 것이 적절하다. 따라서 정답은 '~외에, ~뿐만 아니라'를 뜻하는 (B) Besides이다.

번역   우 씨는 영업 경력 외에 대외 홍보 경력도 있다.

어휘   background 경력   public relations 대외 홍보(부)

10

해설   '처음부터 끝까지'라는 의미가 적절하므로 'from A to B' 구조를 써야 한다. 따라서 정답은 (B) from이다.

번역   에어 필터를 직접 교체하려 시도하기 전에 설명서를 처음부터 끝까지 읽으십시오.

어휘   attempt to ~하려고 시도하다   replace ~을 교체하다

11

해설   '지원서를 받은 후에 면접자를 결정할 것이다'라는 의미가 적합하므로 정답은 (C) After이다.

번역   그 관리직에 대한 모든 지원서를 받은 후에, 추대 위원회는 면접 볼 사람들을 결정할 것이다.

어휘   application 신청서   managerial position 매니저직, 관리직   determine 결정하다

12

해설   largely 이하에서 해외 투자가 지난 5년간 꾸준히 증가해 온 이유에 대해 언급하므로 (D) because of가 정답이다.

번역   해외 투자가 지난 5년간 꾸준히 증가해 왔는데, 이는 주로 몇몇 주요 세계 시장에서 경제가 호전되었기 때문이다.

어휘   steadily 지속적으로, 꾸준히   upturn 개선, 향상   global market 세계 시장

13

해설   '길이가 10페이지를 넘으면 안 된다'는 말이 들어가는 것이 알맞다. in length는 '길이가, 길이에 있어서'라는 의미이므로, 정답은 (B) in이다.

번역   〈신촌 리뷰〉에 게재되려면 제출되는 기사들은 길이가 10페이지를 넘으면 안 된다.

어휘   submit 제출하다   no more than ~을 넘지 않는

14

해설   '가설과는 다르게 결과는 ~했다'가 적합하므로 대조를 나타내는 (A) Contrary to가 정답이다.

번역   가설과는 달리, 그 연구 결과는 두 집단의 총 수면 시간에는 큰 차이가 없었음을 보여 주었다.

어휘   hypothesis 가설, 가정   significant 중요한, 상당한   difference 차이   even though 비록 ~일지라도   except for ~을 제외하고   in place of ~ 대신에

15

해설   빈칸 뒤에 '지난 12개월'이라는 기간이 있으므로 '~에 걸쳐'라는 뜻의 기간 전치사 (C) over가 정답이다.

번역   레드버리 타운 도서관은 지난 12개월에 걸쳐 거의 5천 유로를 기부금으로 받았다.

어휘   nearly 거의   contribution 공헌, 기부   above ~ 위의   along ~을 따라

16

해설   '정부 계약을 (따기) 위해 경쟁하다'라는 의미가 적절하므로 목적을 나타내는 전치사인 (B) for가 정답이다.

번역   정부 계약을 수주하려고 경쟁하는 운송업체의 수가 지난 10년 동안 급격히 감소했다.

어휘 transport company 운송 회사　contract 계약
decrease 감소하다　sharply 급격히

17
해설 '모든 계좌(all accounts)'를 지칭하고 있으므로 '계좌의
종류에 상관없이'라고 연결하는 것이 적합하다. 따라서 '~
에 상관없이'라는 뜻의 (D) regardless of가 정답이다.
번역 합병의 결과, 센트랄라 은행의 모든 계좌들이 그 종류에 상
관없이 클라러스 트러스트사로 이양되었다.
어휘 as a result of ~의 결과로　merger 합병　account
계좌, 거래　transfer 이전[이양]하다　prior to ~ 이전에
except for ~을 제외하고　instead of ~ 대신에

18
해설 빈칸 뒤에 '지난 10년'이라는 기간이 있으므로 '내내'라는
기간 전치사 (A) Throughout이 정답이다. 참고로, for,
during, over, in도 '~ 동안'이라는 의미로 이 자리에 올
수 있다.
번역 지난 10년 동안 루엘렌 병원은 모범적인 환자 관리와 혁신
적인 기술로 인정받고 있다.
어휘 recognize 인정하다　exemplary 모범적인
progressive 진보적인, 혁신적인

19
해설 '얼마 되지 않는 과학자들 사이에'가 적합하므로 (C) among
이 정답이다. 주어가 among 뒤에 있는 명사들 중에 속한
다는 의미로 be동사 뒤에서 among이 자주 출제된다.
번역 굽타 씨는 쿠퍼슨 협회와 헨리 과학 위원회 모두에게 상을
받은 몇 안 되는 과학자에 속한다.
어휘 few 얼마 안 되는　honor 존경하다, 상을 주다

20
해설 '성명을 발표할 계획이다(plans to issue a statement)'
라고 했고, 무엇에 관한 성명인지 그 내용이 뒤따르므로 '~
에 대한'이라는 뜻의 (D) about이 정답이다.
번역 그 조직은 오늘 오후에 유명한 마케팅 전략가의 고용에 대
한 성명을 발표할 예정이다.
어휘 organization 조직　issue 발표하다, 발행하다
statement 성명, 진술, 성명서　hiring 고용　well-
known 유명한　marketing strategist 마케팅 전략가

21
해설 '투자자들의 불안(investors' unease)'을 언급하며, 무엇
에 대한 불안인지 그 내용이 뒤따르므로 '~에 대한'이라는
뜻의 (B) with regard to가 정답이다.

번역 전 씨의 발표로 탠델사와의 잠재적 합병을 둘러싼 협상에
대한 투자자들의 우려를 해결하고자 했다.
어휘 address 처리하다, 다루다　investor 투자자　unease
불안, 우려　negotiation 협상　potential 잠재적인;
잠재력　merger 합병　in accordance with ~에 따라
in place of ~ 대신에　by means of ~을 이용하여

22
해설 '면허 만료일 90일 전에 공지를 보낸다'라는 의미가 적합하
므로 '~ 이전에'를 뜻하는 (B) prior to가 정답이다.
번역 차량 면허 교부 기관은 면허 만기일 90일 전에 모든 상업용
트럭 기사들에게 통지를 보낸다.
어휘 vehicle 차량　licensing 면허 [교부]　agency 기관,
대행사　notice 통지　commercial 상업용의; 광고
expiration 만기

23
해설 '번역하다'라는 뜻의 동사 translate는 'translate A into
B' 형태로 쓰여 'A를 B로 번역하다'라는 의미를 나타낸다.
따라서 '5개 언어로 번역했다'라는 의미를 이루는 (C) into
가 정답이다. 참고로, 동사로 온 had는 사역동사로 쓰였으
며 목적어와 목적격 보어 관계가 수동이므로 p.p. 형태인
translated가 왔다.
번역 옵틱스 아이 케어는 보유한 모든 안내 책자들과 기타 인쇄
물들을 5개 언어로 번역해 놓았다.
어휘 brochure 안내책자, 팸플릿　written materials
서면[인쇄] 자료　translate A into B A를 B로 번역하다

24
해설 '모든 지원자에게 응답하기 힘들다'라는 내용으로 보아, '이
력서의 상당한 양을 고려할 때'라는 의미로 연결되는 것
이 자연스럽다. 따라서 '~을 고려해 볼 때'라는 뜻의 (D)
Given이 정답이다. 접속사인 (A) Even if와 (C) Unless
는 올 수 없다.
번역 매달 받는 이력서가 매우 많기 때문에 모든 구직자들에게
응답할 수 없습니다.
어휘 receive 받다　respond 응답하다　applicant 지원자

25
해설 '많은 질문을 받은 후에 공식 발표를 했다'가 적합하므로 '~
후에'를 뜻하는 (A) Following이 정답이다.
번역 주주들의 질문 공세 후, 제임스 홍은 회사가 잘 운영되고 있
다고 공식 발표했다.
어휘 inquiry 질문　shareholder 주주　issue an
announcement 발표하다　formal 공식적인

26

해설 '안전 규정에 따라 보호 장비를 착용해야 한다'라는 내용이 적합하므로 '~에 따라'를 뜻하는 (C) in keeping with가 정답이다. 같은 의미의 in compliance with, in accordance with도 쓸 수 있다.

번역 톰슨 연구소의 직원들은 안전 규정에 따라 연구소 입구의 포스터에 제시된 모든 보호 장비를 반드시 착용해야 한다.

어휘 protective gear 보호 장비 safety regulations 안전 규정 provided that 만약 ~이라면 extend 확장하다, 연장하다 by means of ~을 이용하여

27

해설 '워크숍과 관련된 세부 사항'이라는 의미가 적합하므로 '~에 관련된'이라는 뜻의 (A) pertaining to가 정답이다.

번역 워크숍에 관계된 추가 세부 사항은 참석 의사를 표한 모든 이에게 발송될 것이다.

어휘 additional 추가의 details 세부 사항 express 표현하다

28

해설 '화기 근처에 놓지 말라'는 뜻으로 '근처에'를 의미하는 (D) near가 정답이다.

번역 예민한 전자 부품이 손상될 수 있으니, 고열을 내는 기구 근처에 디지털 저울을 놓지 않도록 하십시오.

어휘 avoid -ing ~하는 것을 피하다 scale 저울 source 근원지, 원천 excessive 과도한 sensitive 예민한 component 부품

29

해설 '온라인 채팅 서비스를 통해 연락할 수 있다'는 내용이 되어야 자연스러우므로 '~을 통해'라는 수단을 나타내는 뜻의 전치사 (A) through가 정답이다.

번역 문의 담당 사서는 하클리 공공 도서관의 온라인 채팅 서비스를 통해 24시간 연락할 수 있습니다.

어휘 reference 문의, 조회 librarian 사서

30

해설 '~에 주안점을 두다, ~을 강조하다'를 의미하는 구문은 place[put] an emphasis on이므로 정답은 (D) on이다.

번역 전략 기획 위원회는 내년에 연구 개발에 더 주안점을 두어야 한다고 권고했다.

어휘 strategic 전략적인 research and development 연구 개발 in the coming year 내년에

기출 **TEST 1**   본책 p. 218

| **1** (D) | **2** (A) | **3** (D) | **4** (B) | **5** (B) |
| **6** (B) | **7** (D) | **8** (C) | **9** (A) | **10** (A) |

1

해설 **형용사 어휘:** '격식을 갖추지 않은 복장(Informal attire)이 적절하지 않다고 여겨진다'라는 의미가 적합하므로 '적절한'을 뜻하는 (D) appropriate이 정답이다.

번역 격식을 갖추지 않은 복장은 광고상 만찬에 부적절하다고 여겨진다.

어휘 consider 고려하다, 여기다 complete 완전한 significant 중요한

2

해설 **명사 어휘:** '반품 및 교환에 관한 정책'이라는 의미가 적절하므로 '정책'을 뜻하는 (A) policy가 정답이다.

번역 온라인 구매 물품의 반품 및 교환에 관한 비스타 의류의 정책은 당사 웹사이트에 자세히 나와 있습니다.

어휘 apparel 의류 regarding ~에 관한 exchange 교환; 교환하다 purchase 구매(품); 구매하다 detail 상세히 알리다; 세부 사항

3

해설 **전치사 어휘:** '대학에서 재직한 시간(her time at the university)'이 기간에 해당하므로 기간 전치사인 (D) During이 정답이다.

번역 르플뤼 박사는 대학에 재직하는 동안 학생들과 교직원 사이에서 뛰어난 리더십으로 탄탄한 명성을 쌓았다.

어휘 build a reputation 명성을 쌓다 solid 탄탄한, 확실한 leadership 지도력, 통솔력 faculty 교직원, 교수진

4

해설 **동사 어휘:** 목적어로 '신청서(an application)'가 있고 전치사 to 뒤에 대상이 있으므로 '신청서를 ~에게 제출하라'가 적절하다. 따라서 정답은 (B) submit이다.

번역 광고부 직책에 고려 대상이 되기를 희망하신다면 인사부 책임자 앞으로 지원서를 제출하십시오.

어휘 position 위치, 일자리 comply with ~을 준수하다 urge 촉구하다 advise 충고하다

5

해설 **명사 어휘:** 빈칸 뒤 광고 예산을 반으로 줄였다는 내용으로 보아, '지출을 줄이려고'와 연결되는 것이 적합하다. 따라서 (B) expenses가 정답이다.

번역 지출 비용을 줄이려는 노력으로 바솜 화장품은 광고 예산을 반으로 줄였다.

어휘 effort 노력 reduce 줄이다 halve 반으로 줄이다, 이등분하다 advertising budget 광고 예산 value 가치 customs 관세 refund 환불; 환불하다

6

해설 **동사 어휘:** 빈칸 뒤에 온 to부정사(to air)와 함께 쓰여 '다음 달 공영 텔레비전에서 방영될 예정이다'라는 의미가 되어야 한다. 따라서 정답은 '예정된'이라는 의미의 (B) scheduled이다. 'be scheduled to부정사'로 암기해 두자.

번역 요리사 링의 요리 쇼가 다음 달 공영 텔레비전에서 방영될 예정입니다.

어휘 air 방송하다, 방송되다 public television 공영 텔레비전, 공영 방송

7

해설 **형용사 어휘:** 명사 demand를 수식하여 '점점 더 늘어나는 수요'가 적합하므로 (D) increasing이 정답이다.

번역 점점 늘어나는 제품 수요에 부응하기 위하여 우리는 최소 4명의 직원을 추가로 고용해야 할 것이다.

어휘 keep up with ~에 뒤지지 않게 부응하다 demand 수요 hire 고용하다 minimum 최소한도 additional 추가의 elaborate 상세히 말하다, 부연하다 track 추적하다 increasing 증가하는

8

해설 **명사 어휘:** 동사 has built의 목적어 자리로, '명성을 쌓다'라는 의미를 이루는 (C) reputation이 정답이다.

번역 지난 10년 동안 〈자메이카 뉴스〉는 카리브해에서 가장 신뢰할 만한 시사 프로그램 중 하나로 명성을 쌓아 왔다.

어휘 reliable 믿을 만한, 신뢰할 만한 privilege 특권, 특혜 consequence 결과, 중요성

9

해설 **형용사 어휘:** 빈칸 뒤의 전치사 to와 함께 쓰여 '~와 동일한'이라는 뜻을 이루는 (A) equal이 정답이다. (B) uniform은 '획일적인'이라는 의미로 동일함을 나타내므로 비교 대상과 동일하다는 것과는 차이가 있다.

번역 신나 모터스의 올해 매출은 그 회사의 가장 성공적인 시기였던 5년 전에 기록한 수치와 거의 동일하다.

어휘 figure 수치 period 기간, 시기 uniform 획일적인, 동일한; 제복 fair 공평한, 상당한

10

해설 **동사 어휘:** '성과(performance)가 분기별로 평가된다'라는 의미가 적절하므로 '평가하다'라는 뜻의 (A) evaluated가 정답이다.

번역 나호아 미디어에서 부편집자들은 분기별로 성과를 평가받는다.

어휘 performance 성과, 실적 editor 편집자 quarterly 분기별로 evaluate 평가하다

기출 **TEST 2**			본책 p. 219	
1 (C)	**2** (A)	**3** (C)	**4** (C)	**5** (B)
6 (D)	**7** (C)	**8** (C)	**9** (B)	**10** (A)

1

해설 **형용사 어휘:** 분야(area)를 수식하여 '특정 분야의 전문성을 토대로'라는 의미가 적합하므로 '특정한'이라는 뜻의 (C) particular가 정답이다.

번역 바나 통신에서는 특정 분야에 대한 전문 지식을 토대로 프로젝트 팀장을 선발한다.

어휘 telecommunication 통신 select 선별[선택]하다, 고르다 based on ~을 토대로, ~에 근거하여 expertise 전문 지식 substantial 상당한

2

해설 **명사 어휘:** detailed의 수식을 받아 '자세한 설명'이라는 뜻을 이루는 (A) instructions가 정답이다. 빈칸 뒤의 on은 '~에 대한'으로 쓰여, '수리에 대한 자세한 설명'이라는 의미로 자연스럽게 연결된다.

번역 고객들은 사용자 설명서에서 무선 문제 수리에 관한 자세한 설명을 볼 수 있습니다.

어휘 customer 고객 detailed 상세한, 자세한 repair 수리하다, 고치다 wireless 무선의; 무선 수신 장치 user manual 사용자 설명서 instructions 설명, 지시 fixing 고정, 설비

3

해설 **형용사 어휘:** '온화한 기후(moderate climate)'와 '훌륭한 노동력(well-qualified workforce)'을 들어 특정 지역을 소개하고 있으므로, '투자하기에 좋은 장소'라고 하는 것이 적합하다. 따라서 '유망한'이라는 뜻의 (C) promising이 정답이다.

번역 온화한 기후와 훌륭한 자질의 노동 인구가 있어 헌츠빌은 투자자들에게 매우 유망한 장소이다.

어휘 investor 투자자 identify 식별하다, 확인하다

4

해설 **부사 어휘:** '두 지원자가 똑같이 자격을 갖춘 것으로 보인다'가 적합하므로 '똑같이'를 뜻하는 (C) equally가 정답이다.

번역 제공된 정보에 근거하면, 두 명의 구직자는 그 직책에 똑같이 자격을 갖춘 것으로 보인다.

어휘 be based on ~에 근거[토대]를 두다 qualified for ~에 자격이 있는, 적임의 punctually 정각에 frequently 자주 lately 최근에

5

해설 **동사 어휘:** 목적어로 '계약(agreement)'이 나오므로 '계약을 갱신하다'라는 뜻을 이루는 (B) renew가 정답이다.

번역 친 렌털스 그룹은 젠킨슨 메인터넌스와의 계약을 갱신하기로 결정했다.

어휘 decide 결정[결심]하다 agreement 합의, 계약 proceed with ~을 진행하다 renew 갱신하다 urge 촉구하다 attract 끌다

6

해설 **명사 어휘:** '구역 출입 허가를 받았다'라는 의미가 적절하므로 '허가'라는 뜻의 (D) permission이 정답이다.

번역 그 여행단은 평소에는 일반인의 출입이 금지된 지역에 들어가는 것을 허락받았다.

어휘 admit 들어가게 하다 off-limits 출입 금지의 decision 결정, 결심 expense 비용 request 요청

7

해설 **부사 어휘:** '복구하기 위해 부지런히 작업 중이다'가 적절하므로 '부지런히'를 뜻하는 (C) diligently가 정답이다.

번역 기술팀은 최대한 빨리 온라인 접속을 복구하기 위해 부지런히 작업하고 있다.

어휘 restore 복구하다, 회복시키다 access 이용, 접근; 이용하다, 접근하다 vastly 엄청나게 variably 일정하지 않게 longingly 갈망하여

8

해설 **동사 어휘:** 목적어로 '시스템 고장(system failure)'이 나오므로 '고장을 방지하기 위해 조치를 취했다'라는 의미가 적합하다. 따라서 '막다, 방지하다'라는 뜻의 (C) prevent가 정답이다.

번역 내셔널 뱅크 임원진은 컴퓨터 시스템 장애의 재발을 막는 데 필요한 조치를 취했다고 발표했다.

어휘 official 공무원, 임원 take steps 조치를 취하다 failure 고장, 장애 ignore 무시하다 improve 개선하다

9

해설 **전치사 어휘:** 동사 check는 전치사 for와 함께 쓰이며, 이때 for의 목적어로는 error나 mistake가 잘 나온다. 따라서 정답은 (B) for이다. 'check A for B'로 암기해 두자.

번역 다니엘은 그룹 관리자에게 제출하기 전에 보고서에 실수가 있는지 점검할 것이다.

어휘 submit 제출하다

10

해설 **형용사 어휘:** 사람(individual)을 수식하여 '뛰어난 인물을 찾고 있다'라는 의미가 적합하므로 (A) accomplished가 정답이다. (D) influenced는 '영향을 받은'이라는 뜻이므로 오답이다. '영향력 있는'이라는 뜻의 influential과 구분해야 한다.

번역 LTD사는 이달 말에 퇴임하는 이사의 후임이 될 뛰어난 인물을 찾고 있다.

어휘 individual 개인, 사람 replace ~의 후임자가 되다, 대체하다 current 현재의 director 이사, 임원 retire 은퇴하다 accomplished 기량이 뛰어난, 숙련된 illustrated 삽화를 넣은 observe 관찰하다, 준수하다

기출 TEST 3				본책 p. 220
1 (A)	2 (D)	3 (B)	4 (D)	5 (D)
6 (A)	7 (B)	8 (C)	9 (D)	10 (B)

1

해설 **동사 어휘:** '수익이 통상 겨울에 감소한다'라는 의미가 적합하므로 (A) declines가 정답이다. 참고로 decline은 자동사로 쓰일 때는 '감소하다', 타동사로 쓰일 때는 '거절하다'로 쓰인다.

번역 랜드그로브 부동산의 수익은 대개 겨울철에 감소하고 봄에 회복된다.

어휘 real estate 부동산 revenue 수익 typically 대개, 보통 recover 회복하다, 복구하다 impact 영향을 주다 impede 지연시키다, 방해하다

2

해설 **전치사 어휘:** 빈칸 뒤의 limits가 핵심 단서로, '제한 이내에'라는 의미를 이루는 (D) within이 정답이다. within은 거리, 기간, 제한 범위와 함께 자주 쓰인다.

번역 회계사는 엄격히 제한된 시간 이내에 상당한 양의 자료를 처리한다.

어휘 accountant 회계사 process 처리하다, 가공하다; 과정, 절차 considerable 상당한 amount 양, 금액 material 소재, 재료, 자료 strict 엄격한 limit 제한; 제한하다

3

해설 **형용사 어휘:** '상하기 쉬운 제품이 부패하는 것을 막기 위해'라는 의미가 적절하므로 '상하기 쉬운'이라는 뜻의 (B) perishable이 정답이다.

번역 우유와 다른 부패하기 쉬운 제품들이 상하는 것을 막기 위해 델리오의 식품 배송 트럭들에는 냉장 장치가 되어 있다.

어휘 **prevent from -ing** ~하는 것을 막다[방지하다]
deteriorate (상태가) 악화되다   **refrigerate**
냉장시키다

4

해설 **동사 어휘:** '포장(packaging)'이 변경되는 목적으로 '더
넓은 해외 시장에 어필하기 위해서'가 적절하므로 '마음을
끌다'를 뜻하는 (D) appeal to가 정답이다.

번역 오지그레인 시리얼의 포장은 더 넓은 해외시장에 어필할 수
있도록 변경될 예정이다.

어휘 **packaging** 포장   **overseas** 해외의   **demand**
요구하다   **call out** 불러내다   **appeal** 어필하다,
호소하다

5

해설 **명사 어휘:** '보험 회사(Insurance)'와 관련하여 claims는
'보험 청구'를 뜻하며, '많은 양의 보험 청구를 처리한다'가
적절하므로 '양'을 뜻하는 (D) volume이 정답이다.

번역 헤이브록 보험은 매일 많은 양의 보험금 청구를 처리하므로
유능한 직원이 필요하다.

어휘 **insurance** 보험   **process** 처리하다, 가공하다; 진행,
절차   **claim** (보상금 등의) 청구, 신청   **daily** 매일
efficient 유능한, 효율적인   **section** 부분, 구역
a high volume of 다량의, 다수의

6

해설 **부사 어휘:** almost의 수식을 받고 deal with를 수식하여
'거의 ~만을 다룬다'라는 의미를 완성하는 '전적으로, 오로
지'를 뜻하는 (A) exclusively가 정답이다.

번역 제인 와이즈먼은 거의 전기만을 취급하는 출판사를 경영하
고 있다.

어휘 **publishing company** 출판사   **deal with**
~을 다루다[취급하다]   **biography** 전기, 일대기
impulsively 충동적으로   **mutually** 서로, 상호간에
generously 관대하게

7

해설 **부사 어휘:** 현재 시제와 함께 쓰여 '현재 47퍼센트 완성되
었다'라는 의미를 이루는 (B) now가 정답이다.

번역 컬러 콜로세움 개조 프로젝트는 현재 47퍼센트의 공사가
완료된 상태이다.

어휘 **construction** 건설, 공사   **complete** 완전한, 완성된;
완성하다   **renovation** 보수[수리], 개조   **once** 한때,
한 번   **quite** 꽤

8

해설 **동사 어휘:** 빈칸 뒤의 수치가 문제 해결의 단서로, 숫자 앞
에서 '총계가 ~에 이르다'라는 의미를 이루는 (C) totaling
이 정답이다.

번역 이그나시오 메탈사는 전체 건평이 총 89,000제곱미터에
이르는 시설 두 곳을 운영하고 있다.

어휘 **operate** 운영[운용]하다   **facility** 시설   **combined**
결합한   **floor space** 건평   **square meter** 제곱미터
earn 얻다   **total** 합계[총] ~이 되다   **complete**
완료하다

9

해설 **명사 어휘:** '품질(quality)'뿐만 아니라 생산성도 향상시켰
다'가 적합하므로 '생산성'을 뜻하는 (D) productivity가
정답이다.

번역 새로 나온 그래픽 디자인 소프트웨어 프로그램은 디자이너
들의 작업 품질뿐만 아니라 생산성도 높였다.

어휘 **improve** 개선하다   **quality** 품질   **as well as** ~뿐만
아니라   **economy** 경제   **harvest** 수확(량)   **measure**
조치, 측정

10

해설 **동사 어휘:** '훈련(training)'의 대상이 누구인지 나타내는
문장이므로 '~을 위해 의도된 것이다'라는 의미를 완성하는
(B) intended가 정답이다. 참고로, 목적을 나타낼 때는 '~
하기 위해 의도된 것이다'라는 뜻으로 'be intended to부
정사'를 쓴다.

번역 내일 교육은 입사한 지 1년 미만인 직원들을 대상으로 마련
된 것이다.

어휘 **base** ~에 근거를 두다   **agree** 동의하다   **invite**
초대하다

기출 **TEST 4**				본책 p. 221
1 (C)	**2** (D)	**3** (B)	**4** (B)	**5** (A)
6 (C)	**7** (D)	**8** (D)	**9** (B)	**10** (D)

1

해설 **형용사 어휘:** '수리 후 마침내 ~할 수 있었다'라는 의미가
적절하므로 '~할 수 있는'이라는 뜻의 (C) able이 정답이
다. 'be able to부정사'로 암기해 두자.

번역 몇 시간의 수리 작업 후 트럭은 마침내 배송 경로를 재개할
수 있었다.

어휘 **repair** 수리, 보수   **resume** 재개하다   **delivery route**
배송 경로   **valuable** 가치 있는, 소중한   **responsible**
책임 있는   **possible** 가능한

2

해설 **명사 어휘:** '~로서 역할을 하다'라는 뜻의 serve as에서 자격의 전치사 as 뒤에는 주체와 동격이 될 수 있는 명사가 와야 한다. '워크숍이 토론의 장 역할을 한다'라는 의미가 적절하므로 workshop과 동격을 이룰 수 있는 '토론장'이라는 뜻의 (D) forum이 정답이다.

번역 지역 문화 회관의 건강 관리 워크숍은 건강에 좋은 습관을 논의하는 토론장 역할을 한다.

어휘 community center 지역 문화 회관 wellness 건강 discuss 논의하다 healthful 건강한 habit 습관 selection 선택 ground 지면 vision 시력, 통찰력

3

해설 **동사 어휘:** '설문 결과를 독자들과 공유할 것이다'가 적절하므로 '공유하다'라는 뜻의 (B) share가 정답이다. 'share A with B'로 암기해 두자.

번역 우리는 다음 주 웹사이트에서 여행 설문 조사 결과를 독자와 공유할 것이다.

어휘 result 결과 poll 여론 조사, 설문, 투표 reader 독자

4

해설 **부사 어휘:** 현재진행 시제와 함께 쓰여 '현재는 받고 있지 않다'라는 의미를 이루는 (B) currently가 정답이다. (D) temperately는 '적당하게'라는 뜻이며 '일시적으로'를 뜻하는 temporarily와 혼동하지 않도록 유의하자.

번역 기술적인 문제 때문에 넬슨 전자 경매는 현재 이메일을 통한 어떠한 사진 제출물도 받지 않고 있습니다.

어휘 auction 경매 submission 제출(물) via ~을 통해 precisely 바로, 정확히

5

해설 **명사 어휘:** 금액과 전치사 in이 문제 해결의 단서로, '2억 5천만 달러를 ~에 투자하기로 합의했다'라는 의미를 이루는 (A) investment가 정답이다.

번역 레이크 파이낸셜은 뉴스 웹사이트인 Everydaylive.com에 2억 5천만 달러를 투자하기로 합의했다.

어휘 make an investment in ~에 투자하다 preservation 보존 requirement 요구, 요건 property 재산, 소유물

6

해설 **동사 어휘:** 목적어인 orders와 호응하는 동사로, '주문을 처리하다'라는 뜻을 이루는 (C) fulfill이 정답이다.

번역 네블러스사는 연말까지 주문을 모두 처리하기를 기대할 경우 직원을 충원해야 할 것이다.

어휘 expect 기대하다 affect 영향을 미치다 contain 함유하다 mention 말하다, 언급하다

7

해설 **부사 어휘:** after와 함께 쓰여 '직후에'라는 의미를 이루는 '즉시'라는 뜻의 (D) promptly가 정답이다. after 앞에서 같은 의미로 soon, shortly, immediately, right, just, directly가 모두 가능하다. 참고로, prefer는 that절과 함께 쓰일 때 that절에서 should가 생략되므로 동사원형인 be submitted가 왔다.

번역 야마나카 씨는 비용이 발생한 직후 직원 지출 보고서가 제출되기를 바랍니다.

어휘 prefer 선호하다 expense report 지출 보고서 submit 제출하다 expense 비용, 경비 incur (비용을) 발생시키다, (손해를) 초래하다 measurably 측정할 수 있게 vaguely 애매하게 uniquely 독특하게

8

해설 **형용사 어휘:** '목재 가격이 틀림없이 오를 것이다'라는 의미가 적절하므로 '반드시 ~하다'라는 뜻의 be bound to 부정사를 완성하는 (D) bound가 정답이다. 참고로, (A) covered는 '~로 덮여 있다'고 할 때 be covered with로 쓰이며, '~에 국한되다'라는 뜻의 be limited to에서는 to가 전치사로 쓰인다.

번역 최근의 건축 호황을 감안하면 목재 가격이 틀림없이 오를 것이다.

어휘 given ~을 고려하면 boom 급등, 벼락 경기 construction 건설, 건축 lumber 목재 climb 오르다

9

해설 **전치사 어휘:** 빈칸 뒤에 요일이 나오므로 '수요일부터'라는 의미를 이루는 (B) starting on이 정답이다. (C) afterward는 '~후에'라는 뜻의 부사이므로 답이 될 수 없다.

번역 직장까지 카풀하는 리카너슨스사의 직원들은 수요일부터 특별 주차 특혜를 받을 수 있을 것이다.

어휘 corporation 기업, 회사 share rides 카풀하다 eligible ~을 받을[가질] 수 있는, 자격이 있는 privilege 특혜

10

해설 **형용사 어휘:** '휴가 혜택을 받을 자격이 있다'가 적합하므로 '~할 자격이 있는'이라는 뜻의 (D) eligible이 정답이다. be eligible for와 be eligible to부정사로 암기해 두자. 참고로, (A) capable은 be capable of로 쓴다.

번역 회사 정책에 따르면, 신입 직원들은 3개월의 상근을 마치면 휴가 혜택을 받을 자격이 있다.

어휘 guideline 지침, 정책 benefits 복리 후생 full-time 전임의 employment 고용 capable ~을 할 수 있는 variable 변동이 심한, 가변적인 flexible 융통성 있는

1 (A)	**2** (B)	**3** (B)	**4** (B)	**5** (A)
6 (D)	**7** (A)	**8** (A)	**9** (A)	**10** (D)

1

해설 **명사 어휘:** '과정을 수료해야 한다(must complete a course)'의 주체가 되어야 하므로 사람명사가 주어로 와야 한다. 따라서 정답은 직원을 뜻하는 (A) personnel이다.

번역 모든 실험실 직원은 매년 안전 실무 과정을 수료해야 한다.

어휘 laboratory 실험실 annually 매년, 해마다 safety 안전 practice 실무, 실습 personnel 직원

2

해설 **형용사 어휘:** '연설자(speaker)'를 수식하여 '회의의 주요 연설자이다'라는 의미가 적합하므로 정답은 '주요한'이라는 뜻의 (B) principal이다.

번역 지속 가능한 토지 이용에 관한 권위자인 아유미 스즈키가 제9차 산림 농업 회의에서 주요 연사로 나설 예정이다.

어휘 authority 권위자, 당국 sustainable 지속 가능한 agroforestry 산림 농업 successive 연속적인 maximum 최대의; 최대 immediate 즉각적인

3

해설 **부사 어휘:** '일정이 변경된(rescheduled)'이라고 했으므로, '대신 토요일에 방영될 것이다'라고 하는 것이 자연스럽다. 따라서 '대신'이라는 뜻의 (B) instead가 정답이다.

번역 뉴스 프로그램의 첫 방영 일정이 변경되어서 이제는 대신 토요일에 방영될 예정이다.

어휘 premiere (영화·연극 등의) 개봉, 초연 reschedule 일정을 변경하다 alike 둘 다 seldom 좀처럼 ~ 않는

4

해설 **동사 어휘:** white and brown이 핵심 단서로, '흰색과 갈색으로 칠해졌다'가 적합하므로 정답은 (B) painted이다. 이때 paint는 5형식 수동태로 쓰여 색상이 paint의 목적격 보어로 온 것이다. 참고로, (A) change는 '~을 …로 바꾸다'를 의미할 때 change A into B로 쓴다.

번역 하우랜드 베이커리가 배송을 위해 처음으로 대형 트럭을 사용하기 시작했을 때, 모든 트럭에는 흰색과 갈색의 칠이 되어 있었다.

어휘 alternate 번갈아[교대로] 하다 transfer 옮기다, 전근[전학] 가다

5

해설 **동사 어휘:** 빈칸 뒤의 전치사 with가 핵심 단서로, '준수해야 한다'라는 의미를 이루는 (A) comply가 정답이다. 나머지 보기들은 모두 타동사로 with와 함께 쓰지 않는다.

번역 식품 판매업자들은 특별 행사 시 판매와 관련된 모든 해당 규정을 준수해야 한다.

어휘 vendor 판매업자, 상인 applicable 적용할 수 있는, 해당되는 policy 규정, 정책 pertaining to ~와 관련된 comply with ~을 준수하다, 지키다 achieve 성취하다 regulate 규제하다, 규정하다 authorize 승인하다, 허가하다

6

해설 **전치사 어휘:** '주차권은 주차장의 가용 공간을 기준으로 하여 발행된다'라는 의미가 되어야 하므로, '~에 근거하여'라는 의미를 지닌 (D) based on이 정답이다.

번역 현장 주차권은 주차장의 가용 공간에 입각하여 발행됩니다.

어휘 onsite 현장의, 현지의 parking pass 주차권 issue 발행하다 availability 이용 가능성 adjacent to ~에 인접한 except for ~을 제외하고

7

해설 **형용사 어휘:** '선착순 50명에게만 제공된다'는 내용으로 볼 때, '공급품이 한정되어 있으므로'와 연결되는 것이 적절하다. 따라서 '제한된'이라는 뜻의 (A) limited가 정답이다.

번역 공급품이 한정되어 있기 때문에 우리는 가게를 찾는 첫 50명의 고객들에게만 이것을 제공할 수 있다.

어휘 supplies 공급품[량] make an offer 제공하다, 제의하다 speedy 신속한 available 이용 가능한 presentable 남에게 내놓을 만한, 볼품 있는

8

해설 **전치사 어휘:** '기밀 문서를 반출하기 전에 서명해야 한다'가 적합하므로 (A) before가 정답이다.

번역 모든 직원은 회사 금고에서 기밀 문서를 반출하기 전에 명부에 서명해야 한다.

어휘 personnel (집합적) 직원 remove 제거하다, 옮기다 confidential 기밀의 organization 조직, 단체 vault 금고, 귀중품 보관실

9

해설 **부사 어휘:** '임대주만이 리모델링을 승인할 수 있다'라는 의미가 적합하므로 '~만'을 뜻하는 (A) only가 정답이다. (D) merely는 '단지, 한낱'이라는 의미이므로 유일함을 강조하는 only와 혼동하지 말아야 한다. 참고로, 부사는 관사가 붙은 명사 앞에서 명사의 의미를 강조할 수 있다.

번역 리베라 씨는 임대주만이 부동산에 대한 개량 공사를 승인할 수 있다는 점을 분명히 했다.

어휘 landowner 임대주 authorize 승인하다 improvement 개량, 향상 property 재산, 부동산, 건물 only 단지, 오직 easily 쉽게 simply 간단히 merely 단지, 한낱

10

해설 **형용사 어휘:** 빈칸 앞의 company를 수식하며 to부정사와 함께 쓸 수 있는 형용사로, '사업 확장을 열망하는 기업'이라는 의미가 적절하므로 (D) eager가 정답이다.

번역 그리폰 솔루션즈는 동아시아에서 사업을 확장하기를 열망하는 성장 일로에 있는 컴퓨터 지원 회사이다.

어휘 expand 확대하다 frequent 잦은, 빈번한 common 흔한, 공동의 eager 열렬한, 간절히 바라는

1

해설 **전치사 어휘:** '서명 없이는 처리할 수 없다'라는 의미가 적합하므로 (D) without이 정답이다.

번역 고객의 서명이 없는 송장은 처리하면 안 된다.

어휘 invoice 송장, 청구서 process 처리하다 signature 서명 except ~을 제외하고 amid ~의 복판에, 한창 ~할 때

2

해설 **형용사 어휘:** '25달러, 혹은 25달러 상당의 금액'이 적절하므로 '동등한, 상당의'라는 뜻의 (A) equivalent가 정답이다.

번역 25달러 미만, 혹은 현지 통화로 이에 상당하는 금액의 주문에 대한 배송비는 환불되지 않는다는 점을 유의하십시오.

어휘 note 주목[주의]하다 shipping charge 배송비 currency 통화, 화폐 nonrefundable 환불이 불가능한 profitable 수익성이 있는 deliberate 고의적인 controlled 통제된

3

해설 **분사 어휘:** revenue를 수식하는 형용사로 '늘어난 수익'이 적합하므로 정답은 (B) increased이다.

번역 릴런드 대로에 있는 수족관이 연간 수천 명의 방문객을 유치해 도시의 수입이 증가할 것으로 전망된다.

어휘 aquarium 수족관 be expected to ~할 것으로 예상되다 draw 끌어들이다, 유치하다 annually 연간 revenue 수익 increased 증가된, 인상된 manage 관리하다, 운영하다 reserve 보유하다, 보존하다

4

해설 **형용사 어휘:** 하룻밤 숙박(one-night stay)을 수식하는 형용사로 '무료로 제공한다'라는 문맥과 자연스럽게 연결되는 '추가적인'이라는 의미의 (D) extra가 정답이다.

번역 그 호텔은 투숙객이 이틀 밤을 예약하면 추가 하룻밤 숙박을 무료로 제공한다.

어휘 offer 제공하다 stay 숙박 free of charge 무료로 book 예약하다 eager 열렬한

5

해설 **동사 어휘:** '초대장을 직접 전달하다'라는 의미가 적합하므로 '전달하다'라는 뜻의 (D) deliver가 정답이다.

번역 이시무라 씨는 초대장을 우편을 통해 발송하지 않고 직접 전달하겠다고 인심 좋게 제의했다.

어휘 generously 관대하게 offer 제의하다, 제안하다 in person 직접 rather than ~보다는 respond to 대답하다, 응하다 benefit 이익이 되다, ~에게 이롭다 commute 통근하다 deliver 전달하다

6

해설 **부사 어휘:** '최근 개장된 주차장'이라는 의미가 적합하므로 (A) recently가 정답이다. recently는 p.p.와 함께 어울려 recently installed(최근에 설치된), recently hired(최근에 고용된) 등으로 활용된다.

번역 최근 문을 연 기즈번즈 주차장의 허가증은 온라인으로 구입할 수 있습니다.

어휘 permit 허가증; 허락하다 parking garage 주차장 purchase 구매[매입]하다; 구매(품) typically 일반적으로, 전형적으로 directly 직접 concisely 간결하게

7

해설 **명사 어휘:** '다양한 요구 사항'이라는 의미로 복수명사 needs를 수식하는 a range of가 적합하다. 따라서 정답은 (C) range이다. '다양한'을 뜻하는 a variety of, an array of, an assortment of도 함께 알아 두자.

번역 그린 앤 버치는 풀 서비스를 제공하는 회계 회사로, 재무 및 사업에 필요한 다양한 요구 사항들을 도와 드릴 수 있습니다.

어휘 accounting firm 회계 회사 assist A with B B에 대해 A를 돕다 financial 금융의, 재무의 deposit 보증금

8

해설 **형용사 어휘:** '첫 번째 줄은 발표자들을 위해 따로 마련된 좌석이다'라는 의미가 적합하므로 '예약된, 따로 잡아 둔'이라는 뜻의 (B) reserved가 정답이다.

번역 워크숍 참가자들은 강당에서 발표자들을 위해 지정된 앞줄의 좌석들을 제외하고 아무 좌석이나 선택할 수 있습니다.

어휘 auditorium 강당 front row 앞줄 chair 의장직을 맡다 substitute 대신하다 perform 공연하다

9

해설 **명사 어휘:** '설문 조사의 결과를 받을 것이다'라는 의미가 적합하므로 정답은 (B) results이다.

번역 목요일에 코나도 씨는 연구개발부가 최근에 실시한 설문조사 결과를 받을 것이다.

어휘 **survey** 설문 조사 **conduct** 수행하다 **matter** 일, 문제

10

해설 **동사 어휘:** '기상 조건이 수산 회사의 영업에 지장을 줄 것이다'라는 의미가 적합하므로 '방해하다'라는 뜻의 (A) interfere with가 정답이다. (D) rely on의 경우, 영업이 기상 조건에 달려 있다고 하는 것이 적절하므로 주체와 대상이 바뀌어야 한다.

번역 보도에 따르면 기상 조건이 아이스하우스 수산 회사의 7월 영업에 지장을 줄 것이라고 한다.

어휘 **report** 보도; 보도하다 **suggest** 나타내다, 암시하다 **weather condition** 기상 조건[상태] **operation** 운용, 영업 **fisheries** 어업 **correspond to** ~와 일치하다, ~에 부합하다 **fall behind** ~에 뒤떨어지다 **rely on** ~에 의존하다

기출 **TEST 7**			본책 p. 224	
1 (B)	**2** (B)	**3** (A)	**4** (D)	**5** (B)
6 (C)	**7** (D)	**8** (D)	**9** (C)	**10** (D)

1

해설 **형용사 어휘:** '문서가 당장 이용 가능하다'라는 의미가 적합하므로 '이용 가능한'이라는 뜻의 (B) accessible이 정답이다.

번역 잿콘 전자 파일 시스템은 부서의 모든 문서를 즉시 이용 가능하게 해 줍니다.

어휘 **ensure** 보장하다, 확실히 하다 **at a moment's notice** 즉시 **competent** 유능한 **constant** 지속적인 **accustomed** 익숙한

2

해설 **동사 어휘:** 목적어인 tickets와 함께 쓰여 '표를 구매하다'라는 의미를 이루는 (B) purchase가 정답이다. (C) achieve는 '목표 등을 달성하다'로 쓰인다.

번역 몇몇 팬들이 음악회 표를 사려고 매표소 밖에서 14시간 동안이나 줄을 섰다.

어휘 **line up** 줄을 서다 **replace** 대신[대체]하다

3

해설 **동사 어휘:** 목적어로 온 tourists와 전치사 to가 함께 쓰여 '관광객을 ~로 끌어들이다'라는 의미를 이루는 (A) attract가 정답이다.

번역 새로 문을 연 과학 박물관은 많은 관광객들을 그 도시로 끌어들일 것으로 예상된다.

어휘 **value** 소중히 여기다 **capture** 붙잡다, 사로잡다 **observe** 관찰하다, 준수하다

4

해설 **명사 어휘:** '많은 심사숙고 후에 결정되었다'라는 의미가 적합하므로 '심사숙고'를 뜻하는 (D) deliberation이 정답이다.

번역 많은 심사숙고 끝에, 회사 야유회는 스위트워터 파크에서 열기로 결정되었다.

어휘 **take place** 일어나다, 발생하다 **outcome** 결과 **precision** 정확성

5

해설 **동사 어휘:** 목적어로 온 '재무 책임자(financial officer)'를 '임명한다'라고 하는 것이 적합하므로 (B) appoints가 정답이다.

번역 이사회는 2년마다 회사의 국내 영업을 총괄할 새 재무 책임자를 임명한다.

어휘 **board of directors** 이사회 **financial** 금융의, 재무의 **oversee** 총괄하다, 감독하다 **domestic** 국내의 **operation** 영업 **deposit** 두다, 예금하다 **predict** 예측하다 **operate** 운영하다

6

해설 **명사 어휘:** '무료 프로그램을 이용하다'라는 의미가 적합하므로 take advantage of를 완성하는 (C) advantage가 정답이다.

번역 회사의 무료 소프트웨어 업그레이드 프로그램을 이용하기 위하여 고객들은 제시된 주소로 영수증 사본을 우편으로 보내야 한다.

어휘 **mail** 우편으로 보내다 **receipt** 영수증, 수령 **merit** 장점 **take advantage of** ~을 이용하다 **improvement** 개선, 향상

7

해설 **부사 어휘:** '관리부가 항상 연락을 받아야 한다'는 의미가 적합하므로 '항상'을 의미하는 (D) always가 정답이다. 참고로, (C) ever는 형용사나 명사 앞에서 또는 ever since(~이래로 줄곧)와 같은 표현에서 '항상'을 의미할 수 있다.

번역 에어컨에 문제가 있으면 항상 관리부에 연락해야 한다.

어휘 maintenance department 관리부 contact
연락하다 exactly 정확하게 evenly 고르게, 균등하게

8

해설 **전치사 어휘:** '동료들과 고객들이 하비브 씨를 존경한다'라
는 문장에서 주체가 행위자로 바뀐 수동태 문장이므로 '동
료들과 고객들에 의해 존경을 받는다'가 된다. 따라서 정답
은 (D) by이다. 만약 수동태를 쓰지 않고 earn respect
와 같이 표현하면 '~로부터 얻다(earn … from)'라는 의미
가 이루어지므로 from이 온다.

번역 하비브 씨는 동료와 거래 고객 모두에게 존경을 받는다.

어휘 respect 존경하다 colleague 동료 business
client 거래 고객, 기업 고객 alike 둘 다

9

해설 **동사 어휘:** 목적어로 사람명사를 받아, '~에게 …하라고 상
기시키다'라는 의미를 이루는 (C) reminded가 정답이다.

번역 한 사람도 낙오되지 않도록 하기 위해 여행 관리자는 모든
방문객들에게 오전 7시까지 정문 로비로 나오라고 신신당
부했다.

어휘 leave behind ~을 두고 가다, ~을 뒤에 남기다
operator 운영자, 관리자 recall 기억해내다, 상기하다
memorize 암기하다 identify (신원을) 확인하다,
식별하다

10

해설 **형용사 어휘:** '안내 책자(directory)'를 수식하여, '종합 안
내 책자'라는 의미를 이루는 '종합적인'이라는 뜻의 (D)
comprehensive가 정답이다.

번역 백스터 컨설팅은 지역 사업체 단일 종합 안내 책자를 제공
하고자 다양한 출처들의 정보를 통합할 계획이다.

어휘 intend to ~할 작정이다 combine 결합하다, 통합하다
source 원천, 출처 variable 변동이 심한 apparent
분명한 redundant 여분의, 불필요한

기출 **TEST 8**				본책 p. 225
1 (C)	**2** (A)	**3** (D)	**4** (A)	**5** (A)
6 (D)	**7** (D)	**8** (D)	**9** (A)	**10** (D)

1

해설 **전치사 어휘:** '~에 노력을 쏟다'는 put effort into로 표현
한다. 따라서 '~에'라는 의미의 (C) into가 정답이다.

번역 윈돈 제약은 자사의 마케팅 도구를 확충하는 데 상당한 노
력을 기울여 왔다.

어휘 pharmacy 약국, 제약(업) significant 상당한
expand 확대하다, 확장하다 tool 수단, 도구

2

해설 **동사 어휘:** 목적어로 '기대(expectations)'를 받아 '기대
치를 뛰어넘다'라는 의미를 이루는 '넘어서다, 초과하다'라
는 뜻의 (A) exceed가 정답이다.

번역 홀덴사는 지속적으로 회사의 기대를 넘어서는 직원들에게
보상한다.

어휘 enterprise 기업, 회사 reward 보상하다; 보상(금)
consistently 지속적으로 describe 설명하다
command 명령하다, 지시하다; 언어 구사력

3

해설 **형용사 어휘:** 명사 addition을 수식하여, '훌륭한 추가물'
이라는 의미를 이루는 (D) great가 정답이다. 참고로,
addition은 '추가 인력'을 뜻하기도 하며, '환영 받는'이라
는 뜻의 형용사 welcome과도 자주 함께 쓰인다.

번역 〈별을 찾아서〉는 아마추어 천문학자의 소장 도서에 훌륭한
추가물이 될 것이다.

어휘 search 찾다, 구하다 make ~이 되다 addition
추가, 추가된 것[사람] astronomer 천문학자, 천문가
collection 수집(품), 소장(품)

4

해설 **동사 어휘:** 'refer to A as B'는 'A를 B라고 일컫다'라는
의미이며, 'A is referred to as B'라는 수동태로 자주 쓰
인다. 따라서 '긴 매장 이름이 흔히 ~라고 불리운다'라는 의
미를 이루는 (A) referred to가 정답이다.

번역 그 매장의 정식 명칭은 〈상상력이 뛰어난 이들을 위한 책으
로의 도피〉이지만, 대개 〈도피〉라고 부른다.

어휘 escape 도피, 탈출; 도피하다 imaginative 상상력이
뛰어난 balance 균형을 유지하다

5

해설 **동사 어휘:** 전치사 from이 핵심 단서이며, '자신을 동료와
차별화하다'라는 의미가 적합하므로 정답은 '차별화하다'라
는 뜻의 (A) differentiated이다. 'differentiate A from
B'와 같은 뜻으로 'distinguish A from B'도 함께 암기해
두자.

번역 박 씨는 우수한 디자인으로 이미 자신을 동료들과 차별화
했다.

어휘 superior 우수한 peer 동료 differentiate 차별하다
designate 지정하다, 지명하다 fashion (손으로) 빚다
feature 특징으로 하다

6

해설 **부사 어휘:** 과거 시점을 나타내는 ago와, and 뒤의 현재 완료 시제(has become)가 핵심 단서이다. since는 전치사, 접속사, 부사로 모두 쓰이며, '5년 전에 시작하여 그 이래로 ~했다'라는 의미를 이루는 (D) since가 정답이다.

번역 크로프트 씨는 5년 전에 중앙 도서관에서 일하기 시작했고 그 이후 도서 관장이 되었다.

어휘 director 관리자, 관장

7

해설 **명사 어휘:** '즉각적인 재정 지원의 필요성'이 적합하므로 (D) need가 정답이다. 'There is a/an (urgent) need for ~'는 '~이 (시급히) 필요하다'는 뜻이다.

번역 환경 위원회는 댐을 보수하기 위해 재정 지원이 즉각적으로 필요하다는 결론을 내렸다.

어휘 environmental 환경의 commission 위원회 conclude 결론을 내리다 immediate 즉각적인 funding 재정 지원 repair 수리하다 dam 댐

8

해설 **형용사 어휘:** '어떤 논문을 게재할지(which articles they publish)'에서 which가 '선택'과 관련된 표현의 단서가 된다. 따라서 선택에서 '(까다롭게) 선별하는'이라는 의미의 (D) selective가 정답이다. '엄격한'을 뜻하는 (C) rigorous는 규칙 적용 등의 엄격함을 나타내며 기준, 표준, 검토, 테스트 등을 수식하여 rigorous standards, rigorous review 등으로 출제된다.

번역 〈카리브해 공학 저널〉 편집자들은 어떤 논문을 게재할지 신중하게 고른다.

어휘 editor 편집자 journal 저널, 학술지 article 논문, 기사 publish 출판[발행]하다, (신문·잡지 등에) 발표하다, 게재하다 prominent 두드러진 punctual 시간을 엄수하는

9

해설 **명사 어휘:** magazines를 수식하여, '50여 개국에 구독자를 보유하고 있다'라는 의미가 적합하므로 정답은 '구독자'를 뜻하는 (A) subscribers이다.

번역 〈마켓 솔루션〉은 50여 개의 나라에 구독자를 보유한 유럽 제일의 국제 비즈니스 잡지이다.

어휘 leading 제일의, 선두의 spectator 관중 witness 목격자; 목격하다

10

해설 **명사 어휘:** '조경의 개선이 구매 의지를 부추길 것이다'라는 의미가 적합하므로 '향상, 개선'을 뜻하는 (D) enhancements가 정답이다. 변화, 변경의 대상에는 전치사 to를 써서,

change to, modification to, revision to 등과 같이 표현한다는 것도 알아 두자.

번역 부동산 중개업자들은 프레스몬트 지역의 조경 개선이 구매자들로 하여금 그곳의 주택 구입을 고려하도록 부추길 것이라고 주장한다.

어휘 real estate 부동산 landscape 조경 continuation 지속, 연속 increment 증가, 이익 deviation 벗어남, 일탈

기출 **TEST 9** 본책 p. 226

1 (B)	2 (B)	3 (D)	4 (B)	5 (A)
6 (B)	7 (A)	8 (A)	9 (B)	10 (B)

1

해설 **동사 어휘:** 빈칸의 동사는 앞에 나온 be동사와 함께 쓰여 수동태를 이루는데, 수동태 뒤에 목적어로 the grand prize가 왔으므로 빈칸에는 4형식 동사가 와야 한다. 따라서 정답은 '수여하다'라는 뜻의 (B) awarded이다. (A) won은 4형식이 가능하나 'won herself the grand prize'와 같은 능동태 형식으로 쓴다.

번역 클라인 씨는 회사 장기 자랑에서 일련의 동작으로 대상을 받았다.

어휘 prize 상 routine (공연의 일부인) 일련의 동작 talent 재능 award 상을 주다; 상

2

해설 **명사 어휘:** 빈칸은 동사 must be submitted의 주체가 되어야 하므로 '후보 추천'을 뜻하는 (B) Nominations가 정답이다. 나머지 보기들은 제출될 수 있는 것이 아니므로 오답이다.

번역 리더스 초이스 어워즈를 위한 지역 업체 추천은 5월 20일까지 〈뉴스-트리뷴〉에 제출되어야 한다.

어휘 award 상 subscription 구독 nomination 지명, 추천 supporter 후원자 venue 장소

3

해설 **형용사 어휘:** '기록(records)'을 수식하여, '정확한 기록을 작성해야 한다'라는 의미가 적합하므로 (D) accurate가 정답이다.

번역 직원들은 환급 요청 시 지연을 피하려면 출장비에 대해 정확한 기록을 작성해야 한다.

어휘 record 기록 travel expense 출장비 avoid 피하다 delay 지연, 지체 request 요청하다 reimbursement 환급, 상환 caring 돌봐 주는, 배려하는 distant 먼

4

해설 **부사 어휘:** 현재진행 시제와 함께 쓰여 '현재 구하는 중이다'라는 의미를 이루는 (B) currently가 정답이다.

번역 우리는 곧 있을 메이피 마케팅 소비자 연구에 참여할 자원봉사자를 현재 모집하고 있다.

어휘 seek 찾다, 구하다   volunteer 자원봉사자
participate in ~에 참여하다   upcoming 다가오는, 곧 있을   consumer research 소비자 연구
significantly 상당히   completely 완전히   slightly 조금, 약간

5

해설 **형용사 어휘:** '기술이 계속 발달하고 있으므로 1년 내내 교육을 제공해야 한다'라고 하여 '끊임없는 발전'과 '1년 내내'를 연결시킬 수 있다. 따라서 정답은 '끊임없는, 지속적인'을 뜻하는 (A) continuous이다.

번역 회사들은 계속되는 기술 향상 때문에 기술 지원 직원들에게 1년 내내 교육을 제공해야 한다.

어휘 year-round 연중 계속되는   technical support 기술 지원   improvement 향상, 개선   prosperous 번영하는   mature 성숙한   straight 곧은, 똑바른

6

해설 **전치사 어휘:** '권 씨가 돌아올 때까지 회의가 연기될 것이다'라는 의미가 적합하므로 (B) until이 정답이다. until은 postpone과 함께 자주 출제된다.

번역 전략 기획 회의는 권 씨가 돌아올 때까지 연기될 것이다.

어휘 strategic 전략적인   planning 기획   postpone 연기하다   return 돌아오다, 돌려 주다

7

해설 **부사 어휘:** '~ 근처에 위치해 있다(be located near)'를 수식하여, '편리한 위치에 있다'는 의미를 이루는 '편리하게'라는 뜻의 (A) conveniently가 정답이다.

번역 라피엣 타운홈 커뮤니티는 그 지역에서 가장 큰 쇼핑몰로 이어지는 철도 노선 인근에 편리하게 입지해 있다.

어휘 community 공동체, 지역사회   region 지역
conveniently 편리하게

8

해설 **명사 어휘:** '실적에 대해 마땅히 인정을 받을 만하다'라는 의미가 적합하므로 '인정'을 뜻하는 (A) recognition이 정답이다. 참고로, (B) accomplishment는 '업적, 성과'를 뜻할 때 가산명사로 쓰인다.

번역 쿠시다 씨의 관리자들은 그녀가 지난 영업 캠페인 동안 올린 실적에 대해 특별한 인정을 받을 자격이 있다고 생각한다.

어휘 deserve ~을 받을 만하다   performance 실적, 성과
sales campaign 영업 캠페인   accomplishment
성취, 성과   capability 능력   balance 균형

9

해설 **명사 어휘:** '새로운 절차의 채택이 중대한 영향을 미쳤다'라는 의미가 적합하므로 정답은 '채택'을 뜻하는 (B) adoption이다.

번역 새로운 재고 관리 절차의 채택은 자원 관리에 큰 영향을 미쳤다.

어휘 inventory 재고품, 재고 조사   process 과정, 절차
have an impact on ~에 영향을 미치다   significant
상당한   management 관리, 경영   resource 자원
trade 거래   reservation 예약

10

해설 **동사 어휘:** '설명서(instructions)'를 목적어로 받아 '설명서를 검토하라'라는 의미를 이루는 (B) review가 정답이다.

번역 새 식기세척기를 설치하기 전에 동봉된 설명서를 검토하십시오.

어휘 enclosed 동봉된   instructions 설명, 지시   attempt
to ~하려고 시도하다   install 설치하다   dishwasher
식기세척기   gather 모으다   program 설정하다

기출 **TEST 10**			본책 p. 227	
1 (A)	**2** (B)	**3** (C)	**4** (C)	**5** (C)
6 (D)	**7** (C)	**8** (A)	**9** (A)	**10** (B)

1

해설 **동사 어휘:** '방법을 시연하다'라는 의미가 적합하므로 '시연하다'라는 뜻의 (A) demonstrate가 정답이다. (B) respond는 respond to, (C) inquire는 inquire about으로 쓴다.

번역 정비 부장은 프라임 SX 자동차의 브레이크 오일을 교체하는 적절한 방법을 시연할 예정이다.

어휘 mechanic 정비사, 기계공   proper 적절한, 알맞은
method 방법, 방식   replace 교체하다, 대체하다
brake fluid 브레이크 오일   respond to ~에 응답하다
inquire about ~에 관해 문의하다

2

해설 **동사 어휘:** 목적어인 way를 받아 '길을 찾는다'라는 의미가 적합하므로 (B) find가 정답이다.

번역 자원봉사자들은 회의 참가자들이 컨벤션 센터 주변의 길을 찾는 일을 도울 것이다.

어휘 volunteer 자원봉사자; 자원하다, 봉사하다
participant 참가자

3

해설 **명사 어휘:** or 앞에 refund가 나오므로 '환불 또는 교체'라고 하는 것이 적절하다. 따라서 정답은 '교환, 교체'를 뜻하는 (C) replacement이다.

번역 스테레오 기기 성능에 만족하지 못한 고객들은 두 달 이내에 환불 또는 교환 신청을 할 수 있다.

어휘 performance 성능 equipment 기기, 장비 complaint 불만 receipt 영수증 promotion 홍보, 승진

4

해설 **형용사 어휘:** 원래 her twelve years of experience as a professor of marketing이 주어, is가 동사, 빈칸부터 candidate까지가 보어인 문장으로, 보어가 문두에 오면서 주어와 동사가 도치되었다. 문맥을 살펴보면, 12년의 마케팅 교수 경력이 윤 씨가 가장 적합한 후보자가 된 주요 이유라고 할 수 있으므로, '주된, 주요한'이라는 의미의 (C) Chief가 정답이다.

번역 윤 씨가 가장 적합한 후보자인 주된 이유는 12년의 마케팅 교수 경력이다.

어휘 reason 이유 qualified 자격이 있는, 적임의 candidate 후보자, 지원자 experience 경험, 경력; 경험하다, 겪다 professor 교수 adept 숙련된, 숙달된 proper 적절한, 올바른 chief 주된, 주요한 straight 곧은, 똑바른

5

해설 **부사 어휘:** '등록할 수 있다(can enroll)'를 수식하여, '온라인으로 쉽게 등록할 수 있다'라는 의미를 이루는 (C) easily가 정답이다.

번역 소비자들은 온라인으로 쉽게 워젯코의 최신 마케팅 연구에 등록할 수 있다.

어휘 consumer 소비자 enroll 등록하다 current 현재의, 최신의

6

해설 **형용사 어휘:** 빈칸 뒤의 to부정사와 함께 쓰여 '~할 만큼 충분한'이라는 의미를 이루는 (D) enough가 정답이다.

번역 도서 〈성공 투자〉의 판매량은 쇼윈도 진열에 포함되는 것이 타당할 만큼 충분하지는 않았다.

어휘 prosperous 번영하는, 성공한 invest 투자하다 warrant 보장하다, 정당한 근거가 되다 inclusion 포함

7

해설 **동사 어휘:** '음식이 상하는 것을 막다'라는 의미가 적합하므로 '막다, 방지하다'라는 뜻의 (C) prevent가 정답이다. 'prevent A from -ing' 형태로 암기해 두자. (D) forbid

는 '금지하다'이며 예방의 의미가 아니므로 혼동하지 않도록 하자.

번역 모든 출장 연회 영리 업체들은 부패를 막기 위하여 상하기 쉬운 음식을 냉장 보관한다.

어휘 commercial 영리의, 상업적인 catering 케이터링, 출장 연회업 refrigerate 냉장 보관하다 perishable 상하기 쉬운 spoil 상하다, 부패하다 remove 제거하다 oppose 반대하다 forbid 금지하다

8

해설 **명사 어휘:** '저자 가족의 허가를 얻어 원고가 출간되었다'라는 의미가 적합하므로 '허가'를 뜻하는 (A) permission이 정답이다. 동사 obtain과 함께 쓰임을 기억해 두자.

번역 제인 톨렌의 원본 원고는 젠슨 북스가 그녀 가족의 허락을 얻은 후 지난해 출판되었다.

어휘 manuscript 원고 publish 발표하다, 발간하다 obtain 얻다 permission 허가, 허용 suggestion 제안, 제의 comparison 비교 registration 등록

9

해설 **부사 어휘:** '이익이 되는(beneficial)'을 수식하여 '상호 이익이 되는'이라는 의미를 이루는 (A) mutually가 정답이다. 연어로 자주 출제되니 암기해 두자.

번역 저희 TPG 재무 기획은 귀하의 사업을 도울 기회를 환영하며 상호 유익한 관계를 고대합니다.

어휘 opportunity 기회 assist 돕다 look forward to ~을 고대하다 punctually 시간을 엄수하여, 정각에 respectively 각자 precisely 정확하게

10

해설 **부사 어휘:** '열심히 일해야 하지만, 가족과의 시간 또한 가져야 한다'로 연결되는 것이 적합하다. 따라서 정답은 '또한, 역시'라는 뜻의 (B) also이다.

번역 우리 회사는 직원들이 항상 열심히 일해야 하지만, 가족을 위한 시간도 가져야 한다고 생각한다.

어휘 altogether 완전히 alone 혼자서

기출 TEST 11				본책 p. 228
1 (B)	2 (C)	3 (B)	4 (C)	5 (A)
6 (B)	7 (C)	8 (B)	9 (A)	10 (A)

1

해설 **명사 어휘:** '그 인턴직은 정규직으로 이어질 가능성이 있다'라는 의미가 적합하므로 '가능성'을 뜻하는 (B) potential이 정답이다.

번역 박 씨는 정규직으로 이어질 가능성이 있으므로 인턴직을 수락했다.

어휘 permanent position 정규직 preference 선호
authority 권한 ambition 야망

2

해설 **명사 어휘:** '최고 경영자의 승인 없이 신입 사원을 채용할 수 없다'는 의미가 적합하므로 '승인'을 뜻하는 (C) approval 이 정답이다.

번역 인사부장은 최고경영자의 승인 없이 신입 영업 사원을 채용할 수 없다.

어휘 personnel 인사 sales executive 영업 사원
approval 승인 benefit 혜택

3

해설 **부사 어휘:** '독특한(unique)'이 핵심 단서로, '다른 곳에서 구할 수 없는'이라는 의미로 연결되는 것이 적합하다. 따라서 '다른 곳에서'를 뜻하는 (B) elsewhere가 정답이다.

번역 울리 시티 크래프트 마켓은 다른 곳에서는 구할 수 없는 독특한 수제 제품을 제공한다.

어휘 available 구할 수 있는 evidently 분명히
thoroughly 철저히

4

해설 **동사 어휘:** 목적어로 rental car가 나오므로 '렌터카를 임대하다'라는 의미를 이루는 (C) lease가 정답이다.

번역 리버사이드 카운티에서 렌터카를 임대하려면 운전자는 최소한 21세 이상이어야 한다.

어휘 at least 최소한

5

해설 **동사 어휘:** '보너스를 직원들에게 나누어 주다'라는 의미가 적합하므로 '나누어 주다'라는 뜻의 (A) distribute가 정답이다. distribute A to B로 기억해 두자.

번역 다음 주에 젝스턴사는 지난해 판매 할당량을 초과한 직원들에게 보너스 1,000파운드를 지급할 예정이다.

어휘 exceed 초과하다 quota 할당량 separate 분리하다
reserve 남겨 두다

6

해설 **동사 어휘:** 목적어로 program이 나오므로 '프로그램을 시행하다'라는 의미가 적절하다. 따라서 정답은 '시행하다'라는 뜻의 (B) implementing이다.

번역 헤이거스빌 시의회는 대대적인 재활용 프로그램을 시행함으로써 도시 쓰레기를 줄이려고 애썼다.

어휘 seek to ~하려고 노력[시도]하다 reduce 줄이다
extensive 광범위한 estimate 추정하다

7

해설 **형용사 어휘:** '경쟁사(competitor)'를 수식하여 '주요 경쟁사'라는 의미를 이루는 (C) main이 정답이다.

번역 컬리스 커뮤니케이션즈는 지난 3년 동안 우리의 주요 경쟁사였다.

어휘 competitor 경쟁사 numerous 수많은 most
대부분의

8

해설 **명사 어휘:** 직원들을 위해 time-management를 주제로 하는 '워크숍을 제공한다'라는 의미가 적합하므로 정답은 (B) workshop이다.

번역 다음 달에 케이티 쿠퍼가 모든 직원들을 위해 시간 관리 워크숍을 제공할 것이다.

어휘 offer 제공하다 time-management 시간 관리
expert 전문가

9

해설 **형용사 어휘:** '품질 좋은 제품을 매력적인 가격에 제공한다'라는 의미가 적합하므로 '매력적인'을 뜻하는 (A) attractive가 정답이다. 참고로, 가격을 수식하는 형용사로 '합리적인'을 뜻하는 reasonable과 '저렴한'이라는 의미의 affordable도 함께 기억해 두자.

번역 헬시 탓츠에서는 우수한 품질의 제품을 끌리는 가격에 제공해 고객의 충성심을 북돋운다.

어휘 encourage 북돋우다 primary 주요한 actual
실제의 fortunate 운 좋은

10

해설 **형용사 어휘:** '최근 합병의 결과로 회사를 개명할 것이다'라는 의미가 적합하므로 '최근의'를 뜻하는 (A) recent가 정답이다.

번역 로진 출판은 최근 버튼 페이퍼사와 합병의 결과로 다음 달에 사명 변경을 발표할 예정이다.

어휘 merger 합병 various 다양한 frequent 잦은

기출 **TEST 12**				본책 p. 229
1 (A)	**2** (A)	**3** (B)	**4** (A)	**5** (B)
6 (C)	**7** (D)	**8** (D)	**9** (A)	**10** (C)

1

해설 **명사 어휘:** '사이트 방문자 수가 늘었다'라는 의미가 적합하므로 '방문자'를 뜻하는 (A) visitors가 정답이다. visit이 명사로 쓰이면 'make a visit to 장소'와 같이 쓰며, '~로의 방문객' 또한 전치사 to와 함께 쓰였다는 것을 기억해 두자.

번역 케일라스 케이터링이 웹사이트를 개선한 이후, 해당 사이트 방문자 수가 증가하였다.

어휘 **improve** 개선하다 **profit** 이익

2

해설 **명사 어휘:** budget과 함께 쓰여 복합명사를 이루는 자리 이므로 '예산 흑자'라는 의미를 이루는 (A) surplus가 정답이다.

번역 레이포드 제조사는 1백만 달러의 예산 흑자로 한 해를 마감할 것으로 예상한다.

어휘 **budget** 예산 **surplus** 흑자, 과잉 **assembly** 의회, 조립 **launch** 출시 **committee** 위원회

3

해설 **부사 어휘:** 부동산 가격 추이를 예견하는 내용의 문장이므로 '아마도 가격이 오를 것 같다'라는 의미를 이루는 (B) likely가 정답이다. likely는 여기서 '아마도'라는 부사로 쓰였는데, 형용사로 쓰여 '~할 것 같다'라는 뜻의 be likely to로도 자주 출제된다.

번역 라 파즈의 휴가용 임대 부동산에 대한 수요로 올해 가격이 아마도 오를 것이라고 분석가들은 말한다.

어휘 **demand** 수요 **property** 부동산 **analyst** 분석가 **firstly** 맨 먼저 **tightly** 단단히 **previously** 과거에

4

해설 **전치사 어휘:** '수령한 지 1주일 이내로'라는 표현으로, 'within + 기간'과 함께 쓰여 사건이 발생한 시간적 위치를 나타낼 수 있는 (A) of가 정답이다. within a week of your order(주문한 지 일주일 이내로) 등과 같이 활용한다.

번역 엑소테린에서는 모든 서신에 수령한 지 1주일 이내에 응답해야 한다.

어휘 **correspondence** 서신 **respond** 응답하다 **receipt** 수령

5

해설 **명사 어휘:** 동사 take와 함께 쓰여 '예방 조치를 취하다'라는 의미를 이루는 (B) precautions가 정답이다. '조치를 취하다'는 표현으로 take와 함께 쓰는 action, step, measure도 알아 두자.

번역 CPC 빌더스의 모든 근로자들은 추운 날씨에 작업할 경우 안전을 위해 예방 조치를 취해야 한다.

어휘 **element** 요소 **take advantage of** ~을 이용하다

6

해설 **동사 어휘:** '결과가 발표된 후 자리를 떠나다'라는 의미가 적합하므로 '발표하다'라는 뜻의 (C) announced가 정답이다.

번역 보통 대부분의 관중들은 경기 결과가 발표되는 직후 텔라소 아레나를 떠난다.

어휘 **typically** 보통 **spectator** (스포츠 행사의) 관중 **shortly after** 직후에 **result** 결과 **tournament** 시합 **reduce** 줄이다 **remove** 제거하다 **continue** 지속하다

7

해설 **동사 어휘:** '검토 후에 알아차렸다'라는 의미가 적합하며, that이 생략된 문장이므로 that과 함께 쓰여 that 이하 내용을 '알아차리다'라는 뜻으로 쓸 수 있는 (D) noticed가 정답이다.

번역 조시 씨는 자신의 계좌 기록을 검토했을 때, 월별 요금이 삭제되지 않았다는 것을 알아차렸다.

어휘 **review** 검토하다 **charge** 요금 **delete** 삭제하다 **glance** 힐끗 보다 **postpone** 연기하다

8

해설 **전치사 어휘:** '수리가 불가능 할 정도로 파손된 부품'이라는 의미가 적합하다. 따라서 '(능력 등을) 넘어서는, ~할 수 없는'이라는 뜻을 가진 (D) beyond가 정답이다.

번역 운송 중에 수리가 불가할 정도로 파손된 자전거 부품은 즉시 보고되고 반환되어야 한다.

어휘 **repair** 수리 **shipment** 운송 **promptly** 즉시

9

해설 **형용사 어휘:** '매력적인'이라는 뜻의 inviting과 더불어 리모델링을 한 뒤 개선된 대기실의 상태를 나타내기에 적절한 형용사를 골라야 한다. 따라서 '편안한'이라는 뜻의 (A) comfortable이 정답이다.

번역 대기실은 리모델링을 해서 환자들에게 더 아늑하고 편안하다.

어휘 **inviting** 매력적인 **competent** 능숙한 **peculiar** 기이한 **familiar** 익숙한

10

해설 **형용사 어휘:** '설문 조사를 제대로 완료하면'이라는 의미가 되어야 하므로 '성공적인'이라는 뜻의 (C) Successful이 정답이다.

번역 온라인 설문 조사를 제대로 완료하면 응답자는 향후 구매를 위한 포인트를 받는다.

어휘 **completion** 완료 **respondent** 응답자 **(store) credit** 포인트 **toward** ~에 대하여 **dependent** 의존하는 **fortunate** 운 좋은 **prosperous** 번영하는

PART 6

CHAPTER 01 | 문법 / 어휘 문제

UNIT 01	대명사 지시어 문제

ETS 예제 본책 p. 232

버즈비 씨께,

5월 2일자 메시지에 감사드립니다. 당사의 기록에 따르면 고객님은 지난 4월 27일 당사 웹사이트를 통해 졸리트 자전거 타이어 2개(제품 JBT1783)를 주문하셨으며 해당 제품은 5월 1일 도착 예정이었습니다. 고객님께서 아직 **그것들을** 받지 못하셨다니 죄송합니다. 배달은 보통 사나흘밖에 걸리지 않습니다.

어휘 indicate 나타내다, 표시하다 be scheduled to ~할 예정이다 delivery 배송, 배달 no more than 고작

ETS CHECK-UP 본책 p. 233

1 (B)	2 (C)	3 (D)	4 (D)	5 (C)	6 (A)
7 (B)	8 (C)	9 (A)	10 (D)	11 (B)	

1 고객 후기

프레시콘 월드와이드 무버스 후기

두 달 전에 뜻밖에도 스웨덴으로 돌아가야 한다는 걸 알게 됐죠. 프레시콘 월드와이드 무버스가 평판이 좋다는 얘기를 들었던 터라 캘리포니아에서 스톡홀름으로 물건을 배송하는 데 이 회사 서비스를 이용하기로 결정했어요.

저와 함께 일했던 고객 서비스 담당자는 훌륭했어요. 내가 보낸 이메일에 전부 즉시 답장했어요. **그의** 답변은 빈틈없고 유용했어요. 그리고 그가 제시한 가격은 꽤 경쟁력이 있었어요.

어휘 unexpectedly 뜻밖에 reputation 평판 representative 담당자 promptly 즉시 thorough 빈틈없는 quote 견적을 내다 competitive 경쟁력 있는

해설 **인칭대명사_소유격:** 빈칸에는 뒤의 명사 answers를 수식하는 말이 필요하다. 빈칸 앞 문장에서 함께 일했던 고객 서비스 담당자를 '그(he)'라고 칭하며 그가 모든 이메일에 답장을 해 주었다고 했으므로 '답변(answers)'은 고객 서비스 담당자 즉, '그(he)'가 한 것임을 알 수 있다. 따라서 he의 소유격인 (B) His가 정답이다.

2 회람

최근 조사 결과 회사 헬스장을 이용하는 직원 수가 지난 6개월 동안 급격히 감소한 것으로 나타났습니다. 매출이 늘면서 직원들의 일이 점점 더 많아지고 있다는 사실을 알고 있습니다. 그래서 헬스장 운영 시간을 연장하기로 결정했습니다. 2월 3일부터 **그것은** 오전 6시에 문을 열어 저녁 8시 30분에 문을 닫을 것입니다. 하루 두 시간 연장 운영함에 따라 직원들이 헬스장이 제공하는 혜택을 충분히 활용할 수 있기를 바랍니다.

어휘 survey 설문 조사 fitness center 헬스장 decrease 감소하다 dramatically 급격히 increasingly 점점 더 therefore 그러므로 operating hours 운영 시간 take full advantage of ~을 충분히 활용하다 benefit 혜택

해설 **인칭대명사_주격:** 오전 6시에 문을 열고 저녁 8시 30분에 문을 닫는 것은 fitness center이므로 이를 지칭하는 (C) it이 정답이다.

3 이메일

파인스트리 북스 온라인의 주문 변경 절차에 대해 문의해 주신 것에 감사드립니다. 답변을 드리자면, 홈페이지를 통해 이뤄진 주문은 일단 발송이 되고 나면 변경할 수 없습니다.

그러나 주문이 아직 처리 중이고 발송되지 않았다면 물품을 추가하거나 취소하실 수 있습니다. **이것들** 중 하나를 하시려면 고객 서비스 담당 직원에게 말씀하셔야 합니다.

어휘 procedure 절차, 과정 make changes 수정하다, 변경하다 process 처리하다 remove 제거하다 representative 직원

해설 **부정대명사:** 문맥상 앞에서 언급된 추가 또는 취소 중 하나(either)의 의미이므로 복수 대명사로 사용할 수 있는 (D) these가 정답이다. (A) each는 각각을 의미하는 대명사로 either와 의미가 중복되고 (B) this와 (C) that은 단수 대명사로 사용되기 때문에 오답이다.

Questions 4-7 보도

대담한 색상의 **⁴가전제품을** 만드는 말레이시아 제조사 켄지 라이사(KLL)는 다음 달 전국 본부를 우타마 가 18번지로 옮길 예정인데, 이곳에 있는 현대적인 10층짜리 사무용 빌딩이 개조되었다. KLL은 이 건물 꼭대기 2개 층을 **⁵사용하게** 될 것이다. 그곳에서 마케팅 및 영업 간부 사원들은 약 35,000제곱미터에 이르는 새로운 사무 공간을 누리게 된다. **⁶또한 KLL은 1층에 소매점을 임대할 예정이다.** "이곳은 당사의 첨단 기술 오븐과 냉장고를 진열할 완벽한 공간이 될 겁니다." 회사 대변인 아이샤 누어는 말했다. 회사 엔지니어링 및 디자인 부서는 **⁷그들의** 원래 위치인 타이핑에 그대로 남는다고 누어 씨는 언급했다.

어휘 manufacturer 제조업체 boldly 대담하게
headquarters 본부, 본사 contemporary 현대의,
동시대의 story 층 renovate 보수[수리]하다,
개조하다 executive 관리직의; 경영진 ideal 이상적인
display 진열[전시]하다 spokesperson 대변인
remain 남다, 머무르다 original 원래의, 최초의
location 위치, 장소 note 언급하다

4

해설 **명사 어휘:** 지문 중반의 'This will be an ideal area to
display our high-tech ovens and refrigerators'
가 문제 해결의 단서로, 켄지 라이사(KLL)는 첨단 기술
의 오븐과 냉장고를 생산하는 업체임을 알 수 있다. 따라서
ovens and refrigerators를 '가전제품'라고 바꾸어 표현
한 (D) appliances가 정답이다.

어휘 fixture 설비, 비품 apparel 의류 wallpaper 벽지
appliance 가전제품, 기기

5

해설 **동사 어휘:** 빈칸 앞에서 켄지 라이사(KLL)는 본사를 이전
할 예정이며, 10층짜리 사무용 빌딩이 개조되었다(a
contemporary ten-story office building has
been renovated)라고 했다. 따라서 'KLL은 이 건물 꼭
대기 2개 층을 사용하게 된다'라는 의미가 되어야 하므로,
빈칸에는 '사용하다, 차지하다'라는 뜻의 (C) occupy가 가
장 적절하다.

6

해설 **문맥에 맞는 문장 고르기:** 빈칸 앞에서 마케팅 및 영업 간부
사원들은 약 35,000제곱미터에 이르는 새 사무 공간을 누
리게 된다고 했으며, 빈칸 뒤에서는 새로운 사무 공간은 자사
의 오븐과 냉장고를 진열할 완벽한 장소(an ideal area to
display our high-tech ovens and refrigerators)가
될 것이라고 했다. 따라서 빈칸에는 앞뒤 문장처럼 사무실
의 용도를 말해 주는 내용이 들어가야 글의 흐름이 자연스
러워진다. 따라서 (A)가 정답이다.

번역 **(A) 또한 KLL은 1층에 소매점을 임대할 예정이다.**
(B) KLL의 제품은 최첨단 에너지 효율이 특징이다.
(C) KLL은 말레이시아에서 일하기 좋은 직장 50위 안에
올랐다.
(D) 이전이 발표된 후 KLL의 주가는 상승했다.

어휘 lease 임대하다 retail 소매의 ground floor 1층
feature 특징을 이루다; 특징, 기능 cutting-edge
최첨단의 energy efficiency 에너지 효율 list
등재되다 stock price 주가

7

해설 **인칭대명사_소유격:** 빈칸에는 뒤에 온 명사구(original
location)를 수식하는 말이 들어가야 한다. 따라서 명사
앞에 쓰여 한정사 역할을 할 수 있는 소유격 인칭대명사인
(B) their가 정답이다.

Questions 8-11 광고

경영 코칭 과정에 등록해, 업체 지도자들이 경영 역량을 신속
하게 기르도록 조언하는 데 필요한 **8기술**을 습득하세요. 경영
코칭의 가장 큰 보상은 사람들을 도울 수 있도록 매우 실용적
인 방식으로 **9당신이** 가진 역량을 발휘하는 것입니다. 의뢰인
이 나쁜 습관을 버리고 직장에서 과제를 **10효과적으로** 처리하
기 시작할 때 느낄 성취감을 상상해 보세요. 저희는 의뢰인이
스스로 해결책을 찾을 수 있도록 뒷받침하는 기술을 코치에게
교육합니다. **11이렇게 함으로써 의뢰인의 역량이 확인됩니다.**
저희의 코칭 철학에 동의하는 모든 사람에게 이 과정은 다음
단계로 나아가는 확실한 방법입니다.

어휘 enroll 등록하다 executive 경영의 managerial
경영의 exercise 행사하다 possess 소유하다
accomplishment 성취

8

해설 **명사 어휘:** 빈칸에 들어갈 명사는 앞의 내용상 경영 코칭 과
정에 등록함으로써 얻을 수 있는 것이고, 뒤의 수식 구문에
서 업체 지도자들이 경영 역량을 신속하게 기를 수 있도록
조언하는 데 필요한 것이라고 했으므로 '기술'이 들어가야
의미가 자연스럽다. 따라서 (C) skills가 정답이다.

9

해설 **인칭대명사_주격:** 빈칸은 명사 the ability 뒤에 목적격
관계대명사 that 혹은 which가 생략된 절에서 동사
possess의 주어 자리이므로 주격 대명사가 들어갈 수 있
다. 또한 동사 possess는 동사원형이므로 3인칭 단수 주
어인 (B) he, (C) she, (D) it은 답이 될 수 없고, (A) you
가 정답이다.

10

해설 **부사 어휘:** 문맥상 성취감을 느낄 수 있으려면 업무를 제대
로 잘 처리한다는 말이 들어가야 하므로 '효과적으로'라는
뜻의 (D) effectively가 정답이다.

어휘 prematurely 너무 이르게 excessively 지나치게
barely 간신히 effectively 효과적으로

11

해설 **문맥에 맞는 문장 고르기:** 빈칸 앞 문장에서 의뢰인이 스스로
해결책을 찾도록 돕는 기술을 코치에게 교육한다(We train
coaches in the art ~ solutions for themselves)며
코칭 방식을 설명했다. 따라서 빈칸에는 이 방식을 따름으
로써 얻을 수 있는 효과에 대한 내용이 뒤따르는 것이 자연
스러우므로 (B)가 정답이다.

번역 (A) 저희 금융 컨설턴트는 찾는 사람이 아주 많습니다.

(B) 이렇게 함으로써 의뢰인의 역량이 확인됩니다.

(C) 당사는 몇 가지 관리직을 충원하려고 합니다.

(D) 그래서 저희는 졸업과 동시에 진로 상담을 제공합니다.

어휘 in high demand 찾는 사람이 많은   in so doing 그렇게 하여 resourcefulness 역량 affirm 확인하다

UNIT 02	시제 문제

ETS 예제
본책 p. 236

수신: 이귀연 〈glee@grandmoonhotel.com〉
발신: 에버럿 킹 〈eking@grandmoonhotel.com〉
날짜: 8월 21일
제목: 안녕하세요

귀연 씨,

곧 승진하신다는 소식을 최근에 들었습니다. 베이징 지점의 총지배인으로서 새 직위는 9월 3일에 **시작되지만** 당장 축하해 주고 싶었어요. 전근은 힘들 수도 있으니 도움이 필요하면 부담 없이 저에게 연락하세요.

어휘 inform A of B A에게 B를 알리다 upcoming 다가오는 position 직위 officially 공식적으로 offer one's best wishes 축하하다, 행운을 빌다 transition 전환, 이동 feel free to 부담 없이 ~하다

ETS CHECK-UP
본책 p. 237

1 (C)	2 (B)	3 (C)	4 (C)	5 (B)	6 (B)
7 (C)	8 (D)	9 (A)	10 (C)	11 (A)	

1 이메일

콤플릿 산업의 웹사이트가 새로운 모습과 향상된 기능을 선보일 예정이라는 것을 여러분께 알리게 되어 대단히 기쁩니다. 휴대용 기기에서도 볼 수 있는 기능과 쌍방향 견학으로 콤플릿 시설을 둘러볼 수 있는 기능 등 여러 가지 업그레이드된 기능이 사이트에 **포함될 예정입니다.** 새로운 웹사이트로의 전환은 3월 31일 토요일로 예정되어 있습니다.

어휘 excitement 흥분, 들뜸 inform 알리다 look 모습 improved 향상된 functionality 기능(성) feature 기능 such as 예를 들면 readability 가독성, 읽기 쉬움 interactive 대화식의, 쌍방향의 transition 전환 occur 발생하다, 일어나다

해설 **동사의 시제 _ 미래:** 빈칸의 앞 문장에서 웹사이트가 새로운 모습과 향상된 기능을 선보일 예정(is to have ~)이라며 예정된 일에 대해 언급하고 있다. 빈칸 뒤 문장에서도 역시 새로운 웹사이트로의 전환은 토요일로 예정되어 있다(is scheduled to ~)고 하며 앞으로의 일정을 언급하고 있다. 앞뒤 문장의 시제 흐름상 웹사이트와 관련된 앞으로의 변화에 대해 이야기하고 있으므로 빈칸도 미래 시제인 (C) will include가 정답이다.

2 기사

하이 스트리트 갤러리의 경이로운 풍경화들
아이라 바슬리

리즈(6월 7일) – 어젯밤 하이 스트리트 갤러리의 최신 전시회가 감상을 즐기는 사람들을 위해 열렸다. 전시회에는 조 우의 유화, 트레버 나이팅게일의 수채화, 케이시 펠드의 파스텔 작품들이 **선을 보인다.** 화풍은 뚜렷이 구별되지만, 이 화가들은 모두 지역 풍경의 아름다움을 포착하는 데 관심을 가지고 있다. 미술품들은 서로를 훌륭하게 보완한다.

어휘 marvelous 경이로운, 멋진 landscape 풍경, 풍경화 exhibition 전시(회) appreciative 감상을 즐기는, 고마워하는 distinct 뚜렷한, 뚜렷이 구별되는 capture 포착하다 local 지역의 complement 보완하다 nicely 멋지게, 잘

해설 **동사의 시제 _ 현재:** The show가 주어, 빈칸이 동사인 문장으로, 어제 개관하여 현재 전시 중인 작품을 소개하는 내용이다. 따라서 현재 시제인 (B) features가 정답이다.

어휘 feature 특징을 이루다, 특별히 포함하다; 특징, 기능

3 편지

11월 5일

크레제브스키 씨 귀하

귀하의 최근 편지에 감사드립니다. 귀하께서는 지난 시즌처럼 에버웨어 의류의 모험가 재킷 연보라색이 있는지 알고 싶어 하셨습니다. 사실, 저희는 그 색상을 **단종시켰습니다.** 그 색상은 더 어두운 색조인 산딸기 색으로 교체되었습니다. 밝은 색보다 짙은 색 옷의 얼룩이 훨씬 덜 눈에 띈다는 고객의 의견에 응해 그렇게 교체했습니다.

어휘 available 구할[이용할 수] 있는 replace 교체하다, 교환하다 in response to ~에 응답[대응]하여 dirt 먼지, 때

해설 **동사의 시제 _ 현재완료:** 동사 자리 뒤에 목적어 that color가 있으므로 능동태를 써야 한다. 또한 빈칸 뒤의 문장에서 해당 색상이 다른 색으로 교체되었다(It has been replaced with ~)는 내용이 나오므로 색상을 단종시킨 것도 이미 발생한 일이다. 따라서 이미 완료된 일을 나타내는 (C) have discontinued가 정답이다.

어휘 discontinue (생산을) 중단하다

PART 6 | UNIT 02

129

Questions 4-7 기사

> **버크포드 박물관의 여성사**
>
> 현재 버크포드 박물관에는 〈역사는 여자가 만든다〉가 전시되고 있습니다. 이 **4전시회**는 미국에서 여성들에게 투표권을 쟁취해 준 지도자들을 기념합니다. 전시회는 또한 과학, 문학, 법률에서 칭송받는 미국 현대사에서 중요한 인물들에 **5초점을 맞추고** 있습니다. 중요한 문서, 사진, 그림이 전시되어 있습니다. 박물관 방문객들은 또한 초창기 연설과 인터뷰를 담은 실제 자료 화면으로 구성된 단편 영화를 **6즐길 수** 있습니다. **7방문해서 이 사건들이 어떻게 역사를 바꾸었는지 알아보세요.** 〈역사는 여자가 만든다〉는 4월 20일까지 계속됩니다.

어휘 **on display** 전시된 **earn** (명성, 지위 등을) 획득하다, 얻다 **acclaim** 찬사, 칭찬; 칭송하다 **footage** (특정한 사건을 담은) 장면, 화면

4

해설 **명사 어휘:** 앞 문장에는 현재 버크포드 박물관에는 〈역사는 여자가 만든다〉가 전시되고 있다고 했고, 빈칸 뒤로는 이 전시회에 대한 설명이 이어지고 있으므로 빈칸에는 '전시회'가 들어가야 적절하다. 따라서 (C) exhibit이 정답이다.

5

해설 **전치사 어휘:** 빈칸에는 동사 focuses와 함께 쓰여 '~에 초점을 맞추다'라는 의미를 나타내는 전치사가 들어가야 한다. 따라서 정답은 (B) on이다.

6

해설 **동사의 시제_현재:** 앞뒤 문맥에서 박물관에서 현재 열리고 있는 전시회를 소개하고 있으므로, 현재 시제로 '박물관 방문객들은 단편 영화를 즐길 수 있다'는 내용이 되어야 자연스럽다. 따라서 (B) can also enjoy가 정답이다.

7

해설 **문맥에 맞는 문장 고르기:** 빈칸 앞에서 방문객들은 초창기 연설과 인터뷰를 담은 실제 자료 화면으로 구성된 단편 영화를 즐길 수 있다고 했으므로, 앞에서 언급된 '초창기 연설과 인터뷰(early speeches and interviews)'를 '이 사건들(these events)'로 받아 어떻게 역사를 바꿨는지 알아보라며 전시회에 방문할 것을 권하는 문장으로 연결되는 것이 가장 자연스럽다. 따라서 (C)가 정답이다.

번역 (A) 박물관은 4월 3일에 정비를 위해 문을 닫습니다.
  (B) 유감스럽게도, 그 영화는 더 이상 볼 수 없습니다.
  (C) 방문해서 이 사건들이 어떻게 역사를 바꾸었는지 알아보세요.
  (D) 자원봉사를 하시려면, 박물관에서 신청서를 작성하십시오.

어휘 **maintenance** 유지, 정비 **available** 이용할 수 있는 **fill out** 작성하다 **application** 신청서

Questions 8-11 이메일

> 수신: dbyeon@mymail.com
> 발신: shipping@anyyouneed.com
> 날짜: 1월 9일
> Re: 주문 #39-AX19Z
>
> 변 씨께,
>
> 휴대용 무선 스피커 두 개를 주문하셨는데 방금 출고됐습니다. 그것은 1월 12일 뉴욕 주 샤오셋 파커 가 387번지로 **8배송될 예정입니다.** 실시간 맵을 **9이용해** 소포 위치를 보고 주문품을 추적할 수 있습니다.
>
> 당사 **10제품이** 고객님의 기대에 부응하기를 바랍니다. **11염려되는 점이 있으면 연락 주십시오.** 오전 7시부터 오후 7시까지 (800) 555-0131번으로 고객상담팀에 연락하시면 됩니다. 거래해 주셔서 감사합니다.
>
> 배송부

어휘 **warehouse** 창고 **expectation** 기대

8

해설 **미래 시제:** 빈칸이 있는 문장에 동사가 보이지 않으므로 빈칸은 동사 자리이다. 이메일이 작성된 날짜는 1월 9일인데, 문장에서 1월 12일에 대해 언급하고 있는 것으로 보아 미래의 일을 이야기하고 있으므로 미래 시제가 필요하다. 따라서 (D) will be delivered가 정답이다.

9

해설 **전치사 어휘:** 문맥상 '실시간 맵을 이용해'라는 의미가 되어야 하므로 (A) by가 정답이다. 'by -ing'는 '~함으로써'라는 뜻으로 빈출 표현이므로 알아 두자.

10

해설 **명사 어휘:** 빈칸이 있는 문장만으로는 정답을 고르기 어려우며, 빈칸 주변의 내용을 확인해야 하는 문제이다. 글의 첫 문장에서 주문하신 휴대용 무선 스피커 두 개가 방금 출고됐다고 한 것으로 보아, 이메일의 작성자는 제품 판매인, 수신자는 제품 구매인임을 알 수 있다. 따라서 '당사 제품이 고객님의 기대에 부응하기를 바란다'는 내용이 되어야 적절하므로 정답은 (C) product이다.

11

해설 **문맥에 맞는 문장 고르기:** 빈칸 뒤 문장에서 연락 가능한 시간과 연락처를 알려 주고 있으므로, 빈칸에는 연락과 관련된 내용이 들어가야 연결이 자연스럽다. 따라서 문제가 있으면 연락하라는 내용의 (A)가 정답이다.

번역 **(A) 염려되는 점이 있으면 연락 주십시오.**
  (B) 현재 지불 기한이 지났다는 점 유념하세요.
  (C) 본 전자우편을 지역 소매점에서 제시하세요.
  (D) 귀하의 신용카드를 처리할 수 없었습니다.

어휘 **overdue** 지불 기한이 지난 **retail store** 소매점

UNIT 03 | 접속부사 문제

ETS 예제

본책 p. 240

바이올렛 스카이 적립

...

포인트는 전 세계 어디에서나 항공권 구입, 호텔 객실 예약, 자동차 대여 등에 사용할 수 있습니다. **게다가** 본 카드는 회원들이 틸레스 항공사로 여행을 예약할 때 무료 수하물 수속과 우선 탑승을 포함한 특전을 제공합니다. 연간 수수료 없이 이러한 모든 혜택을 받으시려면 www.vsrewards.com에서 신청하십시오.

어휘 redeem (현금이나 상품과) 교환하다 purchase 구매(품); 구매하다 reserve 예약하다 perk 특전 priority 우선(권)

ETS CHECK-UP

본책 p. 241

1 (B)	**2** (B)	**3** (D)	**4** (B)	**5** (D)	**6** (A)
7 (C)	**8** (C)	**9** (D)	**10** (A)	**11** (D)	

1 이메일

우리 고객이 오늘 아침에 전화로 이번 목요일 본사 유리 공장에서 있을 회의에 한 명이 더 참석할 예정이라고 알려 왔어요. 이 예기치 못한 변경은 크게 영향을 주진 않을 거예요. 고객들은 기술적인 문제를 상의하기 위해 변경 없이 오전 10시에 도착할 겁니다. 그날 오후 우리는 변경 없이 그들이 흥미롭고 유익한 공장 견학을 하게 할 것입니다. **하지만** 견학을 시작하기 전에 3인이 아닌 4인을 위한 안전 장비를 준비해 주십시오. 안전모와 귀마개, 장화도 추가해야 합니다.

어휘 unforeseen 예기치 못한 affect 영향을 주다 major 주요한 technical matter 기술적인 문제 informative 유익한 safety equipment 안전 장비

해설 **접속부사:** 빈칸 앞 문장에서 그날 오후, 우리는 고객들에게 공장을 견학시켜 줄 것이다(That afternoon, we will take them ~)라는 내용으로 보아 견학이 기존 계획대로 진행될 예정임을 알 수 있다. 빈칸 뒤 문장에서 견학 전에, 3인이 아닌 4인용 안전 장비를 준비해 달라(before we start the tour ~)는 내용으로 보아 기존 계획과 달리 인원 수에 변경이 있음을 알 수 있다. 앞 문장(변경 없음)과 뒤 문장(변경 있음)이 상반된 내용이므로 역접 관계를 나타내는 (B) However가 정답이다.

어휘 instead 대신 besides 게다가 similarly 마찬가지로

2 이메일

에스피노 씨께,

쿄토 미야시타 갤러리의 소유주인 미야시타 씨께서 5월 현대 예술가 축전의 일환으로 귀하의 작품을 흔쾌히 전시해 주셨습니다. 미야시타 씨는 마드리드에서의 일상 생활을 그린 귀하의 멋진 유화 작품집에 특히 감명을 받으셨습니다. 이제 미야시타 씨께서는 9월에 도쿄에 있는 그의 또 다른 갤러리에서 이 작품들을 전시하고 싶어 하십니다. 전시나 판매용으로 그 작품들을 쓸 수 있을까요? 팔리지 않은 작품은 모두 10월에 돌려드릴 것입니다. 관심이 있으신지 저희에게 연락을 부탁드리며, **만일 그렇다면** 보수와 추가 세부 사항을 논의하기 위해 회의 자리를 마련해 드리겠습니다.

어휘 display 전시하다 be impressed with ~에 감명받다 stunning 멋진 oil painting 유화 available 이용 가능한 inform 통지하다 arrange 마련하다, 준비하다 compensation 보상(금)

해설 **접속부사:** 빈칸 앞 문장에서 관심이 있는지 연락해 달라고 했고, 뒤 문장에서는 회의 자리를 마련할 수 있다고 했다. 따라서 빈칸에는 '만일 그렇다면'이라는 표현이 적합하므로 정답은 (B) if so이다. 여기서 so는 you are interested를 대체한 것이다. 다른 보기들은 모두 부사절 접속사이므로 오답이다.

어휘 even if 설사 ~이라고 할지라도 so long as ~이기만[하기만] 하면 in case ~의 경우에 대비하여

3 보도

싱가포르(4월 5일) – 페이틴 타이어는 쿠알라룸푸르와 방콕에 있는 타이어 공장의 창고 용량을 크게 늘릴 계획이다. 더 큰 창고는 연말 무렵에 문을 열 것으로 예상된다. 이 확장 프로젝트는 아시아 전역의 타이어 대리점들에게 서비스를 제공할 수 있는 회사의 능력을 향상시켜 줄 것이다.

"새로운 창고는 우리가 더 효율적으로 일하고 비용을 절약할 수 있게 해 줄 것입니다."라고 페이틴 타이어의 최고경영자인 시아올린 추이는 말했다. "**그와 동시에,** 우리는 우리에게 관심을 보여 주신 아시아 전역의 고객들의 요구를 더 잘 충족시킬 수 있을 것입니다. 이번 행보는 그들의 피드백에 즉각 부응하여 이루어진 것입니다."

어휘 greatly 대단히, 크게 warehouse 창고 capacity 수용량 expansion 확장 serve 서비스를 제공하다 dealer 대리점 efficiently 효율적으로 reach out to ~에게 관심을 보이다 in direct response to ~에 대한 즉각적인 대응으로

해설 **접속부사:** 빈칸에는 페이틴 타이어의 최고경영자인 시아올린 추이가 한 말을 자연스럽게 연결시켜 줄 접속부사가 필요하다. 빈칸 앞 문장에서 새로운 창고는 우리가 더 효율

적으로 일하고 비용을 절약할 수 있게 해 줄 것(The new warehouses will allow us ~)이라고 했고, 뒤 문장에서는 아시아 전역의 고객들의 요구를 더 잘 충족시킬 수 있을 것(we will be able to better meet ~)이라며 두 문장이 창고 확장 계획으로 인해 동시에 얻게 될 긍정적인 효과에 대해 열거하고 있으므로 '그와 동시에'라는 뜻의 (D) At the same time이 정답이다.

어휘   if not 만약 ~이 아니라면   nevertheless 그렇기는 하지만   on the contrary 그와는 반대로

Questions 4-7 이메일

수신: 브라이언 아누루 〈banuru@brightwing.co.nz〉
발신: 프리실라 젠킨스 〈pjenkins@blue-depths.org.nz〉
제목: 정보
날짜: 6월 10일

아누루 씨께,

저희는 블루 뎁스 수족관 전속 사진가 직무에 지원한 귀하의 지원서를 받았습니다. 그 **4자리는** 아직 비어 있습니다. **5여전히 관심이 있으시다면, 다음 단계는 현장 면접이 될 것입니다.**

제가 **6보니** 귀하는 수족관에서 사진가로 일한 경험이 있으셔서, 일부 직무는 친숙할 것입니다. **7하지만** 저희 시설은 여러 면에서 독특하므로 여기서 새로운 절차를 배우셔야 합니다. 6월 17일 오전 11시로 잠정적으로 면접 일정을 잡았습니다. 제 사무실 번호 (09) 362-3351로 전화하셔서 약속을 확정해 주세요. 그럼 그때 뵙기를 고대하겠습니다.

프리실라 젠킨스, 인사과장
블루 뎁스 수족관

어휘   receive 받다   application 지원(서), 신청(서)   photographer 사진작가, 사진사   aquarium 수족관   available (직위) 공석인, 이용 가능한   previous 이전의, 과거의   experience 경력, 경험   facility 시설   unique 독특한   procedure 절차   tentatively 임시로, 잠정적으로   confirm 확정하다, 확인하다   appointment 약속, 예약   look forward to -ing ~하기를 고대하다

4

해설   **명사 어휘:** 바로 앞 문장이 문제 해결의 단서로, '블루 뎁스 수족관 직원 사진가 자리에 지원한 귀하의 지원서를 받았다'고 했으므로, 빈칸에는 a job as staff photographer를 달리 표현한 (B) position이 정답이다.

5

해설   **문맥에 맞는 문장 고르기:** 빈칸 앞 문장에서는 아누루 씨가 지원한 직원 사진가 자리가 비어 있다고 했으며, 이어지는 단락 중반부에서는 6월 17일 오전 11시로 잠정적으로 면접

일정을 잡았다고 했다. 따라서 다음 단계인 면접에 관해 언급하는 것이 자연스러우므로 정답은 (D)이다.

번역   (A) 이 시점에서 보상에 대한 세부사항을 제공해 주시겠습니까?
     (B) 특히, 사진 편집 소프트웨어에 익숙하신가요?
     (C) 시설로 가는 길 안내는 당사 웹사이트에서 찾을 수 있습니다.
     (D) 여전히 관심이 있으시다면, 다음 단계는 현장 면접이 될 것입니다.

어휘   compensation 보상(금)   specifically 특히   directions 길 안내   on-site 현장의

6

해설   **동사의 시제_현재:** 빈칸은 뒤에 온 that절(that ~ familiar to you)을 목적어로 하는 동사 자리이다. 문맥상 '제가 보니 수족관에서 사진가로 일한 경험이 있으셔서 일부 업무는 친숙할 것이다'라는 의미가 되어야 하므로, 보기 중 현재 시제를 사용하는 것이 가장 자연스럽다. 따라서 정답은 (A) see이다.

7

해설   **접속부사:** 빈칸 바로 앞 문장에서는 '귀하는 수족관에서 사진가로 일한 경험이 있어서, 일부 직무는 친숙할 것이다'라고 했고, 빈칸 뒤에서는 '저희 시설은 여러 면에서 독특하므로 여기서 새로운 절차를 배워야 한다'고 했다. 빈칸 앞과 뒤에 온 문장의 관계를 살펴보면, 서로 대조적인 내용이므로 '그러나'라는 의미의 (C) However가 정답이다.

어휘   accordingly 따라서   moreover 게다가   consequently 결과적으로, 따라서

Questions 8-11 기사

11월 30일 – 2년간의 공사 끝에 피츠버그 역사상 가장 큰 호텔이 문을 열 준비가 되었다. 앨러게니 강둑에 위치한 리버탑 호텔에는 방문객을 위한 1,012개의 객실이 마련될 것이다. **8또한 200명까지 단체를 수용할 수 있는 회의실 7개도 갖추게 될 것이다.** 첫 손님들은 의료 기술 회의의 일환으로 12월 12일에 도착할 것이다. 이 프로젝트는 **9건설 중인** 4개의 도심 호텔 중 하나이다. 피츠버그 호텔 및 숙박 협회 회장인 크리스토퍼 월시에 따르면, 이러한 새로운 개발은 **10불가피한 일이다.** "지난 몇 년간 엄청난 방문객이 유입되었습니다." 월시 씨는 말했다. "**11그 결과** 도시의 거의 모든 호텔이 완전히 만원입니다. 분명 호텔 객실이 추가로 필요합니다."

어휘   construction 건설, 건축   medical 의료의, 의학의   lodging 숙박, 숙소   association 협회   massive 대규모의, 거대한   influx 유입   additional 추가의

8

해설 **문맥에 맞는 문장 고르기:** 첫 문장에서 호텔 개장을 알리는 기사문임을 알 수 있으며, 빈칸 앞 문장에서는 객실 수 (1,012 rooms for visitors)를 언급하고 있다. 따라서 빈칸에는 호텔 시설을 소개하는 내용이 이어지는 것이 흐름상 자연스러우므로 (C)가 정답이다.

번역 (A) 호텔이 언제 예약을 받을 준비가 될지 불분명하다.
(B) 건물 보수 공사는 다음 달에 시작될 것이다.
(C) 또한 200명까지 단체를 수용할 수 있는 회의실 7개도 갖추게 될 것이다.
(D) 그 일에 여러 회사가 입찰하고 있다.

어휘 accept 수용하다, 받아 주다   reservation 예약   renovation 보수, 개조   up to ~까지   multiple 다수의   bid 입찰하다

9

해설 **준동사_분사:** 주어(The project)와 동사(is)를 갖춘 완전한 문장으로, 빈칸은 앞에 온 명사 hotels를 수식하는 자리이다. 문맥상 '이 프로젝트는 건설 중인 4개의 도심 호텔 중 하나이다'라는 의미가 되어야 하므로, 명사를 수식할 수 있는 분사이면서 수동의 의미를 지닌 (D) being constructed 가 정답이 된다. 참고로, hotels와 being constructed 사이에 '주격 관계대명사 + be동사'인 which are가 생략된 것으로도 볼 수 있다.

10

해설 **명사 어휘:** 빈칸 뒤에 이어진 월시 씨의 말이 문제 해결의 단서가 된다. 엄청난 방문객이 유입되어 호텔이 거의 만원이었고 추가 호텔 객실이 필요했다고 했으므로, '필요한 것, 불가피한 일'이라는 의미의 (A) necessity가 정답이다.

어휘 necessity 필요한 것, 불가피한 일   nuisance 귀찮은 존재   risk 위험(요소)   bargain 특가품, 흥정

11

해설 **접속부사:** 빈칸 앞에서는 지난 몇 년간 엄청난 방문객이 유입되었다고 했으며, 빈칸 뒤에서는 도시의 거의 모든 호텔이 완전히 만원이라고 했다. 두 문장이 인과관계를 나타내고 있으므로, '결과적으로'를 의미하는 (D) As a result가 정답이 된다.

어휘 on the other hand 반면에   in other words 다시 말해서   in the first place 우선   as a result 그 결과, 결국

UNIT 04 | 어휘 문제

ETS 예제   본책 p. 244

지역 사회 센터는 연중 내내 여러 가지 **야외** 행사를 제공합니다. 가장 규모가 크고 가장 유명한 것은 연례 펀 박람회입니다. 모든 주민들은 올해 4월 12일 브로드 가 부두에서 저희와 함께 시원한 봄바람을 느끼며 지역 최고의 음식과 공예품, 음악 공연을 즐기실 수 있습니다.

어휘 throughout ~ 전역에서   annual 연례의   fair 박람회   pier 부두   craft 공예품   savor 음미하다, 감상하다   breeze 산들바람, 미풍

ETS CHECK-UP   본책 p. 245

1 (D)	2 (B)	3 (C)	4 (C)	5 (A)	6 (D)
7 (D)	8 (A)	9 (B)	10 (C)	11 (B)	

1 공지

도전을 찾고 있는 아마추어 운동선수이신가요? 올해 최고의 시합에 맞춰 준비를 하시기 바랍니다. 랜드버그와 로데포르트, 샌튼 지역의 선수들이 각각의 지역을 대표해 다양한 스포츠 분야에서 수상 경쟁을 벌이게 될 요하네스버그 메트로폴리탄 챔피언스 대회에서 여러분의 능력을 시험해 보세요. 대회는 3월 30일 로데포르트에서 열립니다. 참가 대상은 15세 이상의 선수들입니다. 등록을 원하시면 jmmchampions.co.za를 방문해 주세요.

어휘 athlete 운동선수   premier 최고의   competition 시합, 대회   meet 대회, 경기   represent 대표하다   compete 경쟁하다   a variety of 다양한   take place 열리다, 개최되다

해설 **명사 어휘:** 빈칸 바로 다음 문장에서 올해 최고의 시합에 맞춰 준비를 하라(Get ready for ~)고 했으므로 운동 경기에 대한 공고문임을 알 수 있다. 따라서 빈칸이 포함된 부분은 '도전을 해 보고 싶은 아마추어 운동선수'라는 의미가 되어야 하므로 정답은 (D) challenge이다.

어휘 scholarship 장학금   teammate 팀 동료

2 보도

긴급 보도

트레퍼드 시(11월 18일) – 시 폐기물 관리국(CWMA)은 재활용을 목적으로 전자 쓰레기를 수거하기 위해 지역 재활용 처리 시설인 GDA 폐기물 솔루션즈와 손을 잡았다.

이 **협력 관계**로 주민들은 휴대전화와 노트북 같은 오래된 기기를 퍼 가에 있는 주민센터에 수거용으로 내버릴 수 있게 됐다. 물건은 주민 센터의 정규 운영 시간에 접수 가능하다. 주민들은 센터가 문을 닫은 후에는 센터 밖에 물건을 놓지 말아야 한다. "회수 프로그램은 우리의 새로운 '청정 도시' 캠페인의 일환입니다." CWMA 국장 로이드 잉그램이 말했다.

어휘 **authority** 당국 **team up with** ~와 협력하다
recycling facility 재활용 처리 시설 **collect** 모으다
resident 주민 **drop off** 수거용으로 특정 장소에 버리다 **leave** 놓아 두다

해설 **명사 어휘:** 앞 단락에서 시 폐기물 관리국이 재활용 처리 시설인 GDA 폐기물 솔루션즈와 손을 잡았다(has teamed up with)고 했으므로, '제휴, 협력 관계'라는 의미의 (B) partnership이 정답이다.

어휘 **modification** 수정, 변경 **separation** 분리 **law** 법

3 회람

수신: 전 직원
발신: 회계부
날짜: 2월 4일
제목: 개정된 절차

산업회의 참석에 따른 출장 수당 처리 절차가 변경되었음을 알려 드립니다. **이전에는** 출장비가 출장이 끝난 몇 주 후에 지급되었습니다. 이제 직원들은 출장 최소 30일 전에 예상 출장비 신청서를 제출해야 합니다. 예상 경비가 적정하고 사전 승인을 받았다면 예상 경비 전액이 회사에서 지급됩니다. 일단 출장 요청이 처리되면 해당 직원에게 승인된 자금액을 통보합니다.

어휘 **accounting** 회계 **revised** 개정된, 수정된
compensation 보상(금) **procedure** (처리) 절차
attendance 참석 **modify** 변경하다, 수정하다
travel expense 출장비, 여비 **reimburse** 환급하다
completion 완료 **estimated** 추산되는 **cost** 비용
prior to ~ 전에 **anticipated** 예상되는 **provided that** ~한다면 **reasonable** 합리적인 **preapprove** 사전 승인하다 **process** 처리하다; 진행, 절차
notification 알림, 통지 **approved** 승인된

해설 **부사 어휘:** 빈칸에 적절한 부사를 선택하는 문제이다. 빈칸 앞 문장에서 출장 수당 처리 절차가 변경되었다(the travel compensation procedure ~ has been modified)고 했으며, 빈칸 다음 문장에서는 이제(Now) 직원들은 출장 최소 30일 전에 예상 출장비 신청서를 제출해야 한다는 변경 절차에 대해 설명하고 있다. 따라서, 빈칸이 있는 문장은 변경되기 전의 절차에 대한 내용임을 유추할 수 있으므로, '이전에는'이라는 의미의 (C) Previously가 정답이다.

어휘 **accordingly** 따라서 **similarly** 비슷하게, 마찬가지로

Questions 4-7 기사

로스앤젤레스(4월 22일) – 루네라 커피 로스터스는 올해 한정 기간 동안 브랜드가 **4처음으로** 유명해진 시기인 50년 전의 복고풍 포장으로 제품을 판매할 예정이다. 이러한 일시적인 디자인 변경은 루네라의 기존 커피에만 한정되지는 않을 것이다. 루네라는 계피, 인삼, 다크초콜릿 커피를 선보이면서 향커피 제품군의 규모를 **5두 배로 늘릴** 예정인데, 이들 커피 역시 고전적인 것에 영감을 받은 디자인을 과시할 것이다.

루네라의 루스 오르테가 회장은 이 포장이 브랜드의 역사를 기린다고 말한다. **6또한 이 포장은 더 소박했던 시절을 그리워하는 소비자들의 마음을 사로잡는다.** "이번 캠페인이 오랜 고객과 새 고객 모두에게 반향을 불러일으킬 거라고 생각합니다." 라고 오르테가는 말한다.

루네라의 복고풍 포장은 6월에 매장 진열장에 놓이기 시작할 것이다. 그리고 루네라의 **7신종 상품**은 7월에 첫선을 보인다.

어휘 **limited** 한정된 **roaster** 굽는 사람[기계] **retro** 복고풍의 **packaging** 포장(재) **temporary** 임시의, 일시의 **face-lift** 개조, 새단장 **restrict** 제한하다
existing 기존의 **introduce** 선보이다, 도입하다
cinnamon 계피 **ginseng** 인삼 **flavored** 향기가 있는 **sport** 자랑스럽게 보이다[입다] **vintage** ~년식, 오래됨 **inspire** 영감을 주다 **celebrate** 기념하다
resonate 반향을 불러일으키다 **debut** 데뷔, 첫선

4

해설 **부사 어휘:** 빈칸에 적절한 부사를 선택하는 문제로, 빈칸 앞 문장에서 '50년 전의 복고풍 포장으로(in retro packaging dating from fifty years ago)라고 하며 그 시기를 지칭하고 있으므로 '처음으로 유명해진 때'라고 하는 것이 적절하다. 따라서 정답은 (C) first이다.

5

해설 **준동사_분사:** 빈칸 앞에 주어(The company)와 동사(will be introducing)를 갖춘 완벽한 절이 왔으므로, 빈칸에는 분사구문을 만들 수 있는 분사가 들어가야 한다. 빈칸 뒤에 목적어(the size of its flavored line)가 있으므로, 능동의 의미를 지닌 현재분사 (A) doubling이 정답이다.

어휘 **double** 두 배로 하다

6

해설 **문맥에 맞는 문장 고르기:** 빈칸 앞에서 복고풍 포장이 브랜드의 역사를 기린다고 했으므로, 빈칸은 앞에 나온 the packaging과 관련된 내용이 나오는 것이 자연스럽다. 따라서 the packaging을 대명사 it으로 받아 설명을 추가한 (D)가 정답이다.

번역 (A) 시장조사에 따르면 이 향들이 인기가 있을 것이다.

(B) 전 세계적으로 커피 가격 상승이 예상된다.

(C) 그 점이 루네라가 그토록 유명해진 이유이다.

(D) 또한 이 포장은 더 소박했던 시절을 그리워하는 소비자들의 마음을 사로잡는다.

어휘 market research 시장조사 flavor 맛, 향 popular 인기 있는 be expected to ~할 것으로 예상되다 worldwide 전 세계적으로 appeal to ~의 마음에 들다 long for ~을 그리워하다, 간절히 바라다

7

해설 **명사 어휘:** 빈칸에는 new의 수식을 받아 첫 번째 단락에서 언급된 새로 선보이는 다양한 맛 종류를 지칭할 수 있는 어휘가 들어가야 한다. 따라서 각종 향커피 제품들을 뜻하는 (D) varieties(품종·종류)가 정답이다.

Questions 8-11 보도

긴급 보도　　　언론 문의처: 알버트 이, (808) 555-0147
로파카 그룹 조 가쿠탄 맞아들이다

카폴레이, 하와이(8월 2일) – 로파카 그룹이 조 가쿠탄을 홍보 서비스부 컨설턴트로 영입하게 되었음을 발표하게 되어 **8기쁘다.** 로파카 그룹은 **9마케팅** 조언 제공을 전문으로 하며, 이런 회사들 중에서는 이 주에서 가장 성공한 기업으로 손꼽힌다.

"가쿠탄 씨가 새로 영입된 건 회사로서는 아주 좋은 일입니다." 로파카 그룹의 홍보 및 연구 담당 부사장인 브렌트 시미즈가 말했다. **10"그녀는 기업이 전체 매출을 늘리도록 돕는 일에 탁월합니다.** 그녀는 의뢰인들이 예비 고객에게 성공적으로 광고하는 방법을 찾도록 도울 방법을 알고 있습니다." 시미즈 씨는 계속 말했다. "더욱이 경영 관점에서 상황을 종합적으로 평가함으로써 의뢰인이 필요 **11가장** 적합한 해결책에 도달하도록 도울 수 있습니다."

어휘 addition 새로 추가된 사람 executive vice president 부사장 prospective 예비의 furthermore 더욱이 comprehensive 종합적인 appraisal 평가 standpoint 관점

8

해설 **준동사_분사:** 주어 The Lopaka Group과 호응하는 보어가 필요한 자리로, 문맥상 '로파카 그룹이 ~을 발표하게 되어 기쁘다'라고 주어가 감정을 느끼는 의미가 되어야 자연스러우므로 과거분사인 (A) pleased가 정답이다.

9

해설 **명사 어휘:** 빈칸이 있는 문장만으로는 정답을 고르기 어려우며, 빈칸 주변의 내용을 확인해야 하는 문제이다. 두 번째 문단에서 의뢰인들이 예비 고객에게 성공적으로 광고하는 방법을 찾도록 도울 방법을 알고 있는 가쿠탄 씨의 영입이 회사에 아주 좋은 일이라는 홍보 및 연구 담당 부사장의 언

급이 문제 해결의 주요 단서로, 회사에서 광고 및 홍보를 주업무로 하고 있음을 알 수 있다. 따라서 광고 및 홍보를 바꾸어 표현한 (B) marketing이 정답이다.

10

해설 **문맥에 맞는 문장 고르기:** 빈칸 앞에는 가쿠탄 씨의 영입이 회사에 아주 좋은 일이라고 홍보 및 연구 담당 부사장이 언급했다고 했고, 빈칸 뒤에는 가쿠탄 씨가 의뢰인들의 성공적인 광고를 도울 방법을 알고 있다고 했다. 따라서 빈칸에는 가쿠탄 씨의 사업상 업무 역량을 소개하는 내용이 들어가야 앞뒤 연결이 자연스러우므로 (C)가 정답이다.

번역 (A) 그녀의 은퇴는 사업 파트너들에게 놀라운 일이었습니다.

(B) 그녀는 팀이 새 소프트웨어를 개발하도록 도울 계획입니다.

(C) 그녀는 기업이 전체 매출을 늘리도록 돕는 일에 탁월합니다.

(D) 자신의 팀을 출범하기로 한 그녀의 결정은 적시에 이루어졌습니다.

어휘 retirement 은퇴 overall 전체의

11

해설 **부사 어휘:** 빈칸은 선행사 the solution을 수식하는 관계사절의 주격 관계대명사 that과 동사 fits 사이에서 동사를 수식하는 부사 자리이다. 문맥상 '의뢰인의 필요에 가장 적합한 해결책'이라는 의미가 되어야 자연스러우므로 정답은 (B) best이다. (C) very는 동사를 수식하지 않으므로 답이 될 수 없다.

ETS TEST 　　　본책 p. 248

1 (B)	2 (D)	3 (B)	4 (C)	5 (A)	6 (C)
7 (B)	8 (B)	9 (B)	10 (B)	11 (A)	12 (D)
13 (A)	14 (C)	15 (B)	16 (D)		

Questions 1-4 편지

3월 10일

노마 반스 씨
인사과
클리어뷰 쇼핑몰
던스턴 가 2011번지
오크빌, 온타리오 주 L6H 6P5

반스 씨께,

쇼핑몰 주차 구역의 직원 중 한 분과 있었던 아주 **1긍정적인** 경험을 알려 드리려고 이 편지를 씁니다. 지난 목요일 오후, 저는 물건을 반품하기 위해 쇼핑몰을 방문했습니다. 너무 서두른 나머지 실수로 열쇠를 차 안에 두고 문을 잠갔습니다. 너무 화가

났고 무엇을 해야 할지 몰랐습니다! **2다행히** 주차 안내원이신 워렌 톤 씨께서 저를 도와주러 오셨습니다. 제가 한 번도 본 적 없는 **3도구를 이용해** 몇 분 만에 차 문을 열어 주셨습니다. 그는 수고해 주신 데 대한 어떠한 대가도 받지 않으셨습니다. **4톤 씨는 칭찬받아 마땅합니다.** 제 감사의 뜻을 그 분께 전해 주시겠습니까?

강은주

어휘 experience 경험 attendant 안내원 hurry 서두름
accidentally 우연히, 잘못하여 lock 잠그다 upset
속상한 rescue 구조 tool 도구 accept 받다
gratuity 팁 convey 전하다

1

해설 **형용사 어휘:** 빈칸이 있는 문장만으로는 정답을 고르기 어려우며, 빈칸 뒤의 내용을 확인해야 하는 문제이다. 편지 중반에 주차 안내원이신 워렌 톤 씨께서 저를 도와주러 오셨다(the parking attendant ~ came to my rescue)는 내용과 마지막에 감사의 뜻을 그 분께 전해줄 수 있는지(Could you please convey my thanks to him?)를 묻는 문장이 결정적인 단서로, '주차 구역의 직원 중 한 분과 있었던 좋은 경험'이라는 의미가 되어야 문맥상 자연스러우므로 '긍정적인'이라는 뜻의 (B) positive가 정답이다. 참고로 (C) amuzing은 '재미 있는, 우스운'이라는 의미로 편지 내용과는 맞지 않으므로 오답이다.

어휘 similar 유사한 amusing 재미있는 puzzling
혼란스러운

2

해설 **접속부사:** 빈칸 앞에서 '실수로 열쇠를 차 안에 두고 문을 잠갔다'고 했고 '너무 화가 났고 무엇을 해야 할지 몰랐다'며 자신에게 일어난 난처한 상황에 대해 언급했는데, 빈칸 뒤에 '주차 안내원이신 워렌 톤 씨께서 저를 도와주러 오셨다'고 했다. 문맥상 곤란한 상황이었지만 도움의 손길이 나타나 다행이었다고 연결되어야 자연스러우므로 '다행스럽게도'라는 뜻의 접속부사인 (D) Fortunately가 정답이다.

3

해설 **전치사구:** 빈칸 앞에 완전한 절이 있으므로, 빈칸 뒤의 명사 a tool을 목적어로 취해 '도구를 이용해'라는 의미로 자연스럽게 연결해 줄 수 있는 전치사구 (B) with the use of 가 정답이다. 나머지 보기는 문장 구조가 된다고 해도 어색한 의미가 되기 때문에 오답이다.

4

해설 **문맥에 맞는 문장 고르기:** 빈칸 앞에서 주차 안내원 워렌 톤 씨께서 도와주셔서 차 문을 열 수 있었는데 수고에 대한 어떠한 대가도 받지 않으셨다며 그의 선행에 대해 언급하고 있으므로, 이 일에 대해 그를 칭찬해 주어야 한다는 내용이 뒤따르면 자연스럽다. 따라서 (C)가 정답이다.

번역 (A) 주차 구역은 분명하게 표시되어 있습니다.
(B) 금요일에 또 그 일이 발생했습니다.
(C) 톤 씨는 칭찬받아 마땅합니다.
(D) 그렇게 많은 차량이 있을 거라고 예상하지 못했습니다.

어휘 clearly 분명하게 mark 표시하다 commend
칭찬하다, 추천하다

Questions 5-8 기사

〈맨체스터 데일리 타임즈 저널〉

재계 새 소식

(1월 3일) – 망원경을 비롯한 천체 관측 장비 제조사인 스카이 시크 테크놀러지는 오늘 오랫동안 회장으로 재직해 온 호시 나카타가 오는 9월에 퇴직한다고 발표했다. 나카타 씨는 20년 넘게 스카이 시크를 **5이끌어 왔다.** **6그는 회사 도쿄 지점에서 영업직으로 경력을 시작했다.** 회사 보도에 따르면, 천문학에 대한 지식과 탁월한 조직력 덕분에 그가 관리직의 완벽한 후보자가 될 수 있었다고 한다. **7머지않아** 그는 최고의 자리에 올랐다. 스카이 시크 영업 부사장인 데릭 그리어슨은, 나카타 씨의 통솔하에서 스카이 시크는 고도로 전문화된 시장에서 꾸준히 많은 수익을 거두어 왔다고 말했다. "나카타 씨는 신규 고객을 **8끌어들이는** 놀라운 능력을 지니고 있습니다." 그리어슨이 말했다.

어휘 manufacturer 제조자, 제조업체 telescope
망원경 astronomical 천문학의 instrument 기구,
장비 retire 은퇴하다 press release 언론 보도
astronomy 천문학 superb 탁월한 organizational
조직적인 candidate 지원자, 후보자 consistently
꾸준히 reap 수확하다, 거두다 profit 수익
specialized 전문화된 remarkable 두드러진, 놀라운

5

해설 **동사의 시제_현재완료:** 문맥에 적절한 시제를 선택하는 문제로, for more than 20 years가 문제 해결의 단서가 된다. '나카타 씨는 20년 넘게 스카이 시크를 이끌어 왔다'라는 의미로, 과거부터 현재까지 계속된 행위에 대해 이야기할 때는 현재완료 시제(have[has] p.p.)를 쓴다. 따라서 정답은 (A) has led이다.

6

해설 **문맥에 맞는 문장 고르기:** 퇴임을 앞둔 나카타 씨에 대해 소개하는 기사문이다. 빈칸 앞에서 나카타 씨는 20년 넘게 스카이 시크를 이끌어 왔다는 내용이 왔으며, 빈칸 뒤에는 천문학에 대한 지식과 탁월한 조직력 덕분에 나카타 씨가 관리직 후보자가 될 수 있었다는 내용이 왔다. 따라서 빈칸에는 나카타 씨가 업무를 시작하게 된 것에 관한 내용이 들어가야 글의 흐름이 자연스러워지므로, 정답은 (C)이다.

번역 (A) 영국에서 몇몇 기업이 망원경을 제조한다.
　　　(B) 이 회사는 아마추어와 전문가 모두 아주 좋아한다.
　　　(C) 그는 회사 도쿄 지점에서 영업직으로 경력을 시작했다.
　　　(D) 그는 회사의 부사장과 오랜 친구 사이이다.

어휘 manufacture 제조하다 favorite 선호하는 사람[것]
　　　amateur 아마추어 professional 전문가 branch
　　　지점, 분점

7

해설 **접속부사:** 빈칸 앞에는 나카타 씨가 천문학에 대한 지식과
　　　탁월한 조직력 덕분에 관리직 후보자가 될 수 있었다는 내
　　　용이 왔으며, 빈칸 뒤에는 나카타 씨가 최고의 자리에 올랐
　　　다는 내용이 왔다. 따라서 빈칸에는 '머지않아'라는 의미의
　　　접속부사인 (B) Before long이 정답이다.

어휘 in other words 달리 말하면 on the contrary
　　　반면에

8

해설 **준동사_to부정사:** ability를 수식하는 형용사 역할을 하면
　　　서, '~할, ~하는'이라는 의미로 쓸 수 있는 to부정사구가 오
　　　는 것이 적합하다. 따라서 (B) to attract가 정답이다.

Questions 9-12 공지

> **일요일 자전거의 날**
>
> 자전거와 헬멧을 챙기고 ⁹**친구**를 데리고 피츠버그 거리를 유람
> 할 수 있는 기회를 즐기세요. 10월 ¹⁰**매주 일요일마다** 다른 동
> 네에서 그 동네만의 자전거 길을 선보입니다. 이 길은 오전 10
> 시부터 오후 5시까지 오로지 자전거 이용자들에게만 개방될
> 예정입니다. 길은 매주 ¹¹**바뀝니다.** 지역 자전거 노선 전체 목
> 록을 보려면 www.pittsburghsundays.com을 방문하세
> 요. ¹²**참가하는 후원사들에서 자전거 할인 대여가 가능합니다.**
> 올해는 아야나 사이클스, 프릴 타이어스, 그로텐디크 자전거
> 스튜디오가 여기에 포함됩니다.

어휘 opportunity 기회 solely 오로지

9

해설 **사람 명사와 추상 명사의 구별:** 빈칸 앞에 부정관사 a가 있
　　　으므로 빈칸에는 가산 단수 명사가 필요하다. 또한, 문맥상
　　　'자전거와 헬멧을 챙기고 친구를 데리고'라는 내용이 되어야
　　　자연스러우므로 가산 단수 명사인 (B) friend가 정답이다.

10

해설 **수량 형용사:** 빈칸에는 명사 Sunday를 수식하는 형용사
　　　가 필요하다. '10월 매주 일요일마다'라는 내용이 되어야
　　　자연스러우므로 요일 앞에 붙어 '매 ~요일마다'라는 의미를
　　　만들어 주는 수량 형용사인 (B) Every가 정답이다.

11

해설 **동사 어휘:** 빈칸이 있는 문장만으로는 정답을 고르기 어려
　　　운 문제이다. 빈칸 앞에 10월 매주 일요일마다 다른 동네에
　　　서 그 동네만의 자전거 길을 선보인다는 내용이 있으므로,
　　　'길이 매주 바뀐다'는 내용이 되어야 문맥상 적절하다. 따라
　　　서 정답은 (A) change이다.

어휘 increase 증가하다

12

해설 **문맥에 맞는 문장 고르기:** 빈칸 뒤에서 올해는 아야나 사이
　　　클스, 프릴 타이어스, 그로텐디크 자전거 스튜디오가 여기
　　　에 포함된다고 했으므로, 여기 언급된 후원 업체들에 대한
　　　내용이 들어가야 문맥상 연결이 자연스럽다. 따라서 정답은
　　　(D)이다.

번역 (A) 행사는 날씨에 상관없이 진행됩니다.
　　　(B) 헬멧은 참가자에게 선택 사항으로 간주되지 않습니다.
　　　(C) 행사에 등록은 요구되지 않습니다.
　　　(D) 참가하는 후원사들에서 자전거 할인 대여가 가능합니다.

어휘 rain or shine 날씨에 상관없이 optional 선택의
　　　registration 등록 participate 참가하다

Questions 13-16 이메일

> 수신: csc@dobsons.com
> 발신: efuller@seascape.net
> 주제: 헵워스 산업 할인
> 날짜: 4월 12일
> 첨부: 매장 영수증
>
> 돕슨 고객 서비스 담당자께,
>
> 스타일과 특징에 감탄해 어제 ¹³**귀사** 매장에서 헵워스 고급 기
> 억장치를 구입했습니다. 더욱이 그 품목에 딸린 30퍼센트 제
> 조사 할인도 좋았고요. ¹⁴**가격** 할인을 받으려면 영수증과 연
> 락처를 헵워스 산업으로 보내기만 하면 된다고 들었습니다. 집
> 에 돌아와서 자격 조건을 더 자세히 읽고 나니 판촉 양식도 제
> 출해야 한다는 걸 깨달았습니다. ¹⁵**그건 구매 당시 발행되기로
> 되어 있었습니다.** 아쉽게도 점원이 저한테 그걸 제공하지 않았
> 습니다. 그러므로 양식을 보내 주시길 ¹⁶**요청합니다.** 영수증
> 사본은 이 이메일에 첨부되어 있습니다.
>
> 이 건에 관해 도와주셔서 감사합니다.
>
> 엘리자베스 풀러

어휘 rebate (할인 금액만큼 현금으로 돌려주는) 할인
　　　impressed 감탄하는 storage unit 기억장치
　　　manufacturer 제조사 qualifying 자격을 주는
　　　closely 자세히 submit 제출하다 promotional
　　　판촉의 unfortunately 아쉽게도 therefore 그러므로

13

해설 **인칭대명사_소유격:** 돕슨이라는 업체의 고객 서비스 담당자에게 보내는 글로 빈칸 앞에 달리 언급된 사람이 없으며, '당신의 매장에서 물건을 구입했다'는 내용이 되어야 자연스러우므로 (A) your가 정답이다.

14

해설 **명사 어휘:** 앞 글에서 물건을 구입했는데 제조사 할인 30퍼센트를 받을 수 있어 좋았다며 할인에 대해 언급했으므로, '가격 할인을 받으려면'이라는 내용이 되어야 문맥이 자연스럽다. 따라서 (C) price reduction이 정답이다.

어휘 **survey** 설문조사 **response** 응답 **reduction** 할인

15

해설 **문맥에 맞는 문장 고르기:** 앞 문장에서 판촉 양식을 제출해야 한다는 것을 깨달았다고 했고, 뒤 문장에서는 점원이 그 양식을 제공하지 않았다고 했다. 따라서 양 문장 사이에는 판촉 양식이 누락된 것과 관련된 내용이 들어가야 연결이 자연스러우므로 (B)가 정답이다.

번역 (A) 거기에는 조립 설명서가 포함되어 있었습니다.
(B) 그건 구매 당시 발행되기로 되어 있었습니다.
(C) 제 매니저가 그걸 적극 추천했습니다.
(D) 그건 전자결제에 한해 사용됩니다.

어휘 **assembly** 조립 **instructions** (사용) 설명서 **issue** 발행하다 **purchase** 구매(품) **recommend** 추천하다

16

해설 **현재 시제:** 빈칸은 주어 뒤에서 that절을 목적어로 취하는 동사 자리이다. 이메일을 작성하고 있는 현재 '양식을 보내주시기를 요청한다'는 내용이므로 현재 시제인 (D) request가 정답이다.

CHAPTER 02 | 문장 고르기 문제

UNIT 05 대명사 / 지시어 활용하기

ETS 예제
본책 p. 252

비밀번호 변경

강력한 비밀번호는 최소 10자 길이에 문자와 숫자 조합이 포함되어야 한다는 점 유의하십시오. **이름이나 흔히 사용되는 단어가 들어가면 안 됩니다.** 시스템에서 변경 사항을 수락하면 로그아웃 후 새 비밀번호를 이용해 다시 로그인 하십시오.

어휘 **character** 문자, 인물 **include** 포함하다 **combination** 조합 **letter** 문자 **accept** 수락하다, 받아들이다

번역 **(A) 이름이나 흔히 사용되는 단어가 들어가면 안 됩니다.**
(B) 직원들은 퇴근할 때 반드시 회사 컴퓨터에서 로그아웃 해야 합니다.
(C) 소프트웨어 업데이트가 가능할 때 이메일을 받게 됩니다.
(D) 정보기술부는 5층에 있습니다.

어휘 **contain** 들어 있다, 포함하다 **commonly** 흔히

ETS CHECK-UP
본책 p. 253

1 (C)	2 (A)	3 (B)	4 (A)	5 (A)	6 (D)
7 (B)	8 (D)	9 (C)	10 (A)	11 (C)	

1 광고

저희 식당 세 곳이 모든 취향에 맞게 음식을 즐기는 모험을 선사해 드리는 페블 리버 리조트로 오시기 바랍니다! **가장 격식 있는 저희 식당은 리버뱅크 레스토랑입니다.** 수상 경력을 지닌 이곳 주방장들이 지역 전통의 영향이 남아 있는 고풍스러운 식사 경험을 마련해 드립니다. 만약 일상적인 식사를 선호하시면 올드 샌즈 그릴이 석조 테라스에서 계절에 맞는 음식을 제공해 드립니다. 또한 저희 스위트숍에 오셔서 수제 초콜릿이나 페이스트리를 즐기시기 바랍니다.

어휘 **culinary** 음식의, 요리의 **taste** 취향, 맛 **classic** 전통의, 고전적인 **heritage** 유산, 전통 **fare** 식사, 음식 **feature** ~을 특별히 포함하다, ~을 특징으로 하다 **seasonal** 제철의 **handmade** 수제의 **pastry** 페이스트리(밀가루로 만든 빵이나 케이크)

해설 **문맥에 맞는 문장 고르기:** 빈칸 뒤에 수상 경력을 지닌 이곳 주방장들(Its award-winning chefs)이라는 말이 있는데, 이럴 경우 Its가 가리키는 식당이 앞 문장에 먼저 언급되어야 하므로 정답은 (C)이다.

번역 (A) 식사 메뉴는 매일 바뀝니다.
(B) 사전 예약을 적극 권장합니다.
(C) 가장 격식 있는 저희 식당은 리버뱅크 레스토랑입니다.
(D) 가장 인기 있는 음식에는 특식 디저트도 많습니다.

어휘 **vary** 다르다, 달라지다 **advance reservation** 사전 예약 **formal** 격식 있는 **dish** 요리 **specialty** (식당의) 전문 음식[요리]

2 이메일

배 씨께

고객님의 최근 주문에 감사드립니다. 고객님께서 주문하신 황갈색 리넨 정장이 유감스럽게도 지금은 고객님께 맞는 사이즈로는 없지만 연한 회색으로는 똑같은 스타일이 있습니다. **이런 스타일은 저희가 바로 보내 드릴 수 있습니다.**

만약 지금 주문하시면 전체 주문품에 대한 무료 배송뿐만 아니

라 정장도 15퍼센트 할인해 드릴 수 있으며 고객님께서는 다음 주까지 물건을 받으실 수 있습니다. 만약 관심이 있으시면 저희 고객 서비스 부서로 이메일을 보내 주시고 위에 있는 주문 번호를 말씀해 주시기 바랍니다.

어휘 **tan** 황갈색의 **linen** 리넨, 아마 섬유 **unfortunately** 유감스럽게도 **have ~ in stock** ~이 재고로 있다 **as well as** ~뿐만 아니라 **reference** 참조 사항으로 인용하다

해설 **문맥에 맞는 문장 고르기:** 선행 문장에서 '고객님께서 주문하신 황갈색 리넨 정장이 유감스럽게도 지금은 고객님께 맞는 사이즈가 없지만 연한 회색으로는 똑같은 스타일이 있습니다(Although the ~ light gray)'라고 했다. 따라서 빈칸에는 연한 회색 스타일의 정장은 바로 보내 줄 수 있다고 하는 것이 자연스러운 연결이 되므로 정답은 (A)이다.

번역 **(A) 이런 스타일은 저희가 바로 보내 드릴 수 있습니다.**
(B) 반품해 주셔서 감사합니다.
(C) 다음 시즌 초에 이용하실 수 있습니다.
(D) 새 양복을 더 큰 사이즈로 교환하실 수 있습니다.

어휘 **return** 반품하다 **exchange** 교환하다

3 편지

로마스 씨께,

6월 18일 토요일, 연례 퍼스 시 철인 3종 경기를 위해 오전 8시에서 오후 2시 사이에 크레스웰 가와 쿠카버라 대로의 모든 교통이 통제됩니다. **이는 선수들의 안전을 확보하기 위한 것입니다.**

불편을 끼쳐 드려 죄송합니다. 본 행사는 근년 들어 점점 더 인기를 얻고 있습니다. 본 행사는 지역 홍보와 관광업을 위한 지역사회의 시책을 촉진하는 데 도움이 되며, 지역의 기업들은 이 행사에서 이익을 얻습니다. 여러분의 협조가 퍼스 시 철인 3종 경기의 지속적인 성공에 도움이 될 것입니다.

어휘 **annual** 연례의, 해마다 일어나는 **triathlon** 철인 3종 경기 **apologize for** ~에 대하여 사과하다 **promote** 증진시키다, 홍보하다 **community** 지역 사회 **initiative** (목표를 위한 새로운) 계획, 정책 **regional** 지역의 **publicity** 홍보 **tourism** 관광(업) **local** 지역의, 현지의 **benefit from** ~에서 이득을 보다, ~에서 도움을 받다 **cooperation** 협조, 협력 **continuing** 연속적인, 지속적인

해설 **문맥에 맞는 문장 고르기:** 빈칸 앞에 '철인 3종 경기를 위해 모든 교통이 통제된다'는 내용이 있으므로, 빈칸에는 교통 통제에 관한 내용이 와야 한다. 따라서 교통 통제가 선수들의 안전을 확보하기 위한 것이라는 내용의 (B)가 정답이 된다.

번역 (A) 접수 마감일은 6월 10일입니다.
(B) 이는 선수들의 안전을 확보하기 위한 것입니다.

(C) 모든 주민들에게 요금 인상을 고지하고 있습니다.
(D) 경기를 돕기 위해 자원해 주셔서 감사합니다.

어휘 **registration** 등록, 접수 **ensure** 보장하다, 확실히 하다 **athlete** 선수 **resident** 주민 **notify** 통보하다 **fare** 요금

Questions 4-7 정보

웹사이트에 올버리 일자리가 게시된다

올버리 잡 디렉토리는 새로운 고용 기회를 알리는 온라인 게시판입니다. 올버리 주민들에게 무료로 ⁴제공되며 지역 내 일자리를 찾을 수 있도록 도움을 줍니다. 모든 사업체들은 얼마든지 디렉토리에 무료로 일자리를 게시해도 좋습니다. 이 서비스를 ⁵이용하는 고용주들은 다양한 이유로 디렉토리가 일시적으로 접속 불가능할 수도 있다는 것을 알고 있어야 합니다. ⁶그 범위는 일상적인 유지 보수에서 시스템 오작동까지 이릅니다. 정기 업데이트가 예정되어 있을 때마다, 우리는 이용자들에게 미리 알리도록 최선을 다할 것입니다. ⁷그러나 웹사이트를 전적으로 혹은 부분적으로 이용할 수 없을 경우 올버리 잡 디렉토리는 이에 대한 책임을 지지 않습니다.

어휘 **board** (판자같이 생긴) ~판 **announce** 발표하다, 알리다 **employment** 고용 **opportunity** 기회 **free of charge** 무료로 **resident** 주민 **match** 연결시키다 **job opening** 일자리 **local** 지역의 **post** 게시하다 **charge** 요금 **employer** 고용주 **aware** 아는 **temporarily** 일시적으로 **inaccessible** 접근할 수 없는 **a variety of** 다양한 **periodic** 주기적인 **notify** 알리다 **ahead of** ~보다 앞서 **assume** (책임 등을) 맡다 **liability** 법적 책임 **completely** 전적으로 **partially** 부분적으로 **unavailable** 이용할 수 없는

4

해설 **동사의 태_수동태:** 빈칸은 The Albury Job Directory를 받은 대명사 주어 It의 동사 자리이고, 빈칸 뒤에 목적어가 없으며 의미상 '올버리 주민들에게 무료로 제공된다'는 수동의 의미가 되어야 자연스러우므로 수동태인 (A) is provided가 정답이다.

5

해설 **관계대명사_주격:** Employers가 주어, should be가 본동사인 문장에서 빈칸부터 use the service까지는 주어인 Employers를 수식하는 관계사절이므로 관계사가 필요하다. 또한, 빈칸은 관계사절에서 동사 use의 주어 역할을 하고 있으므로 주격 관계대명사가 (A) who가 정답이다.

6

해설 **문맥에 맞는 문장 고르기:** 빈칸 앞 문장에서 다양한 이유로 디렉토리가 일시적으로 접속 불가능할 수도 있다고 했으므로, 그 이유에 대한 내용이 뒤따르는 것이 문맥상 가장 자연

스럽다. 따라서 그 범위가 일상적인 유지 보수에서 시스템 오작동까지 이른다며 접속이 안 될 수 있는 이유의 범주에 대해 설명한 (D)가 정답이다.

번역 (A) 이 사이트는 올버리 시의 자금 지원을 받습니다.
(B) 자원봉사자들은 지금 훈련을 받는 중입니다.
(C) 기타 항목은 디렉터리 내 별도의 줄에 나올 것입니다.
(D) 그 범위는 일상적인 유지 보수에서 시스템 오작동까지 이릅니다.

어휘 fund 자금을 대다   volunteer 자원봉사자   separate 별도의   range (범위가) ~에 이르다   maintenance 유지   malfunction 고장

7

해설 **접속부사:** 빈칸 앞에는 디렉터리가 일시적으로 접속 불가능할 수도 있다고 알리며 접속이 안 될 수 있는 경우 중 하나인 정기 업데이트 때마다 미리 알리도록 최선을 다하겠다고 했는데, 빈칸 뒤에는 웹사이트를 이용할 수 없을 경우에 대해 책임지지 않는다며 상반된 내용이 왔다. 따라서 '그러나, 하지만'의 의미로 반대나 대조의 의미를 지닌 두 문장을 연결하는 접속부사 (B) However가 정답이다.

Questions 8-11 공지

엑셀시오르 서점은 5월 11일 화요일 오후 7시에 사토시 다나카를 모시고 다음 '저자와의 만남' 행사를 열게 된 것을 발표하게 되어 기쁩니다. **8다나카 씨의 작품으로는 20여 편의 소설이 있으며 6월 5일에는 자서전 〈저술에 바친 인생〉을 내놓을 예정입니다.** 다나카 씨는 **9이번에 나올** 책의 발췌문을 읽는 것 외에, 평론가 발레리 스테일리와 집필 경력 전반에 대해 인터뷰도 진행합니다. **10청중의 질문도 받을 예정입니다.**

행사 입장은 참가 인원 100명으로 제한됩니다. 참석하실 분은 www.excelsiorbooksellers.com에서 미리 신청하면 무료로 **11좌석**을 예약할 수 있습니다.

어휘 announce 알리다, 발표하다   author 저자, 작가   include 포함하다   novel 소설   release 출시하다, 공개하다; 출시   autobiography 자서전, 전기   excerpt 발췌, 인용   critic 평론가   admission 입장, 인정   limit 제한하다   participant 참가자   reserve 예약하다   in advance 미리   free of charge 무료로

8

해설 **관계대명사_소유격:** Mr. Tanaka가 주어, will be releasing이 동사이며, 빈칸부터 work includes over twenty novels는 관계사절로 주어이자 선행사인 Mr. Tanaka에 대해 부연 설명을 하고 있다. 빈칸은 관계사절에서 뒤에 온 명사 work를 수식하는 형용사 역할을 해야 하므로, 소유격 관계대명사인 (D) whose 가 정답이다.

9

해설 **형용사 어휘:** 빈칸이 있는 문장만으로 정답을 고르기는 어려우며, 전체적인 글의 맥락을 파악해야 풀 수 있는 문제이다. 바로 앞 문장의 will be releasing his autobiography, *A Lifetime in Writing*, on June 5가 문제 해결의 단서로, 〈저술에 바친 인생〉은 앞으로 출시될 자서전이므로, 빈칸에는 '앞으로 나올'이라는 의미의 (C) upcoming이 정답이다.

10

해설 **문맥에 맞는 문장 고르기:** 바로 앞 문장에서 평론가 발레리 스테일리와 집필 경력 전반에 대해 인터뷰도 진행한다고 했으므로, 빈칸에는 인터뷰에 관련된 내용이 들어가야 글의 흐름이 자연스러워진다. 따라서 '인터뷰에서 청중의 질문도 받을 예정'이라는 (A)가 정답이다.

번역 **(A) 청중의 질문도 받을 예정입니다.**
(B) 그는 국립대학교에서 글쓰기를 공부할 계획입니다.
(C) 그 책은 할인된 가격에 구입할 수 있을 것입니다.
(D) 출간일은 발표되지 않았습니다.

어휘 audience 청중, 관객   available 이용[입수] 가능한   discount 할인

11

해설 **명사 어휘:** 바로 앞 문장이 문제 해결의 단서로 행사 입장은 참가 인원 100명으로 제한된다고 했다. 따라서 '웹사이트에서 미리 신청하면 무료로 좌석을 예약할 수 있다'는 내용이 되어야 하므로, 빈칸에는 '좌석'이라는 의미의 (C) seat이 가장 적절하다.

UNIT 06	정관사 활용하기

ETS 예제   본책 p. 256

소중한 고객님께

델미어 뱅크 바인 가 지점이 4월 5일과 6일 문을 닫는다는 점을 알려 드립니다. 이 기간 동안 꼭 필요한 건물 보수공사를 합니다. 이번에 창구 전화선과 거래 카운터도 개선할 것입니다. **불편을 끼쳐 죄송합니다.**

어휘 advise 알리다   branch 지점   undergo 겪다, 거치다   much-needed 꼭 필요한   improvement 개선, 향상   teller 은행 창구직원   transaction 거래

번역 (A) 모든 거래를 일찍 완료해 주시기 바랍니다.
(B) 원래 있던 바닥재는 그대로 두었습니다.
(C) 양식은 로비에서 받을 수 있습니다.
(D) 불편을 끼쳐 죄송합니다.

ETS CHECK-UP

본책 p. 257

1 (C)	2 (A)	3 (D)	4 (B)	5 (B)	6 (C)
7 (D)	8 (B)	9 (D)	10 (C)	11 (D)	

1 기사

홀트 시 공립도서관 중고책 판매는 이번 주 금요일부터 일요일까지 정규 도서관 운영 시간에 개최될 예정이다. 홀트 시 지역 위원회(HCCC)는 이번 연례 행사를 위해 7월부터 중고책을 수집하고 있다. **책 판매는 이제 여덟 번째 해를 맞는다.** "우리 판매 행사는 해가 갈수록 점점 더 인기를 끌고 있습니다." 기획자인 제인 라리시오가 말했다. "책을 사랑하는 분들에게 아주 좋은 기회입니다."

어휘 used book 중고책 regular 정기적인 annual 연례의 popular 인기가 있는 organizer 주최자, 기획자 opportunity 기회

해설 문맥에 맞는 문장 고르기: 빈칸 앞 문장에서 연례 행사를 위해 7월부터 중고책을 수집하고 있다(The Holt City Community Council ~ since July for this annual event)고 했고, 뒤 문장에서 해가 갈수록 점점 더 인기를 얻고 있다(Our sales get ~ more popular each year)고 했으므로, 이제 여덟 번째 해를 맞고 있다는 내용이 앞뒤를 자연스럽게 연결한다. 따라서 (C)가 정답이다.

번역 (A) 공무원들은 모든 자원봉사자에게 감사를 표했다.
(B) 구매자들은 도시 곳곳에서 왔다.
(C) 책 판매는 이제 여덟 번째 해를 맞는다.
(D) 이 할인은 자동으로 적용된다.

어휘 official 공무원 volunteer 자원봉사자 apply 적용하다, 신청하다 automatically 자동으로

2 이메일

졸단 씨께,

2월 19일에 당신이 우리 마케팅팀을 대상으로 진행할 곧 있을 제품 발표와 관련해 글을 쓰고 있습니다. 유감스럽게도, 저는 이 일정을 연기해야 합니다. 현재, 예산상 제약 때문에 밀러튼의 가정용품 부서는 새로운 상품을 고려할 입장이 아닙니다.

제 영업팀과 제가 이 미팅을 고대하고 있었다는 것을 알아주십시오. 모두들 당신의 수입 도자기와 바구니에 대해 더 많이 알아보는 데 관심을 가졌습니다. 그것들은 아마 우리 점포에서 아주 잘 팔릴 유형의 가정용 장식용품입니다. 우리는 6개월 후에 당신과 다시 연락하고 싶습니다.

어휘 upcoming 곧 있을 regrettably 유감스럽게도 postpone 연기하다 budget restriction 예산 제약 merchandise 상품 imported 수입된 pottery 도자기 do well 성공하다 reconnect 다시 연락[연결]하다

해설 문맥에 맞는 문장 고르기: 빈칸 앞에는 예산 문제로 미팅이 취소되었음을 알렸고, 빈칸 뒤에는 모두가 새 상품에 대해 알아보고 싶어 했음을 전하고 있다. 빈칸에는 취소된 미팅과 모두가 가졌던 관심을 자연스럽게 연결할 수 있는 내용이 들어가야 하므로, 모두가 미팅을 고대하고 있었음을 알리는 내용의 (A)가 정답이다.

번역 **(A) 제 영업팀과 제가 이 미팅을 고대하고 있었다는 것을 알아주십시오.**
(B) 제 사무실은 현재 3층에 있다는 것을 기억하십시오.
(C) 일요일에는 매장이 문을 열지 않는다는 점에 유의하십시오.
(D) 아시다시피, 우리는 다양한 스포츠웨어를 갖추고 있습니다.

어휘 note that ~을 주목[주의]하다 be aware that ~을 인지하다 stock (상품을 갖추고) 있다

3 전단지

팜데일 공공 도서관에서 컴퓨터 강좌 제공

팜데일 공공 도서관은 올봄에 바렌 컴퓨터 서비스가 후원하는 무료 컴퓨터 강좌를 제공한다는 소식을 발표하게 되어 기쁩니다. 강의 주제에는 인터넷 조사, 문서 작성 기술 강화, 기본적인 컴퓨터 문제 해결이 포함됩니다. 수업은 매주 토요일 오후 2시에 열립니다. 18세 이상의 팜데일 주민은 등록할 수 있지만 자리는 제한되어 있습니다. 도서관 안내 데스크에서 정규 영업시간 중 아무 때나 등록하십시오. **첫 수업은 3월 20일입니다.** 첫 수업이 끝난 후 간단한 다과가 제공됩니다.

어휘 library 도서관 sponsor 후원하다 research 연구, 조사 refine 개선하다 basic 기본적인 troubleshooting 문제 해결 resident 주민, 거주민 register 신청하다, 등록하다 limited 제한된, 한정된 sign up 등록하다 operating hours 영업시간 refreshments 다과, 간식

해설 문맥에 맞는 문장 고르기: 빈칸 앞에는 수업 등록 장소 및 시간(Sign up at the library's front desk anytime during regular operating hours)에 대한 내용이 왔으며, 빈칸 뒤에는 첫 수업이 끝난 후 간단한 다과가 제공된다(Light refreshments will be served following the opening class)는 내용이 왔다. 따라서 빈칸에는 첫 수업 날짜에 관해 언급하는 내용이 와야 글의 흐름이 자연스러워진다. 따라서 정답은 (D)이다.

번역 (A) 사서가 곧 요청에 답할 것입니다.
(B) 대체 책상이 금요일에 배송될 예정입니다.
(C) 암호는 컴퓨터실 문에 게시되어 있습니다.
(D) 첫 수업은 3월 20일입니다.

어휘 librarian 사서 replacement 대체, 교체 deliver 배송하다 post 게시하다

Questions 4-7 웹페이지

잠자라스 기념품 및 골동품점 – 진귀한 물건으로 가득 찬 독특한 가게!

우리 가게에 오셔서 가구, 보석, 장난감, 인형 외 갖가지 진귀품을 골라 보세요. 수작업으로 정성껏 만든 제품으로 수백 년간 ⁴끄떡없을 물건들입니다. 선반에는 지역 출신인 35명 장인들의 작품을 진열합니다.

⁵**우리는 "토산품을 구매하는 것"이 옳다고 확신합니다.** 우리는 또한 다양한 "녹색" 계획도 지지하며, 재활용 소재로 만든 많은 상품도 판매합니다. ⁶**환경** 의식을 가지고 오늘 우리 가게에서 친환경적인 선물을 구매하세요! 그리고 골동품 판매대를 둘러보는 것도 잊지 마세요. 이 멋진 컬렉션은 오직 ⁷진품으로만 채워져 있습니다. 우리는 복제품이나 모조품은 절대 팔지 않습니다.

어휘   collectible 수집품   one of a kind 유례를 찾기 힘든   treasure 보물   carefully 정성껏, 신중하게   craft 공예품을 만들다   artisan 장인   initiative 계획, 발전 방안   recycled 재활용된   conscious 의식하는, 자각하는   eco-friendly 친환경적인   browse 둘러보다   antique 골동품   marvelous 믿기 어려운, 멋진   consist of ~로 구성되다   reproduction 복제품   replica 모조품, 복제품

4

해설   **동사의 수 일치:** 관계사절의 동사는 선행사에 일치시킨다. 선행사가 the kinds of items로 복수이므로 복수동사인 (B) last가 정답이다.

어휘   last 계속되다

5

해설   **문맥에 맞는 문장 고르기:** 빈칸 앞에서 '선반에는 지역 출신인 35명 장인들의 작품을 진열한다'고 했으므로 빈칸에는 토산품을 구매하는 것이 옳다고 믿는다는 말이 이어지는 것이 자연스럽다. 따라서 (B)가 정답이다.

번역   (A) 강습반은 아직 등록을 받고 있습니다.
    (B) 우리는 "토산품을 구매하는 것"이 옳다고 확신합니다.
    (C) 경품은 매년 10월에 증정됩니다.
    (D) 저희는 수리비 명목으로 약간의 수수료를 부과합니다.

어휘   registration 등록   believe in ~이 옳다고 믿는다   hand out 나눠 주다   charge 청구하다

6

해설   **부사 어휘:** 빈칸 앞에서 '다양한 "녹색" 계획도 지지하며, 재활용 소재로 만든 많은 상품도 판매한다'고 했으므로, 문맥상 '환경 의식을 가지라'는 내용이 되어야 한다. 따라서 '환경적으로'라는 의미의 부사인 (C) environmentally가 정답이다.

어휘   centrally 중심으로   mutually 상호 간에   collaboratively 협력으로

7

해설   **형용사 어휘:** 빈칸 뒤에서 복제품이나 모조품은 절대 팔지 않는다(We never sell any reproductions or replicas)라고 했다. 따라서 '이 멋진 컬렉션은 오직 진품으로만 채워져 있다'라는 의미가 되어야 하므로, '원래의, 원본의'라는 의미의 (D) original이 정답이다.

어휘   modern 현대의, 현대적인   imitation 모조품   flawed 결함이 있는

Questions 8-11 공지

3월 3일 게재

프놈펜 외국어대학교에서 불어학과를 ⁸**이끌어 주실** 경험 있는 불어 강사를 찾고 있습니다. ⁹**불어학과에는 현재 세 명의 전임 강사가 있습니다.** 적임자는 이 작은 팀의 팀장으로 관리자 역할을 할 수 있고, 새로운 강사들을 훈련할 수 있어야 합니다. 지원자의 교육학 학위 소지 ¹⁰**여부는** 경력보다 중요하지는 않습니다. 이상적인 지원자는 최소 5년 이상의 강의 경험이 있어야 합니다. 관심 있으신 분은 이력서와 자기소개서를 chastain@ppsfl.ca.ed로 루벤 채스테인 앞으로 ¹¹**제출하십시오**. 추천인 명단은 현 채용 단계에서는 필요하지 않습니다.

어휘   seek 구하다, 찾다   experienced 경험 있는   instructor 강사   department 학과, 부서   successful candidate 적임자, 합격자   assume (책임을) 떠맡다   managerial 관리자의   applicant 지원자   ideal 이상적인   résumé 이력서   a letter of introduction 자기소개서   reference 추천인, 신원 보증인   recruitment 채용

8

해설   **동사 어휘:** 강사 구인 공지이므로 '우리 불어학과를 이끌어 줄 경험 있는 불어 강사'라는 의미가 되어야 한다. 따라서 (B) lead가 정답이다.

어휘   lead 이끌다   assess 평가하다

9

해설   **문맥에 맞는 문장 고르기:** 빈칸 앞에서는 불어학과를 이끌어 줄 불어 강사를 찾고 있다고 했으며, 빈칸 뒤에서는 적임자의 자격에 대해 설명하고 있다. 따라서 보기 중 현재 불어학과에 세 명의 전임 강사가 있다는 (D)가 들어가야 글의 흐름이 자연스러워진다.

번역   (A) 우리 학생들은 다양한 배경을 갖고 있습니다.
    (B) 불어는 지구촌 언어로서 중요성이 점점 커지고 있습니다.
    (C) 우리는 이네즈 로버트가 새로운 직책을 맡은 것을 축하합니다.
    (D) 불어학과에는 현재 세 명의 전임 강사가 있습니다.

어휘 **diverse** 다양한 **increasingly** 점점 더
congratulate 축하하다

10

해설 **명사절 접속사:** 빈칸부터 education까지가 이 문장의 주어이고 is가 동사인 문장이다. 문맥상 '지원자의 교육학 학위를 소지했는지 아닌지의 여부는 경력보다 중요하지는 않다'는 의미가 되어야 하므로, '~인지 아닌지'라는 의미를 지닌 명사절 접속사인 (C) Whether가 정답이다.

11

해설 **동사의 시제_미래:** Interested parties가 문장의 주어이고, 빈칸이 동사이며, a résumé and letter of introduction이 목적어인 문장이다. 문맥상 '관심 있으신 분은 이력서와 자기소개서를 제출해야 한다'는 의미가 되어야 하므로, (D) should send가 정답이다.

UNIT 07 | 접속부사 활용하기

ETS 예제 본책 p. 260

분실된 도서관 서적, 〈윈드미어 미스테리〉에 관한 회원님의 전화 메시지에 감사드립니다.

(중략)

저는 누군가 해당 서적을 발견해서 반납했을 경우에 대비해, 오늘 아침 직원들에게 서가를 확인하라고 했습니다. **아쉽게도 책은 찾지 못했습니다.**

회원님이 9월 1일까지 책을 찾지 못하시면 저희는 새 책을 주문할 예정입니다.

어휘 **missing** 분실된 **shelf** 서가, 선반 **in case** ~인 경우에 대비하여 **locate** 찾아내다 **copy** (책 등의) 1부, 1권, 복사(본)

번역 (A) 도서관 회원은 누구나 참석해 주시기 바랍니다.
(B) 저희 도서 목록은 온라인으로 볼 수 있습니다.
(C) 아쉽게도 책은 찾지 못했습니다.
(D) 하지만 화요일에는 늦게까지 개관합니다.

어휘 **patron** 고객, 손님 **access** 이용하다, 접근하다

ETS CHECK-UP 본책 p. 261

1 (C) **2** (C) **3** (B) **4** (D) **5** (D) **6** (C)
7 (C) **8** (D) **9** (A) **10** (C) **11** (B)

---

1 이메일

인사 고과 시기가 다시 돌아왔습니다. 늘 그러하듯, 여러분이 직접 관리하는 직원과 일대일로 면담을 나누어 주셨으면 합니다.

여느 때처럼 여러분은 직원들에게 피드백을 제공해야 합니다.

직원들을 만나기 전에, 자신의 실적을 요약해서 보내 달라고 요청하십시오. 이렇게 하면 직원들은 면담에 대비하고, 자신이 회사에 기여한 바에 대해 자신감을 가질 수 있습니다. **또한 여러분이 직원들의 실적을 기억하는 데도 도움이 될 겁니다.**

어휘 **performance review** 인사고과 **supervise** 관리하다 **directly** 직접 **as usual** 여느 때처럼 **summary** 요약 **accomplishment** 업적, 성취 **confidence** 자신, 확신 **contribution** 기여, 공헌

해설 **문맥에 맞는 문장 고르기:** 빈칸 앞에서 직원들이 자신의 실적을 요약해 보면 면담에 대비하고 자신이 회사에 기여한 바에 대해 자신감을 가질 수 있다고 했다. 따라서 빈칸에는 직원들이 자신의 실적을 요약하는 것에 대한 이점을 덧붙여 부연 설명하는 내용이 들어가야 글의 흐름이 자연스러워지므로 정답은 (C)이다.

번역 (A) 아시다시피, 이 영역은 간부 직원으로 제한되어 있습니다.
(B) 안타깝게도 신임 부장 채용이 예상보다 늦어지고 있습니다.
(C) 또한 여러분이 직원들의 실적을 기억하는 데도 도움이 될 겁니다.
(D) 신입직원들이 채용되었고 다음 주부터 업무를 시작합니다.

어휘 **restrict to** ~로 제한하다 **senior staff** 간부 직원 **additionally** 추가로 **achievement** 업적, 실적 **hire** 채용하다

2 기사

크림슨 베이 지역 극장은 에드나 라일리의 연극 〈몬테레이의 겨울〉 공연을 연장할 예정이다. 3월 2일 개막 공연 뒤 평론가들이 쓴 혹독한 평가를 고려할 때, 이러한 변화는 놀라운 것이다. **초기 박스 오피스 판매 역시 저조했다.** 하지만 이 연극은 온라인 정보원에서 소식을 접하는 젊은이들에게 갑자기 인기를 얻게 되었다. 이들은 연극이 경제 문제와 진로 선택을 탐색한다는 점에서 관심이 있는 것으로 보인다.

어휘 **regional** 지역의 **extend** 연장하다, 늘리다 **run** (연극·영화 등의) 연속 공연 **harsh** 가혹한, 냉혹한 **critic** 평론가, 비평가 **apparently** 보아[듣자]하니 **exploration** 탐사, 탐험

해설 **문맥에 맞는 문장 고르기:** 바로 앞 문장에서 개막 공연 뒤 평론가들에게 혹평(the harsh reviews written by critics)을 받았다고 했으며, 빈칸 뒤에서는 하지만 연극이 젊은이들에게 인기를 얻게 되었다(The show, however, has suddenly ~)고 했다. 따라서 빈칸에는 반전이 있기 전까지에 해당하는 부정적인 내용이 와야 한다. 따라서 초기 박스 오피스 판매가 저조했다는 내용의 (C)가 정답이다.

번역 (A) 연극 배우들은 지역 주민들이다.
(B) 초연에는 지역의 재계 지도자들이 참석했다.
(C) 초기 박스 오피스 판매 역시 저조했다.
(D) 게다가 그 극단은 몇 년째 활동하고 있다.

어휘 **local** 지역의 **resident** 주민, 거주민 **premiere** 시사회, 초연 **initial** 최초의, 초기의 **weak** 저조한, 약한 **moreover** 게다가

3 이메일

> 베로니카 제티시가 자신의 최근 영화에서 감독 겸 배우로 두 가지 역할을 한 것에 대한 기사를 써 주시기로 하셔서 감사드립니다. 이번 주말까지 제티시 씨와의 인터뷰를 어떻게 진행할지 설명하는 요약문을 제출하시기 바랍니다. 일단 저희 편집자들이 카렌 씨의 제안서를 승인하게 되면 꼭 저희 전속 사진작가 중 한 명과 인터뷰 날짜와 시간을 확인하시기 바랍니다. 기사에 영화 제작 시 제티시 씨가 맡은 두 가지 역할을 비교해서 담으면 아주 좋을 것 같습니다. **더 나아가 그녀가 각각의 측면에서 사용했던 별개의 기술을 언급해야 합니다.** 궁금한 점이 있으시면 제가 이번 주 내내 시간을 낼 수 있습니다.

어휘 **agree to** ~하기로 동의하다 **work on** ~에 대한 작업을 하다 **director** 감독 **submit** 제출하다 **overview** 개관, 개요 **editor** 편집자 **approve** 승인하다 **proposal** 제안 **staff photographer** 전속 사진작가 **ideal** 이상적인 **compare** 비교하다 **production** 제작 **available** 시간을 낼 수 있는 **throughout** ~ 내내

해설 **문맥에 맞는 문장 고르기:** 빈칸 앞에서 기사에 영화 제작 시 제티시 씨가 맡은 두 가지 역할을 비교해서 담으면 아주 좋을 것 같다(It would be ideal ~ the film)고 했다. 이어지는 문장에서 기사에 추가로 담을 내용을 언급하는 것이 자연스러우므로 정답은 (B)이다.

번역 (A) 예를 들어 그녀의 일정에 있는 다음 프로젝트에 대해 질문할 수도 있을 겁니다.
(B) 더 나아가 그녀가 각각의 측면에서 사용했던 별개의 기술을 언급해야 합니다.
(C) 간단히 말해서 당신의 작업은 2주 만에 완료되어야 합니다.
(D) 또한 기사는 4월호에 실릴 겁니다.

어휘 **distinct** 뚜렷한, 분명한 **aspect** 측면 **in short** 즉, 간단히 말해서 **issue** (잡지·신문의) 호

Questions 4-7 이메일

> 수신: 모든 이용자 〈patronlist@fflibrary.net〉
> 발신: 박다라 〈d.park@fflibrary.net〉
> 날짜: 9월 3일
> 제목: 변경 사항
>
> 이용자분들께,
>
> 풀튼 폴스 도서관 위원회를 대표하여, 저희 서비스의 몇 가지 변경 사항에 **⁴대해** 알려 드리고자 합니다. 한정된 예산과 직원 채용 문제로 인해 정규 **⁵프로그램** 일부를 없애기로 결정했습니다. 월간 커뮤니티 북클럽뿐 아니라 어린이를 위한 주간 스토리 타임도 **⁶계속 진행할 수** 없습니다. 1월에 새로운 예산안이 승인될 예정인데, 그때 자금이 증가하기를 바랍니다. **⁷한편 기존 서비스를 개선할 수 있는 방법을 알려 주시기 바랍니다.** 우리는 항상 새로운 아이디어를 듣는 것에 관심이 있습니다.
>
> 풀튼 폴스 도서관을 지원해 주시는 모든 이용자 여러분께 감사드립니다.
>
> 박다라 위원회장
>
> 풀튼 폴스 도서관

어휘 **patron** 이용자, 고객 **on behalf of** ~을 대표하여 **board** 위원회 **reach out** 연락을 취하다 **offering** 제공된 것 **budget** 예산 **limitation** 제한 **staffing** 직원 채용 **challenge** 도전 **regular** 정기적인 **community** 주민, 지역사회 **approve** 승인하다 **increase** 증가 **funding** 자금 **support** 지원

4

해설 **전치사 어휘:** 빈칸 뒤 명사구 some changes는 도서관 이용자들에게 이메일을 쓰고 있는 목적, 즉 이메일의 주제이므로 '몇 가지 변경 사항에 대해 알리고자'라는 의미로 연결되어야 자연스럽다. 따라서 '~에 대하여'라는 의미의 전치사 (D) regarding이 정답이다.

5

해설 **명사 어휘:** 뒤 문장에서 월간 커뮤니티 북클럽과 어린이를 위한 주간 스토리 타임을 진행할 수 없게 되었다며 도서관 프로그램에 대해 언급하고 있으므로, 빈칸이 있는 문장은 '정규 프로그램 일부를 없애기로 결정했다'는 내용이 되어야 한다. 따라서 (D) programs가 정답이다.

6

해설 **준동사_to부정사:** 빈칸 앞에 'are unable to(~할 수 없다)'가 있고, be (un)able 뒤에는 to부정사가 연결되어야 하므로 빈칸에는 동사원형이 들어가야 한다. 따라서 (C) continue hosting이 정답이다.

어휘 **continue** 계속하다 **host** 주최하다

7

해설 **문맥에 맞는 문장 고르기:** 빈칸 앞에서는 예산과 자금에 대해 언급했는데 빈칸 뒤에서는 새로운 아이디어를 듣고 싶다며 화제가 바뀌어 있다. 따라서 화제의 전환을 자연스럽게 연결하는 접속부사인 in the meantime(한편)과 함께, 뒤 문장의 새로운 아이디어와 연관성이 있는 '기존 서비스의 개선 방법'을 언급한 문장인 (C)가 정답이다.

번역 (A) 도서관은 정확히 26년 전에 대중에게 문을 열었습니다.
(B) 하지만, 변경된 일정은 예고 없이 변경될 수 있습니다.
(C) 한편 기존 서비스를 개선할 수 있는 방법을 알려 주시기 바랍니다.
(D) 지연에 대한 저희의 사과를 받아 주십시오.

어휘 revised 수정된 be subject to ~하기 쉽다 notice 공고 in the meantime 한편 improve 개선하다 existing 기존의 accept 받아 주다 apology 사과 delay 지연

Questions 8-11 회람

수신: 코발리스 모터스 영업 사원 전원
발신: 알리사 제이신스, 최고 제조 책임자
날짜: 4월 12일
Re: TM300의 새로운 색상

소비자의 요구에 ⁸**부응하여** 당사는 TM300 스포츠유틸리티 차량의 외관과 내부에 새로운 색상을 도입하고 있습니다.

지금까지 TM300은 검정색, 흰색, 은색, 빨간색으로만 출시됐습니다. 하지만 오늘부터 감청색과 청록색 버전도 생산에 들어갑니다. 3주 이내에 이 ⁹**추가** 색상으로 차량을 구입할 수 있습니다.

또한 다음 달부터 이 모델에 새로운 내부 색상도 도입할 예정입니다. ¹⁰**구체적으로 베이지색과 회색이 출시될 것입니다.** ¹¹**제공될** 외부와 내부의 색상 조합은 내부 웹사이트에서 확인하세요.

어휘 in response to ~에 부응하여 consumer 소비자 demand 요구 sport utility vehicle 스포츠유틸리티차량(SUV)

8

해설 **전치사 어휘:** 빈칸 앞에 온 in response가 문제 해결의 단서로, in response는 전치사 to와 함께 쓰여 '~에 대한 반응으로'라는 의미를 나타낸다. 따라서 (D) to가 정답이다.

9

해설 **형용사 어휘:** 빈칸 앞 문장에서 지금까지 TM300은 검정색, 흰색, 은색, 빨간색으로만 출시됐지만 오늘부터 감청색과 청록색 버전도 생산에 들어간다며, 구매 가능한 제품의 색상이 추가되었음을 언급하고 있다. 따라서 색상(colors)을 수식하는 형용사 어휘로는 문맥상 '추가의'라는 의미가

들어가야 하므로 (A) additional이 정답이다.

어휘 additional 추가의 combined 결합된 complimentary 무료의 adjustable 조절 가능한

10

해설 **문맥에 맞는 문장 고르기:** 빈칸 앞 문장에서 다음 달부터 해당 모델에 새로운 내부 색상을 도입할 예정이라고 했으므로, 새롭게 소개될 색상에 대한 내용이 뒤따르는 것이 자연스럽다. 따라서 (C)가 정답이다.

번역 (A) 실제로, TM300의 가격은 5퍼센트 인상됐습니다.
(B) 5월 1일 판매 콘테스트가 예정되어 있습니다.
(C) 구체적으로 베이지색과 회색이 출시될 것입니다.
(D) TM300 엔진은 내년에 개선되어야 합니다.

어휘 specifically 구체적으로

11

해설 **동사의 태 + 시제:** 빈칸은 선행사 exterior and interior colors를 수식하는 관계사절의 동사 자리이다. 빈칸 뒤에 목적어가 없으므로 수동태이어야 하고, 앞 문장의 내용에 따르면 다음 달부터 도입될 색상에 대해 이야기하고 있으므로 미래 시제인 (B) will be offered가 정답이다.

UNIT 08	어휘 활용하기

ETS 예제
본책 p. 264

열차 운행 변경 사항에 대해 말씀을 드리겠습니다. 이번 4월부터 노스-사우스 급행열차는 더 이상 그린 가 역에 정차하지 않습니다. 이것은 급행열차 운행에만 해당됩니다. 완행열차는 그린 가 역을 포함해 북남 노선의 모든 역에서 계속 운행됩니다.

어휘 starting ~부터 express train 급행열차 no longer 더 이상 ~가 아닌 stop 정차하다 affect 영향을 끼치다 local train 완행열차 service 운행 uninterrupted 중단되지 않는

번역 (A) 몬테고 메트로는 요금 인상을 발표할 예정입니다.
(B) 그린 가 역이 곧 폐쇄될 것입니다.
(C) 새로운 역 시설들이 이 노선에서 이용 가능합니다.
(D) 열차 운행 변경 사항에 대해 말씀을 드리겠습니다.

ETS CHECK-UP
본책 p. 265

1 (D)	2 (B)	3 (D)	4 (B)	5 (A)	6 (C)
7 (A)	8 (D)	9 (A)	10 (C)	11 (B)	

1 웹페이지

베스키나 호텔 예약 규정

당사 예약 및 취소 정책을 꼼꼼히 읽어 보십시오. 다음은 여러분이 우리 호텔에서 보낼 휴가 계획을 세우는 데 도움이 될 것입니다. 정가 예약은 이유에 상관없이 취소할 수 있습니다. **할인실은 예약 시 전액 결제가 필요하며 취소할 수 없습니다.** 표준 예약의 경우 최소 도착일 72시간 전에 취소 통보가 필요합니다. 이 경우 전액 환불해 드립니다.

어휘 reservation 예약 policy 정책, 규정 cancellation 취소 regularly priced 정가의 notice 통보 require 요구하다, 필요하다 prior to ~ 전에 full refund 전액 환불

해설 **문맥에 맞는 문장 고르기:** 빈칸 앞 문장에서는 정가 예약은 이유에 상관없이 취소할 수 있다고 했으며, 빈칸 뒤에서는 표준 예약의 경우에 최소 도착일 72시간 전에 취소 통보가 필요하다고 했다. 따라서 빈칸에는 예약 취소에 관한 내용이 들어가는 것이 가장 자연스러우므로, 할인실 예약 취소에 대해 설명한 (D)가 정답이다.

번역 (A) 특정 숙박 요청은 호텔의 수용 능력에 따라 이행될 것입니다.
(B) 베스키나 적립 포인트는 특별 절약 패키지에는 적용되지 않습니다.
(C) 모든 객실 요금은 2인 1실 기준이며, 성인 추가 시 요금이 부과됩니다.
(D) 할인실은 예약 시 전액 결제가 필요하며 취소할 수 없습니다.

어휘 specific 구체적인 accommodation 숙박, 수용 honor 이행하다 depending on ~에 따라 capacity 수용력 rate 요금, 비율 occupancy (건물 등의) 사용 incur (비용을) 발생시키다 payment 지불, 납부

2 이메일

회원 여러분께,

데브레이 시 역사박물관은 새로운 "디지털 탐험관"을 공개하게 되어 자랑스럽습니다. 이것은 지역사회에 무료 교육용 자원을 제공하기 위해 제작된 양방향 온라인 박물관입니다. 이 사이트에 접속하기 위해서는 간단히 웹사이트 www.d-museum.org에 접속하시고 "탐험관 입장하기"를 클릭하십시오. 온라인 박물관의 갤러리를 열람하시려면 메뉴로 가서 "소장품 둘러보기"를 클릭하십시오. **그러면 가상 박물관을 견학하실 수 있습니다.** 전시품 아래에 있는 카메라 아이콘을 클릭하면 특정 전시품을 클로즈업으로 보실 수도 있습니다.

어휘 unveil 공개하다 interactive 상호작용을 하는 resource 자원 particular 특정한 exhibit 전시품

해설 **문맥에 맞는 문장 고르기:** 빈칸 앞에 온라인 박물관의 갤러리를 열람하려면 메뉴로 가서 "소장품 둘러보기"를 클릭하라는 내용이 나오고, 빈칸 뒤에 클로즈업으로도 볼 수 있다는 내용이 나오므로, 빈칸에는 클릭 후에 어떤 것이 가능한지를 설명하는 내용이 와야 글의 흐름이 자연스러워진다. 따라서 (B)가 정답이다.

번역 (A) 회원들의 후원금으로 그 보수 공사의 자금을 댔습니다.
(B) 그러면 가상 박물관을 견학하실 수 있습니다.
(C) 모든 갤러리에서 사진 촬영은 금지되어 있습니다.
(D) 행사 입장권은 곧 매진될 것입니다.

어휘 fund 자금을 대다 virtual 가상의 photography 사진 촬영 allow 허용하다

3 기사

발머 산업의 신임 수장

스위스의 선도적인 제약 회사 중 하나인 발머 산업은 어제 리시아 챠오를 신임 CEO에 임명한다고 발표했다. 이번 발표는 현 발머의 책임자인 이돈 두리안이 연말에 은퇴할 것임을 공개적으로 밝힌 지 거의 2개월 만에 나온 것이다. **두리안은 7년간 회사를 이끌었다.** 챠오는 여러 소규모 제약 회사를 성공적으로 지휘한 것으로 업계에 잘 알려져 있다. 발머에서의 직책은 이런 규모의 국제적인 회사의 경영자로서 그녀가 맡게 될 첫 번째 자리일 것이다. 현재 바젤에서 거주 중인 챠오는 11월 28일에 취리히에서 근무를 시작하게 된다.

어휘 head 책임자, 지도자; ~을 이끌다 pharmaceutical 제약의 appointment 임명 make public that ~을 공개적으로 밝히다 well-known 잘 알려진, 유명한 be at the helm of ~의 우두머리이다 reside 거주하다

해설 **문맥에 맞는 문장 고르기:** 빈칸 앞 문장에서 현 발머의 책임자인 이돈 두리안이 연말에 은퇴할 것(he will ~ the year)이라고 했다. 그리고 뒤 문장에서는 새롭게 임명된 챠오의 경력을 소개하고 있다. 따라서 빈칸에는 두리안의 회사 경력을 먼저 언급하고 챠오에 대한 소개로 이어지는 것이 흐름상 자연스러우므로 (D)가 정답이다.

번역 (A) 회사는 현재 그 자리에 대한 면접을 진행 중이다.
(B) 신임 CEO는 11월에 발표될 것이다.
(C) 발머는 이제 본사를 바젤로 옮길 계획이다.
(D) 두리안은 7년간 회사를 이끌었다.

어휘 currently 현재 headquarters 본사

Questions 4-7 편지

9월 5일

레이첼 허친슨
우즈 서클 8451번지
스프링필드, 인디애나 주 62704

허친슨 씨께,

최근에 구매하신 제품에 대해 알려 주셔서 감사합니다. 주문하신 텔레비전이 완벽한 상태로 도착하지 못해 죄송합니다. 고객님의 **4기대에** 부응하기 위해, 판매사원을 파견하여 추가 비용 없이 불량품을 수거하고 교환 제품을 보내 드리겠습니다. **5정확히 똑같은 모델을 받게 되실 것입니다.** 217-555-0121로 사무실로 전화하셔서 배송 시간을 **6정해 주십시오**.

저희는 모든 고객분들의 만족을 위해 노력하고 있으며, 이 **7해결책이** 만족스러우시기를 바랍니다.

감사합니다

잭슨 앨러티
고객 서비스
패런든 일렉트로닉스

어휘 **inform** 알리다 **purchase** 구입하다 **order** 주문하다 **condition** 상태 **sales representative** 판매사원 **defective** 결함이 있는 **replacement** 교체(물) **additional** 추가의 **strive** 분투하다 **satisfactory** 만족스러운

4

해설 **소유격 + 명사:** 소유격 다음에는 소유격의 수식을 받는 명사가 반드시 필요하므로 명사 (B) expectations가 정답이다.

어휘 **expectation** 기대

5

해설 **문맥에 맞는 문장 고르기:** 빈칸 앞 문장에서 불량품을 수거해 가고 교환 제품을 보내 주겠다고 했으므로, 교환 제품에 대한 내용이 뒤따르는 것이 자연스럽다. 따라서 정확히 똑같은 모델을 받게 될 것이라며 교환 제품에 대해 설명한 (A)가 정답이다.

번역 **(A) 정확히 똑같은 모델을 받게 되실 것입니다.**
(B) 잘못된 인증번호입니다.
(C) 당사의 모든 텔레비전은 에너지 효율 인증을 받았습니다.
(D) 해당 제품은 더 이상 보증이 적용되지 않습니다.

어휘 **exact** 정확한 **serial number** 일련번호 **invalid** 인식 불가능한 **certify** 증명하다 **efficient** 효율적인 **cover** (보험 등으로) 보장하다 **warranty** 보증

6

해설 **동사 어휘:** 앞에서 판매사원을 파견해 불량품을 수거하고 교환 제품을 보내 주겠다는 내용이 나왔으므로, '사무실로 전화해 배송 시간을 정해 달라'는 의미가 되어야 자연스럽다. 따라서 '(미리) 정하다'라는 뜻의 동사 (C) arrange가 정답이다.

7

해설 **명사 어휘:** 글의 앞 내용을 보면 텔레비전이 완벽한 상태로 도착하지 못해 죄송하다고 사죄하며, 판매사원을 파견해 추가 비용 없이 불량품을 수거하고 교환 제품을 보내겠다고 고객이 겪고 있는 문제에 대한 해결책을 제시하고 있다. 따라서 문맥상 '이 해결책이 만족스럽기를 바란다'는 내용이 되어야 자연스러우므로 '해결책'을 뜻하는 명사 (A) resolution이 정답이다.

Questions 8-11 이메일

수신: carmen.speranza@wyomines.edu
발신: mstiveson@blaufeld.com
날짜: 11월 20일
제목: 방문 가능성

스페란자 씨께,

지난주 **8광업총회에서** 큰 가르침을 준 귀하의 발표가 끝난 후 만나 뵙게 되어 기뻤습니다. 귀하의 연구는 무척 **9흥미진진했습니다**. 제가 그때 언급했듯이, 블로펠드 미네럴스를 방문해 이곳 간부 직원을 상대로 발표해 주셨으면 합니다.

물론 휴일과 휴가 기간이 다가오고 있습니다. 따라서 올해 남은 기간에 방문 일정을 맞추기는 **10어려울** 것 같습니다. 곧 논의해서 1월 1일 이후에 적당한 날짜를 잡으면 어떨까 합니다. **11다음 주에 전화로 의논할 수 있을지 알려 주십시오.**

맥스웰 스티브슨
블로펠드 미네럴스 회장

어휘 **enlightening** 깨우침을 주는 **presentation** 발표 **mining** 광산, 광업 **conference** 총회, 회의 **research** 연구 **fascinating** 환상적인, 흥미진진한 **mention** 언급하다 **present** (연구 내용 등을) 진술하다, 발표하다 **senior staff** 간부 직원 **fit in** 맞추다, 정하다 **remainder** 나머지 **settle on** ~에 대해 결정하다 **suitable** 적당한, 알맞은

8

해설 **전치사 어휘:** 빈칸에 적절한 전치사를 선택하는 문제이다. 빈칸 뒤에 온 the mining conference가 문제 해결의 단서로, 문맥상 '지난주 광업총회에서 큰 가르침을 준 귀하의 발표'라는 의미가 되어야 한다. 따라서 장소 앞에 쓰여 '~에서'라는 의미를 나타내는 (D) at이 정답이다.

9

해설 **과거 시제:** 바로 앞 문장의 last week이 문제 해결의 단서로, 지난주 발표를 통해 스페렌자 씨의 연구가 흥미롭다고 생각하게 되었으므로 과거 시제가 쓰여야 한다. 따라서 정답은 (A) found이다.

10

해설 **형용사 어휘:** 빈칸 앞 문장에서는 휴일과 휴가 기간이 다가오고 있다고 했고, 빈칸 뒤에 온 문장에서는 논의해서 1월 1일 이후에 적당한 날짜를 잡자고 했다. 따라서 글의 흐름상 '올해 남은 기간에 방문 일정을 맞추기는 어려울 것 같다'고 하는 것이 자연스러우므로, 정답은 (C) difficult이다.

어휘 insignificant 중요하지 않은, 사소한 attractive 매력적인 acceptable 받아들일 만한, 만족스러운

11

해설 **문맥에 맞는 문장 고르기:** 빈칸 앞에서 함께 논의하여 1월 1일 이후에 적당한 날짜를 잡자고 했다. 따라서 빈칸에는 일정 논의에 대해 언급하는 것이 자연스러우므로 정답은 (B)이다.

번역 (A) 저는 가족들과 함께 휴일을 아주 즐겁게 보내고 있습니다.

(B) 다음 주에 전화로 의논할 수 있을지 알려 주십시오.

(C) 회신이 너무 늦어서 다시 한 번 사과 드립니다.

(D) 요청하신 자료를 드리게 되어 기쁩니다.

어휘 apologize for ~에 대해 사과하다 include 포함하다 request 요청하다; 요청

ETS TEST 본책 p. 268

1 (D)	**2** (A)	**3** (C)	**4** (B)	**5** (D)	**6** (D)
7 (A)	**8** (A)	**9** (D)	**10** (A)	**11** (B)	**12** (D)
13 (B)	**14** (C)	**15** (A)	**16** (A)		

Questions 1-4 공지

> **4월 14일**
>
> 진행 중인 공사 때문에 건물 뒷문을 이용해 주세요. 도착하면 문 옆에 있는 벨을 누르세요. **¹누군가** 최대한 빨리 나와서 들여보내 줄 겁니다. 이는 안전을 보장하기 위해 **²시행되는** 임시 조치임을 이해해 주세요. 6월 1일부터 **³입구가** 정상 가동하리라 예상합니다. **⁴불편을 끼쳐 드려 죄송합니다.**
>
> 벌산사

어휘 ongoing 진행 중인 construction 공사 temporary 임시의 measure 조치 functional 가동하는

1

해설 **부정대명사:** 앞에서 you를 제외하고는 달리 언급된 사람이 없으며, 문맥상 '누군가 최대한 빨리 나와서 당신을 들여 보내 줄 것'이라는 내용이 되어야 하므로 정답은 (D) Someone이다.

2

해설 **준동사_분사:** '주어(this) + 동사(is) + 보어(a temporary measure)'로 이루어진 완전한 절 뒤에 빈칸이 있으므로, 빈칸에는 명사 measure를 뒤에서 수식하는 수식어가 들어가면 된다. 빈칸 뒤에 목적어가 없고 '안전을 보장하기 위해 시행되는 임시 조치'라는 의미가 되어야 자연스러우므로, 명사를 수식할 수 있는 분사이면서 수동의 의미를 지닌 (A) implemented가 정답이다.

어휘 implement 시행하다

3

해설 **명사 어휘:** 빈칸이 있는 문장만으로는 정답을 고르기 어려우며, 앞의 내용을 확인해야 하는 문제이다. 글의 첫 문장에서 진행 중인 공사 때문에 건물 뒷문을 이용해 달라고 했으므로 현재 출입구를 이용할 수 없음을 알 수 있으며, '6월 1일부터 입구가 정상 가동하리라 예상한다'는 내용이 되어야 자연스러우므로 '출입구'라는 의미의 (C) entrance가 정답이다.

4

해설 **문맥에 맞는 문장 고르기:** 공사 때문에 출입구를 사용할 수 없으니 그에 따른 임시 방편으로 뒷문을 이용해 달라고 요청하는 글의 전체적인 내용상, 그에 따른 불편함에 대해 사과하는 내용으로 마무리되는 것이 자연스럽다. 따라서 (B)가 정답이다.

번역 (A) 답변 감사합니다.

(B) 불편을 끼쳐 드려 죄송합니다.

(C) 다음 주 오후 3시 이후 방문객들이 오리라 예상됩니다.

(D) 지금이 일년 중 우리가 가장 좋아하는 시기입니다.

어휘 inconvenience 불편

Questions 5-8 이메일

> 수신: p.cooper@slixmail.net
> 발신: orders@desertwillowteas.com
> 날짜: 5월 24일
> 제목: 감사합니다
>
> 쿠퍼 씨께,
>
> 최근에 저의 특제 혼합 홍차를 구매해 주셔서 감사합니다. 고객님께서 그 차를 즐기고 계시길 바랍니다! 만약 그러시다면, 제 웹사이트에 긍정적인 후기를 써 주실 것을 **⁵부탁드리고 싶습니다.** **⁶하지만** 만약 그 차가 고객님의 기대에 미치지 못한다면, 그것을 개선하기 위해 제가 할 수 있는 일을 알려 주시기 바랍니다. 고객님이 주시는 어떤 **⁷의견도** 환영합니다.
>
> **⁸제 웹사이트를 보면 아시겠지만, 저는 기업 판매자가 아닙니다.** 이 일은 제가 열정을 가지고 시간을 쪼개서 즐기는 취미입니다. 저는 고객님처럼 입소문을 내 주시고 약초와 과일 맞춤 혼합차를 꾸준히 개선하도록 도와주시는 고객님들을 믿고 있습니다.

다시 한 번 거래해 주셔서 감사합니다.

나오미 텔크스
데저트 윌로우 티즈

어휘 specialty 특수성, 특제품 blend 혼합 positive 긍정적인 review 평가, 후기 meet expectation 기대에 부응하다 improve 개선하다 be willing to 기꺼이 ~하다 passionate 열정적인 rely on ~에 의존하다 spread 퍼뜨리다 continually 지속적으로 custom 맞춤의

5

해설 **준동사 _to부정사:** 빈칸 앞의 would가 문제 해결의 단서로, 문맥상 '그 차를 즐기고 있다면 웹사이트에 긍정적인 후기를 줄 것을 부탁한다'는 의미가 되어야 한다. 따라서 조동사 would와 함께 쓰여 '~하고 싶다, ~하는 것을 바라다'라는 의미를 나타내는 'would like to부정사' 형태가 되어야 하므로, 정답은 (D) like to ask이다.

6

해설 **접속부사:** 빈칸 앞에는 '차를 즐기고 있다면 긍정적인 후기를 적어 달라'는 내용이, 빈칸 뒤에는 '차가 기대에 미치지 못한다면, 개선하기 위해 할 수 있는 일을 알려 달라'는 내용이 왔다. 따라서 '그러나, 하지만'의 의미로 반대나 대조의 의미를 지닌 두 문장을 연결하는 접속부사 (D) however가 정답이다.

어휘 in other words 달리 말하면, 즉 therefore 그러므로

7

해설 **명사 어휘:** 앞 문장의 please let me know what I can do to improve them이 문제 해결의 단서로, '개선을 위해 자신이 할 수 있는 것이 무엇인지에 대한 의견을 알려 달라'고 했다. 따라서 '의견, 피드백'이라는 뜻의 (A) feedback이 정답이다.

어휘 feedback 의견, 피드백 evidence 증거 ingredient 재료, 성분 donation 기부(금)

8

해설 **문맥에 맞는 문장 고르기:** 빈칸 뒤에 온 문장의 a part-time hobby가 문제 해결의 단서로, '이 일은 내가 열정을 가지고 시간을 쪼개서 즐기는 취미이다'라고 했다. 따라서 빈칸에는 전문 판매자가 아니라는 내용이 와야 글의 흐름이 자연스러우므로, (A)가 정답이다.

번역 **(A) 제 웹사이트를 보면 아시겠지만, 저는 기업 판매자가 아닙니다.**
(B) 저는 아주 다양한 차를 비축해 두고 있어서 대량 주문을 받을 수 있습니다.
(C) 고객님의 주문품 배송에 착오가 있었다면 사과드립니다.
(D) 저의 제품은 온라인뿐만 아니라 대형 소매점에서도 찾을 수 있습니다.

어휘 tell 알아보다, 확인하다 corporate 기업 seller 판매자 a wide variety of 아주 다양한 in stock 재고가 있는 accommodate 수용하다, 맞추다 bulk 대량의 apologize 사과하다 retail 소매의; 소매

Questions 9-12 이메일

수신: kayla_jenson@gorbencorp.com
발신: meredith.lehman@trackerxpress.com
날짜: 10월 7일
제목: 트랙커 엑스프레스
첨부: 소책자

젠슨 씨께,

트랙커 엑스프레스에 관해 문의해 주셔서 감사합니다. 당사의 강력한 소프트웨어는 기업들이 채용 절차를 간소화하여 시간과 돈을 9 **절약하도록** 도움을 줍니다.

첨부된 사례 연구를 10**검토해** 주십시오. 사례 연구에는 트랙커 엑스프레스의 도움을 받은 유명한 회사 세 곳이 소개되어 있습니다. 보시다시피, 키워드를 토대로 이력서를 검색하는 기능이 그 회사들에게 특히 유용했습니다. 11**예를 들어,** 당사 소프트웨어는 특정 도시에 살거나 특정 회사에서 일해 본 적이 있는 모든 지원자들을 쉽게 찾을 수 있도록 해 줍니다. 게다가 모든 분류가 디지털 방식으로 이루어지므로 종이가 어수선하게 널려 있는 일도 없습니다. 12**모든 이력서가 전산화된 데이터베이스에 깔끔하게 정리됩니다.**

이 문제에 대해 언제 더 논의할 수 있는지 알려 주십시오.

메러디스 리먼
트랙커 엑스프레스 마케팅 담당자

어휘 inquiry 문의 streamline 합리화[간소화]하다 recruitment process 채용 절차 attached 첨부된, 딸린 case study 사례 연구 well-known 유명한 benefit from ~에서 이득을 보다 ability 능력, 기능 browse 검색하다 particularly 특히 candidate 후보자, 지원자 specific 구체적인, 특정한 additionally 게다가 sorting 분류 digitally 디지털 방식으로 clutter 어질러진 물건; 어지르다

9

해설 **준동사 _분사:** 빈칸 앞에 완전한 절이 왔고, 접속사와 주어가 생략된 채 빈칸 뒤에 명사구(time and money)가 왔으므로, 빈칸이 포함된 부분은 분사구문이 되어야 한다. 빈칸 뒤에 동사 save의 목적어인 time and money가 왔으므로, 능동의 의미를 지닌 현재분사 (D) saving이 정답이 된다.

10

해설 **동사 어휘:** 빈칸은 명령문의 동사 자리로, 뒤에 온 목적어 the attached case studies와 함께 어울려 쓸 수 있는 동사가 들어가야 한다. 이어지는 문장에서 사례 연구에 대해 설명하고 있으므로, 빈칸이 있는 문장은 '첨부된 사례 연구를 검토해 주세요'라는 의미가 되어야 한다. 따라서 '검토하다'라는 의미의 (A) review가 정답이다.

어휘 prepare 준비하다 discuss 논의하다 disregard 무시하다

11

해설 **접속부사:** 빈칸 앞에는 '검색 기능이 여러 회사에 유용했다'는 내용이 왔으며, 빈칸 뒤에는 '소프트웨어가 유용한 구체적인 실례'를 제시하고 있다. 따라서 '예를 들어'라는 의미의 접속부사인 (B) For example이 정답이다.

어휘 afterward 그 후 as long as ~하는 한 in keeping with ~와 조화하여

12

해설 **문맥에 맞는 문장 고르기:** 빈칸 바로 앞 문장에서 '모든 분류가 디지털 방식으로 이루어지므로 종이가 어수선하게 널려 있는 일도 없다'고 했으므로, 빈칸에는 전산화된 데이터베이스의 장점에 대한 내용이 이어져야 글의 흐름이 자연스러워진다. 따라서 정답은 (D)이다.

번역 (A) 지원자들은 이력서를 온라인 또는 직접 제출할 수 있습니다.
(B) 다음 소프트웨어 업데이트로 이 문제가 해결될 것입니다.
(C) 자리에 맞는 적임자를 구하기가 어려울 수 있습니다.
(D) 모든 이력서가 전산화된 데이터베이스에 깔끔하게 정리됩니다.

어휘 applicant 지원자, 신청자 submit 제출하다 in person 직접 address 처리하다 issue 문제, 쟁점 qualified 자격이 있는, 적임의 position 직위, 자리 neatly 깔끔하게 organize 정리하다, 조직하다

Questions 13-16 기사

나자스 아이스크림 웨스트 사이드에 오다

프라비던스 – 나자스 아이스크림이 웨스트 사이드까지 ¹³확장할 것이다. 이번 주 초 대표인 나자 코월스키는 7월 1일 세 번째 지점을 ¹⁴유서 깊은 로즈 빌딩에 문을 연다고 발표했다. "고객들이 웨스트 사이드 매장을 열어 달라고 요청했지만, 처음에는 적당한 건물을 찾을 수 없었습니다." 코월스키 씨가 말했다. ¹⁵딱 맞는 장소를 물색하는 힘든 작업이 끝났다. 작지만 100년이 된 로즈 빌딩은 따뜻한 날씨에 열 수 있는 큰 창문이 특징이며 여름에는 추가로 고객용 좌석을 놓는 데 쓸 수 있는 야외 공간이 있다. 회사는 또한 내년부터 식료품점에서 아이스크림 제품을 판매할 계획이다. "이 모든 ¹⁶성장에 아주 벅찬 마음입니다." 코월스키 씨가 말했다.

어휘 location 장소, 위치 feature 특징을 이루다; 특징, 기능 additional 추가의, 추가적인 grocery store 식료품점

13

해설 **동사의 시제_현재진행:** 빈칸은 동사 자리인데 빈칸 다음 문장에서 미래 시제(will open July 1)가 등장하므로, 정해진 미래를 나타낼 수 있는 현재진행 시제가 정답이다. 따라서 정답은 (B) is expanding이다.

어휘 expand 확대하다, 확장하다

14

해설 **형용사 어휘:** 중반부의 the 100-year-old Rhodes Building이 문제 해결의 단서이다. 보기 중 '100년 된' 건물과 가장 자연스럽게 어울릴 수 있는 형용사는 '유서 깊은, 역사적인'이라는 뜻의 historic이므로 정답은 (C) historic이다.

어휘 temporary 일시적인 deteriorated 악화된

15

해설 **문맥에 맞는 문장 고르기:** 빈칸 앞에는 처음에는 적당한 건물을 찾을 수 없었다(we couldn't find the right building at first)는 내용이 왔으며, 빈칸 뒤에는 로즈 빌딩의 장점에 대해 언급하고 있다. 따라서 빈칸에는 딱 맞는 장소를 찾았다는 내용이 들어가야 글의 흐름이 자연스러워진다. 따라서 정답은 (A)이다.

번역 **(A) 딱 맞는 장소를 물색하는 힘든 작업이 끝났다.**
(B) 그들은 지금 새로운 맛을 개발하고 있다.
(C) 도시의 동쪽 지역은 경쟁이 치열하다.
(D) 다행히 여름에는 대체로 경기가 호전된다.

어휘 challenging 어려운, 힘든 search 찾기, 수색 perfect 완벽한 flavor 맛 competition 경쟁 fortunately 다행히, 운 좋게도 improve 개선되다, 향상되다

16

해설 **명사 어휘:** 공지문 첫 문장에서 나자스 아이스크림이 웨스트 사이드까지 확장하고 있다고 했으며, 빈칸이 있는 문장 바로 앞에서 회사는 또한 내년부터 식료품점에서 아이스크림 제품을 판매할 계획이라고 했다. 따라서 이러한 내용을 대변할 수 있는 '성장'이라는 뜻의 (A) growth가 정답이다.

어휘 relief 안도, 안심 talent 재능 value 가치

PART 7

CHAPTER 01 | 질문 유형별 공략

UNIT 01	주제 / 목적 문제

ETS 예제
본책 p. 274

수신: 후아나 레자 〈juana.reza@delboroughschools.org〉
발신: 알레어 콜링스 〈acollings@mansfordsports.com〉
제목: 기부
날짜: 4월 7일

레자 씨께,

멜버러 학구를 대표하여 저희에게 연락해 주셔서 감사합니다. 아시다시피, 맨스포드 스포츠는 우리 지역에서 열리는 많은 스포츠 관련 활동의 자랑스러운 후원자입니다. **우리는 귀하께서 요청하신 대로 무료 농구공 25개를 학구에 제공하게 되어 기쁩니다.** 당신은 4월 14일 목요일 오후 2시에 카운티 라인 로에 있는 우리 본점에서 농구공을 가져가실 수 있습니다. (중략)

알레어 콜링스, 마케팅 담당 이사
맨스포드 스포츠

어휘 on behalf of ~을 대신[대표]하여 district 지역, 구역 proud 자랑스러운 township 지역

Q. 이메일의 목적은?
(A) 피드백을 요청하는 것
(B) 요청에 응답하는 것
(C) 실수에 대해 사과하는 것
(D) 신제품을 홍보하는 것

주제/목적	기출 유형 연습하기		본책 p. 275
1 (B)	2 (B)	3 (B)	4 (B)	5 (A)

크롤린의 구 시가지에는 기념품 가게가 많고 어렵지 않게 찾을 수 있다. 안타깝게도, 기념품 가게들은 종종 값을 비싸게 매기기도 한다. 관광객들은 **도시 중심부의 길가에 늘어선 가판대에서 물건을 파는 개인 노점상인들에게** 멜레도니아의 전통 수공예품을 **구입하는 것이 더 낫다.**

어휘 souvenir 기념품 plentiful 풍부한 locate 위치를 찾다 overpriced 비싸게 매겨진 traditional

전통적인 handcraft 수공예(품) individual 개인의, 각각의 vendor 판매자, 노점상 stall 가판대 line ~을 따라 늘어서다

1 발췌문은 주로 무엇에 대해 다루는가?
(A) 가격을 흥정하는 방법
(B) 구매할 장소

국제 건축 보존 협회를 대표하여, 8월 31일부터 9월 3일까지 부다페스트에서 열리는 저희 회의에서 **개막식 기조 연설을 부탁하고자 합니다.** 연설은 회의가 열리는 다뉴브 호텔에서 8월 31일 오후 2시에 거행됩니다.

어휘 on behalf of ~을 대신[대표]하여 architectural 건축의 preservation 보존 society 협회 keynote address 기조 연설

2 편지는 왜 쓰여졌는가?
(A) 건축 계획을 요청하려고
(B) 누군가에게 연설을 부탁하려고

플레즌트 산 고속도로에 대한 운전자 경고: **4월 12일 월요일부터 시작해서 다음 15개월 동안 계속해서 플레즌트 산 고속도로에 보수 공사가 진행될 것입니다.** 이 40년 된 도로는 수년간 수리가 절실히 필요한 상태였습니다. 특히, 프런트 가 주변 교차로가 주로 보수되며, 프런트 가 출구는 나들목이 교체되는 약 3주 동안 폐쇄될 것입니다.

어휘 motorist 운전자 undergo 겪다 in need of ~을 필요로 하다 in particular 특히 exit 출구 exit ramp 나들목(국도에서 고속도로로 연결되는 진출입로)

3 공지의 목적은?
(A) 새 도로 개통 보도
(B) 프로젝트 시작 발표

저희 〈헬씨 리빙〉 소식지의 **1호 구독을 환영합니다.** 여러분이 보시기에 주제들이 재미있고 유익했으면 합니다. 소식지는 두 달에 한 번 발행되며 특별한 관심사를 다룬 기사, 최신 의료 서비스 관련 최근 정보, 그리고 **이곳 타나카 병원에서 근무하는 훌륭한 전문 의료진에 관한 소개가 실리겠습니다.**

어휘 edition (잡지의) 호 entertaining 재미있는 beneficial 유익한 outstanding 뛰어난 professional 전문가; 전문적인

4 이메일은 왜 보내졌는가?
(A) 새 출판물을 위한 기사를 요청하려고
(B) 병원에 의해 제공되는 새로운 서비스를 소개하려고

적색 노선의 철도 보수 작업이 3월 11일에 시작될 것입니다. 닐센과 보에렌 사이(페사크와 크로익스 포함)의 철도 구간은 **3월 12일부터 3월 25일까지 운행하지 않을 것입니다.** 동부행 열차들은 닐센에서 **운행을 중지할 것이며** 승객들은 노선의 남은 세 역들 중 한 곳에 가기 위해 무료 셔틀을 이용하실 수 있습니다. 보에렌, 크로익스, 또는 페사크에서 서쪽으로 이동하고자 하는 승객들도 닐센 역까지 무료 버스를 탈 수 있습니다.

어휘 **rail** 철도 **renovation** 보수 **section** 구간 **eastbound** 동부행의 **remaining** 남아 있는

5 안내되고 있는 것은?

(A) 철도 서비스의 제약

(B) 새 철도 역들을 위한 계획

ETS PRACTICE
본책 p. 276

1 (B)   **2** (D)

기사

이번 주 펠허스트

(5월 28일) – 린필드 유틸리티즈는 월요일부터 펠허스트 시내와 인근의 약 5킬로미터에 이르는 지하 가스관을 보수할 예정이다. 낡은 주철 파이프는 내구성 있는 플라스틱 또는 표면 처리된 강관으로 교체된다. "이 지하 파이프는 앞으로 오랫동안 안전하고 안정적인 가스 시스템을 보장해 줄 것입니다." 린필드 유틸리티즈 영업 이사 임재민이 말했다.

6주간의 프로젝트 기간에 린필드 유틸리티즈는 시 교통 담당 공무원 및 공공 사업부와 긴밀하게 협력해 공사를 조정할 계획이다. 펠허스트 경찰이 교통 통제를 지원하지만, 지역 주민들은 바쁜 출퇴근 시간 교통 체증에 대비해야 한다.

린필드 유틸리티즈 작업반은 오렌지색 원뿔대, 도로 표지판, 바리케이드를 사용해 표준 안전 조치를 취할 예정이다. 펠허스트 운전자들은 주행 속도를 줄이고 공사 현장 주변의 우회로 표지판에 유의해야 한다.

어휘 **utility** (수도·전기·가스 등) 공익 서비스 **underground** 지하의 **cast iron** 주철, 무쇠 **replace** 교체하다 **durable** 내구성이 좋은 **reliable** 신뢰할 수 있는 **transit** 수송, 교통 **official** 간부, 공무원; 공식적인 **signage** 신호 (체계)

1 무엇에 관한 기사인가?

(A) 거리 미화 프로젝트

(B) 지하 파이프 교체

(C) 교통량 감소 계획

(D) 지역 기업의 채용 필요성

해설 **주제/목적:** 첫 단락에서 펠허스트 시내와 인근의 약 5킬로미터에 이르는 지하 가스관을 보수할 예정(Linfield Utilities will be repairing ~ starting on Monday)이라고 하며 낡은 파이프가 내구성 있는 파이프로 교체될 것(will be replaced)이라고 했으므로, 지하 파이프 교체에 관한 기사문임을 알 수 있다. 따라서 정답은 (B)이다.

어휘 **beautification** 미화 **replacement** 교체 **reduction** 감소 **initiative** 계획

이메일

발신: 프리티 파텔 〈ppatel@desantech.com〉

수신: 전 직원

날짜: 10월 9일

제목: 도색

내일 10월 10일 화요일에 로비에 도색 작업이 있다는 것을 모든 분께 상기시키고자 이메일을 씁니다. 작업은 오전 8시에 시작해서 오후 4시에 끝내는 것으로 예정되어 있습니다. 모든 직원은 페인트공들이 작업하는 동안에는 로비에 출입하지 마십시오. (주차장에서) 후문을 통해 건물에 출입하시고 출입구 오른쪽에 있는 계단을 사용하시기 바랍니다.

여러분의 협조에 감사드립니다. 문의 사항이 있으면 내선 431번으로 연락하십시오.

프리티 파텔

시설과 부장

어휘 **avoid** 피하다 **rear door** 후문 **staircase** 계단 **cooperation** 협력, 협조 **extension** 내선(번호)

2 이메일의 목적은?

(A) 새로운 작업 일정 배포

(B) 컴퓨터 프로그램 설명

(C) 업무 제안서 발송

(D) 중요 정보 반복

해설 **주제/목적:** 지문의 remind everyone that the lobby will be painted tomorrow에서 내일 있을 도색 작업에 대한 정보를 다시 제공하는 것이 목적임을 알 수 있으므로 정답은 (D)이다.

어휘 **distribute** 배포하다

패러프레이징

지문의 remind ➡ 보기의 repeat

ETS TEST
본책 p. 277

1 (C)	**2** (D)	**3** (A)	**4** (D)	**5** (C)
6 (D)	**7** (B)	**8** (D)		

Question 1-2 직원 공지

니시오 전자

연수

- [1]연수는 정시에 시작되고 끝난다.
- [1]연수 전 기간에 걸쳐 회사 유니폼을 입어야 한다.
- [1]연수자는 연수 초반에 정해진 안전 예방책을 모두 준수해야 한다. 연수 진행자는 교육이 시작되기 전에 연수자와 예방책을 검토해야 한다.
- [1]음식 반입은 휴게실로 제한된다. 연구소, 생산 구역, 기타 연수 장소에는 어떤 음식도 허용되지 않는다.
- 연수 참가자는 교육실을 청결하게 유지해야 한다. 진행자는 각 세션이 끝날 때 모든 장비와 작업대가 청소될 수 있도록 해야 한다.
- [2]휴대폰 사용은 업무 관련 전화로 제한된다. 사적인 전화는 허용되지 않는다. 교육 중에 휴대폰은 진동 모드로 설정해야 한다.

어휘 observe 준수하다 precaution 예방 조치 established 정해진, 수립된 restrict 제한하다 permit 허용하다 laboratory 연구소 participant 참가자 tidy 청결한 ensure 확실하게 하다 work surface 작업대

1 일람의 목적은?

(A) 연수 강좌의 학습 목표 기술하기
(B) 연수생에게 연구소 절차에 대해 통보하기
(C) 연수 활동과 관련된 규칙 전달하기
(D) 교육 장비 작동법 설명하기

해설 **주제/목적:** '연수(Training Sessions)'라는 제목 아래 연수 시간, 복장 규정, 안전 예방 조치 준수 의무, 음식물 반입 제한 등 연수 기간 동안 지켜야 할 규칙에 대해 열거하고 있으므로 (C)가 정답이다.

어휘 describe 기술하다 notify 알리다 procedure 절차 communicate 전달하다

2 휴대폰 통화에 관해 명시된 것은?

(A) 연수 중 전화는 실외에서 받아야 한다.
(B) 참가자가 전화를 받는 동안은 연수가 중단되어야 한다.
(C) 연수실에 들어가는 즉시 휴대폰을 꺼야 한다.
(D) 연수 중에는 근무 상황과 관련된 전화만 받을 수 있다.

해설 **Not/True:** 공지문의 마지막 목록에서 휴대폰 사용은 업무 관련 전화로 제한되며(Cell phone use is restricted to business-related calls) 사적인 전화는 허용되지 않는다(Taking personal calls is not permitted)고 했으므로 정답은 (D)이다.

패러프레이징
지문의 Cell phone use is restricted to business-related calls ➡ 보기의 Only calls related to work situations can be taken

---

Questions 3-5 편지

기용 보험
스쿨하우스 22번길
워링턴, 펜실베이니아 주

7월 3일

잭 리 씨
오크힐스 가 541번지
샬폰트, 펜실베이니아 주 18914

리 씨께,

기용 보험의 월간 청구서가 이제 온라인으로 이용 가능합니다. [3]8월 3일까지 7월 자동차 보험료 97달러를 납입해 주세요.

잔금을 이미 지불하신 경우에는 더 이상의 조치가 필요하지 않습니다.

[4]고객님 명세서의 인쇄용 사본을 확인하시거나, 종이 사본을 요청하시거나, 계정 결제 설정을 관리하시거나 자동 결제 시스템에 등록하시려면, [5]www.guilloninsurance.com/mypolicy를 방문하세요. 고객님의 계정으로 로그인하라는 메시지가 뜰 것입니다. 아직 작성하시지 않았다면, 사용자 프로필을 작성하셔야 할 수도 있습니다.

기용 보험을 선택해 주셔서 감사합니다.

데니스 호지스
기용 보험 청구 보조

어휘 insurance 보험 bill 청구서 available 이용할 수 있는 submit 제출하다 balance 잔금 further 더 이상의 printable 인쇄 가능한 statement 명세서 manage 관리하다 account 계정 enroll in ~에 등록하다 prompt 촉구하다

3 호지스 씨가 리 씨에게 연락한 이유는?

(A) 지불을 상기시키기 위해
(B) 청구 오류에 대해 알리기 위해
(C) 보험료 할인을 제안하기 위해
(D) 빠진 계정 정보를 요청하기 위해

해설 **주제/목적:** 첫 단락 두 번째 문장에서 8월 3일까지 7월 자동차 보험료 97달러를 납입하라(Please submit your July car insurance payment of $97 by August 3)고 보험료 납입을 요청하고 있으므로 (A)가 정답이다.

어휘 remind 상기시키다 inform 알리다 offer 제안하다 missing 빠진

패러프레이징
지문의 submit your ~ payment
➡ 보기의 make a payment

4 편지에 따르면, 리 씨가 온라인에서 할 수 없는 것은?

(A) 청구서의 인쇄용 버전에 접근하는 것
(B) 청구서 사본을 요청하는 것
(C) 자동 납부 시스템에 등록하는 것
(D) 납부 기한을 연장하는 것

해설 **Not/True:** 세 번째 단락에서 명세서의 인쇄용 사본을 확인하거나 종이 사본을 요청하거나 계정 결제 설정을 관리하거나 자동 결제 시스템에 등록하려면 www.guillon-insurance.com/mypolicy를 방문하라(To view a printable copy ~ visit www.guilloninsurance.com/mypolicy)며 안내한 온라인에서 할 수 있는 것들에 보기 (A), (B), (C)의 내용이 모두 포함되어 있다. 하지만 납부 기한 연장에 대한 내용은 언급되지 않았으므로 (D)가 정답이다.

5 [1], [2], [3], [4]로 표시된 곳 중에서 다음 문장이 들어가기에 가장 적합한 위치는?

"아직 작성하시지 않았다면, 사용자 프로필을 작성하셔야 할 수도 있습니다."

(A) [1]   (B) [2]
(C) [3]   (D) [4]

해설 **문장 삽입:** 제시된 문장은 '아직 작성하시지 않았다면, 사용자 프로필을 작성해야 할 수도 있다'며 사용자 계정 관리에 대해 이야기하고 있으므로 이와 관련된 내용이 나오는 문맥에 들어가야 자연스럽다. [3] 앞에 있는 문장에서 웹사이트 방문(To view a printable copy ~ visit www.guilloninsurance.com/mypolicy)과 계정 로그인(You will be prompted to log in to your account)에 대해 언급하고 있어 제시된 문장이 들어가기에 적절하므로 (C)가 정답이다.

Questions 6-8 이메일

수신: 캐서린 마수르 〈kmasur@worthco.com.au〉
발신: 하림 오스만 〈baharucarrentals.com.my〉
제목: 자동차 대여
날짜: 10월 23일

마수르 씨께,

바하루 렌터카에서 차를 대여해 주셔서 감사합니다. **⁶결제 문제를 해결하도록 도와드리겠습니다.** 현재 대여 총 요금은 RM375입니다. 여기에는 보험료 RM50과 추가된 긴급출동 서비스 비용 RM25가 포함됩니다.

⁶이 금액을 고객님 개인 신용카드로 환불하고 귀사로 요금을 다시 청구하려면 별도의 전자 송장을 보내야 합니다. 귀사에서 대금을 받는 즉시 환불해 드리겠습니다. **⁷제가 송장을 보내야 할 사람의 이메일 주소를 알려 주시겠어요?**

또한 귀사에서 당사와 거래할 수 있는 계좌를 만들면 고객님과

회사 직원 전원에게 원활한 대여 서비스를 제공할 수 있음을 알려 드립니다. 사실, **⁸다음 달에는 저희와 거래 계좌를 새로 만드는 모든 업체에 한 달 이내 어떤 차량이든 대여하면 50퍼센트 할인해 드립니다.**

하림 오스만
바하루 렌터카
말레이시아 쿠알라룸푸르

어휘 insurance 보험 roadside assistance 긴급출동 서비스 separate 별도의 invoice 송장 seamless 원활한

6 이메일의 목적은?

(A) 안전 문제 해결하기
(B) 고객 송장 승인하기
(C) 지역 업체 추천하기
(D) 고객 환불 돕기

해설 **주제/목적:** 첫 단락 두 번째 문장에서 결제 문제를 해결하도록 도와드리겠다(I will be assisting you in resolving your payment issue)고 했고, 두 번째 단락에서 이 금액을 고객님 개인 신용카드로 환불하고 귀사로 요금을 다시 청구하려면 별도의 전자 송장을 보내야 한다(In order to refund the amount ~ separate electronic invoice)며 대금을 받는 즉시 환불해 주겠다(As soon as payment is received from your company, I can issue your refund)고 했다. 전체적으로 자동차 대여 서비스의 환불과 관련된 결제 문제에 대해 설명하고 있으므로 (D)가 정답이다.

7 마수르 씨가 요청 받은 일은?

(A) 보험회사에 전화하기
(B) 연락처 제공하기
(C) 보증금 입금하기
(D) 신청서 작성하기

해설 **세부 사항:** 두 번째 단락 마지막에 송장을 보내야 할 사람의 이메일 주소를 알려 줄 수 있는지(Could you please supply an e-mail address for the person to whom I should send the invoice?)를 묻고 있으므로 (B)가 정답이다.

어휘 security deposit 보증금 fill out ~을 작성하다

8 마수르 씨의 회사가 거래 계좌를 개설하면 제공되는 혜택은?

(A) 1회 차량 업그레이드
(B) 무료 차량 대여
(C) 긴급출동 서비스 요금 인하
(D) 일정 기간 차량 대여 할인

해설 **세부 사항:** 세 번째 단락 마지막에 다음 달 저희와 거래 계좌를 새로 만드는 모든 업체에 한 달 이내 어떤 차량이든 대여하면 50퍼센트 할인해 준다(next month we are offering a 50 percent discount ~ business that opens an account with us)고 했으므로 (D)가 정답이다.

어휘 complimentary 무료의

패러프레이징

지문의 within the month ➲ 보기의 limited-time

UNIT 02 | 세부 사항 문제

ETS 예제 본책 p. 280

아쿠아스티 연구소

아쿠아스티 연구소는 정수 처리 기술을 전문으로 합니다. 저희는 가정용과 산업용 정수 처리 모두에 적합한 최첨단 연수제와 정수 장비를 제공합니다.

저희 검사 시설은 귀하의 구체적인 요구에 가장 적합한 장비를 결정하도록 설비되어 있습니다. **가장 정확한 추천을 해 드리기 위해 저희는 수중 pH(페하)와 철분 함량을 측정하는 수질 분석을 실시합니다.** 그리고 지금, 7월 1일부터 30일까지 저희는 모든 고객께 **이 서비스를 무료로 제공합니다.**

(후략)

어휘 specialize in ~을 전문으로 하다 treatment 처리 state-of-the-art 최첨단의 softener 연화제 household 가정 industrial 산업(용)의 facility 시설 equipped 장비를 갖춘 determine 알아내다, 결정하다 suited 적합한 specific 구체적인 accurate 정확한 conduct 실시하다 analysis 분석 determination 결정, 측정 pH 페하 iron 철분 content 함유량

Q. 무엇이 무료로 제공되고 있는가?

(A) 실험실 분석 서비스
(B) 신제품 설명회
(C) 식수 용기 배달
(D) 정수 처리 장비 교체

세부 사항 | 기출 유형 연습하기 본책 p. 281

1 (B) **2** (B) **3** (B) **4** (A) **5** (B)

재래식 식기 세척기는 사용할 때마다 200–300리터의 깨끗한 물을 소비합니다. 워시웨이브는 매 사이클마다 재사용을 위해 탱크 안에 있는 물을 여과합니다. **탱크 속의 물은 격주로 갈아 주기만 하면 됩니다.** 이로 인해 보통 가정이라면 연간 25만 리터에서 50만 리터의 물을 절약할 수 있습니다.

어휘 conventional 재래식의, 전통적인 dishwasher 식기 세척기 consume 소비하다 per ~마다 every other week 격주로 average 평균의; 평균 household 가정 annually 연간

1 워시웨이브 안의 물은 얼마나 자주 갈아야 하는가?

(A) 주 1회 (B) 격주 1회

콤텍스 카드 사용자로서 고객님께서는 자동으로 구매자 보호 방안의 대상이 되셨습니다. 이는 여러분의 **신용카드로 구매한 것에 대해 구매일로부터** 90일 내내 보험을 적용 받을 수 있는 방안입니다. 구매자 보호 방안은 전 세계 어디서든 여러분의 신용카드로 구매한 물품에 대한 손실, 도난, 돌발적 피해에 대한 보험을 제공합니다.

어휘 cardholder 카드 소지자 automatically 자동적으로 cover 보상하다, 보장하다 protection 보호 plan 제도 insure 보험에 들다, 보증하다 insurance 보험 loss 분실 theft 도난 accidental 돌발적인, 우연한 damage 피해 anywhere 어디서나

2 보험 보장은 언제 적용되는가?

(A) 신용카드가 발급되고 90일 후
(B) 신용카드로 물품을 구매한 그날

벡 씨 귀하,

샌안토니오에서 열렸던 2월 소기업 솔루션 콘퍼런스의 회의록이 원래 예정된 9월이 아니라 8월에 출간됩니다. 이것은 제가 **모든 기고자들께 회보 5권을 무료로 곧 발송한다**는 의미입니다. 그래서 저는 **귀하의 책자를 어디로 보내야 하는지 알고 싶습니다.**

어휘 proceeding (회의 등의) 공식 기록, 회의록 publish 출간하다 originally 원래 volume 책, 권 contributor 기고자

3 벡 씨는 누구인가?

(A) 잡지 편집자 (B) 출판 기고가

편집자들이 제출 작품의 검토를 끝마치면 출판 여부를 알려 드립니다. 제출 후 6개월 이내에 통보될 것입니다. 검토 결과를 알아보고자 편집국에 연락하지는 마십시오. **작품이 잡지의 최종본에 실리면 작가들은 장당 20달러를 지불받습니다.**

어휘 editor 편집자 submission 제출(물) notify 알리다 notification 통지 editorial 편집의 compensate 보상하다 rate 가격 appear 나오다, 발간되다

4 작품이 선택되면 작가들은 무엇을 받게 되는가?

(A) 작품 분량에 따른 보수

(B) 우편 비용의 상환

> 테레사 모디 씨가 새 지점의 매니저로 임명되었습니다. 로스앤젤레스로 오기 전에 모디 씨는 프라임 국제 은행의 리우데자네이루 지점을 맡고 있었습니다. 미국 사업부의 상무 레지날드 **샤오 씨는 신설 지점 개장을 축하하고 지역 재계 인사들과 만나기 위해 로스앤젤레스에 있을 것입니다.**

어휘 **name** 임명하다 **in charge of** ~을 담당하는 **senior vice president** 상무, 전무

5 샤오 씨는 왜 로스앤젤레스 여행을 계획하는가?

(A) 채용 결정을 하려고

(B) 사업 관계자들과 접촉하기 위해

ETS **PRACTICE**

본책 p. 282

1 (C)   **2** (D)

회람

> **회람**
>
> 수신: 모든 시간제 직원
> 발신: 마리사 고메즈, 사장
> 날짜: 12월 15일
> 전달: 급여 처리
>
> 1월 2일경에 회계부는 직원 정보를 새로운 온라인 근무 시간 기록 시스템으로 옮길 예정입니다. 온라인 시스템은 2월 1일부터 운영되니 이날부터 **전 직원은 온라인으로 본인의 근무 시간을 매일 기입해야 합니다.** 1월 31일은 회계부가 이전의 시간 기록표 용지를 받는 마지막 날입니다.
>
> 1월 15일에 크리스토퍼 반 펠트가 새 온라인 시스템 사용에 대한 교육을 진행합니다.
> 참가하려면 내선 478번으로 그에게 연락하십시오.

어휘 **hourly** 시급제의 **transfer** 전송하다, 이동하다 **timekeeping** 시간 기록 **operational** 사용할 수 있는 **timesheet** 시간 기록표 **tutorial** 교습, 개별 지도 **sign up** ~에 참가하다, 등록하다

1 직원들은 무엇을 하라고 요청되는가?

(A) 다른 방식으로 종이 주문하기

(B) 개인 소지품들을 새로운 장소로 옮기기

(C) 직원 정보를 온라인으로 제출하기

(D) 회계부에 신규 작업 스케줄 요청하기

해설 **세부 사항:** 부탁이나 요구를 나타내는 표현을 집중해서 찾아야 한다. 전 직원은 온라인으로 본인의 근무 시간을 매일 기입해야 한다(all employees must enter their work hours into the online system daily)라고 했으므로 정답은 (C)이다.

패러프레이징

지문의 enter their work hours into the online system
➡ 보기의 Submit employee information online

정보

> **모닝 딜라이트**
>
> 모닝 딜라이트는 햇볕을 좋아하는 식물로 매혹적인 꽃을 피웁니다. 고객님의 식물을 아주 조심스럽게 포장해서 배송했지만 안전하게 도착했는지 식물을 살펴보세요. 식물이 건강하게 자라도록 하려면 아래 단계를 따르세요.
>
> 지면에 15센티미터 깊이의 구덩이를 파세요. 구덩이가 준비되면 상자에서 식물을 꺼내되 뿌리까지 전부 꺼내세요. 구덩이에 식물을 놓고 주위에 흙을 지그시 눌러 주세요.
>
> **모닝 딜라이트는 온화한 날씨에는 이틀에 한 번 물을 주면 되지만 실외 기온이 높을 때는 매일 물을 주어야 합니다.**

어휘 **produce** 생산하다 **attractive** 매력적인, 마음을 끄는 **pack** (물건을) 포장하다 **ship** 배송하다 **care** 주의, 돌봄 **inspect** 점검하다 **determine** 판단하다, 결정하다 **following** 다음의 **ensure** 보장하다 **dig** 파다 **carton** 상자 **gently** 부드럽게 **press** 누르다 **every other day** 이틀에 한 번 **mild** 온화한 **outdoor** 실외의 **temperature** 기온, 온도

2 정보에 따르면 모닝 딜라이트 식물에 특별히 주의를 기울여야 하는 때는 언제인가?

(A) 꽃을 잘라낼 때

(B) 꽃이 필 때

(C) 건조한 보관 시설에 둘 때

(D) 날씨가 더울 때

해설 **세부 사항:** 마지막 단락에서 모닝 딜라이트는 온화한 날씨에는 이틀에 한 번 물을 주면 되지만 실외 기온이 높을 때는 매일 물을 주어야 한다(but must be watered daily when outdoor temperatures are high)고 했으므로, 실외 기온이 높을 때 특별히 주의를 기울여야 한다는 것을 알 수 있다. 따라서 정답은 (D)이다.

어휘 **bloom** 꽃이 피다; 꽃 **storage** 저장, 창고 **facility** 시설

패러프레이징

지문의 when outdoor temperatures are high
➡ 보기의 When the weather is hot

1 (A)	2 (B)	3 (A)	4 (D)	5 (D)
6 (B)	7 (C)	8 (A)	9 (A)	

Questions 1-2 전단지

페리만 마켓 쇼핑객 여러분께,

페리만 마켓의 충실한 고객이 되어 주셔서 감사합니다. 우리 회사는 직원들과 양질의 제품 및 서비스에 큰 자부심을 갖고 있습니다. **1우리는 여러분이 이곳에서의 쇼핑 경험에 만족하실 수 있도록 노력하고 있습니다. 2**5개의 짧은 질문에 답해 주시고 우리 매장에서 사용할 수 있는 100달러짜리 상품권 다섯 장 중 하나에 당첨될 수 있는 자격을 부여받으세요. 설문조사는 영업시간, 채용 공고 및 매장 내 할인에 관한 정보와 함께 우리 웹사이트 www.perriman.com에서 확인하실 수 있습니다.

어휘 loyal 충실한 pride 자부심 quality 양질[고급]의 strive 노력하다 ensure 보장하다 satisfied 만족하는 experience 경험 eligible 자격이 되는 survey 설문조사 along with ~와 함께 regarding ~에 관하여 job opening 일자리

1 페리만 마켓에서 주장하는 것은?

(A) 고객 만족에 신경 쓴다.
(B) 지역에서 가격이 가장 낮다.
(C) 사업이 성장하고 있다.
(D) 배송 서비스를 시작할 예정이다.

해설 **세부 사항:** 페리만 마켓에서 작성한 전단지의 세 번째 문장에서 우리는 여러분이 이곳에서의 쇼핑 경험에 만족할 수 있도록 노력하고 있다(We strive to ensure that ~ shopping experience here)고 했으므로 (A)가 정답이다.

2 전단지는 읽는 사람에게 무엇을 하라고 권장하는가?

(A) 입사 지원
(B) 일련의 질문에 응답
(C) 상품권 구매
(D) 시장 행사 참석

해설 **세부 사항:** 네 번째 문장에서 5개의 짧은 질문에 답하고 매장에서 사용할 수 있는 100달러짜리 상품권 다섯 장 중 하나에 당첨될 수 있는 자격을 부여받으라(Please answer five short questions ~ use in our store)며 설문 조사에 응해줄 것을 권하고 있으므로 (B)가 정답이다.

패러프레이징

지문의 answer five short questions
➡ 보기의 Respond to a set of questions

Questions 3-5 기사

캘리스타 커피, 리버사이드로 이전하다

리버사이드(7월 7일) – 10년 전, 데니엘 모레는 리버사이드에서 커피 원두를 직접 로스팅하는 최초의 커피숍인 럭스 카페를 설립했다. 이제는 리버사이드의 커피 로스팅 동향의 창시자로 여겨지는 그는 신규 진입자들을 두 팔 벌려 환영한다. "저는 점점 더 많은 커피 로스터들이 우리 지역으로 옮기고 있다는 사실이 좋습니다"라고 모레 씨는 말한다.

3수사나 가르시아는 이러한 신규 진입자들 중 한 명으로, 더 합리적인 부동산 가격을 찾아 오스틴에서 이곳으로 가업을 옮겨 왔다. 1년 동안 찾은 결과 가르시아 씨와 그녀의 캘리스타 커피는 리버사이드에 정착했다.

4가르시아 씨의 아버지는 3년 전 은퇴할 때까지 캘리스타의 **CEO로 일했다.** 가르시아 씨는 아직 10대이던 시절 방과 후에 로스팅 과정을 돕기 시작했고, 20대에는 주니어 관리직을 맡았으며, **4**아버지가 은퇴했을 때 자리를 물려받았다.

5(A)캘리스타 커피는 서점 카페와 기타 소규모 업체들을 위해 유기농 커피를 로스팅하고 갈고 포장하는데, **5(C)**내년에는 호텔에 공급을 시작하려고 계획하고 있다. **5(B)**리버사이드 상공회의소는 가르시아 씨가 커피 로스팅을 위해 개조할 아이리스 가에 위치한 2,500 제곱피트의 건물을 찾는 것을 도왔다. 가르시아 씨는 40만 달러를 투자하고 궁극적으로는 수십 개의 새로운 일자리를 만들겠다고 약속했다.

어휘 found 설립하다 movement 동향, 움직임 declare 분명히 말하다 newcomer 신참 relocate 이전하다 attempt 시도 reasonable 합리적인 real estate 부동산 search 찾기 land 도착시키다 retirement 은퇴 process 과정 assume (책임을) 맡다 management 경영진 retire 은퇴하다 grind 갈다 package 포장하다 supply 공급하다 Chamber of Commerce 상공회의소 renovate 개조하다 invest 투자하다 eventually 결국 dozens of 수십 개의

3 가르시아 씨는 왜 오스틴에서 이전하기로 결정했는가?

(A) 돈을 절약하기 위해
(B) 모레 씨를 위해 일하기 위해
(C) 아버지와 더 가까이 살기 위해
(D) 가족에게 한 약속을 이행하기 위해

해설 **세부 사항:** 두 번째 단락의 첫 문장에서 수사나 가르시아는 이러한 신규 진입자들 중 한 명으로 더 합리적인 부동산 가격을 찾아 오스틴에서 이곳으로 가업을 옮겨 왔다(One such newcomer is Susana Garcia ~ find more reasonable real estate prices)고 했다. 따라서 가르시아 씨가 더 저렴한 부동산을 찾아 업체를 이전했다는 것을 알 수 있으므로 (A)가 정답이다.

어휘 **fulfill** 이행하다

패러프레이징

지문의 find more reasonable ~ prices

➲ 보기의 save money

4   가르시아 씨의 현재 직업은?

(A) 마케팅 전문가

(B) 견습생

(C) 서점주

(D) 회사 임원

해설 **세부 사항:** 세 번째 단락의 첫 문장에서 가르시아 씨의 아버지는 3년 전 은퇴할 때까지 캘리스타의 CEO로 일했다(Ms. Garcia's father served as Calista's CEO ~ ago)고 했고, 같은 단락의 마지막 부분에 아버지가 은퇴했을 때 자리를 물려받았다(took over for her father when he retired)고 했으므로 가르시아 씨는 현재 CEO임을 알 수 있다. 따라서 (D)가 정답이다.

패러프레이징

지문의 CEO ➲ 보기의 Company executive

5   가르시아 씨가 리버사이드에서 하려는 일이 아닌 것은?

(A) 소규모 업체에 공급하기

(B) 대형 건물 보수 공사하기

(C) 호텔에 커피 판매하기

(D) 신사업에 수익금 투자하기

해설 **Not / True:** 네 번째 단락에서 캘리스타 커피는 서점 카페와 기타 소규모 업체들을 위해 유기농 커피를 로스팅하고 갈고 포장하는데 내년에는 호텔에 공급을 시작하려고 계획하고 있다(Calista Coffee ~ plans to start supplying hotels next year)고 했으므로 (A)와 (C)는 사실이다. 또한, 리버사이드 상공회의소는 가르시아 씨가 커피 로스팅을 위해 개조할 건물을 찾는 것을 도왔다(The Riverside Chamber of Commerce ~ to be renovated for coffee roasting)고 했으므로 (B)도 사실이다. 마지막 문장에서 가르시아 씨가 40만 달러를 투자한다(Ms. Garcia has promised to invest $400,000)고는 했으나 신사업에 대한 이야기는 언급되지 않았으므로 (D)가 정답이다.

Questions 6-9 안내 책자

당신의 기술에 대한 수요가 항상 있을 것입니다
배관공과 전기공을 위한 배리스 직업 학교를 다니세요

⁶타이론 카운티의 배관 및 전기 작업 종사자들이 분야를 막론하고 최저 실업률과 최고 수준의 직무 만족도를 보고하고 있다는 것을 아십니까?

단 10개월(선행 학점 취득 시 더 짧음) 동안 파트타임으로 공부하면 수습 배관공이나 수습 전기공 자격을 획득할 수 있다는 것을 아십니까?

배리스 직업 학교에서는 다음과 같은 서비스를 제공합니다:

❖ 기존 근무 일정에 맞춘 편리한 주 2회 수업
   – A조: 월요일과 수요일, 저녁 6시부터 10시까지
   – B조: 토요일과 일요일, 오전 7시 30분부터 11시 30분까지

❖ ⁷타이론 카운티 또는 인근 카운티 거주 증명 시 등록금 인하

❖ 자격증을 소지한 전문가 작업 참관, 당사 전용 비디오 게임 교육용 도구로 게임하기, ⁸구직 면접 기술 연습하기 등을 포함한 흥미로운 일련의 수업 활동. 수업 시간의 75%가 실습 학습에 할애된다고 보장합니다.

❖ ⁹졸업 후 첫 3년간 취업을 돕기 위한 당사의 취업 전문가 서비스 이용

우리 지역의 일반적인 전기공 혹은 배관공이
얼마나 버는지 궁금하십니까?

	평균 초년 급여	평균 5년차 급여
전기공	43,025달러	48,089달러
배관공	41,379달러	49,012달러

자세한 정보는 www.barrystradeschool.com으로 웹사이트를 방문하시거나 1 (402) 555-0183으로 전화 주십시오.

어휘 **plumber** 배관공 **electrician** 전기공
unemployment 실업 **satisfaction** 만족 **field** 분야
earn 취득하다 **credit** 학점 **qualification** 자격
apprentice 수습생 **existing** 기존의 **tuition rate**
수업료 **proof of residence** 거주 증명 **surrounding**
인근의 **an array of** 일련의, 다양한 **professional**
전문가 **be dedicated to** ~에 전념하다, 할애되다
hands-on 실습의, 직접 해 보는 **secure** 얻어 내다

6   안내 책자에 따르면, 배관공이나 전기공직의 장점은?

(A) 유연한 일정

(B) 쉬운 구직

(C) 필요한 공구 및 비품이 저렴함

(D) 보장된 연봉 인상

해설 **세부 사항:** 첫 문장에서 타이론 카운티의 배관 및 전기 작업 종사자들이 분야를 막론하고 최저 실업률과 최고 수준의 직무 만족도를 보고하고 있다는 것을 아는지(Do you know that employees in plumbing and electrical work ~ job satisfaction of any field?) 묻고 있는 것으로 보아 배관공이나 전기공은 쉽게 취직할 수 있음을 알 수 있다. 따라서 (B)가 정답이다.

어휘 **flexible** 유연한 **ease** 용이함 **supply** 비품; 공급하다
guaranteed 보장된

패러프레이징

지문의 the lowest unemployment rates
➡ 보기의 Ease of finding jobs

7 인하된 수업료에 자격이 있는 사람은 누구인가?

(A) 복학생
(B) 자격증을 소지한 전문가
(C) 그 지역에 거주하는 사람들
(D) 선행 학점을 보유한 학습자

해설 **세부 사항:** 배리스 직업 학교에서 제공하는 서비스 목록 두 번째에 타이론 카운티 또는 인근 카운티 거주 증명 시 등록금 인하(Lower tuition rates with proof of residence in Tyron County or surrounding countries)라고 나와 있으므로 (C)가 정답이다.

패러프레이징

지문의 Lower tuition rates ➡ 질문의 reduced class cost
지문의 residence in Tyron County or surrounding countries ➡ 보기의 live in the area

8 안내 책자에 따르면, 수업에 대해 무엇이 강조되는가?

(A) 면접 기술을 포함하고 있다.
(B) 온라인상으로 열린다.
(C) 자격증 시험을 위한 광범위한 복습을 제공한다.
(D) 학생들에게 교과서를 사용하도록 한다.

해설 **세부 사항:** 배리스 직업 학교에서 제공하는 서비스 목록 세 번째에 흥미로운 일련의 수업 활동(An exciting array of class activities)으로 구직 면접 기술 연습하기(practicing job interview skills)가 포함되어 있으므로 (A)가 정답이다.

어휘 **extensive** 광범위한 **textbook** 교과서

패러프레이징

지문의 skills ➡ 보기의 techniques

9 배리스 직업 학교에 의해 제공되는 것은?

(A) 취업 알선 지원
(B) 집에 가져갈 수 있는 교육용 비디오
(C) 졸업 후 인턴직
(D) 불만인 학생에게 등록금 환급

해설 **세부 사항:** 배리스 직업 학교에서 제공하는 서비스 목록 마지막에 졸업 후 첫 3년간 취업을 돕기 위한 당사의 취업 전문가 서비스 이용(Access to the services of our employment ~ three years after graduation)이라고 나와 있으므로 (A)가 정답이다.

어휘 **reimbursement** 환급 **dissatisfied** 불만을 느끼는

패러프레이징

지문의 help you secure employment
➡ 보기의 Job-placement assistance

| UNIT 03 | NOT / TRUE 문제 |

ETS 예제   본책 p. 286

설치 설명
퀵시컵 프로
모델 번호: GCM-1624
전압: 120Vac, 50-60Hz
전력량: 최대 1800와트
용량: 20컵

1. 기계를 단단하고 평평한 표면에 똑바로 놓고, 콘센트에 **플러그를 끼운다.**
2. 필터 바구니를 비운 채로 제자리로 밀어 넣는다.
3. 물통에 찬물(최대 2리터)을 붓는다.
4. 빈 **유리 주전자를 열판** 위에 놓는다.
5. "끓이기" 버튼을 누르면 "사용 중" 표시등이 켜진다.
6. 유리 주전자가 뜨거운 물로 채워질 때까지 4~5분 기다린다.
7. 뜨거운 물을 버리고 이 과정을 두 번 반복한다. 이를 통해 뜨거운 물로 사용 전 기계의 내부 부품을 세척할 수 있다.

(후략)

어휘 **installation** 설치 **instruction** 설명 **upright** 똑바른; 똑바로 **surface** 표면 **insert** 끼우다, 삽입하다 **outlet** 콘센트 **slide** 밀어 넣다 **pour** 붓다, 따르다 **reservoir** 통 **carafe** 유리 물병 **plate** 판 **brew** 끓이다 **illuminate** 불이 들어오다 **dispose of** 버리다 **process** 과정 **internal** 내부의

Q. 기계의 부품이 아닌 것은?

(A) 발열체   (B) 냉각 팬
(C) 유리 용기   (D) 전기 플러그

Not/True | 기출 유형 연습하기   본책 p. 287
1 (B) **2** (A) **3** (B) **4** (B) **5** (A)

어메이징 크루즈는 알래스카의 강과 호수에서 4일간의 보트 여행과 연어 낚시, 그리고 **캠프파이어 주변에서 갓 잡은 고기로 저녁 식사를 즐기는 경험을 제공합니다.** 이 여행에서 참가자들은 오직 보트로만 이동하고 강과 호수를 따라 설치된 텐트에서 숙박합니다.

어휘 **salmon** 연어 **fresh-caught** 갓 잡힌 **alongside** ~을 따라

1 어메이징 크루즈의 특징으로 언급되지 않은 것은?

(A) 캠프파이어 주변에서 식사하기
(B) 빙하 방문하기

PART 7 | UNIT 03

세계 각 지역이 다른 배송 요금을 요구하므로, 배송료는 별도로 계산될 것입니다. 지역의 배송 요금으로부터 발생하는 추가 요금은 주문이 처리된 후 발송되는 메일에 제시된다는 점에 주의해 주십시오. **온라인 주문은 처리하는 데 최대 3일까지 소요됩니다.**

어휘 region 지역 shipping charge 배송료 calculate 계산하다 separately 별도로 result from ~의 결과로 발생하다 process 처리하다

2 온라인 주문에 대해 언급된 것은?

(A) 3일 후나 혹은 더 빨리 처리된다.

(B) 구매자에게 더 저렴한 배송 요금을 허용한다.

저희에게 고객님의 건강은 소중하기 때문에 지금이 정기 건강 검진을 할 시간이라고 알려 드리고 싶습니다. 조만간 뵙길 바랍니다!

고객님의 예약일은, 9월 12일 월요일 오전 10시 30분입니다. **예약을 지키지 못할 경우 24시간 전에 사전 통보해 주시길 바랍니다. 그렇지 않으면 수수료가 부과됩니다.**

어휘 remind 상기시키다 examination 검사 appointment 예약 advance notice 사전 통보 charge 청구하다

3 병원에 대해서 언급된 것은?

(A) 방문 24시간 전에 사람들에게 연락한다.

(B) 늦게 취소하면 수수료가 부과된다.

박람회 장소의 기반 시설을 고려했을 때 전시 참가 비용은 경쟁력이 있는 편입니다. 현장에서 전시관 주변의 전시 제품 운반을 위해 지게차 기사를 무료로 이용할 수 있습니다. 지게차로 운반하지 못하는 중장비는 **적은 비용에 기중기로 운반될 수 있습니다.** 각 전시 업체는 모든 전시관 내의 각 부스에 무료 전기와 수도를 보장 받습니다.

어휘 competitive 경쟁력 있는 considering ~을 고려할 때 infrastructure 기반 시설 venue 장소 forklift 지게차 operator 기사 pavilion 전시장

4 출품자에게 무료로 제공되지 않는 것은?

(A) 전기 (B) 기중기 서비스

9월 1일은 메도우 레이크스에 있는 쇼어라인 플레이하우스의 제20회 공연 시즌의 시작을 알리는 날로서, 불과 1년 전만 해도 이 행사가 열릴 것이라고 생각한 사람은 거의 없었습니다. 가까운 무어랜드 시티에 필드 극장이 개관한 것은 이제는 이 지역의 단골 관람객들에게 쇼어라인 플레이하우스가 유일한

목적지가 아니라는 것을 의미했습니다. 게다가 **월터스 재단이 필드 극장에 준 넉넉한 보조금으로 그들은 보다 폭넓게 어필한 대규모 작품들을 만들었습니다.**

어휘 mark 나타내다, 기념하다 theatrical 연극[공연]의 nearby 인근의 no longer 더 이상 ~ 아닌 destination 목적지 theatergoer 연극 애호가 generous 후한, 넉넉한 grant 보조금 foundation 재단 scale 규모 production 작품 broad 폭넓은

5 필드 극장에 대해 사실인 것은?

(A) 상당한 액수의 돈을 받았다.

(B) 레이크 가에 위치해 있다.

ETS **PRACTICE** 본책 p. 288

1 (A) **2** (B)

공지

쓰레기 방지 – 여러분이 동참할 수 있는 방법

복사

- 문서들을 공유 디렉토리에 저장함으로써 불필요한 복사를 없애라.
- 파일 사본을 간직하지 말고 중앙 파일 관리 시스템을 만들어라.
- 당신의 컴퓨터에서 직접 팩스 전송이 가능한 프로그램을 구입하라.
- **서식과 보고서를 다시 디자인하여 여백(그리고 필요한 복사본의 수)을 줄여라.**
- **글이 긴 문서들의 요약본을 준비하라.** 요청하는 경우에만 문서의 전문을 제공하라.
- 사내 메시지는 이메일이나 음성 메일을 사용하라.
- 복사 대신 게시판에 정보를 게시하라.

어휘 photocopy 복사(물) eliminate 없애다, 제거하다 shared 공유된 directory (컴퓨터의) 디렉토리 instead of ~대신에, ~하지 않고 maintain 간수하다, 유지하다 duplicate 사본의; 복사하다 transmission 전송, 송신 redesign 다시 디자인하다 margin 여백 executive summary (보고서나 제안서의) 요약(본) lengthy 긴, 장황한 on request 요청하는 경우에 interoffice 부서 간의, 회사 내의 post (안내문 등을) 게시[공고]하다 bulletin board 게시판 make copies 복사하다

1 복사를 줄이기 위해 제안된 방법이 아닌 것은?

(A) 복사에 대한 일련의 지침들을 게시한다.

(B) 공유 문서 디렉토리를 사용한다.

(C) 요약본을 작성한다.

(D) 문서의 여백을 줄인다.

해설 **Not/True:** 문서들을 공유 디렉토리에 저장하여 불필요한 복사를 없애라(Eliminate unnecessary photocopies by storing documents on a shared directory)에서 (B)를, 서식과 보고서를 재디자인하여 여백과 복사본 수를 줄여라(Redesign forms and reports to reduce margins (and the number of copies required))에서 (D)를, 글이 긴 문서들의 요약본을 준비하라(Prepare executive summaries for lengthy documents)에서 (C)를 해당 내용으로 찾을 수 있다. 마지막 항목(Post information on a bulletin board instead of making copies)은 복사 대신 정보를 게시판에 게시하라는 의미이지 복사 지침들을 게시하라는 의미가 아니므로 복사를 줄이기 위해 제안된 방법이 아니다. 따라서 정답은 (A)이다.

어휘 post 게시하다, 고시하다 guideline 지침

패러프레이징
지문의 reduce margins ➡ 보기의 Decrease margins

안내문

물품을 반품하려면

1. 품목을 조심스럽게 싼 다음 상자 안에 넣으세요.
2. www.breezybeluga.co.uk/forms에서 배송 송장을 출력해 포장 전면에 붙이세요. 접착식 송장을 추천합니다. **테이프를 써서 송장을 고정한다면 테이프가 바코드를 가리지 않도록 하세요.**
3. 배송 전에 포장이 제대로 됐는지 확인하세요.
4. www.breezybeluga.co.uk/track에서 주문 번호를 사용하면 소포를 추적할 수 있습니다.

이 설명서는 국내 반품에만 적용된다는 점 유의하세요. 해외 반품은 고객서비스부 0113-496-0836으로 문의하세요.

어휘 self-adhesive 접착식의 domestic 국내의

2 송장에 관해 명시된 것은?

(A) 반드시 테이프로 상자에 부착해야 한다.
(B) 바코드가 뚜렷이 보이도록 해야 한다.
(C) 손으로 작성할 수 있다.
(D) 상자 어디에나 붙일 수 있다.

해설 **Not/True:** 2번 목록에서 배송 송장을 출력해 상자 전면에 붙이라고 했으므로 (C)와 (D)는 답이 될 수 없고, 접착식 송장을 추천한다고 했으므로 (A) 역시 답이 될 수 없다. 테이프로 송장을 고정할 경우 바코드를 가리지 않도록 하라(If tape is used to secure the label, make sure that the tape does not cover the bar code)고 했으므로 (B)가 정답이다.

패러프레이징
지문의 does not cover the bar code
➡ 보기의 must clearly show the bar code

ETS TEST
본책 p. 289

1 (B)	2 (C)	3 (C)	4 (D)	5 (C)
6 (A)	7 (D)	8 (B)		

Questions 1-2 이메일

수신: 카라 라일리 〈carareilly@rphost.ie〉
발신: 리암 캐시디 〈lcassidy@iaw.ie〉
날짜: 3월 4일
제목: RE: 지난 대화에 뒤이어

메시지를 보내 주셔서 감사합니다. ¹저는 3월 2일부터 9일까지 사무실을 비우고, 국제 운동용품 교역 박람회를 위해 스페인 바르셀로나에 있을 예정입니다. 이 기간 동안, 저는 이메일 접속이 제한적일 것입니다. ²즉각적인 도움이 필요하시면 **mdolan@iaw.ie**로 매리 돌란에게 연락하셔서 판매 및 고객 요청과 관련된 모든 문제를 문의해 주십시오. 그렇지 않으면 3월 10일 제가 돌아오고 나서 제 회신을 기다려 주십시오.

리암 캐시디
아이리시 운동복 영업 이사

어휘 international 국제적인 athletic 체육의 goods 제품 trade 교역 limit 제한하다 access 접근 immediate 즉각적인 assistance 도움 matter 문제 related to ~와 관련된 request 요청 otherwise 그렇지 않으면 response 회신 director 이사

1 캐시디 씨에 대해 명시된 것은?

(A) 최근에 영업 이사로 임명되었다.
(B) 정기적으로 이메일을 확인할 수 없을 것이다.
(C) 자택에서 근무하고 있다.
(D) 전에 바르셀로나를 방문한 적이 있다.

해설 **Not/True:** 두 번째 문장에서 캐시디 씨는 3월 2일부터 9일까지 사무실을 비우고 박람회를 위해 바르셀로나에 있을 예정(I will be out of the office ~ Goods Trade Show)이라면서, 이 기간 동안 이메일 접속이 제한적일 것(During this time, I will have limited access to my e-mail)이라고 했다. 이는 이메일을 정기적으로 확인하기 어렵다는 뜻이므로 (B)가 정답이다.

어휘 appoint 임명하다 regularly 정기적으로

패러프레이징
지문의 have limited access to my e-mail
➡ 보기의 unable to check his e-mail regularly

2 메시지 수신자는 무엇을 하라고 권고되는가?

(A) 교역 박람회 주최측에 이메일을 보낼 것
(B) 행사 일정표를 확인할 것
(C) 캐시디 씨의 동료에게 연락할 것
(D) 영업부에 반품할 것

161

세부 사항: 네 번째 문장에서 캐시디 씨가 수신자에게 도움이 필요하면 mdolan@iaw.ie로 매리 돌란에게 연락해 판매 및 고객 요청과 관련된 모든 문제를 문의하라(For immediate assistance, please contact ~)고 권하고 있으므로 (C)가 정답이다.

어휘 recipient 수령인 organizer 주최자 coworker 동료

Questions 3-4 기사

> 재계 소식: **3웨딩업계 지역 회사들 협업**
>
> 티모니 웨딩 의상은 최근 웨딩업계 다른 업체들과 손잡고 협업 체계를 구축했다. **4지역에서 매우 아름다운 꽃다발과 테이블 배치로 유명한 브라이스 플로리스트**와 장식 서비스 업체 로열 이벤트 디자이너스는 모두 결혼 축하 행사의 모든 요소가 원활하게 진행되도록 하는 합작 사업에 참여하기로 합의했다. 이 업체들은 루이스버그 다운타운 플라자에 위치해 있다. **4사진작가, 미용실, 출장 연회 업체를 포함해 더 많은 업체들이 곧 이 그룹에 합류할 계획이다.**

어휘 attire 의상 collaborative 협업 exquisite 정교한, 매우 아름다운 enterprise 사업 seamlessly 원활하게 caterer 출장 연회 업체

3 기사가 설명하는 것은?

(A) 다가오는 결혼식

(B) 성공적인 인수

(C) 업체간 협업

(D) 투자자들의 협업

해설 **주제/목적:** 제목은 글의 전체적인 내용을 압축해서 보여주므로 글의 주제를 파악하는 데 훌륭한 단서가 된다. 기사의 제목이 웨딩업계 지역 회사들 협업(Local Companies in the Wedding Business to Collaborate)이고, 본문에서도 티모니 웨딩 의상의 협업에 대해 설명하고 있으므로 (C)가 정답이다.

어휘 acquisition 인수

패러프레이징

지문의 Collaborate ➡ 보기의 partnering

4 기사에 언급되지 않은 웨딩 서비스 유형은?

(A) 음식   (B) 꽃

(C) 사진   (D) 오락

해설 **Not/True:** 두 번째 문장에서 지역에서 매우 아름다운 꽃다발과 테이블 배치로 유명한 브라이스 플로리스트(Brice Florists, locally known for exquisite bouquets and table arrangements)를 언급했고, 마지막 문장에서 사진작가, 미용실, 출장연회 업체를 포함해 더 많은 업체들이 곧 이 그룹에 합류할 계획(More businesses are planning to join ~ a photographer, a hairstyling salon, and a caterer)이라고 했다. 꽃 장식, 사진, 출장

연회 업체들에 대해서는 언급을 했지만 오락에 대한 이야기는 없으므로 (D)가 정답이다.

Questions 5-8 기사

> **달아오르는 호텔 경쟁**
>
> 젠슨빌 공항 확장 이후로, 시의 호텔들은 투숙객을 늘리기 위해 경쟁하고 있다. 한때 젠슨빌 시청이었던 건물에 새로운 마룬 2 호텔이 문을 열면 곧 경쟁은 더욱 거세질 전망이다.
>
> 12년 전, 시청이 도심에서 역사지구의 모닝 플라자로 이전한 후, 한 투자 그룹이 옛 시청 건물을 구입해서 사무용 공간으로 개조했다. 그 후 2년 전에 그 건물은 마룬 2 호텔 그룹에 매각되었다.
>
> **8마룬 2는 지난 2년 동안 이 건물을 호텔로 개조하고 수십 년 동안 감춰져 있던 초기 시청의 역사적인 측면을 복원해 왔다.** 예를 들어, 5(D), 8여러 겹의 벽지로 덮여 있던 5(A)시의 창건에 관한 벽화는, 5(B)이제 로비를 환하게 밝히고 있다. 또한 중앙 원형홀의 돔 천장이 원래 상태로 완전히 복구되었다.
>
> **7시에서 유일하게 100개 이상의 객실을 보유한 다른 호텔 두 곳 또한 최근 구조에 변화를 주었다. 6객실 120개를 갖춘 소네터즈 호텔은 지난달에 체력단련실을 추가했으며,** 소네터즈에서 모퉁이를 돌면 있는 제너럴스 인에는 이제 옥외 정원 식당과 수영장이 들어섰다. 이 세 개의 호텔 중, 객실 146개를 보유한 마룬 2가 결국 가장 규모가 큰 호텔이 될 예정이다.
>
> 총지배인 디에고 코르디요는 마룬 2 브랜드는 개조에 들인 돈이 옳았음을 증명할 만큼 손님을 충분히 유치할 것이라고 확신한다.
>
> "마룬 2 브랜드라고 하면 사람들이 떠올리는 모든 특징이 여기 있을 것입니다." 그는 말했다. "고급스러운 가운, 세련된 시트, 그리고 물론, 감탄이 나오는 서비스 같은 것을 말이죠."

어휘 competition 경쟁 heat up 뜨거워지다, 활기를 띠다 expansion 확장, 확대 jostle for ~을 위하여 다투다 be about to 막 ~하려고 하다 intense 강렬한, 거센 downtown 시내 historic 역사적인 investment 투자 convert A to B A를 B로 전환하다, 개조하다 edifice (큰) 건물, 조직 restore 복원하다, 복구하다 historical 역사(학)의 aspect 측면, 관점 hidden 감춰진 mural 벽화 founding 설립, 창립 layer 층 undergo 받다, 겪다 structural 구조적인, 구조의 courtyard 뜰, 정원 end up -ing ~하게 되다, 결국 ~이 되다 sizable 상당한 크기의, 넓은 confident 자신 있는, 확신하는 attract 유치하다, 끌어들이다 justify 타당성을 입증하다 cost 비용 renovation 보수[수리], 개조 attribute 특징, 속성 associate 연결 지어 생각하다 plush 안락한, 고급의 robe 가운 exquisite 정교한, 세련된 phenomenal 경이적인, 경탄이 나오는

5 벽화에 관해 명시되지 않은 것은?

(A) 역사적인 사건을 묘사한다.

(B) 호텔 로비에 있다.

(C) 개조 기간에 제작되었다.

(D) 오랫동안 볼 수 없었다.

해설 **Not / True:** 세 번째 단락에서 벽화에 관해 언급되어 있다. 여러 겹의 벽지로 덮여 있던(had been covered by layers) 시의 창건에 관한 벽화(the mural of the city's founding)는, 이제 로비를 환하게 밝히고 있다(is now a brightly colored feature of the lobby)고 했다. 따라서 벽화는 개조 기간 전에 이미 제작되었던 것임을 알 수 있으므로, 정답은 (C)이다.

어휘 **depict** 묘사하다, 설명하다   **view** 둘러보다

패러프레이징

지문의 the city's founding

➡ 보기 (A)의 a historical event

지문의 is now a brightly colored feature of the lobby

➡ 보기 (B)의 It is located in the hotel's lobby.

지문의 had been covered by layers

➡ 보기 (D)의 It had not been viewed for many years.

6 기사에서 소네터즈 호텔의 새로운 특성으로 언급된 것은?

(A) 헬스장   (B) 수영장

(C) 확장된 로비   (D) 옥외 식당

해설 **세부 사항:** 네 번째 단락 두 번째 문장에서 소네터즈 호텔은 지난달에 체력단련실을 추가했다(The 120-room Sonnetters Hotel added an exercise room last month)고 했으므로, 정답은 (A)이다.

어휘 **fitness room** 헬스장   **expand** 확장하다, 확대하다   **outdoor** 실외의

패러프레이징

지문의 an exercise room ➡ 보기의 A fitness room

7 세 호텔 모두에 관해 명시된 것은?

(A) 밝은 색이다.

(B) 역사 지구에 위치하고 있다.

(C) 한때 사무용 건물이었다.

(D) 100개가 넘는 객실을 보유하고 있다.

해설 **추론:** 네 번째 단락 첫 문장에서 시에서 유일하게 100개 이상의 객실을 보유한 다른 호텔 두 곳 또한 최근 구조에 변화를 주었다(The city's only two other hotels that have more than 100 rooms have recently undergone structural changes as well)고 했으므로, 세 호텔 모두 100개 이상의 객실을 보유하고 있음을 추론할 수 있다. 따라서 정답은 (D)이다.

8 [1], [2], [3], [4]로 표시된 곳 중에서 다음 문장이 들어가기에 가장 적합한 위치는?

"또한 중앙 원형홀의 돔 천장이 원래 상태로 완전히 복구되었다."

(A) [1]   (B) [2]

(C) [3]   (D) [4]

해설 **문장 삽입:** 제시된 문장의 Also가 문제 해결의 단서이다. 제시된 문장은 '또한 중앙 원형홀의 돔 천장이 원래 상태로 완전히 복구되었다'라는 의미이므로, 제시된 문장은 복원에 대한 내용 뒤에 들어가야 한다. 따라서 벽화 복원에 대한 내용 바로 뒤인 [2]에 들어가, 벽화 복원에 부가적으로 중앙 원형홀의 돔 천장 복원을 언급하는 것이 문맥상 자연스러우므로 정답은 (B)이다.

어휘 **dome** 둥근 지붕을 달다; 둥근 지붕   **ceiling** 천장   **rotunda** 원형의 홀, 원형 건축물   **completely** 완전히, 전적으로   **original** 원래의, 독창적인   **state** 상태

UNIT 04	추론 문제

ETS 예제   본책 p. 292

2월 15일

츠루미 이토

알몬트 가 11번지

로스앤젤레스 캘리포니아 주 90103

이토 씨 귀하:

저희 기록에 따르면, 귀하는 지난 12개월 동안 저희 계절별 상품 카탈로그에서 주문을 하지 않으셨습니다. 이전에 저희 고객이셨던 분들과의 관계를 유지하는 데 정성을 다하는 회사로서 저희는 이 편지에 적힌 날짜로부터 30일간 귀하께 모든 전화 주문이나 우편 주문에 대해 20퍼센트 가격 할인을 해 드리고자 합니다. (중략)

브렌다 메이슨

고객 관리부 부사장

어휘 **seasonal** 계절에 따른   **be dedicated to** ~에 전념하다   **maintain** 유지하다

Q. 이토 씨에 대해 알 수 있는 것은?

(A) 과거에 이 회사에서 제품을 구입했다.

(B) 작년에 로스앤젤레스로 이사했다.

(C) 브렌다 메이슨을 위해 일했었다.

(D) 우편 배달 신청용 카탈로그를 요청했다.

보존 협회는 박사님의 도시에 있는 오페라 타워즈의 최근 복원 작업에서 박사님의 리더십에 감동했습니다. **이렇게 중요한 역사적인 건물의 건축학적 요소를** 보존하려는 박사님의 헌신은 유적 보호 운동가들이 애써 매진하는 최선의 노력을 보여 주는 훌륭한 본보기입니다.

어휘　preservation 보존　society 협회　restoration 복원　commitment 헌신　preserve 보존하다 architectural 건축학적인　element 요소 preservationist 유적 보호 운동가　strive 노력하다, 분투하다　put forth 발휘하다

1　오페라 타워즈에 대해 암시된 것은?

　(A) 역사적인 중요성을 지니고 있다.

　(B) 현재 공사 중이다.

마닉 바타가 향후 학교들의 박물관 단체 방문 일정을 검토했다. 그는 방문 일정을 짜는 일을 도와줄 수 있는 비벌리 톰슨을 추가 직원으로 고용했는데, 이로써 **그는 학습 프로그램을 위한 커리큘럼 개발과 초빙 강사 초청에 집중할 수 있게 되었다.**

어휘　upcoming 곧 있을　concentrate on ~에 집중하다 curricula 교과 과정, 커리큘럼　lecturer 강연자

2　바타 씨는 누구이겠는가?

　(A) 큐레이터

　(B) 교육 책임자

리 씨 귀하:

바텔의 음식 포장 기술에 대한 귀하의 관심에 감사드립니다. 전화 통화에서 의논했던 것처럼 서튼 실은 **중대형 식품 가공 회사의 수요에 적합합니다.** 서튼 실은 많은 양을 처리할 수 있도록 설계되었으며, 거의 모든 크기나 모양의 음식에 맞게 주문 제작될 수 있습니다.

어휘　processing 처리　handle 처리하다　volume 양 customize 주문 제작하다

3　리 씨는 어떤 업계에서 일하겠는가?

　(A) 대규모 농업

　(B) 식품 가공

동봉된 3개짜리 새 UM-3 건전지들을 표시에 나타난 대로 양극 (+)과 음극 (−)이 향하도록 끼워 넣으세요. **이 건전지들이 정**전이나 전기 어댑터에서 플러그가 뽑혀 있을 때 금전 등록기의 메모리에 저장되어 있는 거래 정보들을 보호해 줍니다. 기계 사용 전 이 건전지들을 꼭 설치하십시오.

어휘　as indicated 표시된 대로　transaction 거래　store 저장하다　register (금전) 등록기　power failure 정전

4　건전지에 대해 알 수 있는 것은?

　(A) 기계에 전력이 차단되었을 때 사용된다.

　(B) 기계의 뒷면에 있는 수납 칸에 들어간다.

팔레 호텔이 최고의 주방장을 맞이하다

내부자들 사이에서는 홍콩의 숨겨진 보석으로 알려진 팔레 호텔이 이제 매우 유명해질 기세다. 호텔의 제이드 레스토랑에서 새로운 총괄 주방장이자 요리 전문가이며 탁월한 요리사인 메이 이 간을 고용했다. 지난달에 레스토랑에 부임해 간 주방장은 자신의 유명 요리를 메뉴에 올림으로써 벌써 명성을 떨쳤다.

어휘　hidden 숨겨진　be about to 막 ~하려는 참이다 executive chef 총괄 주방장　extraordinaire 탁월한 take over 인계 받다　make one's mark 이름을 떨치다　signature dish 가장 유명한 요리

5　팔레 호텔에 대해 암시된 것은?

　(A) 식당이 크다.

　(B) 현재는 널리 알려지지 않았다.

후기

http://www.productreviews.com/outdoor_lighting

소비자 후기: 옥외 조명 장치

후기 게시자: 토니 위벨

내 이웃은 도토노 동작 감지 전등을 작동시키기 위해 D사이즈 배터리에 매달 30달러를 지불한다. 밝은 빛을 뿜어내기는 하지만, 운영비가 놀라웠다. 대안으로, 나는 환불을 보장해 주는 F&Q 조명을 사용해 봐야겠다고 생각했다. 시험 삼아 써보려고 실외 벽등을 한 개만 구입했다. 그것을 햇볕에 놓아 두고 세 시간 동안 충전했는데, 밤새 불을 밝히기에 충분했다! 또한 어떠한 움직임에도 매우 민감했다. **내가 선택했지만 턱없이 부족했다. 더 많이 있어야 든든하리라 확신한다.**

어휘　motion-activated 동작 감지의　emit 내뿜다 alternative 대안　experiment 시험 삼아 해 보다 sensitive 민감한

1 위벨 씨는 후기를 쓴 뒤 아마 무엇을 했겠는가?

(A) F&Q에 환불을 요청했다.

(B) 이웃에게 불평했다.

(C) F&Q 조명을 추가로 구입했다.

(D) 도토노 조명을 시험했다.

해설 **추론:** F&Q 조명에 대한 후기의 마지막에 내가 선택했지만 턱없이 부족했다(I've made my choice, and it wasn't even close)며 더 많이 있어야 만족스러울 것(I'm sure I'll be happy with more)이라고 했으므로 조명을 더 구입할 것임을 짐작할 수 있다. 따라서 (C)가 정답이다.

기사

말레이시아 영화, 수상하다

어제 인도 뭄바이에서 열린 뭄바이 국제 영화제는 최고의 영예를 말레이시아 감독 뉴 탄의 장편 영화 〈작은 언덕에서〉에 안겨 주었다. 중국어로 된 이 영화는 시골인 고향을 떠나 도시로 가는 한 청년의 이야기를 보여 준다. 영화 전편에 걸쳐 그의 고향을 둘러싼 산맥은 그가 겪는 어렵고 '힘겨운' 정서적 여정에 대한 은유로 사용된다.

뉴 탄 감독은 작품상을 수상하는 자리에서 "제 영화가 이렇게 영예를 얻게 되어 감사드립니다"라는 말과 함께 자신의 영화를 계기로 **"말레이시아 및 주변국들의 원숙한 영화 제작 산업에 진작에 받았어야 할 온 세계인의 관심이 모이기 바란다"**고 덧붙였다.

어휘 **top honor** 최고의 영예, 1위 **director** 감독 **feature-length film** 장편 영화 **entitle** 제목을 붙이다 **foothill** 작은 언덕 **rural** 시골의 **metaphor** 은유, 비유 **uphill** 힘겨운 **emotional** 정서의, 감정의 **undergo** 겪다 **grateful** 고마워하는 **honor** 영예를 주다 **draw attention to** ~로 이목[주의]을 끌다 **long-overdue** 진작에 했어야 할, 오랫동안 기다려 온 **masterful** 원숙한, 거장다운 **neighboring** 인접한

2 탄 씨가 말레이시아 영화에 대해 암시하는 것은?

(A) 흔히 소설을 기반으로 한다.

(B) 특히 인도에서 인기 있다.

(C) 많은 상을 수상했다.

(D) 세계적으로 더 인정받을 가치가 있다.

해설 **추론:** 두 번째 단락에서 진작 받았어야 할 온 세계의 관심이 모이기 바란다(she hopes her film will draw "long-overdue, international attention ~)고 했으므로 정답은 (D)이다.

어휘 **numerous** 수많은 **deserve** ~을 받을 만하다, 누릴 자격이 있다 **recognition** 인식, 인정

패러프레이징

지문의 long-overdue, international attention

➡ 보기의 deserve more international recognition

ETS TEST
본책 p. 295

1 (D)	**2** (A)	**3** (A)	**4** (A)	**5** (D)
6 (A)	**7** (D)	**8** (C)	**9** (A)	

Questions 1-2 온라인 채팅

윈스턴 후앙(오전 9:12)
안녕, 알리샤. [1]매딩리 가에 건설되고 있는 신축 학교 건물에 관한 기사 때문에 조사를 시작했어요.

알리샤 에르난데스(오전 9:14)
잘됐네요, 이렇게 지체 없이 시작해 줘서 고마워요!

윈스턴 후앙(오전 9:15)
기사가 얼마나 길어야 되죠?

알리샤 에르난데스(오전 9:18)
[2]기사가 인쇄물로 출판될지, 온라인으로만 나올지 결정하지 않아서 아직 단어 제한이 어떻게 될지는 모르겠어요. [2]오전 10시 편집자 회의 때 결정할 거예요.

윈스턴 후앙(오전 9:20)
[2]알겠어요, 결정되면 알려 주세요. 오전 11시에 병원에 예약이 있어서 갔다 와서 쓰려고요.

알리샤 에르난데스(오전 9:21)
그럼요!

어휘 **promptly** 지체 없이 **appointment** 예약

1 후앙 씨와 에르난데스 씨는 어디에서 일하겠는가?

(A) 연구소   (B) 건설회사

(C) 진료실   (D) 잡지 출판사

해설 **추론:** 9시 12분 후앙 씨의 메시지에서 신축 학교 건물에 관한 자신의 기사 건으로 조사를 시작했다(I've started doing research for my article on the new school building)는 내용을 시작으로 출판물에 게재할 기사에 대해 논하고 있으므로 (D)가 정답이다.

2 오전 9시 21분에 에르난데스 씨가 "그럼요!"라고 쓴 의도는?

(A) 나중에 후앙 씨에게 연락할 것이다.

(B) 지금 회의에 참석하러 가고 있다.

(C) 후앙 씨는 즉시 일을 시작해야 한다.

(D) 후앙 씨는 매딩리 가에 가야 한다.

의도 파악: 9시 18분에 에르난데스가 기사가 인쇄물로 출판될지 온라인으로만 나올지(whether that article will be published in the print edition or only online) 편집자 회의 때 결정할 것(We'll be deciding during our editors' meeting)이라고 했고, 9시 20분에 후앙이 알겠다(OK)며 결정되면 알려 달라(let me know after you decide)고 하자 9시 21분에 에르난데스가 '그럼요!(Absolutely!)'라고 답했다. 따라서 '그럼요!'는 결정이 나면 후앙에게 알려 주기 위해 연락하겠다는 뜻이므로 (A)가 정답이다.

어휘 immediately 즉시

Questions 3-5 이메일

발신: 재닌 맥켄지 〈jmckenzie@romengoair.com〉
수신: 오스카 잭 〈ojach@mertacompany.com〉
제목: 아담 쿠니 추천서
날짜: 4월 19일

잭 씨께,

³귀하의 전 직원인 아담 쿠니 씨가 로멘고 항공사의 품질 분석가직에 지원했고 귀하의 이름을 추천인으로 제시했습니다. 그의 지원서를 처리하기 위해 추천을 확인하고 싶습니다.

쿠니 씨에 대한 평가를 저희와 공유해 주시기를 요청합니다. 쿠니 씨를 얼마나 오래 알고 지내셨으며 당시 쿠니 씨가 어떤 능력을 발휘했는지 알고 싶습니다. **⁴그의 역량, 직무, 급여 이력, 팀의 일원으로 일할 수 있는 능력과 관련된 자세한 내용을 제공해 주세요.** 공유하신 모든 세부 사항은 극비로 처리됩니다.

쿠니 씨 건을 빨리 결정하고 싶습니다. **⁵제가 언제 직접 통화해서 이 이메일에 관한 후속 조치를 취할 수 있을지 되도록 빨리 회신해서 알려 주세요.**

도와주셔서 감사합니다.

재닌 맥켄지
선임 엔지니어, IT 품질 보증

어휘 analyst 분석가 reference 추천인, 추천서
evaluation 평가 capacity 능력 pertaining to ~와 관련된 with the strictest confidence 극비로

3 잭 씨에 관해 암시된 것은?
   (A) 한때 쿠니 씨를 고용한 적이 있다.
   (B) 로멘고 항공에서 일했다.
   (C) 품질 분석가직에 지원했다.
   (D) 온라인에 구인 광고를 올렸다.

해설 **추론:** 첫 문장에서 이메일의 수신인인 잭 씨에게 귀하의 전 직원인 아담 쿠니 씨가 로멘고 항공사의 품질 분석가직에 지원했고 귀하의 이름을 추천인으로 제시했다(Mr. Adam Cooney, one of your former employees, ~ has

given your name as a reference)고 했으므로 잭 씨는 쿠니 씨의 전 고용인임을 알 수 있다. 따라서 (A)가 정답이다.

지문의 Mr. Adam Cooney, one of your former employees ➡ 보기의 He once employed Mr. Cooney.

4 쿠니 씨에 대한 정보로 맥켄지 씨가 요청하지 않은 것은?
   (A) 마지막 근무일
   (B) 직무상 책임
   (C) 능력
   (D) 급여

해설 **Not/True:** 두 번째 단락 세 번째 문장에서 쿠니 씨의 역량, 직무, 급여 이력, 팀의 일원으로 일할 수 있는 능력과 관련된 자세한 내용을 제공해 달라(Please provide details pertaining to his skills, job duties, salary history, and ability to work as part of a team)고 했고, 근무일에 대해서는 언급한 사실이 없으므로 (A)가 정답이다.

지문의 job duties ➡ 보기의 job responsibilities

5 맥켄지 씨가 하고 싶다고 명시한 것은?
   (A) 잭 씨를 직접 만나기
   (B) 잭 씨에게 후속 이메일 보내기
   (C) 잭 씨에게 자신의 회사에 일자리 제공하기
   (D) 잭 씨와 통화하기

해설 **Not/True:** 세 번째 단락 두 번째 문장에서 맥켄지가 언제 직접 통화해서 이 이메일에 관한 후속 조치를 취할 수 있을지 알려 달라(Please reply ~ with a personal phone call)고 했으므로 맥켄지는 잭 씨와 전화로 이야기하기를 원한다는 것을 알 수 있다. 따라서 (D)가 정답이다.

어휘 in person 직접

지문의 with a personal phone call ➡ 보기의 by phone

Questions 6-9 제품 평가

http://www.barclay.com

홈	아웃도어	의류	등산화

현명한 쇼핑객을 위한 바클레이의 안내

등산화를 찾고 계신가요? 선택의 여지가 많습니다. 롤링 마운틴 같은 몇몇 회사는 몇 대째 영업하고 있습니다. 모아 퀘스트 같은 다른 회사들은 신생 기업으로 최신 합성 소재가 특징입니다.

⁶진정한 등산 애호가는 항상 겨울용 등산화와 여름용 등산화를 따로 장만합니다. 여러분이 정말 등산을 좋아하신다면 한 켤레 추가 구입을 고려하십시오.

저희가 선택한 최상의 상품에 대한 후기입니다. 대체로 온라인 매장 사이에 가격이 조금 차이가 있다는 점에 유의하십시오.

트렉 라이프 $$$*

이 등산화는 최고급품 시장에 단단히 자리를 잡고 있다. 가죽, 합성 소재, 단단한 고무로 제조되어 울퉁불퉁한 지형에서 편안하며 여러 해 신을 수 있다. 등산을 자주 하는 사람이라면 최상의 선택이다. 유일한 단점은? 가격이다.

스티브도어 TX $$

양질의 가죽과 합성 소재로 만들어진 방수 등산화로 눈길을 지나는 힘든 등산에도 끄떡없다. **⁷아쉽게도 많이 신으면 밑창이 수명만큼 오래 가지 않는다.**

모아 퀘스트 $

가벼운 소재로 만든 등산화로 더운 날씨에 아주 적합하며 비교적 평평한 지형에서 단시간 등산할 때 이상적이다. **⁸등산을 시작한 지 얼마 안 되는 사람에게는 좋은 선택이지만** 따뜻하고 방수가 되는 등산화를 찾는 사람에게는 적합하지 않다.

롤링 마운틴 3R $

가격에 속지 말라. **⁹이 등산화는 가성비가 아주 좋다.** 가죽, 나일론, 두꺼운 고무로 만들어져 있으며 물이 들어가지 않는다. 그렇다면 뭐가 문제일까? 유연성이 떨어져 여러 번 신은 뒤에도 뻣뻣하다.

* 가격대:

$ = 100달러 미만
$$ = 100~150달러
$$$ = 150~200달러

어휘 feature 특징을 이루다; 특징 latest 최신의 synthetic 합성의 material 소재, 자료 enthusiast 열성 팬 separate 분리된 pick 선택한 것[사람]; 선택하다 vary (서로) 다르다, 다양하다 slightly 약간 firmly 단단하게 leather 가죽 solid 단단한 rubber 고무 rugged 울퉁불퉁한 terrain 지형 last 오래가다, 지속되다 bet 선택한 것[사람], 방책 downside 단점 quality 양질의; 품질 waterproof 방수의 unfortunately 아쉽게도, 안타깝게도 sole 밑창 lightweight 가벼운 relatively 비교적 flat 평평한 fool 속이다 value for money 값어치를 하는 flexible 유연한 stiff 뻣뻣한 price range 가격대, 가격 범위

6 등산을 많이 하는 구매자들이 받는 조언은?

(A) 등산화 두 컬레 구입하기
(B) 오랫동안 영업한 회사에서 구입하기
(C) 방수 등산화만 구입하기
(D) 해마다 새 등산화 구입하기

해설 **세부 사항:** 두 번째 단락에서 진정한 등산 애호가는 항상 겨울용 등산화와 여름용 등산화를 따로(separate pairs of

boots for winter and summer) 장만한다면서, 등산을 정말 좋아한다면 한 컬레 추가로 구입하라(consider buying an extra pair)고 조언하고 있다. 따라서 정답은 (A)이다.

패러프레이징
지문의 an extra pair ➡ 보기의 two pairs of boots

7 스티브도어 TX 등산화의 한 가지 문제는?

(A) 너무 무겁다.
(B) 평가된 등산화 중 가장 비싸다.
(C) 편하지 않다.
(D) 내구성이 떨어진다.

해설 **세부 사항:** Stevedore TX boots를 키워드로 잡고, Stevedore TX boots가 언급되는 부분에서 답을 찾아야 한다. 스티브도어 TX 등산화에 대해 설명한 다섯 번째 단락의 마지막 문장에서 스티브도어 TX 등산화는 아쉽게도 많이 신으면 밑창이 오래 가지 않는다(Unfortunately, with heavy use the soles do not last as long as they should)고 했으므로, 내구성이 떨어진다는 것을 알 수 있다. 따라서 정답은 (D)이다.

어휘 expensive 비싼 durable 내구성이 좋은, 튼튼한

패러프레이징
지문의 do not last as long as they should
➡ 보기의 are not very durable

8 등산 초보자에게 최상의 등산화는 무엇이겠는가?

(A) 트렉 라이프
(B) 스티브도어 TX
(C) 모아 퀘스트
(D) 롤링 마운틴 3R

해설 **세부 사항:** Moa Quest에 대해 설명한 단락의 두 번째 문장에서 모아 퀘스트는 등산을 시작한 지 얼마 안 되는 사람에게 좋은 선택(A good choice for those who are just starting out)이라고 했다. 따라서 정답은 (C)이다.

패러프레이징
지문의 those who are just starting out
➡ 질문의 a new hiker

9 롤링 마운틴 3R에 관해 암시된 것은?

(A) 가격이 적당하다.
(B) 아주 가볍다.
(C) 방수가 안 된다.
(D) 온라인에서 구입할 수 없다.

해설 **추론:** Rolling Mountain 3R boots를 키워드로 잡고, Rolling Mountain 3R boots가 언급되는 부분에서 답을 찾아야 한다. 롤링 마운틴 3R에 대해 설명한 단락의 첫 두 문장에서 가격에 속지 말라(Don't let the price fool you)면서, 롤링 마운틴 3R은 가성비가 아주 좋다(These boots are a great value for the money)고 했다. 따라서 롤링 마운틴 3R은 가격이 비싸지 않고 적당하다는 것을 추론할 수 있으므로, 정답은 (A)이다.

어휘 reasonably 적당히, 합리적으로 purchase 구매하다; 구매(품)

패러프레이징
지문의 a great value for the money
➡ 보기의 reasonably priced

| UNIT 05 | 문장 삽입 문제 |

ETS 예제   본책 p. 298

수신: 전 직원
발신: 오드리 캐논
제목: 다음 특집 기사
날짜: 10월 2일

여러분도 들으셨겠지만, 우리는 신문의 일요일판에 실릴 새로운 특집 기사를 시작합니다. 이 특집은 우리 지역에서 일어난 희망적이고 고무적인 **기사들을** 중점적으로 다룰 것입니다. 지면이 허락하면 그 기사들은 사진과 같이 같이 실릴 것입니다. 본 결정은 그런 특집을 원하는 수많은 독자들의 요청에 따른 것입니다. 이 섹션은 지면 및 온라인판 양쪽 모두에 게재될 것이므로, 신문의 나머지 부분과 동일한 높은 기준을 충족시켜야 합니다. 저는 리아 세코 기자의 도움을 받아 이 섹션을 편집할 예정입니다. 현재, 우리는 아직 이 섹션에 적합한 이름을 찾지 못하고 있습니다. 그러므로, 기사 아이디어와 함께 이름도 자유롭게 제출해 주시기 바랍니다.

어휘 launch 시작하다 feature 특집 edition 판, 호 highlight 강조하다 uplifting 희망적인 inspiring 고무적인 region 지역 motivate 동기를 부여하다 assistance 도움, 지원 have yet to 아직 ~하지 않다 come up with ~을 생각하다 suitable 적합한

Q. [1], [2], [3], [4]로 표시된 곳 중에서 다음 문장이 들어가기에 가장 적합한 위치는?

"지면이 허락하면 기사에는 사진이 같이 실릴 것입니다."

(A) [1]   (B) [2]
(C) [3]   (D) [4]

| 문장 삽입 | 기출 유형 연습하기   본책 p. 299 |

1 (B)   **2** (A)   **3** (B)   **4** (B)   **5** (A)

저는 5월 10일 부교수 직책에서 사임하려고 합니다. -[1]-. 우리 학교에서 가르치는 것을 굉장히 좋아한 만큼 번스타인 음악 학교에서 물러나고자 하는 그 결정은 상당히 어려웠습니다. -[2]-. 몬태규에서의 직책이 **그러한 성장에** 기회를 제공해 줄 것이라 믿습니다.

어휘 resign 사임하다 senior lecturer 부교수 extremely 극히 tremendously 엄청나게 such 앞에 이미 언급한, 그런[그러한]

1 그러나 저는 제 음악 경력의 다음 단계로 넘어갈 시점이라고 생각합니다.

(A) [1]   (B) [2]

12월 10일 플라스켓 출판사의 **편집자들을 대상으로 전화 회의가** 있을 예정입니다. -[1]-. 877-555-1600으로 샐리 그레이엄에게 12월 5일까지 연락하여 접근 코드를 받으세요. -[2]-. 또한, 콘라드 바이스가 프로젝트 관리와 관련해 컴퓨터 워크숍을 진행하는 1월 12일을 달력에 표기하세요.

어휘 editor 편집자 obtain 얻다, 획득하다 mark 표시하다 management 관리

2 이는 뉴욕 본사 직원들과 필라델피아 공장 직원들을 포함합니다.

(A) [1]   (B) [2]

이 식당이 제공하는 경험은 맛있는 음식 그 이상이다. -[1]-. 내가 방문하여 착석하자마자 **오페라 가수 안토니오 베르톨리가 노래를 시작했다.** -[2]-. 사장이 말하길 만약 이런 음악 공연이 인기가 있을 시 더 많은 저녁 공연을 추가할 계획이라고 한다.

어휘 prove ~임이 드러나다 performance 공연

3 그의 공연 이후 베르톨리 씨가 테이블로 와서 식당 손님들에게 자신을 소개했다.

(A) [1]   (B) [2]

리스터즈 푸드 마켓 대변인은 올해 12월의 스완지 시가를 시작으로 향후 2년간 5곳의 새 매장을 열 것이라고 어제 발표했다. -[1]-. 그 다음으로는 리버풀에 5월 개점할 것이다. -[2]-. **마지막 매장의 위치는** 아직 결정되지 않았다.

어휘 spokesperson 대변인 determine 결정하다

4 내년 여름까지 맨체스터와 에든버러에 두 곳 더 개장할 예정이다.

(A) [1]   (B) [2]

리어 하이츠는 대학(공공기관)과 엑스너 그룹(지역 부동산 개발 업체)이 합작한 투자 사업이다. **이는 주상 복합 건물 7동으로 구성될 것이다.** -[1]-. 엑스너는 부지를 개발하고 소매점 운영을 관리할 것이다. "최근까지 대다수 학생이 통학했습니다." 아폴라얀 씨가 말했다. "현재 캠퍼스 주택을 요청하는 지원자 수가 급격하게 증가하고 있습니다." -[2]-.

5 각 동 1층에는 소매점, 2, 3층에는 학생 아파트가 들어설 예정이다.

(A) [1]   (B) [2]

ETS **PRACTICE**   본책 p. 300

1 (A)   **2** (C)

기사

시내 경제 단신

크레스트 서점이 웨스트포드의 라크 가 112번지에 있는 가게의 원래 건물 옆 소매점을 매입했다. 이 인기 있는 시내 가게는 절실하게 필요한 확장 공사에 새로운 공간을 사용할 예정이다.

"우리는 3년 전에 문을 열었고 순조롭게 운영했죠." 설립자이자 공동 소유주인 애나 리가 말한다. **"독립 서점이 더 이상 예전만큼 성공적이지 않다고들 했죠.** 우리는 그 반대가 사실이라는 것을 발견했습니다."

리 씨에 따르면 개조된 크레스트 서점은 원래 서점의 두 배가 넘는 면적이 될 것이다. "재개장은 10월 12일에 합니다." 리 씨가 말한다. "추가 공간 때문에 아주 들떠 있어요. 이제 작가 출연, 도서 사인회, 그리고 아주 인기 많은 크레스트 독서 클럽 모임 같은 행사를 더 많이 열 수 있으니까요."

어휘 purchase 구매하다; 구매(품) retail 소매의; 소매
original 원래의, 독창적인 premises 부지, 구내
downtown 시내 fixture 정착물, 고정물 much-needed 절실하게 필요한 expansion 확장, 확대
hit the ground running 순조롭게 진행하다, 잘 되어 가다 founder 설립자 co-owner 공동 소유주
independent 독립적인 no longer 더 이상 ~이 아닌 used to (과거에 한때) ~했다 revamp 개조하다
double 두 배가 되다, 두 배로 만들다 take place 일어나다, 발생하다 excited 들뜬, 흥분한 host 주최하다 author 저자 appearance 출연, 외관

1 [1], [2], [3], [4]로 표시된 곳 중에서 다음 문장이 들어가기에 가장 적합한 위치는?

"우리는 그 반대가 사실이라는 것을 발견했습니다."

(A) [1]   (B) [2]
(C) [3]   (D) [4]

해설 **문장 삽입:** 제시된 문장은 '그 반대(the opposite)가 사실이라는 것을 발견했다'는 의미이므로, 서로 반대의 의미를 지닌 두 문장 사이에 들어가야 한다. [1] 앞에서는 독립 서점이 더 이상 예전만큼 성공적이지 않다(independent bookstores are no longer as successful as they used to be)는 내용이 왔으며, [1] 뒤의 다음 단락에서는 개조된 크레스트 서점은 원래 서점의 두 배가 넘는 면적이 될 것(the revamped Crest Bookstore will be more than double the size of the original)이라는 반대되는 내용이 왔다. 따라서 제시된 문장이 [1]에 들어가야 글의 흐름이 단절되지 않고 자연스러워지므로, 정답은 (A)이다.

어휘 opposite 정반대의 것; 정반대의

후기

저는 상업용 고층 빌딩의 로비를 디자인하고 있습니다. 프로젝트에는 소파, 안락의자 여러 개를 포함해 실내장식품이 꽤 많이 필요했습니다. 제가 주로 같이 작업하는 실내장식품 회사는 일을 아주 잘하지만 제 의뢰인의 예산을 벗어나서 다른 회사에서 견적을 받아 보기로 했습니다. **갱글리 실내장식이 경쟁 업체들보다 훨씬 낮은 금액의 견적을 보내 줘서 같이 작업하기로 결정했습니다.** 좀 더 현명했어야 했습니다. **확실히 싼 게 비지떡입니다.** 작업을 예상보다 일찍 끝내기는 했지만 일은 무척 엉성했습니다. 제가 선택한 천은 희미한 검정색과 금색 체크무늬였습니다. 천 조각을 같이 꿰맬 때 무늬가 정확하게 맞지 않았습니다. 이 회사에는 더 이상 일을 맡기지 않을 생각입니다.

– 디브야 아그라왈

어휘 commercial 상업적인, 영리의 high-rise 고층빌딩
fairly 꽤, 공정하게 multiple 다수의 couch 소파
lounge chair 안락의자 upholstery (가구 덮개 등의) 실내장식(품) normally 보통, 평소 budget 예산(안)
estimate 견적(서) competitor 경쟁사, 경쟁자
sloppy 날림의, 엉성한 faint 희미한 sew 바느질하다, 꿰매다 match up 맞다 correctly 정확하게

2 [1], [2], [3], [4]로 표시된 곳 중에서 다음 문장이 들어가기에 가장 적합한 위치는?

"좀 더 현명했어야 했습니다."

(A) [1]   (B) [2]
(C) [3]   (D) [4]

해설 **문장 삽입:** I should have known better는 '좀 더 현명했어야 했다, 그러지 말았어야 했다'라는 의미로, 과거의 일에 대한 후회나 유감을 나타내는 표현이다. 따라서 제시된 문장은 가장 낮은 금액을 제시한 갱글리 실내장식과 작업하기로 결정했다(Ganguly Upholstery gave me a quote that was far below that of its competitors, so I decided to go with them)는 내용과 싼 게 비지떡

이었다(Clearly, you get what you pay for)고 후회하는 내용 사이인 [3]에 들어가야 글의 흐름이 자연스러워지므로 정답은 (C)이다.

1 (A)	2 (D)	3 (B)	4 (C)	5 (C)	6 (A)
7 (D)	8 (A)	9 (A)	10 (B)	11 (C)	

Questions 1-3 이메일

수신: 다니엘 비셋 〈dbisset@goldbear.ca〉
발신: 세시 존스 〈sjones@greenfieldtheatre.ca〉
제목: 정보
날짜: 4월 3일

비셋 씨께,

¹최근 그린필드 극장의 〈벨르 인 화이트〉 온라인 티켓을 구매해 주셔서 감사드립니다. 그레이스 티옹이 세계에서 처음 선보이는 공연으로 기대가 큰 행사입니다. 5월 1일 저녁 8시 공연 티켓 2매는 매표소에 보관됩니다. **²,³공연 시작 30분 전에 매표소로 오십시오.** 티켓을 수령할 때 신분증 제시를 요청 받게 됩니다. **³만약 학생 할인으로 구매하셨다면 최근 학생증을 제시해 주세요.** 공연이 시작되고 10분이 지나면 누구도 착석할 수 없습니다.

그린필드 극장 회원이 되시는 것을 고려해 보세요. 특별 행사 초대는 물론이고 티켓과 주차비도 할인 받으실 수 있습니다. 저희 웹사이트 www.greenfieldtheatre.ca/subscription 에서 더 많은 정보를 보실 수 있습니다.

세시 존스
매표소 관리자

어휘 purchase 구매(품); 구매하다　theatre 극장
premiere 초연, 개봉　anticipate 기대하다
performance 공연　present 제시하다　current
최근의, 현재의　subscriber 구독자, 회원　invitation
초대

1 이메일을 보낸 이유는?

(A) 주문 확정
(B) 여배우 홍보
(C) 특별 학생 작품 광고
(D) 새 주차 구역 알리기

해설 **주제/목적:** 첫 단락 첫 문장을 보면 〈벨르 인 화이트〉 온라인 티켓을 구매해 줘서 감사하다(Thank you for your recent online ticket purchase for ~)는 통상적인 인사말로 구매 내역을 확인해 주고 있다. 따라서 온라인 티켓 주문을 확인해 주기 위해 보낸 이메일임을 알 수 있으므로 정답은 (A)이다.

어휘 confirm 확인하다　promote 홍보하다　bring
attention to ~으로 관심을 끌다

패러프레이징
지문의 your recent online ticket purchase
➡ 보기의 an order

2 이메일에서 비셋 씨에게 무엇을 하라고 조언하는가?

(A) 회원 자격 갱신하기　(B) 할인 쿠폰 가져오기
(C) 날짜 바꾸기　　　　　(D) 일찍 도착하기

해설 **세부 사항:** 첫 번째 단락 중반부에서 존스 씨는 비셋 씨에게 공연 티켓 2매는 매표소에 보관된다면서 공연 시작 30분 전에 매표소로 오라(Please come to the box office 30 minutes before the show starts)고 조언하고 있다. 따라서 정답은 (D)이다.

어휘 renew 갱신하다　subscription 가입, 구독

패러프레이징
지문의 come ~ 30 minutes before the show starts
➡ 보기의 Arrive early

3 [1], [2], [3], [4]로 표시된 곳 중에서 다음 문장이 들어가기에 가장 적합한 위치는?

"티켓을 수령할 때 신분증 제시를 요청 받게 됩니다."

(A) [1]　　　　　　　　(B) [2]
(C) [3]　　　　　　　　(D) [4]

해설 **문장 삽입:** 제시된 문장의 when you pick up your tickets가 문제 해결의 단서로, '티켓을 수령할 때 신분증을 제시해야 한다'는 의미이다. 티켓 수령은 매표소에 도착한 후에 일어나는 일이므로, 주어진 문장은 매표소 도착 시간에 대해 언급한 후인 [2]에 들어가야 글의 흐름이 자연스러워진다. 또한 제시문의 신분증과 관련하여 학생증에 대한 언급이 [2] 뒤에서 이어지므로 내용이 자연스럽게 연결된다. 따라서 정답은 (B)이다.

어휘 identification 신원 확인, 신분증

Questions 4-7 기사

몇 가지 구직 면접 전략
스콧 프리드먼

축하합니다! 면접 준비를 하고 계시는군요. 여기 자신감을 높이고 일자리를 제안받을 확률을 높이는 데 도움이 되는 몇 가지 전략이 있습니다.

첫째, **⁴잠재 고용주를 조사하세요. 회사의 사명, 가치 및 목표, 그리고 회사가 업계에 어떻게 기여하는지 알아보십시오.** 현재 진행 중인 프로젝트도 알아보세요. 회사의 어떤 점이 인상 깊었는지 이야기할 수 있도록 준비하세요. 채용 관리자에 대해 알아보면 공감대를 형성하는 데 도움이 됩니다. 회사가 어떤 곳이고 회사에서 어떤 역할을 하고 싶은지 이해하고 있다는 것을 보여 주십시오.

둘째, ⁵전형적인 면접 질문들에 대한 답변을 연습하십시오. 채용공고에 있는 핵심 단어들을 식별하고 답변에 포함시키세요. 해당 직책에 필요한 기술을 보유하고 있음을 보여 주도록 과거에 상황을 어떻게 처리했는지 예시를 준비해 두세요.

셋째, 채용 담당자에게 물어볼 질문을 준비하세요. 여기에는 어떤 승진 기회가 있는지, 지원하는 직책에는 어떤 유형의 사람이 성공하는지 등이 포함됩니다. 또한 ⁶어떻게 평가 받을지, 그 직책에 출장이 필요한지, 혹은 멘토링이 가능한지도 물어볼 수 있습니다. 급여 및 휴가 기간에 대한 질문은 제기하지 마십시오. 해당 질문은 두 번째 면접을 위해 남겨 두세요.

면접은 긴장될 수 있습니다. ⁷불안감을 덜려면 면접장까지 넉넉하게 시간 여유를 두고 출발하고 15분에서 20분 일찍 도착해 자리를 잡도록 계획하세요. 여러분이 보는 모든 사람들에게 따뜻하게 인사하고 시간을 내준 것에 감사하세요. 침착하고 자신감을 가지세요. 해낼 수 있다고 스스로 믿으십시오. 면접관도 반드시 그 사실을 알도록 하세요.

어휘 **strategy** 전략 **line up** 줄을 서다 **confident** 자신감 있는 **increase** 높이다 **potential** 잠재적인 **contribute to** ~에 기여하다 **typical** 전형적인 **identify** 식별하다 **incorporate** 포함하다 **evaluate** 평가하다 **callback** (2차 면접 등을 위한) 재통보 **reduce** 덜다 **anxiety** 불안, 염려

4 잠재 고용주를 조사하는 이유로 언급된 것은?

(A) 경쟁업체가 어디인지 알기 위해
(B) 고객 유치 방법을 확립하기 위해
(C) 업계에서 갖는 중요성을 판단하기 위해
(D) 직원을 성의 있게 대하는지 알아보기 위해

해설 **세부 사항:** 두 번째 단락 첫 문장에서 잠재 고용주를 조사하라(research the potential employer)고 한 뒤, 회사의 사명, 가치 및 목표, 그리고 회사가 업계에 어떻게 기여하는지 알아보라(Find out the company's mission ~ how it contributes to the industry)며 조사할 때 중점적으로 살펴볼 항목을 설명한 것으로 보아 (C)가 정답이다.

어휘 **competitor** 경쟁업체 **attract** 유치하다 **determine** 판단하다 **loyalty** 충성(도)

5 구직 면접자가 조언 받은 일은?

(A) 채용담당자와 면담 일정 잡기
(B) 면접관에게 감사 편지 보내기
(C) 일반적인 질문에 대한 답변 준비하기
(D) 작업 샘플 제출하기

해설 **세부 사항:** 세 번째 단락 첫 문장에서 전형적인 면접 질문들에 대한 답변을 연습하라(practice answers to typical interview questions)고 조언하고 있으므로 (C)가 정답이다.

패러프레이징
지문의 practice answers to typical ~ questions
➡ 보기의 Prepare responses to usual questions

6 기사에 따르면, 지원자가 첫 번째 면접에서 묻지 말아야 하는 것은?

(A) 일자리의 보수
(B) 실적 평가 방법
(C) 멘토 제공 여부
(D) 출장 필요성 여부

해설 **Not/True:** 네 번째 단락 세 번째 문장에서 어떻게 평가 받을지, 그 직책에 출장이 필요한지, 혹은 멘토링이 가능한지도 물어볼 수 있다(You may also ask how you would be evaluated ~ mentoring is available)고 했으므로 (B), (C), (D)는 질문 항목에 속한다. 하지만 바로 다음 문장에서 급여 및 휴가 기간에 대한 질문은 하지 말고 두 번째 면접을 위해 남겨 두라(Do not raise questions about salary and vacation time; save those for your callback interview)고 했으므로 (A)가 정답이다.

어휘 **performance** 실적 **assess** 평가하다

패러프레이징
지문의 salary ➡ 보기의 How much the job pays

7 [1], [2], [3], [4]로 표시된 곳 중에서 다음 문장이 가장 적합한 위치는?

"면접은 긴장될 수 있다."

(A) [1]   (B) [2]
(C) [3]   (D) [4]

해설 **문장 삽입:** 제시된 문장은 '면접은 긴장될 수 있다'며 면접 시 느낄 수 있는 심리 상태에 대해 이야기하고 있다. 따라서 불안감을 덜려면 면접장까지 넉넉하게 시간 여유를 두고 출발하고 15분에서 20분 일찍 도착해 자리를 잡도록 계획하라(To reduce your anxiety, ~ twenty minutes early to get settled)며 면접자가 긴장감을 완화할 수 있는 방법에 대해 조언하고 있는 문장 앞에 들어가면 글의 흐름이 자연스러우므로 (D)가 정답이다.

Questions 8-11 기사

글래스턴빌(9월 2일) – 에클렉틱스 엔터테인먼트는 오늘 다가오는 오픈 슬레이트 축제 장소가 변경되었다고 발표했다. 이 행사는 이제 10월 22일과 23일에 글래스턴빌에 있는 누자 콜라 음료 공장에서 열린다. ⁸이번 변경으로 축제 무대는 이전에 계획된 대로 오후 10시에 문을 닫지 않고 자정 12시까지 열린다.

누자 콜라 음료공장은 지난 30년 동안 글래스턴빌 스카이라인의 일부였다. 이 공장은 8년 전 상징적인 공간에 현대적인 편안

함과 공업시설의 매력을 결합해 다채로운 행사를 개최할 수 있는 공연장으로 새롭게 단장됐다. ¹¹**공연장에 가는 길은 빠르고 편리하다.** 운전자들은 I-9 간선도로를 타고 32번 출구로 나가면 공연장에 도착할 수 있다. ¹¹지하철 이용자는 적색 노선을 타고 호스트라 가 역으로 가서 공연장까지 동쪽으로 세 블록을 걸어야 한다.

^{9, 10}**오픈 슬레이트 축제는 올해로 5회를 맞이하고 있으며, 세계에서 가장 인기 있는 순회공연 밴드들이 출연한다.** 팝 돌풍을 일으키고 있는 패티 피넷이 금요일 밤 주무대에 등장하고, 토요일 밤에는 급부상하고 있는 스타 코로나스와 재즈계의 전설 클리본 벨이 공연할 예정이다.

올해 오픈 슬레이트 축제의 사전 예약 할인 티켓은 www.eklectix.com/openslate/tickets에서 구입할 수 있다.

어휘 **bottling plant** 음료 공장 **previously** 이전에 **refurbish** 새로 단장하다 **breakout star** 급부상하는 스타 **bill** (공연 등) 프로그램

8 **장소가 바뀐 이유는?**

(A) 더 긴 기간 공연할 수 있게 하려고
(B) 참석자에게 더 많은 공간을 제공하려고
(C) 축제를 대중교통과 가깝게 옮기려고
(D) 축제 예산을 절감하려고

해설 **세부 사항:** 첫 문단 마지막에 이번 변경으로 축제 무대는 이전에 계획된 대로 오후 10시에 문을 닫지 않고 자정 12시까지 열린다(This change will allow the festival ~ open until 12:00 midnight, instead of closing at 10:00 P.M.)고 했으므로 공연 시간 연장을 위해 행사장이 변경되었음을 알 수 있다. 따라서 (A)가 정답이다.

어휘 **attendee** 참석자 **reduce** 절감하다 **budget** 예산

9 **축제는 언제 시작되었는가?**

(A) 5년 전   (B) 8년 전
(C) 10년 전   (D) 30년 전

해설 **세부 사항:** 세 번째 문단의 첫 문장에서 오픈 슬레이트 축제는 올해로 5회를 맞이한다(The Open Slate festival celebrates its fifth anniversary this year)고 했으므로 (A)가 정답이다.

10 **오픈 슬레이트 축제의 특징은?**

(A) 국제 영화   (B) 음악 공연
(C) 지역 예술가   (D) 패션 디자이너

해설 **세부 사항:** 세 번째 문단의 첫 문장에서 오픈 슬레이트 축제는 세계에서 가장 인기 있는 순회공연 밴드들이 출연한다(The Open Slate festival celebrates ~ featuring some of the hottest touring bands in the world)고 했으므로 축제가 음악 공연으로 구성되어 있음을 알 수 있다. 따라서 (B)가 정답이다.

---

11 **[1], [2], [3], [4]로 표시된 곳 중에서 다음 문장이 가장 적합한 위치는?**

"운전자들은 I-9 간선도로를 타고 32번 출구로 나가면 공연장에 도착할 수 있다."

(A) [1]   (B) [2]
(C) [3]   (D) [4]

해설 **문장 삽입:** 제시된 문장은 '운전자들은 I-9 간선도로를 타고 32번 출구로 나가면 공연장에 도착할 수 있다'며 공연장에 차로 가는 방법을 안내하고 있다. 따라서 공연장 가는 길에 대해 언급하고 있는 공연장에 가는 길은 빠르고 편리하다는 문장과 지하철 이용자가 공연장에 가는 방법을 안내하는 문장의 사이인 [3]에 들어가는 것이 글의 흐름상 자연스러우므로 (C)가 정답이다.

UNIT 06   동의어 문제

에디슨, 〈손끝의 금융 소식〉
맥스웰 존스톤
리젠트 산업단지 600번지, 스위트 25
그랜트, 뉴욕 주 18387

4월 1일

존스톤 씨께,

시간이 빠르게 지나가서, 매달 〈에디슨〉을 받아 보신 지 이제 거의 1년이 되었습니다. 당신은 이 구독을 통해 금융계의 최신 소식을 계속 접하실 수 있었습니다. 그러나 지금 결정하지 않으시면 한 달 뒤, 당신은 **마지막 호**를 받게 되실 겁니다. 우리는 당신이 중단 없이 계속해서 독자가 되어 주시기를 바랍니다.

어휘 **pass** 지나가다 **nearly** 거의 **subscription** 구독 **informed** 잘 아는 **issue** 호 **unless** ~하지 않는 한 **readership** 독자(층) **interruption** 중단

Q. 편지에서 첫 번째 단락 5행의 "issue"와 의미상 가장 가까운 단어는?

(A) 계산서   (B) 혜택
(C) 발행물   (D) 문제

동의어 | 기출 유형 연습하기				본책 p. 305
1 (B)	**2** (B)	**3** (A)	**4** (A)	**5** (B)
6 (B)	**7** (B)	**8** (B)	**9** (A)	**10** (B)

신분증에 기재된 이름과 예약된 이름이 **일치해야** 합니다.

어휘 match 일치하다

1 (A) 경쟁하다 (B) 일치하다

타이어에 사용된 고무가 너무 빨리 **마모될** 수 있다.

어휘 rubber 고무 be subject to ~되기 쉽다, ~의 대상이다
premature 너무 이른, 정상보다 빠른

2 (A) 옷 (B) 손상

시민들은 캠페인을 통해 상당한 액수의 기부금을 **모았습니다.**

어휘 raise 모으다 significant 상당한 donation 기부

3 (A) 모았다 (B) 들어올렸다

보다 상세한 정보는 13페이지에서 시작하는 **다음** 섹션에서 제공됩니다.

어휘 detailed 상세한 succeeding 다음의

4 (A) 다음의 (B) 달성하는

최대 30일까지 누적된 휴가를 허용하는 방침이 여전히 **시행된다는** 것에 유의하십시오.

어휘 accumulate 모으다, 축적하다 leave 휴가 in place 시행되는

5 (A) 필요한 (B) 시행되는

두 항공사에서 이미 구입한 항공권은 그대로 **인정될** 것이다.

어휘 airline 항공사 honor 존중하다, (유효성을) 인정하다

6 (A) 보상되다 (B) 인정되다

빌랙스 자산 관리가 6월 15일에 상 파울로 아파트 단지에 대한 책임을 **맡게** 될 예정임을 알려 드립니다.

어휘 assume 떠맡다 responsibility 책임, 책무
complex 복합 건물, 단지

7 (A) 가정하다 (B) 인계 받다

그 가이드북은 꼭 가 봐야 하는 유명 관광지뿐만 아니라 거의 알려지지 않은 장소도 **다루고** 있다.

어휘 sight 명소[관광지]

8 (A) 보호하다 (B) 포함하다

제때 이 문제를 **처리해** 주셔서 감사합니다.

어휘 attend to 처리하다, 다루다 in a timely manner
시기 적절하게

9 (A) 처리 (B) 참석

주인 셰릴 페어리는 공원이 조성된 이후로 사업이 급격히 **성장하는 것을** 보았다고 말한다.

어휘 pick up 회복[개선]되다, 더 강해지다 dramatically
급격히

10 (A) 모으다 (B) 증진하다

ETS PRACTICE 본책 p. 306

1 (C) **2** (D)

기사

저는 최근 몇 년간 수십 곳의 제조 공장을 방문했고, 정보를 더 잘 알게 되었다기보다는 부담스럽다고 느끼며 시설을 나서기 일쑤였습니다. 일반적인 견학은 여러 복잡한 기계들을 관찰하고 많은 관리자와 근로자들을 소개받는 일을 포함하고 있습니다. 많은 견학 가이드들은 너무 많은 정보를 제공합니다. 게다가, 그들은 방문객들을 혼란스럽게 할 수 있는 지나치게 기술적인 용어를 사용합니다.

이러한 견학을 통해 가장 많은 이득을 취하려면, 다음 제안 사항들을 염두에 두세요. 첫째, 견학 당일에 앞서 공장에 관해 사전 조사를 하세요. 이렇게 하면, 공장 운영에 대해 **초점이 맞춰진** 질문을 하실 수 있습니다. 두 번째, 당신의 회사로부터 제조 장비를 실제로 사용하는 직원들 즉, 생산 관리자뿐 아니라 고위 관리직 등 적절한 사람을 데려오도록 하세요.

어휘 dozens of 수십 개의 facility 시설 overwhelmed
압도된, 부담을 느끼는 informed 잘 아는 typical
전형적인 observe 관찰하다 complex 복잡한
present 제시하다 confuse 혼란스럽게 하다
benefit from ~로부터 이득을 얻다 keep ~ in
mind ~을 염두에 두다 preliminary 예비의 this
way 이렇게 하여 representative 대표자 senior
management 고위 관리직 production operator
생산 관리자 manufacturing 제조업

1 **기사에서 두 번째 단락 3행의 "focused"와 의미상 가장 가까운 단어는?**

(A) 주의를 기울이는 (B) 어려운

(C) 구체적인 (D) 최종의

해설 **동의어:** 공장 견학 전에 사전 연구를 하라(do preliminary
research on plant ~)며 이렇게 하면, 공장 운영에 대해
좀 더 초점이 맞춰진 질문을 할 수 있다고 했으므로, 막연하
지 않고 구체적인 질문을 할 수 있다는 의미로 쓰였다. 따라
서 정답은 (C) specific이다.

편지

무탐비 씨께,

6월 2일 개점 예정인 프라임 내셔널 뱅크(PNB) 더반 채츠워스 지점 지점장직에 제가 적합한지 검토해 주셨으면 합니다. 아시다시피 저는 지난 5년 동안 케이프타운 벨빌에 있는 PNB 지점에서 이 직위에 근무해 왔습니다.

지식과 기량 외에도 저는 다른 사람들과 달리 지점장직에 특별한 **특성**을 도입하고 있습니다. 바로 재계 및 지역사회 지도자들을 비롯해 많은 지역 주민들과 대인 관계를 맺는 것입니다. 2년 전까지 부모님이 채츠워스에 인기 식당을 소유하고 계셔서 많은 지역 주민들과 알고 지냈습니다. 따라서 저는 고객 기반을 구축함으로써 회사에 귀중한 기여를 할 수 있습니다.

고려해 주시면 감사하겠습니다. 회신 고대하겠습니다.

어휘 consider 고려하다 scheduled to ~할 예정인 capacity (공식적인) 지위[역할] apart from ~ 이외에 knowledge 지식 particular 특별한 dimension 차원, 관점, 특성 personal 개인적인 numerous 많은 resident 거주민 community 지역 사회, 공동체 own 소유하다 therefore 그러므로 valuable 귀중한 contribution to ~에 대한 기여[공헌] client base 고객 기반 consideration 고려, 배려

2 편지에서 두 번째 단락 1행의 "dimension"과 의미상 가장 가까운 단어는?

(A) 결정   (B) 비율
(C) 쟁점   (D) 특징

해설 **동의어:** I bring a particular dimension to the position that others may not은 '다른 사람들과 달리 지점장직에 특별한 특성을 도입하고 있다'는 의미로, 편지 발신인이 자신만이 가진 특성에 대해서 이야기하고 있는 것을 알 수 있다. 따라서 '특성, 특징'을 뜻하는 (D) characteristic이 정답이다.

어휘 determination 결정, 결심 proportion 비율, 부분 issue 쟁점 characteristic 특징

ETS **TEST** 본책 p. 307

| 1 (C) | 2 (C) | 3 (A) | 4 (D) | 5 (B) |
| 6 (B) | 7 (D) | 8 (A) | 9 (C) | 10 (D) |

Questions 1-3 회람

회람

수신: 엘크스턴 시 직원
발신: 그레이스 오카로
날짜: 8월 9일

제목: 새 웹사이트

[1]새 웹사이트가 처음 공개되어 기쁩니다. 이제 엘크스턴 주민과 관광객 모두 정부 서비스와 우리 시에서 보고, 체험할 수 있는 재미있는 것들에 대한 정보를 더 쉽게 찾을 수 있게 됐습니다. 그러나 [2]새로운 웹 플랫폼의 결정적인 장점은 이전에 비해 악성 코드와 사이버 공격에 대비해 훨씬 더 많은 보호 기능을 제공한다는 점입니다.

처음 로그인 페이지에 갈 때 새 암호를 설정하려면 거기에 표시되는 단계를 따르기만 하면 됩니다. 시스템에 계속 접근하려면 6개월마다 암호를 변경해야 합니다. [3]6개월 수준이 가까워지면 시스템에서 자동으로 알림 이메일을 보냅니다.

어휘 rollout 공개 critical 결정적인 protection 보호 malware 악성 코드 previously 이전에 maintain 계속하다 approach 가까워지다

1 회람에 따르면, 웹사이트에 접속하는 이유는?

(A) 상품을 주문하려고
(B) 서비스 예약을 요청하려고
(C) 방문 장소로 인기 많은 곳에 대해 알아보려고
(D) 웹사이트 설계 방법에 대해 알아보려고

해설 **세부 사항:** 첫 문장에서 새 웹사이트를 공개(We are pleased with the rollout of our Web site)하며, 엘크스턴 주민과 관광객 모두 정부 서비스와 우리 시에서 보고, 체험할 수 있는 재미난 것들에 대한 정보를 더 쉽게 찾을 수 있게 됐다(Elkston residents and tourists alike will have easier access ~ information about fun things to see and do in our city)고 했으므로 (C)가 정답이다.

어휘 merchandise 상품 appointment 예약

2 오카로 씨가 암시하는 것은?

(A) 그녀는 소셜 미디어 사이트에 광고할 계획이다.
(B) 그녀는 직원들이 자신의 이메일에 답장하기를 원한다.
(C) 그녀는 온라인 보안에 대해 우려해 왔다.
(D) 그녀는 직원에게 사용자 이름을 새로 만들라고 권유한다.

해설 **추론:** 첫 문단의 마지막 문장에서 오카로 씨가 새로운 웹 플랫폼의 결정적인 장점은 이전에 비해 악성 코드와 사이버 공격에 대비해 훨씬 더 많은 보호 기능을 제공한다는 점(The most critical advantage ~ provides far more protection from malware and cyberattacks than we previously had)이라고 강조한 것으로 보아, 그동안 웹사이트의 보안 상태에 대해 걱정해왔다는 것을 알 수 있다. 따라서 (C)가 정답이다.

어휘 concern 우려

패러프레이징

지문의 protection from malware and cyberattacks
➡ 보기의 online security

3 두 번째 단락 4행의 "mark"와 의미상 가장 가까운 단어는?

(A) 한도　　　　　　(B) 기호

(C) 규칙　　　　　　(D) 개념

해설　**동의어:** 의미상 6개월 '수준'이라는 뜻으로 쓰인 것이므로 정답은 (A) limit이다.

Questions 4-6 이메일

수신: 솔리다드 오르테가

발신: 크리스 해리스

날짜: 1월 20일 월요일

제목: GSBE 런치앤런 세션

오르테가 씨께,

⁴2월에 개최되고 그랜지우드 기업경영자협회(GSBE)가 주최하는 세 차례의 런치앤런 세션 중 첫 번째 세션이 2월 3일 월요일 정오에 열립니다. 장소는 브리즈 여관의 헬리코니아 룸입니다. 이 협회회원 전용 행사의 비용은 1인당 15달러입니다. 등록이 필요합니다. 1월 31일 금요일까지 웹사이트 www.gsbe.net/lal/registration에서 등록하세요.

⁴이번 행사의 발표자는 찰스 피어스 시장입니다. 피어스 시장은 이제 막 첫 ⁵**임기**를 시작했으며 우리 시의 경제를 발전시키기 위한 자신의 비전을 공유하고자 매우 열심입니다. 이 흥미로운 세션에 우리와 함께해 주시기를 바랍니다. ⁶**이 모임에 참석할 수 없는 경우, 다른 런치앤런 세션들 중 하나에 참여하는 것을 고려해 보십시오.** 다른 세션은 2월 19일 수요일과 2월 27일 목요일로 예정되어 있습니다. 자세한 내용은 www.gsbe.net/lal/info를 방문해 주세요.

크리스 해리스

그랜지우드 기업경영자협회 행사 진행자

어휘　session (특정 활동을 위한) 시간[기간]　host 주최하다　executive 경영 간부　take place 열리다　location 위치　per ~당　registration 등록　register 등록하다　mayor 시장　eager 열심인　vision 비전　interesting 흥미로운　gathering 모임　coordinator 진행자

4 2월 3일 행사에 대해 언급된 것은?

(A) 일반인에게 공개된다.

(B) 무료로 참석할 수 있다.

(C) GSBE의 사무실에서 열린다.

(D) 정부 관계자가 출연한다.

해설　**세부 사항:** 첫 단락의 첫 문장에서 2월에 개최되고 그랜지우드 기업경영자협회가 주최하는 세 차례의 런치앤런 세션 중 첫 세션이 2월 3일 월요일 정오에 열린다(The first of three lunch-and-learn sessions ~ February 3, at noon)고 했고, 두 번째 단락의 첫 문장에서 이번 행사의 발표자는 찰스 피어스 시장(The speaker at the

upcoming event will be Mayor Charles Pierce)이라고 안내하고 있다. 따라서 2월 3일 행사에 시장이 발표자로 나오고, 시장은 정부 관계자이므로 (D)가 정답이다.

패러프레이징

지문의 Mayor ⊙ 보기의 government official

5 두 번째 단락 2행의 "term"과 의미상 가장 가까운 단어는?

(A) 단어　　　　　　(B) 기간

(C) 조건　　　　　　(D) 종점

해설　**동의어:** 의미상 '임기'라는 뜻으로 쓰인 것이므로 정답은 (B) time period이다.

6 두 번째 런치앤런 세션은 언제 열리는가?

(A) 월요일　　　　　(B) 수요일

(C) 목요일　　　　　(D) 금요일

해설　**세부 사항:** 두 번째 단락의 네 번째 문장에서 이 모임에 참석할 수 없는 경우 다른 런치앤런 세션들 중 하나에 참여하는 것을 고려하라(In the event you cannot make it to this gathering ~ our other lunch-and-learn sessions)고 권유하며, 다른 세션은 2월 19일 수요일과 2월 27일 목요일로 예정되어 있다(They are scheduled for Wednesday ~ February 27)고 알려 주고 있다. 다음 세션 즉, 두 번째로 열리는 세션은 2월 19일 수요일로 예정되어 있으므로 (B)가 정답이다.

Questions 7-10 기사 발췌

플로트닉 공원 새단장한다

로라 도리엇

아라모어(6월 17일) - ⁷**아라모어 시의회는 8년 된 플로트닉 공원을 개조하기 위한 결의안을 만장일치로 승인했다.** 공원 개조는 2년 전에 처음 제안된 이후로 계속 검토되고 있었다. 그러나 마야 클라크 시장이 취임하고 나서야 변경이 마침내 승인되었다. "저는 시에 이것이 제 임기 내 주요한 첫 활동이 될 것이라고 말했고, 약속을 지킬 ⁸**생각입니다.**" 시장은 인터뷰에서 말했다.

공원이 조성된 후 ⁹**호수를 따라 이어지는 3킬로미터의 가로수 길은 아라모어 주민들의 오후 산책 장소로 선택되었다.** 하지만 머지않아 가족들은 이 공원이 아이들에게는 이상적이지 않다는 점을 깨닫게 되었다.

"⁹**우리는 주기적으로 산책로를 이용하지만,** 애들은 공을 차고 싶어 해요." 시 주민인 리암 엘리스는 말한다. "공원에는 아이들이 마음껏 뛸 수 있는 공터가 부족해요. 게다가 종종 공원에 소풍 도시락을 가지고 갈까 생각했지만, 탁자도 벤치도 없어요."

이 프로젝트를 위해 야외 활동을 위한 넓은 녹지 공간을 조성하려면 상당한 면적의 초목을 개간해야 한다. ¹⁰**놀이터, 피크**

닉 테이블, 야외 배구 네트도 반가운 추가물이 될 예정이다. 시의회는 공원 산책로를 따라 가로등을 설치하는 것에도 동의했다. ¹⁰이는 저녁 늦게까지 운동하는 것을 좋아하는 사람들의 요구에 부응하기 위해 시의 달리기 동호회가 요청한 것이다. 겨울 몇 달 동안 개조 공사가 진행될 예정이며, 내년 봄이면 공원은 다시 이용할 수 있도록 준비될 것이다.

어휘 renovate 보수[수리]하다, 개조하다 town council 시의회 unanimously 만장일치로 approve 승인하다 resolution 결의안, 해결 renovation 보수[수리], 개조 initially 처음에 propose 제안하다 under consideration 고려 중인 mayor 시장 come into office 취임하다 intend to ~할 의도이다 path 오솔길, 길 resident 거주민 stroll 산책 realize 알아차리다, 깨닫다 ideal 이상적인 trail 오솔길, 산길 lack 모자라다; 결핍 call for ~이 필요하다, ~을 요구하다 clearing 개간, 빈터 growth (초목 등이) 자란 것 make way for ~을 위해 길을 내어 주다 outdoor 야외의 addition 추가된 것[사람] request 요청 accommodate 부응하다, 수용하다 prefer to ~하기를 선호하다

7 공원 개조에 관해 명시된 것은?
   (A) 내년 봄에 시작된다.
   (B) 클라크 시장이 처음 제안했다.
   (C) 완공하는 데 2년이 걸릴 것이다.
   (D) 의회 의원 전원이 동의했다.

해설 **Not / True:** 첫 단락 첫 문장에서 아라모어 시의회는 8년 된 플로트닉 공원을 개조하기 위한 결의안을 만장일치로 승인했다(Aramore's town council has unanimously approved a resolution to renovate eight-year-old Plotnick Park)고 했으므로, 정답은 (D)이다.

어휘 complete 완성하다; 완성된 council member 의원

패러프레이징
지문의 Aramore's town council has unanimously approved a resolution ➡ 보기의 All the council members agreed to it.

8 첫 번째 단락 10행의 "intend"와 의미상 가장 가까운 단어는?
   (A) 계획하다   (B) 동의하다
   (C) 시도하다   (D) 의사소통하다

해설 **동의어:** I told the town that this would be my first major act in office, and I intend to keep that promise는 '나는 시에 이것이 임기 내 주요한 첫 활동이 될 것이라고 말했고, 약속을 지킬 생각이다'라는 의미이다. 여기에서 intend는 '~할 생각이다, 의도하다'라는 의미이므로, 정답은 (A) plan이다.

어휘 attempt 시도하다 communicate 의사소통하다, (정보 등을) 전달하다

9 주민들은 공원을 어떻게 활용해 왔는가?
   (A) 점심을 먹는다
   (B) 운동을 한다
   (C) 산책한다
   (D) 호수에서 수영한다

해설 **세부 사항:** 두 번째 단락에서 공원이 조성된 후 호수를 따라 이어지는 3킬로미터의 가로수길은 아라모어 주민들의 오후 산책 장소로 선택되었다(~ became Aramore residents' place of choice for an afternoon stroll)고 했다. 또 세 번째 단락 첫 문장의 We use the trail regularly에서도 주민들이 공원을 산책로로 이용했다는 단서를 찾을 수 있다. 따라서 정답은 (C)이다.

어휘 go for a walk 산책하러 가다

패러프레이징
지문의 an afternoon stroll ➡ 보기의 To go for walks

10 [1], [2], [3], [4]로 표시된 곳 중에서 다음 문장이 들어가기에 가장 적합한 위치는?

"시의회는 공원 산책로를 따라 가로등을 설치하는 것에도 동의했다."
   (A) [1]   (B) [2]
   (C) [3]   (D) [4]

해설 **문장 삽입:** 제시된 문장의 has also agreed to have lampposts installed가 문제 해결의 단서이다. also로 미루어 보아 주어진 문장 앞에는 동의된 가로등 설치 외에 시의회에서 추가로 하기로 동의한 내용이 와야 하며, 뒤에는 가로등과 관련된 내용이 와야 함을 유추할 수 있다. 따라서 놀이터, 피크닉 테이블, 야외 배구 네트 설치(A playground, picnic tables, and an outdoor volleyball net will be welcome additions)에 대한 내용 뒤에, 그리고 가로등 설치의 목적(to accommodate those who prefer to exercise later in the evening)에 대한 내용 앞인 (D)가 정답이다.

어휘 agree to ~하는 데 동의하다 lamppost 가로등 install 설치하다

CHAPTER 02 | 지문 유형별 공략

| UNIT 07 | 이메일 / 편지 |

ETS 예제

수신: 마리오 곤잘레스 〈mgonz@protemp.com〉
발신: 에스텔라 모랄레스 〈emorales@caixadirectcorp.com〉
제목: 지원
날짜: 7월 20일

곤잘레스 씨 귀하,

카익사 다이렉트의 하급 회계직에 지원해 주신 것에 감사드립니다.

두 명의 선임 직원이 첫 번째로 모든 지원서와 이력서를 검토합니다. **검토 후 면접 대상자로 선정되면 인사부 담당자 리카도 마르티네즈가 연락해서 약속 시간을 잡을 것입니다.** 그때, 추천인 세 명의 이름과 연락처를 요청할 것입니다.

첨부된 파일은 귀하께서 요청하신 우리 회사의 최신 연례 보고서 사본입니다. 카익사 다이렉트사에 관심을 가져 주신 것에 다시 한 번 감사드립니다.

사무실 관리자 에스텔라 모랄레스 드림
카익사 다이렉트사

어휘 accounting 회계 personnel officer 인사 담당자 set up ~을 세우다, 정하다 reference 추천인

ETS TEST

본책 p. 319

| 1 (C) | 2 (B) | 3 (D) | 4 (B) | 5 (D) |
| 6 (B) | 7 (D) | 8 (B) | 9 (A) | 10 (B) |

Questions 1-2 이메일

수신: 멜린다 라이트 〈mwright@xmail.com〉
발신: 안토니오 로시 〈antoniorossi@citadelhp.com〉
날짜: 11월 19일
제목: 에이컨 가 220번지

라이트 씨께:

¹우리는 공사를 위해 페인트를 구입했고 화요일부터 시작하리라 예상했습니다. ¹·²하지만 일기 예보에 비가 많이 올 것 같다고 하니 하루나 이틀 정도 미뤄야 할 것 같습니다. 화요일 오전까지 연락드려서 확정하도록 하겠습니다. 궁금한 점이 있으시면 이메일이나 전화 주세요. 제 휴대폰 번호는 202-555-0162입니다.

안토니오 로시
시터들 하우스 페인터스

어휘 anticipate 예상하다 forecast 일기 예보 wet 비가 오는 postpone 미루다

1 이메일의 목적은?

(A) 가격 견적서 수정하기
(B) 의견에 답변하기
(C) 새로운 소식 제공하기
(D) 주문 확인하기

해설 **주제/목적:** 첫 문장에서 우리는 공사를 위해 페인트를 구입했고 화요일부터 시작하리라 예상했다(We have purchased the paint for your project and anticipate starting on Tuesday)고 했는데 하지만 일기예보에 비가 많이 온다고 하니 하루나 이틀 정도 미뤄야 할 것 같다(However, the forecast looks very wet ~ postpone a day or two)며 작업 진행 상황과 일정에 대한 근황을 이야기하고 있으므로 (C)가 정답이다.

2 로시 씨가 공사에 관해 명시하는 것은?

(A) 반쯤 끝났다.
(B) 비 때문에 지연될 수도 있다.
(C) 화요일에 끝났다.
(D) 추가로 도장작업이 필요하다.

해설 **Not/True:** 두 번째 문장에서 로시 씨가 일기예보에 비가 많이 온다고 하니 하루나 이틀 정도 미뤄야 할 것 같다(the forecast looks very wet ~ postpone a day or two)고 했으므로 (B)가 정답이다.

패러프레이징
지문의 postpone ➡ 보기의 delayed

Questions 3-6 이메일

수신: m.chae@newmail.co.uk
발신: info@fantastisoft.co.uk
날짜: 2월 15일
제목: 판타스티소프트 프리미엄 가격 책정

채 씨께,

³귀하는 판타스티소프트 프리미엄의 과거 구독자이시므로 지금이 당사의 제품을 다시 살펴보고 소프트웨어에 대한 지식과 협업 능력을 키우기에 최적의 시기임을 알려 드리고 싶었습니다. ⁴이제 사용자는 중요한 실무 기술을 위한 교습에 중단 없이 접속할 수 있는 스마트폰 앱 같은 몇 가지 놀라운 새 기능을 이용할 수 있습니다. 이제 학습자는 더 광범위한 주제를 다루는 교습, 미리 녹화된 동영상과 게임도 선택할 수 있습니다.

그런데 이런 멋지고 새로운 기능과 함께 가격이 새롭게 책정됩니다. **⁵4월 12일부터 월 구독료는 현재처럼 9파운드가 아닌**

PART 7 | UNIT 07

12파운드이며, 연간 구독료는 90파운드에서 110파운드로 인상됩니다. 수정된 가격은 판타스티소프트 프리미엄이 학습자에게 제공하는 가치를 제대로 반영하고 있습니다. 4월 12일 이전에 www.fantastisoft.co.uk/premium을 방문하시면, 오늘처럼 더 저렴한 가격으로 판타스티소프트 프리미엄을 구독하실 수 있습니다!

판타스티소프트 프리미엄 고객의 의견을 읽어 보십시오:

"**⁶저는 몇 달 전에 판타스티소프트 프리미엄으로 업그레이드했고, 교습이나 게임은 곧 매일 하는 일과의 일부가 되었습니다.** 저는 정말 새로운 역량을 많이 배웠고, 직장에서 승진하게된 것도 틀림없이 그 덕분이라 생각해요. 프리미엄은 그만한 값어치가 있습니다!" – 구스타프 롤런드

"**⁶판타스티소프트 프리미엄 사용자가 된 이후, 저는 매일 아침 판타스티소프트 수업을 시작해 제 역량이 녹슬지 않도록 합니다.** 자신감이 부쩍 커졌어요. 프리미엄은 제 사업을 한 단계 도약시키는 데 큰 도움이 되었습니다." – 모니카 타흐신

판타스티소프트 팀

어휘 subscriber 구독자 increase 늘리다 soft skills (남들과 소통하며 일하는) 협업 능력 feature 기능 on-the-go 끊임없는 a range of 다양한 feature 기능 annual 연간의 routine 일과 promote 승진시키다 confident 자신감 있는

3 **이메일의 목적은?**

(A) 다가오는 할인 광고하기
(B) 고객 추천사 수집하기
(C) 현재 사용자에게 빠른 결제 요청하기
(D) 이전 사용자에게 재가입 독려하기

해설 **주제/목적:** 이메일의 첫 문장에서 귀하는 판타스티소프트 프리미엄의 과거 구독자이시므로 지금이 당사의 제품을 다시 살펴보고 소프트웨어에 대한 지식과 협업 능력을 키우기에 최적의 시기임을 알려 드리고 싶었다(Because you are a past subscriber ~ knowledge of software and soft skills)며 예전에 서비스 이용자였던 수신자에게 재가입을 고려할 것을 권하는 말로 시작한 뒤, 재가입 시 누릴 수 있는 이점에 대해 열거하고 있으므로 (D)가 정답이다.

어휘 testimonial 추천서, 추천의 글

4 **최근 판타스티소프트 프리미엄에 추가된 기능은?**

(A) 기량 연습을 위한 가상 상대
(B) 교습 접근 용이성
(C) 그래픽이 향상된 교육용 게임
(D) 실황 실무 동영상

해설 **세부 사항:** 첫 단락의 두 번째 문장에서 이제 사용자는 중요한 실무 기술을 위한 교습에 중단 없이 접속할 수 있는 스마트폰 앱 같은 몇 가지 놀라운 새 기능을 이용할 수 있

다(Our users now have access to ~ on-the-go access to lessons for essential business skills)며 새로 추가된 기능에 대해 언급하고 있으므로 (B)가 정답이다.

5 **4월 12일 이후 판타스티소프트 프리미엄 연간 비용은?**

(A) 9파운드   (B) 12파운드
(C) 90파운드   (D) 110파운드

해설 **세부 사항:** 두 번째 단락 두 번째 문장에서 4월 12일부터 월 구독료는 현재처럼 9파운드가 아닌 12파운드이며 연간구독료는 90파운드에서 110파운드로 인상된다(Starting on 12 April ~ annual subscription will increase to £110 from £90)고 했으므로 (D)가 정답이다.

6 **롤런드 씨와 타흐신 씨에 대한 설명으로 옳은 것은?**

(A) 자영업을 한다.
(B) 매일 판타스티소프트 프리미엄을 이용한다.
(C) 최근에 승진했다.
(D) 판타스티소프트 프리미엄이 더 저렴해야 한다고 생각한다.

해설 **Not/True:** 이메일 후반부의 고객 후기에서 롤런드 씨는 몇 달 전에 판타스티소프트 프리미엄으로 업그레이드했고 교습이나 게임은 곧 매일 하는 일과가 되었다(I upgraded to Fantastisoft Premium ~ my daily routine)고 했고, 타흐신 씨는 판타스티소프트 프리미엄 사용자가 된 이후 매일 아침 판타스티소프트 수업을 시작해 역량이 녹슬지 않도록 한다(Since I became a Fantastisoft Premium user ~ keep my skills fresh)고 했다. 두 사람 모두 매일 프리미엄을 활용하고 있다고 공통적으로 이야기하고 있으므로 (B)가 정답이다.

패러프레이징

지문의 daily & every morning ➡ 보기의 every day

Questions 7-10 편지

모어하우스 서플라이어즈
리즈, 영국

고객님께,

최근 주문하신 물품을 배송하게 되어 기쁩니다. **⁷첨부된 배송 전표에 나와 있는 모든 물품이 포장물에 동봉되어 있는지 확인해 주세요.**

수선 서비스를 이용하셨으므로 옷에 붙은 치수 라벨이 현재 치수를 더 이상 반영하지 못하는 점 유의하세요. 또한 **¹⁰저희가 줄인 셔츠 소매가 요청보다 1.5센티미터까지 길어 보일 겁니다. 이것은 실수가 아닙니다.** ¹⁰통상 줄어드는 정도를 감안했습니다. **⁸소매를 원하는 길이로 만드려면 셔츠를 세 번 세탁하세요.**

앞으로 주문을 위해, 당사는 아래 표준 주문 제작 서비스를 모두 제공하니 유념하세요:

- **⁷소맷부리 글자도안 추가**
- 호주머니 추가
- 바지 길이 줄이기
- 소매 길이 줄이기
- 단추 교체(대부분 품목)

⁹가격과 제약 조건 등 수선 서비스 전체 목록은 봄이나 겨울 카탈로그 뒷면에 있는 차트를 보세요. 가장 최근 카탈로그를 받으시려면 웹사이트 고객서비스란에서 우편 발송용 주소를 제공할 수 있는 양식을 이용하세요.

감사합니다.

프레데릭 가르자
재단 책임자

어휘 **take advantage of** ~을 이용하다 **alteration** 수선 **garment** 옷 **measurement** 치수 **shrinkage** 줄어드는 정도 **assume** 형태를 띠다 **customisation** 주문 제작 **monogram** 글자 도안 **restriction** 제약

7 모어하우스 서플라이어즈는 어떤 업체인가?

(A) 건설 자재 생산업체
(B) 미술용품점
(C) 가구 제조업체
(D) 의류업체

해설 **추론:** 첫 단락에서 첨부된 배송 전표에 나와 있는 모든 물품이 포장물에 동봉되어 있는지 확인하라(Please ensure that all items ~ are included in this package)고 했고, 세 번째 단락에 있는 서비스 목록이 모두 옷에 관련된 것이므로 모어하우스 서플라이어즈는 의류업체임을 알 수 있다. 따라서 (D)가 정답이다.

8 가르자 씨가 고객에게 제안한 일은?

(A) 제품 결함 확인하기
(B) 여러 번 세탁하기
(C) 가격표 제거하기
(D) 서비스에 대한 의견 제출하기

해설 **세부 사항:** 두 번째 단락 마지막 문장에서 소매를 원하는 길이로 만들려면 셔츠를 세 번 세탁하라(To enable the sleeves ~ put the shirt through the laundry cycle three times)고 구체적으로 할 일을 제안하고 있으므로 (B)가 정답이다.

어휘 **defect** 결함 **remove** 제거하다

패러프레이징
지문의 put the shirt through the laundry cycle three times ➡ 보기의 Wash an item several times

9 편지에 따르면, 고객들이 수선 서비스에 대한 세부 내용을 얻을 수 있는 곳은?

(A) 카탈로그
(B) 웹사이트
(C) 판촉용 이메일
(D) 동봉된 운송 전표

해설 **세부 사항:** 네 번째 단락에서 수선 서비스 전체 목록은 봄이나 겨울 카탈로그 뒷면에 있는 차트를 보라(For a complete list of our alteration services ~ see the chart at the back of either our Spring or Winter catalogues)고 안내하고 있으므로, (A)가 정답이다.

10 [1], [2], [3], [4]로 표시된 곳 중에서 다음 문장이 가장 적합한 위치는?

"이것은 실수가 아닙니다."

(A) [1]   (B) [2]
(C) [3]   (D) [4]

해설 **문장 삽입:** 제시된 문장은 '이것은 실수가 아니다'는 의미이므로, 실수나 오류처럼 보일 수 있는 상황에 대해 언급한 내용 뒤에 들어가야 한다. [2] 앞에서 저희가 줄인 셔츠 소매가 요청보다 1.5센티미터까지 길어 보일 것이라며 수선 결과가 요청 사항과 차이가 있다는 내용이 왔고, [2] 뒤에는 통상 줄어드는 정도를 감안한 것이라며 오차가 발생한 이유를 설명하고 있으므로 제시된 문장은 [2]에 들어가면 자연스럽게 연결된다. 따라서 (B)가 정답이다.

UNIT 08	광고

ETS 예제   본책 p. 322

아티스틱스사 개점!

아티스틱스사가 새로운 거점인 웰리 가 2416번지에서 재개점하였음을 자랑스럽게 알려 드립니다. **저희는 계속해서 명함, 전단, 포스터, 메뉴, 카탈로그 및 기타 홍보 자료를 전문적으로 취급할 것입니다.** 아울러 이제는 매장이 더 커졌으므로 시각적 매력의 극대화를 위해 여러분과 함께 제품 구상 및 디자인 작업을 할 수 있는 **보강된 그래픽 디자이너팀의 서비스를 제공해 드릴 수 있게 되었습니다.**

저희 매장을 방문하셔서 수백 개의 견본용 명함, 우송 광고지 및 안내 책자를 살펴보시기 바라며, 이 모든 것은 고객님의 특정 상품이나 서비스에 맞도록 주문 제작이 가능합니다. **만약 4월에 200달러 이상 인쇄 서비스를 이용하시면 무료로 100장들이 명함 한 통(25달러 상당)을 받으실 수 있습니다.**

어휘 **grand opening** 개점 **specialize in** ~을
전문으로 하다 **business card** 명함 **flyer** 전단
promotional materials 홍보 자료 **expanded**
확장된 **conceptualize** 구상하다 **achieve**
달성하다 **visual** 시각적인 **appeal** 매력 **mailer**
(우편으로 보내는) 광고지 **customize** 주문 제작하다
complimentary 무료의 **value** 가격, 가치

ETS **TEST**   본책 p. 325

1 (B)	**2** (C)	**3** (B)	**4** (D)	**5** (A)
6 (C)	**7** (B)	**8** (C)	**9** (A)	

Questions 1-2 광고

> ### 유로 텔레토크
>
> **1유럽에 있는 동안 당신의 고객들에게 연락하시려고요?** 유로 텔레토크는 계약이나 숨은 요금 없이 즉시 모바일 서비스를 제공합니다! **2낮게는 40달러부터 시작하는 요금제들로, 모든 예산에 맞출 수 있는 여러 옵션을 갖고 있습니다.**
>
> 먼저 euroteletalk.ca를 방문해 계정을 활성화시키고 **1여행의 필요에 적합한 요금제를 선택하기만 하면 됩니다.** 그런 다음 1.99달러짜리 앱을 휴대폰에 다운로드하여 사용자 프로필에 들어가고 해외에서 일하는 동안 유로 텔레토크의 통화, 문자, 데이터 패키지의 편리함을 즐기세요. 결제가 누락되는 불편한 상황을 피하시려면 계정을 자동 지불로 설정하세요. 위약금 걱정 없이 언제든 취소하세요.
>
> www.euroteletalk.ca

어휘 **immediate** 즉각적인 **contract** 계약 **hidden**
숨겨진 **fee** 요금 **fit** 맞다 **budget** 예산 **activate**
활성화시키다 **account** 계정 **suit** ~에 맞다 **access**
접근하다 **convenience** 편리함 **overseas** 해외에
skip 건너뛰다 **hassle** 귀찮은 상황 **miss** 놓치다
penalty 위약금

1 광고는 누구를 대상으로 하는가?

(A) 대학생
(B) 출장자
(C) 공무원
(D) 휴가 중인 사람

해설 **추론:** 첫 단락 첫 문장에서 유럽에 있는 동안 고객들에게 연락하려 하는지(Are you looking to ~ while in Europe?)를 묻고 있고, 두 번째 단락 첫 문장에서 여행의 필요에 적합한 요금제를 선택하기만 하면 된다(simply choose the plan that suits your travel needs)고 했으므로 광고는 사업차 출장을 다니는 사람을 대상으로 한 것임을 짐작할 수 있다. 따라서 (B)가 정답이다.

2 유로 텔레토크에 대해 명시된 것은?

(A) 계약이 필요하다.
(B) 취소 수수료가 있다.
(C) 다양한 요금제 옵션을 제공한다.
(D) 무료 휴대전화기가 포함되어 있다.

해설 **Not / True:** 첫 단락 세 번째 문장에서 낮게는 40달러부터 시작하는 요금제들로 모든 예산에 맞출 수 있는 여러 옵션을 갖고 있다(With plans starting as low as $40, we have options to fit every budget)고 했으므로 다양한 가격대의 요금제를 구비하고 있음을 알 수 있다. 따라서 (C)가 정답이다.

패러프레이징
지문의 options to fit every budget
⊙ 보기의 a variety of plan options

Questions 3-5 광고

> ### 와서 함께하세요!
>
> 빅토리아 호스피탤리티 디럭스가 경력을 중시하는 사람들을 찾고 있습니다. 멜버른에 있는 세계 본사에 영업 및 마케팅, 홍보, 정보 기술 분야에 공석이 있습니다. 그리고 **3, 4이곳 호주와 전 세계 각국 호텔에는 요리, 조경 디자인, 행사 서비스, 시설 관리 직종에 공석이 있습니다.**
>
> 뒤지지 않는 급여 및 복리 후생과 함께 이전 비용 지원, 건강관리 프로그램 및 리더십 교육도 제공합니다. 1800-160-401로 전화해 팀원이 되기 위한 첫걸음을 내디디세요. 팀원 한 사람 한 사람 모두 당사 성공에 **5없어서는 안 됩니다.**

어휘 **hospitality** 환대 **career-minded** 경력[성공]을
중시하는 **public relations** 홍보 **culinary** 요리의
facility 시설 **competitive** 뒤지지 않는 **benefits**
package 복리 후생 제도 **relocation** 이사, 이전
wellness 건강(관리) **vital** 없어서는 안 되는

3 빅토리아 호스피탤리티 디럭스에 관해 암시된 것은?

(A) 조직 개편 중이다.
(B) 전 세계에 호텔을 소유하고 있다.
(C) 본사를 이전했다.
(D) 직원들에게 무료 호텔 숙박을 제공한다.

해설 **추론:** 첫 단락 마지막 문장에서 호주와 전 세계 각국에 있는 우리 호텔(at our many hotels here in Australia and in countries across the globe)이라고 한 것으로 보아 세계 각지에 호텔이 여러 곳 있음을 알 수 있다. 따라서 (B)가 정답이다.

어휘 **reorganize** (조직을) 개편하다

패러프레이징
지문의 across the globe ⊙ 보기의 around the world

4 광고에 제일 관심이 있을 만한 사람은 누구이겠는가?

(A) 전기 기술자
(B) 의료 기사
(C) 운동 트레이너
(D) 제빵사

해설 **추론:** 첫 단락 마지막 문장에서 호주와 전 세계 각국에 있는 호텔에는 요리, 조경 디자인, 행사 서비스, 시설 관리 직종에 공석이 있다(at our many hotels here ~ culinary arts, landscape design, event services, and facility management)고 했다. 광고에 언급된 여러 직종 중 (A), (B), (C)과 관련된 직종은 없고, 요리 분야에 대한 언급은 있으므로 (D)가 정답이다.

패러프레이징
지문의 culinary arts ➡ 보기의 pastry

5 두 번째 단락 3행의 "vital"과 의미상 가장 가까운 단어는?

(A) 필수적인
(B) 설득력 있는
(C) 활력 있는
(D) 문자 그대로인

해설 **동의어:** 의미상 '없어서는 안 되는'이라는 뜻으로 쓰인 것이므로 정답은 (A) essential이다.

어휘 essential 필수적인 persuasive 설득력 있는
energetic 활력 있는 literal 문자 그대로인

Questions 6-9 광고

⁶사기 전에 빈러 피트니스 제품을 사용해 보세요!

⁷노련한 운동선수든 열의가 넘치는 입문자든, 새로운 피트니스 장비는 값비싼 투자가 될 수 있습니다. 하지만 이제는 빈러 피트니스의 편리한 장비 대여 프로그램을 통해 장기 계약이나 부담스러운 선약금 없이 자기만의 개인 체육관에서 훈련하는 것이 어떤 것인지 경험할 수 있습니다. 최고급 브랜드의 러닝머신, 일립티컬, 프리웨이트 등과 같은 다양한 유형의 운동 기계를 대여해서 집에서 편안하게 사용할 수 있습니다.

그 외 우리 독점 프로그램의 몇 가지 중요한 특징은 다음과 같습니다:
- 단 3개월에서부터 시작하는 유연한 임대 계약
- ⁸⁽ᴮ⁾언제든지 장비를 구입하거나 임대 기간을 연장할 수 있는 옵션
- ⁸⁽ᴰ⁾구매 가격에 반영되는 대여료
- ⁸⁽ᴬ⁾장비의 배송 및 설치를 위한 전문가 팀
- 장비 구매 시 지속적인 보증 및 서비스 옵션 제공

여러분이 피트니스 목표를 달성하는 데 도움이 될 수 있는 수백 가지 아이템이 준비되어 있습니다. ⁹오늘 당장 온라인으로 www.binlerfitness.com.au에 방문하셔서 우리의 제품 목록을 둘러보세요!

어휘 seasoned 노련한 athlete 운동선수 enthusiastic 열성적인 equipment 장비 pricey 값비싼 investment 투자 hassle-free 편리한 rental 대여 experience 경험하다 commitment 약속 up-front 선불의 expense 비용 numerous 다양한 treadmill 러닝머신 comfort 편안함 feature 특징 exclusive 독점적인 flexible 유연한 agreement 계약 term 기간 extend 연장하다 apply 적용하다 professional 전문가 warranty 보증(서) explore 분석하다 inventory 물품 목록

6 광고의 대상은 누구인가?

(A) 신규 고객을 찾고 있는 개인 트레이너
(B) 이제 막 체육관에 가입한 사람들
(C) 새로운 피트니스 장비를 써 보는 데 관심 있는 사람들
(D) 피트니스 카탈로그를 받고 싶어 하는 사람들

해설 **추론:** 제목에서 사기 전에 빈러 피트니스 제품을 사용해 보라(Try Binler Fitness products before you buy!)고 했으므로 피트니스 제품 사용에 관심이 있는 잠재 고객들을 대상으로 하는 광고임을 알 수 있다. 따라서 (C)가 정답이다.

어휘 private 개인 소유의 in search of ~을 찾아서

패러프레이징
지문의 fitness products ➡ 보기의 fitness equipment

7 첫 번째 단락 1행의 "seasoned"와 의미가 가장 가까운 단어는?

(A) 맛을 첨가한
(B) 경험이 풍부한
(C) 주기적인
(D) 부드러워진

해설 **동의어:** 의미상 '노련한 운동선수'라는 뜻으로 쓰인 것이므로 정답은 (B) experienced이다.

8 프로그램의 특징으로 언급되지 않은 것은?

(A) 장비가 집으로 배달된다.
(B) 계약을 쉽게 연장할 수 있다.
(C) 개인 트레이너가 운동 시간을 지도해 줄 수 있다.
(D) 이전 대여료가 구매에 반영될 수 있다.

해설 **Not / True:** 두 번째 단락에 열거된 프로그램의 특징 중 언제든지 장비를 구입하거나 임대 기간을 연장할 수 있는 옵션(An option to purchase ~ rental at any time)은 (B), 구매 가격에 반영되는 대여료(Rental payments are applied to purchase price)는 (D), 장비의 배송 및 설치를 위한 전문가 팀(A team of professionals ~ set up your equipment)은 (A)의 내용과 일치하지만, 개인 트레이너가 지도해 준다는 언급은 없으므로 (C)가 정답이다.

광고에 따르면, 제품에 대한 정보는 어떻게 구할 수 있는가?

(A) 웹사이트에 접속해서

(B) 매장 전시장에 가서

(C) 고객 서비스 라인에 전화해서

(D) 회원가입 시 홍보 이메일 수신을 수락해서

해설 **세부 사항:** 광고의 마지막 문장에서 오늘 당장 온라인으로 www.binlerfitness.com.au에 방문해 제품 목록을 둘러보라(Visit us online www.binlerfitness.com.au and explore our inventory today!)고 권유하고 있으므로 웹사이트를 방문함으로써 제품 정보를 찾아볼 수 있음을 알 수 있다. 따라서 (A)가 정답이다.

패러프레이징

지문의 Visit us online ➡ 보기의 accessing a Web site

UNIT 09	공지 / 회람

ETS 예제
본책 p. 328

코로스트 철강회사 시상식 만찬

코로스트 철강회사의 시상식 만찬이 계획대로 6월 1일 월요일 오후 6시에서 9시 30분까지 진행됩니다. 그러나 **공사로 인해 행사 장소가 변경되었습니다.** 행사는 콜로나 빌딩이 아니라 셰리든 가 휘트웰 센터에서 열립니다.

코로스트 본사에서 오시는 길:
말린 가에서 남부 방향으로 진출하여 크레센트 가로 진입하십시오. 아서 가에서 우회전해 여섯 블록을 쭉 지나 셰리든 가에서 좌회전합니다. 오른쪽 첫 번째 552번 건물이 휘트웰 센터입니다. 만찬은 2층에서 열립니다.

주차 정보:
주차는 휘트웰 센터 전용 구역을 이용할 수 있습니다. 전용 구역 입구는 건물 오른편에 있습니다. **주차료를 납부하는 일이 없도록 시상식 만찬 초대장을 지참하여 주차 요원에게 제시하십시오.**

어휘 **as planned** 계획한 대로, 예정대로 **no longer** 더 이상 ~이 아닌 **directions** 길 안내 **headquarters** 본사 **entrance** 입구 **invitation** 초대(장) **attendant** 안내원

ETS TEST
본책 p. 331

1 (A)	**2** (D)	**3** (C)	**4** (A)	**5** (A)
6 (D)	**7** (A)	**8** (B)	**9** (B)	**10** (D)

Questions 1-3 공지

도일사 고객들께 알려 드립니다

[1]건축 및 엔지니어링 회사인 도일사는 본사 사옥 완공을 기다리는 동안 9월 1일부터 사무실을 아래편 길로 이전합니다. [2]메인 가 1102번지에서 메인 가 813번지로의 이전은 임시적입니다(오데사 비즈니스 센터에 회사의 본사 사옥이 완공될 때까지만 있을 예정). 업무는 평상시와 같이 지속될 것이며 현재 진행 중인 프로젝트가 사무실 이전 때문에 지연되는 일은 없을 것임을 약속드립니다. [3]단, 이번 여름에는 저희의 대학교 건축학과 인턴 프로그램 참여가 연기되며 내년이 되어야 재개됨을 참고하시기 바랍니다.

어휘 **permanent** 영구적인 **as of** ~부터 **temporary** 임시의, 잠정적인 **assure** 장담하다 **as usual** 평상시처럼 **involvement** 참여, 관여 **postpone** 연기하다 **resume** 재개되다

1 공지되고 있는 내용은?

(A) 회사 이전

(B) 대학교 개교

(C) 회사 폐업

(D) 두 조직의 합병

해설 **주제/목적:** 첫 문장에서 본사 사옥 완공을 기다리는 동안 사무실을 이전한다(While waiting for its permanent headquarters ~ will be moving it offices)고 했으므로 정답은 (A)이다.

어휘 **relocation** 이전, 재배치 **merger** 합병

2 도일사의 사무실은 현재 어디에 있는가?

(A) 지역 대학교

(B) 메인 가 813번지

(C) 오데사 비즈니스 센터

(D) 메인 가 1102번지

해설 **세부 사항:** 두 번째 문장에서 메인 가 1102번지에서 메인 가 813번지로 임시 이전한다(The move from 1102 Main Street to 813 Main Street will be temporary)고 했으므로 현재 위치는 메인 가 1102번지임을 알 수 있다. 따라서 정답은 (D)이다.

3 무엇이 지연될 것인가?

(A) 비즈니스 센터 건설

(B) 건축 계획 완성

(C) 회사의 프로그램 참여

(D) 회사의 연례 회의

해설 **세부 사항:** 공지의 마지막 문장에서 여름에는 대학교 건축학과 인턴 프로그램 참여가 연기된다(our involvement with the university's architectural intern program will be postponed)고 했으므로 정답은 (C)이다.

패러프레이징
지문의 postponed ➡ 질문의 delayed
지문의 involvement with ~ program
➡ 보기의 participation in a program

Questions 4-6 공지

납품 거부 통지

다음 품목(들)에 대한 당사의 거부 의사를 명백히 하기 위해 이 통지서를 제출합니다.

[5]납품일	제품	송장	배송지 주소
4월 2일	클로렙 라텍스 페인트, 감청색, 10갤런	8996510	포츠우드 건설 머리디언 가 367번지 케치칸, 알래스카 주 99901

당사 기록에 따르면 귀사는 아래와 같이 품목(들)에 대한 결제를 수락했습니다:

날짜	신용카드	금액	지급처
3월 30일	끝 번호 4617	230.50달러	브랜치 페인트사

이유:

[4, 5]3월 15일 주문 시 3월 28일 이전까지 배송을 약속했습니다. 다른 페인트 공급자를 찾았습니다.

거부된 물품을 귀사의 비용으로 반품하는 건에 관해 당사에 알려 주십시오. [6]페인트 및 배송비 전액을 영업일 기준 10일 이내에 환불해 주시기 바랍니다.

웨스틴 슬로언
회계 담당자
포츠우드 건설

어휘 rejection 거부, 거절 verify 확인하다 reject 거부하다, 거절하다 expense 비용 refund 환불 fee 요금 business day 영업일

4 페인트에 관해 명시된 것은?

(A) 3월에 주문되었다.
(B) 고객의 집으로 배송되었다.
(C) 슬로언 씨가 납품했다.
(D) 두 개의 용기에 담겨 배송되었다.

해설 **Not/True:** 통지서의 이유란을 보면 페인트를 3월 15일에 주문했다(the order was placed on March 15)고 했으므로, 정답은 (A)이다.

패러프레이징
지문의 the order was placed on March 15
➡ 보기의 It was ordered in March.

5 납품이 거부된 이유는?

(A) 너무 늦게 도착했다.
(B) 예상보다 비쌌다.
(C) 물품이 파손되었다.
(D) 물품이 누락되었다.

해설 **추론:** 주문 시 3월 28일이나 그 전에 배송을 해 주기로 약속했는데(delivery was promised on or before March 28), 납품일(Delivery date)을 보면 4월 2일(April 2)이다. 따라서 약속한 납품일보다 늦게 배송되었기 때문이라는 것을 추론할 수 있으므로, 정답은 (A)이다.

6 통지에 따르면 브랜치 페인트사는 무엇을 해야 하는가?

(A) 지불 기한 연장하기
(B) 즉시 다른 배송 보내기
(C) 문제에 대해 설명하기
(D) 반품 배송비 지급하기

해설 **세부 사항:** 마지막 문장에서 페인트 및 배송비 전액을 영업일 기준으로 10일 이내에 환불해 달라(A full refund for the paint and the delivery fee is expected within 10 business days)고 했으므로, 정답은 (D)이다.

어휘 extend 연장하다 immediately 즉시 explanation 설명 shipping charge 배송비

패러프레이징
지문의 A full refund for ~ the delivery fee
➡ 보기의 return shipping charges

Questions 7-10 회람

회람

수신: 신제품 개발부
발신: 포커스 그룹 진행자, 아리아나 리
날짜: 10월 12일
제목: 포커스 그룹 번호 4829

[7]10월 10일, 저는 여름 특별 상품으로 개발된 새로운 아이스티 병 음료 네 개의 공식 시음 테스트를 실시했습니다. 테스트한 맛은 서머 라즈베리와 프레시 민트, 레몬이 섞인 프레시 민트, 힌트 오브 피치입니다. [7]여러분 중 몇 분이 시음 테스트에 대해 문의해 와서, 간단하게 요약해 드리겠습니다.

현지에서 온 각각 12명의 참가자들로 구성된 [9(A)]두 그룹을 [9(C)]무작위로 선정했습니다. 10월 10일 낮에 [9(D)]회사 밖에서 만났습니다. 첫 번째 그룹의 참가자들에게 각각의 맛의 샘플을 주고 1부터 10까지의 단위로 각각의 샘플을 [8]평가하라고 했습니다. 1은 음료가 전혀 맛이 없다는 것을 의미하고, 10은 음료가 아주 맛있다는 것을 의미합니다. 두 번째 그룹의 참가자들

에게는 같은 샘플을 줬지만, 샘플에 이름표를 붙였습니다. 그 후에 두 가지 기준에서 1부터 10까지 평가해 달라고 요청했습니다. 즉, 음료수가 얼마나 맛있는지와 이름을 보고 예상한 기대치를 얼마나 만족시켰는지에 대한 평가입니다. 이 테스트의 목적은 음료의 맛이 실제로 제품명이 불러일으킨 기대치와 잘 맞는지 알아내기 위한 것이었습니다.

¹⁰그룹 시음 테스트의 결과는 정리 및 분석 중에 있으며, 다음 주에 나올 것입니다. 항상 그렇듯이 결과는 기밀 사항으로, 이 메일 첨부 파일로 보내는 것이 아니라 제 비서가 여러분 사무실로 보고서 사본을 한 부 직접 건네드릴 것입니다. 우리 경쟁 업체에서 이 결과를 무척 알고 싶어 한다는 것에 유념하십시오. 우리 부서 외 다른 사람과 어떤 세부 사항이라도 공유할 필요가 있다고 생각하시면 저에게 먼저 말씀해 주십시오.

어휘 coordinator 진행자 conduct 실시하다, 수행하다 formal 공식적인 taste test 시음(회) flavor 풍미, 맛 at random 무작위로 off-site (어느 특정한 장소에서) 떨어진[져], 부지 밖의[에서] scale 척도, 기준 signify 의미하다 enjoyable 즐길 수 있는 label 라벨을 붙이다 expectation 기대, 예상 determine 알아내다, 결정하다 match ~와 어울리다 process 처리하다 as always 언제나처럼 confidential 기밀의 hand-deliver 직접 건네다

7 이 회람의 목적은?

(A) 제품 테스트에 대한 세부 사항을 공유하려고
(B) 한 음료수에 대한 의견을 제공하려고
(C) 고객 만족도 조사 결과를 설명하려고
(D) 포커스 그룹 절차에 대한 변경 사항을 건의하려고

해설 **주제/목적:** 첫 번째 단락 첫 번째 문장에서 신제품 시음 테스트를 했다(I conducted a formal taste test of the four new bottled iced tea drinks)고 밝히고, 이어서 같은 단락 마지막 문장에서 간단하게 요약하겠다(I'd like to provide a brief summary)고 했으므로 정답은 (A)이다.

어휘 customer satisfaction survey 고객 만족도 조사

8 두 번째 단락 3행의 "rate"와 의미상 가장 가까운 단어는?

(A) 값을 매기다   (B) 평가하다
(C) 받을 만하다   (D) 이해하다

해설 **동의어:** 참가자들이 각각의 샘플을 '평가하도록' 요청 받았다는 의미이므로 정답은 (B) judge이다.

9 조사 내용에 대해서 언급되지 않은 것은?

(A) 참가자들을 그룹으로 나누었다.
(B) 리 씨의 비서가 실시했다.
(C) 참가자들은 무작위로 선정되었다.
(D) 회사 사무실에서 떨어진 곳에서 시행되었다.

해설 **Not/True:** 두 번째 단락의 첫 두 문장에서 정답의 단서를 찾을 수 있다. (A)와 (C)는 Two groups with twelve participants each from the local area were selected at random을, (D)는 an off-site location 을 바꿔 표현한 것이다. 따라서 지문에 언급되지 않은 (B)가 정답이다.

패러프레이징
지문의 at random ➡ 보기 (C)의 by chance

10 회람에 의하면, 다음 주에 무슨 일이 있을 것인가?

(A) 더 많은 사람들이 음료수를 시음할 것이다.
(B) 음료수를 시장에 내놓을 것이다.
(C) 절차를 재설계할 것이다.
(D) 연구 결과가 나올 것이다.

해설 **세부 사항:** next week가 키워드로, next week가 언급되는 부분에서 답을 찾도록 한다. 마지막 단락 첫 번째 문장 Results of the group taste test are being processed and analyzed and will be available next week에서 다음 주에 조사 결과가 나올 것임을 알 수 있다. 따라서 정답은 (D)이다.

어휘 sample 시식하다, 시음하다 redesign 재설계하다

패러프레이징
지문의 Results of the group taste test
➡ 보기의 Results of the study

UNIT 10 | **기사/안내문**

ETS 예제 본책 p. 334

제프리즈 새롭게 단장하다

토론토(7월 16일)–2년 전, 캐나다의 디자인 회사인 인텔리가미는 제프리즈를 다시 단장하는 임무를 부여받았다. **제프리즈는 미주 및 카리브해 전역에 걸쳐 60개의 지점을 두고 있는 체인형 매장이다.** 지난주 멕시코시티에 있는 제프리즈 매장은 22번째로 인텔리가미에 의해 개조되었고, 내년 1월까지 모든 매장이 재단장될 예정이다.

새로 바뀐 제프리즈 매장을 찾은 방문객들은 식료품 코너가 매장 전면으로 이동된 모습을 보면 놀라면서도 기분이 좋을 듯하다. 이러한 변화는 식품만 사기 위해 들르는 많은 고객들에 의해 높이 평가 받고 있다. 재단장 노력의 다른 요소들은 질서 있고 열린 공간이라는 느낌을 준다. **바닥은 타일을 벗겨 내고 콘크리트를 드러내 반짝이게 윤을 냈다.** 벽은 참나무 판자로 덮여 있다. 그리고 LED 조명이 눈에 거슬리는 형광등을 대체했다. 이러한 변화들은 모두 더 즐겁고 효율적인 쇼핑 경험을 만들어 낸다.

어휘 undergo (변화, 절차 등을) 겪다, 거치다 makeover
변신 project 나타내다 strip 벗겨내다 polish 윤을
내다 gleaming 반짝이는 replace 대체하다 harsh
(빛 등이) 눈에 거슬리는 fluorescent light 형광등
efficient 효율적인

ETS **TEST**   본책 p. 337

| **1** (A) | **2** (B) | **3** (B) | **4** (D) | **5** (C) |
| **6** (A) | **7** (B) | **8** (C) | **9** (D) | **10** (A) |

Questions 1-3 보도

긴급 보도   연락처: 실리아 퍼킨스,
                            +27 11-555-1823

요하네스버그(5월 3일) – ¹오래된 남아프리카공화국 항공사인 서든 오션스 항공사(SOA)는 남아프리카공화국 더반과 호주 퍼스를 연결하는 최신 노선을 발표하게 되어 자부심을 느낍니다.

³6월 3일에 비행을 시작해 활기찬 두 도시를 잇는 유일한 직항 서비스를 제공하고 수많은 출장 여행자들의 시간을 절약해 줄 것입니다. 휴가를 즐기는 분들에게도 도움이 될 것입니다. 호주 여행자들은 세계적으로 유명한 더반의 해변에 쉽게 갈 수 있으며 남아프리카공화국 여행자들은 퍼스의 뛰어난 수상 스포츠 현장을 즐길 수 있을 것입니다.

SOA 72편은 매일 16시에 더반을 출발해 익일 11시 45분 퍼스에 도착합니다. 회항 비행기인 SOA 73편은 매일 14시 30분에 퍼스를 출발해 당일 19시 30분에 더반에 도착합니다. 양방향 비행 모두 현대적인 에코 와이드바디 EW-1555 항공기로 오가며 비즈니스 클래스에 52명, 이코노미 클래스에 216명의 승객을 태울 수 있습니다.

²아프리카에서 가장 성장 속도가 빠른 항공사이자 세계에서 성장 속도가 빠르기로 손꼽히는 SOA는 정시 출발로 세계 항공사들 중 선두에 선 것을 자랑스럽게 생각합니다.

어휘 carrier 항공사, 운수회사 link 연결하다; 연결, 연계
vibrant 활기찬 access 접근, 이용 outstanding
탁월한, 우수한 passenger 승객 departure 출발

1 무엇에 관한 보도인가?

(A) 신규 국제 항공 노선
(B) 기내 접대 개선
(C) 요하네스버그 공항 개조
(D) 항공사의 최신 수하물 정책

해설 **주제/목적:** 첫 단락에서 서든 오션스 항공사(SOA)는 남아프리카공화국 더반과 호주 퍼스를 연결하는 최신 노선을 발표하게 되어 자부심을 느낀다(Southern Oceans Airlines (SOA) ~ is proud to announce its latest

route linking Durban, South Africa, with Perth, Australia)고 했으므로 정답은 (A)이다.

어휘 improvement 개선, 향상 in-flight 기내의
entertainment 접대, 여흥, 오락 renovation 개조
luggage 수하물, 짐 policy 규정, 정책

패러프레이징
지문의 its latest route linking Durban, South Africa, with Perth, Australia ➡ 보기의 A new international airline route

2 SOA는 무엇으로 유명한가?

(A) 저비용
(B) 드문 지연
(C) 경량 항공기 설계
(D) 많은 승객 수

해설 **세부 사항:** 마지막 단락 마지막 문장에서 SOA는 정시 출발로 세계 항공사들 중 선두에 선 것을 자랑스럽게 생각한다(SOA is proud to lead among world carriers in on-time departures)고 했다. 따라서 정답은 (B)이다.

어휘 lightweight 가벼운, 경량의

패러프레이징
지문의 on-time departures ➡ 보기의 Few delays

3 [1], [2], [3], [4]로 표시된 곳 중에서 다음 문장이 들어가기에 가장 적합한 위치는?

"휴가를 가시는 분들에게도 도움이 될 것입니다."

(A) [1]   (B) [2]
(C) [3]   (D) [4]

해설 **문장 삽입:** 제시된 문장의 will also benefit이 문제 해결의 단서로, 제시된 문장 앞에는 어떤 이점이 오고 이어서 휴가를 가는 사람들에게도 도움이 될 것이라고 부가적으로 (also) 언급되는 것이 문맥상 자연스럽다. 따라서 수많은 출장 여행자들의 시간을 절약해 줄 것(saving time for thousands of business travelers)이라는 이점이 언급된 다음인 (B)가 정답이다.

어휘 vacationer 행락객, 휴가를 즐기는 사람

Questions 4-6 정보

타카시 후지오카
〈황혼의 교토〉
캔버스에 유화
114.3cm X 99.06cm

이 작품은 국제적으로 인정 받은 타카시 후지오카의 연작 〈황혼의 교토〉의 첫 번째 작품이다. 이 연작 회화들은 도쿄 모토 현대미술관, 뉴욕 시 폰테인–쉴즈 갤러리, 런던 스타리트 아트 갤러리 등을 포함한 전 세계 박물관과 미술관에서 전시되어 왔다. ⁶⁽ᶜ⁾〈황혼의 교토〉는 작품이 완성된 그 해 〈현대 미술〉

지 표지에 실렸다. ^{4, 5, 6(B)}이 작품은 4년 전 토마스 체스터 게인즈가 개인 소장용으로 구매했다가 2년 전 영구 소장용으로 클락슨 – 워커 미술관에 판매되었다. 이후 이곳 우리 미술관이 소장하고 있다. ^{6(D)}후지오카 씨가 이 그림을 "나의 전성기"라고 부른 것으로 유명하다.

어휘 **recognition** 인정, 인식 **exhibit** 전시하다 **feature** 특징을 이루다; 기능, **collection** 수집(품), 소장(품) **permanent** 영구적인

4 이 정보문은 어디에 게시되었는가?

(A) 모토 현대미술관
(B) 폰테인 – 쉴즈 갤러리
(C) 스타리트 아트 갤러리
(D) 클락슨 – 워커 미술관

해설 **세부 사항:** 지문 후반부에서 〈황혼의 교토〉는 2년 전 영구 소장용으로 클락슨 – 워커 미술관에 판매되었으며 그 이후 이곳 클락슨 – 워커 미술관에서 소장하고 있다(was sold to the Clarkson-Walker Museum for our permanent collection ~ here with us since)고 했다. 따라서 클락슨 – 워커 미술관에 게시된 정보임을 알 수 있으므로 정답은 (D)이다.

5 게인즈 씨는 누구이겠는가?

(A) 화가   (B) 미술 평론가
(C) 미술품 수집가   (D) 전시 책임자

해설 **추론:** Mr. Gaines를 키워드로 지문에서 답을 찾아야 한다. 지문 후반부에서 게인즈 씨는 4년 전에 〈황혼의 교토〉를 개인 소장용으로 구입했다(It was bought four years ago by Thomas Chester Gaines for his private collection ~)고 했으므로, 게인즈 씨는 미술품 수집가임을 알 수 있다. 따라서 정답은 (C)이다.

어휘 **critic** 평론가, 비평가 **collector** 수집가

6 〈황혼의 교토〉에 관해 언급되지 않은 것은?

(A) 화가가 2년에 걸쳐 창작했다.
(B) 지금까지 소유자가 둘 이상이었다.
(C) 〈현대 미술〉지 표지에 실렸다.
(D) 화가가 자신의 가장 훌륭한 작품 중 하나로 여긴다.

해설 **Not/True:** 보기에 언급된 내용을 지문에서 찾아 하나씩 확인해 본다. 게인즈 씨가 개인 소장용으로 구매했다가 미술관에 판매했다(It was bought ~ by Thomas Chester Gaines for his private collection ~ was sold to the Clarkson-Walker Museum ~)고 했으므로 소유자가 둘 이상이었음을 알 수 있다. 세 번째 문장에서 〈황혼의 교토〉는 작품이 완성된 그 해 〈현대 미술〉지 표지에 실렸다(~ was featured on the cover of *Modern Painting* magazine)고 했으며, 마지막 문장에서 후지오카 씨는 〈황혼의 교토〉를 '자신의 전성기'라고 했다(Mr.

Fujioka famously called this painting "my finest hour")고 했으므로 화가가 자신의 작품 중 훌륭한 작품으로 여긴다는 것을 알 수 있다. 따라서 언급되지 않은 (A)가 정답이다.

패러프레이징
지문의 was featured ◉ 보기 (C)의 appeared
지문의 my finest hour ◉ 보기 (D)의 one of his best works

Questions 7-10 기사

복잡함을 보여 주는 연구 결과

7월 20일 – ^{7, 10}최근 보고서에 따르면, 하버 포인트 시의 사무실 및 창고 임대료는 전국 평균보다 24% 가까이 높다. 임대료가 전국에서 가장 높다. ⁷연구는 최근 몇 년간 기술 회사의 유입으로 공간에 대한 높은 수요가 발생하고 있다는 것을 발견했다. 동시에, 지역 경제의 불확실성으로 많은 건설업자들이 새로운 건설 프로젝트에 착수하지 못하고 있다. 예를 들어, 지난 2년 동안 하버 포인트에서 완료된 신규 개발은 단 7건뿐이었다. 게다가 ⁸건설 프로젝트는 부분적으로 더 엄격해진 환경 요건 때문에 완수하는 데 더 오랜 시간이 걸리고 있다. 이러한 복합적인 요인들이 공급을 제한하고 임대료를 끌어올리고 있다.

⁹인접한 서밋과 미드빌도 하버 포인트의 뒤를 따르는 추세다. 지난 9개월 동안 두 도시에서는 상업용 임대료가 각각 10%와 8.5% 상승했다.

어휘 **warehouse** 창고 **nearly** 거의 **average** 평균 **influx** 유입 **demand** 수요 **simultaneously** 동시에 **uncertainty** 불확실성 **regional** 지역의 **discourage** 단념하게 만들다 **launch** 시작하다 **development** 개발 **strict** 엄격한 **environmental** 환경의 **requirement** 요건 **combination** 조합(물) **factor** 요인 **restrict** 제한하다 **supply** 공급 **raise** 올리다 **nearby** 인근의 **commercial** 상업의 **respectively** 각각

7 기사는 무엇을 설명하고 있는가?

(A) 환경 규제의 축소
(B) 상업용 공간의 부족
(C) 미완성 건축 프로젝트
(D) 너무 고가인 아파트

해설 **주제/목적:** 도입부에서 하버 포인트 시의 사무실 및 창고 임대료는 전국 평균보다 24% 가까이 높다(office and warehouse rents ~ 24 percent above the national average)고 했고 연구는 최근 몇 년간 기술 회사의 유입으로 공간에 대한 높은 수요가 발생하고 있다는 것을 발견했다(The study found that ~ high demand for space)며 상업 공간에 대한 높은 임대료 및 수요에 대해 언급하고 있으므로 이 기사는 상업용 부동산이 수요 대비

충분하지 않다는 주제에 관한 것임을 알 수 있다. 따라서 (B)가 정답이다.

어휘 reduction 감소 restriction 규제 shortage 부족

패러프레이징
지문의 office and warehouse, firms ➡ 보기의 commercial space

8 기사에 따르면, 하버 포인트에서 건축 프로젝트를 완수하는 데 시간이 더 걸리는 이유는?

(A) 기술이 현대화되어야 한다.
(B) 도급업자들의 예약이 이미 초과된 상태이다.
(C) 일부 규정이 변경되었다.
(D) 많은 작업현장이 접근하기 어렵다.

해설 세부 사항: 기사 중반부에 건설 프로젝트는 부분적으로 더 엄격해진 환경 요건 때문에 완수하는 데 더 오랜 시간이 걸리고 있다(construction projects now take longer ~ stricter environmental requirements)고 했으므로 환경 관련 규정이 변경되어 건설 프로젝트가 지연되고 있음을 알 수 있다. 따라서 (C)가 정답이다.

9 기사를 통해 하버 포인트, 서밋, 미드빌에 대해 알 수 있는 것은?

(A) 소득 성장률이 전국 평균을 웃돈다.
(B) 인구가 감소하고 있다.
(C) 건설업이 번창하고 있다.
(D) 같은 지역에 있다.

해설 추론: 마지막 단락 첫 문장에서 인접한 서밋과 미드빌도 하버 포인트의 뒤를 따르는 추세(Just behind Harbor Point in the trend are the nearby cities of Summit and Midville)라며 서밋과 미드빌을 하버 포인트와 인접한 도시라고 소개하고 있으므로 (D)가 정답이다.

어휘 decline 감소하다 population 인구

패러프레이징
지문의 nearby ➡ 보기의 in the same region

10 [1], [2], [3], [4]로 표시된 곳 중에서 다음 문장이 들어가기에 가장 적합한 위치는?

"임대료가 전국에서 가장 높다."

(A) [1]   (B) [2]
(C) [3]   (D) [4]

해설 문장 삽입: 제시된 문장은 '임대료가 전국에서 가장 높다'며 임대료에 대해 언급하고 있으므로 '임대료'가 주요 단서가 된다. 기사의 첫 문장에서 보고서에 따르면 하버 포인트 시의 사무실 및 창고 임대료는 전국 평균보다 24% 가까이 높다(According to a recent report, office and warehouse rents ~ 24 percent above the av national average)며 시의 임대료가 전국과 비교했을 때 얼마나 높은지 구체적인 수치를 들어 보여 주고 있으므로 전국 대비 임대료 수준에 대한 결론을 언급하는 제시된

문장이 그 뒤에 들어가면 글의 흐름이 자연스럽다. 따라서 (A)가 정답이다.

UNIT 11	웹 페이지 / 기타 양식

ETS 예제   본책 p. 340

베타페이직 솔루션즈
헤이워드 가 965 번지
디모인, 아이오와 주 50047

고객 유형: 신규
고객명: 리징웬
전화번호: 515-555-0144
이메일 주소: jlee@comptravel.com
프로젝트명: 컬러 전단지
선호 연락수단: 이메일
이곳에 사양서를 첨부해 주십시오:
COMPTRAVEL_AD

이곳에 추가 정보를 기입해 주십시오:

> 저는 최근에 컴프 트래블이라는 여행사를 시작했고, 제 사업을 홍보하기 위해 다음 달에 무역 박람회에 갈 예정입니다.
>
> 무역 박람회에서 배포할 수 있도록, 고급 컬러 인화지로 첨부한 파일 250장이 필요합니다. 이 작업에 대한 견적서를 보내 주십시오.

어휘 boulevard 도로 대로 flyer 전단지 preference 선호 trade show 무역 박람회 promote 홍보하다 attach 첨부하다 price estimate 견적서

ETS **TEST**   본책 p. 343

1 (C)	**2** (D)	**3** (D)	**4** (B)	**5** (C)
6 (C)	**7** (D)	**8** (D)	**9** (C)	

Questions 1-2 웹사이트

http://www.colinsdrive.co.uk

콜린스 드라이브 앤 플라이

홈	안내	자주 묻는 질문	연락처

콜린스 드라이브 앤 플라이에 오신 것을 환영합니다. 당사는 공항에서 가까운 거리에 있으며 편리한 셔틀 서비스를 제공합니다. **¹아래 양식을 작성해 차량 자리를 예약하세요.** 수용 공간에 제한이 있으므로 미리 예약하시기 바랍니다. **²A 터미널과 B 터미널로 가는 무료 셔틀이 10분마다 출발합니다.** 양식 작성에 도움이 필요하시면 고객지원 담당 직원에게 문의하세요.

PART 7 | UNIT 11

187

또한 추가 정보는 웹페이지 www.colinsdrive.co.uk/FAQ 자주 묻는 질문에서 확인하세요.

이름:	제이콥 랭
항공기 출발일:	11월 17일
주차 추정 시간:	오전 5:30
항공기 도착일:	11월 23일
차량으로 돌아오는 추정 시간:	오후 4:15

어휘 **distance** 거리 **convenient** 편리한 **capacity** 수용력 **complimentary** 무료인 **approximate** 대략적인

1 양식의 용도는?

   (A) 호텔 교통 서비스 요청

   (B) 공항 마중을 위한 운전기사 예약

   (C) 주차 장소 예약

   (D) 서비스에 대한 의견 제공

해설 **추론:** 세 번째 문장에서 아래 양식을 작성해 차량 자리를 예약하라(fill in the form below to hold a space for your car)고 했으므로 주차 공간을 예약하기 위한 양식임을 알 수 있다. 따라서 (C)가 정답이다.

패러프레이징
지문의 hold a space for your car
➡ 보기의 Reserving a parking location

2 셔틀에 관해 명시된 것은?

   (A) 각 터미널에서 10분 대기한다.

   (B) 추가 요금이 있다.

   (C) 좌석은 하루 전에 예약해야 한다.

   (D) 한 시간에 여러 차례 운행된다.

해설 **Not/True:** 글의 중반부에 A 터미널과 B 터미널로 가는 무료 셔틀이 10분마다 출발한다(Complimentary shuttle rides to Terminals A and B depart every ten minutes)고 했으므로 셔틀이 한 시간에 6번씩 운행된다는 것을 알 수 있다. 따라서 (D)가 정답이다.

패러프레이징
지문의 every ten minutes
➡ 보기의 multiple times an hour

Questions 3-5 양식

스타 교통
★★★★★★
스타 교통을 이용해 주셔서 감사합니다. ³저희 고객님을 더 잘 모시기 위한 결연한 노력으로 저희는 가장 최근 경험에 대한 고객님의 의견을 듣고 싶습니다. 잠깐만 시간을 내시어 다음 설문지를 작성하시고 동봉된 반신용 우표 부착 봉투에 넣어 5월 28일까지 저희에게 부쳐 주시기 바랍니다.

날짜: 5월 20일	고객 이름: V.N. 첸

전화번호: 603-555-0143

서비스 날짜 및 내역:

4월 12일 – 캐롤사에서 프랭클린 공항까지 이동

4월 25일 – 프랭클린 공항에서 뉴햄프셔 센터빌에 있는 집까지 이동

⁴1에서 4까지의 척도로 다음 사항을 평가해 주시되, 1은 '형편 없음'을, 4는 '훌륭함'을 나타냅니다.

서비스

친절함	1	2	3	④
예약 과정	1	2	③	4

차량

널찍함	1	2	③	4
⁴청결함	1	2	3	④

저희 서비스를 다시 이용하시겠습니까?   예 아니오 ⑭마도⑮

다른 사람들에게 저희 서비스를 추천하시겠습니까?
                                예 아니오 ⑭마도⑮

의견
저는 출장 때문에 스타 교통을 자주 이용하며 항상 만족해 왔습니다. ⁵이번에 제가 페루 리마에서 장시간 비행을 한 후 프랭클린 공항에 도착했을 때는, 운전기사가 어디에도 없었습니다. 비행기가 예정과는 다른 터미널에 도착하긴 했지만 기사가 훨씬 미리 항공편의 도착 상황을 확인했어야죠. 버스를 탈 수도 있었지만 결국 기사를 기다려야 했습니다.

어휘 **transportation** 교통 **concerted** 합심한, 결연한 **serve** (서비스 등을) 제공하다 **take a moment** 잠깐 시간을 내다 **fill out** 작성하다 **following** 다음의 **enclosed** 동봉된 **self-addressed** 반신용의 **stamped** 우표가 붙은 **rate** 평가하다 **scale** 척도 **spaciousness** 널찍함 **business travel** 출장 **nowhere to be found** 어디에도 없는 **status** 상태, 상황 **well** (부사 앞에 써서) 훨씬 **beforehand** 미리 **end up -ing** 결국 ~하다

3 스타 교통은 양식에서 모은 정보를 어떻게 사용하겠는가?

   (A) 효과적인 마케팅 자료를 만들기 위해

   (B) 시간 절약형 운전 노선을 설계하기 위해

   (C) 직원 승진을 결정하기 위해

   (D) 고객 서비스를 향상시키기 위해

해설 **추론:** 양식 상단에 저희 고객님을 더 잘 모시기 위한 결연한 노력으로 가장 최근 경험에 대한 고객의 의견을 듣고 싶다(In a concerted effort to better serve ~ recent experience with us)고 했으므로 정답은 (D)이다.

패러프레이징
지문의 better serve our customers
➡ 보기의 improve customer service

4 첸 씨는 차량에 대해 어떻게 말하는가?

(A) 차량은 버스였다.

(B) 매우 깨끗했다.

(C) 너무 컸다.

(D) 운전하기 어려웠다.

해설 **Not / True:** 양식에서 첸 씨가 차량의 청결함(Cleanliness) 항목에서 4에 표시를 했으므로 정답은 (B)이다.

5 첸 씨는 자신이 받은 서비스에 대해 어떻게 이야기하는가?

(A) 센터빌에서 오는 여행이 너무 오래 걸렸다.

(B) 예약 과정이 헷갈렸다.

(C) 운전기사가 예정보다 늦게 도착했다.

(D) 차량이 너무 작아 그의 짐을 넣을 수 없었다.

해설 **Not / True:** 마지막 문장에서 첸 씨는 버스를 탈 수도 있었 지만 결국 운전기사를 기다렸다(I ended up waiting ~ taken a bus)고 했으므로 정답은 (C)이다.

Questions 6-9 보고서

간달 패션

[7]**3월 12 - 17일 주간 현황 보고서**
작성자: 샘 호지킨즈, 프로젝트 관리자

이번 주 실적:

- 핸드백 제조 경험이 있는 인도 구자라트 소재 제조회사 5곳 연락했음. [6]**신상품 가방 디자인 스케치를 제공하고** 최소 주 문량, 제조 비용과 배송비, 소요 시간 질문했음.
- [7, 9]**최초 응답을 토대로, 카드산 산업이 우리 수요에 가장 적합한 제조사로 보임.** 다른 회사들만큼 크지는 않지만, 우 리 주문 전량을 납품하기 위해 직원을 추가로 채용할 의향 이 있음. 또한 경리부장인 둘라리 로이가 바로 전화했음. [8]**그녀는 무척 전문가답고 호감이 가며 내가 한 모든 질문에 솔직하게 답변해 주었음. 그녀와 좋은 거래 관계를 발전시 킬 수 있을 듯함.**
- [7]**연락해 본 다른 회사 4곳은 우리 일정을 맞출 수 없거나 우리 가격 조건에 맞출 수 없었음. 따라서 이 회사들은 더 이상 고려 대상이 아님.**

3월 20 - 24일 주간 계획:

- 프로젝트에 필요한 것과 지불 조건에 관해 계속 카드산 산 업과 논의.
- 디자인팀에게 최종 치수, 직물, 색상을 문서로 만들어 달라 고 요청하고 생산 과정의 단계를 대략 설명하도록 요청. 시 제품을 만들 수 있도록 이 정보를 카드산 산업에 전달.

어휘 **status** 진행 상황, 지위 **accomplishment** 업적, 실적 **contact** 연락하다; 연락(처) **manufacturing** 제조업 **minimum** 최소한의; 최소 **quantity** 양 **turnaround** 작업을 완료해서 회송하는 데 걸리는 시간 **initial** 최초의 **response** 응답 **manufacturer** 제조업체 **suited** 적합한 **personable** 호감이 가는, 매력적인

straightforward 솔직한, 간단한 **accommodate** 맞추다, 수용하다 **requirement** 요건 **measurement** 치수, 측량 **submit** 제출하다

6 간달 패션에 관해 암시된 것은?

(A) 인도로 이전하고 있다.

(B) 프로젝트 관리자를 뽑고 있다.

(C) 신제품을 개발하고 있다.

(D) 다른 회사와 합병하고 있다.

해설 **추론:** 첫 단락 첫 항목에서 신상품 가방 디자인 스케치를 제 공했다(Provided them with drawings of our new bag design)고 했으므로, 간달 패션에서 신제품을 개발 하고 있음을 알 수 있다. 따라서 정답은 (C)이다.

어휘 **relocate** 이전하다 **merge** 합병하다

패러프레이징
지문의 our new bag ➡ 보기의 a new product

7 보고서에 따르면 호지킨즈 씨는 3월 12일 주간에 무엇을 했 는가?

(A) 배송 일정을 짰다.

(B) 건축 허가증을 받았다.

(C) 임시직 공장 직원들을 교육했다.

(D) 가능성 있는 협력업체들을 평가했다.

해설 **세부 사항:** 3월 12일에서 17일까지의 주간 업무 보고의 두 번째 항목에서 카드산 산업이 수요에 가장 적합한 제조 사로 보이며(Kadsan Industries seems to be the manufacturer that is best suited to our needs) 세 번째 항목에서 다른 회사 네 곳은 일정이나 가격 조건에 서 고려 대상이 아니다(The four other companies ~ they will no longer be considered)라고 했다. 따라 서 정답은 (D)이다.

어휘 **acquire** 얻다, 획득하다 **permit** 허가증; 허락하다 **temporary** 일시적인, 임시의 **evaluate** 평가하다

8 로이 씨에 관해 언급된 것은?

(A) 호지킨즈 씨를 직접 만났다.

(B) 디자인팀 일원이다.

(C) 많은 질문을 했다.

(D) 같이 일하기 편하다.

해설 **Not / True:** Ms. Roy를 질문의 키워드로 잡고 지문에서 답을 찾아야 한다. 첫 단락 두 번째 항목에서 경리부장인 둘라리 로이와 통화했는데, 무척 전문가답고 호감이 가며 모든 질문에 솔직하게 답변해 주었으며(She was very professional, personable, and gave me straight- forward responses to all my questions) 좋은 거래 관계를 발전시킬 수 있다(I can see us developing a good business relationship with her)고 했으므로, 정답은 (D)이다.

9 [1], [2], [3], [4]로 표시된 곳 중에서 다음 문장이 들어가기에 가장 적합한 위치는?

"다른 회사들만큼 크지는 않지만, 우리 주문 전량을 납품하기 위해 직원을 추가로 채용할 의향이 있음."

(A) [1]   (B) [2]

(C) [3]   (D) [4]

해설 **문장 삽입:** 제시된 문장은 주문 수요를 맞추기 위해 직원을 추가 채용할 의향이 있다는 내용이므로, 수요에 대해 언급한 내용(Kadsan Industries seems to be the manufacturer that is best suited to our needs) 뒤인 [3]에 들어가야 글의 흐름이 자연스러워진다. 따라서 정답은 (C)이다.

UNIT 12	문자 메시지 / 온라인 채팅

ETS 예제
본책 p. 346

앤 대니얼스 [오전 11:00] 안녕하세요, 케네스. 오늘 고객들에게 최신 설문조사지를 보내고 있어서 알려 드리려고요.

케네스 주트라스 [오전 11:03] 훌륭해요! **지난번에 설문조사를 했을 때, 우리는 다양한 품목들, 특히 주방용품과 의류를 구비하고 있다는 점에서 높은 평가를 받았어요. 하지만 우리 탈의실은 비좁고 어수선하다고 묘사되었죠.**

앤 대니얼스 [오전 11:04] 리모델링이 완료되었으니 평가를 살펴보죠. 경영진이 일을 대충하지 않을 거라고 장담했어요.

케네스 주트라스 [오전 11:05] 지금 탈의실은 정말 근사해 보여요.

앤 대니얼스 [오전 11:06] 저도 그렇게 들었어요. 저는 아직 직접 보지는 못했어요.

케네스 주트라스 [오전 11:07] 어제 보석에서 전자제품 쪽까지 전 구역을 걸어 다녔어요. 모두 훌륭해 보여요!

어휘 **rating** 순위[평가] **in stock** 재고가 있는 **particularly** 특히 **apparel** 의류 **cramped** 비좁은 **cluttered** 어수선한 **assure** 확신시키다 **cut corners** 대충하다 **entire** 전체의

ETS TEST
본책 p. 349

1 (D)	2 (C)	3 (C)	4 (C)	5 (D)
6 (B)	7 (C)	8 (B)	9 (A)	10 (B)

Questions 1-2 문자 메시지

필립 스마이스(오전 9:16)
안녕하세요, 조지앤. 오늘부터 승차 공유 서비스에서 새로운 운전 업무를 시작했어요! 벌써 세 명의 고객이 예약되어 있어요.

조지앤 컬런(오전 9:18)
잘됐네요. 첫날 행운을 빌어요.

필립 스마이스(오전 9:21)
질문이 있는데요. 경험상, **¹얼마나 자주 세차를 해야 하나요?**

조지앤 컬런(오전 9:23)
¹저는 매주 해요. ¹,²셰리던 가에 아주 저렴한 곳이 있어요. 내부 및 외부 세차를 30달러에 할 수 있고, 아니면 훨씬 적은 비용으로 그들의 용품을 가지고 직접 할 수도 있어요.

필립 스마이스(오전 9:24)
좋은 팁이네요. **²정말 고마워요.**

어휘 **ride-sharing** 승차 공유 **affordable** (가격이) 알맞은 **exterior** 외부 **supply** 지급(품)

1 컬런 씨에 따르면 스마이스 씨가 셰리던 가에서 할 수 있는 것은?

(A) 물품 구매
(B) 주차 구역 찾기
(C) 승객 태우기
(D) 세차

해설 **세부 사항:** 9시 21분에 스마이스 씨가 얼마나 자주 세차를 해야 하는지(how often should we get our vehicles cleaned?) 묻자, 컬런 씨가 자신은 매주 한다(I do it weekly)며 셰리던 가에 아주 저렴한 곳이 있다(There's a place on Sheridan Avenue that's very affordable)고 세차할 수 있는 장소를 알려 주고 있다. 따라서 (D)가 정답이다.

패러프레이징
지문의 get our vehicles cleaned
➡ 보기의 Have a car washed

2 오전 9시 24분에 스마이스 씨가 "좋은 팁이네요"라고 쓴 의도는?

(A) 고객으로부터 여분의 돈을 받았다.
(B) 컬런 씨의 회사에서 자신을 고용해서 기뻐한다.
(C) 컬런 씨가 조언해 준 것에 감사한다.
(D) 이번 주에 승객을 차에 태울 수 있다.

해설 **의도 파악:** 9시 23분에 컬런 씨가 세차를 저렴하게 할 수 있는 곳을 알려 줬고, 9시 24분에 스마이스 씨가 좋은 팁이네요(Great tip)라고 답하며 정말 고맙다(Thanks so much)고 했다. 따라서 (C)가 정답이다.

Questions 3-6 온라인 채팅

피비 드폴[오전 8:18] 안녕하세요. ³기술 지원부서가 어제 제가 보낸 이메일을 받았는지 확인하려고 다시 연락드려요.

닉 리스[오전 8:19] 안녕하세요, 드폴 씨. 예, ³퇴근 무렵에 읽었어요. 더 빨리 답장 못해서 죄송해요. 컴퓨터 모니터가 문제죠?

피비 드폴[오전 8:20] 맞아요. 어제 오후 늦게 화면이 갑자기 몹시 밝아졌어요. 일하기가 정말 불편해서 알려 드리기로 했죠.

닉 리스[오전 8:21] 부장님을 대화상대에 추가해도 괜찮을까요?

피비 드폴[오전 8:22] 괜찮아요.

닉 리스[오전 8:23] 안녕하세요, 이후이 부장님. 지금 모니터 때문에 피비 드폴과 채팅 중이에요. ⁴모니터가 유달리 밝다고 하는데, 구식 디스플레이 드라이버 때문인 것 같아요.

이후이 리[오전 8:24] 그럴 수도 있어요. ⁴드폴 씨, 디스플레이 설정을 조절해 보셨나요?

피비 드폴[오전 8:25] 어제 해 봤는데 안 되더군요. 오늘 아침에 출근해서 ⁵동료인 안 씨에게도 도움을 요청했어요. 안 씨가 기계를 잘 다루는데도 문제가 그대로 있네요.

이후이 리[오전 8:28] ⁶닉, 디스플레이 드라이버를 다시 설치하세요. 꼭 처리해 주시겠어요?

닉 리스[오전 8:32] ⁶그럼요-감사합니다, 이후이 부장님. 드폴 씨, 그렇게 하려면 10분이 더 걸려요. 지금 시간 있으세요?

어휘 extremely 몹시 uncomfortable 불편한 unusually 유달리 outdated 구식인 adjust 조절하다 see to 반드시 ~하도록 (조처)하다

3 드폴 씨의 문제를 가장 먼저 통보 받은 사람은 누구이겠는가?

(A) 그녀의 비서
(B) 그녀의 부장
(C) 리스 씨
(D) 안 씨

해설 **추론:** 8시 18분에 드폴 씨가 기술 지원부서가 어제 자신이 보낸 이메일을 받았는지 확인하려고 다시 연락한다(I'm just following up ~ got my e-mail from yesterday)고 하자, 8시 19분에 리스 씨가 퇴근 무렵에 읽었는데(I read it at the end of the day) 더 빨리 답장 못해 미안하다(Sorry for not getting back to you sooner)며 컴퓨터 모니터가 문제인 것이 맞는지(The problem is your computer monitor, right?) 확인하고 있다. 따라서 드폴 씨의 문제를 가장 먼저 알게 된 사람은 리스 씨이므로 (C)가 정답이다.

4 오전 8시 24분에 리 씨가 "그럴 수도 있어요"라고 쓴 의도는?

(A) 리스 씨가 이메일에 즉시 회답했으면 한다.
(B) 안 씨가 드폴 씨를 도울 수 있다고 믿는다.
(C) 여전히 모니터 문제의 원인이 무엇인지 확신하지 못한다.
(D) 새 모니터를 구입해야 한다고 생각한다.

해설 **의도 파악:** 8시 23분에 리스 씨가 드폴 씨의 모니터가 유달리 밝다고 하는데 구식 디스플레이 드라이버 때문인 것 같다(She says it's unusually bright ~ could be an outdated display driver)고 문제의 원인을 추정하자, 8시 24분에 리 씨가 '그럴 수도 있어요(Possibly)'라고 답한 뒤 드폴 씨에게 디스플레이 설정을 조절해 봤는지(have you tried adjusting the display settings?)를 물으며 문제의 원인이 될 수 있는 다른 가능성에 대해 더 알아보려 하고 있다. 따라서 '그럴 수도 있다'는 대답은 리스 씨가 말한 것이 문제의 원인이 맞는지 확신할 수 없다는 의도이므로 (C)가 정답이다.

어휘 promptly 즉시

5 드폴 씨가 안 씨에 관해 암시한 것은?

(A) 최근에 자신의 모니터를 수리했다.
(B) 깜박하고 프로그램을 설치하지 않았다.
(C) 그녀가 사용할 수 있는 여분의 모니터를 가지고 있다.
(D) 해결책을 찾을 수 없었다.

해설 **추론:** 8시 25분에 드폴 씨가 동료인 안 씨에게도 도움을 요청했는데(I even asked my colleague Mr. Ahn for help) 안 씨가 기계를 잘 다루는데도 문제가 그대로 있다(He's great with technology, but the problem is still there)고 한 것으로 보아 안 씨가 문제를 해결하지 못했음을 알 수 있다. 따라서 (D)가 정답이다.

패러프레이징

지문의 the problem is still there
➡ 보기의 unable to find a solution

6 리스 씨는 다음에 무엇을 하겠는가?

(A) 모델 번호 확인하기
(B) 소프트웨어 다시 설치하기
(C) 기기에 문제가 있는지 시험하기
(D) 드폴 씨의 하드웨어 교체하기

해설 **추론:** 8시 28분에 리 씨가 리스 씨에게 드폴 씨의 디스플레이 드라이버를 다시 설치해 달라(I suggest that you reinstall her display driver)고 요청하자 곧바로 리스 씨가 그러겠다(Sure)고 답했으므로 (B)가 정답이다.

패러프레이징

지문의 display driver ➡ 보기의 software

Questions 7-10 문자 메시지

헨리 디어링스[오후 9:22] 브리아나, **7여기 공장 3번 라인 컨베이어가 멈췄어요. 크렐러 문구점을 위한 생산 가동이 끝난 듯한데요.** 다음 라인 가동을 시작할까요?

브리아나 페머[오후 9:24] 가동이 완전히 끝났는지, 아니면 다른 이유로 멈춘 건 아닌지 확인해야 해요.

헨리 디어링스[오후 9:26] 알겠어요, **8그건 해본 적이 없는데. 어떻게 확인하죠?**

브리아나 페머[오후 9:28] **8주통제 패널 화면에서 3번 라인을 보세요.** 뭐라고 돼 있죠?

헨리 디어링스[오후 9:31] "가동 완료 2,500"이라고 돼 있어요.

브리아나 페머[오후 9:34] 화면 위에 오늘 생산 가동이 모두 열거된 출력물이 붙어 있는데 그걸 봐야 해요. 화면에 있는 숫자가 크렐러 생산 가동 수량과 일치하나요?

헨리 디어링스[오후 9:36] 예, 2,500이네요.

브리아나 페머[오후 9:38] 그러면 완료된 거예요. **9차트에서 아랫줄에 있는 다음 생산라인을 보세요. 8, 9제가 이중으로 검수하기 위해 찰스에게 막 문자를 보냈어요.**

찰스 마커스[오후 9:41] **8, 9다음 가동은 후아니타 밀러의 주문이에요. 9품번 345 파란색 1,500개.**

헨리 디어링스[오후 9:42] 정확해요.

브리아나 페머[오후 9:45] 좋아요. 이제 가동 시작하세요. 내일 저녁까지 포장을 마쳐야 해요. **101시간쯤 있으면 그리로 돌아갈게요. 전 여기 창고에 할 일이 좀 있거든요.**

어휘 stationery 문구점 run 가동 match 대등하다
quantity 수량

7 글쓴이들은 어떤 업계에서 일하는가?

(A) 여행 (B) 금융
(C) 제조 (D) 통신

해설 **추론:** 9시 22분 헨리 디어링스의 메시지에서 여기 공장 3번 라인 컨베이어가 멈췄다(the conveyer on line 3 here at the factory has stopped)고 했고 크렐러 문구점을 위한 생산 가동이 끝난 듯하다(I think the production run for Kraler Stationery has finished)고 한 것으로 보아, 메시지 작성자들은 문구류를 생산하는 제조업체에서 일하고 있음을 알 수 있다. 따라서 (C)가 정답이다.

패러프레이징
지문의 production ➡ 보기의 Manufacturing

8 회사에 가장 최근 입사한 직원은 누구이겠는가?

(A) 후아니타 밀러 (B) 헨리 디어링스
(C) 찰스 마커스 (D) 브리아나 페머

해설 **추론:** 9시 26분에 헨리 디어링스가 업무를 해 본 적이 없다(I haven't done this before)며 어떻게 확인하는지(How do I check?) 묻자 9시 28분에 브리아나 페머가 주통제 패널 화면에서 3번 라인을 보라(Look at the screen ~ for line 3)고 답했고, 그 뒤에서도 페머 씨는 업무에 대해 설명하고 디어링스 씨는 배우는 내용의 메시지가 계속된다. 9시 38분에 페머 씨가 이중으로 검수하기 위해 찰스에게 막 문자를 보냈다(I just texted Charles to double-check it)고 한 것으로 보아 찰스 마커스는 페머 씨와 업무 파악도가 비슷한 사람임을 알 수 있으며, 9시 41분에 마커스 씨가 다음 가동은 후아니타 밀러의 주문(The next run is for Juanita Miller's order)이라고 했으므로 후아니타 밀러는 직원이 아닌 의뢰인 측임을 알 수 있다. 따라서 가장 최근에 입사한 직원은 업무를 배우고 있는 헨리 디어링스라고 추정되므로 (B)가 정답이다.

9 오후 9시 42분에 디어링스 씨가 "정확해요"라고 쓴 의도는?

(A) 마커스 씨가 제공한 정보를 보고 있다.
(B) 화면과 출력물의 숫자가 일치한다.
(C) 페머 씨에게 수정된 정보를 보낼 것이다.
(D) 컨베이어가 예상대로 작동하고 있다.

해설 **의도 파악:** 9시 38분에 페머 씨가 디어링스 씨에게 차트에서 아랫줄에 있는 다음 생산라인을 보라(Look at the next line down on the chart ~ the next production run)면서 이중으로 검수하기 위해 찰스에게 막 문자를 보냈다(I just texted Charles to double-check it)고 했고, 9시 41분에 마커스 씨가 다음 가동은 후아니타 밀러의 주문(The next run is for Juanita Miller's order)이고 품번 345 파란색 1,500개(1,500 of item 345 in blue)라고 확인해 주자 디어링스 씨가 정확해요(Precisely)라고 했다. 따라서 디어링스 씨는 페머 씨가 일러준 대로 차트를 보고 있다가 마커스 씨가 확인해 준 수치가 차트와 일치한다는 뜻으로 한 말이므로 (A)가 정답이다.

10 페머 씨는 문자 메시지를 쓸 때 어디에 있는가?

(A) 집 (B) 창고
(C) 공장 작업장 (D) 문구점

해설 **세부 사항:** 9시 45분에 페머 씨가 1시간쯤 있으면 그리로 돌아가겠다(I'll be back there in about an hour or so)며 여기 창고에 할 일이 좀 있다(I have a little more work here at the warehouse)고 했으므로 현재 페머 씨는 창고에 있음을 알 수 있다. 따라서 (B)가 정답이다.

어휘 factory floor 공장 작업장

192

UNIT 13	이중 연계 지문

ETS 예제 본책 p. 358

파텔 씨께:

고객님께서 9월 18일 팀페인 스타 시드니 호텔에서 최근 겪으신 일을 듣게 되어 유감입니다. 예약이 확정되었음에도 예약한 방을 쓰실 수 없었다고 들었습니다. 하지만 전담 프런트 직원들이 대체할 숙소를 찾았다고 하니 다행입니다.

제가 알아본 바에 따르면 컴퓨터 소프트웨어가 오작동해 사실은 이미 예약되어 있는 특정 객실들이 비어 있는 방으로 등록되었다고 합니다. 고객님이 시드니를 방문하신 기간과 호텔 부근에서 열리는 국제회의 2개가 겹치는 바람에 투숙객이 유난히 많았습니다. 안타깝게도 이런 이유로 의도치 않게 일부 초과 예약이 생겼습니다.

불편을 끼쳐 드려 죄송하며 팀페인 호텔을 대표해 호주 내 어느 지점(시드니, 퍼스, 멜버른, 브리즈번)에서나 묵을 수 있는 **무료 1일 숙박권을 드리고자 합니다.** 자세한 사항은 첨부한 이용권에 있습니다.

서맨사 존스턴, 고객 서비스부 부장
팀페인 호텔 사

어휘 confirm 확정하다, 확인하다 reservation 예약 book 예약하다 dedicated 전용의, 헌신하는 alternative 대체의, 대안의 accommodation 숙박, 수용 discover 발견하다 malfunction 오작동, 고장 cause 유발하다, 초래하다 particular 특정한 list 목록을 작성하다, 목록에 포함하다 reserve 예약하다 coincide with ~와 동시에 일어나다 result in (결과로) ~이 되다 unusually 유달리, 특히 unintentional 의도치 않은 overbooking 초과 예약 inconvenience 불편 on behalf of ~을 대신[대표]하여 complimentary 무료의 voucher 이용권, 쿠폰 vice president 부(서)장, 부사장

팀페인 호텔 이용권 # X3445

이 쿠폰은 팀페인 스타 시드니, 팀페인 씨뷰 퍼스, 팀페인 하이 스퀘어 멜버른, 팀페인 게스트 스위트 브리즈번 중 한 곳의 **일반실 1일 무료 숙박에 유효합니다.** 객실은 미리 예약하셔야 합니다. 식사는 포함되지 않습니다.

고객 서명 _____ 날짜 _____

문의 사항 있으시면 고객 서비스부로 연락하십시오.

이메일: guestservices@timpanehotels.com.au
전화: 1800-160-401
우편: 체슬러 가 14번지, **브리즈번**, 퀸즐랜드 주 4000, 호주

어휘 good 유효한 in advance 미리, 사전에 signature 서명

1 존스턴 씨가 이메일을 보낸 이유는?
(A) 예약을 확인하려고
(B) 불만 사항에 대응하려고
(C) 회의 준비를 도우려고
(D) 파텔 씨의 계획에 대해 문의하려고

2 존스턴 씨는 9월 18일에 무슨 일이 있었다고 명시하는가?
(A) 호텔 직원들이 문제를 해결했다.
(B) 호텔 직원들이 새로운 소프트웨어를 설치했다.
(C) 파텔 씨가 예상보다 일찍 도착했다.
(D) 새로운 안내 데스크 직원이 교육을 받았다.

3 파텔 씨에 대해 암시되는 것은?
(A) 회의에 참석하려고 시드니에 있었다.
(B) 객실 변경을 요청했다.
(C) 객실을 미리 예약했다.
(D) 이전에 팀페인 호텔에 숙박한 적이 있다.

4 쿠폰에서 첫 번째 단락 1행의 "good"과 의미상 가장 가까운 단어는?
(A) 고품질의
(B) 행운의
(C) 품행이 바른
(D) 유효한

5 존스턴 씨의 사무실은 어디에 위치해 있겠는가?
(A) 시드니
(B) 퍼스
(C) 멜버른
(D) 브리즈번

ETS PRACTICE 본책 p. 361

1 (A)	2 (A)	3 (A)

편지 + 스케줄

WHKK 라디오 담당자께,

지난 화요일 오전 10시경에 차 안에서 라디오로 정말 좋은 교향곡을 들었습니다. 그런데 프로그램 진행자가 작곡가와 곡명을 이야기하기 전에 그만 회사에 도착해 버렸어요. 이 음악이 담긴 앨범이 아내 생일 선물로 아주 좋을 것 같아서 꼭 좀 알고 싶습니다.

쓰는 김에 덧붙이자면 제가 최근에 이 지역으로 이사를 왔는데, 귀하의 방송국에서 틀어 주는 다양한 음악을 듣는 것이 저에겐 큰 기쁨입니다. 아울러 방송 프로그램과 시간대가 담긴 목록을 받아볼 수 있을까요?

조셉 버나드

WHKK 라디오 7월 방송 일정표

	월요일 – 금요일	토요일과 일요일
오전 8시 – 오전 11시	**토드 햄프턴의 모닝 클래식**	지역 및 전국 뉴스
오전 11시 – 오후 1시	로저 프리드의 클래식 재즈	호세 캄포의 라틴 리듬
오후 1시 – 오후 5시	록(진행자 고정되어 있지 않음)	고전 음악
오후 5시 – 오후 7시	전국 뉴스	랜들 타일러의 심야 토크쇼

프로그램에서 방송된 음악에 대해 더 자세히 알고 싶으시면 본 방송국 555-9765로 전화하셔서 프로그램 진행자를 찾으십시오. 콘서트 및 기타 행사를 사전 공지받으시려면 555-9766으로 전화하셔서 본 방송국의 소식지를 구독하십시오.

1 버나드 씨는 더 많은 정보를 얻기 위해 누구에게 이야기해야 하는가?

   (A) 토드 햄프턴
   (B) 로저 프리드
   (C) 랜들 타일러
   (D) 호세 캄포

해설 **연계:** 일정표의 마지막 부분 For more information about the music played on any program, call station at 555-9765 and ask to speak to the host of the program에서 더 많은 정보를 얻으려면 해당 프로그램 진행자와 통화를 하라고 했는데, 편지 첫 문장(I heard a wonderful ~ around 10 A.M.)에서 버나드 씨가 오전 10시에 라디오를 들었다고 했고, 일정표를 보면 그 프로그램은 Morning Classical with Todd Hampton으로 진행자는 Todd Hampton이다. 따라서 (A)가 정답이다.

공지 + 일정표

점심시간 걷기 동호회

5월 17일 애셔 레크리에이션 위원회는 애셔 근린공원에서 점심시간 걷기 동호회 설립을 승인했습니다. **걷기 동호회는 월요**

일부터 금요일까지 정오에서 오후 1시에 모이며 1년 내내 지속적으로 계속됩니다. 동호회는 헌터 가에 있는 공원 북측 입구 옆 기점에서 만날 예정입니다. 모든 참가자는 편안한 워킹화를 신고 식수 한 병을 가져와야 합니다. 관심 있는 주민은 공원 레크리에이션 사무소로 전화하시거나 방문하셔서 등록하십시오. 최소 인원인 7명의 회원이 모이면 동호회는 공식 모임을 갖게 됩니다. 최신 정보 또는 변경 사항이 있는지 일정표를 확인하십시오. 자세한 정보를 원하면 동호회 코디네이터 슈레야 캄다르에게 215-555-0193으로 전화하십시오.

애셔 근린공원 7월 주간 활동 일정표

월요일	오후 12:00 오후 5:30	**점심시간 걷기 동호회**(북쪽 산책로) 지역 주민 배구(서쪽 코트)
화요일	오후 12:15	"점심시간에 배우기": 나비들(별관) 비용 7달러, 점심 포함
수요일	오후 12:00 오후 5:30	**점심시간 걷기 동호회**(북쪽 산책로) 지역 주민 배구(서쪽 코트)
목요일	오후 12:15 오후 5:30	"점심시간에 배우기": 버섯류(별관) 비용 7달러, 점심 포함 탐조(둘째 주와 넷째 주)(레크리에이션장)
금요일	오후 12:00 오후 5:30	**점심시간 걷기 동호회**(북쪽 산책로) 지역 주민 배구(서쪽 코트)
토요일	오전 10:00 오후 2:00	"자연과 예술": 그림 그리기(레크리에이션 건물) 비용 10달러, 용품 포함 애셔 공원 호수 투어(보트 창고) 보트 임대료 15달러

위 행사들에 관한 상세한 정보를 원하면 공원 레크리에이션 사무소 215-555-0102로 전화하십시오.

2 7월 걷기 동호회에 관해 암시된 것은?

   (A) 당초 계획보다 모이는 횟수가 적다.
   (B) 코디네이터가 교체되고 있다.
   (C) 참가자에게 생수를 제공한다.
   (D) 매일 다른 장소에서 모인다.

해설 **연계:** 공지문 두 번째 문장에서 걷기 동호회는 월요일부터 금요일까지 매일 정오에서 오후 1시에 모일 예정(The walking club will meet from Monday through Friday, noon-1 P.M.)이라고 했는데, 일정표를 보면, 월요일, 수요일, 금요일에만 열렸다. 따라서 당초 계획보다 모이는 횟수가 적었다는 것을 알 수 있으므로 정답은 (A)이다.

기사 + 이메일

**주간 뉴 비즈니스 집중 조명:
리바이털라이즈 레노베이션즈**

존 니콜스와 브래들리 니콜스의 1년 된 기업, 리바이털라이즈 레노베이션즈가 시드니 중심부의 부동산 시장의 판도를 바꾸어 놓고 있다. 이 작은 회사는 시의 기존 건물주들과 협력하여 낡은 아파트를 단장한다. 이 2인조 컨설턴트는 부동산을 평가하여 어떤 부분을 개선하면 가장 효과적으로 가치를 높이고 잠재적 임대 소득을 늘릴지 판단한다. 그 다음에 리바이털라이즈 레노베이션즈는 실외 조경에서 실내 바닥 설치에 이르기까지, 프로젝트를 완수하는 데 숙련된 작업자들을 선별하고 관리한다. **지금까지 그들의 작업은 모두 시드니 중심가에 집중되어 있었다.**

지역 건물주인 휘트니 그레이는 최근 니콜스 형제와 계약해 그녀의 도심 아파트 건물을 개조했다. "리바이털라이즈 레노베이션즈와 작업하고 난 뒤, 세입자 수요 증가와 전력 및 용수 비용 절감 덕분에 임대 수익이 11퍼센트 증가했습니다. 새로 설치한 옥상 테라스에서 신선한 공기와 파노라마 같은 전망을 맘껏 즐기고 있다는 전화를 많은 세입자들로부터 받았습니다. 분명히 리바이털라이즈 레노베이션즈에게 다시 조언을 구할 겁니다." 그레이는 말했다.

웹사이트 revren.com.au를 통해 니콜스 형제에게 연락할 수 있으며, 관심있는 관계자들은 그곳에서 회사에 대해 더 많은 것을 알고 제안된 프로젝트의 세부 사항을 제출할 수 있다.

어휘 revitalize 새로운 활력을 주다, 되살리다 renovation 보수[수리], 개조 climate 풍조, 경향, 기후 real estate 부동산 existing 기존의 landlord 건물주, 지주 refurbish 재단장하다, 정비하다 evaluate 평가하다 property 부동산, 토지 determine 결정[결심]하다, 판단하다 improvement 개선, 향상 efficiently 효과적으로 value 가치 rental 임대(료), 임대물 income 수입 potential 잠재력; 잠재적인 outdoor 옥외의 landscaping 조경 indoor 실내의 installation 설치 manage 관리하다, 운영하다 skilled 숙련된 laborer 작업자, 근로자 complete 완성하다; 완전한, 완성된 concentrate 집중하다 profit 수익 tenant 세입자 demand 수요 numerous 많은 panoramic 파노라마 같은 view 전망, 견해 rooftop 옥상 certainly 분명히, 확실히 seek 구하다 interested party 이해 당사자, 관심있는 사람 proposed 제안된

발신: 타니아 페레이라 〈tferreira@quintext.com.au〉
수신: 존 니콜스 〈jnichols@revren.com.au〉
내용: 새로운 개조안 제안
날짜: 1월 2일

니콜스 씨께,

제가 최근에 시드니 인근 해변 마을인 포인트 파이퍼에 있는 건물을 구입했기 때문에 메일을 씁니다. 당신이 그 프로젝트에 관심이 있을지도 모른다고 생각했어요. 그 건물은 현재 거주 가능한 상태가 아니어서 매매가가 굉장히 저렴했어요. 하지만 대중교통이 가까운데 이는 큰 장점이죠. 몇 달 안에 이 건물을 멋진 생활공간으로 만들어서 건물 내 아파트 15채를 임대로 내놓고 싶습니다.

제가 건축에 대한 경험이 부족해 당신의 도움이 크게 유익할 것 같습니다. 덧붙여 새로운 에너지 지침 준수에 대해서 알고 싶고, 이것이 잠재적인 전기 배선 개선에 어떤 영향을 미칠지 알고 싶습니다. 이 문제에 대해 저와 의논할 시간이 되신다면 알려 주십시오.

감사합니다.

타니아 페레이라

어휘 habitable 주거할 수 있는 public transportation 대중교통 major 주요한, 큰 advantage 장점 put ~ up for rent ~을 임대로 내놓다 limited 제한된 construction 건설, 공사 benefit from ~로부터 이익을 얻다 additionally 덧붙여, 게다가 compliance (법규 등의) 준수 guideline 지침 affect 영향을 미치다 electrical wiring 전기 배선

3 페레이라 씨의 제안이 리바이털라이즈 레노베이션즈의 통상적인 업무와 다른 점은?

(A) 시드니 밖에서 작업이 이루어진다.
(B) 페레이라 씨가 공사를 준비한다.
(C) 공사가 시작되기 전에 비용이 지불된다.
(D) 엄격한 시간 제한이 있을 것이다.

해설 **연계:** 이메일 첫 단락 첫 문장에서 페레이라 씨는 최근에 시드니 인근 해변 마을인 포인트 파이퍼에 있는 건물을 구입했다(I am writing because I recently purchased a building in Point Piper, a seaside town near Sydney)고 했다. 그런데 기사문 첫 단락 마지막 문장에서 지금까지 리바이털라이즈 레노베이션즈의 작업은 모두 시드니 중심가에 집중되어 있었다(So far, all of their work has been concentrated in central Sydney)고 했다. 따라서 정답은 (A)이다.

어휘 organize 준비하다, 기획하다 strict 엄격한 constraint 제한, 제약

패러프레이징
지문의 Point Piper, a seaside town near Sydney
➡ 보기의 outside Sydney

1 (A)	**2** (A)	**3** (D)	**4** (B)	**5** (C)
6 (B)	**7** (B)	**8** (C)	**9** (A)	**10** (B)
11 (B)	**12** (C)	**13** (B)	**14** (A)	**15** (D)
16 (C)	**17** (D)	**18** (C)	**19** (B)	**20** (A)
21 (C)	**22** (A)	**23** (B)	**24** (A)	**25** (A)
26 (C)	**27** (D)	**28** (A)	**29** (D)	**30** (B)
31 (D)	**32** (A)	**33** (B)	**34** (B)	**35** (D)

Questions 1-5 이메일 + 온라인 양식

수신: 미공개 수령인
발신: 린다 보이트
날짜: 4월 30일
제목: 피드백 요청

좋은 오후입니다.

¹4월 13일 금요일부터 15일 일요일까지 오리니 이벤트 센터에서 열리는 리즈 기술 콘퍼런스에 참석해 주셔서 감사합니다. 모든 사람들의 열띤 호응과 기록적인 참석자 수에 정말 즐거웠습니다.

잠시 시간을 내어 ltc.co.uk/feedback의 온라인 후기를 작성해 주십시오. 내년 회의를 개선하는 데 여러분의 답변을 활용할 것입니다. ², ⁴귀하의 솔직한 의견에 감사드리기 위해 5월 31일까지 후기를 제출하시면 저명한 의사이자 수상 경력이 있는 작가인 찰리 휘틀리 박사의 금요일 기조 연설 영상을 무료로 다운로드 받으실 수 있습니다.

린다 보이트
회의 주최자

어휘 undisclosed 밝혀지지 않은　recipient 수령인　seek 구하다　thrilled 매우 신이 난　enthusiasm 열광　attendee 참석자　complete 작성하다　response 답변　appreciation 감사　honest 솔직한　input 의견, 조언　submit 제출하다　keynote address 기조 연설　renowned 유명한　physician 의사　author 작가

---

https://www.ltc.co.uk/feedback

아래 양식을 작성하신 후 "제출"을 클릭하십시오.

이름: 야시르 시디크

후기: 저는 콘퍼런스 내내 머무르지는 않았지만 리즈에서의 콘퍼런스는 즐거웠습니다. ³, ⁴회사에서는 제가 제 업무와 관련 있는 토요일 오전 세션 두 개에 참석하기를 원했지만, 유일한 입장권 구입 옵션은 주말 전체를 위한 것뿐이었습니다. 두 번째 토요일 세션이 끝난 직후 바로 떠났기 때문에 일일 입장권을 살 수 있었다면 좋

았을 것 같습니다. 또한, ⁵두 세션 중 하나는 길고 좁은 회의실인 201호에서 열렸는데, 그곳에서는 발표자의 말이 잘 들리지 않았습니다. 우리 중 몇몇은 의자를 앞쪽으로 옮겨야 했고, 그것이 도움이 되었습니다. ⁵더 좋은 마이크와 스피커 시스템이 있었다면 도움이 되었을 것이라고 생각했습니다.

제출

어휘 entire 전체의　session (특정 활동을 위한) 시간　applicable 적용되는　ticketing 매표　narrow 좁은　presenter 발표자

1 이메일에 따르면, 가장 최근의 콘퍼런스는 이전의 콘퍼런스와 어떻게 달랐는가?

(A) 참석자가 더 많았다.
(B) 더 많은 주제를 다루었다.
(C) 더 큰 건물에서 열렸다.
(D) 하루 더 지속되었다.

해설 **세부 사항:** 이메일의 첫 문장에서 4월 13일 금요일부터 15일 일요일까지 오리니 이벤트 센터에서 열린 리즈 기술 콘퍼런스에 참석해 주셔서 감사하다(Thank you for attending ~ through Sunday, 15 April)며 모든 사람들의 열띤 호응과 기록적인 참석자 수에 정말 즐거웠다(We were thrilled by everyone's enthusiasm and by the record number of attendees!)고 했으므로, 가장 최근에 열린 콘퍼런스의 참석자 수가 최고 기록을 이루었음을 알 수 있다. 따라서 (A)가 정답이다.

어휘 attendance 참석　cover 다루다　last 지속되다

패러프레이징
지문의 the record number of attendees
➡ 보기의 more people in attendance

2 이메일에 따르면 피드백의 대가로 무엇이 제공되는가?

(A) 발표자의 녹화 영상
(B) 서명된 책 한 권
(C) 내년 입장권 할인
(D) 특별행사 초대

해설 **세부 사항:** 이메일의 두 번째 단락 세 번째 문장에서 귀하의 의견에 감사드리기 위해 5월 31일까지 후기를 제출하시면 찰리 휘틀리 박사의 금요일 기조 연설 영상을 무료로 다운로드 받으실 수 있다(To show our appreciation ~ Dr. Charlie Whitley)고 했으므로 (A)가 정답이다.

3 시디크 씨가 온라인 양식에 적은 불만 사항은?

(A) 강의실 중 하나가 찾기 어려웠다는 점
(B) 참석한 세션이 업무와 관련이 없었다는 점
(C) 일정이 더 일찍 끝났어야 했다는 점
(D) 일일 입장권을 구할 수 있어야 했다는 점

해설 **세부 사항:** 양식의 두 번째 문장에서 회사에서는 제가 업무와 관련 있는 토요일 오전 세션 두 개에 참석하기를 원했지만 유일한 입장권 구입 옵션은 주말 전체를 위한 것뿐이었다(My company wanted me to attend ~ only ticketing option was for the entire weekend)며, 두 번째 토요일 세션이 끝난 직후 바로 떠났기 때문에 일일 입장권을 살 수 있었다면 좋았을 것 같다(It would have been nice ~ Saturday session ended)고 했다. 시디크 씨는 일일 입장권 옵션이 없었다는 점을 아쉬워하고 있으므로 (D)가 정답이다.

어휘 **relevant to** ~에 관련된   **finalize** 끝내다

패러프레이징
지문의 It would have been nice to be able to buy a daily ticket ➡ 보기의 a one-day ticket should have been available

4 시디크 씨에 대해 판단할 수 있는 것은?

(A) 4월 15일에 콘퍼런스를 떠났다.
(B) 휘틀리 박사의 강의에 참석하지 않았다.
(C) 몇몇 동료들과 함께 콘퍼런스에 참석했다.
(D) 콘퍼런스에서 보이트 씨와 대화를 나누었다.

해설 **연계:** 이메일의 후반부에는 후기를 제출하면 저명한 의사이자 수상 경력이 있는 작가인 찰리 휘틀리 박사의 금요일 기조 연설 영상을 무료로 다운로드 받을 수 있다(if you submit comments ~ Dr. Charlie Whitley)고 했고, 온라인 양식에는 시디크 씨가 회사에서 자신이 토요일 오전 세션 두 개에 참석하기를 원했다(The company wanted me to attend two Saturday morning sessions)며 두 번째 토요일 세션이 끝난 직후 바로 떠났다(I left right after the second Saturday session ended)고 했다. 따라서 시디크 씨는 토요일에만 콘퍼런스에 참석했고 휘틀리 박사는 금요일에 연설했다는 것을 알 수 있으므로 (B)가 정답이다.

어휘 **lecture** 강의   **colleague** 동료

5 양식에서 시디크 씨는 201호에 대해 무엇을 언급하는가?

(A) 메인홀에서 멀리 떨어져 있었다.
(B) 자리가 편했다.
(C) 더 나은 오디오 시스템이 필요했다.
(D) 너무 따뜻했다.

해설 **Not / True:** 양식의 후반부에 두 세션 중 하나는 길고 좁은 회의실인 201호에서 열렸는데 그곳에서는 발표자의 말이 잘 들리지 않았다(one of those sessions took place in room 201 ~ it was difficult to hear the presenter)고 했고, 마지막 문장에서 더 좋은 마이크와 스피커 시스템이 있었다면 도움이 되었을 것이라고 생각했다(A better microphone and speaker system

would have been helpful, though)고 직접적으로 언급하고 있으므로 (C)가 정답이다.

패러프레이징
지문의 microphone and speaker ➡ 보기의 audio system

Questions 6-10 표 + 이메일

캠페인명	날짜	설명	Social Friend.com 공유 횟수	VoteTally. com 투표 횟수	Goldencrunch. com 방문 횟수
건강상 이점	4월 29일 – 5월 20일	팝업 광고로 고객이 연간 정기 검진을 받고 헬시 바이트 크래커를 더 많이 먹도록 일깨웠다.	92	자료 없음	1,112
6새로운 맛	**65월 23일 – 6월 14일**	**6고객에게 6가지 크래커 양념 컨셉을 제안하고 그중 하나에 투표하도록 권유했다.**	자료 없음	873	34
8퍼즐 도전	6월 20일 – 7월 29일	제품 상자에 퍼즐 단서를 주고 고객에게 온라인에 정답을 올리도록 요청했다.	**81,865**	자료 없음	216
무료 상자	8월 1일 – 8월 31일	고객이 헬시 바이트 크래커를 친구에게 소개할 때마다 무료로 한 상자를 제공했다.	430	자료 없음	889

골든 크런치 스낵사 – 마케팅 캠페인 분석

어휘 **annual** 연간의   **checkup** 건강 검진   **clue** 단서

수신: dbenson@gcsnackco.com
발신: lcortez@multiplicityadvisors.com
날짜: 9월 6일
제목: 신규 캠페인

벤슨 씨께,

9**10월 마케팅 캠페인**에 대한 아이디어를 보내 주셔서 감사합니다. 언뜻 봐도 좋아 보이네요. 8, 9**과거에 도전 유형의 캠페인에 고객들의 호응이 좋았어요.** 9**더욱이 헬시 바이트 크래커를 개인 운동과 연계한 점이 브랜드 이미지에 정말 잘 어울립니다.**

그런데 한 가지 명심해야 할 7**고려 사항**이 있어요. 대체로 웹페이지 트래픽이 반드시 높은 매출로 전환되는 건 아니라는 점을 알게 되었습니다. 그리고 과거 캠페인 데이터도 이 사실을 증명합니다. 8**이 통계는 판매와 소셜 미디어 참여 사이의 밀접한 상관관계를 나타냅니다.** 따라서 웹페이지를 활용해서 다음 캠페인을 시작하는 건 하지 않는 게 좋겠습니다. 8**SocialFriend.com 또는 VoteTally.com 같은 소셜 미디어 플랫폼에 캠페인을 선보이는 것이 더 효과적일 수도 있습**

니다. 고객이 온라인으로 의견을 제시하고 말하면 이는 최고 단계의 브랜드 충성도로 이어질 수 있습니다.

그런데 ¹⁰제품 연구팀의 에린 듀프리와 상의해 보는 것이 좋을 듯합니다. 에린 듀프리는 보건 전문가로, 과거 우리를 위해 대단한 지략을 발휘한 바 있습니다.

리넷 코테즈
다양성 자문단

6 5월에 시작된 마케팅 캠페인 기간에 고객들이 요청 받은 일은?

  (A) 독창적인 맛 제안하기
  (B) 여러 제품 아이디어 중 선택하기
  (C) 건강에 관한 설문지에 답하기
  (D) 어려운 퍼즐 풀기

해설 세부 사항: 차트에 따르면, 5월에 23일에 시작한 새로운 맛 (New Flavors) 마케팅 캠페인에서 고객들에게 6가지 크래커 양념 컨셉을 제안하고 그중 하나에 투표하도록 권유했다(Customers were invited to vote for one of six ~ concepts)고 했으므로 (B)가 정답이다.

어휘 come up with 제안하다

패러프레이징
지문의 vote for one of six ~ concepts
➡ 보기의 Choose between several ~ ideas

7 이메일에서 두 번째 단락 1행의 "consideration"과 의미상 가장 가까운 단어는?

  (A) 친절   (B) 요소
  (C) 명상   (D) 지급

해설 동의어: 의미상 '고려 사항'이라는 뜻으로 쓰인 것이므로 정답은 (B) factor이다.

8 어떤 마케팅 캠페인이 가장 매출을 많이 올렸겠는가?

  (A) 건강상 이점
  (B) 새로운 맛
  (C) 퍼즐 도전
  (D) 무료 상자

해설 연계: 이메일의 첫 단락에서 과거에 도전 유형의 캠페인에 고객들의 호응이 좋았다(Your customers have responded well to challenge-style campaigns before)고 했고, 통계가 판매와 소셜 미디어 참여 사이의 밀접한 상관관계를 보여 준다(Those statistics indicate ~ sales and social media engagement)며 SocialFriend.com 또는 VoteTally.com 같은 소셜 미디어 플랫폼에 캠페인을 선보이는 것이 효과적일 것(A more effective strategy ~ like SocialFriend.com or VoteTally.com)이라고 권유하고 있으므로 소셜 미디어 플랫폼을 통한 도전 유형 캠페인의 실적이 좋았음을 알 수 있다. 차트에 따르면, SocialFriend.com에서 이루어진 퍼즐 도전 캠페인의 공유 횟수가 가장 높으므로 가장 높은 매출을 올렸을 것으로 짐작할 수 있다. 정답은 (C)이다.

9 10월에 계획된 마케팅 캠페인에 관해 암시된 것은?

  (A) 개인의 신체단련 도전이 포함될 것이다.
  (B) 스포츠 역사와 관련된 질문이 포함될 것이다.
  (C) 잡지와 신문에 실릴 것이다.
  (D) 이전 캠페인에서 수집된 정보를 배포할 것이다.

해설 추론: 이메일의 첫 단락에서 10월 마케팅 캠페인에 대해 언급하며 과거에 도전 유형의 캠페인에 고객들의 호응이 좋았고(Your customers have responded well to challenge-style campaigns before), 헬시 바이트 크래커를 개인 운동과 연계한 점이 브랜드 이미지에 정말 잘 어울린다(it really suits your brand image to link ~ to individual exercise)고 했다. 따라서 10월 캠페인에는 고객의 개인 운동과 관련된 도전이 수반될 것임을 알 수 있다. 따라서 (A)가 정답이다.

패러프레이징
지문의 individual exercise ➡ 보기의 personal fitness

10 코테즈 씨는 다음에 무엇을 하고 싶어 하는가?

  (A) 마케팅 설문조사 실시하기
  (B) 보건 전문가에게 연락하기
  (C) 회사 웹사이트 재설계하기
  (D) 보건 데이터 검토하기

해설 세부 사항: 이메일의 마지막 단락에서 코테즈 씨가 제품 연구팀의 에린 듀프리와 상의할 것을 권하며(I recommend that we consult with Erin Dupree on our product research team), 그녀가 보건 전문가이자 과거 우리를 위해 대단한 지략을 발휘한 바 있다(she is a health expert ~ for us in the past)고 소개하고 있으므로 (B)가 정답이다.

패러프레이징
지문의 consult with ➡ 보기의 contact

Questions 11-15 이메일 + 직원 근무 시간표

발신: 알레한드라 퀸타나
수신: 르 웨이 창
¹¹제목: 근무 시간 기록부 수정
날짜: 12월 10일 월요일

창 씨께,

지난 급여 기간의 근무 시간 기록부를 정시에 제출해 주셔서 감사합니다. ¹¹양식을 급여부서로 보내기 전에 수정했다는 점 알려 드리고자 메일을 보냅니다. ¹⁵지난주에 유급 휴가로 반차를 내셨는데 근무 시간 기록부에 이 내용이 반영되지 않았습니다. 한 주의 모든 시간이 001 프로젝트 시간, 002 사무 시간 또는 003 비프로젝트 시간으로 분류되어 있었습니다. 앞으로 참조하시도록 말씀드리면, ¹⁵유급 휴가를 낼 때마다 해당 시간을 "급여 코드" 열에 있는 관련 코드 004로 청구하세요.

¹²이번에는 제가 양식을 수정했습니다. 시간 있을 때 변경 사항을 확인하세요. ¹⁴그로스버그 컨설팅의 정규직 재무 자문으로서, 융통성 있게 독자적으로 일정을 ¹³정하실 수 있으며 1년 동안 유급 휴가는 열을 낼 수 있습니다.

탁월한 업무 수행에 대해 감사를 표하고 싶습니다. ¹⁴지난 2주 동안 의뢰인들과 일을 순조롭게 시작하셨고, 그로스버그 컨설팅에서 매끄럽게 직책을 전환하셨습니다.

알레한드라 퀸타나, 전무이사
그로스버그 컨설팅

어휘 paid time off 유급 휴가 reference 참조 amend 수정하다 flexibility 융통성 entitled to ~할 자격이 있는 seamless 매끄러운

그로스버그 컨설팅 직원 근무시간 기록부
르 웨이 창 – 재무 자문, 살렘 사무소

급여 코드	월 12월 3일	화 12월 4일	수 12월 5일	목 12월 6일	¹⁵금 12월 7일	급여 기간 총계
[001]	3.00	7.75	6.50	7.75	4.00	29.00
[002]	4.00		1.00			5.00
[003]	1.00	0.25	0.50	0.25		2.00
¹⁵[004]					¹⁵4.00	4.00

11 퀸타나 씨가 창 씨에게 연락하는 이유는?

(A) 그의 휴가 요청을 승인하려고
(B) 그가 저지른 실수에 대해 알려 주려고
(C) 그를 다른 팀에 다시 배치하려고
(D) 그의 승진을 축하하려고

해설 **주제/목적:** 이메일의 제목이 근무 시간 기록부 수정(Time sheet adjustment)이고, 두 번째 문장에서 양식을 급여부서로 보내기 전에 수정했다는 점을 알리고자 이메일을 보낸다(I am writing to let you know that I made an adjustment ~ to payroll)고 했으므로 창 씨의 실수에 대해 알려 주려고 연락했음을 알 수 있다. 따라서 (B)가 정답이다.

어휘 **approve** 승인하다 **alert** 알리다 **reassign** 다시 배치하다

패러프레이징
지문의 let you know ➡ 보기의 alert

12 퀸타나 씨가 창 씨에게 요청하는 일은?

(A) 급여 부서에 근무일정 변경 사항 통보하기
(B) 매일 근무한 시간이 나타나도록 일정 수정하기
(C) 근무 시간 기록부 변경 사항이 정확한지 확인하기
(D) 의뢰인에게 제안서를 제출해 승인 받기

해설 **세부 사항:** 두 번째 단락에서 퀸타나 씨가 이번에는 본인이 양식을 수정했다(I've amended your form for you this time)며 시간 있을 때 변경 사항을 확인하라(Please confirm the change when you have a spare moment)고 창 씨에게 요청하고 있으므로 (C)가 정답이다.

어휘 **verify** 정확한지 확인하다

패러프레이징
지문의 confirm the change ➡ 보기의 Verify a change

13 이메일에서 두 번째 단락 3행의 "set"과 의미상 가장 가까운 단어는?

(A) 위치에 두다   (B) 정하다
(C) 놓다   (D) 얻다

해설 **동의어:** 의미상 '일정을 정하다'라는 뜻으로 쓰인 것이므로 정답은 (B) arrange이다.

14 창 씨에 관해 암시된 것은?

(A) 그로스버그 컨설팅에서 최근 정규직 사원으로 합류했다.
(B) 허용된 것보다 더 많은 날을 쉬었다.
(C) 인사 전문가이다.
(D) 다른 그로스버그 컨설팅 지점으로 옮겼다.

해설 **추론:** 이메일의 두 번째 단락에서 창 씨를 그로스버그 컨설팅의 정규직 재무 자문(a full-time financial advisor with Grossberg Consulting)이라고 했고, 마지막 문장에서 창 씨가 지난 2주간 의뢰인들과 일을 순조롭게 시작했고 그로스버그 컨설팅에서 매끄럽게 직책을 전환했다(You've gotten off to a great start ~ transition to your position here at Grossberg Consulting)고 했다. 따라서 창 씨는 2주 전에 그로스버그 컨설팅의 정규직 재무 자문이 되었음을 알 수 있으므로 (A)가 정답이다.

15 창 씨는 언제 유급 휴가를 냈는가?

(A) 월요일   (B) 수요일
(C) 목요일   (D) 금요일

해설 **연계:** 이메일의 세 번째 문장에서 창 씨가 지난주에 유급 휴가로 반차를 냈다(you took half a day as paid time off last week)고 했고, 유급 휴가를 낼 때마다 해당 시간을 "급여 코드" 열에 있는 관련 코드 004로 청구하라(whenever you take paid time off ~ associated code 004 under the "Pay Code" column)고 요청하고 있다. 직원 근무 시간 기록부에 따르면, 급여 코드 004에 표기된 날은 12월 7일 금요일이므로 창 씨는 금요일에 유급 휴가를 냈다는 것을 알 수 있다. 따라서 (D)가 정답이다.

Questions 16-20 이메일 + 카탈로그 목록

> 발신: 피터 윌리엄스 〈pwilliams@arbenlogistics.com〉
> 수신: 전 직원 〈staff@arbenlogistics.com〉
> 날짜: 5월 20일 월요일 오전 8:50
> 제목: 직원 휴게실 물
>
> 안녕하세요, 여러분,
>
> 직원 휴게실에 있는 정수기를 다시 채워야 합니다. ¹⁹**스프링스위프트가 어제 교체용 물통을 배달했고** 정수기 옆에 있습니다. 공교롭게도 저는 지금 손목 부상으로 25리터짜리 통을 들어올려 정수기 위에 놓을 수 없습니다. ¹⁷**오늘 관리팀 중 저만 근무를 하고 있으므로,** ¹⁶, ¹⁷**한 분이 물통을 정수기 위에 올려 주시면 감사하겠습니다.** ¹⁷**아니면 마이크 프레틀로우가 내일 아침 교대 근무를 시작할 때 할 수 있습니다.**
>
> 빈 물통은 이미 ¹⁸**버렸으니** 참고하시기 바랍니다.
>
> 이 건에 대한 여러분의 도움에 감사드립니다.
>
> 피터 윌리엄스
> 관리부, ¹⁹**아벤 물류**

어휘 **replacement** 교체(품) **unfortunately** 공교롭게도 **wrist** 손목 **injury** 부상 **maintenance** 관리 **discard** 버리다

> **스프링스위프트 식수**
>
> **스프링스위프트** 식수는 엄격한 10단계 품질보증 절차를 거치며 건강하고 신선한 물을 보장하기 위해 미네랄을 살짝 보강했습니다.
>
> **스프링스위프트** 식수는
> - 통에 담은 날짜로부터 2개월 동안 안심하고 보관 및 섭취할 수 있습니다.
> - ²⁰**밀봉되어 쉽게 조작할 수 없는 25리터 물통으로 나옵니다.**
> - 오존수와 미네랄(황산마그네슘, 탄산수소칼륨)이 들어 있습니다.
>
> 당사의 편리한 식수 배송 서비스를 신청하세요. 선택하신 날짜에 매달 한 번씩 물통을 갖다 드립니다. 고객님은 냉장고에 넣기만 하면 됩니다.
>
> ¹⁹**유의: 배송 서비스는 웰링턴에서 15킬로미터 이내 지역만 가능합니다.**

어휘 **undergo** (변화, 절차 등을) 겪다, 거치다 **rigorous** 엄격한 **quality assurance** 품질 보증 **enhance**

보강하다 **consume** 소비[섭취]하다 **sealed** 봉인을 한 **tamper-proof** 쉽게 조작할 수 없는 **ozonated water** 오존수 **subscribe to** ~을 신청하다 **cooler** (음료 보관용) 냉장고

16 이메일의 목적은?

(A) 물품 배송 문의
(B) 작업일정 변경 공지
(C) 작업 지원 요청
(D) 직원에게 새로운 규정 통지

해설 **주제/목적:** 이메일 작성자인 피터는 누군가 물통을 정수기 위에 올려 주면 감사하겠다(I would appreciate it if one of you would be so kind as to load the bottle of water onto the dispenser)고 했으므로 정답은 (C)이다.

17 이메일에서 프레틀로우 씨에 관해 암시하는 것은?

(A) 고장 난 정수기를 수리한다.
(B) 손목을 다쳤다.
(C) 보통 밤에 일하는 일정이다.
(D) 관리팀 일원이다.

해설 **추론:** 오늘은 관리팀 중 자신만 근무한다(I am the only member of the maintenance staff on duty today)며 누군가 대신 물통을 올려 주지 않는다면 마이크 프레틀로우가 내일 아침 교대 근무를 시작할 때 그 일을 할 수 있다(Or Mike Pretlow can do it tomorrow morning when his shift begins)고 한 것으로 미루어 프레틀로우 씨 또한 관리팀 일원임을 알 수 있다. 따라서 정답은 (D)이다.

18 이메일에서 두 번째 단락 1행의 "discarded"와 의미상 가장 가까운 단어는?

(A) 무시했다   (B) 거부했다
(C) 버렸다   (D) 반입했다

해설 **동의어:** 빈 물통을 버렸다는 뜻이므로 정답은 (C) thrown away이다.

19 아벤 물류에 관해 암시된 것은?

(A) 최근 물 배송 서비스를 시작했다.
(B) 웰링턴에서 15km 이내에 위치한다.
(C) 사무실에 정수기가 여러 대 있다.
(D) 관리 인력을 모집하고 있다.

해설 **연계:** 이메일에서 아벤 물류로 생수를 배달한 것이 스프링스위프트사임을 알 수 있고(A replacement bottle was delivered yesterday by Springswift), 카탈로그 목록의 맨 마지막 줄에 유의 사항으로 배송 서비스는 웰링턴에서 15킬로미터 이내 지역만 가능하다(Note: Delivery service is only available within 15 kilometers of Wellington)라고 했으므로 정답은 (B)이다.

어휘 **multiple** 많은, 다양한 **recruit** 모집하다

20 스프링스위프트 식수의 특징으로 언급된 것은?

(A) 보호용 포장

(B) 저렴한 가격

(C) 맛 선택권

(D) 다양한 크기

해설 **Not / True:** 카탈로그 목록에서 스프링스위프트 식수는 밀봉되어 쉽게 조작할 수 없는 25리터 물통으로 나온다 (comes in a sealed, tamper-proof 25-liter bottle) 고 했으므로 정답은 (A)이다.

어휘 **protective** 보호용의 **affordable** 저렴한

Questions 21-25 정보 + 허가증

걸버턴 공원 관리국

21행사 허가증 받기

21걸버턴 시내 공원에서 행사를 개최하려면 걸버턴 공원 관리국에 신청서를 제출해 허가증을 받아야 합니다. 행사를 계획하고 필요한 허가 신청서를 작성할 때 아래 규정에 유의하십시오.

- **22도시는 다양한 규모와 유형의 행사를 위해 장소들을 지정해 놓았습니다.** 가끔 요청 받은 장소가 해당 행사의 성격으로 미루어 보았을 때 적합하지 않다고 여겨질 때가 있습니다. 이 경우 시의 재량으로 대체 장소를 선정해 승인을 내줄 수도 있습니다.

- 최소한 행사 30일 전에 신청서를 제출해야 합니다. **23늦게 제출된 신청서는 "긴급 요청"으로 간주되어 50달러의 수수료가 부과되며 이 돈은 환불이 안 됩니다.**

- **24라이브 음악이나 옥외 식품 판매상이 있는 행사는 추가 허가증이 필요합니다.** 이 허가증은 시의 다른 부서에서 발급하는데 승인을 얻는 것은 귀하의 책임입니다. 이에 대한 지침이나 기타 문의는 parksmanagement@gulverton.gov로 걸버턴 공원 관리국에 연락하십시오.

어휘 **obtain** 얻다, 취득하다 **permit** 허가증 **submit** 제출하다 **application** 지원, 신청 **fill out** (양식을) 작성하다 **pay attention to** ~에 주의[주목]하다 **policy** 규정, 정책 **designate** 지정하다 **occasionally** 가끔 **deem** 간주하다, 생각하다 **unsuitable** 부적합한 **approval** 승인, 허가 **grant** 주다, 수여하다 **alternate** 대체의, 대안의 **prior to** ~ 전에 **nonrefundable** 환불이 안 되는 **vendor** 판매업체, 판매상 **additional** 추가의 **issue** 발행하다 **responsibility** 책임, 책무 **guidance** 지침, 지도

걸버턴 시

행사 허가 번호: 4571

23현황: 긴급 요청

25걸버턴 공원 관리국은 본 계약의 약관에 의거하여 **쿠엔틴 펠레티어**가 대표로 있는 **스타라이트 멜로디즈 재단**에 아래와 같이 시설 사용을 허가합니다.

행사 정보

행사 신청자: 쿠엔틴 펠레티어 **전화:** 228-555-0132

행사 명칭/상세 사항: 24**"스타라이트 사운즈"**는 일반인에게 개방된 무료 야외 저녁 콘서트이다. 행사에는 세 가지 다른 무대와 라이브 음악 공연이 포함된다.

예상 참석자 수: 800~1,000명

위치: 메이어 콜린스 공원 – 오션사이드 산책로

사용 날짜와 시간:

24**시작: 10월 12일 토요일 오후 5시**

종료: 10월 12일 토요일 오후 10시

25**승인자:** 리오나 오자키

승인 날짜: 9월 23일 수요일

어휘 **permission** 허가, 승인 **facility** 시설 **subject to** ~의 대상인, ~해야 하는 **terms and conditions** 약관 **agreement** 계약, 합의 **applicant** 신청자, 지원자 **estimated** 추정되는, 예상되는 **attendance** 참석자 수 **promenade** 산책로

21 이 정보문은 누구를 대상으로 하겠는가?

(A) 공원 관계자

(B) 걸버턴 방문자

(C) 행사 진행자

(D) 지역 음악가

해설 **추론:** 정보문의 제목이 Obtaining event permits(행사 허가증 받기)이며, 첫 문장에서 걸버턴 시내 공원에서 행사를 개최하려면 걸버턴 공원 관리국에 신청서를 제출해 허가증을 받아야 한다(To hold an event at any public park within the city of Gulverton, you must submit an application for a permit with ~)고 했으므로, 행사 진행자들을 위한 정보문임을 추론할 수 있다. 따라서 정답은 (C)이다.

22 걸버턴 시에 관해 명시된 것은?

(A) 행사 장소가 여러 곳이 있다.

(B) 인기 있는 관광지이다.

(C) 최근 공원관리국을 확대했다.

(D) 음악 축제로 유명하다.

해설 **NOT / True:** 정보문 규정의 첫 항목에서 걸버턴 시는 다양한 규모와 유형의 행사를 위해 장소들을 지정해 놓았다 (The city has designated areas for events of different sizes and types)고 했으므로, 행사 장소가 여러 곳임을 알 수 있다. 따라서 정답은 (A)이다.

어휘 **popular** 인기 있는 **tourist destination** 관광지, 관광 명소 **recently** 최근에 **expand** 확대하다, 확장하다

패러프레이징

지문의 designated areas for events
➲ 보기의 has several event venues

23 펠레티어 씨에 관해 암시된 것은?

   (A) 티켓 800장을 팔아야 한다.
   (B) 수수료 50달러를 청구 받았다.
   (C) 걸버턴에 산다.
   (D) 오자키 씨와 회의를 했다.

해설 **연계:** 허가증을 보면 긴급 요청(Status: Rush Request) 표시가 되어 있으며, 정보문 규정의 두 번째 항목에서 늦게 제출된 신청서는 "긴급 요청"으로 간주되어 50달러의 수수료가 부과된다(Late applications are considered to be "rush requests" and require a nonrefundable $50 fee)고 했다. 따라서 정답은 (B)이다.

패러프레이징

지문의 require a nonrefundable $50 fee
➲ 보기의 was charged a $50 fee

24 10월 12일 이전에 스타라이트 멜로디즈 재단이 해야 하는 일은?

   (A) 추가 허가증 받기
   (B) 만료된 인가증 갱신하기
   (C) 더 넓은 장소로 옮기기
   (D) 식품 판매상 모집하기

해설 **연계:** 허가증을 보면 "스타라이트 사운즈"는 무료 야외 저녁 콘서트("Starlite Sounds" is an outdoor evening concert)이며, 행사일은 10월 12일(Starting: Saturday, October 12 5:00 P.M.)이다. 정보문 세 번째 항목에서 라이브 음악이나 옥외 식품 판매상이 있는 행사는 추가 허가증이 필요하다(Events that feature live music or outside food vendors will require additional permits)고 했다. 따라서 정답은 (A)이다.

어휘 **renew** 갱신하다 **expired** 만료된

25 오자키 씨는 어디에서 일하는가?

   (A) 걸버턴 공원관리국
   (B) 메이어 콜린스 공원 식당
   (C) 오션사이드 산책로
   (D) 스타라이트 멜로디즈 재단

해설 **세부 사항:** 걸버턴 공원 관리국(The Gulverton Parks Management Division hereby grants ~)의 허가증을 보면, 승인자가 리오나 오자키(Approved by: Riona Ozaki)임을 알 수 있다. 따라서 오자키 씨는 걸버턴 공원 관리국에서 근무한다는 것을 알 수 있으므로 정답은 (A)이다.

Questions 26-30 메모 + 카탈로그 페이지

타겐스 서점
여름 카탈로그

고객님들께 드리는 메모:

저희 최신 카탈로그를 즐겁게 보시기 바랍니다. ²⁶3페이지에서 시작하는 "여행과 관광" 코너에서 이번 여름에 어디를 가시든 여러분을 도와줄 상용 회화집과 여행 가이드를 보실 수 있습니다. 5페이지의 "음식" 코너에는 음식 애호가들과 크고 작은 가정용 주방을 가진 아마추어 요리사들을 위한 흥미로운 도서 제목들이 있습니다. 7페이지부터 시작하는 "건축과 디자인" 도서들에서는 손꼽히는 전문가들이 주택 및 상업용 건축의 새로운 경향을 강조합니다. ²⁹"비즈니스와 경영" 코너에 있는 최신 도서들에서는 헨더슨 상 수상작인 〈비즈니스 마케팅 백과사전〉을 비롯해 저희가 선별한 교재와 참고 자료를 보실 수 있습니다 (8페이지).

이 카탈로그는 저희가 가장 최근에 구입한 제품의 일부만 뽑은 것입니다. 전체 도서 목록을 보시려면 www.tagensbooks. com을 방문하세요. 미네올라 지역에 계시다면 꼭 매장에 오셔서 웹사이트에서 볼 수 없는 수백 권의 책을 비롯해 ²⁷수많은 추가 도서들을 보세요.

타겐스 서점

어휘 **phrase book** (여행 등에 쓸 만한) 상용 회화집 **no matter where** 어디를 ~하든 **include** 포함하다 **title** 제목 **amateur** 아마추어 **expert** 전문가 **highlight** 강조하다 **trend** 경향, 동향 **residential** 거주의 **commercial** 상업의 **selection** 선택, 선택된 것[사람] **encyclopedia** 백과사전 **acquisition** 매입, 인수 **a wealth of** 수많은, 풍부한

〈경영 분석 교재〉
스티븐 Y. 코레이아, 제인 S. 야마시로 지음

재정 관리에 대한 명확하고 읽기 쉬운 입문서로, 추천 학습 활동과 ³⁰⁽ᴰ⁾핵심 요점을 설명하는 재미있는 만화가 가득하다. ³⁰⁽ᴬ⁾교사들은 단체 활동을 위해 자유롭게 페이지들을 복제할 수 있다. ²⁸상태: 사용 흔적이 별로 없어 아주 좋음. 49.95달러

〈새로운 세기의 재무 운용〉
아멜리에 고란손 지음

이 귀중한 책은 탄탄한 재무 이론과 현실적인 적용을 결합하고 있다. 고란손은 ³⁰⁽ᶜ⁾실제 예시와 사례 연구로 이론적 원칙을 강조한다. 학생과 사업주 모두에게 추천한다. ²⁸상태: 신품과 유사. 34.95달러

〈중소기업 회계〉
앨리샤 D. 고 지음

직접 회계와 납세 의무를 처리하고 싶은 중소기업 소유주의 필독서. ²⁸**상태: 보통으로 모서리와 가장자리 닳음. 29.95달러**

²⁹**〈비즈니스 마케팅 백과〉**
앤드류 오팔린스키 지음

어떤 초보도 이해할 수 있는 책으로, 비즈니스와 마케팅 핵심 용어 2,500개 이상이 정의되어 있음. 비즈니스에 입문하려는 모든 이들에게 꼭 필요한 책. ²⁸**상태: 양호하며 표지에 닳은 흔적 있음. 35.95달러**

타겐스 서점

어휘 readable 읽기 쉬운 finance 금융, 재무
entertaining 재미있는, 즐거움을 주는 illustrate 설명하다 essential 핵심적인, 필수적인 reproduce 복제하다 sheet 종이 activity 활동 limited 제한된, 한정된 sign 표시, 흔적 century 세기 invaluable 귀중한 combine A with B A와 B를 결합하다 practical 실용적인, 현실적인 application 적용, 응용 case study 사례 연구 take care of ~을 처리하다 accounting 회계 obligation 의무 fair 괜찮은 wear 닳음, 마모 edge 모서리 novice 초보자 definition (개념이나 단어 등의) 정의

26 메모를 토대로, 타겐스 서점은 어떤 책을 재고로 보유하고 있겠는가?

(A) 유명한 사진가의 전기
(B) 우주 여행의 역사
(C) 유럽 최고의 휴양지에 대한 평가
(D) 전문 요리사들을 위한 교재

해설 **추론:** 메모 첫 단락에서 타겐스 서점의 최신 카탈로그(our latest catalog)를 소개하고 있는데, 두 번째 문장에서 '여행과 관광' 코너에서 이번 여름에 어디를 가든 여러분을 도와줄 상용 회화집과 여행 가이드를 볼 수 있다(in our "Travel and Tourism" section, you will find phrase books and travel guides to help you no matter where you go this summer)고 했으므로, 정답은 (C)이다.

어휘 biography 전기 photographer 사진가 space 우주, 공간 spot 장소 professional 전문적인, 직업의

패러프레이징
지문의 travel guides to help you no matter where you go ➡ 보기의 A review of top vacation spots in Europe

27 메모에서 두 번째 단락 3행의 "wealth"와 의미가 가장 가까운 단어는?

(A) 가치   (B) 비용
(C) 재산   (D) 풍부함

해설 **동의어:** be sure to visit our store for a wealth of additional books는 '꼭 매장을 방문해서 수많은 추가 도서들을 보라'는 의미로, wealth는 '풍부, 다량'의 의미로 쓰였다. 따라서 (D) abundance가 정답이다. a wealth of는 '풍부한, 수많은'의 의미로 자주 쓰이는 표현이다.

어휘 value 가치 expense 비용 fortune 재산 abundance 풍부함

28 카탈로그에 관해 암시된 것은?

(A) 중고 서적을 광고한다.
(B) 종합적인 목록이다.
(C) 주로 학술 도서가 포함된다.
(D) 1년에 한 번 발행된다.

해설 **추론:** 각 서적의 상태(Condition)를 설명하는 부분을 보면, '사용 흔적이 별로 없어 아주 좋음(Very good with limited signs of use)', '신품과 유사(Like new)', '보통으로 모서리와 가장자리 닳음(Fair with some wear to corners and edges)'과 '양호하며 표지에 닳은 흔적 있음(Good with signs of cover wear)'으로 보아 중고 서적임을 알 수 있다. 따라서 정답은 (A)이다.

어휘 advertise 광고하다 used 중고의, 사용한 comprehensive 포괄적인 mainly 주로 academic 학술적인 publish 발행하다, 발간하다

29 누가 상을 받았는가?

(A) 코레이아 씨
(B) 고란손 씨
(C) 고 씨
(D) 오팔린스키 씨

해설 **연계:** 메모 첫 단락 마지막 문장에서 '비즈니스와 경영' 코너에 있는 〈비즈니스 마케팅 백과사전〉은 헨더슨 상 수상작(the *Encyclopedia of Business Marketing*, winner of the Henderson Prize)이라고 했다. 카탈로그의 마지막 항목을 보면 〈비즈니스 마케팅 백과사전〉의 저자는 앤드류 오팔린스키(*Encyclopedia of Business Marketing* by Andrew Opalinsky)이므로, 정답은 (D)이다.

패러프레이징
지문의 winner of the Henderson Prize
➡ 질문의 received an award

30 카탈로그 페이지의 책에 대한 설명 중 언급되지 않은 특징은?

(A) 복사할 수 있는 교재
(B) 신규 업체 설립 시 점검 사항
(C) 실생활에서 끌어낸 예시
(D) 요점을 분명하게 설명하기 위한 그림

해설 **Not/True:** (A)와 (D)는 Business Analysis Textbook 설명에서 교사들은 단체 활동을 위해 자유롭게 페이지들

을 복사할 수 있다(Teachers are free to reproduce sheets for group activities)와 핵심 요점을 설명하는 재미있는 만화들(entertaining cartoons illustrating essential points)에서 언급되었으며, (C)는 *New Century Finance Management* 설명에서 실제 예시와 사례 연구(real-life examples and case studies)라고 언급되었다. 따라서 언급되지 않은 (B)가 정답이다.

어휘 **photocopy** 복사하다 **checklist** 점검 사항 **example** 예시 **draw from** ~에서 끌어내다 **real life** 실생활 **drawing** 그림 **clarify** 분명하게 설명하다 **key point** 요점

패러프레이징
지문의 reproduce ➡ 보기 (A)의 be photocopied
지문의 real-life examples ➡ 보기 (C)의 Examples drawn from real life
지문의 entertaining cartoons illustrating essential points ➡ 보기 (D)의 Drawings to clarify key points

Questions 31-35 표 + 이메일

Nydoka.com 웹사이트 - 6월 1일 주간 방문자 분석

웹페이지	이 페이지 이후 웹사이트를 나간 손님의 비율	손님이 다른 페이지를 방문하지 않을 만한 이유
³²홈	46%	홈페이지에 광고 링크가 너무 많음
제품	34%	조악한 페이지 구성
문의	31%	한정된 고객 서비스 시간
판매	13%	제품을 구매하지 않은 채로 두는 고객들에 대해 후속 조치를 하지 않음
³¹계산	5%	성공적인 거래

어휘 **analysis** 분석 **percentage** 비율 **reason** 이유 **advertisement** 광고 **layout** 배치 **limited** 한정된 **checkout** 계산 **transaction** 거래

수신: ernest_bram@nydoka.com
발신: lservin@nydoka.com
날짜: 6월 12일
제목: RE: 웹사이트 방문자 분석

어니스트 씨께,

웹사이트 방문자 분석 보고서를 보내 주셔서 감사합니다. 데이터로부터 제가 파악할 수 있었던 것을 제안하고자 합니다. 내일 만나서 제 의견에 대해 이야기할 수 있겠네요.

• ³²가장 긴급한 일은 링크 문제를 해결하는 것이라고 생각합니다. 방문자들을 머무르도록 하기보다는 다른 사이트로 보내

우리와 멀어지게 만들고 있는 것 같습니다. 마케팅 부서와 이 문제에 관해 이야기해 보겠습니다.

• 제품 페이지 문제의 한 가지 가능한 해결책은 유사한 제품을 함께 보여 주기보다는 따로 분리해 나열하는 것입니다. 예를 들어, ³³오디오 기기를 위한 제품 페이지에 헤드폰과 스피커를 별도로 나열해 볼 수 있습니다. ³⁴웹디자이너인 비제이 라자스탄에게 페이지를 수정하라고 하겠습니다.

• ³⁵고객들이 웹페이지를 나가려고 할 때 가상 장바구니에 물건이 있다는 것을 떠올릴 수 있도록 웹개발자인 우메카 다츠노에게 판매 페이지에 팝업 메시지를 추가해 달라고 요청하고자 합니다.

우리의 토론을 기대하며,

리디아 서빈

어휘 **forward** 전달하다 **insight** 통찰력 **derive** 얻다 **observation** 관찰, (관찰에 따른) 의견 **pressing** 긴급한 **address** 다루다 **alienate** 멀어지게 만들다 **rather than** ~보다는 **communicate** 소통하다 **solution** 해결책 **device** 장치 **separately** 별도로 **modification** 수정 **virtual** 가상의

31 웹사이트의 방문자 중 몇 퍼센트가 물건을 구입하는가?
(A) 46%   (B) 34%
(C) 31%   (D) 5%

해설 **세부 사항:** 웹사이트 방문자 분석 차트에 따르면, 계산, 즉 고객이 웹사이트를 방문해 성공적인 거래까지 완료한 항목이 5%라고 나와 있으므로 (D)가 정답이다.

32 서빈 씨는 어느 웹페이지에 대해 가장 걱정하는가?
(A) 홈   (B) 제품
(C) 문의   (D) 판매

해설 **연계:** 이메일의 두 번째 단락에서 서빈 씨는 가장 긴급한 일은 링크 문제를 해결하는 것이라고 생각한다(I think the most pressing need is to address the links issue)고 했고, 차트에 따르면 홈페이지에 광고 링크가 너무 많다(Too many links to advertisements on the home page)며 링크와 관련된 문제를 언급하고 있다. 따라서 서빈 씨가 가장 걱정하는 웹페이지는 링크 문제가 있는 홈페이지이므로 (A)가 정답이다.

33 니도카사에서 판매하는 제품은 무엇이겠는가?
(A) 의류 및 액세서리
(B) 음향 기기
(C) 주방용품
(D) 사무용품

해설 **추론:** 이메일의 세 번째 단락 두 번째 문장에서 오디오 기기를 위한 당사의 제품 페이지에 헤드폰과 스피커를 별도로 나열해 볼 수 있다(on our products page for audio devices, we could list headphones and speakers separately)고 했으므로 니도카사는 음향 기기를 판매하는 곳임을 알 수 있다. 따라서 (B)가 정답이다.

패러프레이징
지문의 audio devices ➡ 보기의 Sound equipment

34 라자스탄 씨는 무엇을 할 것 같은가?

(A) 링크 몇 개를 손본다.
(B) 페이지 구성을 다시 디자인한다.
(C) 계약을 수정한다.
(D) 새로운 연구에 착수한다.

해설 **추론:** 이메일의 세 번째 단락 세 번째 문장에서 서빈 씨가 웹디자이너인 비제이 라자스탄에게 페이지를 수정하라고 하겠다(I'll have our Web designer Vijay Rajasthan make modifications to the page)고 했으므로 라자스탄 씨는 서빈 씨의 요청을 받아 웹페이지를 다시 디자인할 것임을 알 수 있다. 따라서 (B)가 정답이다.

어휘 revise 수정하다 launch 착수[시작]하다

패러프레이징
지문의 make modifications to the page
➡ 보기의 redesign a page layout

35 다츠노 씨는 무엇을 만들라고 요청받을 것인가?

(A) 이메일 회신
(B) 눈길을 사로잡는 로고
(C) 새로운 지불 옵션
(D) 자동 알림 메시지

해설 **세부 사항:** 이메일의 네 번째 단락에서 서빈 씨가 고객들이 웹페이지를 나가려고 할 때 가상 장바구니에 물건이 있다는 것을 떠올릴 수 있도록 웹개발자인 우메카 다츠노에게 판매 페이지에 팝업 메시지를 추가해 달라고 요청하고자 한다(I'd like to request that Web developer Umeka Tatsuno ~ when they try to leave the Web page)고 했으므로 다츠노 씨는 곧 자동 팝업 메시지를 만들어 달라고 요청받을 것임을 알 수 있다. 따라서 (D)가 정답이다.

어휘 response 응답 eye-catching 눈길을 끄는
automated 자동의 alert 경보

패러프레이징
지문의 a pop-up message
➡ 보기의 An automated alert

UNIT 14	삼중 연계 지문

ETS 예제 본책 p. 378

오클랜드(2월 1일) – 호주의 Z&W 푸드가 사업을 확장하고 있다. **이 슈퍼마켓 체인은 내년 내내 뉴질랜드와 남아프리카에 새로운 점포 20곳을 열 것이라고 발표했다.** "Z&W는 전 세계에 매장을 여는 데 전념하고 있습니다. **우리의 가격 책정 관행이 신규 및 기존 시장에서 우리에게 경쟁 우위를 가져다줄 것으로 믿습니다**"라고 마야 카필 대변인은 전화 인터뷰에서 말했다.

게다가, Z&W 푸드의 신임 지역 부사장인 다니엘 스티븐슨은 기존 점포 여러 곳을 리모델링할 예정이라고 말했다. "우리는 매장이 좀 더 현대적이고 매력적인 디자인을 갖추고 친환경적인 기능을 구현하는 것을 목표로 하고 있습니다."라고 그는 설명했다. 가까운 곳으로는, **오클랜드의 호킨스 가에 있는 Z&W 푸드 매장이 3월 1일 개보수 공사를 위해 문을 닫을 것으로 예상된다. 5월 18일에 다시 문을 열 예정으로 약 3개월간 휴점할 예정이다.**

어휘 expand 확장하다 be committed to ~에 전념하다
pricing 가격 책정 practice 관행 competitive
경쟁적인 advantage 이점, 우위 existing 기존의
spokesperson 대변인 regional 지역의 vice
president 부사장 remodel 개조하다 aim for ~을
목표로 하다 inviting 매력적인 implement 시행하다
feature 특징; 특징으로 하다 environmentally
friendly 친환경적인

그랜드 재개점 기념식 Z&W 푸드
오클랜드 호킨스 가 673번지   5월 2일 토요일

오전 9시, 리본 커팅식에 로즈 에노카 매니저와 직원들과 함께 주십시오. 경품 당첨 기회와 함께 무료 간식, 케이크, 음료수를 즐기십시오. 4번 가 학교 어린이 합창단이 오전 10시에 공연할 예정입니다.

우리가 만들어 낸 상점의 변화를 보러 오십시오.

• 리모델링된 수프 앤 샐러드 바
• **현장 베이커리, 주 7일 영업**
• 확장된 고객 서비스 구역
• 상담 공간이 있는 새로운 약국
6월 예정 – 매장 내 카페와 커피 바!

어휘 complimentary 무료의 along with ~와 함께
choir 합창단 expanded 확장된 pharmacy 약국
consultation 상담

PART 7 | UNIT 14

205

구인

Z&W 푸드

오클랜드 호킨스 가 673번지

- 매장 내 카페 카운터 직원
- 야간 근무조 제빵사(경력 요망)
- 출납원, 상근 또는 파트타임
- 유지 관리

세부 사항은 매장 관리자에게 문의하십시오.

어휘 in-store 매장 내의 overnight shift 야간 근무
maintenance 유지 관리

1 기사의 목적은?

(A) 임원 승진 논의

(B) 일부 신제품에 대한 강조

(C) 회사의 계획에 대한 보고

(D) 지역 비즈니스 동향 설명

2 기사는 Z&W사의 제품에 대해 타 업체 제품과 비교해서 어떻다고 암시하는가?

(A) 덜 비싸다.

(B) 품질이 더 높다.

(C) 더 다양한 선택을 제시한다.

(D) 친환경적이다.

3 전단지에서 추론할 수 있는 것은?

(A) 기념식은 일반인에게 비공개로 한다.

(B) 다과류는 행사 기간 중 할인 판매될 것이다.

(C) 학교 합창단이 상을 받았다.

(D) 보수 공사 프로젝트가 일정보다 앞서 완료되었다.

4 전단지가 상점에 대해 명시하는 것은?

(A) 더 이상 약을 취급하지 않는다.

(B) 제과점은 매일 영업한다.

(C) 가격이 인하되었다.

(D) 영업시간이 바뀌었다.

5 누가 구직자들에게 더 자세한 내용을 제공할 수 있는가?

(A) 스티븐슨 씨   (B) 에노카 씨

(C) 수석 제빵사   (D) 선임 출납원

ETS **PRACTICE**					본책 p. 381
1 (A)	**2** (B)	**3** (A)	**4** (C)	**5** (B)	**6** (C)

웹페이지 + 광고 + 이메일

서비스	**사람**	언론	인재 채용

플림턴 파이낸셜 서비스

국가: 미국   지사: 댈러스

더 자세한 내용을 위해 선도적인 전문가 중 한 명과 연락을 하시려면 이메일을 보내 주십시오.

등기 이사: b.green@plimptonfs.com

[1]이사: j.waters@plimptonfs.com

감사 관리자: k.bean@plimptonfs.com

선임 회계사: l.framel@plimptonfs.com

어휘 leading 선도적인 expert 전문가 partner 등기이사
audit 감사 accountant 회계사

신입 세무사

플림턴 파이낸셜 서비스에서 댈러스에 있는 국제팀에 합류할 신입 세무사를 찾습니다. 지원자는 국제 세무 회계 서류를 준비해 본 경험이 있고 팀에 잘 협력해서 일하는 사람이어야 합니다. 2개 국어를 구사하는 지원자는 우대합니다. 저희는 우수한 의료 복리후생과 승진 기회를 제공합니다. **[1,2]이력서와 자기소개서, 세 통의 추천서를 j.waters@plimptonfs.com으로 재니스 워터스에게 보내 주십시오.**

어휘 entry-level 신입직, 초보자의 tax accountant
세무사 candidate 지원자 team player (회사에서)
다른 사람들과 잘 협력해서 일하는 사람 preparation
준비 bilingual 2개 국어를 쓰는 preferred 선호되는
benefits 복리 후생 opportunity 기회 career
advancement 승진 cover letter 자기소개서
reference 추천서

발신: 모리스 윌리엄스 〈maury@gomail.com〉

수신: 재니스 워터스 〈j.waters@plimptonfs.com〉

제목: 세무사 직위

첨부파일: 서류

워터스 씨께,

저는 신입 세무사직에 관련하여 이 이메일을 씁니다. 저는 제가 그 자리에 적임자라고 믿습니다. 런던에 있는 체스터필드 파이낸셜 그룹에서 현재 제가 하는 직무가 세무 회계 쪽이기 때문입니다. 일단 저는 이번 인턴십이 끝나면 2월 2일에 댈러스로 돌아갑니다. **[2]요청하신 보충 서류는 모두 첨부했습니다.** 그럼 소식 기다리겠습니다.

모리스 윌리엄스 드림

어휘 in regards to ~에 관하여 a good match 적임자
current 현재의 duty 직무 complete 마치다,
완료하다 attach 첨부하다 support document
보충 서류

1 플림턴 파이낸셜 서비스에서 재니스 워터스 씨의 직위는?

(A) 이사   (B) 선임 회계사

(C) 등기 이사   (D) 감사 관리자

해설 **연계:** 광고의 마지막 문장에 보면 이력서와 자기소개서, 세 통의 추천서를 j.waters@plimptonfs.com으로 재니스 워터스에게 보내 달라는 내용이 있는데, 웹 페이지에서 해당 이메일을 찾아보면 재니스 워터스의 직위가 이사(Director)임을 알 수 있으므로 정답은 (A)이다.

2 윌리엄스 씨가 이메일에 첨부하지 않은 것은?

(A) 추천서   (B) 납세 증명서
(C) 이력서   (D) 자기소개서

해설 **연계:** 광고의 마지막 문장에 보면 이력서와 자기소개서, 세 통의 추천서를 j.waters@plimptonfs.com으로 재니스 워터스에게 보내 달라는 내용이 있는데, 이메일 마지막 부분에 보면 요청한 보충 서류를 모두 첨부했다(I have attached ~ you requested)는 내용이 있으므로 윌리엄스 씨가 이력서, 자기소개서, 추천서를 보냈으리라 짐작할 수 있다. 납세 증명서는 언급이 없으므로 정답은 (B)이다.

웹페이지 + 기사 + 편지

제목: 〈1페니를 은행에 넣어라〉   ³⁽ᴰ⁾**저자: 하퍼 라이언스**
책 소개
하퍼 라이언스의 두 번째 책은 아버지가 들려준 현명한 조언으로 시작한다. "은행에 넣은 모든 돈은 미래의 투자를 위한 돈이다." 그녀의 아버지는 말한다. 라이언스는 아버지의 충고에 따라 돈을 성공적인 사업과 주식에 투자했다. 신간에서 ³⁽ᴮ⁾**라이언스는 투자에 대한 그녀의 생각, 전략, 주의할 점을 들려준다.**

제품 소개   형태: 양장본
³⁽ᴬ⁾**가격: 19.99달러**   출시일: 11월 4일

어휘 penny 페니, 센트   investment 투자   stock 주식
strategy 전략

하퍼 라이언스, 신간 발매

보스턴 – ³⁽ᴰ⁾**베스트셀러 〈1달러로 할 수 있는 일〉의 저자 하퍼 라이언스**가 큰 기대를 모은 책 〈1페니를 은행에 넣어라〉를 마침내 출간했다. 현명하게 돈을 투자하는 법을 설명하는 ³⁽ᶜ⁾**187쪽 분량의 이 책은** 벌써 백만 부 이상이 팔렸다. 경제학자 에이든 헨리에 따르면, 라이언스는 "사람들이 공감할 수 있고 배울 수 있는" 책을 써냈다.

다음 달에 라이언스는 2주간의 일정으로 책 홍보 전국 투어를 시작할 예정이다. ⁴**라이언스의 보스턴 일정으로는 12월 4일 마고 서점이 예정되어 있다.** 투어에 관해 더 자세히 알고 싶다면 아울 앤 패럿 출판사 웹사이트에 접속하면 된다.

어휘 release 출시하다, 공개하다   author 저자   highly anticipated 큰 기대를 모은   wisely 현명하게
economist 경제학자   relate to ~을 공감하다, ~에 관련되다   embark on ~에 착수하다   be scheduled to ~할 예정이다

11월 17일

라이언스 씨께,

귀하의 책 홍보 투어가 12월 1일에 시작될 예정임을 알려 드리게 되어 기쁩니다. 귀하의 일정 최종본을 첨부합니다. 귀하께서 마지막으로 일정을 확인하신 이후 두 가지 세부 사항이 추가되었음을 양지하십시오.

⁴**12월 4일 마고 서점 방문 일정에 책 사인회가 추가되었습니다.** 사인회는 〈1페니를 은행에 넣어라〉의 한 부분을 발췌해 낭독하신 후에 진행됩니다. 아울러 라디오 프로그램인 〈벤추라 뉴스〉와의 인터뷰도 확정되었습니다. 따라서 12월 12일 로스앤젤레스행 항공편이 일정에 추가되었습니다. 혹시 궁금한 점이 있으시면 주저하지 말고 저에게 연락주세요.

로건 파킨슨, 경제 금융 분야 편집자
아울 앤 패럿 출판사

어휘 promotional 홍보의   be set to ~할 예정이다
finalized copy 최종본   itinerary 여행 일정
appearance 출현, 등장   excerpt 발췌   confirm
확인하다   agenda 의제, 일정   hesitate 주저하다

3 〈1페니를 은행에 넣어라〉에 대해 언급되지 않은 사실은?

(A) 20달러 이상으로 판매된다.
(B) 독자들에게 투자 조언을 제공한다.
(C) 200페이지 미만이다.
(D) 베스트셀러 작가가 썼다.

해설 **연계:** 웹페이지에서 저자가 투자에 대한 그녀의 생각, 전략, 주의할 점을 들려준다(Lyons shares her thoughts, strategies, and warnings on investing money)고 한 데서 (B)를, 기사에서 187쪽의 분량(The 187-page book)이라고 한 데서 (C)를, 웹페이지의 저자명(Author: Harper Lyons)과 기사의 베스트셀러 저자 하퍼 라이언스(Harper Lyons, the best-selling author of What a Dollar Can Do)라고 한 데서 (D)를 알 수 있다. 웹페이지 하단 부분에서 책 가격은 19.99달러로 나오므로 정답은 (A)이다.

4 보스턴에서 무슨 일이 있겠는가?

(A) 홍보 투어가 시작될 것이다.
(B) 한 저자가 〈1달러로 할 수 있는 일〉의 한 부분을 발췌해 낭독할 것이다.
(C) 한 작가가 신간에 사인을 해줄 것이다.
(D) 라디오 인터뷰가 녹음될 것이다.

해설 **연계:** 기사 마지막 부분에서 저자의 보스턴 일정이 12월 4일 마고 서점(Lyons is scheduled to be in Boston ~ Margot Bookstores)임을 알 수 있는데, 편지 두 번째 단락에서 마고 서점 방문 일정에 책 사인회가 추가되었다(On December 4, a book signing event ~ Margot Bookstores)고 했으므로 정답은 (C)이다.

이메일 + 공지 + 후기

수신: 티아고 프랑코 〈franco@cooperdenton.com〉
발신: 자이나브 와셈 〈wasem@cooperdenton.com〉
제목: 웹사이트 공지
날짜: 5월 31일

티아고 씨께,

우리 박물관 웹사이트에 게시해 줬으면 하는 공지 사항이 몇 개 있어요. 첫 번째로 **5에드거 홀에서 하는 세 달짜리 특별 전시회 〈위대한 비행〉을 홍보해야 합니다.** 내 사무실에 그 항공 전시회에 대한 세부 자료가 있으니, 되도록 빨리 자료를 받아 가세요. 아울러 방문객들에게 라이트 홀 폐쇄도 공지해 주세요. 감사합니다.

자이나브 와셈 드림
쿠퍼 덴턴 박물관장

어휘 post 게시하다 publicize 홍보하다 exhibition 전시회 aviation 항공(술) at one's earliest convenience 되도록 빨리 notify 통지하다 closure 폐쇄

공지

게시일: 6월 5일

6 7월 1일부터 라이트 홀이 지속적인 보존 프로젝트의 일환으로 임시 폐쇄됩니다. 박물관은 그 전시관에 있던 소장품을 보호하고 보존할 것입니다. 박물관의 나머지 부분은 여전히 대중에게 개방될 것입니다. 라이트 홀은 8월 1일에 다시 문을 엽니다.

어휘 temporarily 일시적으로 ongoing 지속적인 preservation 보존 protect 보호하다 conserve 보존하다 object 물건 accessible 접근 가능한

평가: ★★★☆
게시자: 가브리엘 이

저는 지난주에 쿠퍼 덴턴 박물관에 다녀왔는데, 아주 좋은 시간을 보냈습니다. 우리 인솔자였던 나탈리 씨는 지식이 풍부하고 친절했어요. 〈위대한 비행〉은 탐사에 사용된 각종 항공기를 보여 주는 볼거리가 풍부한 전시회였어요. **5일반 입장권 외에 별도로 표를 구매해야 했는데,** 충분히 값어치가 있었어요. **6유일하게 아쉬운 점은 우주 비행사들이 우주에서 사용한 우주복과 장비를 볼 수 없었다는 점이에요.** 그것들을 전시한 라이트 홀이 임시 폐쇄되었기 때문이죠.

어휘 knowledgeable 지식이 풍부한 spectacular 볼 만한, 화려한 showcase 전시하다 aircraft 항공기 exploration 탐험, 탐사 downside 단점, 불리한 점

---

space suit 우주복 equipment 장비 astronaut 우주 비행사

5 에드거 홀에서 하는 전시회에 대해 사실인 것은?

(A) 티아고 프랑코가 마련했다.
(B) 추가 입장료가 있다.
(C) 아동을 위한 것이다.
(D) 영상 전시회를 특징으로 한다.

해설 **연계:** 이메일에서 에드거 홀에서 하는 세 달짜리 특별 전시회 〈위대한 비행〉을 홍보해야 한다(we should publicize our special three-month exhibition, *Great Flights*, in Edgar Hall)고 했고 후기에서 〈위대한 비행〉을 보기 위해 일반 입장권 외에 별도로 입장권을 구매했다(I had to buy another ticket to get in)는 내용이 있으므로 정답은 (B)이다.

6 어느 달에 이 씨가 박물관을 방문했는가?

(A) 5월   (B) 6월
(C) 7월   (D) 8월

해설 **연계:** 세 번째 지문에서 가브리엘 이 씨가 라이트 홀이 임시 폐쇄되었기 때문에 우주복과 장비를 볼 수 없었다(I couldn't see ~ temporarily closed)고 했다. 그리고 공지에서 7월 1일부터 라이트 홀이 임시 폐쇄된다(Starting July 1, Wright Hall will ~ project)고 명시되어 있으므로 정답은 (C)이다.

ETS TEST 본책 p. 384

1 (D)	**2** (A)	**3** (B)	**4** (C)	**5** (C)
6 (C)	**7** (C)	**8** (D)	**9** (B)	**10** (C)
11 (B)	**12** (D)	**13** (D)	**14** (C)	**15** (B)
16 (B)	**17** (A)	**18** (C)	**19** (B)	**20** (D)
21 (A)	**22** (D)	**23** (B)	**24** (C)	**25** (A)
26 (B)	**27** (D)	**28** (A)	**29** (C)	**30** (D)
31 (C)	**32** (A)	**33** (B)	**34** (C)	**35** (A)

Questions 1-5 이메일 + 일정표 + 이메일

발신: 아그네스 하펜던
〈aharpenden@findleycommunitycentre.ca〉
수신: 케빈 벅맨 〈kbockman@westbanklaw.ca〉
제목: 후원 기회
날짜: 12월 14일

벅맨 씨께,

1수년간 귀하는 법률 사무소 웨스트뱅크 법률 사무소를 대표해 핀들리 주민 센터에서 지역 사회 주민들에게 무료로 제공하는

여러 교육 기회를 위해 자금 지원을 인가해 주셨습니다. 2이제 다가오는 2월과 3월에 있을 연례 강연 시리즈의 기업 후원자가 되는 것을 고려해 주셨으면 합니다. 이 강연은 저희가 6년 동안 주최했습니다만 해마다 참석자가 많았다고 확실히 말씀드릴 수 있습니다. 2만약 이번 강연 시리즈에 재정을 지원하기로 선택하시면, 관련 출판물과 팻말에 귀사의 후원 사실을 자랑스럽게 표시하겠습니다. 답변 기다리겠습니다.

아그네스 하펜던
행사 총괄담당자
핀들리 주민 센터

어휘 authorize 인가하다   on behalf of ~을 대표해   well attended 참석자가 많은   publication 출판(물)

2핀들리 주민 센터 수요일 강연 시리즈
웨스트뱅크 법률 사무소 후원

2월 6일: 아스트리드 쿨롬
지역 의류매장 아스트리드 터치 주인인 쿨롬 씨가 패션 업계와 업주가 경험하는 문제와 즐거움에 대해 논의합니다.

2월 20일: 루카스 캐럴
전문적으로 훈련 받은 요리사인 캐럴 씨가 식당에서 일하고, 식당을 소유한 경험에 대해 이야기합니다.

43월 6일: 하이르 카타나
어레인지먼츠 포 유의 주인 카타나 씨가 꽃집 프랜차이즈 사업을 창업해 성공한 방법을 공유합니다.

3월 20일: 에바 루비오
자격증을 갖춘 금융설계사인 루비오 씨가 은퇴를 위한 예산 수립과 저축 등 금융 문제를 논의합니다.

모든 행사는 오후 6시 30분 핀들리 주민 센터 대강당에서 시작하며 일반에게 공개됩니다. 입장은 무료이지만 등록해야 합니다. 3커피, 차, 가벼운 간식이 무료로 제공됩니다. 시리즈에 대한 더 자세한 정보는 행사 총괄담당자인 아그네스 하펜던에게 416-555-0179, 내선번호 43으로 연락하거나 〈aharpenden@findleycommunitycentre.ca〉으로 이메일을 보내세요.

어휘 certified 자격(증)을 갖춘   retirement 은퇴   complimentary 무료의

발신: 히로지 이와오 〈hirojii5@mailserve.net.ca〉
수신: 아그네스 하펜던
      〈aharpenden@findleycommunitycentre.ca〉
제목: 강연 시리즈 문의
날짜: 3월 25일

하펜던 씨께:

지난 두 달 동안 강연 시리즈에서 제공하신 모든 주제가 무척 흥미로웠습니다. 4제가 참석할 수 있었던 강연이 정말 즐거웠

지만, 꽃 사업에 특별히 관심 있는 터라 더 많이 가지 못해 서운했습니다. 5아쉽게도 저는 수요일 저녁이면 늦게까지 일하기 때문에 다른 강의에는 참석하지 못했습니다. 더 많은 사람이 참석할 수 있도록 향후 행사를 다양한 날짜와 시간에 제공할 계획이 있으신가요?

히로지 이와오

어휘 intrigued 흥미로운

1 첫 번째 이메일에서 핀들리 주민 센터에 관해 언급된 것은?

(A) 마케팅 회사를 고용해 서비스를 홍보할 계획이다.
(B) 강연할 의사가 있는 강사를 찾는 데 어려움을 겪고 있다.
(C) 판매업체가 현장에서 참석자들에게 제품을 판매하도록 권유한다.
(D) 지난 몇 년 동안 여러 강연 시리즈 행사를 개최했다.

해설 **Not / True:** 첫 이메일의 첫 문장에서 수년간 귀하는 웨스트뱅크 법률 사무소를 대표해 핀들리 주민 센터에서 지역 사회 주민들에게 무료로 제공하는 여러 교육 기회를 위해 자금 지원을 인가해 주셨다(Over the years ~ several of the educational opportunities that we at Findley Community Centre have offered free of charge to residents of our community)고 했으므로 (D)가 정답이다.

어휘 vendor 판매업체

패러프레이징
지문의 the educational opportunities
➡ 보기의 the lecture-series events

2 벅맨 씨에 관해 판단할 수 있는 것은?

(A) 수요일 강연에 재정 기부를 승인했다.
(B) 국제 기업에 법률 자문을 제공한다.
(C) 주기적으로 하펜던 씨를 만난다.
(D) 주민 센터에서 수업할 것이다.

해설 **연계:** 첫 이메일의 두 번째 문장에서 웨스트뱅크 법률 사무소의 벅맨 씨에게 다가오는 2월과 3월에 있을 연례 강연 시리즈의 기업 후원자가 되는 것을 고려해 주셨으면 한다(we are inviting you to consider ~ this coming February and March)면서, 네 번째 문장에서 이번 강연 시리즈에 재정을 지원하기로 선택하시면 관련 출판물과 팻말에 귀사의 후원 사실을 자랑스럽게 표시하겠다(If you should choose to financially support ~ identify your firm's sponsorship on all related publications and signs)고 했다. 일정표를 보면 핀들리 주민 센터 수요일 강연 시리즈(Findley Community Centre Wednesday Lecture Series)라는 제목 아래에 웨스트뱅크 법률 사무소 후원(Sponsored by Westbank Law Partners)이라고 표시되어 있으므로, 벅맨 씨가 강연 시리즈를 후원하기로 결정했음을 알 수 있다. 따라서 (A)가 정답이다.

3 강연 시리즈에 관해 명시된 것은?

(A) 참석하려면 수업비가 필요하다.
(B) 무료 음식이 포함된다.
(C) 원래 위치가 변경되었다.
(D) 목표 청중은 변호사다.

해설 **Not / True:** 일정표의 마지막 단락 세 번째 문장에서 커피, 차, 가벼운 간식이 무료로 제공된다(Complimentary coffee, tea, and light snacks are provided)고 했으므로 (B)가 정답이다.

패러프레이징
지문의 complimentary coffee, tea, and light snacks
➡ 보기의 free food and drinks

4 이와오 씨는 누구의 발표회에 참석했겠는가?

(A) 쿨롬 씨   (B) 캐럴 씨
(C) 카타나 씨   (D) 루비오 씨

해설 **연계:** 두 번째 이메일의 두 번째 문장에서 이와오 씨가 꽃 사업에 특히 관심 있는 터라 참석할 수 있었던 강연이 정말 즐거웠다(While I really enjoyed the one ~ a special interest in the flower business)고 했고, 일정표에 따르면 꽃 사업과 관련된 강연은 3월 6일에 있었던 하이르 카타나 씨의 강연이므로 (C)가 정답이다.

5 이와오 씨가 언급하는 문제는?

(A) 행사에 늦게 도착했다.
(B) 주문한 물품을 받지 못했다.
(C) 수요일 저녁에는 대개 바쁘다.
(D) 작품이 별로 다양하지 않다.

해설 **세부 사항:** 두 번째 이메일의 후반부에 이와오 씨가 아쉽게도 수요일 저녁이면 늦게까지 일하기 때문에 다른 강의에는 참석하지 못했다(Unfortunately, I normally work late on Wednesday nights ~ the other lectures)고 했으므로 (C)가 정답이다.

패러프레이징
지문의 work late on Wednesday nights
➡ 보기의 busy on Wednesday evenings

Questions 6-10 구인 목록 + 이메일 + 이메일

카피라이터 – 큐어리어스 캣 애널리틱스
큐어리어스 캣 애널리틱스에서 역동적인 팀과 함께할 재능 있는 마케팅 카피라이터를 찾고 있습니다. 우리 카피라이터들은 당사의 브랜드와 서비스를 홍보하기 위해 간결하고 매력적인 컨텐츠를 제작합니다.
책무
  • **6기사, 블로그 게시물, 이메일용 컨텐츠의 작성 및 편집 업무로 마케팅 팀과 협업**

  • 큐어리어스 캣 애널리틱스만의 목소리를 개발하면서도 스타일 가이드 유지

요구 자격
이상적인 지원자는 다음과 같습니다.
  • **8최소 3년 이상의 마케팅 경력 소지**
  • **8강력한 작문 및 편집 능력 보유**
  • **8빠른 템포의 환경에서 팀 작업 수행**

7관심 있는 구직자는 schow@cca.com으로 사라 차우에게 자기소개서와 이력서를 보내세요.

어휘 analytics 분석 정보 talented 재능 있는 dynamic 역동적인 concise 간결한 engaging 매력적인 promote 홍보하다 collaborate 협업하다 maintain 유지하다 qualification 자격 ideal 이상적인 candidate 지원자 possess 갖추고 있다 fast-paced 빠른 속도의 job seeker 구직자 cover letter 자기소개서

발신: 제바 싱 〈j.singh@swiftbox.com〉
수신: 사라 차우 〈schow@cca.com〉
날짜: 12월 18일
제목: 카피라이터 자리
첨부: ⬚ 이력서

차우 씨께,

큐어리어스 캣 애널리틱스의 마케팅 카피라이터 자리에 지원하려고 이메일을 씁니다. **8오랜 여행 작가이자 야외 단체 여행 인솔자로서, 저는 팀에 생산적이고 획기적인 공헌자가 되리라 확신합니다.** 첨부해 드린 저의 이력서를 확인해 주십시오.

저의 여행 블로그인 원더 어스는 많은 팔로워가 있어 제 글의 효력을 보여 주며 10년 이상 된 여행 작문 경험을 나타내 줍니다. 저는 다른 문화와 풍습에 대한 저의 강한 호기심을 보여 주는 새로운 게시물을 매주 서너 개씩 지속적으로 작성하고 있습니다.

또한 저는 강한 팀빌더입니다. **9, 10저는 3년 동안 시 트래블에서 투어 그룹을 이끌고 프로그램을 편성했으며, 고객들이 편안함을 느낄 수 있도록 돕는 한편 다양한 배경을 가진 사람들 사이에서 관계를 구축하는 데 탁월합니다.** 귀하를 만나 제가 큐어리어스 캣 애널리틱스에 기여할 수 있는 점에 대해 알아볼 수 있기를 기대합니다.

제바 싱

어휘 apply for ~에 지원하다 excursion 여행 productive 생산적인 innovative 획기적인 contributor 기여자 effectiveness 효과적임 represent 나타내다 decade 10년 custom 풍습 coordinate 편성하다 excel 탁월하다 forge 구축하다 explore 알아보다 contribution 기여

싱 씨께,

카피라이터직에 지원해 주셔서 감사합니다. 우리 고용 위원회는 당신의 자기소개서와 이력서에 깊은 인상을 받았습니다. **10당신의 추천인인 던바 씨는 당신과 함께 베트남에서 배낭여행을 인솔했던 경험을 근거로 당신을 매우 높이 평가했습니다.**

이 직책에 대한 후보자로서 다음 단계로 넘어가는 과정에서 목표 시장 도달을 위한 검색 엔진 최적화 활용의 중요성에 대해 500자 정도의 블로그 게시물을 작성해 제출할 것을 요구합니다. 제출하신 내용을 검토한 후, 면접 가능성에 대해 연락 드리겠습니다.

사라 차우

어휘 hiring committee 고용 위원회 impressed 인상 깊게 생각하는 reference 추천인 particularly 특히 speak highly of ~을 칭찬하다 candidacy 입후보 자격 compose 작성하다 optimization 최적화 submission 제출 potential 가능성이 있는

6 구인 목록에 따르면, 싱 씨가 채용될 경우 해야 할 일은?

(A) 다른 도시로 이사하기
(B) 대부분 혼자 작업하기
(C) 저작물 중 일부를 온라인에 게시하기
(D) 잠재 고객과의 영업 회의 주최

해설 **세부 사항:** 구인 목록의 책무에 마케팅 팀과 협업하여 기사, 블로그 게시물, 이메일용 컨텐츠 작성 및 편집하기 (Collaborate with our marketing team by writing and editing content for articles, blog posts, and e-mails)라고 나와 있으므로 (C)가 정답이다.

어휘 post 게시하다 potential client 잠재 고객

7 차우 씨는 어떤 종류의 일을 하는 것 같은가?

(A) 제품 개발
(B) 재무 분석
(C) 직원 채용
(D) 고객 서비스

해설 **추론:** 구인 목록 마지막에 관심 있는 구직자는 schow@cca.com으로 사라 차우에게 자기소개서와 이력서를 보내라(Interested job seekers should send a cover letter and resume to Sara Chow, schow@cca.com)고 한 것으로 보아 차우 씨는 채용 담당자라는 것을 알 수 있다. 따라서 (C)가 정답이다.

8 싱 씨가 해당 직책에 고려되지 못할 수 있는 요인은?

(A) 자기소개서를 늦게 제출했다.
(B) 학력이 부족하다.
(C) 자기소개서가 엉뚱한 사람에게 발송되었다.
(D) 마케팅 경력이 부족하다.

해설 **연계:** 구인 목록에서는 최소 3년 이상의 마케팅 경력 소지 (have at least 3 years of marketing experience), 강력한 작문 및 편집 능력 보유(possess strong writing and editing skills), 빠른 템포의 환경에서 팀 작업 수행(enjoy working on a team in a fast-paced environment)의 3가지 자격을 요구하고 있다. 그런데 싱 씨의 이메일 첫 문단에서 오랜 여행 작가이자 야외 단체 여행 인솔자로서 자신이 팀에 생산적이고 획기적인 공헌자가 되리라 확신한다(As a longtime travel writer and outdoor group excursion leader ~ contributor to your team)며 3가지 요건 중 마케팅 경력을 제외한 작문 능력과 팀 작업 수행 능력에 관해서만 언급하고 있다. 따라서 (D)가 정답이다.

9 첫 번째 이메일에서, 싱 씨에 대해 암시된 것은?

(A) 블로그 작성을 그만두었다.
(B) 다른 사람들과 일하는 것을 즐긴다.
(C) 해외여행을 가본 적이 없다.
(D) 데이터 분석에 경험이 있다.

해설 **추론:** 첫 이메일의 세 번째 단락에서 싱 씨가 3년 동안 시 트래블에서 투어 그룹을 이끌고 프로그램을 편성했으며 고객들이 편안함을 느낄 수 있도록 돕는 한편 다양한 배경을 가진 사람들 사이에서 관계를 구축하는 데 탁월하다 (I spent three years coordinating programs ~ helping clients feel at home)고 했으므로 싱 씨는 사람들과 일하는 것에 자신이 있다는 것을 알 수 있다. 따라서 (B)가 정답이다.

10 던바 씨에 대한 설명으로 가장 사실에 가까운 것은?

(A) 고용 담당자이다.
(B) 최근에 승진했다.
(C) 시 트래블에서 싱 씨의 동료였다.
(D) 큐어리어스 캣 애널리틱스의 카피라이터이다.

해설 **연계:** 첫 이메일 세 번째 단락에서 싱 씨는 3년 동안 시 트래블에서 투어 그룹을 이끌고 프로그램을 편성했다(I spent three years coordinating programs and leading tour groups for SEA Travel)고 했고, 두 번째 이메일 첫 단락에서는 싱 씨에게 당신의 추천인인 던바 씨는 당신과 함께 베트남에서 배낭여행을 인솔했던 경험을 근거로 당신을 매우 높이 평가했다(Your reference, Ms. Dunbar, spoke ~ in Vietnam with you)고 했다. 따라서 던바 씨는 시 트래블에서 싱 씨와 함께 근무했다는 것을 알 수 있으므로 (C)가 정답이다.

Questions 11-15 기사 + 웹페이지 + 인터뷰 녹취록

판촉 제품, 고객을 끌어모으다

회사에서 판촉 제품을 왜 활용해야 할까? 이유는 많다. **11대기업은 오랫동안 무료 증정품을 효과적으로 활용해 왔다.** 스웨트 셔츠 같은 일부 제품은 중소기업에겐 너무 비싸지만 달력 같은 더 싼 제품을 나눠 주면 많은 잠재 고객을 잡을 수 있다. 제품에 회사 로고를 넣으면 브랜드 인지도를 쌓을 수 있다. 제품에 연락처 정보를 표기하면 명함 역할을 하기도 한다.

14어떤 유형의 제품을 살지 결정할 때는 반드시 고객이 여러 달 동안 매일 쓸 수 있는 제품을 선택해야 한다. 예산이 많은 회사는 좀 더 창의적인 제품을 시도해 볼 수 있다. 선물은 누구나 받고 싶어 한다. 선물로 사업에 도움을 얻자!

어휘 promotional 판촉의 giveaway 무료 증정품 effectively 효과적으로 expensive 비싼 potential 잠재적인 recognition 인지도 budget 예산

---

http://www.worldpromo.com/products/pens

홈	소개	**제품**	여러분을 위한 아이디어	연락처

월드 프로모
고품질 볼펜

스크립 라이트가 제조하는 최고 인기 제품인 고품질 볼펜으로 이름을 외부에 알리세요! 이 펜은 잉크가 번지지 않고 잉크가 없어질 때까지 계속 쓸 수 있다는 점, 보증합니다.

12(D)수량	단가
1*	무료
2-249	0.88달러
250-499	0.73달러
155 00-999	**0.62달러**
1000+	0.54달러

* 모든 주문에 제품당 무료 샘플 하나가 추가될 수 있습니다.
12(C)배송비는 추가입니다.

12(A)셔츠, 컵, 토트백, 달력 등 더 많은 월드 프로모 제품을 보시려면 제품 메인 페이지로 돌아가세요.

어휘 manufacture 제조하다 smudge 잉크가 번지다

10월 18일 라디오 방송 〈비즈니스 투데이〉 녹취록. 진행자 니다 바마가 리뉴 위드 루빈 기업주 알 루빈을 인터뷰했다.

바마 씨: 사업에 대해 얘기해 주시죠.
루빈 씨: 우리는 주방을 설계하고 설치합니다. 고객과 협력해 고객이 감당할 수 있는 가격에 고객이 원하는 모습을 창조하죠.
바마 씨: 고객층은 어떻게 늘리시나요?
루빈 씨: 대부분 입소문이죠. 하지만 건축 박람회, 무역 박람회, 지역 축제도 참가합니다.

바마 씨: **13오랜 세월, 그러니까 40년 넘게 사업을 하셨는데요.** 신생 기업에 조언을 해주신다면요?
루빈 씨: 수익이 나려면 시간이 걸리기도 합니다. 사람들과 교류하세요. **14사람들이 갖고 싶어 하고 매일 쓰는 품목을 무료로 나누어 주세요.**
바마 씨: 판촉용 무료 증정품 말씀인가요?
루빈 씨: 맞습니다. 사실 **15우리는 월드 프로모에서 펜 600개를 주문해서** 지난번 무역 박람회에 갖고 갔는데, 전부 다 나눠 줬습니다. 많은 사람들이 단지 펜을 받으려고 우리 부스에 왔어요! 그 사람들이 우릴 만날 때는 새 주방을 설치할 생각이 아니더라도, 회사 이름이 적힌 펜을 주면 그럴 마음이 들 때 우리를 기억할 겁니다.

어휘 afford (돈을) 감당할 여유가 되다 word-of-mouth 입소문의 profitable 수익이 나는

---

11 기사에서 중소기업이 무료로 나눠줄 수 있다고 나타내는 것은?

(A) 스웨트 셔츠 (B) 달력
(C) 명함 (D) 홍보 동영상

해설 **세부 사항:** 기사의 세 번째 문장에서 대기업은 무료 증정품을 효과적으로 활용해 왔다(Large corporations ~ giveaways)며, 일부 제품은 중소기업에겐 너무 비싸지만 달력 같은 더 싼 제품을 나눠 주면 많은 잠재 고객을 잡을 수 있다(Although some items ~ by giving out cheaper products, such as calendars)고 했으므로 (B)가 정답이다.

12 웹페이지에 명시된 것은?

(A) 펜은 월드 프로모에서 이용할 수 있는 유일한 품목이다.
(B) 다양한 결제 방식을 수용한다.
(C) 구매 가격에 배송비가 포함된다.
(D) 대량이면 가격이 저렴하다.

해설 **Not/True:** 웹페이지에 나온 표에 따르면 주문 수량이 많을수록 제품 단가가 낮아지므로 (D)가 정답이다. 배송비는 추가라고 했으므로 (C)는 틀린 보기이고, 펜 외에도 셔츠, 컵, 토트백, 달력 등의 월드 프로모 제품에 대해 언급하고 있으므로 (A)는 답이 될 수 없다. (B)의 결제 방식에 대해서는 언급된 것이 없으므로 알 수 없다.

13 인터뷰에서 루빈 씨의 업체에 관해 명시된 것은?

(A) 무역 박람회를 주관한다.
(B) 이름을 변경할 계획이다.
(C) 처음부터 수익을 올렸다.
(D) 40여 년 전에 설립되었다.

해설 **Not/True:** 바마 씨가 세 번째 대사에서 루빈 씨에게 40년 넘게 사업을 하셨다(You have been in business a long time, more than four decades)고 언급했으므로 (D)가 정답이다.

패러프레이징

지문의 more than four decades

➲ 보기의 over 40 years

14 기사 작성자와 루빈 씨는 어떤 조언에 동의하는가?

(A) 상품을 선물 포장용으로 포장하라.

(B) 로고 디자인은 최대한 단순하게 하라.

(C) 정기적으로 사용하는 물품을 나누어 주라.

(D) 물품에 명함을 넣어라.

해설 **연계:** 기사 작성자는 어떤 유형의 제품을 살지 결정할 때는 반드시 고객이 여러 달 동안 매일 쓸 수 있는 제품을 선택해야 한다(When deciding what type of item ~ use daily for many months)고 했고, 루빈 씨는 인터뷰의 세 번째 대사에서 사람들이 갖고 싶어 하고 매일 쓰는 품목을 무료로 나누어 주라(Give away items ~ use on a daily basis)고 했다. 두 사람 모두 매일 쓰는 제품을 나누어 주라고 했으므로 (C)가 정답이다.

패러프레이징

지문의 daily ➲ 보기의 regularly

15 리뉴 위드 루빈이 펜 하나에 지불한 돈은?

(A) 54센트

(B) 62센트

(C) 73센트

(D) 88센트

해설 **연계:** 루빈 씨가 인터뷰의 마지막 대사에서 월드 프로모에서 펜 600개를 주문했다(we ordered 600 pens from World Promo)고 했고, 웹페이지의 표에 따르면 수량이 600개, 즉 500~999개 사이일 때는 단가가 62센트라고 나와 있으므로 (B)가 정답이다.

Questions 16-20 공지 + 온라인 양식 + 기사

> **몬테고 베이 운송 회사**
> **16전자 발권기 도입**
>
> 몬테고 베이 운송 회사(Mobay Transcorp)는 월간 버스 이용권과 더불어 전자 발권기(ETM)의 도입 또한 고려하고 있습니다. 통근자를 위한 이 두 가지 옵션은 이 나라의 수도인 킹스턴 도시 교통국(KUTA)이 현재 사용하고 있는 것과 유사할 것입니다. 17지난달로 서비스를 제공한 지 50년이 된 것을 기념하며 몬테고 베이 운송 회사는 보다 편리한 발권 서비스를 제공함과 동시에 고객과의 상호작용을 개선하고자 합니다.
>
> 16, 19전자 발권기와 월간 버스 이용권의 도입 날짜는 10월 1일입니다. 16주민 여러분께 www.mbtc.com.jm/etmprop에서 제안된 사업 계획에 대한 세부 사항을 보고 의견 및 제안을 제출해 주실 것을 요청드립니다.

모든 의견은 공개될 것이므로, 응답자들은 의견이나 제안에서 개인 정보를 생략하는 것이 좋습니다. 기밀 정보를 포함하기를 원하시는 분은 서면으로 의견을 제출하셔야 하며, 몬테고 베이 핸더슨 가 123번지, 몬테고 베이 운송 회사의 데니스 사무다 홍보 이사 앞으로 보내시면 됩니다. 서면 및 전자 제출은 3월 30일 오후 11시 59분까지 수신되어야 합니다.

어휘 transport 운송 corporation 기업 introduction 도입 electronic 전자의 commuter 통근자 urban 도시의 transit 운송 authority 당국 capital 수도 mark (중요 사건을) 기념하다 desire 바라다 interaction 상호작용 convenient 편리한 proposed 제안된 resident 주민 initiative 계획 suggestion 제안 respondent 응답자 omit 생략하다 confidential 기밀의 address 보내다 submission 제출(물)

> www.mbtc.com.jm/etmprop
>
> 이름: 올랜도 그렌지
>
> 날짜: 3월 9일
>
> 의견 또는 불만 사항:
>
> 저는 전자 발권기의 도입으로 수반되었을 수도 있는 의도치 않은 결과를 직접 경험했습니다. 지난달 가족모임을 위해 킹스턴에 있으면서, 바로 작년에 전자 발권기를 도입했던 킹스턴 도시 교통국(KUTA)이 운영하는 버스를 탔습니다. KUTA 운전기사는 승객이 티켓을 발권받기 전에 전자 발권기에 특정 코드를 입력해야 합니다. 그런데 18제가 탔던 버스의 전자 발권기가 고장 나면서 운전기사는 꽤 여러 승객들을 위해 그 코드를 반복적으로 입력해야 했습니다. 그 결과 저는 모임에 계획보다 10분 늦게 도착했습니다. 만약 면접을 보러 가는 상황이었더라면 이 지체 상황이 저에게 어떤 영향을 미쳤을지 상상해 보십시오. 게다가 20저는 장비 수리가 시간이 많이 걸리는 경향이 있다는 것을 알고 있습니다. 특히 기술자가 수리를 수행할 수 있는 적절한 훈련이 부족할 경우에 말이죠. 따라서 저는 몬테고 베이 운송 회사가 현행 버스 승차권 발권 방식을 고수할 것을 촉구하는 바입니다.
>
> 제출

어휘 firsthand 직접 consequence 결과 gathering 모임 operate 운영하다 punch in 입력하다 issue 발행하다 malfunction 제대로 작동하지 않다 repeatedly 반복적으로 affect 영향을 미치다 equipment 장비 tend ~하는 경향이 있다 time-consuming (많은) 시간이 걸리는 particularly 특히 lack 부족하다 adequate 적절한 perform 수행하다 urge 촉구하다 method 방법

몬테고 베이 운송 회사, 전자 발권 시스템 정비

몬테고 베이(9월 24일) – ¹⁹**12월 1일, 몬테고 베이 운송 회사에서 전자 발권기(ETMs)를 선보인다.** 이 회사는 이 기기들이 돈만 많이 투자하고 별로 득될 것은 없다고 걱정하는 현지 시민들의 우려에도 불구하고 변화를 실행하고 있다. 몬테고 베이 운송회사가 대중들로부터 받은 많은 의견들은 킹스턴 도시 교통국(KUTA)이 전자 발권기 시스템으로 겪고 있는 문제들을 인용하고 있다.

몬테고 베이 운송 회사의 데니스 사무다 홍보 이사는 전자 발권기로 발생할 수 있는 문제를 최소화하기 위한 일련의 조치를 실행해 왔다고 말했다. 장비의 마모를 줄이고 발권 절차를 더욱 간소화하기 위해 회사는 일일, 주간, 월간 버스 이용권을 도입할 예정이다. 또한, ²⁰**사내 기술자들은 장비 고장이 적시에 해결되도록 전자 발권기 수리에 관한 광범위한 교육을 받았다.**

몬테고 베이 운송 회사는 네덜란드의 다국적 기업인 담스코 통합 시스템과도 제휴를 맺어 3년마다 새로운 전자 발권기를 공급받기로 했다. 내년 4월에는 양사가 새로운 발권 시스템의 효과를 평가하고 필요에 따라 조정을 할 예정이다.

어휘 **overhaul** 점검[정비]하다 **debut** 데뷔하다 **concern** 우려 **express** 나타내다 **costly** 많은 돈이 드는 **investment** 투자 **benefit** 이득 **reference** 참조문으로 인용하다 **state** 말하다 **implement** 시행하다 **measure** 조치 **minimize** 최소화하다 **pose** 제기하다 **wear and tear** 마모 **simplify** 간소화하다 **process** 절차 **extensive** 광범위한 **failure** 고장 **address** 다루다 **in a timely fashion** 적시에 **multinational** 다국적의 **supply** 공급하다 **evaluate** 평가하다 **efficacy** 효과 **adjustment** 조정

16 공지의 목적은?

(A) 웹사이트 출범 발표
(B) 시민 의견 요청
(C) 직원 문제 해결
(D) 버스 노선 변경 안내

해설 **주제 / 목적:** 공지의 소제목이 전자 발권기 도입 (Introduction of Electronic Ticketing Machines)이고 첫 단락에서 이에 대해 간단히 설명한 뒤, 두 번째 단락에서 전자 발권기와 월간 버스 이용권의 도입 날짜는 10월 1일(The proposed introduction date ~ is 1 October)이라며 주민 여러분께 www.mbtc.com.jm/etmprop에서 제안된 사업 계획에 대한 세부 사항을 보고 의견 및 제안을 제출해 주실 것을 요청드린다(Residents are invited to view details ~ comments and suggestions at www.mbtc.com.jm/etmprop)고 했으므로 공지의 주요 목적은 새로 도입할 서비스에 대한 주민들의 의견을 요청하는 것임을 알 수 있다. 따라서 (B)가 정답이다.

어휘 **launch** 시작 **commentary** 논의, 비판 **route** 노선

패러프레이징
지문의 comments and suggestions
➔ 보기의 commentary

17 공지에 따르면, 몬테고 베이 운송 회사는 최근에 무엇을 했는가?

(A) 창립 50주년을 기념했다.
(B) 데이터 기록 방식을 변경했다.
(C) KUTA와 제휴했다.
(D) 몬테고 베이 거주자만 고용하기로 결정했다.

해설 **세부 사항:** 공지의 첫 단락 세 번째 문장에서 지난달로 서비스를 제공한 지 50년이 된 것을 기념하며 몬테고 베이 운송 회사는 보다 편리한 발권 서비스를 제공함과 동시에 고객과의 상호작용을 개선하고자 한다(Marking five decades of service just last month ~ provide more convenient ticketing)고 했으므로 (A)가 정답이다.

패러프레이징
지문의 Marking five decades of service
➔ 보기의 celebrated its fiftieth year of service

18 그렌지 씨에 대해 사실인 것은?

(A) 정기적으로 회의에 참석한다.
(B) 최근에 취업 면접을 보았다.
(C) 이동 정체를 겪었다.
(D) KUTA 버스 운전사였다.

해설 **Not / True:** 온라인 양식의 중반부에 그렌지 씨는 자신이 탔던 버스의 전자 발권기가 고장 나면서 운전기사가 꽤 여러 승객들을 위해 그 코드를 반복적으로 입력해야 했다(since the ETM on the bus ~ repeatedly for quite a few passengers)며 그 결과 저는 모임에 계획보다 10분 늦게 도착했다(As a result, I arrived ten minutes later than planned at that gathering)고 했으므로 (C)가 정답이다.

패러프레이징
지문의 arrived ten minutes later
➔ 보기의 experienced a delay

19 몬테고 베이 운송 회사에 대해 알 수 있는 것은?

(A) 홍보 이사를 교체했다.
(B) 전자 발권기를 원래 계획보다 늦게 도입한다.
(C) 버스 이용권의 가격을 인상했다.
(D) 담스코 통합 시스템과 2년 계약을 체결했다.

해설 **연계:** 공지의 두 번째 단락에서 전자 발권기와 월간 버스 이용권의 도입 날짜는 10월 1일(The proposed introduction date of the ETMs ~ is 1 October)이라고 했는데, 기사의 첫 문장에 따르면 12월 1일에 몬테고 베이 운송 회사에서 전자 발권기를 선보인다(On 1 December, Mobay Transcorp will debut electronic ticketing machines on its buses)고 했으므로 몬테고 베이의 전자 발전기 도입이 계획보다 두 달 정도 늦춰진 것을 알 수 있다. 따라서 (B)가 정답이다.

20 몬테고 베이 운송 회사가 대처한 그렌지 씨의 우려 사항은?

(A) 잘못된 코드   (B) 노후된 장비
(C) 과도한 비용   (D) 직원 교육

해설 **연계:** 온라인 양식의 후반부에 그렌지 씨가 특히 기술자가 수리를 수행할 수 있는 적절한 훈련이 부족할 경우에 장비 수리에 시간이 많이 걸리는 경향이 있다는 것을 알고 있다(I understand ~ technicians lack adequate training to perform repairs)고 했는데, 기사의 두 번째 단락 세 번째 문장에서 사내 기술자들은 장비 고장이 적시에 해결되도록 전자 발권기 수리에 관한 광범위한 교육을 받았다(company technicians have received extensive training ~ in a timely fashion)고 했다. 따라서 몬테고 베이는 그렌지 씨가 언급한 기술자의 훈련 부족 시 발생할 수 있는 문제에 대처하기 위해 직원 교육을 실행했음을 알 수 있으므로 (D)가 정답이다.

어휘 outdated 구식인 excessive 과도한

Questions 21-25 웹페이지 + 보도 + 기사

http://www.timewisetele.com

| **타임와이즈란?** | 자주 묻는 질문 | 연락처 |

²¹**타임와이즈 텔레비전 서비스에 가입하시면 방해하는 광고 없이 고품질 방송편성을 이용할 수 있습니다.** 1달 요금에는 전체 채널이 포함되므로 새로운 프로그램을 시청하려고 상급으로 변경 가입할 필요가 없습니다. 주요 채널로는 아래와 같이 오랫동안 고객들에게 인기가 높은 채널들이 있습니다.

- ²⁵**업 로켓:** 세계에서 가장 흥미진진한 사람들을 만나는 토크쇼 및 심층 인터뷰. 최고의 텔레비전 토크 채널에서 〈딥 다이브〉, 〈토크 투나잇〉 등 인기 프로그램을 시청하세요.

- **와이어 TV:** 정치 및 경제 뉴스, 스포츠, 날씨 등 전국 및 전 세계 소식을 일주일 내내, 24시간 전하는 가장 정확한 최신 뉴스 보도

- **네트워크 RP:** 다큐멘터리 영화, 과학 프로그램, 교육 프로그램으로 견문을 넓히세요. 방영 임박: 〈깊은 바닷속〉

- ²²**기가 10:** 하루 종일 웃게 해 주는 최고의 코미디 프로그램들로, 〈그냥 이웃이야〉, 〈끝에서 두 번째〉 같은 시리즈물과 함께 실황 코미디 특집, 장편영화도 방영합니다.

²¹**오늘 가입하세요!**

어휘 subscription 가입, 구독 get access to ~을 이용하다 interruption 방해 accurate 정확한 coverage 보도 expand 넓히다

긴급 보도

3월 18일 – ²²**WTB 스튜디오는 히트 시리즈인 〈무슨 일이야〉가 또 다른 시즌으로 개편됐다고 발표했다.** 지난 10년 동안, 이 인기 쇼는 별난 인물과 날카로운 재치로 많은 팬들을 웃게 만들었다. 제나 저비스와 안와르 사이드가 유쾌한 주인공 안나와 루카스로 돌아온다. ²³**이 쇼는 또한 새로운 스타 데니스 램을 맞이할 예정인데, 램은 이 커플의 옆집에 새로 온 이웃 역할을 맡는다.** 시즌 첫 방송은 9월 9일 오후 8시로 예정되어 있으며, 텔레비전 구독 서비스인 타임와이즈를 통해 시청할 수 있다.

어휘 quirky 별난 hilarious 유쾌한 premiere 첫 방송, 초연

데니스 램 근황

4월 5일 – 데니스 램은 그동안 바빴다. 약 10년 전 할리우드로 이사한 후, ²⁴**그는 인기 텔레비전 쇼 〈끝에서 두 번째〉에서 농구 스타로 주역을 차지했다.** 몇 시즌 후, 그는 다른 기회를 탐색하기 위해 그 역할에서 하차했다. 램 씨의 재능은 다양하다는 것이 입증되었다. 그는 두 편의 장편영화에 출연했고 이어서 센차 극장을 위해 각본도 썼다. ²⁵**램 씨는 최근 이달 말에 업 로켓의 〈딥 다이브〉에서 지금 맡고 있는 일을 그만둔다고 발표했다.** 그는 인기 프로그램인 〈무슨 일이야〉에서 자신만을 위해 만들어진 역할로 연기 복귀를 계획하고 있다.

"다시 연기하기를 고대하고 있습니다"라고 램은 말했다. "매우 훌륭한 쇼라서 빨리 그 쇼에 참여하고 싶습니다." 올 가을 처음 방영되는 〈무슨 일이야〉에서 램 씨를 찾아보세요.

– 카탈리나 바로스

어휘 land 차지[획득]하다 explore 탐색하다 diverse 다양한

21 웹페이지에 게시된 정보의 목적은?

(A) 신규 고객 유치하기
(B) 상급 변경 시 할인 홍보하기
(C) 텔레비전 광고 시간 판매하기
(D) 최근 추가된 채널 알리기

해설 **주제/목적:** 웹페이지의 첫 문장에서 타임와이즈 텔레비전 서비스에 가입하시면 방해하는 광고 없이 고품질 방송편성을 이용할 수 있다(With a subscription to the ~ without the interruption of advertisements)고 했고 마지막 문장에서도 오늘 가입하라(Start your subscription today!)며 서비스에 가입할 것을 권유하고 있으므로 (A)가 정답이다.

어휘 attract 유치하다 offer (단기간) 할인

22 타임와이즈는 어떤 채널에서 〈무슨 일이야〉를 방영하겠는가?

(A) 업 로켓   (B) 와이어 TV
(C) 네트워크 RP   (D) 기가 10

연계: 웹페이지의 마지막 채널 목록에 기가 10은 하루 종일 웃게 해 주는 최고의 코미디 프로그램들로 〈그냥 이웃이야〉, 〈끝에서 두 번째〉 같은 시리즈물과 함께 실황 코미디 특집, 장편영화도 방영한다(Giga 10: the best comedy programs ~ comedy specials and feature films)고 채널을 소개하고 있다. 보도의 첫 문장에서 WTB 스튜디오는 히트 시리즈인 〈무슨 일이야〉가 또 다른 시즌으로 개편됐다고 발표했다(WTB Studios has announced ~ another season)며 지난 10년 동안 이 인기 쇼는 별난 인물과 날카로운 위트로 많은 팬들을 웃게 만들었다(For the past decade ~ quirky characters and sharp wit)고 했으므로 〈무슨 일이야〉는 코미디 프로그램이라는 것을 알 수 있다. 따라서 〈무슨 일이야〉는 코미디 전문 채널인 기가 10에서 방송되는 것이 적합하므로 (D)가 정답이다.

패러프레이징
지문의 explore other opportunities
➡ 보기의 try other jobs in his field

25 램 씨가 현재 하는 일은 무엇이겠는가?

(A) 토크쇼 진행자

(B) 영화감독

(C) 뉴스 기자

(D) 극장 지배인

해설 **연계:** 기사의 첫 단락 후반부에 램 씨는 이달 말에 업 로켓의 〈딥 다이브〉에서 지금 맡고 있는 일을 그만둔다고 최근 발표했다(Mr. Lam recently announced ~ *Deep Dive* at the end of the month)고 했다. 웹페이지의 첫 채널 목록에서는 업 로켓(Up Rocket)을 세계에서 가장 흥미진진한 사람들을 만나는 토크쇼 및 심층 인터뷰 채널(talk shows and in-depth interviews ~ people)이라고 소개한 뒤, 최고의 텔레비전 토크 채널에서 〈딥 다이브〉, 〈토크 투나잇〉 등 인기 프로그램을 시청하라(Watch *Deep Dive* ~ number-one television talk channel)고 했다. 따라서 업 로켓의 〈딥 다이브〉는 토크쇼이고, 램 씨가 〈딥 다이브〉 일을 관둔다고 했으므로 램 씨는 토크쇼 진행자라는 것을 알 수 있다. 그러므로 (A)가 정답이다.

23 보도에 따르면 가을에는 〈무슨 일이야〉가 어떻게 달라지는가?

(A) 할리우드를 배경으로 할 것이다.

(B) 새로운 인물이 등장할 것이다.

(C) 〈딥 다이브〉 후 텔레비전에 나올 것이다.

(D) 방송 시간이 변경될 것이다.

해설 **세부 사항:** 보도의 중반부에 이 쇼는 새로운 스타 데니스 램을 맞이할 예정인데 램은 이 커플의 옆집에 새로 온 이웃 역할을 맡는다(The show will also welcome a new star ~ new next-door neighbor)고 했고, 시즌 첫 방송은 9월 9일 오후 8시로 예정되어 있다(The season premiere is scheduled for September 9 at 8:00 P.M.)고 했으므로 가을에 방영하는 새로운 시즌에 새로운 인물이 등장할 것임을 알 수 있다. 따라서 (B)가 정답이다.

패러프레이징
지문의 welcome a new star
➡ 보기의 introduce a new character

24 기사에 따르면, 램 씨가 〈끝에서 두 번째〉를 떠난 이유는?

(A) 쇼에서 맡은 역할이 끝났다.

(B) 가족이 다른 도시로 이사했다.

(C) 자기 분야에서 다른 일을 해 보고 싶었다.

(D) 농구 경력을 쌓기로 결심했다.

해설 **세부 사항:** 기사의 두 번째 문장에서 램 씨는 인기 텔레비전 쇼 〈끝에서 두 번째〉에서 농구 스타로 주역을 차지했다(he landed the leading role as a basketball star on the popular television show *Next to Last*)고 했고, 몇 시즌 후 그는 다른 기회를 탐색하기 위해 그 역할에서 하차했다(After several seasons, he left that role to explore other opportunities)고 했으므로 (C)가 정답이다.

Questions 26-30 이메일 + 주문서 + 비평

수신: 리암 두건

발신: 데어드레 코리건

날짜: 9월 15일 목요일 오전 9:15

제목: 장 보기

첨부: 주문서

리암 주방장님께,

²⁶오늘 아침 피넌 가 시장에서 장을 보고 주문서를 첨부했으니 확인하세요. 오늘 저녁 수프에 쓸 파스닙이 다 팔리고 시장에 없어서 대신 당근 수프로 바꿔야 해요. ²⁹이제 저는 당근 수프에 넣을 나머지 재료를 사려고 맥커운 식료품점으로 가고 있어요. 그런데 ²⁸피넌 가 시장에서 잎채소를 할인된 가격에 팔고 있어서, 두 가지 다른 종류를 각 5킬로그램씩 샀어요. 유용하게 쓰셨으면 합니다. 요청하신 다른 것들은 다 찾았어요.

오늘 저녁에 봐요.

데어드레

어휘 **parsnip** 파스닙(배추 뿌리같이 생긴 채소) **remaining** 남아 있는 **ingredient** 재료 **leafy** 잎으로 된

피넌 가 시장
주문서

구매자: 카페 드 리암
날짜: 9월 15일

품목	수량	킬로그램당 가격	총계
²⁸시금치	**5킬로그램**	1.00유로	5.00유로
²⁸녹색잎 상추	**5킬로그램**	1.00유로	5.00유로
무화과	18킬로그램	4.00유로	72.00유로
붉은 감자	20킬로그램	2.00유로	40.00유로
당근	25킬로그램	1.50유로	37.50유로
²⁷양파	**30킬로그램**	0.95유로	28.50유로
총계			188.00유로

식당 후기: 계속 감탄하게 되는 카페 드 리암
브리짓 트레이너

킬라니(9월 16일) – 카페 드 리암은 킬라니에서 오랫동안 숨겨진 보석 같은 식당이다. 이제, 주방장 리암의 베스트셀러 채식 요리책 덕분에, 식당에 테이블 예약이 늘고 길게 줄을 서기 시작했다. 그 결과 카페에서 내놓는 음식의 품질이 떨어졌는지 확인하기 위해 나는 어젯밤에 카페를 방문했다. 새로 얻은 유명세에도 불구하고 카페 드 리암이 품질에 대한 관심을 조금도 놓지 않았다는 소식을 전하게 되어 기쁘다.

전채 요리인 버터와 무화과 잼을 곁들인 갓 구운 빵은 훌륭했고, ²⁹코코넛 요구르트를 넣은 카레 당근 수프는 특히 맛있었다. 메인 요리인 구운 포도를 곁들인 푸짐한 옥수수 수플레도 좋았다. ³⁰하지만 진짜 갈채를 보내고 싶은 요리는 캐러멜 소스를 곁들인 대추 케이크였다. 이렇게 간단한 요리가 이렇게 맛있을 줄은 예상하지 못했다.

멋진 저녁 외출을 원한다면 카페 드 리암을 진심으로 추천한다. 예약은 020-912-0155번으로 카페에 전화하거나 웹사이트 cafedeliam.ie를 방문하면 된다.

어휘 **gem** 보석 **reservation** 예약 **suffer** 나빠지다
newfound 새로 얻은 **flavourful** 맛있는 **hearty**
푸짐한 **showstopper** (공연) 갈채를 받는 연기[배우]

26 **코리건 씨가 이메일을 보낸 이유는?**

(A) 주방장에게 조리법을 요청하려고
(B) 주방장에게 문제점을 알리려고
(C) 가게에 대한 의견을 전달하려고
(D) 요리법을 제안하려고

해설 **주제/목적:** 이메일의 첫 문장에서 오늘 아침 피넌 가 시장에서 장을 보고 주문서를 첨부했으니 확인하라(Please find attached my invoice ~ morning's shopping trip)면서 오늘 저녁 수프에 쓸 파스닙이 다 팔리고 시장에 없어서 대신 당근 수프로 바꿔야 한다(The market was completely sold out ~ switch to carrot soup

instead)고 장 보기 임무를 수행하면서 생긴 문제점에 대해 보고하고 있으므로 (B)가 정답이다.

27 **주문서에 따르면, 카페는 양파를 몇 킬로그램 샀는가?**

(A) 18 (B) 20
(C) 25 (D) 30

해설 **세부 사항:** 주문서에 보이는 품목 중 맨 마지막 줄에 양파(Onions)를 30킬로그램(30 kilos) 샀다고 나와 있으므로 (D)가 정답이다.

28 **할인된 가격으로 판매된 품목은?**

(A) 시금치 (B) 무화과
(C) 감자 (D) 당근

해설 **연계:** 이메일의 네 번째 문장에서 피넌 가 시장에서 잎채소를 할인된 가격에 팔고 있어서 두 가지 다른 종류를 각 5킬로씩 샀다(Finnan Street Market was selling leafy greens at a marked-down price, so I bought 5 kilos each of two different kinds)고 했고, 주문서에 따르면 시금치와 녹색잎 상추를 각각 5킬로그램씩 샀으므로 이 두 품목이 할인되고 있음을 알 수 있다. 보기에는 시금치만 나와 있으므로 (A)가 정답이다.

29 **코리건 씨가 매커운 식료품점에서 구입했을 것 같은 당근 수프 재료는?**

(A) 버터 (B) 잼
(C) 요구르트 (D) 당근

해설 **연계:** 이메일의 세 번째 문장에서 코리건 씨는 이제 당근 수프에 넣을 나머지 재료를 사려고 매커운 식료품점으로 가고 있다(I'm heading over now to ~ for the carrot soup)고 했고, 후기의 두 번째 단락 첫 문장에는 코코넛 요구르트를 넣은 카레 당근 수프가 특히 맛있었다(the curried carrot soup with coconut yogurt was especially flavourful)고 나와 있다. 따라서 코리건 씨는 매커운 식료품점에서 당근 수프에 넣은 요구르트를 구입했음을 알 수 있으므로 (C)가 정답이다.

30 **후기를 쓴 사람이 가장 좋아한 음식은?**

(A) 전채 요리 (B) 수프
(C) 메인 요리 (D) 디저트

해설 **세부 사항:** 후기의 두 번째 단락 마지막에 하지만 진짜 갈채를 보내고 싶은 요리는 캐러멜 소스를 곁들인 대추 케이크였다(But the real showstopper was the date cake with caramel sauce)며 이렇게 간단한 요리가 이렇게 맛있을 줄은 예상하지 못했다(I never would have expected such a simple dish to be so delicious)고 디저트로 나온 케이크에 찬사를 보내고 있으므로 (D)가 정답이다.

Questions 31-35 공지 + 이메일 + 이메일

겨울 폭풍에 대비하여 안전을 기하세요!

잰즈 엔지니어링 직원 여러분께 알립니다:

현재 우리는 가장 추운 시기의 계절에 접어들고 있어 기상 여건이 힘들어질 수 있습니다. **³¹24시간 안에 대형 겨울 폭풍이 예보되면, 퇴근할 때 노트북 컴퓨터와 모든 중요한 서류를 집으로 가져가는 것을 기억하세요.** 이는 폭풍이 진행됨에 따라 이동 여건이 안전하지 않게 될 경우에 대비하기 위함입니다.

덧붙여 회의 일정을 조정하거나 화상 회의를 실시하기 위한 모든 노력을 기울여 주세요. 개별 상황에 따라 취할 수 있는 몇 가지 옵션이 있습니다. 그 옵션은 바로 이동이 안전할 경우 사무실로 출근하거나, 재택근무를 하거나, 근로 보상 휴가를 사용하는 것입니다. **³²무엇보다도 안전을 유지하고 당신의 계획을 직속 상사에게 알리세요.**

어휘 **attention** 알립니다 **challenging** 힘든 **forecast** 예보하다 **projected** 예상된 **critical** 중요한 **in case** ~하는 경우에 대비해서 **progress** 진행하다 **conduct** 수행[실시]하다 **individual** 각각의; 개인 **earned vacation** (연장 근무 등에 대한) 보상 휴가 **immediate** 직속의 **supervisor** 상관

수신: 파리드 아데 〈fadeh@janzengineering.com〉
발신: **³³대릴 피터슨 〈dpeterson@janzengineering.com〉**
날짜: 1월 7일
제목: 일정 업데이트

안녕하세요, 아데 씨,

³²회사 방침에 따라 내일의 예상 날씨 때문에 집에서 근무할 계획이라는 것을 알려 드리려고 합니다. 그리고 우리가 내일로 계획했던 회의는 어떻게 진행하시겠습니까? **³⁴화상 회의를 준비할까요, 아니면 다른 날로 회의를 연기할까요?** 제 일정은 다음 주 월요일, 화요일, 목요일, 금요일이 비어 있습니다.

또한 **³³닉 개리티가 우리 회사를 떠난 터라 패로우 리버 프로젝트의 진행 상황이 궁금합니다.** 그의 후임자 채용 상황은 어떻습니까? 프로젝트가 여전히 5월 완료를 목표로 잘 진행되고 있는지요?

감사합니다.

대릴 피터슨

어휘 **predict** 예측하다 **proceed with** ~을 진행하다 **arrange** 마련하다 **postpone** 연기하다 **wonder** 궁금하다 **status** 상황 **replacement** 후임자 **on track** 제대로 진행되고 있는

수신: 대릴 피터슨 〈dperterson@janzengineering.com〉
발신: 파리드 아데 〈fadeh@janzengineering.com〉
날짜: 1월 7일
제목: RE: 일정 업데이트

안녕하세요, 피터슨 씨,

³⁴다음 주에 직접 만나기로 계획을 짭시다. 회사 밖으로 몇 군데 방문을 해야 해서 화요일과 수요일에만 사무실에 있을 예정입니다. ³⁵패로우 리버 프로젝트의 진행 상황에 대해 적절한 질문을 했군요. 구직자 몇 명의 면접을 진행했고 구인 범위를 3명으로 좁힌 상태입니다. 일자리 제의가 곧 이루어질 예정이라 이달 말 즘에는 새로운 프로젝트 매니저가 합류해 **³⁵당초 계획대로 프로젝트가 진행될 것입니다.**

파리드 아데

어휘 **in person** 직접 **off-site** 밖의 **candidate** 지원자 **narrow** 좁히다 **search** 찾기 **extend** 주다 **originally** 원래

---

31 악천후에 대한 예보가 있을 경우 직원들은 무엇을 해야 하는가?

(A) 중요한 서류를 사무실에 두고 간다.
(B) 일찍 출근하도록 계획한다.
(C) 컴퓨터를 집에 가져간다.
(D) 대중교통을 이용한다.

해설 **세부 사항:** 공지의 두 번째 문장에서 24시간 안에 대형 겨울 폭풍이 예보되면 퇴근 시 노트북 컴퓨터와 모든 중요한 서류를 집으로 가져가는 것을 기억하라(When a major winter storm is forecast ~ with you as you leave the workplace)고 당부하고 있으므로 (C)가 정답이다.

32 아데 씨는 누구일 것 같은가?

(A) 부서장　　　　　(B) 회사 연수생
(C) 잰즈 엔지니어링 고객　(D) 급여조정관

해설 **연계:** 공지의 마지막 문장에서 무엇보다 안전을 유지하고 당신의 계획을 직속 상사에게 알리라(Above all, stay safe and keep your immediate supervisor informed of your plan)고 했는데, 첫 이메일에서 피터슨 씨가 회사 방침에 따라 내일의 예상 날씨 때문에 집에서 근무할 계획이라는 것을 알려 드리려고 한다(Per company policy, I just wanted to let you know ~ I am planning to work from home)며 아데 씨에게 자신의 근무 계획을 보고하는 것으로 보아 아데 씨는 피터슨 씨가 근무하는 부서의 상관임을 알 수 있다. 따라서 (A)가 정답이다.

33 개리티 씨에 대해 암시된 것은?

(A) 현장에서 작업을 감독할 것이다.
(B) 잰즈 엔지니어링의 전 직원이다.
(C) 중요한 프로젝트를 완수했다.
(D) 예비 매니저들의 면접을 보고 있다.

해설 **추론:** 첫 이메일 두 번째 단락에서 이메일 작성자인 피터슨 씨는 닉 개리티가 우리 회사를 떠난 터라 패로우 리버 프로젝트의 진행 상황이 궁금하다(I was wondering about the ~ Nick Garrity has left our company)고 했으므로 개리티 씨는 퇴사했음을 알 수 있다. 또한, 피터슨 씨의 이메일 주소가 dpeterson@janzengineering.com인 것으로 보아 피터슨 씨가 근무하는 회사는 잰즈 엔지니어링이므로 (B)가 정답이다.

어휘 oversee 감독하다 former 예전의 prospective 장래의

패러프레이징
지문의 left our company ➡ 보기의 a former employee

34 피터슨 씨와 아데 씨는 다음 회의를 언제 열 것 같은가?

(A) 월요일 (B) 화요일
(C) 목요일 (D) 금요일

해설 **연계:** 첫 이메일 첫 단락에서 피터슨 씨가 화상 회의를 준비할지 아니면 다른 날로 회의를 연기할지(Would you like me to arrange a ~ postpone the meeting to another day?)를 물으며 자신의 일정은 다음 주 월요일, 화요일, 목요일, 금요일이 비어 있다(My schedule is open on Monday, Tuesday, and Friday next week)고 했다. 두 번째 이메일에서 아데 씨는 다음 주에 직접 만나기로 계획을 짜자(Let's plan to meet in person next week)며 회사 밖으로 몇 군데 방문을 해야 해서 화요일과 수요일에만 사무실에 있을 예정(I will be in the office only on Tuesday ~ make several off-site visits)이라고 했다. 아데 씨는 화요일과 수요일에 사무실에 있을 계획이고, 피터슨 씨는 두 날 중 화요일에 시간이 된다고 했으므로 다음 회의는 화요일에 열릴 것임을 알 수 있다. 따라서 (B)가 정답이다.

35 두 번째 이메일에서 패로우 리버 프로젝트에 관해 명시된 것은?

(A) 예상대로 완료될 것이다.
(B) 회사의 비용이 많이 들었다.
(C) 특이한 공학적 설계를 수반한다.
(D) 5월에 시작할 것이다.

해설 **Not / True:** 두 번째 이메일 세 번째 문장에서 패로우 리버 프로젝트의 진행 상황에 대해 적절한 질문을 했다(You ask a good question about the status of the Farrow River project)며 마지막 문장에서 당초 계획대로 프로젝트가 진행될 것(the project will proceed as originally planned)이라고 단언했으므로 (A)가 정답이다.

어휘 costly 많은 비용이 드는 involve 수반하다 unusual 특이한

패러프레이징
지문의 proceed as originally planned
➡ 보기의 be completed as expected

101 (A)	**102** (A)	**103** (D)	**104** (B)	**105** (D)
106 (D)	**107** (B)	**108** (C)	**109** (D)	**110** (C)
111 (D)	**112** (D)	**113** (B)	**114** (C)	**115** (C)
116 (C)	**117** (D)	**118** (B)	**119** (C)	**120** (B)
121 (A)	**122** (A)	**123** (D)	**124** (A)	**125** (A)
126 (B)	**127** (C)	**128** (C)	**129** (B)	**130** (C)
131 (A)	**132** (B)	**133** (C)	**134** (D)	**135** (C)
136 (A)	**137** (D)	**138** (A)	**139** (A)	**140** (D)
141 (A)	**142** (B)	**143** (B)	**144** (A)	**145** (B)
146 (D)	**147** (B)	**148** (D)	**149** (A)	**150** (B)
151 (C)	**152** (B)	**153** (D)	**154** (D)	**155** (C)
156 (A)	**157** (B)	**158** (C)	**159** (B)	**160** (A)
161 (B)	**162** (B)	**163** (D)	**164** (B)	**165** (C)
166 (A)	**167** (D)	**168** (C)	**169** (B)	**170** (A)
171 (D)	**172** (B)	**173** (D)	**174** (D)	**175** (D)
176 (D)	**177** (C)	**178** (D)	**179** (A)	**180** (D)
181 (D)	**182** (A)	**183** (C)	**184** (B)	**185** (B)
186 (C)	**187** (B)	**188** (C)	**189** (C)	**190** (D)
191 (C)	**192** (A)	**193** (C)	**194** (D)	**195** (B)
196 (B)	**197** (D)	**198** (A)	**199** (C)	**200** (A)

PART 5

101 인칭대명사_주격

해설 빈칸은 접속사 because가 이끄는 절에서 동사 has의 주어 자리이다. 따라서 앞에 언급된 Ms. Yu를 대신하는 주격 인칭대명사인 (A) she가 정답이다.

번역 유 씨는 그날 다른 약속이 있어서 영업 회의에 참석하지 않을 것이다.

어휘 commitment 약속

102 부사의 역할_동사 수식

해설 등위접속사 and 뒤에 주어(The Jin Zan Group)가 생략되어 있고 동사 will contact, 목적어 her에 수식구까지 붙은 완전한 절 뒤에 빈칸이 있으므로 동사 will contact를 수식할 부사가 들어가야 한다. 특히 shortly는 '곧'이라는 뜻으로 미래 시제와 잘 어울리므로 (A)가 정답이다.

번역 진 잰 그룹은 엘리베 씨의 지원서를 받았고 곧 그녀에게 연락해 그 직책에 대해 논의할 것이다.

어휘 application 지원(서) shortly 곧

103 동사 어휘

해설 빈칸 뒤 unexpectedly strong revenue growth를 목적어로 취해 '의외로 높은 매출 신장을 보고했다(reported)'는 뜻이 되어야 자연스러우므로 (D) reported가 정답이다. (B) insisted와 (C) commented는 'on + 명사'로 쓰고, (A) wrote는 의미상 부적절하므로 오답이다.

번역 대럴 사는 3분기에 예상외로 높은 매출 성장을 기록했다고 보고했다.

어휘 unexpectedly 예상외로 revenue 매출 insist 주장하다

104 복합명사

해설 '매장 진열대에 놓일 예정이다'라는 문맥이 되어야 하므로 빈칸에는 store(매장)와 함께 '매장 진열대'라는 복합명사를 만들 수 있는 명사인 (A) shelf나 (B) shelves가 들어가면 된다. 매장 진열대는 가산명사인데 store 앞에 한정사가 보이지 않으므로 복수 형태가 되어야 한다. 따라서 (B) shelves가 정답이다.

번역 컬스 갤로어 헤어 제품군은 4월에 시판될 예정이다.

105 형용사 어휘

해설 or 앞에 '회의실을 예약하려면'이라는 내용이 있으므로 뒤에도 이에 상응하는 '어떤 방을 쓸 수 있는지 알아보려면'이라는 내용이 되어야 문맥이 자연스럽다. 또한 (A) widespread와 (B) consistent, (C) instructive는 '방(rooms)'이라는 명사와는 의미상 어울리지 않으므로 답이 될 수 없다. 따라서 (D) available이 정답이다.

번역 회의실을 예약하거나 어떤 방을 쓸 수 있는지 알아보려면 빌딩 서비스에 문의하세요.

어휘 reserve 예약하다 widespread 널리 퍼진 consistent 지속적인 instructive 유익한 available 쓸 수 있는

106 전치사 어휘_자동사+전치사

해설 빈칸에는 동사 refer와 함께 쓰여 '~을 참고하다'라는 의미를 나타내는 전치사가 들어가야 한다. 따라서 정답은 (D) to이다.

번역 보상 포인트로 티켓을 구매하려는 카드 소지자는 홈페이지의 제한 사항 목록을 참고해야 한다.

어휘 purchase 구매하다; 구매(품) reward 보상 refer to ~을 참고하다 restriction 제한

107 부사 어휘

해설 '숙련된(Experienced)' 등산객이라고 했으므로 등산로를 '쉽게' 다닐 수 있다는 내용이 되어야 문맥상 자연스럽다. 따라서 '쉽게, 수월하게'라는 뜻의 (B) easily가 정답이다.

번역 숙련된 등산객은 호핑 산 등산로를 쉽게 다닐 수 있다.

어휘 experienced 숙련된 trail 등산로 sharply 날카롭게, 갑자기 precisely 정확하게

108 동사 자리

해설 앞에 있는 The CEO가 주어이므로 빈칸은 동사 자리이고, 빈칸 뒤에 명사절 that절이 목적어 자리에 있으므로 능동형이 들어가야 한다. 따라서 (C) believes가 정답이다. (A) was believed는 수동형이고, (B) to believe와 (D) a belief는 동사 역할을 할 수 없으므로 답이 될 수 없다.

번역 하트포드 프로듀스 CEO는 모든 저장시설의 운용절차를 표준화하는 것이 최우선 과제라고 믿는다.

어휘 standardize 표준화하다 protocol 운용절차 storage 저장 facility 시설 priority 우선 과제

109 명사 어휘

해설 신 씨의 일을 축하하기 위해 팀이 모인다는 내용이므로, 빈칸에는 축하할 수 있는 좋은 일을 나타내는 의미의 명사가 들어가야 한다. 따라서 '승진'이라는 뜻의 (D) promotion이 정답이다.

번역 신 씨의 승진을 축하하기 위해 팀은 금요일 정오 더 센터 비스트로에 모일 예정이다.

어휘 in honor of ~을 축하하기 위해 revision 수정 adjustment 조정 refinement 개선

110 인칭대명사_소유격

해설 administration team은 전치사 with의 목적어로, 빈칸에는 명사구(administration team)를 수식할 수 있는 소유격이 들어가야 한다. 따라서 (C) our가 정답이다.

번역 CEO 알마 카바낙이 다음 주 화요일에 저희 행정팀과 만날 예정입니다.

어휘 administration 행정

111 동사 어휘

해설 문맥상 '광고 전문가들이 아이디어를 요약해 주었다'는 내용이 되어야 자연스러우므로 '요약하다'는 뜻의 (D) summarized가 정답이다. 전체 문맥을 살피지 않더라도 (A) measured, (B) afforded, (C) based는 their best ideas를 목적어로 취하는 동사로는 의미상 어울리지 않는다.

번역 기획 세션에 이어, 호바트 미디어 그룹의 광고 전문가들이 고객을 위한 최고의 아이디어들을 요약했다.

어휘 following ~에 이어 measure 측정하다 afford 여유가 되다 base 기초를 두다

112 명사의 역할_주어

해설 빈칸은 동사 begins와 can be completed의 주어 자리이므로 명사가 들어가야 한다. '회의 등록은 5월 1일에 시

작한다'는 내용이 되어야 자연스러우므로 '등록'이라는 의미의 명사 (D) Registration이 정답이다. (A) Register도 명사이기는 하나 '명부'라는 뜻으로 문맥에 어울리지 않고, 가산명사라서 앞에 한정사가 필요하므로 답이 될 수 없다.

번역 회의 등록은 5월 1일에 시작하며 웹사이트에서 완료할 수 있다.

어휘 register 등록하다; 명부, (금전) 등록기

113 전치사 어휘

해설 문맥상 '분석가 자리에 적격인 지원자'가 되어야 하므로 '~용의, ~에 적합한'이라는 용도의 의미를 나타내는 전치사인 for가 들어가야 자연스럽다. 따라서 (B) for가 정답이다.

번역 앤도버 소프트웨어는 품질 보증 분석가 자리에 적격인 지원자를 찾고 있다.

어휘 qualified 적격인 candidate 지원자 quality assurance 품질 보증 analyst 분석가

114 부사의 역할_형용사 수식

해설 빈칸은 be동사 was와 형용사 complete 사이에서 형용사를 수식하는 부사 자리이다. '디자인이 거의 끝났었다'는 내용이 되어야 자연스러우므로 '거의'라는 뜻의 부사 (C) nearly가 정답이다.

번역 티셔츠 디자인이 거의 완성되었을 때 고객이 막바지 변경을 위해 전화했다.

어휘 last-minute 막바지의

115 부사절 축약

해설 빈칸 뒤에 현재분사 loading이 있으므로 부사절 접속사 (C) After나 (D) Since와 결합할 수 있다. '트럭에 물건을 실은 뒤, 허가를 받아야 한다'는 내용이 되어야 자연스러우므로 '~한 뒤에'라는 뜻의 (C) After가 정답이다.

번역 트럭에 화물을 적재한 후 운전자는 국경 너머로 자재를 운송할 수 있는 허가를 받아야 한다.

어휘 load 적재하다 permit 허가(증) transport 운송 border 국경

116 관계대명사_주격

해설 주어는 the employee, 동사는 will receive이며 빈칸부터 sales figures까지는 주어이자 선행사인 the employee를 꾸미는 관계절이다. 빈칸 뒤에 동사(has)가 왔으므로, 주격 관계대명사인 (C) who가 정답이다.

번역 매월 매출액이 가장 높은 직원은 상을 받을 것이다.

어휘 sales figure 매출액

117 부사 어휘

해설 '문제에 부딪히면 기술 팀에 알리세요'라는 내용에 어울리는

부사를 골라야 한다. 문제 발생 시 즉각 보고하라는 뜻이 적합하므로 '즉시'라는 뜻의 (D) immediately가 정답이다.

번역 소프트웨어 응용 프로그램을 사용할 때 문제에 부딪히면 즉시 기술 팀에 알리세요.

어휘 encounter 부딪히다 issue 문제 notify 알리다 commonly 흔히 formerly 이전에 unnecessarily 쓸데없이

118 수동태 관용 표현

해설 문맥상 '승객들은 물건을 가져오도록 권장된다'는 수동의 의미가 되어야 한다. 'encourage + 목적어 + to부정사' 구문을 수동태로 고치면 'be encouraged + to부정사'의 형태가 된다. 따라서 (B) encouraged가 정답이다.

번역 승객들은 고래관찰 시 비디오카메라와 쌍안경을 가지고 오시기 바랍니다.

어휘 binocular 쌍안경

119 명사 어휘

해설 빈칸에는 방문객이 입장 전에 프런트에 제시해야 할 것을 뜻하는 명사가 들어가야 한다. 보기 중 '신분증'이 가장 적합하므로 (C) identification이 정답이다.

번역 모든 방문객은 건물 안으로 들어가기 전에 프런트에 유효한 신분증을 제시해야 한다.

어휘 present 제시하다 valid 유효한 communication 통신 reception 환영회 graduation 졸업

120 과거분사 + 명사

해설 빈칸은 to see의 목적어인 명사 results를 수식하는 형용사 자리이다. 보기 중 명사 앞에서 명사를 수식할 수 있는 것은 과거분사인 improved뿐이고 '개선된 결과'라는 뜻으로 의미도 자연스럽다. 따라서 (B) improved가 정답이다.

번역 오카베 씨는 모리 애널리틱스의 다음 데이터 보고서에서 개선된 결과를 보기 원한다.

어휘 result 결과 improve 개선하다 improved 개선된

121 명사절 접속사

해설 빈칸은 동명사 determining의 목적어 자리이고, 뒤에 주어와 동사를 갖춘 절이 왔으므로 명사절 접속사가 필요하다. 따라서 '~인지 아닌지'라는 의미를 나타내는 명사절 접속사인 (A) whether가 정답이다.

번역 새로운 직원 평가 절차는 직원이 기준에 부합하는지 여부에 대한 판단을 간단하게 만든다.

어휘 evaluation 평가 simplify 간단하게 만들다 determine 판단하다

122 부사의 역할_동명사구 수식

해설 빈칸은 완전한 문장에서 주어 자리에 있는 동명사구인 Cleaning the parts를 수식하는 부사 자리이다. 따라서 '주기적으로'라는 의미의 (A) periodically가 정답이다.

번역 주기적으로 부품을 청소하면 커피 메이커의 추출 품질과 수명이 모두 향상된다.

어휘 increase 향상시키다 life span 수명 periodically 주기적으로

123 형용사의 역할_명사 수식

해설 빈칸은 전치사 including의 목적어로 온 명사 pens, brochures, and stickers를 수식하는 형용사 자리이다. 따라서 '맞춤형인'이라는 뜻의 분사형 형용사인 (D) customized가 정답이다.

번역 당사는 맞춤형 펜, 안내책자, 스티커 등 다양한 고급 판촉용품을 제공한다.

어휘 a range of 다양한 promotional 판촉의 customize 맞춤형으로 만들다 customized 맞춤형인

124 전치사 자리

해설 빈칸은 완전한 절에 명사구 the next several months를 연결하는 자리이므로 전치사가 필요하다. 보기 중 전치사 within이 들어가면 '향후 몇 달 내에'라는 내용으로 글의 흐름도 자연스러우므로 (A) within이 정답이다.

번역 와이싱어 부동산은 향후 몇 달 내에 신규 사무소 지점 세 개를 열 계획이다.

어휘 realty 부동산

125 준동사_to부정사

해설 빈칸 앞에 완전한 절이 있으므로 동사는 들어갈 수 없고, 빈칸 뒤에 남아 있는 명사구를 연결시켜 줄 연결어가 필요하다. 빈칸 이하를 이끌어 '무공해 비누를 제조할'이라는 의미로 명사 scientists를 수식할 수 있는 (A) to formulate가 정답이다.

번역 클린 서드사는 공해 없는 비누를 제조하는 과학자들을 고용함으로써 환경을 중시한다.

어휘 environment 환경 nonpolluting 공해 없는 formulate 제조하다

126 부사절 접속사 vs. 전치사

해설 전치사구 in flight를 자연스럽게 문장에 연결해 줄 연결어를 골라야 한다. 문맥상 '비행하는 동안 휴대전화 사용을 허용할 예정이다'는 내용이 되어야 하므로 빈칸에는 '~하는 동안'이라는 뜻의 부사절 접속사 (B) while이 정답이다. 빈칸 뒤에 in flight만 남아 있는 것으로 보아 부사절 접속사 절의 주어와 be동사가 생략되고 보어 자리의 전치사구만 남아 있는 것을 알 수 있다.

번역 핀치 항공은 6월부터 비행 중 휴대전화 사용을 허용할 예정이다.

어휘 flight 비행

127 형용사 어휘

해설 주어 자리의 명사구 Turnet Tea's new location을 수식하기에 적절한 형용사를 골라야 한다. 수식 받는 명사가 장소를 나타내는 말이므로 '넓은'이라는 뜻의 spacious가 가장 잘 어울린다. 따라서 (C) spacious가 정답이다.

번역 겔람 레인에 있는 터넷 티의 새 위치는 원래 있던 뱅크 가 매장보다 훨씬 넓다.

어휘 urgent 긴급한 spacious 넓은 gradual 점진적인

128 동사 어휘

해설 문맥상 '바이오말즈사는 개선하고자 한다'는 내용이 되어야 하므로 빈칸에는 진행형으로 쓰여 '(~하려고) 노력하다'는 의미를 나타내는 동사 look이 들어가면 가장 적절하다. 따라서 (C) looking이 정답이다. 참고로, (A) regarding과 (B) viewing은 타동사로 뒤에 목적어가 필요하므로 답이 될 수 없다.

번역 바이오말즈사는 라이브 채팅 기능을 추가해 온라인 고객 서비스 경험을 개선하고자 한다.

어휘 enhance 개선하다 feature 기능

129 부사의 역할_동사 수식

해설 빈칸은 have와 p.p. 사이에 있으므로 동사를 수식하는 부사 자리이다. 부사 just가 들어가면 '방금 전에 발표했다'는 내용이 되어 자연스러우므로 (B) just가 정답이다. (A) plus(게다가)와 (C) but(오직)도 간혹 부사로 쓰이기는 하나 문맥에 어울리지 않는다.

번역 로이그 재단은 얼마 전 도시의 독서 프로젝트에 자금을 지원하겠다고 발표했다.

어휘 fund 자금을 지원하다

130 접속부사

해설 등위접속사 and 뒤에 주어가 생략된 완전한 절이 왔으므로 빈칸은 부사 자리이다. and 앞은 트렌드를 빠르게 수용했다(quickly embraced new trends)는 내용이고 뒤는 업계 매출을 선도했다(led the industry in sales)는 내용이므로, 빈칸에는 인과 관계를 나타내는 접속부사가 필요하다. 따라서 (C) therefore가 정답이다. 참고로, then(그 다음에), therefore(따라서), thus(그러므로)와 같은 접속부사는 and와 함께 어울려 and then, and therefore, and thus와 같이 자주 활용된다.

번역 서적 출판사 피트너 프레스는 인기 소설의 새로운 트렌드를 빠르게 수용했고, 따라서 작년에 이 업종에서 판매를 선도했다.

어휘 embrace 수용하다

Part 6

131-134 이메일

수신: 전 직원

발신: 로지타 고메즈

날짜: 9월 30일

Re: 파쇄 행사

귀하의 민감한 정보를 보호하기 위해 10월 30일에 반 윙클 슈레딩과 함께 하는 현장 파쇄 행사를 마련했습니다. 이 ¹³¹**서비스**는 전 직원에게 무료로 제공됩니다. 반 윙클이 방문하기 전에 개인 문서를 담을 수 있는 상자를 최대 3개까지 받습니다. ¹³²제공된 상자만 사용하세요. 늦어도 10월 30일 정오까지 ¹³³**당신의** 사무실 밖에 놓으세요. 오후 1시에서 2시 사이에 반 윙클 직원들이 건물을 돌아다니며 파쇄할 자료를 ¹³⁴**수거할** 예정입니다. 회사 기밀 문서는 복사기 구역에 있는 안전한 파란색 용기를 계속 사용할 것을 요청합니다.

로지타

어휘   shred 파쇄하다   sensitive 민감한   arrange 마련하다   no later than 늦어도 ~까지   confidential 기밀의

131 명사 어휘

해설   빈칸은 앞 문장에서 언급한 반 윙클 슈레딩과 함께 하는 현장 파쇄 행사를 지칭하는 것으로, 직원들에게 무료로 제공된다고 했으므로 보기 중 '서비스'가 빈칸에 가장 적합하다. 따라서 (A) service가 정답이다.

어휘   experience 경험   performance 실적, 공연

132 문맥에 맞는 문장 고르기

해설   빈칸 앞에는 개인 용지를 담을 상자를 최대 3개까지 받을 것이라는 내용이 왔고, 뒤에는 그 상자들을 사무실 밖에 두라는 내용이 왔다. 앞뒤 문장 모두 상자에 대한 안내 사항을 공지하고 있으므로 빈칸에도 역시 상자와 관련된 지침이 들어가야 글의 흐름이 자연스럽다. 따라서 제공된 상자만 사용하라는 내용의 (B)가 정답이다.

번역   (A) 정보 침해는 대가가 뒤따를 수 있다.

       (B) 제공된 상자만 사용하세요.

       (C) 5월에 또 파쇄 행사가 열립니다.

       (D) 반 윙클 슈레딩은 40년 이상 사업을 해 왔습니다.

어휘   breach 침해   costly 대가가 있는

133 인칭대명사_소유격(2인칭)

해설   빈칸이 있는 문장은 명령문으로 주어(You)는 생략되었으나 이메일 수신자(you)가 해야 할 일을 언급하고 있다. 앞 문장에서도 다른 인물에 대한 언급은 없고 이메일 수신자가 하게 될 일에 대해 안내하고 있다. 따라서 (C) your가 정답이다.

134 동사 어휘

해설   앞 문장에서 용지가 담긴 상자들을 사무실 밖에 내놓으라고 했으므로, 반 윙클 직원들이 건물을 돌아다니며 파쇄를 위해 당신이 내놓은 자료들을 '수거해' 갈 것이라는 내용이 되어야 자연스럽다. 따라서 '수거하다'는 뜻의 (D) collect가 정답이다.

어휘   produce 생산하다   develop 개발하다   promote 승진시키다   collect 수거하다

135-138 광고

폰빌 홀세일 리넨에서는 사람들에게 숙면을 제공하는 것이 우리 일입니다. ¹³⁵**보통** 호텔, 여관, 리조트에만 판매합니다. 그러나 4월 한 달 내내 온라인 매장을 일반에게 개방합니다. 일반적으로는 당사에서 제공하지 않는 소비자들에게는 고품질의 시트, 베개, 이불, 담요를 ¹³⁶**갖출 수 있는** 좋은 기회입니다. 당사는 다양한 사이즈, 색상, 소재를 제공합니다. ¹³⁷여러분의 스타일과 선호도에 맞는 건 무엇이든 틀림없이 찾으실 겁니다. 그러니 집안의 모든 ¹³⁸**침대**에 당사 고급 제품을 갖출 수 있는 이번 제안을 활용하세요!

어휘   wholesale 도매   opportunity 기회   comforter 이불   outfit (장비 등을) 갖추다

135 부사 어휘

해설   뒤 문장에서 '그러나' 4월에는 온라인 매장을 일반인에 개방한다고 했으므로 보통 때는 일반에 개방하지 않고 호텔, 여관, 리조트에만 판매한다는 내용이 되어야 흐름상 자연스럽다. 따라서 빈칸에는 '보통'이라는 뜻의 부사인 (C) Normally가 정답이다.

136 준동사_to부정사

해설   명사 opportunity는 to부정사와 함께 '~할 기회'라는 표현으로 자주 쓰인다. opportunity 뒤에 목적격 관계사가 생략된 관계사절(we do not typically serve)의 수식을 받고 있는 의미상 주어 for consumers가 있고, '소비자가 당사의 고품질 제품들을 갖출 기회'라는 의미가 되어야 하므로 빈칸에는 to부정사가 들어가야 한다. 따라서 (A) to stock up이 정답이다.

어휘   stock up on 구비하다

137 문맥에 맞는 문장 고르기

해설   앞 문장에서 당사는 다양한 사이즈, 색상, 소재를 제공한다며 제품의 다양성을 강조했으므로 원하는 것은 무엇이든 찾을 수 있을 것이라는 내용이 들어가면 자연스럽다. 따라서 (D)가 정답이다.

번역 (A) 올해로 10주년이 되었습니다.
(B) 모든 물품이 잘 포장되었는지 확인하시기 바랍니다.
(C) 당사 제품은 순수 에센셜 오일의 천연 혼합 향이 납니다.
(D) 여러분의 스타일과 선호도에 맞는 건 무엇이든 틀림없이 찾으실 겁니다.

어휘 scented 향이 나는 be guaranteed to 틀림없이
~하다 preference 선호

138 명사 어휘

해설 빈칸이 있는 문장만으로는 답을 고르기 어려우므로 앞 글에서 단서를 찾아야 한다. 첫 문장에서 폰빌 홀세일 리넨에서는 사람들에게 숙면을 제공하는 것이 우리의 일이라고 했고, 네 번째 문장에서 취급 제품으로 시트, 베개, 이불, 담요를 언급했으므로 폰빌 홀세일 리넨은 침대 용품 회사임을 알 수 있다. 따라서 '모든 침대에 당사 제품을 갖추라'는 내용이 되어야 적절하므로 (A) bed가 정답이다.

139-142 이메일

수신: 라메시 난디라주 〈rnandiraju@tsag.in〉
발신: 프라티마 다르마푸리
〈pratima@dharmapurievents.in〉
날짜: 2월 21일
제목: 체육관 임대

난디라주 씨께,

타워링 스포츠 앤드 짐네이지엄을 빌릴 수 있는지 알고 싶습니다. 저는 139**행사 기획자로**, 한 기업 고객이 회사의 연례 가족행사를 체육관과 피크닉장에서 열고자 합니다. 140**특히**, 제 고객은 경기를 할 수 있는 농구 코트와 기타 실내외 활동을 할 수 있는 시설을 찾고 있습니다. 141귀사 시설이 이들 기준에 완벽하게 부합합니다.

제 고객은 5월 둘째 주나 셋째 주 일요일에 행사를 열고 싶어 합니다. 이 계획이 142**가능한**지 알려 주세요. 만약 그렇다면, 오전 11시부터 오후 4시까지 진행되는 행사의 비용을 알려 주세요.

프라티마 다르마푸리
다르마푸리 행사 기획

어휘 gymnasium 체육관 corporate 기업의

139 시제_현재

해설 앞 문장에서 체육관을 빌릴 수 있는지 알고 싶다며 현재 이 메일을 쓰고 있는 이유를 설명했고, 뒤에서는 한 기업 고객이 회사의 연례 가족행사를 체육관과 피크닉장에서 열고자 한다고 상황 설명을 하고 있다. 따라서 현재 시제로 '저는 행사 기획자이다'라고 자신을 소개하는 내용이 되어야 문맥에 어울리므로 (A) am이 정답이다.

140 접속부사

해설 빈칸 앞에서 한 기업 고객이 회사의 연례 가족행사를 체육관과 피크닉장에서 열고자 한다고 했고, 뒤에서는 그 고객은 경기를 할 수 있는 농구 코트와 기타 실내외 활동을 할 수 있는 시설을 찾고 있다며 앞에서 말한 고객이 제시한 조건을 구체화한 내용을 말하고 있다. 따라서 '특히, 구체적으로 말하면'이라는 뜻을 가진 (D) Specifically가 정답이다.

어휘 as you expected 예상했던 대로 unfortunately 안타깝게도 in any case 어쨌든 specifically 특히

141 문맥에 맞는 문장 고르기

해설 이메일의 첫 문장에서 수신인의 체육관을 빌릴 수 있는지 알고 싶다고 했고, 빈칸의 바로 앞 문장에서는 경기를 할 수 있는 농구 코트와 기타 실내외 활동을 할 수 있는 시설을 찾고 있다며 원하는 체육관 시설에 대한 구체적인 기준을 제시하고 있다. 빈칸에 귀사의 시설이 제시한 기준에 딱 들어맞는다는 내용이 들어가면 해당 체육관의 임대를 원하고 있는 합당한 이유가 되므로 (B)가 정답이다.

번역 (A) 귀하의 제안에 대해 논의하도록 연락 주세요.
(B) 귀사 시설이 이들 기준에 완벽하게 부합합니다.
(C) 그들은 귀하의 사업에 투자하는 것을 고려하고 있습니다.
(D) 귀사의 특별한 행사를 기꺼이 관장하겠습니다.

어휘 meet 부합하다 criteria 기준

142 형용사 어휘

해설 빈칸 앞에서 고객이 5월 둘째 주나 셋째 주 일요일에 행사를 열고 싶어 한다고 했으므로 아직 행사 일정을 조율 중임을 알 수 있다. 따라서 제시한 일정이 가능한지 알려 달라는 내용이 되어야 문맥상 자연스러우므로 빈칸에는 '가능한'이라는 뜻의 형용사 (B) possible이 정답이다.

어휘 possible 가능한 avoidable 피할 수 있는
underway 진행 중인

143-146 편지

**윈슬로우 파이낸셜 어드바이저스 · 31번 가 4215번지 ·
뉴욕, 뉴욕 주 10003**

11월 1일

웬디 겐델만
E 가 22번지
뉴욕, 뉴욕 주 10009

겐델만 씨께,

벌어들인 돈을 지키는 것은 매우 중요합니다. 윈슬로우 파이낸셜 어드바이저스가 제공하는 지식과 도구가 143**있으면** 돈을 관리해 고객님의 생활방식을 뒷받침하고 미래를 위해 저축할 수 있습니다. 144저희는 고객님의 요구에 귀를 기울입니다. 당

224

사는 고객님이 제공하는 그 정보를 활용해 투자를 안전하게 분산할 수 있도록 개인 맞춤형 재무계획을 설계합니다. 모든 ^{145}옵션에 대해 설명해 드립니다. 여기에는 투자, 저축, 보험 및 세금 전략이 포함됩니다.

안전하고 ^{146}정보에 입각한 금융 결정을 시작하려면 지금 (212) 555-0100으로 윈슬로우 파이낸셜 어드바이저스에 문의하세요.

바락 카마라, 재정 고문

어휘 safeguard 지키다   earn 벌다   personalized 개인 맞춤형인   spread out 분산하다   investment 투자   insurance 보험   strategy 전략

143 전치사 어휘

해설 문맥상 '윈슬로우 파이낸셜 어드바이저스가 제공하는 지식과 도구가 있으면 돈을 관리할 수 있다'는 내용이 되어야 자연스럽다. 따라서 '~가 있으면'이라는 조건의 의미를 나타내는 전치사인 (B) With가 정답이다.

144 문맥에 맞는 문장 고르기

해설 빈칸 뒤에서 당사는 고객님이 제공하는 '그 정보'를 활용해 투자를 안전하게 분산할 수 있도록 개인 맞춤형 재무계획을 설계한다고 했으므로, 빈칸에는 회사가 고객으로부터 받는 정보와 관련된 내용이 들어가야 글의 흐름이 자연스럽다. 따라서 고객의 요구 사항(needs)을 '고객이 제공하는 그 정보'로 받아서 연결할 수 있는 (A)가 정답이다.

번역 (A) 저희는 고객님의 요구에 귀를 기울입니다.
　　 (B) 당사는 많은 신규 고객을 돕고 있습니다.
　　 (C) 저렴한 주택에 대해 알려 드리겠습니다.
　　 (D) 돈을 절약하는 것은 매우 어렵습니다.

어휘 affordable 저렴한

145 명사 어휘

해설 빈칸 뒤에서 빈칸의 명사를 대명사 These로 받아 여기에는 투자, 저축, 보험 및 세금 전략이 포함된다며 재무 계획과 관련한 선택 사항들에 대해 나열하고 있다. 따라서 빈칸에는 '선택 사항'이라는 의미를 나타내는 (B) options가 정답이다.

146 형용사의 역할_명사 수식

해설 빈칸은 safe와 함께 명사구 financial decisions를 수식하는 형용사 자리이다. 따라서 '정보에 입각한'이라는 뜻의 형용사 (D) informed가 정답이다. 참고로, '형용사 + 명사' 앞에는 또 형용사가 올 수 있으며 이때 앞에 붙는 형용사는 당연히 명사를 수식한다.

어휘 informed 정보에 입각한

Part 7

147-148 이메일

수신: 전 직원 〈allstaff@celianfinancial.com〉
발신: 시오도라 헝 〈t.heng@celianfinancial.com〉
날짜: 8월 5일 월요일
제목: 건물 내 전기기술자들

동료 여러분께:

골로빈 일렉트릭 전기기술자 팀이 내일부터 건물 도처에서 조명 설비를 교체할 예정이니 유념하시기 바랍니다. ^{147}**이들은 오전 8시 30분 건물이 문을 열기 전 공용장소에서 작업한 뒤 동관 직원 사무실로 이동합니다.** 서관에서 일하는 사람들은 수요일에 이들을 보게 될 예정입니다. ^{148}**금요일 업무 마감까지 모든 작업이 끝납니다.** 도급업자들은 일하는 동안 방해를 최소화하기 위해 전력을 다할 것입니다.

궁금한 점이나 우려되는 점이 있으면 언제든지 연락 주세요.

시오도라 헝, 시설 부팀장

어휘 replace 교체하다   light fixture 조명 설비   contractor 도급업자   disruption 방해

147 Not/True

번역 예정된 작업에 관해 명시된 것은?
　　 (A) 동관에만 영향을 미칠 것이다.
　　 (B) 건물이 문을 열기 전에 시작할 것이다.
　　 (C) 헝 씨의 부서 직원이 수행한다.
　　 (D) 직원들이 다른 장소로 이동해야 한다.

해설 두 번째 문장에서 전기기술자 팀이 오전 8시 30분 건물이 문을 열기 전 공용장소에서 작업한 뒤 동관 직원 사무실로 이동한다(They will be working in the public areas before the building opens ~ the east wing)고 했으므로 (B)가 정답이다.

어휘 affect 영향을 미치다   carry out 수행하다

148 세부 사항

번역 작업은 언제 완료되는가?
　　 (A) 월요일
　　 (B) 화요일
　　 (C) 수요일
　　 (D) 금요일

해설 네 번째 문장에서 금요일 업무 마감까지 모든 작업이 끝난다(The entire job will be finished by the close of business on Friday)고 안내했으므로 (D)가 정답이다.

149-151 광고

> **팜 프론드 모텔에 묵으세요**
>
> ¹⁴⁹벤슨 가족은 몇 대에 걸쳐 팜 프론드 모텔로 손님들을 따뜻하게 맞았습니다. ¹⁵⁰40번 U.S. 간선도로에서 차로 불과 2분 거리인 팜 프론드 모텔은 편안한 침대, 대형화면 텔레비전, 커피 메이커로 객실을 더 좋게 꾸몄습니다. 무료 와이파이와 주차 외에도 저렴한 가격에 현장 세탁 서비스도 제공합니다. ¹⁵¹추가 요금을 내시면 소형 반려동물도 환영합니다.
>
> 760-555-0157로 전화하시거나 reservations@palmfrondmotel.com에서 온라인으로 예약하세요.

149 추론

번역 팜 프론드 모텔에 관해 암시된 것은?

  (A) 수 년째 운영되고 있다.
  (B) 풀서비스 식당이 있다.
  (C) 객실 2개짜리 스위트룸을 임대한다.
  (D) 비즈니스 회의를 주최한다.

해설 광고문의 첫 문장에서 벤슨 가족은 몇 대에 걸쳐 팜 프론드 모텔로 손님들을 따뜻하게 맞아 왔다(The Bentson family has been ~ for generations)고 했으므로 모텔이 여러 해 동안 운영되어 왔음을 알 수 있다. 따라서 (A)가 정답이다.

패러프레이징
지문의 for generations ➡ 보기의 for many years

150 세부 사항

번역 팜 프론드 모텔은 어디에 있는가?

  (A) 공항 인근
  (B) 간선도로 부근
  (C) 테마파크
  (D) 도심

해설 두 번째 문장에서 40번 U.S. 간선도로에서 차로 불과 2분 거리인 팜 프론드 모텔(Located just a two-minute drive from U.S. Highway 40, the Palm Frond Motel)이라고 소개하고 있으므로 (B)가 정답이다.

패러프레이징
지문의 just a two-minute drive from
➡ 보기의 Close to

151 세부 사항

번역 투숙객들이 추가로 지불해야 하는 것은?

  (A) 와이파이 접속
  (B) 커피 서비스
  (C) 반려동물 숙박
  (D) 차량 주차

해설 첫 단락의 마지막 문장에 추가 요금을 내면 소형 반려동물도 환영한다(Small pets are welcome for an additional fee)고 했다. 따라서 반려동물을 동반할 경우 숙박비를 추가로 지불해야 한다는 것을 알 수 있으므로 (C)가 정답이다.

어휘 accommodation 숙박

152-153 도서 제안서

> **도서 제안 개요**
>
> **제목:** 〈하인스부르크의 설계자〉
> **저자:** 셀레스테 세르
>
> **설명:** ¹⁵²이 책은 제가 채널 10 뉴스 기자로 취재했던 이야기를 바탕으로 할 예정입니다. ¹⁵³책은 마리아나 델이라는 여성의 일생을 추적하는데, 그녀의 가족은 1897년 하인스부르크 시로 이사했습니다. 부모는 시 외곽에 농장을 샀고 지역 정가에서 활발히 활동했습니다. 델 씨는 마침내 하인스부르크 시장에 선출됐고 시의 유명한 식물원을 조성하는 일에 앞장섰습니다. 델 씨는 아주 중요한 역사적 인물이지만 잘 알려지지 않았습니다. 제 조사에는 시 기록, 하인스부르크 공공 도서관에 보관된 예전 신문 기사, 지역 역사학자들 대상 인터뷰가 포함될 것입니다.

어휘 architect 설계자, 건축가 trace 추적하다 outskirts 외곽 politics 정가 eventually 마침내 spearhead 앞장서다 crucial 아주 중요한 figure 인물 municipal 시의 archive 보관하다

152 추론

번역 세르 씨의 직업은?

  (A) 사서   (B) 건축가
  (C) 정원사   (D) 기자

해설 첫 문장에서 글의 작성자인 세르 씨가 이 책은 자신이 채널 10 뉴스 기자로 취재했던 이야기를 바탕으로 할 예정(This book will be based on a story I covered as a reporter for Channel 10 News)이라며 자신이 기자라고 밝혔으므로 (D)가 정답이다.

패러프레이징
지문의 reporter ➡ 보기의 Journalist

153 세부 사항

번역 어떤 종류의 책을 제안하고 있는가?

  (A) 전기
  (B) 추리소설
  (C) 여행 가이드
  (D) 개인 에세이 시리즈

해설 두 번째 문장에서 책은 마리아나 델이라는 여성의 일생을 추적한다(It traces the life of Mariana Dell)고 했으므로 마리아나 델의 전기라는 것을 알 수 있다. 따라서 (A)가 정답이다.

154-155 이메일

수신: 마케팅 팀 배포 목록

발신: 에릭 무심바

제목: 휴가

날짜: 6월 12일

마케팅 팀에게:

¹⁵⁴저는 6월 26일부터 휴가를 가서 7월 10일에 돌아옵니다. 이 기간 동안 인터넷 접속이 제한되므로 이메일을 확인하지 않을 겁니다.

¹⁵⁴제가 자리를 비운 동안 지원 면에서는, 예나이 첸이 저를 대신할 예정입니다. ¹⁵⁵첸 씨는 현재 진행 중인 프로젝트에 대한 최신 정보를 알고 있으므로 제 이메일과 음성 메시지에 답할 것입니다. 해결되지 않은 고객 문제가 있으면 그녀에게 직접 연락하세요. 제가 주요 고객들에게 부재중임을 알릴 겁니다. 그리고 부재를 알리는 이메일 답신에 관련 연락처를 포함시키겠습니다.

데이터파인 테크놀러지스 발표회에서 행운을 빕니다. 돌아오면 발표회 얘기를 듣고 싶습니다.

에릭 무심바

마케팅 부장

어휘 in terms of ~ 면에서는 up-to-date 최신 정보를 아는 unresolved 해결되지 않은 absence 부재

154 주제 / 목적

번역 무심바 씨가 이메일을 보낸 이유는?

(A) 인터넷 장애에 관해 팀에게 알리기

(B) 데이터파인 테크놀러지스 발표회에 관한 최신 정보 제공하기

(C) 새로운 휴가 규정 설명하기

(D) 부재 시 계획 설명하기

해설 이메일의 첫 단락에서 무심바 씨는 6월 26일부터 휴가를 가서 7월 10일에 돌아온다(I will be on vacation ~ July 10)고 휴가 계획을 알리며 이 기간 동안 인터넷 접속이 제한되므로 이메일을 확인하지 않을 것(I will have limited access ~ during this time)이라고 했다. 또한 두 번째 단락 첫 문장에서도 자리를 비운 동안 지원 면에서는 예나이 첸이 자신을 대신할 예정(In terms of support while I am away, ~ covering for me)이라고 부재 시 대비책을 설명하고 있으므로 (D)가 정답이다.

155 Not / True

번역 첸 씨에 관해 명시된 것은?

(A) 곧 휴가에서 돌아올 것이다.

(B) 이메일보다 음성 메시지를 더 좋아한다.

(C) 현재 진행 중인 팀 프로젝트를 잘 알고 있다.

(D) 중요한 신규 고객을 확보했다.

해설 두 번째 단락의 두 번째 문장에서 첸 씨는 현재 진행 중인 프로젝트에 대한 최신 정보를 알고 있다(Ms. Chen is up-to-date on our ongoing projects)고 했으므로 (C)가 정답이다.

패러프레이징

지문의 up-to-date on our ongoing projects

➡ 보기의 familiar with current team projects

156-157 온라인 채팅

마유미 타마키 (오전 9:20)

안녕하세요. 회계사직에 다섯 사람을 면접했어요. 두 사람은 다음 주에 추가 면접을 합니다. ¹⁵⁶로버트 플레처가 한 지원자를 아주 선호하는데 저는 다른 사람이 끌리네요. ¹⁵⁷두 사람 면접에 참석하실래요?

헨리 크루스 (오전 9:22)

¹⁵⁷제가 여기 있으면요. 내일 브뤼셀로 가거든요. 다음 주 수요일에 돌아옵니다. 면접이 언제죠?

마유미 타마키 (오전 9:23)

아직 정확한 날짜는 없어요. 하지만 ¹⁵⁷둘 다 출장을 피해서 일정을 잡을 수 있어요. 최종 결정을 내리기 전에 당신 의견을 꼭 듣고 싶어요.

헨리 크루스 (오전 9:24)

너무 좋죠.

어휘 accountant 회계사 follow-up 후속의 lean 끌리다 sit in on ~에 참석하다 input 의견

156 Not / True

번역 타마키 씨에 관해 명시된 것은?

(A) 지원자에 관해 플레처 씨와 의견이 다르다.

(B) 더 많은 지원서를 검토하고 싶어 한다.

(C) 플레처 씨에게 업무차 브뤼셀에 가 달라고 요청했다.

(D) 새로운 구인광고를 준비하고 있다.

해설 9시 20분 타마키 씨의 메시지에서 로버트 플레처가 한 지원자를 아주 선호하는데 저는 다른 사람이 끌린다(Robert Fletcher strongly prefers one candidate, and I'm leaning toward the other)고 했으므로 지원자에 대한 둘의 의견이 일치하지 않는다는 것을 알 수 있다. 따라서 (A)가 정답이다.

157 의도 파악

번역 오전 9시 24분에 크루스 씨가 "너무 좋죠"라고 쓴 의도는?

(A) 플레처 씨와 회의 일정을 잡는 데 동의한다.

(B) 면접에 포함된 것에 고마워한다.

(C) 제안된 날짜에 시간이 있다.

(D) 여행 계획을 확정하고 있다.

9시 20분에 타마키 씨가 두 면접에 참석할지(Would you like to sit in on both interview?) 묻자, 9시 22분에 크루스 씨가 자신이 여기 있으면(If I'm here)이라며 내일 브뤼셀로 가서(I'm going to Brussels tomorrow) 다음 주 수요일에 돌아온다(I'll be back next Wednesday)며 출장 일정이 있다고 알렸다. 그러자 9시 23분에 타마키 씨는 두 면접 다 출장을 피해 일정을 잡을 수 있다(I can schedule both around your trip)며 최종 결정을 내리기 전에 의견을 꼭 듣고 싶다(We'd really like to get your input before we make a final decision)고 제안했고, 이에 대해 크루스 씨가 9시 24분에 '너무 좋다(Perfect)'고 답했다. 따라서 크루스 씨가 '너무 좋다'고 한 말은 자신의 출장 일정까지 고려해 가며 면접에 참여해 달라는 타마키 씨에게 고마움을 표하는 의도로 한 말임을 알 수 있으므로 (B)가 정답이다.

158-160 이메일

수신: 밀버리 사무소 직원
발신: 기술팀
날짜: 5월 18일 월요일
제목: 네트워크 서버

1585월 22일 금요일에는 밀버리 사무실 서버가 수리를 위해 오프라인 상태가 됨을 알려 드립니다. 따라서 이 위치에 있는 직원들은 인터넷이나 해당 서버에 있는 파일에 접근할 수 없습니다.

159밀버리 사무실 직원들은 그날 재택 근무가 허용됩니다. 아니면 노스버러 사무실에 직원들이 있을 만한 공간이 있습니다. 어느 쪽을 선택할지 늦어도 **5월 20일 수요일까지 관리자에게** 알려 주세요. 5월 25일 월요일에는 모두 정상적으로 **160진행 되리라** 예상됩니다.

기술팀

어휘 **repair** 수리 **alternatively** 아니면 **accommodate** 공간이 있다 **properly** 정상적으로

158 세부 사항

번역 이메일에 언급된 문제에 영향을 받는 사람은?
(A) 원격 근무 직원만
(B) 기술팀 팀원만
(C) 밀버리 사무소 직원
(D) 노스버러 사무소 직원

해설 첫 단락에서 5월 22일 금요일에는 밀버리 사무실 서버가 수리를 위해 오프라인 상태가 됨을 알린다(Please be advised ~ off-line for repair)고 했고 따라서 이 위치에 있는 직원들은 인터넷이나 해당 서버에 있는 파일에 접근할 수 없다(As a result ~ files on that server)고 했으므로 (C)가 정답이다.

159 세부 사항

번역 이메일에 제공된 것은?
(A) 불편에 대한 사과
(B) 직원에게 주는 지시
(C) 기여에 대한 감사
(D) 용역비 견적

해설 두 번째 단락에서 밀버리 사무실 직원들은 그날 재택 근무가 허용된다(Millbury office staff ~ work from home that day)고 했고 아니면 노스버러 사무실에 직원들이 있을 만한 공간이 있다(Alternatively, staff can ~ Northborough office)며 어느 쪽을 선택할지 늦어도 5월 20일 수요일까지 관리자에게 알려 달라(Please inform your manager ~ option you will choose)고 지시 사항을 전하고 있으므로 (B)가 정답이다.

어휘 **inconvenience** 불편 **instruction** 지시 **contribution** 기여 **estimate** 견적(서)

160 동의어

번역 두 번째 단락 3행의 "run"과 의미상 가장 가까운 단어는?
(A) 기능하다   (B) 서두르다
(C) 흐르다   (D) 변하다

해설 의미상 서버 수리가 끝난 뒤 인터넷이나 파일 접속 등의 작업이 제대로 '진행되다'라는 뜻으로 쓰인 것이므로 정답은 (A) function이다.

161-163 이메일

수신: 연구개발과
발신: 에바 탕겐
날짜: 7월 20일
제목: 팀워크

안녕하세요, 여러분.

161오늘 송별회를 열어 주신 모든 분들께 감사드립니다. 깜짝 파티에 얼마나 기분 좋았던지요! **162**제가 지난 **14년간 산메르케에서 일하면서 가장 즐거웠던 것이 무엇인지 다시 한 번 깨우쳐줬어요.** 바로 걸출한 팀입니다.

작별 인사를 하기가 힘들기는 하지만, 업계의 규정 분야로 옮기면서 제 경력에서 새로운 단계를 시작하게 되어 설렙니다. **162새로운 직책에서 제가 맡은 책임은 우리가 이곳에서 수행하는 의료 업무와 연관이 있으므로** 앞으로도 많은 분들과 만날 거예요.

계속 연락하고 싶어요. **163제 개인 이메일 주소가 가장 좋은 연락 방법이 될 거예요**: eva.tangen@lmnmail.com.

에바 탕겐
연구개발부사장
산메르케 산업

어휘 gratitude 감사 extraordinary 특별한 phase 단계 regulation 규정 responsibility 책임 related to ~와 연관 있는

161 주제/목적

번역 이메일의 목적은?

(A) 행사를 연 동료들에게 감사하기

(B) 직원에게 사규 환기하기

(C) 신규 직원 채용 알리기

(D) 프로젝트 지원 요청하기

해설 이메일이나 편지, 공지 등에서는 보통 글의 주제나 목적이 전반부에 제시되어 있다. 첫 단락의 첫 문장에서 오늘 송별회를 열어 주신 모든 분들께 감사드린다(I wanted to express my gratitude to you all for hosting my farewell party today)며 감사의 뜻을 전하는 것으로 글을 시작한 것으로 보아 (A)가 정답이다.

패러프레이징

지문의 express my gratitude to you

➡ 보기의 thank colleagues

162 Not/True

번역 탕겐 씨에 관해 명시된 것은?

(A) 은퇴할 것이다.

(B) 10년 이상 의료계에서 일했다.

(C) 산메르케 산업 설립자이다.

(D) 산메르케 산업의 새 지사를 관리할 것이다.

해설 첫 단락의 세 번째 문장에서 탕겐 씨는 자신이 지난 14년간 산메르케에서 일하면서 가장 즐거웠던 것이 무엇인지 다시 한 번 깨우쳤다(It was a reminder of ~ Sanmerke these past 14 years)고 했고, 두 번째 단락의 두 번째 문장에서 새로운 직책에서 맡은 책임이 우리가 이곳에서 수행하는 의료 업무와 연관이 있다(Since the responsibilities ~ health-care work we do here)고 밝혔다. 탕겐 씨는 의료 관련 업체인 산메르케에서 14년간 근무한 것이므로 (B)가 정답이다.

어휘 retire 은퇴하다 decade 10년 founder 설립자

패러프레이징

지문의 past 14 years ➡ 보기의 over a decade

163 문장 삽입

번역 [1], [2], [3], [4]로 표시된 곳 중에서 다음 문장이 가장 적합한 위치는?

"계속 연락하고 싶어요."

(A) [1]   (B) [2]

(C) [3]   (D) [4]

해설 제시된 문장은 '계속 연락하고 싶다'며 동료들과 연락하며 지내고 싶은 바람을 이야기하고 있다. 따라서 개인 이메일을 통한 연락을 제안하며 이메일 주소를 알려 주고 있는 문

장 바로 앞에 들어가는 것이 글의 흐름상 자연스러우므로 (D)가 정답이다.

164-167 구인 공고

국내 최대 스포츠 로펌 중 하나인 러하인 파트너스는 재능 있고 의욕 넘치는 소셜미디어 전문가를 찾고 있습니다. 164당사는 특히 운동선수와 계약 협상에 적용되는 스포츠 법을 전문으로 합니다. 당사는 스포츠 산업에 대한 당사의 관심과 법률적 전문 지식이 소셜 미디어 영향력을 통해 드러나기를 바랍니다. 채용 과정에서 두 분야 모두에 경력 있는 지원자들이 우대 받습니다.

165지원자는 커뮤니케이션 또는 언론학 학사학위와 소셜미디어 분야에서 최소 5년의 경력이 있어야 합니다. 다양한 스포츠에 정통하면 더 좋지만 필수 요건은 아닙니다. 법조계에 대한 지식은 이점이 됩니다. 166, 167관심 있는 지원자들은 이력서와 자기소개서를 admin@lehinepartners.com으로 보내시기 바랍니다. 직장 추천인 2인의 연락처 정보가 반드시 포함되어야 합니다. 최종 결정을 내리기 전에 선발된 지원자들과 개인 면접을 실시합니다.

어휘 driven 의욕 넘치는 expert 전문가 athlete 운동선수 contract 계약(서) negotiation 협상 presence 영향력 reflect 반영하다 expertise 전문지식 engagement 참여, 관심 priority 우선(권) candidate 지원자 bachelor 학사 familiarity 정통함 a range of 다양한 prefer 선호하다 required 필수의

164 추론

번역 러하인 파트너스에 관해 알 수 있는 것은?

(A) 비교적 작은 로펌이다.

(B) 계약 협상에서 선수를 대변한다.

(C) 몇 가지 스포츠만을 전문으로 한다.

(D) 소셜미디어 정책을 수정해야 한다.

해설 첫 단락의 두 번째 문장에서 당사는 특히 운동선수와 계약 협상에 적용되는 스포츠 법을 전문으로 한다(We specialize in sports law ~ athletes and contract negotiations)고 했으므로 계약 협상에서 운동선수의 대리인 역할을 하는 스포츠 로펌임을 알 수 있다. 따라서 (B)가 정답이다.

어휘 represent (이익을) 대변하다

165 세부 사항

번역 직책에 필요한 요건은?

(A) 법학 학위

(B) 스포츠 분야 경력

(C) 소셜미디어 분야의 과거 직업

(D) 법적 절차에 정통함

229

두 번째 단락의 첫 문장에 지원자는 커뮤니케이션 또는 언론학 학사학위와 소셜미디어 분야에서 최소 5년의 경력이 있어야 한다(Candidates must have ~ experience in social media)고 했으므로 (C)가 정답이며 (A)는 답이 될 수 없다. 두 번째 문장에서 (B)는 좋지만 필수 요건은 아니라고(preferred but not required) 했고, 세 번째 문장에서 (D)는 우대 사항(a plus)이라고만 했으므로 답이 될 수 없다.

어휘 **prior** 과거의

패러프레이징

지문의 professional experience ➡ 보기의 A prior job

166 세부 사항

번역 관심 있는 지원자들은 이 일자리에 어떻게 지원해야 하는가?
  (A) 이메일에 지원 자료를 첨부해서
  (B) 온라인 신청서를 작성해서
  (C) 작업 샘플을 웹사이트에 업로드해서
  (D) 개인면접을 신청해서

해설 두 번째 단락의 네 번째 문장에서 관심 있는 지원자들은 이력서와 자기소개서를 admin@lehinepartners.com으로 보내야 한다(Interested candidates should send ~ admin@lehinepartners.com)고 했으므로 (A)가 정답이다.

패러프레이징

지문의 a résumé and a cover letter
  ➡ 보기의 application materials

167 문장 삽입

번역 [1], [2], [3], [4]로 표시된 곳 중에서 다음 문장이 가장 적합한 위치는?

"직장 추천인 2인의 연락처 정보가 반드시 포함되어야 합니다."
  (A) [1]   (B) [2]
  (C) [3]   (D) [4]

해설 제시된 문장은 '직장 추천인 2인의 연락처 정보가 반드시 포함되어야 한다'며 지원자가 제출해야 할 자료에 대한 주의 사항을 이야기하고 있다. 따라서 지원자가 보내야 할 서류와 함께 이메일 주소를 알려 주고 있는 문장 바로 뒤에 들어가는 것이 글의 흐름상 자연스러우므로 (D)가 정답이다.

168-171 회람

회람

수신: 전 직원
발신: 키스 아이른
날짜: 5월 4일
제목: 알림

[168]사무실 이전 날짜인 이번 주 금요일 5월 8일이 다가오고 있습니다. 파일, 사무용품, 책, 공예품이나 식물 같은 개인 물품 포장은 직원에게 책임이 있습니다. [168, 169]컴퓨터 본체, 모니터, 키보드는 있는 장소에 그대로 두면 됩니다. 이것들은 이전 팀이 포장할 것입니다. 5월 7일 목요일 업무시간까지 상자를 전부 포장해서 [170]표시해 주십시오. 이름과 새로운 위치가 명확한지 확인하세요. 포장되지 않은 물건은 금요일 오전에 모두 폐기하겠습니다.

[171]이전하는 날은 회사 휴일이니 긴 주말을 즐기세요. 5월 11일 월요일에 평소처럼 사무실에 오시면 됩니다. 그날을 활용해 소지품을 풀고 상자를 분해해 주세요. 빈 상자는 관리 직원이 가져갈 수 있도록 반드시 작업장소나 사무실 밖에 두도록 하십시오.

키스 아이른
사무소장, 팜비사 홍보

어휘 **responsible for** ~에 책임이 있는 **dispose of** ~을 폐기하다 **belonging** 소지품 **empty** 빈 **maintenance** 유지 관리 **public relations** 홍보

168 주제/목적

번역 회람의 목적은?
  (A) 특수 프로젝트 지원자 요청하기
  (B) 회사 장비 개선 설명하기
  (C) 향후 이전 계획 알리기
  (D) 직원들에게 예정된 청소 작업 상기시키기

해설 첫 단락에 사무실 이전 날짜인 이번 주 금요일 5월 8일이 다가오고 있다(Our office moving day is coming up this Friday, May 8)고 사무실 이전을 상기시키며, 파일, 사무용품, 책, 공예품이나 식물 같은 개인 물품 포장은 직원에게 책임이 있다(Employees are responsible ~ artwork or plants)고 했고 컴퓨터 본체, 모니터, 키보드는 있는 장소에 그대로 두면 된다(Computer tower ~ remain where they are)고 하는 등 이전 준비에 관한 사항들을 직원들에게 공지하고 있다. 따라서 회람은 직원들에게 사무실 이전과 관련한 계획을 알리려고 쓴 것이므로 (C)가 정답이다.

169 세부 사항

번역 직원들이 제자리에 두어야 하는 품목은?
  (A) 책
  (B) 전자기기
  (C) 사무용품
  (D) 공예품

해설 첫 단락의 세 번째 문장에서 컴퓨터 본체, 모니터, 키보드는 있는 장소에 그대로 두면 된다(Computer tower ~ remain where they are)고 지시했으므로 (B)가 정답이다.

지문의 computer towers, monitors, and keyboards

➡ 보기의 Electronic equipment

170 동의어

번역 첫 번째 단락 5행의 "marked"와 의미상 가장 가까운 단어는?

(A) 라벨이 부착된　　(B) 개정된

(C) 등급을 매긴　　(D) 제안된

해설 의미상 상자에 '표시된'이라는 뜻으로 쓰인 것이므로 정답은 (A) labeled이다.

171 세부 사항

번역 회람에 따르면 직원들은 언제 쉬는가?

(A) 월요일　　(B) 화요일

(C) 목요일　　(D) 금요일

해설 두 번째 단락의 첫 문장에서 이전하는 날은 회사 휴일이니 긴 주말을 즐기라(The day of the move is ~ enjoy the long weekend)고 했고, 5월 11일 월요일에 평소처럼 사무실에 오면 된다(We expect you to ~ Monday, May 11)고 했다. 따라서 금요일이 휴가라는 것을 알 수 있으므로 (D)가 정답이다.

172-175 온라인 채팅

> **벨라 보토프(오전 8:45)** 모두 안녕하세요. 172제가 공유 드라이브에 "예비 고객" 폴더를 만들었어요. 거기에는 잠재 고객들 목록과 당사 인터넷 마케팅 서비스 개요를 담은 슬라이드 프레젠테이션이 들어 있어요.
>
> **그레그 이바라(오전 8:50)** 173제가 봤는데 클릭하면 제 개인 문서가 전부 들어 있는 폴더로 다시 돌아가요.
>
> **캐시 암브러스터(오전 8:54)** 이상하네요, 그레그. 전 폴더가 열려요.
>
> **그레그 이바라(오전 8:56)** 저한테 그렇게 할 권한이 없는 것 같아요. 파일 공유 설정을 바꿔야 할지도 모르겠어요.
>
> **캐시 암브러스터(오전 9:01)** 174그레그, 방금 슬라이드 프레젠테이션 사본을 이메일로 보냈어요. 좀 있으면 크로노스 보석상과 회의가 있는데 필요할지도 몰라서요.
>
> **그레그 이바라(오전 9:03)** 사실 그 회의를 위해 추가로 문서가 필요한데 알려 드릴게요.
>
> **벨라 보토프(오전 9:05)** 그레그가 제일 잘 알 거예요. 제가 알기로 이미 몇 차례 그들과 이야기를 나눴잖아요.
>
> **캐시 암브러스터(오전 9:08)** 175베크 패션을 위한 마케팅 캠페인 데이터를 공유하는 게 어떨까요? 우리와 협업하기 전과 후 그들의 수익을 보여 주는 유용한 그래프가 있어요. 그들은

> 제 고객이니 우리가 그 그래프를 공유해도 되는지 그쪽에 물어볼게요.
>
> **그레그 이바라(오전 9:12)** 고마워요. 크로노스 보석상이 우리와 함께하도록 하려면 바로 그런 세부 사항을 제시해야 해요.
>
> **캐시 암브러스터(오전 9:14)** 알았어요! 베크 패션에 오늘 메시지를 보낼게요.

어휘 prospective 예비의　potential 잠재적인 authorization 권한　revenue 수익　on board with ~와 함께하다

172 추론

번역 글쓴이들은 어떤 회사에서 일하겠는가?

(A) 기술지원 서비스 업체

(B) 마케팅 대행사

(C) 인터넷 서비스 공급자

(D) 소프트웨어 개발 회사

해설 오전 8시 45분에 벨라 보토프가 공유 드라이브에 "예비 고객" 폴더를 만들었다(I have created a folder ~ on our shared drive)며 거기에는 잠재 고객들 목록과 당사 인터넷 마케팅 서비스 개요를 담은 슬라이드 프레젠테이션이 들어 있다(It includes a list of ~ our Internet marketing services)고 했으므로 글쓴이들은 인터넷 마케팅 서비스 업체임을 알 수 있다. 따라서 (B)가 정답이다.

173 세부 사항

번역 이바라 씨는 무엇을 하는 데 어려움을 겪고 있는가?

(A) 고객에게 연락하기

(B) 폴더에 접근하기

(C) 제품 조사하기

(D) 비밀번호 기억하기

해설 오전 8시 50분에 이바라 씨는 자신이 봤는데 클릭하면 개인 문서가 전부 들어 있는 폴더로 다시 돌아간다(I saw that, but ~ personal documents are)고 했으므로 앞서 언급된 폴더를 열지 못하고 있음을 알 수 있다. 따라서 (B)가 정답이다.

174 의도 파악

번역 오전 9시 5분에 보토프 씨가 "제가 알기로 이미 몇 차례 그들과 이야기를 나눴잖아요"라고 쓴 의도는?

(A) 결정이 예상보다 오래 걸리고 있다.

(B) 때때로 잠재 고객에게 여러 차례 알림을 보낼 필요가 있다.

(C) 이바라 씨는 정보를 더 효율적으로 수집하도록 노력해야 한다.

(D) 크로노스 보석상은 이미 회사의 서비스에 익숙하다.

9시 1분에 암브러스터 씨가 그레그에게 방금 슬라이드 프
레젠테이션 사본을 이메일로 보냈다(I just e-mailed ~
slide presentation)며 좀 있으면 크로노스 보석상과 회
의가 있는데 필요할지도 모른다(You might need it ~
Chronos Jewelers)고 했고, 9시 5분에 보토프 씨가 그
레그에게 이미 몇 차례 그들과 이야기를 나눴다고 알고 있
다(I know you've already spoken with them a
few times)고 했다. 따라서 그레그는 크로노스 보석상과
의 회의를 준비 중이라는 것을 알 수 있고, '이미 몇 차례 그
들과 이야기를 나눴다고 알고 있다'는 말은 크로노스 보석
상이 이미 그레그와의 사전 대화를 통해 회사의 서비스에
대해 알고 있다는 의도로 한 말이므로 (D)가 정답이다.

175 세부 사항

번역 암브러스터 씨가 자신의 고객 중 한 명에게 연락하는 이유는?
(A) 계약 재협상하기
(B) 긍정적인 소식 들려주기
(C) 최근 수익 통계 확인하기
(D) 정보를 공유해도 되는지 허락 구하기

해설 9시 8분에 암브러스터 씨는 베크 패션을 위한 마케팅 캠페
인 데이터를 공유하는 게 어떨지(what about sharing
data ~ Bech Fashion?)를 제안했고, 우리와 협업하
기 전과 후 그들의 수익을 보여 주는 유용한 그래프가 있다
(I have a great graph ~ partnered with us)며 그들
은 자신의 고객이니 우리가 그 그래프를 공유해도 되는지
그쪽에 물어보겠다(Since they're my client ~ could
share that graph)고 했다. 따라서 수익 그래프를 공유해
도 되는지 묻기 위해 고객에게 연락하는 것이므로 (D)가 정
답이다.

어휘 relate 들려주다 statistics 통계 permission 허락

패러프레이징
지문의 that graph ➡ 보기의 some information

176-180 회람 + 이메일

회람

수신: 영업팀
발신: 사라 랜서스, 영업부장
날짜: 3월 30일
제목: 필라벅스사 발표

영업팀 모든 팀원은 4월 7일 수요일 오전 9시에 회의에 참석해
야 합니다. 그때, ^{176, 177}**아드난 마흐무디 회장이 텍사스 주
댈러스에 있는 리바스 내셔널과 예정된 합병에 대해 중대 발표
를 할 예정입니다.** ^{177, 180}**회장님은 또한 데일 이전 서비스 담
당자를 소개할 예정인데 이 사람이 댈러스로 순조롭게 이전하
기 위한 계획에 대해 설명할 것입니다.**

회의는 아넷 빌딩 회의실에서 열립니다.
참석은 의무입니다.

어휘 anticipated 예정된 merger 합병 relocation
이전 representative 담당자 seamless 순조로운
mandatory 의무인

발신: dan@dalerelocation.com
보냄: 4월 10일
수신: slancers@philabux.com
¹⁷⁸**제목: 예약**

안녕하세요, 랜서스 씨:

¹⁷⁸**앞서 준비된 대로, 4월 12일 수요일 오전 9시 15분에 필
라델피아 오클랜드 가 457번지에서 주택 점검 및 매각 상담
을 받기로 예약되어 있습니다.** ¹⁸⁰**저희는 집을 빨리 팔기 위한
가격 책정을 논의하고 시장에 내놓기 전에 큰 수리를 완료해야
할 필요는 없는지 확인하겠습니다. 그런 다음 새 집을 찾기 위
해 어디에 집중해야 할지 얘기하면 됩니다.**

저는 고객님의 시간을 ¹⁷⁹**소중히 여깁니다.** 따라서 비는 시간
이 바뀔 수도 있다는 점, 이해합니다. 이 예약을 변경해야 할
경우 사무실로 전화해 접수 담당자와 직접 이야기하세요.

4월 12일에 뵙기를 기대합니다.

댄 월렌스키
데일 이전 서비스
(301) 555-0186

어휘 arrange 준비하다 appointment 예약 repair 수리

176 Not/True

번역 필라벅스사에 관해 명시된 것은?
(A) 곧 CEO를 새로 뽑는다.
(B) 마케팅 전략을 바꿀 가능성이 높다.
(C) 시설 개보수를 계획하고 있다.
(D) 다른 회사와 합병을 준비하고 있다.

해설 회람의 두 번째 문장에서 아드난 마흐무디 회장이 텍사스
주 댈러스에 있는 리바스 내셔널과 예정된 합병에 대해 중
대 발표를 할 예정이다(company president Adnan ~
merger with Livas National in Dallas, Texas)라고
했으므로 (D)가 정답이다.

177 Not/True

번역 회람에서 회의에 관해 언급한 것은?
(A) 월례행사다.
(B) 한 시간 정도 지속될 것이다.
(C) 회장이 주도할 것이다.
(D) 이사회 임원 몇 명이 포함될 것이다.

해설 회람의 두 번째 문장에서 아드난 마흐무디 회장이 텍사스
주 댈러스에 있는 리바스 내셔널과 예정된 합병에 대해 중
대 발표를 할 예정이다(company president Adnan
~ merger with Livas National in Dallas, Texas)
라고 했고, 곧이어 회장님은 또한 데일 이전 서비스 담

당자를 소개할 예정(He will also introduce a Dale Relocation Services representative)이라고 했다. 따라서 마흐무디 회장이 회의를 주로 이끌 것임을 알 수 있으므로 (C)가 정답이다.

패러프레이징
지문의 company president
➡ 보기의 the head of the company

178 주제/목적

번역 이메일의 목적은?
(A) 잇따른 예약 잡기
(B) 알림 발송
(C) 회의 일정 변경하기
(D) 연락처 확인하기

해설 이메일의 제목이 예약(Appointment)이고, 첫 문장에서 앞서 준비된 대로 4월 12일 수요일 오전 9시 15분에 필라델피아 오클랜드 가 457번지에서 주택 점검 및 매각 상담을 받기로 예약되어 있다(As previously arranged, you have a scheduled appointment ~ April 12, at 9:15 A.M.)며 고객에게 예약 사항에 대해 상기시키고 있다. 따라서 (B)가 정답이다.

어휘 verify 확인하다

179 동의어

번역 이메일에서 두 번째 단락 1행의 "appreciate"와 의미상 가장 가까운 단어는?
(A) 소중하게 여기다   (B) 증가하다
(C) 이해하다   (D) 칭찬하다

해설 의미상 '소중히 여기다'라는 뜻으로 쓰인 것이므로 정답은 (A) value이다.

180 연계

번역 랜서스 씨에 관해 암시된 것은?
(A) 집을 수리하기 위해 회사를 고용했다.
(B) 4월 12일에 일정이 겹친다.
(C) 데일 이전 서비스 직원이다.
(D) 댈러스로 이사할 것이다.

해설 회람의 세 번째 문장에서 랜서스 씨는 회장님이 데일 이전 서비스 담당자를 소개할 예정인데 이 사람이 댈러스로 순조롭게 이전하기 위한 계획에 대해 설명할 것(He will also introduce ~ move to Dallas)이라고 했고, 이메일의 첫 단락 두 번째 문장에서 데일 이전 서비스 담당자인 월렌스키 씨는 랜서스 씨에게 집을 빨리 팔기 위한 가격 책정을 논의하고 시장에 내놓기 전에 큰 수리를 완료해야 할 필요는 없는지 확인하겠다(We will discuss pricing your house to sell ~ putting it on the market)며 그런 다음 새 집을 찾기 위해 어디에 집중해야 할지 얘기하면 된다(Then we can talk about ~ for your new home)고

했다. 따라서 랜서스 씨는 회사가 이전함에 따라 댈러스로 이사할 것임을 알 수 있으므로 (D)가 정답이다.

어휘 scheduling conflict 일정 겹침

181-185 청구서 + 이메일

타미노 그룹

회사: 골든 크라운 교육 컨설턴트
주문 날짜: 11월 22일   주문 확인: No.432886

품번	품목	가격	수량	총	배송 방법	배송 예상일
TG433	타이탄 스타 프린터용 재켁스 토너 (모델 433x)	98.49 달러	2상자	196.98 달러	육로-특송	11월 25일
185 TG214	185카켈 종이(A4 사이즈)	32.99 달러	4케이스	131.96 달러	육로-일반	11월 29일
TG558	몬탄 스테이플(표준 사이즈)	3.49 달러	6팩	20.94 달러	육로-이코노미	12월 4일
TG232	181퍼커 종이클립(중)	2.49 달러	12상자	29.88 달러	육로-이코노미	18112월 4일
		배송		50.00 달러		
		총		429.76 달러		

어휘 estimated 예상되는   expedited 특송의

발신: 앨버트 후앙 〈albert.huang@goldencrownec.com〉
수신: 업무 지원 부서 〈help@taminogroup.com〉
날짜: 11월 23일 오전 11:00
제목: 주문번호 432886

관계자께:

183폐를 끼쳐서 죄송하지만, 182제 주문에 몇 가지 실수가 있었던 것 같습니다. 182, 184아까 고객 서비스 담당자에게 전화했더니 업무 지원 부서에 이메일을 보내서 제가 담당자에게 말한 변경 사항을 확인하게 하고, 코드 입력을 요청해 품목 중 하나에 대한 배송 방법을 변경하라고 하더군요.

귀사의 온라인 주문 시스템을 사용하는 건 이번이 처음이라, 메뉴에서 프린터를 잘못 선택한 것 같습니다. 433x 프린터 말고 430x 프린터 모델의 토너가 필요합니다. 185덧붙여 종이가 토너와 함께 도착하도록 지금 바로 종이 주문을 "지상-특급"으로 속도를 높이고 싶습니다. 또 스테이플 2팩을 더 넣어서 총 8팩으로 주시고 그에 따라 총 가격을 조정하세요. 도움에 감사드립니다.

앨버트 후앙, 사무국장
골든 크라운 교육 컨설턴트

어휘 **apparently** 보아하니 ~인 듯하다 **adjust** 조정하다
accordingly 그에 따라

181 세부 사항

번역 청구서에 따르면 종이클립은 언제 배송되는가?

(A) 11월 22일 (B) 11월 25일
(C) 11월 29일 (D) 12월 4일

해설 청구서에 있는 표의 마지막 줄에 퍼커 종이클립(중)(Perker paper clips (medium))은 12월 4일(December 4)에 배송된다고 나와 있으므로 (D)가 정답이다.

182 주제 / 목적

번역 이메일의 목적은?

(A) 주문 변경 확인 요청하기
(B) 특정 사무용품 배송 취소하기
(C) 종이 케이스 추가 주문하기
(D) 회사 웹사이트 정보 얻기

해설 이메일의 첫 단락에서 주문에 몇 가지 실수가 있었던 것 같다(I made a few errors on my order)고 했고, 아까 고객 서비스 담당자에게 전화했더니 업무 지원 부서에 이메일을 보내서 제가 담당자에게 말한 변경 사항을 확인하게 하고 코드 입력을 요청해 품목 중 하나에 대한 배송 방법을 변경하라고 했다(I spoke to a customer service representative ~ shipping method for one of the items)며 고객 서비스 담당자에게 안내 받은 대로 주문 변경 사항의 확인을 요청하고 있으므로 (A)가 정답이다.

183 동의어

번역 이메일에서 첫 번째 단락 1행의 "trouble"과 의미상 가장 가까운 단어는?

(A) 경고하다
(B) 재촉하다
(C) 귀찮게 하다
(D) 혼란스럽게 하다

해설 의미상 '폐를 끼치다'라는 뜻으로 쓰인 것이므로 정답은 (C) bother이다.

184 Not / True

번역 후앙 씨에 관해 명시된 것은?

(A) 배송 속도가 더뎌서 화가 났다.
(B) 타미노 그룹 직원과 이야기했다.
(C) 자신이 갖고 있는 프린터가 어떤 모델인지 확실히 모른다.
(D) 전화상으로 받은 서비스에 만족하지 못했다.

해설 이메일의 첫 단락 두 번째 문장에서 후앙 씨가 아까 고객 서비스 담당자에게 통화했다(I spoke to a customer service representative on the phone earlier)고 했으므로 (B)가 정답이다.

패러프레이징
지문의 representative ➡ 보기의 employee

185 연계

번역 후앙 씨가 더 빨리 배송해 달라고 요청한 품목의 번호는?

(A) TG433 (B) TG214
(C) TG558 (D) TG232

해설 이메일의 두 번째 단락 세 번째 문장에서 종이가 토너와 함께 도착하도록 종이 주문을 "지상-특급"으로 속도를 높이고 싶다(I would now like to speed up the paper order ~ arrive with the toner)고 했다. 청구서의 표에 따르면 종이(Cakel paper)의 품목번호는 TG214이므로 (B)가 정답이다.

186-190 기사 + 공지 + 이메일

와일드포트, 새 감독 선임

스프링데일(5월 21일) – 스프링데일에서 인기 높은 미술 공간인 와일드포트 갤러리는 어제 렐 매논 씨가 관장으로 임명됐다고 발표했다. 가장 최근, 매논 씨는 로치데일 예술학교 시각예술학과 부교수이자 해당 학과 학과장이었다.

매논 씨는 매트린대학교를 졸업했는데 조각을 공부했다. 그녀의 작품들은 전 세계 갤러리와 박물관에 전시되었다. 가장 최근에 지난 1월에 열린 전시회를 위해 말레이시아 쿠알라룸푸르로 갔다.

[186]그녀는 또한 근현대 미술에 관한 책 몇 권과 기사들을 썼으며 여러 영화 및 연극 작품의 세트를 위해 자문 역할을 담당했다.

어휘 **recently** 최근에 **chair** 학과장 **sculpting** 조각
contemporary 현대의 **theatrical** 연극의

와일드포트 갤러리가
여름날들을
선사합니다

멀티미디어 전시회에서 다음 작품들이 선보입니다:

- 알리야 수할리 – 추상 조각품(6월 8-26일 전시)
- [188]헨리 홀란드 – 수채화(7월 5-24일 전시)
- 아벨 은고지 – 도자기 식기류(8월 9-28일 전시)
- 마사 토레스 – 흑백 사진(9월 6-25일 전시)

[187]각 전시회마다 예술가의 환영사가 있는 개막 축하연이 열립니다. 갤러리 운영시간: 월-금, 오후 12:30-8:30, 토요일, 오전 10:00-오후 6:00.
입장은 무료입니다.

이스트 히코리 가 221번지 | [190]스프링데일 | 555-0179 |
www.wildportgallery.com

어휘 **abstract** 추상적인 **tableware** 식기류

수신: 렐 매논 〈rmanon@wildportgallery.com〉
발신: 스테판 웨버 〈sweber@laa.edu〉
날짜: 5월 29일
제목: 기쁜 소식

렐에게,

로치데일 예술학교에서 더 이상 교수진에 계시지 못하신다니 섭섭합니다. 하지만 189, 190**와일드포트 갤러리 관장으로서 새로운 시도에 행운이 깃드시길 기원합니다.** 189**여기서 저희와 함께하실 때처럼 똑같은 열정과 결단력, 전문성을 새로운 역할에 쏟으시리라 확신합니다.**

그런데 헨리 홀란드가 관장님 갤러리에서 작품을 전시한다는 소식을 듣고 정말 기뻤습니다. 홀란드는 25년 전 이곳 학교에서 제 제자였거든요. 188, 190**10년 전 홀란드가 스프링데일을 떠나 런던으로 이사한 이후 그의 전시회에 가본 적이 없기 때문에, 이번 단독 전시회에 꼭 참석하려고 합니다.** 홀란드의 기법과 기량이 10년 동안 어떻게 발전했는지 궁금합니다.

끝으로, 새로운 직책에서 모든 일이 잘되기를 기원합니다.

스테판 웨버
로치데일 예술학교 총장

어휘 faculty 교수진 endeavor 시도 enthusiasm 열정 determination 결단(력) incidentally 그런데 definitely 꼭 practice 기량 evolve 발전하다

186 세부 사항

번역 기사에 따르면, 매논 씨의 과거 직업들 중 하나는?
(A) 갤러리 주인 (B) 대학교 총장
(C) 영화 컨설턴트 (D) 영화배우

해설 기사의 마지막 문장에서 매논 씨가 근현대 미술에 관한 책 몇 권과 기사들을 썼으며 여러 영화 및 연극 작품의 세트를 위해 자문 역할을 담당했다(She is also the author ~ adviser on the sets of several film and theatrical productions)고 했으므로 (C)가 정답이다.

패러프레이징
지문의 adviser ➡ 보기의 consultant

187 Not/True

번역 전시회에 관해 명시된 것은?
(A) 여러 언어로 된 음성 가이드를 갖추고 있다.
(B) 돈을 내야 참석할 수 있다.
(C) 첫날에 연설이 포함될 것이다.
(D) 일주일 내내 일반에게 개방된다.

해설 공지의 후반부에 각 전시회마다 예술가의 환영사가 있는 개막 축하연이 열린다(An opening reception, with welcome remarks from the artist, will be held for each exhibit)고 했으므로 (C)가 정답이다.

어휘 multilingual 여러 언어로 된

패러프레이징
지문의 remarks ➡ 보기의 speech

188 연계

번역 웨버 씨는 와일드포트 갤러리에서 열리는 전시회에 언제 참석하겠는가?
(A) 6월 (B) 7월
(C) 8월 (D) 9월

해설 이메일의 두 번째 단락 세 번째 문장에서 웨버 씨는 10년 전 홀란드가 스프링데일을 떠나 런던으로 이사한 이후 그의 전시회에 가본 적이 없기 때문에 이번 단독 전시회에 꼭 참석하려고 한다(I haven't been to an exhibit ~ attend his solo show)고 했고, 공지의 전시회 목록 두 번째에 헨리 홀란드의 수채화(Henri Holland-water-color paintings)를 7월 5-24일에 전시(on view July 5-24)한다고 나와 있다. 웨버 씨는 홀란드의 전시회가 열리는 7월 중에 전시회에 참석할 것이므로 (B)가 정답이다.

189 주제/목적

번역 이메일의 목적은?
(A) 취업기회 문의
(B) 미술품 구매에 대한 관심 표현
(C) 성취한 일 축하하기
(D) 향후 전시 관람권 요청

해설 이메일의 첫 단락 두 번째 문장에서 웨버 씨는 매논 씨에게 와일드포트 갤러리 관장으로서 새로운 시도에 행운이 있길 기원한다(we wish you all the best ~ Wildport Gallery)며 여기서 함께할 때처럼 똑같은 열정과 결단력, 전문성을 새로운 역할에 쏟으리라 확신한다(I'm sure you will bring ~ during your years with us)고 했다. 따라서 이메일은 매논 씨가 갤러리 관장직을 맡게 된 것을 축하하고 성공을 기원하려고 쓴 것이므로 (C)가 정답이다.

190 연계

번역 홀란드 씨에 관해 암시된 것은?
(A) 매논 씨와 같은 반이었다.
(B) 혁신적인 기법을 사용하는 것으로 유명하다.
(C) 25년 전에 전문 경력을 쌓기 시작했다.
(D) 매논 씨가 현재 일하고 있는 도시에 한때 살았다.

해설 이메일의 첫 단락 두 번째 문장에서 웨버 씨가 매논 씨에게 와일드포트 갤러리 관장으로서 새로운 시도에 행운이 있길 기원한다(we wish you all the best ~ the Wildport Gallery)고 했으므로 매논 씨는 현재 와일드포트 갤러리에서 일하고 있다는 것을 알 수 있다. 또한 두 번째 단락 세 번째 줄에서 10년 전 홀란드가 스프링데일을 떠나 런던으로 이사했다(he left Springdale and moved to London about ten years ago)고 했는데, 와일드포

트 갤러리의 공지에 따르면 마지막 줄에 주소가 스프링데일 (Springdale)이라고 나와 있으므로 홀란드 씨는 매논 씨가 근무하는 와일드포트 갤러리가 있는 도시에 거주했었음을 알 수 있다. 따라서 (D)가 정답이다.

191-195 편지 + 이메일 + 광고

라우처 업무 단지

제이드 가 456번지, 멍크턴, 뉴브런즈윅 E1G 9Z9

¹⁹¹업주님께,

¹⁹¹**장기 계약, 높은 월세, 비싼 장비 대여와 작별하세요.** 작지만 번성하는 업체는 이제 편리한 도심 입지에 필요에 따라 쓰는 공유 사무공간을 임대할 수 있습니다. 프린터/복사기, 인터넷 접속, 편안한 회의실 등 기반이 잘 갖춰진 회사 시설의 이점이 모두 있는 현대적 빌딩을 아주 적당한 월세로 누리실 겁니다. 노트북만 가지고 오시면 사업 준비는 완료입니다!

교대 업무 시간	1인용 사무실	¹⁹³2인용 사무실	3인용 사무실
주간(오전 7시 – 오후 6시)	350달러	500달러	750달러
저녁(오후 6시 – 자정)	250달러	400달러	550달러
야간(자정 – 오전 7시)	150달러	300달러	450달러
¹⁹³24시간	600달러	¹⁹³900달러	1,300달러

506-555-0163번 또는 arthur@raucherofficecomplex.ca로 연락해 필요한 사항을 논의하세요.

아서 라우처

어휘 **costly** 값비싼 **equipment** 장비 **benefit** 이점 **comfortable** 편안한 **reasonable** (가격이) 적당한

수신: arthur@raucherofficecomplex.ca
발신: mlangenbach@frogpod.ca
날짜: 4월 20일
제목: 프로그 팟

라우처 씨께,

¹⁹²그곳에서 공간을 임대하고 있는 마리아 셸비를 통해 라우처 업무 단지에 대해 알게 됐습니다. 저도 공간을 임대하는 데 관심이 있습니다. 사장님과 만나 사무실 공간을 색다르게 사용하는 건에 관해 논의하고, 수용할 의향이 있으신지 알고 싶습니다.

^{194, 195}제 계획은 프로그 팟이라고 부르는 팟캐스트 센터 서비스를 제공하는 것입니다. 기본적으로, ^{193, 194, 195}저는 2인용 사무실을 24시간 빌려서 사무실 하나에 기본 녹음장비를 설치하고 싶습니다. ^{194, 195}그런 다음, 오디오나 비디오를 직접 제작하고자 하는 사람에게 이 미니 녹음 스튜디오를 한 시간 단위로 다시 빌려주려고 합니다. 어떻게 생각하시는지 알려주세요.

감사합니다.

마크 랑겐바흐

---

¹⁹⁴**프로그 팟**

제이드 가 456번지, 멍크턴, 뉴브런즈윅 주 E1G 9Z9

방송 활동을 시작하세요! 프로그 팟에 편승해 여러분만의 팟캐스트를 녹음하세요.

¹⁹⁴**1단계: 한 시간 단위로 녹음 공간을 임대하세요. 당사는 라우처 업무 단지에 있습니다.**

2단계: 팟캐스트를 만드세요. 스포츠, 예술, 연예, 뉴스 등 무엇이나 원하는 주제에 관해 이야기하세요.

3단계: 편안히 쉬시면서 나머지 일은 프로그 팟에 맡기세요! 저희가 팟캐스트를 중요한 소셜미디어 플랫폼에 전부 퍼뜨리겠습니다!

자세한 내용은 frogpod.ca를 방문하세요!

어휘 **distribute** 퍼뜨리다

---

191 주제/목적

번역 라우처 씨 편지의 목적은?
(A) 사무 공간 개조 문의
(B) 멍크턴 시내 임대료 조사
(C) 업주에게 서비스 홍보
(D) 멍크턴에서 일하는 이점 설명

해설 편지의 수신인이 업주(Business Owner)이며 장기 계약, 높은 월세, 비싼 장비 대여와 작별하라(Say good-bye to long leases, high rents, and costly equipment rentals)며 작지만 번성하는 업체는 이제 편리한 도심 입지에 필요에 따라 쓰는 공유 사무공간을 임대할 수 있다(Your small but growing business ~ convenient downtown location)고 소규모 업체의 업주들에게 사무 공간을 홍보하고 있으므로 (C)가 정답이다.

192 Not/True

번역 셸비 씨에 관해 명시된 것은?
(A) 라우처 업무 단지에 공간을 임대하고 있다.
(B) 멍크턴에 사무용 건물을 소유하고 있다.
(C) 랑겐바흐 씨의 직원이다.
(D) 팟캐스트를 즐겨 듣는다.

해설 이메일의 첫 문장에서 그곳에서 공간을 임대하고 있는 마리아 셸비를 통해 라우처 업무 단지에 대해 알게 됐다(I learned about the Raucher Office Complex from Maria Shelby, who is renting space there)고 했으므로 (A)가 정답이다.

패러프레이징
지문의 is renting ➡ 보기의 leases

193 연계

번역 랑겐바흐 씨는 원하는 업무 공간을 위해 매달 얼마를 지불하겠는가?

(A) 400달러   (B) 600달러

(C) 900달러   (D) 1,300달러

해설 이메일의 두 번째 단락 두 번째 문장에서 랑겐바흐 씨는 2인용 사무실을 24시간 빌려서 사무실 하나에 기본 녹음 장비를 설치하고 싶다(I would like to rent a double office for 24 hours a day and outfit one of the offices with my basic recording equipment)고 했고, 편지의 표에 따르면 2인용 사무실(Double Office)을 24시간(24 hours a day) 빌리는 요금은 900달러($900)라고 나와 있으므로 (C)가 정답이다.

194 연계

번역 라우처 씨는 4월 20일에 받은 질문에 어떻게 대답했는가?

(A) 새 프린터를 구입했다.

(B) 임대료를 낮췄다.

(C) 인터넷 제공업체들을 바꿨다.

(D) 제안에 동의했다.

해설 랑겐바흐 씨는 4월 20일에 보낸 이메일의 두 번째 단락에서 자신의 계획은 프로그 팟이라고 부르는 팟캐스트 센터 서비스를 제공하는 것(My plan is to offer ~ called Frog Pod)으로 2인용 사무실을 24시간 빌려서 사무실 하나에 기본 녹음장비를 설치하고 싶다(I would like to rent ~ recording equipment)고 했고 그런 다음, 오디오나 비디오를 직접 제작하고자 하는 사람에게 이 미니 녹음 스튜디오를 한 시간 단위로 다시 빌려주려고 한다(Then I would sublet ~ video productions)며 어떻게 생각하는지 알려 달라(Please let me know what you think)고 했다. 그리고 프로그 팟(Frog Pod)의 광고문의 1단계(Step 1)에 따르면 한 시간 단위로 녹음 공간을 임대하라(Rent our recording space by the hour)며 당사는 라우처 업무 단지에 있다(We are located at the Raucher Office Complex)고 설명하고 있다. 따라서 라우처 씨는 4월 20일에 받은 랑겐바흐 씨의 제안에 동의했다는 것을 알 수 있으므로 (D)가 정답이다.

195 세부 사항

번역 프로그 팟이 주로 제공하는 것은?

(A) 방송인을 위한 교재

(B) 미디어 제작 장비 이용

(C) 사무공간 매입자금 조달

(D) 웹사이트 설계 및 유지관리

해설 이메일의 두 번째 단락에서 랑겐바흐 씨는 자신의 계획이 프로그 팟이라고 부르는 팟캐스트 센터 서비스를 제공하는 것(My plan is to offer ~ called Frog Pod)으로 2인용 사무실을 24시간 빌려서 사무실 하나에 기본 녹음장

비를 설치하고 싶다(I would like to rent ~ recording equipment)고 했고 그런 다음, 오디오나 비디오를 직접 제작하고자 하는 사람에게 이 미니 녹음 스튜디오를 한 시간 단위로 다시 빌려주려고 한다(Then I would sublet ~ video productions)고 했다. 따라서 프로그 팟은 팟캐스트 제작자에게 제작에 필요한 장비와 공간을 제공하는 업체이므로 (B)가 정답이다.

패러프레이징

지문의 recording equipment

➡ 보기의 media production technology

196-200 발표문 + 이메일 + 편지

산스포어사

싱가포르 – 뉴욕 – 토론토

인사 분야 경영 교육 프로그램

[196]산스포어사가 올 9월부터 시작하는 6개월 인사 분야 경영 교육 프로그램에 지원을 받습니다. 교육에는 회사 전반에 걸친 다양한 업무(순환제)가 포함됩니다. 프로그램을 성공리에 수료하면 교육생들은 당사 정규직인 인사과 부팀장직에 고려 대상이 됩니다. 프로그램 교과과정에는 다음이 포함됩니다.

프로그램 월	순환 주제
9월	일반적인 정책과 채용
10월	보상과 급여
11월	고용법과 분규
12월	복지혜택
[199]1월	**통신산업**
2월	커뮤니케이션과 마케팅

자세한 정보와 지원은 mnguyen@sanspore.com 민 응우옌에게 연락하세요.

어휘 application 지원 involve 포함되다 assignment 업무 encompass 포함하다 compensation 보상 dispute 분규

수신: 존 로사노 〈jrossano@otil.com〉

발신: 민 응우옌 〈mnguyen@sanspore.com〉

날짜: 5월 27일

제목: 경영 교육 프로그램

첨부: 🔗 지원서

로사노 씨께,

산스포어사의 경영 교육 프로그램에 대한 문의에 감사드립니다. [197, 198]귀하의 심리학과 학위는 인사 분야 경력을 쌓을 수 있는 탄탄한 기반을 제공합니다. [198, 199]부전공 분야로 이수한 통신 과정 역시 유리하며, 순환제 주제에서 해당 기간 동안 참여를 면제받을 수도 있습니다. [200] 이 이메일에 첨부한 지원서를 작성해 7월 18일까지 교과과정 성적증명서와 추천서 두

장을 첨부해 제출해 주세요. 8월 10일까지 지원자들에게 결정 사항을 통지할 예정입니다.

민 응우옌 인사부장

어휘 solid 탄탄한 foundation 기반 excuse 면제하다
transcript 성적증명서 recommendation 추천
notify 통지하다 applicant 지원자

---

²⁰⁰⁷**7월 18일**

민 응우옌 씨
산스포어사
46번 가 12번지
뉴욕, 뉴욕 주 10017

응우옌 씨께,

귀사의 경영 교육 프로그램에 존 로사노를 적극 추천하고 싶습니다. 저는 로사노 씨를 4년 동안 알고 지냈습니다. 그는 하트랜드대학교에서 공부하는 동안 우리 회사에서 파트타임으로 일했습니다.

그는 저를 위해 특별 프로젝트를 완수하면서, 학습이 빠른 사람이라는 사실을 입증했으며 다른 사람들과 잘 협력하고 시스템 개선에 효과적인 아이디어로 기여했습니다. 수년간 많은 직원들을 관리한 사람으로서, 저는 로사노 씨가 귀사의 프로그램을 성공적으로 완수할 수 있는 탁월한 장래성을 지니고 있다고 믿습니다.

엘린 캐런 피터스, 회장

EKP 컨설팅 사

어휘 demonstrate 입증하다 contribute 기여하다
effective 효과적인 supervisor 관리자
outstanding 탁월한

196 주제/목적

번역 발표문의 목적은?
(A) 업계 회의에 구직자 초청
(B) 특별 프로그램에 잠재 직원 모집
(C) 직원에게 직무능력 개발 요건 환기시키기
(D) 연속 강좌 변경 사항 알리기

해설 발표문 첫 단락에 산스포어사가 올 9월부터 시작하는 6개월 인사 분야 경영 교육 프로그램에 지원을 받는다(Sanspore Corporation invites ~ September of this year)고 했고, 교육에는 회사 전반에 걸친 다양한 업무(순환제)가 포함된다(The training involves ~ throughout the company)며 프로그램을 성공리에 수료하면 교육생들은 당사 정규직인 인사과 부팀장 직에 고려 대상이 된다(Upon successful completion ~ human resources officers in our company)고 했

다. 따라서 발표문은 수료 시 나중에 직원이 될 수도 있는 경영 교육 프로그램에 참여자를 모집하기 위해 작성된 것이므로 (B)가 정답이다.

어휘 potential 잠재적인, 나중에 ~이 될 수도 있는
publicize 알리다

197 세부 사항

번역 로사노 씨가 중점적으로 연구한 것은?
(A) 경영
(B) 기업금융
(C) 통신
(D) 심리학

해설 이메일의 두 번째 문장에서 로사노 씨의 심리학과 학위는 인사 분야 경력을 쌓을 수 있는 탄탄한 기반을 제공한다(Your university degree in psychology ~ in human resources)고 했다. 로사노 씨는 대학에서 심리학을 주전공으로 공부했으므로 (D)가 정답이다.

198 추론

번역 이메일에서 로사노 씨에 관해 암시하는 것은?
(A) 산스포어사 교육 프로그램의 요건을 충족한다.
(B) 이전에 산스포어사 일자리에 지원했다.
(C) 5월 27일에 지원서를 제출했다.
(D) 응우옌 씨와 함께 대학에 다녔다.

해설 이메일의 두 번째 문장에서 로사노 씨의 심리학과 학위는 인사 분야 경력을 쌓을 수 있는 탄탄한 기반을 제공한다(Your university degree in psychology ~ in human resources)고 했고, 로사노 씨가 부전공 분야로 이수한 통신 과정 역시 유리하다(The coursework you completed ~ your secondary field of study, is an advantage)고 한 것으로 보아 로사노 씨는 산스포어사의 교육 프로그램에 지원 자격이 된다는 것을 짐작할 수 있다. 따라서 (A)가 정답이다.

199 연계

번역 로사노 씨는 몇 월에 순환제에서 면제되겠는가?
(A) 9월   (B) 10월
(C) 1월   (D) 2월

해설 이메일의 세 번째 문장에서 로사노 씨가 부전공 분야로 이수한 통신 과정이 유리하며 순환제 주제에서 해당 기간 동안 참여를 면제받을 수도 있다(The coursework you completed ~ month of that rotation topic)고 했고, 발표문의 프로그램 교과과정에 따르면 순환 주제 중 통신산업(The Telecommunications Industry)은 1월(January)에 배정되어 있으므로 로사노 씨는 1월에 순환제 프로그램에서 면제될 수도 있다. 따라서 (C)가 정답이다.

200 연계

번역 편지에 관해 사실인 것은?

(A) 지원 마감일에 발송되었다.

(B) 작업 샘플과 함께 발송되었다.

(C) 응우옌의 과거 교수에 의해 제출되었다.

(D) EKP 컨설팅사의 채용 제안이 포함되어 있다.

해설 이메일의 후반부에 이 이메일에 첨부한 지원서를 작성해 7월 18일까지 교과과정 성적증명서와 추천서 두 장을 첨부해 제출해 달라(Please complete the application form ~ letters of recommendation)고 했는데, 편지 상단에 보면 작성일이 7월 18일(July 18)이라고 나와 있으므로 편지는 지원 마감일에 발송되었음을 알 수 있다. 따라서 (A)가 정답이다.

어휘 **former** 과거의

토익 정기시험
기출종합서 RC

토익 시험, 문제는 적중률!
시험에 나온 **기출 문제** 그대로,
출제기관이 만든 **진짜 문제**로
빠르고 확실하게 대비하라!